Teaching English as a Second or Foreign Language

FOURTH EDITION

MARIANNE CELCE-MURCIA

DONNA M. BRINTON

MARGUERITE ANN SNOW

EDITORS

Australia • Brazil • Japan • Korea • Mexico • Singapore • Spain • United Kingdom • United States

Teaching English as a Second or Foreign Language, Fourth Edition
Marianne Celce-Murcia,
Donna M. Brinton,
and Marguerite Ann Snow

Publisher: Sherrise Roehr

Acquisitions Editor: Tom Jefferies

Director of Global Marketing: Ian Martin

Senior Product Manager:
Barbara Quincer Coulter

Director, Content and Media Production:
Michael Burggren

Content Project Manager:
Andrea Bobotas

Print Buyer: Mary Beth Hennebury

Cover Designer: Gina Petti

Cover Image: Joel Sartore/National
Geographic Image Collection

Compositor: MPS Limited

ISBN-13: 978-1-111-35169-4

ISBN-10: 1-111-35169-4

National Geographic Learning
20 Channel Center Street
Boston, MA 02210
USA

Cengage Learning is a leading provider of customized learning solutions with office locations around the globe, including Singapore, the United Kingdom, Australia, Mexico, Brazil, and Japan.

Cengage Learning products are represented in Canada by Nelson Education, Ltd.

Visit National Geographic Learning online at **elt.heinle.com**

Visit our corporate website at **www.cengage.com**

Printed in the United States of America
2 3 4 5 6 7 16 15 14 13

Contents

UNIT III. Skills for Teachers

UNIT IV. Integrated Approaches

Credits

Chapter 3
TEXT: 'Instructed Second Language Acquisition' by Rod Ellis. Copyright © by Rod Ellis. Reprinted by permission of the author.

Chapter 4
Figure 1: Sato, K. & Takahashi, K. (2008). Curriculum revitalization in a Japanese high school: Teacher-teacher and teacher-university collaboration. In D. Hayes & J. Sharkey (Eds.), Revitalizing a curriculum for school-age learners (pp. 205–238). Alexandria, VA: TESOL.

Figure 2: Agosti, C. (2006). Seizing the Opportunity for Change: The Business Preparation Progam, a New Pathway to Gain Direct Entry into Macquarie University. In M. A. Snow & L. Kamhi-Stein (Eds.), Developing a new course for adult learners (pp. 99–122). Alexandria, VA: TESOL.

Figure 3: Sharkey, J. & Cade, L. (2008). Living things are interdependent: An ecological perspective on curriculum revitalization In D. Hayes & J. Sharkey (Eds.), Revitalizing a curriculum for school-age learners (pp. 179–204). Alexandria, VA: TESOL.

Figure 4: Adapted from Graves, K. (2006). Preface to P. McKay (Ed.), Planning and teaching creatively within a required curriculum for school-age learners (pp. v–vii). Alexandria, VA: TESOL

Chapter 6
Figure 1: Teaching and learning second language listening: metacognition in action by Vandergrift, Larry; Goh, Christine Chuen Meng. © 2012. Reproduced with permission of TAYLOR & FRANCIS GROUP LLC - BOOKS in the format Textbook via Copyright Clearance Center.

Appendix B: Teaching and learning second language listening: metacognition in action by Vandergrift, Larry; Goh, Christine Chuen Meng. © 2012. Reproduced with permission of TAYLOR & FRANCIS GROUP LLC - BOOKS in the format Textbook via Copyright Clearance Center.

Chapter 7
Table 1: Vandergrift, L. (1997). The comprehension strategies of second language (French) listeners: A descriptive study. Foreign Language Annals, 30(3), 387–409. ©John Wiley & Sons. This material is reproduced with permission of John Wiley & Sons, Inc.

Figure 1: Flowerdew, John and Miller, Lindsay (1995), Academic Listening, Figure 6.1, page 86. Cambridge University Press.

Figure 2: http://en.wikipedia.org/wiki/File:Human_skeleton_front_en.svg

Figure 3: http://en.wikipedia.org/wiki/File:Human_skeleton_front_en.svg

Chapter 9
Figure 1: Touchstone level 1 students book with Audio CD/CD-ROM, by Michael J. McCarthy, Jeanne McCarten and Helen Sandiford. © 2005 Cambridge University Press. Reprinted with permission.

Figure 2: From Collins/Maples, *Time Zones 1: Student Book*, 1E. © 2010 Cengage Learning

Figure 3: From Frazier/Frazier, *Time Zones 2 with MultiROM,* 1E. © 2011 Cengage Learning

Figure 4: Four Corners Level 2 Students Book with Self-study CD-ROM, by Jack C. Richards and David Bolke. © 2005 Cambridge University Press. Reprinted with permission.

Chapter 10
Figure 1: Adapted from Teaching Pronunciation: A Course Book and Reference Course (2nd ed.) by M. Celce-Murcia, D. M. Brinton, & J. M. Goodwin, 2010, p. 61. © 2010, Cambridge University Press. Reprinted with the permission of Cambridge University Press.

Figure 2: Adapted from Teaching Pronunciation: A Course Book and Reference Course (2nd ed.) by M. Celce-Murcia, D. M. Brinton, & J. M. Goodwin, 2010, p. 61. © 2010, Cambridge University Press. Reprinted with the permission of Cambridge University Press.

Figure 3: Adapted from Teaching Pronunciation: A Course Book and Reference Course (2nd ed.) by M. Celce-Murcia, D. M. Brinton, & J. M. Goodwin, 2010, p. 61. © 2010, Cambridge University Press. Reprinted with the permission of Cambridge University Press.

Figure 4: Adapted from Teaching Pronunciation: A Course Book and Reference Course (2nd ed.) by M. Celce-Murcia, D. M. Brinton, & J. M. Goodwin, 2010, p. 61. © 2010, Cambridge University Press. Reprinted with the permission of Cambridge University Press.

Chapter 12
Figure 1: Grabe, William; Stoller, Fredricka L., Teaching and researching: Reading, 2nd edition, © 2012. Reprinted by permission of Pearson Education, Inc., Upper Saddle River, NJ.

Figure 2: Grabe, William; Stoller, Fredricka L., Teaching and researching: Reading, 2nd edition, © 2012. Reprinted by permission of Pearson Education, Inc., Upper Saddle River, NJ.

Figure 3: Grabe, William; Stoller, Fredricka L., Teaching and researching: Reading, 2nd edition, © 2012. Reprinted by permission of Pearson Education, Inc., Upper Saddle River, NJ.

Figure 16: Grabe, William; Stoller, Fredricka L., Teaching and researching: Reading, 2nd edition, © 2012. Reprinted by permission of Pearson Education, Inc., Upper Saddle River, NJ

Figure 17: Adapted from Day, R., & Bamford, J. (1998). Extensive reading in the second language. New York, NY: Cambridge University Press.

Chapter 21
Figure 5: Gottlieb, M., Katz, A., & Ernst-Slavit, G. (2009). Paper to practice: Using the TESOL English language proficiency standards in PreK-12 classrooms. Alexandria, VA: TESOL.

Appendix B: Used with permission.

Chapter 22
Figure 9: © jmoor17/iStockphoto

Chapter 27
Figure 5: Snow, M.A., & Kamhi-Stein (Eds.). (2006). Developing a new course for adult learners. Alexandria, VA: TESOL

Figure 7: Lopriore, L. (2009). Content learning in English: Issues and perspectives. In K. Graves & L. Lopriore (Eds.), Developing a new curriculum for school-age learners (pp. 173–196). Alexandria, VA: TESOL.

Chapter 28
Figure 6: Adapted from a task in Nunan, D. 1995. ATLAS: Learning-Centered Communication. Boston MA: Heinle & Heinle. p. 97

Chapter 29
Figure 6: Based on Bitterlin, G., Johnson, D., Price, D., Ramirez, S., & Savage, K. L. (2008a). Ventures student book 1. New York, NY: © 2008, Cambridge University Press. Reprinted with permission

Figure 8: Based on Bitterlin, G., Johnson, D., Price, D., Ramirez, S., & Savage, K. L. (2008a). Ventures student book 1. New York, NY: © 2008, Cambridge University Press. Reprinted with permission.

Chapter 32
Short narrative "John and Bobby": Heyer, Sandra, True stories in the news: A beginning reader, 2nd edition, ©1996. Reprinted by permission of Pearson Education, Inc., Upper Saddle River, NJ.

TEXT: A Coral Reef: Lahav, D., Barzel, S., & Shrire, S. (2003). Earth matters: English outline series., p. 35. Tel Aviv, Israel: Center for Educational Technology. © All rights are reserved.

Chapter 33
Text: Purpura, James E; Pinkley, Diane, On Target 1, Intermediate, 2nd edition, © 2000. Reprinted by permission of Pearson Education, Inc., Upper Saddle River, NJ.

Figure 1: Rebecca Oxford, Teaching & Researching: Language Learning Strategies, p. 24. Reprinted with permission from Pearson Education.

Chapter 36
Figure 4: © Amy Eckert/Getty Images

Chapter 37
Figure 4: Pasternak, M., & Bailey, K. M. (2004). Preparing nonnative and native English-speaking teachers: Issues of professionalism and proficiency. In L. D. Kamhi-Stein (Ed.), Learning and teaching from experience: Perspectives on nonnative English-speaking professionals (pp. 155–175). Ann Arbor, MI: University of Michigan Press.

Chapter 38
Figure 1: Sintagma: Action Research by Van Lier, L. (1994) from Sintagma, 6, 31–37. Reprinted with permission.

Preface

Introduction

This is the fourth edition of *Teaching English as a Second or Foreign Language*, Cengage Learning's comprehensive textbook for use in courses designed to prepare teachers of English as a second language (ESL) or English as a foreign language (EFL). Although designed primarily as a textbook for a preservice teaching English as a second/foreign language methods course, this volume is also a useful reference and guide for those who are already teaching ESL or EFL without having had specific training and for practicing teachers who received their training some time ago and are looking to update their knowledge of the field. The field of Teaching English to Speakers of Other Languages is dynamic and constantly evolving, and the many developments between 2001 (the publication date of the third edition of the text) and 2013 have demonstrated the need for this new edition. The latest research findings are included and integrated with time-tested features of classroom practice.

Purpose in Preparing the Text

Our purpose in preparing this fourth edition of *Teaching English as a Second or Foreign Language* (also known as the "Apple Book") remains the same as for the first (1979), second (1991), and third (2001) editions: to produce the best and most comprehensive introduction to the teaching of English to speakers of other languages. Our conceptual approach has been to reflect the most recent findings of current approaches to the teaching and learning of second languages, and to maintain a balance between theory and practice—that is, between providing necessary background information and relevant research, on the one hand, and offering many classroom suggestions and resources for teachers, on the other.

Organization of the Book

This edition covers all areas that are critical to successful language instruction and is organized into six units:

1. **Foundations of Methodology**: an overview of past and present teaching approaches and related research
2. **Language Skills**: the treatment of and techniques for teaching the four language skills (including pronunciation) plus grammar and vocabulary, along with guidance on how to assess these skills through large-scale and classroom-based assessment
3. **Skills for Teachers**: a close examination of skills that teachers need to be effective
4. **Integrated Approaches**: options for integrating the teaching of language skills with content
5. **Focus on the Learner**: information on language learners relevant to classroom instruction
6. **Focus on the Teacher**: issues for the professional development of language teachers

As editors, we have worked to produce an introduction to the field that is of sufficient depth and breadth to be suitable for students with some previous teaching experience yet straightforward enough not to needlessly bewilder the novice.

Features

Each chapter begins with key questions that preview the content of the chapter. Next is an "experience," or example of how the topic at hand plays out in the classroom or in the life of an ESL/EFL learner or teacher. This is followed by a section that defines the topic and introduces readers to key concepts and terminology. These early sections frame the chapter and are referred to when appropriate. Chapters continue with a discussion of conceptual underpinnings (i.e., research and theory) followed by classroom applications. The body of each chapter ends with a section on future trends, a conclusion, and a bulleted summary. Following the body of the chapter are discussion questions, suggested activities, and recommendations for further reading. These supplementary materials suggest ways in which the chapters can be used in methodology courses to stimulate critical thinking, application of the material presented, and further exploration of the topic.

New to this Edition

This new edition covers more topics and has more contributing authors than the previous ones:

- First edition (1979): 31 chapters, 27 contributors;
- Second edition (1991): 32 chapters, 36 contributors;
- Third edition (2001): 36 chapters, 40 contributors;
- Fourth edition (2013): 40 chapters, 46 contributors.

Twenty-three of the 40 authors who contributed to the third edition have also contributed to this volume (often—but not always—on the same topic). Eighteen of the chapters appearing in this edition are revised and updated versions of chapters in the third edition, and in most cases, the revisions have been substantial. Eleven chapters have been completely rewritten by new authors. The following 11 chapters are on topics that appear for the first time in this edition:

> Principles of Instructed Second Language Learning (Rod Ellis)
>
> Teaching English in the Context of World Englishes (Marianne Celce-Murcia)
>
> Fluency-Oriented Second Language Teaching (David Bohlke)
>
> Developing Engaged Second Language Readers (Neil J Anderson)
>
> Spoken Grammar (Michael McCarthy & Anne O'Keeffe)
>
> Assessment in Second Language Classrooms (Anne Katz)
>
> Tools and Techniques of Effective Second/ Foreign Language Teaching (Donna M. Brinton)
>
> Teaching Language through Discourse (Marianne Celce-Murcia & Elite Olshtain)
>
> Task-Based Teaching and Learning (David Nunan)
>
> Motivation in Second Language Learning (Zoltán Dörnyei)
>
> Teaching Young Learners in English as a Second/Foreign Language Settings (Joan Kang Shin)

Many of these topics were suggested by users of the third edition and by reviewers commissioned by the publisher to provide feedback for the fourth edition. This feedback guided our decisions as we planned the new edition and led to revisions and expansion of the scope and content. In addition, the fourth edition has been greatly enriched by the addition of a more international focus—both in terms of the diverse settings in which the authors work and teach, and in the examples from second and foreign language classrooms they used to illustrate their topics.

Ancillary Materials

A new feature of this edition is the companion website (http://www.NGL.Cengage.com/tesfl), which accompanies this text. For each chapter, there is a list of Internet links with useful information to help the reader explore related research and teaching suggestions. There are also expanded biographical statements for all the authors to supplement the list of contributors and their affiliations on pp. x–xi. Perhaps the most important feature of the website is the glossary, which defines the hundreds of key terms introduced in the book. We have prepared this glossary as a tool to assist the reader.

Editors/Authors

This fourth edition benefits greatly from having three co-editors: Donna Brinton and Ann Snow have joined with Marianne Celce-Murcia to bring their expertise and knowledge of the field to the task of compiling this edition. Marianne Celce-Murcia is professor emerita of applied linguistics at the University of California, Los Angeles (UCLA) and served as the editor of the previous three editions of this book. Donna Brinton is a retired member of the TESL and applied linguistics faculty at UCLA, and has also served on the faculty of the University of Southern California and Soka University of America; she brings extensive expertise as an author and editor. Ann Snow is professor of education at California State University, Los Angeles; she has significant experience as an author, researcher, series consultant, and editor. (See longer biographies for all three editors on the companion website [http://www.NGL.Cengage.com/tesfl].)

Suggestions on How to Use the Book

Our goal in compiling this volume has been to produce a comprehensive introduction to the field—one that would serve both as a course text and as a resource for the ESL/EFL teacher's professional library. As a result, the book may contain too much material for a single methods course. Thus, we advise instructors using this volume as a course text to be selective and to focus on the chapters most relevant to preparing their students as classroom teachers; alternatively, instructors may consider dividing up the content of the text over two or more courses. Different instructors and different teacher-preparation programs emphasize different topics and organize courses differently. This is understandable, and thus there is flexibility in how instructors will choose to use the book.

There are many options available for using *Teaching English as a Second or Foreign Language.* Using it as a course text, instructors can tailor the reading list to the anticipated needs of their students, taking into account the length of the course and its focus. In addition to simply assigning chapters to be read, many instructors assign pairs or small groups of students to present and lead a discussion on individual chapters of their choice. Instructors with access to a course management system may also wish to have students respond to selected end-of-chapter discussion questions by posting their answers in the online discussion forum section and also by responding to their peers' contributions. Any chapters that are not covered in a course as a result of time constraints will become useful reference materials for the teacher in training, whose interests, needs,

and target student population may well change after the completion of the methods course and the teacher education program. Finally, the book can serve as a single, comprehensive reference for language methodology—just as it is useful to have a comprehensive dictionary or a comprehensive reference grammar.

We welcome comments and feedback on this edition. In our role as teachers, we all have much to learn from one another.

Acknowledgments

Many colleagues, students, and friends have been of invaluable assistance in the preparation of this volume. Our greatest debt is to all the colleagues who graciously accepted our invitation to write or rewrite chapters for this fourth edition. The breadth and depth of their expertise make this collection truly unique.

We are especially indebted to many people at National Geographic Learning/Cengage Learning who have supported the production of this edition. Thanks, first of all, to our editor Tom Jefferies, who has shepherded this project from the initial planning to final production and who has been extremely helpful and supportive. We are also most grateful to our content project manager Andrea Bobotas and to our copy editor, Julie Nemer. Thanks also to those who have helped to prepare the authors' contracts (Vanessa Richards, David Spain, and Timothy Paquet), to obtain permissions (Julie Berggren, Kavitha Kuttikan, Catherine Pare, Gabriel Feldstein, and Miranda Paquet), and to ready the manuscript for production (Liza Ruano). We also thank Sarah Barnicle for her feedback on many chapters.

Finally, we have greatly appreciated the patience and encouragement of friends and family throughout the lengthy preparation process. We accept full responsibility for any errors or shortcomings due to our actions or inactions as editors.

Marianne Celce-Murcia, University of California, Los Angeles (emerita)
Donna M. Brinton, University of California, Los Angeles (retired)
Marguerite Ann Snow, California State University, Los Angeles

Contributors

Note: To see full biographies of the contributors, please consult the companion website for this book (NGL.Cengage.com/tesfl).

Neil J Anderson is professor of linguistics and English language at Brigham Young University in Provo, Utah.

Kathleen M. Bailey is professor of applied linguistics at the Monterey Institute of International Studies and also a professor in the Teaching English to Speakers of Other Languages (TESOL) Master's Program of Anaheim University in California.

David Bohlke is a materials writer, editor, and teacher educator who has taught English as a foreign language, has worked in publishing as an editor, and now also does international teacher training.

Donna M. Brinton is an educational consultant who has held academic and/or administrative positions at the University of California, Los Angeles; Soka University of America; and the University of Southern California.

Pat Byrd is professor emerita in the Department of Applied Linguistics and English as a Second Language at Georgia State University in Atlanta.

Marianne Celce-Murcia is professor emerita of applied linguistics at the University of California, Los Angeles.

JoAnn (Jodi) Crandall is former co-director of the MA TESOL Program and director of the Language, Literacy and Culture PhD Program at the University of Maryland, Baltimore County.

Zoltán Dörnyei is professor of psycholinguistics in the School of English Studies at the University of Nottingham, United Kingdom.

Patricia A. Duff is professor of language and literacy education at the University of British Columbia, Canada.

Anne M. Ediger is professor of TESOL and applied linguistics at Hunter College of the City University of New York.

Rod Ellis is professor in the Department of Applied Language Studies and Linguistics at the University of Auckland in New Zealand; he is also a professor at Anaheim University in California and visiting professor at Shanghai International Studies University.

Janet L. Eyring is professor of TESOL in the Department of Modern Languages and Literatures at California State University, Fullerton.

Shannon Fitzsimmons-Doolan is a consultant based in Corpus Christi, Texas, doing professional development of kindergarten through 12th-grade (K–12) teachers on sheltered instruction for organizations such as the Center for Applied Linguistics in Washington, DC.

John Flowerdew is professor of English at the City University of Hong Kong.

Jan Frodesen is director of the English for Multilingual Students Program in the Department of Linguistics at the University of California, Santa Barbara.

Christine C. M. Goh is professor of linguistics and language education at the National Institute of Education at Nanyang Technological University in Singapore.

Janet Goodwin is lecturer at the University of California, Los Angeles, where she coordinates the International Teaching Assistant Program.

William Grabe is Regents' Professor of Applied Linguistics in the English Department at Northern Arizona University in Flagstaff.

Kirby Grabowski is lecturer in linguistics and language education at Teachers College, Columbia University in New York City.

Kathleen Graves is associate professor of education practice in the School of Education at the University of Michigan, Ann Arbor.

Eli Hinkel is professor in the Department of Anthropology at Seattle University, where she teaches courses in linguistics and applied linguistics.

Ann M. Johns is professor emerita of linguistics and writing studies at San Diego State University in California.

Lía D. Kamhi-Stein is professor of education in the TESOL MA Program at California State University, Los Angeles.

Anne Katz is a consultant who has taught graduate courses in curriculum and learner assessment at the Graduate Institute of the School for International Training in Brattleboro, Vermont, and at the New School in New York City.

Antony John Kunnan is professor of education and TESOL at California State University, Los Angeles.

Diane Larsen-Freeman is professor of linguistics and of education in the English Language Institute and faculty associate in the Center for the Study of Complex Systems at the University of Michigan, Ann Arbor. She is also a distinguished research fellow at the School for International Training in Brattleboro, Vermont.

Anne Lazaraton is associate professor of second language studies at the University of Minnesota in Minneapolis.

Michael McCarthy is professor emeritus of applied linguistics at the University of Nottingham, United Kingdom; adjunct professor of applied linguistics at the University of Limerick, Ireland; and visiting professor of applied linguistics at the University of Newcastle, United Kingdom.

Mary McGroarty is professor of English at Northern Arizona University in Flagstaff.

Sandra Lee McKay is professor emeritus of English at San Francisco State University.

Susan Finn Miller is a consultant and teaches at the University of Pennsylvania in Philadelphia and at Eastern Mennonite University in Harrisonburg, Virginia.

Lindsay Miller is associate professor in the Department of English at City University of Hong Kong.

John M. Murphy is professor in the Department of Applied Linguistics and ESL at Georgia State University in Atlanta.

David Nunan is professor emeritus of applied linguistics at the University of Hong Kong, vice president for academic affairs at Anaheim University in California, and professor of education at the University of New South Wales in Sydney, Australia.

Anne O'Keeffe is senior lecturer at Mary Immaculate College at the University of Limerick in Ireland.

Elite Olshtain is professor emerita of language education at Hebrew University in Jerusalem, where she was also director of the National Council of Jewish Women's Research Institute for Innovation in Education and held the Wollens Chair for Research in Education.

Donna Price is associate professor of ESL in the Continuing Education Program at San Diego Community College.

Kitty B. Purgason is professor of applied linguistics and TESOL in the Cook School of Intercultural Studies at Biola University, Los Angeles area.

James E. Purpura is associate professor of linguistics and education at Teachers College, Columbia University in New York City.

Cynthia Schuemann is professor of ESL and linguistics at Miami Dade College in Florida.

Joan Kang Shin is the director of the TESOL Professional Training programs at the University of Maryland, Baltimore County.

Marguerite Ann Snow is professor of education at California State University, Los Angeles, where she teaches in the TESOL MA Program.

Maggie Sokolik is a lecturer in the College Writing Programs at the University of California, Berkeley.

Fredricka L. Stoller is professor of English in the MA TESL and Applied Linguistics PhD programs at Northern Arizona University.

Sara Cushing Weigle is professor of applied linguistics and chair of the Department of Applied Linguistics and ESL at Georgia State University in Atlanta.

Cheryl Boyd Zimmerman is professor of TESOL in the Department of Modern Languages and Literatures at California State University, Fullerton.

To our colleagues, who encouraged
us to undertake this new edition, and
to our contributors, who made it possible

UNIT I

Foundations of Methodology

1 | An Overview of Language Teaching Methods and Approaches

MARIANNE CELCE-MURCIA

KEY QUESTIONS

➤ What are the methods and approaches that language teachers have used over the years to teach foreign or second languages?

➤ What are the current methodological trends and challenges?

➤ Where does language teaching methodology appear to be heading?

EXPERIENCE

A committee of professors reviewing applications for their graduate program in TESOL come upon the statement of another applicant who declares in his statement of purpose that he wishes to be admitted to discover or (more ambitiously) to develop the one best method for teaching English as a second or foreign language. Several committee members utter words of impatience and disappointment:

"Oh, no! Not another one!"
"Here we go again!"

The reasons for the committee's reactions to this statement of purpose will become clear in the course of this chapter.

WHAT IS A METHOD OR AN APPROACH TO LANGUAGE TEACHING?

Anthony (1963) was one of the first applied linguists to distinguish the terms *approach, method,* and *technique* as they apply to language teaching.[1] For Anthony, an approach reflects a theoretical model or research paradigm. It provides a broad philosophical perspective on language teaching, such as found in the justifications for the direct method, the reading approach, or the communicative approach (all are discussed in this chapter). A method, on the other hand, is a set of procedures for Anthony. It spells out rather precisely in a step-by-step manner how to teach a second or foreign language. Examples of methods are the Silent Way, Community Language Learning, and Suggestopedia (all of which are also described here). A method is more specific than an approach but less specific than a technique. Anthony's methods are typically compatible with one (or sometimes two) approaches. A technique in Anthony's system is a specific classroom activity; it thus represents the most specific and concrete of the three concepts that he discusses. Some techniques are widely used and found in many methods (e.g., dictation, listen and repeat drills, and read the passage and fill in the blanks); other techniques, however, are specific to or characteristic of a given method (e.g., using cuisenaire rods in the Silent Way) (Gattegno, 1976).

A more recent framework for discussing language teaching methodology has been proposed by Richards and Rodgers (2001); it is presented in Figure 1. Richards and Rodgers use *method* as the most general and overarching term. Under method, they have the terms *approach, design,* and *procedure.* Their use of the term *approach* is similar to Anthony's use, but their concept is more comprehensive and explicit. It includes theories of the nature of language (including units of language analysis) and the nature of language learning with reference to psychological and pedagogical principles. The design portion of Richards and

2

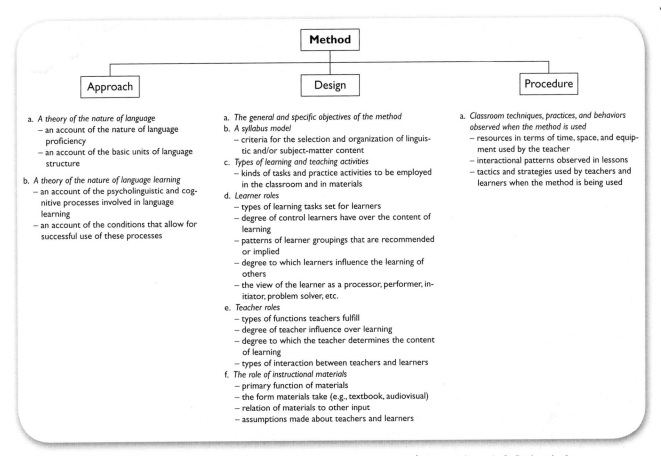

Figure 1. Summary of elements and subelements that constitute a method (adapted from J. C. Richards & T. S. Rodgers, 2001).

Rodgers's framework entails the curriculum objectives and syllabus types (e.g., structural, notional-functional, or content-based). (See Graves, this volume.) It also includes learning and teaching activities and spells out the roles of teachers and learners. Finally, it includes instructional materials along with their form, function, and role in the teaching-learning process. The term *procedure* for Richards and Rodgers refers to techniques, practices, behaviors, and equipment observable in the classroom. The interactional patterns and the strategies used by teachers and students are also part of their procedural component. (See Brinton, this volume.)

CONCEPTUAL UNDERPINNINGS

The field of second language (L2) teaching has undergone many fluctuations and shifts over the years. In contrast to disciplines like physics or chemistry, in which progress is more or less steady until a major discovery causes a radical theoretical revision (referred to as a paradigm shift by Kuhn, 1970), language teaching is a field in which fads and heroes have come and gone in a manner fairly consistent with the kinds of changes that occur when people jump from one bandwagon to the next (M. Clarke, 1982). One reason for the frequent swings of the pendulum is that very few language teachers have a sense of history about their profession and are thus unaware of the linguistic, psychological, and sociocultural underpinnings of the many methodological options they have at their disposal. It is hoped that this overview will encourage language teachers to learn more about the origins of their profession. Such knowledge will ensure some perspective when teachers evaluate any so-called innovations or new approaches to methodology, developments that will surely arise in the future.

Pre-twentieth-century trends: A survey of key approaches

Prior to the twentieth century, language teaching methodology vacillated between two types of approaches: getting learners to use a language (i.e., to speak and understand it) and getting learners to analyze a language (i.e., to learn its grammatical rules). Both the classical Greek and medieval Latin periods were characterized by an emphasis on teaching people to use foreign languages. The classical languages, first Greek and then Latin, were used as lingua francas (i.e., languages used for communication among people speaking different first languages). Higher learning was conducted primarily through these languages all over Europe. Manuscripts and letters were written in these languages. They were used widely in philosophy, religion, politics, and business. Thus the educated elite became fluent speakers, readers, and writers of the classical language appropriate to their time and context (Prator, 1974).

We can assume that during these earlier eras language teachers or tutors used informal and more or less direct approaches to convey the form and meaning of the language they were teaching and that they used aural-oral techniques with no language textbooks per se; instead, they probably had a small stock of hand-copied written manuscripts of some sort, perhaps a few texts in the target language (the language being learned), or crude dictionaries that listed equivalent words in two or more languages side by side.

During the Renaissance, the formal study of the grammars of Greek and Latin became popular through the mass production of books made possible by Gutenberg's invention of moveable type and the printing press in 1440. In the case of Latin, it was discovered that the grammar of the classical texts was different from that of the Latin then being used as a lingua franca—the latter subsequently being labeled vulgate Latin (the Latin of the common people). Major differences had developed between the classical Latin described in the Renaissance grammars, which became the formal object of instruction in schools, and the Latin being used for everyday purposes. This occurred at about the same time that Latin was gradually beginning to be abandoned as a lingua franca. No one was speaking classical Latin as a first language anymore, and various European vernaculars (languages with an oral tradition but with little or no written tradition) had begun to rise in respectability and popularity; these vernacular languages, such as French and German, had begun to develop their own written traditions (Prator, 1974).[2]

Since the European vernaculars had grown in prestige and utility, it is not surprising that people in one country or region began to find it necessary and useful to learn the language of another country or region. Thus during the early seventeenth century the focus on language study shifted from an exclusive analysis of the classical languages back to a focus on utility. Perhaps the most famous language teacher and methodologist of this period is Johann (or Jan) Amos Comenius, a Czech scholar and teacher, who published books about his teaching techniques between 1631 and 1658. Some of the techniques that Comenius used and espoused were:

- Use imitation instead of rules to teach a language.
- Have your students repeat after you.
- Use a limited vocabulary initially.
- Help your students practice reading and speaking.
- Teach language through pictures to make it meaningful.

Thus Comenius, perhaps for the first time, made explicit an essentially inductive approach to learning a foreign language (i.e., an approach based on exposure to the target language in use rather than through rules), the goal of which was to teach the use rather than the analysis of the language being taught (Kelly, 1969).

The next section of this chapter outlines the major approaches that still resonate and influence the practice of language teaching today—some to a greater and some to a lesser degree.

The grammar-translation approach. Comenius's progressive views held sway for some time; however, by the beginning of the nineteenth century, the systematic study of the grammar of classical Latin and of classical texts had once again taken hold in schools and universities throughout Europe. The analytical grammar-translation approach became firmly entrenched as a way to teach not only Latin but also, by extension, the vernaculars that had become modern languages as well. Grammar-translation was perhaps best codified in the work of Karl Ploetz (1819–1881), a German scholar who had a tremendous influence on the language teaching profession during his lifetime and afterward. The following is a synthesis of the key elements of the grammar-translation approach (Kelly, 1969):

- Instruction is given in the native language of the students.
- There is little use of the target language for communication.
- The focus is on grammatical parsing, that is, the forms and inflections of words.
- There is early reading of difficult texts.
- A typical exercise is to translate sentences from the target language into the mother tongue (or vice versa).
- The result of this approach is usually an inability on the part of the student to use the language for communication.
- The teacher does not have to be able to speak the target language fluently.

The direct method. The swinging of the pendulum continued. By the end of the nineteenth century, the direct method, which once more stressed as its goal the ability to use rather than to analyze a language, had begun to function as a viable alternative to grammar-translation. François Gouin, a Frenchman, began to publish his work on the direct method in 1880.[3] He advocated exclusive use of the target language in the classroom, having been influenced by an older friend, the German philosopher-scientist Alexander von Humboldt, who had espoused the notion that a language cannot be taught, that one can only create conditions for learning to take place (Kelly, 1969). The direct method became very popular in France and Germany, and even today it has enthusiastic followers among language teachers in many countries (as does the grammar-translation approach). Key features of the direct method are:

- No use of the mother tongue is permitted (i.e., the teacher does not need to know the students' native language).
- Lessons begin with dialogues and anecdotes in modern conversational style.
- Actions and pictures are used to make meanings clear.

- Grammar is learned inductively (i.e., by repeated exposure to language in use, not through rules about forms).
- Literary texts are read for pleasure and are not analyzed grammatically.
- The target culture is also taught inductively.
- The teacher must be a native speaker or have native-like proficiency in the target language.

The influence of the direct method grew; it crossed the Atlantic in the early twentieth century when Emile de Sauzé, a disciple of Gouin, traveled to Cleveland, Ohio, to see to it that all foreign language instruction in the public schools there implemented the direct method. De Sauzé's endeavor, however, was not completely successful (in Cleveland or elsewhere) since at the time there were too few foreign language teachers in the United States who were highly proficient speakers of the language they were teaching (Prator, 1974).

The reform movement. In 1886, during the same period that the direct method first became popular in Europe, the International Phonetic Association was established by scholars such as Henry Sweet, Wilhelm Viëtor, and Paul Passy. They developed the International Phonetic Alphabet—a transcription system designed to unambiguously represent the sounds of any language—and became part of the reform movement in language teaching in the 1890s. These phoneticians made some of the first truly scientific contributions to language teaching when they advocated principles such as the following (Howatt, 2004):

- The spoken form of a language is primary and should be taught first.
- The findings of phonetics should be applied to language teaching.
- Language teachers must have solid training in phonetics.
- Learners should be given basic phonetic training to establish good speech habits.

The work of these influential phoneticians focused on the teaching of pronunciation and oral skills, which they felt had been ignored in grammar-translation. Thus, although the reform movement is not necessarily considered a full-blown pedagogical approach to language teaching, its adherents did have a significant influence on certain subsequent approaches, as we will see.

Early and mid-twentieth-century approaches

The reading approach. In the early decades of the twentieth century, the Modern Language Association of America, based on the Coleman Report (Coleman, 1929), endorsed the reading approach to language teaching. The report's authors felt that, given the skills and limitations of most language teachers, all that one could reasonably expect was for students to come away from the study of a foreign language being able to read the target language, with emphasis on some of the great works of literature and philosophy that had been produced in that language. As reflected in the work of Michael West (1941) and others, this approach held sway in North America until the late 1930s and early 1940s. Elements of the reading approach are:

- Only the grammar useful for reading comprehension is taught.
- Vocabulary is controlled at first (based on frequency and usefulness) and then expanded.
- Translation is once more a respectable classroom procedure.
- Reading comprehension is the only language skill emphasized.
- The teacher does not need to have good oral proficiency in the target language.
- The first language is used to present reading material, discuss it, and check understanding.

The audiolingual approach. Some historians of language teaching (e.g., Howatt, 2004) believe that the earlier reform movement played a role in the simultaneous development of both the audiolingual approach in the United States and the oral-situational approach in Britain (discussed next). When World War II broke out and made it imperative for the U.S. military to quickly and efficiently teach members of the armed forces how to speak foreign languages and to understand them when spoken by native speakers, the U.S. government hired linguists to help teach languages and develop materials: the audiolingual approach was born (Fries, 1945). It drew on both the reform movement and the direct method but added features from structural linguistics and behavioral psychology. Structural linguistics begins with describing minimally distinctive sound units (phonemes), which then form lexical and grammatical elements (morphemes), which then form higher structures such as phrases and clauses/sentences (Bloomfield, 1933). In behavioral psychology, learning is based on getting learners to repeat behaviors (verbal or nonverbal) until they become fully learned habits (Skinner, 1957). The audiolingual approach became dominant in the United States during the late 1940s, 1950s, and 1960s. Its features include:

- Lessons begin with dialogues.
- Mimicry and memorization are used, based on the assumption that language learning is habit formation.
- Grammatical structures are sequenced and rules are taught inductively (through planned exposure).
- Skills are sequenced: first listening and speaking are taught; reading and writing are postponed.
- Accurate pronunciation is stressed from the beginning.
- Vocabulary is severely controlled and limited in the initial stages.
- A great effort is made to prevent learner errors.
- Language is often manipulated without regard to meaning or context.
- The teacher must be proficient only in the structures, vocabulary, and other aspects of the language that he or she is teaching, since learning activities and materials are carefully controlled.

The oral-situational approach. In Britain the same historical pressures that prompted the development of the audiolingual approach gave rise to the oral or situational approach (Eckersley, 1955). It arose as a reaction to the reading approach and its lack of emphasis on listening and speaking skills (Howatt, 2004). This approach was dominant in Britain during the late 1940s, 1950s, and 1960s; it drew on the reform movement and the direct approach but added features from Firthian linguistics (Firth, 1957)[4] and the emerging professional field of language pedagogy. It also drew on the experience that Britain's language educators had accrued in oral approaches to foreign language teaching (e.g., Palmer, 1921/1964). Although influenced by, but less dogmatic than, its American counterpart (the audiolingual approach), the oral-situational approach advocated organizing structures around situations (e.g., "at the pharmacy" or "at the restaurant") that provided the learner with maximum opportunity to practice the target language. However, practice often consisted of little more than pattern practice, choral repetition, or reading of texts and memorization of dialogues. Features of the oral-situational approach include:

- The spoken language is primary.
- All language material is practiced orally before being presented in written form (reading and writing are taught only after an oral base in lexical and grammatical forms has been established).
- Only the target language should be used in the classroom.
- Efforts are made to ensure that the most general and useful lexical items are presented.
- Grammatical structures are graded from simple to complex.
- New items (lexical and grammatical) are introduced and practiced situationally (e.g., "at the post office," "at the bank," "at the dinner table").

More recent approaches to language teaching

In addition to the above approaches whose historical developments have been sketched here, there are four other discernible approaches to foreign language teaching that developed and were widely used during the final quarter of the twentieth century; some of them continue into the early twenty-first century. In this section, I briefly describe key features of the cognitive, affective-humanistic, comprehension-based, and communicative approaches.

The cognitive approach. This approach was a reaction to the behaviorist features of the audiolingual approach, influenced by cognitive psychology and Chomskyan linguistics. Cognitive psychology (Neisser, 1967) holds that people do not learn complex systems like language or mathematics through habit formation but through the acquisition of patterns and rules that they can then extend and apply to new circumstances or problems. Likewise, in Chomskyan linguistics (Chomsky, 1959, 1965),

language acquisition is viewed as the learning of a system of infinitely extendable rules based on meaningful exposure, with hypothesis testing and rule inferencing, not habit formation, driving the learning process. Features of the cognitive approach include:

- Language learning is viewed as rule acquisition, not habit formation.
- Instruction is often individualized; learners are responsible for their own learning.
- Grammar must be taught, but it can be taught deductively (rules first, practice later) and/or inductively (rules can either be stated after practice or left as implicit information for the learners to process on their own).
- Pronunciation is deemphasized; perfection is viewed as unrealistic and unattainable.
- Reading and writing are once again as important as listening and speaking.
- Vocabulary learning is again stressed, especially at intermediate and advanced levels.
- Errors are viewed as inevitable, to be used constructively for enhancing the learning process (for feedback and correction).
- The teacher is expected to have good general proficiency in the target language as well as an ability to analyze the target language.

The affective-humanistic approach. This approach developed as a reaction to the general lack of affective considerations in both the audiolingual approach and the cognitive approach (e.g., Curran, 1976; Moskowitz, 1978).[5] It put emphasis on the social climate in the classroom and the development of positive relationships between the teacher and the learners and among the learners themselves. It argues that learning a language is a social and personal process and that this has to be taken into account in the methods and materials used. Following are some of the defining characteristics of the affective-humanistic approach:

- Respect for each individual (students and teachers) and for their feelings is emphasized.
- Communication that is personally meaningful to the learner is given priority.
- Instruction involves much work in pairs and small groups.
- The class atmosphere is viewed as more important than materials or methods.

- Peer support and interaction are viewed as necessary for learning.
- Learning a second or foreign language is viewed as a self-realization process.
- The teacher is a counselor or facilitator rather than the ultimate source of knowledge.
- The teacher should be proficient in the target language and in the students' native language since translation may be used heavily in the initial stages to help students feel at ease; later, it is gradually phased out.

The comprehension-based approach. This is an outgrowth of research in first language (L1) acquisition that led some language methodologists to assume that second language (L2) learning is very similar to L1 acquisition and that extended exposure and comprehension (i.e., listening with understanding) must precede production (i.e., speaking (Asher, 1996; Krashen & Terrell, 1983; Postovsky, 1974; Winitz, 1981). The best-known of the comprehension-based approaches is Krashen and Terrell's Natural Approach (1983). The characteristics of the comprehension-based approach are:

- Listening comprehension is very important and is viewed as the basic skill that will allow speaking, reading, and writing to develop spontaneously over time, given the right conditions.
- Learners should begin with a silent period by listening to meaningful speech and by responding nonverbally in meaningful ways before they produce language themselves.
- Learners should not speak until they feel ready to do so; such delayed oral production results in better pronunciation than if the learner is expected to speak immediately.
- Learners progress by being exposed to meaningful input that is just one step beyond their level of proficiency.
- Rule learning may help learners monitor (or become aware of) what they do, but it will not aid their acquisition or spontaneous use of the target language.
- Error correction is seen as unnecessary and perhaps even counterproductive; what is important is that the learners can understand and can make themselves understood.

- If the teacher is not a native (or near-native) speaker, appropriate audiovisual materials must be available online and in the classroom or lab to provide the appropriate input for the learners.

The communicative approach. This approach is an outgrowth of the work of anthropological linguists in the United States (e.g., Hymes, 1971) and Firthian linguists in Britain (e.g., Firth, 1957; Halliday, 1973, 1978), all of whom view language as a meaning-based system for communication. (See Duff, this volume, for an extended discussion.) Now serving as an umbrella term for a number of designs and procedures (to use Richards and Rodgers's terminology) the communicative approach includes task-based language teaching and project work, content-based and immersion instruction, and Cooperative Learning (Kagan, 1994), among other instructional frameworks. (See also chapters by Nunan and Snow, this volume.) Some of the salient features and manifestations of the communicative approach are:

- It is assumed that the goal of language teaching is the learners' ability to communicate in the target language.
- It is assumed that the content of a language course will include semantic notions and social functions and that they are as important as linguistic structures.
- In some cases, the content is academic or job-related material, which becomes the course focus with language learning as a simultaneous concern.
- Students regularly work in groups or pairs to transfer and negotiate meaning in situations in which one person has information that the other(s) lack.
- Students often engage in role play or dramatization to adjust their use of the target language to different social contexts.
- Classroom materials and activities often consist of authentic tasks and projects presented and practiced using segments of preexisting meaningful discourse, not materials primarily constructed for pedagogical purposes.
- Skills are integrated from the beginning; a given activity might involve reading, speaking, listening, and also writing (this assumes the learners are educated and literate).

Table 1. Central Principles of Four Current Approaches to Language Teaching

Approach	Central Principle
Cognitive approach	Language learning is rule-governed cognitive behavior (not habit formation).
Affective-humanistic approach	Learning a foreign language is a process of self-realization and of relating to other people.
Comprehension approach	Language acquisition occurs if and only if the learner receives and comprehends sufficient meaningful input.
Communicative approach	The purpose of language (and thus the goal of language teaching and learning) is communication.

- The teacher's role is primarily to facilitate communication and secondarily to correct errors.
- The teacher should be able to use the target language fluently and appropriately.

To sum up, we can see that certain features of several of the pre-twentieth-century approaches arose in reaction to perceived inadequacies or impracticalities in an earlier approach or approaches. The more recent approaches developed in the twentieth century and expanded in the early twenty-first century also do this to some extent; however, each one is based on a slightly different theory or view of how people learn or use second languages, and each has a central principle around which everything else revolves, as summarized in Table 1.

Designer methods. In addition to the four approaches already discussed, several other methods proliferated in the 1970s and 1980s; these have been labeled designer methods by Nunan (1989b). These methods were rather specific in terms of the procedures and materials that the teacher, who typically required special training, was supposed to use. They were almost always developed and defined by one person. This person, in turn, trained practitioners who accepted the method as gospel and helped to spread the word. Several of these methods and their originators follow with brief descriptions:

Silent Way. (Gattegno, 1976) Using an array of visuals (e.g., rods of different shapes and colors, and charts with words or color-coded sounds), the teacher gets students to practice and learn a new language while saying very little in the process. The method is inductive, and only the target language is used.

Community Language Learning. (Curran, 1976) Sitting in a circle, and with the session being recorded, students decide what they want to say. The teacher as counselor-facilitator then translates and gets learners to practice in the target language the material that was elicited. Later at the board, the teacher goes over the words and structures the class is learning and provides explanations in the L1 as needed.

Total Physical Response. (Asher, 1996) The teacher gives commands, "Stand up!" "Sit down!" and so on and shows learners how to demonstrate comprehension by doing the appropriate physical action as a response. New structures and vocabulary are introduced this way for an extended time. When learners are ready to speak, they begin to give each other commands. Only the target language is used.

Suggestology, Suggestopedia, or Accelerated Learning. (Lozanov, 1978) In a setting more like a living room than a classroom, learners sit in easy chairs and assume a new identity; the teacher, using only the target language, presents a script two times over two days, accompanied by music. This is followed by group or choral reading of the script on the first day, along with songs and games. On the second day, the students elaborate on the script to tell an anecdote or story. The learners have copies of the script along with an L1 translation juxtaposed on the same page. The process continues with new scripts.

The lockstep rigidity found in such designer methods led some applied linguists (e.g., Richards, 1984) to seriously question their usefulness. This aroused a healthy skepticism among language educators, who argued that there is no such thing as a "best" method; Strevens (1977) was among the earliest to articulate skepticism about the various proliferating methods:

> the complex circumstances of teaching and learning languages—with different kinds of pupils, teachers, aims, and objectives, approaches, methods, and materials, classroom techniques and standards of achievement— make it inconceivable that any single method could achieve optimum success in all circumstances. (p. 5)

Adamson (2004) also critiques language teaching methods and suggests that attention now be turned "to the teacher and the learner, and the ways in which they can operate effectively in their educational context, instead of offering generalized, pre-packaged solutions in the shape of teaching materials and strategies" (p. 619).

The post-methods era

Building on the professional consensus that no method could claim supremacy, Prabhu (1990) asks *why* there is no best method. He suggests that there are three possible explanations: (1) different methods are best for different teaching/learning circumstances; (2) all methods have some truth or validity; and (3) the whole notion of what is a good or a bad method is irrelevant. Prabhu argues for the third possibility and concludes that we need to rethink what is "best" such that classroom teachers and applied linguists can develop shared pedagogical perceptions of what real-world classroom teaching is.

Coming from the perspective of critical theory (Foucault, 1980), Pennycook (1989) also challenges the concept of method:

> Method is a prescriptive concept that articulates a positivist, progressivist and patriarchal understanding of teaching and plays an important role in maintaining inequities between, on the one hand, predominantly male academics and, on the other, female teachers and language classrooms on the international power periphery. (p. 589)

Many applied linguists, while not holding as radical a view as that of Pennycook, nonetheless agree that we are in a post-methods era. Beyond what Strevens, Prabhu, and Pennycook have noted, H. D. Brown (2002), in his critique of methods, adds the following two observations: (1) so-called designer methods seem distinctive at the initial stage of learning but soon come to look like any other learner-centered approach; and (2) it has proven impossible to empirically (i.e., quantitatively) demonstrate the superiority of one method over another. Brown (2002) concludes that classroom teachers do best when they ground their pedagogy in "well-established principles of language teaching and learning" (p. 17).

So what are these well-established principles that teachers should apply in the post-methods era? One of the early concrete proposals comes from Kumaravadivelu (1994), who offers a framework consisting of the 10 following macro strategies, which I summarize briefly:

1. *Maximize learning opportunities.* The teacher's job is not to transmit knowledge but to create and manage as many learning opportunities as possible.
2. *Facilitate negotiated interaction.* Learners should initiate classroom talk (not just respond to the teacher's prompts) by asking for clarification, by confirming, by reacting, and so on, as part of teacher-student and student-student interaction.
3. *Minimize perceptual mismatches.* Reduce or avoid mismatches between what the teacher and the learner believe is being taught or should be taught as well as how learner performance should be evaluated.
4. *Activate intuitive heuristics.* Teachers should provide enough data for learners to infer underlying grammatical rules, since it is impossible to explicitly teach all rules of the L2.
5. *Foster language awareness.* Teachers should get learners to attend to and learn the formal properties of the L2 and then to compare and contrast these formal properties with those of the L1.
6. *Contextualize linguistic input.* Meaningful discourse-based activities are needed to help learners see the interaction of grammar, lexicon, and pragmatics in natural language use.
7. *Integrate language skills.* The separation of listening, reading, speaking, and writing is artificial. As in the real world, learners should integrate skills: conversation (listening and speaking), note-taking (listening and writing), self-study (reading and writing), and so on.

8. *Promote learner autonomy.* Teachers should help learners to learn on their own by raising awareness of effective learning strategies and providing problems and tasks that encourage learners to use strategies such as planning and self-monitoring.

9. *Raise cultural consciousness.* Teachers should allow learners to become sources of cultural information so that knowledge about the culture of the L2 and of other cultures (especially those represented by the students) becomes part of classroom communication.

10. *Ensure social relevance:* Acknowledge that language learning has social, political, economic, and educational dimensions that shape the motivation to learn the L2, determine the uses to which the L2 will be put, and define the skills and proficiency level needed in the L2.

Based on these 10 guiding macrostrategies, Kumaravadivelu (1994) suggests that teachers should have the independence to design situation-specific micro strategies, or materials and procedures, to achieve their desired learning objectives. (See Brinton, this volume, for specific instructional strategies.)

Kumaravadivelu (2001, 2006) further elaborates on his 1994 paper, acknowledging that this post-methods era is a transitional period and that post-method pedagogy is a work in progress. He argues that language teachers need to become principled pragmatists, shaping their students' classroom learning through informed teaching and critical reflection. The post-methods teacher is characterized as reflective, autonomous and self-directed (Nunan & Lamb, 1996), and able to elicit authentic pedagogical interaction (van Lier, 1996). Ideally, such teachers will engage in research to refine their practices. (See also chapters by Murphy and Bailey, this volume.)

The post-methods teacher educator moves away from transmitting an established body of knowledge to prospective teachers and, instead, takes into account their beliefs, voices, and visions to develop their critical thinking skills. The goal is to help them develop their own effective pedagogies that will create meaningful collaboration among learners, teachers, and teacher educators (Kumaravadivelu, 2001).

Not all applied linguists are fully convinced that the idealistic proposals that have emerged to date in the post-methods era will work in all settings. Adamson (2004), for example, reviews Kumaravadivelu's 10 macro strategies and notes that this framework might not be applicable where the syllabus and teaching materials are fixed and external examinations are prescribed. In such cases, he feels that teachers may not have sufficient autonomy to implement a post-methods approach. He adds that teachers may also lack access to the professional knowledge that will allow them to develop an approach truly responsive to their learners and their context.

CLASSROOM APPLICATIONS

Recall the TESOL-program applicant described in the opening Experience section, who wanted to discover or develop the one best method to the consternation of the professors on the graduate admissions committee. What is the solution for dealing with this prospective ESL/EFL teacher? The best way for him or her to learn to make wise decisions is to gain knowledge about the various approaches, methods, and frameworks currently available and to identify practices that may prove successful with the learners in the context in which he or she is, or will be, teaching (Larsen-Freeman & Anderson, 2011). This chapter's overview just scratches the surface. Further information is available in the remainder of this volume and in many other books, in journal articles, in presentations and workshops at professional conferences, and on the Internet.

There are at least five things that our applicant to the MA TESOL program should learn to do to make good pragmatic decisions concerning the judicious application of an approach, a design, or a method (including teaching materials) and its techniques or procedures:

1. Assess student needs: Why are they learning English? For what purpose?

2. Examine the instructional constraints: time (hours per week, days per week, and weeks per term), class size (nature of enrollment), materials (set syllabus and text, or completely open to teacher?), and physical factors (classroom size, available audiovisual and technological support). Then decide what and how much can reasonably be taught and how.

3. Determine the attitudes, learning styles, and cultural backgrounds of individual students

to the extent that this is possible, and develop activities and materials consistent with the findings.

4. Identify the discourse genres, speech activities, and text types that the students need to learn so that they can be incorporated into materials and learning activities.

5. Determine how the students' language learning will be assessed, and incorporate learning activities that simulate assessment practices into classroom instruction.

In the course of doing all these, the applicant (having completed his or her training) will be in a position to select the most useful techniques and procedures and to design a productive course of study by drawing on existing research findings and assessing the suitability of available approaches, syllabus/curriculum types, and teaching materials. Clifford Prator, a professor and former colleague of mine, summed up the professional ESL/EFL teacher's responsibility aptly (personal communication):

Adapt; don't adopt.

Our MA program applicant will certainly be in a better position upon graduation to follow Prator's advice if he or she is familiar with the history and the state of the art of our profession as well as with all the options available to the teacher and his or her learners.

FUTURE TRENDS

Finding ways to integrate all that we now know is the challenge for current and future language teachers and for the profession at large. We must build on our past and present knowledge of what works to refine and improve existing language teaching practices and, it is hoped, develop other practices that will be even better and more encompassing. We cannot be satisfied with the current, in-progress state of affairs but must seek out new ways to provide learners with the most effective and efficient language learning experiences possible, taking into account the learners' goals, interests, and learning contexts. Language teachers must also become familiar with the research in the field of instructed second language acquisition. (See Ellis, this volume.) This research offers insights into the teaching and learning of grammar, vocabulary,

and pronunciation, as well as the language skills (listening, speaking, reading, and writing).

Canagarajah (2006) suggests that research into the following six areas could result in new methodological paradigms:

1. *Motivation:* How does the nature and extent of the learner's motivation affect language learning? (See Dörnyei, this volume.)

2. *Learner variability:* How can teachers best accommodate students with different strengths and weaknesses in the same class?

3. *Discourse analysis:* How does the discourse of the classroom and of the materials used by the teacher and generated by the learners contribute to language learning? (See Celce-Murcia & Olshtain, this volume.)

4. *Corpus-based research:* To what extent can corpus-based data be used by teachers and learners to enhance the learning process? (See McCarthy & O'Keeffe, this volume.)

5. *Cognition:* How do the learners' cognitive styles and cognitive strategies influence their language learning and language use? (See Purpura, this volume.)

6. *Social participation:* To what extent can group work, pair work, Cooperative Learning, and well-structured tasks enhance student participation and learning? (See chapters by Brinton and by Nunan, this volume.)

To this list, we add a seventh area—new technologies—since we are only beginning to understand how wide access to and use of the Internet and social media can advance language pedagogy and accelerate language learning. (See Sokolik, this volume.)

CONCLUSION

This is an exciting time to be teaching English as a second or foreign language. The spread of English around the world has created a growing need for qualified teachers—native and non-native speakers. In many countries, children are starting to learn English at an ever-younger age. There is more need than ever for teachers who can deal with English in the workplace. The ever-growing use of English as a lingua franca and the proliferation of varieties of English require careful linguistic description and appropriate pedagogies.

Continual advances in digital technology are opening new channels for teaching and learning. Language teachers must be ready to continually adapt to new and changing circumstances since there is no fixed body of knowledge that one can master and say, "Now I know everything!"

SUMMARY

➤ Many different approaches and methods for L2 instruction have been proposed and developed over the centuries.

➤ New approaches and methods are often developed in direct response to perceived problems with or inadequacies in an existing popular approach or method and/or to the learning theory prevalent at that time.

➤ There has never been and will never be one approach or method that works best in all possible teaching/learning contexts.

➤ Ideally, L2 teachers will develop (with full knowledge of available options and in collaboration with their students) the goals, methods, materials, and activities that work best in their particular contexts.

➤ Some applied linguists claim that we are in a transitional post-methods era in which teachers have opportunities to creatively apply new findings and fine-tune effective past practices to develop, reflect on, and continuously improve their classroom teaching.

DISCUSSION QUESTIONS

1. Which of the approaches discussed in the chapter have you personally experienced as a language learner? What were your impressions, and what is your assessment of the effectiveness of the approach(es)?

2. What is the position regarding the teaching of: (a) pronunciation; (b) grammar; and (c) vocabulary in the many approaches discussed in this chapter? Has there been a swinging of the pendulum with respect to the teaching of these areas? Why or why not?

3. What changes have occurred regarding the relative emphasis on spoken language or written language in the various approaches discussed in this chapter? Why?

4. What has been the role of the native language and the target language in the various approaches and methods?

5. Do you agree or disagree that we are currently in a post-methods era? Explain.

SUGGESTED ACTIVITIES

1. Select an integrated-skills ESL/EFL text that you have used or expect to use. Examine its contents to determine which approach it seems to follow most closely. Support your decision with examples. Discuss any mixing of approaches that you observe.

2. Observe an ESL or EFL class, and make a list of all the procedures that the teacher uses. Based on these observations, hypothesize the main features of the approach and design that the procedures imply.

3. Demonstration of teaching method: In groups, use the Internet and other available sources to research a teaching method/approach from the list that follows. Then plan a lesson illustrating the key features of this method. Be prepared to: (a) present a brief demonstration of the method to your classmates; and (b) explain its key features using the Richards and Rodgers framework. Suggested topics:

• Audiolingual approach	• Natural Approach
• Task-based learning	• Content-based instruction
• Total Physical Response	• Silent Way
• Cooperative Learning	• Oral/situational approach
• Community Language Learning	• Direct method (Berlitz method)
• Project work	• Suggestopedia

FURTHER READING

Howatt, A. P. R. (with Widdowson, H. G.). (2004). *A history of English language teaching* (2nd ed.). Oxford, UK: Oxford University Press.

This book covers the teaching of English from 1400 to the present day.

Kelly, L. G. (1969). *Twenty-five centuries of language teaching*. New York, NY: Newbury House.

This volume goes back to the Greeks and Romans and covers the teaching of all foreign languages (not just English).

Larsen-Freeman, D., & Anderson, M. (2011) *Techniques and principles in language teaching* (3rd ed.). New York, NY: Oxford University Press.

This is a good source for a more detailed look at many of the teaching methods mentioned in this chapter.

Richards, J. C., & Rodgers, T. S. (2001). *Approaches and methods in language teaching: A description and analysis* (2nd ed.). New York, NY: Cambridge University Press.

This text presents a thorough description and analysis of past and current second language teaching approaches.

ENDNOTES

[1] Versions of the first part of this chapter were published in Prator with Celce-Murcia (1979) and Celce-Murcia (2001). This expanded and updated version also draws on Madsen (1979) and Brinton (2011a).

[2] Examples of such written texts are the Gutenberg Bible in German and the *Chanson de Rolande* in French.

[3] The term *direct method* is more widely used than *direct approach*; however, the former is a misnomer, since this is really an approach, not a method, if we follow Anthony's (1963) terminology or that of Richards and Rodgers (2001).

[4] Firthian linguistics is best codified in the work of Firth's best-known student, M. A. K. Halliday (1973), who refers to his approach to language analysis as systemic-functional grammar. Halliday's approach is very different from Chomsky's generative grammar, a highly abstract extension of structuralism and an approach to language that paid explicit attention to the description of linguistic features (Chomsky, 1965). In addition to form and meaning, Halliday also takes social context into account in his theory and description. Halliday's system extends beyond the sentence level, whereas Chomsky's does not. Thus many applied linguists find Halliday's framework better for their purposes than Chomsky's.

[5] The term *humanistic* has two meanings. One refers to the humanities (i.e., literature, history, and philosophy). The other refers to that branch of psychology concerned with the role of the socio-affective domain in human behavior. It is the latter sense that I am referring to here. However, see Stevick (1990) for an even broader perspective on humanism in language teaching.

2 | Communicative Language Teaching

PATRICIA A. DUFF

KEY QUESTIONS

➤ What is communicative language teaching?
➤ How is this approach related to other proficiency-based approaches to language teaching?
➤ How relevant or adaptable is communicative language teaching to language teaching contexts worldwide?

EXPERIENCE

Experience 1: Teaching young adult learners in an ESL context

It is Monday morning and a group of young adult English as a second language (ESL) learners have just arrived for their language class. The teacher starts the class by asking the students about their weekend:

Teacher: So what did you do this weekend?
Student 1: I ran my first marathon!
Teacher: Wow! Did you finish?
Student 1: Yes, eventually. . . . But I can barely walk today!
Several students: Congratulations! Way to go!
Student 2: I saw the latest Harry Potter movie!
Student 3: How did you like it?
Student 2: It was great but not as good as the last one.
Teacher: Did anyone else do anything interesting?
Student 4: I stayed home and finished today's assignment—ha, ha!
Several students: Groan. . . .)

The discussion continues for a few more minutes and one student finally asks the teacher if she had a good weekend. She replies and then announces the focus of today's class: producing personal narratives in the past tense.

WHAT IS COMMUNICATIVE LANGUAGE TEACHING?

Communicative language teaching (CLT) is an approach to language teaching that emphasizes learning a language first and foremost for the purpose of communicating with others. Communication includes finding out about what people did on the weekend, as in Experience 1, or on their last vacation and learning about classmates' interests, activities, preferences, and opinions and conveying one's own. It may also involve explaining daily routines to others who want to know about them, discussing current events, writing an email message with some personal news, or telling others about an interesting book or article or Internet video clip. Although the concept of communication underlying CLT may seem self-evident as a goal for language education, a generation ago (and still in many parts of the world today) teaching and learning another language were often more concerned with language analysis, literary text analysis, memorization, translation, or high-stakes multiple-choice language testing. Instead of describing one's own weekend, students might have read a passage and changed all present tense forms to past tense or translated the passage into their first language (L1). Learning how to express and interpret ideas in speech or in writing in their second language (L2) and getting to know classmates or other L2 users better were not priorities. Often people did not imagine ever needing to communicate with others using the language being taught. Or the educational culture they were in and theories of learning at the time placed a premium on linguistic knowledge, such as the ability to analyze grammar and vocabulary, rather than the ability to use the language to speak or write to others about topics of mutual concern.

In this chapter, I examine the principles and history of CLT, how and why it has evolved, what it represents today, and directions for CLT in the future. The relationship between CLT and other proficiency- or competency-based approaches to language education is also considered. Finally, I consider how communicative competence might be reconceptualized for the purposes of language education given the changes in the nature of communication in the twenty-first century. This involves a growing assortment of new media and interfaces for communicating and sharing information, especially using English.

Reflections on your own experiences as a language learner

Think of your own experiences of learning another language through formal instruction. Was the language you learned a modern language that is used in everyday communication in some region of the world? Or was it a classical language, such as Latin, learned more for the study or reproduction of particular sacred or literary texts but not widely spoken in society? What were your goals for learning the language? Did the instructional methods used support those goals? Did you have opportunities to interact with others in the classroom using the language or in other contexts outside of class or online? Or did the instruction place much more emphasis on memorizing lists of vocabulary items, grammatical forms, sentence patterns, and rules mainly for the purpose of using those structures appropriately on tests of grammar, vocabulary, and translation?

Historically, classical and modern languages were often required courses at school and university and taught as a form of intellectual and literary enrichment, with no expectation that students would ever have the opportunity to use the language for either face-to-face communication or to correspond with other readers and writers of the language for their own purposes. In some

contexts, however, the requirements might be much more rigorous, involving speaking and listening and not just reading and writing, beginning with primary education and continuing throughout one's educational and professional career. Yet many such programs place considerable emphasis on grammatical and lexical sophistication and accuracy with much less emphasis on fluency and the ability to use the language for meaningful communication with others.

The traditional grammar- and text-based approach to teaching and learning language for the sake of engaging with literary works or mastering the grammatical conventions of language is still cultivated in many institutions and can constitute important intellectual and metalinguistic activity (i.e., building an awareness of how language functions as a system). However, people have many other reasons for learning languages than the study of grammar and classical literary texts; these reasons relate to the increasing levels of immigration and transnationalism worldwide, migrant worker programs, and opportunities for travel and international education. In addition, the Internet, globalization, more knowledge-based economies, and new information and communication technologies have all had an impact on language learning and use as well as on perceptions about its significance in people's lives. Learners may need to learn and use a second or foreign language such as English to participate in public education; to obtain employment; to communicate with relatives, friends, or colleagues who speak that language; to travel to regions of the world where the language is spoken; or to communicate with newcomers in their own neighborhoods who speak the language.

Experience 2: CLT in a secondary school English as a foreign language class

It has sometimes been argued that CLT is more appropriate in ESL curricular contexts, as in Experience 1, where English is spoken more widely in the local community, than in English as a foreign language (EFL) settings, where it is not the dominant local language. Indeed, there has sometimes been resistance to CLT in EFL contexts (Littlewood, 2011). Yet there are still ways that the principles of CLT can be applied, adopted, or adapted in EFL contexts. This was apparent in a 40-minute lesson I observed in 2009 in a well-resourced, urban, public secondary school classroom in China with over 50 grade 11 (senior year 2) students.

The topic is art and architecture, based on a unit in the textbook *Senior English for China, Student Book 2A* (PEP Curriculum Team, 2003b, Unit 3). The teacher begins by asking the students to generate words or phrases that they associate with the word *art* (e.g., they volunteer *beauty, creative, opera, music, architecture,* and *culture*). Using a PowerPoint (PPT) presentation, she then shows them images of some famous works of both modern and classical art (e.g., the *Mona Lisa* and a famous Chinese painting) and then iconic architectural landmarks from around the world, such as the Eiffel Tower. The teacher asks students to guess the name and location of the works shown and to decide what they have in common. They offer such responses as *They are special . . . beautiful . . . creatively designed . . . famous.* The linguistic goal of the lesson is to introduce and review vocabulary related to art and architecture, and also the grammatical structures for expressing a preference for one artistic or architectural style over another, such as the advantages and disadvantages of traditional versus modern Chinese houses. Guided by the teacher, students compare images of modern houses (apartments) and more traditional courtyard-style houses. Then, in groups of four, the students discuss which housing style they would want to live in and why. Students exchange their personal preferences and compare the different layouts of traditional and modern housing and ways of describing them. Finally, for the main task of the lesson, which takes 10–15 minutes, the students, in small groups again, discuss and design their "dream house" and then present it to the class, after which others give their impressions of the dream house. The lesson ends with a summary of the main conceptual and linguistic points of the lesson (modern versus traditional architecture; shapes and styles of housing; and building materials, such as concrete or wood).

In their lesson the following day, they continue with this theme, discussing a reading about some of the buildings designed for the Beijing 2008 Olympics, such as the "Bird's Nest" national stadium. Most of the class is conducted in English.

What aspects of this class are consistent with CLT? First, like the teacher in Experience 1, this teacher has students communicating in English, to the extent possible or desirable, about their personal experiences, opinions, and interests. Second, they discuss students' knowledge and understandings of art and architecture. They also discuss their preferences for certain kinds of artistic form. Third, a great deal of interaction (questions, responses, and requests for more information and for their opinions) occurs between the teacher and students. Fourth, to encourage additional oral language practice and a more personalized discussion of the topic, the teacher has students work together, here in groups of four, to create the prototype of their "dream house." They are therefore communicating with one another—negotiating meanings and preferences and showing their creativity through drawings—and then communicating with others in the class, as well. Finally, the students are asked to explain why they chose certain features and not others. There are many points of intersection between the curriculum and the students' own lives, their background knowledge, perspectives, and even hopes or dreams.

The teacher's approach to teaching this lesson is constrained by a number of factors in addition to class size: lesson length, prescribed textbook materials (supplemented by the teacher's PPT slides), and learning outcomes. Teachers and students are held accountable for the curriculum with monthly examinations for all classes in the same grade, culminating in their final year with the high-stakes College Entrance Examination, which determines students' higher education prospects and places considerable emphasis on English grammar. Even so, this very experienced teacher has managed to find ways of engaging students in interactions about the topic and has also highlighted both the language structures required to complete the task effectively that were also in the textbook (e.g., nouns: *architecture, balcony, furniture,* adjectives: *classical, modern;* expressions of preference: *I'd rather . . . , In my opinion, . . . , What I like is . . .*) and the grammar (past participles used as object complements: *We want traditional materials [to be] used;* hypothetical conditionals: *If I were to build a house, I would . . .*). The students seem genuinely interested in the lesson and are able to express themselves. The teacher espouses CLT but concedes that she must provide balanced instruction given the very language-focused curriculum mandated by the province.

CONCEPTUAL UNDERPINNINGS OF CLT

The CLT movement, often also referred to as the communicative approach, began in the 1970s to address shifting priorities in both education and society associated with socioeconomic trends at the time in continental Europe, the United Kingdom, and the United States. Addressing the needs of mobile or migrant language learners wishing to convey and interpret meanings in actual social contexts became paramount. These learners often had very practical needs like getting a job, buying groceries, finding housing, or speaking to neighbors. Giving learners the tools to communicate and some choice regarding what they might want to say or write as well as the freedom to experiment with language use distinguished CLT from other widely used approaches based on pattern drilling, recitation, and grammatical analysis (Richards & Rodgers, 2001).

An important parallel development taking place within theoretical linguistics was an emphasis on understanding the functions of language in a variety of social contexts. This included analyzing the kinds of adaptations that competent speakers know how to make when speaking to others of higher versus lower status, when speaking formally versus informally, when talking about technical or academic topics versus everyday subjects, and when interpreting others' speech and writing, among other facets of sociolinguistics (the study of language use in society). Savignon (1983, 2001, 2005, 2007), an American proponent of CLT, documented some of these shifts in European and British functional linguistics and also their impact on language teaching internationally since then.

The growing convergence in social and functional orientations in linguistics, along with the needs of learners seeking practical language skills for social, academic, occupational, and other purposes in the United Kingdom and continental Europe, gave rise to a very pragmatic and learner-centered approach to language teaching and learning. In the United States, similarly, a more socially oriented linguistics was proposed by Hymes (1971). He argued that to function in society, to be able to use language appropriately in social situations, speakers must know how to produce and interpret language for a wide range of purposes, as part of different types of activities in many settings, and with a variety of interlocutors. This ability to use language effectively, which native speakers of a language often take for granted, is known as *communicative competence.* Communicative competence was contrasted with idealized, abstract representations of grammatical knowledge (linguistic competence) or intuitions that native speakers have about language (e.g., Chomsky, 1965) with little reference to the observed real-world linguistic behaviors, needs, or intentions of speakers.

In addition to changes in society and linguistics that gave rise to the new field of sociolinguistics, psychological theories of learning were also evolving from more behavioral to more cognitive and social approaches. New insights about the nature of L1 and L2 learning, skill acquisition, comprehension, production, and memory, in particular, acknowledged the interplay of multiple factors in successful language learning and education, going well beyond rote skills. Among the many insights generated by the newer learning theories was that learners need to be actively and socially engaged in constructing meaning (either as readers/listeners or as speakers/writers) by interacting with both their textual environment (e.g., linguistic and nonlinguistic material, ideas, and texts) and with other language users. They need to attend simultaneously to the basic building blocks of language, such as morphemes (the smallest units of meaning or structure in language), words (which may include more than one morpheme), and grammatical structures (a bottom-up approach to processing information), and also to the larger meanings and types of discourse being conveyed (a more top-down holistic approach).

In our earlier examples, students were engaged in discourse about past events and leisure activities (Experience 1) and preferred types of art, architecture, and housing (Experience 2). Students need to become effective communicators in their L2 using many kinds of language (or discourse)—to compare and contrast items, describe sequences in a complicated process or narrative, categorize and classify information, present the causes and effects of different actions or events, provide evaluations, persuade people by making a good argument, or use language creatively to express themselves. Thus, the ability to learn and use grammar effectively, though clearly important, is only part of being able to communicate well. Appropriate registers or styles of speech (academic, nonacademic; formal, informal) and other socially appropriate ways of engaging in oral or written communication (making requests, complimenting others, complaining, apologizing, and expressing humor or passion) are also required in particular situations.

To develop communicative abilities, it was argued, learners need to experience or practice communicating in the language they are learning by negotiating meanings with others (e.g., Scarcella, Andersen, & Krashen, 1990). The term *negotiation of meaning* comes up often in discussions of CLT, and it refers to efforts to make oneself understood and to understand others—to convey messages or meanings—by asking such questions as "Is this what you mean?" and "Do you understand what I'm trying to say?" After all, communication—and learning—cannot occur if people do not understand what others have tried to express. The first wave of research in the new subfield of second language acquisition (SLA) also provided compelling evidence that learners do not simply learn what they are taught or are exposed to, especially if the grammatical and lexical (vocabulary) structures are too complicated or too numerous, or if students are not cognitively (mentally) ready to acquire them (R. Ellis, 1994b). (See also Ellis, this volume.)

In Canada, French immersion researchers Canale and Swain (1980) began to operationalize communicative competence for the purposes of instructing and assessing English-speaking learners of French in special programs in which most of the instruction was delivered in French. They sought to compare students' ability to communicate in their L2, French, with that of native French speakers or of learners of French in more traditional L2 programs. In addition to grammatical competence, long the hallmark of language teaching internationally, the following three components were added: sociolinguistic competence, strategic competence, and later, discourse competence (Canale, 1983). These four kinds of competence represent interrelated aspects of speakers' being able to use language effectively for purposes of communication both inside and outside classrooms.

Whereas *grammatical competence* refers to the ability to use and interpret sentence-level features of language effectively, including vocabulary (lexis), syntax (grammar), morphology (word construction), semantics (meaning), and phonology (the mapping of structure and meaning onto sound patterns), the other three domains of competence operate across different levels of language—from the word or sentence level to the larger social and discourse contexts. These larger units of language involve strings of phrases, sentences, or spoken utterances and the ability to cope with communicative needs in interactional contexts in strategic ways. An example of strategic language use is speakers' being able to paraphrase or find a synonym when unable to retrieve a word or other desired expression. So, if learners cannot think of the English word *enormous* but produce *very large, huge,* or *gigantic,* they have strategically managed their communication by finding a similar expression.

These additional, newly elaborated, and tested kinds of competence under the larger umbrella of communicative competence were important because they signaled to teachers, administrators, textbook writers, testers, and language learners themselves that learning phrase-level or sentence-level grammar and vocabulary alone does not enable one to communicate well across a variety of contexts. Furthermore, people must learn to create and comprehend cohesive and coherent oral and written texts on different topics (reflecting discourse competence); that is, they must produce language that makes sense, with ideas tied together in a logical, smooth manner so the relationship between ideas and sentences is clear, involving neither too much repetition nor too much disconnected switching between topics or other things being discussed. They must also learn to produce and interpret different genres or types of language use (e.g., a dialogue, a short narrative, a news or weather report, a personal letter, or a research paper) and in different disciplines or content areas (e.g., in the sciences versus the humanities). Nevertheless, learners cannot be expected to know everything there is to know about language across disciplines—not even native speakers do—since language learning, including L1 learning, is a lifetime process guided by need and opportunity.

Other aspects of language education not originally given prominence in CLT include critical thinking (e.g., Benesch, 1993) and critical literacies (e.g., Pennycook, 1999), which are now sometimes folded into CLT as well. *Critical thinking* is the ability to analyze information rationally, solve problems, and discern and evaluate implicit assumptions, values, and points of view while considering alternative perspectives; *critical literacies* are similar analytic skills applied to various kinds of texts—reading between the lines—to expose issues of bias (both explicit and implicit), misrepresentation, and possible manipulation of readers and listeners by texts and to consider alternative interpretations or versions of the same texts.

Despite CLT's origins in the teaching of European languages in Europe, the United Kingdom, and North America, its current reach is much more global, with educators worldwide recognizing the importance of a more functional and practical approach to language education. CLT is by no means a uniform method, however. If anything, like the term *democracy*, CLT is used to describe an increasingly diverse array of practices, principles, and contexts.

Indeed, many scholars have wondered whether the term CLT has outlived its usefulness because of the many different ways it has been interpreted and applied. However, Littlewood (2011) argues that "CLT still serves as a valuable reminder that the aim of teaching is not to learn bits of language but to 'improve the students' ability to communicate'" and that "every country needs people who can communicate internationally" (p. 542). He also asserts that both analytical and experiential aspects of language learning are valuable. Therefore, CLT should emphasize learners' experiences with language, life, and the curriculum *and* language analysis.

As I have suggested, the implementation of CLT is very context-dependent, based on local language education policies, educational cultures, assessment practices, and the availability of proficient and trained teachers and resources (e.g., textbooks, multimedia, classroom layouts, and number of students per class). Local demographics, languages, and the primary purposes for which languages are being taught and learned must be considered. No two countries or contexts are identical.

According to J. Richards (2006a), language instruction and learning in the early decades of CLT focused on fluency and the integration of language skills, rewarding learners' efforts to speak or write even if errors resulted. Many kinds of instructional activities were recommended, from mechanical language practice initially, involving the entire class or individuals, to much more open-ended communicative practice, some of it

requiring either one-way or two-way exchanges of information through activities in which partners need to share and consolidate information to carry out the task. These principles still apply. However, now other types of activities, such as inductive discovery-oriented learning, are also encouraged where students try to find patterns in language texts and data sets (e.g., common collocations of words) and guess their meanings or usage. The teacher's role is to create a nurturing, collaborative learning community and worthwhile activities for students. Richards's own English language textbooks embody CLT principles as well (e.g., *New Interchange*, J. Richards, 2012; *Passages*, Richards & Sandy, 2008). The existence of a flexible curriculum (over which the teacher and students have a fair amount of control and input), small class sizes, and relatively little formal assessment is assumed in much CLT pedagogy, unlike the situation in Experience 2.

How does CLT relate to other proficiency-based approaches to language teaching?

As CLT was developing, particularly for adult English language teaching, other highly compatible theoretical frameworks were being developed. Three are discussed in this section.

American Council on the Teaching of Foreign Languages Standards. The first related proficiency framework or model that arose alongside CLT was the American Council on the Teaching of Foreign Languages (ACTFL) *Standards for Foreign Language Learning for the 21st Century*, also known as the Five Cs model. This model consisted of the following components:

1. *Communication:* fostering communication within and across cultures (oral and written)
2. *Cultures:* encouraging the development of deep cultural understanding and insight
3. *Connections:* forging connections with other disciplines and information sources
4. *Comparisons:* facilitating metalinguistic and metacultural understanding by comparing one's own and the target language
5. *Communities:* making connections with multilingual communities of target-language

speakers near and far and becoming lifelong learners (American Council for the Teaching of Foreign Languages, n.d.)

Each component represents an interlocking knowledge domain for language education, although communication (the first C) is part of all of them. This model, which evolved in the late twentieth century, is widely used in postsecondary and, increasingly, elementary and secondary foreign language ("world language") programs across the United States (Omaggio Hadley, 2001; Shrum & Glisan, 2010). Like CLT, the ACTFL Standards movement stresses contextualizing language itself, contextualizing learning activities and language use, fostering communication, and integrating the learning of language, culture, communication, and (academic) content of different types within and across communities. An emphasis on oral-aural language, particularly at lower levels, was a remedy to earlier approaches devoted to written literary text analysis and interpretation at the expense of a wider range of functional oral abilities on the part of college-level learners in particular (Higgs & Clifford, 1982).[1]

Also like CLT, learning theories informing the model underscored both top-down and bottom-up orientations to learning and processing language. People must be able to attend to global meanings and structures of texts (What is the overall purpose and meaning of the text, and what cultural or other background knowledge is relevant?) and to details (What vocabulary or grammatical forms are involved, and what meanings are being conveyed by these?) at more or less the same time (see Shrum & Glisan, 2010). However, when first exposed to oral or written texts, students may need to focus initially on more holistic, top-down strategies that enable them to understand the linguistic elements used. In addition, the three primary modes of communication cultivated by this proficiency-based approach are known as *interpersonal* (e.g., conversing, and exchanging ideas or information with others), *interpretive* (providing impressions or understandings of content), and *presentational* (e.g., communicating through oral or written reports and public speaking). Assessment, according to ACTFL guidelines, includes determining the functional level of students as Novice, Intermediate, Advanced, or Superior.[2]

Common European Framework of Reference for Languages. The second framework or model with communicative ability and proficiency at its core originated in Europe and is now spreading to other parts of the world. It is known as the Common European Framework of Reference for Languages (CEFR, 2011). Developed under the direction of the Council of Europe, CEFR is an impressive functional approach to task-based teaching and assessment designed for at least 20 languages across a broad spectrum of proficiency levels (Broeder & Martyniuk, 2008; Little, 2007). CEFR now guides language teaching policies, planning, and assessment in countries in the European Union and is gaining ground in the Asia-Pacific region, Canada, and elsewhere. CEFR encourages learners, teachers, and teacher educators to collect evidence of learners' proficiency and language learning biographies through various media, including multimedia personal learning portfolios that include statements and illustrations of what learners can *do* in the various languages that are part of their L2 or multilingual repertoire (Duff, 2008; Little, 2007).

Like ACTFL, which provides descriptors of different levels of proficiency, CEFR is based on a common template that enables people working in different program contexts to have the same (i.e., common) frame of reference for what is meant by a Basic, Independent, and Proficient user (to use the CEFR labels). Functional descriptors help direct pedagogy by focusing teachers' and students' attention on practical competencies and serve as a means of assessing students' abilities and progress. Having a shared framework that is understood by other end users also allows for greater mobility and information sharing as learners move across or through different institutions and countries. Increasingly, programs adopting one or the other scale (i.e., ACTFL or CEFR) also specify the expected learning outcomes in terms of the level students are expected to reach after specified types and amounts (hours or years) of instruction. For example, a Basic A2-level learner, according to CEFR (2011), can (or is expected to) do the following:

Can understand sentences and frequently used expressions related to areas of most immediate relevance (e.g. very basic personal and family information, shopping, local geography, employment). Can communicate in simple and routine tasks requiring a simple and direct exchange of information on familiar and routine matters. Can describe in simple terms aspects of his/her background, immediate environment and matters in areas of immediate basic need. (p. 24)

At a much higher level, on the other hand, a Proficient C1-level learner is described as:

> Can understand a wide range of demanding, longer texts, and recognise implicit meaning. Can express him/herself fluently and spontaneously without much obvious searching for expressions. Can use language flexibly and effectively for social, academic and professional purposes. Can produce clear, well-structured, detailed text on complex subjects, showing controlled use of organisational patterns, connectors and cohesive devices. (p. 24)

Canadian Language Benchmarks. The third communicative, proficiency-based framework embodying the principles of CLT is the Canadian Language Benchmarks (CLB) 2000 (Centre for Canadian Language Benchmarks, 2000) project for adult ESL learners in Canada. The theoretical rationale for the document, which includes benchmarks and tasks for diagnostic/placement, instructional, and assessment purposes, makes its CLT foundations very clear (Pawlikowska-Smith, 2002):

> The Canadian Language Benchmarks is based on a functional view of language, language use, and language proficiency. Such a view relates language to the contexts in which it is used and the communicative functions it performs. The focus of the Canadian Language Benchmarks is thus on communication and communicative proficiency in English as a second language. (p. 5)

The five communicative components promoted through the CLB 2000 also bear a direct relationship to the early theoretical development in Canada and elsewhere (e.g., Bachman, 1990) regarding features of communicative competence that can be assessed: linguistic competence, textual competence (coherence and cohesion), functional competence (ability to "convey and interpret communicative intent"), sociocultural competence (related to sociolinguistic appropriateness), and strategic competence (managing actual communication across all components).

Other curricular program types compatible with CLT

Several other developments in language education that have had an impact on CLT are dealt with in more depth by other authors in this volume. Here I briefly introduce a few of them.

Content-based language teaching. One curricular trend favors attention to content learning together with language learning. Known as content-based language teaching (or content and language integrated learning in Europe), this type of curriculum is usually found at the intermediate to advanced levels of study and appears to be gaining in popularity worldwide, particularly in programs where English is the medium of instruction but not the language of the wider community or the L1 of the students. Content-based teaching is often adopted after students have participated in the equivalent of a year of intensive communication-based language instruction or several years of regular L2 coursework incorporating theme-based and task-based discussions and activities. However, these students have not yet studied a particular content area over a sustained period using the L2. Content-based approaches can also be used at lower proficiency levels, such as early immersion or bilingual programs in which students study curricular subjects (content) through the L2 following an initial period in which language arts and literacy are introduced in that language. (See also Snow, this volume.)

The rationale for content-based approaches is that students must communicate (read, write, speak, and listen) in the L2 to make meaning and construct knowledge about topics using "authentic" texts, which are core principles in CLT. *Authentic*, a synonym for *genuine* (versus *contrived*, *bookish*, or *artificial*), refers to language naturally produced by speakers or writers of the target language; it also refers to the kinds of communication that people might normally engage in when using the language. Very often the test of authenticity has been whether the language forms, texts, or types of interaction used for instructional purposes represent contemporary oral or written language produced or used by native speakers for purposes other than language teaching.

Academic/professional purposes language teaching. Closely related to content-based instruction is an increasing focus on learning to communicate more effectively in another language for academic or professional purposes. (See Johns & Price, this volume.) Teaching languages (especially English) for specific occupational, vocational, scientific, and academic purposes was an early priority of CLT internationally for engineers, pilots, graduate students, hotel workers, and other groups. However, as more English learners worldwide participate in academic programs requiring high levels of oral and written communication, advanced CLT typically extends into academic study as well. Since learner-centered pedagogy has influenced academia in recent years as well, in lieu of transmission-based approaches in which teachers lecture and students passively take notes, students now work together to solve problems, create projects, and investigate real-world issues of interest to them.

Work from Australia that integrates sociocultural, functional, and communicative aspects of learning language for academic purposes has also had great traction (see Byrnes, 2006), especially in advanced language and literacy education. Much like Hymes's (1971) conceptualization of communicative competence but with a more fully elaborated application to education, Halliday's systemic functional linguistics (e.g., Halliday & Hasan, 1989) focuses on text types, different registers and genres of language (e.g., in academic spheres), particular audiences or interlocutors in various social contexts, and the linguistic resources or choices available to produce or interpret specific meanings.

Task-based language teaching. CLT spawned important developments in task-based language teaching and learning in the late 1970s that continue to be researched in terms of theory, pedagogy, and task and curriculum design. (See Nunan, this volume.) Now there is an increasing focus on more elaborate, multiskill, and multimodal collaborative project work that involves many subtasks over an extended curricular period (e.g., Beckett & Miller, 2006).

Service learning. An additional area of increased curricular and extra-curricular activity for the development of communicative competence and community well-being is (community) service learning. Students are encouraged to use the language they are learning to assist other speakers of that language living within their own community, thereby gaining genuine language practice but also contributing to society by helping others. Service learning is now included in many language programs' community outreach and global citizenship efforts, for which students can receive course credit (e.g., Wurr & Hellebrandt, 2007). It is sometimes combined with content-based language learning where issues related to immigration, housing, or social justice, for example, are dealt with in course readings and discussion. This academic content provides advanced linguistic material and helps students better understand the learning contexts they are in. In the United States, for example, learners of Spanish might reach out to local (Spanish-speaking) Latino communities, or ESL learners in Canada might spend time at soup kitchens feeding local homeless people or interact with English-speaking seniors at a local nursing home. Thus, a growing number of approaches to contemporary language teaching stress communication skills, intercultural sensitivity, and social action, together with language and content learning.

CLASSROOM APPLICATIONS: ADDITIONAL EXAMPLES OF CLT IN TESOL

Two additional examples of English teaching informed by CLT are provided next; these involve young children in an EFL context (Experience 3) and students in an academic preparation program at a Canadian university (Experience 4).

Experience 3: Teaching young learners in an EFL context

In an elementary school in China, an enthusiastic English teacher is teaching 9-year-old students a lesson about discussing the weather. She begins by asking the students about the weather outside that day. Individual students reply: *It's warm . . . cloudy . . . sunny . . . fine,* and so on. The teacher continues by asking about the weather in other parts of China, for example, up north, where it is much colder.

She even pretends that she has caught a cold, shivering and sneezing, and asks the students to guess what is wrong. She then goes over a dialogue about two characters named Zip and Zoom, one of whom has traveled up north, where the weather is cold, and has caught a cold. The students do role plays of the dialogue seated in pairs and then perform it at the front of the class. Later they sing a song about the weather. In subsequent classes, the teacher asks students about the weather at the beginning of class.

In other chapters, the colorful textbook series used at the school, *PEP Primary English* (PEP Curriculum Team, 2002, 2003a), has students talk about their school, their families, their friends, their own personal characteristics (height, size, health, and likes and dislikes), holidays, and how they spent the last weekend. The curriculum aims to prepare students for language use that relates to their own lives and interests and not just those of the human and animal characters in the textbook. Section headings in each lesson also reflect CLT principles: Let's Learn, Let's Play, Let's Try, Let's Talk, Group Work, Let's Read, Pair Work, Task Time, Let's Sing, Story Time, and Let's Chant.

However, as in all educational contexts, the same textbook and lesson content can be used in many different ways by different teachers, some much more effectively than others. This teacher tries to make the lesson as meaningful as possible to the children, relating the content to their lives and settings, and she also gives them opportunities to practice the lesson content in a variety of social participation formats (whole class, pairs, and groups of four), despite the large class size (60–70 students).

Experience 4: Fostering communication in English for academic purposes classes

Now consider what CLT principles might look like when applied to a completely different educational context, in an English for academic purposes (listening and speaking skills) class at a university in western Canada.

In addition to espousing principles of CLT, the instructor incorporates into the curriculum a social justice orientation to teaching known as critical pedagogy, which raises students' awareness of and seeks to redress various forms of oppression and unfairness in society (e.g., Benesch, 2001; Norton & Toohey, 2004). The students here are lower-advanced international and immigrant students. Students reflect on, discuss, and listen to news reports and watch and discuss films about social issues (e.g., discrimination) of different types, based on race, gender, class, sexuality, and certain political and cultural ideologies (see Royal, 2010).

First, the instructor engages the students in a negotiated curriculum (Breen & Candlin, 1980), in which students have some choice regarding the topics to be included in the course or aspects of assignments. This level of student involvement is not uncommon in CLT and, particularly, in ESL classes with adult immigrant students to make the instruction relevant to the students and to give them a sense of ownership of the curriculum. One class activity early in the course asks students to discuss "the five most serious problems facing the world and then the five most serious concerns in their own lives." The purpose is not only to broach social justice at the macro-societal level (about which students needed to reach a group consensus and make a short presentation to the class later) but also to deal with students' own lives and to give them a chance to discuss their perspectives with others in small groups. In the process, they get to know one another better, practice speaking English and listening to others, and offer advice and feedback to one another about homesickness, parental pressure, and the lack of opportunities to practice English outside of class. They also report back to the class the world problems they have identified. The curriculum involves problem solving and role plays related to academic life and discussions about cultural issues in the community (e.g., arranged marriages).

The students later report that they appreciated being able to discuss real-life problems, learn more about Canadian society and culture, talk about issues that are personally meaningful to them, and consider human rights, critical media literacy, and social and political issues not talked about in their countries of origin. These aspects are all clearly connected with learning to use English for both everyday and academic communication. The learning objectives include listening and speaking subskills, content objectives related to social justice, and employability skills, such as being able to take part in discussions, presentations, and interviews (for course purposes and job-seeking).

Although the contexts and goals for these two courses are completely different, both aim to make clear connections between the topics being discussed and the world outside the classroom. Both help build up students' linguistic knowledge, enabling them to produce and interpret oral, written, and multimedia texts; use language actively; and relate topics to their own lives, interests, and understandings, whether they are children or young adults.

Challenges in CLT

CLT in theory versus practice.   In an influential early study on CLT, Spada (1987) documents how teachers might say they were using a particular teaching method, especially a popular one such as CLT, but observations of their classroom teaching revealed wide disparities between their self-reports and actual practice. Some of the teaching processes the teachers characterized as "CLT" in her study were not at all communicative and seemed indistinguishable from earlier, more traditional approaches to language teaching.

My observations have also revealed how differently the same curriculum materials and objectives are taken up by individual teachers; some were more focused on recitation and rote work, and others were more focused on truly communicating about topics in addition to working on language structures and skills. The teachers' confidence and competence in teaching and using English, managing class time, and covering the curriculum are major factors.

Sometimes teachers simply need additional mentoring and constructive suggestions from trusted colleagues to help them extend the language practice in more personally meaningful directions. In one elementary school EFL classroom I observed, for example, an enthusiastic young teacher was teaching a lesson based on transportation and specifically about how people get to school. The class energetically rehearsed and even acted out statements in their textbook lesson such as *I go to school by bus* and *I go to school by taxi*; they also sang songs and chanted relevant

lyrics and seemed fully engaged with the material. However, the teacher never asked any of the students how *they themselves* traveled to school—on foot, by bus, bicycle, or by other means? By moving beyond the structures and prompts in the textbook, PPTs, and audio recordings, the teacher could quite easily have helped students make connections between the English expressions being taught and their own routines. This extension of the lesson would have taken relatively little time and would have made the language more engaging and memorable.

One strategy to help preservice or in-service teachers learn concrete new ways of making their teaching more consistent with desired or mandated methods is to invite them to take part in lesson study, an instructional approach in which sample lessons taught by highly effective teachers are video-recorded (with permission) and then analyzed for professional development purposes by groups of teachers.[3]

Even teachers who subscribe to the principles of communicative methodology must sometimes compromise their own beliefs about instruction to prepare students for the high-stakes assessment that might reward very traditional forms of knowledge, such as grammar and detection of written errors. This negative effect of assessment practices on teaching, known as *negative washback*, plagues language teaching all over the world; when written examinations do not match the curriculum, short shrift is typically given to oral, integrative communication skills because they are more expensive and logistically challenging to assess than grammatical or lexical knowledge.

Teachers embracing a communicative orientation usually need to be resourceful, constantly looking for current print-based and multimedia materials of potential interest to the class and for new formats for activities. Sometimes students are asked to bring in relevant materials as well. For example, the lessons in the Chinese English-teaching materials for middle school students that I examined dealt with a number of topics that students said appealed to them, such as "heroes" (e.g., great women, freedom fighters), the "Special Olympics," "Australia," "World Englishes," "pop culture" (e.g., movies, music), "new technologies," and "advertising." Sometimes students were asked to do Internet searches before class to contribute examples for the different topics.

CLT and language education reforms. Savignon (2007) offers examples of curricular reform in the direction of more communicative language education in Asia and Central America. She also documents some of the factors conspiring against a more truly communicative approach related to testing or teacher development, teachers' L2 proficiency, and their epistemologies. Such challenges are particularly salient when teaching is extended to new contexts with inadequate preparation of teachers, such as in elementary schools in many regions of the world where the age of initial English education has been lowered and teachers are expected to teach English with insufficient training and L2 proficiency. Similarly, Hasanova and Shadieva (2008) describe the challenges of implementing CLT in Uzbekistan. An online search of research on CLT yields a long list of dissertations around the world that have examined its relevance, utility, implementation, effectiveness, and reception on the part of teachers, parents, administrators, students, and other stakeholders, along with some of the challenges facing language education reform.

CLT and English as a lingua franca. Teaching in contexts where English is a lingua franca (a widely used language among speakers of mutually unintelligible languages) also raises interesting challenges for CLT in terms of the desired accuracy-fluency balance that CLT now embraces (see Kirkpatrick, 2007). For example, many learners of English, even advanced speakers, often produce similar sorts of ungrammatical features (e.g., deleting third person –s, producing *he go* instead of *he goes*) and yet can understand one another quite well. The argument goes: Why insist on accuracy in such structures when they are pervasive and do not seem critical to mutual understanding? However, some forms of ungrammatical language use can have serious consequences for L2 users. The issue, then, is how to determine what levels of accuracy are appropriate (and worth attaining) and for what purposes.

Classroom management and social organization. Finally, while CLT can be a very promising way of helping students learn and learn to use language, the social organization of activities must also be carefully considered and monitored to ensure its effectiveness. How students are perceived, referred to, or even grouped in class by themselves, by teachers, or by classmates in terms of their abilities, identities, proficiency level, and cultural backgrounds can have a direct impact on their learning and retention in courses (Duff, 2012).

FUTURE TRENDS

How and why is CLT evolving in the twenty-first century?

Proponents of CLT maintain that, although it might not be possible to create exactly the kind of learning environment described by J. Richards (2006a) for a variety of cultural and institutional reasons, much can nevertheless be learned from CLT to make learning under other conditions more meaningful, effective, and rewarding. CLT is evolving in response to contextual constraints, priorities, technological possibilities, and preferences. As Savignon (2007) points out, although certain aspects of CLT are commonly observed in Western teaching contexts, especially those involving European target languages, CLT does not or need not involve primarily oral or face-to-face communication and small-group work, nor should CLT preclude the development of students' metalinguistic or metacommunicative awareness (i.e., understanding and being able to discuss both the nonverbal and verbal elements of communication). Spada (2007) and Littlewood (2011) concur strongly with this view. Spada also notes that avoidance of the learners' L1 is not a necessary feature of CLT, although in early CLT that practice was common because migrant learners in the same class might come from diverse language backgrounds and not share a common language apart from the L2. Furthermore, the goal was to have learners practice using the L2 as much as possible in all four skills.

In CLT, contextualization, meaning making, and the usefulness of the language being learned and the activities being engaged in should be very evident in curriculum and instruction, keeping in mind that communication takes place in different ways, using different media. For example, I might read an online article in my L2 about the environment but never discuss it with others. Yet I am interacting with the text and with its author. I might also write a journal in my L2 that is not intended for anyone but myself. But that too is certainly a form of communication and self-expression.

Information and communication technologies and CLT

Contemporary educational policy, curriculum, and pedagogy have been profoundly affected by the impressive new global information and communication technologies used in many sectors of society. Twenty-first-century competencies include being able to collaborate with others in processes of problem solving, data mining and induction, textual co-construction and negotiation, and cooperative report production and presentation even when working in different locations and connected only by these new technologies. Language education is no exception. With growing access to Internet resources in many parts of the world, English language learners have a wealth of authentic oral, written, and multimodal texts at their disposal, as well as linguistic corpora and concordance programs, to help them solve linguistic puzzles of their own choosing and to work on projects with others elsewhere. (See chapters by McCarthy & O'Keeffe and Sokolik, this volume.) They can take part in the interactive creation or analysis of Internet video clips, or they can read or respond to blogs with English language users worldwide who share their interests (Dudeney, 2007; Dudeney & Hockly, 2007). Indeed, one of the benefits of developing communicative competence in more than one language is precisely to tap into such resources for a variety of interpersonal, informational, and creative purposes.

In addition, forms of delivery and venues for CLT or communication-driven learning activities now increasingly include both in-class and out-of-class online programs involving websites, Internet-based project work, email, chat, blogs, wikis, Skype (a free means of teleconferencing or video-chatting with others via the computer), podcasts, and electronic portfolios. Moreover, as new online tools and devices (e.g., mobile phones and small portable tablet computers with wireless capability) become more widely available and more versatile, new possibilities will exist for people to access and produce language in innovative ways online.

One particular innovation that is likely to evolve further is virtual or simulated worlds for educational purposes, such as Second Life.[4] Three-dimensional online sites ("worlds") such as Second Life allow users to create different personas or identities for themselves. They can then interact with others (real people using their personas in that same virtual space) by means of the L2 and tools for building a simulated physical or cultural environment, which they also co-create. Language practice in such a game-like environment often appeals to adolescents and young adults accustomed to video gaming. However, virtual worlds such as Second Life are more than games. They provide a site for social, cultural, and intellectual networking mediated by language, and increasingly, they are being used in university education to support problem solving, improved communication, and creativity (e.g., Bradley, 2009).

Live tutoring systems and other social networking tools that enable language learners to practice using language with others around the world are another growing phenomenon made possible by the Internet.[5] Indeed, the Internet, Skype, and other digital tools provide endless possibilities for teachers and students to connect with other L2 users for a variety of meaningful purposes, including the creation or analysis of pop culture (see Duff & Zappa-Hollman, 2013). (See also Sokolik, this volume.) Online discussion forums and distance learning, furthermore, are increasingly part of language courses and (other) academic courses as well, providing students with alternative means of participating in and contributing to discussions outside class (e.g., Yim, 2011). Students and classes in different locations can meet online via email, Skype, or other programs through formal or informal class exchanges or partnerships.

However, having access to a wealth of resources and new communication media does not in itself lead to learning; nor does it constitute sound pedagogy. Teachers (and learners in more self-directed learning contexts) must carefully select sites, activities, and texts to ensure that they are appropriate for the cognitive, social, and linguistic levels of their students. For example, WebQuests[6] allow students to engage in tasks or projects involving sets of (authentic) online materials and media carefully preselected in advance by teachers. Alternatively, students can design the WebQuest themselves and preselect sources for their peers (see the example in Dudeney & Hockly, 2007, on how to be a responsible consumer of running shoes). But these activities should not just be a low-cost substitute for textbooks or printed handouts. Because of their multimodality (e.g., images, text, sound, and links) and the ease of providing updates and thus timeliness of the materials, students can easily access important media materials for analysis, synthesis, evaluation, transformation, and presentation.

CONCLUSION

Whereas early CLT focused on functional (oral) language ability in which fluency and comprehensibility were key, CLT now typically also integrates formal attention to language features in a variety of ways, from direct instruction and metalinguistic awareness-raising to more inductive learning through the use of language-corpus data (e.g., Spada, 2007). (See also McCarthy & O'Keeffe, this volume.) In addition, a wider range of learning and communication formats now exists. Clearly CLT cannot offer a common template or prescription for all L2 teaching and learning contexts, all the different ages and stages of learners, or all the different purposes for learning. However, making connections between formal instruction and students' own lives, interests, prior knowledge, and existing linguistic and sociocultural knowledge is a central tenet not just of CLT but of current learning theory and pedagogy.

Developments in digital information and communication technologies, moreover, offer students almost limitless access to language input, interaction, and output; they also offer real purposes for communicating. Yet, like other innovations, the actual learning, skills, and forms of participation should be monitored carefully to ensure that they are compatible with learning objectives of the students and the programs. That is, novel interaction formats may initially engage students' interests but soon wear off if the content is unsubstantial and motivation is not sustained in meaningful ways. (See Dörnyei, this volume.)

There is a renewed emphasis in education on teaching for global citizenship, intercultural understanding, and lifelong learning and not only for the development of language proficiency across skill areas for more immediate, local purposes. However, there is also a greater wariness of educational colonialism and orthodoxies that export language curricula, materials, tests, and methods to very diverse parts of the world but that might be incompatible with local priorities, purposes, and sensibilities. Moreover, new understandings of how communication takes place among speakers of English (as an L2 and lingua franca) suggest that a priority in language teaching (and teacher education), quite in keeping with the original focus of CLT, should be to maximize the speakers' (or writers') intelligibility and comprehensibility—that is, their functional ability in real contexts of need and use—and not to focus relentlessly on grammatical accuracy or on any one culture's notions of cultural or sociolinguistic niceties.

In addition, according to sociocultural and critical pedagogical perspectives, the goals of language education should be to help learners find an appropriate "voice" and identity in their target language and feel confident enough as legitimate users of the language to pursue their own educational, career, and personal aspirations (Duff, 2012). After all, as we learn additional languages, we learn possibly as much about ourselves and our own languages and cultural frames of reference as we do about those of others (Kramsch, 1993). As Rifkin (2006) has pointed out, however, learners, programs, and those who make language education policies often underestimate how much time, exposure, and instruction are required to help learners achieve high levels of proficiency or communicative competence. The instruction needs to take place over a well-articulated, multiyear period and must be very carefully planned and delivered, with students having ample opportunities to use the language.

SUMMARY

➤ CLT focuses on helping language learners communicate effectively in another language by enabling them to convey and interpret messages and meanings of various types for various real, or realistic, purposes.

- ➤ Some core principles of CLT include developing learners' confidence, fluency, resourcefulness (strategies), and autonomy in the L2; making language practice interesting and social; and teaching language skills, content, and forms that are useful, relevant, and meaningful.

- ➤ Teachers must ensure that learning is contextualized in discourse that is relevant to learners and appropriate to the curriculum; that the language appears in the kinds of genres or text types normally associated with a particular activity; and that activities are structured (designed or modeled) in such a way that students have the means, motivation, and assistance to carry out tasks on their own and with others.

- ➤ CLT has evolved over the past four decades and has been adapted for use in a wide variety of curricular and cultural contexts and with new information and communication technologies.

DISCUSSION QUESTIONS

1. Answer the questions in the section "Reflections on your own experiences as a language learner" (p. 16), and compare your experiences with those of two classmates.

2. What kinds of topics, communication activities (e.g., activities, role plays, presentations, and debates), and participation formats (teacher-fronted, pair, or small-group) did you most enjoy using as a language learner, and why? Which did you enjoy least? Did the instruction enable you to use the language later in noninstructional situations? Can you recall any activity or project that integrated listening, speaking, reading, and writing?

3. How do (or might) you use technology for language teaching and learning in your context? What constraints do you face? Do you think that you as a language learner or your (future) students would want to engage in virtual or simulated learning environments online? Why or why not? What possibilities might there be for other non-face-to-face interactions (via chat, email, or online discussion groups) as a way of developing learners' communicative competence? What advantages do those have over more traditional print-based or face-to-face instruction and practice?

4. Is it reasonable to assume that CLT can be implemented in the same sort of curriculum and manner in EFL contexts (where students may never need or be able to interact in the target language) as students do in ESL contexts (where English is the dominant language in the wider community)? How might you motivate students in EFL contexts to use English to take part in communicative activities?

5. How might the principles of CLT be applied or adapted to meet the challenges posed by the following sorts of contexts? Choose three situations from the list below to discuss with a classmate:

   a. Learners have limited access to new information and communication technologies or to authentic samples of oral or written language.

   b. Existing teaching materials represent a very different orientation to teaching.

   c. The goals of the course are much more traditional, for example, to help students pass high-stakes language tests like TOEFL.

   d. Class sizes are very large, and acoustics are poor.

   e. Students seem to be shy and unaccustomed to discussing topics of a personal or social nature with one another, and the teaching approach is very teacher-centered.

   f. Teachers (and students) have difficulty teaching using the L2 primarily due to a lack of proficiency in it.

SUGGESTED ACTIVITIES

1. Consider the generic topics: (1) my community; (2) technology in modern life; and (3) popular culture and education. With a partner, brainstorm possibilities for creating a lesson plan (or possibly a whole unit) related to one of these topics, comprising several lessons. Include possible tasks that would allow you, as a teacher using CLT, to engage learners of specific ages and proficiency levels in a variety of stimulating, integrated oral and written activities related to the topic.

a. What strategies would you use initially to arouse students' interest in the topic?

b. What vocabulary and grammatical structures might be useful? How would you teach them?

c. What images or multimedia might further arouse students' interest in the topic? What kind of pair- or small-group work would you have them do (if any)?

d. What core task might be the focus?

e. How might you adapt your teaching of these themes for more academic purposes?

f. What cultural themes might be incorporated?

g. How might you adapt the topic further if you wanted to address community issues more critically?

h. What kind of project could students do if an entire unit or course focused on the topic?

i. What kinds of literacy activities and assessment might you include?

2. Observe a language class, and note which aspects of CLT seem to be present. Discuss ways in which the same lesson could be taught (even) more communicatively. If the original lesson was already consistent with CLT, discuss some alternate activities that you could use if you were to teach the same lesson.

3. For the lessons described in Examples 1 to 4 in the chapter, how might you adapt the topics for students of different ages (much younger or much older) and proficiency levels (much lower or much more advanced)?

FURTHER READING

Brandl, K. (2008). *Communicative language teaching in action: Putting principles to work.* Upper Saddle River, NJ: Pearson/Prentice Hall.

This is a very user-friendly, practical book especially suitable for novice foreign language teachers. Many examples of classroom activities are included.

Savignon, S. (1997). *Communicative competence: Theory and classroom practice* (2nd ed.). New York, NY: McGraw Hill.

The author's approach to CLT, to theoretical understandings of communicative competence in language education, and to the professional development of teachers are worth examining.

Savignon, S. (Ed.). (2002). *Interpreting communicative language teaching: Contexts and concerns in teacher education.* New Haven, CT: Yale University Press.

This edited volume examines some of the challenges of implementing CLT in language classrooms in different parts of the world, addressing issues of technology, learner autonomy, the misplaced emphasis on the native speaker as teacher, and problems with high-stakes assessment that thwarts communicative teaching.

Spada, N. (2007). Communicative language teaching: Current status and future prospects. In J. Cummins & C. Davis (Eds.), *International handbook of English language teaching* (pp. 271–288). New York, NY: Springer.

The author's observations of CLT as a teacher educator and researcher are very insightful.

ENDNOTES

[1] In addition, in the post–World War II period (and again in the post–9/11 era), U.S. personnel in the military, foreign service, and other federal domains were found to be relatively ill-prepared for the high levels of functional proficiency required across a range of critical languages. Grammar was recast as one tool among many others required for effective communication, and not simply an end in itself, and this has paved the way for a wider implementation of CLT in the United States.

[2] The ACTFL proficiency guidelines for speaking and writing are available at http://www.actfl.org/i4a/pages/index.cfm?pageid=4236

[3] I learned about this initiative when participating in the Asia-Pacific Economic Cooperation (APEC) Education Network meeting in Xian, China, in January 2008. Examples using mathematics education in Japan were modeled, and lesson study was recommended for international modern language education as well. See http://hrd.apec.org/index.php/Projects

[4] See http://www.secondlife.com (Caution: Sections of this website contain adult content.)

[5] Livemocha is one such online peer tutoring system, http://www.livemocha.com

[6] See http://www.WebQuest.org

3 | Principles of Instructed Second Language Learning

ROD ELLIS

KEY QUESTIONS

➤ How do you think about teaching? Do you think about it in terms of what and how you will teach? Or do you think about it in terms of how you can create the conditions for successful second language learning?

➤ If you were asked to state general principles that could help teachers create the conditions for successful learning in the classroom, what would they be?

➤ How can you tell that students are successfully learning in the second language in your classroom?

EXPERIENCE

All teachers have a theory of how teaching can assist learning. However, the theory that teachers hold may be more or less explicit. That is, teachers may base their teaching on intuitive notions of what works rather than on explicit principles of how they can best promote learning in their students. Intuitive notions can result in highly successful teaching—and are probably necessary to enable a teacher to take the countless instant decisions needed to accomplish a lesson—but they may not promote critical reflection. If teachers are to undertake a thoughtful evaluation of their own teaching, they need to make the principles that inform their actions explicit. A major goal of this chapter is to offer a set of principles that can inform such an evaluation. Let us look at how one teacher undertook a principled evaluation of her own teaching.

Juanita Watts (2009) elected to plan, teach, and undertake an evaluation of an information-gap task (i.e., spot the difference). This required the students (upper-intermediate learners in a private language school in Auckland, New Zealand) to work together in pairs to identify the changes evident in two pictures of the same location 100 years apart. Each student held only one of the pictures. The main goal of Juanita's evaluation was to determine to what extent the task resulted in the kinds of interaction that have been hypothesized to promote language learning—in particular the negotiation of meaning that occurs when a communication problem arises. To help with this evaluation, she recorded two pairs of students performing the task and then transcribed their interactions.

Juanita identified a number of negotiation-and-meaning sequences in both pairs' interactions. Interestingly, all the sequences arose from problems having to do with vocabulary or pronunciation. There was no negotiation focused on grammatical problems. She also reported some differences in how the two pairs undertook the task. One pair engaged much more extensively in negotiation than the other and also worked harder to resolve the communication problems that arose and was more successful in doing so. There was also a difference in how the two pairs negotiated. The pair that negotiated extensively did so by means of clarification requests, whereas the other pair employed confirmation checks. The two examples that follow illustrate these differences. In Example 1, the two students persist until they successfully resolve their communication problem with Student 2 (S2) repeatedly requesting clarification. In Example 2, Student 4 (S4) uses a confirmation check to address a vocabulary problem, but even though Student 3 (S3) indicates that Student 4

(S4) has not understood, no further attempt is made to resolve the problem.

Example 1

S1: on the left, I can see um lam – post. Lam-post.
S2: wh-pardon? What? (= clarification request)
S1: lam – sorry. Lam post.
S2: name post? (= clarification request)
S1: /leim/ post /laem/ post post post
S2: L – A? (= clarification request)
S1: L-A-M lam
S2: Ah, lamp. Ah lamp post (successfully resolved)

Example 2

S3: And . . . can you see the, can you say, electronic lines
S4: road? (= confirmation check)
S3: no, no
S4: no (not resolved)

Juanita concluded that the task was successful in generating interaction that created opportunities for learning. She noted, however, that the task resulted in very different behavior in the two students. She suggested this was because S1 and S2 had different first languages (L1s) whereas S3 and S4 shared the same L1. She also suggested that they differed in terms of the extent to which they worked together collaboratively. S1 and S2 displayed a high level of mutuality, but S3 assumed a dominant role and S4 a more passive role, reflecting differences in their English proficiency.

Juanita's evaluation drew on a number of the principles of instructed language learning discussed later in this chapter. Principle 8 states: *The opportunity to interact in the L2 is central to developing L2 proficiency.* This principle motivated her to investigate one specific aspect of interaction—the negotiation of meaning. Principle 9 states: *Instruction needs to take account of individual differences in learners.* Juanita found that the two pairs of learners reacted very differently to the task and sought explanations for why this was. Principle 4 states: *Instruction needs to be predominantly directed at developing implicit knowledge of the L2 while not neglecting explicit knowledge.* Juanita elected to use an information-gap task because this caters to the kind of incidental acquisition that fosters implicit knowledge. However, in the conclusion to her evaluation, she states that her lesson would have benefited from some explicit attention to language and suggests that this could have been provided in the form of a post-task activity that focused directly on the errors the students were making.

Evaluation is a key element of good teaching. For evaluation to be effective, it needs to draw on a set of explicitly formulated principles of instructed language learning. It also needs to subject these principles to critical scrutiny in the light of a teacher's reflection on her teaching. Juanita's task evaluation is a good example of how this can be undertaken.

WHAT IS INSTRUCTED SECOND LANGUAGE LEARNING?

Second language acquisition (SLA), as a subdiscipline of applied linguistics, is still a very young field of study. While it may not be possible to identify its precise starting point, many researchers agree that the late 1960s marked the onset of an intense period of empirical and theoretical interest in how second languages are acquired. While some researchers have been concerned with purely theoretical issues of little direct relevance to language pedagogy, others have addressed how instruction can assist SLA. There are now numerous studies that have investigated the effects of instruction on learning. Norris and Ortega (2000), for example, identified a total of 79 such studies and there have been many more since. Also, much of the theorizing about SLA has been specifically undertaken with language pedagogy in mind; for example, Krashen's Monitor Model (Krashen, 1981), Long's Interaction Hypothesis (Long, 1996), DeKeyser's Skill-Acquisition theory (DeKeyser, 1998), VanPatten's Processing Instruction theory (VanPatten, 1996, 2002), and my own theory of instructed language learning (R. Ellis, 1994a) all address the role of instruction in SLA.

However, the research and theory do not afford a uniform account of how instruction can best facilitate language learning. There is considerable controversy (see R. Ellis, 2006). In particular, there is no agreement as to whether instruction should be based on a traditional *focus-on-forms* approach, involving the systematic teaching of grammatical features in accordance with a structural syllabus, or a *focus-on-form* approach, involving attention to linguistic features in the context of communicative activities derived from a task-based syllabus, or some combination of the two. Nor is there agreement about the efficacy of teaching explicit knowledge or about what type of corrective feedback to provide or even when explicit grammar teaching should commence. These controversies reflect the complexity of the object of enquiry (instructed language acquisition), its contextual nature, and the fact that what constitutes the most effective approach for one learner may not do so for another.

Given these controversies, it might be thought unwise to attempt to formulate a set of general principles of instructed language acquisition. Hatch's (1979) warning—"apply with caution"—is as pertinent today as it was over 30 years ago.

Nevertheless, I think there is a need to try to draw together a set of generalizations that might serve as the basis for language teacher education. I am not alone in this; Lightbown (1985, 2000) felt and responded to a similar need. If SLA is to offer teachers guidance, there is a need to bite the bullet and proffer advice, as long as this advice does not masquerade as prescriptions or proscriptions (and there is always a danger that advice will be so construed). The guidance provided by this chapter should be viewed as tentative, in the form of what Stenhouse (1975) calls "provisional specifications."

I have chosen to present my own provisional specifications in the form of principles.[1] I have based these largely on a computational model of SLA (Lantolf, 1996). This model, which has informed the bulk of the research that has investigated instructed language learning, views acquisition as taking place in the mind of learners as a result of attending to and processing the input that they are exposed to. I do not expect that all SLA researchers or all language teachers will agree with the principles, not least because the computational model is disputed by researchers who view acquisition as more of a social than a cognitive activity. I hope, though, that they will provide a basis for argument and for reflection.

Principle 1: *Instruction needs to ensure that learners develop both a rich repertoire of formulaic expressions and a rule-based competence.*

Proficiency in a second language (L2) requires that learners acquire a rich repertoire of formulaic expressions, which cater to fluency and immediate functional needs. Formulaic chunks such as: *What's the time?*, *I don't know*, *Can I have a __?*, and *I'm very sorry* are part of a native speaker's linguistic repertoire and are also important for L2 learners. L2 proficiency, however, also requires that learners develop a rule-based competence consisting of knowledge of specific grammatical rules in order to understand and produce novel utterances of greater complexity and accuracy (Skehan, 1998).

There is now widespread acceptance of the importance played by formulaic expressions in language use. Advances in corpus linguistics have made it possible to identify the formulaic sequences in specific language registers and testify to their frequent use (e.g., see Simpson-Vlach & Ellis's [2010] *Academic Formulas List*). Native speakers have been shown to use a much larger number of formulaic expressions than even advanced L2 learners (Foster, 2001). Formulaic expressions may also serve as a basis for the later development of a rule-based competence. N. Ellis (1996), for example, has suggested that learners bootstrap their way to grammar by first internalizing and then analyzing fixed sequences into their component parts. Classroom studies by R. Ellis (1984), Myles, Mitchell, and Hooper (1998, 1999), and Myles (2004) demonstrate that learners often internalize rote-learned material from the input they are exposed to as chunks and then break them down for analysis later on.

Traditionally, language instruction has been directed at developing rule-based competence (i.e., knowledge of specific grammatical rules) through the systematic teaching of preselected structures, what Long (1991) has referred to as a focus-on-forms approach. While such an approach certainly receives support from research that has investigated direct intervention in interlanguage development, curriculum designers and teachers need to recognize that this type of instruction may result in students learning rote-memorized patterns rather than internalizing underlying rules (Myles, 2004). This need not be seen as an instructional failure, however, as such patterns are clearly of value to the learner. It points, instead, to an acknowledgment of what can be realistically achieved by a focus-on-forms approach, especially with young beginner learners.

If formulaic chunks play a large role in early language acquisition, it may pay to focus on these (and, more generally, on vocabulary) with beginner learners, delaying the teaching of grammar until later, as I propose in R. Ellis (2002). Lewis (1993) has argued that "language is grammaticalised lexis, not lexicalised grammar" (p. vi) and has developed his lexical approach to prioritize formulaic chunks at first. One way of achieving this is by means of a notional-functional approach. This lends itself perfectly to the teaching of routines (i.e., expressions that are completely formulaic, such as *I don't know*) and prefabricated patterns (i.e., expressions that are partly formulaic but have one or more empty slots, such as *Can I have a __ ?*), and may provide an ideal foundation for direct intervention in the early stages of language learning. Clearly, though, a complete language curriculum needs to ensure that it caters to the development of both formulaic expressions and rule-based knowledge.

Principle 2: *Instruction needs to ensure that learners focus predominantly on meaning.*

The term *focus on meaning* is somewhat ambiguous. It is necessary to distinguish two different senses of this term. The first refers to the idea of semantic meaning (i.e., the meanings of lexical items or of specific grammatical structures). For example, *can* in the sentence *I can swim* expresses a semantic meaning (i.e., ability). The second sense of *focus on meaning* relates to pragmatic meaning (i.e., the highly contextualized meanings that arise in acts of communication). *Can* also encodes pragmatic meaning, as when it is used in requests such as *Can you pass the salt?* To provide opportunities for students to attend to and perform pragmatic meaning, a task-based (or, at least, a task-supported) approach to language teaching is required. It is clearly important that instruction ensures opportunities for learners to focus on both types of meaning, but arguably, it is pragmatic meaning that is crucial to language learning.

There is an important difference in the instructional approaches needed for semantic versus pragmatic meaning. In the case of semantic meaning, the teacher and the students can treat language as an object and function as pedagogue and learners. But in the case of pragmatic meaning, they need to view the L2 as a tool for communicating and to function as communicators.[2] In effect, this involves two entirely different orientations to teaching and learning.

The opportunity to focus on pragmatic meaning is important for a number of reasons:

- In the eyes of many theorists (e.g., Prabhu, 1987; Long, 1996), only when learners are engaged in understanding and producing messages in the context of actual acts of communication are the conditions created for acquisition to take place.
- To develop true fluency in an L2, learners must have opportunities to create pragmatic meaning (DeKeyser, 1998).
- Engaging learners in activities during which they are focused on creating pragmatic meaning (and, therefore, treating language as a tool rather than as an object) is intrinsically motivating.

In arguing the need for a focus on pragmatic meaning, theorists do so not just because they see this as a means of activating the linguistic resources that have already been developed but because they see it as the principal means by which the linguistic resources themselves are created. This is the theoretical position that has informed many highly successful immersion education programs around the world (see Johnson & Swain, 1997). However, in advocating this principle, I do not wish to suggest that instruction needs to be directed exclusively at providing learners with opportunities to create pragmatic meaning but only that, to be effective, instruction must include such opportunities and that, ideally over an entire curriculum, they should be predominant.

Principle 3: *Instruction needs to ensure that learners also focus on form.*

There is now a widespread acceptance that acquisition also requires that learners attend to form. Indeed, according to some theories of L2 acquisition, such attention is necessary for acquisition to take place. Schmidt (1994a), for example, has argued that there is no learning without conscious attention to form.[3]

Again, though, the term *focus on form* is capable of more than one interpretation. First, it might refer to a general orientation to language as form. Schmidt (2001) dismisses this global attention hypothesis, arguing that learners need to attend to specific forms (e.g., the *−s* on a plural noun). Second, the term might be taken to suggest that learners need to attend only to the graphic or phonetic instantiations of linguistic forms. However, theorists such as Schmidt and Long are insistent that focus on form refers to form-function mapping (i.e., the correlation between a particular form and the meaning[s] it realizes in communication). For example, –s on a noun conveys the meaning "more than one." Third, *focus on form* might be assumed to refer to the awareness of some underlying, abstract rule. Schmidt, however, is careful to argue that attention to form refers to the noticing of specific linguistic items as they occur in the input to which learners are exposed, not to an awareness and understanding of grammatical rules.

Instruction can cater to a focus on form in a number of ways:

- through grammar lessons designed to teach specific grammatical features by means of input or output processing. An inductive approach to grammar teaching is designed to encourage the noticing of preselected forms; a deductive approach seeks to establish an awareness of the grammatical rule by providing learners with an explicit explanation
- through structure-based comprehension and production tasks (i.e., tasks that require learners to comprehend and process specific grammatical structures in the input, and/or to produce the structures in the performance of the task)
- through consciousness-raising tasks that assist learners to discover grammatical rules for themselves and to develop an explicit representation of them (e.g., see Eckerth, 2008a)
- through methodological options that induce attention to form in the context of performing a task; two methodological options that have received considerable attention from researchers are: (1) the provision of time for strategic and online planning (Foster & Skehan, 1996; Yuan & Ellis, 2003); and (2) corrective feedback (Lyster, 2004)

Instruction can seek to provide an *intentional* and *intensive* focus on preselected linguistic forms (as in a focus-on-forms approach or in a lesson built around a structure-based production-comprehension task or consciousness-raising task), or it can offer *incidental* and *extensive* attention to form through corrective feedback in task-based lessons. There are pros and cons for both intensive and extensive grammar instruction. Some structures may not be mastered without the opportunity for repeated practice. Harley (1989), for example, finds that Anglophone learners of L2 French failed to acquire the distinction between the *preterite* and *imparfait* past tenses after hours of exposure (and presumably some corrective feedback) in an immersion program but were able to improve their accuracy in the use of these two tenses after intensive instruction. However, intensive instruction is time consuming (in Harley's study the targeted structures were taught over an eight-week period!), and thus there will be constraints on how many structures can be addressed. Extensive grammar instruction, on the other hand, affords the opportunity for large numbers of grammatical structures to be addressed. Also, more likely than not, many of the structures will be attended to repeatedly over a period of time. Further, because this kind of instruction involves a response to the errors that each learner makes, it is individualized and affords the skilled teacher communicative opportunities for the kind of contextual analysis that Celce-Murcia (2002) recommends as a basis for grammar teaching. Ellis, Basturkmen, and Loewen (2001) report that extensive instruction occurred relatively frequently in communicative adult ESL lessons through both preemptive (i.e., teacher- or student-initiated) and reactive (i.e., corrective feedback) attention to form. Loewen (2005) shows that learners who experienced such momentary form-focused episodes demonstrated the subsequent learning of the forms addressed in both immediate and delayed tests. However, it is not possible to attend to those structures that learners do not attempt to use (i.e., extensive instruction cannot deal with avoidance). Also, of course, it does not provide the in-depth practice that some structures may require before they can be fully acquired. Arguably, then, instruction needs to be conceived of in terms of both approaches.

Principle 4: *Instruction needs to be predominantly directed at developing implicit knowledge of the L2 while not neglecting explicit knowledge.*

Implicit knowledge is procedural, is held unconsciously, and can be verbalized only if it is made explicit. It is accessed rapidly and easily and thus is available for use in rapid fluent communication.

In the view of most researchers, competence in an L2 is primarily a matter of implicit knowledge. Explicit knowledge "is the declarative and often anomalous knowledge of the phonological, lexical, grammatical, pragmatic and socio-critical features of an L2 together with the metalanguage for labelling this knowledge" (R. Ellis, 2004, p. 244). It is held consciously, is learnable and verbalizable, and is typically accessed through controlled processing when learners experience some kind of linguistic difficulty in the use of the L2. A distinction can be made between explicit knowledge as analyzed knowledge and as metalingual explanation. The former entails a conscious awareness of how a structural feature works, while the latter consists of knowledge of grammatical metalanguage and the ability to understand explanations of rules. Thus a person can possess explicit knowledge even though he or she lacks the metalanguage needed to express it. Neurolinguistic research (e.g., Ullman, 2001) indicates that different neural structures are involved in acquiring and storing these two types of knowledge.

Given that it is implicit knowledge that underlies the ability to communicate fluently and confidently in an L2, it is this type of knowledge that should be the ultimate goal of any instructional program. How, then, can it be developed? There are conflicting theories regarding this. According to Skill-Acquisition theory (DeKeyser, 1998), implicit knowledge arises from explicit knowledge when the latter is proceduralized through practice. In contrast, *emergentistism* (Krashen, 1981; N. Ellis, 1998) sees implicit knowledge as developing naturally from meaning-focused communication, aided, perhaps, by some focus on form. Irrespective of these different theoretical positions, there is consensus that learners need the opportunity to participate in communicative activities to develop implicit knowledge. Thus, communicative tasks need to play a central role in instruction directed at implicit knowledge.

The value in teaching explicit knowledge of grammar has been and remains today one of the most controversial issues in language pedagogy. To make sense of the different positions relating to the teaching of explicit knowledge, it is necessary to consider two separate questions:

1. Is explicit knowledge of any value in and of itself?
2. Is explicit knowledge of value in facilitating the development of implicit knowledge?

Explicit knowledge is arguably of value only if it can be shown that learners are able to use this type of knowledge in actual performance. Again, there is a controversy. One position is that this use is very limited. Krashen (1982) argues that learners can use explicit knowledge only when they monitor and that this requires that they be focused on form (as opposed to meaning) and have sufficient time to access the knowledge. Other positions are possible. It can be argued that explicit knowledge is used in both the process of formulating messages and in monitoring, and that many learners are adroit in accessing their explicit memories for these purposes, especially if the rules are, to a degree, automatized. Some current approaches to teaching grammar emphasize the importance of ensuring that learners develop clear and scientifically explicit rules. Systemic-functional instruction (see Lantolf & Thorne, 2006) is based on three fundamental principles: (1) the instruction needs to be organized around full and precise descriptions of the rules to be learned (as opposed to the kinds of rules of thumb that figure in many pedagogical grammars); (2) it needs to provide a material instantiation of the target concepts by means of charts and diagrams; and (3) learners need to verbalize the concept-based explanation to foster a full understanding and internalization of the concepts.

Irrespective of whether explicit knowledge has any value in and of itself, it may assist language development by facilitating the development of implicit knowledge. This involves a consideration of what has become known as the *interface hypothesis*, which addresses whether explicit knowledge plays a role in L2 acquisition. Three positions can be identified. According to the non-interface position (Krashen, 1981), explicit knowledge and implicit knowledge are entirely distinct, with the result that explicit knowledge cannot be converted into implicit knowledge. This position is supported by research that suggests that explicit and implicit memories are neurologically separate and do not interact with each other (Paradis, 1994). The interface position argues the exact opposite. Drawing on Skill-Acquisition theory (DeKeyser, 1998), this position argues that explicit knowledge becomes implicit knowledge if learners have the opportunity for plentiful communicative practice. Systemic-functional instruction is similarly premised on the assumption that properly formulated explicit knowledge serves as the foundation for developing implicit knowledge. The weak interface position (R. Ellis, 1993) claims that explicit knowledge primes a number of key acquisitional processes, in particular *noticing* and *noticing the gap* (Schmidt, 1994a). That is, explicit knowledge of a grammatical structure makes it more likely that learners will attend to the structure in the input and carry out the cognitive comparison between what they observe in the input and their own output. These positions have not been resolved empirically and so continue to be argued at a theoretical level.

The three positions support very different approaches to language teaching. The non-interface position leads to a *zero grammar* approach, that is, one that prioritizes meaning-centered approaches such as task-based teaching. The interface position supports the idea that a grammatical structure should be first presented explicitly and then practiced by means of, first, controlled and, then, free production activities (i.e., an approach known as PPP) until it is fully proceduralized. The weak interface position has been used to provide a basis for consciousness-raising tasks (R. Ellis, 1991). These provide learners with data that illustrate a specific grammatical feature and guide learners to a discovery of the underlying rule. There has been considerable research (e.g., see Eckerth, 2008b) that has investigated whether such tasks are effective in helping learners develop explicit knowledge and whether they are subsequently able to use this in L2 production.

This principle, then, asserts that instruction needs to be directed at developing *both* implicit and explicit knowledge, giving priority to the former. However, teachers should not assume that explicit knowledge can be converted into implicit knowledge because the extent to which this is possible remains controversial and it is clear that it does not always happen. Teachers also need to recognize that different types of instructional activities are needed to develop the two types of knowledge.

Principle 5: *Instruction needs to take into account the learner's built-in syllabus.*

Early research into naturalistic SLA showed that learners follow a natural order and sequence of acquisition (i.e., they master different grammatical structures in a relatively fixed and universal order, and they pass through a sequence of stages of acquisition en route to mastering each grammatical structure). This led researchers like Corder (1967) to suggest that learners have their own "built-in syllabus" for learning grammar as implicit knowledge. By and large, the built-in syllabus is universal (i.e., it is the same irrespective of the learner's age or L1). Nevertheless, the L1 has been found to have some influence. For example, Japanese learners of English may master plural *–s* somewhat later than Spanish learners because there is no equivalent structure in Japanese whereas there is in Spanish.

Krashen (1981) famously argues that grammar instruction plays no role in the development of implicit knowledge (what he calls *acquisition*), a view based on the conviction that learners (including classroom learners) automatically proceed along their built-in syllabus as long as they have access to comprehensible input and are sufficiently motivated. He argues that grammar instruction can contribute only to explicit knowledge (i.e., *learning*).

A number of empirical studies were conducted to: (1) compare the order of acquisition in instructed and naturalistic learners (e.g., Pica, 1983); (2) compare the success of instructed and naturalistic learners (Long, 1983); and (3) examine whether attempts to teach specific grammatical structures resulted in their acquisition (White, Spada, Lightbown, & Ranta, 1991). These studies show that, by and large, the order and sequence of acquisition is the same for instructed and naturalistic learners (e.g., R. Ellis, 1989a; Pienemann, 1989), that instructed learners generally achieve higher levels of grammatical competence than naturalistic learners, and that instruction is no guarantee that learners will acquire what they have been taught. This has led to the conclusion that it is beneficial to teach grammar but that it is necessary to ensure it is taught in a way that is compatible with the natural processes of acquisition.

How, then, can instruction take account of the learner's built-in syllabus? There are a number of possibilities:

Zero grammar approach. Adopt a zero grammar approach, as proposed by Krashen; that is, employ a task-based approach that makes no attempt to predetermine the linguistic content of a lesson.

Developmental readiness. Ensure that learners are developmentally ready to acquire a specific target feature. However, this is probably impractical because teachers have no easy way of determining which level individual students have reached and it would necessitate a highly individualized approach to cater to differences in developmental levels among the students. Also, as we noted earlier, such fine-tuning may not be necessary. While instruction in a target feature may not enable learners to "beat" the built-in syllabus, it may serve to push them along it as long as the target structure is not too far ahead of their developmental stage.

Explicit knowledge. Focus the instruction on explicit rather than implicit knowledge because explicit knowledge is not subject to the same developmental constraints as implicit knowledge. While it is probably true that some declarative facts about language are easier to master than others, this is likely to reflect their cognitive rather than their developmental complexity, which can be taken into account more easily in deciding the order of instruction. Traditional structural syllabuses, in fact, are graded on the basis of cognitive complexity.[4]

It should be noted, however, that not all researchers accept the universality and inviolability of the built-in syllabus. Skill-learning theory, for example, is premised on the assumption that *declarative knowledge* of a grammatical structure can be converted into *procedural knowledge* at any time given the right amount and type of practice. Similarly, the adoption of Vygotskian sociocultural theory "would require that we . . . eradicate the assertion that SLA progresses along a predetermined mental path" (M. Johnson, 2004, p. 172). However, these researchers do not offer evidence to support their claims—at least, not where the development of implicit knowledge is concerned.

Principle 6: *Successful instructed language learning requires extensive L2 input.*

Language learning, whether it occurs in a naturalistic or an instructed context, is a slow and laborious process. Children acquiring their L1 take between two and five years to achieve full grammatical competence, during which time they are exposed to massive amounts of input. Ellis

and Wells (1980) demonstrate that a substantial portion of the variance in speed of acquisition of children can be accounted for by the amount and the quality of input they receive. The same is undoubtedly true of SLA. If learners do not receive exposure to the target language, they cannot acquire it. In general, the more exposure they receive, the more and the faster they will learn. Krashen (1981, 1994) adopts a very strong position on the importance of input. He points to studies that have shown that length of residence in the country where the language is spoken is related to language proficiency and to other studies that that have found positive correlations between the amount of reading reported and proficiency or literacy. For Krashen, however, the input must be made *comprehensible*, either by modifying it or by means of contextual support. Other researchers (e.g., Swain, 1995) disagree with Krashen's claim that comprehensible input (together with motivation) is all that is required for successful acquisition, arguing that learner output is also important (see Principle 7), but there is wide agreement about the importance of input for developing the highly connected implicit knowledge that is needed to become an effective communicator in the L2.

How can teachers ensure their students have access to extensive input? In a second language teaching context, learners can be expected to gain access to plentiful input outside the classroom, although, as Tanaka (2004) has shown in a study of adult Japanese students learning English in Auckland, not all such learners are successful in achieving this. In a foreign language teaching context (as when French or Japanese is taught in schools in the United Kingdom or United States), there are far fewer opportunities for extensive input. To ensure adequate access, teachers need to do the following:

Maximize use of the L2 inside the classroom. Ideally, this means that the L2 needs to become the medium as well as the object of instruction, especially in a foreign language setting.[5] A study by Kim and Elder (2005) reveals that foreign language teachers of French, German, Japanese, and Korean in Auckland secondary schools varied enormously in the extent to which they employed the L2 in the classroom (i.e., between 22 and 88% of the total input).

Create opportunities for students to receive input outside the classroom. This can be achieved most easily by providing extensive reading programs based on carefully selected graded readers, suited to the level of the students, as recommended by Krashen (1989). Elley (1991) reviews studies that show that L2 learners can benefit from both reading and from being read to. Also, ideally, if more resources are available, schools need to establish self-access centers that students can use outside class time. Successful foreign language learners seek out opportunities to experience the language outside class time. Many students are unlikely to make the effort unless teachers: (1) make resources available; and (2) provide learner training in how to make effective use of the resources.

Much L2 learning is incidental rather than intentional, and this requires access to massive amounts of input. It can be claimed with confidence that, if the only input students receive is in the context of a limited number of weekly lessons based on some course book, they are unlikely to achieve high levels of L2 proficiency.

Principle 7: *Successful instructed language learning also requires opportunities for output.*

Contrary to Krashen's insistence that acquisition is dependent entirely on comprehensible input, most researchers now acknowledge that learner output also plays a part. Skehan (1998), drawing on Swain (1995), summarizes the contributions that output can make:

- Production serves to generate better input through the feedback that learners' efforts at production elicit.
- It forces syntactic processing (i.e., obliges learners to pay attention to grammar).
- It allows learners to test hypotheses about the target language grammar.
- It helps to automatize existing knowledge.
- It provides opportunities for learners to develop discourse skills (e.g., by producing "long turns").
- It is important for helping learners to develop a "personal voice" by steering conversation to topics they are interested in contributing to.

R. Ellis (2003) adds one additional contribution of output:

- It provides the learner with "auto-input" (i.e., learners can attend to the input provided by their own productions).

The importance of creating opportunities for output, including what Swain (1985) has called *pushed output* (i.e., output where the learner is stretched to express messages clearly and explicitly), constitutes one of the main reasons for incorporating tasks into a language program. Controlled practice exercises typically result in output that is limited in terms of length and complexity. They do not afford students opportunities for the kind of sustained output that theorists argue is necessary for interlanguage development. Research (e.g., Allen, Swain, Harley, & Cummins, 1990) has shown that extended talk consisting of a clause or more in a classroom context is more likely to occur when students initiate interactions in the classroom and when they have to find their own words. This is best achieved by asking learners to perform oral and written tasks.

Principle 8: *The opportunity to interact in the L2 is central to developing L2 proficiency.*

While it is useful to consider the relative contributions of input and output to acquisition, it is also important to acknowledge that both co-occur in oral interaction and that both cognitive-interactional (e.g., Long, 1996) and sociocultural (e.g., Lantolf & Thorne, 2006) theories of SLA have viewed social interaction as the matrix in which acquisition takes place. As Hatch (1978) famously put it, "one learns how to do conversation, one learns how to interact verbally, and out of the interaction syntactic structures are developed" (p. 404). Thus, interaction is not just a means of automatizing existing linguistic resources but also of creating new resources. According to the Interaction Hypothesis (Long, 1996), interaction fosters acquisition when a communication problem arises and learners are engaged in negotiating for meaning. The interactional modifications arising help to make input comprehensible, provide corrective feedback, and push learners to modify their own output when they repair their errors. In sociocultural theory, interaction serves as a form of mediation, enabling learners to construct new forms and perform new functions collaboratively (Lantolf, 2000). According to this view, learning is first evident on the social plane and only later on the psychological plane. In both theories, while social interaction may not be viewed as necessary for acquisition, it is viewed as the primary source of learning.

What then are the characteristics of interaction that are deemed important for acquisition? In general terms, opportunities for negotiating meaning and plenty of scaffolding (assistance from experts) are needed. K. Johnson (1995) identifies four key requirements for interaction to create an acquisition-rich classroom:

1. creating contexts of language use where students have a reason to attend to language
2. providing opportunities for learners to use the language to express their own personal meanings
3. helping students to participate in language-related activities that are beyond their current level of proficiency
4. offering a full range of contexts that cater for a full performance in the language

Johnson suggests that these are more likely to occur when the academic task structure (i.e., how the subject matter is sequenced in a lesson) and the social participation structure (i.e., how the allocation of interactional rights and obligations shapes the discourse) are less rigid. Once again, this is more likely to be provided through tasks than through exercises. R. Ellis (1999) suggests that a key to ensuring interaction that is beneficial to acquisition is giving control of the discourse topic to the students. This, of course, is not easily achieved given that teachers have a duty to ensure that classroom discourse is orderly, which, in turn, is most easily achieved by taking control of the discourse topic by means of IRF (teacher initiates–student responds–teacher provides feedback) exchanges. Thus, creating the right kind of interaction for acquisition constitutes a major challenge for teachers.

One solution is to incorporate small-group work into a lesson. When students interact among themselves, acquisition-rich discourse is more likely to ensue. Learners speak more and use the L2 for a wider range of language functions (Long & Porter, 1985). However, there are a number of dangers in group work that may militate against this (e.g., excessive use of the L1 in monolingual groups and exposure to interlanguage errors), and some educators (e.g., Prabhu, 1987) have argued that it is more important to ensure that learners are exposed to well-formed L2 input from teacher-class interaction.

Principle 9: *Instruction needs to take into account individual differences in learners.*

While there are identifiable universal aspects of L2 acquisition, there is also considerable variability in the rate of learning and in the ultimate level of achievement. In particular, learning will be more successful when:

■ The instruction is matched to students' particular aptitude for learning.
■ The students are motivated.

It is probably beyond the abilities of most teachers to design lessons involving the kind of matching instruction employed in Wesche's (1981) study. This used language aptitude tests to identify different learning styles and then sought to match the kind of instruction provided to the learners' preferred approach to learning. However, teachers can cater to such variation in their students' aptitudes by adopting a flexible teaching approach involving a variety of learning activities. They can also make use of simple learner-training materials (e.g., Ellis & Sinclair, 1989) designed to make students more aware of their own approaches to learning and to develop their awareness of alternative approaches. Good language learner studies (e.g., Naiman, Fröhlich, Stern, & Todesco, 1996) suggest that successful language learning requires a flexible approach to learning. Thus, increasing the range of learning strategies at the learners' disposal is one way in which teachers can help them to learn. Such strategy training needs to foster an understanding that language learning requires both an experiential and an analytical approach and to demonstrate the kinds of strategies related to both approaches. School-based students often tend to adopt an analytical approach to learning (even if this does not accord with their natural aptitude) because this is the kind of approach generally fostered in schools (Sternberg, 2002). They may have greater difficulty in adopting the kind of experiential learning required in task-based language teaching. Some learner training, therefore, may be essential if learners are to perform tasks effectively.[6]

Dörnyei's research has shown the kinds of teaching strategies that teachers can employ to develop and maintain their students' intrinsic motivation. Dörnyei (2001) also makes the obvious point that "the best motivational intervention is simply to improve the quality of our teaching" (p. 26). Dörnyei and Csizér (1998) conducted a study of 200 high school teachers in Hungary and, based on their self-reported use of motivating strategies, identified "10 commandments" for motivating learners. Examples are "create a pleasant and relaxed atmosphere in the classroom" and "increase the learners' goal-orientedness." Guilloteaux and Dörnyei (2008), in a study of EFL classrooms in Korea, find a significant positive correlation between the teacher's motivational practice and the learners' motivated behavior. These studies show that motivation is not just something learners bring to the classroom but something that can be generated inside the classroom. Teachers also need to accept that it is *their* responsibility to ensure that students are motivated and stay motivated. While it is probably true that teachers can do little to influence students' extrinsic motivation, there is a lot they can do to enhance their intrinsic motivation.

Principle 10: *In assessing learners' L2 proficiency, it is important to examine free as well as controlled production.*

Norris and Ortega's (2000) meta-analysis of studies investigating form-focused instruction demonstrates that the extent of the effectiveness of instruction is contingent on the way it is measured. They distinguish four types of measurement:

1. metalinguistic judgment (e.g., a grammaticality judgment test)
2. selected response (e.g., multiple choice)
3. constrained constructed response (e.g., gap-filling exercises)
4. free constructed response (e.g., a communicative task)

They find that the magnitude of effect was greatest in Types 2 and 3 and least in Type 4. Yet, arguably, it is Type 4 that constitutes the best measure of learners' L2 proficiency because

it is this measure that corresponds most closely to the kind of language use found outside the classroom. The ability to get a multiple-choice question right amounts to very little if the student is unable to use the target feature in actual communication.

Free constructed responses are best elicited by means of tasks. The performance elicited by means of tasks can be assessed in three ways (R. Ellis, 2003): (1) a direct assessment of task outcomes; (2) discourse analytic measures; and (3) external ratings. Method 2 is not practical for busy classroom teachers because it requires transcribing speech and then painstakingly calculating such measures as number of error-free clauses and clause complexity. Method 3 is practical, but it requires considerable expertise to ensure that the ratings of learner performance are valid and reliable. Method 1 holds the most promise for classroom testing. However, it is possible only with closed tasks (i.e., a task for which there is a single correct outcome), such as a spot-the-difference task, where learners are asked to interact to find a specified number of differences in two similar pictures. In this task, assessment consists of establishing whether learners were able to successfully identify the differences.

FUTURE TRENDS

The 10 principles were first formulated in 2005 as part of a report for the New Zealand Ministry of Education, entitled *Instructed Language Acquisition: A Literature Review.*[7] At that time, my work in SLA was largely informed by the computational model of learning, so the principles were mainly based on this model. Since then, SLA has been increasingly influenced by more socially oriented theories of learning, in particular sociocultural theory. This theory differs from the computational model in a number of important ways, most significantly in how it views learning. In the computational model, learning occurs inside the head of the learner; the role of instruction, therefore, is to prompt the internal cognitive processes required for learning to take place. In sociocultural theory, learning is a social phenomenon; it occurs *in* the social interactions in which learners participate. Interaction, in other words, is not just a source of input but a powerful means for mediating learning. Furthermore, research based on sociocultural theory has provided a much richer account of how interaction can assist learning than does the computational model. It has shown, for example, that the collaborative talk that learners engage in when they experience linguistic problems helps them not only to resolve these problems in targetlike ways while they are talking but also to remember the solutions and use them independently in their own language use at a later date. In short, talking about language leads to learning. Social learning is the precursor to individual learning.

The insights provided by sociocultural theory feed into a number of the existing principles, as I have indicated in this chapter (e.g., see Principle 8). But they also point to a new principle:

Principle 11: *Learners need to engage collaboratively in talk about linguistic problems and try to agree on solutions to them.*

This principle can be seen as an extension of Principle 7 (*Successful instructed language learning also requires opportunities for output*) but it is, arguably, so important that it should be stated as a separate principle.

I am also aware of another gap. In general, the principles assume a universalistic view of L2 learning; they view language learning as involving cognitive processes that are common to all learners. To a large extent, this is true. We know, for example, that all learners follow a very similar order and sequence of acquisition (see Principle 5), and certainly having plenty of input and having the opportunity to interact in the L2 are key to successful learning for all. I have acknowledged the role of learner factors such as language aptitude and motivation in language learning (see Principle 9), but I have so far made no mention of one important area of individual difference in learners—the subjective nature of language learning. Learning a new language is not just a question of developing linguistic or communicative ability but also, potentially at least, an opportunity to acquire a new symbolic form. Learners have the opportunity to develop their subjective selves by taking on new identities and even a new personality. Learning an L2 can change how people view reality and how they see the world around them. Thus, I see a need for an additional principle:

Principle 12: *Instruction needs to take into account the subjective aspect to learning a new language.*

This principle indicates the need for instructional activities that encourage learners to engage in language play and to form an emotional identification with the target language. One way this can be achieved is through the introduction of literature and creative writing into the L2 curriculum.

Finally, I emphasize that the 12 principles I have proposed are not cast in stone. As I have just shown, they will be subject to modification as a result of new theoretical perspectives on L2 learning.

CONCLUSION

These general principles have been derived from my understanding of SLA. I have drawn on a variety of theoretical perspectives, although predominantly from the computational model of L2 learning. I am aware that this model has its limitations and is open to criticism; in particular, it is not socially sensitive because it fails to acknowledge the importance of social context and social relations in the language learning process (for an extended critique along these lines, see Block, 2003). Clearly, it would be useful to formulate a set of principles based on the broader conceptualization of SLA of the kind advocated by Block and others, but this is not my aim here. There will always be a need for a psycholinguistic account of how learners internalize new linguistic forms and how they restructure their linguistic knowledge during the process of acquisition. Social theories emphasize language use, but language use is *not* language acquisition, only a means to it. To my mind, the computational model, along with sociocultural theory, provides a solid foundation for developing a set of principles that articulate the relationships among instruction, language use, and language acquisition. It also constitutes a metaphor that teachers can easily relate to.

SUMMARY

This chapter draws together findings from a range of second language acquisition studies to formulate a set of general principles for language pedagogy. These principles address such issues as:

➤ the nature of second language competence as formulaic and rule-based knowledge
➤ the contributions of both focus on meaning and focus on form
➤ the need to develop both implicit and explicit second language knowledge
➤ the problems posed by the learners' built-in syllabus
➤ the roles of input, output, and interaction in learning
➤ the importance of catering to individual differences in learners
➤ the need to assess language learning in terms of both free and controlled production

The principles are offered as provisional specifications for a learning-centered language pedagogy.

DISCUSSION QUESTIONS

1. Do you agree that formulaic sequences and vocabulary are more important than grammar in the early stage of L2 learning?
2. Explain the difference between semantic meaning and pragmatic meaning, and think of one instructional activity for each.
3. The chapter describes four ways of focusing on form (see p. 35). What do you see as the advantages and limitations of each way?
4. Given that the main goal of teaching should be to help students acquire implicit L2 knowledge, how do you think this can be best achieved?
5. What are your own views about the value of teaching explicit L2 knowledge?
6. Make a list of ways in which you can maximize the input that your students are exposed to (a) inside the classroom and (b) outside the classroom.
7. "Controlled practice exercises typically result in output that is limited in terms of length and complexity" (p. 39). Do you agree with this statement? Do you see any advantages of such exercises?
8. In many classrooms, students have only limited opportunities to interact using the L2. Why is this? What can you do to provide students with more opportunities to interact?

SUGGESTED ACTIVITIES

1. Observe a lesson of a teacher whom you know well. Your aim is to investigate to what extent the lesson manifests the principles of instructed language learning. You can use these questions to help you carry out your observation:

Principle 1: Do the students use formulaic chunks in the target language during the lesson? Do the students produce utterances in the target language that contain complex constructions?

Principle 2: Are there opportunities for students to focus on pragmatic meaning during the lesson? Does the lesson contain any communicative tasks? What proportion of the lesson time engages learners in processing pragmatic meaning?

Principle 3: What evidence is there of attention to form in any of these ways?

▪ through grammar/vocabulary/pronunciation lessons designed to teach specific linguistic features
▪ through focused tasks
▪ through methodological options designed to induce attention to form (e.g., planning, preemptive attention to form, and reactive attention to form)
▪ through an intentional (intensive) and incidental (extensive) approach to lessons

Principle 4: What opportunities are there for the learners to develop implicit L2 knowledge? Does the teacher attempt to teach explicit knowledge of the target language? If so, how?

Principle 5: If the lesson takes a focus-on-forms approach, what specific grammatical structure is the target of the lesson? How did the learners appear to handle this grammatical structure: (a) very easily, (b) with some difficulty, (c) with great difficulty, (d) not at all?

Principle 6: How extensive is the input that the learners are exposed to in the lesson? What does the teacher do to try to make the target language input comprehensible?

Principle 7: When the students speak in the target language, how long are their utterances typically: (a) single words, (b) short phrases, (c) full clauses, (d) multiple-clause sentences?

Principle 8: What evidence is there that negotiation of meaning is taking place? What evidence is there that the teacher is scaffolding students' attempts to use the target language? Do the students work in groups? If they do, do they use English or their L1?

Principle 9: To what extent are the instructional activities designed to take into account differences among the students? How intrinsically motivated do the students seem to be during the instructional activities? What indicators are there of their motivation or lack of it?

2. When you have finished your observation, discuss your findings with the teacher and ask him or her to comment on them.

3. Choose an ESL or EFL textbook that you know well. To what extent do the methodological approach and the activities in the textbook accord with the principles discussed in this chapter?

4. "While it is probably true that teachers can do little to influence students' extrinsic motivation, there is a lot they can do to enhance their intrinsic motivation" (p. 41). Note the difference between extrinsic motivation (efforts made by the learner in anticipation of external rewards) and intrinsic motivation (efforts made by the learner when there are are possible internal rewards). Drawing on your own experiences as a language learner or as a teacher, make a list of the strategies that teachers can use to enhance their students' intrinsic motivation.

FURTHER READING

Ellis, R. (1999). Making the classroom acquisition rich. In R. Ellis (Ed.), *Learning a second language through interaction* (pp. 211–229). Amsterdam, The Netherlands: John Benjamins.

Ellis discusses how opportunities for language learning are more likely to arise when the students have the chance to initiate topics and control their development in classroom discourse.

Erlam, R., & Sakui, K. (2006). *Instructed second language acquisition: Case studies.* Wellington, New Zealand: Ministry of Education.

This report presents the results of a study that investigated the classroom practice of teachers of foreign languages in terms of the extent to which this conformed to Ellis's ten principles.

Gibbons, P. (2007). Mediating academic language learning through classroom discourse. In J. Cummins & C. Davison (Eds.), *International handbook of English language teaching* (pp. 701–718). New York, NY: Springer.

Gibbons identifies four conditions that need to be met for what she calls "progressive discourse" to take place in the classroom.

Gray, S. (2009). From principles to practice: Teachers' uptake of principles from instructed learning to plan a focus on language in content lessons. *System, 37,* 570–584.

This article describes how a pair of secondary content teachers used Ellis's principles in an action research project to focus on form when planning a task-based lesson sequence.

Johnson, K. (1995). *Understanding communication in second language classrooms.* Cambridge, UK: Cambridge University Press.

Johnson distinguishes "academic task structures" (i.e., how the subject matter is sequenced in a lesson and the sequential steps involved) and "social participation structures" (i.e., how the allocation of interactional rights and obligations shapes the discourse).

Walsh, S. (2002). Construction or obstruction: teacher talk and learner involvement in the EFL classroom. *Language Teaching Research*, 6, 3–24.

Walsh identifies ten features of typical language classroom discourse and then suggests ways in which teachers can both enhance and impede learners' participation in the classroom.

ENDNOTES

[1] This chapter is an expanded version of an article first published as: Ellis, R. (2005). Principles of instructed language learning. *System*, *33*(2), 209–224.

[2] It is also possible to teach pragmatic meaning as an "object." That is, specific pragmatic meanings (e.g., requesting or apologizing) can be identified and instructional materials developed to teach learners the linguistic means for performing these strategies. See Kasper and Rose (2002) for examples of studies that have investigated the effectiveness of this approach. Such an approach constitutes a version of "focus on forms," discussed on p. 33. Here, however, I wish to emphasize the need to create materials that allow students to create their own pragmatic meanings through communication.

[3] The extent to which attention to form is *necessary* for learning remains controversial, however. A number of researchers (e.g., Williams, 2005) have provided evidence to demonstrate that some learning takes place without awareness. Schmidt (2001) has modified his position somewhat to allow for the possibility of nonconscious registration of linguistic form, arguing only that "more attention results in more learning" (p. 30).

[4] A good example of where cognitive complexity and developmental complexity can be distinguished is subject-verb agreement in English. This is typically introduced very early in structural courses, but it is invariably mastered only at a very advanced stage of development.

[5] In advocating use of the L2 as the medium of instruction, I do not wish to suggest that the learners' L1 has no role to play in the classroom. Polio and Duff (1994) have identified a number of ways in which the L1 can be used in the L2 classroom.

[6] Foster (1998) reports that the adult ESL learners she investigated engaged in very little negotiation of meaning when performing tasks because they failed to take them seriously. They viewed them as "games" and eschewed negotiation because it would detract from the "fun."

[7] See http://www.educationcounts.govt.nz/publications/schooling/5163

4 Syllabus and Curriculum Design for Second Language Teaching

KATHLEEN GRAVES

KEY QUESTIONS

➤ What is the relationship between syllabus and curriculum design?
➤ What are the challenges involved in designing a language-learning syllabus?
➤ What is the role of teachers and learners in curriculum design?

EXPERIENCE

The English Language Studies [ELS] program was less of an organized program, and more of a hodge-podge of courses. Staffed initially by adjuncts, these courses were a series of attempts to address the needs of international and immigrant students on campus, but there was no central plan or means of assessing effectiveness. . . . For the ELS faculty, there was a pervading sense that the program was stagnant. (Petro, 2007, p. 119)

I've just found out that I [will be] teaching a one month intensive course for adults to be held in Quito, Ecuador, next January. . . . I can't quite envision what it is I am going to do for one hundred hours with the same class. I mean, I can't even begin to plan a course if I don't know what the students are going to have to do in and with the language. (Blyth, 1996, pp. 86–87)

EFL [English as a foreign language] learners in China have many opportunities to learn English and to use the language in their daily lives. Even so, some EFL learners may not know about or take advantage of those resources or opportunities. . . . My motivation for revitalizing the curriculum for my classes stemmed from the realization that the existing curriculum did not take advantage of the available resources and opportunities to help students use English in a context beyond school. (Zhang, 2008, p. 293)

After more than fourteen years' experience teaching, I am still learning how to work effectively to meet the needs of English as an additional language [EAL] learners in the inner-city south London school in which I teach. . . . A critical factor is that there is no separate EAL curriculum, and government authorities that deal with the issue of making the curriculum accessible for learners of EAL provide very little guidance for coordinators [of EAL instruction]. (Waters, 2006, pp. 101–102)

The teachers, administrators, and coordinators quoted here describe their motivation and challenges as they sought to design or redesign courses and programs for language learners in very different contexts. In this chapter, we explore what is involved in syllabus and curriculum design, and how to meet such challenges in ways that are responsive to the needs of learners and the context.

WHAT IS A SYLLABUS?

A syllabus provides information about a course. It can include a range of information. Figures 1 and 2 represent two different English language–focused courses. Figure 1 is a syllabus, and Figure 2 is part of a syllabus. The title of each course has intentionally been omitted to show that what is in a syllabus depends on who the learners are, their purposes for learning, and the context in which the course takes place. Each syllabus provides clues to the learners, their purposes, and the context. You are invited to take a moment to study them to see if you can provide a title or a context for each course.

Figure 1 provides the following clues to the nature the course. The topics (e.g., "smoking" and "cyber-love") suggest the learners are adults or young adults, since they are not appropriate for children.

Title of course: _____

Goals
- Improve communication skills (focus on speaking and writing skills)
- Develop awareness about language learning

Objectives
- Enable students to have 4-minute discussions about social topics
- Enable students to write a five-paragraph essay about social topics
- Enable students to think logically and express their opinions in a debate
- Enable students to be autonomous learners through peer editing, self-assessment, and portfolio assessment

Topics (from *Impact Topics*, Day & Yamanaka, 1999)
- I Can't Stop (Unit 4; discussion)
- My Pet Peeves (Unit 19; discussion)
- Smoking (Unit 3; discussion)
- Living Together before Marriage (Unit 10; debate)
- English Should Be a Second Official Language in Japan (Lesson 7: English and the Filipinos, from the textbook in English Reading class; debate)
- Cosmetic Surgery (from *Impact Issues*, Day & Yamanaka, 1998; debate)
- Cyber Love (Unit 8; debate)

Assessment Components:
- Term examination (40%)
- Assignments (15%)
- Speaking test (20%)
- Fun essay (20%)
- Portfolio (5%)

Figure 1. Syllabus 1 (Sato & Takahashi, 2008).

One topic focuses specifically on Japan, which suggests that the learners are Japanese. The students appear to be at an intermediate level because the objectives require a four-minute discussion and a five-paragraph essay. The assessment includes a term examination, which suggests the context for the course is an academic setting. The purposes for learning focus on speaking and writing using the genres of discussions, debates, and an essay; these purposes also suggest the setting is academic. The topics are from course books, which suggests that the course focuses on general English rather than on specific content. One objective is for learners to become autonomous, which suggests they may not be accustomed to being self-directed learners. The assessment includes a "fun essay," so the course may not be completely academic. The course appears to be extensive because seven chapters are addressed in one term.

Figure 2 provides the following clues to the type of course and who the learners are. The first aim mentions preparing students for university, which suggests the learners are university age. Their level of language appears to be advanced because they are expected to listen to lectures and take notes, write argumentative essays, and prepare annotated bibliographies. The mention of a specific university in the first aim suggests the context is a university or linked to it and that the purpose for learning is to be able to participate in university courses. The course seems highly academic because it focuses on academic text types, tutorials, lectures, and critical reading. The course appears to be intensive, since it meets every day for 10 weeks. Topics are not specified, so it is possible the learners choose their own topics.

The two courses have similarities. They are for young adults or adults, rather than children. They seem to be taking place in academic settings. Both focus on writing and speaking (although the second one also focuses on listening and reading). There are also striking differences. The learners are at different levels of language proficiency. One course takes place at an English-medium university; the other is in Japan. One is topic-focused and uses a course book; the other is focused on academic preparation and uses authentic texts. One is extensive; the other is intensive. In fact, Figure 1 is the syllabus for a writing course for students in their final year of high school in Japan

Title of course: _____

Course Aims:

- To facilitate the active development of skills needed to function successfully within the particular discourse community in which learners will participate at Macquarie University
- To introduce learners to the text types they are likely to encounter during their university studies
- To facilitate the development of communication skills, both verbal and nonverbal
- To encourage learners to focus on planning skills and developing a study plan as a valuable strategy for future studies
- To familiarize learners with the dynamics used in tutorials and lectures regarding the setting of assignments and tutorial discussions

Excerpt from 10-Week Timetable

Week	Monday	Tuesday	Wednesday	Thursday	Friday
2	Oral discussion techniques Tutorial discussion Group presentations	Reading skills: Inference Written argumentation techniques Group presentations	Individual consultations Group presentations	Listening to lectures: Signposts Group presentations	Connectives Class meeting Homework: Critical reading and summary Group presentations
3	Tutorial discussion Case studies Group presentations	Group presentations Case studies	Individual consultations Group presentations Case studies	Listening to longer talks Group presentations	Class meeting Homework: Critical reading and summary Group presentations
4	Tutorial discussion Essay and exam questions, and assignment instructions Group presentations	Essay structure Group presentations	Individual consultations Group presentations	Annotated bibliography and reference list Group presentations	Class meeting Homework: Critical reading and summary Group presentations

Figure 2. Syllabus 2 excerpts (Agosti, 2006).

(Sato & Takahashi, 2008). Figure 2 is an English for academic purposes (EAP) course that prepares students to enter the Department of Economics and Financial Studies at Macquarie University in Australia (Agosti, 2006).

The syllabus in Figure 3 comes from yet a different context, with different learners and purposes for learning. It is markedly different from the first two in that it identifies content objectives, content concepts, and supplementary materials that are not related to language learning per se. These suggest that it is an academic course that focuses on science and the environment. Evidence that the unit is intended for or geared toward language learners is the presence of language objectives, vocabulary, and adaptation of content. Clues to the learners for whom it is intended may not be apparent until the description of the activities, which include songs

and snack time. These suggest that the learners are in primary school. It is also different because it is for a unit, not for a course or a semester, which is typical of how the curriculum of primary school classes is organized.

Like the other two academic courses, this syllabus focuses on speaking skills, specifically, giving a presentation. It also focuses on listening and questioning skills. The principal outcomes of the unit, however, are not only language skills but an understanding and mastery of content. In fact, the course is for fifth-grade learners (ages 10–11) in a public sector school in the United States (Sharkey & Cade, 2008). The context is a self-contained English as a second language (ESL) classroom, although it could also be a mainstream classroom that includes both mother-tongue English speakers and English language learners.

4-Week Interdisciplinary Biomes Unit

Content objectives:
Students will demonstrate an understanding that all
  biomes depend on the relationships of living things
  within that ecosystem.
Students will work in groups to create a diagram that
  illustrates the interdependence of plants and animals
  within a specific biome.

Language objectives:
Students will give an oral presentation of their biome
  project, appropriately using target vocabulary.
Students will evaluate each other's group projects
  through listening and questioning.

Content concepts:
An ecosystem is a group of interdependent organisms
  together with the environment that they inhabit and
  depend on.
A biome is an ecosystem that covers a large area of land.
Plants and animals within a particular ecosystem have
  interdependent relationships.
A food chain is a series of steps showing the transfer of
  energy among living things.

New vocabulary:
*Ecosystem, habitat, producer, consumer, decomposer,
  omnivore, herbivore, carnivore*

Supplementary materials:
Posters of biomes and food chains
Wall charts of plant and animal classification
Nonfiction books about biomes (at a variety of reading
  levels)
Overhead transparencies of food webs (downloaded
  from various websites)
Poster board and markers for students
Printouts of information about different animals (from
  various websites)

Adaptation of content:
Charts
Books
Songs (e.g., "Habitat")
The ways in which students use the maps and charts
  from the textbook

Meaningful activities:
Computer searches for information on assigned biomes
Group work creating biomes posters
Read alouds during snack time and other transition times
Class discussions
Vocabulary classification activities
Singing content songs at the end of each day

Figure 3. Syllabus 3 excerpt (Sharkey & Cade, 2008).

The information in Figures 1, 2, and 3 shows that syllabus design requires a good understanding of the learners, their purposes for learning, and the resources and constraints of the context in which they are learning. These understandings, which the syllabus designer finds out via needs assessment and context analysis, allow her or him to set goals as to what will be learned, how, and why; to choose or design materials, activities, and assessment tasks; and to organize them within the time frame available. These processes are discussed in detail in the next sections.

WHAT IS A CURRICULUM?

A curriculum is a dynamic system of interconnected, interrelated, and overlapping processes. The three main curricular processes are planning, enacting, and evaluating. (The second process is also called "implementing." The distinction between enacting and implementing will be explored later in the chapter.) These processes are in play at every curricular level, whether it is a lesson, unit, course, or program. They are carried out by people and may result in an array of curriculum products such as syllabuses, lesson plans, and assessment instruments.

At the lesson level, a teacher plans a lesson for a class. The process of lesson planning results in a product: a detailed written plan, a set of notes, marginal notes in the textbook, or a mental plan. Teacher and learners enact the lesson, which may go according to plan or may diverge from it, depending on a variety of factors. As the lesson is enacted, the teacher makes adjustments depending on what happens in the classroom. During and after the lesson, the teacher (sometimes in conjunction with the learners) evaluates its effectiveness and makes decisions that affect the planning and enactment of the next lesson or future lessons.

At the program level, a person or group of people designs a curriculum plan for an educational program. Teachers and learners enact the curriculum over time (which may follow or diverge from the plan). Its effectiveness is then evaluated informally, if not formally. Unlike the lesson level, where the teacher is usually the planner of the lesson, at the program level there are degrees of separation between the different people who conduct the processes and create the products of planning, enacting, and evaluating. Because of this separation among participants, communication and mutual understanding are essential to a coherent curriculum (R. K. Johnson, 1989; Markee, 1997).

Between the micro level of a lesson and the macro level of a program are in-between levels such as units and courses. Typically, a teacher (or group of teachers) makes a plan for a course, teacher and students enact the course, and teachers and others evaluate the effectiveness of the course to improve it. The process of planning a course results in a written plan called a syllabus. At its most basic, then, a syllabus describes what will be taught in a course. Curriculum is a broader concept than syllabus in two ways: it applies to the program level, which subsumes courses, units, and lessons; and it is more comprehensive than a syllabus because it includes not only planning but also enacting and evaluating. Curriculum and syllabus are similar because both involve similar planning processes, although at different levels of scale.

In summary, at its most basic, a syllabus describes what will be taught in a course. Curriculum is a broader concept than syllabus because it goes beyond planning and beyond the course level. That said, the term *syllabus* is also used to refer to the content of a program, as in "the program syllabus," especially in British-influenced English language teaching. The term *curriculum* is also used to refer to the instructional content of a course, as in "the curriculum for my course," especially in American-influenced English language teaching.

CONCEPTUAL UNDERPINNINGS

Syllabus types

In the field of language teaching, the term *syllabus* has both practical and theoretical meanings. In a practical sense, a syllabus is an actual plan for a course. In a theoretical sense, it refers to "a specific way to conceptualize what language is and how language is learned so that materials can be selected or prepared for the classroom" (K. Graves, 2008, p. 161). This focus on syllabus, rather than on the broader concerns of curriculum, appears to be unique to the field of language teaching (J. C. Richards, 2001a). One reason for this emphasis on syllabus is that language is not inherently a subject to be learned in school, like science or history. Rather, it is a tool that humans use to express themselves, to think, to communicate, to construct knowledge, and so on. The *study* of language,

linguistics, is not the *learning* of language. To turn language into something that can be learned in a classroom, we need ways to define and package it so it can be taught (K. Graves, 2008). The different ways it has been packaged emerge in different types of syllabuses. The syllabus types described next chart a history of how applied linguists and practitioners in the field of language teaching have defined what we teach. Each type provides a lens through which to understand the complex phenomenon of language as something that can be learned and taught.

Grammatical, formal, or structural syllabuses. The grammatical syllabus is organized around the grammatical structures of the language: verb tenses, question formation, types of clauses, and so on. It focuses on grammatical patterns as the building blocks of language, usually at the sentence level. The grammatical syllabus has been criticized because learners learn *about* the language and its systems, not *how to use* the language to express themselves, construct knowledge, communicate, and so on (Breen, 1987a). Nevertheless, it continues to be the operating system of many courses.

Notional-functional syllabus. The notional-functional syllabus (Wilkins, 1976) is organized around the communicative purposes, called functions, for which people use language (e.g., to obtain information or to apologize) and the notions that are being communicated (e.g., time and space). Unlike for the grammatical syllabus, which could be designed without reference to learners, for the notional-functional syllabus it is important to find out about the learners' needs for using the language—with whom, where, and why. The Common European Framework of Reference (Council of Europe, 2001) grew out of the work on the notional-functional syllabus.

Task-based syllabus. The task-based syllabus is organized around tasks. By doing tasks together, learners use whatever language they have to negotiate the task, and through that negotiation, they acquire the language (Breen, 1987a, 1987b; Nunan, 1989a). Tasks can range from real-world tasks to pedagogic tasks, from open-ended tasks to tasks that have one solution, and from tasks that target certain language use to those that encourage general language use (J. R. Willis, 2004). (See also Nunan, this volume.)

Skills-based approaches. Skills-based approaches are organized around the four macro skills of speaking, listening, reading, and writing. A focus on using the skills in context so learners can cope with authentic language is the basis for proficiency-oriented instruction (Omaggio Hadley, 2001). The skills are further broken down into micro skills (e.g., reading for details or using transitions in writing) and strategies. The syllabus is built around situations and communicative interactions as well as around tasks that enable learners to learn the micro skills and use the strategies.

Lexical syllabus. A lexical syllabus is based on a mini-corpus of common, pragmatically useful language items and language patterns drawn from spoken and written language corpora. (See McCarthy & O'Keeffe, this volume.) The lexical items in the corpus are embedded in authentic language texts, and learners work inductively to understand the patterns of usage. This enables them to learn large amounts of useful vocabulary (Lewis, 2001; D. Willis, 1990).

Genre or text-based syllabus. The text-based syllabus is organized around genres. Genres are spoken or written texts, such as recounts, lectures, and critical reviews, structured in particular ways to achieve particular social purposes. Texts are selected according to learners' educational and social needs (Burns, Joyce, & Gollin, 1996; Feez, 1998, 2001). Learners analyze texts to identify particular linguistic moves, specialized vocabulary, and so on to produce or participate in the texts effectively.

Project-based language learning. Project-based language learning uses a project or projects as the backbone of the syllabus. Learners engage in individual and cooperative investigative and production-based tasks to complete a project. The work is meant to be self-directed, with the teacher as resource. The projects result in an end product such as a research report, a performance, or a presentation (Beckett, 2006; Stoller, 2006). (See also Nunan, this volume.)

Content-based instruction and content and language integrated learning. Content-based instruction (CBI) and content and language integrated learning (CLIL) syllabuses are organized around subject-specific content (e.g., history or science)

in addition to or as a means to learning language (Lopriore, 2009; Snow & Brinton, 1997; Stoller, 2002b). Approaches vary as to the relative emphasis on content or language. When the emphasis is on content, learners are expected to learn the content in the target language and may be assessed on their mastery of the content. When the emphasis is on language, the content is a means for language learning, not an end in itself. (See also Snow, this volume.)

Negotiated syllabus. The negotiated or process syllabus grew out of the task-based syllabus, in the sense that it is through processes of negotiation in interaction with others that one uses and acquires language (Breen, 1987a, 1987b). It contrasts with product-based syllabuses, which focus on the knowledge and skills that are the products of learning (Nunan, 1988) and in which decisions about what will be learned are made prior to meeting the learners. The negotiated syllabus has itself shifted from a thing—a type of syllabus—to an educational process—a negotiation in which teacher and learners share decision making in the classroom. Breen and Littlejohn (2000) call this procedural negotiation: "Procedural negotiation in the language classroom comprises overt and shared decision-making . . . so that the teaching-learning process within a class can be as effective as possible" (p. 9).

Two views of curriculum

The notion that negotiation is vital to effective classroom processes is congruent with an enactment view of curriculum, in which the curriculum is seen as the educational experiences jointly created by teacher and learners in the classroom (Eisner, 1985; Snyder, Bolin, & Zumwalt, 1992). The enactment view contrasts with an implementation view, in which a curriculum is designed by curriculum specialists and is implemented by the teachers and learners. That is, the processes of planning and implementing are seen as sequential stages, each carried out by different specialists in a hierarchical manner (R. K. Johnson, 1989). Policymakers set curriculum policy; a curriculum committee analyzes needs, decides on methodology, and produces a curriculum plan; materials writers produce materials according to the plan; teacher trainers train the teachers to use the materials; and the teachers and learners use the materials in the classroom. The implementation view of curriculum puts the learners whom the curriculum is meant to serve, and the teachers who teach them, at the end of the chain of decisions. If there are problems in implementation, the fault is often seen as the teacher's for not following the curriculum plan faithfully or for being resistant to change. In this view, the curriculum *plan* is the key to a successful curriculum, and teachers are expected to faithfully implement it. As Schwartz (2006) notes, this view is problematic because:

> Teachers are seen as taking their materials and making them "practical". However, curriculum writers cannot expect to relate to the teacher's classroom experience, or the "inward journey" that students experience as a result of their exposure to the ideas and activities of any curriculum. What happens in the learning experience is an outcome of the original, creative, thinking-on-your-feet efforts of the teacher —which often lead the class in directions far, far away from the anticipated goals of the curriculum writers. (p. 450)

Another way to conceptualize the three curriculum processes of planning, enacting, and evaluating is as recursive processes that overlap and mutually influence each other. Figure 4 depicts the processes in terms of their relationships to each other. The purpose of planning is to guide and support enactment and to provide a basis for evaluation. The purpose of evaluating is to determine the effectiveness of the learning and teaching in the classroom so that it can become more effective. The findings of the evaluation affect future planning, which in turn affects enactment. In this view, enactment—learning and teaching in the classroom—is the key to a successful curriculum and so is placed at the center of the diagram.

Decisions about curriculum center on the teacher and learners who enact it. Teachers are well informed about the plan, value the plan, and have the skills to use it.

The implementation view of curriculum (i.e., that curriculum is a plan to be implemented) is widespread. As a result, when we talk about "a curriculum," we usually mean a design or plan for an educational program, not the enacted curriculum, the teaching and learning experiences in the classroom. The distinction between design and enactment is important. Without enactment, the design is simply a document or a set of ideas, and there is no actual curriculum. For this reason, design needs to be closely allied with the teaching and learning processes that happen in the classroom (real or virtual). The curriculum enacted in the classroom is guided or influenced to a greater or lesser degree by the design. For a design to support successful teaching and learning, it should be realistic for the target users—learners and teachers. The aims of the curriculum need to be appropriate for the learners, given the time frame and resources. This does not mean that a curriculum plan should not be ambitious or challenge the status quo; it means that teachers need to understand the design and how to use it successfully. They need to see it as a tool that can help them support student learning. When curriculum developers are removed from the classroom and fail to take into account the nature of the context, they risk developing a curriculum that describes unrealistic outcomes, thus setting up teachers and learners for failure to achieve the outcomes. Curriculum planning needs to go hand in hand with teacher involvement.

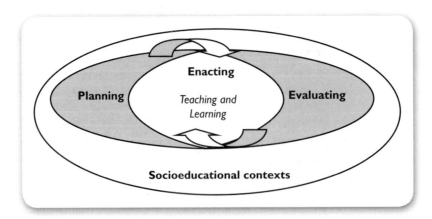

Figure 4. Curriculum as a dynamic system (adapted from K. Graves, 2006).

Curriculum planning

The purpose of curriculum planning is to provide a framework for course and unit development, to guide and support teaching and learning in the classroom, and to provide a basis for the evaluation of program effectiveness. Successful curriculum planning is built around three foundational processes: articulating the guiding principles on which the curriculum is based, analyzing contextual factors that have an impact on the success of the curriculum, and assessing the needs of the learners for whom the curriculum is intended. These three processes provide the basis for determining educational goals (also called outcomes or aims) that are clear and realistic. To achieve the outcomes, decisions are then made about the program—deciding what the content should be, how to organize it, and how to monitor and assess achievement. These processes, outlined in Figure 5, are described in broad terms in this section. In the next section, I explain them in detail at the level of syllabus design for a course.

Articulating guiding principles. Guiding principles state the views of learning, learners, and subject matter on which the curriculum is based. They are responsive to the social and educational contexts of the curriculum, derive from sound educational theory, and are appropriate for the learners and teachers who will enact the curriculum. The two examples that follow are from very different educational contexts. The curriculum framework for English language education for learners ages 6–14 in Bahrain (Bahrain Directorate of Curriculum, 2004) is based on the following five principles:

1. Learners learn language when they are involved in meaningful and purposeful activities which require them to communicate using the target language.
2. Learning is not a linear process.
3. Learning is enhanced by the development of learning strategies and the gradual introduction of activities and tasks where learners begin to take more responsibility for their own learning.
4. Learning is an active process.
5. Learning of English is not an isolated event.

The Massachusetts Adult Basic Education Curriculum Framework for English for Speakers of Other Languages (Massachusetts Department of Education, Adult and Community Learning Services, 2005) is based on seven principles, including:

> 2. Adult learners come to ESOL programs with a variety of motivations for learning English; a range of personal, educational and career goals; and differing expectations about the learning process. It is important that teachers, program staff, and students work together to identify learners' goals and expectations to ensure that each program's curriculum, instruction, and assessment address learners' immediate and long-term goals. (p. 9)

> 5. Language learning requires risk-taking. Adult learners will benefit from a classroom community that supports them in taking risks in authentic communication practice. (p. 12)

Articulating guiding principles	→	What beliefs about learners and learning, teaching, and subject matter undergird the curriculum?
Analyzing contextual factors	→	What social, economic, political, educational, and institutional factors impact the curriculum?
Assessing learner needs	→	What are the learners' abilities, needs, and purposes for learning?
Determining program goals	→	What knowledge, skills, and dispositions will learners attain?
Deciding program content	→	What should be taught and in what ways so that learners can attain the goals?
Organizing program content	→	How will the content and materials be organized and sequenced?
Designing an assessment plan	→	In what systematic ways will learning be monitored and assessed?

Figure 5. Processes of curriculum planning.

The principles in these two examples differ because each set describes the views of learners, learning, language, and language acquisition that are appropriate for the particular educational context. A set of coherent principles provides a common focus for different stakeholders in the curriculum development process.

Guiding principles ensure that the curriculum will be based on understandings of effective learning and teaching. Context analysis and needs assessment ensure that the design is grounded in the actual needs of the learners and the context for learning so that it is realistic and feasible for the target learners.

Analyzing contextual factors. Context analysis, also called situation analysis (J. C. Richards, 2001a) and environment analysis (Nation & Macalister, 2010), is the process of identifying the social, economic, political, and institutional factors that may have an impact on the curriculum (J. C. Richards, 2001a). For example, when designing the materials for a new standards-based curriculum for early primary students in Egypt, the designers had to consider factors such as an educational system that relies heavily on exams, parent expectations about literacy, the teacher's comfort with managing student output, and the limited amount of weekly time available for English (Thornton, Touba, Bakr, & Ianuzzi, 2009). If these factors were ignored, the resulting materials would not be a good fit with the context and would not serve the aims of the curriculum.

Assessing learner needs. Needs assessment (also called needs analysis) focuses on the learners. It is the process of gathering information about the learners and then analyzing it to formulate clear goals and make decisions about what to teach. This information includes the learners' needs and purposes for learning, their current abilities, and what they are expected to know and do with the language at different stages of the program. For example, university language centers in universities in the United States often have two types of learners: those who are there for a short period to improve their general English skills and those who are there to prepare to enter the university (Bollati, 2007; Bonfanti & Watkins, 2007). These two types of learners have different needs that the program design must account for.

Determining program goals. A sound understanding of learners' needs and contextual resources and constraints provides a basis for determining achievable goals for the curriculum. Achievable goals describe in broad terms the types of knowledge, skills, and dispositions that learners are expected to gain as a result of their experience in the program. According to J. C. Richards (2001a), the statement of goals (which he calls aims) serves the following purposes:

- to provide a clear definition of the purposes of a program
- to provide guidelines for teachers, learners and materials writers
- to help provide a focus for instruction
- to describe important and realizable changes in learning (p. 120)

For example, Potts and Park (2007) describe how a Korean university language center conducted an extensive needs analysis through focus-group interviews with students in its program. The needs analysis revealed that students wanted to know how to talk in English so that they would not feel silenced when engaging in English conversation. They also wanted to know how to measure their language learning progress. The goals for the six levels were rewritten based on the four dimensions of Canale and Swain's (1980) model of communicative competence. (See also Duff, this volume.) Each level had goals related to grammatical competence, discourse competence, strategic competence, and sociolinguistic competence, gradually shifting from an emphasis on learning about features of English conversation to participating in conversations. The goals for each level served as a basis for student self-assessment.

Deciding and organizing program content. Clear goals provide a basis for making decisions about the program content: what will be taught and how to organize it so that learners can achieve the goals. Deciding on program content and how to organize it involves making decisions about:

- what should be taught over the span of the program
- how the content will be divided into courses or modules
- what should be emphasized in each course
- how courses will complement or build on each other
- how courses will be leveled and sequenced

Decisions must be made about both the horizontal curriculum, that is, what is studied within one level, and the vertical curriculum, that is, what is studied across levels (Eilam & Ben-Peretz, 2010). In public and state school contexts, program content may be guided or mandated by standards that have been created for each subject and each grade level.

Designing an assessment plan. A curriculum plan includes an assessment plan that monitors and assesses students' learning. It should help to chart student progress and achievement throughout the program. (Note that assessment is different from evaluation. Program evaluation judges the effectiveness of the program using a variety of measures, one of which is assessment data.) At the program level, the assessment plan includes proficiency tests and placement tests, a variety of assessments to determine progress and achievement within courses, and some kind of benchmarks for each level. For example, Royal, White, and McIntosh (2007) describe the development of an assessment program at a university-based intensive English program in Canada. Assessment had not been carried out systematically within that program. However, this was critical both for students' progression from one level to the next and also for exit testing to determine students' entry into the university. Course descriptions and assessments were revised "with the goal of standardizing course objectives and assessment measures across the curriculum" (2007, p. 72). Placement testing, classroom assessment, and exit testing were put into place. Clearly defined objectives for each course were developed so there was a progression from one level to the next. The course objectives were also aligned with the Canadian Language Benchmarks (Centre for Canadian Language Benchmarks, 2000). (See also Duff, this volume.) The comprehensive assessment plan contributed to the cohesion and effectiveness of the program.

CLASSROOM APPLICATIONS: HOW TO DESIGN A SYLLABUS

In this section, I explore how to design a syllabus for a course. The processes of designing a course syllabus are similar to those of designing a curriculum for a program, but on a smaller scale.

What does a syllabus include?

As we have seen in Figures 1, 2, and 3, a syllabus for a language course may include the overall goals for the course and specific learning objectives, topics to be explored, specific skills to be used or learned (e.g., academic skills), subject-specific content and concepts to be mastered, and grammar or vocabulary to be studied; the timetable; materials used; assignments; types of in-class interactions and activities; and the assessment and grading scheme. Figure 6 provides a template for a syllabus. It includes a brief description of the course; the goals for the course (and the objectives, if not too numerous); how learners will be assessed and graded; the materials that will be used (e.g., course books and readings); and an outline of the course content and sequence (what will be learned or done and in what order), which may include the timetable. Teachers need to have all this information, but what actually goes into the syllabus document depends on the intended audience. There may be different versions of the syllabus depending on whom it is for. For example, the syllabus for the Japanese high school course (see Figure 1) was originally written in Japanese and given to the learners as a way to inform them about what they could expect to do and learn in the course.

Name of course:

Brief description of course

Course goals (and objectives)

Assessment scheme

Materials

Outline or timetable of course content and sequence

Figure 6. Syllabus template.

Processes of designing a syllabus

Designing a syllabus forces us to think about both the whole and all the parts of a course—how the trees make up the forest. We can think of planning processes as working from two different points: a starting point of *what is* and an ending point of *what is desired*. We then map what should happen between those two points to create a bridge from one to the other. We also develop ways to determine whether the end point has been reached. Defining the starting point (*what is*) involves context analysis and needs assessment. Defining the ending point (*what is desired*) involves needs assessment and formulating goals and objectives. Creating a bridge between the two points involves deciding on content and activities and on how to organize them. Determining how one will know whether the desired point (as well as intermediate points) has been reached involves making decisions about assessment.

Although I describe the processes in sequential fashion here, in reality they overlap and complement each other. Most practitioners experience aspects of the processes simultaneously (K. Graves, 2000). For example, if in a needs assessment we find out the genres that the students need to be familiar with or the tasks they will perform, we are already conceptualizing the goals and content of the course in terms of genre or task. When we describe goals and objectives, we are already thinking about assessment because objectives describe what we want learners to achieve and, therefore, what we need to assess.

We begin here with context analysis and needs assessment because each course has a different starting point and different ending point— different learners with different needs in different contexts. The three syllabus examples in Figures 1, 2, and 3 are not interchangeable. It would be inappropriate to include developing an annotated bibliography in a course for Japanese high school students, just as it would be inappropriate to include singing content songs in a business-preparation program.

Context analysis

The purpose of context analysis is to ensure that the course is realistic for the learners and teachers so that they can be successful. This kind of analysis is "an important part of curriculum design because at its most basic level it ensures that the course will be usable" (Nation & Macalister, 2010, p. 14). The process of context analysis involves identifying the resources and constraints that will have an impact on the course and making decisions about how to account for factors that are particularly challenging. If challenging factors are ignored, the course may not be realistic. Nation and Macalister suggest listing the factors that will have an impact on the curriculum, ranking them from those having the most to the least impact and then choosing which ones to address explicitly.

Figure 7 is a list of some of the factors to consider in a context analysis. Any one of these factors may be either a resource or a constraint, depending on the nature of the course (K. Graves, 1996, 2000; Nation & Macalister, 2010).

Needs assessment

The purpose of needs assessment is to have as much information as possible about the learners, their needs, and their purposes to set realistic learning targets. Needs assessment involves gathering the necessary information through a variety of means, such as in-class observation of students, interviewing or surveying students and other stakeholders, diagnostic and placements tests, document analysis, and target situation analysis (i.e., where, how, with whom, and why learners will use the language). An

Factors	Examples
Time	When, how often, how long, schedule, preparation time
Physical resources	Location, availability of materials, classroom space, equipment
Human resources	Role of/support from teachers, staff, administrators, and parents
Educational requirements	The curriculum framework (national/state/provincial standards, alignment with other courses), testing, materials, other institutional requirements
Social, cultural, and political factors	Expectations of the wider community and other stakeholders, policies that affect the course

Figure 7. Factors to consider in a context analysis.

important consideration when assessing language learners' needs is whether they have a target situation in which they will use the language. If they do, needs analysis involves gathering information about the target situation. In cases where students have no immediate need for using the language, a context of use must be created within the classroom.

Figure 8 lists the types of information that can be gathered in needs assessment. The students in the Australian EAP course (see Figure 2) needed to develop academic skills to successfully complete university studies. The course designers conducted an extensive needs analysis by interviewing professors in the Department of Economics and Financial Studies, obtaining lists of texts and assignments, and analyzing examples of written assignments by international students to identify common problems that the course could address. Having learned that the learners needed to listen to lectures and take notes, write critical reviews of articles, and undertake research, the designers constructed the course around these specific targets. They also designed the course so that students undertook weekly self-assessments to keep them focused on their targets. The students were highly motivated learners for whom success in the course had implications for their professional learning path.

In contrast, the students in the Japanese high school course (see Figure 1) had no immediate target situations in which they would use English. They had more general needs, and so the learning targets were internal to the course, in that the language outcomes, such as being able to write a five-paragraph essay, did not have an immediate application. The independent learning skills outcomes, on the other hand, could be used in other settings. The teachers and university advisor who designed the course knew a great deal about the learners because they had long experience teaching them. They took into account the kinds of topics that interest students in their teens. They also considered the need to change the classroom culture to encourage more independence and autonomy on the part of the learners.

The learners in the fifth-grade class (see Figure 3) were *in* the target situation. They were in school, not preparing to be in school. These learners were simultaneously learning English and learning content *in* English and *through* English (Gibbons, 2006b). The learners not only had language and content needs, but they were also at different levels of language proficiency, and so the teacher had to meet a variety of language needs while also instructing them in the content.

Types of information	Purposes for gathering information
Demographic information: *Age, gender, nationality, first and other languages*	To choose appropriate content
Educational background information: *Length, place, and focus of education; expectations of teacher/learner roles*	To develop appropriate content and activities; to anticipate and overcome resistance
Language proficiency level: *Speaking, listening, reading, writing*	To ensure the material and activities are at the appropriate language level
Interests and life experience	To engage learners and draw on their expertise
Purposes for study	To get a sense of students' expectations to avoid potential mismatches
Target situation analysis: *What students are expected or want to do with and in English; where they will use English, with whom and for what purpose.* *Texts they will read or write* *Spoken interaction they will engage in* *Listening they will engage in* *Tasks they will perform in daily, work-related, or academic life* *Subject-specific content and concepts they will need to master*	To be able to choose the type of texts, interactions, tasks, and subjects that learners encounter or will encounter

Figure 8. Types of information that can be gathered in a needs assessment.

With information from context and needs assessment, the syllabus can be designed to account for contextual factors and what is known about the learners and the target situation to provide a path from what learners know or are able to do at the start of the course to what they are expected to know or be able to do by the end of the course.

Determining syllabus content

As we discussed in the section on syllabus types, the nature of language and language learning makes defining goals and deciding on the content that will enable learners to achieve the goals challenging. Is language a set of skills? The texts we produce and interpret? The grammar that underlies it? The vocabulary? It is all of these. Does language learning involve interacting with others? Using grammar rules? Performing tasks? Interpreting texts? Using strategies? It involves all of these. To design a conceptually coherent course, we need to make reasoned choices among these different ways of understanding how language is learned.

Syllabus content consists of what students are expected to learn and learn how to do in the course. The purpose of determining the content is to ensure that what the course focuses on is appropriate for the students, meets their needs, and is realizable within the time frame of the course. Determining the content involves making decisions about what and how learners will be taught, which aspects of language and learning to emphasize. The categories in Figure 9 have considerable overlap because they are different ways of looking at the same complex phenomenon—language and how one learns it. Deciding which categories to emphasize should be based on what we know about the learners' needs and purposes and the available resources.

Deciding on goals and objectives

Goals (also called aims or outcomes) state what the learners will know and be able to do by the end of the course. Goals are broken down into subgoals, called objectives. Learners reach a goal by achieving each of the associated objectives. The purpose of goals and objectives is to define clear outcomes for learning so that the course can be planned to effectively help learners achieve the outcomes.

We plan the goals of the course based on what we know about learners' needs and the context, and based on our own understandings of

Categories	Examples
Macro skills: Reading, listening, speaking, writing, and associated subskills	Extensive listening/reading, predicting, inferring Pronunciation, interactional skills, communication strategies Drafting, editing
Topics, themes	*Topics:* family, food, weather *Themes:* modern families, nutrition and health, global warming
Specific content areas	Algebra, history, economics, science
Text types (genres)	Journal articles, scientific reports, presentations, classroom discussions
Tasks	Interviewing, prioritizing a list, making a timetable
Projects	Conducting academic research, creating a guidebook
Metacognitive skills and learning strategies	Study skills, self-assessment skills
Grammar	Verb tenses, question formation, types of clauses
Vocabulary	Specific vocabulary, strategies for learning vocabulary
Cultural/pragmatic knowledge and skills	Differentiating forms of address, choosing appropriate topics of conversation, analyzing appropriate behavior
Sociopolitical skills	Navigating the health system, advocating for one's legal rights

Figure 9. Possible syllabus content categories.

language, learning, and language learning. The most straightforward way to write goals is to formulate each one so that it targets an important focus of the course, for example, a genre or one or more macro skills, projects, or content. Goals are broad statements about the aims of the course and can be written in general terms.

Objectives are specific statements of what learners will know and be able to do. They are obtainable and measurable to the extent that learners should have some way of knowing whether the objective has been reached. For this reason, objectives are written with verbs that describe activities or processes that can be assessed (J. D. Brown, 1995).

In the case of the Australian EAP course (see Figure 2), the course designers wrote goals related to the major focuses of the course, which had been identified through needs analysis and also through the lens of their own understanding and theories of language learning. Two of the course goals were:

1. To facilitate the active development of skills needed to function successfully within the particular discourse community in which learners will participate at Macquarie University

2. To introduce learners to the text types they are likely to encounter during their university studies

These are broad statements about what the learners will learn or know about as a result of the course. The course as a whole will be successful in meeting learners' needs if the goals are achieved, that is, if learners develop skills, encounter the text types, and so on. The objectives tell us more specifically what learners must be able to do to achieve each goal. The course designers wrote objectives under the four macro skills and study skills, with a heavy emphasis on writing (particularly writing critical reviews of articles in the students' field) and a secondary emphasis on reading. Here are three objectives:

1. Can identify and comprehend main ideas and viewpoint, and evaluate business texts written for native speakers

2. Can effectively write a critical review based on the critical reading of a text

3. Can present a written assignment in an appropriate manner (specified in a rubric) (Agosti, 2006, pp. 117–118)

The objectives were written as learner "can do" statements, or competencies. The advantage of

writing them in this way is that they can be measured or assessed.

The teacher of the fifth-grade social studies/science unit (see Figure 3) was guided by state educational standards in developing the unit objectives. Educational standards describe, for each subject and each grade level, what all learners in a grade should know about the subject and the skills they should be able to perform with respect to the subject. "The major benefit of standards is that they set out clear expectations for all involved in the educational enterprise, including the public" (Katz & Snow, 2009, p. 67). Standards are meant to guide the local development of instructional goals and objectives, which describe outcomes for a particular instructional setting.

The fifth-grade teacher chose the relevant state standards for social studies and life sciences in planning the unit objectives. She describes the process (Sharkey & Cade, 2008):

> The planning started by working with the standards (i.e., state curriculum frameworks, grade-level concepts) and then thinking about ways to make them accessible to students. This was a subtle but significant shift from thinking about general topics and themes to asking "What kinds of things can students do with these topics?" It meant bringing students up to the content rather than watering down the content for the students. (p. 185)

She used the Sheltered Instruction Observation Protocol (Echevarria, Vogt, & Short, 2012) planning processes to organize her syllabus to include content objectives, content concepts, and language objectives. Students in the course chose a specific biome, such as the desert or the rainforest and, through carefully scaffolded research for their group presentations, mastered the content concepts and achieved the unit objectives.

Organizing the course

Organizing a course involves deciding how to integrate and organize or sequence the main focuses or strands of the course. The purpose of organizing a course is to give it a structure that will allow learners to learn in a purposeful, systematic, and holistic way. There is no exact science about how to organize elements within a syllabus. We first need to identify the core curriculum elements of the course, for example, tasks, projects, one or more of the macro skills, topics, subject-specific content, and strategies. Once core elements have been identified, they can be broken down into subelements that can be taught.

In the Australian EAP course, academic reading and writing skills and academic genres were the core curriculum elements. The course began with an introduction to critical reading so that learners could write critical reviews, a core genre of the course. Unpacking the critical review revealed that it includes both a summary of the main arguments and a critique of the article. Each week, students were to read an article and write a summary. So that students learned how to write both parts of the review, the course focused on the reading skill of inferencing; it also focused on written argumentation techniques, integration of statistics and graphs, providing data and commentary, and integrating examples and quotations. The course developers determined an order for learning these skills that made sense to them. The learning was purposeful, systematic, and holistic in that it resulted in the ability to write a critical review. In essence, this approach starts with the whole, breaks it down into parts, and then teaches the parts to realize the whole. The parts are taught in relation to the whole, not separated from it.

Once the subelements have been identified, decisions about how to sequence them within a strand is based on factors such as complexity, length/quantity, and scaffolding. Simpler tasks or genres are taught before more complex ones. Tasks that scaffold later tasks are taught first. For example, the Japanese high school course was organized around the strands of speaking and writing essays about social topics. Speaking was broken down into discussions and debates. Students learned to discuss topics before they learned to debate them because discussions are more open-ended than debates but build skills that can be used in debates.

Another element of course organization involves deciding whether there are regular routines in the way the course is organized. For example, the Australian EAP course had several weekly features: on Mondays, tutorial discussions; on Wednesdays, individual consultations; and on Fridays, a class meeting in which the learners met without the teacher to talk about what they had learned during the week and express their needs. Minutes of the meeting were given to the teachers, who then would "tailor the course to their learners' needs" (Agosti, 2006, p. 102). There were almost daily group presentations and a weekly written assignment given on Friday.

Making decisions about assessment

Assessment is the gathering and interpreting of information about or evidence of learning. Through assessment, we find out whether and to what extent learners are learning the content as set out in the goals and objectives. The purpose of assessment is to provide reliable feedback to learners and teachers about the learners' progress and achievement so that learners know what they have accomplished or need to improve and so that teachers can adjust the instruction to help them. (See also Katz, this volume.) Assessment addresses the following questions (Wiggins & McTighe, 2005):

- What is the learner supposed to learn/be able to do?
- What is evidence of that learning?
- What kinds of tasks will enable learners to provide that evidence?
- How will the evidence be evaluated?
- What will happen with the results?

Clear objectives provide answers to the first question. In the Australian EAP course, each of the reading, writing, speaking, and listening objectives was assessed through tasks that were as authentic as possible to provide the needed evidence. For example, students listened to taped lectures, took notes, summarized their notes, and answered questions; they read articles and then they wrote essays about the articles. For each task, the students were provided with the criteria on which the task would be assessed and how the results would be graded. The task was assessed according to the criteria, and the results were shared with the learners. Midway through the course, there were counseling sessions with learners who had not been able to meet the criteria for passing to help them find an alternate means into university.

Effective assessments are practical to use and transparent to learners. They are both formative (they provide evidence along the way) and summative (they provide culminating, integrated evidence of learning). In her fifth-grade biome unit, Lynn Cade wanted to involve students in assessment and create more opportunities for formative assessment. She and her co-author describe how assessment was used (Sharkey & Cade, 2008):

> The first step in this process was making sure students knew what the learning objectives were, why those objectives were important and then consistently encouraging students to identify and reflect on what they were learning and how they were learning it. The learning objectives, key vocabulary and concepts were posted in a prominent position in the classroom, and students became accustomed to referring to them at different points of the day and throughout the week. (p. 186)

For larger projects, the teacher explained the criteria for evaluation to the students. When students gave presentations, for example, the teacher and the students completed the same rubric.

In all three courses used here as exemplars, connecting the assessment to the goals and objectives was an important part of syllabus design. The connection between goals and assessment is indicative of the way in which all the processes of syllabus design interrelate and influence each other.

FUTURE TRENDS

Focusing on learners' needs, capacities, and potential has enlarged our vision of what is possible in the language classroom. Rather than focusing narrowly on language, syllabuses for language courses increasingly include challenging content and learning activities that mine learners' capacities for thoughtful, investigative learning. Promising directions include the use of authentic content via print, Internet, and electronic media; involving learners in investigative tasks and projects both in and outside the classroom; and involving learners in assessment.

A greater role for teachers in curriculum decisions and curriculum thinking promotes integration between curriculum planning and enactment. Teachers have to learn to "think curricularly." Designing a syllabus is a constructive way for teachers to become knowledgeable about and instrumental in curriculum development and educational innovation. Teachers who design the courses they teach are uniquely able to use theory in their practice and to transform it through practice.

Teachers and teacher-educators can work together in complementary and mutually supportive ways to design innovative curriculums, research their enactment, and evaluate their effectiveness. Such collaboration grounds teachers' education in the reality of teaching contexts, validates teachers' knowledge, and reinvigorates the practice of both teacher-educators and teachers. Ultimately, such collaboration benefits learners.

CONCLUSION

This chapter has explored the relationship between syllabus and curriculum design, the challenges in designing a language-learning syllabus, and the roles of the teacher and learners in curriculum. Just as effective classroom practice is a negotiated process among learners and between learners and teacher, effective syllabus and curriculum design is a negotiated process among stakeholders. Curriculum designers need to stay close to the life of the classroom so that they can create designs that are useful, usable, and generative for teachers and learners.

SUMMARY

➤ A curriculum is the dynamic interplay of planning, enacting, and evaluating an educational program. A syllabus is a plan for a course. The curriculum and the syllabus are both designs for learning but at different levels.

➤ The history of syllabus design in language teaching characterizes the ways in which language and language learning have been conceptualized to teach language in the classroom.

➤ Effective curriculum and syllabus design are based on understanding learners' needs and purposes for learning and the factors in the context that influence the enactment of the program or course.

➤ Clear goals and objectives and program/course organization go hand in hand with assessment to support learning.

DISCUSSION QUESTIONS

1. How have you experienced the relationship between curriculum planning and curriculum enactment?

   a. If you have been involved in curriculum and syllabus planning, how did you take into account the teachers and learners who would use the plan?

   b. If you have been a classroom teacher, how did the curriculum plan or syllabus inform, constrain, or support your teaching?

2. Consider a recent course you designed, taught, or are familiar with. Consult Figure 9, which lists possible syllabus content. What were the major strands of content in your course? Why were they chosen? How did they interrelate?

3. Choose one of the syllabuses described in Figures 1, 2, and 3. Could you prepare to teach the course based on the syllabus? What else would you want to know?

4. What role should learners play in curriculum and syllabus design?

5. Who should a syllabus be for? Why?

SUGGESTED ACTIVITIES

1. Find three language course syllabuses that are aimed at different groups of learners (from your place of work, online, or in course books, or use the syllabuses in Figures 1, 2, and 3). Create a chart or graphic display that shows how the syllabuses are similar and how they are different. What accounts for the differences?

2. You have been asked to evaluate a new curriculum plan for a language institute. Write a letter to the language institute in which you explain to them what you will need to evaluate the plan.

3. Create your own template for a syllabus.

4. Rewrite a syllabus from one of your courses (or a course that you are familiar with), incorporating ideas and information from this chapter.

FURTHER READING

Graves, K. (2000). *Designing language courses: A guide for teachers.* Boston, MA: Heinle & Heinle.

This book is written for teachers, with explanations of how to carry out each of the curriculum development processes, illustrated with examples from teachers.

Nation, I. S. P., & Macalister, J. (2010). *Language curriculum design.* London, UK: Routledge.

This book provides a systematic approach to understanding curriculum design, mainly at the course level, with examples throughout. It also includes chapters on syllabus negotiation and materials design.

Richards, J. (2001). *Curriculum development in language teaching.* New York, NY: Cambridge University Press.

The author argues for a broad curriculum approach, rather than a narrow syllabus-based approach. The book provides an overview of curriculum processes, with a wide variety of examples.

TESOL Language Curriculum Development Series

Each book in this series includes a variety of practitioner accounts in curriculum design, renewal, and innovation. Contributors describe their context, the motivation for the curriculum innovation or adaptation, the processes (including successes and missteps), sample curriculum products, and what they learned from their experience. The series addresses both school-age learners and adult learners.

Burns, A., & de Silva Joyce, H. (Eds.). (2007). *Planning and teaching creatively within a required curriculum for adult learners.* Alexandria, VA: Teachers of English to Speakers of Other Languages.

Carroll, M. (Ed.). (2007). *Developing a new curriculum for adult learners.* Alexandria, VA: Teachers of English to Speakers of Other Languages.

Graves, K., & Lopriore, L. (Eds.). (2009) *Developing a new curriculum for school age learners.* Alexandria, VA: Teachers of English to Speakers of Other Languages.

Hayes, D., & Sharkey, J. (Eds.). (2008). *Revitalizing an established curriculum for school age learners.* Alexandria, VA: Teachers of English to Speakers of Other Languages.

McKay, P. (Ed.). (2006). *Planning and teaching creatively within a required curriculum for school age learners.* Alexandria, VA: Teachers of English to Speakers of Other Languages.

Rice, A. (Ed.). (2007). *Revitalizing an established program for adult learners.* Alexandria, VA: Teachers of English to Speakers of Other Languages.

Snow, M. A., & Kamhi-Stein, L. (Eds.). (2006). *Developing a new course for adult learners.* Alexandria, VA: Teachers of English to Speakers of Other Languages.

5 | Teaching English in the Context of World Englishes

MARIANNE CELCE-MURCIA

KEY QUESTIONS

➤ What does the term World Englishes refer to?
➤ What are some pedagogical consequences of including World Englishes in an English as a second or foreign language curriculum?
➤ How should a teacher decide which variety or varieties of English to teach to a given group of second or foreign language learners?

EXPERIENCE

Susan is an American Peace Corps volunteer working at a regional teacher-training college in Nigeria. With a BA in linguistics and some training in teaching English to speakers of other languages, Susan has been teaching advanced English language courses and some methods classes to Nigerians preparing to teach English in middle school.

The principal of Susan's college, a Nigerian, gave her a class set of English pronunciation textbooks based on British Received Pronunciation (RP) and told her to teach a course in pronunciation to all the prospective English teachers since, in his opinion, their pronunciation was dreadful. Susan is the only native speaker of English in her department, but she is not a native speaker of British English. Susan does her best, trying to imitate the well-known British actress Helen Mirren, as she takes her students through the highly controlled exercises in the textbook. However, as soon as she speaks naturally, she reverts to her native General American pronunciation. Her students notice the difference and tell her, "You teach us 'waw-ta' but you say 'waw-der' [for *water*]." Susan tries to explain her dilemma to the students, who are not particularly interested in modifying their regional English pronunciation to better approximate either the British or the American standard.

We will come back to this situation later to reconsider how Susan might have responded.

WHAT ARE WORLD ENGLISHES?

In the past, the field of English language teaching was divided into teaching English as a second language (ESL) and teaching English as a foreign language (EFL). ESL was for immigrants to English-speaking countries or for citizens of countries where English was a widely used second language (L2). EFL was taught as a foreign language in countries where English had no official internal use (i.e., it was an academic subject at school). It is now necessary to go well beyond the English as a second versus foreign language distinction. English has, over the past century, gradually become the most widely taught language in the world. It has also become the most widely used language for most purposes of communication in international diplomacy, business, science, education, and entertainment. English is also more widely dispersed geographically than any other language. These facts prompted Ferguson (1971) to claim that English has become a language of wider communication, or (in more recent terminology) what S. L. McKay (2012) calls English as an international language (EIL).

World Englishes are regionally distinct varieties of English that have arisen in areas of Asia, Africa, and Oceania, where there is a long (often colonial) history of English being widely used in education, commerce, and government. Over time this widespread use of English (spoken side by side with local languages) has given rise to local varieties of English with their own standards. Examples of World Englishes are Indian English, West African English, Filipino English, and Singapore English.[1] Examples of features of these varieties of English include more frequent use of the progressive aspect (*be . . . –ing*) in Indian English (e.g., *Whatever you are wanting, I am not having*), the use of *isn't it?* as the invariant tag in Nigerian English (e.g., *Our team won the football game, isn't it?*), and the use of *lah* as a marker of solidarity in Singapore English (e.g., *No problem lah. I go there anyway*).

English has long been used as a language of wider communication in countries with historical colonial ties to Great Britain or the United States, especially in countries where many different native languages have existed alongside English (e.g., India, Nigeria, and the Philippines). People in these countries often use English to communicate with fellow nationals who speak another first language (L1). However, what is now happening on a large scale is that English is also becoming the dominant lingua franca (the language used among speakers lacking a common L1) on the European continent. Seidlhofer, Breiteneder, and Pitzl (2006) note that English is used by native speakers of languages such as French, German, Dutch, Spanish, and Italian to communicate with each other. According to Kirkpatrick (2007), this phenomenon is also occurring on a large scale in the member countries of the Association of Southeast Asian Nations (ASEAN), which includes Indonesia, Thailand, Singapore, the Philippines, Malaysia, Vietnam, Brunei, Myanmar, Cambodia, and Laos.

Although English can be used as the lingua franca between a native English speaker and a non-native speaker, the prototypical use of English as a lingua franca (ELF) occurs in communication between two non-native speakers of English who do not share a common L1. Furthermore, in a majority of environments, it is now more common to have an English teacher who is a non-native speaker than a teacher who is a native speaker. (See Kamhi-Stein, this volume.) It is thus often more realistic in such contexts to teach English so that learners can communicate with other non-native speakers rather than with native speakers. This represents a fundamental shift in orientation in that most previous EFL instruction assumed that communication with native speakers was the primary learning objective (Seidlhofer, 2004).

English as a native language

We need to begin our discussion concerning varieties of English by acknowledging that there is a great deal of variation both within and among the native varieties of English spoken in England, Scotland, Wales, Ireland, the United States, Canada, Australia, New Zealand, South Africa, and the Caribbean (Trudgill & Hannah, 2008). While there are a few other places where English functions as an L1, these are the major locations. Who are native speakers of English? Cook (1999) defines *native speakers* as people who use the language they were born and raised with. Traditionally, native speakers have been valued as ideal language teachers and as models of norms. However, several applied linguists (Canagarajah, 1999; Cook, 1999; Seidlhofer, 2004) have questioned the central role of native speakers in the teaching of English as an international language and as the gate-keepers of linguistic norms. In much of the remainder of this chapter, I elaborate on what Canagarajah calls the "native speaker fallacy."

CONCEPTUAL UNDERPINNINGS

World Englishes

The most influential early argument in favor of recognizing the existence of regional standards where English is used as an intranational and international language, rather than as a native language, comes from B. B. Kachru (1985). His well-known representation of three concentric circles of English (see Figure 1) makes the following distinctions:

- *the inner circle* (the smallest circle at the center): the countries and regions where English is the native language of the majority
- *the outer circle* (actually the middle circle surrounding the inner circle): countries where English has had a long history of use and where local L2 varieties have developed and become codified through extensive use
- *the expanding circle* (the outermost circle): countries where English is a dominant foreign language used in limited domains but is beginning to become or has become a lingua franca

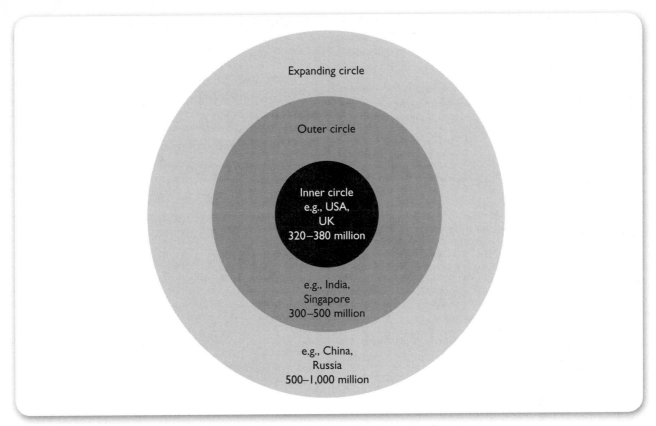

Figure 1. Kachru's three circles of English (adapted from Crystal, 2003, p. 61).[2]

B. B. Kachru's major concern (and that of many of his colleagues) has been the varieties of English that have developed in outer-circle countries—the various World Englishes. These are relatively stable varieties of English that can and have been described in terms of their grammar, lexicon, and phonology (e.g., Kirkpatrick, 2007; Trudgill & Hannah, 2008). The users of these varieties range in proficiency from expert to novice, generally depending on the user's level of education. The expert users have taken full possession of their variety of English and use it alongside their native language for many purposes, such as a medium of instruction in schools, a language of commerce, and a language for media (newspapers, television, movies, and Internet). The expert users not only write school assignments, reports, business letters, or news articles in their variety of English, they also use it to write literature (novels, plays, and poems). They have acquired full control of their variety of English and use it freely for communication and self-expression in most of the same ways that native speakers do.

This is why B. B. Kachru and his colleagues have argued that these well-established World Englishes are fully legitimate varieties that deserve to be recognized alongside the native varieties of English.

The one major problem that has been raised with respect to these established varieties is that they are often not fully intelligible to users of other varieties of English. Kirkpatrick (2007) proposes a scale that characterizes this problem. At one extreme, we have the goal of national or regional identity; people use a regional variety of English with its specific grammar, lexicon, and phonology to affirm their own national or ethnic identity. At the other end of the scale, we have the goal of intelligibility; users of a regional variety should ideally still be readily intelligible to other users of English everywhere else in the world to fully participate in the use of English as an international language. The challenge is to find a good balance between the identity-intelligibility extremes on Kirkpatrick's scale. Effective users may engage in a certain amount of code-switching (i.e., using English and another language in the same discourse unit). Based on the situational context, they may use a strongly local version of the regional variety to communicate with fellow users of the local variety and a weaker, more formal version when communicating with users of other varieties, when international intelligibility is necessary.

English as a lingua franca

When English is used as a lingua franca in B. B. Kachru's expanding circle, the situation is somewhat different. Although English is often deployed by these users for a variety of purposes, their range of uses for English and the amount of English they use does not match what the inner- and outer-circle users do with English. A native speaker of French living in France or a native speaker of Japanese living in Japan is unlikely to use English to converse with a colleague at work, to write a novel, or to make a film. Nevertheless, that they may often use ELF (e.g., to write to each other) is beginning to have an impact on the English that they do speak and write, and the study of the English used in ELF contexts has begun to be seriously studied. Seidlhofer (2004) makes the following four statements with respect to ELF:[3]

1. Using native-speaker norms is questionable.
2. Language variation is pervasive in all different communities of use.
3. The need to examine the attitudinal and linguistic implications of the global spread of English is urgent.
4. The description and codification of ELF are needed.

Seidlhofer and her colleagues have been amassing a corpus of spoken English produced by users of ELF in Europe, and they have identified some preliminary grammatical tendencies that they have observed in their data (Seidlhofer, 2004, p. 230):[4]

- dropping third person singular −s in simple present tense

  Paul *go* to school every day.[5]

- using the relative pronouns *who* and *which* interchangeably

  Mary is the teacher *which* they hired.

- omitting articles where they are used in L1 English and inserting them where they are not used by native speakers

  Stan was __ first person to leave.
  I enjoy studying *the* literature.

- using fixed forms as tag questions

  The student arrived late, *isn't it?*

- inserting redundant prepositions

  I was seeking *for* Jack's address.

- overusing verbs of high semantic generality (e.g., *do, have, make, put, take*)

  We need to *do* a meeting. (instead of *call, hold,* or *organize*)

Seidlhofer concludes that such ELF features do not seem to cause communication problems.

Given the potentially large number of minor deviations from L1 norms in much of the ELF communication (in terms of accents and pragmatics as well as lexicon and grammar), other researchers such as S. L. McKay (2002) discuss the need for *comity* (the efforts that interlocutors make to maintain cordial relations with fellow ELF interlocutors). Comity also includes special strategies that are said to be needed for speakers to develop solidarity with and provide support for listeners; it results in a joint willingness and patience to negotiate and confirm understandings.

Pronunciation (or accent) was found by Jenkins (2000, 2002) to be the cause of communication breakdowns in about 70% of the L2 cases of breakdown that she examined. Jenkins (2000, 2006a) has been a leader in the attempt to develop a lingua franca core or identify a reduced set of English pronunciation features that are needed for effective communication. Based on Jenkins (2006a) and Walker (2010), the following aspects that are typically a part of the ESL/EFL pronunciation curriculum are deemed unnecessary in the ELF pronunciation curriculum:

- the two *th* sounds: /θ/ as in *thing* and /ð/ as in *that*
- dark *l* [ɫ], which occurs in words such as *doll* or *milk*
- exact differences in vowel quality, as in /ɪ/ *ship* versus /iy/ *sheep*
- pitch movement or tone, as in *Do you prefer coffee*↗ *or tea?*↘

- word stress (the placement of primary or secondary stress within words), as in the verb *reFUSE* versus the noun *REFuse*
- stress-timing (the tendency in English to place prominence on content words and to unstress words that carry grammatical meaning, such as articles or prepositions), as in *TAKE a BUS to the BEACH*

In the case of Examples 1 and 2, ELF researchers believe that these sounds are both difficult to teach and are largely unnecessary for intelligibility among lingua franca speakers of English. For Example 3, they make the case that among the many L1 varieties of English there are great fluctuations in vowel quality; therefore, the focus should be placed on assisting ELF users to make consistent vowel contrasts (long/tense vs. short/lax vowels) to distinguish words like *sheep* and *ship* instead of producing such words with native-like vowel qualities. Finally, regarding Examples 4, 5, and 6, some researchers feel that the time spent to teach these aspects of English pronunciation is not warranted in terms of the overall rewards in increased intelligibility. In sum, in the ELF pronunciation curriculum, the goal of intelligibility replaces the traditional goal of having the learner strive for a native-like accent in English.

There are, of course, critics of the positions that Jenkins and Seidlhofer have taken with regard to describing and encouraging pedagogical adaptation to expanding-circle ELF norms (e.g., Berns, 2008; Dauer, 2005). Dauer, based on her training as a phonetician and also her classroom teaching, challenges some of the content of Jenkins's lingua franca core. Dauer argues that several features that Jenkins has not included in the core should be included (e.g., word stress because it is often critical for comprehension), that several should be changed (e.g., substitute /t/ and /d/ but not /f/ and /v/ for /θ/ and /ð/ because they are easier to teach), or that several items should be omitted (the vowel /ʊ/ in *put* because of its low frequency). Dauer concludes that substantial further research is needed to refine and validate Jenkins's ELF core.

Berns (2008) argues that the ELF movement, which focuses on non-native to non-native communication, marginalizes native speakers, who are in fact an integral part of World Englishes (i.e., part of both the inner circle and outer circle). All possible combinations of native and non-native English speakers of different varieties are part of World Englishes—and learners should be exposed to them for comprehension (not necessarily for production). Berns believes that the variability and dynamics of international communication make it questionable to try to isolate the linguistic features of any variety of English without also taking into account the user's strategic, sociocultural, and discourse competence. Facilitating the comprehension and tolerance of varieties of English that differ from one's own is more important for Berns than teaching a simplified core of linguistic features. Clearly, this is a debate that will be part of our professional discourse for the foreseeable future. In fact, we note that there is now an annual international conference dealing with ELF issues.[6]

CLASSROOM APPLICATIONS

Most applied linguists now agree that teacher trainers must become better sensitized to the many varieties of English being used in the world today and that they should be prepared to make their trainees aware of this reality. Y. Kachru (2005) goes a step further and emphasizes that teachers need both awareness and training to be equipped to make their learners cognizant of the rich variation that exists in English internationally. She recommends that learners in all three circles (inner, outer, and expanding) should be given the tools "to educate themselves further about using their English for effective communication across varieties" (p. 166).

Other educators also offer advice for teaching English in the context of World Englishes. S. L. McKay (2002) suggests that teachers be taught to think globally but act locally when teaching English as an international language. She also recommends that "decisions regarding teaching goals and approaches be given to local educators" (p. 129). McKay gives two reasons for this recommendation:

1. Local educators are in the best position to understand what their learners need to know.
2. Local educators can take their place as valid users of their variety of English.

Other language experts echo McKay's concern for local practice and teacher autonomy in determining course content. Snow, Kamhi-Stein, and Brinton (2006) emphasize the importance of "implementing language teaching methodologies that are sensitive to local socio-cultural and institutional beliefs" (p. 264). This means that the Western version of communicative language teaching may well need to be modified to better fit other educational cultures and contexts. Jenkins (2006), referring specifically to the teaching of pronunciation, puts the onus squarely on the teacher, saying that ELF pronunciation "will only be taken up if teachers themselves ultimately see an ELF identity as providing their students with accents which will enhance rather than damage their future social and economic prospects internationally" (p. 43).

In most models of teacher training and teacher evaluation, the teacher's proficiency in the target language is a criterion for judging teacher effectiveness (Snow, Kamhi-Stein, & Brinton, 2006). However, one must decide on the linguistic norm or variety to use for judging the teacher. Normally, if the teacher is a native speaker of an established standard variety, this variety is the norm. However, given the fact that about 80% of English language teachers worldwide are not inner-circle native speakers (Canagarajah, 1999), one must deal with the issue of which variety of English the teacher should be modeling for his or her learners. In ESL contexts where immigrants are learning English in an English-speaking country, the local variety of English should serve as the norm in most cases. In outer-circle contexts where there are established varieties of English, one can argue that the local variety should be the norm as long as intelligibility with other varieties of English is maintained. In ELF contexts, the regional ELF variety might be used as the norm. However, it is possible that the ELF variety developing in Europe and the ELF variety developing in ASEAN countries are different in interesting ways due to the L1s of the speakers in each region who use their ELF variety to communicate mainly with other ELF speakers in their region. Are the ELF speakers from these two groups able to communicate as effectively with each other, across the two ELF varieties, as they are within each ELF variety? Other considerations are raised by S. L. McKay (2012), who suggests that an appropriate pedagogy for teaching English as an international language would include examples of L2-L2 interactions and that explicit recognition should also be given to the L1s spoken by the interlocutors.

FUTURE TRENDS

The future will involve greater sensitivity to and explicit training in varieties of English in inner-circle, outer-circle, and expanding-circle countries. The focus will be on intelligibility and communication with the degree of attention to accuracy and norms being determined by local needs. A doctoral student writing a dissertation will need a much higher proficiency level and greater accuracy than someone who needs English only to bargain in the local marketplace with speakers of another L1 (e.g., an Ibo L1 Nigerian who needs English to bargain with a Yoruba L1 vendor in Lagos).

In her discussion of the future of English as an international language, D. Davies (2005) points out that many non-native speakers of English in places like Singapore control two varieties of English: a local nativized variety and an "international" variety that they use in formal settings as well as with users of other varieties. Such complexity in outer-circle usage needs further description and discussion since it appears that distinct varieties often exist side by side. For the expanding circle, Davies acknowledges the new spoken-ELF norms proposed by Jenkins for pronunciation (2000, 2002) and Seidlhofer for lexicon and grammar (2001, 2004). In contrast to these new ELF varieties of English, Davies cites Crystal (2003), who points out that World Standard Printed English has few regional variations beyond the occasional spelling differences or the use of lexical items from other languages. However, Davies feels that World Standard Printed English may in the future exhibit greater differences across varieties, in which case there may be a need to establish outer-circle norms and a lingua franca core for written English as is now being done for spoken English.

D. Davies (2005) also echoes S. L. McKay (2002) when suggesting that negative attitudes toward the English language and English-speaking nations could, in the future, negatively impact the spread of English. Finally, she cites Graddol (1997), who argues that the world's social, economic, and political ills will not be solved by everyone being able to use English and that published teaching materials intended for global use will become increasingly irrelevant as more appropriate local materials are developed and used in outer-circle and expanding-circle classrooms.

CONCLUSION

Let us now return to Susan's dilemma, presented at the beginning of this chapter. Given what we now know, what could Susan have done with her Nigerian teacher trainees in the pronunciation class that her principal assigned her to teach? Keep in mind that the textbooks were based on British Received Pronunciation (RP) and that Susan was a native speaker of General American (GA) English.

Since the drills and exercises in the textbook consisted of word lists and short sentences for repetition and practice, Susan could have done comparative work with the students, making them aware of the difference between the British RP version (in the textbook) versus the GA version (the teacher) and then asking the class to provide the Nigerian English version (the students). Such an approach might have been more collaborative and less frustrating for all concerned. A concurrent discussion of intelligibility issues (e.g., Is Nigerian English readily intelligible to speakers of other varieties?) might be sufficient to encourage the prospective teachers to make minor adjustments in their pronunciation in favor of greater cross-varietal intelligibility. In fact, all teachers must grapple with the same language-variety issues that Susan should have faced more directly and sensitively. The norm or model selected for instruction will depend on who the students are, what they need to do in English, and who they need to interact with, among other factors.

It is probably seldom appropriate to teach RP or GA pronunciation to students like Susan's, who speak an outer-circle variety of English. The decision needs to be a local one that will satisfy the school system, the teacher, and the students. In Susan's case, there was a problem with the principal, who wanted her to teach RP; she should have discussed her dilemma with the principal and proposed a course curriculum that included but went well beyond the RP-based textbooks that he had given her in hopes that she could convince him of her alternative approach.

SUMMARY

➤ English has become a world language and is the language most widely used and taught in the world today.

➤ There are many varieties of English, both native and non-native. Awareness of this reality needs to become part of teacher training and of English language instruction generally.

➤ Non-native varieties of English include either World Englishes (established outer-circle varieties) and ELF (emerging expanding-circle varieties).

➤ The needs and attitudes of students, teachers, and administrators often have an influence on the norm or standard adopted for instruction; it is thus best that local norms be respected whenever possible.

DISCUSSION QUESTIONS

1. Brainstorm with a partner and list at least five countries that belong in each of Kachru's inner, outer, and expanding circles.
2. Which variety of English is best to use as a norm for the students you (expect to) teach, and why?
3. Do you think it is useful in some contexts to teach ELF varieties of English grammar and lexicon or ELF pronunciation (e.g., Jenkins's lingua franca core)? Why or why not?
4. What do L2 learners of English need to know about varieties of English, and to what extent should that knowledge be receptive or productive?
5. What do L2 teachers of English need to know about varieties of English? Does it make any difference whether they are native or non-native speakers?

SUGGESTED ACTIVITIES

1. Try to find at least two consultants from each of these three groups: inner circle, outer circle, and expanding circle. Give each the same task to do (e.g., write a paragraph on a given topic). What are the similarities and differences in their use of English on this task?
2. Write down some ideas for teaching the receptive use of an unfamiliar variety of English to

language learners. Compare your ideas with those of your classmates, and compile a list of suggestions for future reference.

3. Give the same speaking prompt (e.g., "Tell me about your home town") to both a native and an advanced non-native speaker of English (record them if possible). Reflect on any differences you can detect in their intelligibility, fluency, and length of description and any differences in your own comprehension of and reaction to what they said.

4. Find and bring to class one or two examples of code-switching (instances of a speaker switching from one language to another in the same discourse unit). Share your example(s) with a group of fellow students. Did the speaker seem to switch codes to (a) compensate for a lexical or grammatical gap in his or her L2, (b) display group identity or solidarity, or (c) make a stylistic or playful choice?

FURTHER READING

Crystal, D. (2003). *English as a global language* (2nd ed.). Cambridge, UK: Cambridge University Press.

Crystal provides the definitive discussion of why and how English has assumed the role of a global language.

Kirkpatrick, A. (2007). *World Englishes: Implications for international communication and English language teaching.* Cambridge, UK: Cambridge University Press.

This book is a comprehensive introduction to varieties of English, World Englishes, and English as a lingua franca. It includes a CD with sample recordings of the varieties.

McGroarty, M. (Ed.). (2006). Lingua franca languages [Special issue]. *Annual Review of Applied Linguistics, 26.*

This is a special issue of *ARAL* with several relevant articles on English as a lingua franca.

McKay, S. L. (2002). *Teaching English as an international language.* Oxford, UK: Oxford University Press.

This is a sound monograph-length introduction to the major issues raised in this chapter.

ENDNOTES

[1] See Kirkpatrick (2007) for a comprehensive discussion of World English varieties.

[2] Note that the figures given for the number of English speakers in each of the three circles are from 2003; thus they are dated.

[3] It is interesting to note that most of these points were also raised by B. B. Kachru (1985) and his colleagues when they initially argued for the legitimacy of outer-circle varieties of English.

[4] In a description of the English vernacular spoken by the Cajun French community in the southern United States, Dubois and Horvath (2003) also cite several of the features that Seidlhofer and her colleagues ascribe to ELF users in Europe.

[5] Note that these examples are original to this chapter and not given in Seidlhofer. Many second language acquisition researchers consider this omission to be a common developmental error and a late-acquired form.

[6] This annual conference, the International Conference of English as a Lingua Franca, was first held in Helsinki in 2008.

UNIT II

Language Skills

Listening

6 | Second Language Listening Comprehension: Process and Pedagogy

CHRISTINE C. M. GOH

KEY QUESTIONS

➤ What is the state of listening pedagogy?
➤ What should teachers know about the listening process?
➤ How can teachers help English as a second or foreign language learners improve their listening comprehension and long-term listening development?

EXPERIENCE

Listening is a demanding skill for many language learners, and it is also a skill that many teachers find challenging to teach. The following excerpts from the reflections of a learner and a teacher illustrate some of the challenges with listening.

Learner A

We heard a talk from the librarian about how to do research work on the computer. I could not keep up with her because of the speed and some academic words, especially some words used in computer language. . . . I have a routine listening plan. Usually I can't catch what is said the first time. I have to repeat it again until I can make most sentences clear. On an average, the recording should be repeated 4 or 5 times. Of course, I'm not pleased with the result. I hope that one day I can understand something as soon as I hear it. I find the target is so hard to achieve that I sometimes lose hope. No matter how hard I practise my listening, I still stay at the original level.

Teacher Z

Back in my country, teaching listening is a simple affair. We just play the recording and ask the students to choose the correct answers to the accompanying listening comprehension questions. Looking back, there was hardly any real teaching because there wasn't much that we could teach. We just corrected their answers in class. We just hoped that the repeated exercises would help them become better eventually. . . . Sometimes we prepared them by telling them the title of a listening passage and to guess what it was about. We didn't know how to teach listening because we didn't know how to help our students like the way we helped them with pronunciation, grammar or writing.

The challenges facing learners and teachers are due partly to a lack of understanding of what listening entails and how comprehension is achieved. As a result, the learners may have unrealistic expectations of their listening development and the teachers may think that there is little they can do to teach listening because the processes that learners engage in during listening cannot be directly observed and controlled. It is not surprising therefore that for a long time listening activities in the classroom focused on the product of comprehension. Lessons typically involved listening to passages, answering questions, and checking answers. As G. Brown (1987) observes, listening pedagogy was heavily influenced by practices in the teaching of reading, with little allowance made for the complex nature of the listening process and the unique features of spoken language. Listening activities were also often a disguised form of testing because learners were expected to demonstrate their comprehension without receiving any real support (Sheerin, 1987). To help learners develop their listening, teachers need to understand how comprehension is achieved and recognize factors that can influence its outcome for language learners. Like other areas of language learning, learning to listen can benefit from curricula and activities that are planned in a theoretically principled manner and delivered systematically. This chapter assists teachers to acquire important theoretical perspectives about the listening process and to consider their implications for teaching listening. It also offers practical ideas for designing listening tasks to enhance learners' cognitive processes and ability to manage their overall listening development.

WHAT IS INVOLVED IN LISTENING?

Listening is not just hearing. It is an active process that may begin even before the first speech signal is recognized, and it may go on long after the input or spoken information has stopped. Meaning cannot be simply extracted from the sound signals, and understanding is the result of active construction occurring at all levels of text (sounds, grammar, lexis, and discourse structure) and context (the topic, the participants, the communication purpose, and the place or setting for the interaction). An *active listener,* according to G. Brown (1990), "is someone who constructs reasonable interpretations on the basis of an underspecified input and recognises when more specific information is required. The active listener asks for the needed information" (p. 172). This definition captures learners' limitations in listening where input is often incomplete because of their inability to recognize every word they hear. It also underscores the contribution that learners themselves can potentially bring to their comprehension process. In face-to-face interactions, meaning construction can be facilitated by cooperative processes between listeners and speakers (e.g., asking questions and offering clarifications). Where direct interaction is absent, listeners have to resort to other means of completing the gaps in their understanding. Like all language communication skills, listening is goal-directed

and purposeful. As Rost (1990) notes: "people listen for a purpose and it is this purpose that drives the understanding process" (p. 7). This is an important principle to bear in mind when planning lessons and activities for listening.

Active listening can therefore take place in *one-way* (nonparticipatory) or *two-way* (interactive and participatory) listening contexts. In one-way listening, listeners have few or no opportunities to interact directly with the speaker and have to rely almost exclusively on their linguistic knowledge, experience, and factual knowledge to make sense of what they hear. Examples include listening to and/or viewing recorded materials in a textbook, radio programs and songs, films, television programs, large lectures, and to some extent live speeches and presentations. In two-way listening, listeners are participants in an interaction where they alternate between the role of the listener and the speaker. Examples include casual conversations, telephone conversations, videoconferencing, formal or semi-formal interviews, one-to-one and group discussions, and some speeches and presentations where there are spontaneous interactions between speakers and the audience.

Listening skills and strategies

Language learners who are active listeners use a range of skills and strategies to direct and manage their listening processes according to their communication goals. (See Purpura, this volume, for a general discussion of learner styles and strategies.) Listening skills are acquired abilities that enable a person to listen without a great deal of deliberate effort or conscious planning. They are the result of actions that have been practiced frequently in varied situations, and through prolonged experience, the actions have become automatized. For example, decoding skills for perception and parsing can become automatized as language learners become increasingly sensitized to the phonological patterns of English through frequent exposure and develop greater awareness of its linguistic features through noticing.

Listening strategies, on the other hand, are ways of listening that are planned and consciously adopted to improve comprehension and communication as well as cope with listening difficulties. Strategies that direct attention to the input and coordinate various cognitive processes are often known as metacognitive strategies. They broadly consist of strategies for planning, monitoring, and evaluation, and they can be used before, during, or after listening. During face-to-face interactions, learners can use strategies to manage the communication and discourse. Strategies can have a social dimension and are used to enhance the interaction process through eliciting the speakers' cooperation. Following the conceptualization of reading skills and reading strategies by Afflerbach, Pearson, and Paris (2008), listening strategies can also be expected to develop into automatized listening skills with time. More critically, learners will also constantly move between skills and strategies while listening to different kinds of discourse with different levels of challenge. This is something that even competent listeners have to do at times.

CONCEPTUAL UNDERPINNINGS

Historical overview

Like other language skills, the teaching of listening has understandably been influenced by changes in approaches to language teaching methodology. A criticism of the audiolingual approach in the 1960s and 1970s was that the drills and dialogues did not prepare learners to comprehend authentic speech by native speakers (Belasco, 1971, as cited in Morley, 2001). In the mid to late 1970s, when the communicative and the related task-based approaches became popular, listening was given more systematic attention and the teaching of listening focused on the understanding of spoken discourse for functional and interactional purposes (Flowerdew & Miller, 2005). (See chapters by Duff and Nunan, this volume, for discussions of the communicative and task-based approaches, respectively.) Rather than being restricted to drills and dialogues, listening was practiced in face-to-face communication with native speakers or through communicative tasks (Morley, 2001). Materials were selected mainly from authentic communication instead of scripted for language learning, and learners used the information they processed for larger communication goals. Teachers were given guidelines on developing materials and designing tasks for practice in authentic or simulated communication (e.g., Geddes, 1981). Lists of listening comprehension skills were also proposed (J. C. Richards, 1983; Rixon, 1981). Although the psychological reality of dividing listening up into component skills has been questioned, such descriptions continue to be useful references for teachers to plan and organize listening practice (Field, 2008).

The place of listening was reinforced by second language acquisition (SLA) theories that foregrounded the role of input (Gass & Madden, 1985; Krashen 1981) and evidence that supported the claim that listening comprehension, coupled with delayed speaking, could facilitate language acquisition (Gary & Gary, 1981; Postovsky 1974). Discussions about listening pedagogy were further informed by theories in cognitive psychology concerning the constructive nature of text comprehension. Text comprehension, it was shown, did not result from a linear sequence of sounds being decoded and interpreted in an additive manner; instead, it was the outcome of interactions between prior knowledge retrieved from long-term memory and the sounds that are processed in working memory. Informed by cognitive theories, pre-listening activities were proposed to help learners anticipate words that they might hear and make appropriate inferences (Anderson & Lynch, 1988; Underwood, 1989; Ur, 1984). Research into learner listening also made significant gains, with Dunkel (1991) calling for a closer examination of the role of listening comprehension skill development in the beginning stages of language learning, the roles of participatory and nonparticipatory listening in second language acquisition, factors that affect comprehension, dynamic processes involved in L2 listening, and specific instructional tasks and activities that could enhance listening skill development.

The last two decades have seen further developments in listening instruction through the strategy approach (Mendelsohn, 1995). This approach focused on helping learners use strategies to enhance their listening processes and develop their metacognitive awareness about listening. It also aimed to empower learners to take control of their comprehension process in various listening contexts. Teachers were advised to model the metacognitive strategies of planning, monitoring, and evaluating comprehension (Chamot, 1995), along with cognitive strategies for verifying informed guesses (Field, 1998). Teacher modeling was assumed to help demystify the seemingly complex processes that listening involved and make the hidden processes of skillful listening explicit to language learners. Precommunication activities were recommended for raising learners' awareness about listening processes (G. Buck, 1995). These activities introduce learners to strategies for coping with listening difficulties and for using long-term memory resources to construct their understanding. Learners are also encouraged to develop their metacognitive knowledge about listening with the help of reflection tools such as listening diaries (Goh, 1997) and prompts for group dialogues (Cross, 2010). Some aspects of this knowledge could also be developed by sensitizing learners to the phonological features of speech and practicing their abilities to perceive sounds and segment a steam of speech into meaningful words or lexical items (Field, 2008).

Vandergrift (2004) made the teaching of cognitive processes during listening more direct by proposing the use of a metacognitive sequence whereby metacognitive processes such as verification and evaluation are integrated with listening at specific stages. This helps to raise metacognitive awareness and, at the same time, give learners the much needed scaffolding (i.e., support) while working with listening texts. According to the research conducted, learners who were successfully taught to use strategies through such a lesson sequence also experienced greater motivation to learn listening skills (Liu & Goh 2006; Mareschal, 2007), better awareness of effective strategies (Cross, 2010), and improvement in their performance (Vandergrift & Tafaghodtari, 2010). Vandergrift and Goh (2012) built on the strengths of the strategy approach by proposing a pedagogical framework underpinned by a theory of metacognition. They propose a pedagogy that combines metacognitive development with communicative task-based learning. In this approach, learners get plenty of listening practice to develop their listening skills and also engage in metacognitive processes such as planning, monitoring, and evaluation to be more self-regulated in their listening development. A metacognitive approach is particularly relevant for listening instruction because teachers need a way of making visible to learners the processes of comprehension and learning to scaffold these processes more effectively for the learners.

In spite of the many developments in second language listening pedagogy, the role of the listening teacher in some English as a second/foreign language (ESL/EFL) situations has remained largely that of the controller of the playback device and listening materials, as is the case with Teacher Z at the beginning of the chapter. For this reason, in some language programs teachers are deemed to be no longer needed for listening lessons and listening is taken out of curriculum time. Learners practice listening on their own by using self-access materials and online resources. Some commentators have suggested that, rather than teach learners how to listen strategically, it may be more beneficial simply to provide interesting materials for learners to practice their listening in class. Any kind of extensive listening is clearly useful, but leaving learners literally to their own devices may overlook an important principle about language teaching—namely that the teacher has an important role in scaffolding learning so that learners can achieve more than they can achieve on their own. To begin to do this well, teachers need to understand the different processes that take place during listening and how to support them in the process of learning to listen.

Cognitive processes

Much of our current understanding of how individuals process spoken signals and construct meaning from them has been illuminated by theoretical perspectives from cognitive psychology. A classic model of comprehension proposed by J. R. Anderson (1995) outlines three recurrent and overlapping phases—perception, parsing, and utilization—that can explain the function of cognitive processes during listening. Perception occurs as listeners match the sounds they hear to words they know. Also referred to as decoding and sound-script recognition, this process focuses on recognizing words in a stream of speech. Decoded words are almost simultaneously analyzed in larger units according to grammar or lexical cues in a process known as parsing. Comprehension is not achieved until a higher-level process known as utilization takes place; information processed at the phonological, grammatical, and lexical levels is related to the listeners' prior knowledge of the facts and listening context to enable them to interpret the meaning and functions of the utterances. If the constructed meaning is not needed immediately, it is transferred to long-term memory and stored there to be retrieved at an appropriate time. In interactive listening, however, listeners generally have to hold the meaning longer in their working memory while they formulate a response. For first language speakers, perception and parsing typically occur in an automatized manner;

that is, listeners need not exert any special effort in decoding the sounds of the words and analyzing the grammatical function of the utterances. Nevertheless, more effortful processing is usually needed during utilization for higher-level inferences and interpretations to take place.

Cognitive processes during listening are complex, but they can occur harmoniously as sound signals interact with learners' prior knowledge and as different knowledge sources are drawn on and connected throughout the process. The connectionist model, which posits the simultaneous processing of input, shows how this is done through the activation of interconnected or associative neural networks in the brain (Bechtel & Abrahamsen, 1991). In other words, when we receive input in the form of speech, our brain starts to match the sounds to words we know, as well as working toward an overall understanding of the spoken message by drawing on lexical and grammatical knowledge and on other stored knowledge about facts and experiences. In these processes, the working memory plays a central role by attending to the aural inputs through the phonological or articulatory loop (Baddeley, 2000). The phonological loop is a system that holds verbal information in our working memory long enough for it to be processed by reviving the memory traces of the information that has been perceived to prevent it from decaying too rapidly. Another working memory system that manages the processing of aural information is the central executive. This system is responsible for directing attention to the inputs, coordinating cognitive processes to ensure that they work harmoniously, and controlling them such that, when an individual's attention starts to wander, his or her attention is redirected back to the input. The working memory also integrates the processed information into a single mental representation through a system known as the episodic buffer so that the sound signals that are perceived and parsed are also interpreted semantically, thus enabling the individual to arrive at an understanding of the overall message for utilization. In the information-processing literature the term *bottom-up processing* is often used to describe the way meaning is built up from the sounds that have been decoded, while *top-down processing* is used to describe the way meaning is inferred and constructed from the application of prior knowledge about language

and the world stored in long-term memory. All of these processes are directed by the listener's metacognition, which is the ability to think about these processes and manage them (see Figure 1).

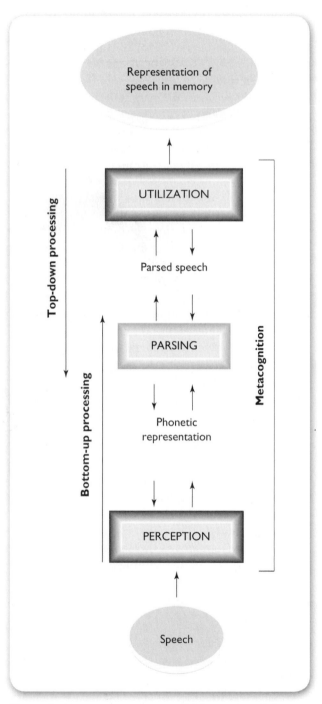

Figure 1. Cognitive processes in L2 listening and their interrelationships (based on Vandergrift & Goh, 2012).

An accumulation of literature over the decades strongly supports the theory that both bottom-up and top-down processes are needed for listening comprehension and that successful listening in a second or foreign language depends to a large extent on a learners' ability to engage in both sets of processes effectively. Many language learners, like Learner A at the beginning of the chapter, however, often experience difficulty because they may mishear key words due to inaccurate pronunciation and an inability to segment individual words in a stream of speech (S. Graham, 2006; Harada, 1997/8). They also have problems remembering key words long enough for meaning to be constructed or transferred to long-term memory (Goh, 2000). Lower-proficiency language learners' working memory is often overloaded as they juggle low- and high-level processes. Information in their limited-capacity memory is constantly being replaced by new input that they need to attend to, and they may have to rely heavily on their prior knowledge to achieve some comprehension. The use of background knowledge has been shown to assist learner comprehension in a large number of listening studies (Macaro, Graham, & Vanderplank, 2007), but it sometimes distracts learners and leads them to ignore useful cues in the text (Field, 2004); it also limits their interpretations (Tsui & Fullilove, 1998).

Types of knowledge that support listening comprehension

Language learners rely on different kinds of knowledge to facilitate their comprehension. The most common kind referred to in the literature on listening is *schema*, or background knowledge about the world that is derived from personal experiences and learning. This type of knowledge allows listeners to process information in a top-down manner, where gaps in comprehension are filled by what they know about the topic. To facilitate top-down as well as bottom-up processes, knowledge of the language system, discourse, and pragmatics are all equally important.

Knowledge of language. Learners' knowledge of the English language system is an important contributory factor for successful comprehension. One aspect of this knowledge is phonological knowledge, or knowledge about the sounds of English, which facilitates perception. At the segmental level, that is, the level of discrete sound elements, learners need to know how vowels and consonants combine to produce words. At the suprasegmental level, that is, the level beyond individual sounds, learners need to know that words in English have different stress patterns. Knowing a word in the written form does not guarantee that learners will recognize it in speech. If the learners' own pronunciation of certain words is inaccurate, perception of these words will be affected. For example, someone who pronounces *hostel* with the same stress pattern as *hotel* may not recognize *hostel* when it is spoken. In addition, if learners are unfamiliar with the stress-timed rhythm and intonation of spoken English, where only some words are stressed in continuous utterances, they may expect to hear every word. (See Goodwin, this volume, for a discussion of rhythm and intonation.)

For effective parsing to occur, learners must rely on their knowledge of how meaning is represented syntactically. Grammatical knowledge, however, goes beyond the written language. Spoken language, particularly casual and informal speech, is organized differently from written prose; it is organized through spoken grammar, which includes features such as ellipsis (*Lemonade?* Instead of *Would you like a lemonade?*) and question tags (*That can't be right, can it?*) (Carter & McCarthy, 1997). Furthermore, natural speech is messy, with incomplete utterances, repetitions, and redundancies. Learners' knowledge of the grammar and features of spoken language will facilitate their listening comprehension of authentic speech.

Vocabulary knowledge also has a significant impact on listening comprehension, a factor that many language learners recognize themselves. In addition to individual words, learners may also be unfamiliar with formulaic expressions or prefabricated lexical "chunks" (e.g., *the long and short of it* or *over the hill*) that are commonly used by native or competent speakers of English. Thus even when learners are able to decode individual words correctly, they may still have problem processing the meaning of colloquial expressions and idioms, and this can affect their overall understanding of what they hear.

Knowledge of discourse and language use. Listening is carried out in a wide variety of places, such as schools, colleges, shops, clinics, and workplaces. In each of these contexts, learners can expect to encounter different kinds of discourse, or extended pieces of language created during an interaction. Each type of discourse is patterned differently, and knowledge about how specific discourses are structured can enhance listening comprehension. For example, in short exchanges, there will usually be three conversational turns, as the next example illustrates:

A: Going to the party this Saturday?
B: Nope. Got to hand in my term paper on Monday.
A: Too bad, but the paper's more important, I guess.

Learners' discourse knowledge about short exchanges will lead them to expect at least two turns or adjacency pairs (i.e., where one speaker asks a question or makes a comment and the listener responds). They may also know that when someone answers a question with a negative response, the response is typically accompanied by a reason. In addition, learners will expect to hear a third utterance, where the person who asks the questions rounds off the exchange with a comment.

In one-way listening contexts, such as lectures, learners will find it helpful to know how a lecture typically begins, develops, and ends; they also need to understand the role of discourse markers such as *next* and *on the other hand* in signaling the way a lecture unfolds. (See also Flowerdew & Miller, this volume.) Knowledge about the structure of other common kinds of genres or communicative events (e.g., news reports, announcements, interviews, and jokes) will also help learners during listening.

Rost (2011) observes that listeners have "an intention to complete a communication process to some degree" (p. 79). Not only do listeners aim to understand the words that are said, but they also want to grasp the function of an utterance and its intended effect (e.g., whether the speaker is disagreeing politely or expressing disbelief). Knowledge of language use or pragmatic knowledge is particularly crucial during the utilization phase of comprehension, where the listener interprets what is said or formulates appropriate responses. Pragmatic knowledge enables learners to go beyond the literal meaning drawn from successful decoding and parsing of the input to draw conclusions about the speaker's intention. Because English is spoken by people from different sociocultural backgrounds, listeners will also have to know the sociocultural rules of use that are appropriate for the people that they are interacting with. This is perhaps the most challenging aspect of pragmatic knowledge development, and learners may have to rely on resources beyond the language classroom.

CLASSROOM APPLICATIONS

Listening skills and strategies

As mentioned, the literature on second/foreign language listening contains long lists of listening skills and subskills. J. C. Richards (1983) presents over 30 subskills, ranging from ones for decoding words (e.g., the ability to distinguish word boundaries) to those needed for understanding of discourse (e.g., the ability to detect causes and effects from events). (See Appendix A.) Field's (2008) lists of decoding and meaning-building processes bear some similarities to many of these listening subskills, but by calling them processes, Field highlights the cognitive complexities involved in listening. G. Buck (2001) emphasizes different abilities for understanding both literal meanings and implied meanings in spoken input.

As a guide for teachers to plan listening tasks, Vandergrift and Goh (2012) identify six core skills that are integral to the listening process:

1. *Listen for details.* Identify specific information that is relevant to the listening goal, such as key words, numbers, names, dates, and places.
2. *Listen selectively.* Pay attention to particular parts of the listening text and ignore others that are not relevant to listening goals or that contain too much information to attend to at the same time.
3. *Listen for global understanding.* Understand the overall general idea, such as the theme, topic, and purpose.
4. *Listen for main ideas.* Understand the key points or propositions in a text, such as points in support of an argument, directions for doing something, and important events in a story.
5. *Listen and infer.* Make up for information that is missing, unclear, or ambiguous in the listening text by using different resources, such as background knowledge, visual clues, and speaker's tone.

6. *Listen and predict.* Anticipate what is going to be said before or during listening by using clues from the context, from background knowledge, or knowledge about the speaker.

Competent listeners typically use these skills to direct and adjust their attention productively to the spoken input according to their listening purpose. Each skill is operationalized by the activation of the cognitive processes discussed earlier. The use of the core listening skills is influenced by the purpose for listening. It determines which skill or skills are more relevant at a specific point in the listening event. Because listening purposes may change throughout the duration of a communicative event, listeners too will modify the skills they use. For example, someone who listens to the news on the radio or television does not use all six skills equally. At the start of the broadcast, the listener may try to get all the details in the headlines. The person may then listen selectively and pay attention to only those items that are of interest. If a news item is something he or she is not interested in, the person may go to the kitchen to get something to drink but return to catch another news item. The person may miss hearing some words because the phone rings or there is some distraction. To fill in the gaps, he or she may use the film footage to get an overall idea of what is being presented. The core skills are also applied similarly in face-to-face listening. Listeners may find it is either too tiring or just unnecessary to focus on all the details in a conversation and may decide to listen for global understanding. They may also tune in and tune out selectively depending on attention span or interest. If they are engaged in a discussion, however, they may want to listen closely to the points that the speaker is presenting and use cues from the speaker's body language and suprasegmental features (e.g., intonation and stress) to infer information that is not conveyed explicitly through language.

Second/foreign language learners will find it useful to develop the core listening skills so that they can vary their level of attention and not expect to hear all the details in every utterance. However, the process will still largely be effortful and deliberate, and the learners need to use appropriate listening strategies. For example, when they realize that they do not recognize many words in a message, they may consciously listen for global understanding. Learners may also decide to listen for key words and use the words to construct their understanding of the message in a largely top-down manner. Where possible, some language learners may also do some forward planning before they start listening. Research has shown that there are differences in the quality and the frequency of strategies used by successful and less successful listeners, with some studies suggesting that strategy instruction may improve listening performance (Macaro, Graham, & Vanderplank, 2007). There is also evidence that the better listeners not only used strategies that were more appropriate and effective but were also better at orchestrating the use of several strategies and substrategies or tactics to construct reasonable interpretations of what they heard (Vandergrift, 2003).

Research on strategy use in second language listening has produced a number of strategy taxonomies. Vandergrift and Goh (2012) identify 12 strategies that occur across many of these taxonomies:

1. *Planning:* developing an awareness of what needs to be done and an action plan to overcome possible difficulties
2. *Focusing attention:* heeding the spoken input in different ways and avoiding distractions
3. *Monitoring:* checking, confirming, or correcting one's comprehension during the task
4. *Evaluation:* checking the outcomes of listening and listening plans
5. *Inferencing:* using different kinds of prior knowledge to guess unfamiliar words and fill in missing information
6. *Elaboration:* using different kinds of prior knowledge to extend and embellish an interpretation
7. *Prediction:* anticipating the contents of what one is going to hear
8. *Contextualization:* placing what is heard in a specific context to assist further comprehension
9. *Reorganizing:* transferring what is understood into another form to facilitate further understanding, storage, and retrieval
10. *Using linguistic and learning resources:* relying on knowledge of first language or additional languages, and referring to available resources that support listening and learning
11. *Cooperation:* working with others to get their assistance in comprehension and learning

12. *Managing emotions:* being aware of one's negative emotions and finding ways to prevent them from affecting comprehension and learning

A process-oriented listening pedagogy

Learners' knowledge of the language, discourse, and language use will enable them to decode speech signals as well as make predictions or inferences to construct reasonable interpretations. Cognitive and social processes, however, are complex and can be problematic for learners, but teachers can provide appropriate kinds of guidance and scaffolding to help them manage their process of learning to listen. Valuable proposals have been made regarding ways to teach listening that develop bottom-up and top-down processes (see Field 2008; Lynch, 2009; Rost, 2011) and that also address complex dimensions of authentic listening, such as individual-variation, cross-cultural, social, intertextual, strategic, affective, and critical dimensions (Flowerdew & Miller, 2005).(See also Flowerdew & Miller, this volume.)

There are two complementary methods for planning lessons to teach listening: (1) *task-based metacognitive instruction*, which combines one- and two-way communicative listening tasks with metacognitive development activities; and (2) *metacognitive pedagogical sequence*, which integrates strategy-based instruction to guide learners through metacognitive processes of listening as they listen to a text. As shown in Figure 2, both methods aim to develop learners' metacognitive awareness about listening while offering them plenty of listening practice at the same time. The tasks and lessons allow learners to practice the core listening skills, develop their explicit knowledge of second language listening, and adopt strategies for managing their listening comprehension and overall development of listening skills.

Task-based metacognitive instruction. This instructional strategy integrates task-based learning with metacognitive instruction. It builds on the strengths of communicative task-based learning, which encourages learners to listen and respond actively to texts that have a high degree of authenticity. In this section, I first describe two types of listening tasks—one-way (nonparticipatory) listening tasks and two-way (interactive and participatory) listening tasks—and then explain how metacognitive activities can be integrated into these tasks.

Task-based instruction for listening emphasizes the importance of communication goals between speakers and listeners, and focuses on the comprehension of meaning according to learners' purpose for listening. For example, if the learners' purpose is to identify times and dates from the text, they need to concentrate on attending to the details. If they need to get the gist of a long segment of discourse, learners can ignore the details and concentrate on using clues such as key words to construct a global understanding of the text. Listening tasks are seen as useful opportunities for learners to practice listening to a variety of discourses and to use listening strategies whenever they are needed. Learners are told their purpose for listening or are given an opportunity to define the purpose and anticipated outcomes themselves. The specification of a communicative purpose and an outcome are essential features of language learning tasks (J. R. Willis, 1996). One-way (nonparticipatory) and two-way (participatory) listening tasks are further integrated with appropriate metacognitive activities before and after listening to guide learners in regulating and appraising their own listening comprehension processes and efforts at learning to listen (Goh, 2010).

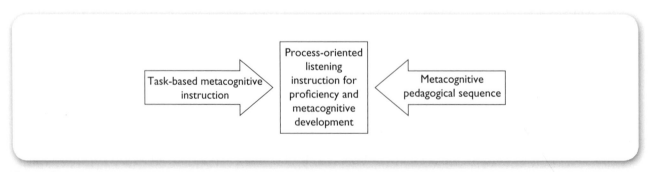

Figure 2. Process-oriented instruction for listening fluency and metacognitive development.

One-way (nonparticipatory) listening tasks. The goal of one-way listening is for learners to obtain information from the listening text with minimal or no interaction with the speaker. One-way listening tasks require learners to understand the meaning of what is said without the need to give immediate responses. Learners listen to different kinds of spoken texts that are recorded or read aloud by the teacher. They then use this information to achieve a variety of listening outcomes or products, such as lists, categorized information, edited texts, diagrams, pictures, summaries, notes, questions, and individual or group responses. Table 1 presents examples of one-way listening tasks that help learners practice different listening skills for a specific product. Each example outlines the procedures and forms the basis for developing a complete lesson where metacognitive activities are also incorporated.

Two-way (interactive and participatory) listening tasks. Two-way listening tasks engage learners in interactions where they alternate between the roles of listener and speaker. They usually have to respond directly to what they hear, either to provide the necessary information or to ask the speaker about what was said. Spoken interaction takes two forms: (1) conversations, which are interpersonal in purpose; and (2) encounters, which are transactional in purpose (Burns, Joyce, & Gollin, 1996). Applied to teaching listening, the tasks could involve learners in conversations of either an informal or a formal nature in which ideas, information, and thoughts are shared. Responses will also be affected by the perceived power relationships between learners and other participants in the interaction. In listening tasks that involve transactional interactions, learners are asked to obtain information, goods, or services from other participants in the interaction. Listeners may seek further clarifications, and their use of language will be affected by the perceived degree of familiarity between them and the speaker.

Unlike one-way listening tasks, which make use of monologic texts, two-way listening tasks require learners to listen to discourse of a dialogic nature, one that is jointly constructed by them and other participants in an interaction. Listening outcomes may be similar to the ones in one-way listening, but the process of achieving those outcomes tends to be collaborative. Table 2 presents examples of two-way interactive listening tasks that give learners opportunities to practice different listening skills as well as discourse strategies that can enhance listening comprehension during an interaction. In addition to practicing different ways of attending to the spoken input, learners should also learn to use cooperation strategies to help improve their comprehension. Teachers might find it useful to preteach some relevant questions or phrases that learners can use to seek help and clarification (e.g., *Could you say that again, please?*).

Incorporating metacognitive activities

Although listening tasks provide learners with valuable listening practice, the learners' experience is not complete without opportunities to step back from the activities to think about their learning. These opportunities are found in the use of metacognitive activities before, during, or after listening, as well as at appropriate times during a language course. By incorporating metacognitive activities into task-based instruction, teachers can develop learners' knowledge about ESL/EFL listening processes and the contribution they themselves can make to enhance the comprehension and learning process.

Metacognition is our ability to think about our own thinking and learning (Flavell, 1979). It enables us to move away from doing an activity to analyzing the way we do it, and it is central to the learning process (Alexander, 2008; Borkowski, 1996). Metacognition plays a key role in language learning as it enables learners to plan, monitor, and evaluate how they process information in a new language; it also directs the way they do it (Wenden, 1991). The role of metacognition is crucial to the development of second and foreign language listening because listening comprehension, as a largely hidden process that happens inside the head of the learners, cannot be modified or corrected unless these processes are made visible. Not only are teachers unable to observe learners' development and the problems the learners face; the learners themselves are often unclear about how they listen because they quickly forget the processes that they engage in unless there are opportunities for them to reflect on these processes, document them, and learn from these reflections. Metacognitive activities in class can raise learners' awareness of the processes of comprehension, encourage them to adopt appropriate strategies and skills and to evaluate and improve their learning processes. Through metacognitive

Table I. One-Way (Nonparticipatory) Listening Tasks

Task	Skills	Product	Materials	Procedure
Listen and restore	Listening for global understanding; listening for details	An amended text in print	Different types of listening texts, such as narratives and information reports; the transcript of a text with incorrect details	1. Students work individually or in pairs to read the printed text. 2. They discuss the gist of the text and listen to the text once. 3. When they listen again, they correct the details in the written texts by changing, adding, or deleting words.
Listen and sort	Listening for main ideas; listening for details	A rearranged sequence of text or pictures	A text that describes a sequence, a procedure, a chronological event, or items in ranked order; sets of jumbled up texts and/or pictures	1. Students work in pairs to examine the jumbled texts or pictures. 2. They discuss what the text might be about and sort the texts/pictures according to their speculations. 3. They listen to the text and use the information to sequence the texts/pictures.
Listen and compare	Listening for main ideas; listening for details	A list of similarities and differences	Several short texts that have a common theme or topic	1. Students listen individually to the texts and identify similarities and differences. 2. They compare their answers with another student to confirm what they have identified. 3. The class listens to the texts again and students check their answers.
Listen and match	Listening for global understanding	Texts matched to themes	Several short texts that have different themes; theme cards (small cards with a single word written on each one, e.g., recycling, marriage, health). *Note*: Teachers should prepare more theme cards than the number of texts.	1. The teacher checks that students understand the meaning of the words in the theme cards. 2. Students listen individually to the texts and identify the most appropriate theme for each text.
Listen and combine	Listening for main ideas; listening selectively	A combined summary based on information from different sources	A fairly long text (e.g., a news broadcast, narrative, or procedure) divided into several parts	1. Students listen to one part of the text individually. 2. They make notes of what they hear. 3. In small groups, they report to one another and reconstruct a summarized form of the original text.
Listen and compose	Listening and predicting; listening and making inferences	The beginning or conclusion of a text	A narrative text (e.g., a short story) with either the beginning or the end missing	1. Students listen to the text in pairs or in a small group. 2. They discuss what the text is about and what the missing part should be like. 3. They write the missing part and a representative reads the part aloud to the rest of the class.
Listen and evaluate	Listening for details; listening for main ideas; listening and making inferences (depending on the criteria for evaluation)	A list of items based on their relative merits	Several short texts on a common theme or topic	1. Students listen to the texts individually and assess the information or message based on predetermined criteria, such as clarity, interest level, accuracy, and effectiveness. 2. In groups or pairs, they explain their choices.
Listen and reconstruct	Listening for global understanding; listening for main ideas; listening for details	A text that is reconstructed based on the content of the original text	A short text (e.g., an information report, procedures, or exposition of a viewpoint)	1. Students listen individually to the text once. 2. They listen to it again and take notes of key content words or key points in a text (e.g., problems, solutions, and recommendations). 3. They use their notes to produce a text that is close in meaning to the original one.

Table 2. Two-Way (Participatory) Listening Tasks

Task	Skills	Product	Materials	Procedure
Dictate and complete	Listening for details, listening selectively	A restored and complete text	Different types of listening texts (e.g., narratives and information reports); versions A and B of the text with blanks inserted in different parts of the text	1. Students read their version of the incomplete text individually. 2. They take turns dictating their version without showing it to their partners. Listeners must ask for clarification and repetition where necessary. 3. They write down the missing words in their version of the text.
Describe and draw	Listening for main ideas; listening for details	Pictures, maps, sketches, and objects	Pictures of scenery and objects, plans, and maps	1. Students work in pairs, with one of them describing the content of a picture. 2. The other student draws it or completes a similar picture that is incomplete. 3. Listeners must ask for clarification and repetition where necessary.
Simulate and discuss	Listening for main ideas; listening for details; listening and inferring; listening and predicting	Views and recommendations	Cards with scenarios for simulations, roles, or statements of a problem and an issue and the required outcome, such as a set of recommendations	1. Students form small groups to discuss a problem or an issue in the simulation. 2. A moderator or the chairperson in the simulation is assigned to ask questions, elicit views, challenge assumptions, and clarify understanding. 3. Students in their respective roles listen to one another's views, make notes, respond to views, and seek clarifications. 4. They agree on a set of outcomes following the discussion.
Take notes and clarify	Listening for global understanding; listening for main ideas; listening for details; listening and making inferences	A set of notes; a list of questions for clarifying understanding of the content	Presentations by students or guest speakers	1. Students listen to a presentation and take notes. 2. They review their notes and prepare some questions about the content of the presentation to ask the presenter.

instruction, learners become more self-directed (knowing what to do to develop their listening) and self-regulated (knowing how to manage challenges and opportunities). Metacognitive activities in the listening classroom can include the use of one or more of the following:

Self-directed listening guide. This is a set of questions and prompts that learners respond to before and after they listen to materials selected for individual listening practice (see Appendix B).

Listening diaries. Entries are made into a journal or specially prepared reflection sheets that learners complete individually by answering *what, when,*

how, why, and *who* questions about a specific listening event.

Process-based discussions. Students are given prompts similar to the ones for listening diaries. They can also be specific ones that refer to the listening skills that the lesson aimed to develop. Learners form pairs or small groups to discuss how they have approached a listening task and their goals, comprehension, achievement, problems, and strategies.

Self-report checklist. Learners have a set of checklist questions that they consider at the end of every listening lesson. They can also include short comments.

Developing task-based metacognitive lessons. Teachers can select one or more of the listening tasks described to develop complete listening lessons. This can be done by using a three-stage lesson structure of pre-listening, while-listening, and post-listening. In the pre-listening stage, teachers can prepare learners to listen by using activities that focus on the content of the text and/or the language in the text. These activities may include brainstorming, researching, reading, viewing pictures or photographs, and discussing. While-listening activities can take the form of one-way and two-way listening tasks that develop listening skills and fluency. Post-listening activities should enable learners to make use of the meaning they have derived from listening to the text or participating in an interaction. For example, learners can write a letter or an email to someone to share their reactions to the text. Post-listening activities can also help learners focus on the language in the text to develop better decoding skills. For example, learners listen to the pronunciation of unfamiliar words again or they listen to the whole text with the help of a transcript.

The types of pre- and post-listening activities mentioned so far will help learners engage with the content or meaning of the text before and after listening. These activities should also aim to develop learners' metacognitive awareness, which in turn can support and enhance both comprehension and overall listening development. More specifically, pre- and post-listening activities can focus on learners' metacognitive knowledge about themselves as ESL/EFL listeners, the nature and demands of ESL/EFL listening, and the strategies that can assist learners in coping with listening difficulties and enhancing comprehension. By incorporating task-based instruction with metacognitive activities, teachers will help learners practice their skills at comprehending listening texts while taking greater control over their listening development.

Pre-listening activities can also help learners to define what the task requires and set appropriate goals. Learners can plan what they are going to do when they listen and prepare for it by considering what strategies they may need and how they can make use of their background knowledge appropriately. They can predict what they are going to hear and, in the process, learn words that the text might contain and how the words are pronounced. Post-listening activities can include a variety of guided reflections that can encourage learners to attend to implicit listening processes and consider what they have learned about listening. Students can also share with one another their reflections and learn new ways of approaching the task of listening. Post-listening metacognitive activities need not be exclusively retrospective in nature. Learners can look ahead to the next task or lesson and do some forward planning. They can think back to the listening task or experience and then think about how they can enhance their listening performance in similar tasks in future, whether in class or on their own.

To keep planning and reflection activities relevant and enjoyable, teachers can vary the ways in which they are done by selecting from the list of four metacognitive activities suggested earlier. These are also metacognitive tools that document the learners' listening experience during and after class, and the output can be developed into a listening portfolio for self-assessment. Teachers can also learn about how their students are managing their out-of-class listening development and, if appropriate, can use the completed guides as part of a formative assessment of the students' listening development. By including metacognitive activities in a listening lesson, teachers can help direct learners' efforts at planning, monitoring, and evaluating their listening and learning experiences. Learners who have experienced a task-based metacognitive instruction approach in the classroom are more likely to carry out extensive listening activities more independently and productively.

Metacognitive pedagogical sequence for listening

The metacognitive pedagogical sequence proposed by Vandergrift (2004) is a strategy-based instructional method that weaves metacognitive processes into a listening lesson to support learners' listening. It works well with one-way listening, where learners listen to a text several times and go through selected processes with each listen. The teacher scaffolds learners' individual use of strategies and at the same time provides opportunities for learners to collaborate with one another. The design of the sequence is based on the four metacognitive processes that are considered to be crucial to successful listening development: (1) planning for the activity; (2) monitoring comprehension; (3) solving comprehension problems; and (4) evaluating the approach and outcomes. The sequence has five stages in which teachers guide students to apply strategies such as making inferences, elaboration, predicting, monitoring, evaluation, directed attention, and selective attention. Learners listen to the text three times in all. Each time, learners verify their understanding of the text, thereby increasing their understanding of the text content and awareness of the metacognitive processes involved. An intended outcome of the metacognitive pedagogical sequence is for learners to increase their control over their listening processes gradually. Figure 3 shows how these stages are organized.

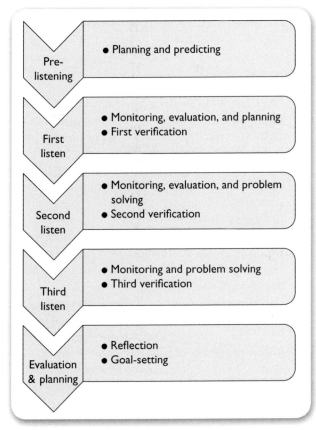

Figure 3. A metacognitive pedagogical sequence for listening (based on Vandergrift, 2004).

The sequence provides a framework for planning listening lessons that offers teachers the flexibility to vary the activities according to the strategies that they intend to focus on. The next example shows how the metacognitive pedagogical sequence proposed by Vandergrift (2004) can

be used so that it includes peer discussions and teacher modeling. It allows teachers to give just-in-time input on strategy use and learners to practice all appropriate strategies to process the input on their own. It also includes support for developing sound-script recognition to develop the students' decoding skills after listening.

Planning. Students define their listening goals and share with others what they know about the topic. Together they predict the information and words/phrases in the text. They write this down in English; however, the teacher can also allow them to include some words in their first language if they are unable to think of the English words. In addition to the text, they also try to anticipate potential difficulties and prepare themselves to use some coping strategies.

First listen. As they are listening to the text, students write down words that they have predicted and recognized. With a partner, they compare what they have understood so far and describe the strategies they have used. They identify problems and tell each other what they need to pay special attention to when they listen again. The teacher models thinking aloud of how he or she would listen selectively to problematic parts of the text.

Second listen. Students listen selectively to those parts they found problematic. They make notes of any new information they hear. The teacher leads a discussion to check students' comprehension. He or she elicits from students the strategies that they used and models some selected ones.

Third listen. Students decide individually what strategy or strategies they would like to use and try them out when they listen again. As a follow-up activity, students listen to the text one more time and follow along with a transcript, paying attention to how some problematic words and utterances sound.

Evaluation and planning. Students write their reflections on the lesson in their listening diaries. They also summarize what they have learned and understood from the listening text.

FUTURE TRENDS

The teaching of listening has gone through several paradigm shifts in the last five decades. In the process, the types of listening materials used have also changed from long written passages recorded or read aloud to a wide range of authentic materials from the media and the Internet. Special activities are now planned so that teachers can scaffold learners as they engage in various kinds of cognitive and social processes during listening. The systematic use of metacognitive activities is a relatively new development, and we can expect to see an expanded role for such activities in instructional tasks and activities. We are likely to see a better balance between the emphasis given to the development of top-down and bottom-up processes. Listening instruction will continue to highlight the role that learners' metacognition plays in the learning process.

In research, we can expect to see further work that investigates the efficacy of metacognitive approaches through experimental studies and in-depth case studies of second language listeners in different learning and cultural contexts. Research is also likely to examine more closely the role of discourse knowledge on listening performance, an area that has hitherto received little attention. The teaching of listening to young learners is also an area of interest, but research on it is likely to be done in the context of two-way participatory listening, such as the types of listening (and interaction) that occur in English-medium classrooms. In academic contexts, a focus on more demanding listening skills such as critical listening will be useful.

CONCLUSION

Listening can take place independently of speaking or in conjunction with speaking. To be an effective listener, learners have to adapt to the different roles that they play and apply various types of knowledge to facilitate the processing of the text in different contexts. Because listening proficiency depends on the speed and accuracy of the processing of spoken input, an important aim of listening instruction is to help learners enhance the interconnected networks of their cognitive processes through better linguistic knowledge and effective use of skills and strategies. While teachers cannot directly manipulate these processes, they can provide the necessary conditions for learners to learn about these processes and practice them frequently so that their performance can improve with time. Learning activities

should direct learners' attention to the input and provide the conditions where learners can engage successfully in at least some amount of decoding and analysis of the signals. It should also enable learners to make use of different kinds of prior knowledge to act on the information as it is being processed. Being supported to find small successes can be immensely motivating to learners, particularly to less able listeners. Last but not least, metacognitive activities are needed to help learners develop self-knowledge as ESL/EFL listeners, understand the nature and demands of the listening process, and become familiar with using strategies to support their own listening. Finally, it is hoped that from the discussion in this chapter, we can see that, far from being redundant, teachers are needed more than ever to help learners develop their listening skills.

SUMMARY

➤ Over the past five decades, the focus of listening lessons has shifted from a demonstration of the product of listening (accurate comprehension of listening texts) to a development of knowledge, skills, and strategies that can facilitate the cognitive and social processes of comprehension.

➤ Listening involves complex cognitive processes of perception, parsing, and utilization, which can be controlled and modified by learners through an enhancement of their knowledge of the language system, discourse, and how language is used; it can also be enhanced through the application of their prior knowledge of the text and context.

➤ Social processes of listening require the cooperation between learners and speakers to clarify meaning and intentions during an interaction, and the processes can provide valuable support to learners who experience the pressure to formulate appropriate responses.

➤ Process-oriented pedagogy for listening combines the strengths of task-based learning and a metacognitive approach to develop learners' listening fluency and accuracy and promote greater metacognitive awareness in them about the nature and demands of L2 listening and their individual contribution to their overall listening development.

DISCUSSION QUESTIONS

1. Read the two individual reflections at the beginning of the chapter, and identify the specific challenges that the learner and the teacher each face. Discuss what could have contributed to these challenges and what can be done to support them in their respective tasks.

2. Do you agree with the distinction between skills and strategies offered in this chapter? Drawing from your own experience as a language learner or the experience of someone you know, discuss how a listener may move between skills and strategies in the process of listening. What are the implications of this for teaching listening to ESL/EFL learners?

3. Compare the listening subskills in J. C. Richards's (1983) taxonomy (see Appendix A) to the six core skills by Vandergrift and Goh (pp. 78–79). Wherever possible, match the subskills to the appropriate core skills. To what extent can a detailed list of subskills and broad categories of listening core skills be useful for teachers and learners?

4. Discuss the extent to which the development of a knowledge of language and discourse is related to learners' metacognitive awareness about second/foreign language listening. Why would learners who have good metacognitive knowledge about the nature and demands of listening feel more confident about their listening?

SUGGESTED ACTIVITIES

1. This activity allows you to experience some of the cognitive processes that learners engage in when listening. Select a listening text based on a subject matter that your classmates are unlikely to be familiar with. Play the recording, or read the text out loud to your classmates. Do not at any time tell them what the text is about. At the end of the listening, have each person reflect on the experience, telling the others what they think the text is about and how they tried to make sense of what they heard. Review some of the cognitive processes explained in this chapter, and use your understanding to explain what your classmates were trying to do.

2. Select a one-way listening task and a two-way listening task presented in the chapter. For each task, plan a one-hour listening lesson for a group of students you have in mind, decide what listening skills are being practiced and what listening outcomes are appropriate for the task, and then explain what type of listening text or interaction scenarios you would use for the lesson. Your lesson should include a pre-listening and a post-listening activity. One of the activities must include a clear metacognitive dimension. Write the outline of the lesson in the format that is recommended in your course. If you have access to an ESL/EFL class, present the lesson in the class and share with your classmates how the lesson went.

3. Learners need to use cooperation strategies to seek clarifications from speakers or to check and confirm their comprehension. Make a list of useful questions and phrases that you can teach your students to say when they need to ask for: (a) repetition; (b) explanation; (c) verification; (d) rephrasing; and (e) examples. Compare your ideas, and discuss how these questions and phrases are relevant to the two kinds of spoken interaction explained in the chapter—namely conversations and encounters. Consider the appropriateness of these expressions for different levels of formality and power relations.

4. Work with a partner to select a listening/viewing text. Refer to *A Learner Guide for Self-Directed Listening/Viewing* in Appendix B and use it with the text. Listen/view the text, and make notes individually. Then share your notes with each other, and identify differences and similarities in what you thought and did. Discuss the reasons for these similarities and differences, and identify one or two things you have learned about the listening process through this activity. Share your ideas with the rest of the class.

FURTHER READING

Fields, J. (2008) *Listening in the language classroom.* Cambridge, UK: Cambridge University Press.

The book gives an overview of the teaching of listening and provides in-depth discussions of a number of important issues related to listening. It also proposes a number of useful activities that can be used to develop learners' decoding skills.

Goh, C. (2008). Metacognitive instruction for second language listening development: Theory, practice and research implications. *RELC Journal, 39*(2), 188–213.

Reviewing theories and research about metacognition, this article argues for the importance of metacognition in listening development, explains approaches to metacognitive instruction, and identifies areas of research.

Lynch, T. (2009). *Teaching second language listening.* Oxford, UK: Oxford University Press.

The book gives a useful summary of developments on L2 listening instruction, offers useful guidelines on selecting and using authentic materials for listening, and demonstrates how listening can be integrated with other language skills.

Vandergrift, L., & Goh, C. C. M. (2012). *Teaching and learning second language listening: Metacognition in action.* New York, NY: Routledge.

This book provides a detailed explication of theories related to the listening process and the construct of metacognition and applies them to practical ideas for teaching listening in and beyond the classroom.

APPENDIX A: TAXONOMY OF MICRO-SKILLS FOR CONVERSATIONAL LISTENING

1. ability to retain chunks of language of different lengths for short periods
2. ability to discriminate among the distinctive sounds of the target language
3. ability to recognize the stress patterns of words
4. ability to recognize the rhythmic structure of English
5. ability to recognize the functions of stress and intonation to signal the information structure of utterances
6. ability to identify words in stressed and unstressed positions
7. ability to recognize reduced forms of words
8. ability to distinguish word boundaries
9. ability to recognize typical word order patterns in the target language
10. ability to recognize vocabulary used in core conversational topics
11. ability to detect key words (i.e., those which identify topics and propositions)
12. ability to guess the meanings of words from the contexts in which they occur
13. ability to recognize grammatical word classes (parts of speech)
14. ability to recognize major syntactic patterns and devices
15. ability to recognize cohesive devices in spoken discourse
16. ability to recognize elliptical forms of grammatical units and sentences
17. ability to detect sentence constituents
18. ability to distinguish between major and minor constituents
19. ability to detect meanings expressed in differing grammatical forms/sentence types (i.e., that a particular meaning may be expressed in different ways)
20. ability to recognize the communicative functions of utterances, according to situations, participants, goals
21. ability to reconstruct or infer situations, goals, participants, procedures
22. ability to use real world knowledge and experience to work out purposes, goals, settings, procedures
23. ability to predict outcomes from events described
24. ability to infer links and connections between events
25. ability to deduce causes and effects from events
26. ability to distinguish between literal and implied meanings
27. ability to identify and reconstruct topics and coherent structure from ongoing discourse involving two or more speakers
28. ability to recognize markers of coherence in discourse, and to detect such relations as main idea, supporting idea, given information, new information, generalization, exemplification
29. ability to process speech at different rates
30. ability to process speech containing pauses, errors, corrections

31. ability to make use of facial, paralinguistic, and other clues to work out meanings

32. ability to adjust listening strategies to different kinds of listener purposes or goals

33. ability to signal comprehension or lack of comprehension, verbally and nonverbally

Source: J. C. Richards, 1983, pp. 228–229

APPENDIX B: A LEARNER GUIDE FOR SELF-DIRECTED LISTENING/VIEWING

My Self-Directed Listening/Viewing Guide

Name:

Listening text:

Source:

Date and time of practice:

Setting my listening goal

Why did I choose this recording?

What is my goal?

To achieve my goals, how many times do I plan to listen/view this recording? Why?

Preparing to listen

What do I know about this topic?

What difficulties can I expect?

What type of information can I expect to hear (and view)?

What words can I expect to hear? (Use a dictionary, if necessary.)

What strategies should I use when I encounter these difficulties?

Evaluating my listening

Was this recording what I expected?

Was I able to make use of my prior knowledge about the topic?

Did I achieve my goal? Why or why not?

Am I satisfied with what I have understood? Why?

Was my listening plan useful?

What difficulties did I face?

Were my strategies useful?

7 | Dimensions of Academic Listening

JOHN FLOWERDEW AND LINDSAY MILLER

KEY QUESTIONS

➤ What distinguishes academic listening from other forms of listening?
➤ How can we help learners develop their academic listening ability?
➤ How can the dimensions of the listening model presented in this chapter be applied to the classroom?

EXPERIENCE

In universities in the Middle East, many subjects, especially those related to science and technology, are taught through the medium of English. Students, therefore, need academic listening skills. Students arrive at these largely English-medium universities still needing more English than they have received in secondary school, especially English for science and technology, to bring them up to the level required by university study. Students in this context have difficulties in the classroom with issues such as adapting to the speed of extensive second language monologue; dealing with different lecturer accents (lecturers come from all over the world); dealing with a heavy vocabulary load; recognizing the overall structure of the lecture, its main ideas and supporting details; taking effective notes; dealing with the examples used by the international lecturers to illustrate their main points, many of which may be unfamiliar to the students; and many other issues. In addition, students may have interactional difficulties that involve listening, such as asking and answering questions. Furthermore, students may have difficulties discussing issues outside the class with their foreign lecturers or teaching assistants. Although interactional skills are outside the scope of this chapter, they can nevertheless be considered an academic listening skill.

WHAT IS ACADEMIC LISTENING?

Academic listening can be defined as the processing of spoken language in academic contexts. Most work on academic listening has focused on lectures, but interactive contexts such as seminars, tutorials, and online media may also be included. Academic listening is concerned with the transmission and acquisition of knowledge, although that is not to say that the interpersonal dimension of meaning is not also important. Academic listening may thus also concern the transmission and comprehension of attitudes, beliefs, values, and culture. Alongside the acoustic signal, academic listening furthermore involves the comprehension of paralinguistic features such as body language. Typical goals for the processing of academic discourse of various types, including lecture and seminar discourse, are "to impart knowledge, teach skills and practices, induct learners into discourse communities, promote critical thinking and encourage a positive attitude towards learning . . ." (Crawford Camiciottoli, 2007, p. 16).

In academic settings, listening takes place primarily in the contexts of lectures and seminars. These contexts have their own distinctive features, for example, understanding extensive monologue, processing technical and subtechnical lexis (i.e., vocabulary such as *composition, function, procedure,* and *relation,* that may be used across various content areas), note-taking, and questioning, among many others. These distinctive features are reviewed in the next section, which deals with the research literature on academic listening.

CONCEPTUAL UNDERPINNINGS OF ACADEMIC LISTENING

In this section, we explore some of the approaches to researching second language (L2) listening. The research agenda into L2 listening offers us insights into what may, or may not, be important when considering how to teach listening to second language learners, especially within an academic context. Until the 1970s, listening, per se, was not seen as a language skill that required much attention. There were several reasons for this: (1) speech and grammar were considered more important than listening; (2) listening was considered a skill that could be "picked up" without overt instruction; and (3) because language teachers and researchers themselves had probably never been taught how to listen in a second language, they did not see the need to explicitly teach this skill or conduct research into it (Gilman & Moody, 1984). As we moved into the 1970s and realized that listening was a core language skill that should have its own pedagogical approach and be taught, a research agenda began to appear. This agenda was later extended to listening in academic contexts, J. C. Richards (1983) being an early example and J. Flowerdew (1994a) being the first volume specifically devoted to academic listening.

We provide here a brief overview of a selection of the areas of research into academic listening. Four specific methodological approaches to researching academic listening can be identified: psychometric experiments, discourse analysis, research into listening strategies, and ethnographic investigations.

Psychometric research into listening to lectures

Some researchers have adopted a positivist, psychometric approach to investigate listening, using tests to measure the effects on levels of comprehension created by variation in the input presented to learners. Research involving a psychometric approach include speech rate and pausology (e.g., Derwing & Munro, 2001), the effect of syntactic and discourse level modification (e.g., Chaudron & Richards, 1986; Flowerdew & Tauroza, 1995), lexis (e.g., Crawford Camiciottoli, 2007), foreign accents (e.g., Derwing & Munro, 2005), and comparisons of different types of listening support (Chang & Read, 2006). It is notable that, even though we have cited the most recent references, not a lot of research of this type has been conducted in recent years.

Discourse analysis research into listening to lectures

A second main approach to conducting research into L2 students' listening skills is discourse analysis. Using this approach, spoken texts are examined in detail to discover the features that listeners need to be able to identify to aid their listening. Work by discourse analysts has focused on lexical phrases (e.g., Low, Littlemore, & Koester, 2008); propositions or main ideas in a text (e.g., Rost, 1994); length of texts and silent periods (e.g., Crawford Camiciottoli, 2005); discourse patterns in talk (e.g., Fortanet-Gomez, 2004; Crawford Camiciottoli, 2010); non-relevant information in talk, such as asides (Strodt-Lopez, 1991); the use of pronouns (e.g., Fortanet, 2004; Gomez, 2006); and slang expressions (Huang, 2004).

Research into listening strategies

Researchers have attempted to identify the listening strategies that L2 learners use and to assess how efficient these strategies are. Studies into listening strategies use a variety of research tools, including the analysis of listening tests and questionnaires (e.g., Chien & Wei, 1998); the analysis of students' listening diaries (e.g., Goh, 2000); the use of students' talk-aloud procedures (e.g., Vandergrift, 2003); and strategy instruction sessions (Carrier, 2003; Goh & Taib, 2006; Vandergrift & Goh, 2009). Through these different tools, researchers have identified certain types of learner strategies, the relationships between types of strategies and language proficiency, and some of the learners' problems when using listening strategies.

One of the most active researchers in the area of identifying listening strategies is Vandergrift (1997). His listening strategy taxonomy shows the range of strategies learners can access when listening to a spoken text (see Figure 1).

Metacognitive strategies
  Planning: advanced organization, directed attention, selective attention, self-management
  Monitoring: comprehension monitoring, auditory monitoring, double-check monitoring
  Evaluation: performance evaluation, problem identification
Cognitive strategies
  Inferencing: linguistic, voice, paralinguistic or kinesthetic, extra-linguistic, inferencing between parts
  Elaboration: personal, world, academic, questioning, creative, imagery
  Summarization
  Translation
  Transfer
  Repetition
  Resourcing
  Grouping
  Note-taking
  Deduction/induction
  Substitution
Socioaffective strategies
  Questioning for clarification
  Cooperation
  Lowering anxiety
  Self-encouragement
  Taking emotional temperature

Figure 1. Listening strategies taxonomy (adapted from Vandergrift, 1997, pp. 392–395).

Before learner strategies research hit its stride, J. C. Richards (1983) had already put forward a taxonomy of academic listening skills (Figure 2). Although not the same thing as strategies, skills (or micro skills) are still a useful way to think about the academic listening process and are useful in the preparation of academic listening materials. (See Purpura, this volume, for an expanded discussion of learner skills and strategies.)

The research agenda into listening strategies is ongoing. However, more research needs to be conducted into learning strategies, in general, and into listening strategies, in particular. Such research needs to isolate the different types of effective listening strategies that learners use;

- Ability to identify purpose and scope of lecture
- Ability to identify topic of lecture and follow topic development
- Ability to identify relationships among units within discourse (e.g., major ideas, generalizations, hypotheses, supporting ideas, examples)
- Ability to identify role of discourse markers in signaling structure of a lecture (e.g., conjunctions, adverbs, gambits, routines)
- Ability to infer relationships (e.g., cause and effect, conclusion)
- Ability to recognize key lexical items related to subject/topic
- Ability to deduce meanings of words from context
- Ability to recognize markers of cohesion
- Ability to recognize function of intonation to signal information structure (e.g., pitch, volume, pace, key)
- Ability to detect attitude of speaker toward subject matter
- Ability to follow different modes of lecturing (e.g., spoken, audio, audiovisual)
- Ability to follow lecture despite differences in accent and speed
- Familiarity with different styles of lecturing (e.g., formal, conversational, read, unplanned)
- Familiarity with different registers (e.g., written vs. colloquial)
- Ability to recognize irrelevant matter (e.g., jokes, digressions, meanderings)
- Ability to recognize function of nonverbal cues as markers of emphasis and attitude
- Knowledge of classroom conventions
- Ability to recognize instructional and learner tasks (e.g., warnings, suggestions, recommendations, advice, instructions)

Figure 2. Taxonomy of academic listening skills (adapted from J. C. Richards, 1983, pp. 228–230).

it also needs to examine the ways that learners acquire listening strategies and the constraints that different variables have on learners. Until a much wider database of research findings is available, the promotion of listening strategies to L2 students may continue to be done on an ad hoc basis.

Ethnographic research into academic listening

The fourth main approach to investigating listening skills is ethnography, the study of the behavior and beliefs of groups, in this case L2 students who need to listen in their L2. Although still not widely used to investigate listening skills, ethnographic research is generally becoming more popular in second language research. There are, however, some challenges in employing ethnographic methodology, among which are that: (1) a variety of research instruments is required to ensure triangulation of the data; (2) ethnographies often take a long time to complete; and (3) usually two or more researchers have to be involved to ensure data verification.

We can include here our own ethnographic work undertaken into L2 lecture comprehension. In this work, we conducted a long-term ethnographic study of academic listening in a Hong Kong university where Cantonese first language (L1) students studied through the medium of English. Ethnographic data were collected over a period of eight years. Findings of the study are reported in three papers (Flowerdew & Miller, 1992, 1996a; Flowerdew, Miller, & Li, 2000) that together report on the perceptions, problems, and strategies of L2 students and lecturers participating in lectures in English. The findings of these studies broadly show that students and lecturers shared some perceptions about lectures in English. In particular, both students and their lecturers agreed that the type of English used when lecturing to L2 students had to be modified, that examples were a very important way of presenting information, and that handouts were highly valued. In contrast, the students felt that their lecturers sometimes presented the lectures using fast speech, but the lecturers often said that they slowed down their delivery rate; students were also of the opinion that it was the duty of the lecturers to impart knowledge to them, while most lecturers wanted to have an interactive style of lecture presentation that involved students in thinking about and discussing issues. There were also several gray areas where each group had differing perceptions of the lecturing event. For instance, although most of the lecturers reported that they enjoyed lecturing and that lectures were of central importance to conveying information to the students, the students had had minimal experience of attending lectures prior to university and so did not seem to appreciate the importance that their lecturers attached to lectures. This mismatch in perceptions can obviously lead to a lack of preparation for listening to academic discourse and to loss of comprehension on the part of students. It also can lead to frustration on the part of lecturers.

In other papers, we report on the different dimensions of lecturing to L2 listeners identified in our ethnographic research—ethnic culture, local culture, academic culture, and disciplinary culture (Flowerdew & Miller, 1995)—and on different sociocultural features such as the purpose of lectures, the roles of lecturers, styles of lecturing, simplification, listener behavior, and humor (Flowerdew & Miller, 1996b). Separately, L. Miller (2002) tracked a group of engineering students over a three-year period to discover the problems they had comprehending their science and technology lectures. A model for lecturing in a second language was developed based on the findings (L. Miller, 2002). This model is based on the following four premises:

1. L2 listeners belong to a community of learners; in their academic lectures, they are being initiated into a community of practice (involving the genres of the academic lecture, the behavior and pedagogy of the lecturer, etc.).
2. Students' comprehension of a given lecture is based not only on their level of language skill but also on their previous learning experiences (i.e., familiarity with the genre of the academic lecture) and expectations of what will occur in the lecture.
3. Lecturers' negative expectations of L2 students' linguistic ability and their attempts to address this (e.g., by creating extensive lecture notes for the students) may have the adverse consequence of having students rely on the notes alone and cease to pay attention to the lecture.
4. Lecturers need to create a bridge between the students' community of learners and the community of practice into which they are initiating students such that a new community of learning is created.

A pedagogical model for second language listening

Based on a review of the research into L2 listening and academic listening in particular, Flowerdew and Miller (2005) develop a pedagogical model to aid teachers and textbook writers in preparing learners for second language listening. Here we briefly present the main features of the model.[1] After this review of the model, we then return to the situation cited at the outset of the chapter to illustrate how the model can be used to design more effective listening material in that particular context.

At the heart of the model we see the main cognitive characteristics of listening, as outlined in Figure 3:

- *Bottom-up processing*. Listeners build understanding by making reference to the smallest units of the acoustic message, individual sounds, or phonemes. These are then combined into words, phrases, clauses, and sentences. Listening is developed in a serial or hierarchical fashion.
- *Top-down processing*. This type of listening relies on activating previous knowledge about the language, text, or culture. Personal or world knowledge is brought to the text to make sense of it.
- *Interactive processing*. This involves making use of both bottom-up and top-down processing. In this type of parallel processing, phonological, syntactic, semantic, and pragmatic information interact with each other.

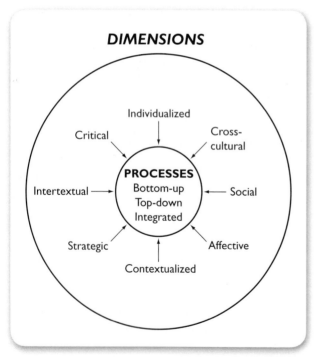

Figure 3. A pedagogical model for second language listening (based on Flowerdew & Miller, 2005, p. 86).

In addition to these three main types of processing, our model also has distinct dimensions

of listening that give it a more complex structure, taking into account pedagogical considerations. According to this model, listening is:

- *Individualized.* Each learner approaches a listening task in a unique way Learners have their own ways of learning, so any model must try to accommodate each learner's preferred learning styles.
- *Cross-cultural.* The ways in which learners comprehend depends to a certain extent on their cultural background This is related not only to ethnicity, nationality, and language but also gender, age, social and professional position, attitudes, values, and beliefs.
- *Social.* Listening is interactive, whether it be a monologue or dialogue. Therefore, learners need to make use of a range of pragmatic devices to interact with the speaker. An example of a social element of comprehension is *back channeling*, where the listener signals that he or she is listening to the message (e.g., *Ah, ha!*). In the context of a lecture, this might be where the lecturer asks rhetorical questions (e.g., *Now you understand this, don't you? Of course you do*) or signposts the structure of the lecture for the listener (e.g., *Today's lecture is divided into four parts. . . . Now moving onto the next section of today's lecture. . . .*).
- *Affective.* Listeners also have to have the right motivation to listen, have a positive attitude toward the speakers or subject matter, and feel that they want to listen for the message to be transmitted effectively.
- *Contextualized.* Listening is often integrated with other language activities (reading, writing, or speaking). An example of this is when students listen to a lecture, view PowerPoint slides, and make notes.
- *Strategic.* From the extensive work that has already been done into the use of strategies, we know that some ways of listening provide learners with better comprehension than other ways of listening.
- *Intertextual.* Comprehension is based on our past linguistic experience, how aspects of text we hear (or read) relate to text we have heard before. If a text is closely related to what we have heard before, then we may be more likely to comprehend it.
- *Critical.* Effective listeners do not simply process the messages they hear; they also actively

evaluate them in a critical light, considering the content in terms of strength of evidence, contradictions with previous materials, lecturer bias, and their wider social implications.

CLASSROOM APPLICATIONS

In this section we return to the instructional setting described in the Experience section at the beginning of this chapter and provide a case study of a unit of academic listening material that could be used in that situation, based on the pedagogical model presented in the previous section. The format of the case study is based on a previous case study published in Flowerdew and Miller (2005), and the reader is referred there for a comparison with the case developed here. Our focus here is on material designed to help the students with their lecture listening comprehension, although this material is not seen in isolation from the other language skills. (See also Goh, this volume, for a more in-depth discussion of the general process of listening.)

We have chosen this context of the transition from L1 school instruction to English as the medium of instruction at the university level because this is a very typical context for English as a foreign language (EFL) academic listening, not only in the Middle East but increasingly worldwide (the Far East, Africa, and Europe) as well as in English L1 contexts such as the United States, Great Britain, and Australia, where foreign students go to study through the medium of English for the first time.

The course in question was developed following an extensive needs analysis. (See Johns & Price, this volume, for information on needs analysis.) This included surveying the level of the English and study skills of the entering students when they left their L1 school, interaction with the faculty members of the university's College of Science to find out their requirements, and familiarization with and analysis of the sorts of texts (both written and spoken) that the students were likely to need to access. This analysis revealed that the College of Science was planning to run an introductory common core "foundation" program for all its students in their first year and that this course would be organized around a series of lectures in biology, chemistry, and physics.

One of the decisions that needs to be made in all academic listening courses is that of how subject-specific the material should be. Should it be *wide-angle* (i.e., focused on a broad range of subject matter and more general language features) or should it be more *narrow-angle* (i.e., more tightly focused on a narrow range of subject matter, perhaps limited to one discipline, and more specific language features)? In general terms, the authors of this chapter favor a more narrow-angle approach, where possible. This is based on the very straightforward argument that language varies according to discipline (Flowerdew & Peacock, 2001 although see Hutchinson & Waters, 1987, for a counterargument). Where students come from a given subject area, it makes sense to target their specific needs. In many cases (typically in intensive English programs in the United States, pre-sessional courses in the United Kingdom, and "foundation" or preparatory programs in many EFL settings, for example), this decision is made for the course designers because the students come with varied disciplinary requirements; some may be humanities students, some science students, and some business students. The course designers have no choice other than to prepare a wide-angle course[2] for such heterogeneous groups of learners (see Hafner & Miller, 2011, for an example of such a course). It is only when students come from a single disciplinary background, such as those described in the papers by Dudley-Evans and Johns (1981) and Johns and Dudley-Evans (1985) in the context of specialist courses for MA degree students of transportation and plant biology at the University of Birmingham, that narrow-angle courses are possible.

Our context in the Middle Eastern university was in fact between the two extremes just described. The students were enrolled in particular disciplines (e.g., math, biology, chemistry, physics, agriculture, and medicine), but, on the other hand, they were concurrently taking a fairly generic science foundation course. This actually worked in our favor because it allowed us to prepare learning material in science and hence have a degree of specificity. At the same time, because the level of the material was very elementary, we did not need to deal with very content specific texts. One of the challenges with specific purpose material is that it may be beyond the technical expertise of language teachers (Flowerdew & Peacock, 2001). In our case, because of the elementary nature of our target goal, this problem did not arise. We were thus able to have specific purpose material but at a level of content accessible to nonspecialist language teachers.

Based on the needs assessment, a decision was made to develop a 15-week listening course based on lectures that would replicate those that the students would be receiving in their foundation science course but at a level that was as accessible to the students as possible. With this aim in mind, a group of content lecturers was enlisted to give a series of video-recorded mini-lectures in their given disciplines of biology, chemistry, and physics. Their task was for them to each create a video-recording of a mini-lecture lasting up to 15 minutes on an elementary topic in their field. The idea was that the material would be authentic, in the sense that it would convey material of the sort that students would need in their future courses, but would at the same time be accessible to the students (and language teachers) and suitable for language development work. To create materials that were as natural as possible, the lecturers were asked not to read from a prepared script but to speak from notes in a conversational style (J. Flowerdew, 1994b). They were also asked to use some visual aids to provide some contextualization. Figure 4 lists the topics for the mini-lectures.

1. Laboratory Glassware
2. The Skeletal System
3. The Periodic Table
4. The Sand Dollar
5. Proof by Contradiction
6. Structure of the Leaf
7. The Solar System
8. Molecular Models

Figure 4. Mini-lecture topics.

The aims and objectives of the course were set out as follows:

General aims. Students will develop the ability to comprehend, record, and apply the information presented in short lecture-style monologues of up to 15 minutes duration on topics of general scientific interest.

Objectives. In relation to spoken texts, students will be able to demonstrate the ability to:

- understand the overall information structure (e.g., introduction, conclusion, and main points)
- understand the speaker's purpose as it develops during the talk, (e.g., introducing a topic, concluding a topic, giving an

example, making an analogy, defining, describing a process, and classifying)
- complete outline notes based on the lectures
- reconstitute notes into speech and writing

Here, we demonstrate how an academic listening lecture might be developed, based on one of these lectures: The Skeletal System. In the lecture, the speaker used a skeleton as a visual aid. Incorporated into the videotaped listening material

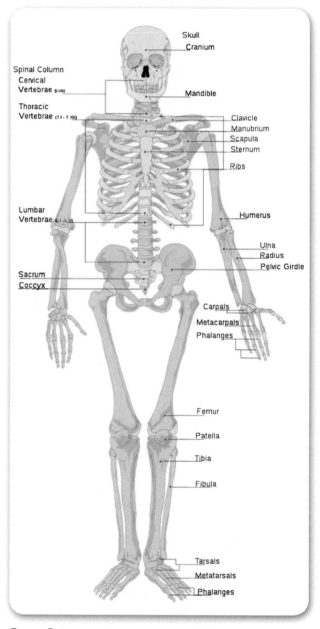

Figure 5. Diagram of the skeletal system. *Source:* http://en.wikipedia.org/wiki/File:Human_skeleton_front_en.svg

was a similar picture of a skeleton (Figure 5). Also, for the purpose of further contextualizing the listening, a written text could be incorporated into the material (Figure 6). Figure 7 is a transcript of the actual lecture.

The human skeleton consists of both fused and individual bones supported and supplemented by ligaments, tendons, muscles, and cartilage. It serves as a scaffold that supports organs, anchors muscles, and protects organs such as the brain, lungs, and heart. The biggest bone in the body is the femur in the thigh, and the smallest is the stapes bone in the middle ear. In an adult, the skeleton comprises around 30–40% of the total body weight, and half of this weight is water.

Fused bones include those of the *pelvis* and the *cranium*. Not all bones are interconnected directly: there are three bones in each *middle ear* called the *ossicles* that articulate only with each other. The *hyoid bone,* which is located in the neck and serves as the point of attachment for the *tongue,* does not articulate with any other bones in the body, being supported by muscles and ligaments.

Figure 6. Written text to accompany mini-lecture. *Source:* http://en.wikipedia.org/wiki/File:Human_skeleton_front_en.svg

Sample teaching unit based on the pedagogical model

The following sample listening unit has eight stages.

Stage 1: First warm-up stage.   As a warm-up to listening to the lecture, the teacher develops a discussion about the importance of looking after one's body. The purpose here is to integrate discussion skills with listening. Focus questions may be:

- Why is it important to take care of your body?
- What types of exercise are good for different parts of your body?
- How often is it recommended to do exercise?

As another, or alternative, warm-up the teacher is encouraged to use the diagram (Figure 5) and short text (Figure 6) to introduce the topic. Some interactive questions here may be:

- Are you familiar with the human skeleton?
- Can you name any of the parts on the diagram that you already know?

The skeletal system is a good example of how form and function relate to each other in the body.

Firstly, form. Let us look at the skeleton, which is comprised of many sizes and shapes of bone. Bone must be known to you all, you must have seen it lying around in the countryside. What you see is the hard part of the bone comprised of calcium and phosphorus. It lasts for long periods of time without obvious deterioration. Mature bone is very hard, it will not bend but it will break. While it is developing, and the bone is laid down, the calcium and phosphorus is laid down in cartilage which is quite flexible and will bend, but under a microscope looks very similar to bone.

If we look at the skeletal system we see first of all that there is a vertebral column. The vertebral column is made up of many pieces of bone. There is the body of the vertebra, which is a solid piece of bone, and then there is an arch on behind the body. The bodies sit one on top of the other to give the vertebral column. The arches form a canal in which the spinal cord runs. The skull sits on top of the vertebral column, it is also comprised of two parts, the cranium, which is a round box containing the brain, and the facial bones, which contain openings for the eyes, the nose and the mouth, there is the lower jaw which is mobile here and allows you to open the mouth.

Here is the rib cage, it is comprised of long flat curved bones most of which are attached in the front to the sternum directly, there are other ribs which are attached indirectly lower down. On the top of the rib cage is the shoulder girdle and it is through the shoulder girdle that the arms are attached to the vertebral column. At the lower end of the vertebral column is the pelvis and it's through the pelvis that the legs are attached.

Now that is a rapid description of the form of the skeleton, let us look at its functions. The first function is rigidity. All the bones give a rigidity to the form of the body, without it we would not be able to stand as this diagram shows a man standing, we would just be like jelly fish. Then there is movement, muscles are attached to various bones which allow movement at joints between the bones. Then the skeleton acts as protection for various vital organs, we have the cranium which protects the brain. There is the rib cage protecting the heart and lungs. There are the vertebral arches protecting the spinal column and the fourth function is that of a container. These long bones of your legs and arms are not solid, they have a cavity inside or they would be too heavy to move around, in that cavity is the bone marrow and it is in the bone marrow that blood is formed.

So in summary then, the skeleton has a definite form, it is made up of bones of many shapes and sizes. It also has definite functions, that of rigidity, movement, protection and as a container.

Figure 7. Mini-lecture transcript.

In addition, the teacher may ask students a few comprehension questions on the reading, such as *What is the purpose of a skeleton? How are bones connected?* The purpose of this stage is to activate students' relevant background knowledge to help them comprehend the lecture.

Stage 2: Second warm-up stage. This stage, another warm-up stage, is designed to develop further background knowledge and to integrate listening with spoken interaction. It might take the form of elicitation, discussion, or group or pair work and start from the topic of the human body in general or the systems of the body, developing toward the specific topic of the skeletal system. Students are likely to already have some knowledge of the skeletal system, or, at least, of the human body, and so there should not be much problem in eliciting and building up background knowledge. If the stage is done as group or pair work, students can compare the knowledge they already have about the relevant topics. If this information is written down, it can form a starting point for the Stage 4 listening phase and students can be asked to compare the information they have noted with what the speaker says.

Stage 3: Open-ended learner-centered stage. This is an open-ended learner-centered stage where students are asked to view and listen to the video-recording and apply whatever bottom-up and top-down strategies they have to their listening and note-taking. After the students have attempted this, they are asked to discuss any difficulties they had in following the lecture. Based on this feedback, the teacher can ask the students what strategies they might use to overcome these difficulties. Based on our experience, areas of difficulty may include:

- lecturer speaks too fast
- difficult concepts
- overall structure of the lecture not grasped
- speaker's purpose not clear
- difficult sentence structures

Stage 4: Key vocabulary. The teacher shows PowerPoint slides (Figure 8) with the key vocabulary items on them and asks students to explain them or try to guess what they each mean with reference to the diagram of the skeleton (Figure 5). The teacher then discusses possible

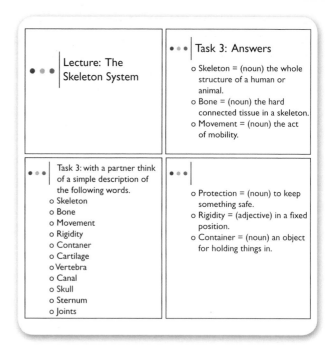

Figure 8. PowerPoint slides accompanying the lecture.

Key vocabulary	Possible definitions
Skeleton	the whole structure of a human or animal (noun)
Bone	the hard connected tissue in a skeleton (noun)
Movement	the act of mobility (noun)
Protection	to keep something safe (noun)
Rigid	in a fixed position (adjective)
Container	an object for holding things in (noun)
Cartilage	flexible, soft tissue inside the bones (noun)
Vertebra	the parts that make up the spine (noun)
Canal	a tube that something (blood) can pass through (noun)
Skull	the bone part or skeleton of the head (noun)
Sternum	the flat bone in the middle of the chest (noun)
Joints	the connection between two bones in the body (noun)

Figure 9. Key terms and possible definitions.

simple definitions with the class (Figure 9). The idea here is to make sure that students are prepared with the key semi-technical and technical vocabulary they will need for their academic listening.

Stage 5: Global comprehension. In this stage, the teacher explains that, when students listen to a lecture, they will usually find that it can be divided into a number of sections. He or she gives the following instructions to the students: *Listen to the video-recording about the skeletal system and decide how many sections there are (there are not many). Decide what a suitable title would be for each section.* Possible answers that students might provide to these questions are:

> Number of sections: 4
> Suitable titles:
>
> 1. Introduction
> 2. Form
> 3. Function
> 4. Conclusion

For the next task, the teacher gives the following instructions: *Look at the following list of terms used in the lecture. Try to organize them into two groups, according to the sections of the lecture.*

bone	protection	legs
rib cage	shoulder girdle	pelvis
movement	container	arms
vertebral column	skull	rigidity

The teacher then instructs students to listen to the lecture again and put the terms into the sequence in which they are mentioned by the lecturer. The correct answers in this example are:

1. bone		7. pelvis
2. vertebral column		8. leg
3. skull		9. rigidity
4. rib cage		10. movement
5. shoulder girdle		11. protection
6. arms		12. container

Stage 6: Recognizing the speaker's purpose. In this stage, the students are instructed that when speakers give lectures they use certain expressions to indicate the purpose of what they are saying. For example, they may be introducing a new topic; they may be moving from one topic to another; they may be giving some examples; they may be comparing two things; or they may be defining, describing the steps in a process, or classifying. To provide practice in identifying the lecturer's purpose, the students are asked to listen again to the lecture and try to recognize what expressions the speaker uses to do the following (answers follow the exercise):

1. to indicate that he is using the skeletal system as an example
2. to tell the listener to look at the skeleton
3. to direct the listener's attention to the skeletal system again
4. to indicate the rib cage
5. to indicate that he has finished talking about the form of the skeleton
6. to indicate that he is going to tell the listener about the functions of the skeleton
7. to give a list of the functions of the skeletal system (there are several expressions here)
8. to indicate that he is going to finish his lecture and give the main ideas to the listener again

Answers:

1. *The skeletal system is a good example of . . .*
2. *Let us look at the skeleton . . .*
3. *If we look at the skeletal system . . .*
4. *Here is the rib cage . . .*
5. *Now that is a rapid description of the form . . .*
6. *Let us look at its functions.*
7. *The first function . . . then . . . then . . . there is . . . there are . . .*
8. *So in summary then . . .*

Stage 7: Note-taking. This stage gives students practice in note-taking. Students are instructed to listen again to the first main section of the lecture and to complete the incomplete lecture notes (see Figure 10), which provide information about various parts of the skeleton. The approach to note-taking here is inductive, the aim being to raise students' consciousness about note-taking formats. Individual teachers may spend time on presenting the material more deductively, showing students how to create good notes, but the whole issue of note-taking is rather controversial because, in their content classes, students often put pressure on their lecturers to give them detailed handouts, thereby obviating the need for students to take notes.

In the final activity in this stage, students are instructed to listen again to the second main part of the lecture and fill in the answer key (see Figure 11) indicating which parts of the skeleton protect which vital organs.

Bone

Composition
    calcium and phosphorus

Properties
    lasts for a very long period
    very hard
    does not bend (rigid)
    breaks (brittle)

Vertebral column

Parts
    many pieces of bone
    bodies and arches

Skull

Location
    on top of vertebral column

Parts
    Cranium
    facial bones

Rib cage

Parts
    long flat curved bones

Location
    most *attached to sternum in front directly*
    others *attached indirectly lower down*

Figure 10. Incomplete lecture notes. Student answers are indicated in cursive.

Part of skeleton	Answer
cranium	*brain*
rib cage	*heart and lungs*
vertebral arches	*spinal column*

Figure 11. Answer key. Student answers are indicated in cursive.

Stage 8: Note reformulation. In this stage, the teacher asks students to practice reformulating their notes from the previous note-taking exercise into complete spoken or written texts.

The teaching material and the pedagogical model

In this section we evaluate the unit of material just presented with regard to the eight dimensions of the pedagogical model presented earlier in Figure 3. It should be noted that there is probably more material here than would be needed for the short lecture that is the focus of the listening exercise. However, we have provided this extra material to show various possibilities.

Dimensions of the model covered

Individualized dimension. This dimension of the model applies in the before-listening group work. A lot of this material is controlled by the teacher. However, there are opportunities for individualized learning. In the group work suggested at the beginning of the unit, students are encouraged to provide their individual input. This video-recording of the lecture was also made available for individual listening in the self-access learning center (see Gardner & Miller, 1999, for descriptions of such centers). It was found that many students took the opportunity to listen to the mini-lecture over and over to develop their bottom-up listening skills.[3]

Cross-cultural dimension. At first sight, there does not seem to be a cross-cultural element in this text and supporting learning material. It could be argued that science is a universal subject and so there is no need to develop cross-cultural awareness. However, if we look carefully, we do find that the Western expatriate lecturer is sensitive to the local Omani culture. Near the beginning of the lecture, he refers to bones that can be found in the countryside. This is a very appropriate example in the context of Oman, where the lecture was delivered. Oman is a desert country and well-preserved bones are to be found all over the place. In addition, the majority of the students at the university come from rural backgrounds. We could not imagine giving this example in the very urban context of Hong Kong, where the two authors of this chapter currently reside.

Social dimension. Given that lectures are monologues, we might not expect much social interaction in a video lecture, if any at all. However, as demonstrated in Stage 2 (recognizing the speaker's purpose), the lecturer is constantly indicating to the audience how to interpret the direction the lecture is taking. Recognizing the speaker's purpose is a very important skill for students when listening to lectures.

Affective dimension. Here we are interested in what might motivate the students in this unit. It can be argued that the choice of topic—something that the students can relate to and that is at the same time related to their field of studies—is motivating here. Notice, too, how the lecturer introduces the topic by relating it to the students' personal experience: *Bone must be known to you all, you must have seen it lying around in the countryside.*

Contextual dimension. The contextual element comes into this unit in: (1) the use by the lecturer of the visual aid of the skeleton diagram; and (2) the preliminary discussion, supporting text, and visual aid provided with the listening material. In an authentic learning situation, any given lecture is likely to come as part of a series and each lecture is likely to help listeners contextualize what they will hear in the next one. In this sense, the listening course discussed in this chapter is rather artificial, insofar as each mini-lecture is a one-off (a single, unrepeated event) and therefore decontextualized. This is the rationale, of course, for the supporting visual aid and text and for encouraging the learners to draw on their preexisting knowledge. Some language teachers, however, might argue for a series of lectures on a given topic rather than one-offs, on the grounds that this will provide greater contextualization.

Strategic dimension. A number of specific listening strategies are focused on in this unit of material. These include focusing on key words, recognizing the discourse structure of the lecture, recognizing the speaker's purpose, and note-taking.

Intertextual dimension. There are various elements of intertextuality in this material. The language used in this lecture is very typical of the field of biology, which, like the text of the lecture, is all about structure and function. The very formulaic patterns of language used here are likely to be found in other biology-related texts. Figure 12 lists some of the typical structures that are likely to occur in just about any biology text. Students of biology are likely to come across these patterns regularly in their lecture listening and reading. In fact, in later course materials, attention is drawn to these patterns and students are shown how they typically occur repeatedly in their lectures and reading material.

Relating to structure
- is comprised of
- if we look at
- is made up of
- the arches form a canal
- The arms are attached to the vertebral column.
- At the lower end of the vertebral column is the pelvis.

Relating to function
- The first function is rigidity.
- Muscles are attached to various bones, which allow movement at joints between the bones.
- The skeleton acts as protection.
- We have the cranium, which protects the brain.
- There is the rib cage protecting the heart.

Figure 12. Formulaic patterns of language in biology texts.

Critical dimension. The critical element here comes in Stage 1, where the teacher introduces the discussion about the importance of looking after one's body. The class talks about how people treat their bodies and what are good (e.g., well-balanced diet, exercise and sports) and bad practices (e.g., high-fat diet, alcohol abuse, lack of exercise).

Traditional models of listening and pedagogic listening materials are limited in their scope and, in our opinion, leave a lot out, failing to cater to all the complexities of the listening process. This is particularly true with regard to academic listening. As we have shown, our pedagogic model, with its multidimensional character, can help students overcome these deficiencies.

FUTURE TRENDS

In an earlier publication (Flowerdew & Miller, 1997), we noted that there was a lack of authentic material used in textbooks that claimed to prepare students for academic listening. In a recent review of published textbooks for this chapter, we found that the situation has not changed much. Although many textbooks maintain that they prepare students for listening to lectures in English, we found that many of the texts used were scripted or semi-scripted, and that the type of tasks suggested in these books were similar to the tasks found in general listening textbooks: gap-filling, choosing correct answers, and recognizing intonation or stress.

Nevertheless, there have been some changes to textbooks on academic listening. For instance, Lebauer (2010) employs authentic lectures from different subject areas (e.g., biology, geology, anthropology, and food science) to teach listening strategies and reinforce the structure of the academic lecture. Alternatively, instructors can use the provided outline-style notes to deliver the lecture themselves. By having the lecture delivered in such a way, the students are exposed to more authentic features of spoken texts, as outlined in the pedagogical model. Lynch's (2004) materials employ speakers from different countries to deliver the lectures, exposing students to different accents. Students are introduced to each speaker before listening to the text: (e.g., *He is from the south of Scotland* . . . [p. 63]); and special features of each talk are highlighted for the listener (e.g., (1) *He makes use of his voice* . . . ; (2) *He speeds up when he is giving less important information;* (3) *He used two extended examples* . . . [p. 63]). This contextualization of the speaker can be an important feature in students' overcoming difficulties in listening to unfamiliar voices. Further, Lim and Smalzer (2005) include DVDs of the lectures being delivered. Through the use of the DVDs, students are able to focus on aspects of spoken delivery, such as gestures, that are missing from audio-only materials. And Salehzadeh (2009) includes activities such as recognizing hedging,[4] recognizing specific features of spoken text, and humor.

Online self-access materials that support academic listening are also now available. For example, *Essential Academic Skills in English: Listening to Lectures*[5] allows the users to view a range of authentic lectures given at the University of Warwick and to practice a range of academic listening skills via computer. This type of material is motivating because learners have complete control over the material they are viewing and can focus on the aspects of the lectures that cause them most difficulties, from sentence level to discourse level.

While some materials are now available that encourage a more multidimensional approach to teaching academic listening, we maintain that more attention still needs to be given to preparing students for the sort of authentic listening that is required in academic settings. Such materials could be prepared by applying the pedagogical model presented in this chapter.

CONCLUSION

In this chapter, we have reviewed and highlighted the specific features of academic listening, also providing our own pedagogical model for teaching. We have then demonstrated how this model might be applied to the development of teaching materials. As well as the traditional bottom-up and top-down listening skills, our model, and the materials based on it, emphasizes further dimensions that lead to a more comprehensive treatment of the skills that are needed in effective academic listening.

SUMMARY

➤ Academic listening refers to the processing of spoken language in academic contexts; it is primarily concerned with the transmission and acquisition of content knowledge.

➤ Four main methodological approaches to researching academic listening can be identified: psychometric experiments, discourse analysis, research into listening strategies, and ethnographic investigations.

➤ In the pedagogical model proposed in this chapter, top-down, bottom-up, and interactive processing are integrated.

➤ The model takes into account the eight dimensions of listening: individualized, cross-cultural, social, affective, contextualized, strategic, intertextual, and critical.

➤ In the future, it is hoped that classroom and self-access materials for academic listening practice will aim for authenticity of content and delivery. It is also hoped that these materials will help focus learners on aspects of spoken delivery, such as the use of gestures, hedging, and humor.

DISCUSSION QUESTIONS

1. In what ways are general listening skills similar to academic listening? Is academic listening different from everyday listening? Give specific examples.

2. For a group of students you are familiar with, what main academic listening problems do they usually encounter?

3. To what extent do the eight dimensions in the proposed pedagogical model enhance the more traditional top-down and bottom-up approaches to listening?
4. Which of the dimensions in the pedagogical model would it be easy to develop materials for, and which might be more difficult? Why?.

SUGGESTED ACTIVITIES

1. Locate an English as a second language (ESL) or EFL student who is taking courses through the medium of English. Interview this student about the academic listening challenges that he or she encounters.
2. Search for lectures on the Internet. You could try, for example, MIT Open Courseware (http://ocw.mit.edu/index.htm) or Open Yale Courses (http://oyc.yale.edu/). Record a short extract of a lecture and transcribe it.
3. Based on your lecture transcription from Activity 2, identify the features that characterize it as an academic text.
4. Design some additional tasks or activities that might accompany the lecture text used in this chapter.

FURTHER READING

Crawford Camiciottoli, B. C. (2007). *The language of business studies lectures: A corpus-assisted analysis*. Amsterdam, The Netherlands: John Benjamins.

This book is specifically about lectures in business studies. It focuses on the ever-increasing demands for university courses in business, especially now that English is widely used as the lingua franca of the business world.

Flowerdew, J. (1994). *Academic listening: Research perspectives*. Cambridge, UK: Cambridge University Press.

This edited volume brings together researchers and practitioners from around the world to discuss issues relevant to academic listening.

Flowerdew, J., & Miller, L. (2005). *Second language listening: Theory and practice*. Cambridge, UK: Cambridge University Press.

This book outlines important issues related to listening and presents the pedagogical model referred to in this chapter. It then applies the theoretical concepts of listening to practical contexts, including academic listening.

ENDNOTES

[1] A more detailed account of the model can be found in Flowerdew and Miller (2005).
[2] Wide-angle courses are also sometimes referred to as broad-angle courses.
[3] Students may also be referred to websites at this stage. For example, material on the human body at http://www.kidinfo.com is designed primarily for children and therefore uses simple language that may be more accessible for learners at lower levels of proficiency.
[4] Hedging involves the use of certain word or expressions to give a sense of imprecision or lack of commitment to what is being said. Examples of words used in hedging include *sort of*, *more or less*, and *roughly*.
[5] See http://www2.warwick.ac.uk/fac/soc/al/learning_english/leap/listeningandspeaking

UNIT II

Language Skills

Speaking

Second Language Speaking

ANNE LAZARATON

KEY QUESTIONS

➤ In teaching speaking, which is more important, a focus on fluency or on accuracy?

➤ How can the teacher promote authentic oral communication in the second language class?

➤ What considerations go into planning and teaching a speaking course?

EXPERIENCE

An English as a second language tutor, in the journal she is keeping for her methods class, writes the following:

> I am tutoring a student from South America who hired me to help him improve his oral accuracy. Although he feels he is making great progress, I feel that he pays attention only to his fluency and has made no progress at all with his grammatical accuracy. I have pointed this out to him, have tried using more accuracy-based activities, and have even talked to his classroom teacher but to no avail. Is there anything I can do to keep my expectations in line?

WHAT IS INVOLVED IN TEACHING SECOND LANGUAGE SPEAKING?

When queried about competence in other languages, it would certainly sound odd to be asked, "How many languages do you write?" A question such as "How many languages can you understand (or read)?" makes more sense, but overwhelmingly the question put to us is "How many languages do you *speak?*" In fact, speaking is considered by many to be the *fundamental* skill in second language (L2) learning. In what are often referred to as the productive approaches to language teaching (e.g., communicative language teaching, Silent Way, and even the audiolingual approach), speaking is the main skill by which a language is acquired, and it is almost certainly so at the beginning level. Likewise, much second language acquisition (SLA) research is based on data collected from L2 learners speaking to each other or to native speakers to ascertain the role of input, interaction, and corrective feedback in their acquisition of the L2. An entire academic field is devoted to the analysis of *talk-in-interaction* in attempts to understand the nature of conversation and other forms of institutional talk.

The act of speaking is staggeringly complex. According to H. D. Brown (2007), a number of the characteristics of speaking lead to this complexity. These include clustering (i.e., speech is segmented into thought groups rather than single words, and even single words may be contracted); hesitation markers and pausing; colloquial language, including slang and idioms; and suprasegmental features including stress, rhythm, and intonation. (See also Goodwin, this volume.) Moreover, because speech almost always involves interaction with at least one other speaker, these multiple demands are in place at the same time: monitoring and understanding the other speaker(s), thinking about one's own contribution, producing that contribution, monitoring its effect, and so on. It is certainly not a coincidence that speaking is also perhaps the most perplexing of the traditional four skills to assess.

This chapter discusses current issues in oral skills pedagogy, the nature of the oral skills class, various classroom activities that promote L2 speaking development, and the evaluation of speaking skills.

CONCEPTUAL UNDERPINNINGS

This section considers four factors that are at the foundation of competent L2 speaking: fluency, accuracy, appropriacy, and authenticity. It is intended to contextualize the more practical issues in the teaching of L2 speaking that follow.

Fluency versus accuracy

Through the years, the then-current positions taken on various dichotomies have guided (or confused) the teacher of L2 speaking. For example, which is more important, a focus on fluency or on accuracy? Should one come before the other? How does this decision depend on the learners involved and their backgrounds, needs, and proficiency levels?

Simple definitions of *accuracy* and *fluency* have been proposed by Edge and Garton (2009): accuracy is "conforming to the language system itself," while fluency is "operating the [language] system quickly" (p. 15). According to H. D. Brown (2007), "The fluency/accuracy issue often boils down to the extent to which our techniques should be **message oriented** (or, as some call it, teaching language use) as opposed to **language oriented** (also known as teaching language usage)" (p. 324, emphasis in the original).

A related concern is choosing between speaking tasks that engender controlled language production or those that encourage freer, more communicative speech. Although we might expect recommendations for a balanced approach to accuracy and fluency concerns, H. D. Brown's (2007) teaching methodology text and others used in training preservice English as a second language (ESL) or English as a foreign language (EFL) teachers imply that this controversy is, more or less, settled. Parrish points to "fluency as the goal of instruction" (2004, p. 100); Ur's (2012) methodology text states, "in most cases, the primary aim [in teaching speaking] is to improve students' fluency in informal conversational interaction" (p. 117). Nation and Newton (2009) suggest that "as a rough rule, language-focused learning should not make up more than about 25% of the whole range of contact that learners have with the language" (p. 148). They go on to remark that in an ESL setting, where there are many out-of-class opportunities for exposure to and practice with the L2, more time in class could be devoted to [...] based speaking activities. In contrast [...] these opportunities are limited (as in an EFL setting), fluency-based, meaning-focused tasks merit more attention. Of course, other factors come into play when making decisions about teaching L2 speaking (or any other skill), and a needs assessment should be the first step in designing and teaching an oral skills course (this issue is discussed later in the chapter). In either circumstance, it behooves the L2 teacher to look beyond the traditional classroom setting for these speaking opportunities.

Appropriacy

Appropriacy is all about sociocultural context, or pragmatics. It is not enough for L2 speakers to be accurate and fluent; they must also be competent socially and culturally. That is, L2 learners need to be able to communicate "with the proper politeness, directness, and formality. . . . [They] also need to know what not to say at all and what to communicate nonverbally" (Ishihara & Cohen, 2010, p. 4). The most researched area of pragmatics in applied linguistics is speech acts, which describe "the ways in which people carry out specific social functions" (p. 6) like greetings, thanking, and disagreeing. Speech acts are composed of various strategies that speakers draw on to convey their intended meaning, and the selection of particular strategies will depend on a variety of sociocultural factors (e.g., social distance, social status, and the nature of the speech act itself).

The importance of pragmatic appropriacy is fairly well established in ESL/EFL teaching, and the vast majority of student textbooks and teacher training resources show a greatly heightened awareness about these issues of language use. This may be due in part to Celce-Murcia and Larsen-Freeman's adoption of the tripart grammar "pie" for language teaching and learning. (See Larsen-Freeman, this volume.) The form-meaning-use slices of the pie are differentially weighted for particular grammar structures, both in *The Grammar Book* (Celce-Murcia & Larsen-Freeman, 1999) and in the *Grammar Dimensions* series edited by Larsen-Freeman (2007). The when and why of language use are questions about appropriateness. As we see later

...n the chapter, empirical support for claims about language appropriacy is now available through studies of large language corpora.

Authenticity

A final sticking point for the teacher of L2 oral skills is the matter of authenticity at all stages of instruction. The construct of authenticity itself is slippery—authentic for whom, for what purpose, and in what contexts? Other questions present themselves in this area: How and how much can the teacher of L2 speaking provide meaningful contexts for authentic language use? Should controlled simple language be at the center of beginning-level instruction, with the introduction of authentic materials, tasks, and language use gradually presented as proficiency level increases? Or should all input be authentic regardless of level, following what I always tell my students— simplify the task, not the text? Tentative answers to questions like these are put forward in Roberts and Cooke's (2009) study of linguistic-minority migrant adults. They point to two meanings of authenticity: the first having to do with authentic teaching materials and the second referring to issues of "self-expression and the development of authentic voice" (p. 621). After examining some workplace English materials (e.g., *Skills for Life* [2003], developed by the Department of Education and Skills in England), Roberts and Cooke conclude that L2 adults who have actual experience in the workplace do not benefit from such artificially created pedagogical material; rather, "comparative, research-based materials" that are "authentic in both content and interactional environment" are necessary for adults to become competent L2 speakers (p. 639).

It is unfortunate, therefore, that even today the vast majority of published pedagogical materials that teachers of L2 speaking use contain scripted dialogues that are free of speaker errors (consistent with Gilmore's [2004] analysis of pre-2000 books) and represent the speech from some often unspecified variety of native-speaker English. How can this situation be rectified? One promising direction is corpus-based L2 teaching.

Corpus-based L2 teaching. In a review of research in the teaching of L2 speaking, McCarthy and O'Keeffe (2004) contend that, while there have

not been any major shifts in L2 teaching methodology and practice, "our knowledge concerning spoken language has indeed changed, mainly through developments in spoken corpus linguistics." One such development has been an increasing interest in *spoken grammar* as contrasted with *written grammar*. Work in this area is united by "the belief that spoken grammars have uniquely special qualities that distinguish them from written ones" (McCarthy & Carter, 2006, p. 29).

McCarthy and Carter propose 10 baseline principles as a guide in the development of a spoken grammar. (See McCarthy & O'Keeffe, this volume, for a thorough treatment of these principles.) For example, we do not speak in sentences, but in phrasal chains that demonstrate the clustering of words and phrases and that are connected by simple conjunctions like *and* and *but*. Spoken grammar contains language that would be considered ungrammatical (or at least register inappropriate) in writing, such as the elliptical forms *Wanna go with?* instead of *Do you want to go with me?*; *I gotta go* rather than *I must go*; and clipped forms like *ad* for *advertisement*. Both hesitation markers (forms like *um*, *uh*, *sorta*, *y'know*, *well*, and *like*) and discourse markers (like *cuz* and *oh*) are ubiquitous in spoken language and do not appear in writing, nor do they show up in many scripted dialogues presented in ESL/EFL teaching materials.

Further explication of the spoken grammar of English (SGE) was undertaken by Mumford (2008), who maintains that a working knowledge of SGE can improve both the fluency and appropriacy of L2 speaker speech. Mumford claims that student work on fluency "is desirable in any context" because our goal as teachers is to help our learners "transmit the[ir] message as quickly and efficiently as possible" (p. 142). Mumford is enthusiastic in endorsing the empirical study of and pedagogical materials based on spoken language corpora:

> *Cambridge Grammar of English* [CGE; Carter & McCarthy, 2006] is a significant contribution to our knowledge of English because of size of the corpus used and its detailed analysis. We can now see that SGE consists of a range of different structural and lexical items with a variety of functions. As it is purely descriptive, it is not the purpose of CGE to give an indication of whether, which features of, or how this

new information should be taught. However, it gives new impetus to the productive teaching of SGE by collating and codifying it. (p. 143)

Mumford provides a useful summary of many data-driven findings regarding spoken (British) English and strongly argues for teaching SGE forms for production as well as reception. It is true that a number of the features that are documented in analyses of SGE have been on our radar for years, but in the past, statements about their use and frequency were often based on intuitions (see also Ishihara & Cohen [2010] on this point with regard to pragmatics instruction) or on the sort of very small-scale corpus studies that were possible before computerized analysis of authentic spoken language became widespread.

As a result of large-scale corpus-based research on the features of SGE, materials developers and teachers of L2 speaking are better equipped to discern practical applications from such scholarly investigation. For example, Shin and Nation (2008) analyzed the spoken portion of the British National Corpus (BNC) to determine the top 100 expressions that would be most important for beginning-level L2 learners. It turns out that *you know* and *I think* were by far the most prevalent collocations, while greetings like *Good morning* were noticeably absent from the inventory of the top 100 expressions. Shin and Nation use this particular fact to caution L2 teachers to think about frequency of occurrence as only one of several variables that should be considered in designing a speaking activity, lesson, or syllabus. Learners' needs and their level of proficiency, for example, may dictate pedagogical choices based on criteria other than frequency.

Likewise, Fung and Carter (2007) scrutinized an L2 learner corpus from Hong Kong and relevant parts of the CANCODE corpus (the Cambridge University Press and Nottingham University Corpus of Discourse in English) and indicate a general paucity of SGE features in the Hong Kong corpus as well as a very limited range in their use (mostly connecting expressions like *but* or *because* rather than pragmatically flexible expressions like *really* or *sort of*). The authors make a number of recommendations for L2 classroom teachers, one of which is the explicit incorporation of information about and practice with these forms. The authors argue that, rather than being peripheral

to the development of speaking skills, discourse markers are of central importance, constituting the interactional fabric of the L2 classroom. Some of the discourse functions that they perform are interpersonal (e.g., helping to build solidarity), referential (e.g., marking cohesive relationships), structural (organizing discourse), and cognitive (illuminating thought processes about the message itself) (p. 435).

To what degree have empirical findings about spoken grammar been incorporated into published teaching materials for teaching L2 speaking? Cullen and Kuo's (2007) analysis of 24 British textbooks published from 2000 to 2006 hones in on three SGE phenomena: (1) "productive grammatical constructions;" (2) "fixed lexicogrammatical units;" and (3) grammatical structures that are "incorrect" based on prescriptive (written) grammar rules (p. 365). Examples from their analysis in Category 1 include left dislocations (e.g., *Grace, I like her*) and structures derived from ellipsis (e.g., *Got a day off?*). Category 2 includes discourse markers (*you know, I mean*) and hedges (*sort of*). Category 3 includes the loss of the subjunctive in spoken English (e.g., *If I was you . . .* in place of *If I were you . . .*). Their findings indicate that almost half of the books made no mention of structures or expressions from these three categories, a shortcoming particularly evident in the beginner-level books. Features included in their Category 2 (discourse markers) were the most apparent, although not prevalent. The authors argue that teaching spoken language use grounded in empirical data gives learners exposure to and explicit practice with features of SGE, thus making it less likely they will avoid certain structures or resort to transferring nonidiomatic counterparts from their first language (L1).

Thus, it is a welcome development when ESL materials writers do use large-scale searchable corpora to inform the creative process. One such textbook series has as its foundation facts derived from corpus studies, Cambridge University Press's *Touchstone* (McCarthy, McCarten, & Sandiford, 2005/2006), which is based on the 1 billion-word Cambridge International Corpus of spoken and written North American English. One of the main objectives of *Touchstone* is to explicitly teach and relate facts about *actual* English usage; the grammar, vocabulary, and conversation strategies are chosen from the corpus.

Nevertheless, the fact that few ESL/EFL textbooks specifically target SGE features and, more generally, conversation seems to bear out this lacuna in authentic speaking materials (one exception is an older text, *Speaking Naturally* [Tillitt & Bruder, 1985]; see also Riggenbach, 1999). This is rather ironic given that conversation or, more accurately, talk-in-interaction is the "core root of sociality itself" (Schegloff, 2007, p. xiii).

Conversation analysis. Conversation analysis (CA) has been a locus of scholarly interest for over 40 years. Briefly, CA is "a sociological approach that attempts to uncover the systematic properties of sequential organization of talk and the social practices that are displayed by and embodied in talk-in-interaction" (Lazaraton, 2002, p. 29). *Talk-in-interaction* refers to different kinds of talk and their accompanying body language that occur in daily life across settings from casual to institutional contexts" (Wong & Waring, 2010, p. 2). Specifically, CA is concerned with the organization systems that underlie conversation and other forms of spoken language, including overall structural organization (openings, closings, and transitions), turn-taking (the structure and distribution of turns), sequence structure (the linking of turns to the performance of actions like requesting, greeting, etc.), and repair (mechanisms for rectifying problems of hearing and understanding in conversation).

In terms of L2 pedagogy, Wong and Waring (2010) put forward many ideas on how CA can inform L2 speaking instruction: "CA not only enriches our knowledge of *what* to teach, it also sharpens our understanding of *how* to teach" (p. 251). That is, knowledge of the interactional practices encoded in language can inform instructional practices surrounding the learning of that language. One such application comes from empirical descriptions of the nature of pedagogical repair (i.e., repair that takes place in the L2 classroom), which can inform complex decisions about error correction. For example, should errors in speaking be ignored or repaired? This topic has been exhaustively studied by second language acquisition researchers; a review of that literature is beyond the scope of this paper but can be found in Tarone and Swierzbin (2009). In the area of error correction, the teacher of L2 speaking is given plenty of advice on "considerations in deciding when to correct learner errors" (Parrish, 2004, p. 78) as well as techniques for providing correction. H. D. Brown's (2007) coverage of error treatment spans seven pages in his methodology book, including charts, lists of options, and a very visually appealing "model for treatment of classroom speech errors" (p. 349). He suggests that, if the teacher chooses to correct an error, other decisions must be made: when to correct the error (immediately or later), who should correct the error (the teacher, another student, or the speaker), and how the error should be corrected (e.g., by indicating the existence of an error, by pointing out its location, by modeling the correct form, by indicating the type or source of error, or by providing a metalinguistic explanation).

In this case, conversation analysis research provides important information about specific classroom error correction techniques. Seedhouse (2004; as cited in Wong & Waring, 2010, p. 257) found that direct correction is generally avoided in favor of other, less direct strategies, including: (1) indirect indication of an error (*Excuse me?*); (2) partial repetition of the error (*The what?*); (3) repetition of the original question that generated the error; (4) repetition of the error with rising intonation (*Luggages?*); (5) provision of a "correct" version (*Do you mean luggage?*); (6) indication of why an error is an error rather than calling it one; (7) acceptance of the incorrect form and then giving the correct form; and (8) the invitation to other students to do the repair. I return to error correction in the next section.

To summarize, the long-standing concerns about fluency, accuracy, appropriacy, and authenticity in teaching L2 speaking are still with us, but work in the areas of corpus linguistics and conversation analysis has prompted a reconsideration of our more traditional understanding of these notions. Whatever standards of accuracy and appropriacy are adopted for spoken English, they cannot (and should not) be based solely on the norms of written language. Our new knowledge about the nature of SGE and conversation should encourage, rather than discourage, teachers of L2 speaking to explicitly teach these forms, designing and implementing activities that contain them. In other words, true authenticity of tasks, materials, and language is promoted when teachers make pedagogical decisions not by intuition only but on the basis of data-driven findings that have become more widely available.

CLASSROOM APPLICATIONS

Before getting into the specifics of teaching L2 speaking, it is worth considering the understandable questions that ESL/EFL teachers have about appropriate teaching methodologies in an L2 speaking class. The concept of method has taken somewhat of a beating in recent years; authors such as Pennycook (1989) have gone to great lengths to show how confining the concept method is. Kumaravadivelu (2003) has proposed a post-method pedagogy, while other scholars (e.g., Akbari, 2008; Rajagopalan, 2007) have put forward their own critiques of the post-method condition. (See also Celce-Murcia's methods chapter, this volume.)

As intellectually intriguing as these polemics may be, a more immediate and concrete concern has to do with the *how* of teaching speaking skills. H. D. Brown (2007) puts forward a number of concrete principles for teaching speaking skills including:

> Focus on both fluency and accuracy; provide intrinsically motivating techniques; encourage the use of authentic language in meaningful contexts; provide appropriate feedback and correction; capitalize on the natural link between speaking and listening; give students the opportunities to initiate oral communication; and encourage the development of speaking strategies. (pp. 331–332)

Another framework for creating and implementing speaking activities is presented by J. C. Richards (2008), who poses questions that the ESL/EFL teacher should consider in addressing the nuts and bolts of defining objectives, preparing instructions, providing necessary language support, selecting appropriate materials, and considering the when and how of feedback. Obviously, these considerations are fundamental for teaching any language skill, not just speaking.

The oral skills class

(Speaking & listening)

Nowadays, L2 speaking-skills classes at all levels are often structured around functional uses of language. In a nonacademic context, these might involve basic greetings, interacting with school personnel, looking for employment, and the like.

With adults in an academic context, authentic practice in activities and skills required in post-secondary school classrooms would be central: giving oral presentations, listening to content lectures, reading academic texts, and the like. A needs assessment should also consider the real-world tasks that the target students are confronted with.

In addition to learner needs, another basic consideration is the proficiency level of the students. Level is often determined by some form of assessment, whether it be a large-scale language test such as the Test of English as a Foreign Language (TOEFL) (Educational Testing Service, 2012b), an in-house diagnostic test, or an in-class assessment designed by the teacher. Needs can also be determined by means of a student information sheet on which learners report the amount of time they spend speaking English; their future goals; their goals for the course; and a self-assessment (perhaps on a 4-point scale from poor to excellent) of their overall speaking ability, confidence in speaking English, and skills in pronunciation, conversation, and listening.

With low-level adults, the teacher may need to find helpers who speak the students' L1s to assist in getting information on student experiences, educational background, and needs. It will be especially important with this student group to build on learners' experiences, to share expertise, and to use hands-on learning activities (such as realia) to keep learning as concrete as possible. More often than not, oral skills courses for nonacademic adults focus on survival English, basic vocabulary, and communication functions, along with a strong structural component (that may be presented explicitly or implicitly).

On the other hand, learners of academic English will need practice with different sorts of activities, including participation in class and discussions, interaction with peers and professors, and asking and answering questions related to the academic content. The *Q: Skills for Success* series (e.g., Craven & Sherman, 2011) targets this group with an activity-packed reading-writing book as well as a listening-speaking book. The listening-speaking books engage (pre-)academic learners in tasks that develop speaking strategies, promote critical thinking, and reinforce content vocabulary on general academic topics such as psychology, interpersonal communication, advertising, and finance. Extensive listening practice with these topics leads to group discussions and presentations that empha-size relevant speaking skills, such as asking for clari-fication and practicing and using recap techniques. Notably, there is a strong language component that is integrated with the many communicative activities in the series, such as using modal verbs to give advice, practicing tag question intonation, and linking consonants and vowels.

Some academic learners may be facing an exit examination at the conclusion of their course that will determine whether they are competent to teach English (as is the case with international teaching assistants [ITAs]) or to take other academic courses for credit. As a result, these learners take their course work seriously and have high expectations of their teacher. Even so, many of these students can probably benefit from (and may even ask for) some instruction on and practice with the more interpersonal aspects of oral communication.

Published materials for teaching L2 speaking

Usually language teachers are given a textbook or materials for teaching the L2 speaking class. It is extremely important that teachers and textbook-selection committees take a close critical look at these materials, since not all of them live up to their claims about what they promote or teach in terms of language content, teaching methodol-ogy, and task or textual authenticity (as discussed earlier in the chapter). Questions such as the fol-lowing could guide this critical evaluation: What buzzwords (e.g., on the book's back cover) try to sell you on the material? Is the text appropri-ate for the level/audience being taught? What sorts of content/topics are used, and are they appropriate for this group of students? Does the text require authentic language use? How do you know? Another possibility when selecting text-books is to consult reviews of teaching materials in professional journals, such as the online *TESOL Journal*, *TESL-EJ* electronic journal, or *ELT Journal*. Obviously, the reviews themselves should be taken with a grain of salt, but they are useful for locat-ing descriptions of book content as well as opin-ions about a book's strengths and shortcomings. However, even when using an assigned text, ESL teachers can choose content and activities from a variety of print and digital resources and can create their own materials as well.

Discussions and group work

Discussions are probably the most commonly used activity in the L2 speaking class. Often, the stu-dents are introduced to a topic via a reading or listening passage and then divided into pairs or groups to discuss a related topic to come up with a solution, a response, or ideas for a writing assign-ment. Teachers must take care in planning, setting up, implementing, and evaluating discussions.

The first aspect of group work that the teacher must consider is whether the students have the interactional skills necessary for task completion. That is, an earlier lesson should be devoted to working with the functional language required for stating opinions, agreeing and disagreeing, inter-rupting, and clarifying. Promoting competence in these metaskills, rather than assuming they are already there, can go a long way toward ensuring successful group work.

Next, the L2 speaking teacher must make decisions about grouping and pairing students for class discussions. In some cases, planned (versus random) pairing or grouping may be necessary to ensure a successful discussion outcome. While there is no one right way to group students, consider-ations such as first language, ethnicity, proficiency level, and talkativeness may come into play. To foster a student-centered classroom, Jones (2007) suggests groups of three for talkative students and groups of four or five for the more reticent students. Other factors such as class size, mixed proficiency, and monolingual settings require that the oral skills teacher develop a set of principles for pair, group, and whole-class discussions. Before the discussion task begins, students need to self-select or be assigned clear explicit roles for these activities. Specific responsibilities such as time-keeper, note taker, and group reporter should be chosen by the students themselves.

Finally, L2 learners need to know *what* they are going to discuss, *why* they are discussing it, *how long* they have for the activity, and *what outcome* is expected. In other words, it is insufficient to tell the class, "Get in groups and discuss this topic." There should be guidance beforehand and follow-up afterward. It is also worth thinking about how success or comple-tion will be defined for the activity and observed in the groups. Activities in which participation opportunities are approximately equal and students seem motivated to produce a lot of language that is sufficiently accurate, meaningful, and appropriate indicate that the discussion activity has most likely met its objectives. Not so successful speaking activities are characterized by "shyness and inhibition . . . low participation of individuals" or "L1 use" (Ur, 2012, p. 118), and the oral skills teacher should carefully evaluate what happened in order to have a more satisfactory outcome the next time.

The instructor's role during group discussions is to monitor the activity to ensure that students are on task, that they have equal opportunities to participate, and that they are speaking in English. At the conclusion of the activity, it is important for the teacher to provide feedback to and, at times, elicit reactions from the class. This may involve reviewing answers, commenting on and consolidating ideas, or linking discussion outcomes to future class activities or assignments. In other words, it is important to plan for wrap-up time.

Presentations

Presentations are another frequent activity in L2 speaking classes. Topics for presentations will vary depending on proficiency level and the particular focus of the class, but in any case, students should be given some leeway in determining the content of their talks. In other words, teachers can provide the structure for the presentation—its rhetorical genre (description, persuasion, etc.) and its time restrictions—while the students select the content, ideally with teacher guidance or input. Whenever possible, students should be encouraged to talk about ideas, experiences, or information that is meaningful to them. Guidance for structuring oral presentation tasks can be found in textbooks such as the *Present Yourself* series (Gershon, 2008), which is aimed at low-intermediate- to intermediate-level adults learning American English. Each of the six chapters takes students through the oral presentation process, from brainstorming ideas, practicing expressions that are useful for talking about presentation content, and creating a presentation outline to examining a model presentation on the topic, practicing presentation skills, delivering the talk, and then finally students' using a self-evaluation form to critique their own performances.

Presentations can be frightening for the speaker and, after a while, boring for the listeners, so it is a good idea to ensure that the listeners take on some responsibilities during the presentation.

This is an excellent opportunity for peer evaluation, guided by evaluative criteria that the teacher, the students, or both develop. These criteria should be put into a written form that guides the listening. At the end of the presentation, the evaluators can be asked to summarize content, note strengths and weaknesses, or relate the presentation topic to personal experience.

Videotaping the presentations allows all evaluators (speakers, peers, and teacher) to do a more in-depth critique at a later time by viewing the digitized presentation. Again, the evaluative guidelines can be developed by the teacher, the class, or, with guidance, individually by each presenter. Students are often surprised to see how they appear and sound, and they can often come up with their own ideas about how to improve their performances. Videotaping also allows for some of the language analysis activities described next to encourage students to notice their own abilities in pronunciation, grammar, fluency, vocabulary, and nonverbal behavior. Taping class presentations allows the teacher to direct more sustained attention to both the content and language than real-time evaluation does. Evaluation criteria should be consistent with the goals of the class. Categories of performance may include: content and organization (Was it easy to locate and understand the main point of the presentation? Was there an appropriate introduction and conclusion?); language use (What issues were there with grammar, vocabulary, pronunciation, and fluency?); and interaction and rapport with the audience (How effective were the nonverbal aspects of the presentation: eye contact, posture, gestures, and composure?).

Group presentations may be the only choice for presentations, given class size and time restrictions. The benefits of students working in pairs or groups to prepare presentations are much the same as for discussions (negotiation of meaning, interaction in an authentic context, collaborative learning, etc.), and as such, there is much to recommend them. The oral skills teacher, however, must plan these assignments carefully by considering questions such as: How will the groups be constituted (i.e., by the teacher, randomly, by interest, or self-selection)? How can the teacher ensure that effort and participation will be equal? How can the teacher evaluate the contribution of individuals to the process? It has been my experience that it is best to offer options to the class. For example, a particular student may insist on working alone; in this case, the teacher can plan for several such presentations, with an option for one of them to be a solo effort. For group-project evaluations, it is beneficial to have each group member state his or her contribution to the process, whether the work was divided fairly, and what grade the individual and the group deserve.

Related to oral presentations are impromptu speeches, which can serve several purposes in the L2 speaking class. An impromptu speech offers students more actual practice with speaking the language, but it also compels them to think, and speak, on their feet without the benefit of notes or memorization. A variation on this activity can be part of a lesson on the use of hesitation markers, such as *um, well, sort of,* and *like.* In this activity, students are told that using hesitation markers is an acceptable, if not preferred, speaking strategy to avoid periods of silence, which may cause embarrassment, confusion, and even loss of the speaking floor. After the teacher goes over a list of hesitation markers and the students practice their pronunciation and intonation, each student is assigned a topic that he or she is likely to know little about. For example, in university academic English courses, topics such as how to find a derivative in mathematics or how to describe the molecular structure of carbon are likely to be unfamiliar to at least some members of the class. For pre- or nonacademic learners, suitable topics might be how to preserve fruit or how to change the spark plugs in a car. Once students understand the task and are familiar with hesitation markers, they are given a strip of paper with the topic on it just before they begin to speak. The one-minute, unprepared response should contain as many hesitation markers as possible while at the same time avoiding silence and giving as little actual content information as possible. This is actually quite a humorous activity that students enjoy; it can be expanded by having students who *do* know about the topics give a short explanation of their own after each attempt.

Role plays

Another popular speaking activity is the role play, which is particularly suitable for practicing the sociocultural variations in speech acts, such as complimenting, requesting, and refusing. Depending on the students' level, role plays

can be performed from prepared scripts, created from a set of prompts and expressions, or written using and consolidating knowledge gained from instruction or discussion of the speech act and its variations. *Speaking Naturally* (Tillitt & Bruder, 1985) is an excellent older textbook that provides a framework of ordered steps for teaching speech acts. First, a diagnostic assessment is useful for determining what students already know about the act(s) in question. A model dialogue, presented aurally or in written form, serves as language input, after which the class is encouraged to evaluate the role-play situation to understand the factors that affect pragmatic and linguistic choices made in the dialogue. Students can listen to and practice prototypical phrases used in the speech act and then perform the role play (after considering appropriate information about the participants and their ages, relationships, etc.) as a final activity.

Conversations

An important tool in the repertoire of the teacher of L2 speaking is the use of tasks that require students to analyze and evaluate the language that they and others produce (for many additional ideas along these lines, see Riggenbach, 1999). In other words, it is not always enough to have students produce a great deal of language; they must also become more metalinguistically aware of the many features of spoken language to become more competent speakers and interlocutors in English. While the importance of noticing in SLA research is a generally accepted fact for sentence-level features of language input, it is only recently that applied linguists have suggested that an analysis of the interactional features of conversation is crucially important as well. Nearly all L2 students can benefit from instruction on the nature of informal conversation and practice with its fundamental features, whether they are in a classroom context or in a tutorial setting like the Experience scenario at the beginning of the chapter. A conversation assignment can be helpful in this regard.

One way to approach this activity is to assign students to find a fluent speaker of English that they know—a friend, roommate, or colleague— and record a 20- to 25-minute interaction with this person. Of course, not all the discourse that results from this encounter will be technically natural conversation; the fluent speaker may fall into the role of interviewer and ask all the questions while the student merely responds. Therefore, the teacher should encourage students beforehand to come up with a few questions to ask their interlocutor. In any case, the resulting interaction will provide a sample of spontaneous production from (and for) the student to analyze.

The next step is for the students to transcribe a portion of the interaction. Transcription involves a faithful reproduction of what was said on paper and provides a genuine awareness of what speech is really like. In this way, students can "see" speech, and they are often surprised that nearly everyone's speech is far from perfect. Students are given some basic instructions on how to transcribe this talk; they are reminded not to correct grammar or pronunciation errors, and to include the hesitation markers, false starts, and pauses that occur.

Once the transcript is produced, there are various activities that can be pursued. One that works well is to have students find several instances of communication difficulties. They can be asked to describe and exemplify a few and then determine what happened, why, and how the difficulty could have been avoided or repaired. In a more advanced class where students feel comfortable with each other, transcripts can be exchanged and critiqued; the teacher may also use these critical incidents for whole-class activities on communication breakdown and repair. Another activity is to have students analyze such incidents selected by the teacher and determine why the teacher chose to point them out. A variation of this assignment is to have students conduct interviews with fluent English speakers on a topic of their choice and then present their results to the class, which can be evaluated using the techniques suggested earlier (videotaping, self-evaluation, and peer evaluation).

Evidence for the efficacy of student transcription is reported by Stillwell et al. (2011). University EFL students in Japan created posters on film genres and then, in pairs, improvised an oral presentation based on questions from a peer. The pairs then transcribed their three-minute talks, correcting errors when they were apparent. The instructor also corrected errors. Post-task questionnaires required the students to calculate rough measures of accuracy, fluency, and complexity, as well as to rate their satisfaction with different aspects of the transcription process. Students showed improvement in their ability to correct errors as well as expressing generally positive attitudes toward the transcription tasks themselves.

Dialogue journals

The activities discussed so far have emphasized fluency and meaning negotiation over accuracy. One popular assignment that lends itself well to both fluency and accuracy is the oral dialogue journal. Ordinarily, the teacher starts the journal dialogue by giving directions for the assignment and suggesting a topic and a time limit for the first audio exchange. The student then reacts to the teacher prompt, via either a sound file, a CD or audiotape, or a voice-based technology tool. Finally, the teacher provides an audio response. In a small class, it is not unrealistic for the teacher to listen to all the journals and to assign them on a regular basis. In a large class, on the other hand, this is not always feasible, so other options are possible. The journals can be submitted on a rotating basis, some students submitting their journals one week and others the next. Alternatively, students can exchange journals and provide feedback to peers after some guidance from the teacher.

Like written journals that are used extensively in writing classes, the oral dialogue journal has much to offer both teachers and students; it is one format where practice with fluency and attention to accuracy can be accomplished at the same time. Teachers should be sure to remind students to speak extemporaneously and should explain why. Some students will want to write out their entries and read them so they can sound "perfect"; this defeats the purpose of the assignment, which is to work on *unplanned* speaking. It is always a good idea for teachers to comment on the content of the response to reinforce that *what* is said is as important as *how* it is said. Overall, the student recordings are an excellent resource for the teacher to provide individual feedback and instruction on pronunciation or grammar problems, since students have a recording of their speech to which they can refer.

Accuracy-based speaking activities

Look again at the Experience at the beginning of this chapter, where the tutor is concerned with the lack of improvement in her student's accuracy skills. There is no reason that communicative activities cannot also address accuracy concerns. Drills, which were a hallmark of language teaching during the audiolingual era, have, for the most part, fallen out of favor in language teaching, but they should not be shunned out of hand. (See the discussion of methods in Celce-Murcia, this volume, for information on the audiolingual approach.) H. D. Brown (2007) suggests that if drills are to be used, they should be short, simple, and snappy; they should be used sparingly; and they should lead to more authentic communicative activities. Sources such as *Grammar Practice Activities* (Ur, 2009) recommend many communicative tasks that at the same time focus on particular structural features.

Activities that promote students getting acquainted with each other lend themselves to practice with *yes-no* and *wh*-questions and the appropriate responses to them. For example, in a *Find someone who* . . . activity, students match personal characteristics listed on a sheet of paper (e.g., runs marathons, plays the trumpet, has a tattoo) with at least one classmate who can answer *yes* to the question "Do you . . . ?" The first student to "find someone who" can answer *yes* to each question wins the game. A variation of this activity, much like Twenty Questions, has students take on a new identity (e.g., a celebrity, a type of vegetable, a color) and then have others try to guess the identity by asking a series of *yes-no* and/or *wh*-questions.

Before I close this section, a word about error correction is in order. In the more meaning centered activities discussed in this section, explicit error correction will probably be out of place because it interrupts the communication that is going on (unless, perhaps, the errors occur in a particular structure being targeted in the activity). Teachers may note these errors for later remediation with the class as a whole or with individual students, as necessary. During accuracy-based activities, the basic decision to be made is whether to treat any actual error or to ignore it; the decision will depend on several factors, including the type of error being made and the context in which it occurs. In the activities suggested here, problems with question formation should be remediated, while subject-verb agreement errors may not be. Some teachers choose to correct only errors that impede communication (such as word order) and ignore less serious errors (such as third person singular *–s* confusion). H. D. Brown (2007) recommends that teachers determine (perhaps in consultation with the class) *how* these errors should be corrected and *by whom*. Teachers should strive for optimal feedback, which shows that the learners' contributions are valued in their own right rather than representing "bad" English.

Teaching speaking in an EFL context

This chapter is primarily written with the ESL teacher in mind, working with a heterogeneous class (by L1 and ethnicity) in an English-speaking context. However, homogeneous EFL classes, where all students speak the same L1 and outside class exposure to English is limited, present certain additional challenges for the teacher of L2 speaking, including motivation, the use of the first language, and getting students to speak (especially in cultures where speaking in class is prohibited unless called on). An innovative effort in China to address learner reticence is reported by Zhang and Head (2009); this entailed including their EFL students in designing the English course and creating course materials and activities. The authors found that over the course of one year, the students had improved attitudes, motivation, and self-confidence as a result of this student-centered approach. In addition, large classes are often the norm in both ESL and EFL settings, limiting student opportunities to talk and teacher opportunities to provide individual feedback (see also Hess's, 2001, book-length treatment on teaching large multilevel classes). EFL curricula may not stress speaking skills or may view them only as an avenue to grammatical accuracy; furthermore, if the teacher is a non-native speaker of English, he or she may not be fully competent or confident in speaking and teaching English.

While solutions to these problems are beyond the scope of this chapter, one general suggestion can be made. When teaching speaking skills, EFL teachers need to be particularly adept at organizing class activities that are authentic, motivating, and varied. Digital technology now allows access to an almost limitless number of movies and TV shows (via YouTube and other sources of streaming video), as well as to distance communication with other speakers across the world (using Skype or other voice over Internet protocols). There are numerous websites where EFL learners can find partners to speak English with, particularly if the partner is trying to learn the EFL student's first language. It goes without saying that the Internet and digital technologies have forever changed the landscape for teaching speaking. Some of these technologies merit a brief mention.

Technology tools

One reason that digital technologies are important for teaching L2 speaking is that they give students the opportunity not only to practice in real time but also to reflect on what they produce at some later time. These technologies also afford instructors a way to give pointed feedback to students. The following are some tools to consider.[1]

Videoconferencing tools. These tools simultaneously open up and shrink the world, making connections with native speakers even easier. When teaching in an area where there are few native English speakers, one of the videoconferencing tools can be used to connect with native speakers in different countries. In a context where contact with native speakers is plentiful, video-recording tools are still useful. Ask students to record themselves giving a presentation; this can be followed by any of the evaluation techniques mentioned earlier.

Podcasts. Podcasts, or digital audio and/or video files, are a great free source for finding authentic or instructional audio and video materials. Many podcasts contain a series of files that are released in episodes and can be downloaded for later viewing or listening. Instructors and students can subscribe to podcasts to have new content delivered to their computer, mp3 players, or smartphones. Often, podcasts link to a supporting website, so there is a wealth of information to be found to support the audio or video content. In fact, students can study the rhetorical style of a podcast and then create their own using one of the voice-based technology tools.

Voice-based technology tools. A voice-based tool that is available at many North American universities is Wimba, which is very intuitive and easy to use. Via Wimba, synchronous (real-time) and asynchronous voice recordings can be incorporated into oral skills teaching, as can threaded discussions,[2] chat sessions, oral interviews, voice email, and voice presentations. While Wimba is quite costly, Audacity is a free audio recorder and editor that can be downloaded and installed on a Mac or Windows machine. These are useful tools for teachers who want to develop their own listening activities and for students who want to record their voices. In addition to using the program for recording, the teacher can import audio files from other sources and create more advanced audio clips with background sounds; it is ideal for creating audio content for podcasts. Both Wimba and Audacity can provide a permanent, portable, and sharable record of speaking performance.

Assessment

The teacher of L2 speaking may be required to make decisions about two kinds of oral assessment. The first, evaluation of classroom performance, has been discussed with reference to various class activities. Unfortunately, there is still too little guidance for classroom teachers on creating, implementing, and evaluating formative and summative assessments of speaking (or other skills, for that matter). It has been over 30 years since Nic Underhill published his practical and user-friendly book, *Testing Spoken Language* (1987). Luoma's (2004) *Assessing Speaking* is a more recent book that details practical principles and techniques in spoken language assessment. Perhaps because classroom-based assessment remains a murky area for teachers of L2 speaking, there appears to be a trend for ESL/EFL teaching materials to contain an assessment component. For example, the *Touchstone* series mentioned earlier includes a testing program with quizzes and tests that match the material presented in each student book. The quizzes are both oral and written, and tap the various skills taught at each level. Teachers are given guidance on preparing for and administering these assessments. They are also provided with guidance in rating communication, grammar, vocabulary, conversation strategies, and fluency using a 5-point scale, from poor (1) to excellent (5).

A second assessment situation with which the teacher of L2 speaking may be confronted is preparing students to take or interpret the results from large-scale speaking tests; successful performance on these tests has increasingly become a common requirement for admission to universities, a minimum standard for ITAs, and a qualification for various types of employment. The speaking components from three international testing organizations are described next; interested readers should consult the organization websites for additional information. (See also Kunnan & Grabowski, this volume.)

Cambridge ESOL has offered a speaking component for nearly all of its examinations from its inception. All components of its "Main Suite" series, which correlates with the Common European Framework of Reference (Common European Framework of Reference, 2011) at all five levels, have speaking sections that count toward final marks. For international testing, the International English Language Testing System (University of Cambridge ESOL Examinations, 2009–2011) offers a face-to-face speaking task in which a test taker and an interviewer interact for approximately 11–14 minutes. The three parts of the test (Introduction-Interview, Long Turn, and Discussion) tap different interaction patterns, task input, and test-taker output. The language produced is rated on four criteria—fluency and coherence, lexical resource, grammatical range and accuracy, and pronunciation—which are equally weighted in determining the final band score, from 1 to 9.

The Educational Testing Service (2012c) administers the Internet-Based Test of English as a Foreign Language (iBT), which assesses the four skills in an academic context using an Internet format. The speaking test is a semi-direct measure because test takers do not interact with a live interlocutor; instead, they respond to computer-generated prompts and tasks by speaking into a microphone. The speaking section is approximately 20 minutes long and consists of six questions, some of which are independent speaking tasks that require test takers to draw on their own ideas, opinions, and experiences in their responses; the integrated speaking tasks require an integration of English language skills (listening and speaking, or listening, reading, and speaking), much like what occurs in or outside a university classroom. Human raters evaluate the language produced, and scores are reported on a 120-point scale.

A third large-scale oral assessment, administered by the American Council on the Teaching of Foreign Languages (ACTFL), is the ACTFL Oral Proficiency Interview (OPI), which is used extensively in both English and foreign language assessment (American Council on the Teaching of Foreign Languages, n.d.). The 20- to 30-minute recorded interview is administered (either over the telephone or face to face) by a trained OPI tester, who carefully structures the interaction to elicit the best possible performance from the test taker. The interviewer and a different examiner rate the tapes by comparing the language produced with the *ACTFL Proficiency Guidelines* (American Council on the Teaching of Foreign Languages, 2012), which define proficiency at nine levels, from superior to novice-low. The guidelines provide an extensive description of what speakers can do in various settings and in various tasks at each of the nine levels.

FUTURE TRENDS

One additional area that deserves attention from teachers of L2 speaking concerns the sociopolitical issues involved in language pedagogy. We must consider the complex relationships between factors such as the social value of the L2 and the historical relationships of power involving gender, ethnicity, and class. Much scholarship has been devoted to issues of English as an international language, English as a lingua franca, and the covert mechanisms of marginalization and oppression that are embedded in the construct of the native speaker (e.g., Jenkins, 2000; Kamhi-Stein, 2004; McGroarty, 2006). These issues raise more practical questions concerning English language varieties (i.e., World Englishes), the standards of spoken (and written) international English, and by whom these norms should be set. S. L. McKay (2002) reminds us that "the evidence clearly suggests that the use of EIL [English as an international language] will continue to grow, an international language that belongs, not just to native speakers, but to all of its users" (p. 129).

CONCLUSION

L2 speaking skills are not only critical for communication within the L2 classroom but they are necessary for communication both inside and outside the English-speaking world. As a result, ESL/EFL teachers will want to do whatever they can to advance the development of fluent, accurate, appropriate, and authentic language on the part of their learners. This effort will require an understanding of the nature of speaking fluency, the principles of error correction, the elements of pragmatic appropriacy, and the findings from corpus-based research so that they are able to plan and deliver lessons and activities that promote oral communication skills in the second language. They will also want to gain expertise in selecting appropriate teaching materials, using technology tools, and creating meaningful assessments to enhance the learning experience of their students. Finally, they will need to be cognizant of the sociopolitical aspects of language pedagogy so that issues such as English language varieties and international English standards can be addressed in a sensitive, contextually suitable manner.

SUMMARY

➤ Teachers of L2 speaking should continue to focus on promoting the development of fluent, accurate, appropriate, and authentic language.

➤ Recent findings from corpus-based studies of the SGE and CA have prompted a reconsideration of both the structural and interactional features of spoken English.

➤ The decisions of L2 teachers about the choice of speaking activities depend on a variety of learner and contextual factors.

➤ Speaking assessment continues to be a challenge for classroom teachers, and there are differing ideas about the best way to assess oral proficiency on high-stakes examinations.

DISCUSSION QUESTIONS

1. Think about a foreign or second language that you have studied. How were oral skills addressed? How do you judge your speaking ability as a result of the class? How could the class have been improved so that your ultimate attainment might have been better?

2. What considerations go into grouping or pairing students for speaking activities?

3. What would you tell a student who asks you to correct all of her oral language errors (pronunciation, grammar, lexical choice) in all of her spoken production work?

4. What role, if any, should the first language play in the ESL oral skills class? Would your answer change if the class were taught in an EFL context?

SUGGESTED ACTIVITIES

1. You teach an ESL oral skills class where some students, perhaps due to their personalities and/or cultural backgrounds, are the most talkative and dominate class discussions while others never speak up in class and, even when called on, merely agree or claim they have no opinion. This seems to happen particularly with the women, who in general tend to be more reticent than the men. What are some ways to encourage everyone to participate and practice conversing with each other, and to help the women, especially, feel more comfortable expressing their ideas?

2. Imagine that you have access to digital recordings of authentic conversations, such as the excerpts from recorded telephone conversations shown here. What sorts of activities could be developed based on this type of material?

(Part A:) *Brother and sister (native speakers)*

1. B: Okay, Viola, I'm gonna get going.
2. S: okay.
3. B: alright?
4. S: alright.
5. B: see you this evening.
6. S: okay, bye bye.
7. B: bye.
8. (clicks)

(Part B:) *MA TESL student (native speaker [NS]) and university ESL-course student (non-native speaker [NNS])* (from Bargfrede, 1996, p. 36). (Note: numbers in parentheses in the transcript refer to the length of the pauses in seconds.)

1. **NS:** right. Right. Well it'll come. Don't worry.
2. **NNS:** okay, thank you. (0.5). Oh alright. I will (0.8) finish my conversation.
3. **NS:** okay
4. **NNS:** okay? Uh have a good time.
5. **NS:** okay
6. **NNS:** bye bye
7. **NS:** bye
8. (clicks)

3. Imagine you have been assigned to teach a university-level orals skills class for future ITAs.

You are required to cover material specifically tailored to their future teaching needs, but you find that nearly all the students need practice with and ask for more class time on informal conversation. What should you do in this situation? Ask two experienced ESL/EFL teachers what they would do. Were the solutions offered similar to yours?

4. You suspect that the classroom textbook you have been assigned to use in your oral skills class presents dialogues containing stilted, awkward language. How can you test this assumption? In other words, what criteria can you use to evaluate dialogue authenticity?

FURTHER READING

Ishihara, N., & Cohen, A. D. (2010). *Teaching and learning pragmatics: Where language and culture meet.* Harlow, UK: Pearson.

This is a practical introduction to pragmatics and sociocultural context as they relate to L2 teaching and learning. Much of the book consists of suggestions for systematic materials development, instruction, and assessment of pragmatics.

Jones, L. (2007). *The student-centered classroom.* Cambridge, UK: Cambridge University Press.

Although this pamphlet does not focus exclusively on teaching L2 speaking, the excellent suggestions regarding pair and group work as well tips on classroom management, fostering motivation, and taking on a teacher-as-facilitator role make it a highly valuable addition to any language teacher's library.

Nation, I. S. P., & Newton, J. (2009). *Teaching ESL/EFL listening and speaking.* New York, NY: Routledge.

This up-to-date treatment offers both theoretical principles for teaching speaking and suggestions for promoting oral proficiency by means of a large variety of pedagogical techniques.

Underhill, N. (1987). *Testing spoken language: A handbook of oral testing techniques.* Cambridge, UK: Cambridge University Press.

This volume is a practical, teacher-friendly guide to the testing process that covers numerous assessment techniques and suggests how to elicit and rate spoken language and how to evaluate tests themselves.

Wong, J., & Waring, H. Z. (2010). *Conversation analysis and second language pedagogy: A guide for ESL/EFL teachers.* New York, NY: Routledge.

This textbook explains conversation analysis (CA) to the nonresearcher; it highlights key CA concepts, presents authentic tasks for analysis of conversational data, and puts forward a number of practical teaching activities.

ENDNOTES

[1] I am grateful to Alyssa Ruesch (personal communication, January 18, 2011) for sharing these ideas with me.

[2] A threaded discussion refers to online discussion postings that relate to a certain assignment or topic. The first message posted by a teacher or a student receives responses from others in the form of subsequent messages. This group of messages forms a thread.

9 Fluency-Oriented Second Language Teaching

DAVID BOHLKE

KEY QUESTIONS

➤ What does it mean to be fluent in a language?
➤ What factors make speaking a second or foreign language easy or difficult?
➤ How can teachers help language learners develop their oral fluency?

EXPERIENCE

Three second language students in three different classes all responded to a question asked by a teacher. Consider these scenarios.

Jason is asked what he is going to do after class. He pauses and thinks intently. He looks down, his lips moving silently as he formulates a halting but grammatically perfect sentence. The teacher asks him a follow-up question, and he continues in the same way. His second answer has an error with subject-verb agreement that he self-corrects.

Lucy is asked what she watched on television over the weekend. She immediately talks about a reality show she saw and mentions how stupid she thought it was, adding that she is looking forward to a new show that is previewing the following weekend. She speaks fairly quickly, using conversational fillers like *um* and *you know*. She speaks confidently, but her speech is full of grammatical errors.

Alex is asked to describe the people in his family. He describes them with ease, speaking faster than he normally speaks in class. He has answered this question before in other English classes with other teachers and always answers in more or less the same way. When the teacher asks him what person in his family he is most like and why, he is at a loss for an answer.

Which of the three students do you think speaks the best? How you answer may depend on what objective you think the teacher had in mind when asking the question. It may depend on what context the question was asked in and during which part of the lesson. It may also depend on

what you understand fluency to mean and how important you think fluency is.

In this chapter, I discuss what happens when we speak a language, including how speech is processed and the conditions that can make speaking easy or difficult for learners. I explore what it means to speak fluently. I look at ways of improving oral fluency and the conditions that can aid its development. Finally, I suggest practical classroom activities that can assist in making students sound more fluent when they speak.

WHAT IS FLUENCY?

Fluency is often discussed in relation to accuracy. While most second language professionals tend to agree on what it means to be accurate in a language, the concept of fluency is not as easy to define. Hartmann and Stork (1976) state that a person is fluent when he or she uses the language's structures accurately while at the same time concentrating on meaning, not form. The fluent speaker uses correct patterns automatically at normal conversational speed. Interestingly, here accuracy is seen as a major part of fluency.

An early advocate of the fluency-accuracy polarity was Brumfit (1984). He contrasts the two in pedagogical contexts and makes the distinction that "accuracy will tend to be closely related to the syllabus, will tend to be teacher-dominated, and will tend to be form-based. Fluency must be student-dominated, meaning-based, and relatively unpredictable towards the syllabus" (p. 121).

Brumfit further points out that fluency is meant "to be regarded as natural language use, whether or not it results in native-speaker-like language comprehension or production" (p. 56). It involves maximizing the language so far acquired by the learner by creating natural use in the classroom as much as possible.

Fillmore (1979) proposes that fluency includes four abilities: (1) the ability to talk without awkward pauses for relatively long periods of time; (2) the ability to talk in coherent and semantically dense sentences that show mastery of syntax and semantics; (3) the ability to say appropriate things in a variety of contexts; and (4) the ability to use language creatively and imaginatively. These are abilities that language users all possess to varying degrees. Fillmore's categories are interesting in that they relate to language but also to personality. They also show that there is an interaction between language use and knowledge of the world. In particular, this is seen in the third and fourth characteristics.

Hedge (1993) describes fluency as "the ability to link units of speech together with facility and without strain or inappropriate slowness or undue hesitation" (p. 275). Similarly, Richards and Schmidt (2010) describe fluency as "the features which give speech the qualities of being natural and normal, including native-like use of pausing, rhythm, intonation, stress, rate of speaking, and use of interjections and interruptions" (p. 222). These descriptions emphasize a smoothness of language delivery, without too many pauses or hesitations. They suggest natural language use, not necessarily speaking quickly.

Thornbury (2005) describes features of fluency centered primarily around pausing. A speaker's rate of speech is important, but it is not the only factor or even the most important one. Research on listeners' perceptions of a speaker's fluency suggests that pausing is equally important. Thornbury's four features of fluency are:

1. Pauses may be long but not frequent.
2. Pauses are usually filled.
3. Pauses occur at meaningful transition points.
4. There are long runs of syllables and words between pauses.

Fluency as a concept, it seems, includes many perspectives, and the features that make it up are still being debated. Koponen and Riggenbach (2000) conclude that "there can ultimately be no single all-purpose definition of fluency" (p. 19). Despite the subjectivity involved in defining fluency, the notion of fluency has already been shown "to be a useful concept *as is*" (p. 20). This is evident in that fluency is an important rating consideration for many oral language tests. It is also a high priority for many language learners even after they complete their formal language study. There are many reasons for this. Learners want to feel more confident in speaking to others. The use of English in business, research, and technology remains strong. For many learners, there is a need to receive a high score on the Test of English as a Foreign Language (TOEFL) (Educational Testing Service, 2012c), Test of English for International Communication (TOEIC) (Educational Testing Service, 2012d), or other exams that require spoken English. There is, therefore, pressure on teachers to show that their students can actually speak and can do so with a high degree of fluency. Many teachers thus want to find ways to incorporate more fluency development in their classes. How can these teachers create learning conditions where fluency can be developed?

CONCEPTUAL UNDERPINNINGS

What happens when we speak?

What factors make speaking a second or foreign language easy or difficult? Speaking is a complicated endeavor, no doubt, but an appreciation of what is involved in speaking can help a teacher provide the best conditions possible for fluency to develop.

Speech processing. We can look to cognitive science for models of speech processing. These processes of what happens when we speak can provide important insights to the language teacher. What may come naturally to a native speaker may be quite challenging to the language learner. Citing Levelt (1989), Bygate (2001) describes what happens in the planning and production phases of speaking. First, the mental process in which ambiguous or imprecise notions are made clear and more precise is called *conceptualization*. The information to be conveyed is selected based on the speaker's conceptual knowledge and other types of prior knowledge. What the speaker wishes to say may exist only vaguely. The conceptualized information is then conveyed through the *formulation* of utterances. Meaning is expressed through forms, and at this time the speaker must give attention to grammar and lexis. The concepts are realized when the words are put together in the correct syntactic order. A speaker may depend on formulaic expressions and chunked language, such as collocations, functional expressions, and idiomatic expressions. Finally, the utterance is spoken, or *articulation* occurs. It is phonologically encoded through the activation of certain muscle groups of the articulatory system.

These three functions are what produce speech; in daily speech, they happen more or less at the same time. Success also depends on automation, "to some degree in conceptualization, to a considerable degree in formulation, and almost entirely in articulation" (Bygate, 2001, p. 16). It is challenging for beginning second language (L2) learners to manage speech fluency, since they lack automation. It is therefore difficult for them to pay attention to and process these speech processes simultaneously.

Speaking competence. For L2 learners to communicate effectively, they must have a reasonable command of grammar and vocabulary. But this knowledge alone is insufficient. Learners need to develop a wide range of other skills. Four skill areas of speaking competence are required for effective communication (Goh, 2007). (See also Goh, this volume.)

1. *Phonological skills.* Learners need to be able to blend the phonemes of the language they are learning. In addition, they must use appropriate stress and intonation.
2. *Speech function skills.* Learners need to achieve specific communicative functions in social and transactional exchanges, such as agreeing with someone, asking for clarification, or offering a reason.
3. *Interactional skills.* In face-to-face exchanges, learners must manage interactions by regulating turn-taking, redirecting the topic, and negotiating meaning, in addition to initiating, maintaining, and closing a conversation.
4. *Extended discourse skills.* Learners must often produce long stretches of uninterrupted language, and they need to structure what they say so it is easy for others to follow. This requires the use of established conventions for structuring different kinds of extended spoken language, such as narrative, procedural, expository, or descriptive discourse.

In addition to these four skills, the use of conversation management strategies can lead to more effective speaking. These may be strategies for enhancing one's message, such as asking questions in two ways to be less direct or dealing with communication breakdowns, such as rephrasing to clarify meaning. Such strategies have been identified and categorized and are now part of the syllabi of several language textbooks. In Figure 1, the use of *I mean* as a strategy for repeating or expanding on a topic is explicitly taught.

Speech conditions. The conditions under which speaking occurs play a major role in determining the degree of fluency a speaker may be capable of. These factors have been isolated and divided into three categories: cognitive, affective, and performance. Thornbury (2005) provides a useful summary.

Figure 1. Using "I mean" as a conversation strategy (based on McCarthy, McCarten, & Sandiford 2005, p. 49).

Cognitive factors.

■ *Familiarity with the topic.* The more familiar something is, the easier it is to talk about. Learners usually find it easier to talk about their family, friends, school, or work than it is to talk about something unfamiliar or less personal. As seen in the Experience section at the beginning of the chapter, this may be why Alex was able to speak quite fluently on the topic of family, although he faltered when presented with a question he had not encountered before.

■ *Familiarity with the genre.* Speech genres are "particular language events, which unfold in predictable and institutionalized ways and move, stage by stage, toward a recognizable completion" (McCarthy, 1998, p. 62). Giving a speech or participating in a debate, for example, will be easier if students are already familiar with these particular genres.

■ *Familiarity with the interlocutors.* In general, the more familiar speakers are with the people they are talking with, the easier the conversation will be. A certain amount of shared knowledge can be assumed.

■ *Processing demands.* Certain speaking activities may involve complex mental processing. For example, if a student is describing how to operate a complicated machine, a diagram will generally make the description more comprehensible.

Affective factors.

■ *Feelings toward the topic or participants.* If the speaker has a positive feeling or attitude toward the topic or other people involved, speaking will generally be easier.

■ *Self-consciousness.* Some learners lack confidence about their speaking skills. They can become anxious or stressed if called on randomly or put on the spot by the teacher. In the Experience section, Jason spoke haltingly and seemed more concerned with accuracy than fluency. This could possibly be attributed to his being put on the spot. He may perform better on the same task, for instance, in a smaller group.

Performance factors.

■ *Mode.* Speaking face to face rather than over the phone is easier for many speakers because they can rely on gestures and body language.

■ *Degree of collaboration.* Peer support can often make things easier. For many, presenting on a topic with others is easier than doing it on their own.

■ *Discourse control.* On the other hand, being able to control the direction of events can be easier than being subject to others' control. As seen in the Experience section, when Lucy spoke at length about the topic with relative ease, she was able to answer the question posed but was also given freedom by the teacher to expand her answer.

■ *Planning time.* The more time the speaker has to plan and prepare, the easier the task will be.

■ *Time pressure.* The more urgent the task, the more pressure there will be. This can increase the difficulty for the speaker.

■ *Environmental conditions.* Students tend to perform better in a relaxed and noise-free classroom.

The interaction of cognitive, affective, and performance factors with personality. To a large extent, these cognitive, affective, and performance conditions also interact with personality, so it is not always possible to predict exactly how easy or difficult any speaking activity will be for a particular speaker. Being put on the spot, for example, can have a positive effect on some people's speaking performance. Some people find that working alone will produce better results than collaborating with others. In any event, these conditions provide a useful template for gauging how fluently a speaker may perform on a particular activity. They also give us a window into the complexity of speaking for second and foreign language learners.

Developing fluency

One the most challenging aspects about teaching a second or foreign language is finding ways to help learners improve their oral fluency. This is especially true in EFL contexts or ESL settings where there is little exposure to the L2 outside the classroom or where learners share a common language. Many students, even after years of study and an extensive knowledge of grammar and vocabulary, have difficulty achieving a desired level of fluency. Inevitably, many learners feel they lack the ability to speak and suffer from frustration and low motivation. But by using their latent abilities to focus on getting their meaning across, these learners can become successful speakers of the language.

Supporting learners. Goh (2007) suggests three ways to support learners during fluency activities. She proposes these as ways to reduce the cognitive load of students so as not to overburden them. The first is through *language support*. For example, the teacher may choose to review or preteach key vocabulary before certain activities. The second is through *knowledge support*. At times, the teacher may choose to introduce an unfamiliar concept into a lesson. The teacher will need to provide key background knowledge to assure that the learners have something to speak about and that the activity is successful. The third kind of support is *strategy support*. Using oral communication strategies can keep the students on task. One example of this is paraphrasing. If students do not know a word, they may paraphrase to get their point across. The teacher will need to teach and model these strategies and then allow students to practice them.

Pretask planning. Skehan (1998) suggests that fluency, accuracy, and complexity (the use of a wide range of structures to form more varied sentences) all demand mental capacity, and a trade-off occurs when one is emphasized more than another during a language activity. Increasing attention to accuracy, for example, is likely to hamper fluency and/or complexity. In an effort to increase fluency, a learner may rely more on language chunks, producing less accurate or less complex speech. Encouraging learners to experiment with new expressions and combinations of words may have a negative effect on accuracy and fluency.

But what happens when learners are given adequate time to plan what they want to say? Does this improve performance? And if so, which aspects of speaking show improvement—accuracy, fluency, or complexity? The research, as summarized by Goh (2007), shows that planning time does not improve all three aspects at the same time, but it does help with certain aspects of oral performance. Pretask planning provides learners with an opportunity to give attention to language areas that have not yet been automatized. It also encourages learners to use appropriate grammar forms to communicate certain kinds of meaning. When learners have sufficient time to formulate their message, they demonstrate greater language complexity. The effect on accuracy, however, remains inconclusive.

According to Skehan (1998), the pretask planning phase can have multiple purposes. This stage can introduce new language, assist learners in organizing their ideas, activate existing knowledge, recycle known language, ease the speech processing load, and encourage learners to interpret tasks in more demanding ways. Planning can be guided or unguided. In guided planning, the teacher tells the students what to focus on. In unguided planning, learners decide how best to use the planning time.

Some studies indicate that learners focus more on the content than the language when provided with planning time. Research on pretask planning indicates the following effects on oral performance (Skehan, 1998):

- greater fluency
- improved accuracy in select tasks
- more experimentation in expressing complex ideas
- more complex content as a result of deeper interpretation of task demands
- improved self-monitoring during the task

Task selection criteria. The type of tasks the teacher chooses also has an effect on fluency development. Thornbury (2005) puts forth the following criteria for selecting tasks with the aim of increasing autonomous language use. When selecting a language activity for an oral skills class, the teacher may want to consider how many of these criteria the activity fulfills.

Interactivity. An activity that focuses on building fluency should have an interactive element to it. Discussions, conversations, and role plays are interactive fluency activities, but interactivity can also be made a part of activities that at first glance are non-interactive in nature. For example, if one student is giving a speech, others who are listening should be assigned a task, such as asking questions or providing their own point of view.

Productivity. The activity needs to be productive in terms of the amount of language spoken by the learner. To achieve this, the activity needs to be designed and set up in a way that allows or even requires participants to use a large amount of language to complete it. An activity such as a survey may be done in pairs with little or even no language, or done in the mother tongue, and it is up to the teacher to assure that students are using the target language to complete the tasks. This can be achieved through careful monitoring and encouragement by the teacher or even other students. Ideally, too, each participant should contribute to the successful completion of the task, a key characteristic of Cooperative Learning.

Challenge. In an activity that is focused on fluency, it is important for the learners to be challenged. They should be able to undertake and complete the activity with the knowledge and resources at hand. By drawing on these communicative resources, the learner will feel a sense of achievement and pride. It is up to the teacher to provide just the right amount of challenge. If the activity is too demanding, the results can be disheartening to the student.

Safety. Learners should be challenged, but at the same time they need to feel safe in their undertakings. The learners expect to take some risks, but at the same time they must know that taking such risks, and perhaps failing, is part of the process of learning and will not incur any judgment from the teacher or other learners. The teacher should set up a nurturing classroom environment of trust, respect, and even protection.

Purposefulness. The reason or outcome of an activity should be apparent to the learners. An activity in which they must work together to achieve a common aim can be very effective and motivating, such as the need to agree on the best solution to a problem. Learners appreciate knowing exactly what is expected of them. At the same time, students may be more willing to participate or complete an activity if they know they will be asked to share their ideas with another group or summarize it for the class.

Authenticity. Teachers should strive to choose or develop classroom activities that bear some relation to language use outside the classroom. Real-life language use is unpredictable, and at times learners should be put in positions where they must be spontaneous and rely on what they have at hand. At the same time, what the students discuss and learn should be of relevance to their lives. Role plays are, in effect, classroom simulations of real-life experiences and can provide students with

a learning experience that is meaningful, focused, and relevant to their needs.

Task repetition. As discussed, preplanning tasks can help enhance fluency during a language activity. Another way to enhance fluency is through task repetition. When learners are exposed to the same task and context, they become more familiar with its expectations and performance is improved. One of the reasons that language learners struggle with the skill of speaking is because it is unpredictable. By repeating a task, the expectation becomes more predictable. Just as rehearsals can improve a pianist's performance, task repetition allows the learner to practice and improve, to have a second chance. And with these rehearsals, the cognitive demands are lessened, with some processes such as conceptualizing becoming more automatized.

Nation and Newton (2008) describe the well-researched 4/3/2 technique first devised by Maurice (1983). The technique requires the learners to repeat the same story or talk to three successive listeners spending four minutes for the first telling, three minutes for the second, and two minutes for the third. Nation and Newton attribute the success of this technique to three factors. First, the speaker must process a large amount of language. The speaker talks without interruption and does so three separate times. Second, the speaker plans the talk and chooses its content and language, thereby increasing the level of control over the delivery. This allows fluency to be a primary goal of the activity. And third, the speaker is helped to perform well by repeating the same message three times but with the challenge of an ever-decreasing time limit.

Bygate (2001) discusses a study in which students repeated a task, first immediately upon completing the task and then ten weeks later. The language produced by the students repeating the task after ten weeks was more fluent and complex than the language the students produced when they repeated the task on the same day. Task repetition thus provides "the basis for learners to integrate their fluency, accuracy, and complexity of formulation around what becomes a familiar conceptual base" (Bygate 2001, p. 17). Task repetition, pretask planning, and careful task selection all provide ways for the teacher to assist students in enhancing their speaking skills, thereby increasing their fluency. As noted by P. Nation (2002), a word of caution is in order, however:

The more something is repeated, the less likely it will continue to be seen as a message-focused activity. The teaching methodology solution to this is to balance the ease provided by the repetition against a challenge provided by new but similar material, reducing time, a new audience, and increasing complexity. (p. 270)

We do not want task repetition to backfire. While the 4/3/2 technique can be an effective approach to task repetition, some learners may tire of repeating the same message, even just three times. In addition, in some cases the teacher may not want the exact same message repeated. It is then the teacher's responsibility to assure the repeated task is different enough to engage and motivate the students. Here are some ways to change the task so it is not exactly the same. The first two use two principles of the 4/3/2 technique, but the task is more interactive in nature. The repeating of the task could occur in the next or subsequent class.

- *Reducing time.* The teacher gives pairs one minute to perform a role play about shopping. The teacher then has the pairs repeat the role play, but this time in 45 seconds.
- *A new audience.* Students tell their group about an embarrassing moment, allowing listeners to ask questions. The students then tell the story again to a new group.
- *New but similar material.* A group agrees on a list of rules for the student cafeteria after they agree on a list of classroom rules.
- *Increasing the complexity of the task.* Groups have $50 to spend for a class party that includes the teacher. The students decide how they will spend the money on food, drinks, and entertainment. The teacher then tells the groups they only have $25, and the school director will also be attending.

Feedback and correction. During an activity that is focused more on accuracy than fluency, there are generally two steps that take place. First, the teacher alerts the student to the fact that an error has been made. Second, the teacher moves to the correction stage. In some cases, the teacher may need to help the student correct the error. Harmer (2007b) describes techniques that show students that an error has been made. By showing incorrectness, we generally hope that the students can correct themselves. If they cannot, the teacher has other options, such as peer correction, although this must be handled very delicately so no one student feels like he or she is the only one who does not know something. The following are all ways of alerting a student to an error:

- *Repeating.* The teacher can simply ask for repetition by saying "Once again, please," or "Can you say that again?" If using this technique, the teacher should use intonation or facial expressions that also indicate he or she is asking for repetition due to hearing an error rather than simply not hearing something.
- *Expressions or gestures.* The teacher can change facial expression, such as raising his or her eyebrows, or make a hand gesture to show that an error has been made. The teacher may even choose to demonstrate gestures for specific points, such as wrong word order or missing final –s.
- *Hinting.* The teacher can provide a simple hint using metalanguage. Saying the word *article* or *preposition*, for example, may be enough to get a student to self-correct.
- *Echoing.* The teacher can repeat what a student said, emphasizing the error. Saying "He BUYED a new phone?" with a questioning intonation can be a very efficient way of alerting a student to a precise error.
- *Reformulation.* The teacher can say something correctly without making a big issue of the error. If the learner says, "I'm more tall than my brother," the teacher might say something like "Oh, you're taller than your brother! That's interesting." The teacher may or may not require the student to provide the correction. In any case, reformulation is a gentle and unobtrusive method of error correction that focuses on the form while reacting to the message.

During a fluency activity, it is generally accepted that the teacher should not interrupt students to point out a grammar or vocabulary error, or to correct pronunciation. Doing so stops the communication that is taking place, shifting the focus from meaning to form. There is value when a student has to attempt to get meaning across in different ways, and interference by the teacher, though well-intentioned, may cause stress levels to rise and learning to stop. If a teacher does choose to intervene, when should that be? Lynch (1997) feels "the best answer to the question of when to intervene in learner talk is: as late as possible" (p. 324).

Generally our tolerance of errors will be higher during fluency activities. Many teachers feel that the only appropriate time to focus on error correction is after the activity is completed. After the activity, a few minutes might be set aside to focus, as a class, on the errors the teacher noted during the activity. But there may be times when teachers *do* want to intervene. Many students want and expect correction, even during fluency work. Correction is a delicate area, and much depends on classroom atmosphere, teacher-student rapport, group dynamics, and student preferences. During a fluency activity, the teacher may find it is imperative to intervene, especially if communication is at risk.

Some of Harmer's (2007b) correction techniques that are appropriate for accuracy work are also suited for fluency work, in particular echoing and reformulation. Here, if the teacher is alerting students to errors during an activity, any correction is done gently, tactfully, and selectively. An important difference is that the teacher may well choose not to go on to the second step, that of actually requiring the correct form.

CLASSROOM APPLICATIONS

Fluency activities are often the language activities that we find in the back of textbooks or listed only in teacher's manuals or resource books. This is unfortunate as these activities, because of their placement, often get overlooked. They may be seen as less important or as optional activities that are worth doing but only if there is enough time. The following types of activities are all useful in helping develop fluency.

Information-gap activities

When we communicate with one another, we often need information we do not possess. This happens in the real world when, for example, we ask someone on the street for directions. This situation can be replicated in the classroom using the information-gap technique. "More authentic communication is likely to occur in the classroom if students go beyond the practice of language forms for their own sake and use their linguistic and communicative resources in order to obtain information" (J. C. Richards, 2006a, p. 18). Classroom information-gap activities are those in which a student has information another does not have. There is a knowledge gap between the students, and they must communicate to close the gap. In the process, they negotiate meaning. The following classroom examples all make use of the information-gap technique. For each one, the teacher divides students in A-B pairs. While these examples are pair activities, others can be done in groups.

Complete the missing information. In this information-gap activity, there is missing information that the students must work together to complete. For example, Student A has a map of a neighborhood in a city. Some buildings are already identified, but others are not. Student B has the same map, but the buildings that are already identified are different from those in Student A's map. Student A and Student B sit back to back and take turns describing and/or asking each other questions (e.g., "On your map, what's next to the post office?") to identify the information missing from their maps. In this activity, the two maps are the same, but each has information missing. Vocabulary and the required grammatical structures can be pretaught. Figure 2 shows an example of this type of activity.

Find the differences. In this activity, two students are given pictures that are similar but not the same. The students work together to find the differences. Student A has a picture, for example one of a group of people at a party. Student B has a similar picture, but it contains some differences from Student A's picture. Student A and Student B take turns describing and/or asking questions (e.g., "In my picture, Jeff is wearing a sweater and jeans. What's he wearing in your picture?") to identify the differences. Figure 3 shows an example of this type of activity.

Role play. In this activity, students simulate a real-world task in the classroom. Student A and Student B prepare to perform a role play between a hotel front-desk agent and a tourist. Student A first takes the role of the front-desk agent and looks at a card that lists the room types, room availability,

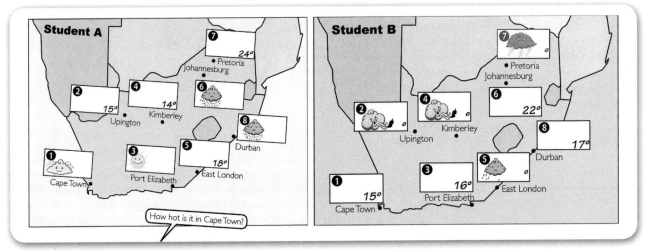

Figure 2. Sample "Complete the Information" activity. Source: *Time Zones,* pp. 55, 122, Heinle Cengage.

room prices, and check-in and checkout times. Student B takes the role of the tourist and looks at a card that lists the type of room desired, the price the tourist is willing to pay, and a request for a late checkout. They then role-play the situation without looking at each other's information. Later, they switch roles using new information. For this particular activity, the role-play cards can be created by the teacher, or to make them more authentic and personalized, Student B can add his or her own preferences and use that information.

While information-gap activities may appear to be accuracy focused, a student needs to draw on available grammar, vocabulary, and communication strategies to complete the activity. This emphasizes fluency. R. Ellis (2010) offers a useful distinction between focused and unfocused tasks. A *focused* task is one that is meant to elicit a certain linguistic structure; an *unfocused* task, on the other hand, is meant to elicit general samples of language use. Unfocused tasks are not designed to elicit a specific linguistic feature, although it is possible to predict a cluster of linguistic features that a learner is likely to need to perform the task. To emphasize fluency, it may be helpful to create or design tasks that are more unfocused than focused.

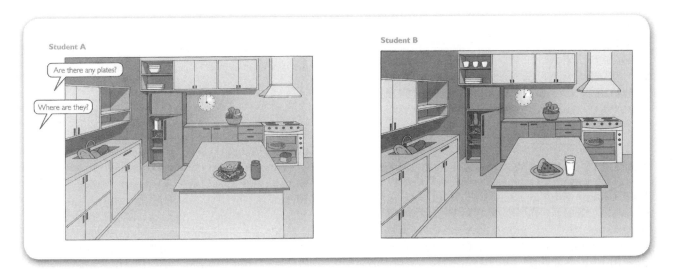

Figure 3. Sample "Find the Differences" activity. Source: *Time Zones,* pp. 65, 119, Heinle Cengage.

Jigsaw activities

These types of activities also use the information-gap principle. Each student in a group is provided with only a part of the information needed to complete an activity. As a group, students share their information to create the whole. Students work together orally until everyone has completed the activity. Success depends on each person contributing to the completion of the activity. Jigsaw activities use strategies of Cooperative Learning, where each student first becomes an "expert" on something before he or she shares or teaches it to others. Because much of the learning is student to student, the teacher's role is very much that of organizer and facilitator. These two classroom examples both use the jigsaw technique.

Jigsaw reading. In a *jigsaw reading*, a story is divided into four equal parts. Then the class is divided into Groups A, B, C, and D. Each group receives one part of the story and works together to understand it. If someone does not understand something, he or she should first try to get help from the group. If this does not work, the teacher helps. In the next step, a student from Group A and a student from Group B form a pair and share their two parts of the story. A student from Group C and a student from Group D do the same. They cannot look at each other's stories but must share the information orally. In the final step, new groups are formed, each group consisting of one student each from Groups A, B, C, and D. Students continue to share their parts of the story orally until everyone understands it and the parts can be placed in the right sequence. During each step, the teacher can provide guiding discussion questions or other tasks. And because this is based on Cooperative Learning, the teacher should be able to call on any student at random to answer a question about the story or even to retell it.

Jigsaw listening. In this activity, three different audio clips containing different perspectives are prepared, for example, one containing an interview with someone who has witnessed an accident, one interviewing someone who has seen a UFO, and one about someone who has been involved in a natural catastrophe. Then the class is divided into three groups: Groups A, B, and C. Each group goes into a different part of the room and listens to its part of the interview. Each group completes a task, such as answering comprehension questions or filling in a chart. Next, new groups are formed, each containing one student each from Groups A, B, and C. The three students in each new group now report what they heard or role-play the person describing the scene. As a group, the students then decide who the most reliable witness is.

Other jigsaw formats. These activities are just two ways to use the jigsaw technique to build fluency. There are variations to the technique, such as a four-part jigsaw listening, a three-part jigsaw reading, or a reading activity where two different groups read similar texts and later pair up to compare and discuss them. And while an activity may be called a jigsaw reading or a jigsaw listening, it is clear that more than one skill is being practiced, especially speaking. This integration of skills is one of the many benefits of this activity. Other benefits include:

- Jigsaw activities provide an efficient way to learn.
- Students are active in the learning process.
- Each individual has a unique contribution to make.
- Students take responsibility for their own learning.
- Learning revolves around student-to-student interaction.
- There is built-in task repetition.
- Students gain fluency with each retelling.
- Students are held accountable by their peers.
- Working together builds interpersonal skills.

Consensus-building activities

In consensus-building activities, participants work together to come to an agreement on something. They may present points of view, argue, listen, consider, weigh options, and compromise. Students involved in a consensus-building activity do not have to share the same ideas or opinions, but they do need to try to agree on a solution. A key indicator of success is that everyone is satisfied with the final outcome. In these activities, how the students get to the outcome (and, of course, the language they use to do so) is more important than the outcome itself. A task can have one answer (a closed task) or more than one answer (an open task). If a task is open, the teacher may want to alert the students that more than one answer is possible. It can be discouraging for students to ask the teacher for "the right answer" only to be told there is more than one acceptable answer.

Problem solving. A problem-solving activity can be as simple as completing a word puzzle. It may require no oral output. The kinds of problem-solving activities that are communicative, discussion-based, group-oriented, and open-ended, and are thus fluency-oriented, are those like the classic "dinner party" activity. Here learners are presented with the names, personalities, and other background information of various people who will be attending a dinner party. The group must work out a seating plan that will assure an interesting and successful dinner party for everyone involved. Since there is no one correct answer, the teacher may wish to specify a time limit. When the group members find an acceptable solution, they present and defend their choices to other groups.

Ranking. A ranking activity is a form of consensus building whereby students rate something according to its relative importance to something else. It involves three steps. First, students work individually to choose from a list the most important characteristics of something, for example, the qualities of a good roommate (see Figure 4). Of the choices given, each person chooses the eight most important. In the second step, each student joins a partner to form a pair. They compare and discuss their ideas,

A good roommate is . . .	You	Pair	Group
Respectful			
Responsible			
Friendly			
Patient			
Quiet			
Hardworking			
Clean			
Reliable			
Honest			
Considerate			
_____ (your idea)			

Figure 4. Sample ranking activity.

agreeing on the six most important qualities. In the third and final step, each pair joins another pair to form a group of four. They then agree on the four most important qualities, ranking them from most important to least important.

Fluency circle

In a fluency circle, the learners practice a dialogue in a fun and active way. The aim of the activity is not to memorize a dialogue but to internalize its structures to help make speaking easier and more fluid. The technique is useful for a variety of objectives, such as practicing a certain grammar point, reviewing vocabulary, previewing a structure inductively, or working on pronunciation, stress, and intonation. The teacher prepares a dialogue that can be personalized and gives a copy to each student. For example:

A: How are things going?

B: Not bad. How about you?

A: Pretty good, thanks. I'm a little sleepy, though.

B: How come? Did you go to bed late?

A: No, but I got up early. I didn't want to be late today.

B: What time did you get up?

A: 6:30.

B: Wow, that *is* early. I got up at 7:45. I got here in plenty of time.

A: How did you get here? Did you drive?

B: No, I took a taxi.

A: Well, that explains it! I took the bus. I had to wait forever!

B: Why don't we share a cab tomorrow?

There are three steps to the activity (see Figure 5).

Step 1. The teacher organizes the students into two circles: an outer one and an inner one. Students in the inner circle face out, and those in the outer circle face in. The teacher then models the dialogue, and the students practice it in pairs. The students in the inner circle take the role of Student A, and those in the outer circle take the role of Student B. The students can read the dialogue as they practice; meanwhile, the teacher monitors the pair work. When the pairs finish the dialogue, they start over, so there is continuous speaking. Next, the teacher signals for the students in the outer circle to rotate one person to the left. The students in the inner circle do not

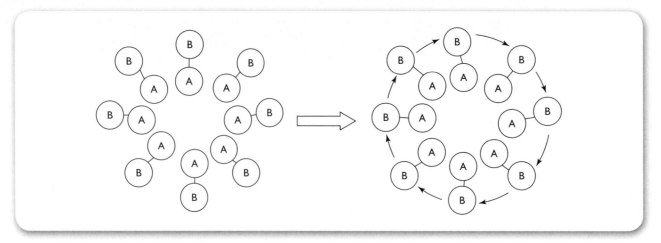

Figure 5. Fluency circle diagram.

move. The pairs then practice the dialogue with a new partner while the teacher monitors the pair work. The teacher continues to signal for the outer-circle students to rotate, so each speaker has multiple partners. To signal, the teacher stands in the middle of the inner circle and holds up a flag or raises his or her arms.

Step 2. After the students have practiced the dialogue with several partners, the teacher stops the activity and gives new instructions. This time, the teacher tells the students to use the "look up and say" technique. The students can refer to the dialogue but should not read it. Instead, they look at their partner when they speak. The teacher continues to signal for the students to rotate.

Step 3. After the students have practiced the dialogue with several more partners, the teacher stops the activity once again and gives new instructions. This time, the teacher tells the students to personalize the dialogue to make it their own. They should not use the dialogue on the paper but have a similar conversation using their own information. Some students will likely stick to the script, but others may choose to open up the dialogue. The goal is for students to have a real, natural conversation.

Using fluency circles. This technique works well for scripted dialogues and role plays, and it is also effective for question-answer exchanges or "quick interviews." For example, in the activity "speed dating," students try to get to know a large number of potential dates in a short period of time by asking and answering personal questions such as "What type of music do you like?" and "How would you describe your personality?"

Board games

Many textbooks and resource books contain question-answer or discussion activities disguised as board games. See Figure 6 for a game that practices questions and answers with *be*. There often is not a real winner in these activities, and they appear competitive but are not. Questions or discussion topics are simply seen in the form of a game to make the activity appear more fun and interesting to the students. Although questions may focus on a certain structure, such as the simple present or present perfect, these games focus on both accuracy and fluency. But, as with any activity, the use of a game must be clear to the teacher as well as to the students. It is important to let the students know why they are doing what they are doing.

Projects

Projects have been used in various educational disciplines for many years, and English language educators have exploited this tradition. In fact, project work is now part of the English language curriculum in many contexts. (See Nunan, this volume.) Projects are an extended assignment that usually lasts longer than a single lesson. There are many possible areas for project work in both ESL and EFL settings. Some examples include creating a class newspaper, designing a health poster, compiling a recipe book, creating a webpage, designing an informational brochure, and creating an advertising campaign.

Favorites

Group work Play the game. Put a small object on *Start*. Toss a coin.

Move 1 space.   Move 2 spaces.

Heads   Tails

Use the correct form of *be* to ask and answer questions. Can you answer the questions? Take turns.

Yes. → Move ahead.   No. ← Move back.

A: *Are you interested in travel?*
B: *Yes, I am. I'm interested in new places.*

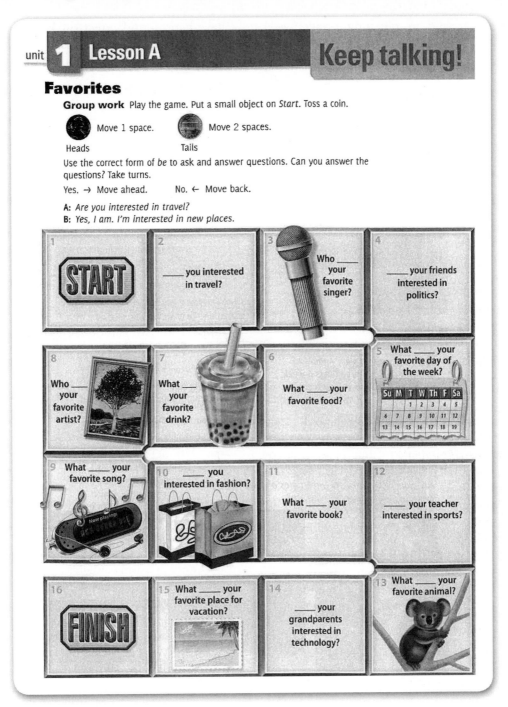

Figure 6. Sample board game (based on Richards & Bohlke, 2012, p. 125).

Hedge (1993) outlines a number of features common to most projects:

- the study and use of authentic English language materials
- an emphasis on student group-centered experiences and deemphasis on teacher-directed work
- a sequence of activities over a period of time, such as planning, fieldwork, preparation of information, and presentation
- the use of a range of skills
- activity outside the classroom on the students' own time

For those interested in pursuing project work, Harmer (2007b) suggests a step-by-step approach that includes deciding on the topic, generating ideas, gathering data, planning, drafting and editing, and unveiling the finished project. See Harmer (2007b) for a more detailed explanation of how to manage project work.

The use of projects has many benefits. Project work involves the integration of language skills and encourages creativity, collaboration, responsibility, discipline, research and information-gathering skills, and, at times, cross-curricular work. In some situations, however, there simply will not be enough time for project work. In addition to there being sufficient time, the success of any project will depend on other factors, such as access to authentic materials and the receptiveness of participants. But if project work is undertaken, it can result in a highly satisfying learning experience. At the end, the students have work they can proudly show as well as a sense of achievement.

FUTURE TRENDS

One area of future study that needs more attention is how the sequencing of fluency, complexity, and accuracy activities works within a larger language activity. What do different combinations of these activities result in? Bygate (2001) points out several possible scenarios that can be researched. One involves starting with an accuracy activity and moving on to fluency, putting learners under increased time pressure in an attempt to achieve more automacity. A second sequence might start with fluency activities and later progress to getting learners to integrate more accurate features into their fluency base. A third sequence could move from accurate and/or fluent speech into more complex language. Is there a best order and placement for these activities in a learning cycle?

Similarly, the notion of task repetition deserves further study. Task repetition provides learners with the chance to do something again, to do it better. While any task can be repeated, what types benefit the most from repetition? It remains unclear when it is the best time to repeat a task. Should a teacher repeat a task immediately, a few days later, or even a few weeks later? It may depend on the task types, the learners, and the results of the first task. This is an area that may

have a profound effect on how course materials are written and how curricula are planned.

CONCLUSION

Fluency is not an absolute value that learners either have or do not have. It is, rather, a matter of degree. All learners can achieve a level or degree of fluency, and the teacher has an opportunity as well as a responsibility to help his or her students develop this important area of communication. The teacher has a wide range of activities and resources to draw from for classroom learning. Some tasks may be focused on accuracy, others on fluency, and others on both. The activities that the teacher chooses for oral work are part of the equation. Also important are the teacher's attitude and demeanor in the classroom and his or her rapport with the students. For many learners, an improvement in fluency comes about more easily when they are relaxed and in an environment that is nurturing and nonjudgmental.

SUMMARY

➤ Fluency involves learners communicating meaning as best they can, using whatever resources are available.

➤ Cognitive, affective, and performance factors all play a major role in determining the degree of fluency a speaker may be capable of.

➤ There are ways that the teacher can foster fluency in learners, such as by providing the necessary language, knowledge, and strategy support.

➤ The types of activities that a teacher chooses will affect fluency development. The criteria for choosing effective tasks types for enhancing fluency development are interactivity, productivity, challenge, safety, purposefulness, and authenticity.

➤ Many fluency-oriented activity types are available for the teacher, such as information-gap tasks, jigsaws, consensus-building tasks, fluency circles, games, and projects.

DISCUSSION QUESTIONS

1. What foreign language have you studied that you feel you are the most proficient in? Do you consider yourself fluent? Why or why not?

2. What should the role of the teacher be while students are engaged in a fluency-oriented language activity?
3. What activity types have you experienced as a student or a teacher that were fluency-oriented? What made them so? Which of the criteria discussed by Thornbury (2005) (interactivity, productivity, challenge, safety, purposefulness, authenticity) might have been involved in choosing activity types?
4. Think of an accuracy-focused classroom activity. What could be done to the activity to make it more fluency-oriented?

SUGGESTED ACTIVITIES

1. Find an activity in a language textbook that you feel is fluency-oriented. Read the teaching instructions in the teacher's manual. Would you follow the teaching steps as described? How might you further enhance the learner's fluency? Rewrite the notes.
2. Choose a language activity you have recently taught or experienced as a learner. Revise it based on one of P. Nation's (2002) criteria: (a) reducing the time; (b) a new audience; (c) new but similar material; or (d) an increase in complexity. Teach it again. List the differences that you noticed in the students' performance.
3. Observe a class of language learners. After class, interview three of the most fluent speakers in the class. Ask them how fluent they feel they are or are not. Investigate what they think they need to do to improve their fluency.
4. Look at the rating systems of two or more exams that assess oral language such as the TOEFL or the International English Language Testing System. Find the similarities and differences among them. Determine what role fluency should play in assessing the speaker. Create a new rating system for assessing speaking. How could you use this as a classroom-based assessment?

FURTHER READING

Baker, J., & Westrup, H. (2003). *Essential speaking skills: A handbook for English language teachers.* London, UK: Continuum.

This handbook provides practical activities to help teachers develop their students' fluency skills and is particularly useful for teachers who teach large classes with limited resources.

Folse, K. (1996). *Discussion starters: Speaking fluency activities for advanced ESL/EFL students.* Ann Arbor, MI: University of Michigan Press.

Folse, K., & Ivone, J. (2002a). *First discussion starters: Speaking fluency activities for lower-level ESL/EFL students.* Ann Arbor, MI: University of Michigan Press.

Folse, K., & Ivone, J. (2002b). *More discussion starters: Activities for building fluency.* Ann Arbor, MI: University of Michigan Press.

In most of the activities of this three-textbook classroom series, students must work together to reach a conclusion about a topic or solve a problem.

Nation, I. S. P., & Newton, J. (2009). *Teaching ESL/EFL listening and speaking.* New York, NY: Routledge.

Grounded in theory made accessible to the reader, this book offers practical suggestions for teaching listening and speaking in both ESL and EFL contexts and contains a discussion on how to develop fluency in the classroom.

Thornbury, S. (2005). *How to teach speaking.* Harlow, UK: Pearson Longman.

This book begins with a description of what happens when someone speaks a foreign language and continues with an extended discussion of how to approach the teaching of speaking. It is a practical, readable guide for teachers who want to improve their understanding of and develop their skills in this area.

10 | Teaching Pronunciation

JANET GOODWIN

KEY QUESTIONS

➤ What does teaching pronunciation involve?
➤ What can teachers learn from research on pronunciation?
➤ What are the most effective techniques for teaching pronunciation?
➤ How can teachers assess pronunciation?

EXPERIENCE

In a questionnaire distributed at the beginning of a pronunciation course, learners were asked to describe their experiences with English pronunciation. Here are excerpts from two responses.

> I feel that I am judged by my way of talking English. In other classes, teachers often treat me as inferior or academic disability because of my muttering English. (Undergraduate student in an ESL pronunciation course)

> Sometime when I speak to native American, I guess because of my Chinese asense or mispronunciate the word, they ask me what did you say, can you repeat, or I beg your pardon. Sometime my face turn red, and become so embarrassed in front of them. I remembered once my tears were in my eyes. (Graduate student in an ESL pronunciation course)

Accent is a filter through which second language (L2) speakers are viewed and frequently discriminated against (Lippi-Green, 1997; Munro, 2003). These two comments reveal the frustrations that our learners feel, the discrimination they experience, and the very human element present in the teaching and learning of pronunciation.

WHAT IS INVOLVED IN TEACHING PRONUNCIATION?

The sound system of English is broadly divided into two categories: consonant and vowel sounds (known as the *segmental* features) and more global aspects such as stress, rhythm, and intonation (known as the *suprasegmental* features, or *prosody*). Traditionally, the sound system has been described and taught in a building-block fashion:

sounds → syllables → phrases → extended discourse

Although this makes sense from an analytical point of view, this is not how our learners experience language. As speakers, we usually do not think about what we are saying sound by sound, or even syllable by syllable, unless communication breaks down. So the bottom-up approach of mastering one sound at a time and eventually stringing sounds together has been replaced by a more top-down approach in which the sound system is addressed as it naturally occurs—in the stream of speech. We start with the big picture of speech by addressing macro features such as stress and intonation; yet, whenever this "picture" becomes unclear, we "zoom in" to examine micro features, such as how a final consonant sound can be linked to the following syllable. This approach acknowledges that suprasegmental and segmental features function as an interdependent system.

Viewing pronunciation in terms of how it serves the listener highlights the role pronunciation plays in spoken interaction. Speakers use pauses and intonation to divide speech into listener-friendly chunks. In each chunk, we draw the listener's attention to the most important word through extra stress and a rise or fall in pitch. Additional meaningful words in the chunk may be stressed, but any words that we think listeners will be able to understand through context or grammar are usually just squeezed into the intervals between stressed syllables. The resulting pattern of stressed and unstressed syllables creates a rhythm that listeners use to comprehend what they hear, predict what will come next, form ongoing hypotheses about the overall meaning, and fill in any gaps in comprehension. And although we think of words as being pronounced with a fixed sequence of consonants and vowels, the dictionary pronunciation may well represent only the stressed (i.e., citation) version of a word. The unstressed form, if even recognizable as an individual word, may sound quite different in the stream of speech. Let us now take a more detailed look at these basic features of English pronunciation.

Thought groups

Just as writers use punctuation to help readers decode text, speakers use pauses to divide speech into meaningful chunks, called *thought groups* (also referred to as *tone groups* or *intonation units*). Since thought groups usually represent a meaningful grammatical unit, the utterance that follows could be divided up like this:

> *I was speaking to him / on the phone yesterday.*

but not like this:

> *I was speaking to / him on the / phone yesterday.*

Thought group boundaries can vary; in casual conversation, speakers tend to pause less and have longer thought groups. Alternatively, a speaker might have a clear communicative purpose for pausing after each word, for example, a frustrated parent talking to a recalcitrant child:

> *Come / here / right / now!*

This variability can lead to misconceptions about fluency and intelligibility. Some learners believe if they talk rapidly without pausing they will sound fluent; others are convinced that pronouncing each word separately and distinctly is the key to intelligibility.

How can we help learners un[...] apply the concepts of pausing and th[...] appropriately? Ambiguous phrase[...] way to illustrate how pausing af[...] Consider the following phrase: *w[...] man is nothing.* One set of pauses produces [...]

> *Woman / without her man / is nothing*

But if we move one of the pauses slightly, we have:

> *Woman / without her / man is nothing*

Once learners understand the concept and importance of pauses, they can be asked to identify logical breaks in the spoken texts that are used for oral practice. Learning to package our speech in meaningful chunks is an essential part of intelligibility.

Prominence

Within each thought group, there is generally one element that stands out from the rest, the *prominent* word or syllable. Other common terms for this element include *sentence focus, tonic syllable,* and *nuclear stress.* Speakers use prominence to:

- signal new information: *Did you hear that John moved to ChiCAgo?*
- highlight contrasting information: *I don't think he MOVED to Chicago; I think he's just VISiting there.*
- show emphasis: *No, he DID move there—he's already bought a HOUSE!*

Notice how prominence can shift depending on context:

- *What are you doing? I'm READing.* (focus on the action)
- *Who's reading? I'M reading.* (focus on the agent)
- *Why aren't you reading? I AM reading!* (contradict a mistaken assumption)

A study by Hahn (2004) showed that prominence plays a significant role in intelligibility. Because it depends so heavily on context, prominence needs to be taught through longer stretches of discourse, not through short isolated sentences.

Intonation

Prominence is accompanied by a rise or fall in pitch, creating a melodic line, or what we call

...ution. Learner textbooks use various conventions to represent this feature, such as:

Arrows: *She flew to PARis.* ↗↘

Contours: *She flew to PARis.* ⌐

Intonation patterns have traditionally been associated with particular grammatical forms. Research has shown, however, that grammar is not a reliable key to intonation (Levis, 1999). Note how the prominence and intonation vary in the next examples, not due to the grammatical structure—both are the same *wh*-question—but, rather, due to the speaker's communicative intent:

Request for information:

When are you LEAVing?

Clarifying a mishearing or misunderstanding; double-checking:

WHEN are you leaving?

    Although intonation patterns do vary somewhat among varieties of English, certain general patterns prevail. By offering learners continued exposure to authentic speech, we help them to develop an awareness of the contextual meaning of intonational choices. For more on how speakers use intonation in discourse, see Celce-Murcia, Brinton, and Goodwin (2010) and Chun (2002).

    One challenge for L2 speakers is their lack of pitch variation, resulting in flat-sounding intonation (O. Kang, 2010; Wennerstrom, 1994). Having learners perform a gesture while speaking—such as rising on their toes for a rise in pitch and bending at the knee for a fall in pitch—can help them to imitate these same patterns in their speech. Another promising resource for helping learners modify their intonation is speech analysis software. These tools allow the user to see pitch contours on a computer screen and then try to match them (Levis & Pickering, 2004).

Rhythm

The rhythm of English is created by the alternation of longer (stressed) syllables and shorter (unstressed) syllables, similar to meter in poetry. Content words (e.g., nouns, main verbs, adverbs, and adjectives) are typically stressed, while function words (e.g., determiners, pronouns, and prepositions) generally are not:

● ●   ●   ● ●   ● ● ●   ● ● ●

She atTENDS the uniVERsity of MARyland.
(13 syllables but only 3 are stressed)

A point of clarification should be made here. Rhythm, also called *sentence stress*, refers to *all* the syllables that receive stress in a thought group, while prominence (previously discussed) refers to *one* of those stressed elements (the one that receives the most emphasis):

● ●   ●   ● ●   ● ● ●   ● ● ●

*She atTENDS the uniVERsity of **MAR**yland.*
(of the three stressed syllables, the third is prominent)

English speech rhythm is usually referred to as *stress-timed;* that is, stresses or beats occur at semiregular intervals. This contrasts with what are often called *syllable-timed* languages, such as Spanish and Korean, in which each syllable receives roughly the same timing and length. In reality, natural English speech is not perfectly stress-timed, and the "one syllable, one beat" explanation for syllable-timed languages is an oversimplification too. Nonetheless, the highlighting of certain syllables over others through length, vowel quality, and pitch is an important clue for the listener. Learners can practice rhythm patterns while clapping, tapping, or stretching a rubber band on stressed syllables. Shadowing tasks, in which learners recite while listening to a spoken model, also promote rhythmic awareness and fluency.

Word stress

Similar to rhythm in phrases, each multisyllabic word in English exhibits a pattern of stressed and unstressed syllables, known as *word stress* (also called *syllable stress* or *lexical stress*). One syllable in the word receives the primary, or strongest, stress; other syllables receive either secondary or very weak stress. Common ways of depicting word stress are:

●	●	●	●	(bubbles)
e	*co*	*nom*	*ic*	
e	co	NOM	ic	(upper and lower case letters, small capitals)
è	*co*	*́nom*	*ic*	(superscript and subscript accent marks preceding the stressed syllable)

To make stressed syllables stand out for the listener, speakers make them longer, louder, and/or higher in pitch. Vowel quality is also key—stressed syllables contain a full, clear vowel, but unstressed syllables usually have a reduced, or weakened, vowel. Notice the difference in vowel quality between the stressed and unstressed syllables in two related words: (1) *PHOtoGRAPH*, in which only the syllables *pho* (which sounds like *foe)* and *graph* are spoken with a clear vowel; and (2) *phoTOGrapher*, in which only the stressed syllable *tog* has a full, clear vowel. The vowels in the remaining unstressed syllables of both words are reduced.

Research has shown that correct word stress is crucial for intelligibility (Field, 2005). Specifically, we need to help learners make stressed syllables stand out unambiguously from the syllables surrounding them and to pronounce the sounds in those stressed syllables accurately (Zielinski, 2008). Moreover, learning vocabulary involves more than knowing the definition, usage, and spelling of a word—learners also need oral repetition practice to acquire its stress pattern.

How can learners determine which syllables are stressed? Stress patterns in English depend on several factors, including the historical origin of a word, the part of speech, and affixation. In very general terms:

- Stress falls more often on the root and less often on a prefix or suffix:

   beLIEVE, TEACHer, unHELPful

- Compound nouns tend to take primary stress on the first element and secondary stress on the second:

   AIRPLANE, BUS STOP, comPUter SCREEN

- Suffixes may:

   - have no effect on the stress pattern

      BEAUty → *BEAUtiful*

      deLIVer → *deLIVerance*

      perFORM → *perFORMer*

   - take the primary stress themselves (many of these are from French):

      trusTEE, enginEER, balLOON

   - cause the primary stress in the stem to shift to a different syllable:

PERiod → *periODic*

ORganize → *organiZAtion*

ACtive → *acTIVity*

A more detailed explanation of English word stress can be found in Celce-Murcia et al. (2010) and Teschner and Whitley (2004).

Connected speech

In rapid English speech, a variety of modifications can occur, causing the boundaries between words to seem blurred:

- Syllables can be linked together by a sound:

   an egg (sounds like *annegg*)

- A final consonant may shift to the next syllable:

   She logged off. (sounds like *log-doff*)

- Two sounds may blend together, creating a new sound:

   Can't you make it? (sounds like *can-chu*)

- Sounds may disappear:

   I love her a lot. (sounds like *lover*)

- Unstressed function words are reduced in multiple ways:

   That must have been fun. (sounds like *must-of* or *musta*)

These modifications help speakers to squeeze unstressed syllables into the space between stressed syllables, an important feature of English rhythm. Although these shortcuts ease communication for the speaker, words that non-native listeners comprehend easily in isolation can become unrecognizable in connected speech.[1] Learners' repeating longer stretches of connected speech at a natural speed will help them improve their rhythm in spoken English as well as their listening comprehension.

Consonants

Consonant sounds are characterized by *place of articulation* (where the sound is made), *manner of*

Manner of Articulation	Place of Articulation						
	Bilabial	Labiodental	Dental	Alveolar	Palatal	Velar	Glottal
Stop voiceless voiced	/p/ /b/			/t/ /d/		/k/ /g/	
Fricative voiceless voiced		/f/ /v/	/θ/ /ð/	/s/ /z/	/ʃ/ /ʒ/		/h/
Affricate voiceless voiced					/tʃ/ /dʒ/		
Nasal voiced	/m/					/ŋ/	
Liquid voiced				/l/ (/r/)	/r/	/ɬ/	
Glide voiceless voiced	(/hw/) /w/				/y/		

Figure 1. Sample chart of North American English consonants (adapted from *Teaching Pronunciation: A Course Book and Reference Course*, 2nd ed., by M. Celce-Murcia, D. M. Brinton, & J. M. Goodwin, 2010, p. 61).

articulation (how the sound is made), and *voicing* (whether the vocal cords are vibrating or not). For classroom teaching purposes, these three dimensions are commonly summarized in a consonant chart (see Figure 1).

To further assist learners, the articulatory organs are usually illustrated in a diagram such as the one in Figure 2.

Because English does not have a strict sound-to-spelling correspondence, symbols are used to represent sounds, usually a modified version of the International Phonetic Alphabet (IPA), as shown in Figure 3.

Most consonant symbols are easy to learn because the letter used in common spellings is the same as the phonetic symbol. However, for certain consonant sounds (*this, thumb, shop, decision, butcher, pageant, long*), a single letter that represents the sound is not available in English, so we use the following IPA symbols:

this /ð/, *thumb* /θ/, *shop* /ʃ/, *decision* /ʒ/, *butcher* /tʃ/, *pageant* / ʤ /, *long* /ŋ/

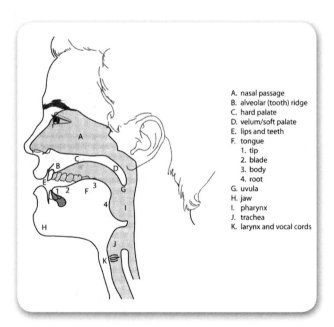

A. nasal passage
B. alveolar (tooth) ridge
C. hard palate
D. velum/soft palate
E. lips and teeth
F. tongue
  1. tip
  2. blade
  3. body
  4. root
G. uvula
H. jaw
I. pharynx
J. trachea
K. larynx and vocal cords

Figure 2. The articulatory organs (adapted from *Teaching Pronunciation: A Course Book and Reference Course*, 2nd ed., by M. Celce-Murcia, D. M. Brinton, & J. M. Goodwin, 2010, p. 57).

Sound	Examples		Sound	Examples
I. The consonants of North American English				
1. /b/	boy, cab		13. /ʒ/	leisure, beige
2. /p/	pie, lip		14. /ʃ/	shy, dish
3. /d/	dog, bed		15. /h/	his, ahead
4. /t/	toe, cat		16. /tʃ/	cheek, watch
5. /g/	go, beg		17. /dʒ/	joy, budge
6. /k/	cat, back		18. /m/	me, seem
7. /v/	view, love		19. /n/	no, sun
8. /f/	fill, life		20. /ŋ/	sing(er), bang
9. /ð/	the, bathe		21. /l/	long, full
10. /θ/	thin, bath		22. /r/	run, car
11. /z/	zoo, goes		23. /w/	win, away
12. /s/	see, bus		24. /hw/	which, what
			25. /y/	you, soya
II. The stressed vowels of North American English				
1. /iy/	pea, feet		8. /ow/	pole, toe
2. /ɪ/	pin, fit		9. /ʊ/	put, foot
3. /ey/	pain, fate		10. /uw/	pool, stew
4. /ɛ/	pen, fed		11. /ay/	pine, fight
5. /æ/	pan, fad		12. /aw/	pound, foul
6. /ɑ/	pot, doll		13. /ɔy/	poise, foil
7. /ɔ/	bought, talk		14. /ʌ/	pun, cut
			15. /ɜʳ/	bird, third
III. The unstressed vowels of North American English				
1. /ə/	focus, allow		4. /ɪ/	music, coping
2. /əʳ/	father, bitter		5. /o/	hotel, narrow
3. /i/	city, prefer		6. /u/	into, igloo
IV. Other frequently used symbols and diacritical markings				
[ʔ]	glottal stop			_uh-_oh
[Cʰ]	aspirated consonant			time, pick, kitchen
[ɫ]	velarized or dark /l/			ball, told, coal
[ɾ]	flap allophone			little, butter, put on
[V:, C]	lengthening			pa, bid, June night
[C˚]	unreleased consonant			but, cap, back
[C̩]	syllabic consonant			kitten, riddle, battle

Figure 3. Modified phonetic alphabet (adapted from *Teaching Pronunciation: A Course Book and Reference Course,* 2nd ed., by M. Celce-Murcia, D. M. Brinton, & J. M. Goodwin, 2010, inside cover).

Although the IPA uses the symbol /j/ to represent the initial sound in *young* or *unity,* many modified IPA alphabets for teaching English simply use the symbol /y/, which reflects the most common spelling.

Together, the three tools presented in Figures 1, 2, and 3 assist teachers in helping learners understand how to produce the consonants of

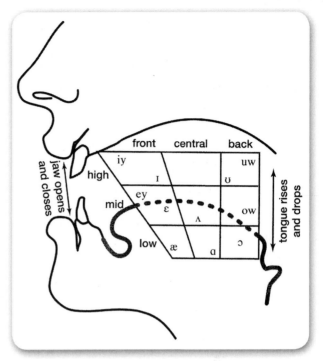

Figure 4. Example vowel chart for North American English (adapted from *Teaching Pronunciation: A Course Book and Reference Course,* 2nd ed., by M. Celce-Murcia, D. M. Brinton, & J. M. Goodwin, 2010, p. 116).

English; Figures 2 and 3 also apply to our understanding and teaching of vowels.

Vowels

Vowels are distinguished by tongue position (front/central/back), tongue and jaw height (high/mid/low), degree of lip rounding/spreading, and the relative tension of the muscles involved (tense/lax vowels). For English language learners, this information is typically conveyed in a vowel chart that situates the vowels within the oral cavity, as in Figure 4.

Learners who are used to a strict sound-to-spelling correspondence in their L1 will often be misled by the spelling of English vowel sounds (note that the words *turn, bird, worm, heard,* and *were* all contain the same vowel sound, /ɜʳ/). Since the phonetic symbols used to represent vowels can vary widely among dictionaries and ESL textbooks, Morley (1979) recommends associating each vowel symbol with a key word (see Figure 5).

1	2	3	4	5		6	7	8		9	10	11	12		13	14	15
/iy/	/ɪ/	/ey/	/ɛ/	/æ/		/ɜʳ/	/ʌ/	/ɑ/		/uw/	/ʊ/	/ow/	/ɔ/		/ay/	/aw/	/ɔy/

FRONT VOWELS   CENTRAL VOWELS   BACK VOWELS   DIPHTHONGS

Figure 5. Morley's (1979) key word associations for vowel symbols, p. 116.

Students repeat the two-word phrases chorally until they can remember them. A number can also be attached to each key word (as shown in the example) instead of using phonetic symbols. It is easier to refer to the *it* vowel or the #2 vowel than to the /ɪ/ vowel, since many listeners will not be able to distinguish /iy/ and /ɪ/ when hearing either sound in isolation. Common color words can also be used to represent many vowel sounds, for example, *green* for /iy/, *red* for /ɛ/, and *purple* for /ɜʳ/.

A learner-friendly resource showing how consonants and vowels are articulated can be found at the University of Iowa's *Phonetics: Sounds of American English* website.[2] However, learning to pronounce sounds accurately in isolation is not enough; learners need practice producing sounds *in context* using authentic materials. Only then does it become clear how crucial a sound or distinction is to intelligibility.

CONCEPTUAL UNDERPINNINGS

As Derwing and Munro (2005) emphasize in their review of the literature, L2 pronunciation teaching has suffered from a lack of empirical research as well as from the insufficient application of research findings to classroom practice. Although additional studies are needed, a number of key questions that pertain to pronunciation teaching have been addressed.

Is it true that only children can learn to pronounce an L2 without an accent?

This has long been an issue of debate among L2 researchers. Some linguists suggest that there is a critical or sensitive period after which the learner cannot achieve a native-like accent (Long, 1990),

while other linguists point out cases of adult L2 learners who have managed to do so (e.g., Scovel, 2000).[3] Evidence does suggest that the younger one begins learning an L2, the better one's accent will be. However, this may be due less to biological constraints than differences in the learning situation. One crucial factor is motivation (Moyer, 2004; Piller, 2002). What these findings mean for teachers is that, although a target-like accent may be possible for certain highly motivated adult learners, a more realistic goal is intelligibility in the real contexts in which learners need to speak.

How is pronunciation influenced by a learner's L1?

The fact that we can often identify a speaker as having a particular accent, such as French, Vietnamese, or Farsi, reveals the influence of the learners' L1 on their pronunciation in the L2. What is also true—but less evident—is that the L1 also influences perception skills. So, for example, because the distinction between /r/ and /l/ does not exist in Japanese, a Japanese learner of English usually has difficulty perceiving the difference as well as producing it.

A *contrastive analysis*, a study of the differences between two languages, can be a useful guide for teachers regarding the difficulties that a speaker of a particular L1 might have understanding and pronouncing English. For contrastive information regarding several language groups, see Swan and Smith (2001). For an overview of research on *phonological transfer* (how L1 pronunciation patterns can influence or interfere with L2 speech), see Major (2008).

How is accent related to identity?

Accent, in our first or second language, is tied to our perception of ourselves. It can indicate our ethnic affiliation (Gatbonton, Trofimovich, & Magid, 2005) or a sense of belonging to a particular reference group. In the dynamics of a language classroom, it may not be "cool" to try to sound like the target model or it may even make some learners feel disloyal to their ethnic group.

In an interesting study of advanced L2 users who reported being able to pass for native speakers (Piller, 2002), one subject revealed that she always makes it clear early on that she is not a native speaker: "'If I don't,' she says, 'some reference to something every German knows will come up, and I won't understand, and they'll think I'm stupid'" (p. 195). This example illustrates a rarely discussed negative consequence of acquiring a native-like L2 accent—the expectation of a native-like understanding of the culture as well.

Not all learners fear a loss of identity when using their L2, and many do express a desire for native-like pronunciation (Scales, Wennerstrom, Richard, & Wu, 2006). Nonetheless, studies exploring the relationship between accent and identity reveal the complex social and psychological variables involved in teaching pronunciation. If we are sensitive to both ends of the continuum—the downside for some learners of sounding too native-like versus the embarrassment of being misunderstood—we are better able to support learners in the goals that they set for themselves.

What does it mean to be intelligible?

Munro and Derwing (1995) examined three different dimensions of spoken production: accentedness, comprehensibility, and intelligibility. The participants (native listeners) in Munro and Derwing's study sometimes rated a non-native speech sample as heavily accented (accentedness) but were able to transcribe it perfectly (intelligibility) and judged it easy to understand (comprehensibility). If the goal of pronunciation instruction is successful communication, then it is essential to understand that being *intelligible* is not synonymous with being *accent-free.*

After reviewing research on international intelligibility, Smith and Nelson (1985) draw the following conclusions: (1) intelligibility does not reside solely in the speaker or the listener but, rather, in the interaction between the two; and

(2) if listeners expect to understand a speaker, they are more likely to find the speaker intelligible (p. 333).

The second point touches on the role of listener bias as it relates to intelligibility. In a landmark study by D. Rubin (1992), subjects who thought they were listening to an Asian-looking lecturer rated a speech sample as more heavily accented; they also performed less well on a post-listening comprehension test than did subjects who thought they were listening to a Caucasian-looking lecturer. Yet both sets of listeners had heard the exact same recording, that of a native speaker of American English.

These studies reveal that intelligibility cannot simply be equated with accentedness and that it can vary according to audience, context, and expectations. As A. Brown (1991b) observes, "a speaker may be more intelligible or less intelligible to a listener, depending on who the particular listener is, rather than on the clarity of the speech itself" (p. 45).

Do all sounds carry an equal load in communication?

One way of setting priorities in the teaching of segmentals is *functional load*, how many words a sound contrast in a language distinguishes (A. Brown, 1991a; Catford, 1987). For example, the contrast /d, z/ (as in *road* versus *rose*) distinguishes a large number of words and thus carries a high functional load. A study by Munro and Derwing (2006) found that high-functional-load errors affected accentedness and comprehensibility of L2 speech more than low-functional-load errors (p. 529). These findings should discourage teachers from spending too much time on low-functional-load items like the two *th* sounds in *thigh* /θ/ and *thy* /ð/.

What role does gesture play in pronunciation?

Condon (1982) talks about *self-synchrony,* how speakers move in rhythm with their own speech, and *interactional synchrony,* how listeners tend to coordinate their movements in rhythm with the speaker. As pronunciation teachers, we understand that speakers use vowel length and pitch to indicate stressed or prominent syllables. However, speakers also use hand gestures, head nods, and eyebrow movements to indicate stress. Researchers have found that, when speakers were asked to make a gesture while saying a particular word in a longer phrase, they articulated that word with more emphasis (Krahmer & Swerts, 2007). In the same experiment, when listeners saw a speaker make a gesture while articulating a word, they perceived that word as more prominent than when they did not see the gesture. Cognitive research is finding that the listener's brain is more active when viewing speech accompanied by prosodically linked gestures than speech without gestures (Hubbard, Wilson, Callan, & Dapretto, 2009). These findings support teaching learners how a well-placed gesture can make a prominent syllable more salient to the listener.

Which aspects of L2 speech contribute most to a lack of intelligibility?

Numerous studies have revealed the importance of suprasegmental features in intelligible speech (Derwing, Munro, & Wiebe, 1998; O. Kang, 2010). However, segmental issues can affect intelligibility as well (Zielinski, 2006). Specific features shown to cause a lack of intelligibility include:

- misplaced or missing prominence (Hahn, 2004)
- incorrect word stress (Field, 2005)
- insufficient differentiation in syllable duration between stressed and unstressed syllables, thereby creating an unnatural speech rhythm (Setter, 2006)
- lack of clearly articulated consonants, both in final position (Zielinski, 2006) and in stressed syllables (Zielinski, 2008)
- speaking too slowly and/or too fast (O. Kang, 2010; Munro & Derwing, 2001)
- too many pauses and/or pauses that are too long (O. Kang, 2010)
- too little variation in pitch (O. Kang, 2010)

Derwing, Munro, and Wiebe (1998) recommend that teachers focus primarily on suprasegmental training, which was shown to improve spontaneous spoken production, but include segmental training, which may increase a learner's ability to self-correct in the case of a misunderstood word or phrase.

Does instruction lead to pronunciation improvement?

Although further research is needed, several studies have shown that pronunciation instruction can be effective (Couper, 2003, 2006), specifically:

Computer-assisted instruction. Several studies showed positive results with computer-based training, much of which was self-directed (Hardison, 2004; Tanner & Landon, 2009).

Listening instruction. Perception work has led not only to better listening comprehension but also to improved pronunciation (Bradlow, Pisoni, Akahane-Yamada, & Tokhura, 1997; Trofimovich, Lightbown, Halter, & Song, 2009).

Contextualized instruction. Subjects in one study received no direct instruction on sounds at all—only prosodic training—yet their pronunciation of sounds improved, showing a benefit to learning segmental features in context (Hardison, 2004). In another study, learners who received intonation instruction that was contextualized through the use of drama, video, and mirroring techniques reported a deeper knowledge of real-world pronunciation, an increased awareness of body language, and a greater awareness of their own pronunciation (Goodwin, 2005).

Form-focused instruction. Several studies have found evidence supporting an explicit focus on form in pronunciation instruction, both drawing learners' attention to L2 pronunciation features and helping learners to notice the gap between their own production and that of a competent user. J. K. Park (2000) compared the effect of three different types of instruction on word stress accuracy: (1) form-focused; (2) meaning-focused; and (3) both form-and meaning-focused. Although both groups receiving form-focused instruction showed improvement, the group receiving both form- and meaning-focused instruction demonstrated significant improvement. A study by Saito and Lyster (2011) has found that form-focused instruction needed to be accompanied by corrective feedback to be effective.

In sum, pronunciation instruction has been shown to be effective, particularly if it is contextualized, addresses both form and meaning, includes feedback, contains a strong listening component, and makes effective use of technology.

CLASSROOM APPLICATIONS

Teaching pronunciation in a principled way involves several key steps: setting realistic goals; having an overall plan for instruction; incorporating a variety of techniques, tools, and technology; and assessing learners' proficiency and progress.

Setting realistic goals

Morley (1999) outlines four important goals for pronunciation instruction: functional intelligibility, functional communicability, increased self-confidence, and speech monitoring abilities.

For our purposes, *intelligibility* is defined as spoken English in which an accent, if present, is not distracting to the listener. Our goal is not to "fix a broken accent" but, rather, to promote intelligibility between speakers in a particular context. Since no one accent is dominant in every context, neither teachers nor learners need to sound like idealized native speakers.

Communicability is the learners' ability to understand and be understood in the situations they engage in. Notice how the following aspects of verbal communication (Dalton & Seidlhofer, 1994) intersect with pronunciation:

- *Prominence:* how to make salient the important points we make
- *Topic management:* how to signal and recognize where one topic ends and another begins
- *Information status:* how to mark what we assume to be shared knowledge as opposed to something new
- *Turn-taking:* when to speak, and when to be silent, how (not) to yield the floor to somebody else (p. 52)

If we teach learners to recognize and employ pauses, pitch movement, and stress to achieve these communicative goals, they will increase their functional communicability.

As learners gain communicative skill, they also need confidence in their ability to speak and be understood. By designing practice materials around the situations learners face, we help them rehearse for the real world. Ideally, materials spring from authentic recordings of the target situations, such as a friendly conversation, a job interview, or a marketing presentation—whatever is appropriate and useful. Addressing learners' specific needs is the key to building their confidence.

Finally, by teaching learners to pay attention to their own speech as well as that of others, they will make better use of the input they receive. Good learners attend to certain aspects of the speech they hear. Speech-monitoring activities help to focus learners' attention on such features both in the instructional context and beyond it.

Planning instruction

Celce-Murcia et al. (2010) present a communicative framework for planning pronunciation instruction in five stages: description and analysis, listening discrimination, controlled practice, guided practice, and communicative practice.[4] This framework does not presuppose that pronunciation is a stand-alone subject; on the contrary, pronunciation can and should be integrated not only with speaking instruction but also with listening, grammar, vocabulary, and spelling (for more on integrating pronunciation with other skills, see Celce-Murcia et al., 2010; Levis & Grant, 2003).

Description and analysis. Initially, the teacher presents a feature showing when and how it occurs, perhaps with the use of charts or diagrams. For instance, the teacher can either present the rule first or provide multiple examples and ask the learners to figure out the rule themselves.

Listening discrimination. Pronunciation-focused listening activities involve both discrimination and identification. Common discrimination exercises make use of contextualized minimal pairs, such as in this example from Gilbert (2012); the speaker secretly chooses which sentence to pronounce (a or b), and the listener responds with the appropriate rejoinder.

a. *Is it light?*　　*No, it's heavy.*

b. *Is it right?*　　*No, it's wrong.* (p. 147)

In another discrimination exercise, learners pay attention to the difference between two intonation patterns for tag questions: falling if the speaker is fairly sure the statement is true and rising if the speaker is less sure.

In identification exercises, learners often work with a transcript of the listening passage and are asked to mark occurrences of a particular

	Sure ↘	Unsure ↗
Your name's Bob, isn't it?		
You live far from here, don't you?		

feature as they hear it, such as pauses between thought groups or linking between vowels. In general, the listeners' task should be clearly defined and limited. At this stage, we want to focus learners' attention directly on a feature that they might not be recognizing yet.

The three final stages, which involve practice and production, progress on a continuum. The important point here is not to define an exercise as strictly controlled, guided, or communicative but, rather, to sequence our oral production activities so that they move forward systematically.

Controlled practice. At this stage, the learner's attention should be focused almost completely on form. Any kind of spoken text can be used for choral repetition or reading-aloud practice. If possible, choose speech that reflects learners' needs and interests. For some learners, a transcript of a phone conversation between friends would be valuable; for others, a sample job interview would be beneficial. During controlled practice, it is helpful to have learners make a gesture on stressed syllables and to highlight problematic segmental features.

Guided practice. In guided activities, the learner's attention is no longer entirely on form. The learner now begins to focus on meaning, grammar, and communicative intent as well as on pronunciation. Bridging activities help learners to shift their attention gradually to a new cognitive task while attempting to maintain control of the pronunciation target. For example, learners might be asked to interview a partner and report on the interview while focusing on –s endings and linking: *My partner, Raoul, likes to play soccer and watch movies on the weekend.*

Communicative practice. In this stage, activities strike a balance between form and meaning. Examples include role plays, debates, interviews, simulations, and drama scenes. As the activities become more communicative, the learners' attention should still be focused on one or two features at a time. It is overwhelming to suddenly monitor all pronunciation features at once. Set an objective and let students know it in advance, for example: "When performing this role play, pay special attention to linking between words." Feedback should then be focused on the stated objective.

Techniques, tools, and technology

Traditional classroom techniques for teaching pronunciation include imitation ("Repeat after me"), articulatory explanations ("Touch your tongue to the roof of your mouth"), minimal pair exercises (*ship* versus *sheep*), and reading-aloud activities. More recent techniques include the use of kinesthetic reinforcement and drama. In addition, many of the gadgets, games, songs, and other items that are part of every language teacher's toolbox have been adapted for teaching pronunciation. Last but not least, technology continues to enhance pronunciation instruction through access to models, opportunity for practice, and feedback for the learner.

Kinesthetic reinforcement

Not every learner will be able simply to hear a sound or phrase and imitate it. Learners can be made aware of the physical sensation associated with producing a sound (e.g., "Feel how your throat vibrates when you pronounce /zzzzz/ but not /sssss/"). In imitation of what English speakers do nonverbally, we can have learners nod, raise their eyebrows, or move their entire bodies in time with the stress and intonation patterns of what they are saying, thereby helping them rehearse an essential component of authentic speech.

As a way of helping learners internalize rhythm patterns, L. Grant (2009) suggests having learners stand up and take a step in synchrony with each stressed syllable in a phrase while repeating it. Steps are taken at regular, natural intervals regardless of the number of syllables between beats, for example:

> *WHAT did you THINK of the MOVie?*
> (step 1)   (step 2)   (step 3)

Teachers can also employ gestures to represent a specific pronunciation feature and then make use of it later as a silent correction technique:

■   *Word stress.* Hold up the number of fingers corresponding to the number of syllables in a word and point to the finger that corresponds to the stressed syllable.

- *Word stress or rhythm.* Open your palm for stressed syllables, and close it for unstressed ones.
- *Linking.* Make a circle with the thumb and forefinger of each hand. Join the circles together like links in a chain.
- *Intonation.* Hold the hand flat with palm down making a sweeping upward movement for rising pitch and a downward movement for falling.
- *Articulatory position.* Use one hand cupped, palm down, to represent the roof of the mouth and the other underneath it to show the position of the tongue. This is particularly useful for consonant contrasts where articulators touch for one sound but not for the other (e.g., the tongue touches the ridge behind the upper front teeth for initial /l/ but not /r/).

Drama and imitation techniques

Drama and imitation techniques provide discourse-level practice with stress, rhythm, intonation, and connected speech. Imitation techniques include shadowing, where learners speak along with or slightly after a speaker model, and mirroring, in which learners not only repeat the lines but also imitate the body movements, gestures, and facial expressions of the speaker (Hardison & Sonchaeng, 2005).

Drama is an effective tool for pronunciation teaching because various components of communicative competence (discourse intonation, pragmatic awareness, and nonverbal communication) can be practiced in an integrated way. Goodwin (2005) uses short drama scenes on video as the focus of study over several class periods.[5] Initially, learners listen intensively to each line several times and mark pauses, prominence, intonation, and noticeable gestures on a script of the scene. While looking at the marked-up script, the class recites the scene chorally multiple times. Learners then rehearse in pairs while the teacher moves around the room providing individual feedback. If the scene is available on the web, learners can do additional rehearsal outside class. In a subsequent class, pairs perform the scene. Ideally, the performances are video-recorded so that learners can review them outside of class and complete a self-evaluation guide. The teacher is then able to evaluate learners both in terms of their pronunciation improvement and their self-awareness.

Tools for teaching pronunciation

Pronunciation practitioners make use of a variety of objects to enhance student learning. An inexpensive pocket mirror can be used to check whether lip position and mouth movements match a visual model. Gilbert (1994), a strong proponent of pronunciation teaching aids, popularized the use of thick rubber bands and kazoos.[6] The learners stretch the rubber band when pronouncing a stressed syllable and relax it on each unstressed syllable. When the learners hum a line of dialogue or speak it through a kazoo, intonation patterns can become more salient because the pitch is clear but the words are obscured (Gilbert, 1994). Aspiration can be made visible by learners' holding a facial tissue or strip of paper in front of their mouth (in English, this extra puff of air accompanies /p, t, k/ at the beginning of words or stressed syllables; the first *p* in *paper* is aspirated and the second is not).

Cartoons and comic strips contain dialogue that illustrates how pronunciation features are a part of everyday speech. Comics often include examples of reduced speech such as *gonna, wanna,* and *hafta.* Prominence is usually indicated by capital letters, boldface font, or both.

Songs exhibit an engaging form of rhythm, linking, stress, or sound patterns. Songs that have clear lyrics, a catchy tune, and multiple occurrences of the targeted feature work best for pronunciation practice (for examples of pronunciation exercises using songs, see S. Miller, 2006).

Games provide both a sense of fun and competitiveness in the classroom. Pronunciation bingo can be used for practicing sound contrasts, substituting minimal-pair words for numbers. One board can be cut into individual word squares in advance and shuffled into a stack. The "bingo-master" (either the teacher or, later, a learner) picks up one word at a time from the stack and reads it. Listeners mark the word they hear on their board. If the boards are identical (see Figure 6 for an example), all students should get bingo (a row across, down, or diagonally) at the same time.

In conventional dominoes, players match tiles with the same number of dots. Hancock (1995) has created pronunciation versions, in which players match either rhythm patterns or

bed	sad	mess	mat	lend
tan	dead	pest	met	fed
said	past	FREE	dad	bad
ten	mass	men	man	bland
blend	land	fad	Brad	bread

Figure 6. Sample bingo board for /ɛ/ vs. /æ/ contrast.

vowels. For example, *How do you do?* could be placed next to *Where did he go?* or *weigh* could be placed next to *great*.

Nursery rhymes, limericks, and poems often have strong patterns of stressed and unstressed syllables that help learners hear (and to a certain extent feel) the rhythm of English. One well-known use of rhythmic chants is Carolyn Graham's *Jazz Chant* series (e.g., *Small Talk* [1986]). These short easy-to-learn chants have a strong beat and engage adults as well as children.

Knock-knock jokes can be used to illustrate and practice linking and reduced speech:

A: Knock Knock.
B: Who's there?
A: Jamaica.
B: Jamaica who?
A: *Jamaica* mistake? (= *Did you make a* mistake?)

In this case, the joke is based on the similarity of pronunciation between *Jamaica* the place and a fast speech rendition of *did you make a*.

Technology

Instructional technology, consisting of audio, video, software, and Internet resources, provides valuable support to the pronunciation classroom. Although technology does not replace a teacher, it can clearly enhance instruction.

Audio. Audio-recordings, essential tools in teaching pronunciation, allow learners to: (1) listen to multiple pronunciation models; (2) monitor their own speech; (3) receive individual feedback; and (4) control the pace, amount, and type of practice. Learners can periodically record a homework exercise, a short free speech exercise, or something individualized that relates to their personal communicative needs. Teachers can better manage response time by limiting feedback to a few features and clarifying in advance what these features are. Ideally, teachers should note errors on a checklist, transcript, or written text of an exercise and then record their feedback so learners can review it as often as they wish. A learner's self-review can also function as a basis for targeting feedback.

If learners have access to pronunciation tutoring, encourage them to record the session. Tutoring can be very effective, but without a recording of the advice and corrections, it will be difficult for learners to continue working with the feedback on their own.

Video. Video-recordings for teaching pronunciation are available through DVDs, video podcasts, speech analysis displays, and video-sharing websites such as YouTube. Commercial video programs offer complete pronunciation courses designed for learners as well as teacher resource videos that demonstrate teaching and tutoring techniques. The wide availability of inexpensive pocket camcorders allows teachers to record a video and upload it easily to a website. Student presentations or role plays can be captured on video, creating a powerful tool for self, peer, and instructor feedback.

Pronunciation software. Many pronunciation software programs function much like a traditional language lab. The student records his or her voice and then presses a button to play it back, but the student is still using his or her own perception to hear the difference between the production and the model utterance.

Other programs provide some type of visual feedback, but it can hard for students to interpret. Most teachers who use computerized visual feedback stress that it is not necessarily useful in and of itself—the learner must be trained to make effective use of it. The weakest aspect of most pronunciation software is its inability to let users know what they did wrong and how to improve (Levis, 2007). As instructional technology continues to advance, the capability to view a visual representation of intonation, whether a target utterance or one's own attempt to imitate it, promises to be a valuable tool. Godwin-Jones (2009) gives a detailed overview of speech tools and technologies.

Internet. The Internet provides access to sound, video, and sophisticated graphics. Virtual multimedia labs can be created through online courses or supplementary course websites using course management systems. (See Sokolik, this volume.) As a complement to face-to-face instruction, a supplementary course website can become a repository for resources and information tailored to a specific group of learners and a place where they can receive individualized peer and instructor feedback.

The number of free websites targeting pronunciation is increasing rapidly. Learners can see how sounds are produced, watch video pronunciation lessons, practice distinguishing sounds, hear the pronunciation of words in online dictionaries, and practice imitating real speakers.

Assessing pronunciation

In this section, three types of pronunciation assessment are discussed: diagnostic evaluation (how we discover what learners' needs are), ongoing feedback (how we guide them toward improvement), and classroom achievement testing (how we determine the progress they have made).

Diagnostic evaluation. At the beginning of a course, teachers often have learners record a diagnostic passage, which is usually designed to contain a variety of features and sounds that might not occur naturally in a short speech sample. Teachers may also elicit a free speech sample, prompted by a topic, a series of questions, or an illustration to describe. The first task, reading aloud, allows a singular focus on pronunciation, but the words and/or phrasing may be awkward for a given learner. In the second, more authentic task, the words are chosen by the learners, but their attention is divided among pronunciation, word choice, and grammar.

Ongoing feedback. Feedback during instruction gives learners a sense of their progress and indicates where they need to focus their attention for improvement. With a growing awareness of progress, learners also gain confidence in their pronunciation.

Awareness raising and self-monitoring. One way to guide learners to self-correct is to point out their errors silently (rather than simply pronouncing it correctly for them). Correction can be cued through:

Gestures. As mentioned earlier, hand gestures can represent different aspects of pronunciation (e.g., number of syllables, linking, or rising or falling intonation).

Pronunciation correction signs. Signs can be placed around the room, displaying the features that have been taught. Once learners understand what is meant by each sign, it becomes shorthand for error correction. One sign might read *–ed*, which cues the learners to think about past tense endings in their speech (which they might have either omitted or pronounced incorrectly). Other signs might read:

| –s | intonation | linking | stress |

Charts. If a vowel chart has been introduced and a large version of it is hanging in the classroom, teachers can use it to guide learners toward raising or lowering their jaw, gliding, or spreading or rounding their lips to better approximate a particular vowel.

Another way to encourage self-monitoring is to record student speech, in either audio or video format. Learners can monitor their own performance by filling out a self-monitoring guide. This is particularly effective if the learners' first task is to transcribe their speech (not with phonetic symbols, just with regular orthography). Working with their transcript while listening to their recording, learners can monitor for a specific feature, such as linking or word stress. For more on self-monitoring in pronunciation instruction, see Ingels (2010).

Peer feedback. During a traditional minimal-pair activity, rather than working only in pairs (one speaker and one listener), learners can be placed in groups of four. In this scenario, the first speaker reads one of the two minimal-pair options (e.g., *Don't slip/sleep on the floor*) and the three other group members each tell the speaker what they heard. If this is done as a pair activity, only one listener gives the feedback, so it is less reliable and convincing to the speaker since that listener might have difficulty hearing that particular distinction.

If a role play between two learners is recorded, they can transcribe it together and also fill out the analysis form together. In this case, it is good to pair students together who do not necessarily share the same pronunciation difficulties. Learning from someone who is only a little further along than you can be an effective alternative to instructor feedback alone.

Teacher feedback. During class, the teacher can use gestures or pronunciation correction signs to provide feedback silently. Out-of-class feedback can be provided through an exchange of recordings.

Which errors should we correct? Rather than overwhelming the student, teachers should focus on errors that:

- cause a breakdown in communication
- occur as a repeated pattern, not as isolated mistakes
- relate to the pronunciation points being taught

The last point should not be viewed as the least important; it is related to the first two in an integral way. It is the *errors* that learners make that guide us toward what to teach.

Classroom achievement tests. Classroom achievement tests evaluate learners' progress according to what has been taught, and they are consequently more focused than diagnostic assessment. The testing tasks should resemble the classroom teaching tasks to reduce the effect of an unfamiliar format on learners' performance.

Any oral performance to be evaluated for a grade should be recorded, if possible. This not only makes the teacher's evaluation of it easier but also allows the learner to review and revise the recording before turning it in. In fact, since one of our goals is to help learners monitor their own speech, this step is crucial. Although our ultimate goal is intelligibility during spontaneous speech, for assessment purposes it is also valuable to know whether learners can control their pronunciation during a communicative task when they are monitoring for specific features. The ability to determine what might have gone wrong in their pronunciation allows learners to recover from a communication breakdown in real life. In other words, when they notice someone's puzzled look or blank stare, they can mentally run through what they just said and, in all likelihood, reformulate the same utterance more intelligibly.

FUTURE TRENDS

What does the future hold for the teaching of pronunciation? First, more attention needs to be paid to pronunciation in teacher preparation programs—either as a part of teaching oral skills or as a stand-alone phonetics/phonology course. Second, the field needs additional research related to pronunciation learning and teaching, particularly in the areas of: (1) intelligibility, which is clearly a complex issue; (2) effective classroom practices; and (3) addressing the needs of learners in diverse contexts. Third, advances in pronunciation software need to focus on helping learners figure out what is wrong with their speech and how to improve. In sum, the important trends ideally include an increased focus on teacher preparation, additional research that is useful and accessible to teachers, and software that provides better feedback to users.

CONCLUSION

Effective pronunciation teaching is measured by what the learners are able to achieve: the ability to understand and be understood in the communicative situations they face, the confidence to enter these communicative situations with ease, and the ability to monitor their speech to make adjustments and improvements based on input from the environment. If we consider the frustration expressed by the learners quoted at the beginning of this chapter, we now have tools to respond to their pronunciation needs in a systematic and principled way.

SUMMARY

➤ Pronunciation consists of both segmental and suprasegmental features that function as interdependent systems.

- ➤ Research related to pronunciation offers insights into what intelligibility is and the complex factors that influence it.
- ➤ The goal for pronunciation improvement is successful communication in a particular context, not a perfect nativelike accent.
- ➤ Effective pronunciation teaching involves a systematic progression of tasks that include a focus on form, targeted feedback, lots of context, a strong listening component, and the use of technology with a clear pedagogical rationale.
- ➤ Diagnostic assessment, ongoing feedback, and classroom achievement tests are essential components of teaching pronunciation.

DISCUSSION QUESTIONS

1. Think about a foreign language you have learned. How good is your accent? In what ways have your age, your L1, or your feelings of identity contributed to how well you pronounce this language?
2. Who is better equipped to teach pronunciation: a non-native who speaks the L1 of his or her learners or a native English teacher who does not? What factors might influence your answer?
3. Which aspect of pronunciation is the hardest to teach? Why?
4. Which types of technology do you think are most effective for teaching pronunciation? What advances do you envision for the future?
5. Do you think that learners pronounce an L2 better when taking on the role of a character in a drama scene? What are the advantages and disadvantages of using drama, role play, and imitation?

SUGGESTED ACTIVITIES

1. Consult a reference containing contrastive analyses such as Swan and Smith (2001), and summarize the information for a language that you know well (other than English). What pronunciation errors in English does this reference predict for learners of that language background? How does this compare with your knowledge of the two sound systems?

2. Choose one pronunciation teaching point (e.g., word stress in compound nouns, /l/ vs. /r/, one rhythm pattern). Develop one or two activities for each of the five stages of the communicative framework discussed on pp. 147–148) to teach this point.
3. Interview a non-native speaker of English who has a good accent. How did this person achieve this level of pronunciation?
4. Examine a textbook for teaching pronunciation, and evaluate it in terms of:
   a. Layout: Is it user-friendly? Are the diagrams, charts, and explanations clear?
   b. Use of phonetic symbols
   c. Focus: Does it cover segmentals, suprasegmentals, or both?
   d. Exercises: Is there a logical progression from controlled to communicative? Are the instructions clear? Is the language authentic?

FURTHER READING

Celce-Murcia, M., Brinton, D., & Goodwin, J. (with Griner, B). (2010). *Teaching pronunciation: A coursebook and reference guide* (2nd ed.). New York, NY: Cambridge University Press.

This textbook, which provides a detailed description of the sound system of North American English and numerous teaching techniques, also addresses curriculum, assessment, technology, phonological research and the intersection of pronunciation with other language areas. It includes two audio CDs with authentic samples of native and non-native speaker speech.

Hancock, M. (1995). *Pronunciation games.* Cambridge, UK: Cambridge University Press.

This photocopiable resource book contains ready-to-use activities and teacher instructions. The focus is on British English, but many games are not accent-specific or are easily modified.

Hewings, M. (2004). *Pronunciation practice activities: A resource book for teaching English pronunciation.* Cambridge, UK: Cambridge University Press.

This resource text includes a wide variety of pronunciation activities and a CD with listening support material.

Kelly, G. (2000). *How to teach pronunciation.* Essex, UK: Pearson Education.

This practice-oriented handbook, which has a predominantly British English focus, summarizes the basic features of pronunciation and includes a variety of teaching techniques as well as an audio CD.

Swan, M., & Smith, B. (Eds.). (2001). *Learner English: A teacher's guide to interference and other problems* (2nd ed.). Cambridge, UK: Cambridge University Press.

This volume provides a description of typical learner errors in English for speakers of 22 different languages. It covers grammar as well as pronunciation and includes an audio CD with examples of the various accents.

ENDNOTES

[1] For examples of how the pronunciation of a word can vary in connected speech, go to Cauldwell's Speechinaction website, http://www.speechinaction.org/

[2] This resource is available at http://www.uiowa.edu/~acadtech /phonetics/english/frameset.html

[3] For an overview of the research regarding age and the critical period hypothesis, see Marinova-Todd, Marshall, and Snow (2000).

[4] These stages are not necessarily meant to occur in one 50-minute lesson. They simply represent a pedagogical sequence that could take place over several lessons.

[5] Many short one- to three-minute scenes are available at a free language learning website EnglishCentral http://www.englishcentral.com/ videos#!/index

[6] A kazoo is a toy musical instrument consisting of a short hollow pipe (often made of plastic) with a small hole on top covered by wax paper. Humming into one end of the kazoo creates a buzzing sound. If one speaks into it, rather than hums, the buzzing effect distorts the individual words and makes the intonation or pitch of the speech more noticeable.

Language Skills

Reading

11 | Teaching Second/Foreign Language Literacy to School-Age Learners

ANNE M. EDIGER

KEY QUESTIONS

➤ In what ways is developing literacy in a second language similar to or different from developing literacy in one's first language?

➤ Which aspects of language and literacy should teachers focus on when teaching children English?

➤ What kinds of teaching practices grow out of what we know about literacy development for English language learners?

EXPERIENCE

Ms. Lee picked up a book she had already read to her third-grade intermediate English as a Second Language (ESL) class several times and said, "Today we're going to read *The Paper Bag Princess* (Munsch, 1980) again. This time though, afterwards, I want you to tell me in your own words what happened in the story, so listen carefully." The last time they had read it, they had talked about princes and princesses, castles, forests, and even caves. They had seen pictures of a dragon with fiery breath and also discussed that many fairy tales illustrate a moral. They had already read several other fairy tales, too, as part of a collection of stories they were reading.

When she finished reading, Ms. Lee turned to her class and asked, "So, who can tell me what happened first?" "The dragon burn up Elizabeth's house!" said Leyla. "The dragon took Ronald," said Osvaldo. "OK, let's write both of those down," said Ms. Lee, as she wrote on the poster paper the exact words the children had said. The class continued working together to describe the events, and Ms. Lee wrote them down as each child recounted what had happened. When they finished the story, together the whole class read each sentence as she

pointed to each word. Some of the children stumbled over a few of the words, but after reading each sentence several times, most of them were able to say the whole sentence.

That evening, Ms. Lee typed up the story and made two copies for each child. One copy had the whole story on one page; the other had each sentence on a separate line, which she cut up into strips. She put the sets of strips into an envelope for each child—their task tomorrow would be to order the strips to re-create the story. She took a couple of the envelopes and cut those sentence strips up further into individual words—these would be special challenges for those students who were already reading well.

The next day, Ms. Lee handed out the papers with the entire story to the class, and they read through it all together. She then asked the class to turn the story over on their desks, and she handed out the envelopes containing the story strips. "In your envelope you will find your story of *The Paper Bag Princess* cut into strips. Now I would like each of you to work with a partner to see if you can put the strips in order so that they tell your story." Ms. Lee walked around the room, helping each pair of students put the story together.

When they all finished, they read the story together again. "Now, I would like each of you to take your complete story and draw a circle around all of the words that begin with a *P*." When they all finished doing this (with a little bit of help from Ms. Lee), she asked, "What words did you find that begin with this sound?" The children came up with words like *prince*, *princess*, *paper*, and *pretty*, and Ms. Lee wrote these words down on the board and the class read the list again.

WHAT IS SECOND LANGUAGE LITERACY FOR YOUNG ENGLISH LANGUAGE LEARNERS?

The notion of literacy has undergone profound changes in recent years, particularly in response to recent technological developments. For many years, *literacy* has referred not only to reading and writing skills but also to a host of other related skills: the oral language skills used to talk about and support reading and writing development; critical thinking for real-life and academic purposes; critical reading, that is, understanding how reading and writing are used for political purposes and views of literacy as a phenomenon that is closely connected to power, social identity, and ideologies (Gee, 1996); and visual literacy, the judgments and skills involved in interpreting and producing visual content and text for a wide variety of contexts and social uses. Reading and writing are clearly critical skills for life needed for understanding road signs, communicating via email, filling out official documents, evaluating statements on a sample ballot, understanding instructions on how to use a new piece of equipment, thinking critically about advertisements we see, finding information about our favorite music, or just for enjoyment.

More recently, along with developments in technological media, the "new literacy" now includes such skills and functions as the ability to find, identify, evaluate, use, and communicate using a wide variety of resources, including text, visual, audio, and video (Leu et al., 2007). Online and other technology-based uses of reading and writing are leading researchers to identify new features and to view literacy as increasingly collaborative, distributed, and participatory (Lankshear & Knobel, 2006); as blurring the notions of authorship in such co-constructed online contexts as blogs and wikis (Bloch, 2007); and, as asking readers/writers to use the Internet and other media to "identify important questions, locate information, critically evaluate the usefulness of that information, synthesize information to answer those questions, and then communicate the answers to others" (Leu, Kinzer, Coiro, & Cammack, 2004, p. 1570).

So, if we are concerned with the development of reading and writing skills by English language learners (ELLs) in kindergarten through grade 8 (K–8), along with the oral skills that support this development, as viewed within the context of ESL and English as a foreign language (EFL), what do teachers need to focus on? In K–8 learning contexts, teachers and schools face different challenges in teaching literacy to young ELLs who are often learning literacy skills for the first time, as opposed to teaching literacy to older children who are more likely to be transitioning to a second language (L2) from their first language (L1) and possibly L1 literacy abilities, as might be the case for middle school, high school, or adult ELLs. In this context, not only do young ELLs need to learn to navigate the literacy demands of their first languages but also that of their second, along with the uses of language across a growing range of technological media.

Today, given the expectations that ELLs must keep pace (or sometimes, catch up) with their native English-speaking (NES) peers in all areas of the curriculum, many K–8 classroom teachers are expected to take the approach of teaching students to read and write in content and language integrated learning environments (also called content-based instruction [CBI]). CBI is a popular learning approach that is increasingly common in both ESL and EFL contexts for K–8 learners around the world, and it includes both learning to read/write and reading/writing to learn. (For more information on CBI, see Snow, this volume; for more information on teaching young learners, see Shin, this volume.) Thus, when we speak about literacy instruction for school-age ELLs, it is helpful to think of it in terms of the need to develop language and literacy skills while simultaneously learning content in social studies, math, science, and English language arts.

Thus, for the purposes of this chapter, we view literacy as the necessary oral, written, and visual skills involved in using text (whether in print or on a screen) for purposes of creating and interpreting meaning (including messages) for various purposes.

CONCEPTUAL UNDERPINNINGS: THE RESEARCH BASE FOR SECOND LANGUAGE LITERACY

Over the years, research has shown us that when people read or write, they bring a whole host of skills together into a seamless process for making and creating meaning through text. In the past 10–20 years, research focusing on understanding how ELLs learn to read and write has grown considerably (for reviews of this literature, see California Department of Education, 2010; Genesee, Lindholm-Leary, Saunders, & Christian, 2006; August & Shanahan, 2006), although some areas, including the development of second or foreign language writing by ELLs, have been relatively less explored (see Manchon, 2009, for recent work on L2 writing in EFL contexts). Only in the last few years have researchers begun to look in depth at ELLs beyond the early grades or at students with limited or interrupted formal education and L1 literacy instruction (see DeCapua, Smathers, & Tang, 2009). Fundamentally, we know that children need instruction to learn to read and write, whether informally at home or more formally in school; it does not just come automatically from being exposed to the language. But what can we say about that process?

Several key theories, based on beliefs about the L1-L2 relationship in literacy and language development, have greatly influenced the research on literacy for young ELLs. Cummins's (1981, 1984, 2000) notion, originally developed as part of his developmental interdependence hypothesis, is that learning to read and write in one's L2 involves developing academic language, as distinguished from informal, oral, everyday communication. In informal oral language, speakers can make use of shared background knowledge, as well as elements in their surrounding physical context to make meanings clear and can get immediate feedback about what they do or do not understand. Then, further clarification can be made if necessary. In academic language, on the other hand, a different type of language is involved; according to Cummins, this language is more "cognitively demanding" and "context reduced."

For example, if two people are discussing a song they are listening to, they share the common experience of hearing it, they can watch each other's faces, hear each other's tones of voice, and use a variety of gestures to indicate what they mean. All these factors decrease the amount of specificity they need to communicate through the actual choice of words and the language structures they use. In reading and writing, however, the ability to give that immediate feedback and the use of nonverbal communication, not to mention the ability to make assumptions about shared background knowledge and experience, are no longer possible. Instead, the reader and the writer have to put all their meaning into the specific words and language forms that they choose to convey their meaning. They can no longer look to see if the other person understands or if the person needs additional information. The demanding requirement of academic language proficiency is "the ability to make complex meanings explicit . . . by means of language itself rather than by means of contextual support or paralinguistic cues" (Cummins, 2000, pp. 68–69).

Cummins proposes that academic language is related to a "common underlying proficiency," a set of skills and knowledge that, if learned in one's L1, can also be used in the development of skills in one's L2. When children begin school in an L2, it is this academic language that they need to develop, both for engaging in discussions and for the critical analysis of complex ideas and, especially, for learning to read and write critically, the means through which they will encounter many of the new concepts they learn in school.

In recent years, there has been considerable discussion of what exactly academic language involves (for further discussion of this concept, see A. Bailey, 2007; Lyster, 2007; Rolstad, 2005; Scarcella, 2003; Schleppegrell, 2004) and how it differs from informal oral social language; nevertheless, researchers generally agree about its importance in the development of language and literacy for schooling (see Snow & Katz, 2010, for suggestions on designing instruction for developing academic language for young children). Although there are various definitions, Chamot and O'Malley (1994) define *academic language* as "the language that is used by teachers and students for the purpose of acquiring new knowledge and skills . . . imparting new information, describing abstract ideas, and developing students' conceptual understanding" (p. 40). However, A. Bailey (2007) cautions us:

against believing that there is something inherent in social language that makes it less sophisticated or less cognitively demanding than language used in an academic context. . . . [T]hus, it is perhaps most accurate to speak of [it] . . . as differences in the relative frequency of complex grammatical structures, specialized vocabulary, and uncommon language functions. In some regard, it is not meaningful to conceive of *language* as either social or academic, rather it is the *situation* that is either predominantly social or academic. (p. 9)

In recent years, the demand has increased for evidence-based instruction of literacy skills. In 2001, the National Literacy Panel on Language-Minority Children and Youth, composed of expert researchers, was convened to conduct a comprehensive, evidence-based review of the research literature on the development of literacy in L2 learners, ages 3 to 18. The panel produced a report evaluating and synthesizing this research literature to guide educational practice, inform educational policy, and help establish an agenda for future research. During nearly the same period, a group of researchers associated with the Center for Research on Education, Diversity, and Excellence conducted a similar study. The findings of these groups, although they used somewhat different standards and methods, are remarkably similar in many ways (for reviews of these results, see August & Shanahan, 2006, 2010; Genesee et al., 2006; Goldenberg, 2008; Saunders & Goldenberg, 2010). These studies suggest a number of implications for K–8 literacy instruction.

L2 literacy is similar to L1 literacy in certain basic ways; thus, ELLs' L1 literacy background is helpful for developing L2 literacy. Studies investigating the development of both word-level (word reading and spelling) and text-level (reading comprehension and writing) skills have found that "although some L2 learners may progress at slower rates than native speakers, their growth in literacy generally follows similar developmental paths" (August & Shanahan, 2010, p. 211). Researchers generally agree that many of the same skills used to read and write in one's L1 are also involved in one's L2. Children who already know how to read and write in their L1 can use it in a variety of ways to learn to read and write English more quickly and easily than children who do not have that knowledge (August & Shanahan, 2006, 2010; Riches & Genesee, 2006). Reese, Garnier, Gallimore, and Goldenberg (2000) reinforce this point:

[E]arly literacy experiences support subsequent literacy development, regardless of language, and time spent on literacy activities in the native language whether it takes place at home or in school is not time lost with respect to English reading acquisition. . . . (p. 633)

Being taught to read and write in their L1 serves as a significant asset for children developing L2 literacy (Schecter & Bayley, 2002), and children are able to maneuver within two languages without becoming confused. In fact, Schecter and Bayley have found that the L2 children they studied surpassed their monolingual peers because they had the resources of literacy in two languages.

When learning to read and write in a second or foreign language, children are able to build on whatever knowledge they have about their L1—both their language, in general, and literacy skills, in particular (Samway, 2006). They use what they know about the sound system to figure out how to sound out and spell words in the L2; how letters or symbols in the printed text represent words, ideas, and meanings; and how different genres of text use language in specific ways and present information using different systems of organization and for different purposes. Children find it easier to write in genres of text they have been exposed to previously, a good argument for introducing them to a variety of reading genres—they can then reflect and build on this when they write.

Also, like L1 literacy, reading and writing are easier when one knows something about the topic and reads or writes from experience or knowledge of that topic. In the language experience approach (LEA) (Dixon & Nessel, 1983) lesson described in the Experience, Ms. Lee did exactly that by providing her students with multiple exposures and a chance to develop extensive content knowledge of the fairy-tale genre by reading a variety of different fairy tales. If teachers are aware of this L1-L2 relationship, they can use it in various ways to help the ELLs in their classes.

Like their NES peers, ELLs' literacy development benefits from explicit teaching of multiple components of literacy in deliberate and balanced ways. Similar to findings for NES children learning to read in English, research tells us that ELLs benefit from instruction in the essential literacy component skills of phonemic awareness, decoding and encoding, vocabulary, fluency, comprehension strategies (including "ways of thinking during reading"), and writing (August & Shanahan, 2010).

We have long known that reading and writing involve the use of lower-order (or bottom-up) skills related to understanding sound-letter relationships, word recognition and understanding, spelling, and an awareness of grammar and sentence structure. They also require higher-order (top-down) skills, including bringing world knowledge and knowledge of the various ways we use texts in society to the understanding, analysis, or creation of a text, as well as using strategies in reading and writing to help learners understand, monitor, or perform these skills more effectively. The skills involved in reading and writing efficiently are not used one at a time; rather, they involve the integration of multiple skills, and the more one is able to perform them quickly and almost without thinking (called automaticity), the stronger they will be. While the lower-order skills are critical foundational skills for other skills, a focus on meaning and comprehension is important for learners at every level and cannot be set aside (Gersten et al., 2007):

> In monitoring student progress in phonological processing, phonics, and reading fluency, instruction in the development of comprehension and higher order thinking skills may be overlooked. But these skills should not be neglected. Instruction in comprehension and higher order skills should receive attention in the earliest phases of reading development. The challenge for schools will be to maintain a strong instructional focus on both higher and lower order skills. (p. 14)

Writing, too, has multiple components and is not a simple linear process (see Figure 1); in fact, it includes multiple subprocesses (I. S. P. Nation, 2009). We know that good writers plan, revise, and edit at various points in the process. In the composing stage, writers often are still planning and reworking their original ideas, and they may do this again and again later in the process. These various stages in the writing process can also occur in varying orders, and writers often come back to previous steps in a recursive process. Thus, teachers who know this can be careful not to oversimplify writing, present steps in a linear fashion, or provide only a single opportunity to perform parts of the process in a lock-step order.

L2 literacy also differs from L1 literacy development in important ways. At the same time, developing L2 literacy is not the same as developing it in one's L1. Although a good starting point may involve using some of the instructional approaches that work for NESs, using exactly the same techniques with L2 learners is not the most effective approach. Some of the ways in which ELLs differ in their development of literacy skills from NESs include:

- ELLs bring different background and world knowledge to literacy processes; NES children, while they too are broadening their background knowledge and are learning to apply it to the literacy process, typically share more of the background knowledge needed for comprehending material they read.
- When NES children first begin learning to read and write, they already have substantial oral language ability and vocabularies of several thousand words in that language (I. S. P. Nation, 2009). Beginning-level ESL readers and writers, in contrast, do not have those same oral skills or vocabulary knowledge in English and are often developing literacy skills at the same time as they are developing basic oral language and vocabulary.
- ELLs are able to able to match their NES peers in developing decoding skills, but significant gaps still exist in their achievement of higher-level reading skills, including comprehension, making inferences, and writing (August & Shanahan, 2010; Gersten et al., 2007).
- One advantage that ELLs have is that they also bring their L1 literacy skills to L2 literacy development (and in some cases are older when they begin) and may be able to transfer some literacy knowledge from their L1 to the L2.

Because ELLs come from many language and learning backgrounds that differ from those of NES children, a child's L2 literacy needs depend on his or her prior experiences and

Subprocesses	Examples
Having/considering a goal or purpose for writing	To learn, convey, or signal something; to inform; to convince or persuade; to entertain; to maintain contact; to store or document or remember information
Considering the type of writing	A note; formal letter; summary or paraphrase; narrative; description; exposition, analysis, definition, classification, or argument; literary text; advertisement; journal or personal writing
Considering who the readers are, and what they know about the topic	Are they encountering these ideas for the first time? Or are they experts in the field?
Gathering ideas and information	By brainstorming, researching, making lists
Organizing ideas	By constructing a web, outlining
Composing/putting ideas down	By free-writing, gathering ideas in a journal
Reviewing what one has written	By obtaining self-, teacher, or peer feedback; by using checklists
Revising what one has written	By rewriting parts that one has gotten feedback on, by restating something using different words, by adding examples or explaining in more vivid detail
Editing what one has written	By using a checklist, a chart of grammar or vocabulary that is updated with areas the learner needs to work on
Publishing or sharing what has been written	By making books that students have written, posting on the Internet, sharing with or sending to another person

Figure 1. Subprocesses of writing, with examples.

stage of literacy development. Teachers who are aware of this know the importance of conducting formative assessments of ELLs on phonological processing (segmenting the phonemes in a word, sound blending, and rhyming), alphabetic or letter knowledge (measures of speed and accuracy in letter naming and phonological recoding), word and text reading and writing (measures of single-word reading and phonics rules for younger children, and measures of reading and writing connected text and reading/writing fluency for higher grades) to determine which areas they need further work in (Gersten et al., 2007).

ELLs need early, constant, and deep instruction in vocabulary. Research also tells us that one of the areas ELLs need a lot of instruction in throughout their schooling is vocabulary development (August, Carlo, Lively, McLaughlin, & Snow, 2006):

Knowing a word means knowing many things about a word—its literal meaning, its various connotations, the sorts of syntactic constructions into which it enters, the morphological options it offers, and a rich array of semantic associates, such as synonyms and antonyms. (p. 97)

ELLs benefit from daily explicit instruction in vocabulary, which should also be emphasized in all areas of the curriculum in addition to reading and writing, including math, science, and social studies. Optimal instruction goes further than just teaching ELLs to learn definitions of words; they need to be able to explain meanings in their own words, as well as to use the new words when talking about their reading and writing. Research tells us that readers need 8–12 encounters with a word to remember or be able to use it. Furthermore, word knowledge is critical for reading and writing. For ELLs to truly comprehend what they read, they need to understand close to 98% of the words in what they read (I. S. P. Nation, 2009). ELLs have enormous challenges—to catch up with their peers by the time they graduate from high school, they need to know at least 50,000 words (M. F. Graves, 2006). The importance of vocabulary learning for ELLs cannot be overemphasized.

In addition to high-quality literacy instruction, ELLs also benefit from simultaneous development of their oral language proficiency—and of academic language in particular. The oral language knowledge of ELLs plays a major role in their development of literacy. The level of ELLs' oral language is not necessarily a good indicator of their literacy skills—an ELL may be able to communicate fluently in oral English without being able to read and write well. Nevertheless, ELLs' English reading comprehension and writing skills are closely related to having well-developed oral proficiency in English—their broader language abilities serve to support their ongoing literacy development. Thus, it is vital that ELLs continue to develop their oral language together with their reading and writing. While the development of literacy skills does not need to wait for oral language to develop (Cloud, Genesee, & Hamayan, 2009), the underlying basis of literacy lies in children's broader overall language competence and abilities to use it communicatively for both social and academic purposes. In fact, "oral English proficiency and the skills that allow accurate and effortless recognition of printed words are essential factors in comprehension development" (August & Shanahan, 2010, p. 215).

However, it is not just any language that ELLs need to develop—what is critical for their development is academic language (Gersten et al., 2007):

> In reading, knowledge of academic English helps students gain perspective on what they read, understand relationships, and follow logical lines of thought. In writing, knowledge of academic English helps students develop topic sentences, provide smooth transitions between ideas, and edit their writing effectively. Reading, discussing, and writing about texts needs to be a central part of the English language development instruction dispersed throughout the day. (p. 24)

Again, teachers who understand the value of oral academic language development can provide instruction in ways that particularly enrich this area of language for ELLs.

CLASSROOM APPLICATIONS: CHILDREN'S L2 LITERACY INSTRUCTION

Teachers of ELLs who want to provide rich, challenging literacy instruction to their ELL students can build on these findings in a variety of ways. The research on L2 literacy already discussed suggests a number of principles and practices for literacy instruction.

Support knowledge and skills learned in and from the L1, and teach children to use these resources in the L2

Children developing L2 literacy vary greatly in the L1 language, literacy, and educational backgrounds they bring to their schooling. Thus, one of the first steps teachers need to take is to determine who their ELLs are and to identify what knowledge and skills they already have (see Figure 2). Some of the kinds of knowledge ELLs may bring to the development of L2 literacy skills include those listed in Figure 3.

Depending on the country, state, province, or school district, formal assessments probably already exist for identifying the knowledge and skills ELLs bring. However, in addition, teachers will probably want to assess their ELLs using various informal methods of oral and written language assessment.

In bilingual and EFL classrooms where the children all share the same L1 background, literacy development in the L1 can be supported right along with that of the L2. However, once teachers know the backgrounds of their students, even those with children from multiple language backgrounds in their classes can support and encourage learners' L1 literacy development while teaching L2 literacy. Enabling children to make use of their L1 and culture is important because they can build on what they already know. L1 literacy knowledge is a valuable resource that

1. Age and grade level
2. Level of English language proficiency when they enter class
3. Prior education and content knowledge
4. Prior literacy knowledge in L1 or L2, at home or in school
5. Similarities/differences between L1 and L2 language and culture
6. Level of education and literacy of family members

Figure 2. Important information to learn about ELL students.

1. Knowledge of the alphabetic principle (that letters of the alphabet represent different sounds)

2. Knowledge that writing in English flows from left to right and from the top of the page to the bottom

3. Understandings about phonemic awareness, such as the recognition that deleting a sound from a word yields a different word (e.g., removing the first sound from *stop* gives us *top*)

4. Knowledge that we read a book in English by holding the binding on the left and the open pages on the right; we turn the pages from the right side to the left side

5. Knowledge that when we write in English, we leave a space between words

6. Knowledge that when we read or write, the words in a text convey meaning

7. Knowledge that when we tell stories (narratives), they often follow common patterns

8. Knowledge that different genres have different formats, use language in certain ways, and contain certain types of information

Figure 3. Types of literacy knowledge that can be transferred to the L2.

should be used to achieve the challenging goal of closing the literacy achievement gap for ELLs. Some of the ways teachers can use the L1 include:

- Asking ELLs to read and write in their L1 to learn about what they already know about literacy. Even if teachers are not fluent in the L1, there is a great deal that they can observe about how fluently children are able to use their L1 literacy skills. This information can then be helpful for designing future instruction.

- Showing through their attitudes and opportunities in class that they appreciate the L1 culture, and prior experiences of all children in the class. This can facilitate the application of L1 knowledge to L2 development.

- Encouraging ELLs to share information with classmates about how they say or spell words in their L1; later, building on students' understandings of such knowledge directly by using this information to teach explicitly some differences between learners' L1 and L2. Encourage students to use their knowledge of these differences in their reading, writing, and even spelling (Samway, 2006).

- Encouraging parents or caregivers, especially those with L1 literacy skills, to become involved in class activities. They can serve as a valuable source of L1 literacy information, a resource for all members of the class.

Teach multiple literacy skills, but keep constant focus on meaning-making

Within an evidence-based approach to L2 literacy, ELLs at early literacy levels need explicit reading instruction in phonics and phonemic awareness, as well as in vocabulary, comprehension, and fluency, all within meaningful contexts. When providing early learners with explicit instruction in decoding and sound-symbol correspondences, whether for sounding out words, letter formation, or spelling, the instruction should be systematic. Teachers need to assess the specific needs of their ELLs and then focus on those areas giving learners the most difficulty, based on a knowledge of the entire sound system. Depending on the composition of the class, the systematic order for teaching the sound-symbol relationships of English shown in Figure 4 can be used.

However, even when focusing on teaching these low-level skills, instruction should not be done in isolation but should always occur within a context that is meaningful, interactive, and interesting. Activities for helping children identify individual sounds and their combinations, dividing words into syllables, and sight recognition of high-frequency words that do not follow common sound patterns (e.g., *one, of, have, the*) should be done keeping the following six principles in mind:

1. After students initially read a text or book to understand or discuss what it says, or for some other authentic communicative purpose, the class should return to that same text to focus on phonics or word work using words from that text.

2. Teachers should do phonics work with ELLs using L2 words they already know (or go back to a text they read previously for meaning) to introduce words that have new sound patterns, word structures (prefixes, suffixes, word roots), or word classes.

3. Whenever possible, teachers should make connections to words and sound patterns in

Consonants	Pattern	Examples
for which there is a single sound		*b, d, f, j, k, l, m, n, p, r, s, t, v, z*
for which there is more than one sound		*c, g, h, w, y*
which occur in two-letter combinations, or "blends"	with *l*	*bl, cl, fl, gl, pl, sl*
	with *r*	*br, cr, dr, fr, gr, pr, tr*
	with *s*	*sc, sk, sm, sn, sp, st, sw*
which occur in three-letter blends		*scr, spr, str, squ*
which combine to form a new sound, or digraph		*ch, sh, th, wh, gh, −nk, ng*
Vowels		
long vowels	CV	*be*
	(C)VCe	*ate, like, note*
	CVVC	*paid, boat*
short vowels	VC or CVC	*it, hot*
r-controlled vowels	Vr or CVr	*art, car, her*
digraphs/diphthongs	VV	*saw, book; boil, out*

Figure 4. One systematic order for teaching sound-symbol relationships in English. (Note that C stands for consonant, V for vowel, and e for "silent e.")

the ELLs' L1 as well as to other similar L2 words that they already know.

4. Teachers should keep word work short, focused, and interesting, using a variety of activities that foster this awareness in children, including songs, rhymes, and poetry. This work should be done using big books, shared reading, or collaborative writing activities.

5. Teachers should keep in mind that the point of such instruction is to facilitate comprehension of what is read, not to recite rules.

6. Teachers should remember that, ultimately, the goal of all reading instruction is to develop independent readers.

Because ELLs particularly struggle to catch up with NES peers in the development of higher-level literacy skills, including comprehension, making inferences, critically analyzing what they read, and communicating their ideas effectively through writing, the real challenge for teachers is delivering instruction that moves students toward higher-level skills. There are many activities that can help ELLs develop comprehension skills (see Roit, 2006). When doing these activities, teachers should remember to relate the discussion to specific language and portions of the text that signal the meaning or point being discussed. Also, providing students with sentence starters (sample structures

or sentences for conveying particular meanings) can help scaffold the language that ELLs need for talking and writing about their reading and writing. Some activities that support ELLs' reading comprehension include those listed in Table 1.

Teach reading, writing, speaking, and listening in an integrated manner

When teaching L2 literacy, there are many benefits to teaching reading, writing, speaking, and listening together. First, as previously explained, starting with informal oral language, teachers can gradually introduce students to more formal language used in reading and writing. By explicitly teaching language functions, another component of academic language, teachers can help students make links between oral and written language (for more information on teaching language functions, see Gibbons, 2009; and Gottlieb, Katz, & Ernst-Slavit, 2009). Some of the most common language functions used in CBI classrooms include those listed in Figure 5.

Next, talking about reading helps learners make sense of what they read; similarly, talking about writing can let them try out their ideas for writing or give them ideas for improving their writing. Talking can be used as an entry point into writing by generating ideas through discussion or explaining tentative ideas. Talking can serve as an entry point

Table 1. Activities for Fostering ELLs' Reading Comprehension

Activity	Description/Explanation of Activity	Sentence Starters
Have ELLs draw pictures of what they have read.	Sometimes beginning-level ELLs are able to show what they have understood better through drawing than through words; afterward, ask the children to explain what their pictures show.	*My picture shows . . . from the story. This is a. . . . I drew this because. . . .*
Retell events and discuss what happened.	After reading a passage, share understandings in class about what class members understood. Combine information from all class members to recount the entire story or event.	*First, . . . happened. Then, . . . did. . . . I think . . . because. . . . . . . because on page. . . .*
Clarify any unclear information.	Encourage questions by class members and clarify any unclear areas; be sure to refer specifically to the place in the text where the event in question happened so that students can focus on the language involved.	*Why did the author write . . . ? What does . . . mean? How did you know . . . ? What happened on page . . . ?*
Use reading strategies.	Spend time in class talking about strategies the class members used to understand a text: What did the student do? Why did he or she do that? Some common strategies include: • Predicting: Before reading or at various points, stop and predict what happens next. Then read on to check your predictions. • Visualizing: Imagine what a scene looked or felt like. Have students close their eyes to do this. • Question the author: What information does the text make readers want to know more about?	Predicting: *I think . . . is going to happen because. . . . I think . . . will do . . . next.* Visualizing: *I see. . . . I feel. . . .* Questioning the author: *Why did you . . . ? What happened next? What kind of person is . . . ? Why didn't . . . do . . . ?*
Make connections from the text to the children's experiences and to other texts they have read.	Talk about how something the class is reading or writing about relates to ELLs' real-world knowledge, previous personal experiences, and other books/texts they have read. Make connections to ELLs' previous knowledge, and help them connect to things they already know. Remember to tie connections to specific information in a text to check or facilitate comprehension of specific language in the text.	*This is just like . . . because. . . . This reminds me of. . . . . . . made me remember. . . . (Character) . . . is like. . . . This story is like my experience because. . . .*
Think aloud through the process used to understand what was read.	Think-alouds put into words the ways in which a reader thinks about or solves the problem of understanding. Mention and describe the specific strategy used and adapt this explanation to the level of the ELLs in the class. Think-alouds can be used for summarizing, comprehending, understanding unknown vocabulary, making inferences, or finding the main idea of a passage.	*When I didn't understand this word, I tried to understand it from the context by. . . . When I saw the word, I thought about. . . .*

- Agreeing/disagreeing
- Asking for assistance
- Classifying
- Comparing
- Contrasting
- Describing
- Defining
- Evaluating
- Expressing a position
- Explaining
- Giving instructions
- Hypothesizing
- Identifying
- Offering/refusing
- Predicting
- Reporting
- Sequencing
- Suggesting

Figure 5. Some common classroom language functions.

into reading through such activities as the LEA lesson described at the beginning of this chapter. Many of the activities described in the previous section for building comprehension skills can simultaneously be used for modeling academic language and providing practice for academic language skills. Talking about literature can open learners' ideas to alternate interpretations of a text. For both reading and writing, talking plays an important role in the development of fluency, both for students' language in general and for their L2 literacy. Children need to be provided with opportunities to talk meaningfully about their reading and writing, not just given worksheets to practice subskills over and over.

In particular, reading and writing benefit from being taught together for multiple reasons:

Reading as a model for writing. After students read a text, going back to highlight vocabulary, look at various literary techniques the author used (as a model for ELLs' own writing), and notice how grammatical structures used for various purposes can serve as important steps in developing language competence.

Writing for themselves. Writing for themselves can help readers see what went into a reading that they are trying to make sense of. ELLS can gain insight into how the reading and writing processes are related.

Writing as a response to reading. Writing is an excellent way to respond to material that has just been read. It provides opportunities for ELLs to use new vocabulary items that have been recycled through multiple texts they have read on the same topic (see Cloud et al., 2009, for further suggestions).

Bringing together oral language, reading, and writing. Reading interesting material can motivate a writer to try to write in a similar style or voice. Various activities can be used to bring together oral language, reading, and writing in ways that can inspire ELLs to continue reading and writing practice, an important element in the development of fluency; these include reader's theater (in which each student takes the part of a character and reads/acts out the part), choral reading (in which the entire class reads a passage out loud together, with feeling), poetry reading and writing, and literature circles (in which a group of students all read the same book and then discuss various aspects of it).

Reading a variety of genres. Readings in various genres can provide models and texts for analysis to aid in the process of developing the written competence to produce those genres of text in the future. Seeing how the language features of texts change from genre to genre is an effective method for teaching ELLs to produce those same discourse features themselves (see Gibbons, 1991, 2002, 2009 for language features of various genres).

Build deep understandings of academic vocabulary constantly

Building an ELL's storehouse of academic vocabulary is one of the greatest challenges facing teachers and learners. Not only do ELLs need to know basic everyday words that their NES peers arrive at school with, but to close the gap on content and literacy knowledge, they also need to develop a large, active, deep, academic vocabulary. Part of what makes vocabulary difficult is that often the same word can take on multiple meanings in different contexts and subject areas (see Figure 6). Even if ELLs develop a large vocabulary of high-frequency words, it is often their alternate meanings that give them difficulty. Also, if words are used differently in different subject areas, ELLs need exposure to those areas to see words used in context in those specific ways. Thus, teaching academic vocabulary needs to follow a multi-pronged approach, with explicit teaching, along with large amounts of extensive reading. Both of these are discussed in more depth later in the chapter.

Effective vocabulary instruction provides multiple exposures to target words over multiple days and across various reading, writing, and speaking opportunities. One of the best ways to do

Not related to specific subject/field	Used in different fields, but having a particular meaning in specific subjects/fields	Used only in a particular subject/field
adjacent, amount, commonly, directly, constant, superior, pair, structure, associated, protects, assume, concept	*factor, method, function, intonation, morphological, irregular (verb), token, proportion, compounds, pivot*	*transmitter, bacteria, stimulant, morpheme, beaker, lipids, adrenaline, least common denominator, fulcrum*

Figure 6. Different types of academic vocabulary.

this is through sustained reading and writing on a single topic, what Cloud et al. (2009) call "text sets":

A text set is a collection of reading materials that is organized around themes—be it literary (African folktales) or informational (nutritional foods). A good text set includes a wide variety of written texts and materials that vary in length, difficulty, and structure, and encompasses texts that are interesting, relevant, and accessible to most students. A good text set gives students options for independent reading and provides students with opportunities to practice new reading strategies and to learn content information. (pp. 54–55)

By reading about a single content theme across multiple texts, some easier, some harder, ELLs get exposure to key vocabulary repeatedly, as required for learning new words. Reading multiple texts enables ELLs to build up their knowledge on a topic over a sustained period of time, giving them the understanding they need to talk and write about it confidently and fluently. Reading multiple books on a single topic further enables ELLs to see how certain words are used repeatedly with the same words or structures and how those words are used in various contexts and grammatical structures. The multiple fairy tales that Ms. Lee's students were reading are an example of this type of sustained content reading. ELLs benefit most from rich, intensive vocabulary instruction that emphasizes student-friendly definitions (definitions using their own words or words they can easily understand). Some activities that encourage students to use words meaningfully in reading, writing, speaking, and listening and also provide review and recycling of those words on a regular basis can be seen in Figure 7.

1. Teach only a small number of words in intensive ways at any one time; depending on students' ages and proficiency levels, focus on two to eight words per day, constantly providing review and extension.

2. Teach early on that many words have multiple meanings; knowing this can often help ELLs realize that a word used in one context may not mean the same as the word they have encountered elsewhere. When words come up in reading or writing, ask the students if the words have the same or different meanings from their encounters with those words previously.

3. Along with academic vocabulary, emphasize the acquisition of meanings of everyday words that native speakers know and that are not necessarily part of the academic curriculum. ELLs need to know these words too.

4. Teach actively, and constantly focus on vocabulary in shared reading or when reading aloud to the class.

5. Encourage students to become language detectives, in which part of the goal is to notice and have fun with words (and language in general) and appreciate their form and meaning.

6. Call attention to cognates (L1 words that are similar to words in the L2 and have similar meanings, e.g., *produce* in English/*producir* in Spanish) as well as loanwords (words in the L1 that have been borrowed from the L2, e.g., *computer* in English/*kompyuta* in Japanese) as shortcuts to learning new words. Warn students to be careful of false cognates (e.g., *molestar/molest* [bother] in Spanish versus *molest* in English) or loanwords whose meanings changed when they were borrowed (e.g., *boyfriend* [a romantic relationship] in English vs. *boifurendo* [a male friend] in Japanese).

7. Do not just have children memorize definitions; work to help them understand words conceptually and deeply and to be able to explain the meanings of vocabulary (with their multiple meanings) in their own words.

8. Call attention to new words and new meanings within a text where they appear, noting what other words they frequently appear with (collocations) and what other words share meaning relationships (antonyms and synonyms) or word roots with them.

9. Teach vocabulary in multiple ways. Sometimes, preteach vocabulary that the class will encounter in a reading. Other times, discuss vocabulary that caused difficulties for the class after reading. At yet other times, stop in the middle of reading a story aloud to check if students understand a word, if they can explain it in their own words, or if they can give an example of it.

10. Encourage ELLs to keep vocabulary journals in which they write down new words they want to remember and try to use them in their writing and speaking later, along with the sentences in which they saw them used and other noteworthy characteristics of the word.

11. Follow up with word analysis skills after reading (prefixes, suffixes, and roots).

12. Write new words on word walls around the classroom; use large printing so ELLs can look up and see them when they are speaking or writing and want to use them.

Figure 7. Ways to foster active vocabulary learning for ELLs.

Develop a program of sustained, extensive reading and writing at the level of each student

One of the most important elements of building reading and writing fluency is simply doing it a lot. Children learning to read and write benefit from constant exposure to words of all kinds, texts of all kinds, and language of all kinds. As described earlier, using text sets on themes of interest to children will provide multiple reading texts on a topic, providing them with lots of material to read and write about. However, be careful to select reading material with no more than a couple of unknown words per page; otherwise, learners will become bogged down in unknown vocabulary and struggle with comprehension. Since the ultimate goal of any L2 literacy program is to develop independent readers and writers, independent reading needs to be encouraged and modeled, even during classroom time. If the teacher models this too, reading right along with the students, and encourages them to share and write about what they have read, an important message can be conveyed. Figure 8 lists some other teaching strategies for fostering fluency for ELLs.

FUTURE TRENDS

Recent research has given us the beginnings of what constitutes effective instruction for L2 literacy, suggesting some concrete ideas for teaching ELLs. However, there is clearly still much to do as the number of ELLs needing to develop L2 literacy continues to increase. To address their

---

1. Build fluency, background knowledge, and academic language by using culturally sensitive reading materials (A. Freeman, 2000), and texts that relate to ELLs' own backgrounds and personal experiences. These texts can help to increase interest and motivation of ELLs and encourage them to keep on reading, a critical factor in developing fluency.

2. Help students read extensively in a wide range of genres, both fiction and nonfiction. Children find it easier to write in genres they have been exposed to previously, a good argument for introducing them to a variety of genres through their reading. In class, talk about how different genres of text use language in particular ways and present information for different purposes. Students can then reflect and build on this when they write.

3. Make reading and writing independently a regular part of your class. Making it a consistent part of the class will reinforce how important it is.

4. Scaffold ELLs' independent reading/writing so that it does not become tedious. Take a few moments of class time here and there to talk about a specific book they have read or a particular essay they wrote. Encourage them to say what they particularly enjoyed about the book or the essay.

5. To model reading as an enjoyable activity, read regularly to the class. For this purpose, use books that are a little bit above the independent reading level of the class as an opportunity to:
   - show the enjoyment that can come from reading a book
   - highlight new academic language
   - model how the teacher uses strategies for making meaning
   - use the ELLs' L1 to support reading and writing wherever useful through fostering positive attitudes toward it and by using it to build L1 literacy skills that later can be transferred to and practiced in the L2
   - for low-level ELLs, use wordless books to model how language can be used to describe what is in a picture; this will enable children at any level to provide the language to describe what is in the book
   - use techniques like LEA to make connections between oral language and written text
   - use dialogue journals to provide extensive writing practice where the focus is on conveying meaning. Later the teacher can make notes about vocabulary, grammar, or other language areas the students need work on, and can address them in an appropriate contextualized activity in class.
   - use dictations and dictocomps[1] to help ELLs make connections between the language they hear and the ways we represent those words in written text
   - set up class-to-class exchanges between your class and another one in a different location to provide an authentic purpose for communicating (via the Internet or email) in writing through such activities as "buddy reading" or cross-age tutoring. Talk with the class about how to make meanings clear to someone who is far away from you.
   - consider setting up a class blog for the purpose of sharing reviews of books students have read or discussing issues they are dealing with in their writing

Figure 8. Ways to foster fluency for ELLs.

needs better, more teachers need an intimate understanding not only of who their ELLs are but also of the most promising ways to increase their L2 literacy abilities and approach the levels of NES readers and writers.

To support the broader preparation of effective teachers of ELLs, much more research is needed on little-known areas of L2 literacy development, such as the social and affective factors of literacy and writing. More needs to be known about what exactly constitutes academic language and how it varies across different content areas. New and ongoing research is also needed on long-term ELLs (those who continue to need L2 instruction even after many years in ESL/EFL classes), and ELL students with interrupted formal education. Finally, we also need to continue to expand conceptualizations and instruction for developing literacies "that link conventional school-based and academic tasks to new technologies, multimedia communications and diverse notions of literacy at work and in society" (Cumming, 2009a, p. 226).

CONCLUSION

An L2 literacy classroom has the potential to be a dynamic active place where issues related to using written and oral language in students' L2 can be wrestled with to learn new information. We need more teachers who are committed to learning and understanding ELLs better and who recognize that they bring great amounts of prior experience of the world to their learning. If the literacy needs of ELLs continue to evolve along with technological developments and new ways of and purposes for communicating, literacy instruction will also need to continue to evolve. This will bring great challenges to teachers and classrooms that can be embraced with interest and enthusiasm.

SUMMARY

➤ Based on important findings that L1 literacy is similar to L2 literacy in certain basic ways, it is helpful whenever possible to build on ELLs' L1 literacy backgrounds when developing L2 literacy.

➤ Like L1 learners, ELLs benefit from the explicit teaching of multiple skills, including phonological awareness, decoding/encoding, vocabulary, comprehension, fluency, and writing.

➤ However, L2 literacy also differs from L1 in that ELLs often need to develop their oral language and content knowledge at the same time as they are encountering literacy, and they do not bring the same background knowledge as NESs to their reading/writing.

➤ ELLs need integrated instruction in reading, writing, speaking, and listening that develops multiple sub-areas of literacy through a constant focus on making meaning.

➤ ELLs need instruction specially adapted to their varying needs and levels that focuses explicitly on developing their academic language, including language functions and vocabulary.

➤ Young ELLs benefit from being exposed to texts of all kinds, spanning a wide variety of genres and illustrating large amounts of language in different contexts.

DISCUSSION QUESTIONS

1. Look back at the description of Ms. Lee's LEA lesson at the beginning of this chapter and answer the following questions:
   a. What were the steps the teacher followed in this activity? If the children in that class already know what happened in the story, is this really reading? Explain. In what ways does this type of activity scaffold the literacy challenges for beginning-level ELLs?
   b. In the scenario, the teacher did not correct the errors in the sentences dictated by some of her students. Why might a teacher in this situation *not* want to correct her students' errors? What are some other times when teachers might not want to correct students' errors?
   c. How could technology be used to enhance Ms. Lee's LEA activity if her class had access to it? What are some other ways not mentioned in the chapter that L2 literacy skills could be developed using technology? Which reading or writing skill(s)

would that particular technology application enhance? Make a list of these ways.

2. How might encountering vocabulary through a text set (a collection of fiction and nonfiction books and readings on a single theme or topic; described on p. 165) help ELLs learn new vocabulary? What about having the students read on several topics? Which do you think is better: deeper vocabulary knowledge on fewer different topics or broader (but shallower) vocabulary knowledge from a wide range of topics? Give arguments for both approaches to teaching vocabulary.

3. Review the various adaptations to literacy instruction recommended in this chapter for school-age ELLs. What sorts of patterns do you see among them? What are some principles underlying the different adaptations recommended for ELLs?

4. What are some of the ways you can find out about the L1 and L2 language and literacy abilities that a class of ELLs brings with them? What assessments already exist in your area for doing this? What informal assessments might you also want to do yourself to find out about the backgrounds and abilities of your students?

SUGGESTED ACTIVITIES

1. With a classmate, do a think-aloud in which you describe the steps in your mental processes for doing one of the following:
   a. identifying the main idea of a passage
   b. making an inference from something you read
   c. figuring out the meaning of a sentence that contains an unknown word

2. Together with a classmate, put together a text set of children's books on a single theme or topic, including both fiction and nonfiction and books at multiple reading levels, that you can use to develop the vocabulary and content knowledge of children at a particular grade level. Then present your text set to your classmates or post it to a course website so your entire class can see it.

3. Look up on the Internet or find other sources to learn more about the LEA (e.g., Dixon &

Nessel, 1983). What are the various steps in this approach? What are some of the kinds of experiences that can be used for an LEA activity? Then design a L2 literacy lesson in which you incorporate an LEA activity.

4. a. Research more about what academic language involves. What are its characteristics? What do we know so far about the language demands of schooling?
   b. Not everyone agrees with the distinction between informal oral language and academic language. Research and discuss the difference between the two. Do you agree that this is a helpful distinction? If so, why? If not, why not?
   c. Sit in on a content-based L2 literacy class for several days that focuses on a unit in math, science, or social studies. From that class (with the permission of the teacher), gather together copies of the textbooks, reading materials, and reading and writing assignments. Then analyze the language used in them to identify what the academic language requirements are for that unit. Identify the technical and subtechnical vocabulary; also identify grammatical structures, language functions, and characteristics of specific genres of materials in the lesson, among other aspects of language. After you complete this, what can you say about your findings? What sorts of academic language did you find were involved?

FURTHER READING

California Department of Education. (Ed.). (2010). *Improving education for English learners: Research-based approaches.* Sacramento, CA: Standards, Curriculum Frameworks, and Instructional Resources Division, California Department of Education.

This is a very accessible and thorough review of research-supported practices for teaching all aspects of language to school-aged ELLs, with many concrete examples for teachers; it includes a chapter focusing specifically on research-based literacy instruction for ELLs.

Cloud, N., Genesee, F., & Hamayan, E. (2009). *Literacy instruction for English language learners.* Portsmouth, NH: Heinemann.

This textbook provides an overview of effective, evidence-based teaching practices and suggestions for L2 literacy development of K–8 ELLs.

Gibbons, P. (2009). *English learners, academic literacy, and thinking.* Portsmouth, NH: Heinemann.

This practical guide for teachers explains how to provide "high challenge and high support" instruction that fosters literacy and language development for ELLs in the middle grades of school.

Samway, K. (2006). *When English language learners write: Connecting research to practice, K–8.* Portsmouth, NH: Heinemann.

This work is a practical, hands-on guide to teaching writing to K–8 ELLs.

Scarcella, R. (2003). *Accelerating academic English: A focus on the English learner.* Oakland, CA: Regents of the University of California. Available from http://exstream.ucsd.edu/UCPDI/webtool/html/publications/ell_book_all.pdf

This is a review of the various aspects of academic English and how to facilitate its acquisition by ELLs.

Young, T., & Hadaway, N. (Eds.). (2006). *Supporting the literacy development of English learners.* Newark, DE: International Reading Association.

This collection of articles by well-known teacher educators on various aspects of L2 literacy development provides helpful suggestions for K–8 teachers of ELLs.

ENDNOTE

[1] In the dictocomp technique (also known as a reproduction), students hear a short text read several times by the teacher and then attempt to reproduce it, maintaining the meaning but using their own words.

12 | Developing Engaged Second Language Readers

NEIL J ANDERSON

KEY QUESTIONS

➤ What does it mean to be an engaged reader?

➤ How is an engaged reader different from other readers?

➤ What can classroom teachers explicitly do to help learners become more engaged readers?

EXPERIENCE

Brad has just accepted a full-time position as an English as a foreign language (EFL) teacher. He graduated with an MA degree in teaching English to speakers of other languages (TESOL) from a university in the United States. The program from which he received his degree provided a solid balance of theoretical and application-based coursework; it also included a practicum class where he was able to do practice teaching. Since graduating with his degree two years ago, he has held various part-time teaching positions. He regularly reviewed job listings online and found several that he was interested in applying for. After an intense round of interviews, Brad received three offers. He selected a position at a well-known university outside of the United States. Although Brad considers himself to be a novice professional, he is confident that with his teaching experience and his academic training he will be successful. He is motivated and ready to use his knowledge and experience. After the first week of classes, Brad sits in his office to reflect on his initial experiences in the classroom. Here is the entry from his teaching journal:

> What a week! Graduate school never fully prepared me for this. The reality of teaching four classes, with four separate preparations has been overwhelming. I'm so pleased that I've been assigned to teach two reading classes, a writing class, and an oral skills development class. This combination allows me to see how

I might make suggestions for improving the integration of courses in the curriculum.

The learners in my reading classes are not anything like those I worked with while in my graduate program. Am I expecting too much of them? I have high expectations of them, but I don't think they have high expectations of themselves. They seem to be more concerned about "passing the iBT"[1] than about learning to be good readers. I was well prepared as I went to class each day, but we were never able to make it through the lesson plan because of the slow reading rates of the students. Even after taking twice as much time to complete the reading passage as I had allocated in my lesson plan, the students were not able to complete the comprehension activities that I had prepared. I carefully explained our purpose for reading, but the students resisted trying the reading strategies that I was teaching. I recall a discussion in one of the graduate courses in which we discussed establishing a culture of reading. There is definitely not a culture of reading in this university EFL program.

Am I overwhelmed? Absolutely! Am I discouraged? Yes! Will I give up? No! I understand that things are not going to go smoothly all of the time, and I know that I cannot measure my success after only one week on the job. I look forward to applying the aspects of my philosophy for teaching reading that can help the learners to be more engaged readers.

WHAT IS ENGAGED READING?

Five characteristics define engaged readers: (1) they read widely with different purposes; (2) they read fluently and use their cognitive capacity to focus on the meaning of what they read; (3) they develop their comprehension by using what they read; (4) they are metacognitively aware as they use a variety of reading strategies; and (5) they are motivated readers. Understanding the key aspects of these five characteristics will lead us to be more thoughtful about the theoretical rationale for each.

This chapter focuses specifically on adult readers at the intermediate level of language proficiency. In particular, I invite readers to think of the *struggling* readers at this level of proficiency and to use this chapter to provide guidance in helping those learners to become engaged readers. Teaching at this level of language proficiency presents certain challenges. The greatest challenge is helping learners get through what has been labeled the "intermediate-level slump" (N. J. Anderson, 2008). This slump was first identified by Chall (1967) as the fourth-grade slump for first language (L1) readers. This slump is characterized by learners who are mastering the basic principles of reading and are moving from learning to read to reading to learn. *Learning to read* requires learning what the shapes and lines on the page mean. Readers must learn the conventions that writers use to convey information. Narrative texts, or stories, are typically used to teach learners *how* to read. Once the conventions of reading have been learned, learners transition to *reading to learn*. In this stage, readers use information to increase knowledge. Expository texts, or information-based texts, are typically used to learn content. Chall labeled this the fourth-grade slump because in the U.S. education system, this is typically the point when children move from learning the conventions of reading (learning to read) to gaining new knowledge from what they read (reading to learn).

Learners caught in the intermediate-level slump experience a slowing of progress. A partial reason for the slowing of progress is that learners at this level of language proficiency have more to learn. This is best explained by viewing the amount of material to learn as an inverted pyramid. As students achieve higher levels of language proficiency, there is an increase in the amount of material available to learn. Learning a language is not a linear process where the amount of material is consistent as one progresses up the proficiency scale. At this stage of language development, the learners' oral language skills have grown significantly. They can often engage in conversations with others, who compliment them on their use of English. There are even some learners at this level of reading proficiency who believe that they are more advanced than they really are. This can lead to the learners' being overconfident in their reading ability.

In the initial stages of learning to read, learners can measure their progress quickly. They are able to complete basic tasks in reading that not long ago they could not do. They are encouraged by what they can read, mostly because the texts that they are reading are simple, short, and include basic levels of vocabulary. The texts are often narrative in nature, and they are able to follow the story line successfully. Engaging readers at the intermediate level of language proficiency is critical to their ultimate success. Many of them want to continue making progress so that they can get to the point where they can read academic texts. (See Grabe & Stoller, this volume, on teaching reading for academic purposes.)

What can we expect from readers at the intermediate level of language proficiency? At this level of reading ability, learners move from reading primarily narrative texts to adding expository texts to their repertoire. The Common European Framework of Reference (CEFR) for languages (Council of Europe, 2001) provides a tool for comparing what learners of any European language (e.g., Bulgarian, Czech, French, German, Italian, Polish, Portuguese, Spanish, or Swedish) can do in the language at various stages of language development. The framework therefore provides a standard way of comparing levels of language ability across languages. The CEFR indicates that at the intermediate level readers are able to read personal letters, newspaper articles on familiar topics, basic instructions for a piece of equipment, and contemporary prose (Morrow, 2004). The vocabulary demands increase from what readers were accustomed to at beginning levels of proficiency. The structure of the writing also changes at this level. Readers are now expected to engage in identifying main ideas, separating main ideas from details, scanning, separating facts from opinions, and identifying conclusions. The reading begins to take on more academic characteristics.

Perhaps the greatest mistake that a teacher can make at this level is to expect too much from the readers. This is not to suggest that teachers should not have high expectations but that those expectations should be focused on moving the reader from learning to read to reading to learn. To avoid making this mistake, and to guide teachers in helping learners through the intermediate-level slump, this chapter provides direction on the five characteristics of engaged readers.

What are the purposes for which we read?

Engaged readers have a purpose for reading, or in other words, they have a specific goal. What are the typical purposes for reading? We read for pleasure. We read for information. We read to learn something new. These three reasons seem to capture the primary purposes for reading.

Teachers who desire to engage their learners as readers should have clearly articulated goals for reading and make sure that the goals are explicitly stated. Effective teachers will go one step further in making sure that the learners understand what the goals are and that the learners begin to make the goals their own. As Grabe (2009) observes:

> sometimes students do not fully understand the goals for a given reading text or reading task, and perform poorly. The problem may not be an inability to comprehend but a lack of awareness of the real goal for the reading task. (p. 19)

Engaged readers are able to describe *why* they are reading a particular text. They are actively involved in reading both narrative and expository texts. They read daily from a variety of text types and for a variety of purposes.

Teachers should understand that there are differences between narrative and expository texts. Grabe (2002) reports on research that indicates that narrative and expository texts require different reading goals. D. Gardner (2004) questions the curricular balance between narrative and expository text. He asks:

> is it possible that an overemphasis on narrative fiction (or conversely, an underemphasis on expository materials) in the literacy training of ESL learners "builds in" much of the

noted disparities between the development of basic language skills ("easy narratives") and more complex cognitive abilities ("more difficult expositions")? (p. 29)

This line of thinking certainly lends support to the notion of an intermediate-level slump. Perhaps the overemphasis on easy narrative texts and the underemphasis on expository texts contribute to the slump. Teachers (and curricula) desiring to develop engaged readers will explicitly examine the balance between narrative and expository materials to provide appropriate exposure to both types of texts and help L2 readers expand their reading purposes.

Our reading purposes or goals determine the amount of effort and time we will invest in getting the information we need from a text. This connects directly to the aspect of motivation and reading, which I address in more depth later in the chapter.

What is fluent reading?

Recall Brad's experience, which opened this chapter. One of the challenges that he faced was that the students read very slowly, with the result that he was not able to reach his instructional objective. Reading fluency, or more important, the lack of reading fluency, is a reality in most classrooms. I contend that the reason for this reality is that teachers do not know what to do to help learners improve their reading fluency.

Engaged readers read fluently. For adult L2 readers, N. J. Anderson (1999, 2008, 2009) defines *reading fluency* as reading at 200 words per minute (wpm) with 70% comprehension. Fluency is a combination of both reading rate and reading comprehension. Few researchers on reading include both rate and comprehension in their discussions of reading fluency. Samuels (2006) is one exception. He states that "reading fluency is the ability to decode and to comprehend the text at the same time" (p. 9). Some may argue that reading rate can be slower for beginning- and intermediate-level readers. Anderson (2009) suggests that, regardless of the level of language proficiency, this target should be sought. Beginning- and intermediate-level readers should seek to be reading 200 wpm with at least 70% comprehension while reading texts that are level appropriate.

Automaticity in word recognition is one key element in fluent reading. Readers must develop rapid, automatic word recognition skills to be fluent readers. *Automaticity* is defined as the ability to perform a task easily, with little or no conscious attention. Automaticity is developed through extensive practice. One aspect of automaticity in word recognition that requires more attention from L2 reading teachers is the bottom-up process of reading. *Bottom-up reading* focuses on building meaning starting from the smallest units and leading to larger units—from letters, letter-sound correspondences, syllables, words, multiword expressions, phrases, sentences, paragraphs, to entire texts. This means that we need to be prepared to teach learners how to decode and connect a meaning to the word. I am sure that we have all heard that English is a difficult language to learn because "there are no rules for spelling and pronunciation." That is not entirely true. There are many decodable words in English. A *decodable word* is one where there is one sound for each letter or letter combination. To cite just one example, the word *provide* is a decodable word. The *pr–* is a blend. Each letter produces one sound each. The vowel *o* is the long-o sound because it occurs at the end of a syllable. The letter *v* produces one sound. The letter *i* produces the long sound because it occurs between two consonants (*v* and *d*) and there is an *e* at the end of the word. The *d* produces one sound. The *e* is silent because it occurs at the end of the word. When you know the rules for decoding, it is easy to crack the code. We need to teach learners decoding strategies so that they can crack the code and read the words that are decodable. There are many phonics-based programs available to help train teachers and learners how to use decoding effectively. One such program that is available online is *Reading Horizons*.[2] Keep in mind that our goal in teaching learners how to decode a word is that they will be able to engage in rapid, fluent word recognition.

How do we recognize reading comprehension?

Engaged readers read with comprehension and are able to do something with what they read. The doing something with what they read often results in readers critically evaluating what was read and determining ways that they can demonstrate their new knowledge. "We never know what we've read until we are forced to perform as readers—as though we know what we've read" (Bartholomae & Petrosky, 1986, p. 19). This implies a direct connection between reading comprehension and reading purpose. Teachers need to encourage readers to know their purpose to be able to demonstrate their comprehension.

The suggestion to readers from I. A. Richards (1942) given 70 years ago is still appropriate today. He suggested that when we are challenged to comprehend a difficult text we should "read it as though it made sense and perhaps it will" (p. 41). This requires that we be more metacognitively aware while we are reading.

What does it mean to be metacognitively aware of reading strategies?

Engaged readers are metacognitively aware of the reading strategies available to support their reading. (See Purpura, this volume, for a discussion of learner styles and strategies.) N. J. Anderson (2005) defines *strategies* as "the *conscious* actions that learners take to improve their language learning. . . . Because strategies are conscious, there is active involvement of the L2 learner in their selection and use" (p. 757). Anderson (in press) points out that metacognitive awareness requires: (1) *preparing* and *planning* for effective learning; (2) deciding *when to use* specific strategies; (3) knowing how to *monitor* the use of strategies; (4) learning how to *combine* various strategies; and (5) *evaluating* the effectiveness of strategy use. The conscious awareness of what is taking place within the mind of an individual reader is best monitored by the individual reader. If we want metacognitively aware learners, we must have metacognitively aware teachers. This means that L2 reading teachers need to be more aware of ways to help learners become aware of their strategies.

What can teachers do to motivate readers?

Engaged readers are motivated. The topic of motivation is not new to language teaching and learning. One question that receives considerable attention is, whose responsibility is it to motivate second language learners? Dörnyei (2001) notes:

> the current situation is not very promising in this respect: by-and-large, promoting learner motivation is nobody's responsibility. Teachers are supposed to teach the curriculum rather than motivate learners, and the fact that the former cannot happen without the latter is often ignored. . . . My guess is that it is every teacher's (responsibility) who thinks of the *long-term* development of his/her students. (p. 27)

If we want engaged readers, all teachers should consider ways to motivate their students.

Dörnyei and Ottó (1998) provide the following comprehensive definition that applies specifically to the context of second language teaching and motivation:

> motivation can be defined as the *dynamically changing cumulative arousal in a person that initiates, directs, coordinates, amplifies, terminates, and evaluates the cognitive and motor processes whereby initial wishes and desires are selected, prioritised, operationalised, and (successfully or unsuccessfully) acted out.* (p. 64)

What makes this definition particularly relevant to the context of L2 teaching is the emphasis on the dynamic nature of language learning. Language learning is not a quick and easy process. Motivation is central in the language learning process. (See also Dörnyei, this volume.)

Dörnyei and Ottó's definition of *motivation* (1998) underscores why it is so important for classroom teachers to be concerned with it. We receive additional insight from Dörnyei (2001) who points out that:

> learners with sufficient motivation can achieve a working knowledge of an L2, regardless of their language aptitude or other cognitive characteristics. Without sufficient motivation, however, even the brightest learners are unlikely to persist long enough to attain any really useful language. (p. 5)

For the past 25 years, I have used a simple definition of motivation to guide me in my preparation for teaching reading classes. The definition comes from Schramm (1956):

$$\text{motivation} = \frac{\text{expectation of reward}}{\text{effort required}}$$

This mathematical formula provides an ideal way to approach reading instruction and motivation: Teachers need to look for ways to increase the expectation of reward while at the same time decreasing the effort required on the part of the reader.

I emphasize at this point that developing engaged readers is not simply a matter of applying any one of the five characteristics in isolation but rather integrating them into our teaching so that all are present. There is a synergy resulting from integrating all these characteristics that makes for a truly engaged reader. The five characteristics of engaged readers overlap and reinforce each other. Reading purpose (the first characteristic) and goals direct the strategies we select and use. Engaged readers know why they are reading the particular text in front of them. As discussed, having a purpose for reading can make all the difference between readers engaging meaningfully with a text, and thus comprehending it, and readers simply going through the motions of reading and running the risk of not understanding. The purpose for reading also determines in part what strategies readers will engage in to accomplish their purpose. Metacognitive awareness of reading strategies gives the reader more control. As Linderholm and van den Broek (2002) indicate, "reading for coursework most certainly requires a different kind of processing, and different strategies, than reading for relaxation" (p. 778).

CONCEPTUAL UNDERPINNINGS

With the basic foundation of the five characteristics of engaged readers, we now review the theoretical rationale for each.

Reading purposes

Ediger (2006) asserts that reading purpose is addressed in reading research but that "few go the next step to spell out *how* to focus reading toward accomplishing the purpose that one has set" (p. 312). She continues:

> in real-life reading, generally one *starts out* with a goal or purpose for which one is going to read, a reason for taking up a text in the first place, and then one uses various strategies to determine how to proceed with reading in order to get the information necessary for *accomplishing* that purpose. (p. 313)

Linderholm and van den Broek (2002) provide input on this issue by asking, "to what extent do readers actually alter cognitive processes and strategies in accordance with their reason for reading?" (p. 778). To answer this question, they gathered data from 29 L1 readers who were each assigned to one of two reading purposes: reading for pleasure or reading for information. Their research, which focused on nine strategy differences, helps clarify that readers use different comprehension processes depending on the purpose for reading. The researchers point out that "successful reading includes the ability to adjust processing in such a way that learning goals, as a function of reading purpose, are met" (p. 778).

A second research study by Noji, Ford, and Silva (2009) can also guide us in developing engaged readers who understand the importance of reading purpose. Noji, Ford, and Silva argue that there is a lack of alignment between classroom materials and purposeful reading instruction. They support the two common ways of thinking about reading instruction: learning to read and reading to learn. However, they express concern that the instructional strategies used in these two contexts are not interchangeable and, specifically, that the instructional strategies used for learning to read should not be used in classrooms where reading to learn is the goal.

Noji, Ford, and Silva's research (2009) consisted of a quasi-experimental study in China with 300 high school L2 readers who were divided into three groups: the main-idea group, the purpose group, and the control group. The focus of the research was to determine whether the readers could be taught how to select the most important information from three reading passages. The main-idea group received explicit instructions on locating the main idea in sentences. The purpose group received a specific purpose for reading the text. The control group received neither. The findings indicate that the readers in the purpose group were able to identify the important information in the texts significantly better than the readers in the main-idea and the control groups. Immediately following the test, the readers were asked to rate the perceived difficulty of the reading passages, using a 10-point scale (1 = easy, 10 = difficult). The main-idea group rated the text difficulty as 5.0, and the control group rated the text difficulty as 4.3. The purpose group rated the perceived text difficulty as 3.25. Noji, Ford, and Silva draw two important conclusions from their research: (1) "when students have a purpose, they are more able to read and understand material in the same way" and (2) "having a purpose made it much easier for the students to read and comprehend these passages" (p. 10). Given the challenge of getting readers through the intermediate-level slump, these ideas should play a more important role in directing classroom instruction. (More on what can be done in this area is addressed in the Classroom Applications section.)

Carver's research (1990, 1992, 2000) with L1 readers acknowledges that one's reading rate varies depending on the reading purpose. He suggests that if our reading purpose is to scan a text to find specific information, the target words per minute is 600. If we are skimming to get a general idea of the information in the text, the reading rate target is 450 wpm. "Rauding" (a term that Carver coins that is a blend of reading and auding [listening]) occurs at 300 wpm. Carver defines *rauding* as "attending to each consecutive word in sentences and comprehending each consecutively encountered thought in a passage; operating the rauding process and comprehending about 75% or more of the thoughts in a passage" (p. 467). This process happens when we are reading or listening. When we read to learn, the target rate is 200 wpm; and if we are memorizing, the target rate is 138 wpm. These data suggest that there is an interaction between purpose and rate and that there is a need for more data from L2 readers to determine how reading purpose influences reading rate.

These studies have important implications for developing engaged L2 readers. First, we must make sure that L2 readers understand that reading for different purposes requires the use of different reading strategies. For struggling intermediate-level readers, grasping this concept will help them to move forward in their development of language skills. Next, our readers must set a purpose for reading. Engaged readers are not those who wait to be directed by a teacher or someone else; they establish a reason for reading and use that purpose to guide them through the text. Finally, teachers need to tie reading purpose with the explicit teaching of reading strategies so that readers are aware of how to expand their strategies to accomplish their purpose.

Fluent reading

Fluency begins with the development of word-decoding skills. For the struggling intermediate-level reader, the lack of decoding skills is a contributing factor to poor reading fluency. With strong bottom-up reading skills, L2 readers can draw on top-down reading skills (i.e., building meaning by making predictions or inferences and using background knowledge to understand a text) to integrate both in comprehending text. Readers can then read at an appropriate rate with adequate comprehension.

Birch (2007) proposes an interactive model of the reading process that gives equal importance to both top-down and bottom-up elements. The model consists of three primary components: the text being read, processing strategies, and the reader's knowledge base. The processing strategies component comprises two subcategories: cognitive processing strategies and language processing strategies. The cognitive processing strategies equate to the top-down elements of reading. These strategies allow readers to make predictions about what they anticipate will happen in the text, to make inferences using various pieces of knowledge from the text, to solve problems while reading, and to make meaning from the text. The language processing strategies equate to the bottom-up elements of reading. These strategies consist of recognizing letters, associating each letter in English with its appropriate sounds, identifying individual words, tying meaning to the word, and chunking words into meaning phrases.

The knowledge base also consists of two subcategories: world knowledge (top-down) and language knowledge (bottom-up). Birch (2007) emphasizes that our world and cultural knowledge constitutes essential elements that function at the top of the model. Our knowledge of people, places, events, and activities comprise our world knowledge. Without this knowledge, fluent reading could not occur. At the bottom of the model, we have language knowledge, which consists of our knowledge of sounds, letters, words, phrases, and sentences and how each of those parts of the English language is used to make meaningful texts. The elements from the top and the bottom are both essential for fluent reading to take place. Our reading fluency is slowed if we do not have sufficient world knowledge

or appropriate cognitive processing strategies (top-down elements of reading). Likewise, our reading fluency is slowed if we lack knowledge of the basics of the language and the corresponding language processing strategies (bottom-up elements of reading). Figure 1 illustrates my interpretation of Birch's model of these essential components for reading fluency.

Birch (2007) brings to our attention the vital importance of understanding the bottom-up elements of interactive models of reading. She summarizes key research on brain-activation studies. Summarizing the work of Nakada, Fujii, and Kwee (2001), Paulesu et al. (2000), Siok, Zhen, Fletcher, and Tan (2003), and Tan et al. (2001), Birch states that "human brains . . . acquire different patterns of activation based on the language that they learn to read" (p. 167). She then emphasizes:

> L2 readers may require direct instruction in English letter-to-sound conversions, onsets and rimes,[3] and ample practice with easy readings and steadily increasing vocabulary to build up their facility with English reading strategies. To change the L1 knowledge and strategies, we must expect a more lengthy acquisition period; we must allow learners to acquire automaticity in reading English before requiring the comprehension of difficult texts. (p. 168)

The research on reading fluency has clear implications for teachers of L2 reading working with learners at the intermediate level of language

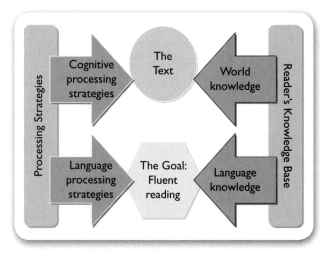

Figure 1. Representation of Birch's (2007) Interactive Model of the Reading Process.

proficiency. We must be more patient with our learners. We must teach them to be more patient with themselves. We must help our intermediate-level L2 readers understand the lengthy process of learning to be more fluent readers in English. The process will not be completed in a single 16-week university or college semester, in a short reading course received in an adult education program, or in an intensive English program. Extensive practice with a wide variety of texts and reading purposes is what must be provided for learners at this level, and this takes time.

Reading comprehension

We tend to speak about reading comprehension as if it were a unitary concept. However, research by Kendeou, van den Broek, White, and Lynch (2007) indicates that reading comprehension is:

> a family of skills and activities. A general component in many definitions of comprehension is the interpretation of the information in the text. . . . At the core of comprehension is our ability to mentally interconnect different events in the text and form a coherent representation of what the text is about. (pp. 28–29)

Some of the key components of comprehension include decoding skills, vocabulary knowledge, grammar knowledge, world knowledge, short-term memory, and inferential knowledge (Prater, 2009). We focus our attention here on one of these components of reading comprehension, vocabulary knowledge.

Many reading studies have consistently shown that vocabulary knowledge is one of the best predictors of a reader's comprehension (Folse, 2010; Laufer & Ravenhorst-Kalovsky, 2010; I. S. P. Nation, 2008). One study that has significant implications for reading comprehension and L2 teachers of intermediate-level readers is Schmitt, Jiang, and Grabe (2011). This research builds on previous research by Laufer (1989) and Hu and Nation (2000) to determine the percentage of vocabulary that L2 readers must know to comprehend a text. Schmitt, Jiang, and Grabe (2011) studied 661 L2 readers from eight countries. The language proficiency of these participants, who were studying in intensive

English programs as well as in undergraduate and graduate programs at universities, ranged from intermediate to very advanced. Three tasks were completed by the participants:

Task 1. They completed a vocabulary knowledge test with 120 words drawn from the texts that they would read. These words were carefully chosen from the first 500 most frequent words (10 words), from the second 500 most frequent words (10 words), and from the 1000–2000 and the 2000+ most frequent words. In addition to the 120 words drawn from the texts they were to read, 30 nonsense words were randomly inserted into the vocabulary test, for a total of 150 words to be tested. These words were then grouped into 15 lists of 10 words each, roughly in frequency order. The readers simply checked yes or no to indicate whether they knew the words.

Task 2. They read two expository academic-type passages of equal difficulty. One passage was entitled "What's Wrong with Our Weather?" (757 words in length) and the second passage was entitled "Circuit Training" (582 words in length). Schmitt and his colleagues emphasize that these passages are longer than typical reading research passages but that this was an intentional element of the research design. They wanted the test passages to mirror more authentic types of reading that readers moving into academic contexts have to be able to read.

Task 3. For each of the two reading passages, the participants responded to a reading comprehension test of two parts. Part 1 required them to respond to 14 multiple-choice (MC) questions that focused primarily on the ability to make inferences. To maintain independence among the tasks that the participants had to complete, the MC questions did not ask about vocabulary. Part 2 of the comprehension measure asked the readers to respond to 16 items from a graphic organizer (GO). A GO that visually represented the organization of the text was developed for each reading passage in which some information was included and other information was left blank. The readers' task was to complete the missing information in the GO. The researchers indicate that this part of the test is very innovative and requires readers to engage in more cognitive processing than the standard reading comprehension test.

The results of the research indicate a strong linear relationship between knowledge of vocabulary and reading comprehension: the greater a reader's knowledge of vocabulary, the higher the score on the comprehension measures. Readers who indicated that they knew 90% of the vocabulary words scored 50% on the comprehension tests. Readers reporting knowledge of 100% of the vocabulary words scored 75% on the comprehension tests.

I see two very important implications for L2 reading teachers of intermediate-level readers. First, understanding 100% of the vocabulary does not mean that a reader will understand 100% of the text. There is more to reading comprehension than just knowing the meanings of the words being read. Certainly the bottom-up aspects of decoding a word and encoding its meaning are important, but the higher-order top-down aspects of reading are also essential to comprehension. Readers must be able to make inferences and use their world knowledge to make connections between the text and their knowledge. Readers must also be able to make predictions and build knowledge from the combinations of words they encounter in a text. Meaning does not reside in the meaning of the individual words in a text; it is the combination of the text and the reader's cognitive processing strategies that allows meaning to emerge. This is a vital skill for intermediate-level readers to acquire. Perhaps the intermediate-level slump would not be such a traumatic event for language learners if they understood this principle early in the learning process. A second important implication of this research is that reading teachers should have an explicit plan for addressing vocabulary learning in the classroom. Here I have one caution. Keep in mind that teachers do not teach vocabulary. Students learn vocabulary. The vocabulary-learning needs of individual students vary. What we can do in the classroom is teach appropriate vocabulary-learning strategies that learners can then apply to their own circumstances to move forward with vocabulary learning. (See also Zimmerman, this volume.)

Metacognitive awareness of reading strategies

The research on metacognitive awareness consistently points to the value of learners who can step back from their learning and reflect on what is happening. Macaro (2001) summarizes major research studies on metacognition and concludes that the learners who are most effective in language learning are those who use metacognitive strategies, understand the effort required in learning a language, and take responsibility for learning. Chamot (2009) helps us understand that learners who are metacognitively aware have the ability to reflect on their thinking and their learning. These learners are aware of what it takes to successfully engage in a language learning task, and they use a variety of strategies to accomplish it.

O'Malley and Chamot (1990) emphasize the importance of metacognition when they state, "students without metacognitive approaches are essentially learners without direction or opportunity to plan their learning, monitor their progress, or review their accomplishments and future learning directions" (p. 8). Teachers who are trying to develop engaged readers should establish an environment where readers learn to be self-directed learners who are making significant progress because they are aware of and take charge of their learning. Metacognitive awareness is central to this success.

Part of the reason that metacognition is so important is that, for those readers who are struggling to increase their reading abilities and reach their language learning goals, awareness of how they best learn and awareness of the strategies they engage in to improve their reading are vital to success. Metacognitive awareness of one's learning makes the learning process conscious and allows the learner to reflect on identifying what the learning challenge is and evaluate which strategies can best be implemented to solve the learning challenge.

Motivation

Motivation plays a central role in the development of positive reading habits and attitudes. (See Dörnyei, this volume.) The research shows clearly that motivated readers are more engaged readers. ESL/EFL teachers play a central role in the development of motivated readers, yet there is a lack of training in and development of exactly what teachers can do to accomplish this important role in the classroom.

Perhaps the most important message from the research on motivation and language learning is that motivation cannot be isolated to a learner alone (intrinsic motivation) or to a teacher (extrinsic motivation). It is the combination of what the learner and the teacher can do together that should be our focus in the reading classroom. Guilloteaux and Dörnyei (2008) help us understand the importance of this dual responsibility in their definition of *motivational strategies* for improving language learning. They state that: "*motivational strategies* refer (a) to *instructional interventions* applied by the *teacher* to elicit and stimulate *student* motivation and (b) *self-regulating* strategies that are used purposefully by individual *students* to manage the level of their own motivation" (p. 57). Note the clear emphasis on the role of both the teacher and the student in this definition of motivational strategies. I am intrigued that Guilloteaux and Dörnyei chose to list the teacher's responsibility first in their definition.

There are clear indications in the research literature that teachers play an important role in motivating learners. Guilloteaux and Dörnyei (2008) point out that "the teacher's motivational practice does matter" and that "student motivation is related to the teacher's motivational practice" (p. 72). We also learn from McCardle, Chhabra, and Kapinus (2008) that "the role of the teacher is central to the development and sustainability of motivation, especially in reading development" (p. 219). During the struggles of the intermediate slump, the teacher may be the most important factor in keeping the reader motivated.

CLASSROOM APPLICATIONS

Given the points that have been addressed up to this point, we can now move to a discussion of the teaching implications. What are the specific pedagogical tasks that teachers can use to develop engaged L2 readers? To assist in this process, look carefully at Figure 2.

This figure provides a visual representation of a balanced reading curriculum. The development of reading skills must be connected to the other language skills of listening, speaking, and

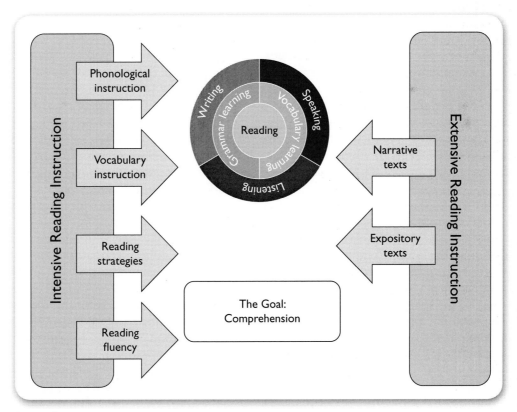

Figure 2. A model for a balanced reading curriculum.

writing. Reading must also be connected to grammar and vocabulary learning. Even in a skills-based curriculum, reading must be integrated with all other aspects of language use. Both teachers and readers must remember that comprehension is the goal of reading. To reach this goal, both intensive and extensive reading must occur during instruction. Intensive reading includes, but is not limited to: instruction in phoneme-grapheme correspondences, the bottom-up aspects of reading; vocabulary instruction; strategy instruction, especially the importance of metacognitive awareness; and reading fluency, which includes both reading rate and reading comprehension. Intensive reading focuses on reading small chunks of text with the explicit purpose of learning a new reading skill or learning new vocabulary, while extensive reading focuses on reading larger amounts of text.

What a balanced model of reading instruction suggests is that there should be a specific link between the intensive and extensive instruction. After explicitly practicing a new strategy for vocabulary learning, there should be natural opportunities to practice that strategy during extensive reading. This suggests that extensive reading is more than just encouraging students to read a lot of material. Especially at the intermediate levels of reading instruction, there should be pedagogical ties between the two types of reading. In this way, learners are guided more carefully in their reading instruction.

How do the five characteristics of an engaged reader tie into this model for balanced instruction? What can teachers do to develop the five characteristics of an engaged reader?

Reading purposes

At all points of reading instruction, teachers must keep readers focused on the question of *why*? Teachers should encourage readers in class to always be prepared to explain why they are reading a paragraph from their textbook. Why are they reading a newspaper or magazine article? Why are they reading a novel? Why are they reading an academic text? Teachers will help learners stay focused on their reading purpose by keeping the *why* question front and center during reading instruction. One way that this can be accomplished is by incorporating a purposeful reading activity into the teaching plan.

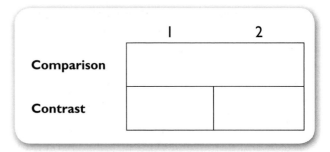

Figure 3. Sample purposeful reading activity.

Figure 3 is an example of instructions that the teacher can give readers for a purposeful reading activity. Additional purposeful reading activities for students include reading in preparation for talking with a peer about what they have read, reading and gathering information to support their opinions, and reading in preparation for writing a summary.

In this reading activity, we will read two short paragraphs about environmental concerns in Kenya and in Costa Rica. Your reading purpose is to be prepared to complete the comparison and contrast graphic organizer after reading the two paragraphs. While you are reading, the teacher can stop you at any point and ask you, *why are we reading this*? What will your answer be?

Fluent reading

One key methodological issue that teachers and materials developers need to pay particular attention to is the selection of level-appropriate texts. For readers to develop appropriate levels of fluency, the text they are using must not be too difficult. Reading materials need to provide texts of varying levels of difficulty. But in my experience, in far too many reading classrooms around the world the texts that students are asked to read are at a difficult level of reading. Perhaps this is a factor that contributes to why so many students report not liking to read.

One simple reading fluency practice that teachers can use to build reading fluency is called rate build-up reading. In rate build-up reading, students are given 60 seconds to read as much material as they can. I specifically ask students to mark a ① in the text where they finished reading after the first minute. They then begin reading the text again from the beginning and are given an additional 60 seconds. They are to read more material during the second 60-second period than they did during the first. After the second time through the same material, I ask them to mark a ② where they are in the text when I say stop. The drill is repeated a third and a fourth time. The purpose of this activity is to reread "old" material quickly, gliding into the new. As the eyes move quickly over the "old" material, the students actually learn how to get their eyes moving at a faster reading rate. The exercise involves more than simply moving the eyes quickly: the material should be processed and comprehended. As students participate in this rate-building activity, they learn to increase their reading rate.

After each reading, I take the opportunity to conduct some type of a comprehension check to help strengthen readers' comprehension. I may ask them to turn to a partner and describe one thing they liked about what they read. Or I may ask them to identify any vocabulary words that are new to them. Or I may ask them to complete a graphic organizer for the key ideas in the text.

Also, after the second reading and the third reading, I have the readers set a reading fluency goal. I ask them to look at where the number ① is in the text and where the number ② is. I then ask them where they hope the number ③ will be after they read the text the third time. I have them write the number ③ in the text and draw a circle around the number. They then read for the third time, and I ask them if they have reached their goal. I usually know whether they reached the goal based on the moans or exclamations of excitement when I say stop. I repeat the same goal-setting process between the third and fourth times through the text.

This activity takes no more than 10 minutes of class time. Once students understand the goal of building the amount of text that is read during each 60-second period, they want to engage in this activity to push themselves to be more fluent readers. After introducing this activity in class, I ask the students to follow the same instructions on their own outside of class during their extensive reading. This provides students the opportunity to practice on their own something that we have done in class during intensive reading.

Grabe (2009) argues that "fluency practice cannot be an afterthought in instructional planning; rather, it needs to become an equal partner with comprehension practice in reading instruction" (p. 105). I encourage teachers to explicitly build more fluency practice into their instructional practices. In addition to rate build-up reading, ideas on how to build reading fluency include shadow reading, repeated reading, class-paced reading, and self-paced reading (N. J. Anderson, 1999, 2009).

Shadow reading has five steps. First, students listen to the reading passage. Second, students listen and follow the text with their eyes. Next, students listen and speak along with the text. Fourth, students read the text silently. Finally, students read the text aloud. After each of these steps, the teacher should engage the students in a comprehension check so that the focus is not just on reading rate. Also, any of these steps may be repeated as many times as is necessary to achieve fluent reading.

Repeated reading is somewhat similar to rate build-up reading in its purpose but not in how it is carried out. Students read a short passage over and over again until they achieve criterion levels of reading rate and comprehension. For example, they may try to read a short 100-word paragraph four times in two minutes. The criterion levels may vary from class to class, but reasonable goals to work toward are criterion levels of 200 wpm at 70% comprehension.

During a class-paced reading activity, the class sets a reading rate goal (i.e., 200 wpm). Once that goal is established, the average number of words per page of the material being read is calculated. It is then determined how much material needs to be read in one minute to meet the class goal. For example, if the class goal is to read 200 wpm and the material being read has an average of 100 words per page, the class would be expected to read one page every 30 seconds. As each 30-second period elapses, the teacher indicates to the class to move to the next page. Students are encouraged to keep up with the established class goal. Of course, those who read faster than 200 wpm are not expected to slow down their reading rate. As long as they are ahead of the designated page, they continue reading.

During a self-paced reading activity, each student determines his or her own reading-rate goal. The student then determines how much material needs to be read in a 60-second period to meet the rate. For example, suppose a student's objective rate is 180 wpm and the material being read has an average number of 10 words per line. The student would need to read 18 lines of text in 1 minute to meet the goal. The activity proceeds nicely by having each student mark off several chunks of lines and silently read for a period of 5–7 minutes with the instructor calling out minute intervals. Students can then determine if they are keeping up with their individual reading-rate goal.

READING COMPREHENSION

As part of the preparation for engaging L2 readers, teachers can build into their planning an explicit reading comprehension activity. Trabasso and Bouchard (2002) point out that, in spite of the significant research available on the importance of teaching reading comprehension strategies, very little of this research gets applied in pedagogical practice. They also emphasize that, unless teachers have been prepared to explicitly teach comprehension strategies, they are likely not to do so.

Since vocabulary acquisition is a major key to reading comprehension, explicit vocabulary instruction is essential for readers at all levels of proficiency but especially for learners at the intermediate level. One way to help learners move through the intermediate-level slump is to provide explicit vocabulary instruction. Learners can easily measure progress and development in their language abilities through studying and using new vocabulary. Folse (2010) points out that the teacher in a language classroom may be the best source of input for vocabulary acquisition.

Specifically, what can the teacher do in the language classroom to provide explicit vocabulary instruction? One activity that can be used to help learners build vocabulary knowledge and automaticity in word recognition is a rapid word-recognition exercise. In preparing for this activity, I encourage teachers to identify 10 vocabulary words that will appear in a reading passage that students are going to read. Those 10 words are then recycled five times on the rapid word-recognition activity sheet. An example of one such sheet appears in the Appendix.[4] Notice that the 10 vocabulary words are recycled in groups of 10 (1–10, 11–20, 21–30, etc.).

Students are given a specific time limit (not too long and not too short) to look at the word on the left and identify its corresponding mate on the right of the vertical line. Notice how the distractors have been carefully selected so that the exact word must be identified. I usually start this activity by giving the student 50 seconds (1 second for each of the 50 words on the worksheet) to quickly complete the exercise and mark a line through the match for the target word.

Following the timed activity, I conduct a vocabulary learning exercise in class with the 10 words. This activity is a modified version of one proposed by Allen (1999). Using the rapid word-recognition worksheet (see the Appendix), I have the learners look at the vocabulary listed in 1–10. I then provide them with the following instructions:

> How well do you know the words 1–10 from this rapid word-recognition activity? To the left of the number on the worksheet, write one of the four numbers to indicate how well you know each word.
>
> 0 = I do not know this word.
> 1 = I think I have seen this word before, but I do not know what it means.
> 2 = I have seen this word before, and I think I know the definition, but I'm not sure.
> 3 = I know the definition of this word.

Once they have completed this activity, I ask them to circulate among their classmates to find someone who knows the vocabulary that they do not know. If they wrote the number 0, 1, or 2 next to a word on the list, they are to look for someone who wrote a 3 next to that word. This allows students to teach each other the meanings of the vocabulary they are about to encounter in the reading that will follow. If there are any words on the list that no one has written a 3 next to, I know that I need to engage in explicit vocabulary instruction for those words.

Just prior to reading the passage that contains these 10 vocabulary words, I have the students turn their rapid word-recognition exercise page over to the reverse side, where I have provided an identical copy of the activity. I give the students an additional 50 seconds to see how many of the words they can match. I have the learners compare how many words they were able to identify in the first exercise compared to the second exercise. Following this second activity, we move to the reading passage where the students will see the words in the context of a reading passage. The students then read the passage. As a post-reading exercise, I have them skim the reading passage to find and circle the 10 words in the reading. We look at the context in which the word is used. If needed, we repeat the rapid word-recognition activity during this class session or the next class session. This is a useful example of how reading comprehension exercises can be integrated into the lesson with a focus on the rapid word recognition of vocabulary.

Metacognitive awareness of reading strategies

I like the title of a resource for reading teachers entitled *Comprehension Shouldn't Be Silent* (Kelley & Clausen-Grace, 2007). Kelley and Clausen-Grace outline a four-phase framework for teaching readers to be more metacognitively aware of their strategies. Although it was written for elementary school teachers, it has useful applications to L2 reading instruction. The Metacognitive Teaching Framework is designed to assist teachers in helping readers to make their comprehension visible. The four phases are think-aloud, refining strategy use, letting strategy use gel (or come together), and self-assessment and goal setting. A valuable section of the textbook outlines five reading strategies that readers can engage in to practice being more metacognitively aware: predicting, making connections, questioning, visualizing, and summarizing.

Kelly and Clausen-Grace (2007) emphasize that writing a strong summary depends on the reader's comprehension of the text, thus illustrating the integrative nature of strategy instruction and reading comprehension from the balanced model in Figure 2, explained earlier. One activity that they suggest is the preparation of a summarizing rubric. The rubric they provide lists three categories: completeness, correctness, and quality of the summary. They then provide four levels for scoring the summary for each of these three categories: intervention, instructional, independent, and advanced. An advanced rating indicates that the reader/writer has all the correct information included in the summary. A rating of independent indicates an adequate summary that the reader/writer was able to complete on his or her own. An instructional rating indicates that the reader/writer needs more instructional time on writing summaries to produce a stronger summary. Finally, an intervention rating signifies that the teacher needs to intervene with the reader/writer for more explicit one-on-one assistance to produce a stronger summary. By providing the readers with the rubric before the reading and explaining how to write a summary, we can model how we use the rubric to produce a strong summary. For the reader's summary to receive a rating of advanced, it must have the following characteristics in each category:

- *Completeness.* It includes the most important ideas, details, facts, and important vocabulary.
- *Correctness.* It clearly and correctly states the main idea and all the key information.
- *Quality of writing.* It is written in the students' own words and contains a smooth flow of information from one idea to another.

The value of providing the summarizing rubric is in getting the students to use it while they are writing and then to verbalize how they are using it. The verbalization of the strategies highlights that comprehension is not silent and assists the students to be more metacognitively aware of what they are doing while reading to produce a strong summary. Table 1 provides an example scoring rubric that I have created based on Kelly and Clausen-Grace (2007).

Motivation

Dörnyei (2001) has prepared a list of 20 motivational strategies specifically designed around his model for motivation in the L2 classroom. (See also Dörnyei, this volume, Figure 1.) These strategies are listed in four categories: (1) creating the basic motivational conditions; (2) generating initial motivation; (3) maintaining and protecting motivation; and (4) encouraging positive retrospective self-evaluation. I encourage teachers to keep this list of strategies in front of them while they are planning their lessons. If we do this, we can explicitly plan how we can weave "motivational moments" into our lessons. A motivational moment is a opportunity for the teacher to motivate the readers. I recommend that a motivational moment last no longer than 60 seconds. For example, the first strategy Dörnyei lists, under the category of creating the basic motivational conditions, is to "demonstrate and talk about

Table 1. Summary Scoring Rubric.

	Rubric		
Scoring Level	**Completeness**	**Correctness**	**Quality**
Intervention	Your summary is missing information and/or adds information not included in the original.	Your summary does not state the main idea. Some of the information is not correct.	Your summary is copied from the text.
Instructional	Your summary is not complete. You are missing important information and/or you added information not included in the original.	Your summary has the main idea, but it is only partly correct. Some of the information is not correct.	Your summary is written in your own words, but it is not presented as connected text.
Independent	Your summary includes some of the most important ideas, details, facts, and important vocabulary.	Your summary expresses the main idea and includes correct facts.	Your summary is written in your own words, but the flow of the information needs more attention.
Advanced	Your summary includes the most important ideas, details, facts, and important vocabulary.	Your summary includes a clearly stated main idea, and all the information included in the summary is correct.	Your summary is written in your own words, and it flows smoothly from one idea to another.

(Adapted from Kelly and Clausen-Grace, 2007.)

your own enthusiasm for the course material, and how it affects you personally" (Dörnyei, 2001, p. 33). Usually on the first day of a reading course, I take a minute to tell my students how excited I am about reading and how it makes me a better world citizen. I tell them that I read regularly in my second language (Spanish) to maintain my language skills. When students hear the teacher talk about the excitement of reading in a second language, it helps them also want to read.

FUTURE TRENDS

There are two areas that I see as vital in helping to move forward our work as ESL/EFL reading teachers and to assist struggling readers to overcome the intermediate-level slump: teacher preparation and curriculum development. Janzen (2007) shares the concern for teacher development. She worked closely with six teachers in her research to identify how they could be better prepared to address the needs of learners. Her work provides six categories of concerns:

1. dealing with a wide range of learner proficiencies in the classroom
2. determining appropriate use of materials
3. developing effective instructional practices in the areas of decoding skills, vocabulary, writing, and thematic teaching
4. developing a love of reading
5. cooperating and coping with mainstream teachers and with school demands
6. working with students who have limited or no school in their L1 and/or with students who have limited proficiency in their L1 (pp. 711–712)

The trend for the future must be effective teacher preparation programs that explicitly prepare teachers to address the concerns identified by Janzen (2007). I am particularly hopeful that Category 3 will be adequately addressed in teacher preparation programs. If we expect teachers to be prepared to teach decoding, there must be an explicit component of our teacher preparation programs that provides the instructional practices that teachers need to do the job. Also, training teachers how to address the issues of vocabulary instruction and integrating reading with writing must receive more attention in teacher preparation programs.

The second future trend is tied to Category 2 identified in Janzen's research (2007)—determining the appropriate use of materials. Evans, Hartshorn, and Anderson (2010) suggest a principled approach to the development of content-based materials for L2 reading. (See also Snow, this volume.) They suggest three curriculum principles to guide teachers in the development of materials: responsiveness, cohesion, and stability. For materials to be responsive, teachers must first conduct a needs analysis. A needs analysis involves determining what the students need to be able to read and do with the information they read. This is most frequently accomplished through a questionnaire directed to individual students or by interviewing those who engage with the students in a context outside the classroom. A reading curriculum must be responsive to the future needs of the students by helping them develop the reading skills they will need when they complete their study of English. When a curriculum is responsive to learners' needs, they see greater value in being more engaged readers.

The curriculum also needs to be cohesive. Cohesion must exist within a single reading course as well as across reading courses. For example, a program curriculum could provide training to all reading teachers to use reading fluency activities in every class. One thing we know about the development of fluency is that it must be a continual focus in the classroom over an extended period of time to sufficiently develop fluency in readers. A cohesive program will have fluency-related goals for each class so that there is a focus on its development within a class and also across classes in the program. In this way, as students progress through a program they will continue to explicitly develop their reading fluency skills.

The final curriculum development principle identified by Evans et al. (2010) is that a reading curriculum should be stable. Changes in a reading curriculum should be deliberate and careful. Sometimes teachers want to change books as soon as they see a new one. Many times, a book is what drives the curriculum and not the learning outcomes, such as the improvement of reading. When a reading curriculum is stable, there is time to evaluate the successes and then, based on the deficiencies, make changes that will lead to a stronger curriculum.

CONCLUSION

Recall Brad's experience, which opened this chapter. His journal entry recorded that he felt overwhelmed and discouraged after his first week of full-time teaching in his new position. However, he was clear that he would not give up. For a reading teacher to improve his or her ability to integrate all the elements that we have discussed in this chapter into teaching will take time. Following the examples in this chapter, teachers can provide purposeful reading activities for each text. They can tie the reading purpose to their reading comprehension objectives. Teachers can encourage the readers to be metacognitively aware of a wider range of strategies that they could be using to accomplish their reading purpose. They can also explicitly build reading fluency by engaging in some of the numerous and varied fluency activities identified in this chapter. By so doing, effective teachers will create a more motivating classroom environment in which learners will want to be engaged readers.

Hudson (2007) put it nicely when he wrote "our long-term goal is to have students who do not stop reading when the reading class is over" (p. 29). Effective preparation on the part of the reading teacher can lead to this result.

SUMMARY

➤ It is crucial to develop engaged L2 readers, especially at the intermediate levels of language proficiency.
➤ Engaged readers are those who:
  ▪ read widely with different purposes
  ▪ read fluently and use their cognitive capacity to focus on the meaning of what they read
  ▪ develop their comprehension by using what they read
  ▪ are metacognitively aware as they use a variety of reading strategies
  ▪ are motivated readers
➤ Teachers play a key role in developing engaged readers. When we carefully prepare ourselves to be better teachers of reading, students will ultimately benefit.
➤ The development of appropriate curricula for teaching reading should be a focus in language programs. A curriculum should be:
  ▪ responsive to student needs
  ▪ cohesive across classes and levels in a program
  ▪ stable; frequent changes in a curriculum suggest that a program is not sure what it hopes to accomplish.

DISCUSSION QUESTIONS

1. Do you know someone you would classify as a strong L2 reader? What are the characteristics of that reader that make him or her strong? Is there a relationship between the characteristics you have identified and the five characteristics of an engaged reader identified in this chapter?

2. Do you know someone you would classify as a weak L2 reader? What are the characteristics of that reader that make him or her weak? Is there a relationship between the characteristics of the weak reader you have identified and the five characteristics of an engaged reader identified in this chapter?

3. Why is motivation such an important aspect of language teaching and learning? Who bears the responsibility for motivation? What role could you play as the teacher in motivating students to be more engaged readers?

SUGGESTED ACTIVITIES

1. List five areas you would like to improve in your teaching of L2 reading that you have learned about in this chapter. Choose one thing at a time, and focus on improving that aspect of your teaching. Share with others what you are doing to become a better teacher of reading. Remember that it will take time to fully develop the ability to integrate improvements into your teaching.

2. Rank the five characteristics of an engaged reader in terms of their importance to you as a teacher or future teacher. Compare your ranking with others. Discuss why you each have the order you do.

3. Carefully review the steps for conducting a rate build-up fluency exercise as described in this chapter. Carry out the activity at least five times over the course of two weeks with your students or with student volunteers. After each time you use the activity, record in a teaching journal what went well and what did not go well. After using it a fifth time, ask the students if they like the activity and why or why not. Make a final journal entry, and then discuss your experience of using the activity with a trusted colleague.

4. Review Figure 2, the model for a balanced reading curriculum. Based on your experience as a reader, do you think there are any things that could be added to the list for intensive reading instruction? Is there anything you could add to the list for extensive reading?

FURTHER READING

Cohen, R. (2009). *Explorations in second language reading*. Alexandria, VA: Teachers of English to Speakers of Other Languages, Inc.

This book is part of the TESOL Classroom Practice Series, which focuses on strengthening classroom teaching. This volume in the series emphasizes reading *in* the classroom and encourages teachers to reemphasize the ways that reading can strengthen learning in all language skill areas.

Hudson, T. (2007). *Teaching second language reading*. New York, NY: Oxford University Press.

This volume is particularly valuable in providing L2 teachers with a solid theoretical foundation to the issues and concepts related to L1 and L2 reading. Reading skills, metacognition, content schema, genre, and reading-writing relationships are a few key issues addressed by Hudson.

Mikulecky, B. S. (2011). *A short course in teaching reading: Practical techniques for building reading power* (2nd ed.). White Plains, NY: Pearson.

This textbook for teachers addresses in more detail issues identified in this chapter. See particularly Mikulecky's treatment of improving bottom-up reading, developing reading fluency, vocabulary building, text structure, and comprehension.

APPENDIX: RAPID WORD RECOGNITION

Instructions

This activity provides practice in rapid word recognition. The words that you see below are from the passage we will read in class today. You will see a target word following by a |. Following the | you will see four or five other words that are similar to the target word. Your task is to draw a line through the word that matches the target word. Work as quickly as possible. You will have 50 seconds to complete this activity.

Two examples are done for you.

Examples		
A. healthy	|	wealthy healthier heady handy ~~healthy~~
B. harmful	|	brimful handful ~~harmful~~ hurtful harmed

1. simple	|	simply sample symbol simple subtle
2. harmful	|	brimful harmed handful hurtful harmful
3. encourage	|	entourage encourage engage enrage
4. collect	|	correct contact collect connect context
5. chef	|	chief cheat chef chat check
6. serve	|	serve curve savvy swerve salve
7. simple	|	simple symbol sample sample subtle
8. healthy	|	healthy wealthy healthier heady handy
9. kitchen	|	kitchen kitten kindle kicking kites
10. harmful	|	brimful handful harmful harmed hurtful
11. weight	|	waste wait weight whet white
12. healthy	|	healthier wealthy heady healthy handy
13. collect	|	correct connect contact context collect
14. serve	|	curve swerve savvy serve salve
15. encourage	|	engage entourage encourage enrage
16. chef	|	chief chef chat cheat check
17. weight	|	weight waste wait whet white
18. kitchen	|	kitten kindle kitchen kicking kites
19. harmful	|	brimful harmful hurtful harmed handful
20. junk food	|	dog food junk food cat food junk yard
21. chef	|	chief cheat chat check chef
22. harmful	|	harmful handful hurtful brimful harmed
23. encourage	|	entourage enrage encourage engage
24. simple	|	sample simple symbol simply subtle
25. collect	|	contact correct connect collect context
26. serve	|	curve serve savvy salve swerve
27. kitchen	|	kitten kindle kicking kitchen kites
28. weight	|	waste wait whet weight white
29. simple	|	simply sample subtle symbol simple
30. junk food	|	cat food dog food junk yard junk food
31. harmful	|	brimful handful hurtful harmful harmed
32. healthy	|	wealthy healthier healthy handy heady

33. chef	check cheat chat chef chief
34. collect	correct collect context contact connect
35. serve	savvy swerve curve salve serve
36. encourage	encourage enrage entourage engage
37. weight	waste weight wait whet white
38. junk food	dog food junk yard junk food cat food
39. kitchen	kitten kindle kicking kites kitchen
40. junk food	junk food junk yard dog food cat food
41. healthy	wealthy handy healthier heady healthy
42. collect	collect connect correct contact context
43. encourage	entourage engage enrage encourage
44. simple	simply sample simple symbol subtle
45. chef	chef cheat chief chat check
46. serve	curve swerve serve savvy salve
47. kitchen	kitten kitchen kindle kicking kites
48. healthy	handy healthy wealthy healthier heady
49. junk food	junk food dog food junk yard cat food
50. weight	waste wait whet white weight

ENDNOTES

[1] This refers to the computerized version of the international Test of English as a Foreign Language (TOEFL) examination that is typically required of non-native speaking applicants to U.S. universities.

[2] See http://www.readinghorizons.com/

[3] A *rime* is a vowel together with any following consonant(s) in the same syllable.

[4] This rapid word-recognition exercise sheet is based on a reading from *ACTIVE Skills for Reading: Book 1* (N. J. Anderson, 2007), *Jaime Oliver's School Dinners* (Unit 1, Chapter 1).

13 | Teaching Reading for Academic Purposes

WILLIAM GRABE AND FREDRICKA L. STOLLER

KEY QUESTIONS

> ➤ What are the key component abilities that contribute to reading for academic purposes?
> ➤ How can teachers prepare English for academic purposes students for the reading demands that they will face in future classes?
> ➤ How can English for academic purposes teachers supplement traditional textbooks to develop more effective reading instruction?

EXPERIENCE

Picture an English for academic purposes (EAP) reading class. You have completed a pre-reading task, directed students to skim pages 17–21 for main ideas, and just asked students to stop skimming. For homework, students will reread the same pages for a different purpose. Four students have raised their hands and made the following statements. All but one of the statements are characteristic of EAP classes with reading skills development goals. Which is the uncharacteristic one?

S1: What? Read pages 17–21! That's too much, teacher. Can we have extra time to read those pages? Or can you make the assignment shorter?

S2: What means this word, teacher? I cannot find the meaning in my dictionary.

S3: Read for details? What do you mean?

S4: Ohhh (sadly). Stop now? Teacher, can we have five more minutes (to read)?

Statement S4 is the unusual one. How often do EAP students ask for more time to read? Yet that is exactly what should happen for reading skills development to occur. In this chapter, we offer pedagogical suggestions that can help students develop the abilities and motivation needed to read more and to read more skillfully.

WHAT IS INVOLVED IN READING FOR ACADEMIC PURPOSES?

The ability to read well may be the most important second language (L2) academic skill needed by EAP students. In academic contexts, students' success depends in large part on their grasp of information learned through reading. In such settings, students are typically required to read a lot and for different purposes. Students need to, at a minimum, be able to identify main ideas and details; distinguish between fact and opinion; draw inferences; determine author stance and bias; and summarize, synthesize, and extend textual information to new tasks (e.g., class projects, oral presentations, and examinations). That reading provides a major source of input for further student learning of both language and content is indisputable.

The mastery of academic reading skills requires not only the integration of comprehension abilities but also the development of a very large vocabulary and a reasonably good command of grammar resources (Shiotsu, 2010). Furthermore, to handle academic reading loads, students need a repertoire of reading strategies and plenty of conscious practice using strategies in meaningful combinations to achieve reading goals. In this way, students can work toward overcoming the challenges associated with reading a lot, untangling dense texts, understanding new concepts, and making connections across texts.

Many EAP students enter our classes with limited L2 reading experience and, oftentimes, little if any practice reading for academic purposes in their first languages (L1s). Fortunately for our students, explicit instruction in reading skills development can make a difference (Grabe, 2009) and establish the foundations for ongoing reading skills improvement and lifelong reading abilities.

CONCEPTUAL UNDERPINNINGS

Reading is a complex skill, as revealed by syntheses of L1 and L2 reading research (e.g., Grabe, 2009; Han & Anderson, 2009; Koda, 2005). Research on L1 and L2 reading suggests that skilled reading requires, at a minimum, the abilities outlined in Figure 1. The first three abilities listed suggest the need for rapid and automatic word recognition and fluent recognition processing of phrase and clause structures to support comprehension. These abilities argue for fluency practice, extensive reading (i.e., reading a lot of relatively easy material), and time spent on the development of a large recognition vocabulary. Abilities 4 and 5 signal

the importance of developing main-idea comprehension using all levels of language knowledge, including discourse structure awareness. Abilities 6–10 identify strategic processing as a means for improving comprehension of more difficult texts and carrying out academic tasks that require the application of text information. Abilities 11 and 12 highlight the importance of reading fluency development, reading practice for extended periods of time, and student motivation.

An effective reading curriculum interprets the findings in Figure 1 from the perspectives of institutional and teacher goals; students' abilities and proficiency levels; and constraints imposed by time, costs, resources, and teacher preparedness. Nonetheless, a general set of nine curricular principles (Figure 2) can be proposed to assist teachers, materials writers, and curriculum developers in translating research findings into instructional practices appropriate for EAP reading classrooms. (Note that Figure 2 is not intended

1. Decoding graphic forms for efficient word recognition
2. Accessing the meanings of a large number of words automatically
3. Drawing meaning from phrase- and clause-level grammatical information
4. Combining clause-level meanings into larger networks of text comprehension
5. Recognizing discourse structures that build and support comprehension
6. Using reading strategies for a range of academic reading tasks
7. Setting goals for reading, monitoring comprehension for reading goals, adjusting goals as needed, and using text information to achieve reading goals
8. Using inferences of various types
9. Drawing on prior knowledge as appropriate
10. Evaluating, integrating, and synthesizing information for critical reading comprehension
11. Maintaining these processes fluently for extended periods of time
12. Sustaining motivation to persist in reading

Figure 1. Skilled-reader abilities that have implications for L2 reading instruction.

1. Integrate reading skill instruction with extensive practice and exposure to print.
2. Use reading resources that are interesting, varied, attractive, abundant, and accessible.
3. Give students some choice in what they read.
4. Introduce reading skills and provide students with practice opportunities by first drawing on course book passages.
5. Connect readings to students' background knowledge.
6. Structure lessons around pre-, during, and post-reading tasks.
7. Provide students with opportunities to experience comprehension success.
8. Build expectations that reading occurs in every lesson.
9. Plan instruction around a curricular framework that integrates goals for the development of reading abilities. To do so,
   • promote word recognition efficiency
   • assist students in building a large recognition vocabulary
   • create opportunities for comprehension skills practice
   • build students' discourse-structure awareness
   • develop the strategic reader
   • build students' reading fluency
   • provide consistent extensive reading opportunities
   • motivate students to read
   • integrate content- and language-learning goals

Figure 2. Nine curricular principles for EAP reading instruction.

to map explicitly onto Figure 1 because research findings represent only one contribution, among many, to curricular principles.) Additional principles could be proposed, and some of these nine may not apply to every EAP context, but these nine provide a strong foundation for EAP reading instruction.

These nine curricular principles help frame EAP reading instruction that develops students' reading comprehension abilities. First, and perhaps most important, students build reading abilities through consistent practice and exposure to print. There are simply no short cuts. EAP students improve their reading abilities by reading—and reading a lot. Unfortunately, students do not typically read a lot in EAP classes. Instead, we commonly devote time to a review of comprehension questions and vocabulary exercises, but we do not ask our students to engage in much reading. Such conventional practices need to change if students' reading improvement is to become a curricular priority.

Second, students are more likely to engage in reading (and reading instruction) when text materials are interesting, varied, abundant, attractive, and easily accessible. If mandated textbook readings are not inherently interesting, the teacher should determine ways to frame them so that they are (more) interesting to students. Third, allowing some level of student choice in reading material and activities typically leads to student engagement, motivation, and autonomy, three keys to reading improvement. Fourth, instruction should build reading skills development activities around the main passages in students' textbooks. If important skills, comprehension strategies, and language features cannot be exemplified initially with the texts assigned for the class, then either the textbook does not address the skills that students need (and should be reevaluated) or the skills, strategies, and language features targeted for instruction may not be as important as assumed.

Fifth, students need to call up appropriate background knowledge to support their comprehension efforts. While drawing on loosely related background knowledge is not always helpful, the activation of specific and directly relevant background information improves main-idea comprehension and strategic processing. Sixth, reading lessons should be structured consistently around a pre-, during-, and post-reading framework that prepares students for reading, helps them while reading, and then guides them in reconsidering texts (and text information) for a variety of purposes (Figure 3; see also Hedgcock & Ferris, 2009).

Seventh, EAP students need to experience success when reading; a steady stream of frustrating reading experiences inevitably leads to student disengagement, exactly what we do not want as we work to prepare students for future reading demands. Eighth, some actual text reading should be included in *every* class session; too often, this point is overlooked. Finally, students benefit from EAP reading curricula that consistently integrate the instructional goals required for the development of skilled reading (listed under Principle 9 in Figure 2). These goals, explored in more detail throughout this chapter, suggest the need for explicit comprehension instruction along with the development of the strategic reader, and for student involvement and motivation for reading. While these nine goals may not be granted equal time in all instructional contexts, consistent attention to the most important ones, for a given context, will contribute to students' reading comprehension development.

CLASSROOM APPLICATIONS

The goals for reading instruction listed under Principle 9 in Figure 2 translate into practice in various ways. In the sections that follow, we explore each goal and offer instructional tips that have proven effective in a range of instructional settings. EAP teachers may not have the opportunity to adapt every idea presented here for immediate use. Nonetheless, we suggest that EAP teachers identify those practices that might realistically be incorporated into the reading components of their EAP curricula.

Promote word recognition efficiency

Most EAP students, at secondary and tertiary levels, enter our classes with reasonable control over basic word- and phrase-recognition abilities. Over time, students improve their word-recognition skills when engaged in vocabulary development activities, reading fluency practice, and extensive reading. Yet many EAP students benefit from

Reading lesson stage	Objectives
Pre-reading	• Establish a purpose for reading. • Tap prior knowledge. • Provide information needed for comprehension (e.g., key vocabulary, important concepts). • Set up expectations. • Stimulate interest. • Build confidence and motivation. • Explore text organization. • Model and practice common pre-reading strategies (e.g., identifying reading goals, previewing the text, predicting main ideas).
During reading	• Guide reading to facilitate comprehension (e.g., by asking students to fill in a graphic organizer—that is, a visual display of information, such as in a table, chart, graph, or time line—that reflects relationships among ideas in the text). • Help students construct meaning and monitor comprehension. • Give students opportunities to connect what is read with what they know so they can evaluate what is being read. • Support ongoing summarization. • Model and practice common strategies used at this stage (e.g., monitoring comprehension, identifying difficulties, repairing faulty comprehension). • Promote discussions that support comprehension and strategy development.
Post-reading	• Check comprehension. • Explore how text organization supports comprehension. • Provide opportunities for reading fluency development (e.g., rereading activities). • Ask students to summarize, synthesize, evaluate, integrate, extend, and apply text information. • Ask students to critique the author and aspects of the text (e.g., writing, content). • Establish and recognize comprehension successes (e.g., completing written summaries, lining up a set of main-idea statements in the correct order, distinguishing between main ideas and details). • Model and practice common post-reading strategies (e.g., reflecting on what has been learned through reading, making connections across texts).

Figure 3. Objectives at each stage of the pre-, during-, and post-reading framework.

word-recognition practice through oral paired rereading (explained later in the chapter), word matching, word- (and phrase-) recognition exercises, and flashcards. Flashcards, while sometimes considered passé, can prove effective not only for vocabulary building and vocabulary collecting but also for word-recognition practice (Nicholson, 2000). Three activities that promote word- and phrase-recognition speed and accuracy, and that support reading fluency, are described next.

Word- and phrase-recognition exercises. Most EAP reading textbooks do not include word- or phrase-recognition exercises, although a few exceptions exist (e.g., Folse, 2004; Jeffries & Mikulecky, 2009a, 2009b). Fortunately, teachers can easily create recognition exercises, also called timed word-selection exercises (Folse, 2004), with vocabulary from the texts that students are reading. Common recognition-exercise formats are shown in Figures 4 and 5. Students generally enjoy recognition exercises in a timed recognition or "beat-the-clock" fashion and with record-keeping charts for tracking progress. Through such exercises, students develop a heightened awareness of the role that rapid word recognition plays in reading. Fortunately, relatively little class time is needed to incorporate, let us say, three recognition exercises per textbook chapter (for suggestions on using recognition exercises in class, see M. Crawford, 2005; Stoller, 1993).

Timed semantic-connection exercises. Another way to provide practice in quick lexical access is to create exercises with words that are already familiar to students. Under timed conditions, students consider the key word (on the left) and multiple choices (to the right), and select the one word (or phrase) that: (1) has something in common with

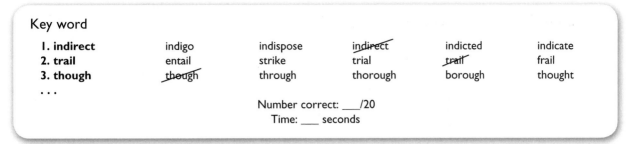

Figure 4. Common word-recognition exercise format.

Key word					
1. indirect	indigo	indispose	~~indirect~~	indicted	indicate
2. trail	entail	strike	trial	~~trail~~	frail
3. though	~~though~~	through	thorough	borough	thought
...					

Number correct: ___/20
Time: ___ seconds

Figure 5. Common phrase-recognition exercise format.

Key phrase				
1. in conclusion	to conclude	~~in conclusion~~	in consultation	in retribution
2. as required	~~as required~~	as reported	in retirement	as registered
3. on the one hand	on the other hand	on the other band	in the one hand	~~on the one hand~~
...				

Number correct: ___/20
Time: ___ seconds

the key word; (2) is similar in meaning; or (3) is a common collocate of the key word (see Figure 6).

Lexical access fluency exercise. More advanced EAP students benefit from lexical access fluency exercises (Figure 7). A variation on the timed semantic-connection task (Figure 6), these exercises require the matching of key words (in boldface, on the left) with their definitions or synonyms under timed conditions. Students progress through three sets of the same key words and definitions, with definitions scrambled in each set (see Figure 7) and with less time allowed for the completion of each set (e.g., 60, 50, and 40 seconds). These exercises take little class time and one three-part set could easily be created for each assigned reading.

Build a large recognition vocabulary

It is generally agreed that vocabulary knowledge is closely related to reading abilities (e.g., Laufer & Ravenhorst-Kalovski, 2010; I. S. P. Nation, 2008; Pulido & Hambrick, 2008). Evidence also suggests that: (1) students need to recognize at least 95% of

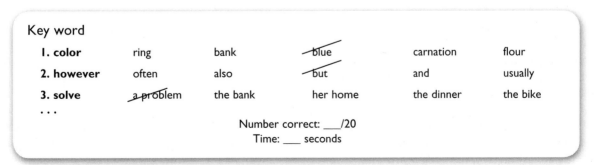

Key word					
1. color	ring	bank	~~blue~~	carnation	flour
2. however	often	also	~~but~~	and	usually
3. solve	~~a problem~~	the bank	her home	the dinner	the bike
...					

Number correct: ___/20
Time: ___ seconds

Figure 6. Sample timed semantic-connection exercise.

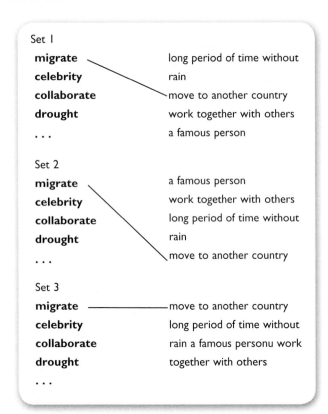

Set 1

migrate	long period of time without
celebrity	rain
collaborate	move to another country
drought	work together with others
. . .	a famous person

Set 2

migrate	a famous person
celebrity	work together with others
collaborate	long period of time without
drought	rain
. . .	move to another country

Set 3

migrate	move to another country
celebrity	long period of time without
collaborate	rain a famous personu work
drought	together with others
. . .	

Figure 7. Sample lexical access fluency exercise.

the words that they encounter for adequate comprehension in instructional contexts; and (2) more fluent reading and comprehension generally occur when a reader recognizes 98–99% of the words in a text (Laufer & Ravenhorst-Kalovski, 2010; I. S. P. Nation, 2006; Schmitt, Jiang, & Grabe, 2011). The number of words needed for 95% coverage of most texts seems to lie somewhere between 10,000 and 15,000 words; 98–99% of coverage for most texts probably requires a recognition vocabulary of about 35,000–40,000 words (e.g., Schmitt, 2008).

A realistic goal for more advanced reading is an L2 recognition vocabulary above 10,000 words. Of course, the argument that students need to know the first 2,000 most frequent word families still remains a key goal for vocabulary instruction (I. S. P. Nation, 2001). At the same time, direct vocabulary practice with large sets of words may be essential to increase L2 recognition vocabulary knowledge. To institute an active vocabulary development framework that guides EAP teachers, materials designers, and curriculum developers, the following eight resources should be in place:

(1) systematic procedures for selecting target words; (2) techniques for introducing new words and encouraging students to use words meaningfully; (3) activities to practice word-meaning connections and work with large sets of words; (4) tasks for building students' word-learning strategies; (5) approaches for creating a vocabulary-rich classroom environment; (6) tasks that guide students in becoming independent word collectors; (7) ways to build student motivation for word learning; and (8) the recycling of texts and vocabulary. Next, we introduce three ideas for building a strong vocabulary development framework. These techniques are more effective for building a vocabulary instruction framework than simply asking students to memorize words (and be tested on them), a technique mentioned frequently by teachers as their predominant vocabulary teaching technique.

Procedures for selecting words that merit explicit instruction. For EAP students to build a large receptive vocabulary, teachers need a systematic way to decide *which* words to focus on because we simply cannot teach students all the words that they need to know. Textbooks often preteach key vocabulary, but there are usually other words worthy of explicit attention, including the most important words for text comprehension, the most helpful words for working with other vocabulary, and the most useful words beyond the immediate text. One systematic way for teachers to select vocabulary for explicit attention is by categorizing unfamiliar words from an assigned reading into one of four types (Table 1). Words falling into the + + category deserve direct instruction; words falling into the – – category are not worth instructional time. Teachers need to decide how much time to devote to words falling into the + – and – + categories.

Concept-of-definition map for introducing vocabulary. One way to introduce a new key word and connect it to what students already know is to build a concept-of-definition map with the class (Figures 8 and 9). In this approach, students view a key word from four vantage points, providing them with multiple perspectives for building their understanding of the word.

Approaches for creating vocabulary-rich classroom environments. Teachers can promote vocabulary learning by creating vocabulary-rich environments. They can do so by placing students' written work,

Table 1. Systematic Way for Teachers to Identify Words Worthy of Explicit Attention

Vocabulary Categories	Words Critical for Text Comprehension	Words Useful Beyond the Text Being Read
Plus–plus (+ +)	+	+
Plus–minus (+ −)	+	−
Minus–plus (− +)	−	+
Minus–minus (− −)	−	−

interesting magazine articles, information from the web, book covers from new library acquisitions, and popular song lyrics on the walls and bulletin boards of their classrooms and school corridors. Another option is to place key words and phrases from core readings on the classroom wall (or on a poster board or bulletin board). Of course, the simple display of words (selected by the teacher and/or students) does not guarantee vocabulary learning. The key is to return to the word wall and engage students in tasks that involve the meaningful use of the words on the wall. To assist students in learning the words, teachers can ask students to move words around on the wall to create meaningful word clusters (e.g., words that belong to a particular content area, antonyms, words from the same parts of speech, words with positive or negative connotations, and collocations). They can also have students engage in activities (e.g.,

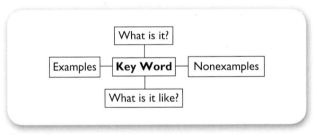

Figure 8. Generic concept-of-definition map.

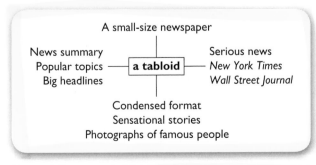

Figure 9. Concept-of-definition map for the word *tabloid*.

speed writes, ranking activities, spontaneous speaking tasks, and role plays) that promote the meaningful use of word-wall items (Eyraud, Giles, Koenig, & Stoller, 2000; Green, 2003). (See also Zimmerman, this volume.)

Create opportunities for comprehension skills practice

The ability to understand a text underlies all reading tasks; yet it is not a simple ability. Comprehension requires a reasonable knowledge of basic grammar, an ability to identify main ideas in the text, an awareness of discourse structure, and strategic processing. Reading comprehension instruction should direct some attention to grammar, particularly at the beginning and low-intermediate levels. In certain cases, teaching a key grammar point will support students' reading comprehension. However, most EAP reading instruction occurs beyond the beginning levels, and it is not necessary for a reading course to review grammar extensively. Certainly, a reading course is not the place in which to embed a grammatical syllabus. At the same time, it is important not to ignore grammatical knowledge as a resource for more advanced reading comprehension abilities (I. S. P. Nation, 2009).

Main-idea comprehension should be at the core of reading instruction. Typically, however, teachers *assess* comprehension (through post-reading comprehension questions) rather than *teach* it (N. J. Anderson, 2009). Main-idea comprehension is effectively developed through class conversations during which students identify and explore main ideas in the texts that they are reading. During those discussions, students can be guided to note connections across parts of the text, between two or more texts, or between the text and their own background knowledge. Class conversations centered on main-idea comprehension may start with post-reading comprehension questions, but students should be invited to follow up initial responses with further elaboration, during which students: (1) explain why an answer is appropriate; (2) point out where the text supports their answers; and (3) engage in discussions about how to understand the text better, thereby building their reading strategies (Grabe, 2009).

Main-idea comprehension can also be developed by identifying where main ideas are stated in the text, as well as the words that signal these parts of the text. Asking students to summarize what they have read, or some segment of a longer text, also provides them with helpful practice in identifying main ideas, articulating these ideas clearly (orally or in writing), and establishing links across main ideas and supporting details. To assist students in summarizing, teachers can start out by asking students to fill in a partially completed summary (or outline) while consulting the text. Finally, main-idea comprehension develops from instruction that emphasizes discourse structure awareness through, in particular, the use of graphic organizers.

Many other techniques can be used to promote main-idea comprehension. For example, with the questioning the author (QtA) technique (e.g., Beck & McKeown, 2006), questions not only address text comprehension, but they may also lead to hypotheses about author's purpose, critiques of the author's writing, identification of author bias and tone, and students' stance on the usefulness of text information. Typical questions asked in QtA interactions (Beck & McKeown, 2006) are listed in Figure 10.

Consistently orchestrated, teacher–whole class and student-group conversations about the text can also promote main-idea comprehension (Pressley, 2006). Next, we provide details about two other approaches to main-idea comprehension instruction.

Elaborative interrogation. Elaborative interrogation (e.g., Ozgungor & Guthrie, 2004; Pressley, 2006) is a more gentle approach to main-idea comprehension than its label suggests. In this approach, comprehension questions are followed by *why* questions that oblige students to return to the text, reread, and then explain their answers. When done well, usually in small, consistent doses, student responses generate class discussion and students learn to defend their answers and explain the strategies used for deciding on an answer. *Why* questions lead to an exploration of main ideas in addition to text recall, inferencing (i.e., reading between the lines), and coherence building (i.e., making connections across parts of the text). For elaborative interrogation to work well, students need teacher guidance initially, time to discuss their answers with classmates, and lots of practice.

Comprehension monitoring. Comprehension monitoring, often identified as a reading strategy that improves main-idea comprehension (Grabe, 2009), involves much more than the recognition of main ideas and the identification of difficulties being experienced while reading. Strategies identified as playing a major role in comprehension monitoring are listed in Figure 11. Teachers can support reading comprehension development (and monitoring) by modeling these strategies, discussing them, guiding students in using them, and leading students in discussions about when the students used the strategies, what purpose(s) they served, and how they helped (see N. J. Anderson, 2008).

- What is the author talking about?
- What do you think the author wants us to know?
- That's what the author said, but what did the author mean?
- Does that make sense given what the author told us before?
- But does the author tell us why?
- Why do you think the author tells us this now?
- How is the author making you feel about [X]?
- How has the author let you know that something has changed?

Figure 10. Questions typical of the questioning the author approach (adapted from Beck & McKeown, 2006).

- Having a reason for reading and being aware of it
- Recognizing text structure
- Identifying important and main-idea information
- Relating the text to background knowledge
- Recognizing the relevance of the text to reading goal(s)
- Recognizing and attending to reading difficulties
- Reading carefully
- Rereading as appropriate
- Clarifying misunderstandings

Figure 11. Comprehension monitoring strategies used by skilled readers (from Grabe, 2009).

Build students' discourse-structure awareness

It is well established that reading comprehension depends on a reader's awareness of discourse structure (e.g., Hudson, 2007). Good readers recognize how textual information is organized and the signals that provide cues to this organization; readers use this information (e.g., words that signal rhetorical patterns or topic shifts, transition phrases, headings, and paragraphing) to achieve comprehension. Yet few EAP reading curricula focus on discourse-structure awareness as a consistent instructional feature.

Instruction that aims to raise students' discourse-structure awareness engages students in regular discussions about how texts are structured and how discourse structure is signaled (e.g., Grabe, 2009; Jiang & Grabe, 2009). To show the pervasiveness of discourse structure, teachers should use texts that students are already reading for other purposes, rather than bringing in "special texts." Graphic organizers serve as effective tools for raising students' discourse-structure awareness (Jiang & Grabe, 2007, 2009). Common tasks for exploring discourse structure at different points in a reading lesson are explained in the following sections.

Building discourse-structure awareness at pre-reading stage. At pre-reading stages, teachers can guide students in: (1) examining text headings and subheadings; and (2) hypothesizing what each section is about. The goal is for students, over time, to take these steps independently, without being directed to do so. Students can also be asked to preview preselected text sections and highlight key words that signal discourse structure. Similarly, students can examine predetermined paragraphs and decide their function in the text (e.g., to offer a counterargument, propose a solution, make a comparison, or provide an elaborated definition). These activities not only raise students' discourse awareness but also reinforce automatic behaviors of good readers.

Raising students' awareness of discourse structure at during-reading stage. Textbooks do not often include while-reading activities; thus, teachers must create them to bring text organization features to students' conscious attention. Depending on the nature of the text being read, teachers can ask students to do the following *while* reading:

- Complete an outline of the text (at one or more points, depending on the length and nature of the text) that reveals main text units. As part of post-reading discussion, students can explain what makes each unit identifiable as a separate unit.
- Fill in a graphic organizer (e.g., Venn diagram or time line). As part of the post-reading discussion, students can explain how the information placed in the graphic organizer was signaled in the text.
- Underline lexical clues that indicate major organizational patterns (e.g., cause–effect, comparison–contrast, problem–solution).
- Highlight transition words and phrases that signal new sections (e.g., *And finally* used to signal not only continuation but also the last item in a series; *conversely* used to signal a contrast). As part of post-reading discussion, students can describe what they think the phrases and words signal.
- Assign a brief main-idea label to each paragraph (or sets of paragraphs) in the margin. As part of post-reading discussion, students can compare labels and explore the function of different paragraphs.

Building discourse-structure awareness at post-reading stage. Discourse-structure awareness can be developed further in post-reading discussions and rereading tasks. Many of the during-reading activities just noted can be converted into post-reading tasks. Students can also be asked to reread a text to match main ideas and supporting information across two columns. Also effective are tasks that require students to reorganize the scrambled paragraphs or sentences of a text or to create a good summary. Students can also be given a teacher-generated summary with inappropriate sentences or segments included and be asked to remove inappropriate parts, followed by a whole-class discussion that explores why the discarded parts do not belong.

Develop the strategic reader and promote strategic reading

Good readers typically employ multiple strategies (Figure 12) to achieve their reading comprehension goals. When they encounter challenging texts, they employ strategies with a heightened level of

- Planning and forming goals before reading
- Forming predictions before reading
- Reading selectively according to goals
- Rereading as appropriate
- Monitoring reading continuously
- Identifying important information
- Filling in gaps in the text through inferences and prior knowledge
- Making guesses about unknown words to be able to continue reading without major disruptions
- Using discourse-structure information to guide understanding
- Integrating ideas from different parts of the text
- Building interpretations of the text while reading
- Building main idea summaries
- Evaluating the text and the author, and forming feelings about the text
- Attempting to resolve difficulties
- Reflecting on information in the text

Figure 12. Strategies employed by good readers while reading for comprehension (drawn from Pressley, 2002, pp. 294–296).

metacognitive awareness. These strategies, often applied in combination, support each other to achieve comprehension. Initially, good readers apply some subset of strategies without a lot of conscious thought. It is when the initial set of default strategies does not lead to successful comprehension that a much more conscious problem-solving mode of attention is activated. At this point, good readers may reread the text, reconsider initial predictions, reexamine discourse markers, or try to unravel complex phrases, among other fix-up strategies.

EAP textbooks oftentimes introduce reading strategies, but these are rarely introduced in purposeful combinations to achieve meaningful reading goals. Reading curricula that focus on strategic-reader training, as opposed to isolated strategy instruction, are likely to benefit EAP readers the most (N. J. Anderson, 2008; Grabe & Stoller, 2011; Hedgcock & Ferris, 2009). Teaching for strategic reading involves a number of important steps. First, teachers should introduce a strategy and talk about how, when, and why to use it. The strategy can be added to a "permanent" list (e.g., on a classroom bulletin board or wall) that can be easily consulted by the class (Janzen, 1996). After the strategy has been introduced, it should be practiced and revisited multiple times, with accompanying whole-class discussions. Second, teachers can model combinations of strategy uses while reading

aloud to the class and making explicit the strategies being used. Over time, students should be encouraged to verbalize the strategies that they are using and then discuss them as ways to understand texts. Third, teachers need to promote ways to monitor comprehension. Options for students include asking if the text is making sense, rethinking goals for the particular reading, and deciding at certain points what the main ideas of the text are.

Goals for the development of strategic reading should include: (1) student use of multiple strategies in combination for better comprehension; and (2) student familiarity with strategic responses to texts, which, with practice and teacher reinforcement, become more automatic. Teaching students to become more strategic readers should be central to comprehension instruction (Pressley, 2006). Additional approaches for incorporating strategic reading into reading curricula are described in the following sections.

Directed reading-thinking activity. With directed reading-thinking activity (DR-TA), students are guided in thinking like good readers: anticipating, predicting, confirming, or modifying their ideas as they read and then summarizing (Blachowicz & Ogle, 2008). DR-TA guides students in relating background knowledge to the text, determining goals for reading, and engaging in a series of prediction and summarizing tasks at set pause points. It is during prediction practice, and accompanying classroom discussion, that students develop monitoring strategies, text-evaluation abilities, and main-idea comprehension (Blachowicz & Ogle, 2008; Kern, 2000). The prediction cycle involves asking students to: (1) make predictions about what they think is coming next; (2) read to confirm or refute their predictions; (3) discuss predictions and reformulate them using text information; and (4) summarize what they have read before moving on to the next text segment. Questions commonly asked to guide such discussions (with adaptations for different student proficiency levels) include:

- What do you predict will happen?
- What are your reasons for these predictions?
- What do you think now? How accurate were your predictions?
- What made you change your mind?
- Can you find information in the text to support or challenge your predictions?

- What is the main idea of this section?
- What do you think will happen next?

When students have difficulties adjusting their predictions as they proceed through the text (possibly because they are unable to make good inferences or connect text segments), the teacher can ask students to reread particular segments to find information that will improve their predictions.

One key to successful DR-TA activities is the teacher's determination of *how much* text should be read between pauses, during which students revisit, evaluate, and adjust their predictions. The teacher needs to be sure that "there is enough information for the students to check likely predictions, and also enough new information for further predictions to be made" (Blachowicz & Ogle, 2008, p. 140). Another key to successful DR-TA implementation is the realization that prediction is real only when the whole class is reading the material for the first time. Pausing at page breaks or at the end of a well-defined section might lessen students' temptation to read ahead.

KWHL chart. The KWHL chart (Figure 13) is commonly used for promoting strategic reading and motivating students to read by having them discover what they have learned from reading. The approach combines activating background knowledge, goal setting, monitoring for important points, evaluating text information, and relating text information to reading goals. With a KWHL chart on the board, the teacher, as part of the pre-reading segment of his or her lesson, asks students what they *know* (K) about the reading topic, what they *want* to know (W) about the topic, and *how* (H) they will accomplish their goals while reading. While discussing the how of reading, the teacher and students can review reading strategies purposefully (Raphael, George, Weber, & Nies, 2009). During the while-reading lesson segment, students can look for the information that they want to learn, using the stated strategies to do so. Toward the end of the post-reading lesson segment, the class can revisit the KWHL chart and report what they have *learned* (L) and which strategies (listed in the H column) were most effective. They can also connect newly learned information (listed in the L column) with already known information (listed in the K column) to consolidate comprehension and long-term retention.

Identification of challenging parts of a text. EAP students are likely to encounter challenging texts on a fairly regular basis in academic classes. Students' academic success will depend, in part, on their ability to make sense of difficult texts. Teachers can ask students to identify a challenging text segment and then guide them in

Topic: Native Americans in the United States			
K	**W**	**H**	**L**
reservations	customs	Preview text to	
tribes	traditions	determine main	
Apache	languages	ideas.	
casinos	religions	Write 2–3 questions	
bows and arrows	medical	that might be	
cowboys and Indians	practices	answered in the	
rain dances	migrations	passage.	
buffaloes	today's	Read passage and	
Geronimo	problems	underline possible	
teepees	education	answers to	
jewelry	government	questions.	
movies	clothes		
Dances with Wolves			

Figure 13. Sample KWHL chart used with a passage on Native Americans in the United States. Sample includes plausible students' pre-reading responses.

- Absence of concrete examples
- Abstract imagery
- Abstract theorizing
- Assumed background knowledge
- Conceptual complexity
- Confusing formatting
- Density of text
- Grammatical complexity
- Lack of clarity in the writing
- Length of sentences
- Length of text
- New conceptual knowledge
- Poorly signaled organization
- Unfamiliar content
- Unfamiliar vocabulary or new meanings

Figure 14. Possible sources of reading difficulty.

identifying the sources of difficulty (Figure 14) and strategies for overcoming the challenges. Instead of skipping over difficult segments and focusing on what students understand, students benefit from working through difficult texts as a class; in these lessons, students discuss the process of making sense of the passage and develop strategies that will, it is hoped, over time carry over to other reading contexts.

Build students' reading fluency

Fluent reading—rapid, accurate, and prosodically appropriate reading—is frequently neglected in EAP curricula (I. S. P. Nation, 2008) and EAP reading textbooks. However, as reading research has demonstrated in the past decade, reading fluency development is a critical component of effective and successful reading instruction (Grabe, 2009; Schwanenflugel & Ruston, 2008). When fluency practice is incorporated as a consistent component of a reading curriculum, students make important gains in their reading comprehension.

Building word- and passage-reading fluency requires a real-time commitment. Students do not become fluent readers by practicing for a month or two, with one or two readings, or on Fridays only. When students begin to understand the need for fluency development, typically they look forward to fluency activities. Developing word-recognition fluency can be carried out through repetition and beat-the-clock practice with flash cards and timed readings of word lists (with words that have already been introduced). Students can also improve their

word-recognition fluency when they are asked to reread texts, read along in a text as the teacher reads aloud, and engage in extensive reading. Passage-level fluency can be developed with: (1) consistent practice in rereading texts, both silently and aloud; (2) extensive reading; and (3) timed- and paced-reading activities. Details on some of these fluency-building activities are explored in the subsections that follow.[1]

Rereading. EAP students are rarely asked to reread texts for additional purposes, despite the fact that the rereading of familiar texts represents: (1) one of the best ways to build reading fluency; and (2) a common practice among skilled readers in academic settings to consolidate content learning. On completion of a textbook chapter, EAP teachers usually direct students to turn to the next chapter instead of giving students a new reason for reading the previously read text at least one more time. And even when in the midst of a textbook unit, students are rarely given a good reason to return to the text, even though so many tasks (Figure 15) can lead to purposeful rereading. Each rereading of a text provides fluency practice as well as vocabulary recycling.

- Confirming an answer to a comprehension question
- Confirming the main idea (skimming)
- Locating details (scanning)
- Preparing for a summary or synthesis task
- Reading between the lines (inferencing)
- Filling in a graphic organizer that reflects text organization
- Determining author stance, bias, and position (and possibly taking a position different from that of the author)
- Locating discourse-structure and main-idea signals
- Finding points of agreement or disagreement with another information source (e.g., a video)
- Connecting information with a previously encountered information source (e.g., another passage, teacher mini-lecture, video, or field trip)
- Preparing for a follow-up activity requiring the use of text information (e.g., a radio report, essay, or debate)
- Reading a full text after a jigsaw activity in which students have read only one part of the text

Figure 15. Rereading tasks that promote reading-fluency development.

Repeated reading. In English L1 settings, repeated reading (not to be confused with rereading) has become an important component of reading curricula (Rasinski, 2010; Rasinski, Blachowicz, & Lems, 2006). Repeated reading, unassisted or assisted, is equally valuable for L2 students in EAP settings. Unassisted repeated reading involves students reading short passages aloud alone (either in class or at home) until they reach a set reading rate. Assisted repeated reading encourages students to read passages: (1) silently along with an audiotape or CD; (2) aloud with an audiotape or CD; (3) with a teacher; or (4) after first listening to the passage and then reading along (among other variations). The nine tips listed here can help teachers initiate a repeated reading routine:

1. Teachers should keep passages to between 70 and 200 words.
2. Teachers should assign only texts for rereading practice that students have *already* read or heard, or that will be easy for students' reading levels.
3. Teachers should limit reading of the same passage to three to four times.
4. Students should read with reasonable accuracy and an effort to pronounce intelligibly.
5. Pronunciation should not be considered a key issue for repeated reading unless the word is pronounced so poorly that it could be confused with a different word.
6. Students can time their reading of a whole passage (from start to finish), or they can read for a set number of seconds (e.g., 60, 90, or 120 seconds), even though in the latter case they may not finish the whole passage.
7. Students can read in pairs, with one student reading and the other listening (and helping out, when necessary).
8. When students read at an improved rate, or when they improve their rate three times in a row with a single passage, they should move to another text.
9. Students chart their progress (time and accuracy) on a record-keeping chart.

Oral paired reading. Oral paired reading, commonly used in L1 settings, should be considered for EAP fluency training. Students work in pairs with passages that they have *already* read for other purposes; in this way, students can focus on reading more fluently instead of focusing on meaning and unfamiliar words. Student A reads the passage aloud for a designated period of time (e.g., 30–60 seconds) as quickly and as accurately as possible. While Student A reads aloud, Student B follows along and assists Student A if necessary. At the end of the designated time period, Student A marks the end point of his read-aloud. Then Students A and B switch roles. Student B reads the exact same passage as Student A, starting at the beginning. After the same designated time period, Student B marks the end point of his read-aloud. The students then repeat the procedure for a second round, rereading exactly the same text from the beginning. The goal of this reading activity is to advance further in the text in the second round. The number of words gained on the second reading is then recorded. After students become familiar with these general procedures and expectations, students typically look forward to these oral paired reading activities because they are fun, but, more important, they contribute to fluency building.

Provide consistent extensive reading opportunities

It should come as no surprise that EAP students can master reading abilities only by reading. It sounds so simple, yet most reading programs do not equate instructional time with actual reading time (Renandya & Jacobs, 2002). One way to ensure that students actually read, and read a lot, is to make extensive reading a regular component of the reading curriculum (I. S. P. Nation, 2009). Extensive reading requires a curriculum-wide commitment if it is to have a major impact on fluency and reading comprehension development. Ten principles for a successful extensive reading program are listed in Figure 16. Additional tips that can enhance an extensive reading program are presented in the section that follows.

Scaffolded silent reading. Teachers can assist students in developing reading abilities by setting aside class time for silent reading. Effective scaffolded silent reading (ScSR), unlike traditional sustained silent reading (SSR), is defined by these practices (Reutzel, Fawson, & Smith, 2008; Reutzel, Jones, & Newman, 2010):

- The teacher schedules ScSR sessions regularly.
- The teacher teaches strategies for the selected reading material.

1. Students read as much as possible, perhaps in and definitely outside the classroom, the latter done when and where students choose.
2. A variety of materials on a wide range of topics is available so as to encourage reading for different reasons and in different ways.
3. Students select what they want to read and can stop reading material that fails to interest them.
4. Purposes for reading, generally related to pleasure, information, and general understanding, are determined by the material and students' interests.
5. Reading is its own reward, yet some level of student accountability is expected.
6. Reading materials are well within students' linguistic competence in terms of vocabulary and grammar. Dictionary use while reading is discouraged because the constant stopping to look up words makes fluent reading difficult.
7. Reading is individual and silent, at each student's own pace.
8. Reading speed is usually faster rather than slower as students read books and material that they find easily understandable.
9. Teachers orient students to the goals of the program, explain the methodology, keep track of what each student reads, and guide students in getting the most out of the program.
10. Teachers explicitly offer students support and assist with comprehension difficulties.

Figure 16. Top ten principles of an extensive reading program (adapted from Day & Bamford, 1998, pp. 7–8; Reutzel, Jones, & Newman, 2010; see also Day & Bamford, 2002).

- Students read student-selected materials and can change reading materials when motivation lags, interest wanes, and/or the text proves too difficult.
- The teacher engages students in short (5- to 10-minute) lessons that explain or model some aspect of fluent reading or a comprehension strategy.
- Students engage in silent reading for a designated period of time.
- The teacher monitors student engagement and text comprehension. Monitoring takes place as the teacher moves around the room and interacts with individual students on a periodic basis.
- The teacher holds students accountable for time spent reading silently (e.g., during teacher-individual student interactions, with completed-book response assignments).

Motivate students to read

Frustrating reading experiences, not uncommon among EAP students, can demotivate students, "a truly unfortunate consequence considering the importance of reading for most of our students" (Komiyama, 2009, p. 32). EAP students benefit from motivational support provided by teachers and the curriculum in numerous ways:

- Teachers share their reading interests with students by talking about what they are reading, why it is interesting, and what other types of reading they engage in. The teacher as role model serves as a powerful motivator.
- Students are encouraged to share what they are reading and why they find it interesting.
- Teachers identify students' interests and then are on the lookout for related readings to bring to class.
- Teachers work toward promoting the development of group cohesiveness so that learners can support each other with challenging reading tasks.
- Teachers increase students' expectancy of success by selecting texts that are within students' ability levels and by devising reading tasks that students are capable of completing. The texts and tasks should involve just enough challenge to require some effort.
- Teachers devise attention-catching introductions to major texts and associated tasks (e.g., by posing provocative questions, connecting students' backgrounds to the text, examining a photo and caption in the text, and connecting the overall theme to students' lives) to build initial interest.
- Teachers build relevance into the curriculum and, by extension, into the assigned readings to motivate students.
- Teachers encourage active student participation.
- Teachers grant students some degree of choice in reading materials whenever possible.
- Teachers help students discover what they have actually learned *from* reading so that students develop an appreciation for the value of reading.
- Teachers, whenever possible, guide students in building real levels of expertise in reading topics (as suggested next in our discussion of content-based instruction).

Integrate content and language learning objectives

One way to build effective EAP reading curricula is to combine emphases on content learning and language learning, an approach often labeled content-based instruction (CBI). (See also Snow, this volume.) The combination of content- and language-learning objectives inherent in CBI (Stoller, 2008) naturally leads to opportunities for extended reading, motivational learning experiences, strategic responses to increasingly complex tasks, greater choices in reading materials, and growing challenges to match expanding skills. CBI naturally lends itself to project-based learning; the recycling of important skills on a regular basis; the rereading of texts; and realistic tasks for interpreting, integrating, and evaluating information from multiple texts. Such activities mirror the types of tasks that EAP students will encounter in academic settings. Teachers interested in integrating content- and language-learning objectives as a way to help students improve their reading skills might want to consider features of two empirically supported curricular frameworks briefly described next.

Concept-oriented reading instruction. Concept-oriented reading instruction (CORI) is a curricular framework that has been used and researched extensively in L1 settings (e.g., Guthrie, McRae, & Klauda, 2007; E. A. Swan, 2003). CORI was initially guided by instructional principles for stimulating student interest and motivation to read. It has since evolved into a more elaborate yet flexible approach organized around four stages: (1) immersion in a main theme through students' personal engagement with the topic and a specific question to pursue; (2) wide reading and information gathering on the theme across multiple information sources; (3) reading-strategy instruction to assist with comprehension; and (4) project work leading to a tangible outcome that demonstrates what students have learned. CORI activities extend well beyond strategy training and include a commitment to vocabulary development, fluency practice, and extensive reading. As students proceed through CORI stages, they engage in content discus-sions and activities that require the purposeful use of multiple strategies, including the following:

- activating background knowledge
- forming and answering questions
- determining main ideas
- monitoring and repairing comprehension
- noting text structure and text characteristics
- paraphrasing
- summarizing
- synthesizing information
- taking notes
- using graphic organizers to integrate information

These strategies are reinforced by consistent teacher modeling, teacher scaffolding, and extensive practice.

Collaborative strategic reading. Collaborative strategic reading (CSR) is based on concepts from reciprocal teaching (Palincsar & Brown, 1984) but is appropriate for L2 learners. It combines reading comprehension–strategy instruction and Cooperative Learning principles to promote content learning, language mastery, and reading comprehension (Klingner & Vaughn, 2000, 2004). During CSR, students work collaboratively in groups to comprehend texts. While working in groups, students apply four strategies to their reading: They preview to predict what the passage might be about; they "click and clunk" to identify difficult words and concepts, and use fix-up strategies to make sense of difficult texts; they read for the gist to restate the most important ideas in portions of the text; and they summarize what has been learned. CSR teachers introduce the four strategies through modeling; role playing; thinking aloud; and discussing why, when, and how to use the strategies. While engaged in these activities, students "activate prior knowledge, make predictions, monitor comprehension difficulties, clarify information, restate important ideas, summarize the text, and form appropriate questions about the text" (Grabe, 2009, p. 233).

FUTURE TRENDS

The coming decades may bring us new ways of reading (e.g., with electronic books and other technologies), but the need to read for academic purposes and the need to read well, strategically, and for different purposes will remain vital for academic success. Because of the importance of reading for academic purposes, we hope to see a greater commitment to reading in language curricula in addition to the teaching (rather than the testing) of comprehension. With a deeper understanding of the complexities of reading, we hope that the field at large, and individual teachers, will pay more attention to the importance of

- vocabulary instruction for a larger recognition vocabulary
- strategy training with the goal of developing the strategic reader
- extensive reading for reading development
- motivation instruction
- teacher training for effective reading instruction

Most important, we hope to see teachers asking their students to actually read in (and outside) class because our students cannot become skilled readers unless they read—and read a lot.

CONCLUSION

A single chapter on teaching reading for academic purposes can only begin to identify the instructional options (and their variations) that can make a difference in EAP students' reading successes. It is our hope that EAP reading teachers, materials writers, and curriculum designers can use the ideas presented here as springboards for change in their approaches to reading instruction. The ultimate goal is that students become the readers that they need to be to succeed in academic contexts.

SUMMARY

➤ Reading is carried out for many purposes and involves many component skills.
➤ Among the component skills that are critical to reading comprehension development are word-recognition efficiency, vocabulary building, discourse-structure awareness, main-idea comprehension practice, reading strategies for academic purposes, reading fluency, extensive reading, and student motivation.
➤ Nine curricular principles are proposed to guide reading instruction.
➤ Implications from reading-related research are translated into specific instructional techniques for EAP reading skills development.

DISCUSSION QUESTIONS

1. Based on what you have read in this chapter, how have your conceptions of L2 reading changed? Identify three ideas from the chapter that you think are particularly important for EAP reading teachers, and rank them in order of importance. Be prepared to provide a rationale for your decisions.
2. Consider the reading demands faced by students who want to pursue academic studies in an L2. How might an EAP reading curriculum differ from a more general L2 curriculum? What should the essential components of an EAP reading curriculum be? Why?
3. In this chapter, Grabe and Stoller suggest that there is a difference between facilitating the development of the strategic reader and teaching reading strategies. How would you explain the distinction that they are making?
4. In what ways might a content-based approach facilitate EAP students' reading skills development? Would you favor such a curricular approach in an EAP program? Why or why not?
5. Consider your own experiences reading for academic purposes. How do you approach lengthy reading assignments? What steps do you take to synthesize information from multiple texts? How do you approach challenging texts? What can you apply from your own reading experiences to help prepare EAP students for the reading demands that they will almost certainly encounter?

SUGGESTED ACTIVITIES

1. Create a graphic organizer that depicts your current views of reading for academic purposes.
2. Select three L2 reading textbooks that might be used in an EAP classroom context. Examine one chapter in each textbook.
   a. To what extent, and how, are the following aspects of reading covered: word and phrase recognition, main-idea comprehension, reading fluency, discourse structure awareness, and vocabulary building.
   b. To what extent, and how, are the following characteristics of effective of reading instruction translated into practice: the pre-, during, post-framework; strategy

training; meaningful rereading; the integration of content- and language-learning goals; and student choice.

3. Select a short text (e.g., from a magazine, newspaper, or the Internet) that might be of interest to an EAP student population.

   a. What aspects of the text might prove difficult for EAP students?

   b. Identify 8–10 words (or phrases) that might be unfamiliar to these students. Place each word into one of the following categories: + +, + −, − +, − −. How would you help students learn the words placed into the + + category?

   c. Design three post-reading tasks that oblige students to return to the text to reread for a meaningful purpose. Each task should focus on a different aspect of reading (e.g., distinguishing between main ideas and details, identifying factual and opinion statements, determining author stance, inferencing, unraveling information in complex sentences, connecting information to another text, or using textual information for another task). Be prepared to explain the aim of each task that you design.

FURTHER READING

Anderson, N. J. (2008). *Practical English language teaching: Reading.* New York, NY: McGraw Hill.

This is an easy-to-read volume with insightful discussions of principles, techniques, and activities for teaching reading to beginning, intermediate, and advanced L2 learners.

Grabe, W. (2009). *Reading in a second language: Moving from theory to practice.* New York, NY: Cambridge University Press.

This comprehensive volume describes the complex cognitive processes that readers employ when reading and explores variation in reading abilities. The author moves from theory to practice when examining reading comprehension in relation to strategies, discourse structure awareness, vocabulary, motivation, fluency, and curricular models.

Grabe, W., & Stoller, F. L. (2011). *Teaching and researching reading* (2nd ed.). New York, NY: Pearson Longman.

This volume helps teachers understand the complex nature of L1 and L2 reading, connects research to evidence-based teaching practices, and showcases an iterative 12-step process for teacher-initiated action research on reading-related topics. Twenty-nine model action research projects are presented to help teachers get started.

Hedgcock, J. S., & Ferris, D. R. (2009). *Teaching readers of English: Students, texts, and contexts.* New York, NY: Routledge.

This volume, dedicated primarily to an exploration of L2 reading instruction, highlights important practical techniques for teaching and assessing L2 reading in secondary and post-secondary contexts.

Jiang, X., & Grabe, W. (2009). Building reading abilities with graphic organizers. In R. Cohen (Ed.), *Explorations in second language reading* (pp. 25–42). Alexandria, VA: Teachers of English to Speakers of Other Languages.

This chapter explores ways in which teachers can use graphic organizers to promote main-idea comprehension and raise students' awareness of discourse organization. The authors describe how teachers can become skilled at making graphic organizers for classroom use.

Nation, I. S. P. (2009). *Teaching ESL/EFL reading and writing.* New York, NY: Routledge.

This volume provides teachers with practical suggestions for teaching and assessing reading (and writing). Special attention is paid to word recognition, intensive reading, extensive reading, and fluency building.

ENDNOTE

[1] For other fluency development activities, see: J. Cohen (2011); Grabe and Stoller (2011); and Rasinski (2010).

UNIT II

Language Skills

Writing

14 | Practical Tasks for Mastering the Mechanics of Writing and Going Just Beyond

ELITE OLSHTAIN

KEY QUESTIONS

➤ How can initial writing activities connect phonology, grammar, and vocabulary, on the one hand, with pronunciation, reading, and writing, on the other, in a beginner's course in English as a second or foreign language?

➤ How can we create a graded program that leads learners from the initial mechanical steps in writing to authentic communication via writing for real-life purposes?

➤ How can we take advantage of the world around us and of the latest technological developments to create interesting writing activities for beginners?

EXPERIENCE

We are visiting a class of 12-year-old children learning English as a foreign language (EFL). Each student is sitting in front of a laptop and doing individual practice using sentences in the present progressive to describe a picture. The summary of the activities requires the students to write their own description of the picture, and one of the students is surprised to find that she did not double the verb's final letter before adding *–ing* in *sitting* and *beginning*. The teacher, using the students' first language, draws their attention to some rules they studied earlier by using the interactive white board:

The pronunciation patterns that we learned when we had words like *sit, hit, slip,* etc., helped us in pronouncing the vowel letter *i* correctly as /ɪ/.

Verbs that have such short syllables ending in one consonant double the final consonant before adding *–ing* (*sitting*).

The same is true for longer verbs that end in a stressed syllable that looks like the short syllables, such as in words like *begin* (*beginning*).

The teacher continues to practice various verbs that students already know, showing them where there is doubling and where there is no need for doubling, as in examples with a verb ending in a silent *e* (*write → writing*).

WHAT IS INVOLVED IN MASTERING THE MECHANICS OF WRITING?

Within a discourse-based approach to language teaching, where the goal of interaction is meaningful communication, the skill of writing enjoys special status. It is via writing that a person can communicate a variety of messages to a close or distant, known or unknown reader. (See Celce-Murcia & Olshtain, this volume, regarding discourse-based approaches to language teaching.) Such communication is extremely important in the modern world, whether the interaction takes the form of traditional paper-and-pencil writing or an up-to-date digital message on a computer, a cell phone, or any other technological device. Writing as a communicative activity needs to be encouraged and nurtured during the language learner's course of study. This chapter focuses on the early stages of English as a second language (ESL) and EFL writing, which are a critical prerequisite to the later development of writing for communication.

What are the important components when learning to write in a new language?

Viewing writing as an act of communication suggests an interactive process that takes place between the writer and the reader via the text. Such an approach places value on the goal of writing as well as on the perceived (or intended) reader audience. These two aspects of the act of writing need to be stressed even at the very beginning level, as soon as students can create the smallest meaningful messages. Teachers need to encourage students to define for themselves the messages they want to send and the audiences who will receive them.

The writing process, in comparison to spoken interaction, imposes greater demands on the text, since most of the time written interaction lacks immediate feedback. The writer should try to anticipate the reader's reactions and produce a text that will adhere to Grice's (1975) *cooperative principle*. According to this principle, the writer is obligated (by mutual cooperation) to try to write a clear, relevant, truthful, and preferably interesting and memorable text. The reader, on the other hand, will interpret the text with due regard for the writer's presumed intention if the necessary clues are available in the text. This is true even for the shortest and most reduced digital text message: All the clues needed by the reader to understand the writer's intention should be included in the text.

In academic or official exchanges in writing, it is important that the linguistic accuracy, clarity of presentation, and organization of ideas support the efficacy of the communicative act, since they supply the clues for interpretation. Accordingly, while the global perspectives of content and organization must be focused on and given appropriate attention, it is also important to present a product that does not suffer from illegible handwriting, numerous spelling errors, faulty punctuation, or inaccurate sentence structure, any of which may render the message unintelligible.

The present chapter focuses on the gradual development of the mechanics of writing, a necessary instrumental skill without which meaningful writing cannot take place. At this early stage of learning, the primary goal is to recognize and reproduce the elements of the target language writing system (the letters or other graphic shapes).

There is, however, another important objective to the writing of graphic shapes—it provides students with support in the acquisition of the mechanics of reading. They gain a sound basis for letter and word recognition when reading.

It is important to remember that in the ESL/EFL context, writing, like the other language skills, needs to be dealt with at the particular level of linguistic and discourse proficiency that the intended students have reached (Raimes, 1985). The proposed sequence of activities will start with primary focus on the mechanical aspects of the writing skill and move on to a more communicative goal.

Writing systems

EFL learners usually acquire the mechanics of writing in English as an extension of their ability to read and write in their first language (L1). It is therefore important to first understand what writing system the students already know to design an efficient program that suits their particular needs.

Our first global consideration is whether the student's L1 has a writing system based on meaning, such as Chinese (the graphic sign is a unit of meaning) or a system based on sounds. In writing systems based on meaning, the graphic sign is linked to a meaning in the real world; in the writing systems based on sounds, the graphic sign is linked to a spoken sound (usually a phoneme as in English) or a syllable (as in the Japanese *katakana* writing system). Many languages in the sound-based writing group use an alphabetic system in which a graphic sign stands, in principle, for a phoneme. In such writing systems, we talk about phoneme-grapheme (or sound-to-letter) correspondences. Korean has basically an alphabetic writing system consisting of consonant and vowel symbols, but when they are put together they form syllables. Some of these alphabetic writing systems are more transparent and consistent in representing these correspondences than others. Italian and Finnish are good examples of transparent and highly consistent alphabetic writing systems (V. Cook, 2008). English, on the other hand, is much less transparent and has complicated rules for linking graphemes with phonemes. We often talk about sound-spelling correspondences in English to capture the complexity of the writing system.

The direction of the writing system can be up and down and in columns (as it is for traditional

Chinese and Japanese) or in lines (as it is for European and Middle Eastern languages). The direction on each line can be left to right for languages with Roman or Cyrillic alphabets or right to left for languages like Arabic, Urdu, and Hebrew. Suitable practice activities need to be developed according to the needs of students who may come from language backgrounds with scripts that have an orientation other than the left-to-right, horizontal writing used for English.

CONCEPTUAL UNDERPINNINGS

Early writing in a new language

Children learning to read and write in their L1 have had prior experience with the language by listening to stories, being read to, interacting with adults and others in their environment, and observing people writing. In fact, many children have developed an understanding of writing before they actually need to learn how to write in school. Most important, they have acquired a large vocabulary in their own language. The EFL learner, on the other hand, usually knows how to read and write in his or her own language but often has to adjust to a new writing system while acquiring the first words in that new language. The acquisition of the new writing system has to be carried out within the linguistic framework of the knowledge newly acquired in the target language. This is an important consideration that will come up at various points along the way.

Learners whose first language employs the Roman alphabet already possess the appropriate direction of reading and writing, they recognize and use letters with the same shapes as those in English, and they are aware of the phonological processing route (V. Cook, 2008). Sometimes the L1 writing system uses a different alphabet such as Cyrillic, used for many Slavic languages, or for Greek, which has its own alphabet. In these cases, learners may have to adjust to a few new phoneme-grapheme correspondences, but mainly they need to focus on the orthographic regularities and irregularities in English, which probably has a less transparent writing system than their L1.

Learners whose L1 employs an alphabetic system that is different from the Roman alphabet need to focus on the appropriate direction of reading and writing, on learning to recognize and produce the actual graphic characters, and on learning both the regularities and irregularities of the English writing system. These early steps will be significant for developing efficient reading and writing strategies at later stages.

Learners whose L1 employs a meaning-based writing system (e.g., Chinese) will have a more difficult task acquiring the English writing system, especially if this is their first encounter with a Roman alphabet. They need careful training in associating a graphic sign with a vocal sound and then recognizing sequences of such graphic signs as words. The phonological process route, which is only partially familiar to them, will need to be enhanced and practiced in the new writing system. Phonemic awareness might require some practice as well. At the same time, these learners must get used to the appropriate direction of reading and writing. Eventually, they too, will need to learn both the regularities and irregularities of the English writing system.

All learners, irrespective of their language background, will need to learn the English punctuation system and the English spelling rules. These will develop along with the acquisition of the language in the first years of studying English, since many of the spelling rules are related to morphological rules and can be learned as part of the morphology. For example, doubling the final consonant of certain verbs can be taught along with regular past tense formation (e.g., *fit, fitted*).

The mechanics of reading and writing

When using the term *mechanics of writing*, we usually refer to the very early stage of letter recognition, letter discrimination, sound-to-letter correspondence, word recognition, and basic rules of spelling. Just beyond this early stage, we continue to expand the spelling rules, focus on punctuation and capitalization, and cover the comprehension and production of sentences and short paragraphs. The time devoted to developing the mechanics of writing serves the acquisition of both reading and writing skills.

The interaction between reading and writing has often been stressed in language teaching, yet it deserves even stronger emphasis at this early stage. To learn how to discriminate one letter from another while reading, learners need to practice writing these letters; to facilitate their perception of words and sentences during the reading process, they might need to practice writing them first. It is therefore the case that writing plays an important role in early reading by facilitating the development of both the reading and writing skills. The importance of this early stage of reading and writing is emphasized in a study by Ke (1996) on the relationship between Chinese character recognition and production at the early stages of learning. With the English alphabet, this stage is much simpler, yet it deserves appropriate attention, especially for learners accustomed to other writing systems and for adult preliterate learners.

Sound-spelling correspondences

English presents the learner with a number of unique difficulties related to its orthographic rules, even in cases in which the learners come from a first language writing system based on the Roman alphabet. Students and teachers alike often throw their hands up in despair, ready to give up on finding reliable rules for English orthography; yet the English writing system is much more rule governed than many realize. In fact, English has a very systematic set of sound-spelling correspondences (Chomsky & Halle, 1968; Schane, 1970; Venezky, 1970). These sound-spelling correspondences enable the ESL/ EFL teacher to combine the teaching of phonetic units with graphic units and to give students practice in pronunciation along with practice in spelling (see Celce-Murcia, Brinton, & Goodwin, 2010).

The English consonants

The first rule to remember about English orthography is that students may tend to look for a one-to-to one correspondence and then discover that they get into a lot of trouble by doing this. For most of the 21 consonant letters, this type of rule works fairly well if we disregard allophonic[1] differences in pronunciation, such as *t* (/t/) being pronounced as an aspirated initial [t^h] (as in *ten*) as opposed to a nonaspirated, unreleased final [t$^-$] (as in *net*) for monosyllabic words in English. Yet there are also consonant letters whose sounds depend on the environment in which they occur:

Thus, the letter *c* can have the sound /k/ when followed by the vowel letters *a, o,* or *u* (e.g., *call, cook, cup*) or by the consonant letters *l, r,* or *k* (e.g., *click, crew, rocker*). However, it has the sound /s/ when followed by the vowel letters *e, i,* or *y* (e.g., *cell, cinch, cyst*). Although these rules may appear confusing to a learner coming from an L1 with a transparent phoneme-grapheme correspondence system, they work quite consistently in English and need to be introduced and practiced from the very start. The story of the letter *c* is not finished, however, and now we come to the part that is less consistent. This occurs when *c* is followed by the letter *h* and can have the sound of /tʃ/ (*chocolate*) or /k/ (*chorus*). There is no help we can give our students in this respect but to tell them to pay special attention to such words and to try to remember their initial sound according to the meaning of the word. The letter *c* also occurs in quite a number of common words followed by the letter *k* (not initially, but in the middle or at the end of words, e.g., *chicken* and *lock*). The sound in this case is /k/, and the correspondence should create no difficulty.

The letter *g* in English demonstrates a similar pattern. When followed by the vowel letters *a, o,* and *u* or the consonant letters *r* and *l*, it is pronounced /g/ as in *gas, go, gun, grass,* and *glow*. However, before the vowel letters *i, e,* and *y*, the letter *g* is pronounced /dʒ/ as in *gin, gem, and gym*. We thus need to alert students to the fact that the correspondence in English is not always between letter and sound but between the letter and its immediate environment and the relevant sound. In many such cases, the correspondences are quite predictable, while in others, the rules do not always work as well. Another helpful generalization for English consonants is related to the letter *h*, which is very powerful in changing the sound of the consonant that it follows. Thus, the letter combinations *ch, sh,* and *th* represent distinct consonant sounds (/tʃ/, /ʃ/, and /θ/ or /ð/, respectively) in words such as *chin, shut,* and *thin* or *then*. Learners need to recognize these graphic clusters as such. Our discussion of the letters *c, g,* and *h* highlights the types of difficulties that learners can encounter with consonant letters in English. There must also be an awareness of common and frequent exceptions. For example, despite the rules, the letter *g* in *get* or *give* is pronounced /g/; the letter *c* in *cello* is pronounced /tʃ/.

Teachers also need to be aware that there are many silent consonants in English, such as these common cases that beginners might encounter:

- *k* or *g* before *n*: *knock, knee, gnaw, gnome*
- *l* after vowels and before final consonants in several contexts: *could, would; walk, talk; calf, half*
- *gh* after vowels: *through, sigh, light, caught*
- word-final *b* and *n* after *m*: *comb, thumb, autumn, column*
- *t* after *s* and before *–en* or *–le*: *whistle, listen*

To summarize, when teaching consonant letters and their sound correspondences to students whose own alphabet is similar to that of English, we need to focus only on the unique features of the English writing system and its irregularities. On the other hand, when teaching students coming from a different alphabetic writing system (e.g., Arabic, Russian, or Korean), a syllable-based system (e.g., Japanese *katakana*), or a meaning-based system (e.g., Chinese), teachers need to emphasize the recognition of every consonant letter. Here learners might have difficulties similar to the ones encountered by young children when they first learn to read and write in English as their mother tongue (such as the distinction between *b* and *d*). Intensive writing practice will help learners with both the reading and the writing skills.

The English vowels

The vowel letters in English present more complex sound-spelling correspondences, but again there is much more consistency and predictability than many learners realize. First, learners need to be made aware of two basic types of syllable environments that are very productive in English orthography: CVC (often the environment for short vowels) and CV or CVCe (the latter ending in a silent *e*; these are the environments for long vowels).[2] The terms *short vowels* and *long vowels* as used in English spelling are rather unfortunate, since they conceal the difference in quality by placing too much emphasis on length. The difference between the vowel sounds in the words *pin* and *pine* is not necessarily one of length (or production time) but one of phonetic quality. A true difference in vowel length can be observed in the words *bit* versus *bid*,

where the quality of the two vowel sounds is similar but the one preceding the voiceless consonant /t/ is shorter than the one preceding the voiced consonant /d/.[3]

Although we often say that the five vowel letters of the English alphabet[4] result in at least 11 or more vowel sounds (depending on the particular English dialect), these sound-spelling correspondences are, at least in part, consistent and predictable. What teachers and learners need to take into account is the fact that in English we must consider both the vowel letter and the environment in which it occurs. Thus, CVC syllables present a rather consistent environment for all five vowel letters *a, e, i/y, o,* and *u* in which they stand for simple, lax (produced with relatively relaxed muscles), nondiphthongized[5] vowel sounds, as in the words *pan, pen, pin, pot,* and *but*. However, the same five vowel letters occurring in the CVCe environment stand for tense (produced with relatively tensed muscles) and diphthongized vowels, as in the words *pane, pine, Pete, rope,* and *cute*. Similarly, most vowels that can occur in the CV or V environment are also tense and usually diphthongized: *go, be, I/my, Lu* (as in *Lulu*). In a CV-type syllable, long *a* needs a following *y*, as in *pay*, or it is pronounced /ɑ/ as in *ma*. Not all these patterns are equally frequent in English orthography. The letter *e*, for instance, does not often occur as the vowel sound in the CVCe environment, and learners have to study its more common spellings as in *meet* and *meat* for the sound /iy/. In other words, there are some basic sound-spelling correspondences in English, the knowledge of which can greatly facilitate the acquisition of reading and writing. But there are also quite a number of exceptions or expansions that need to be learned individually.

In teaching the basic sound-spelling correspondences in English, it is important to emphasize the rules that provide learners with useful generalizations and that therefore help them become effective readers. Once students have assimilated and internalized the basic features of such correspondences—namely, the distinction between CVC and CV or CVCe syllables—they will be able to apply these patterns not only to monosyllabic words but also to polysyllabic ones; in such words, the stressed syllable can act as a monosyllabic environment for letter-sound vowel correspondences (e.g., *open, dispose, reset*).

Furthermore, some of the more advanced spelling rules related to English morphology can be facilitated by this knowledge. In polysyllabic verbs in which the final syllable is stressed, the spelling rules for adding the inflection –*ing* work in the same manner as in monosyllabic verbs. Thus, learners who know the rule for consonant letter doubling when changing *sit* to *sitting* will be able to apply the same rule to any polysyllabic verb that ends with a stressed syllable having the form CVC. Therefore, the verb *begin,* since its final syllable is stressed, will undergo doubling of the last letter in *beginning,* as opposed to the verb *open,* where the final syllable is not stressed and the –*ing* form is *opening.*

However, in spite of all that has been said so far, English orthography has a notorious reputation because, in addition to all these helpful and relatively reliable rules, we must take into account some less productive rules that have a lot of exceptions. These exceptions are often found in some very common words that defy the most basic rules, such as *give, have,* and *love,* where the silent-*e* rule does not work.

There are some additional rules that are quite predictable, such as the occurrence of the letter *a* in front of *l* or *ll,* which (in some dialects) is quite consistently realized as /ɔ/ as in *call,* or the letter *a* in front of the letter *r,* which has the sound of /ɑ/ as in *car.* In general, the letters/sounds *l* and *r* affect the way the preceding vowel letter is pronounced, causing it to represent a more centralized (i.e., pronounced in the center of the mouth) vowel as in the words *world, bird,* and *curd.* Furthermore, the vowel diphthongs have a variety of spellings, such as the following letter combinations, all of which correspond to the same vowel diphthong /iy/: *meat, beet,* and *cede.* So, while it is true that there are quite a few cases in English that need to be learned as individual correspondences, there are far fewer than people imagine (for good sources of rules on sound-spelling correspondences, see Schane, 1970; Venezky, 1970).

In summing up this section dealing with the teaching points relevant to the mechanics of reading and writing, we emphasize that it is important for learners of ESL/EFL to realize from the start that English orthography is by no means a one-to-one letter-sound correspondence system; it has its own consistency embedded in the combinations of letters in their environments, resulting in what we call sound-spelling correspondences.

By introducing the proper pronunciation of sounds in relation to the given spelling patterns, we can provide learners with a good basis for pronunciation as well as for the skills of reading and writing. The three areas of pronunciation, reading, and writing go hand in hand in the very early stages of acquiring another language.

CLASSROOM APPLICATIONS

How do we teach mechanics?

The teaching of the mechanics of reading and writing has three goals: (1) to enhance letter recognition, especially when learners come from a different writing system; (2) to practice sound-spelling correspondences via all four language skills; and (3) to help the learner move from letters and words to meaningful sentences and larger units of discourse.

Recognition and writing drills constitute the first steps in the development of effective reading and writing habits. However, to acquire active mastery of the sound-spelling correspondences, it is necessary for the learners to arrive at relevant generalizations concerning these correspondences. Such generalizations lead to a better understanding of the systematic representation of sounds in English orthography and require learners to master some basic phonological rules in English and develop an ability to recognize the distinctive features of each letter within a spelling pattern.

Three major types of recognition tasks are used at this early stage of reading and writing, each type incorporating an adequate variety of drills: (1) matching tasks; (2) writing tasks; and (3) meaningful sound-spelling correspondence practice. These drills can be carried out using paper and pencil or via computerized/digitalized lessons.

Matching tasks. The major objective of matching tasks is to practice the quick and effective recognition of the English letters. This is particularly important for learners who know a writing system that does not use the Roman alphabet. Many of the drills used here are similar to the drills used for beginning readers of English who are native speakers. Learners need to distinguish a particular letter from other similar letters, they need to match words beginning or ending with the same small or capital letter, and

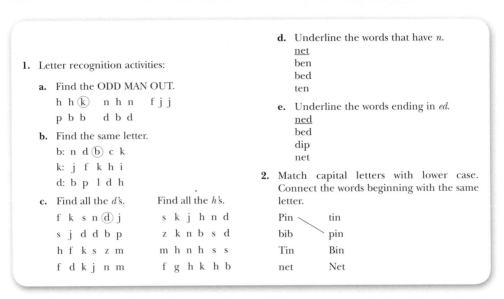

Figure 1. Sample matching tasks (adapted from Olshtain, Crumlish, Goell, & Kneller, 1970).

they need to search for a certain letter within a group of different letters. All these exercises are focused on recognition and do not require either writing or pronouncing the letters or words. When the drills are done digitally, students drag similar letters and words to matching positions or relevant groups or simply click on them. At a slightly more advanced stage, the drill requires students to match words with pictures and even short sentences with pictures. This can be used when students can work with meaning as well as accurate recognition. Figure 1 provides some sample matching tasks.

Writing tasks. The major objective of writing tasks is to allow students to produce the shapes of the letters both as a recognition and a production task. Usually these activities begin with tracing letters that are printed on the page. In this way, students can focus on the detailed characteristics of the letters. This stage is needed only for learners who come from a different writing system; students familiar with the Roman alphabet can move right to writing meaningful words. In computerized activities, students can type out the letters on the keyboard and thus practice using the keyboard as well as the alphabet. Figure 2 provides a sample writing task involving tracing letters, words, and sentences; Figure 3 provides a sample task involving meaningful copying activities.

Sound-spelling correspondence tasks. The major objective of sound-spelling correspondence tasks

is for the learner to match individual sounds or sequences of sounds and words with their written form. The teacher may read the words, or students may listen to a recorded drill. In either case, the focus here is on listening and recognizing the sound corresponding to the relevant written form. The spelling environments are important in these kinds of tasks. The distinction between CVC and CVCe can be practiced in many different ways. In the computerized version, there is a voice accompanying the activities and students choose the written forms according to the sounds they hear. Students can also be asked to pronounce the written forms and thus practice pronunciation. These activities provide learners with a solid basis for all four languages skills: reading, writing, listening, and speaking. Figure 4 provides a sample task that focuses on sound-spelling correspondences.

An important feature of this early stage of writing is the need to accustom learners to using the appropriate capitalization rules in English and some basic rules of punctuation. While practicing sound-spelling correspondences, students can be writing meaningful sentences, or typing them on the keyboard, with proper capitalization and punctuation such as the following simple sentences, which focus on some of the important environments that need practice:

There is a cat on the mat and a cake on the plate.
The ball is near the tall boy next to the wall.

I. Writing Practice: Tracing Letters, Words, and Sentences

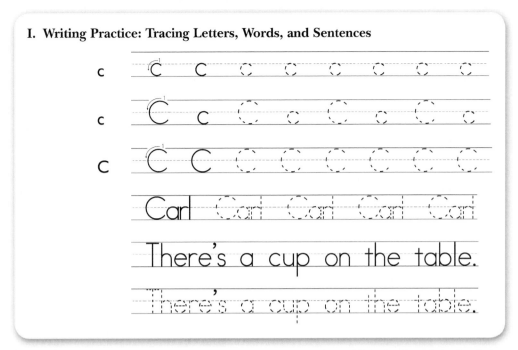

Figure 2. Tracing letters, words, and sentences (adapted from Olshtain, Crumlish, Goell, & Kneller, 1970).

These sentences contain words that exemplify sound-spelling correspondences and that, at the same time, have probably already been learned by the students. Such sentences should be accompanied by pictures to ensure that learners understand the meaning. We may not be able to write a whole story this way, but since our focus is first and foremost on the sound-spelling correspondences, it is an important step toward more meaningful personal writing. Eventually, the discourse units that students write will grow and incorporate more meaningful and interesting texts. The language knowledge the students gain can be the

II. Meaningful Copying Activities

(Adapted from Olshtain et al. 1998, pp. 76, 85, and 157)

1. Read and decide.

Dan wants to win at tennis. He doesn't practice a lot, but when he goes to play he takes a lucky ring with him. He thinks it can help him win. What do you think?

☐ It can help Dan.   ☐ It can't help Dan.

2. Read about Lucky the Rock Star in Exercise 3 below. Then answer these questions.

What is he wearing?

_____

_____

_____

What is he doing?

_____

_____

_____

(continued)

Figure 3. Meaningful copying activities (adapted from Olshtain, Feuerstein, Schcolnik, & Zerach, 1998).

3. **Who is Lucky the Rock Star? Read and check (✔).**

He is wearing 2 necklaces. He is wearing a funny hat. He is wearing huge sunglasses. He is wearing new black shoes. He is wearing old ugly jeans. He is holding a guitar. He is sitting on a black chair.

4. **Read and decide. Where does he live? In South Carolina or Canada?**

He lives in _____ .
He doesn't live in _____ .

Where I live it rains a lot in winter, but there are also many sunny days. Sometimes it is cold, but it doesn't usually snow.

5. **Write about today's weather. These sentences may help you.**

It's very nice.   It's cloudy.   It's hot.   It's warm.
It's cold.   It's windy.   It's rainy.

_____
_____
_____
_____
_____
_____
_____
_____

Figure 3. Meaningful copying activities (adapted from Olshtain, Feuerstein, Schcolnik, & Zerach, 1998). (*Continued*)

Practicing Sound-Spelling Correspondences

1. The letter *a* in *all* and *al*

a. Read the following words out loud.

all	also
ball	always
call	almost
fall	although
wall	
tall	
hall	
small	

but the sound is different in the word—*shall*

b. Use the above words to write the missing letters and then read the sentence.

_ l l t h e s m_ _ _

_ _ l l s f _ _ _.

2. Underline the word your teacher says.

a. tin, tine, tan	**b.** tam, tame, time	**c.** mit, mite, mat
d. bad, bade, bid	**e.** hide, hid, had	**f.** can, cane, cap

Figure 4. Practicing sound-spelling correspondences (adapted from Olshtain, Feuerstein, Schcolnik, & Zerach, 1998).

basis for developing more sophisticated and personally relevant texts.

At this early stage of writing, we need to give learners "plenty of opportunities for copying" (Byrne, 1988, p. 130), either in handwriting or in keyboarding. Such copying activities can be made more challenging by asking students to create sentences for new contexts. One such activity is to provide a bank of sentences and pictures; students copy the proper sentence below the matching picture. Although copying may seem terribly mechanical, it allows students to practice words and sentences while gaining fluency in writing.

More advanced writing tasks

More advanced writing activities that start shifting from a focus on the mechanics of writing to basic process-oriented tasks need to incorporate some language work at the morphological and discourse levels. The activities suggested for this part of the program focus on both accuracy and content, with a clear communicative goal. At this stage, we are still concerned with the beginning level of ESL/EFL, yet the focus shifts toward communication. Three types of writing tasks serve as the framework for communicative writing activities: practical writing tasks, emotive writing tasks, and school-oriented tasks. These activities can all be carried out in handwriting for traditional writing exchanges as well as using email messages, social network postings, or any other digital interaction.

To develop and use these more demanding writing activities in the ESL/EFL classroom, we need to develop a detailed set of specifications that will enable both teachers and students to cope successfully with these tasks. Such a set of specifications should include:

The task description: This description presents students with the goal of the task and its importance. Such a task description will initially be provided by the teacher, and eventually students will provide their own task and define it.

The content description: This description presents students with possible content areas that are relevant to the task. Here again, the teacher will first suggest these areas, but gradually students will become more involved via discussion and brainstorming in suggesting relevant content.

The audience description: This description guides students in developing an understanding of the intended audience, its background, needs, and expectations. Gradually students will be guided to write authentic messages to friends and others.

Format cues: These cues help students in planning the overall organizational structures of the written product. Even for short messages or emails, students should learn to plan the format to ensure effective communication.

Linguistic cues: These cues help students make use of certain grammatical structures and vocabulary choices that are appropriate for the intended message.

Spelling and punctuation cues: These cues help students focus their attention on the spelling rules they have learned and eventually on the need to use a dictionary or a computerized spell check (to check the accuracy of spelling); they also guide students to use acceptable punctuation and capitalization conventions.

Practical writing tasks. These are writing tasks that are procedural in nature and have a predictable format. This makes them particularly suitable for writing activities that focus primarily on spelling and morphology. Writing lists of various types, writing notes, categorizing, labeling, writing short messages, writing simple instructions, and other tasks are particularly useful in reinforcing classroom work.

There are many types of lists: things to do, things completed, things to share with others, and shopping lists. Each of these list types provides teachers with an opportunity to combine some spelling rules with morphological rules and with the logical creation of a meaningful message. Things-to-do lists are useful for practicing verb base forms and reinforcing various sound-spelling correspondences. When assigning an activity, the teacher should indicate whether the list is personal or intended for a group project. The content specification will indicate whether this is a list of things to do in preparation for some event or just a plan for someone's daily routine. For example, a list for a group of students who are preparing a surprise birthday party might look like this:

Things to Do

1. Buy a present for Donna (Sharon).
2. Call Donna's friends (Gail).
3. Write invitations (Dan).

Today it is most likely that a list like this would be sent around to the group members via email or text messages on cell phones. These types of digital activities should become part of classroom work so that students feel that they are learning to function successfully in the new language in relevant and familiar situations.

Following a things-to-do list, we can easily move on to the things-completed list, which specifies which things have already been taken care of; it is therefore useful for practicing the past tense forms of verbs. As part of this activity, students will need to review the regular past tense formation of verbs (in which –ed is added) and its spelling patterns, such as the deletion of a final *e* before adding –ed (as in *live, lived*); the doubling of the last consonant in monosyllabic bases of the form CVC (as in *pat, patted*) and the same doubling rule when the final CVC syllable of a polysyllabic verb is stressed (as in *occur, occurred*; but not when a nonfinal syllable is stressed, as in *open, opened*); and the replacement of *y* with *i* when the base ends in C*y* (as in *try, tried*). Such an activity also enables students to practice the spelling of irregular past tense formations. For example, a list of things completed for the surprise birthday party might look like this:

Things Completed

1. Planned the games for the party
2. Wrote the invitations
3. Bought the present
4. Called Donna's friends
5. Tried to call Donna's mother

Shopping lists provide us with a very good opportunity to practice the spelling of the plural ending of count nouns and the use of quantifiers. The sound-spelling correspondences here consist of the two orthographic forms of the plural inflection with its three phonetic variants:

–*s*, which is pronounced [s] in *nuts, grapes*, and *soft drinks* and is pronounced [z] in *eggs, apples*, and *onions*

–*es*, which is pronounced [əz] or [ɪz] in *peaches, oranges*, and *toothbrushes*

Another type of practical writing task is notes and messages that are left for another person or are sent via cell phone text messages. These allow students to practice brief and simple sentences with proper punctuation and a meaningful message. To make the activities more interesting and personal, students can design their own message headings and then fill them in. Here is an example:

Messages for My Little Sister

1. Wash the dishes in the sink.
2. Feed the dog.
3. Watch your favorite program on TV and have a good time.

Such messages can also be done as "sticky notes" on the computer.

Other types of practical writing activities might include the completion of forms on paper or on the computer and the preparation of invitations, greetings, and thank you notes on paper or on the computer. All these activities, when carried out in class, require the set of specifications already mentioned, with the appropriate focus on orthographic, mechanical, and linguistic accuracy.

Emotive writing tasks. Emotive writing tasks are concerned with personal writing. Such personal writing primarily includes letters to friends and narratives describing personal experiences, messages on social networks, and personal journals and diaries. When teaching letter writing, teachers should emphasize format, punctuation, and spelling of appropriate phrases and expressions. When students write about personal experiences—usually in a narrative format—they can review and practice the spelling of past tense forms. Entries in diaries and journals, both on paper and on the computer, can take the form of personal letters and serve as a review of letter writing in general.

To serve the personal needs of the learners, emotive writing has to be quite fluent. To make these activities real and authentic, teachers should allow students to decide on their own written messages. How can they carry out such tasks in the early stages of acquiring English when their knowledge of the language is limited and their vocabulary does not include all the words they may want to use? It is important at this stage to guide students to use the language that they know. It is always amazing to realize that, even with limited knowledge of a new language, learners can express most of their thoughts if they plan the message carefully. Personal letters and messages can be designed in simple language, reflecting the language that the students know. Teachers can provide sample pieces of writing and encourage students to design their own messages based on the models. Brainstorming activities preceding such writing activities can help develop the task specifications that should guide all students in their work.

School-oriented tasks. One of the most important functions of writing in students' lives is its use in school. Much individual learning goes on while students are writing assignments, summaries, answers to questions, and essay-type passages. In most cases, the audience for these writing tasks is the teacher, but gradually students must learn to write for an unknown reader who needs to receive the information being imparted exclusively via writing. This is true, of course, both in written messages or digital messages. In some schools, students can correspond with their teachers via email or social networks, and they can hand in homework assignments in a digital form.

At the early stages of writing, the assignments and written tasks might be very short and simple. Answers might be single phrases or sentences, summaries (a listing of main ideas, and descriptions), or a sequence of related sentences. All these writing activities should be given attention, both at the linguistic-accuracy level and at the message-transmission level. Students should be guided to take responsibility for developing their writing abilities. Combining content and organization with accepted formal features of writing conventions will help students develop the writing skill needed in their future use of English. This is particularly true of school-oriented tasks.

Dialogue journal writing at the early stages. Dialogue journals enable students and teachers to interact on a one-to-one basis at any level and in any learning context. They are, therefore, also very useful communicative tasks at the early stages of learning to write in a new language. The dialogue journal enables the beginner in English to generate some personal input and receive the teacher's direct feedback on it.

According to Peyton and Reed (1990), both young children who are beginning writers in a second language and nonliterate adults can start a dialogue journal as soon as they are comfortable writing in the classroom. The journal can start as an interactive picture book in which, first, the teacher and, later, the learners label the pictures and provide brief descriptions. Gradually the texts become more detailed as the communication process is enhanced.

The dialogue journal, like any other writing activity, but even more so, can be done via email or on social networks, expanding the communication between teachers and students and also among the students themselves. Students should be encouraged to use the second language as their special code for interacting with classmates. There can be a special discussion forum in which they interact with the teacher as well as with other students. The keyboard, rather than the pen or pencil, can become their most significant writing tool.

All learners in a classroom, school, or any other group can take part in a discussion forum. In this case, the writers will be addressing a wider and more varied audience. They can discuss a topic, share some ideas or experiences, and react to the writing of others. The messages on the forum should be read and judged for content rather than quality of writing (Lahav, 2005), and therefore more students may feel comfortable participating, even if their mastery of language is not perfect. Such a forum provides an authentic setting and an authentic purpose for writing.

FUTURE TRENDS

Taking into account the writing needs of learners in general, more emphasis will be placed on written interaction via digital tools. Yet the ability to produce clear, well-understood messages is important for all students. Students' experiences will expand to include more and more varied types of writing activities. The present chapter sets up the basic framework for beginning students who will eventually become proficient writers in English as an additional language.

While the constantly changing environment will certainly affect the learning and teaching of language in all areas of use, it will also affect research, providing new questions that need to be investigated. The impact of technology on writing needs to be investigated further, with a clear focus on the acquisition of the L2 writing system in its various realizations. Such issues include how many repetitions of computerized recognition activities should be included in a lesson, what mediation is needed for students to work on their own in early-learning writing activities supported by technology, and how certain writing activities affect reading fluency.

CONCLUSION

Teachers should be encouraged to use a variety of writing tasks at all learning levels and particularly at the beginning level. Writing, in addition to being a communicative skill of vital importance, is a skill that enables the learner to plan and rethink the communication process. It therefore provides the learner with the opportunity to focus on both linguistic accuracy and content organization. That the mechanics of writing are particularly important in the initial stage of learning English as an additional language must be emphasized; they help students establish a good basis in and useful mastery of the sound-spelling correspondences that are crucial for reading in English. As I. S. P. Nation (2009) points out: "An essential part of the reading skill is the skill of being able to recognize written forms and to connect them with their spoken forms and their meaning" (p. 9).

The focus on sound-spelling patterns also leads to improved pronunciation and, as such, plays a central role in students' acquiring listening and speaking skills. The importance of carefully planned interaction among these different subskills in the initial stages of learning the language cannot be overemphasized.

When teachers focus on writing, in particular, they should emphasize the importance of a carefully planned presentation, which combines the mechanics of writing with the composing process. Teachers might advise students to prepare a list of guiding questions that they should try to answer in their writing activity. Such questions raise the writers' awareness about the communicative perspective of a written text.

The early stages of an ESL/EFL course of study must provide learners with a good foundation for furthering their knowledge in all language areas and language skills beyond the beginners' course. The present chapter shows how important these early stages are. Yet another perspective of the beginning level, not discussed here, relates to the students' interests and motivation to learn. The use of the target language and writing, in particular, should reflect the learners' real-world and real communicative needs. Since we live in an innovative, high-technology world, it is important to take full advantage of what students need and want to do with their second or foreign language, right from the start.

SUMMARY

➤ By learning how to write letters and words in the new language, students also become better readers.

➤ The sound-spelling correspondences in English provide learners with the basis for reading, writing, speaking, listening, and spelling.

➤ Even in the early stages of learning a new language, once students have acquired the mechanics of writing they should begin writing for communication.

➤ Early writing activities can take digital forms and can be used by students in authentic exchanges with their peers.

DISCUSSION QUESTIONS

1. How would you plan the early writing stage differently for students whose first language uses a Roman alphabet compared to students whose first language has a writing system based on meaning?
2. How should we sequence the teaching of the various sound-spelling correspondences to be most effective? Would using a computer for practice make a difference?
3. Give an example of how the teacher of either beginning-level ESL or EFL students can combine elements of the composing process with elements of the mechanics of writing.
4. How would you use Twitter or any other typical social networking system to have students interact meaningfully at their level?

SUGGESTED ACTIVITIES

1. At the early stages of learning a new language, we focus on some basic grammatical structures and vocabulary items. Design some interesting writing tasks for beginners, such as creating a wanted poster (i.e., a poster of a criminal the police are searching for) with questions that students need to answer using a person's description or creating a lost-pet poster, which requires the description of an animal. Suggest a variety of such activities, and evaluate their usefulness.
2. Prepare a game or a set of cards to practice the difference between the vowels sounds in the environments CVC and CVCe (e.g., *hat, kit* versus *hate, kite*). Incorporate as many words as will be meaningful for the intended student population. You may have to use some words that exemplify this sound-spelling correspondence that are not yet known to your students. How will you present the new words to your students before you practice the spelling patterns?
3. Find pictures that can be used to produce simple descriptions. Develop a number of activities that will enable pairs or small groups to answer a set of questions about each picture. The questions should lead to a concise description of what is in the picture.

FURTHER READING

Ferris, D., & Hedgcock, J. S. (2004). *Teaching ESL composition: Purpose, process, and practice.* London, UK: Routledge.

This book provides teachers with a detailed description of how syllabi for ESL writing programs are developed. A major chapter in the book is devoted to material and task construction that is helpful for expansion activities beyond textbooks that are used. The book also focuses on writing assessment and on developing a community of writers.

Gelb, I. J. (1963) *A study of writing.* Chicago, IL: University of Chicago Press.

A reference for those interested in the history and evolution of human writing systems.

Ivanic, R. (2004). Discourses of writing and learning to write. *Language and Education, 18*(3), 220–245.

This article presents research on writing and writing pedagogy focusing on six types of discourse: a skills discourse, a creativity discourse, a process discourse, a genre discourse, a social practices discourse, and a sociopolitical discourse. Thus the article links the writing course to discourse research and provides approaches to the teaching of writing.

ENDNOTES

[1] The term *allophonic* contrasts with the term *phonemic*. A phoneme is a difference in sound that makes a difference in meaning, such as initial /p/ in *pull* versus initial /b/ in *bull*. An allophone is a difference in sound that is typically environmentally conditioned and does not make a difference in meaning, such as the initial aspirated (breath-releasing) [tʰ] in *tip* versus the unaspirated, unreleased final [t ̚] in *pit*, which are both allophones of the phoneme /t/ in English. Languages differ in that an allophonic difference in one language can be a phonemic difference in another. This can complicate the learning process.

[2] In these formulas C stands for "consonant," V stands for "vowel," and e stands for silent *e*. Thus, the formula for a word like *take* is CVCe.

[3] When consonants are voiced, the vocal cords are vibrating; when they are voiceless, the vocal cords do not move. This can be felt by touching the throat and is perhaps most obvious with the difference between a sustained /z/ sound (which is voiced) versus a sustained /s/ sound (which is voiceless). All vowels in English are voiced.

[4] Sometimes *y* serves as a sixth vowel letter, replacing *i*. This is not very frequent in CVC contexts (e.g., *gym*), but it does occur frequently in CV or CCV position (e.g., *my, sky, try*).

[5] English vowels are diphthongized if there is tongue and lip movement during the production of the sound toward /y/ or /w/. For example, /ey/ as in *bait*, /ay/ as in *bite*, /ow/ as in *boat*, or /aw/ as in *shout* are all diphthongized vowels in North American English. Vowels are simple, or nondiphthongized, if there is no tongue or lip movement during vowel production, as in the vowels in the words *bit* /bɪt/, *bat* /bæt/, or *but* /bʌt/.

15 | Considerations for Teaching Second Language Writing

SARA CUSHING WEIGLE

KEY QUESTIONS

➤ What does it mean to know how to write?
➤ What is the role of writing in the second/foreign language curriculum?
➤ What do English as a second or foreign language teachers need to know about writing to design and teach a writing course?

EXPERIENCE

Elizabeth teaches a writing course in an intensive English program designed to prepare students to enter an American university. Her 16 students come from 11 different countries and are interested in different disciplines, from business to mathematics to the social sciences. As class begins, Elizabeth divides the class into groups of four and gives each group a set of writing assignments from different university courses: one from an undergraduate business course, one from U.S. history, one from environmental science, and one from psychology. Elizabeth reminds the class of the concepts of audience, purpose, and genre and asks the groups to identify each in the set of tasks. The groups quickly get to work; after about five minutes, Elizabeth asks them to report on the similarities and differences among the tasks. She writes their responses on the board and then asks the class to list the verbs used in the assignments (e.g., *discuss, compare, analyze*) and then gives students a handout listing several of such verbs. Students discuss the handout with partners to make sure they understand all the verbs. Then Elizabeth presents the instructions for a writing assignment that students will be working on over the next several weeks. In introducing the assignment, she highlights the verbs in the instructions and then proceeds to go over the details of the assignment.

An observer in this class wanting to learn about teaching writing might notice several features about it. First, it is very much a collaborative class. The teacher controls the pace of the class and directs the activities, but during most of the class the students are interacting with each other. Second, students are using reading as a first step to inform their future writing. In this instance, they are analyzing writing prompts, though in another class they may be reading about and discussing a particular topic that they will be writing about. Third, they are learning that the expectations of readers in different disciplines will be different and that they cannot necessarily transfer everything they know about writing in one subject area to writing in another. Finally, this class involves a consideration of global issues in writing, such as the need to think about one's audience and purpose in writing when deciding how to organize an essay, as well as local issues, such as being able to use specific verb forms appropriately. Even in a very short observation, it is clear that learning to write in a second language (L2) is a complicated endeavor that involves a multiplicity of concerns.

WHAT IS SECOND LANGUAGE WRITING?

Writing has always had a place in the second/foreign language curriculum, but in the twenty-first century the ability to write in an L2 may be even more important than ever. Globalization and technological advances such as the rise of the Internet have made written communication across languages and cultures not only possible but essential in business, education, and many other fields. More and more people are seeing the need to learn to write in a language that is not their mother tongue, whether their purpose is to transact business, interact on social-networking sites, or pursue academic degrees. Thus, whereas writing was once seen as a skill that was primarily taught to reinforce other language skills such as listening, reading, and grammar, in many settings writing has moved to a more central place in the curriculum (Reid, 2001). As a result, many teachers will find themselves needing to teach writing and may not feel well prepared to do so effectively. The purpose of this chapter is to present some of the most important concepts in teaching writing and provide guidance on planning and delivering an effective writing curriculum.

To teach writing effectively, we first need to understand the nature of L2 writing ability. We can look at this ability from two perspectives: as a cognitive ability (i.e., a set of skills and knowledge that reside within an individual) and as a sociocultural phenomenon (i.e., as a means of communication within a particular setting aimed at achieving specific goals). Both of these perspectives are important in the teaching of writing.

From a cognitive perspective, second language writing can be seen as some combination of writing ability (perhaps learned in one's first language [L1]) and L2 proficiency. Even in one's native language, composing a text is a highly complex task that involves the consideration of many factors at the same time. Writers have to keep in mind their overall message, the major points and subpoints to be included, how these points will be organized, and a representation of the likely readers: what they already know or believe about the topic, what sorts of information they will find persuasive, and how they might react. Writers need to be able to plan their writing, monitor and revise what they have already written, and keep focused on the process until they are satisfied with the end product. When an L2 is added to the mix, the picture becomes even more complex because writers need to focus some of their attention on finding the appropriate language to express their ideas clearly and accurately as well. It seems reasonable, and indeed research has shown it to be true, that students who have learned to write in their L1 can transfer these skills to a second language; however, a certain level of language proficiency is required before such transfer can occur. For students at every level of proficiency, a writing course provides opportunities to learn and practice new language forms and structures and thus contributes to language learning. For students with lower language proficiency, this focus on language may need to be emphasized, while for advanced students, more emphasis can be placed on the composition process. In short, both writing ability and language proficiency are important factors in L2 writing ability, and both need to be included in a writing curriculum.

From the sociocultural perspective, writing is seen as part of a socially and culturally situated set of literacy practices shared by a particular community. From this perspective, the process of learning to write is the process of becoming a member of a *discourse community*, a group of people (e.g., biologists, politicians, or even fans of a particular musical genre) who share values and assumptions about using language and also have certain ways of using language (oral or written) for particular purposes. In academic writing, for example, there are different conventions for publishing articles in different disciplines, and certain linguistic or stylistic choices, such as the use of the passive voice, may be considered good writing in one discourse community or discipline but not in another.

Learning to write means learning to participate in one or more discourse communities, whether this means participating in an online social network, writing medical laboratory reports, or writing academic papers. From this perspective, focusing simply on improving language proficiency or studying strategies for composing and revising does not necessarily lead to good writing unless considerations of the broader context in which writing will be used are also taken into account. In addition, a crucial insight from the sociocultural perspective is that written texts do not exist in isolation; rather, the texts that writers produce are shaped by and responsive to other preexisting texts. This notion is important when we consider the role of reading in the writing classroom, discussed later in the chapter.

These two perspectives together provide a useful framework for the consideration of writing instruction. The cognitive perspective helps us remember that individual students need to acquire knowledge and skills—about language and about the process of writing—while the sociocultural perspective reminds us that writing is always done for a purpose, is directed at a specific audience, and is part of a broader set of literacy practices that is shaped by a particular culture and setting.

The cognitive and sociocultural perspectives can also help us understand the difference between speaking and writing, an important distinction for language teachers. From a purely mechanical perspective, the act of writing takes longer than the act of speaking and leaves a physical trace that can be referred to at a later date. Oral communication, at least without the help of technology, typically requires that both participants (speaker and listener) be present at the same time in the same place and allows the use of nonverbal and contextual clues for shared meaning; furthermore, speakers get continuous feedback from their listeners about whether they are being understood and can clarify and repair mistakes if necessary. In writing, these contextual cues and immediate feedback are absent, and thus a writer must choose words more carefully to avoid misunderstandings. The cognitive challenge of speaking is contributing to an ongoing discourse without time to plan out what to say; the cognitive challenge of writing is anticipating and taking into account the existing knowledge, goals, and interests of one's likely readers and tailoring one's choice of words and sentence structures to that audience.

The fundamental differences between speaking and writing in the cognitive domain are responsible to a great degree for differences in the sociocultural domain. First, writing is used for different purposes and functions than speaking; because it can be planned and leaves a permanent record, it tends to be used for functions where precision and accuracy are important, such as contracts. Written language tends to be more formal, use more complex structures, and be more carefully planned than spoken language, which tends to be characterized by shorter sentences or fragments, pauses, and repetitions and repairs. Correctness is more highly valued in writing than in speaking; thus errors that might be permissible in speaking are often more stigmatized in writing. (See McCarthy & O'Keeffe, this volume.)

In summary, writing is not simply speaking in another modality. While the same basic building blocks of vocabulary and grammar are essential to both, writing is frequently used for different purposes; it thus requires different linguistic structures and functions than speaking and calls for a somewhat different set of cognitive and metacognitive strategies. Writing teachers must have an understanding of both perspectives to plan and deliver instruction that addresses the writing needs of their students, whether these students are not literate in their L1 or are transferring advanced L1 writing skills to their L2.

CONCEPTUAL UNDERPINNINGS

Up to this point we have considered the nature of writing ability, its relationship to speaking, and the distinction between language ability and writing ability. In this section, I discuss several areas of research and best practices that teachers should be aware of to teach writing effectively. First, teachers should understand why their students want or need to write, and how certain student characteristics (e.g., L1 literacy) affect their ability to write in an L2. Next, teachers need to be familiar with research on the writing process, that is, how experienced writers go about creating written texts and how to support this process in novice writers. Finally, I discuss two issues that contribute to a growing appreciation of best practices in writing instruction: (1) connections between reading and writing; and (2) the role of grammar and error correction in writing.

Student background and needs

The goals of a writing curriculum must start with the needs of the students. As Leki, Cumming, and Silva (2008) state:

> Curricula for writing are also circumscribed by the purposes for which people are learning. These purposes reflect the status in a society of the language being learned, the functions and values of literacy in that language, as well as the characteristics, intentions, and status of the learners and of the institutions in which they study. (p. 76)

One important factor is the age and educational background of the writers. Children need writing for school and are learning writing skills along with other cognitive skills, whereas adult learners come equipped with many of these cognitive skills but may not actually need writing for their jobs; furthermore, while many adult L2 learners have good or excellent writing skills in their L1, others may not have had much formal schooling and may not be literate in their L1. Such students may need to be taught the basics of writing, starting from practicing how to hold a pencil and learning the alphabet. Another difference that impacts how writing is taught is the difference between L2 learners and foreign language learners. L2 learners either need English for school or work, whereas foreign language learners may be studying English for a variety of reasons: for personal enrichment, as a requirement for school, for further study, or for career reasons.

In the North American context, one distinction that is frequently discussed is the difference between "eye" learners (typically, those who have learned English through formal education and thus primarily through reading and grammar instruction) and "ear" learners (those who have learned English informally through oral interactions; Reid, 1998a). Many ear learners emigrated from their home countries as children and speak a language other than English at home; such learners are sometimes referred to as "Generation 1.5" (Harklau, Losey, & Siegal, 1999). Research suggests that many of these U.S.-educated multilingual writers graduate from high school without the academic reading and writing skills needed for success in higher education (see Doolan & Miller, 2012, for a review and discussion of error patterns made by these writers). Although the eye/ear distinction may be an oversimplification, it is clear that the needs of students with different educational and language learning backgrounds will be quite diverse: "eye" learners have strengths in formal vocabulary and explicit knowledge of grammar, but may lack the fluency and naturalness of ear learners. Teachers will have to adjust their lessons to accommodate the needs of these different learner types.

In addition to considering the background of students and their development as writers in L1 and L2, it is important to distinguish between learners who need to write for academic reasons and those who need to write for professional or career reasons. Much of the pedagogy of second language writing draws on the literature in first language composition (see Matsuda, 2003b, for a historical overview of second language writing instruction, particularly in the North American context). Much of this literature assumes that students are writing for academic purposes; this may not always be the case, however, particularly in English as a foreign language (EFL) contexts. Increasingly, writing is used in the workplace, and students need to learn the appropriate genres and discourse conventions for different areas of work, such as resumes, business letters, emails, and website content.

To summarize, the variety of English language learners throughout the world, their linguistic and educational backgrounds, and their different writing needs make it impossible to prescribe a single approach to the teaching of writing because so much depends on the particulars of the local context. However, there are some general principles of writing that are of value to teachers in all contexts, and it is to these principles we now turn. Specifically, teachers should be aware of research in such areas as what proficient writers do when they write, what distinguishes good writers from weaker writers, and what the specific writing problems of English as a second language (ESL) learners are likely to be. Research (Peñuelas, 2008; Sasaki, 2000; Weigle, 2005) has shown that, for expert writers in particular, writing is not a linear process but involves going back and forth among planning, writing, rereading, and revising. Furthermore, compared to novice writers, expert writers spend more time planning and revising their writing and editing their writing for content and organization than they do making small surface changes to their texts. Expert writers are able to hold in mind numerous considerations simultaneously and have a greater understanding of their own limitations, a greater understanding of the needs and expectations of their audiences, and more highly developed schemata for different genres than novice writers. All this does not mean that writing is less effortful for experts than for novices, however: Expert writers are more likely to set greater challenges for themselves and to use a strategy of "knowledge transforming" (using writing to create new knowledge) rather than "knowledge telling" (expressing what they already know) in writing (Bereiter & Scardamalia, 1987, pp. 9–10).

Comparing L1 and L2 writers, Silva's (1993) extensive review of the literature concludes that L2 writing is "more constrained, more difficult, and less effective" (p. 668) than L1 writing, although the general processes are similar. L2 writers in the studies that Silva reviewed tended to be similar to less experienced native speaking writers in focusing prematurely on sentence-level errors rather than global issues of rhetorical organization and were less likely to engage in knowledge-transforming rather than knowledge-telling strategies (Bereiter & Scardamalia, 1987). Learning to write in a second language is further complicated by the fact that genres differ across languages and cultures, so writers may not be able to transfer their rhetorical knowledge from their first language to English.

The implication of this research for teaching writing is that L2 writers need more of everything: more practice writing, more opportunities to develop effective writing strategies, more familiarity with genres, more practice with vocabulary and grammar, and more feedback. Writing teachers need to be aware that their students will not become experts over the course of a few weeks or months and need to develop realistic expectations regarding what can be accomplished in a single term.

It is well known that language proficiency, as it relates to writing, develops slowly over a number of years and depends on extensive exposure to different texts in different genres. Certain elements of grammar, for example, appear to be resistant to explicit instruction and acquired late, such as the use of relative clauses and the English article system (R. Ellis, 2005). However, other aspects of writing seem to be independent of language proficiency and amenable to instruction with more immediate results. For example, Roca de Larios, Murphy, and Marin (2002) suggest that several writing strategies can be effectively taught within a relatively short time frame, including problem-solving strategies; goal setting and organization; having a sense of audience; and planning, monitoring, and evaluating performance.

The process approach

Research on the writing process has led to what is now the dominant paradigm in writing instruction, the process approach. Historical overviews of writing instruction that have led to the preeminence of process approaches can be found in numerous sources (e.g., Ferris & Hedgcock, 2004; Matsuda, 2003b; Raimes, 1991). Although there are many variations on process approaches, they all have certain features in common. Specifically, instead of producing several different single-draft essays that are turned in for a grade, often with a primary focus on linguistic accuracy, students produce more than one draft of each piece of writing for feedback and evaluation, and emphasis is placed on supporting students through the various stages of writing, including pre-writing (e.g., brainstorming or outlining), drafting, giving and receiving feedback, and revising (see Table 1). How a process approach is implemented in practice is discussed in the next section

Reading and writing connections

Another important theoretical consideration for writing instruction is the connection between reading and writing, skills that scholars now consider complementary elements of literacy rather than separate, discrete skills. This connection between reading and writing is one that has received a great deal of emphasis in recent years (see Belcher & Hirvela, 2001; Carson & Leki, 1993; Hirvela, 2004). There is a growing recognition that reading and writing are intimately connected and that one cannot easily be taught without the other. In fact, problems with student writing can often be traced to problems with reading (Hirvela, 2004); for this reason, the writing teacher must also be prepared to teach certain aspects of reading.

Hirvela (2004) provides a convincing rationale for including reading as an integral component of the writing classroom, primarily through three main areas of reading-writing connections:

Reader response theory. This approach emphasizes the reader's active participation in understanding a text and ways to develop effective reading strategies. For example, instead of asking students simply to discuss their understanding of a particular text, teachers can ask them to reflect on the strategies they use for reading, what problems they encountered, and how they dealt with those problems. In this way students are encouraged to see themselves as active meaning-makers. Reflecting on reading processes can lead to an understanding of composition processes as complementary activities to reading.

Writing to read. This approach involves using writing as a way of interpreting and understanding

Table 1. Phases of the Writing Process

Phase	Definition	Examples of Teaching and Learning Activities
Pre-writing	Structured activities to provide motivation, content, fluency, language practice	Structured language practice, readings, films, discussions, brainstorming, webbing, outlining
Writing	First draft	Focus on content, getting ideas on paper
Response	Reaction of a reader or listener	Peer review, partners or small groups, teacher conferences, written feedback
Revising	Reseeing or rethinking content; second draft	Reorganizing, adding details, adding support for arguments
Editing	Refinement and attention to writing conventions, including grammar and vocabulary; third draft	Checklists, grammar logs, exercises, proofreading practice
Post-writing	What students and teachers do with finished pieces	Display, share online, compile class writing into a booklet
Evaluating	How teachers and/or students assess student writing	Rubrics, conferences, self-evaluation, portfolios

Adapted from California State University, Stanislaus (n.d.).

a text. Examples of writing-to-read activities include writing about a topic in preparation for reading about it and response activities such as journals and response papers. Writing about what they read helps students create a deeper understanding of texts, which will in turn help them in their further writing.

Reading to write. This approach involves using reading as a source of input in creating a written text. In reading to write, students explicitly and actively search for knowledge about writing; this knowledge can be rhetorical (what kinds of organizational patterns are common in this type of writing?), linguistic (what words, phrases, or sentence structures are useful?), or stylistic (how formal/informal is this kind of writing?).

Attribution of sources and plagiarism

In academic writing in particular, an emphasis on reading as part of writing naturally brings up the issue of appropriate attribution of sources and the specter of plagiarism. Students are frequently told to "use your own words" and are warned about the seriousness of plagiarism and its consequences, but teachers are often frustrated because their students seem to have a difficult time knowing when and how to paraphrase. In fact, the issue of

appropriate source use in writing is a much more complicated issue than it first appears to be. There are both cognitive and cultural factors involved, and writing teachers need to understand what these issues are so they can help their students learn to incorporate source materials into their writing appropriately. Students with limited proficiency have limited linguistic resources and may need to rely more heavily on scaffolding (both lexical and grammatical) from source materials because they may not know how to express an idea in a different way. Research suggests that many students have difficulty with sentence simplification and paraphrasing without changing the author's original intent; furthermore, some students consider copying a legitimate strategy for composing (Shi, 2004). Similar cultural issues regarding the use of source text language have been noted by Pennycook (1996), who was among the first to point out that the idea that individuals "own" ideas and words is a peculiarly Western notion that may not be prevalent in other cultures. Commenting on the lack of fit between instructor and student perceptions, Starfield (2007) noted:

> whereas lecturers view the issue as being about the correct referencing of sources, for students plagiarism is linked to their developing identities as writers and their relative lack of

authority vis-à-vis the authority of academic texts and is part of a complex process of learning to write according to unfamiliar norms and conventions in a language that is often not their primary language. (p. 880)

The notion of intertextuality (Bakhtin, 1981; Fairclough, 1992; Starfield, 2007) is frequently invoked to explain students' difficulty with avoiding plagiarism. What is meant by *intertextuality* is that all writing uses words and phrases that are preexisting and combined in new ways, referring to and building on what has come before. Writers constantly draw on and refer to other existing texts in their own writing through a set of conventions that are often implicit and known only to people within a certain discourse community. Beginning writers without extensive experience and without the same history of working with and understanding the important vocabulary and texts in a particular discourse community may have difficulties understanding how to follow their instructors' guidance about using their own words and paraphrasing.

Given these complexities, it is clear that simply teaching students to paraphrase and summarize is only part of the solution to helping them learn acceptable citation practices. Students need to be made aware of the possibilities for censure and be taught strategies for paraphrasing and citing sources; however, these strategies may not be entirely successful given the complexity of issues surrounding textual borrowing (Currie, 1998; Starfield, 2007). Learning to identify and avoid inappropriate textual borrowing is clearly an important part of the writing classroom and teachers should avoid framing it as a moral issue.

The role of grammar and error correction in writing

The last theoretical issue is the role of grammar and the effectiveness of error correction in the writing classroom. Beginning writing teachers tend to take it as a given that one of their main roles is to point out and correct student errors in writing so that students can learn to avoid such errors. At the same time, teachers often become frustrated both by the amount of time that error correction takes and its seeming ineffectiveness. Indeed, the research evidence concerning the effectiveness of error correction is inconclusive (e.g., see Ferris,

2003, for arguments in support of error correction; and see Truscott, 1996, 1999, for arguments against correcting grammar in the writing classroom). Whether grammar instruction is effective in the second language writing classroom, particularly for advanced learners, is similarly a matter of some controversy because it is difficult to draw a straight line between instruction and future performance (e.g., see Ferris, 2003; Frodesen & Holten, 2003). Given the many other issues that writing teachers need to deal with in their classes, asking whether to spend time on error correction is probably less appropriate than asking how to prioritize dealing with grammar instruction and errors along with other equally or more important considerations. (See also Frodesen, this volume.) This issue is revisited later in this chapter.

CLASSROOM APPLICATIONS

In this part of the chapter, I discuss the fundamentals of designing a writing course. Specifically, I discuss objectives and assessment, lesson planning, designing writing tasks, and responding to student writing.

A good place to begin is with Leki, Cumming, and Silva's (2008) statement that a writing curriculum "involves the organization of learning activities for students to develop abilities to produce (a) meaningful, accurate written texts (b) by composing effectively and (c) engaging in the discourse appropriate to specific social contexts and purposes" (p. 72). In other words, there are three main considerations in designing a writing curriculum: the written product, the writing process, and tailoring writing to a specific audience and purpose. Effective teaching involves a balance among these concerns. Focusing too much on accurate texts divorces writing from its communicative function and turns the writing class into a grammar class; on the other hand, focusing exclusively on the writing process with little or no attention to accuracy and precision can result in written products that are inappropriate or that do not communicate clearly. Finally, focusing on process or product without a consideration of the communicative situations in which writing is actually used can lead to lack of motivation because students will not see the relevance of what is being taught in class.

Kroll (2001) notes that the list of tasks that any writing teacher must accomplish is somewhat predictable: designing/implementing a syllabus, planning individual class sessions, providing opportunities for writing, and responding to that writing. The novice teacher often finds it difficult to know how to put this list into practice; the following suggestions may provide some guidance.

The syllabus provides a road map for both students and teachers and also helps to clarify expectations and class policies. Designing a syllabus provides an opportunity to think through the overall goals of the writing course and the major learning activities that serve those goals. For this reason, a critical step in creating a syllabus is articulating learning outcomes or course objectives. As far as possible, learning outcomes should be written in the form of observable behaviors and products so that it is easier to determine whether these objectives have been met by the end of the course. For example, a vague learning outcome such as "Students will improve their writing in this course" is less useful than the following outcome statements (taken from a low-intermediate writing course in an academically oriented intensive English program at a U.S. university):

- Produce organized paragraphs (7 sentence minimum) with topic sentences, supporting details, and concluding sentences through a process of drafting and revision
- Use the language of narration, exemplification, process, comparison/contrast, or description
- Demonstrate coherence using repetition of keywords, pronouns, synonyms, and signal words

Note that these outcomes specify both the product and the process of writing, along with indications of the type of language needed to complete the writing tasks. Students have a clear idea of what is expected of them, and teachers can readily ascertain whether students have achieved these outcomes. Written learning outcomes are also useful in designing scoring rubrics, or written criteria for evaluating the writing, tailored to specific assignments. For example, a rubric for paragraphs based on the outcome statements could include points for content and organization, such as the presence of an effective topic sentence, details that support the main idea, and an appropriate conclusion; it could also include issues of language (such as the use of cohesive devices and the appropriate use of the discourse mode). Finally, the rubric could include a consideration of whether students have successfully incorporated feedback from peers or the teacher in improving their writing. (See the Appendix for an example of a writing rubric used in a low-intermediate composition course in an intensive English program.)

A useful way to begin formulating objectives is to write down in as detailed a fashion as possible what you hope students will know and be able to do by the end of the course and how students will demonstrate their knowledge and skills through observable behaviors or products. Elsewhere (Weigle, 2007) I have suggested an exercise that may help teachers to articulate learning outcomes:

> Imagine the best piece of writing that could come from one of your students, and write an imaginary endnote to a student saying what you like about it. As you do so, you will articulate in words what you are hoping to see in student writing, whether it is precise use of language, vivid details, or a strong thesis with good support. Each of these descriptions can be used to create learning outcomes. (p. 197)

For a writing course, it is useful to think of three components of objectives: (1) a description of the performance itself, or what the student is expected to write (e.g., essays, descriptive paragraphs, or business memoranda); (2) the conditions under which the writing will be done (e.g., at home or in class, and with or without feedback between drafts); and (3) the level of performance that will be deemed acceptable, that is, the criteria for evaluation in terms of such considerations as organization, use of vocabulary, or sentence types (adapted from Mager, 1975, as cited in Ferris & Hedgcock, 2004).

Specifying objectives in this way goes hand in hand with articulating the major assignments for the course and determining how they will be evaluated. For example, in a 14-week term a teacher might assign three or four major papers, depending on the level of student proficiency. The first step in filling out the details of the syllabus, then, is to set deadlines for these major assignments at appropriate intervals during the term.

Outcomes written in this way have the added advantage of helping teachers discern what aspects of writing they need to focus on in their teaching. For example, one learning outcome in an adult ESL setting might be "students will write short informational notes of request to a teacher, landlord, or other community member." Teachers wanting students to meet this outcome will need to make sure students know appropriate basic vocabulary, routine greetings and closings, question formation, writing conventions such as indentation and paragraphing, and politeness strategies. Thinking through these learning points will help teachers determine what activities to focus on in any given lesson.

Lesson planning

Once the major assignments for the course are determined, planning must be done on two levels: in terms of the writing cycle for each major assignment and in terms of the individual lesson. In terms of the writing cycle, there are three phases that need to be considered: pre-writing, writing, and revising/editing. The pre-writing phase includes setting up the assignment; providing input for students to work with in the form of texts, visuals, videos, or other content; introducing and practicing specific points of grammar or vocabulary that are important for completing the assignment; and various activities for brainstorming and idea generation. The writing phase must include time for drafting in class (where appropriate), feedback from peers and/or the teacher, ample time for incubation and rewriting, and continued work on troublesome areas as they come up. Finally, a polished draft must be submitted; teachers need to consider how much time to devote to grading and evaluating, and what other means of dissemination might be appropriate for sharing student work. Specific suggestions for each of these phases are given shortly; first, however, I discuss some general principles of lesson planning.

Most experienced teachers will confirm that a written lesson plan is essential for every class period. A written lesson plan can be as simple as a few notes or quite formal, with each step written out in detail. (See Purgason, this volume, for an extended discussion of lesson planning.) However, as Ferris and Hedgcock (2004) noted, "whatever form a lesson plan takes, it should be readable, convenient to refer to in class when needed, and usable as a future record of what took place" (p. 99). Ferris and Hedgcock divide the typical writing lesson into five phases: activation of prior learning, preview/warm-up, lesson core (instruction, procedures, and participation), closure, and follow-up/reflection. These components are important no matter what phase of the writing process is being focused on in any given lesson. In planning out a lesson, teachers should be mindful of maintaining a balance between teacher-centered and student-centered activities, providing enough time for students to practice and apply concepts, and leaving time at the end to make sure that students understand whatever homework is assigned.

Turning now to a discussion of the types of activities that are appropriate for writing classes, we can divide them into the stages of the writing process: pre-writing, writing, feedback, and revising/editing.

Pre-writing activities

Anyone who has ever stared for hours at a blank sheet of paper or computer screen recognizes that one of the greatest challenges in writing is getting started. Writing teachers need to have a variety of strategies to help students get over their initial anxiety, begin planning out their ideas, and start writing. Pre-writing activities can be targeted toward linguistic development, fluency, idea generation, building up knowledge about a topic, or a combination of all of these. For example, activities such as freewriting (writing for a set period of time without stopping), generating lists of ideas or thoughts associated with a topic, and making a mind map of related concepts are appropriate at all levels of proficiency and experience. Additional pre-writing activities may include targeted lessons on specific aspects of writing, including strategies for using dictionaries or other reference materials in writing, and identifying and analyzing rhetorical structures of texts, such as the activity described in the opening experience section of this chapter. Detailed suggestions for activities for pre-writing activities can be found in Ferris and Hedgcock (2004) and Williams (2005). Such activities serve to help students find a way into the writing topic and to discover for themselves strategies that they find useful and can apply to writing assignments in the future.

In academic settings in particular, it is very common to incorporate readings as a starting place for writing. A substantial amount of pre-writing time will thus be dedicated to encountering written texts of various types. As noted earlier, writing teachers need to think carefully about how they will use readings in their courses; it is not enough simply to ask students to read a passage and then write about it. Some questions teachers may want to ask themselves about readings include:

- What will students do with the reading in their writing? Will they be responding to the reading, using materials from the reading to support an argument, or completing some other writing task?
- What challenges might this reading pose to students? Will the vocabulary, concepts, or background knowledge be an issue? How will I deal with these challenges?
- How can I exploit this reading to teach something about writing? For example, are there organizational patterns that I can call students' attention to? Depending on the level of the student and the stage within the writing process where students will encounter the text, the reading can be used to highlight citation practices, language forms and structures, or organizational patterns, for example; see Hyland (2004c) for specific suggestions for additional activities.

Writing tasks

To help students develop a wide range of writing skills, they should be asked to respond to a variety of tasks, some graded and some not, some impromptu and some planned, in a variety of genres (Ferris & Hedgcock, 2004; A. M. Johns, 1997; S. McKay, 1994). Williams (2005) notes that the nature of writing tasks will depend in part on learners' proficiency and provides a wealth of suggestions for students at different proficiency levels. Activities appropriate for students with lower proficiencies include picture description tasks; giving advice or instructions; and collaborative activities such as dictoglosses, in which students take notes on a short text that is read aloud and then try to reconstruct the text. For students with higher proficiencies, especially in academic contexts, several task types typical of authentic academic writing include summaries, proposals, reading responses, case studies, and annotated bibliographies. For many of these activities, students can be asked to either gather or generate information (from their own personal experience, surveys, observations, or interviews) or to summarize, analyze, or critique information from preexisting sources.

Writing tasks need to be structured carefully to elicit the best writing from students. Reid and Kroll (1995) point out that classroom writing differs from all other writing in the sense that it is not voluntary, the topics are usually assigned, and the writing is evaluated. Even if the assignment specifies an audience and a purpose, students know that their real audience is the teacher and the real purpose is to demonstrate their writing ability. In this sense, a writing assignment is a form of assessment, and teachers thus need to design their writing prompts with as much care as they would for any other assessment. Reid and Kroll provide useful suggestions for designing appropriate tasks. In particular, they note that the content should be accessible to all students and allow for multiple approaches to responding to the prompt, the instructions should be written in clear and unambiguous language, and the task should include the criteria on which the writing will be judged.

For major assignments, where students will go through a process of drafting and revision, some useful guidelines are as follows:

- Make sure that the scope of the task is feasible within the time allotted.
- Structure the task to reduce the possibility of plagiarism.
- Provide appropriate scaffolding of the task.
- Specify the topic, genre, and purpose.
- Provide the scoring criteria at the beginning.
- Specify intermediate deadlines for assignments.

One issue that teachers need to confront in lesson planning is how much class time to devote to actual writing. How much writing is done in the classroom (as opposed to between class meetings at home) depends in great measure on the context; for example, the availability of computers and the time available for out-of-class work are obvious factors that affect this. One argument in favor of devoting substantial time in class to writing is that it reinforces the fact that writing takes a lot of practice and that one cannot be a good writer without writing a lot; another advantage of devoting time to writing in class is that the teacher can be available for one-on-one help while others are working. On the other hand, there are often so many other things to do during the class period itself that many teachers feel they cannot sacrifice class time for writing. Students who are paying for instruction may also feel somewhat slighted if they perceive that the teacher has not prepared instruction for a class period. In this case, teachers will need to communicate their rationale for devoting class time to writing.

Feedback, revision, and editing

In a process approach to teaching writing, once students have a working draft of a paper, they need to receive feedback (the third phase in Table 1) and then revise and edit their paper (for global and local issues, respectively) on the basis of this feedback (the fourth and fifth phases). While there is general agreement among students, teachers, and scholars that good feedback is essential to revision, there is less consensus on how feedback should be given, when, by whom, and what sort of feedback is most useful. Since providing feedback to students is potentially one of the most important yet difficult and time-consuming activities that writing teachers engage in, it is important for teachers to know what experience and research have shown to be the most useful ways to provide feedback to students.

Most resources for writing teachers (e.g., Ferris & Hedgcock, 2004; Williams, 2005) recommend commenting primarily on content before commenting on language issues, despite it being a natural tendency for language teachers to focus on sentence-level accuracy. There are several reasons for this recommendation. As noted earlier, inexperienced writers tend to revise at the sentence level more than at higher levels of organization and often need to be explicitly taught to revise on the rhetorical level. In addition, a premature focus on language may stifle students' processes of idea generation. Furthermore, there is little point in making detailed language comments if the overall content and organization are going to be revised. On the other hand, if language errors impede communication to the extent that it is impossible to discern the meaning, clearly these errors need to be addressed right away.

Based on this notion of content first, a common practice in writing courses is to require three drafts of a paper with two cycles of feedback and revision: the first focusing primarily on global issues of content and organization, and the second (assuming adequate improvements from the first round) on language issues. One or both of these feedback cycles frequently involve peer feedback instead of or in addition to instructor feedback. Peer feedback has the obvious benefit of reducing the teacher's grading workload, but it has other benefits as well. Some of the benefits of using peer response include (adapted from Williams, 2005):

- Students have an authentic audience to write for other than their teacher and can try different writing approaches.
- The process of reading others' work develops critical reading skills that can transfer to students' own writing, in addition to improving other L2 skills.
- Peers may focus on issues that teachers do not have time to comment on or choose not to address.

On the other hand, teachers should be aware of potential drawbacks to the use of peer feedback. Research on peer feedback in L2 classroom has revealed two main issues: (1) students do not always give good feedback; and (2) students frequently resist or disregard peer feedback activities as not useful. Both of these issues can be dealt with by sufficient preparation on the part of the teacher, including rationalizing the procedure, modeling the process, and providing materials such as checklists or peer-response guides that target only certain features for students to fill out while responding to their classmates' writing. Additional guidelines for implementing peer review successfully in the second language writing classroom can be found in Ferris (2003) and Liu and Hansen (2002).

Turning to the specifics of providing feedback, another issue is whether to provide oral comments, written comments, or both. Written feedback, in the form of endnotes or marginal comments, can reinforce the strengths of a paper or indicate areas where improvement is needed. However, written comments can be very time-consuming and are often open to misunderstandings and different interpretations. An alternative is individual conferencing with students during office hours so that teacher and student can discuss the strengths and weaknesses of the paper. However, this may not be possible in some settings, if there are no office hours, or if students are unavailable outside class. Fortunately, new technologies have opened up new possibilities for feedback in the form of podcasts or other digitally recorded means. The advantages of recording comments are several. First, it is often faster and easier for teachers to express their comments orally than in writing. Second, attending to comments provides additional practice in listening comprehension. Students can listen to recorded comments and relisten as often as they need to, unlike in face-to-face conferences. Third, and perhaps most important, the oral-aural channel preserves cues to meaning and intention, such as vocal inflection and pitch, which can help students interpret the comments in a positive light. These options are summarized in Table 2.

Williams (2005) provides a comprehensive list of good practices for giving feedback to student writers. Some of these suggestions involve making explicit to students the goals and process of feedback: explaining feedback procedures, modeling the process to students, and demonstrating to students how to incorporate feedback into their writing. In terms of the actual feedback process, Williams recommends reading the whole text through before making comments, being as clear as possible (avoiding indirectness because students often misinterpret it), and offering concrete suggestions that students can act on. Consistency is important, as is balancing critique with praise. An important part of the feedback process is making students accountable for using feedback; worksheets or checklists that students need to fill out when turning in later drafts can be a useful tool for accountability.

As discussed earlier, one important issue in teaching writing is how to deal with errors in student writing, given that it is virtually impossible to deal with every issue. Many scholars suggest prioritizing errors that interfere with comprehension, errors that are stigmatized, errors that are a current focus of instruction, and errors that occur frequently. Another important distinction to make is whether students can self-correct the errors or need to be taught the correct form directly. In the former case, an indirect approach is usually advised. Many teachers use coding sheets containing symbols and abbreviations to indicate types of errors that students can correct themselves (for example, *W F* for "word form" or *T* for "tense"). However, while this may be an intuitively appealing practice, it has not been shown to be effective (Truscott, 1996); furthermore, such coding systems can be difficult to implement consistently and may overwhelm both teachers and students with their complexity (Ferris & Hedgcock, 2004).

If self-correction is not an option, and particularly when several students are having difficulties with complex structures, it is generally more effective to conduct a grammar mini-lesson in class, consisting ideally of text analysis/discovery activities, a brief deductive explanation of the grammar point in question, and practice and application activities (Ferris & Hedgcock, 2004; Williams, 2005). However teachers may choose to deal with errors, it is important that they be consistent, explain their systems clearly, and be explicit about

Table 2. Advantages and Disadvantages of Different Types of Teacher Feedback on Writing

Type of Feedback	Advantages	Disadvantages
Written comments	Endnotes and margin comments can reinforce strengths of a paper or indicate where improvement is needed.	Writing is time-consuming; written comments are open to misinterpretation.
Individual conferences	These provide an opportunity to clarify and negotiate meaning through discussion; they may be less time-consuming than providing clear written feedback.	Teachers and/or students may not be available outside class; students may not be willing to attend office hours; students may not be willing to admit when they do not understand the teacher's comments.
Recorded oral feedback	May be faster than providing written feedback; provides opportunities for listening comprehension; students can listen to comments multiple times; nonverbal information (inflections and tone of voice) can promote a positive interpretation of comments.	Technology may not be available; some teachers or students may be uncomfortable with recording equipment.

how they want students to respond to feedback on errors; see Ferris (2011) for a thorough discussion of responding to errors.

FUTURE TRENDS

Numerous changes in writing instruction have been brought about by the rapid expansion of technology over the past 20 years. Writing increasingly involves keyboarding, a skill that can be taken for granted in some contexts but may need to be taught in others. Social media networks such as Facebook and online discussion boards, blogs, and wikis can be exploited in the writing classroom, providing opportunities for genuine interaction with an audience that goes well beyond the teacher and fellow students. (See Sokolik, this volume, for an expanded discussion of the role of technology in second language teaching.) Warschauer (2007) discusses three main technological issues with regard to writing instruction: synchronous (real-time) communication, such as chats and instant messaging; asynchronous communication formats, such as emails or web-based bulletin boards; and hypermedia authoring, such as designing webpages. Warschauer notes that, for many second language writers, electronic media provide more access to authentic communication along with expanded opportunities to understand and use a wider range of language functions and structures than does face-to-face interaction. Electronic media can thus be a tremendous asset to writing courses. However, teachers must be trained to use these new technologies to exploit their advantages in the classroom.

In addition to these new media for writing, an important development that has been brought about by the revolution in information technology is the availability of large language corpora, which can be a useful tool for teachers and students to investigate the uses of specific linguistic items. For example, Cortes (2007) and Lee and Swales (2006) describe courses for international graduate students that use corpora as teaching tools for raising awareness about the genres that these students will need to master in their professional lives. (See also McCarthy & O'Keeffe, this volume.) Charles (2007) outlines procedures for using controlled corpus searches to improve students' awareness of and control over specific linguistic choices to fulfill particular rhetorical functions. For example,

online concordances such as the *Virtual Language Centre* (n.d.) can be used to investigate the difference between words like *interested* and *interesting* by providing many examples of how these words are used in authentic texts. Again, this is an area where teacher education is needed so that writing teachers are aware of the possibilities and limitations of using corpus tools for teaching.

Finally, improvements in natural language processing have led to the introduction of automated systems for scoring and providing feedback on writing, a trend with potential to save time and resources but one that is controversial among writing teachers (see Weigle, 2010, for an overview of automated scoring for ESL writing). Proponents of automated assessment (e.g., Shermis, Burstein, Higgins, & Zechner, 2010) point out the increased speed and reliability of using computers to score writing compared to human raters. Ideally, computers could take over some of the more arduous and time-consuming aspects of providing feedback to students, such as identifying grammatical errors, leaving teachers with more time to attend to higher-order concerns such as content development and rhetorical organization. Self-access programs can allow students to submit samples of their writing for automatic feedback without the potential loss of face involved in giving their writing to another person for evaluation, and such feedback can be immediate, allowing the student more opportunities to practice. Indeed, a recent article reports that in at least one institution this is indeed the case: students find turning in multiple drafts to their teachers "corrective, even punitive" and much prefer to revise using e-rater (Jaschik, 2011).

On the other hand, many writing teachers are strongly opposed to the use of automated essay feedback programs because they contradict the very nature of writing, which is a form of communication (e.g., see Cheville, 2004; Herrington & Moran, 2001). Computers obviously cannot read; they can only count things. Thus students writing to a computer are not writing with an audience in mind. Consequently, aspects of writing that can be judged only by getting a sense of a text in its entirety, such as the persuasiveness of an argument or a sense of authorial voice, cannot be judged by a computer. Another objection to automated scoring systems is that they reinforce the notion that errors can be defined objectively instead of contextually. For example, nonstandard linguistic forms such as double negatives, while often inappropriate in academic writing, are perfectly acceptable in some less formal genres.

A similar development with regard to computers and writing is the increasing use of automated software for detecting plagiarism or textual borrowing, such as Turnitin (Turnitin, 2010). While proponents of such software programs note their success in reducing the incidence of wholesale borrowing of source text materials in student writing, some scholars caution against the uncritical use of such programs by educators. Howard (2007), for example, argues that the use of antiplagiarism software frames complicated issues of textual borrowing solely in terms of individual student ethics rather than engaging teachers and students in pedagogies that help students learn to use textual material appropriately in their own writing, as all successful writers do.

Whatever the objections, it is not likely that technological advances such as automated scoring and plagiarism detection will go away; it is up to teachers, then, to educate themselves as to the most appropriate uses of such technology and to guard against misuses.

CONCLUSION

As the world becomes more interconnected, writing is the skill that may ultimately be the most critical, and the need for skilled writing teachers will only increase. It is clear from this brief overview that writing is a complex ability involving consideration of a wide range of issues and subskills, and that teachers need to develop expertise in many different areas to become effective at teaching writing. Writing is perhaps the most challenging and time-consuming skill to teach because of its complexity, but it is also one of the most rewarding.

SUMMARY

➤ Writing is a complex activity that involves both language ability and composing ability.
➤ Writing teachers need to consider both the cognitive (individual) aspects of writing and the sociocultural (contextual) aspects of writing.
➤ Writing teachers need to understand the role of other language skills, particularly reading and grammar, in the writing process.

➤ Writing teachers need to focus on the process of writing as well as on the product, both in instruction and in responding to student writing.
➤ New technologies are already impacting the role of writing in society and the teaching of writing; teachers must be able to understand and evaluate these tools to make the most effective use of them.

DISCUSSION QUESTIONS

1. Why is it important to understand writing from both a cognitive and a sociocultural perspective?
2. What is the relationship between second language proficiency and writing ability?
3. Do you use elements of a process approach in your own writing? How can thinking about your own process be helpful in teaching writing to your students?
4. What are some of the ways in which reading and writing are connected, and what does a writing teacher need to know about reading to teach writing effectively?
5. What are some of the benefits and drawbacks to peer review in a second language writing class?
6. Why is it problematic to correct or point out every grammatical error in a piece of writing?

SUGGESTED ACTIVITIES

1. Look at Table 1 on p. 227.
   a. Design a lesson plan for a writing class that applies the steps of the writing process presented in the table. Be sure to designate the students' proficiency level, assignment deadlines, and so on.
   b. Prepare a scoring rubric that you would give to students to make your grading criteria clear to students at the beginning of the assignment. Refer to the sample rubric in the Appendix for ideas.
2. Work with an ESL/EFL student for two to four sessions on writing. Ask the student to bring samples of his or her writing to work on together. Decide on a strategy for suggesting improvements on both the

rhetorical level (content and organization) and on the sentence level (grammar and vocabulary).

3. If you are working in an academic context, interview several teachers from different content areas about writing in their field and teaching ESL students. Some questions you might ask include:

   a. What types of writing assignments do you give your students?

   b. Are there specific features of writing in your field that students need to know about that they might not learn in a typical English writing class?

   c. To what extent do you grade writing on content, organization, and language? What is most important? Why? Least important? Why?

   d. If you have had non-native speakers of English in your class, are there specific strengths or weaknesses that such students tend to display?

4. If you are currently teaching a writing class, imagine the best possible essay that could come from one of your students. Write an endnote to the student describing the areas in which the student has succeeded, such as the content, the paragraph development, or the use of vocabulary. Using your endnote, draft learning outcomes for your course.

FURTHER READING

Ferris, D. R., & Hedgcock, J. S. (2004). *Teaching ESL composition: Purpose, process, and practice* (2nd ed.). Mahwah, NJ: Lawrence Erlbaum Associates.

This is a comprehensive book that provides practical guidance for teaching composition. It is particularly appropriate for teaching in North American contexts at the university level.

Hirvela, A. (2004). *Connecting reading and writing in second language writing instruction.* Ann Arbor, MI: University of Michigan Press.

This volume provides a theoretical rationale and practical advice for incorporating reading into the writing classroom.

Leki, I., Cumming, A., & Silva, T. (2008). A *synthesis of research on second language writing.* London, UK: Routledge.

This volume is particularly useful for anyone interested in research and its implications for teaching writing, particularly in the ESL context.

Williams, J. (2005). *Teaching writing in second and foreign language classrooms.* Boston, MA: McGraw Hill.

This volume addresses writing issues for both second and foreign language classes. It is fairly short and accessible to teachers in training and practicing teachers.

APPENDIX: SAMPLE SCORING RUBRIC FOR OUT-OF-CLASS PARAGRAPHS, LOW-INTERMEDIATE LEVEL

Scoring rubric (100 points total)

	Rough Draft	Final Draft	Final Grade
Content, organization, and clarity **(50 points)**			
• Paragraph includes specific content points.	__/10	__/10	
• Paragraph includes a topic sentence (a sentence that tells the main idea).	__/10	__/10	
• All the sentences relate to the main idea and are in logical order.	__/10	__/10	
• Ideas are explained clearly.	__/10	__/10	
• Paragraph gives enough information and includes specific examples.	__/10	__/10	
Grammar, mechanics, and format **(50 points)**			
Sentence structure			
• Complete sentences (subject and verb) Problem: _____ no verb _____ no subject	__/10	__/10	
• Correct use of capital letters and periods (.) to divide sentences Problem: _____ run on _____ comma splice	__/10	__/10	
Other grammar for the level/assignment			
• Correct word order	__/5	__/5	
• Correct word forms: nouns, verbs, adjectives, adverbs, plurals, pronouns (subject, object, possessive)	__/5	__/5	

• Correct use of verbs
  Problem: __ verb tense __ incorrect use of *be* = *am, is, are*
  ___verb form ___ subject-verb agreement
	__/10	__/10	

Format			
• Indents the first line of the paragraph and uses correct format for other lines	__/5	__/5	
Spelling and mechanics			
Problem: ___ spelling ___ punctuation ___ capital letters	__/5	__/5	
Final grade **(100 points)**	__/100	__/100	__/100

Note: Points obtained on the rough and final drafts are averaged to arrive at the final grade. If the final draft is not turned in on time, 10 points are subtracted.
Copyright Georgia State University Intensive English Program. Adapted with permission.

16 | Grammar in Second Language Writing

JAN FRODESEN

KEY QUESTIONS

➤ How should grammar be incorporated into writing instruction?
➤ How are the needs of second language writers different from those of native English writers?
➤ How can we apply insights from research on the role of grammar in writing to form-focused activities in the writing class?
➤ How should grammatical errors be viewed and treated?

EXPERIENCE

In a California elementary school, the teacher of a class of bilingual fifth-graders was preparing her students for a standardized English test. The test required that students demonstrate knowledge of English grammar rules by choosing appropriate word forms to fill in the blanks of a set of decontextualized sentences—a typical discrete-item, multiple-choice test. Up to this point in the class, the students had been creating their own illustrated bilingual storybooks about fantastical beasts, writing their texts first in Spanish, their native language, and then in English. To help her students develop their awareness of the need to meet readers' expectations, the teacher had been serving as a careful reader of their stories, letting them know whenever she had a problem understanding their meaning and providing vocabulary and grammar explanation as needed.

As the students pored over example sentences to prepare for the required exam, a task both the teacher and students found tedious (especially compared to their story-writing activity), they encountered one item in which they had to choose the correct pronoun for a subject slot. The choices were the nominative pronoun *she* and the object pronoun *her*. As the teacher was prompting the correct form for the blank, one of the students exclaimed, "But teacher, this is a bad sentence! We don't know who *she* is!"

This story, related by the teacher of this class, Barbara Hawkins, offers an excellent example of helping writers develop knowledge of grammatical systems to convey ideas meaningfully and appropriately. It illustrates how even young second language (L2) learners can discover and apply discourse-level grammatical principles, in this case making clear the referents for pronouns.

Not only *can* students of all ages learn how to use grammar appropriate to specific contexts, but a focus on form appears to be necessary to some extent for optimal L2 learning. When instruction is meaning focused only, learners fail to develop some linguistic features at target-like levels (Doughty & Williams, 1998b). And, of course, in academic or professional contexts, helping learners develop the ability to select and accurately produce structures typical of written registers and genres is an important instructional objective.

WHAT IS THE ROLE OF GRAMMAR IN L2 WRITING INSTRUCTION?

In L2 writing, the role of grammar has generally included two broad areas: (1) instruction and practice in grammatical structures; and (2) response to and correction of errors in students' texts. An example of the former is an explanation of count and noncount nouns in English followed by exercises that give learners the opportunity to distinguish the two types of nouns and use them in a meaningful context. The second type might focus on a specific type of error in student writing, such as verb tense, or might involve attention to an individual writer's most frequent errors.

Both of these areas of grammar have been controversial in writing instruction for many years. One reason for this has been the influence of first language (L1) composition research and pedagogy. In *Research in Written Composition*, a major synthesis of writing studies published in 1963, authors Braddock, Lloyd-Jones, and Schoer state that instruction in formal grammar had little or no effect on helping students improve their writing. In the decades following this report, composition instruction gradually shifted its focus first to individuals' writing processes and later to an emphasis on writing as a situated social activity. As a result, little attention is now given to language issues in L1 writing instruction other than teachers' correction of errors on student papers and referrals to tutoring centers.

The concerns that arose during the last half of the twentieth century about formal grammar instruction failing to improve students' writing development were shared by some L2 writing instructors, especially those trained in L1 composition contexts. Yet grammar instruction and practice remain a central component in many L2 writing classes. As Frodesen and Holten (2003) have discussed, L2 composition teachers hold varying attitudes about the role of focus on form; they note that L2 writing classes have tended to fall into one of two categories: "writing rich, but grammar poor" or the reverse. "Writing rich, but grammar poor" instruction has been influenced not only by L1 pedagogy and research but also by Krashen (1982), who argues that form-focused instruction is not only unnecessary but thwarts natural acquisition processes. Termed the *noninterventionist position* (Long & Robinson, 1998), the rejection of explicit focus on form has characterized for years many L2 classrooms dedicated to developing learners' communicative competence. In contrast to the "writing rich, but grammar poor" class, many "grammar rich, but writing poor" L2 writing classes have used written texts largely as a context for learning and practicing grammatical structures, and, as such, they are better described not as writing but as grammar classes.

Grammar as resource

Although they clearly offer very different types of instruction, both the "writing rich, but grammar poor" and the "grammar rich, but writing poor" classes reflect misconceptions about the role of grammar in the teaching of writing. There is a great difference between the teaching of linguistic forms apart from a meaningful context, on the one hand, and a focus on language forms to develop learners' ability to communicate meaningfully and appropriately, on the other, as Hawkins's bilingual classroom in the opening experience so aptly exemplifies. In the latter view, learners discover how grammar functions as an integral part of language use and how writers use structures to achieve specific purposes such as to emphasize or connect information. Thus, grammar serves as a resource for effective communication, not just an isolated body of knowledge. Learners come to understand grammar as an essential component of language, a system that they can explore and exploit for their communicative needs rather than as a tedious and complicated set of rules to be memorized or as a template to be used solely for identifying and correcting their errors.

With increasing research on L2 writers and their texts, we now have a great deal more evidence of the differences between L1 and L2 writers, processes, and products (Leki, Cumming, & Silva, 2008; Silva, 1993). This research has shown that English as a second language (ESL) writers do not have the same access to intuitions about language that makes overt focus on some types of grammar unnecessary for most native English speakers. Furthermore, for writers of all language backgrounds, developing proficiency in academic English involves acquiring structures that do not exist in learners' repertoire of spoken, conversational forms. As Silva (1993) concludes from his synthesis of L2 writing research, L1 and L2 writing "are different in numerous and important ways" (p. 671). Thus, while L1 composition theory and practices have certainly informed L2 writing pedagogy, teachers of L2 writers must also attend to the special language needs of their learners.

As we reflect on the role of grammar as a resource for creating and shaping effective written communication, it seems clear, then, that focus on form should be an integral part of the instructional design for L2 writing classrooms. This does not mean, however, that all kinds of grammar instruction are useful in this context. Nor does it mean that students will automatically be able to transform input received through explicit grammar instruction into productive output. Awareness of learner and contextual variables can, however, assist teachers in deciding when and how to incorporate grammar into writing instruction.

Treatment of learner error

While a focus on grammar as a linguistic resource puts a more positive face on the role of grammar in writing instruction, any discussion of this role should include attention to learners' writing errors, a significant concern for most L2 writing teachers and their students. For decades, studies and debates on the effectiveness of differing types of error correction and, indeed, of error correction at all, have been a major topic in the L2 writing literature. Central in recent debates include the exchanges between Truscott (1996, 2007), who believes that ESL research does not provide evidence showing that error correction improves writers' accuracy over time, and Ferris (1999, 2011), who, while acknowledging that the research base lacks controlled studies on this topic, nevertheless asserts that studies have indicated short-term improvement. Ferris (2011) has further pointed out that without attention to errors and explicit instruction, adult learners may fail to make progress in correcting patterns of errors in their L2 writing. Indeed, writing teachers in higher education contexts have found that many of their multilingual students enter colleges and universities unaware of frequent error patterns in their writing.

CONCEPTUAL UNDERPINNINGS

Where should teachers begin in deciding what kinds of grammar focus are appropriate and relevant for their students' needs in the writing classroom? Should we start with the learners or with structures? In thinking about any communicative activity, it is, of course, difficult to separate the learners from the goals of the task, not to mention from the other participants (e.g., readers) who may be involved. Writing is a dynamic process in which writers interact with their intended readers and draw on their knowledge of text types in the co-construction of meaning for specific purposes. From this perspective, a starting point involves not merely a choice between learners and structures but, rather, a more holistic consideration of the communicative task. Nevertheless, it will be helpful to consider some of the learner variables that affect how teachers introduce and integrate grammatical concepts into their classrooms.

Second language writer variables

Age is one of the most obvious of learner variables. This chapter began with an example of elementary school bilingual learners who demonstrated to their teacher the importance of having clear referents for pronouns, though they may not have known the terminology for such structures. In recent decades, elementary school academic language development curricula and standards in English-speaking countries such as Australia and the United States have been informed by the work of functional linguists who make explicit the language structures of school genres that young learners are expected to acquire. For example, Gibbons (2006a) describes Australian fifth-graders in a science classroom, including English learners, transitioning from journal entries of experiments in everyday language to the language of science reports, with attention to grammatical features such as the verb tenses used in these reports. In this context, grammar in writing has clearly been expanded beyond the outdated notion of teaching learners explicit rules of morphology and syntax. It begins with meaningful activities to write about and with the young writers' attempts to communicate their experience, followed by work involving models of the academic language to be mastered.

For older learners in secondary schools, higher education, and beyond, Ferris and Hedgcock (2004) note that students in ESL composition classrooms in English-speaking countries are typically a very heterogeneous population, characterized by many differences in backgrounds and abilities, including linguistic, ethnic, and cultural identities as well as cognitive and metacognitive strategy use.

All these differences can influence the ways in which a writing teacher may approach grammar-based activities in classrooms and providing feedback to individual learners.

With the ever-growing population of non-native English-speaking immigrants in English-speaking countries, differences in students' educational backgrounds and English proficiency have become extremely important in developing L2 curricula. One of the most important distinctions in types of L2 learners at higher education levels has been that between international students who have received their education in their native country prior to attending an English-medium school and U.S.-educated ESL students. (In English as a foreign language [EFL] contexts, of course, most students will have educational backgrounds similar to the international students in English-speaking countries.)

International (or EFL) students have typically learned most of their English in the classroom and generally have received considerable explicit grammar instruction. Thus, they are often able to access and explain grammar rules when doing text analysis and to use their metalinguistic knowledge to revise and edit drafts. For example, in editing sessions with teachers or tutors, they can refer to parts of speech such as articles and prepositions, clause structures such as relative or adverbial clauses, and sentence roles such as subjects or direct objects. Their writing may exhibit more non-nativelike features such as unidiomatic phrasing than the writing of permanent residents does. However, it may also demonstrate better skill in producing the complex structures typical of formal academic English.

In contrast to international students, students who have received most of their education in an English-speaking country often acquire English "by ear" from exposure to the language in oral contexts, including, of course, the classroom but in many informal conversational contexts as well (Reid, 1998b). For this reason, and because explicit grammar instruction has often not been a significant part of their English language education, the knowledge that these learners have about English grammar tends to be implicit, similar to that of native English-language speakers. They may know that an ungrammatical form "doesn't sound right" but may not be able to explain why, just as most native speakers would not be able to explain why they use the definite article *the* rather than the indefinite *a* in a given context. Drawing on this same implicit knowledge, immigrant L2 students may regard structures used in formal written English, but seldom occurring in everyday English, as incorrect or sounding "strange," just as many novice native English language writers do. Like developing native English language writers, ESL writers often inappropriately import informal oral expressions and syntactic structures into academic writing contexts (e.g., using *I mean* rather than *that is* before a clarifying statement). Permanent resident students may enter higher education institutions unfamiliar with most grammatical terminology, and they also may be less aware than international students of their error patterns in English morphology and syntax.

One other learner variable that has been discussed in relation to grammar in writing is the extent to which learners are willing to take risks in using unfamiliar structures. The tendency of writers to avoid using structures that are difficult for them was long ago pointed out by Schachter and Celce-Murcia (1977). These findings emphasize that grammatical instruction dealing with errors alone will not address the need to develop writing fluency.

Texts and contexts

While not losing sight of our learners, in this section I consider the rich variety of possibilities for language-based tasks in writing classrooms that arise from examining how writers use linguistic resources for different kinds of writing and for different communicative goals. In addition, I offer questions to consider for some of the challenges developing writers face in working with sources and in developing writing fluency and accuracy.

Written discourse can, of course, include everything from very informal language, such as that used in some email or blog posts, to the formal genres of much academic and professional writing. While in most classroom contexts instruction is focused on the more formal, academic kinds of writing, even these contexts should give students opportunities to examine and compare the grammar of formal and informal registers of written English.

With a course syllabus in hand that defines the kinds of writing students will be reading and writing, writing teachers might consider the following questions to guide their planning, selection, and creation of activities that include some focus on form.

What grammatical structures do writers use to make meaning, create connections, and express stance in particular writing tasks? As Hyland (2004b) points out in *Genre and Second Language Writing*, "The forms students need often remain elusive as they cannot make connections between the grammar they study and the meanings these items express in the context of a particular genre" (p. 68). For Hyland, the term *genre* refers to a way of grouping texts together for the purpose of "representing how writers typically use language to respond to recurring situations" (p. 4). Some examples of genres often assigned in school settings are essays, narratives, procedures, problem-solution texts, lab reports, and research papers. Each of these could, of course, be further classified into subgenres such as the argumentative essay or the history research paper. In business writing contexts, genres include memos, letters, proposals, and personnel and financial reports.

While genre-based approaches to writing involve much more than attention to language structures, some approaches, such as systemic functional linguistics (Halliday & Matthiessen, 2004) and English for specific purposes (Swales, 1990), have described not only the larger structures that make up a text type, such as a chapter from a science textbook or a research paper, but also the linguistic structures involved in expressing form-meaning relationships. For example, Swales and other scholars have identified and provided explanations for patterns of verb tenses and active versus passive verb use in the different sections of research writing across disciplines.

Researchers in corpus linguistics (e.g., Biber, 1988) have identified grammatical features and clusters of features typically used in particular kinds of writing. Biber's analysis, for example, characterizes the grammar of non-narrative writing (i.e., texts that are not temporally organized) as using present tense verbs, past participle clauses, and longer and more elaborate noun phrases than those that occur in narrative communication. Reynolds (2005) found that writers in fifth-through eighth grade ESL classes differed from students in L1 language arts classes in their linguistic fluency, which he defined as "the use of linguistic structures appropriate to rhetorical and social purposes" (p. 19). Proponents of genre-based and corpus-based approaches to grammar in writing stress that a focus on language forms

for particular genres should not be equated with teaching "formulas" for writing or conveying a view of written texts as static sets of language rules. Such a focus simply acknowledges that certain patterns of rhetorical strategies, such as definition, often occur in particular text types and that L2 writers, just like L1 writers, need control of the forms typically used to express these functions.

As for the role of grammar in creating connections between different parts of a text, these connections, commonly referred to as *cohesion*, contribute to coherence at many levels of text structure. Celce-Murcia and Olshtain (2000) point out that, while text coherence involves top-down planning and organization, "a well-written text has to conform to more local and specific features of the text, such as . . . appropriate use of cohesive devices" (p. 152). Grammatical cohesive devices in English include personal pronouns such as *it* and *they*, demonstrative determiners and pronouns such as *this* and *these*, the definite article *the* + [noun], and logical connectors such as *however* and *thus*.

Although most L2 classes deal with these structures at various stages, the structures used to create cohesion vary depending on text types, levels of formality, and goals of information emphasis and focus, posing a significant challenge for ESL writers who may have learned a small set of connectors that they tend to overuse, such as *in addition* and *however*, or that they use inappropriately in a given rhetorical context, such as beginning a sentence with *therefore* to end a paragraph even though the sentence does not express a result. Hinkel (2002) has found that L2 writers tend to rely on simple conjunctions, exemplification markers, and demonstrative pronouns in establishing text cohesion, devices appropriate for personal narratives but less so for other writing tasks. Studies reported by Leki, Cumming, and Silva (2008) have found that L2 writers tended to use more conjunctive ties (e.g., *moreover* and *on the other hand*) and fewer lexical ties (e.g., synonyms, antonyms, and classifier nouns such as *issue* or *solution*). As learners advance in educational levels, they find that their writing tasks involve complex patterns of cohesion, often combining grammatical cohesive devices with lexical ones in structures. For example, the prepositional phrase *contrary to this widely held view* consists of a complex preposition expressing a logical relationship (*contrary to*), a demonstrative pronoun (*this*), and a classifier noun (*view*), all of which serve as cohesive devices linking to previous information. Given the many types of cohesion in general and the complexity of the reference system in particular, L2 writers clearly need to examine how cohesion is used in actual texts and get meaningful practice and feedback with these structures.

A final consideration in the role of grammar to convey meanings and intentions is that of expressing stance and qualifying or hedging assertions. Biber, Johansson, Leech, Conrad, and Finegan (1999) define *stance* as the ways in which writers and speakers "commonly express personal feelings, attitudes, value judgments, or assessments" (p. 966). The type of stance most focused on in ESL writing pedagogy has been epistemic stance, which marks "certainty (or doubt), actuality, precision or limitation" (p. 972). Stance markers and hedging devices used to qualify statements include a wide range of grammatical structures: adjectives (*certain, unlikely*), adverbs (*typically, possibly*), verbs (*seems, appears*), and modals (*may, might*), among others. Hedging qualifiers also include frequency adverbs (*usually, sometimes*) and determiners (*many, some*). Studies on stance in L2 writing have identified problems with appropriate use of hedges to qualify generalizations. Hinkel (2004) noted that such problems may stem from a lack of these kinds of hedges in the writer's L1 rhetorical tradition. She also observed that L2 writers may transfer conversational strategies involving overstatement or exaggeration (e.g., *students always study hard*) that are unacceptable in formal writing. L2 writing teachers have observed that less advanced students may front their sentences with probability hedges such as *maybe* or *perhaps* (e.g., *Maybe unemployment rates will drop by the end of the year*) as a simplification strategy rather than using modal verbs (e.g., *may, might*) or introductory adjective phrases (e.g., *it is possible that*) that are more typically found in academic prose.

How do linguistic features of writing tasks (and associated readings) differ from students' everyday language and other kinds of writing? As discussed earlier in Gibbons's (2006a) study of Australian fifth-graders writing science reports, learners need opportunities to talk about and compare the language they use for their everyday interactions, including both spoken and written (e.g., text messaging) interactions, as well as the language of other kinds of writing with which they

are familiar: blogs on the Internet, newspaper articles, and academic registers. Responding to this question may require some language analysis on the part of the instructor, but the question also suggests that students can themselves become explorers of language differences in different registers and text types.

What kinds of grammatical practice can help develop writers' overall fluency? Grammar also plays an important role in helping writers expand their repertoire of linguistic choices (i.e., their syntactic fluency). Hinkel (2003) presented the findings of a corpus analysis of L1 and L2 college writers' texts, which revealed that the L2 writers "employed excessively simple syntactic and lexical constructions" more often than the L1 writers did in their texts (p. 275). Silva (1993) concludes from his extensive review of L2 writing research that composition teachers need to work with their students on "potentially unfamiliar textual patterns," helping them build their lexical and grammatical resources. Thus, tasks designed to develop linguistic fluency should help learners understand the forms and functions of lexicogrammatical patterns and provide practice in which they can consider options for expressing meaning and principles for their selections. As an example, consider the ways in which writers express causality. Developing writers are usually familiar with the subordinate conjunctions *because* and *since* when combining clauses to express this relationship in sentences such as the following:

> *Because* more people in India are migrating to cities, the demand for automobiles is rising.

In academic writing, however, authors often use a variety of structures to express such meaning, including complex prepositions such as *because of* and *thanks to* and verbs that more precisely express the relationship such as *contribute, force,* or *trigger*. Such choices sometimes require complex constructions that are less familiar in everyday English, as in the following examples that paraphrase the original sentence:

> *Because* of increased migration to cities in India, the demand for automobiles is rising.

> Increasing migration to cities in India *has led to a* rising demand for automobiles.

> A rising demand for automobiles in India *has been triggered by* increased migration to cities.

In these examples, we see that the choices for expressing causality may require denser nominalizations (*increasing migration to cities in India*), prepositions that collocate with particular verbs (*to* with the verb *lead*), or a passive verb (*has been triggered*) when the result is expressed in the subject phrase (*rising demand for automobiles*). While these examples are all simple sentences (in terms of having only one clause), their structure is much more complex than the original complex sentence with the *because* clause.

Writers' choices of structures will depend on many factors, including the topic, the writer's stance toward the topic, and the writer's familiarity with a variety of structural options in academic English.

What kinds of grammar focus can help writers develop their ability to paraphrase and summarize source materials? In many composition classes, especially those focused on academic English, writing assignments require analysis and synthesis of a variety of source materials. Some writers who perform well in writing independent of source materials (for example, in producing a personal narrative) may encounter considerable difficulty in accurately and appropriately paraphrasing and summarizing ideas from source materials.(See also Weigle, this volume.)

Research on ESL writers' paraphrase and summary strategies has shown that they often depend on "patchwork" and near-copying strategies, resulting in unacceptable textual borrowing (Keck, 2006; Pecorari, 2003). While the processes of paraphrasing and summarizing are complex acts, drawing on background/content knowledge, rhetorical skills, and vocabulary knowledge, the ability to change and manipulate lexicogrammatical structures (e.g., changing word forms and using appropriate syntactic collocations) also contributes to this important academic skill. Simply telling learners to "use your own words" or having them study examples of "bad" and "good" paraphrases fails to provide the kinds of guided scaffolding that developing writers need to produce acceptable paraphrases and summaries. Writing instructors should consider guided vocabulary and grammar "pre-paraphrasing" activities for specific writing assignments and for developing learners' lexicogrammatical knowledge base. As illustrated in the Classroom Applications section of this chapter, teachers can ask students to rewrite sentences using a specific word or phrase not in the original that will require changing the syntax of the sentence (e.g., changing the reporting verb *told* to *said*, which will prompt a *that*-clause complement rather than an object + infinitive clause):

> The project director *told them to review the plans.* (*told* → *said*)

> Rewrite: The project director *said that they should review the plans.*

How can the teacher help writers develop grammatical knowledge for linguistic accuracy and strategies for effective editing? The special needs of ESL writers in achieving grammatical accuracy have been the focus of much L2 writing research and grammar-based teaching materials for decades. Silva (1993) concludes that L2 writers may need to draft in stages, separating revising (rhetorical) work from editing. For the most part, this is an area of concern for all writers beyond elementary school level. The learner variables described in this chapter, as well as others, will play an important role in determining what kinds of explicit instruction and activities are most appropriate. As Little (1994) has stated, a high level of correctness is required for effective communication in formal written discourse, and native as well as non-native English speakers often use explicit knowledge, either from memory or reference books, when they are planning, monitoring, and editing formal written discourse. In general, the teacher will want to assess a group's instructional needs or review common errors such as noun number, incorrect verb forms, or modals used for the wrong purposes. In the next section, I offer some specific suggestions for this type of focus.

Whatever the instructional objectives, the goal of developing writing proficiency should be at the forefront in making decisions about an explicit focus on grammar. In general, learners can benefit from activities that help them understand the role of grammatical structures in expressing meaning and creating connections. It bears repeating that an excessive focus on error not only promotes a limited perception of the role of grammar in communication but may create— or reinforce—negative attitudes about this very important component of L2 writing instruction.

CLASSROOM APPLICATIONS

Using grammar terminology in the writing classroom

Since terminology can be useful in providing learners with feedback on error patterns in their writing, teachers may need to assess individual learners' knowledge of basic grammatical terms. The instructor could give students a list of grammatical and syntactic terms (noun, subject, preposition, etc.) and ask the students to indicate in various ways (e.g., stars, checks, and question marks) the ones they know, the ones they have heard of but do not really understand, and the ones with which they are totally unfamiliar.

There will, of course, be some basic terms that the teacher will want all students to be familiar with to help them develop both fluency and editing skills. Terminology in general should be kept as simple as possible. For example, progressive verbs, gerunds, and present participles in adjective and adverb phrases might be distinguished as *–ing* verbs, *–ing* nouns, and *–ing* adjectives or adverbs, respectively. Infinitives could be referred to as *to* + verb. Relative clauses could be referred to as *which/who/that* adjective clauses. Such designations link grammatical functions with actual morphemes or words that students will see in writing so there is less need to memorize terms.

Text-based activities: Noticing and text analysis

Writers at all levels of proficiency can benefit from learning how grammatical features and grammatical systems are used in authentic written texts. On the one hand, text-analysis tasks can help learners who are familiar with prescriptive grammar rules but who still have problems understanding and appropriately using grammatical oppositions such as present perfect and past tense verb forms. On the other hand, text analysis can also benefit learners with a mostly implicit knowledge of grammar rather than an explicit rule-based knowledge; these writers often need to learn more about the ways in which various genres of written English differ structurally from oral English forms. (See also McCarthy & O'Keeffe, this volume.) Text-based activities emphasize the interactions of reading and writing for learners and focus attention on form-function relationships and motivations for choosing particular structures.

In selecting a grammar focus, the writing teacher should consider the proficiency levels of students and the course objectives and writing tasks. The level of difficulty of a grammatical feature should not be far beyond the learners' developmental stages; for example, students struggling to produce well-formed relative clauses with subject relative pronouns (e.g., *the teacher who called me . . .*) will have difficulty with a lesson on object pronoun relative clauses (*the teacher to whom I gave my address*). This is not to say that new structures should never be introduced, but some consideration should be given to students' readiness to give attention to specific structures.

The sources of authentic texts will vary depending on the writing-course syllabus. The teacher can examine assigned texts to see what kinds of grammatical structures, contrasts, or systems are dominant and which contain forms that students will be able to use in their own writing.

In academic writing courses, assigned readings typically include examples of the kinds of writing expected of students. In these courses, the instructor will want to consider what grammatical features characterize these writings. This is true even for the academic writing required of younger learners. For example, descriptive science writing at the elementary level could require modifying phrases after nouns (e.g., a lizard *with a big head*) and possessive phrases (e.g., the *lizard's* tail) (Schleppegrell, 1998).

Assigned novels and short stories can also offer good opportunities for grammar-focused activities. Students can identify grammatical features such as adjective word order, article usage, or sentence types and, in some cases, compare these structures to their usage in other kinds of writing.

The following considerations may serve as guidelines for selecting grammatical points.

- The grammatical features should be appropriate for students' developmental levels.
- The grammatical features should reflect students' writing needs for the course or for future writing.
- When possible, assigned course readings should be sources of text analysis so that grammar focus is integrated with other prewriting activities.

- The lessons should generally be kept brief, especially for less advanced writers.
- The instructor may want to enhance the texts by underlining certain elements or making them boldface, especially those that are not very salient for some learners.

Productive tasks should follow text analysis so that writers have opportunities to practice the explicit knowledge gained from noticing grammatical features in written texts and so that teachers are able to assess what students have learned from the text-analysis tasks.

Sample text-analysis lessons

The following are a few examples of lessons that focus on grammatical features in texts. For each, assume that the guidelines just discussed have been considered.

Tense and time frame shifts. L2 writers are often confused about the motivations for verb tense shifts and believe that they should not change verb tenses (e.g., from present to present perfect) or time frames (e.g., from present to past). Following a review of the reasons why writers shift verb tenses and time frames, the teacher can give students a passage with selected verbs underlined and numbered. Students identify the tense and time frame (e.g., past progressive tense, past time frame) for each underlined verb and explain any verb tense shifts (e.g., to support a claim about the present with examples from the past). They also note adverbs or adverb phrases that signal time frame shifts (e.g., *last year*). As a follow-up, students examine a text they have written recently to identify tense shifts and reasons.

"Unpacking" meanings in sentences in context. When writers encounter densely packed information in their reading assignments, rephrasing the information in less complex ways can help them not only with their reading but also with productive writing tasks, including paraphrasing. Schleppegrell (2009) offers an excellent illustration of this activity using a sentence from an 11th-grade history book:

> The destruction of the buffalo and removal of Native Americans to reservations emptied the land for grazing cattle.

The abstract nominalizations in the subject can be unpacked by teachers (and advanced learners) and expressed as several clauses to interpret the causal meanings, to supply the previously stated information, and to demonstrate how the phrase is used as a linguistic resource for developing an explanation. Schleppegrell offers this paraphrase of the nominalizations in the subject:

> Settlers and hunters killed all the buffalo, and the government forced all the Native Americans to leave their lands and move to reservations.

As a class activity, advanced students could work in pairs or groups to deconstruct the meanings of abstract noun phrases, rewriting them as clauses. Later they might look at their own drafts and consider the reverse process, condensing clauses into abstract noun phrases with modifiers to create links to previous text.

While some may object to the nominalized style of much academic language, English learners continually encounter these and other complex structures in their reading, and these structures are often important in establishing cohesion. In activities that promote noticing structures and the discourse motivations for them that differ from everyday language, learners can build linguistic resources and make selections appropriate for a specific rhetorical context.

Identifying cohesive devices. Using an assigned reading or other passage, the instructor could lead students in identifying the different kinds and chains of cohesion (pronouns, demonstrative pronouns, sentence connectors, lexical cohesion, etc.). Figure 1 provides a brief example, with the cohesive words and phrases in italics.

Another task for developing understanding of cohesive devices asks students to consider several syntactic structures with essentially the same meaning and to choose the structure that best links new information to what has been stated previously. This type of exercise focuses students' attention on how features such as pronouns, partial repetition, and passive voice interact to create information flow.

In the example in Figure 2, students are asked to indicate the best choices with check marks. This activity emphasizes the importance of context in making grammatical choices and shows how cohesion and coherence result from presenting information that is familiar to the reader at the beginning of the sentence, followed by the new information the writer wants to convey.

<table>
<tr><th>Text</th><th>Examples of cohesive devices</th></tr>
<tr><td>It appears that human beings are unique in *their* ability to keep time to music. *This ability* may result from evolutionary adaptation. *In addition, musical timing* may be related to the importance of *timing* in speech sounds. *For example,* music scientist Aniruddh D. Patel notes that the difference between *a B and a P* in English is a difference in *timing* produced by the *sound.*</td><td>Lexical cohesion:
ability, musical timing, timing, a B and a P, sound
Reference words:
their (human beings), *this* (ability), *the* (sound)
Sentence connectors:
in addition, for example</td></tr>
</table>

Figure 1. Examples of cohesive devices (adapted from Belluck, 2011).

To create such mini-exercises, the teacher could select from a text two sentences in which the second one is linked to the first by grammatical cohesion. The second sentence would then serve as one of the two choices (a) or (b); the teacher can simply re-order the information in the original sentence to produce the other option.

Comparing language differences across genres or text types. Students can examine two texts on the same topic but written in different genres to identify what grammatical or lexicogrammatical features distinguish them. Typically these will be texts for different audiences, such as a newspaper article on medical research for a nonspecialist audience contrasted with a medical journal article for specialists in a particular field. For texts whose levels of formality differ distinctly, such as a film review in an informal blog contrasted with one published in a newspaper, differences could include sentence structure types, use of first person, verb types (e.g., one-word vs. phrasal verbs; active vs. passive voice), and nominalizations.

Readings with authentic or fictional oral English, such as interviews or plays, can be rich sources for discussion of differences between spoken and written English, such as the use of fragments in spoken English versus complete sentences in formal written English.

Expressing stance: Hedging. As noted earlier, increasing attention has been given to the ways in which writers qualify assertions. Following instruction on the types of hedging structures, students can look for words and phrases that writers use to qualify their assertions in a variety of texts.

Advanced writers can investigate the use of hedging devices in different genres and disciplines using corpus-based resources, including corpora created from texts in their disciplines and concordances freely available on the Internet, such as the Corpus of Contemporary American English.[1]

Guided production activities

Appropriate guided-writing activities can provide practice in noticing and using language structures that learners find difficult to produce or that they may not produce at all. Some of the guided-writing activities here offer follow-up practice to text analysis activities. Others target kinds of writing tasks that pose challenges to L2 writers, such as paraphrasing from sources or, as in the first sample activity, improving grammatical accuracy.

Dictation. Especially useful for less advanced students, dictation can be an effective way to familiarize students with the ways in which grammar and vocabulary interact in common collocations as well as to address errors in writing that may result

Choose the structure that best links new information to old information.

Decades ago, climatologists predicted that the continual warming of Earth's surface, commonly known as "the greenhouse effect," could have dramatic consequences.

1. ____ (a) The polar ice caps have been melting at a much faster rate than in the 1970s.

    ____ (b) One consequence has been the melting of the polar ice caps at a much faster rate than in the 1970s.

2. ____ (a) This rapid melting has, in turn, caused a rise in ocean levels.

    ____ (b) A rise in ocean levels has, in turn, been caused by this rapid melting.

Figure 2. Sample mini-exercise in coherence.

in part from mismatches between learners' aural perception of English forms and standard English grammar and spelling.

In one dictation procedure, the instructor reads aloud a short text several times, first at a normal pace with the students just listening and then with pauses after each phrase to allow students to write. During a third reading, at a normal pace, students review their texts and make corrections. The teacher then shows students the passage so that they can check their versions with the original and edit them further if needed. If the activity's main objective is error detection and correction, the instructor could give more specific directions, such as to put a circle at the ends of all words with missing –s third person singular or –ed endings. If the goal is to familiarize writers with particular grammatical features, students could be asked to highlight or underline them; the class could then discuss meanings and/or forms.

Creating cohesion. Following cohesion text analysis, the instructor can give students short passages in which the last sentence needs a cohesive phrase to link it to the preceding sentences. Here is an example:

> During the last decade, the use of cell phones while operating a motor vehicle has been a topic of increased concern. In particular, the sending or reading of text messages while driving is regarded as extremely distracting; such activities increase the risk of serious accidents. One experiment showed that texting while driving resulted in greater safety risks than driving drunk. _____, many people, especially teenagers, continue to send and check messages while driving.

In this example, students are asked to supply both a logical connector (e.g., a preposition such as *despite*) plus a reference phrase (e.g., *the dangers of cell phone use*). For less advanced learners, the instructor could create logical relationships that are easier for students to interpret. For example, a final sentence that expresses a result (*because of . . .*) or an addition (*in addition to . . .*) might be less difficult for students to complete. Instructors could also provide several choices of logical connectors and classifier nouns for the reference phrase and have the students select the best ones.

Writers can then look at their own drafts to see if there are places where cohesive links are needed or where existing ones might be revised to be clearer. For example, a phrase such as *these problems* might need a modifying phrase (e.g., *these problems with cyber-bullying on social networks*) to more clearly connect the new information to the preceding text.

Fluency development: Sentence combining. Sentence-combining tasks can help writers develop their repertoire of linguistic strategies for a number of purposes, including highlighting key information, subordinating less important information, and improving overall syntactic fluency. Sentence combining also serves to familiarize students with word co-occurrences needed for academic writing.

One of the most useful applications of sentence combining for advanced ESL writers involves work on revising drafts. With assistance, students can identify passages in their writing in which sentence combining could result in a better flow of information through clearer connections between ideas. As one example, when learning to reference sources by introducing authors and their work, developing writers may use separate sentences such as:

> Oliver Sacks is a neurologist. He wrote the article "Brilliant Light: A Chemical Boyhood." In this article, he describes how his "Uncle Tungsten" influenced his love of science.

A more experienced writer of academic prose would subordinate some of this information:

> In "Brilliant Light: A Chemical Boyhood," neurologist Oliver Sacks describes how his "Uncle Tungsten" influenced his love of science.

In this way, sentence-combining exercises can focus on particular rhetorical moves that students will need to master in academic writing. These moves include introducing sources, focusing information to emphasize key points in structures (e.g., subjects, verbs, and main clauses), and subordinating and embedding less important information (e.g., via modifying phrases and adverb or adjective clauses). To demonstrate this technique, the instructor could select a set of sentences from a student paper for the class to work together on combining. Sentence-combining work could be especially helpful in contexts in which instructors or tutors can meet individually with students for draft revision.

Guided paraphrase. One of the most important skills that students must develop for academic writing is the ability to paraphrase source materials to support claims and develop ideas. ESL/EFL writers often lack the facility with vocabulary and syntax to rephrase ideas in their own words; most experienced teachers are familiar with the distorted paraphrases that result when novice writers "slot" synonyms from a thesaurus into the original sentence without adjusting the grammar.

When we consider the strategies that experienced writers use in paraphrasing, some of them include the following grammatical or lexicogrammatical resources:

- Knowledge of word forms; ability to choose which form is needed for a particular context once a paraphrase has been started (e.g., *contribute* → *contribution; dramatic* → *dramatically*)
- Knowledge of different lexicogrammatical forms that express similar meanings (e.g., *because, as a result of*)
- Knowledge of syntactic collocation patterns such as functions of noun phrases (NPs) (e.g., *told* as a reporting verb followed by NP [someone] + NP [something])
- Knowledge of grammatical collocations such as verbs/adjectives + prepositions or verb + noun + preposition (e.g., *be concerned about, have an influence on*)

Writers can develop knowledge and facility in transforming structures by building word-family knowledge using charts such as in Figure 3, in which the instructor provides one or more forms of a word from an assigned text and students must fill in other forms that exist. More advanced

For each of the following, provide a synonym for the underlined adjective that is appropriate for the noun that follows it (the first one is done for you).

1. an <u>important</u> finding   *significant*

2. <u>potential</u> problems   _____

3. <u>obvious</u> differences   _____

4. a <u>rational</u> excuse   _____

Figure 4. Synonym exercise.

learners can discover for themselves which forms exist and which do not. For less advanced learners, or to save time, instructors can shade the slots that will not have a word filled in.

Students can practice substituting the correct forms for synonyms, given exercises such as the one in Figure 4, which draws its vocabulary from Hinkel's (2004) list of the most common academic adjectives and nouns.

In cued paraphrase exercises, writers transform sentences or parts of sentences from assigned readings using cues as the first step. The cues, which may be words or phrases, are designed to require syntactic restructuring in the paraphrase. Here is an example based on a sociology text about bystander intervention (Darley & Latané, 1973) with a possible transformation:

> <u>Original</u>: Even if a person defines an event as an emergency . . . *(decides)*

> <u>Rewrite</u>: Even if a person decides that an event is an emergency . . .

As students further transform the structure resulting from the guided paraphrase cues, changing vocabulary and structures more fully so that the final version is not too close to the original, this activity becomes a true composing task. Students should then work at transferring these strategies to future paraphrasing tasks.

Treatment of error

The discussion of grammar in writing in this chapter has emphasized the multidimensional aspects of grammar and the importance of form-focused instruction that does not center solely on errors. Grammar issues related to errors will,

Verb	Noun	Adjective	Adverb
	communication		
		successful	
imitate			
	comparison		
			precisely

Figure 3. Word-family exercise chart.

however, arise in almost every ESL/EFL writing class and for ESL writers in mainstream classes as well. Teachers' classroom experiences as well as research have indicated that ESL writers expect and appreciate assistance in improving their language accuracy.

As much as possible, instructors want to focus work related to error correction on the kinds of accuracy problems students encounter in their writing. While this suggests attention to individual students' writing errors, it is often the case that a group of writers will have common problems at the word and sentence levels. Thus, instructors may want to consider not only a *reactive* focus on language errors but also a *proactive* one that targets common writing errors such as verb tenses, subject-verb agreement, noun number, and word forms. As Ferris (2011) noted, even those who oppose error correction by teachers acknowledge that "there may be a legitimate role for strategy training and grammar instruction as an alternative means to helping students edit their writing" (p. 122).

In form-focused instruction related to errors, it is important that student writers consider *why* accuracy is an integral part of effective communication. Some students may regard the need for linguistic accuracy as relatively unimportant or rely on tutors or teachers (or perhaps classmates) to correct their language errors. So initially, the teacher may want to discuss why attention to accuracy in grammatical structures is important in meeting reader expectations for a variety of contexts, both academic and professional.

Editing strategies and techniques. The benefits of focused work on diagnosing errors and developing editing strategies will certainly vary for students, depending on many complex variables involving the learners, the teacher's knowledge and experience in pedagogical grammar, and the writing context. Depending on the students' levels and course objectives, the following kinds of activities may be help students to focus on linguistic accuracy:

- Diagnostic essays administered at the beginning of a class help instructors identify both individual writers' error patterns and errors common to a group of writers, which can then be the focus of explicit instruction during the course.
- Following review of a grammatical structure, students can edit short texts with specific kinds of errors (e.g., plural nouns lacking –s endings and noncount nouns with plural marking).
- The instructor can collect examples of the same type of error, such as verb tense errors, taken from student writing and ask students to identify and correct them as a group activity.
- For errors with a great deal of variation, such as word choices, the instructor can provide explanations of the common sources for such errors. Students can then assess whether these sources are ones they may need to check in their drafts.

Most ESL writers need to devote considerable time and effort to becoming good editors. Otherwise, many will fail to benefit from classroom exercises and practice or even from individual conferences. Students should be encouraged to explore different strategies to find ones that serve them effectively.

Teacher feedback on errors. Another significant issue related to language errors in writing is, of course, teacher feedback on student writing. The following are some general guidelines and suggestions for providing feedback on grammar.

- At the beginning of a course, the teacher can provide students with an error-analysis sheet based on in-class writing that identifies types and error patterns.
- The teacher should use indirect feedback to correct errors, which is generally more useful (and often more desired by students) than the direct correction of errors. Indirect feedback could involve one or more of the following: putting a check in the margin of the lines where errors occur; underlining or highlighting selected errors; coding errors in the margins, above selected errors, or through track changes with symbols such as *vt* for verb tense, *wf* for word form, *art* for article; and attaching a sheet to the writer's draft with a list of several structural errors along with suggested Internet resources to consult for more information on the grammatical system or feature.
- The teacher should not provide feedback on all errors in any one piece of writing—this can be overwhelming to students. Instead, he or she should focus on those most in need of attention. Deciding which errors most

deserve attention requires consideration of many student variables (e.g., metalinguistic knowledge and proficiency level) and the instructional situation. Errors to be pointed out may be those representing an individual's frequent error patterns, those that most seriously affect communication, those that are socially stigmatizing (e.g., use of double negatives), or those that the teacher has focused on in class work.

- While the bulk of teacher feedback on errors should occur in later stages of the writing process, the teacher can alert students to areas of concern in early drafts also so that all the error feedback is not given in the last draft, when many students find they lack sufficient time to address it effectively.

If the teaching environment permits conferencing with students outside of class, conferences are excellent opportunities to provide individual help. Alternatively, the teacher can hold mini-conferences with individuals or small groups in the classroom. In conferences, the teacher can demonstrate directly the difficulties a reader might have as a result of the grammatical errors in the students' writing. This setting allows the teacher to act as a collaborator rather than as an error detector/corrector. He or she can help students identify errors that create reader confusion or misinterpretation, explore the strategies for editing that best fit the writers' learning styles, set goals for improvement, and assess progress in these goals. Students can also provide insight into the sources of error, ones that a teacher might not even have considered, such as interference from a third language or an inaccurately formulated "rule." When students are able to analyze their error sources, the teacher can more effectively suggest editing strategies.

FUTURE TRENDS

ESL/EFL writing pedagogy will certainly continue to change as the result of new research in related areas such as L2 acquisition, rhetoric and composition, linguistics, education, and psychology. And sociopolitical and sociolinguistic developments will no doubt cause us to reconsider long-held views about language and language teaching. Increased globalization and the development of World Englishes are increasingly challenging long-held notions about Standard English(es). The growing non-native English-speaking immigrant populations in English-speaking countries, especially in institutions of higher education, raise questions about what the expectations about "linguistic correctness" should be, even in formal written English. At the advanced academic and professional levels of writing, researchers and educators are increasingly considering the ways in which multilingual writers are contributing to the creation of literary, journalistic, and academic genres and, as such, are changing how we view what is appropriate in different contexts.

Rapidly developing computer technology and applications of corpus linguistics offer resources for form-focused language instruction that were undreamed of in decades past. In particular, corpus linguistics findings have revealed the complex interrelationships between grammar and the lexicon and the variation of lexicogrammatical patterns across registers. All these areas raise issues that writing teachers will need to be aware of and reflect on in making decisions about the role of grammar in their writing classrooms.

CONCLUSION

This chapter's discussion of grammar in writing supports the view that L2 writers need to pay attention to form in developing writing proficiency. Exploring the ways in which writers use language in various genres and text types to create meanings, connections, and voice, combined with meaningful productive practice, can help L2 writers develop their linguistic resources and gain a better understanding of how to use them. In the case of error correction and feedback, L2 writing teachers can help students understand the role of accuracy in effective communication and develop editing strategies that they can carry forward beyond their classroom tasks.

SUMMARY

➤ Given the important role of grammar as a resource for effective communication, focus on form should be an integral part of the instructional design for L2 writing classrooms.

- ➤ Learner variables to be considered in designing grammar-based activities include age and educational backgrounds in learning English.
- ➤ The specific objectives, readings, and writing tasks in a composition class will influence greatly how grammar can be integrated with writing.
- ➤ Because grammar interacts with the lexicon in important ways, focus-on-form instruction should integrate grammar and vocabulary when relevant.
- ➤ Both text analysis and the use of corpora and concordances in class will enhance productive practice and offer learners opportunities to develop grammatical awareness.
- ➤ The treatment of error remains an important concern in L2 writing instruction, especially for writers at more advanced levels; instructors can help L2 writers to be responsible for the discovery and correction of their frequent error patterns.

DISCUSSION QUESTIONS

1. In what ways has the role of grammar in writing instruction been characterized? How do the different attitudes about grammatical instruction in composition reflect different ways of defining what grammar means?
2. How can grammar instruction be considered compatible with approaches that focus on writing as a process or with writing as a social activity?
3. What is the role of text analysis in developing grammatical competence in writing?
4. If one of your students expressed disappointment that you did not correct all the errors in his or her final drafts, how would you respond?
5. What are some advantages of teacher-student conferences in helping students with grammatical problems in writing?

SUGGESTED ACTIVITIES

1. Evaluate one or more grammar-oriented exercises in an ESL composition textbook or workbook. Use the following criteria:
   a. What do the objectives of the exercises appear to be? Do you think they are pedagogically sound?
   b. Is the exercise text-based? If not, do you think it is still appropriate for its purpose?
   c. Does the language seem authentic?
   d. If the exercise is included in a content-based or rhetorical framework (e.g., as part of a unit on persuasive writing), is it clearly and appropriately related to the discourse of that context?
   e. If the exercise is not part of a larger writing context, for what aspect of writing instruction do you think it would be appropriate?
   f. Does the level of difficulty seem appropriate for the intended learners?
   g. Based on the previous criteria and any others you think relevant, summarize the strengths and weaknesses of the exercise or exercises.
2. Write a reflective essay or journal entry on your own experiences with grammar in writing as a second/foreign language learner. To what extent was grammar associated primarily with diagnosing and correcting errors in your own second/foreign language writing? To what extent were you aware of the ways in which expanding your grammatical knowledge helped you improve your linguistic resources to express your ideas?
3. Examine several ESL/EFL compositions that have frequent and varied grammatical errors. For each composition, identify two of the most frequent or serious errors. Using the suggestions in the chapter, describe exercises or activities that will help the writer to address these grammatical problems.
4. Interview ESL writing teachers about the techniques, both oral and written, that they have used to provide feedback on grammatical errors in their students' writing. During what stages of composing processes do they address errors? Which error feedback and/or correction techniques have they found to be most effective? What student variables have affected the success of techniques used?

FURTHER READING

Byrd, P., & Reid, J. (1998). *Grammar in the composition classroom: Essays on teaching ESL for college-bound students.* Boston, MA: Heinle & Heinle.

This is a collection of essays offering theoretical discussion and practical information for incorporating grammar in writing classes. It emphasizes learner-based approaches and selection of grammatical features based on corpus text analysis for teaching academic writing.

Ferris, D. (2011). *Treatment of error in L2 student writing* (2nd ed.). Ann Arbor, MI: University of Michigan Press.

This volume provides a comprehensive overview of research on error feedback and other forms of grammar instruction. It discusses how teachers can prepare themselves to treat student error, describes error correction options, and other error treatment options such as revision and peer editing.

Frodesen, J., & Holten, C. (2003). Grammar in the ESL writing class. In B. Kroll (Ed.), *Exploring the dynamics of second language writing* (pp. 141–161). New York, NY: Cambridge University Press.

This chapter discusses the role of grammar in writing instruction for various stages of writing processes and offers practical suggestions and activities for the writing classroom.

Hinkel, E. (2004). *Teaching academic ESL writing: Practical techniques in vocabulary and grammar.* Mahwah, NJ: Lawrence Erlbaum Associates.

This book reviews and discusses grammatical and lexicogrammatical structures important for academic writing instruction. It offers techniques for teaching writing using corpus-based material, including discourse functions such as text cohesion and hedging.

Schleppegrell, M. J. (2004). *The language of schooling.* Mahwah, NJ: Lawrence Erlbaum Associates.

The author argues for an explicit focus on language in literacy development across disciplines and provides a functional description of school-based genres, describing how grammatical features construct texts in school genres, such as the academic essay, and in disciplinary genres.

ENDNOTE

[1] The Corpus of Contemporary American English (COCA) can be found at http://corpus.byu.edu/coca/

Language Skills

Grammar and Vocabulary

17 | Teaching Grammar

DIANE LARSEN-FREEMAN

KEY QUESTIONS

➤ What is grammar?
➤ How is grammar learned?
➤ How is it taught?

EXPERIENCE

The following brief example is an episode from an imagined classroom, where English is being taught as a foreign language (EFL) to elementary school students, who are beginning their study of English. The teacher has introduced the grammatical topic of question formation. She explains that *yes-no* questions are made in English by inverting the subject of a sentence with the operator in the sentence. In this initial lesson, she defines the operator as some form of the verb *be,* here *are.* She has provided the class with some examples, and she now gives them practice in forming *yes-no* questions. She makes a statement and tells the students to transform it into a question.

Teacher: We are studying English. Class?
Students: Are we studying English?
Teacher: Yes, we are. We are using a new book.
Students: Are we using a new book?
Teacher: No, we aren't. We are making questions.
Students: Are we making questions?

This drill goes on for a few more turns. Later in the morning, a girl turns to the teacher and asks:

We are going outside for recess?

The teacher silently takes note of the student's failure to invert the subject with the operator and vows to drill the students more the next class.

In this brief example, we can find answers to all three key questions posed at the beginning of the chapter. For this teacher, and for many others, grammar is about the form of the language—here, the form being the word sequence in statements and questions. Learning is expected to take place as a result of sufficient practice, but as we see, what has just been practiced immediately is rarely taken up by students. The lesson plan consisted of two phases. During the presentation phase of the grammar lesson, the formation of *yes-no* questions was introduced, and during the practice phase, question formation was practiced in a drill.

I return to this example several times in this chapter as we more fully examine answers to the three questions.

WHAT IS GRAMMAR?

Some semblance of the lesson I have just described has been widely used in language classrooms for many years. Teaching grammar in this way is indeed a time-honored practice. However, in this chapter, I invite readers to entertain a richer and, I think, more accurate conception of grammar.

In the example lesson, grammar was regarded as form. Grammar *is* about the form of the language, but it is also used to make meaning. Significantly, skilled users of grammar not only express themselves accurately and meaningfully but also use their knowledge of grammar to present themselves to others in the way that they wish to be seen. Of course, there are conventional patterns in language, and they need to be learned, but there is a great deal of choice to be made in the way that language users adapt and deploy the patterns. Moreover, if teachers learn to see grammar for the rich system that it is, their attitude gets conveyed to their students; and in turn, the students come to see that grammar matters and that knowledge of it can be empowering. Using language grammatically is not about conforming to some arbitrary standard.

Another point of departure from the view of grammar depicted in the lesson is that grammar is not a static system of rules; grammar is a dynamic system. To realize it as a dynamic system, students have to experience lessons in which grammar is used in meaningful and psychologically authentic ways. Drills have a function, but mechanical drills rob students of the experience of using the system to negotiate their own identities and to express what they want to say. If all they have is a steady diet of mechanical drills, then they are often at a loss when they are in a situation that calls for them to communicate. They cannot activate the forms that are appropriate for the context.

It is also important to recognize that we are teaching students as we are teaching grammar. And, for this reason, we want to create conditions of use in the classroom in which the affordances for learning are there for all students—where all students have an opportunity to learn. We want them to be free to explore the language for their own purposes, but it is also our job to guide our students to focus their attention on the learning challenge and to help them to move beyond it.

One of the reasons that grammar is misunderstood is that the term *grammar* is ambiguous. Indeed, definitions of grammar abound—and therefore contribute to a great deal of misunderstanding. Many people associate grammar with what linguists call prescriptive grammar, the way that a language "ought to" be used. Prescriptive grammars contribute to a general unease—even proficient users of a language fear making mistakes, such as using *me* instead of *I* or choosing *who* when they should have chosen *whom*. Prescriptive grammar has a role in language teaching, especially for those who need to use academic language, but prescriptive grammar is not the central focus of this chapter. Instead, I concentrate here more on descriptive grammar, a description of how speakers of a language actually use the language, even when it does not conform to what prescriptive grammars prescribe and proscribe. For instance, speakers might say either *It is I* or *It is me*. Prescriptive grammarians would frown on the use of *me*, but its use seems natural to many English speakers. The truth is that there is always variation in language usage.

Even if we restrict our treatment of grammar to descriptive grammar, the term grammar still requires further definition. As I have just written, most linguists would agree it has to do with the form of the language, with using and understanding the language accurately. However, what exactly constitutes a form is not entirely clear. For instance, most grammarians would lay claim to inflectional morphemes, such as verb tense markers (e.g., *–ed* on verbs for past tense in English) and plural markers (*–s* for the plural of many nouns). In addition, they would include common syntactic structures, such as negatives and questions.

However, what the morphosyntax (i.e., the morphology and syntax) of traditional grammar overlooks are the thousands on thousands of patterns that make up a speaker's knowledge of a language, such as *Can I come in? Did you have a good time? Have some more. I'm simply amazed* (Pawley & Syder, 1983). With the increased access to large corpora of language data that computers afford, it has become clear that grammatical structures and lexical items occur in a large number of regularly occurring patterns (Biber, Conrad, & Reppen, 1998; Sinclair & Fox, 1990). These sequences are sometimes rather fixed, as in the phrase *by the way*. At other times, the sequences are more open, allowing some substitutions. For example, I can say *My house needs painting* or *Our washer needs fixing*, but there are really few other verbs besides *need* that fit the pattern [*need* VERB–*ing*]. To give another example, if the verb *insist* is used, either *on* or *that* is very likely to follow. The question to be answered is, should such sequences be considered part of grammar or are they more like complex lexical items? The answer is that they are somewhere in between (Nattinger & DeCarrico, 1992). It is theorized that such language patterns emerge from language use (Bybee, 2006; Ellis & Larsen-Freeman, 2009). Through repeated use, they become "sedimented" as fixed or semi-fixed patterns (Hopper, 1998). Thus, one implication of corpus-based research is that teachers of grammar should pay more attention to convention-alized lexicogrammatical constructions (word-based structures and patterns) while not ignoring traditional morphosyntactic structures (Lewis, 1997). These days, many linguists use the term *constructions* to encompass all lexicogrammatical forms, ranging from morphemes and syntactic structures to meaningful phrasal and clausal sequences or patterns (Tomasello, 2003). Thus, the answer to the question "What is grammar?" is that grammar is a system of lexicogrammatical patterns that are used to make meaning in appropriate ways.

CONCEPTUAL UNDERPINNINGS

A three-dimensional grammar framework

Since our goal is to help our students use the language accurately, meaningfully, and appropriately, it will be helpful to have a frame of reference. The framework takes the form of a pie chart (see Figure 1). The pie chart implicitly claims that all constructions can be characterized to different degrees by the three dimensions of: (1) structure or form; (2) semantics or meaning; and (3) use or the pragmatic conditions governing appropriate usage. In the wedge of the pie having to do with form, we have those overt lexicogrammatical patterns and morphosyntactic forms that tell us how a particular construction is put together and how it is sequenced with other constructions in a sentence or text. With certain constructions, it is also important to note the sound (phonemic) and writing (graphemic) patterns (see the discussion of possessives and phrasal verbs next for examples). In the semantic wedge, we deal with what a grammar construction means. Note that the meaning can be lexical (a dictionary definition for a preposition like *down,* for instance) or it can be grammatical (e.g., the conditional states both a condition and an outcome or result).

Pragmatics in the use wedge means "the use of language in context." The context can be social (i.e., a context created by speakers, their relationship to one another, or the setting), or it can be a linguistic discourse co-text (i.e., the language that precedes or follows a particular structure in the discourse, or how a particular genre or register affects the use of a construction). The influence

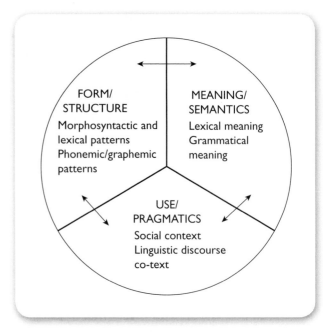

Figure 1. A three-dimensional grammar framework.

of pragmatics may be ascertained by asking two questions:

1. When or why does a speaker/writer choose a particular grammar construction over another that could express the same meaning or accomplish the same purpose? For example, what factors in the social context might explain a paradigmatic choice such as a speaker choosing a *yes-no* question rather than an imperative to serve as a request for information (e.g., *Do you have the time?* versus *Please tell me the time*).

2. When or why does a speaker/writer vary the form of a particular linguistic construction? For instance, what linguistic discourse factors will result in a syntagmatic or word sequence choice such as the indirect object being placed before the direct object (e.g., *Jenny gave Hank a brand-new comb* versus *Jenny gave a brand-new comb to Hank*)?

Despite the permeable boundaries between the dimensions, which is indicated by the bidirectional arrows, it can be very useful to view grammar from these three perspectives, and I trust that the usefulness of this approach will become clearer as we proceed. A teacher of grammar might begin by asking the questions posed in the three wedges of the pie (see Figure 2). For the sake of simplicity, these wedges are labeled form, meaning, and use for any given grammar point.[1]

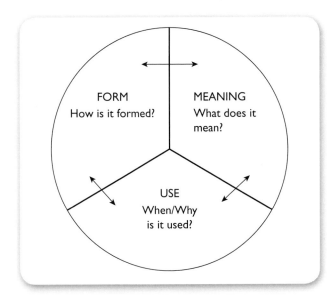

Figure 2. Questions when applying the pie chart.

Let us consider an example. A common construction to be taught at a high-beginning level of English proficiency is the *'s* possessive form (which has the written forms *'s* and *s'*). If we analyze the possessive using our questions, we will fill in the wedges as in Figure 3.

Form of the possessive. This way to form possessives in English is to add *'s* to regular singular nouns and noncount nouns and irregular plural nouns not ending in *s* or to add an apostrophe after the *s*

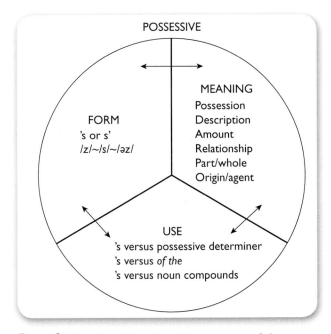

Figure 3. Pie chart describing the grammar of the possessive.

ending of regular plural nouns and after singular/noncount nouns ending in the sound /s/ to form *s'*. This form of the possessive has three allomorphs (or variations of the plural morpheme /–s/): [z], [s], and [əz], which are phonetically conditioned, as in *birds* [z], *bats* [s], and *bridges* [əz].

Meaning of the possessive. In addition to possession, the possessive or genitive form can indicate description (*a debtor's prison, the water's edge*), amount (*two weeks' holiday*), relationship (*Jack's wife*), part to whole (*the woman's hand*), and origin/agent (*Shakespeare's tragedies*). Also, although all languages have a way of signaling possession, they do not all regard the same items as possessable. For example, Spanish speakers refer to a body part using the definite article instead of a possessive form, producing a sentence such as *He broke the arm* (if directly translated). English as a second language (ESL) and EFL students will have to learn the scope of the possessive form in English.

Use of the possessive. Filling in this wedge requires that we ask when the *'s* is used to express possession as opposed to other constructions that can be used to convey this same meaning. For example, possession in English can be expressed in other ways—with a possessive determiner (e.g., *his, her,* and *their*) or with the periphrastic *of the* form (e.g., *the legs of the table*). Possessive determiners are presumably used when the referent of the possessor is clear from the context. While ESL/EFL books will often say that the *of the* possessive is used with nonhuman head nouns and *'s* with human head nouns, there are certain conditions where this generalization does not apply. For example, English speakers often prefer to use the *'s* even with inanimate head nouns if the head nouns are performing some action (e.g., *The train's arrival was delayed*). Finally, students will have to learn to distinguish contexts in which a noun compound (*table leg*) is more appropriate than either the *'s* form or the *of the* form.

Thus, by using a ternary scheme, we can classify the facts that affect the form, meaning, and use of the possessive. Compiling the answers to the questions is only the first step. Teachers would not necessarily present all these facts to students, recognizing that students can and do learn some of them on their own. And certainly no teacher would choose to present all these facts in a single lesson. Nevertheless, distributing the features of the target grammatical construction among the three wedges of the pie can give teachers an understanding of its scope and multidimensionality. In turn, this understanding will guide teachers in making decisions about which facts concerning the possessive will be taught and when and how to do so. Of course, if teachers are not able to fill in all the wedges of the pie on their own, that tells them something, too. When they cannot fill in all the wedges in the pie chart for a given construction, they can consult reference grammars. The pie chart can also be used to spur teachers to do research because many of our grammatical descriptions are incomplete. By exploring the three dimensions of grammar and how to teach them, teachers will continue to develop their professional knowledge base, which will, in turn, benefit their students.

At this point, it might be worthwhile to apply the approach to another construction. This time, let us turn our attention to a pattern—the two- or three-word sequences of phrasal verbs. Phrasal verbs are limited in their constituency but are not as fixed as possessives. By considering the three questions posed earlier, we can compile the following facts about phrasal verbs.

Form of phrasal verbs.   Most phrasal verbs are two-part verbs comprising a verb and a particle (e.g., *look up*). Sometimes, they can be constructed with three parts, with a preposition following the particle (e.g., *keep up with*). A distinctive feature of phrasal verbs is that for many of them the particle can be separated from its verb by an intervening object (e.g., *Alicia looked the word up in the dictionary*). Phrasal verbs also have distinctive stress and juncture patterns, which distinguish them from verb plus preposition combinations:

Alicia looked úp#the word.
Alicia wálked#up the street.

Meaning of phrasal verbs.   There are literal phrasal verbs, such as *hang up*, where it is not difficult to figure out the meaning of the verb-particle combination in a sentence such as *He hung the picture up on the wall.* Unfortunately for the ESL/EFL student, there are far more instances of figurative phrasal verbs (e.g., *run into*, meaning "meet by chance") where a knowledge of the meaning of the verb and of the particle is of little help in figuring out the meaning of the phrasal verb. Moreover, as with single-word verbs, phrasal verbs can have more than one meaning, for example,

come across, meaning "to discover by chance," as in *I came across this old book in the library,* or when used intransitively "to make an impression," as in *Richard's presentation came across well at the convention.*

Use of phrasal verbs.   When is a phrasal verb preferred to a single-word verb that conveys the same meaning (e.g., *put out a fire* versus *extinguish a fire*)? For the most part, phrasal verbs seem to be more common in informal speech than in more formal speech or written discourse.

When is one form of a separable phrasal verb preferred to the other; that is, when should the particle be separated from its verb (e.g., *put out a fire* versus *put a fire out*)? Erteschik-Shir's (1979) principle of dominance seems to work well to define the circumstances favoring particle movement: if a noun phrase (NP) object is dominant (i.e., is a long, elaborate NP representing new information), it is likely to occur after the particle; if the direct object is short and is given information (e.g., a pronoun), it naturally occurs before the particle.

Again, I underscore here that it would not be reasonable for the ESL/EFL teacher to present all this information to students at once. The framework does, however, help to organize the facts (see Figure 4). Furthermore, by doing this, teachers

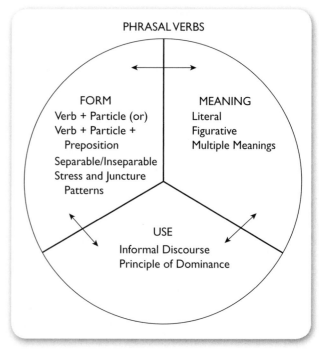

Figure 4. Pie chart describing the three dimensions of phrasal verbs.

can more easily identify where the learning challenge(s) lie for their students, based either on teachers' past experience or on their diagnosis of students' performance. Identifying the challenging dimension(s) is a key step that should be undertaken when planning lessons.[2]

All three dimensions of form, meaning, and use need to be mastered by the learner (although not necessarily consciously). For phrasal verbs, it is the meaning dimension that ESL/EFL students struggle with most. It is often the fact that there is no systematic way of learning to associate the verb and the particle. In this way, they are like lexical items. Adding to the students' woes, new phrasal verbs are constantly being coined. Recognizing where students will likely struggle tells the teacher where to focus work on phrasal verbs. We will amplify this point later. For now, however, it is worth noting that, although we are dealing with grammatical constructions, it is not always the form of the construction that creates the most significant learning challenge. Now that we have a clearer idea of what is meant by *grammar* (constructions in a language, structures and patterns, that have meanings and uses), we can turn to how grammar is learned.

The learning process

However important and necessary it is for teachers to have a comprehensive knowledge of their subject matter, it is equally important for them to understand their students' learning process. This understanding can be partly informed by insights from second language acquisition (SLA) research concerning how students naturally develop their ability to interpret and produce grammatical utterances. Three observations are germane to our topic:

Learners do not learn constructions one at a time. For example, learners do not master the definite article and, when that is mastered, move on to the simple past tense. From their first encounter with the definite article, learners might master one of its pragmatic uses (e.g., to signal the uniqueness of the following noun in a given context). But even if they are able to do this appropriately, it is not likely that they will always produce the definite article when it is needed because learners typically take a long time before they are able to do this consistently. Thus, learning is a gradual process

involving the mapping of form, meaning, and use; constructions do not spring forth in learners' production fully developed and error-free. We saw this phenomenon in our chapter-initial example lesson, where the student who asked the teacher a question did not immediately apply the lesson on inversion in question formation.

Even when learners appear to have mastered a particular construction, it is not uncommon to find new errors being made. For example, the learner who has finally mastered the third-person singular marker on present tense verbs may overgeneralize the rule and apply it to newly emerging modal verbs, thus producing errors such as *She cans speak Spanish*. The point is that learning grammar is not simply adding new knowledge to an unchanging system—it involves changing the system. At some point, the learner's grammatical knowledge will be restructured and well-formedness will be restored. Of course, some students do not aim to adopt target-language norms because their reasons for studying English have more to do with learning English as a lingua franca for international communication than they do with conforming to native speaker norms.

Not surprisingly, language learners rely on the knowledge and the experience they already have. If they are beginners, they rely on their first language (L1) or other languages they know to hypothesize about how the new language works; when they are more advanced, they rely increasingly on the second language (L2). In understanding this, the teacher realizes that there is no need to teach everything about a construction to a group of students; rather, the teacher can build on what the students already know, a step that is facilitated when the students speak a common language.

Successful teaching involves identifying the relevant challenge for a particular group of students, recognizing that the challenge will not necessarily be the same for all students. Successful teachers also recognize that grammar learning is an iterative process; hence they need to return to the same territory again and again. To these three observations, we can add a fourth one that is not to our knowledge treated in the SLA research literature but, rather, is based on our observations and supported by learning theorists (e.g., Gagné & Medsker, 1996).

Different learning processes such as pattern recognition, association, and discrimination are responsible for different aspects of language. Indeed, given that language is as complicated as it is, we would not expect the learning process to be any simpler. It is clearly an oversimplification to treat all grammar learning as resulting from one process. Being aware that different learning processes contribute to SLA suggests a need for the teaching process to respect the differences.

How the nature of the language challenge and the learning process affect teaching decisions is the issue to which I turn next.

CLASSROOM APPLICATIONS

The teaching process

Some educators have questioned whether grammar needs to be taught. For example, Krashen (1982) believes that if the input is understood and there is enough of it, the necessary grammar will unconsciously be acquired, much as young children learn the grammar of their native language. After all, they say, L2 learners often pick up a language from exposure to it. They have also observed that there seems to be little connection between formal knowledge of grammar rules and the ability to deploy them in communication. Moreover, R. Ellis (1993) pointed to the "learnability problem": the fact that grammar is not naturally learned in a linear and atomistic fashion, despite its being taught this way. Often the forms learners use to communicate bear no resemblance to what has been presented to them or what has been practiced. (See Ellis, this volume, for further discussion of instructed SLA.) We saw this in our example lesson with the student's use of an uninverted question.

However, while some learners may be capable of learning a language completely on their own, this is not true of many learners, especially if their time or exposure is limited to the classroom, as is the case when English is taught as a foreign language. Besides, we should not expect our students to learn their L2 as they did their L1. Whereas children learn their language implicitly over a long period of time, focused and explicit attention seems to be desirable in learning/teaching an L2, especially when

learners are a bit older. Indeed, experience with French-immersion programs in Canada shows that, when there is no explicit attention paid to grammatical form, non-native forms often become stabilized (Harley & Swain, 1984), even fossilized (Han, 2004). Giving learners explicit guidance can, but need not, involve using grammatical terminology. It does mean, though, pointing out how the grammar works.

Furthermore, White (1987) made the point that the positive evidence (the input to language learners) is not always sufficient for learners to analyze complex grammatical features. In other words, "while positive evidence contains information about what is possible in the target language, it does not contain information about what is *not* possible" (Spada, 1997, pp. 80–81). Thus, learners are helped by the "negative evidence" that they get from instruction (e.g., corrective feedback) to help them sort out L1 versus L2 differences.

Finally, it is not the case that grammar instruction should emulate natural exposure. We know that learners can indeed generate their own negative evidence (e.g., see Spivey, 2007), but the right kind of grammar instruction should accelerate natural acquisition, not merely imitate it (Larsen-Freeman & Long, 1991). So let us now take up different approaches to grammar instruction that have been proposed as "the right kind."

Present, practice, produce

Traditional grammar teaching has employed a structural syllabus and lessons composed of three phases—presentation, practice, and production (or communication)—often referred to as the PPP approach. (See also Purgason, this volume.) In the first phase, an understanding of the grammar point is provided, sometimes by pointing out the differences between the L1 and L2. In the second phase, students practice the grammar construction using oral drills and written exercises. In the third phase, students are given "frequent opportunities for communicative use of the grammar to promote automatic and accurate use" (R. Sheen, 2003, p. 226). We saw the first two of these phases implemented in the example lesson at the beginning of this chapter.

DeKeyser (1998, 2007) offers J. R. Anderson's (1990) skill-based approach to explain how grammar practice may work in the second phase. Once students are given a rule (declarative knowledge) in the first phase, output practice aids students to proceduralize their knowledge. Continued practice automatizes the use of the rule so that students do not have to think consciously about the rule any longer. As Doughty and Williams (1998a) put it, "proceduralization is achieved by engaging in the target behavior—or procedure—while temporarily leaning on declarative crutches . . ." (p. 49). Countless generations of students have been taught grammar in this way, and many have succeeded with this form of instruction. In support of this, following their meta-analysis of research on the effectiveness of instruction, Norris and Ortega (2000) concluded that "L2 instruction of particular language forms induces substantial target-oriented change . . ." (p. 500).

Focus on form

A different approach to grammar teaching has been proposed by Long (1991), who called for a focus on form within a communicative or meaning-based approach to language teaching, such as task-based or content-based language teaching. Instead of teaching a long list of grammatical constructions in a preemptive PPP way, Long (2007) proposed an essentially reactive approach, whereby learners are primarily engaged in communication with only a brief digression to grammar when necessary (e.g., when learners commit errors). Since there is a limit to what learners can pay attention to, focusing on form may help learners notice constructions (Schmidt, 1990) that would otherwise escape their attention when they are engaged in communication or studying content. Long (1991) hypothesized that "a systematic, non-interfering focus on form produces a faster rate of learning and (probably) higher levels of ultimate second language attainment than instruction with no focus on form" (p. 47). In addition to unobtrusive error correction, various means of focusing on form have been proposed and studied:

Enhancing the input.   By highlighting (e.g., making boldface) certain nonsalient grammatical forms in a reading passage, students' attention will be drawn to them (Sharwood Smith, 1993). The oral equivalent is when a teacher stresses certain forms when speaking with students.

Input flooding.   Choosing texts in which a particular construction or structural contrast is especially frequent will enhance its saliency and thus might promote noticing. One possible function of input flooding, in addition to making certain features in the input more frequent and thus more salient, is that it might prime the production of a particular structure. "Syntactic priming is a speaker's tendency to produce a previously spoken or heard structure" (Mackey & Gass, 2006, p. 173).

Input processing.   Another technique for directing students' attention to form is called *input processing* (VanPatten, 1996). Rather than working on rule learning and rule application, input processing activities push learners to attend to properties of language during activities where the structure is being used meaningfully. The examples the students focus on have been carefully chosen to make salient the differences between the L1 and the L2. For instance, the point that Spanish speakers must pay attention to word order in English might be made by showing students two pictures and asking them to imagine that they are in the picture.[3] Next, they listen to two sentences in English, and they need to point to the picture that corresponds to one of the two sentences.

The man is looking for you.
You are looking for the man.

Since this same distinction is not made using word order in Spanish, this activity is intended to guide the learners to process the input differently.

Te busca el señor.
Tú buscas al señor.

Not everyone is convinced by an input-processing or focus-on-form approach, however. While acknowledging the "carry-over" problem (i.e., the difficulty of achieving simultaneous fluent and accurate spontaneous production), Swan (2005) disputes the claim that the traditional PPP has failed. Further, he admonishes that it does not follow that the issue will be solved by eliminating the first two Ps.

Grammaring

To address the "carry-over" or "inert knowledge problem," whereby students know the rules but do not necessarily apply them when they are communicating, Larsen-Freeman (2003) suggests that grammar instruction needs not only to promote awareness in students but also to engage them in meaningful production (Toth, 2006). Output production pushes students to move beyond semantic processing of the input to syntactic processing (Swain, 1985). Then, too, when students attempt to produce constructions, they have an opportunity to test their hypotheses on how the construction is formed or what it means or when it is used (Shehadeh, 2003). Following these attempts, they can receive feedback on their hypotheses and modify them as necessary. Therefore, Larsen-Freeman maintains that the proper goal of grammar instruction should be *grammaring*, the ability to use grammar constructions accurately, meaningfully, and appropriately. The addition of *-ing* to *grammar* is meant to suggest a dynamic process of grammar using. To realize this goal, it is not sufficient for students to notice or comprehend grammatical constructions or to repeat or transform them, as in the example lesson at the beginning of this chapter. Students must also practice the meaningful use of grammar in a way that takes into account "transfer appropriate" processing (Roediger & Guynn, 1996). This means that, for students to overcome the inert knowledge problem, they must practice using constructions to make meaning under psychologically authentic conditions, where the conditions of learning and the conditions of use are aligned (Segalowitz, 2003).

One way to do this, Gatbonton and Segalowitz (1988) suggest, is "creative automatization," practice that automates control of patterned sequences, ones that would naturally occur in given communicative contexts. Recall the example used earlier in this chapter: *My washer needs fixing*. As part of lesson planning, teachers can design a skit where students get to use such a pattern frequently.

Of course, sometimes a communicative task itself requires that students attend to relevant grammar constructions (Loschky & Bley-Vroman, 1993; Samuda, 2001; R. Ellis, 2009b), such as when using a particular grammatical construction is essential to completing the task. An example of this is when students have to use particular prepositions accurately to give each other directions using a map. When it comes to content-based instruction, lessons should have clear language learning objectives in addition to content objectives. A grammar example might be teaching students to produce stative passives (*X is located between Y and Z*) in geography lessons. Which dimension of a grammar construction is practiced and the way it is practiced will depend on the nature of the learning challenge.

Form.   For instance, if the learning challenge is form, a great deal of meaningful iteration[4] will be required. Students will have to be restricted to using just the particular target form; in other words, structural diversity will not be permitted. Finally, for proceduralization to occur, it is important to concentrate on only one or two forms at a time, although, of course, the target form could be introduced in contrast to forms that the student already controls. An example of an activity that works on form is a language game, such as the one described in Kealey and Inness (1997). Students have to complete a family portrait in which the child's face is missing. To complete the task, they are given clues (e.g., *She has her mother's eyes* or *She has her father's nose*) containing instances of the *'s* possessive.

Meaning.   If the teacher has decided that the challenge of a particular construction lies in the semantic dimension, then a different sort of practice activity should be planned. Meaning seems to call for some sort of associative learning (N. Ellis, 1998), where students are given opportunities to associate the form and the meaning of the particular target construction. It has been my experience that iteration is not needed here to the same extent as it is when teaching form. Sometimes a single pairing of form and meaning suffices, a process known as "fast mapping." Due to memory constraints, it seems prudent to restrict the number of new items being practiced at any one time to between three and six (Asher, 1996). An example of a meaning-based activity is one asking students to mime a series of actions, called "an operation" (Nelson, Winters, & Clark, 2004), such as making a telephone call (using, e.g., *look up, call up, pick up, hang up*). By practicing this operation several times, while they name the action, the students can learn to associate the form and meaning of the phrasal verbs.

Use.   When use is the challenge, it is because students have shown that they are having a hard time selecting the right construction for a particular context. Thus, relevant practice activities will provide students with an opportunity to choose from two or more forms that are roughly semantically equivalent the one best suited for the context and how they wish to position themselves (e.g., in a cooperative way, a polite way, or an assertive way). In some cases, their choice may involve selecting between two options (e.g., when to use a phrasal verb versus a single-word verb with the equivalent meaning). Other times, their choice will be from among an array of options (e.g., which modal verb, *should* or *might*, to use when giving advice to a boss); hence, the number of forms being worked on at one time will be at least two but may involve many more.

Role plays work well when dealing with use because the teacher can systematically manipulate social variables (e.g., increase or decrease the social distance between interlocutors) to have students practice how changes in the social variables affect the choice of form. Then, too, having students work with the same construction in writing and in speaking activities can highlight differences between written and spoken grammars (Carter & McCarthy, 1995).

As was mentioned earlier, the social context is not all that is involved in the choice of which forms to use; often the linguistic discourse co-text also makes a difference, especially in discipline-based writing. Thus, it is very important to consider teaching discourse grammar (Celce-Murcia, 1991; Hughes & McCarthy, 1998). Such is the case with the passive voice. Its use is not particularly sensitive to social factors; nevertheless, students struggle with when to use it versus the active voice. Challenges of this nature call for text-generation or text-manipulation exercises. Students might be given a short text that they have to complete using the appropriate voice. Because some sentences will be better in the passive voice and others in the active voice, students will be making choices, in keeping with a characteristic of practice activities designed to work on the use dimension.

Before leaving our discussion of the passive voice, let me illustrate why I feel that identifying the challenging dimension is a worthwhile step to take before teaching any grammar construction. As I stated earlier, it has been my experience that the greatest long-term challenge for students concerning the passive voice is to figure out when to use it. Keeping this in mind will help us avoid a common practice of ESL/EFL teachers, which is to introduce the passive form as a transformed version of the active (e.g., "Switch the subject with the direct object . . ."). Presenting the passive in this way is misleading because it gives students the impression that the passive is simply a form variant of the active. Moreover, it suggests that most passive sentences contain agents. What we know, in fact, to be the case is that one voice is not a variant of the other; they have different foci. We also know that relatively few passive sentences contain explicit agents. Thus, from the first introduction, the passive should be taught as a distinct construction that occurs in a different context from the active. For example, the teacher can introduce the contexts by asking students where Spanish, or another language, is spoken and students can list and discuss the countries where Spanish is spoken.

Note that many of the activities recommended here are currently being used. What I am advocating is a principled means for dealing with grammar. Choosing a particular dimension of grammar to focus on will enable teachers to adopt or adapt a teaching activity so that students' attention is focused where it will do the most good. Of course, where students choose to put *their* attention is another matter. The point is that teachers should not assume that, just because a textbook activity deals with the target construction, it necessarily addresses the particular learning challenge that their students are experiencing.

Explicit grammar instruction

Consciousness-raising. I said earlier that L2 learners, particularly older ones, might benefit from the explicit teaching of grammatical rules and patterns. One option for explicit rule instruction is to use a consciousness-raising task, in which it is the students' job to induce a grammatical generalization from the data they have been given. For example, Fotos and Ellis (1991) asked students to work out the rule for indirect object alternation in English (e.g., *They gave a gold watch to him* versus *They gave him a gold watch*) by giving the students example sentences where indirect object alternation can and cannot be successfully applied. Indirect object alternation is difficult in English and therefore is an ideal candidate for this sort of explicit rule articulation. Indeed, Carroll and Swain (1993) suggest that when the rules are not that clear-cut, detailed instruction with explicit grammatical feedback may be the most helpful response to student errors.

Garden path. Another option for promoting students' awareness is to use the garden path strategy (Tomasello & Herron, 1988, 1989). As applied to grammar teaching, this means giving students information about a construction without giving them the full picture, thus making it seem easier than it is or, in other words, "leading them down the garden path." If ESL/EFL students were told that the English past tense is formed with *–ed,* for example, this would be leading students down the garden path because there are many irregular verbs in English where this rule will not work. The reason for giving students only a partial explanation is that they are more likely to learn the exceptions to the rule if they are corrected at the moment the overgeneralization error is made than if they are given a long list of "exceptions to the rule" to memorize in advance.

Corpus-informed. Some teachers these days have their students consult online corpora to determine what patterns exist and which of them occur more frequently. Through induction in such a data-driven approach, students can be taught to create their own knowledge of patterned sequences, particularly collocations or words that go together (T. Johns, 1994; Liu & Jiang, 2009). They can do so for both informal and formal language usage, written and spoken.

When using corpora, such as the British National Corpus, the Corpus of Contemporary American English, or specialized corpora, such as the Michigan Corpus of Academic Spoken English, students are exposed to genuine examples instead of invented ones. They also shift their focus from individual words, or empty grammatical structures, to phraseological items (Simpson-Vlach & N. Ellis, 2010; Römer, 2011).

Collaborative dialogues. Donato (1994) has shown that students' participation in collaborative dialogue, through which learners can provide support for each other or scaffold each other's learning by discussing the use of language, has spurred their language development. Other research (Swain & Lapkin, 1998) corroborates the value of language-related episodes that arise during a dialogue where students explicitly discuss grammatical points. Such dialogues serve both as a cognitive tool and as a means of communication that can promote grammatical development.

Other benefits of grammar instruction have been proposed (R. Ellis, 1998, 2006). For instance, grammar instruction can also help students generalize their knowledge to new structures (Gass, 1982). It also helps students "notice the gap" between new features in a construction and how they differ from the learners' own production (Schmidt & Frota, 1986). This last point introduces a very important function of grammar instruction, which is giving students feedback.

Providing feedback

Providing learners with feedback, which they can use to correct their misapprehensions about some aspect of the target language, is an essential function of language teaching. Even such indirect feedback as asking a learner to clarify something he or she has said may be helpful (Schachter, 1986). It has always been a controversial function, however (Larsen-Freeman, 1991). There are, for instance, those who would proscribe it, believing that a teacher's intervention will inhibit students from freely expressing themselves or that there is little evidence demonstrating that learners make use of the feedback they have been given—that is, there is little immediate "uptake" of the correct form. While there are clearly times when such intervention can be intrusive and therefore unwarranted (e.g., in the middle of a small-group communicative activity), at other times focused feedback is highly desirable. Further, immediate uptake cannot be the sole criterion of its usefulness. Negative evidence gives students the feedback they need to reject or modify their hypotheses about how the target language is formed or functions. Students understand this, which explains why they often deliberately seek corrective feedback.

The same pie chart that I used when identifying the learning challenge and creating practice activities can also be a useful aid in diagnosing errors. If the diagnosis is accurate, the remedy may be more effective. More than once I have observed a teacher give an explanation of linguistic form to a student when consulting the pie chart would have suggested that the student's confusion lay with the area of use instead.

As for how the feedback should be provided, there are a number of options available to the teacher. One is recasting, reformulating correctly what a student has said incorrectly. This is a natural thing for most teachers to do in any case, and it is an example of what Long means by unobtrusive focusing on form. In addition, many educators see considerable merit in getting students to self-correct. They might do so by repeating what the student has just said up to the point of the error, in this way signaling to the student that something needs to be changed at the place the teacher has stopped (see Lyster, 2007; Lyster & Ranta, 1997). Giving students an explicit rule is a third way of providing feedback. Some teachers like to collect their students' errors, identify the prototypical ones, and then deal with them collectively in class in an anonymous fashion. Which option is exercised will depend on the teacher's style, the teacher's view of the capacity of the student, the nature of the error, and in which part of the lesson the error has been committed. Giving corrective feedback is complicated, and it should not be studied simply by "extracting behavioral instances of error correction, out of their context in order to classify them into discrete categories . . ." (Ortega, 2012, p. 33).

None of these feedback strategies has to be used exclusively, of course. For instance, Aljaafreh and Lantolf (1994) offer a graduated 12-point scale ranging from implicit to explicit strategies, beginning with students' identifying errors in their own writing, moving to the teacher's isolating the error area and inquiring if there is anything wrong in a particular sentence, and then moving to the teacher's providing examples of the correct pattern when other forms of help fail to lead to a self-correction on the part of the student. (For reviews of research on error correction, see Li, 2010; Y. Sheen, 2010.)

Related pedagogical issues

Sequencing. Earlier we noted that grammar constructions are not acquired one at a time through an additive process (Rutherford, 1987). Rather, different aspects of the form, meaning, and use of a given construction may be acquired at different stages of L2 development. This observation confirms the need for recycling, working on one dimension of a construction and then returning to the construction from time to time as the need arises. To some extent this will occur naturally because the same constructions are likely to be encountered in different communicative tasks and content areas.

However, it is also the case that not all linguistic constructions that students need to learn will be available in the language that occurs in the classroom. Therefore, it is necessary for the teacher to "fill in the gaps" and introduce constructions that do not naturally arise in classroom discourse (Spada & Lightbown, 1993). For this reason, teachers might think in terms of a grammar checklist instead of a grammatical sequence. Rather than adhering to a linear progression, the choice of sequence would be left up to the teacher and would depend on the teacher's assessment of the students' developmental readiness to learn.

Many teachers, of course, have little control over the content or sequence of the material they work on. They must adhere to prescribed syllabi or textbooks, although even in such a situation, it may be possible for teachers not to follow a sequence rigidly. For those teachers who have more flexibility, the research on acquisition orders is germane. Some SLA research has shown that learners progress through a series of predictable stages in their acquisition of particular linguistic forms. One explanation for the order rests on the complexity of the speech-processing strategies required. Thus, all structures processable by a particular strategy or cluster of strategies should be acquired at roughly the same developmental stage. This approach has been shown to account for certain acquisition orders in ESL (Pienemann & Johnston, 1987).

Despite these findings and their potential implications for grammatical construction sequencing, there has been no definitive acquisition order established, and thus teachers are still left to their own judgment on how to proceed. Of course, students chart their own unique learning paths. I should also note that, even if an acquisition order were to be fully specified for English, there might be justification for preempting the acquisition order when students' communicative needs were not being met and when, therefore, certain constructions needed to be taught, at least formulaically. Furthermore, Lightbown (1998) has suggested that even if students are asked to work on structures before they are ready to acquire them, such effort may not be in vain because such instruction might prime subsequent noticing on the part of the students, thereby accelerating acquisition when they are indeed ready.

Inductive versus deductive presentation. An additional choice that teachers face is whether to teach inductively or deductively. An inductive activity is one in which students infer the rule or generalization from a set of examples. In a deductive activity, the students are given the rule, and they apply it to examples. If a teacher has chosen an inductive approach in a given lesson, a further option exists—whether or not to give or have students articulate an explicit rule. While what we are trying to bring about in the learner is accurate performance, not knowledge of the rules themselves, there is no reason to avoid giving explicit rules as a means to this end, except perhaps if the teacher is working with young children. Moreover, stating a rule explicitly can often bring about linguistic insights in a more efficacious manner, as long as the rule is not oversimplified or so obtuse that students must struggle harder to understand the rule than to apply it implicitly (Robinson, 1996).

There are many times when an inductive approach, such as using a consciousness-raising task, is desirable because by using such an approach we are nurturing within the students a way of thinking, through which they can arrive at their own generalizations. In addition, an inductive approach allows teachers to assess what the students already know about a particular construction and to make any necessary adjustments in their lesson plan.

Other times, when students have a particular cognitive style that is not well suited for language analysis or when a particular linguistic rule is rather convoluted, it may make more sense to present a grammar construction deductively. Indeed, Corder's (1973) sensible observations still offer comfort:

> What little we know about . . . second language learning . . . suggests that a combination of induction and deduction produces the best result. . . . The old controversy about whether one should provide the rule first and then the examples, or vice versa, is now seen to be merely a matter of tactics to which no categorical answer can be given. (as cited in Rutherford & Sharwood Smith, 1988, p. 133)

Reasons, not only rules. I have suggested (Larsen-Freeman, 2000) that teachers concentrate on teaching "reasons, not only rules." Many rules appear arbitrary because they are form based, ignoring the meaning and use dimensions. Learning rules puts an additional rote-learning burden on students. Why not tap their cognitive powers instead? For instance, rather than telling students they must use an indefinite noun phrase after the verb in a sentence beginning with existential *there*, such as *There is a snowstorm coming*, help them understand the reason. The function of *there* is to introduce new information. The indefinite article *a* is used in English to mark new information. This is why *a* is used before *snowstorm*. This reason has broader scope and explains a number of English word-order phenomena. Of course, the reason has to be presented in a comprehensible manner. While rules provide some security for learners, reasons give them a deeper understanding of the logic of English and help them make it their own. Besides, reasons are meaning- and use-based and are in keeping with the more robust view of grammar I have been promoting in this chapter.

FUTURE TRENDS

Varieties

A big question in many teachers' minds these days is which grammar they should be teaching. This has always been true to some extent, of course, in the choice between, for example, the grammar of North American English and British English. However, the choices have multiplied with the increasing number of evolving World Englishes such as Singapore English, Nigerian English, and Indian English. These, too, are native Englishes, although they are not always taught as such. Perhaps they should be. Another question these days has been presented by the English as a lingua franca (ELF) scholars (e.g., Seidlhofer, 2001). They point to characteristics of ELF that differ from native speaker varieties. For example, many users of English as an international language drop the third-person singular present tense –*s* marker on verbs. While features of ELF should not necessarily be taught, the question is, should such omissions be considered errors? Even in native speaker grammars, there is more choice than is sometimes perceived (Larsen-Freeman, 2002). For instance, in the example lesson with which I began this chapter, the student who asks about recess uses an uninverted question. Uninverted questions were not the object of this grammar lesson, of course, but native speakers do commonly use uninverted questions in certain situations. Such observations as these have left teachers asking which form of English they should be teaching. Of course, the answer to this question is often more of a socio-political question having to do with attitudes than a linguistic one. The best answer to the question lies in determining what the students' purpose in learning English is and to what ends they will be using their English proficiency in the future.

A complex adaptive system

Another current trend with implications for the future lies in the way we have come to understand the dynamics of language use (Larsen-Freeman, 1997). As Gleick (1987) puts it, "the act of playing the game has a way of changing the rules" (p. 24). Although Gleick was not writing about linguistic rules, this statement captures the facts that language changes all the time and that it does so due to the cumulative innovations that language users make at the local level as they adapt their language resources to new communicative contexts (Larsen-Freeman & Cameron, 2008). The point is that language learners should not be seen as learning to conform to grammatical uniformity. Instead, it is more accurate to say that they are developing the capacity to create and understand meaning by using language, adapting what they know to new situations.

Testing

If grammar is construed as forms that have meanings and uses, testing only grammatical accuracy, as many tests do, is severely limiting (see Larsen-Freeman, 2009; Purpura, 2004). Furthermore, if language is the dynamic system that we claim it to be, no one-time testing procedure will yield a complete picture of what a learner is capable of doing. Finally, language testers will have to wrestle with the vexing matter of which variety of language is to be assessed. All this means that much work needs to be accomplished to reduce dissonance between teaching and testing.

CONCLUSION

Over the centuries, second language educators have alternated between two types of approaches to language teaching: those that focus on analyzing the language and those that focus on using the language. The former teach students the elements of language, including grammar constructions, building students' capacity to use the elements to communicate. The latter encourage students to use the language from the start, however falteringly, to acquire it communicatively. It is not a question of one or the other, however. Educators agree that speaking and writing accurately are important for many students, just as is being able to get one's meaning across in an appropriate manner. Further, it has been observed that, although some learners can "pick up" grammar constructions from exposure to the target language, few learners are capable of doing so efficiently, especially if they are post-pubescent or if their exposure is limited to the classroom, as is the case when English is taught as a foreign language.

However, equating grammar with meaningless forms, decontextualized from use, and equating the teaching of grammar with the teaching of explicit linguistic rules are unduly limiting. I have called them myths (Larsen-Freeman, 1995) that serve only to perpetuate the methodological pendulum swing between language analysis and language use. Opting for the middle ground in this chapter, I have maintained that grammar *is* about form and that one way to teach form is to give students rules; however, grammar is about much more than form, and its teaching is ill-served if students are simply given rules. This is very important to understand, and doing so will make teachers appreciate grammar more than perhaps they have in the past. Their appreciation can help their students see what a powerful tool grammar is in helping them to express their desired meaning accurately and appropriately.

SUMMARY

➤ The term grammar is ambiguous.
➤ Grammar includes both morphosyntactic structures and patterned sequences, which are together called constructions.
➤ Grammar is about form, but more than form, it is about what forms mean and when and why they are used.
➤ It is important for teachers to anticipate the learning challenge for a given grammar point because their doing so has implications for how they allocate time and what activities they use.

> There are some educators who feel that teaching grammar is unnecessary. However, most believe that some combination of awareness raising (devoted to form, meaning, and use), with practice that is meaningful and psychologically authentic and provides for appropriate corrective feedback, is powerful.

DISCUSSION QUESTIONS

1. How does the definition of *grammar* proposed in this chapter compare with others with which you may be familiar?
2. In explaining the pragmatics of phrasal verbs, the principle of dominance was invoked. Explain why the principle of dominance falls in the pragmatic dimension. Then, explain why meaning is claimed to be the greatest long-term challenge for students learning phrasal verbs.
3. The effect of the native language on second language learning has traditionally been seen to be one of interference. How does the observation on p. 261 regarding learners' reliance on their prior knowledge and experience differ in its perception of L1 influence?
4. Why should iteration in a practice activity for learning the form of a construction be meaningful?
5. Why is it important for the teacher to identify the challenge in a particular grammar construction for a particular group of students?

SUGGESTED ACTIVITIES

1. Think of a language teaching approach that tends to favor language use over language form. How could the approach incorporate more language form? Now think of an approach that favors language form over language use. How could a focus on language use be integrated?
2. Analyze restrictive relative clauses in terms of the three dimensions of the pie chart. Which has been the most challenging dimension for the students with whom you have worked?
3. Design practice activities for dealing with the pragmatics of indirect object alternation and presence or absence of existential *there*.

FURTHER READING

Celce-Murcia, M., & Larsen-Freeman, D. (1999). *The grammar book: An ESL/EFL teacher's course* (2nd ed.). Boston, MA: Heinle/Cengage.

The book seeks to guide teachers to an understanding of the grammar of those constructions they will have to teach (their form, meaning, and use in context) and offers teaching suggestions for each.

Doughty, C., & Williams, J. (Eds.). (1998). *Focus on form in classroom second language acquisition.* Cambridge, UK: Cambridge University Press.

The book provides an overview of second language acquisition research that has investigated "focus on form."

Hinkel, E., & Fotos, S. (Eds.). (2002). *New perspectives on grammar teaching in second language classrooms.* Mahwah, NJ: Lawrence Erlbaum Associates.

The book features a variety of approaches to understanding and teaching grammar.

Larsen-Freeman, D. (2003). *Teaching language: From grammar to grammaring.* Boston, MA: Heinle/Cengage.

In this book, Larsen-Freeman argues for a reconceptualization of grammar and the way it is taught, featuring grammar as a dynamic system.

Larsen-Freeman, D. (Series Director). (2007). *Grammar dimensions: Form, meaning, and use.* (4th ed.) Boston, MA: Heinle/Cengage.

This is a communicative grammar textbook series that presents grammar in three dimensions with matching practice exercises and communicative activities.

Willis, D. (2003). *Rules, patterns and words.* Cambridge, UK: Cambridge University Press.

This book demonstrates how patterned sequences provide a link between grammar and vocabulary.

ENDNOTES

[1] Because all three dimensions are present, sometimes it is difficult to distinguish meaning from use. Answering the question "When or why is a grammar structure used?" by saying "when it means such and such" is *not* making the distinction between meaning and use clear. Using the *wh*-questions—asking *what* (meaning) versus *when* or *why* (use)—should help.

[2] Of course, all teachers can do is to anticipate the learning challenge. They need to be prepared to alter their lesson if the anticipated challenge turns out not to be a problem. It is also certainly possible that not all the students in the class will manifest the same learning challenge.

[3] This is based on an example discussed in Doughty and Williams (1998).

[4] *Iteration* means repetition that changes the learner's grammatical resources (Larsen-Freeman, in press).

18 | Spoken Grammar

MICHAEL MCCARTHY AND ANNE O'KEEFFE

KEY QUESTIONS

➤ Is there a distinct spoken grammar separate from written grammar, and, if so, precisely how do they differ? Are there, for example, special rules and forms for speaking that simply do not exist in writing?

➤ Are the meanings of grammatical structures different in speech from their meanings in writing, and why should such differences in meaning exist?

➤ What sorts of communicative functions does spoken grammar perform and how do these contribute to successful spoken interaction?

EXPERIENCE

The following classroom conversation takes place between a male student (a non-native learner of English) and his teacher. The students in this class are all trainees who will work in the international hospitality industry when they complete their training. A good command of spoken English will be very important for their future work.[1]

<student 1> I wanted to experience the different cultures within the hospitality industry as uh, **you know**, you have different people from different backgrounds working within the hotel **like** we have for placement, **I had different, like, around nineteen different** nationalities working within the restaurant itself. So I wanted to **experience** . . . , and, **plus** giving the service to the guest, making them feel important really makes me feel nice about providing good service to a customer **and everything like that**. So that was one key aspect that uh drove me into the hospitality industry, **plus, my father, he planned** to open a hotel in the later stages so he said it's better if you also do something within the hospitality industry so that you can take it forward **and everything**.

So I chose hospitality industry.
[intervening turns]
<teacher> You had mentioned teaching at some stage. **Do you see**+
<student 1> Yeah.
<teacher> +**you teaching** in your future?
<student 1> I had I thought about it but um it's so confusing right now that's **it's not**. . . . But I would love to teach as **like** it's a **total different** experience **I guess** so **you should be knowing** it better.
<teacher> [laughs]
<student 1> [laughs] So I wanted to teach in between because I have been helping my fellow students as well so they are **like**, oh you should try and teach, and and so that's why I wanted to teach in between but if I want to teach I'll be in the finance side as well if ever I plan to teach I have, **so** . . . (Cambridge, Limerick and Shannon Corpus)[2]

This student is asked by the teacher why he chose the hospitality industry as his profession. The teacher (a female native speaker) is also a participant in the conversation. How should she evaluate the student's performance as she listens? Should she focus on accuracy in grammar, or

271

should she be lenient and allow the student to converse fluently? To what extent should the teacher consider whether the grammar is appropriate for speaking in this particular context? Finally, does it matter that she herself, a native speaker, seems to be less than 100% accurate in her use of English? (The words in bold will be of particular interest to our subsequent discussion of spoken grammar.)

We would hardly doubt that the English of the student in the Experience section is both accurate and fluent—his grammar is of a high standard and his language flows without too much hesitation. He has a good command of the vocabulary he needs for this topic. However, the transcript, and in particular the way the transcriber has punctuated it (with commas indicating pauses or boundaries of groups of words), raises some grammatical dilemmas. We can list these:

- The student says *you know,* without any object. Normally the verb *know* is transitive; it requires an object (you know a person or a thing). Is this something that is acceptable in both speaking and writing, or only in speaking, or neither?
- The student uses *like* five times. On two occasions *like* seems to mean "similar to" (*like we have for placement / everything like that*). On two other occasions, *like* seems to act as a marker of pausing to think or to rephrase something (*different, like, around nineteen different / as like it's a total different experience*). On the last occasion, it seems to introduce direct speech (*they are like, oh you should try and teach*). Are all these uses of *like* acceptable in speech and writing, only one, or none of them?
- Some of the student's sentences seem incomplete, breaking off halfway, and the conversation ends with *so. . . .* Should the teacher insist that the students always finish their sentences?
- The student says *and everything like that* and then, later, *and everything.* What do these expressions mean, and are they acceptable or common in writing?
- The student uses *plus* to connect ideas. Is this an acceptable conjunction in all types of English?
- The student says *my father, he planned. . . .* Is it grammatical to have two subjects before the verb (a noun phrase and a pronoun)?

- The teacher says *Do you see you teaching?* Although she is a native speaker, this seems incorrect; it should be *Do you see yourself teaching?* Similarly, the student says *a total different experience* and *you should be knowing it better.* Is the use of *total* instead of *totally* before an adjective acceptable? Is this use of the progressive with a stative verb (*know*) acceptable? Are these errors, or are they normal and acceptable in spoken grammar?

Wherever we look at transcripts of spoken language, whether the speakers are native users, expert users, or learners, we find these and similar dilemmas presenting themselves. To solve the dilemmas, we need to establish whether the apparent grammatical anomalies really are oddities/errors or whether they are a normal part of face-to-face speaking in real time. In short, we need to know what is normal in spoken language before we can evaluate someone's performance and decide what to correct or focus on in teaching.

We illustrate our arguments in this chapter with evidence of how people use grammar in speaking taken from several corpora. Corpora are collections of written and spoken texts, often consisting of tens or hundreds of millions of running words, stored on computers, which can be searched using dedicated software to see exactly what words and patterns of grammar the speakers and writers use most frequently (or, indeed, least frequently), who uses them, and in what contexts. The statistical and contextual evidence the software can provide us with enables us to make more reliable interpretations of speakers' and writers' communicative purposes. For more information about corpora and their uses, see O'Keeffe, McCarthy, and Carter (2007) and O'Keeffe and McCarthy (2010). In this chapter, we look at speech samples taken from the corpora of different varieties of native-speaker English and from the English of learners.

WHAT IS SPOKEN GRAMMAR?

The simplest definition of *spoken grammar* is the grammar we find in regular and repeated use by the majority of native and expert speakers of a language in the majority of their spoken interactions. Most people spend most of their speaking time having ordinary everyday conversations, and they only very rarely engage in special types of speaking such as speeches, interviews, sermons, lectures, and academic presentations. So it is in everyday conversations that we are likely to find the most basic and widespread forms of spoken grammar. This does not mean that all such forms will be applicable to or acceptable in situations such as the classroom context in the Experience at the beginning of the chapter, where a more professionally oriented or formal academic style of speaking may be what the teacher had hoped to encourage. But without knowledge of what constitutes everyday informal spoken grammar, we are hardly in a position to draw the boundaries between it and other, more formal or specialized ways of speaking.

Academic interest in whether there is a spoken grammar and what it consists of was considerably facilitated by the advent of miniaturized recording technology and, later, computerized spoken corpora, which really gave impetus to studies of spoken grammar. In parallel with these technological developments, language teaching was, in the 1970s and 1980s, going through the communicative revolution, where greater emphasis was emerging on the interpersonal functions of language (e.g., requesting, apologizing, and inviting). The functional categories were closely associated with the spoken language rather than the traditional written forms such as literary works and formal writing, which had been the backbone of language teaching for centuries. It is not surprising, therefore, that voices urging a greater understanding of the role of grammar in speaking and interpersonal communication grew louder toward the end of the twentieth century. McCarthy and Carter (2001), for instance, in an article laying out criteria for a spoken grammar, voiced the opinion that speaking-skills pedagogy that did not take into account what we know about the spoken language was hardly adequate. More and more research was published over the next 10 years that offered persuasive evidence of the independence of spoken grammar and its characteristics, and it is to such characteristics that we now turn.

Incomplete clauses and sentences

Many of the features of spoken grammar that we deal with here arise from the nature of face-to-face talk in context and in real time. The first of these

to consider is the status of that most basic unit of grammar, the sentence. The sentence has occupied, and most probably will continue to occupy, a central part in language teaching because it is a good vehicle for illustrating grammar. In sentences, we can see clauses in combination (e.g., main clauses and how they combine with subordinate clauses); the functions of subjects, verbs, objects, and so on and how they relate to one another through various rules and conventions; and how ideas are packaged grammatically. In writing, we have the added benefit of punctuation. Speaking is different. Native speaker conversations seem to unfold naturally and quite happily without always forming complete sentences. In the conversation in Figure 1, two native-speaking co-workers are looking at some documents and talking informally about them.

In Figure 1, Speaker 1 uses an *if*-clause that does not seem to be attached to the typical kind of main clause we find in conditional sentences. This is a common use of freestanding *if*-clauses to make suggestions or to issue polite instructions (e.g., *If you'd like to come this way, please.*). We then have *while I'm er*, an incomplete time clause. Neither clause seems to create any problem of communication in this face-to-face context, but both clauses would look odd "stranded" in this way in a written text. And, obviously, *Right okay okay* is nothing like a complete clause or sentence but performs the crucial function of listener feedback, a point we return to later. The need to speak in full clauses and sentences is not an absolute when speakers clearly understand the meaning in context, and things are often only half-said. Our student in the Experience was doing the same. Although by the standards of written grammar, many clauses in informal speech seem incomplete, to the

<speaker 1> **If you'd like to have a a quick look through those while I'm er**, please ask any questions while you're looking through, and I'll ask any questions that I'll need to here.
<speaker 2> **Right okay okay**.

Figure 1. Use of incomplete clauses (from the British National Corpus).[3]

participants nothing is incomplete or missing; communication is sufficient and efficient.

Main and subordinate clauses

We have noted that *if*-clauses can have a special pragmatic function in spoken language (making polite suggestions and requests, or giving polite instructions). Other subordinating conjunctions also seem to have functions that are more prominent in spoken contexts. *Because* has been shown frequently to have an "I'm justifying what I'm saying to you" function rather than a cause-effect function in conversation (Schleppegrell, 1992), as illustrated in Figure 2, where a teacher is commenting on the talent another teacher has for handling her students in class and the lessons learned from observing her.

In Figure 2, the speaker's use of *cos* is not a reference to cause-effect or to a reason for someone's actions but, instead, means "this is why I am telling you this." From observations of this kind of function in spoken grammar, some linguists have even questioned whether the notion of subordinate clause is viable for everyday spoken language (Blanche-Benveniste, 1995; Schleppegrell, 1992). Much informal spoken language seems to consist of clausal and phrasal units linked together linearly like the cars on a train, which is not surprising since informal speech is created online, in real time. In Figure 3, the speaker is commenting on the difficulties of working unjustifiably long hours and the pressures this puts on a marriage. Notice the use of *plus* with main clauses (clauses that are not dependent on other clauses) to add ideas in this linear way. This usage is extremely rare in a comparable written corpus. So we can see our student in the Experience doing something quite natural in the grammar of

> <speaker 1> What sort of, what sort of things did you learn from her? What were you watching?
> <speaker 2> Well her introduction was good, like, she didn't just launch into things **cos I used to be a bit blunt and just start, launch right in** and you know they're not going to be responsive if you haven't somehow like broached the subject a little bit [laughing].
> <speaker 1> Eased them in a little bit, yeah.

Figure 2. Use of *because* (from the Limerick Corpus of Irish English).[4]

> <speaker 1> It was kind of, it's sort of, it seemed unfair to me to, um, to subject her to that, and **plus**, I mean, the schedule was just starting to take a toll on me as well, and you can only put in so many 80 hour weeks before you kind of break down from it.
> <speaker 2> Uh-huh.
> <speaker 1> **Plus** I really wasn't making the kind of connections that I wanted to make.

Figure 3. Use of *plus* (from the American National Corpus).[5]

spoken language by using the word *plus* to connect main clauses, although we probably do not want to have students writing that way in their essays.

Clause functions: Subjects, objects, and other functions

The student in the Experience said *my father, he planned.* . . . On the face of it, this looks like two subjects (*my father* and *he*) competing for the same verb. Once again, we find this pattern often occurring in the spoken language of native and expert users of English. The speaker in Figure 4 is talking about the decline of neighborhood stores. Twice in this example the speaker doubles the subject, using a noun phrase and a pronoun that refer to the same entity (*the old customers* and *the young people*, respectively).

Using a noun phrase and then repeating it by using a subject pronoun is a way of creating a "headline," or header for the listener, stating, "this person or thing is my topic, what I want to say something about." Again, a structure like this is rare in written texts, and the header pattern seems to be a characteristic of face-to-face interaction. It is also another example of the way spoken grammar arranges its information linearly (for further examples, see Carter & McCarthy, 1995, 2006; Carter, McCarthy, Mark, & O'Keeffe, 2011).

> <speaker 1> Well you know **all the old neighborhood customers they**'ve died. And **the young people they** go to the big supermarkets or the. . . .

Figure 4. Use of double subjects (from the American National Corpus).

Ready-made chunks

It is now widely accepted that much of our language output comes in ready-made chunks, mostly consisting of between two and four to five words (see the many excellent chapters in Schmitt, 2004). Among other terms, these are also referred to as *lexical bundles*, *multiword units*, or *clusters* (see Greaves & Warren, 2010). Chunks are automatically produced strings of words that we use repeatedly. Corpus evidence shows us just how frequent the most commonly used chunks are. By far the most common chunk in everyday conversation is *you know* (which the student in the Experience used). Other common two-word chunks include *I think*, *I guess* (see also the Experience), and *I mean*, all of which signal positions and attitudes between the speaker and the listener: *you know* projects an assumption that speaker and listener are on the same wavelength, *I think* and *I guess* suggest the speaker does not want to be too dogmatic or too direct, and *I mean* suggests the speaker feels the need to explain or elaborate. Once again, these chunks are rare in written texts. The fact that they consist of verbs that normally require objects but do not have objects in these interpersonal uses underlines the fact that the chunks have developed pragmatically specialized meanings in talk. Another aspect of chunks is that they can appear incomplete but many of the seemingly incomplete chunks operate as building blocks or utterance frames. For example, the high-frequency four-word chunk in spoken language *one of the things* appears to be a fragment, but when we look at it in more detail within a spoken corpus, we can see that it performs some important functions as a frame at the beginning of a speaker's turn, when speakers are flagging and framing their ideas, as shown in Figure 5. Clearly, these prefabricated chunks are an important part of how we structure our speaking turns, and a spoken grammar would not be complete without taking into account this phenomenon.

> One of the things I'd like to do. . . .
> One of the things I'd like to know is. . . .
> One of the things we need to think about is. . . .
> One of the things you may notice is. . . .

Figure 5. Use of ready-made chunks: *one of the things* (from the British National Corpus).

Two other notable chunks were displayed in the Experience conversation: *and everything like that* and *and everything*. These chunks are examples of what is often termed *vague language* (see Cutting, 2007), and along with similar chunks such as *(and) things like that*, *(and) that kind of thing*, *or whatever*, *and stuff (like that)*, they form a category of items, extremely common in spoken language but rare in writing, that project to the listener that he or she will be able to fill in the "missing" items in classes of things and actions that are only vaguely referred to. So, the indefinite pronoun *everything* in a statement such as the student's *you can take it forward and everything* is not to be taken too broadly or literally; it simply means "and other actions associated with taking a business forward, which I, the speaker, can assume you, the listener(s) will know." Chunks often contain what seem to be grammatically anomalous forms and meanings, but in their regular use, they acquire pragmatic meanings necessary for the functioning of face-to-face interaction. A spoken grammar must include an inventory of chunks that perform important interactive functions related to the state of knowledge between speakers and listeners, the organization of talk, and the stances and attitudes conversational participants adopt vis-à-vis one another.

Missing elements: Ellipsis

Because real-time conversation characteristically takes place between speakers who are in the same time and place and who often have deeply inter-meshing lives, not everything need be said explicitly in the way that a written text, which has to stand on its own two feet and persist in time and be read in a different place, needs to do. In everyday informal talk, speakers often do not say items that would normally be considered obligatory by the conventions of written grammar. The exchange in Figure 6 is taken from the same type of classroom as the Experience (students training for the hospitality industry). The teacher has set the students a task to evaluate the benefits and downsides of tourism.

In Figure 6, the teacher does not feel the need to say *has/is* before *everybody*; it is obvious that this is a question (partly owing to its rising intonation) and it is one the teacher probably often asks. This is what we call *situational ellipsis*, the

> <teacher> **Everybody finished?**
> <student> Yeah.
> <teacher> So overall do you think tourism is of a benefit to a country or is the, is the negative side too much?

Figure 6. Use of situational ellipsis (from the Cambridge, Limerick and Shannon Corpus).

non-necessity of stating explicitly everything in the situation because one can assume that the listener(s) will simply understand. Auxiliary verbs (*do, be, have*), along with subject pronouns, are often not present in situations like this (*Want a coffee? Going out tonight? You ready yet?*). Situational ellipsis of this type is a very important part of a spoken grammar, one that distinguishes it from written grammatical conventions. Conventional language pedagogy, with its emphasis on written-grammar-based norms, usually does not expose learners to a good deal of situational ellipsis in example dialogues, nor does it offer opportunities for learners to develop the skill of using ellipsis appropriately. For more examples of different types of situational ellipsis, see Carter and McCarthy (2006).

Grammar and the listener

Since face-to-face interaction includes listeners, the role of listener and speaker alternates and listeners are rarely passive, silent participants. There are three things that listeners regularly do that are of interest to anyone wishing to understand the special nature of spoken grammar. First, as seen in Figure 7, listeners often complete a grammatical structure that was only partly or incompletely stated by the speaker (called *sentence completion*).

Second, listeners routinely add extra clauses to the sentences formed by another speaker. Figure 8 shows how a listener adds a *which*–comment clause to a statement made by the speaker. The

> <speaker 1> No they're like, like the pole thing you know they're like the gutter, a pipe, big silver pipes right with like square rectangular extractors like fans
> <speaker 2> On them

Figure 7. Use of sentence completion by listener (from the Limerick Corpus of Irish English).

> <speaker 1> It's st- it's a little, it's a little strange with those parking because I mean were they for, visitors as well or were they for, the faculty, were they assigned?
> <speaker 2> No I think the parking, because there are so few parking spaces they would be assigned spaces. So, we were going to move it to show for, but they're not public. **The public arrive by foot, to this building.**
> <speaker 1> **Which is strange** because what do you do w- with, you know, I mean it's pretty much you get around this campus by car.

Figure 8. Addition of an extra clause by listener (from the Michigan Corpus of Academic Spoken English).[6]

speakers are discussing the allocation of parking spaces on a college campus. We can consider what is happening here to be a kind of joint production of a sentence, with its main clause at the end of the previous speaker's turn and the sentential *which*-clause starting the new speaker's turn. Tao and McCarthy (2001) have observed this phenomenon in spoken corpora and noted that such *which*-clauses enable conversational participants to evaluate events and situations, whether used by the same speaker or by another speaker, as in Figure 8. Joint production of grammatical patterns in this way connects speakers with one another and shapes the conversation as a collaborative artifact. In summary, we may say that the space between two speakers' turns is not like a period/full stop in a written text; in face-to-face dialogue, the grammar can flow across turns, contributing to a sense of confluence, where the whole conversation flows seamlessly (McCarthy, 2010).

The third important aspect of how listeners behave is engaged response. Listeners are not passive, and in their responses, they say more than *yes* or *no* and may offer more than a minimal acknowledgment of what the previous speaker has said. We regularly find listeners responding to another speaker with short turns, often consisting of one or two freestanding words such as *absolutely, wonderful, great, good, cool, right,* and *fine*. Such non-minimal responses show involvement with the speaker and typically express alignment with the speaker's stance and attitudes.[7] The conversation in Figure 9 exemplifies this (the speakers are talking about the city of Chicago).

Exactly and *absolutely* in Figure 9 are, in traditional grammatical terms, *–ly* adverbs. Yet

> <speaker 1> And then you could walk down Navy Pier and it must be a little bit like San Francisco only they don't have, well, they do have people down there making money, but they're mostly drawing people and stuff like that. It is beyond cool! And nobody but, you know, people say they're indifferent or whatever, but not really, it's just that it's a whole different lifestyle!
> <speaker 2> **Exactly! Absolutely.**

Figure 9. Use of non-minimal response tokens (from the American National Corpus).

it is perhaps unhelpful from a spoken-grammar point of view to see them as exemplars of a major word class. They seem to occupy a class of their own, which we have called non-minimal response tokens, and we can list the most common members of that class, which also includes some adjectives (e.g., *definitely, certainly, fine, great,* and *sure*). Just as we need the category header to describe the doubling of a subject (noun phrase plus pronoun), spoken grammar may need a new category called *response token* to reflect the role of a set of common adjectives and adverbs in what we may call good listenership, that is, the ability to respond to and engage with a speaker, something that is essential in face-to-face spoken interaction but rare or nonexistent in writing.

Word order

When we look at spoken transcripts we often see word-order patterns that are rare in writing. One example of this is the positions in the clause that common adverbs typically occupy. In conventional written grammar, adverbs such as *maybe, probably, still, nearly, though,* and *almost* characteristically occupy a position between the subject and main verb or after a first modal or auxiliary verb (*She probably went home / He's still waiting for a decision*). Less frequently, such adverbs may come before the subject (clause-initial position, as in *Probably, I'll leave at 9 a.m.*). In informal speaking, however, they routinely occupy the final position in the clause, something that is, again, rare in writing and that reflects the linear construction of spoken grammar. Figure 10 shows two examples taken from informal academic discussions.

> (discussing an economics graph)
>
> <speaker 1> So if you wanna do the first two steps just take this out. And you have the same picture **still**. See that because this is just a slope. Right? It doesn't affect anything else.
>
> (from a math discussion)
>
> <speaker 1> If you say so Mark how many points is that? I have a hard time believing it **though**. I haven't seen the problem yet. I'm confused.
> <speaker 2> Huh? That's separate points right, that's three points. Find the image of each of these three points. Right? And what is A. . . ? Yeah. Of th- supposed to be points **probably**. Okay. Well that's just so they don't have to write out those coordinates **probably**. Yeah.

Figure 10. Placement of adverbs (from the Michigan Corpus of Academic Spoken English).

In Figure 10, we see the placing of adverbs at the end of the clause, something that is rare or inappropriate in most writing, especially formal and academic writing. Speech offers the possibility of real-time modification of what has just been said, something that in academic writing might misleadingly look like an afterthought or the result of bad planning. In writing, the sentence would simply be rewritten if an afterthought had occurred (e.g., *they **probably** do not have to write out those coordinates*).

The grammatical phenomena that we have illustrated in this section mostly consist of patterns that would be inappropriate in all but the most informal writing and that would certainly be greatly out of place in formal and academic writing. For some of our examples, we have purposefully chosen academic discussions; our reason for this is that people often dismiss the notion of a spoken grammar as the grammar of the street, a corrupted form of "correct" grammar spoken by lazy speakers that is not worthy of serious linguistic analysis and certainly not worthy of inclusion in language teaching syllabi and materials. Almost all the speakers in the examples in this chapter are educated native and expert users of English, who are using the language in natural, efficient, and highly communicative ways, and so we cannot simply dismiss their usage as nonstandard or incorrect or as merely reflecting the pressures of performance.

CONCEPTUAL UNDERPINNINGS

As with any study of grammar, the notions of form and function are central to our understanding. In this chapter so far, we have illustrated a number of forms and their patterns (which, we have argued, show us something about how spoken grammar operates) and have suggested some communicative functions for our chosen examples. What is clear is that there are no unique items or structures that are available only to either the spoken or written grammar. Rather, what we have suggested so far is that the spoken and written grammars may draw on the grammatical resources in different ways, reflecting their different purposes and different contexts of use (see Leech, 2000 for further discussion). In this section, we widen the discussion to consider a broad framework for the interpretation of spoken grammar.

The context of spoken language

A key consideration in understanding the grammar of spoken language is its context of use. As mentioned, speech is produced in real time, typically without the luxury of planning, correcting, revising, and polishing that writing allows (Brazil, 1995). For this reason, complete and well-formed sentences, in the conventional sense, are often not present, nor do they need to be for communicative efficiency. Brazil (1995) puts it succinctly: "In other words, we do not necessarily have to assume that the consideration of such abstract notions as 'sentences' enters into the user's scheme of things at all" (p. 15). We may conclude that, in a spoken grammar, what matters is communicative units and that these may be sentences in the conventional sense or just clauses or verbless phrases (Ricento, 1987).

The other key consideration is that speech is produced for listeners, who are usually present at the time of its production, in contrast to written texts, which are commonly created in one time and place and consumed in another. Listeners are obliged by social convention to actively engage with speakers (Bublitz, 1988); this engagement usually demands both nonverbal and verbal responses. One implication of this is that, in all but the opening turn of any conversation, the primary duty of a next speaker is to show his or her listenership and to respond to what has just been said. Thus the responsive features of spoken grammar (which we have exemplified with the adjectives and adverbs that commonly function as non-minimal responses) are crucial, and the teaching of responses assumes a central role in the teaching of speaking. Above all, the functions of spoken grammar relate to the work speakers and listeners do to create rapport, common understanding, and good relationships; it is these things that enable conversations to achieve their goals.

One important manifestation of the immediacy of shared contexts is the all-pervasive nature of deixis in face-to-face interaction. *Deixis* refers to the way certain features of language point to people and things in the context (Grundy, 2008). At the simplest level, we see deictic items such as *this, that, these, those, here,* and *there* operating to relate the situation to each speaker. *Here* for the speaker might be *there* for the listener (as during a phone call); *this bag* in one speaker's hands might well be *that bag* for a speaker standing a little way off, or it could be *this bag* for both speakers if they are loading it or carrying it together. Likewise, *I* means the person speaking, and *you* means the person listening, and since the roles of speaker and listener alternate in dialogue, the meanings of *I* and *you* shift accordingly, unlike in writing, where the meanings are typically relatively stable as *I* the writer and *you* the reader. Deictic systems vary across languages. Standard English has a binary system for nearness and distance with demonstrative determiners (*this/these* versus *that/those*); Spanish has a three-part system corresponding to the demonstratives (meaning "this here," "that there," and "that a greater distance away"). English *we* can mean "I and you," but it can also mean "I and someone else but not you"; Malay has two separate words for these two meanings.

The spoken grammar can exploit the deictic system to create interpersonal meanings; for example, *we* can be used to create solidarity and a collective sense. McCarthy and Handford (2004) show how powerful individuals in business settings can manipulate the pronoun *we* to alternate between a general, corporate *we* representing the whole corporation and the use of the high-frequency chunk *we need to*, which often has the force of "you must" but without the authoritarian overtones of a command, that is to say, power manifesting itself most effectively and productively as an expression of (pseudo)solidarity (see also Drew & Heritage, 1992).

The all-pervasive nature of deixis can often make it difficult to interpret conversational transcripts. Consider the example in Figure 11.

> <Speaker 1> If I can crawl **under here** < pause > I.
> <Speaker 2> Yes, I **just** wanna have a look at
> < pause > yes you can crawl **under there** to your
> heart's content! < pause > You can unplug **that**
> for the moment. < pause > I'm not really worried
> about it.
> <Speaker 1> No, I **just**, thinking it's easier if I take
> it down **this way**.
> <Speaker 2> Oh alright.
> <Speaker 1> Then I pull it < pause > < unclear >.
> <Speaker 2> Now, < unclear > < pause >
> Ultimately < pause > er < pause > they might
> change the lead on the end of **that** monitor.
> < pause > What's the matter?
> <Speaker 1> **I was wondering** < pause > where
> the socket is. < pause > Oh I see where it's gone!

Figure 11. Use of deixis (from the British National Corpus).

Here we see ample evidence of real-time-ness in the false starts, truncated utterances, and pausing. We see the highly context-dependent nature of *it* and the dependence on deictic references, which are relative to the speaker and listener and the objects in the context in which the interaction is taking place (Speaker 1 says: *If I can crawl under here*; Speaker 2 replies: . . . *you can crawl under there* . . .). We see examples of how the listener responds to what is being said using response tokens (*Oh alright*). We also see how the speakers carefully word what they say so as not to sound too forceful or blunt. For example, *I just wanna have a look* . . . instead of the more direct sounding *I wanna have a look* . . . and *I was wondering where the socket is* instead of saying *where is the socket?*

In looking at how we structure what we say, it is very important to take all the contextual factors into account. Much of what we say and how we say it relates to the face-to-face context in which our interaction takes place. Most of all, we orient what we say to our listeners in context. Next we look in greater detail at the implications of the face-to-face nature of the grammar of spoken language.

Face and politeness and spoken grammar

The field of pragmatics has long concerned itself with how speakers relate to one another in terms of conveying and negotiating meanings and intentions in contexts, and spoken grammar is, par

excellence, the study of grammatical forms and their functions in immediate, shared contexts.

The notion of *face* is a key concept in pragmatics (Brown & Levinson, 1987) and spoken grammar serves this need in face-to-face interaction. The notion of face is concerned with two goals: (1) showing esteem/respect for one's fellow human beings (often referred to as positive face or positive politeness); and (2) not imposing on them (often referred to as negative face or negative politeness). We can show positive face through grammar by using, where available, respectful forms (e.g., many languages distinguish between respectful and familiar forms for *you*). In English, the system of situational ellipsis illustrated earlier plays a part in this (compare *Want a coffee?* with *Do you want a cup of coffee?*), as does the modal verb system. *May I help you?* is considered more oriented toward politeness and respect for the listener than *Can I help you?* Likewise, *Would/Could you help me?* is considered less of an imposition on the listener than *Will/Can you help me?* or just *Help me!*

While the goals of positive and negative politeness pertain to both speaking and writing, there are very important differences. First of all, positive politeness (showing respect or esteem to the person we are speaking or writing to) is particularly important in writing, where how we address our interlocutor can only manifest itself in what we write. For example, addressing a professor as *Hi Jenny* in an email is not normally acceptable. However, it may be acceptable in some face-to-face situations, for example, at an end-of-semester class party where the context is very informal and where first names are generally being used. On the other hand, negative politeness (not imposing on your interlocutor) is important in writing, but it is even more crucial in face-to-face communication. One of the main ways in which we show negative politeness in speaking is by softening or hedging what we say so as not to impose on our listener. This means carefully choosing less direct structures. In terms of grammar, this can be expressed in a number of forms. Figure 12 is an example of someone making a suggestion, using *well, I was thinking, we could, perhaps,* and *if that's okay* to ensure that her suggestion is not seen as too direct by her interlocutor.

Forms like these may also be found in writing (polite letters, emails of inquiry, etc.), but in face-to-face interaction, their presence is even more crucial in the immediate creation of a good relationship between speakers. In this respect, hedges in English often exploit the tense-aspect system (other languages

> **Well, I was thinking we could perhaps** take her to Blagden Hall now that's open . . . **if that's okay**

Figure 12. Forms expressing positive politeness (from the British National Corpus).

may exploit the subjunctive mood or particular types of particles). The English past tense can be used to soften requests and bald statements, and the progressive/continuous aspect can add further softening. In a graduate philosophy seminar (Michigan Corpus of Academic Spoken English corpus), one speaker says, when discussing how we perceive things: *I, I, I'm wanting to make a divi- a a distinction between, the way things seem to us, and the characteristics that give rise to, uh those those those seemings.* In this way, the speaker makes less blunt and less direct the stating of an opinion and, consequently, lessens the threat to face for the listener(s). Softening with forms such as *I was wondering, we were hoping,* and so on is common in speech.

The reverse side of this coin, as we have mentioned, is situational ellipsis, where a very direct and familiar relationship between the speaker and listener(s) is projected. The teacher in Figure 6 who said *Everybody finished?* is projecting a friendlier, more informal relationship with the students than might have been generated by *Has/Is everybody finished?* Situational ellipsis can function only if all the participants are enmeshed in the same situation, and so its forms project just that assumption, that everyone is sharing the context. This is an example of another important concept that underpins spoken grammar: the shared space and assumed shared knowledge within which the conversation proceeds. Conversations rely on many shared assumptions, and the more intimate the participants' relationships, the more that can be assumed. Shared assumptions may be related to the world in general, such that a person who says *Oh, raining now!* may be assumed to be referring to the weather, or very locally to the particular situation, such that someone who says *Kids are home!* may be heard naturally as referring to "our kids/the kids we both know." The converse is also true, and situational ellipsis will be puzzling or inappropriate in a context where the speakers share few, if any, assumptions. It is for this reason that written texts created to be read in a separate situation from that of their creation are likely to be more explicit and elaborated; they can less easily assume the reader has an immediate, shared context with the writer.

Grammar and power relations

Another important factor in the face-to-face context of use that impacts on the grammar we choose is the power relationship between the speakers. For example, previously we referred to the pseudo-solidarity created by the use of we need to by powerful individuals in a business context when they really mean "you need to/you must." A counterexample to this is found in Healy and Onderdonk-Horan (in press), who look at trainer-trainee interactions in the context of a hospitality management degree program. They find that the balder and more face-threatening pattern *you need to* prevails over the more hedged *we need to* pattern. In the context of training, the pragmatic ground rules seem to allow for the more face-threatening form because of the overt power imbalance assumed and accepted in the situation. In Figure 13, trainees are working with a chef. In addition to the more direct you need to, we see other direct, or unhedged, uses of language (shown in boldface), which would, in another spoken context, be face-threatening because of the reprimands and forceful directives.

> The strawberries **should be** kept in the fridge as well, they **shouldn't be** out at room temperature. So **you need to** clean as you go, **you need to** clean as you go, okay? When you're out in the industry, **you'll be lucky** if you have that size of a bench to work on, and if you don't keep it tidy you'll have nowhere to do anything. So **you have to** keep it tidy.

Figure 13. Use of unhedged language (from The Cambridge, Limerick and Shannon Corpus).

CLASSROOM APPLICATIONS

In terms of classroom applications for the teaching of spoken grammar, we are in the early stages. Few pedagogical reference grammars, grammar practice books, or general course books acknowledge that there are important differences between spoken and written grammar, and with few exceptions, the grammar that is taught is that which is codified in the written form. Notable exceptions are two major grammars that do make a clear distinction between spoken and written grammar, *Longman Grammar of Spoken and Written English*

(Biber, Johansson, Leech, Conrad, & Finegan, 1999) and *Cambridge Grammar of English* (Carter & McCarthy 2006), which focus on spoken and written grammar and usage. These two publications recognize that the grammar of writing is not the same as the grammar of speaking. Others who have made progress in this respect include those who have conducted corpus studies highlighting the inconsistencies between the English that is found in textbooks and the English that occurs in both spoken and written corpora (e.g., Gilmore, 2004; McCarthy & Carter, 1995; Römer, 2004). Actual examples of classroom material for the teaching of spoken grammar are few, however. McCarthy, McCarten, and Sandiford (2005, 2006) bring into the general course syllabus for an adult English language program a strong emphasis on the spoken language, and their grammar sections are informed by written and spoken corpus data. Many of the features exemplified in this chapter are illustrated and practiced in natural spoken contexts.

A starting point: Noticing

Schmidt (1994b) talks about raising learner awareness through "noticing." (See also Ellis, this volume.) This is a good starting point for the pedagogy of spoken grammar. Many learners are likely to have an educational background where grammar training was based on written norms. However, language learners already know and use spoken grammar conventions in their first language, so the concepts cannot be entirely new and the first language may need to be brought into service in the classroom to raise awareness of how speech is distinct from writing. Students' ultimate need is to be equipped with how to do things like deixis, ellipsis, responses, and hedging in the target language. Three basic noticing tasks are illustrated in Figure 14 (with suggested answers provided in the Appendix).

This first, noticing stage needs to be followed, as in any learning sequence, by opportunities to articulate what has been noticed and to practice

---

Example task 1: Deixis

The words in bold in the conversation below are being used to point to people, places, objects, and time. Put the words or phrases into the grid. Can you figure out what they refer to? Some examples have been done for you.

Pointing to people	Who?	Pointing to places and objects	Where/what?	Pointing to time	When?
Line 1: *I*	points to speaker: *I*	Line 1: *these*	*the shirts*	Line 3: *another day*	

(A mother and a daughter are shopping for clothes.)
1. <Speaker 1> **I**'ll just have a look at **these** shirts **up here**. **They**'re nice Bev.
2. <Speaker 2> Yeah
3. <Speaker 1> **They**'re nice, aren't **they**? Oh we'll come **down another day** and look.

Example task 2: Ellipsis

The following are real examples of people speaking from recordings of conversations.
(a) If they were written sentences, how would you change them?
(b) What is the effect of the changes?
1. What you going to have?
2. Where you going ice-skating?
3. (to a little child) Think you better go in the bath my love!
4. Where you going now, Chantel?
5. Been to the dentist?

Example task 3: Hedging

In each of the examples from spoken language, take out the hedges. What is the effect?
1. Would you mind describing how you got it up there again cos I thought it was quite a good story?
2. If I could just stop you there for a couple of minutes while we have a break.
3. Here's something that you might like to consider.
4. I was wondering if you'd perhaps like to tell us how you're going to manage the business on your own.

Figure 14. Basic noticing tasks (examples adapted from the British National Corpus).

it in meaningful controlled and freer contexts, as shown in the tasks in Figure 15 (with suggested answers provided in the Appendix).

FUTURE TRENDS

As evidenced in this chapter, the availability of spoken corpora has greatly increased our understanding of spoken grammar. However, there is still much more to be done in this area. There is a need for more data and for these data to be more widely available, especially to language teachers. Teachers also need the skills to examine the data in a corpus to build their confidence in using electronic resources of this kind. This means that introductory skills in corpus linguistics need to be added to initial teacher education programs (for discussion, see McCarthy, 2008; O'Keeffe & Farr, 2003).

Example task 4: Hedging

For each pair of sentences, which is direct, (a) or (b)?

1. (a) Tell me the time. (b) Would you mind telling me the time, please?
2. (a) Could I ask you your name? (b) What's your name?
3. (a) You live in Brussels, do you? (b) So you live in Brussels.
4. (a) Don't forget to lock the door. (b) Lock the door, okay?

Example task 5: Hedging

The email below is from a student to her professor is too direct. Rewrite it so that it is more appropriate.

From: Eniko Varga [mailto:eniko.varga@exeter.ac.uk]
Sent: 14 April 2011 12:38
To: John Holmes
Subject: Essay extension

Dear Prof. John
Please give me more time for my essay. I am very busy because I have a lot of other essays to do at the same time.
Your student,
Eniko

Example task 6: Ellipsis

Remove one or more words from each of the following sentences to make them more informal.

1. Have you seen Gillian?
2. Would you like to go for lunch?
3. I can't go out. It's raining again.
4. Do you need any help with your homework?
5. I don't like cities. They're too noisy, you know what I mean?

Example task 7: Ellipsis

The next email message is from a college student to her mother. The student has just has moved to Canada for summer work. Rewrite this email, leaving out as many words as you can. Then discuss why you deleted certain words and not others.

Dear Mom

I'm getting on really well. I've found a house.
I'm sharing with 3 others. I'm still looking
for work. I'll email again soon.
Agata

Example task 8: Responses

For each example, which is the most appropriate response, (a) or (b), for the second speaker to use in reply?

1. Can we have the bill please? (a) Exactly. (b) Absolutely.
2. This restaurant is really nice, but their service is slow. (a) Fine. (b) Right.
3. Are you going to Paul's party? (a) Not really. (b) Probably.
4. I've lost my phone; I'm going to have to buy a new one! (a) What a nuisance! (b) Surely.

Figure 15. Tasks for articulating and practicing noticing.

Learners as well as teachers can draw benefits from observing corpus data, both spoken and written; data-driven learning (DDL) may be seen as an important bridge between raw data and observation-based learning for students (see Chambers, 2010). In DDL, the corpus data are the material, and learners work toward inductive conclusions regarding rules, patterns, and meanings. Since we have stressed that the key to approaching spoken grammar is training in noticing and awareness (because of the inherent difficulty of reflecting on language produced in real time), DDL seems to be a good vehicle for exercising such awareness. However, it may still be necessary to clean up some of the messiness we find in natural conversational data and to be somewhat selective in our choice of which data to present to learners because we do not want the data to become a distraction in the all-important noticing process. A distinct advantage of DDL is that it typically uses concordance lines, where learners can observe many examples of the target grammar displayed together on the computer screen or printout.

There is also huge potential now in the harnessing of technology to simulate face-to-face interaction in course material where students can interact with recorded speakers and play speaking roles in a nonthreatening, private environment; such interaction offers good opportunities for the practice of many of the features we have highlighted in this chapter, whether in multimedia, online, or blended/hybrid courses, where independent online (students working individually with Internet-based materials) and offline (textbook- and/or classroom-based learning) study are combined.

We are a long way from having a complete grammar of spoken language, and it may not be attainable in any case as a single, monolithic, codified description, given that there are so many varieties of any given language. Written grammars can be more easily described in a more uniform manner because writing in most languages tends to be oriented toward agreed-on norms. Spoken grammar has to take context and variety into account. This also has implications for the assessment of speaking. We need to determine how we can better test learners in terms of their interactional competence rather than their ability to produce monologic speech and in terms of their proficiency on a variety of task types.

Most of all, there is a need to foster an acceptance of spoken grammar and an understanding of why differences between spoken and written grammar exist. Prejudices and worries may be lessened if language educators and learners alike become more aware of how and why educated language users exploit spoken grammar and what the role of spoken grammar is in creating successful interaction.

CONCLUSION

We can conclude that nothing we observe in spoken grammar is totally impossible or completely nonexistent in written grammar. Many styles of writing are highly informal, and writing frequently plunders forms from speaking (e.g., advertising copy, text-messaging, Internet chat and email, direct speech in fiction, and tabloid journalism). The forms that characterize spoken grammar have evolved to serve the special needs of face-to-face communication; they are important and should not be dismissed as being of only marginal interest. Spoken communication has become dominant in language teaching and learning in the past three decades or so, and it is likely to become even more important in a global society where mobility and real-time spoken communication are likely to increase. For this reason, looking at spoken grammar separately from written grammar is linguistically valid and is relevant to and useful for language pedagogy.

In this chapter, we set out to address three key questions related to spoken grammar. The first question asked whether there is indeed such a thing as spoken grammar. The second question asked how, if there is a spoken grammar, it differs precisely from written grammar. Third, we asked why differences exist between spoken and written grammars. We hope to have clearly established the existence of spoken grammar and to have shown how it differs from written grammar in a number of ways. The third question is probably the most important, relating to why the differences exist. Our understanding of the concept of spoken grammar hinges on understanding the difference between writing *to* or *for* someone and speaking *with* someone. Speaking with someone is done in real time and draws greatly on the real-time context of the interaction. There is real-time effort on the part of the speakers to orient what they say to their listeners to enmesh separate but overlapping worlds, to mark and signpost what they say, and to nuance it so that it does not sound too direct. Of course, many of these conditions exist when we sit down to write to someone or to address a particular audience, but as we have discussed, when we write we have the time and space to carefully contemplate and edit. In essence, in the midst of face-to-face conversation, the stakes are higher because we do not often have the comfort of editing and starting all over again.

From a pedagogical perspective, the focus has long been on the codified grammar of the written language. It is neater and easier to package. Until the 1980s, we did not have widespread access to equipment to record everyday spoken language (though many scholars used field notes to great effect). Now we do have large samples of spoken language transcribed and more readily available to materials writers. This has no doubt brought some significant progress, as we have discussed; however, there is a long way to go. We point to the great need within teacher education to raise awareness of the differences between spoken and written grammars and to foster an understanding of why these differences exist. The more aware language teachers are of these differences, the greater the chances of progress for learners' understanding and acquisition of spoken grammar as a natural and essential component of their developing proficiency.

SUMMARY

➤ Many items and structures have greatly different frequencies in spoken and written language, reflecting the demands of the two different modes of communication.

➤ Because most everyday speech is face to face, particular features of grammar have specialized pragmatically to serve the needs of face-to-face communication.

➤ Spoken grammar is produced in real time, without the opportunities for careful composition, reflection, and revision that most writing offers, often giving spoken texts, at first glance, an appearance of incompleteness or incorrectness.

➤ Typical spoken grammar features include ellipsis, a great amount of deixis, forms related to directness and politeness, and forms that create and maintain interpersonal relations.

➤ Introducing spoken language into the classroom requires an initial awareness-raising phase before controlled and free practice can be carried out because students will probably not be familiar with the features characteristic of spoken grammar.

DISCUSSION QUESTIONS

1. If you were teaching at an institution where teachers regularly shared their views about the syllabus, how could you convince a skeptical group of colleagues that introducing spoken grammar into the grammar syllabus was an important step to consider?

2. Where and what would be the best places and situations for you to make useful and relevant audio recordings of people speaking English to use as a resource for spoken grammar? What technical and ethical considerations would you need to take into account?

3. To what extent should a spoken grammar syllabus for English be based solely on the usage of native speakers? Should the spoken English of non-native expert users and learners be incorporated into the syllabus?

4. Fluency and accuracy are often contrasted with each other as two separate skills. Do you think what you have read in this chapter has implications for our understanding of the fluency versus accuracy debate? Why or why not?

5. At what levels of proficiency do you think students could or should be introduced to spoken grammar? Elementary? Intermediate? Only advanced? What are the reasons for your choices?

6. The authors note, referring to the tasks in Figure 14, "This first, noticing stage needs to be followed, as in any learning sequence, by opportunities to articulate what has been noticed and to practice it in meaningful controlled and freer contexts." Discuss how you could create opportunities for practice in controlled and freer contexts.

SUGGESTED ACTIVITIES

1. What features (e.g., ellipsis or deixis) would you choose to present in the first lesson on spoken grammar that you give to a class of intermediate students with mixed first languages? Choose two features, and make a lesson plan for a 10- to 15-minute classroom activity.

2. How could you encourage students to increase their awareness of spoken grammar outside the classroom (e.g., through listening to the target language, using the Internet, or reflecting on their own first language)? Design a homework task or out-of-class activity that will encourage learners to develop awareness of spoken grammar.

3. Access an Internet chat room, email, or a social-networking site in the language you teach. What features typical of spoken grammar can you observe in the messages/postings that people leave? How could you use such material in your own teaching?

4. List some situations (e.g., friends in a café, a TV chat show) where it would be fruitful to make recordings of people speaking so that you and your students could observe the features of spoken grammar. Compare your list with someone else's. What problems do you foresee in collecting such data?

FURTHER READING

Carter, R., & McCarthy, M. (1995). Grammar and the spoken language. *Applied Linguistics, 16*(2), 141–158.

The authors not only argue in favor of many of the features discussed in this chapter but also look at whether and how the popular language teaching texts of the time include them.

Leech, G. (2000). Grammars of spoken English: New outcomes of corpus-oriented research. *Language Learning, 50*(4), 675–724.

This is an important paper that surveys work done to address the broad question of whether there is a spoken grammar and how different it might be from written grammar.

McCarthy, M., & Carter, R. (2001). Ten criteria for a spoken grammar. In E. Hinkel & S. Fotos (Eds.), *New perspectives on grammar teaching in second language classrooms* (pp. 51–75). Mahwah, NJ: Lawrence Erlbaum Associates.

The authors present a list of what they consider to be the 10 most important issues in describing and implementing a spoken grammar (of English) in language pedagogy.

APPENDIX: ANSWER KEY TO TASKS

Example task 1: Deixis (Figure 14)

Pointing to People	Who?	Pointing to Places and Objects	Where/What?	Pointing to Time	When?
Line 1: *I*	points to speaker: *I*	Line 1: *these*	the shirts		
		Line 1: *up here*	points to the place in the shop where the shirts are displayed		
		Line 1: "they"	the shirts		
Line 3: *we*	points to the two speakers	Line 3: *they* (twice)	the shirts	Line 3: *another day*	some day in the future which is not the day on which the speakers are speaking
		Line 3: *down*	to the shop or shopping mall		
Line 10: *I*	points to speaker: *I*				

Example task 2: Ellipsis (Figure 14)

1. What **are** you going to have?
2. Where **are** you going ice-skating?
3. (to a little child) **I** think you **had** better go in the bath my love!
4. Where **are** you going now, Chantel?
5. **Have you** been to the dentist?

The changed sentences sound a little more formal and less friendly.

Example task 3: Hedging (Figure 14)

1. **Describe** how you got it up there again. I thought it was quite a good story.
2. **Stop** there for a couple of minutes while we have a break.
3. Here's something that you **must/have to/need to/should/ought to** consider.
4. **Tell** us how you're going to manage the business on your own.

The changed sentences sound more direct and abrupt, and as if spoken by a person in authority. In Sentence 3, *must, have to,* and *need to* are very direct and assertive.

Example task 4: Hedging (Figure 15)

1. a	2. b	3. b	4. b

Example task 5: Hedging (Figure 15)

Suggested answer. Other answers are possible.

From: Eniko Varga [mailto:eniko.varga@exeter.ac.uk]
Sent: 14 April 2011 12:38

To: John Holmes
Subject: Request for Essay extension

Dear Professor Holmes: [using the professor's family name is more polite]
I would be very grateful if you could give me more time for my essay. At the moment, I am very busy because I have a lot of other essays to do at the same time. I apologise if this inconveniences you in any way, but would be very glad of being able to have a little more time to complete the essay.
I look forward to your reply.

Your student,
Eniko

Example task 6: Ellipsis (Figure 15)

1. Seen Gillian? / You seen Gillian?
2. Like to go for lunch?
3. (I) can't go out. Raining again. [The speaker might retain *I* here if it is not clear who the sentence refers to.]
4. Need any help with your homework?
5. Don't like cities. Too noisy, know what I mean?

Example task 7: Ellipsis (Figure 15)

Dear Mom
Getting on really well. Found a house. Sharing with 3 others. Still looking for work. I'll email again soon.

Agata

I in the first sentence is omitted because Agata can assume that Mom knows that she is referring to herself. In the second sentence, the subject *I* and the auxiliary verb *have* (contracted to *'ve* in the original) can be omitted because they are obvious to the reader in this context. Again in the third sentence, the subject and the auxiliary verb (*I'm*) can be omitted because they are understood in context by Mom (the reader). However, note that the subject pronoun and auxiliary verb (*I'll*) are retained in the last sentence; otherwise the sentence would become a command to the mother to email Agata. (It is also possible to delete just the pronoun, keeping the auxiliary verb *will: Will email again soon.*)

Example task 8: Responses (Figure 15)

1. b	2. b	3. b	4. a

ENDNOTES

[1] The transcription conventions used in the examples are as follows: < > indicates the speaker who is starting his or her turn (e.g., <speaker 1>); . . . indicates a pause longer than a second; [ ] indicates nonlinguistic or nonverbal behavior (e.g., [laughter]); + indicates a "latched" or overlapping turn, where the second + sign indicates a continuation of what the speaker was saying at the first + sign; and - indicates the false start of a word or phrase (e.g., It's st- it's a little). Words set in boldface are discussed in the chapter.

[2] Information on the Cambridge, Limerick and Shannon Corpus is available at http://www.englishprofile.org/index.php?option=com_content&view=article&id=67:top-of-the-clas-new-corpus-to-benefit-english-profile-programme&catid=901:news&Itemid=9

[3] The British National Corpus is available at http://www.natcorp.ox.ac.uk/

[4] The American National Corpus is available at http://americannationalcorpus.org/

[5] The Michigan Corpus of Academic Spoken English is available at http://quod.lib.umich.edu/m/micase/

[6] We call these responses non-minimal, even though they may be brief, because they do more than give a minimal acknowledgment or a *yes* or *no*. They show interpersonal engagement and involvement with what the other speaker has said.

19 | Teaching and Learning Vocabulary for Second Language Learners

CHERYL BOYD ZIMMERMAN

KEY QUESTIONS

➤ What does it mean to know a word?

➤ What do you think is most challenging about vocabulary teaching and learning?

➤ How would you go about selecting the words that you should teach?

EXPERIENCE

Hi dear teacher,

I am writing this in the **intermission** between classes to tell you of my **extolment** for your class. Your group work **rouses a deep sense of admiration and joy** within me. I enjoy **every step of the work** in your class. It **comes without speaking** that your class is the best. I don't know how to **give vent to my feelings**. You help me with the **difficultness** of English. I know other **guys** and I **suggest them** to take your class. I'm **so much happy** to be student of a **sagely teacher** such as you and getting your **advices.** Your help is beyond **valuability.**

    Bye for now,
    Teo

WHAT DOES IT MEAN TO KNOW A WORD?

What is it about the word use in Teo's expressive letter that does not sound quite right, even though we understand its message? It appears that he knows enough about the words to communicate, but there are gaps in his word knowledge. For example, to know a word means to know a considerable amount about its meaning; Teo uses the word *intermission* ("a short period of time between the parts of a play, film, concert, etc.") to apply to the *break* between classes. He knows the literal meaning of *to give vent*

to his feelings but misses the subtle distinction that *vent* is usually used with negative feelings (*I vented my anger*). In addition, to know a word or phrase means to know its *collocations,* or how it is used in combination with other words; for example, although *every step of the way* is a recognizable collocation, **every step of the work* is not. While we understand the meaning of **It comes without speaking,* we are accustomed to the formulaic expression *It goes without saying.* Knowing a word also means to know its grammatical function (e.g., *suggest* is a transitive verb; *advice* is an uncountable noun) and its word parts (e.g., *difficulty* rather than **difficultness,* and *value* rather than **valuability*). Finally, knowing a word means to know its register, or level of formality. *Extolment* is a noun (meaning "enthusiastic praise and admiration"), but it is very formal and infrequently used. Teo also uses several other very formal terms (*rouses a deep sense of admiration and joy*) along with some very informal ones (*guys; Bye for now*).

This letter demonstrates the enormity of the word-learning task; there are many words to know and many details to be known about each word. I. S. P. Nation (1990, p. 31) sheds light on the word-learning task, suggesting that word knowledge includes the mastery of the word's:

- *Meaning(s):* What does the word mean? Are there multiple meanings? Are there connotations (implied additional meanings)?
- *Written form:* What does the word look like? How is it spelled?
- *Spoken form:* What does it sound like? How is it pronounced?

- *Grammatical behavior:* In what patterns does it occur?
- *Collocations:* What words are often used before or after the word? Are there certain words we must use with this word?
- *Register:* Is the word formal or informal? Where can I expect to hear it or use it?
- *Associations:* How does this word relate to other words? What words could we use in place of this one?
- *Frequency:* Is this word common? Is it rare? Old-fashioned?

This knowledge about the aspects of each word is referred to as *vocabulary depth*. But vocabulary depth is not Teo's only concern. In addition, he needs to know an enormous number of words, referred to as *vocabulary breadth*. Word knowledge is further described by distinguishing between *receptive knowledge* (recognizing a word in reading or listening) and *productive knowledge* (using a word in writing and speaking). Teo's letter is a demonstration of his productive knowledge; a reading or listening task would be a demonstration of his receptive word knowledge.

Considerable vocabulary research and methodology illuminate the challenges faced in the word-learning task. In this chapter, I focus on the nature of word learning and on how to facilitate effective word use, beginning with some basic background.

Counting words and managing word counts

How many words are there in English? That seems a simple question, but answers vary greatly. What do we include as a *word?* For example, is *tongue in cheek* or *first of all* one word or three? Are *differ, difference, different,* and *differently* one word or four? How many words do we count for *gross*, as in *gross national product* and *gross* (disgusting) *food?* Do we include proper names such as *Washington, McDonald's,* and *PowerPoint?* And which words count as English words? Do we include words associated with French cooking and Japanese martial arts?

For the same reasons, it is challenging to state how many words a learner should know. Some people answer this question by counting the words in very large dictionaries. For example, the second edition of the 20-volume *Oxford English Dictionary* contains over 180,000 entries. However, this hardly represents the realistic language use of most people. There are more reasonable ways to estimate the number of words a speaker needs to know and to describe the scope of the word-learning task, including the use of word families. A word family includes the base word, its inflections (the word with affixes added according to the requirements of grammar, such as adding *–s* to a verb to mark the third person singular) and its derivatives (the word with affixes that change the word class or part of speech of the word, such as the suffix *–ness*, which changes an adjective to a noun). For example, the word family for *publish* includes the base word (*publish*), its inflections (*publishes, published, publishing*), and its derivatives (*publisher* [noun], *unpublished* [adjective], and *published* [adjective]).

Word families have been used by many researchers to estimate vocabulary size. For example, Zechmeister (1995) estimates that educated first language (L1) speakers of English know about 20,000 word families, not including proper nouns. Roughly speaking, L1 speakers learn about 1,000 word families per year throughout childhood, and some have learned as many as 5,000 words per year (Nagy & Anderson, 1984). This suggests that those who begin learning English after childhood will have a considerable deficit, even if they are able to learn at the L1 rate of 1,000 word families per year once they begin. Word learning is thus a moving target; L1 speakers continue to learn at this rate, while second language (L2) speakers try to keep up while also trying to make up for lost time.

What do L2 word learners need as they approach the word-learning task, and how can we help them? Central interests of language educators today include language use and authentic communication, but these have not always been the priority. Before we focus on the current perspective, let us take a look at history.

A historical look at vocabulary instruction

The role of vocabulary in L2 instruction has changed over time; it has been perceived and prioritized differently. I highlight six of the relatively recent approaches here, focusing on how they viewed and presented vocabulary (Schmitt, 2000). (See Celce-Murcia, this volume, for a more thorough discussion of the history of approaches to language teaching.)

Grammar-translation approach. The primary goals of this approach were to prepare students to study the classics and to pass standardized exams. Students were not expected to use the language for communication. Their skill was evaluated according to their ability to translate from the target language into the mother tongue, to analyze structures, and to conjugate verbs. Words were chosen according to their occurrence in the classics and their usefulness in demonstrating grammatical rules. The teaching of vocabulary primarily covered definitions and etymology (word origins). It was during this time that bilingual dictionaries became commonplace as reference tools. This method dominated language teaching at least as late as the 1920s. It has been challenged on many fronts.

Reform approach. In reaction to grammar-translation, the purpose of the reform approach,[1] a primarily British movement, was the development of phonetic training or *oral language fluency,* defined here as accurate pronunciation of connected passages. Phonetic training and carefully controlled spoken language were emphasized. Isolated words or sentences were avoided. For the first time, emphasis was placed on language associated with reality, not grammatical patterns or isolated words. Target words were selected according to their simplicity and usefulness; students were not to be distracted by interesting words. Since reformers focused on the sentence rather than isolated words, they chose simple, practical, and even dull words (e.g., names of household items and articles of clothing) that would not distract learners from the central task of phonetic training.

Direct method. Another reaction against grammar-translation, the purpose of this approach is to produce students who could communicate in the foreign language. Still used today in the Berlitz method, interaction in the target language is the focus of every lesson and use of the mother tongue is not allowed. Words are chosen for their familiarity and their use in classroom interaction; this includes everyday items that can be fit into classroom exchanges (e.g., objects in the classroom and parts of body). Charts, pictures, and realia came to be used at this time.

Reading approach. This approach was in part a response to the 1929 Coleman report (A. Coleman, 1929), which showed declining reading scores in U.S. schools. It challenged the past by focusing on reading and on a scientific and quantifiable approach to the selection of target-language content. It suggested that reading skill could be improved by the development of vocabulary, and it criticized stressing speech without selecting content in a principled way. One result of this scientific and quantifiable focus was the Vocabulary Control Movement, which was the beginning of word lists based on frequency. Vocabulary was considered primary in language instruction, and words were chosen according to their usefulness and frequency. It was during this period that *A General Service List of English Words* (GSL) was published by Michael West (1953). This list of the 2,000 most frequent words in English is still widely used today in research and course materials.

Audiolingualism. Audiolingualism (ALM) emphasized oral-aural skills and focused on syntax and language structure. It was based on the behaviorist view of habit formation and featured modeling, drills, memorization, and feedback. Charles Fries, a structural linguist and the ALM founder, believed that syntactic structure was the starting point of language learning, and he saw vocabulary as objects used to illustrate grammatical points. He believed that too much focus on words could give learners the false impression that they knew the language because they knew some words. His solution was to choose simple and familiar words so students would not put too much faith in their word knowledge.

Communicative Language Teaching. This term encompasses many differing methods, but the uniting feature is the belief that language is meant for communication. The goal is the ability to communicate rather than the understanding of structures. This goal includes linguistic creativity, which is quite different from the previous approaches based on habit formation. Vocabulary is chosen from authentic materials according to their usefulness. Corpora have recently played a role in identifying target words as they are authentically used. I discuss corpus use in more detail later in the chapter. (For a more thorough discussion of historical trends in second language vocabulary acquisition, see Zimmerman, 1997b.)

Changes in approaches to teaching words. Vocabulary research was once criticized for focusing on teaching rather than word learning and for providing little information about how words are learned (Meara, 1980). Today, we have considerable research that illuminates the word-learning process and that better prepares us for vocabulary instruction. Highlights of that research are discussed next.

CONCEPTUAL UNDERPINNINGS

Intentional and incidental learning

Word learning involves both *intentional learning* (the focused study of words; also referred to as *explicit learning*) and *incidental learning* (as when words are picked up while one's attention is focused on language use). Current teaching methods favor meaning-based approaches, believing that language features are acquired through use rather than only through direct instruction. Nevertheless, research suggests that some features are best acquired incidentally, while others benefit from explicit treatment. I. S. P. Nation (2001) suggests that form, collocation, and word class are best picked up incidentally, while aspects of meaning, register, and other constraints on use are best learned through explicit instruction. Schmitt (2008) sees a broader role for intentional learning, suggesting that many features of vocabulary require explicit attention because learners often do not notice the features of use when their attention is focused on the message (for thorough discussions of intentional and incidental learning, see I. S. P. Nation, 2001; Schmitt, 2008).

One way that incidental word-learning features prominently is in reading. Vocabulary knowledge is widely accepted as a key predictor to reading success (Laufer & Ravenhorst-Kalovski, 2010), and a great deal of vocabulary growth is a direct result of reading (Nagy, Herman, & Anderson, 1985). But the task of benefiting from reading is not an easy one. It is estimated that learners need to know approximately 98% of the words in an oral or written text to comprehend it (Hu & Nation, 2000; Laufer & Ravenhorst-Kalovski, 2010). In a passage of 50 words, knowledge of 98% of the words means that only one word is unknown. This high rate of coverage is needed to guess words in context, make inferences from the clues, and otherwise grasp the content. In addition, to have 98% coverage when reading novels or newspapers, the reader must know 8,000–9,000 word families (plus proper nouns). To have 98% coverage for spoken English, learners must know 6,000–7,000 word families (plus proper nouns). The considerable challenge of reading is referred to as the *beginner's paradox*; beginning readers do not know enough words to comprehend the text, but they need to read to acquire new words (I. S. P. Nation, 1990; see Schmitt, 2008, for a discussion of the research related to vocabulary size).

The incremental nature of word learning

Word learning is *incremental*, that is, information about a word is gathered gradually over time. Considerable attention is needed to address the many details of what it means to know a word. What we might consider an "error" could be an indication of partial knowledge. For example, when Teo wrote in the letter that begins this chapter that he wanted to *give vent to his feelings*, he demonstrated that he knew the basic meaning, the grammatical form, and the collocations of the words. We say his knowledge was partial because he did not know that *vent* usually has a negative connotation. Similarly, when he used *difficultness* and *valuability*, he demonstrated knowledge of the base words (*difficult* and *value*) and of the noun suffixes (*–ness* and *–ity*) but combined the parts inaccurately.

These aspects of word knowledge can be disruptive to a learner's intended meaning and accuracy. Effective vocabulary instruction can address the incremental nature of word learning by including the following.

Repetition. Word learning is dependent on repeated exposure to target words in context because there is so much to learn about a word that the learner needs to meet it several times to gain the information needed. Popular wisdom accepts that learners need to meet a word 7, 10, or even 20 times, but the particulars of this finding are hard to pin down because different researchers have used differing research designs that are difficult to compare. For example, what is meant by having *learned* a word? What is meant by *context*? Citing some of the limitations of earlier studies, Webb (2007) controls for more factors and concludes that: (1) for each repetition of a word, some aspect of at least one feature of word knowledge was gained; and (2) ten repetitions of any unknown word did lead to learning gains, but full word knowledge was apt to take more than 10 encounters.

Spaced repetition.   It is not only the number of times that one encounters a word that is important to learning but also the spacing between the repetitions. Memory research has revealed that most forgetting takes place immediately after the first encounter with new information. That is, the older the piece of knowledge is, the more slowly it will be forgotten. This suggests that the first several encounters should be close together, with later encounters spaced further apart. So, rather than studying a word for one 15-minute period, learners should study it for 3 minutes initially, then for 3 minutes a few hours later, then for 3 minutes the next day, then for 3 minutes 2 days later, and finally a week later. Fifteen minutes spread across several days at progressive intervals will lead to longer retention than 15 minutes spent all at one time (I. S. P. Nation, 2001).

Opportunities to focus on both meaning and form.   As previously discussed, some word learning requires explicit attention, while other learning takes place incidentally when learners are engaged in meaningful interaction. Learners need opportunities to focus on both meaning and form, and they need opportunities to produce the word. I. S. P. Nation proposes what he calls "the four strands," which include a balance between meaning and form: (1) focusing on meaning-focused input; (2) focusing on meaning-focused output; (3) focusing on language-focused learning; and (4) focusing on fluency development. This approach highlights the importance of providing a balanced variety of opportunities for learners to produce the word and to focus on both form and meaning (see I. S. P. Nation, 2008, for further discussion of the four strands).

Engagement.   Engaging topics and tasks lead learners to thoughtful analysis and provide opportunities for them to reflect on words and their use. Research shows that learners are more likely to remember words when they pay attention to them and have to manipulate them. For example, Laufer and Hultstijn (as cited in Schmitt, 2008) find that learners who used target words in a writing task remembered them better than those who saw them only in a reading task, in part because they needed to understand a linguistic aspect of the word to complete the task and they were required to search for the information (see Schmitt, 2008, for a discussion of research related to engagement and vocabulary).

Interaction and negotiation.   Any activity that leads to more exposure, attention, time, and manipulation can add to word learning. Tasks involving oral interaction and negotiation can lead to all of these. When learners discuss the meanings of words in groups, for example, useful information can be exchanged about the words, and all aspects of word knowledge can be called on and discussed (Newton, 1993; Zimmerman, 1997a). For example, Newton (1995) reports that the words that learners acquired were the ones they used most frequently in interactions. For the words that learners saw only on worksheets and did not use in interactions, there was no improvement.

The role of materials in vocabulary instruction

Schmitt (2008) has suggested that there are four partners in the vocabulary learning task: students, teachers, researchers, and materials writers. Textbooks and resource materials guide teachers in which words they teach and how.

Textbooks.   In many cases, textbooks are a source of training for teachers and play an important role in spreading ideas across the English language teaching profession. In a study investigating the nature of vocabulary teaching in nine general English textbooks from the beginning to intermediate levels, D. Brown (2011) concludes that textbooks have a narrow perspective on the word knowledge they present, giving most attention to form and meaning (51.8%) and less to grammatical functions (29%) and spoken form (14.8%); the remaining six aspects (including associations; collocations; word parts; and constraints on use, including register) received very little attention in the textbooks. In light of these findings, think back to the letter written by Teo (at the beginning of this chapter) and remember the difficulties that were reflected in it. Some of the aspects that were a challenge to him (e.g., collocations, word parts, frequency of use, and register) might have never been addressed in his course textbooks.

Dictionary use. Dictionaries are a rich and often underused source of information. They differ greatly in their purposes and intended audiences, so they should be selected carefully. Many English as a second/foreign language dictionaries are based on corpora (large, principled collections of naturally occurring text). Corpus-based dictionaries are rich sources of information for the language learner because they feature information drawn from authentic use, information about contexts, and nuances of meaning. Examples of widely used corpus-based dictionaries are the *Cambridge Dictionary of American English, Longman's Dictionary of Contemporary English,* and the *Oxford American Dictionary for Learners of English.* Learner's dictionaries are designed with the purpose of clearly explaining words and teaching word use to learners of English; they have clear definitions and example sentences that draw on a limited number of words. Unlike dictionaries written for native speakers of English, bilingual dictionaries, and most electronic dictionaries, learner's dictionaries include information about all aspects of word knowledge: collocation, grammatical forms, register, word parts, and more. For example, compare the entries for the noun form of *interior* in Table 1.

Table I Comparison of Dictionary Entries for the Noun *Interior*

Random House Webster's College Dictionary (2001)	Oxford Basic American Dictionary for Learners of English (2011)	Dictionary.com (on cell phone)
interior – n the internal or inner part; space or regions within; inside.	interior – noun [count, usually singular] the inside part: *We painted the interior of the house white.*	In-te-ri-or [in-**teer**-ee-er] inside

Selecting the words to be taught

Even the best teachers in the most ideal settings can never teach all of the words that learners need. Choices need to be made. When deciding which words to address, teachers will find it useful to distinguish between increasing vocabulary (introducing new words) and establishing vocabulary (building on and strengthening partial word knowledge). Both are important. I. S. P. Nation (1990) argues that "old material in any lesson is the most important" (p. 7), in part because of the incremental nature of word learning. It is wise to build on initial investments in word learning by giving known words more attention and giving learners a chance to focus on new aspects of a word in contextualized settings. Therefore, teachers will want to select words that their students have seen before but may not be able to use in their own production. They will also want to select new words that students will need. These choices should be guided by students' needs, including their level of learning and their academic and professional goals. These choices can be informed by: (1) the word's frequency; (2) the word's salience in the course content; and (3) corpus use.

Word frequency. The most important words in any language are those that are most frequent. The GSL, for example, is a high-frequency word list made up of the 2,000 word families that occur most frequently in a variety of domains (conversation, newspapers, novels, news programs, etc.); these high-frequency words make up at least 80% of written texts and 90% of conversation (I. S. P. Nation, 2008). Some frequency lists are designed for specific groups of learners. For example, the Academic Word List (AWL)[2] contains approximately 570 word families that occur most frequently in academic materials across four academic domains (business, the humanities, law, and the physical and life sciences). It is based on a corpus of 3.5 million words and is designed to guide word selection for general academic preparation in all fields. The criteria for inclusion on this list were that the words not appear on the GSL and that they occur frequently and uniformly across the four domains. The AWL is used widely in dictionaries and course materials (see Coxhead, 2000). Other frequency lists identify technical words (words frequently used in specific fields such as science, medicine, or math).[3]

Salience in course content. A word is salient when it is of central importance in a given context. Salience leads to retention of the word both because the learner needs the word to comprehend the meaning of the content and because its central role leads to natural repetitions of the word.

Therefore, when selecting target words from a reading passage (see example in Figure 1), select those that have a central role in the content of the passage. This will allow the learners to use the target words as they read the text, discuss it, complete activities, and write about the text.

> Coober Pedy is a small town in Southern Australia which contains the world's richest sources of opal, a valuable **gem**. In order to **survive** the town's **harsh** heat, dust storms and flies, the **miners** live underground. Three-bedroom homes, hotels, restaurants and churches are all dug into the hills, where the **temperature** is cool and life is comfortable. This **mining** town is now often visited by **hearty** tourists who are interested in this unique story of **survival**.

Figure 1. Example of salient vocabulary in a reading passage.

Corpus use.   Today, we not only have easy access to a variety of frequency lists, but we also have access to extensive authentic written and spoken English through corpus-based research. *Corpora* (the plural form of *corpus*) are "large, principled collections of naturally occurring texts (written or spoken) stored electronically" (Reppen, 2010, p. 2). In vocabulary studies, corpora are used to generate word lists and to help identify word frequency in various domains. In addition, corpus-based investigations can be used by teachers to generate lists of frequent words that students will encounter in specific articles or genres.

Word counts, word lists, and corpus-informed materials are useful as guides, but their use should be tempered by common sense. For example, an English as a second language course for immigrant housewives should at some point deal with vocabulary related to visiting a doctor, whether or not the words appear on a frequency list, in the materials, or in a given corpus. Likewise, an orientation course for international students should include words referring to the campus and campus life, regardless of their inclusion on the academic lists in their fields of study. Before the mid-1980s, there was limited research related to L2 vocabulary learning. Today there is more research available than most of us can manage, but much of it is not reflected in language classrooms. For example, while research demonstrates the complex nature of word knowledge and the incremental process of word learning, teachers too often present words with definitions only and oversimplify the word-learning process. In a rich discussion about the complexity of the mental lexicon and of word learning, Singleton (1999) describes the current state of vocabulary teaching as "address[ing] only the tip of the lexical iceberg" (p. 272). Effective vocabulary teaching addresses the totality of the word-learning process. In the next section, I present activities that are principled, interactive, and meaningful to help teachers facilitate the word-learning process.

CLASSROOM APPLICATIONS

Word-learning activities

Effective activities address the incremental nature of word learning in a variety of ways. They prioritize repetition, engagement, and interaction, and they provide opportunities to focus both on form and meaning. Whenever possible, they provide chances to be content-rich and to elicit authentic language. For our purposes here, activities are divided into three levels:

1. *Word level.* Words are practiced in isolation, focusing on features such as meaning, derivative use, spelling, pronunciation, some grammatical features, associations, and register.
2. *Sentence level.* Words are practiced as they occur in sentences, using collocations and grammatical forms.
3. *Discourse or fluency level.* Words are practiced in paragraphs or longer content-rich segments, often focusing on fluency along with accuracy.

Word-level activities.

Ranking.   Select five to eight target words that are familiar to students but that they have not mastered. Have students rank them according to one of the following, and then compare their answers with a partner.

- Rank words from easy to difficult in spelling, pronunciation, or grammatical form. (How easy is it to put into a sentence?)
- Rank words from frequent to infrequent. (How often do people use this word?)
- Rank words according to importance for work, study, personal relationships, travel, or some other area.

- Rank related words (e.g., a list of appliances, electronic devices, or tools) according to affordability, practicality, dependability, entertainment value, or importance to people in general.

Practice with word parts: A picture tells a story. Write a four-column chart on the board, and label the columns with the parts of speech, as in Table 2. Select a picture (from a book, a magazine, or an Internet source such as Google Images) related to an interesting topic. Select three to five words that could be used to describe or ask questions about the picture. Ask students to place each word in the appropriate column of the chart according to its part of speech; then fill in the remaining cells with word forms derived from the original words. Mark an X in each cell that has no word form that fits. Table 2 presents a sample chart related to the topic of symbolic clothing. In this example, the teacher could use the picture of a bride and groom, a judge in a robe, a student dressed for graduation, or military personnel in uniform.

Table 2. Sample Word Chart for the Activity: A Picture Tells a Story

Noun	Verb	Adjective	Adverb
symbol symbolism	symbolize	symbolic	symbolically
convention	X	conventional	conventionally
importance	X	important	importantly
significance	signify	significant	significantly

How strong are these words? On the board, list several adjective pairs with opposite meanings, chosen according to the students' level (e.g., inept/expert; dumb/brilliant; early/late; apathetic/energetic; compassionate/unfeeling).

- For each word pair, draw a straight line on the board to represent a continuum of word strength, placing one word (e.g., *happy*) at the left of the continuum and its antonym (e.g., *mad*) at the right. Leave space for additional words in between or at the ends of the continuum.

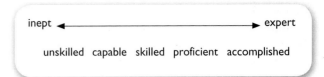

Figure 2. Sample word-strength continuum.

- Have students work in pairs, first copying the continuum onto their own paper. Have them then add three to four words to each continuum, positioning the words according to their relative strengths (e.g., *elated, furious, angry, thrilled, annoyed*). Encourage students to use a thesaurus and to check meanings in a dictionary as needed.
- Have students write the continua on the board. Discuss the answers, noting that they may vary. For example, in Figure 2, there is only a slight difference between *proficient* and *accomplished*.

Phrasal verb practice. Draw a chart on the board similar to the one in Figure 3. Have students copy the chart onto a sheet of paper. Have them work in pairs to complete each phrasal verb with at least one item. For example, for the combination *take* and *on*, they could fill in *(take on) a challenge.* Encourage students to list as many responses as possible. In a class discussion, have students share their results, focusing on the many variations that are possible and how they are used.

	on	in	off	up	down
turn					
bring					
take	a challenge				

Figure 3. Sample phrasal verb chart.

Sentence-level activities.

Strip stories. Choose a short story with transparent sequencing and divide it into sentences. Group students, giving each student a different sentence to memorize. Have each student restate the sentence for the other students in the group, who then decide the order that the sentences should occur in for the story. No writing is allowed. When the ordering is finished, have the group retell the story to the entire class.

A picture tells a story. Refer to the completed four-column chart in Table 2 and the picture used in the word-level activity, "A picture tells a story." Have the students work in pairs, using the target words in questions about or descriptions of the picture.

Discourse-level activities.

How strong are these words? Have students complete the word-level activity "How strong are these words?" that accompanies Figure 2, using words that are suitable for the following scenario. (The teacher explains this scenario to students.)

- Select a university that you would like to attend. Pretend that you have applied to this university and that you have asked a teacher to write a letter of reference for you.
- Now, imagine you are your teacher or an employer: Write a brief letter recommending you for admission to the university. Use as many of the words from the word-strength continuum as possible. Or write a letter that you hope your teacher or employer would *not* write on your behalf. That is, using the idea of word strength, write a letter that describes you in a negative way. For example, "He is quite *inept* at using the computer and is often *late* with his work. He tends to be *apathetic* when given a new task to complete."

Story re-working. Select a short, interesting story or paragraph that is at a suitable level for the students, such as the one in Figure 4. (Possible sources include the course textbook, local or current news sources, or Internet searches on topics such as inventions, famous people, or little-known facts.) Identify three to four appropriate target words. (They should be salient to the story and useful for the students.) Write the words on the board, discuss their meanings, and answer any questions about them. Use any of the following activities with the text. (In the sample paragraph in Figure 4, the target words are in **boldface**.)

- *Hear and retell:* Have half of the class (Group 1) leave the room. Read the sample text to the other half of the class (Group 2) and then encourage students to ask questions to clarify the word use. Have Group 1 return, and pair students who heard the story with those who did not. Have students in Group 2 retell the story to their partner using the

Do you ever worry about having bad breath? Some bad breath is related to eating certain foods. In order to **reduce** bad breath usually **associated** with eating garlic or onions, you should **avoid** eating them at the same time that you eat fatty foods. If you do, the fat will **capture** their smell and **release** it each time you **exhale**.

Figure 4. Sample high-interest text.

target words and accurately transmitting the meaning. Compare the stories in a class discussion.

- *Read and retell:* Similar to the hear and retell exercise, give half the class (Group 1) the sample text to read. Have Group 1 read the text and put it away. Pair students in Group 1 with students who have not read the text (Group 2). Have the students in Group 1 retell the text to their partner. (It would be best to have two sample texts, one for Group 1 and one for Group 2. Have each student in the pair retell his or her text.)
- *Synonym search:* Have pairs of students read the sample text and replace as many words as possible with synonyms. The resulting meaning should be similar to the original text. Compare the results in a class discussion.
- *Register re-word:* As in the synonym search exercise, have pairs work together to replace words in the text with synonyms, but this time with the intent of changing the register of the text. For example, in the fairly formal sample text, have students change as many words as possible to informal words, without changing the meaning of the text.

Dictation. Read the sample text slowly to the class, allowing time for students to write; allow as much repetition as needed for accuracy. Then have partners compare their papers, adjusting spelling and language use as needed. Finally, show a copy of the original text to the students. Discuss with the class which features of the text caused the most challenges.

Games. Vocabulary games allow students to isolate and practice particular features of word knowledge such as spelling, word parts, meaning, or grammatical features. Words for the following games can be selected from a recently studied unit or from a given category such as nouns, verbs, food, or math words.

- *Speller line-up:* Give the first student a word to spell. If the student spells it correctly, the next student says a word beginning with the last letter of the word given. Another student then spells that word. If he or she spells it correctly, a new student then nominates a new word beginning with the last letter of the word just given. If a word is misspelled, the student involved is eliminated from the game. The game continues round-robin style until the last student remaining wins the game. Assuming there is interest on the part of the students, a new round of the game can then begin.
- *Hangman:* Divide the class into two teams. Choose a word, and on the blackboard, draw spaces for the number of letters in a word. Have players from each team take turns guessing the letters. When a student guesses a letter that is in the word, write the letter in the correct space. The team's turn continues until one of the members makes an incorrect guess. When a guess is incorrect, start drawing a stick figure of the man being hanged, one body part per incorrect guess, drawing first the head, then the body, an arm, and so on. The team that guesses the word first receives a point. Then start the game over.
- *Password:* Select target words that are level-appropriate for the students and that lend themselves to multiple synonyms. (Consult a thesaurus for ideas.) Have two students stand in front of the room, facing the class. Write the word on the board or a card so that it is visible to everyone except the two "contestants." One at a time, have the rest of the students volunteer one-word clues to help the contestants guess the target word. Contestants take turns guessing the word until the word is guessed. The contestant who guesses the target word remains at the front of the class; the student who gave the final clue replaces the other contestant. *Variation:* Pair students into teams of two players (one A and one B). Have the A players sit side by side, facing the board, and have the B players sit opposite their partners with their backs to the board. Write the target word on the board so the A players can see it. Taking turns, have the A players give a clue word to their partner, who gets one guess for each clue. Points are given to the team that guesses the word first.
- *Adverbs in action:* Divide the blackboard in two. On one side, write as many verbs as the class can call out; on the other side, write adverbs. Then have one team choose a verb and adverb combination, and have the other team act it out (e.g., *laugh hilariously*). Variation: Have one team choose a verb and adverb combination and the other team write a sentence using the combination.
- *Twenty questions:* Select nouns and verbs for this game. Have teams take turns asking *yes-no* questions such as "Is it something you can do?" and "Is it something you can eat?" The team that guesses the word first receives a point. Then start the game over.

Word-learning strategies

Since students learn only a fraction of the words they need in the language classroom and they often have only a partial knowledge of the ones they learn, it is essential that they are equipped to continue vocabulary development on their own. *Word-learning strategies* are the planned approaches that a word learner takes as an agent of his or her own word learning. They are used to discover a word's meaning (e.g., analyzing parts of speech or word parts, guessing meaning from context, using a dictionary, and asking questions about words). They are also used to establish the use of a word once it has been encountered (e.g., studying and practicing the meaning with classmates, using semantic maps, using word cards or a vocabulary notebook, using spaced repetition in word practice, and using English-language media such as songs, movies, and social media). For a discussion of the research and techniques related to word-learning strategies, see Schmitt (1997).

Research suggests that effective strategy use leads to word-learning success. This requires that learners know a variety of strategies, can select them appropriately, and are able to use them effectively

(I. S. P. Nation, 2001; Schmitt, 1997). Learners benefit when a wide variety of strategies are modeled and used as a regular part of classroom practice. The goal is for the strategies to become useful tools for subsequent independent word learning. Following are some ways to shape opportunities in class for vocabulary strategy practice.

Reflection. Perceptive word learners take the time to think about words and reflect on how they are used. They accurately assess their own understanding of a new word, think about the roles and purposes of the people who use the word, and reflect on the information they need to use the word appropriately. Reflection includes the ability to ask insightful questions that will lead to accurate word use:

■ (if the word is a noun) Is it countable or uncountable?

■ (if the word is a verb) Is there a particular preposition that follows it?

■ Is it a formal word?

■ Does it have positive or negative connotations?[4]

Memory aids: Word cards. Word cards (see sample depicted in Figure 5) provide efficient practice in terms of time and effort. They allow learners to practice linking meaning with form and to use recall as they practice. Word cards are convenient and allow learners to practice often and work at their own pace. They can be customized to include information such as the target word's

translation, part of speech, a sample sentence, pronunciation, collocations, and a picture. I. S. P. Nation suggests that word cards are most effective when kept simple: place the target word on one side and translation on the other side of small cards, adding more information only if it helps the learner remember the word. For example, teachers of young learners often ask students to draw a picture. Word cards allow learners to learn words first receptively and then productively; after practicing the meaning, they can put words in sentences, practicing grammatical features and collocations. As with all word practice, cards are most effective when words are processed deeply and thoughtfully (for more about word-card research and techniques, see I. S. P. Nation, 2008).

Vocabulary notebooks. Vocabulary notebooks are used to promote learner independence. Teachers guide learners in what information should be recorded, but learners select the words and record information they have gathered on their own. Notebook entries should contain the target word and about four other categories, such as a sample sentence ("Write the sentence in which it appeared"), dictionary definition, translation, part of speech, pronunciation, word family members, collocations, other occurrences ("If you have seen or heard the word somewhere else, describe where and show how it was used"), or an original sentence ("Use the word in your own sentence").

Research suggests that, when left on their own, learners do not get as much from this exercise as they might. For example, they tend to draw most of their target words from textbooks or test study guides (such as for the Test of English as a Foreign Language [TOEFL]) rather than the many other sources that might be valuable (e.g., newspapers, campus publications, websites, and ads). Learners also have difficulty distinguishing high-frequency words from others and tend to view all words as having equal importance. Teachers can help by providing guidelines on how to select words from relevant sources. They can encourage students to repeat the words in their own sentences and to focus on a variety of features. The notebooks can be collected every few weeks so teachers can follow students' progress and better understand how perceptive students are about noticing what is important.

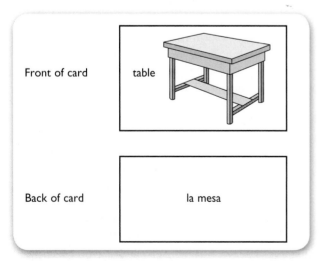

Front of card table

Back of card la mesa

Figure 5. Sample word card.

Teachers do not need to comment on every entry; providing a few suggestions or guiding questions should be enough (e.g., "This is a very useful word. Listen for it in the news or when people are talking about politics" or "Notice the collocations here").

Dictionary use. Dictionary use is not easy; it requires the ability to alphabetize words, incorporate the use of antonyms and synonyms, break a concept down into parts according to its appearance or function, and differentiate similar words. Learners need guidance and practice in using this analytic tool that organizes language. Hands-on dictionary practice is very useful to students, such as the following.

Is that a real word? Pairs of students work together to review a list of words prepared by the teacher, such as the one in Figure 6. (The teacher should be sure that at least some of the words are known to the students.)

Learner's dictionary practice. All students will need a dictionary for this activity. Those who select learner's dictionaries will have an advantage; teachers might use this activity to demonstrate that other dictionaries have less useful information than learner's dictionaries. The teacher should review the aspects of word knowledge and the various symbols used for countable and uncountable nouns, register, and so on. Pairs of students should work together to check how the dictionary might have helped correct the underlined errors in Teo's letter (or another passage).

- I don't know how <u>to give vent</u> to my feelings.
- You help me with the <u>difficultness</u> of English.
- I know other <u>guys</u> and I <u>suggest them</u> to take your class.
- I . . . am happy to be getting your <u>advices</u>.
- Your help is beyond <u>valuability</u>.

Navigating the dictionary: Where is the letter? Students will need a paper dictionary for this activity.[5] Point out that some letters of the alphabet have much larger sections with more words in them than others. Dictate some letters of the alphabet (e.g., *B, E, M, S, Y*), and ask the students to predict which ones might begin the most words in English. Compare the number of pages for the letter *S* with the number of pages for *J* or *K*.

Beyond the planned lesson

No matter how much planning a teacher does, there are always surprises. This is certainly true when one is dealing with the unwieldy nature of words. Effective teachers understand the incremental and often illogical aspects of word knowledge and are willing to analyze their own unconscious knowledge about words as questions and needs arrive. This is a fascinating process and an ongoing endeavor. The following skills will improve with experience and insightful awareness about the nature of word knowledge.

Defining words. A skilled vocabulary teacher can briefly and accurately illuminate the meaning of a new word. First, the teacher should use everyday language and begin the definition by focusing on the basic meaning before moving on to the details. Creating a sample sentence will help the teacher formulate what is important about the word, and the sample sentence will often be clearer to the student because it is less abstract than a definition. Other ways to clarify definitions include:

- Examples (e.g., "Examples of Romance languages are Spanish and French.")
- Negative examples (e.g., "*To slurp* is like *to drink*, but it is noisier, sometimes with a loud sucking sound.")

Put a check mark (✓) beside the words below that are real. Use the dictionary as needed to confirm your guesses. Be prepared to discuss your findings.

procrastinate	cognitive	jastle	cumbersome
retrivane	frugal	impunity	simplistic
eclectic	misdrew	artivious	forensics

Figure 6. Sample dictionary use exercise: Is that a real word?

- Synonyms (e.g., "A synonym for *exhausted* is *very tired*.")
- Antonyms (e.g., "An antonym for *novice* is *expert*.")
- Situational contexts (e.g., "*Sympathy* is what you feel when your friend's father or mother dies or when something else terrible happens to someone.")
- Realia (e.g., food cartons, pictures, toys, and utensils)
- Gesture, pantomime, or demonstration (e.g., When explaining the word *pulse*, the teacher places a hand on his or her own neck and/or wrist and pretends to count.)

In addition, whenever a student asks the meaning of a word, the teacher should find out the context in which the student found the word. The teacher should allow this context to be the guide so that not all possible meanings have to be addressed. For example, if a student asks the meaning of the word *run*, the teacher has many choices of meanings and a summary of them would be very confusing. By asking, "Where did you see the word?" and learning that the student heard the word in reference to a baseball game (as opposed to the act of moving very quickly), the teacher's task of explaining becomes simpler and clearer.

Answering questions about words. Once the definition is clear, the teacher should think beyond the meaning. In what ways could this word cause the students trouble? Is the pronunciation challenging? Is it a transitive verb, therefore requiring an object? For example, the verb *suggest* is often followed by *that*. The teacher should try to anticipate two or three challenging items but select the information to be imparted carefully. He or she should not tell the students everything they need at once; instead, the teacher should learn to understand what is most challenging for word learners. Experience will make these decisions easier. The teacher should not be surprised if students' questions are unexpected. As already mentioned, it is very difficult for a native speaker or a proficient speaker of English to access information that is intuitive or unconscious. The more the teacher can develop his or her own awareness of how words are used, the more the teacher will be able to assist the L2 learners.

FUTURE TRENDS

While vocabulary research once provided little information about how words were learned, much has changed. Considerable research today illuminates the task of word learning and the role of students as agents of their own word learning. Individual learner variables and learner needs are better understood. As research and technology continue to advance, we can expect more access to information about brain function in word learning. We can expect that corpus-based research will continue to help us better understand the nature of authentic language use and will lead to advances in the authentic representation of language in research and instructional materials. Ease of online access should make increasingly targeted information more readily available to classroom teachers. It is hoped that these developments will allow teachers and learners more access to focused and relevant research and information about language use and that the result will be an increase in principled vocabulary instruction in second language classrooms.

CONCLUSION

Just as word learning is daunting for the student, vocabulary teaching may appear intimidating to the instructor. There are so many words! There is so much to know about each word! And there is so little time! Teachers should remind themselves that no single teacher is responsible for covering every word that a student needs or everything a student needs to be know about a word. Students come to class with partial word knowledge that they have picked up on their own or from other teachers. Teachers should be aware of what it means to know a word, and help their students move from this partial knowledge to effective word use. Teachers should use principled instruction as they show learners how to select the new words they invest in, what they need to know about the words, and how to use word learning strategies. And teachers should use every opportunity to demonstrate the importance of repeated exposure to words and of the effective use of word-learning strategies. With a balance of respect for and awareness of the word-learning task, teachers can contribute greatly to the language learning of their students.

SUMMARY

➤ To know a word means to know a great deal about it.

➤ Some aspects of word learning are learned through direct instruction, while others are learned incidentally.

➤ The process of word learning is incremental and includes the development of vocabulary depth, vocabulary breadth, receptive vocabulary, and productive vocabulary.

➤ Teachers should not expect to teach all the words that learners need, but they can equip learners to understand the word-learning process and to effectively use word-learning strategies as independent word learners.

DISCUSSION QUESTIONS

1. As a learner of a second or foreign language, what strategies did you use to learn vocabulary? Which were more successful? Less successful?

2. Some language learners overuse or misuse the dictionary, leading to errors like the use of *extolment* and *sagely* in the letter at the beginning of the chapter. What other types of errors might you expect from the overuse or misuse of a dictionary or a thesaurus?

3. Review the history of second language vocabulary teaching at the beginning of this chapter. Which of the insights from the past do you consider most valuable to us today?

4. In your opinion, what are the primary benefits of using communicative activities to teach vocabulary? Be specific, referring to the four skills of reading, writing, speaking, and listening.

5. As a teacher, are you more concerned about the quality of word learning or the quantity? How will you divide your teaching time between teaching words and teaching word-learning strategies?

SUGGESTED ACTIVITIES

1. Review the letter at the beginning of the chapter. Which of the lexical errors would you correct for this intermediate student? Which would you overlook? Based on this letter, which topic might you prioritize in a future lesson: Collocation? Meaning? Word parts or derivatives? Grammatical forms? Other?

2. Review the meanings of the following terms used in the chapter:

   receptive word knowledge
   productive word knowledge
   vocabulary depth
   vocabulary breath
   word families
   etymology
   explicit instruction
   incidental learning
   increasing vocabulary
   establishing vocabulary
   derivatives
   inflections
   register

   Think about the needs of the word learners in each of the following classroom populations. Select three of the above items that you would prioritize in your instruction for each group.
   a. primary school children in Korea
   b. older adult immigrant Spanish speakers in California, preparing for citizenship
   c. learners preparing for the TOEFL and university entrance
   d. advanced writing students, preparing for a Business English class
   e. other? (Add a setting you are familiar with.)

3. Select a variety of dictionaries, including those that are designed for native speakers of English, designed for learners of English, corpus-based, non-corpus-based, more than 10 years old, and bilingual dictionaries. Look up the following words in each dictionary (or use a list of your choice): *God, interfere, hunger, infer, access, contribute.* Compare the dictionary entries for each word in terms of:
   a. amount of information about each word
   b. clarity and accuracy of definitions
   c. availability and value of sample sentences
   d. availability, accuracy, and usefulness of other information, such as parts of speech, collocations, word parts, register, and

near-synonyms (Note that some of this information changes over time, so the information may vary.)

  e. help with pronunciation
  f. other?

Be prepared to discuss your findings.

FURTHER READING

Leany, C. (2007). *Dictionary activities*. Cambridge, UK: Cambridge University Press.

The aim of this book is to equip teachers to help students know how to select dictionaries and how to make the most of them. It covers relevant topics such as dictionary skill-building, confidence-building, and language-building activities (including vocabulary, grammar, pronunciation, and reading).

Nation, I. S. P. (2001). *Learning vocabulary in another language*. Cambridge, UK: Cambridge University Press.

This is a practical guide to vocabulary instruction that is grounded in a comprehensive and clearly explained collection of research. It is driven by the idea that vocabulary research should be systematically integrated into language instruction.

Zimmerman, C. B. (2009). *Word knowledge: A vocabulary teacher's handbook*. New York: Oxford University Press.

Word Knowledge is written as a handbook for teachers, breaking down the aspects of word knowledge (meaning, collocation, grammatical features, etc.) and showing teachers how to guide students in their mastery of each aspect. It includes examples and activities designed to clarify word teaching and learning.

ENDNOTES

[1] For more information on the reform movement, see Howatt (2004).

[2] Coxhead's *Academic Word List* can be accessed at http://www.victoria.ac.nz/lals/resources/academicwordlist/default.aspx

[3] See Cobb's *The Compleat Lexical Tutor* at http://www.lextutor.ca/ for access to the AWL and the GSL. This site provides useful guidance to teachers in generating their own word lists.

[4] See Zimmerman (2009, p. 117) for more about reflection and for more examples of reflection questions.

[5] This activity is adapted from Leany (2007, pp. 11–12).

Language Skills

Assessing the Language Skills

20 | Large-Scale Second Language Assessment

ANTONY JOHN KUNNAN AND KIRBY GRABOWSKI

KEY QUESTIONS

- ➤ What is large-scale second language assessment?
- ➤ How are large-scale language assessments developed?
- ➤ How do teachers know if an assessment is useful for their purposes?

EXPERIENCE

Sarah is an English as a second language (ESL) teacher in an intensive English program (IEP) in an American university. Many of her students are recent immigrants whose first language is not English. While some of these students are interested in studying in a university after graduation, they have just learned that they must take a large-scale English language proficiency assessment to be considered for admission. They understand the high-stakes nature of the assessment, so Sarah's students want her help in understanding the purpose of the assessment: who the users of the information might be, what the test assessment is like, and how the results are likely to be interpreted. Sarah, therefore, needs a working knowledge of second language assessment theory and practice before she can address their concerns.

Language teachers-in-training are generally required to take courses in language acquisition, teaching methodology, curriculum and materials design, specific teaching skills (e.g., listening, speaking, reading, and writing), pedagogical grammar, discourse analysis, the use of computers, and so on. However, many teachers do not receive much in the way of courses or training in the field of language assessment, either in terms of theory or practical training. A grounded understanding of the principles of language assessment is crucial for teachers in every context of language instruction.

For example, in lesson plans, teachers create teaching or learning targets (or objectives) that need to be met; assessment then helps them figure out whether (and to what extent) those targets have been met. Without assessment, teaching would be incomplete and it would be nearly impossible for students to have any systematic indication of their abilities with respect to what they have been taught. Traditional classroom assessments (e.g., pre-unit checks, essay assignments, homework, midterms, and final exams) are small-scale assessments that teachers need to be familiar with. In addition, both inside and outside school settings, large-scale assessments are increasingly being employed by stakeholders (e.g., teachers, school administrators, employers, and governments) to gather information about what learners know and can do in a second/foreign language. Further, given the wide array of assessments in use today, there are a number of theoretical considerations that teachers-in-training should understand so they can interpret the usefulness and trustworthiness of the data obtained from their own assessments and from those that they may have to use in their teaching contexts. To this end, in this chapter we describe the major theoretical underpinnings of second language assessment and how these concepts support and inform assessment use. We focus here on large-scale assessments in particular; however, most, if not all, of these concepts can, and should, apply to small-scale assessments as well. Our aim is to help classroom teachers better understand the various considerations related to language assessment so that they may make more knowledgeable and effective decisions about instruction and assessment.[1]

WHAT IS LARGE-SCALE SECOND LANGUAGE ASSESSMENT?

Language assessments are ubiquitous and can be found anywhere, from elementary schools to high schools, colleges and universities, the workplace, and even immigration and naturalization contexts, and at all levels, from beginning to advanced levels of language teaching and learning. In these different contexts, the language assessments used could be large-scale assessments (such as those prepared by professionals in testing agencies, a university, or a state board or ministry of education) or small-scale assessments (such as those prepared by a teacher, an assessment development group or committee, or a single immigration or naturalization examiner). Teachers in all these contexts need to understand the main characteristics and advantages and disadvantages of large- and small-scale assessments.

Large-scale versus small-scale assessments

Large-scale language assessments, also known by the traditional term *standardized tests*, are most often used in school contexts for entrance or exit purposes and to monitor student progress through standardized development, administration, scoring, and reporting. Large-scale assessments are also used to collect uniform baseline information from a large group of students, provide diagnostic information to all stakeholders (e.g., teachers, students, parents, and school administrators), and ensure state-level accountability. An example of this type of assessment is the California Standards Test (CST) (Educational Testing Service, 2011) in English language arts and many other subjects, which is administered to school students from grades 2 to 11. The CST is used to "measure students' progress toward achieving California's state-adopted academic content standards in English–language arts . . . which describe what students should know and be able to do in each grade and subject tested" (Educational Testing Service, 2011, para. 1).

Another type of large-scale assessment at the college and university levels is known popularly as the entrance examination. This type of exam is used primarily in the screening and selection of applicants to these institutions, and it typically measures student achievement or language proficiency for accountability purposes, to encourage competition, and to ensure equal opportunities because only the highly able can be rewarded with admission to colleges and universities and job opportunities. In the United States, the Scholastic Achievement Test (SAT) (The College Board, 2012) is an example of an assessment that measures ability in three areas: critical reading, writing, and mathematics. In the area of second language assessment, international examples of large-scale assessments include the Test of English as a Foreign Language: Internet-Based Test (TOEFL iBT) (Educational Testing Service, 2012b); the International English Language Testing System (IELTS) (University of Cambridge ESOL Examinations, 2009–2011); and the Michigan English Language Assessment Battery (MELAB) (Cambridge Michigan Language Assessments, 2012). These three well-known tests measure the English language proficiency of test-takers hoping to study in English-medium universities. A fourth well-known second language assessment, the Test of English for International Communication (TOEIC) (Educational Testing Service, 2012d), is used by employers around the world to measure how well test-takers can comprehend and read workplace English as they listen to and read it. (See the Appendix for descriptions of major large-scale English language proficiency assessments.)

As varied as their purposes are, the main feature of large-scale language assessments is the uniformity (or standardization) of the assessments and testing practices, including development, administration, scoring, reporting, and score interpretation across geographical regions, administration time, and human raters. This has been possible largely because of modern educational measurement (psychometric and statistical) theory and experience with large-scale assessment practices, particularly where test reliability is concerned. More specifically, *reliability* refers to consistency of measurement, usually across test items or tasks, forms, occasions, and raters. For example, if different test forms can be considered equivalent, and if raters assign similar scores to test-taker performance, then the test can be said to have higher reliability. However, due to the numerous resources involved in systematizing test development, administration, and scoring, reliability is more easily maximized in large-scale testing contexts. While the emphasis on uniformity has served large-scale language assessments reasonably well, there have also been criticisms regarding the inflexibility of conceptualization and response format (most of these assessments mainly use the selected-response format, e.g., multiple choice) resulting in inadequate skills diagnosis and feedback to test-takers and score users. This affects the validity of score interpretations of an assessment—whether an assessment is meaningful, relevant, and sufficient for the purpose of the assessment. In response to these criticisms, many large-scale test developers have been working to address these inadequacies in recent years by introducing test tasks that require test-takers to produce written or spoken language. While these types of tasks require more resources and may compromise the reliability of the measurement to some extent, the claims about test-taker ability being made from test performance (the validity of score interpretations) are ultimately more defensible.

In contrast, small-scale language assessments are most often used in school, college, and university settings, where the assessment is used to monitor student progress or achievement, typically by the classroom teacher, or in workplace or immigration and naturalization settings by individuals. Examples from the U.S. context are teacher-made classroom assessments for grade-level students (e.g., unit tests, midterms, and final exams), employer's face-to-face interviews, and immigration examiners' interviews for the U.S. naturalization test. Although this last example is a high-stakes assessment (i.e., a test that informs life- or career-changing decisions), it is still relatively small in scale, typically conducted in one-on-one and face-to-face settings. An obvious advantage of small-scale assessments is that items can be written or delivered by the teacher, instructor, or examiner face to face so that the assessment is directly relevant in terms of the course content or program. In addition, scoring guidelines can be devised with the assessment's specific purpose in mind. And, perhaps most important, direct diagnostic feedback, including strengths and weaknesses regarding the

performance, can be provided to the test-takers on an individual basis. The main disadvantage of this type of assessment is the variability in assessment design across teachers, instructors, and examiners in terms of items, scoring, reporting, and decision making, which may compromise the reliability of the measurement. This lack of uniformity can often make comparison across assessments and assessment contexts quite difficult. (See Katz, this volume, for an in-depth treatment of small-scale or classroom-based assessment.)

Norm-referenced and criterion-referenced approaches

There are two traditionally held frames of reference, or approaches, to large-scale assessments: *norm-referenced* and *criterion-referenced*. Many aspects of assessment (such as development, scoring, reporting, and research) are carried out differently depending on the approach.

To illustrate the difference between norm-referenced testing (NRT) and criterion-referenced testing (CRT) approaches, let us present two different scenarios. First, imagine that a graduate program has 20 scholarships available for newly admitted international students each year. These scholarships are granted to the top 20 students based on their performance on a language proficiency exam. Thus, rather than being determined by a predetermined cut-off score, the scholarships are given to the 20 top-performing students regardless of their numerical score on the assessment. In other words, an absolute level of proficiency (i.e., a certain score) is not required; rather, it is the top 20 test-takers' performance in relation to all other test-takers that determines their relative standing. In fact, the score of the lowest-achieving scholarship grantee could change from year to year, depending on the relative performance of the top 20 test-takers. In this example, the assessment approach is norm-referenced since the interpretation of assessment performance is *relative* rather than absolute.

Compare the first example with a second scenario, which involves the New York State English as a Second Language Achievement Test (NYSESLAT) (New York State Education Department, 2011). ESL students in the public school system in New York state must take the NYSESLAT to track how well they are progressing with English and also to determine whether they are proficient enough to be included in regular English-speaking classrooms. In this case, New York state has a predetermined cut-off score that the students must meet or surpass to be exempt from taking ESL classes. In this case, the cut-off score represents an absolute level of mastery that the students must achieve for them to be considered to be at a high enough level to go directly into regular mainstream classes without additional ESL instruction. In this example, the testing approach is criterion-referenced since the interpretation of test performance is *absolute* rather than relative to other students' performances. Similarly, all teacher-made classroom assessments and immigration and citizenship tests are typically CRTs since it is the ultimate level of mastery of the material on the assessment that is of primary concern rather than the test-takers' relative standing compared to other test-takers. In recent years, many testing agencies have followed suit and adopted a criterion-referenced approach in their large-scale, high-stakes English language proficiency tests. Large-scale test users are gradually coming to an understanding that what they are most interested in is the test-takers' level of mastery rather than one test-taker's performance in relation to another's. Although the type of interpretation of assessment performance (relative vs. absolute) is not the only consideration in determining the distinction between a NRT and a CRT, it is arguably the most salient one in a majority of cases.

CONCEPTUAL UNDERPINNINGS

Assessment development

How is a large-scale language assessment developed? The development of a language assessment, whether it is done by individual teachers or a multinational testing conglomerate, needs careful preparation and expertise in assessment conceptualization, blueprint design, item/task writing, and research. Taking cues from Bachman and Palmer (2010), Fulcher and Davidson (2009), and the example of the TOEFL iBT development (Jamieson, Eignor, Grabe, & Kunnan, 2008), we frame here the cyclical and iterative nature of assessment development in terms of questions and answers so that teachers can understand the purpose of these tests, how they are created, and how they are administered.

We discuss next these relevant questions: What is the purpose of the assessment? Where does assessment development begin? How is assessment format and content planned for in a systematic way? When might technology be used? What does item/task quality control look like? What research is conducted as part of assessment development?

What is the purpose of the assessment? The purpose of large-scale assessment has traditionally been to gather information about test-takers' ability so that placement, proficiency, certification, or achievement decisions can be made. Increasingly, however, information from large-scale assessments is being used for diagnostic purposes—namely, to assess test-takers' strengths and weaknesses so that future teaching (or learning) can be prescribed. Once test users clarify the primary purpose of the assessment, the assessment can be organized to fit the purpose. The general scope of the assessment can then be planned in terms of constructs (i.e., the theory that refers to what is being assessed), skills that need to be assessed (i.e., listening, speaking, reading, writing, and/or integrated skills). In addition, information about the test-takers (ability level, age, gender, and any other salient information) is considered. Finally, teachers need to know how an assessment is scored, interpreted, and used for decision making so that the purpose of the assessment is served. These are essential aspects that need to be identified in the planning stage.

Where does assessment development begin? The first step in answering this question is to gather information regarding the target-language characteristics and tasks that are the focus of the assessment, possibly identified in the content standards or the curricular objectives for the course. Most curricula at the school level have these standards or objectives articulated in school-district scope and sequence documents or at the national level by ministries of education. In other situations, the adopted textbook(s) can be used for this purpose. Test developers identify which of the standards, objectives, or textbook materials need to be part of a particular assessment, keeping in mind the purpose of the assessment. For example, they determine if it is important that the test-takers show a mastery of the standards (as opposed to a sample) to indicate that they have learned the material sufficiently. Another way assessment content is identified is through the characteristics of the target-language use (TLU) domain. Defining the TLU domain involves a specification of how the target language should be used by the test-takers in a particular domain in terms of language tasks and language characteristics. Specifically, the TLU domain can be described in terms of the linguistic features, skills, or functions that the test-takers need to know. Attempts are made at this stage to identify authentic and communicative language items/tasks that relate to the ways in which the test-takers need to use the target language in their real lives. Examples of this include the ability to read for information or to listen to a teacher's introduction to a topic. These considerations are fundamental to the integrity of the test-design phase.

How are assessment format and content planned for in a systematic way? Once the TLU domain is clearly identified, the stage is set for the development of a general blueprint for the assessment. This blueprint can then be taken forward into the writing of specifications that include specific details regarding the constructs, skills, or abilities in terms of task types, the format of the input (e.g., item stems such as an incomplete statement or direct question, reading passages, or lectures), selected-response formats (e.g., multiple choice, true-false, matching information in columns, gap filling), constructed-response formats (e.g., short responses, such as words or phrases, to extended discourse, such as an essay or a speech), the number of tasks, the overall time allotted for the tasks, delivery matters (e.g., paper-and-pencil, computer, or Internet delivery), accommodations for test-takers with disabilities, and administrative aspects (e.g., security issues). These are also an essential part of the design stage. The more detailed the specifications, the easier it will be for the item/task writer; this is particularly important if multiple writers are involved in item construction and review or if more than one form of a test must be created. Once the blueprint and item/task specifications are ready, they can be handed over to the item/task writing group or committee.

A number of approaches are available to writers when planning to write items/tasks for an assessment. One option is to write items based on the item/task specifications (discussed earlier); a second approach is to write items/tasks based on content standards or curriculum objectives already outlined that may be readily available; and a third, but somewhat more difficult approach, is to develop a theory of the language knowledge required for the ability level that the assessment is being constructed to measure (e.g., listening and speaking for air traffic controllers or writing for business or engineering students) and then to operationalize this into items/tasks. Scoring considerations should also be part of the planning so that the actual items/tasks can be scored in an appropriate manner. Specifically, decisions regarding whether the scoring will be based on dichotomous scoring (correct/incorrect), partial credit, or a rubric have to be made. This is a critical component of the operationalizing stage.

When might technology be used? The answer to this question depends on whether test-takers and teachers have access to computers and Internet connections in the test-taking locations and whether the test-takers are familiar with using a keyboard, mouse, and other technological devices. If this is the case, then assessments can be planned and delivered with the help of computers. In terms of assessment materials and response format, computers can be used to include multimedia materials (e.g., text, photographs, audio, and video) in the test and to require test-takers to perform tasks based on the mouse and keyboard, such as keying in a response, speaking into the microphone, and using mouse clicks, screen touch, and drag and drop. Scoring items/tasks can also be automated for the selected-response as well as for longer response formats.

In spite of the allure of using technology in assessment contexts, researchers have raised questions about whether the use of computers has altered the test-taking process. For example, in terms of writing, one question is whether keying in an extended response (with the other advantages of computers, such as cutting and pasting and using the grammar and spell-check functions) is the same as writing on paper (see Kunnan, 1999). Other issues include impersonation, plagiarism, software compatibility, and computer reliability. Perhaps, these questions will become outdated as more academic and professional work is done with the help of computers and the ease of using the relevant technologies takes care of other concerns. In the meantime, however, these are an additional but critical consideration during the design stage.

What does item/task quality control look like? There is usually an extensive content review process that happens when a new test is being developed or when new items/tasks are introduced into an existing test. During this process, expert reviewers, who know the assessment specifications, content standards, or curriculum objectives, have the opportunity to provide comments and suggestions. Their focus typically includes the appropriateness of the materials, task types, and scoring guidelines; they also check for typographical errors and the layout of the items/tasks. The pre-testing of items/tasks is also useful if sample test-takers (who are representative of the target population) are readily available and it is convenient to administer the assessment to these individuals. Performances during pre-testing can then be used to assess several qualities of the items/tasks, including difficulty (how hard or easy an item is), discrimination (how hard or easy an item is for high- and low-performing test-takers), quality of the response choices (if there are multiple-choice items), time allocations for items/tasks, and ease of scoring the tasks (checking for clearly acceptable answers). Once information on all these aspects is available, each item is usually scrutinized before it is accepted, rejected, or revised. If both expert content review and pre-testing are used, the quality of items/tasks should be acceptable. The accepted items/tasks can then be assembled into a single assessment, keeping the general specifications in mind. This is also an essential part of the operationalizing stage.

What research is conducted as part of assessment development? Although research is often considered last in the cyclical process, it is a fundamental part of the development of an assessment. It is part of the operationalizing stage when pre-testing of items and tasks is done. Typically, the main aim of research during pre-testing is to assess the suitability of items/tasks for inclusion in an assessment. This is done based on item/task difficulty and discrimination, two statistical indices that are used for this purpose. In addition, at this stage, research is often conducted on various other components such as timing for each item/task, scoring points, and weights. Similarly, research on test-taker performance (i.e., of the entire sample or of subgroups) can reveal if there are low performances on certain items/tasks or for the whole assessment. Further, if research does not confirm that the overall consequences are beneficial to the test-takers, then the plan and design may need to be reviewed. Ultimately, findings from such focused research studies may result in adjusting or rewriting the basic plan, blueprint, and/or specifications.

Assessment development as a cyclical process. Although the above six questions might seem quite separate, the development of an assessment is an integrated and cyclical process, starting generally with the planning of the assessment and ending with decision making. Figure 1 illustrates the main stages or activities involved in the development of an assessment: planning, designing, operationalizing, using, and researching. It also shows the multi-directionality of the stages in a real assessment development and use cycle.

During the planning stage, the purpose of the assessment is established along with the intended consequences of test use, including the potential decisions that can be made and the impact on test constituents. The designing stage includes identifying the TLU domain and outlining the test blueprint and specifications, including any technology considerations. Item- and task-writing, pre-testing, and revision then follow in the operationalizing stage. Once the test is

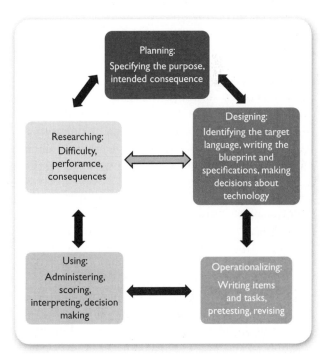

Figure 1. The cyclical nature of assessment development.

ready, it can be administered and scored as part of the using stage. During this stage, score-based inferences can be made, which translate into decisions about individuals or groups. Once test developers get data from a test administration, research on the items or tasks can be performed during the researching stage. Findings from this research can then inform the planning stage in terms of showing support for or evidence against the assessment's intended purpose or the perceived consequences of test use. Research findings can also inform changes to the designing stage for future administrations of the test. Note that, since this process is not linear but, rather, cyclical and iterative in nature, each ensuing stage in the process can also inform prior stages. For instance, pre-testing during the operationalizing stage may uncover issues resulting from the designing stage that need to be addressed before the test can be administered again. Similarly, difficulties revealed during test administration in the using stage may require test developers to modify certain tasks in the operationalizing stage so that listening input, for example, is delivered in a more uniform way.

How do teachers know if an assessment is useful?

If teachers are responsible for choosing or administering a large-scale assessment or if they need to interpret its results in a meaningful way and make decisions based on the scores, they need to understand the fundamental considerations in language assessment research and how this information can be interpreted. Since the selection and evaluation of an assessment should be based on evidence that is available in technical manuals, research reports, or other materials, a firm understanding of test reliability, validity, and fairness is critical. These issues have long been considered foundational evaluative aspects in language assessment research. With some training in understanding language assessment research, teachers should be able to select an appropriate assessment and/or evaluate an assessment being used. To present these concepts, we use here a modified version of the theoretical interpretive and validity arguments (Kane, 1992) and assessment use argument (Bachman & Palmer, 2010) by presenting the notions of claims and evidence.

Claims and evidence. *Claims* are assertions or statements that assessment developers (e.g., teachers, committees, or agencies) make regarding an assessment. These claims are generally stated by testing agencies, but they also serve as a good model for teachers who develop assessments. *Evidence* is defined as any research finding based on the analysis of assessments, assessment performance, and the impact of assessments.

As an example, the TOEFL iBT makes an explicit claim to prospective test-takers about the assessment on its website: "The TOEFL iBT assessment measures your ability to use and understand English at the university level. And it evaluates how well you combine your listening, reading, speaking, and writing skills to perform academic tasks" (Educational Testing Service, 2012c, para. 2). On the other hand, the developer of the California High School Exit Examination (CAHSEE) (California Department of Education, 2011) provides a less explicit claim on its website: "The purpose of the CAHSEE is to improve student achievement in high school and to help ensure that students who graduate from high school can demonstrate grade-level competency in reading, writing, and mathematics" (para. 1).

Regardless of how clearly their claims are stated, assessment developers need to assemble research evidence that supports such claims so that they can justify the use of the assessment. Such evidence could be findings from research that support the many aspects of an assessment. Table 1 presents some example claims, along with acceptable forms of evidence, that an assessment developer might make about an assessment. Once assessment developers have articulated the claims, they need to provide evidence for each of them (or other parties could provide evidence for counterclaims). An example of how this might be done is presented next.

Claim 1: The assessment has beneficial consequences. Kunnan (2004, 2008) notes that all assessments should be beneficial to society and that, in particular, assessments should not be harmful or detrimental. This is especially critical with respect to large-scale assessments, which are often high-stake tests. Arguably the test-takers—the most directly affected stakeholder group—are affected in terms of their preparation (e.g., the change in their cognitive abilities as a result of formal classroom instruction or self-learning), the assessment they

Table 1. Possible Claims and Evidence

Claims	Evidence
1. The assessment has beneficial consequences.	Studies of consequences on the test taker, instructional system, and the wider community
2. The assessment is consistent.	Internal-consistency and external-reliability scores Consistency across different items/tasks, forms, occasions, and raters
3. The assessment interpretations are meaningful.	Content, criterion, and construct validity
4. The assessment is free from bias.	Research showing assessment free from dialect, content, or topic bias Research showing interpretations not biased against any test-taker group
5. The assessment promotes equitable decisions.	Decisions based on appropriate standard-setting procedures Decisions relevant to societal values and legal requirements Decisions equitable to all test-taker groups

take (e.g., in terms of their affective factors), the scores and other feedback (numerical and/or descriptive) they receive, the decisions that are made about their performance (e.g., grades, pass-fail, certification, permission to immigrate, or granting of citizenship), and the life- or career-changing situations they may experience as a result of the assessment decision (e.g., exemption from an ESL requirement or permission to immigrate). In the case of high school students taking the CAHSEE in grades 9 to 12, test-takers have to pass the mathematics and English language components of the assessment to secure a diploma to graduate from high school and go on to college/university or enter the workforce. Therefore, the consequences of a pass or fail grade on the assessment can have a serious impact on the test-takers. This situation makes it crucial that CAHSEE's claims and the supporting evidence for the claims be examined carefully so that the decisions that are made regarding test-takers are justifiable.

Claim 2: The assessment is consistent. The meaningfulness of an assessment's score interpretations (Claim 3) cannot even begin to be investigated without first confirming the consistency, or reliability, of the scores obtained from the assessments. In other words, reliability is a necessary precondition for validity; hence, it is vitally important in determining the trustworthiness of the information obtained from test scores.

As previously mentioned, test *reliability* can be defined as consistency of measurement. If assessment scores are inconsistent (along one or more dimensions), then the trustworthiness of the results, and therefore the inferences that can be made from them, are necessarily called into question. Ideally, assessment scores are representative of the test-taker's true ability as defined in the construct. In other words, scores should be construct-relevant and have as little construct irrelevance as possible. For example, a reading assessment should assess material in the texts and not the background knowledge of the test-taker; background knowledge is construct-irrelevant. However, in assessment contexts, there is always a certain amount of error (i.e., construct-irrelevant variance) that is part of a score. There are a number of possible sources of error that detract from the stability of the assessment. These sources depend on the format and content of the assessment and on the context of the testing situation, including assessment method facets (e.g., raters and occasions). Error can be introduced by factors outside the assessment (e.g., human raters), within the assessment itself (e.g., the items/tasks), or by the test-takers themselves (e.g., a test-taker is ill or has test fatigue). The goal is to minimize the amount of error that is a part of the scores so that the assessment scores represent as accurate a measure of a test-taker's true ability as possible.

Internal-consistency reliability, which is particularly important in justifying the stability of the measurement, relates to the homogeneity of the items/tasks. In other words, internal-consistency reliability asks this question: Do all the items/tasks in the assessment measure the same thing (e.g., grammatical knowledge or speaking ability)? Internal-consistency reliability, though highly related to validity, does not relate to what the items/tasks are measuring; rather, it is primarily concerned with how much of the observed score variance (i.e., the assessment score) can be attributed to the test-takers' true score variance (i.e., the test-taker's theoretical score) rather than error. For example, imagine a 75-question multiple-choice grammar assessment in which there are several items that measure background knowledge rather than grammatical knowledge. These items can compromise the reliability of the assessment since they are introducing construct-irrelevant variance into the scores. In other words, some test-takers who perform very poorly on the grammar items in the assessment may do very well on the five items that have pop-culture references, for which they can draw on their background knowledge (and not grammatical knowledge) to answer these questions correctly. These types of items create anomalies, or inconsistencies, in the test-takers' responses that are unrelated to their grammatical knowledge. This could potentially compromise the reliability of the assessment as a measure of grammatical knowledge. This type of unwanted variability, though it can never be completely eliminated, can be minimized through systematized assessment design and development procedures.

External reliability relates to the factors outside the assessment itself (e.g., different forms or occasions) that have a potential effect on the consistency of the scores. For instance, in large-scale testing, test-takers ideally would receive the same score on an assessment irrespective of which version (Test Form A or B) they took or on which occasion (in January or in June) they took the assessment. If they do, there is evidence that the assessment forms or occasions can be considered interchangeable since these variables introduce little error into the measurement.

Another potential factor affecting external reliability is the lack of consistency among the human raters of extended speaking and writing tasks. Although there is a benefit to performance-based tasks in communicative language teaching contexts, in that test-takers can be engaged in communicative activities similar to those used in the classroom (such as interviews, conversations, and extended writing), human raters are required to score the response samples. These raters inevitably introduce variability into the scores, which can compromise reliability. Rater consistency can be maximized through highly specified domain descriptors in a scoring rubric, extensive rater training/norming, and a deep understanding of the construct being measured. If raters exhibit a high level of consistency, there is evidence that the scores can be interpreted as being a trustworthy indication of the test-takers' true ability. (See Katz, this volume, for examples of analytic and holistic rubrics used for scoring writing assignments.)

Claim 3: The assessment interpretations are meaningful. Once test reliability has been established, arguably the most important quality of an assessment is the extent to which the score interpretations are meaningful. This is commonly known as *validity*, and it is at the core of assessment research. Evidence for validity can be gathered from a variety of sources, but it is not necessary to use all of them. Nevertheless, the more evidence that can be provided, the stronger the argument for the meaningfulness of the interpretations. The three predominant types of evidence that are collected are content-related evidence, criterion-related evidence, and construct-related evidence, though all are often inextricably intertwined.

Content-related evidence of validity, the first type of evidence that is collected to support this claim, is determined based on an assessment's item representativeness (i.e., Does each individual item belong on the assessment?) and domain coverage (i.e., Is a sufficient amount of the content we are trying to measure represented in the assessment?). For example, if the purpose of an assessment is to measure students' mastery of second language reading skills taught at the sixth-grade level, to maximize item representativeness ideally all the assessment items should contribute to making inferences about the test-takers' reading ability at a sixth-grade level. Items that do not measure knowledge of reading ability at a sixth-grade level do not show good item representativeness and therefore compromise the meaningfulness of the assessment score interpretations. With respect to domain coverage, if the purpose of an assessment is to measure knowledge of the linguistic structures covered in Units 1–3 of a given textbook, we want to make sure that a sufficient amount of the Unit 1–3 content is represented in the assessment. Having too little content coverage compromises our ability to make valid inferences about the test-takers' knowledge of those structures. Content experts, including teachers who are familiar with course content or standards, can help determine the adequacy of item representativeness and domain coverage in an assessment.

Criterion-related evidence of validity is collected to support this claim in terms of the capacity of an assessment to predict future performance (e.g., in college or the workplace). For example, if an assessment is used to select high school students for admission into a college or university (such as the SAT in the United States), the expectation is that the SAT is able to predict to some extent the test-takers' readiness for and subsequent performance in college or university courses. If the prediction rate is high, we can state that there is evidence for criterion validity; if the prediction rate is low, we have little evidence for it.

Construct-related evidence of validity is the most important of all types of evidence. Construct validity refers to the extent to which the score-based interpretations are meaningful in terms of the blueprint and specifications, content-standards, curriculum objectives, or theory of knowledge that the test purports to measure. Therefore, a clear and well-defined construct of the ability being measured should be at the heart of every language assessment. Construct definitions can be based solely on a theory of language, or they can be defined in terms of a series of standards or objectives, a syllabus, and/or textbook (all of which are also ideally based on a theory of language). When inferences about test-takers' ability are made based on test scores, evidence is needed that these interpretations are meaningful and appropriate to a given assessment context. Perhaps most notably, construct validity relates to the extent to which the test-taker performance can be generalized to the particular TLU domain that goes beyond the relatively limited scope of the assessment itself. Thus, construct validity involves the ongoing process of justifying the interpretations that we make about test-takers' knowledge in some real-world context based on their scores.[2]

Claim 4: The assessment is free from bias. The topic of unbiased interpretations has been shown in the last few decades to be an essential part of administering a fair assessment. The *Standards for Educational and Psychological Tests and Testing* (from the American Psychological Association, American Educational Research Association, & National Council on Measurement in Education, 1999) first articulated fairness in testing and test use. In his *Test Fairness Framework*, Kunnan (2004) further delineates test fairness in terms of the types of bias assessment developers should focus on: (1) dialect, content, and topic; and (2) group performance. Since potential systematic bias in the dialect, content, or topic can exist in an assessment, an examination of the assessment is necessary to determine if bias exists. When examining each item, we ask this question: Do any of the items/tasks or texts have the potential for systematic bias (given the test-takers)? For example, imagine an English language assessment being used in the United States to determine whether English language learners can be mainstreamed out of their ESL classes in an elementary school. In this assessment, learners listen to texts with conversations from speakers who speak different dialects of English (American English, British English, Australian English, etc.). This is a source of dialect bias if the learners have not previously been exposed to these dialects and they are now being assessed for their ability to understand the conversations. Similarly, imagine an assessment that requires test-takers to read material or write about content or topics that they are unfamiliar with. For example, imagine that students are asked to write an essay about how they enjoyed the Chinese Lunar New Year or *Cinco de Mayo* celebrations. This kind of task is a source of content or topic bias if specific cultural background knowledge is expected and the test-takers do not have it (i.e., are not Chinese or Latino or have never experienced such a celebration). Similar concerns can occur in reading assessments where obscure words that are known by some and not by others (e.g., from pop culture, rocket science, or jazz) are included in the assessment. Content analysis of items/tasks in all sections of an assessment should be conducted before the assessment is administered to ensure the absence of bias. If this is not done, the test-takers will have been unfairly penalized and their scores may not be a meaningful representation of their abilities.

It is also possible that different subgroups of test-takers (e.g., in terms of gender, age, race/ethnicity, or native language) may perform differently on an assessment. What we want to know is whether the difference in performance is based on construct-relevant factors (e.g., grammatical knowledge or writing ability) or irrelevant factors (e.g., gender or socioeconomic status). For example, to examine a high school writing assessment to uncover any gender bias, we would check to see whether the male test-takers have a similar profile of scores as the female test-takers. In some instances, we may find that they do not. For example, a particular item or task that has traditionally male- or female-oriented topical content may turn out to be very easy for one gender group but not for the other. For example, imagine a scenario in which male test-takers are interested in football and female test-takers are interested in golf. In this situation, test content in a reading assessment with information on football would likely favor male test-takers and test content with information on golf would likely favor female test-takers. When such differences occur systematically and are statistically identified as such, these texts and items/tasks are flagged and subject to a content review to ascertain the source of bias, if any. Results from such investigations could result in the review, modification, or deletion of items/tasks if they are found to have bias.[3]

Claim 5: The assessment promotes equitable decisions. Examples of decisions that are made about test-takers based on test scores include whether they succeed in passing a course or program, earning a diploma, being offered employment, securing permission to immigrate, or being granted citizenship. In school, college, or university contexts, setting standards for different levels of performance (e.g., A–F grades or other marking systems) is also important because test-takers need to be awarded appropriate grades based on their performance and instructors/teachers need to know whether they have created classification errors (have given a test-taker a higher or lower grade or placement than was appropriate). Decisions based on test-score interpretations are expected to be equitable based on appropriate standard-setting procedures (e.g., defining a level of achievement or proficiency that corresponds to a certain standard-setting score or cut score), societal values, and also the legal requirements of the community in which an assessment is administered. Again, the higher the stakes of the assessment, the more important equitable decisions become.

Another concern in decision making is whether the decisions that are made are equitable to all test-taker groups. This is particularly important if standard setting and subsequent decision making are not empirically defensible but are carried out following public policy or practice. For example, in a community where meritocracy is the preferred decision-making process, test-takers with the highest scores are the ones who receive the benefits. On the other hand, in a community that has a policy to assist individuals who have been discriminated against in the past, test-takers without the highest scores may be the ones to receive benefits. In many countries, such a policy has resulted in individual standards for different test-taker groups based on race/ethnicity, gender, or religious membership. Any decisions affected by legal requirements (e.g., court rulings, settlements, and precedents) should match the societal values of the community, but all decision making, whether it is merit-based or quota-based, has to stay within the letter and meaning of the law.

Counterclaims. Counterclaims can be articulated by interested parties such as test-takers, schools, parents, and school districts. Some possible counterclaims include that the assessment does not have beneficial consequences, the assessment is not consistent, the assessment interpretations are not meaningful, the assessment is not free of bias, and the assessment does not promote equitable decisions. Evidence that supports each of the counterclaims will then have to be produced in order to arrive at a public or judicial resolution.

CLASSROOM APPLICATIONS

Now let us think back to our IEP teacher Sarah, described in the Experience section of this chapter. Recall that Sarah's students are recent immigrants to the United States and must take a large-scale English proficiency test to be considered for university admission. Now that Sarah has a working knowledge of second language assessment theory and practice, she can better understand the test and help address her students' concerns. We next pose questions that are relevant for Sarah to answer.

What is the purpose and content of the assessment?

The purpose of the high-stakes assessment is to measure non-native test-takers' language proficiency. Language proficiency on the test is defined in terms of how English is heard, spoken, read, and written in the university classroom. The assessment is a large-scale, high-stakes, criterion-referenced test.

How can Sarah interpret the information using what she has learned? Since the assessment is a criterion-referenced test, what is most important is not how well the test-takers do in relation to other test-takers; rather, it is solely the test-takers' proficiency level that determines their score. This means that Sarah's students must ultimately improve their English to do well on the test.

Who are the users of the information that will been gathered from the assessment?

Admissions officers and/or academic departments or programs often require non-native speakers of English to show evidence of their ability to perform at a high enough level to study in the university environment. Thus, they set cut-off scores for these potential non-native-speaking applicants based on the demands of the curriculum to either accept the applicant for admission or to indicate that the applicant needs additional language training.

How can Sarah interpret the information using what she has learned? Cut-off scores are usually set for the entire test, but minimum scores may be required for individual skills sections as well. If test-takers know that they are lacking in one ability or another, it is important for them not only to prepare for the test so that they can surpass the cut-off score but also to improve their language ability so that they can ultimately become a successful student if admitted to a rigorous academic program.

What is the content of the assessment?

The assessment has four sections: reading, listening, speaking, and writing. The speaking and writing sections have both independent and integrated tasks. For the reading section, test-takers will read three or four passages from academic texts and answer multiple-choice questions. For the listening section, test-takers will listen to lectures, classroom discussions, and conversations and answer multiple-choice questions. The multiple-choice questions will assess the students' ability in various reading and

listening skills. The writing and speaking sections of the assessment have two different types of tasks, independent and integrated. In addition to one independent-writing and two independent-speaking tasks where test-takers write or speak in response to a prompt, there are four integrated-speaking tasks and one integrated-writing task that require test-takers to read and/or listen before responding to a question.

How can Sarah interpret the information using what she has learned? Since the purpose of the assessment is to measure academic language proficiency, the test tasks are meant to represent how language is used in the TLU domain—the university context. From the test specifications, it seems that the reading and listening sections, and the independent-speaking and -writing tasks, are fairly straightforward and conventional, and will likely be familiar to the students. Perhaps somewhat unfamiliar, though, are the integrated tasks, which are meant to capture the way academic language skills are combined in an integrated way in the university context. For example, students often read a text for homework, come to class and listen to a lecture about that same topic, and have to summarize that information for a friend who missed class. Or a student might listen to a conversation between two friends about a controversial new university policy and then join the discussion and argue her own point of view. So, in the actual assessment, a test-taker might be asked to read a short passage on an academic subject, listen to a lecture on the same topic, and then respond orally to a question about what he or she has read and heard. Or a test-taker may be asked to listen to a conversation about a problem, summarize that conversation, and then offer his or her solution. These are the types of tasks Sarah's students can expect and should prepare for.

How can users be sure that assessment results are indicative of the test-takers' abilities?

Test-score users want to be sure that the scores obtained are a precise and trustworthy representation of the test-takers' ability. Thus, they are relying on the assumption that the test developers have evidence for the claims they are making about the test, including reliability, validity, and fairness considerations.

The test developer will have a full research program dedicated to making sure that the assessment's scores are precise and that there is sufficient evidence supporting the valid interpretation and use of the test scores. First, the internal-consistency reliability of the assessment could be above 0.90, which is very high. Second, the validity of the assessment could have been a major consideration from the conceptualization and design phases of the test, including the relevance and representativeness of test content, task design and scoring rubrics, the construct definition underlying the test, and the consequences of test use. Last, the test developer routinely investigates any bias present in the test.

How can Sarah interpret the information using what she has learned? The high reliability is, in part, a result of systematic test development procedures, particularly where test specifications are concerned. The test developer also has an extensive and rigorous rater-training program where raters are continually normed. This also undoubtedly contributes to the high precision of test scores. To ensure that the test content is relevant and representative, the test design process includes the analysis of the academic tasks needed for study at English-medium institutions of higher education and the identification of important characteristics of these tasks that can be captured in the test. With respect to test development and scoring design, task types, task characteristics, and the user interface are all important considerations. Perhaps most important, research on the assessment shows evidence that the test measures a complex and multicomponential (i.e., reading, listening, speaking, and writing) construct of ESL/EFL ability, consistent with what the test was designed to measure. In terms of the positive consequences of test use (i.e., positive washback), in preparing to take the test, test-takers may be exposed to the use of test preparation materials and activities that more closely resemble communicatively oriented pedagogy in academic English courses, thus improving their language skills. From a global perspective, the assessment also affords non-native English speakers the opportunity to demonstrate their language ability when applying to English-medium universities.

Thus, Sarah will be better prepared to plan her materials and instruction in her IEP program by keeping these points in mind. She can also make these ideas part of a mini-test preparation course she might plan in addition to her regular course, which could include instruction on how best to approach the test tasks and also practice tasks that are similar to those on the test itself.

FUTURE TRENDS

Computer technology

With the wide availability of computer technology, assessment practice is employing computers and computer technology in various ways. One simple way is to use computers to deliver assessments. In this approach, known as computer-based tests or computer-delivered testing, the computer merely replaces the paper-and-pencil assessment for displaying the test materials and collecting responses. Another approach that is more complex is to use computers to assemble assessments for different test-takers in a tailored fashion; this is known as computer-adaptive testing (CAT). In this approach, items or tasks are matched in difficulty to a test-taker's ability based on the test-taker's previous correct or incorrect responses. Although there are at the time of this writing very few well-known language assessments that use CAT—the Oxford Online Placement Test (OOPT) is one (Oxford University Press, 2011)—this approach is becoming popular in educational assessment. Both these approaches assume that test-takers have access to computers to take the tests.

Another use of computers is in the computerized/automated scoring of constructed-response tasks in both writing and speaking assessments. In writing assessment, computers are trained to score short responses that require a word, phrase, or sentence. Computers are also being programmed to score longer responses such as essays as a way of possibly supplementing or ultimately replacing human raters with computer technology; for example, e-rater® for the TOEFL iBT independent-writing task is currently in use (Educational Testing Service, 2012a). Similarly, in speaking assessments, computer technology is being used to score short spoken responses (see Versant tests for details; Knowledge Technologies, 2011).

A related matter is the issue of whether human readers rate keyed-in or typed versions of essays more favorably than handwritten ones. Research evidence from experimental studies has found that handwritten essays received significantly higher scores than their typed counterparts (Powers & Farnum, 1997; Russell & Tao, 2004). Why human readers rate handwritten versions of essays more favorably than the typed versions is unclear, but perhaps rater expectations may be higher with the typed versions.

In brief, we can expect an increased use of computer technology in language assessments in the next decade. This will also bring new challenges to the profession because we need to be sure that the benefits from technology do not negatively impact assessments and test-taker performance.

New attempts at diagnostic feedback

A recent trend among psychometricians and test developers is to provide diagnostic feedback and profile reports to test-takers. Three large-scale language assessments, TOEFL iBT, IELTS, and MELAB, provide score reports, and surely more tests will follow suit. These reports include individualized test-taker feedback, which is a vast improvement on the basic set of scores that test-takers were provided with in the past. Kunnan and Jang (2008) provide some discussion of the main issues related to diagnostic feedback from large-scale assessments.

Another assessment tool whose primary aim is in diagnosing rather than selecting or certifying language proficiency is DIALANG (Lancaster University, 2006–2012), which is a computer-delivered diagnostic language assessment system. In this system, test-takers can take tests in reading, listening, writing, vocabulary, and grammar in 14 European languages. Test results are reported against the six levels of descriptors of communicative activities in the Common European Framework of Reference for languages (Council of Europe, 2001).

Skills integration

Although most language assessment tasks and response formats have remained the same over many decades, a few innovations have been implemented recently. For example, the TOEFL iBT has integrated-skills tasks (read, listen, and then speak in response to a question; listen and then speak in response to a question; and read, listen, and then write in response to a question). This is a significant change because most assessments have continued to assess language abilities in terms of independent skills (listening, speaking, reading, or writing) despite calls for more authentic assessments that include skills integration.

CONCLUSION

In this chapter, we have presented an introduction to the field of second language assessment with a focus on large-scale assessment. Although the current chapter merely scratches the surface of the field, it is our hope that, at the very least, it provides a foundation in terms of assessment practice and research. A further discussion of test design and development considerations, including test specification and item-writing guidelines, is necessary to understand assessment development more fully. Furthermore, from the research side, both quantitative data-analysis procedures and qualitative data-analysis procedures are certainly necessary for a more complete education in language assessment.[4] Nonetheless, we feel that, given the information in this chapter, teachers-in-training should feel better equipped to make judicious decisions about what assessment practices they choose to use in their own classrooms and to be informed consumers of large-scale language assessments.

SUMMARY

➤ The distinguishing feature of large-scale language assessments is the uniformity (or standardization) of the assessments and testing practice, including development, administration, scoring, reporting, and score interpretation across geographical regions, administration time, and human raters.

➤ Norm-referenced and criterion-referenced testing approaches are different in the way that test performance is interpreted—relative in norm-referenced testing and absolute in criterion-referenced testing.

➤ Assessment development is cyclical and iterative in nature, and includes planning, designing, operationalizing, using, and researching stages.

➤ When assessment developers make claims about an assessment, they also need to assemble research evidence that supports their claims, including (at minimum) reliability, validity, and fairness considerations, so that they can justify the use of the assessment.

➤ Computer technology will undoubtedly influence large-scale assessments in the decades to follow with computer delivery of assessments and automated scoring of constructed-response tasks in writing and speaking.

➤ Diagnostic feedback and skills integration in large-scale language assessments will make a mark in the next decade.

DISCUSSION QUESTIONS

1. What has been your experience with large-scale assessment, either as a test-taker, teacher, or administrator? Did you feel the assessment was fair? Why or why not?

2. Which of the steps in the ESL/EFL assessment development process displayed in Figure 1 might be easy and which difficult to carry out? State your reasons.

3. Define *reliability*. What is the difference between internal and external reliability? In what types of tests do the different types of reliability described apply?

4. Why is it acceptable for a construct definition to be based on a theory of language or based on a series of standards, a syllabus, or textbook when these all seem like very different things?

5. Have you noticed any texts, tasks, or items on tests that caused content, topic, or dialect difficulties for you? Do you think the assessments should or should not have had those materials? Could you claim the assessment was not fair to some students? Would you have sufficient and relevant evidence to justify this claim?

SUGGESTED ACTIVITIES

1. In groups, identify three or four large-scale and small-scale ESL/EFL assessments that you are familiar with. Describe the main characteristics of each.

2. Examine the large-scale and small-scale assessments you described in Activity 1. Identify which of them are norm-referenced and which are criterion-referenced. What characteristics of the assessments make them so?

3. Use a search engine (such as Google or Bing) to look up two ESL or EFL language assessments in an area that you are interested in (such as school or college, workplace, immigration, citizenship). Learn more about the many aspects of the assessment, including development, scoring, reporting, and administration matters. Do you feel that all the information you wanted was available on the assessments' websites? If not, what additional information would you like to see made public on their websites?

4. Imagine you and a colleague are contacted by your principal or language program director to develop a language assessment in the areas of listening and speaking. Also imagine that you have defined your construct and you have written the test specifications. How would you then decide on the listening and speaking materials (input) for your tasks? Search the web for examples of listening or speaking rubrics. How could you adapt them for use with your own students?

5. Choose a language assessment that you are familiar with, and write one argument that the assessment developers might make for each of the following five claims: beneficial consequences, consistent assessment, meaningful interpretations, lack of bias, and equitable decisions. Now consider what evidence you might need for each of the claims. Is it easier to collect some kinds of evidence than others? Why/why not?

FURTHER READING

Bachman, L. F., & Palmer, A. S. (2010). *Language assessment in practice*. Oxford, UK: Oxford University Press.

This book offers the theoretical view that language assessments should be evaluated through a claims and evidence approach.

Brown, J. D., & Hudson, T. (2002). *Criterion-referenced language testing*. Cambridge, UK: Cambridge University Press.

This book presents in one place the criterion-referenced approach to language assessment (CRT). It presents the theoretical, statistical, and practical aspects of developing, analyzing, and reporting CRT assessments.

Fulcher, G., & Davidson, F. (2009). Test architecture, test retrofit. *Language Testing, 26*, 123–144.

This article presents the concepts of test specifications and test development in an innovative way.

Kunnan, A. J., & Carr, N. (2013). Statistical analysis of test results. In C. Chapelle (Ed.), *The encyclopedia of applied linguistics* (pp. 5396–5403). Malden, MA: Wiley-Blackwell.

This article presents information on the statistical analyses that need to be conducted when analyzing test performance data.

APPENDIX: OVERVIEW OF SOME MAJOR LARGE-SCALE ENGLISH LANGUAGE PROFICIENCY ASSESSMENTS

First Certificate in English (FCE)

The FCE is one of Cambridge ESOL's tests, and it measures listening, speaking, reading, writing, and grammar. The purpose of the FCE is to certify that test-takers are able to study, work, or live independently at the intermediate level of English proficiency (B2 in the Common European Framework of Reference [CEFR]). For more information, go to http://www.cambridgeesol.org/exams/fce/index.html

International English Language Testing System (IELTS)

IELTS is one of the Cambridge English for speakers of other languages (ESOL) examinations. There are two versions of the test: general training and academic. Both test modules measure listening, speaking, reading, and writing. IELTS scores are typically used for university admissions. For more information, go to http://www.ielts.org

Michigan English Language Assessment Battery (MELAB)

MELAB, one of the Cambridge Michigan assessments, measures advanced-level English proficiency for individuals applying to educational institutions or for work/training purposes. MELAB measures listening, speaking, reading, and writing. For more information, go to http://www.cambridgemichigan.org/melab

Pearson Test of English (PTE)

PTE, developed by Pearson Education, is a computer-delivered, skills-based language test measuring listening, speaking, reading, and writing. PTE has three versions: academic, general, and young learners. Each version of PTE is used for different purposes. For more information, go to http://www.pearsonpte.com

Test of English as a Foreign Language Internet-Based Test (TOEFL iBT)

TOEFL iBT, developed by Educational Testing Service (ETS), Princeton, is a widely used exam that is administered via the Internet. TOEFL iBT measures academic listening, speaking, reading, and writing through independent- and integrated-skills tasks and is typically used for university admissions. For more information, go to http://www.ets.org/toefl

Test of English for International Communication (TOEIC)

TOEIC, developed by Educational Testing Service (ETS), measures test-takers' English proficiency in the workplace. The test has two versions: one with listening and reading, and the other with speaking and writing. TOEIC is used by employers to determine who can communicate effectively with co-workers and clients when English is the lingua franca. For more information, go to http://www.ets.org/toeic

ENDNOTES

[1] Community college and adult school ESL teachers also need to understand language assessment theory and practice to help their students in citizenship classes take high-stakes assessments such as the U.S. naturalization test, which has an English language component (see Kunnan, 2009a, 2009b).

[2] Evidence of construct validity is very often presented statistically, including estimates of assessment score reliability, variance component estimates, dimensionality, and data-model fit statistics. However, content-related evidence and criterion-related evidence can both serve to help justify and triangulate statistically oriented construct-related evidence because the three are often intertwined.

[3] These analyses are generally called differential item functioning and are statistical in nature (see Ferne & Rupp, 2007; Geranpayeh & Kunnan, 2007).

[4] Quantitative data-analysis procedures typically entail descriptive statistics, inferential statistics, item-response theory, generalizability theory, and structural equation modeling, while qualitative data-analysis procedures entail item-content analysis, discourse analysis, and verbal protocol analysis.

21 | Assessment in Second Language Classrooms

ANNE KATZ

KEY QUESTIONS

➤ What are students learning?
➤ How well are they learning the content of the lesson?
➤ How can assessment help improve learning outcomes for students?

EXPERIENCE

Ms. Aranda has been teaching middle school English learners for nearly 10 years. Although her students take yearly standardized exams intended to determine the effectiveness of the instructional program they are receiving, Ms. Aranda wants to make sure they are prepared to meet—and even exceed—learning expectations, and she wants to gather this information on a regular basis, not just once a year. Just as important, she seeks ways to support students' ongoing development of skills, modify instruction to ensure it meets students' needs, and engage students in reflecting on their own learning efforts. She's been reading materials about new ideas in assessment and trying out some of the ideas. Here are some of the ways she has been incorporating the ideas into her practice. She is:

- integrating assessment into instructional activities on a regular basis
- examining her students' learning processes as well as their outcomes
- designing assessments to support her students' learning
- engaging students as active participants in the assessment of their work
- ensuring that her students are aware of learning expectations *and* criteria for success

In this chapter, I explore fundamental questions about assessment in the classroom. (For information on large-scale assessment, see Kunnan & Grabowski, this volume.) In addition to looking at what assessment is and how it can be used, I ask why second/foreign language teachers need a comprehensive understanding and working knowledge of assessment practices.

WHAT IS CLASSROOM ASSESSMENT?

For many busy teachers planning lessons and teaching classrooms of language learners, assessment may be seen as yet one more task added on to an already crowded agenda of things that "should" be done in the classroom. Other teachers, like Ms. Aranda, however, have discovered that assessment can be a useful instructional tool that provides vital information about the extent of student learning and the effectiveness of their instruction. In this chapter, I address the role of assessment in language classrooms and illustrate how a range of practices can be embedded throughout the lesson to enhance learning opportunities for all students.

The term *assessment* refers to the use of methods and instruments to collect information to inform decision making about learning. In contrast, a *test* is just one of many forms of assessment. Classroom assessment provides useful information for learning and teaching when it is integrated into an instructional framework, often referred to as a *curriculum*, that links assessment to learning targets. The model in Figure 1 represents how both instruction and assessment function together to promote learning within a dynamic educational delivery system.

Effective teachers use classroom assessment for multiple purposes, such as determining their

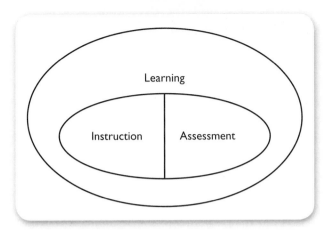

Figure 1. Instruction and assessment as part of learning (adapted from Katz, 2012).

students' learning needs, diagnosing specific learning challenges, monitoring the development of students' skills, and engaging students in their own learning processes. Typically, tests are categorized according to their uses:

- *Placement tests* provide information that is useful for determining students' appropriate levels of instruction within a program or institution.
- *Diagnostic tests* are used to assess students' strengths and weaknesses, providing teachers and students with information that can guide decisions about appropriate instruction to meet students' needs.
- *Proficiency tests* are intended to assess students' ability in a language independent of a curriculum or specific course content.
- *Achievement tests* measure whether a student is reaching instructional objectives. A good deal of the assessment taking place in the classroom is via achievement tests. The discussion in this chapter addresses this last essential use of assessment.

CONCEPTUAL UNDERPINNINGS

As one component in an educational system keyed to learning, assessment reflects theories of learning and the educational approaches tied to those theories. Over time, as these theories have changed, assessment practices have also evolved (Shepard, 2000b). For much of the twentieth century, behaviorist theories of learning dominated

testing culture. According to this paradigm, learning was characterized by the accumulation of bits of knowledge organized according to an instructional sequence that moved, step by step, from simpler to more complex skills. Positive reinforcement such as encouraging feedback at the end of each step enhanced learning by motivating learners to continue their efforts. Testing was a means of verifying that students had learned the lessons. If students did not meet the desired aim, the teacher could reteach, and then retest, until the aim was met (Shepard, 2000b). Newer theories of learning from a social constructivist perspective have broadened the focus of how learning occurs and, consequently, how to describe that learning; in addition to the products of instruction, they include how students process and make meaning within social contexts. Such theories acknowledge the role of prior knowledge and experiences that students bring to bear as they take on new learning experiences, and the theories recognize students as active participants in the learning process. Within this view of learning and assessment as connected and socially constructed activities, teachers, students, and community members participate as partners in the learning process (Arkoudis & O'Loughlin, 2004; Cumming, 2009b; Davison & Leung, 2009).

Congruent with changes in educational theory, changes in language teaching have transformed our understanding of language learning. Methodologies have recognized the importance of not only what knowledge learners have accumulated about language but also how those learners use that knowledge to communicate meaning and achieve their own communicative purposes in a variety of settings and with a range of interlocutors. Not surprisingly, new approaches to language assessment have emerged as alternatives to traditional testing (Brown & Abeywickrama, 2010). Terms such as *authentic assessment* and *alternative assessment* have been used to characterize assessment practices that engage learners in demonstrating their skills in communicative and authentic tasks and that use explicit criteria tied to learning aims to record and interpret student performances. Thus, concurrent with this new understanding has been a move away from an emphasis on indirect testing approaches that attempt to measure students' abilities underlying a specific skill to an increasing reliance on

Traditional Language Testing	Current Approaches to Language Testing
• Focus on language form • Learner produces isolated bits of language that can be scored as right or wrong • Oriented to product • Highly objective scoring • Decontextualized test tasks focused on the right answer	• Focus on communicative effect • Integration of skill areas • Includes process and product • Clear criteria to guide scoring • Open-ended answers • Attention to context

Figure 2. Contrasting features of traditional and current approaches to language testing.

direct testing approaches that require students to perform that skill. To illustrate the difference between these two approaches, consider two different kinds of writing tests. A test that asks students to put a series of sentences into a sequence to make up a coherent paragraph is an indirect measure of the students' ability to write a paragraph. One that asks students to write a paragraph is a direct measure of their writing skill. Both tests can provide information about language learning, albeit about different aspects of that learning.

A view of assessment grounded in current theories of teaching and learning guides the kind of assessment practices envisioned by teachers like Ms. Aranda. Figure 2 contrasts some of the features of these current approaches to language testing with more traditional practices.

Assessment and learning

Teachers new to assessment may have questions about how to choose among the array of assessment tools available for classroom use. Just as there are many useful activities for implementing instruction, there are a number of assessments to support the learning agenda in the language classroom. This section outlines several factors that teachers should consider to make effective choices about incorporating assessment into their classrooms.

Summative and formative purposes for assessment. Busy teachers do not have time to assess their students without first articulating a purpose for assessment. Although tests can be used in several ways (e.g., to make diagnoses or to help with placement), the majority of assessment that takes place in the classroom relates to the achievement of instructional aims. These instructionally aligned assessments serve two main pedagogical purposes.

They are used for summative purposes when they focus on what students have learned as a result of a period of instruction; these are assessments *of* learning. They are used for formative purposes when they help to promote student learning during the process of instruction; these are assessments *for* learning. Figure 3 lists how assessment is used for both summative and formative purposes.

It is important to note that assessment tools in and of themselves are not summative or formative. It is the purpose to which they are put that determines how assessments are characterized. For example, Ms. Aranda uses a rubric when assessing her students' writing. A *rubric* is an assessment tool that includes criteria and levels of performance (examples of rubrics are provided in the section later in this chapter on assessing productive skills). When Ms. Aranda uses the rubric to determine a grade for one of her students on the final draft of a paper, it is being used for summative purposes. When she gives the same rubric to the student at the beginning of the writing process and it is used by the student and perhaps by the student's peers

Summative Purposes: Assessment *of* Learning	Formative Purposes: Assessment *for* Learning
• Document learning • Diagnose learning needs • Provide information for communication linkages among students, families, and teachers • Plan and improve instruction	• Scaffold learning • Provide ongoing feedback during instruction and/or student performances • Engage students in self-assessment

Figure 3. Summative and formative purposes for assessment.

or Ms. Aranda to guide feedback during the writing process, it is being used for formative purposes. Formative uses of assessment have been found to augment learning (Black & Wiliam, 1998). I discuss how this takes place in the classroom at the end of this section.

Types of language assessments. A good deal of the assessment literature focuses on how to construct various forms of assessment tools such as multiple-choice tests, gap-filling texts, rubrics, and checklists; it also provides numerous useful examples of each type (e.g., see Brown & Abeywickrama, 2010; Coombe, Folse, & Hubley, 2007; Hughes, 2003; O'Malley & Valdez Pierce, 1996). One perspective on understanding the range and variety of assessment types examines how students are expected to respond when engaged in a specific type of assessment. Figure 4 presents such a framework, along with examples of each assessment type. The typology is divided into two main divisions: tools that require students to select an answer or response and tools that require students to provide a response using language that they have learned. All the tools listed serve specific kinds of pedagogical purposes. For selected-response tools, students demonstrate learning by choosing a response from among a selection provided by the test maker. Such kinds of assessments are useful, for example, for determining what students know about a particular language structure or text; they are also useful for assessing beginning students who have a limited repertoire of language skills they can call on to interpret a test or produce a response. Multiple-choice and matching tests are the most familiar examples of this type of format.

To get a sense of how students use the language they have been studying, teachers choose assessments that require students to produce a response, ranging from short answers, such as filling in a blank or responding to a partner with words or phrases, to language performances requiring extended text, such as writing an essay or engaging in a role play.

The design of an assessment includes both the way in which a language performance is elicited—via either a selected- or constructed-response format—and a means of scoring that performance. For selected-response assessments, scoring appears fairly straightforward. Such assessments are scored via reference to an answer key that provides the predetermined correct selection for each item. Constructed-response formats require the use of a scoring guide—such as a rubric—to assist in recording and making judgments about a language performance. Because learners can generate a range of responses, it takes more time and expertise to score these assessments. (More discussion on both types of formats can be found in the section on assessing specific language skills.)

Just as each type of assessment serves specific pedagogical purposes, each format also presents specific challenges. As previously noted, selected-response formats provide opportunities for students to show what they know about language but not how effectively they can use that knowledge in

SELECTED-RESPONSE FORMAT	CONSTRUCTED-RESPONSE FORMAT			
	Brief Constructed Response	Performance-Based Assessment		
		Product-focused	Performance-focused	Process-focused
Multiple choice	Gap filling	Essay	Oral presentation	Observation
True/false	Short answer	Story/play/poem	Dramatic reading	Reflection
Matching	Cloze	Portfolio	Role play	Journal
Same/different	Label a visual	Report	Debate	Learning log
Grammatical/ungrammatical	Sentence completion	Video/audiotape	Interview	
	Error correction	Poster session	Online chats	
		Project		

Figure 4. Types of assessment (based on McTighe & Ferrara, 1998).

communicative tasks. The format may also restrict the range of possible language areas to be tested since it is not always possible to come up with an appropriate range of options for possible answers. Given that these items provide a fixed number of answers, guessing has to be factored into how well students perform on these types of tests. Last, a good deal of time and effort is required to construct useful items. For multiple-choice tests, for example, it is important to make sure that only one answer is correct; that each item tests only one bit of language knowledge; and that nothing about the options, such as one response being much longer than the others, provides a clue to the correct response (see Coombe, Folse, & Hubley, 2007, for tips on writing these kinds of tests). To ensure that such tests meet the teacher's intention in using them, they should be tried out beforehand, perhaps by other teachers.

When students are called on to generate language during a constructed-response type assessment, they provide evidence of how they can use that language. Tests that engage learners in producing extended oral and written texts also often engage students in demonstrating higher-order thinking skills. However, this format presents challenges as well. Because it takes longer for students to respond to these kinds of tests, teachers must allot more time to them in the classroom, reducing the number of items that can be included in a test and thus the range of student learning. An essay test, for example, is a one-item test. Scoring the language that students produce also requires a sizable investment of time on the part of the teacher as well as careful attention to the process of providing useful feedback and arriving at a score for the language performance.

Linking assessment to learning. Assessment data provide teachers with information about students' developing skills and the effectiveness of their instruction. However, incorporating assessment into the daily routine of the classroom takes some planning. A useful way to conceptualize and organize activities related to assessment is through a multistep and recursive instructional and assessment cycle (Davison & Leung, 2009; Rea-Dickens, 2001; Teachers of English to Speakers of Other Languages, 2001) in which teachers set up tasks, monitor student engagement and performances during those tasks, collect information about

performances, and then use that information in some purposeful manner. Such a four-step cycle can be found in Figure 5.

Let us look more closely at how teachers can develop a range of assessments linked to learning aims. Before becoming more interested in new assessment practices, Ms. Aranda used to plan her lessons around instructional activities that she felt would help her students learn most effectively. She carefully allotted time for each activity in the class schedule and hoped for the best. While understanding that *what* students do in the classroom is certainly important, Ms. Aranda has come to realize that it is also useful to focus on *why* students are engaging in those activities and to determine whether in fact learning is taking place.

Step 1: Identifying learning aims
- Identify students' proficiency level and language learning needs
- Select learning aims aligned with curriculum guidelines or learning standards that are related to learner needs
- Identify a purpose for the assessment

Step 2: Collecting and recording information about student learning
- Select instructional activities designed to help students meet those aims
- Collect information during and at the end of the unit of instruction
- Use multiple assessments that will provide feedback and record performances
- Prepare scoring tools (e.g., modify or design rubrics for scoring performance assessments, check the accuracy of answer sheets for selected-response assessments)
- Familiarize learners with each assessment format and engage them in self- and peer assessments
- Devise a time line for data collection and analysis

Step 3: Examining the information
- Use a log or record to keep track of student performances
- Review patterns of student performances across time and multiple assessments
- Match student performances against desired outcome levels or benchmarks

Step 4: Using the information
- Modify instructional plans
- Share student progress with students and others (e.g., parents, other teachers)
- Create additional program support for students

Figure 5. Four-step assessment cycle (based on Gottlieb, Katz, & Ernst-Slavit, 2009).

In her planning, she now articulates a learning aim (or standard) as she selects activities so she can choose which ones suit her students' learning needs, and she chooses a variety of assessment types to check on students' progress.

Here is an example of how Ms. Aranda has planned an activity around vocabulary development. Her students have been keeping a vocabulary notebook. They write down words and phrases they would like to know and be able to use. Students are free to choose the vocabulary items from the content covered in class or from other sources related to that content. Although this activity does not reflect a primary learning aim of every daily lesson, it does encourage her students to take more responsibility for their learning as they develop their language skills. To help her plan how assessment will support learning, Ms. Aranda uses an alignment chart like the one in Figure 6 to examine linkages across the learning aim for this activity, details about what students will do, and ways of assessing learning.

The varying role of feedback during lessons: From error correction to reflective logs. Additional support for linkages between assessment and learning has emerged from recent research in educational assessment on the effectiveness of formative assessment, or assessment *for* learning, as a tool to support learning in the classroom (Black & Wiliam, 1998; Rea-Dickens, 2001). Black and Wiliam (1998) found that when teachers provide ongoing feedback to students on their performances and their students use that feedback to move forward in their learning, both high- and low-achieving students make gains in their scores on conventional tests. In more recent work, Black and Wiliam (2009) identify five key strategies for enacting formative assessment:

1. clarifying and sharing learning intentions and criteria for success
2. engineering effective classroom discussions and other learning tasks that elicit evidence of student understanding
3. providing feedback that moves learners forward
4. activating students as instructional resources for one another
5. empowering students as the owners of their own learning. (p. 4)

Moving this work on the importance of feedback to the arena of the language classroom, Rea-Dickens (2001) identifies a continuum of classroom assessment, from "formal" to "informal." This continuum highlights the range of assessment opportunities that teachers can take advantage of in the classroom as they observe and interpret student language performances. It is useful to note that teachers are engaged in processing information and providing feedback about student performances throughout a lesson as, for example, they gauge student engagement during tasks, respond to and build on student interactions, and offer comments on student products. Students can also participate in this processing and feedback loop. Figure 7 illustrates how feedback can be provided at various instructional moments in relation to student language performances.

Merely noting that feedback can play a critical role in supporting student learning is not sufficient for providing guidance since the nature of that feedback can have either a positive or negative effect on student achievement (R. Ellis, 2009a). This means that feedback must move beyond, for example, a grade or mark on a returned piece of student work or a hurried correction during an oral interaction to include substantive information about a specific

Learning Objective	Classroom Activity	Assessment
Students will be able to extend their vocabulary development.	Students will keep a vocabulary notebook. They will create flash cards with the word or phrase on one side and a picture or mnemonic device representing the meaning on the other.	1. Students race against the clock to see how many word or phrases they can name in a minute by looking at the meaning side of the card. Every week they measure themselves against their previous "score" and against the "scores" of their peers. 2. Students fill out a self-assessment form.

Figure 6. Alignment chart linking assessment with learning.[1]

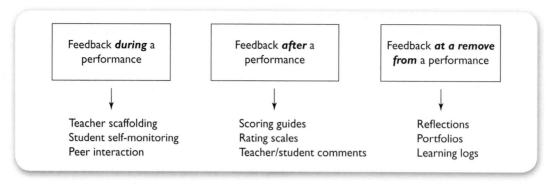

Feedback **during** a performance	Feedback **after** a performance	Feedback **at a remove from** a performance
↓	↓	↓
Teacher scaffolding Student self-monitoring Peer interaction	Scoring guides Rating scales Teacher/student comments	Reflections Portfolios Learning logs

Figure 7. Types of feedback during instruction (adapted from Katz, 2012).

language performance. However, identifying what this feedback may consist of is not so simple (Leung & Mohan, 2004; Rea-Dickens, 2001). Research on various kinds of feedback is helping to pinpoint effective practices in the language classroom (e.g., R. Ellis, 2009a; Ferris, 2011; Lyster & Mori, 2006). Useful feedback leading to more positive outcomes needs to: be frequent; provide students with a clear picture of their current achievement level and how to move forward; and offer encouragement (Marzano, 2006). Moss and Brookhart (2009) offer additional guidance on specific strategies teachers can use in giving feedback:

■ Provide feedback in a timely manner when students are still engaged with the learning aim and can do something with the feedback.

■ Be aware of the amount of feedback being provided; students need enough feedback to know how successful they were on a task or assignment and to have an idea of how to move forward; however, the amount of feedback should not overwhelm students.

■ Include comments on both positive and weak aspects of student performances.

■ Take advantage of multiple modes, written and oral feedback, as well as modeling to demonstrate the learning target (but not all modes for each performance).

CLASSROOM APPLICATIONS

In this section, I examine how teachers can apply current approaches to the assessment of language skills. In classroom activities, oral tasks involve both listening and speaking, while literacy tasks engage students in reading and writing. Additional tasks integrate all four skills as students learn new skills and interact with one another to practice their emerging competencies. However, in this section, I divide the skills into receptive (reading and listening) and productive (speaking and writing) skills to capitalize on the similarities in designing assessments for each pair. I then move on to a discussion of two important tools for classroom assessment of all skills, portfolios and teacher observations, and conclude with a brief examination of some tools for student self-assessment.

Receptive skills: Reading and listening

Reading and listening are often called receptive skills because they share the linguistic feature that students "receive" or take in language sounds and written symbols and then process them to create meaning. Because this processing is not an observable behavior in the same way as speaking or writing a language, teachers must make inferences about the development of these skills. Hughes (2003) explains that the challenge for the assessment of receptive skills is "to set tasks which will not only cause the candidate to exercise reading (or listening) skills, but will also result in behaviour that will demonstrate the successful use of those skills" (p. 136). (See chapters by Anderson, Ediger, Flowerdew & Miller, Goh, and Grabe & Stoller, this volume, for in-depth discussions of reading and listening skills.)

As Figure 4 suggests, there are many types of assessment. Choosing ones that can be used to assess reading and listening depends on factors such as the purpose for collecting the information and the targeted learning aim or language competence that is to be sampled in student performances, as well as the students' language proficiency level. For example, students beginning to read English will need to learn the graphemic symbols that combine to form words carrying meaning. More advanced students may be learning how to scan a text to locate information. A different type of assessment task is needed to capture these two different reading competencies.

Because reading and listening each draw on many components, teachers may choose to assess students' ability using a range of tasks, depending on what they want to know about student learning. The assessment literature provides numerous examples of assessment tasks (e.g., Alderson, 2000; Brown & Abeywickrama, 2010; Buck, 2001; Hughes, 2003). Figure 8 lists a sample of those tasks ordered by a range of selected language performances.

Note that including the assessment tasks in Figure 8 is not meant to suggest that they are the "best" method for testing a particular competence or skill. All tasks have their strengths and weaknesses. Rather, they are illustrative of the variety of assessment tools (both selected- and constructed-response types) that can be used to describe and gauge language development. As Alderson (2000) points out, "No single test method can fulfill all the varied purposes for which we might test" (p. 203).

It is important to remember that whatever task teachers choose to use, it will not be a direct measure of either reading or listening competence since students are processing these skills internally. To tap into that processing, teachers use tasks, such as the ones in Figure 8, that require students to take an action or say or write something that will indicate their developing competence in a particular skill area. Certainly these are useful ways to turn an invisible process into an observable behavior. However, when using one language skill as a means to measure another one, teachers need to make sure the speaking or writing task is itself not another assessment. This caution is particularly salient with students at beginning levels of language proficiency. If students cannot read the directions for a task, for example, they will not be able to carry it out. A general guideline is to write directions and questions at a slightly lower level than that of the targeted language competence.

One way to be more confident in assessing receptive skills is to make sure to use more than one kind of assessment to determine how much

Sample Reading Performances	Sample Assessment Tasks
Learners process the letters, words, and phrases of printed material.	• Picture cued items in which learners identify a word or phrase represented in the picture • Word pairs, such as *hit/hit* or *bit/bait*, in which learners identify which pairs of words or phrases are the same or different
Learners recognize the structures used in texts (from word level to genre level).	• Multiple choice • Matching • Gap filling • Sequencing
Learners interact with the text to interpret meaning.	• Short answer • Summary writing • Sequencing • Information transfer (the learner uses the information in a new setting, e.g., filling in a chart with information gleaned from the reading)
Learners use strategies.	• Reading-strategies checklists • Reading logs • Think-alouds (students verbalize their thoughts as they read to highlight the strategies they are using)

Sample Listening Performances	Sample Assessment Tasks
Learners recognize the components of the sound system.	• Word pairs, both decontextualized and in an utterance • Identification of intonation patterns
Learners listen and respond to relatively short stretches of language.	• Providing an oral response to a question • Body movement in response to a oral command • Picture cued items in which learners listen to an utterance and relate it to a picture
Learners understand the meaning of stretches of discourse.	• Information transfer • Multiple choice • Short answer • Restating the gist • Answering comprehension questions

Figure 8. Sample language competencies and tasks for reading and listening.

students are learning. This guideline, while useful for all assessment practice, is particularly appropriate when assessing receptive skills so the teacher can feel confident about the quality of the information gathered. It is also important that students understand the structure of the task and what they are being asked to do to demonstrate their learning. Typically, tasks for assessment should be based on activities and exercise types that were used for instruction.

Productive skills: Speaking and writing

Speaking and writing are often called productive skills because they require students to produce language and, in doing so, to create meaning. Unlike the receptive skills, language output is an observable behavior, at least in terms of student products such as spoken responses or pieces of writing, and so lends itself to being assessed through direct measures, particularly at more advanced levels of language proficiency. Additional attention is also often paid to the processes inherent in producing these outputs, and like the receptive skills, these processes require more indirect methods of assessment. Figure 9 sets out sample language performances in speaking and writing along with selected tasks for assessing students' proficiency in using those skills. (See chapters by Bohlke, Frodesen, Goodwin, Lazaraton, Olshtain, and Weigle, this volume, for in-depth discussions of speaking and writing skills.)

Once students move away from more controlled language production and begin generating extended texts either in spoken or written performances, teachers are faced with the problem of how to capture and make sense of the language that students are generating. In addition to the assessment task itself—for example, producing a paragraph or engaging in a debate—a consistent means of scoring student performances is needed.

Performance assessments such as these consist of two components: (1) a prompt that sets the task for the assignment; and (2) a way of scoring the language that students produce. Well-crafted prompts do more than instruct the student to write 150 words or take one side of an issue for a debate. They specify the amount

Sample Speaking Performances	Sample Assessment Tasks
Learners produce comprehensible words or phrases.	• Repetition of words and phrases provided by a teacher • Recitation of rhymes and poems • Picture cued items
Learners produce utterances in response to short stretches of language.	• Dialogue completion • Picture cued narratives or descriptions • Pair/group structured tasks
Learners produce longer interactive stretches of discourse.	• Role play • Information gap • Interview
Learners produce monologues.	• Oral presentation • Debate • Retelling stories

Sample Writing Performances	Sample Assessment Tasks
Learners produce letters, words, punctuation, and brief texts.	• Copying letters or words • Spelling tests • Picture cued items • Multiple choice
Learners produce guided writing.	• Picture-cued narratives, sequences, or descriptions • Reordering mixed-up words into a sentence or out-of-sequence sentences into a paragraph • Short answer or sentence completion
Learners produce texts.	• Paragraphs • Texts in various genres (e.g., summaries, book reports, essays)
Learners engage in the writing process.	• Comments on other students' drafts, focusing initially on ideas rather than each grammatical error • Writing conferences

Figure 9. Sample language competencies and tasks for speaking and writing.

or type of information necessary to meet teacher expectations for a satisfactory performance and to generate the desired type of speaking or writing. Additional useful features in a prompt include the identification of an audience, a purpose, and a context for generating language. Here's an example of a prompt for a piece of writing:

> Write a one-page letter to another student in the class about one of the books we've read this year. In your letter, describe what the book is about and why you have chosen to write about this book.

Scoring guides are generally used in assessing the language that students produce. They provide consistency in scoring as well as a clear picture of the criteria that will be used in judging a language performance. In this way, teachers and students can develop a shared understanding of learning aims embodied in the criteria found in the guides and identify what will count as a satisfactory performance. Following are several commonly used types of scoring guides. As with all assessments, there are advantages and shortcomings to each one.

Checklists are one type of assessment tool used in documenting speaking and writing performances. As the name suggests, *checklists* are made up of lists of features of a language performance with a space for noting whether or not that feature is present in a specific performance. Table 1 provides an example of a checklist for a writing assignment. Checklists are simple to use and can be easily adapted to observations of language production during class activities. However, they provide no information about the quality of a performance.

A frequently used scoring guide is a *rating scale,* in which the performance is scored or rated according to a list of features. Some rating scales include only numbers and a brief statement of what the rater should focus on. Ones designed for

Table 1. Writing Checklist

Rating Criteria	Assessment	
	Yes	No
Is the writer's purpose clear?	___	___
Is there a beginning, middle, and end?	___	___
Does each paragraph have a main idea?	___	___
Is each main idea developed?	___	___
Are all the sentences complete?	___	___
Is newly learned vocabulary used appropriately?	___	___

Table 2. Oral Participation Rating Scale

Rating Criteria	Assessment			
Interacts with all members of the group during the task	1	2	3	4
Maintains rapport with other members of the group	1	2	3	4
Uses a range of targeted structures	1	2	3	4
Uses a range of learned vocabulary	1	2	3	4
Pronunciation of learned vocabulary is comprehensible	1	2	3	4

Key: 1 = lowest score; 4 = highest score

younger learners may display a range of graphic "faces" (e.g., from faces with smiles to ones with frowns) that can be circled. Table 2 is an example of a rating scale for assessing the quality of oral participation in a discussion task. Rating scales offer more scoring choices than checklists as well as the opportunity to give more points to some features than others, but the lack of detailed descriptions for each scoring point can lead to differences in scoring the same language performance.

Two additional types of scoring guides are *holistic* and *analytic rubrics.* Unlike the previous scoring guides, both types of rubrics include specific criteria related to various qualities of language proficiency that are aligned with a scale or range of levels. Each score is tied to a set of descriptors. Because of these descriptors, such tools are particularly useful in assessing complex performances such as extended writing or speaking. They also help to ensure more consistency in scoring across performances and across raters by focusing attention on specific aspects of a performance.

Holistic scoring draws on a rater's response to an entire performance produced by a language user. Holistic rubrics generate a single score for a performance. An example of a holistic writing rubric can be found in Figure 10. It was designed to gather information about writing skills in a low-intermediate English as a second language (ESL) class at the secondary level. Holistic tools are useful for quick scoring of a language performance and are used extensively, for example, when assessing numerous writing samples at the end of a marking period or during a placement procedure. They do

5	Well organized with very few errors in grammar to impede comprehension. A wide and appropriate use of vocabulary. Fully comprehensible.
4	Minor problems in content and/or organization. Some errors in grammar and lexical choice that require attention. Generally comprehensible.
3	While some problems in content and/or organization are evident, the paper is comprehensible for the most part. There are obvious errors in grammar and lexical choice that indicate a need for further language development.
2	There are serious problems in content and/or organization. The paper is difficult to understand at times. Errors in grammar and lexical choice are frequent and distracting. Not easy to understand.
1	Unclear content and organization. Overwhelming problems with grammar and lexical choice that make comprehension very difficult.

Figure 10. Sample holistic writing rubric.

not, however, provide specific information about individual components or subskills.

Analytic scales rate the various components of a language performance and provide scores for each one. An example of an analytic writing rubric can be found in the Appendix. It was designed to provide feedback to students in an adult low-intermediate ESL class about their developing skill in paragraph writing. Analytic tools provide specific information about each component of a language performance since each component receives its own score. While it takes more time to use an analytic tool than a holistic one, analytic tools provide information that is useful for discerning a learner's strengths and pinpointing areas for continued efforts. For learning purposes, they provide the kind of formative feedback discussed earlier that can help students see where they are in developing their skills, what is expected from them, where they need to go, and the criteria that will used to gauge the success of their efforts. As a way to

lessen the process of scoring a performance, some teachers use selected segments of analytic tools (i.e., those related to current teaching aims) and then use others at other appropriate times during a unit.

Portfolios

Whether focused on individual language skills or integrated language performances, portfolios capture a more complete picture of where students are in their learning process than any individual assessment can provide. A good deal has been written about portfolios in second language education (e.g., Brown & Abeywickrama, 2010; Genesee & Upshur, 1996; O'Malley & Valdez Pierce, 1996).

Genesee and Upshur (1996) define a *portfolio* as "a purposeful collection of students' work that demonstrates to students and others their efforts, progress, and achievements in given areas" (p. 99). Such work can include samples of writing, including all drafts of a paper to demonstrate the development of students' writing skills during the writing process; reading logs; audio/video-recordings of oral performances; tests; key homework assignments; projects; and self- and peer assessments. In content areas or English for specific purposes classrooms, work products related to the focus of instruction (e.g., lab reports or a business plan analysis) can also be included. To be a useful tool linking learning and assessment, portfolios must be more than a file folder of work products. The contents should reflect learning aims and engage students in the process of both selecting and reflecting on the individual items. Over time, portfolios provide a rich picture of the stages of student learning as they document achievement during the period under consideration.

O'Malley and Valdez Pierce (1996) caution that to be effectively used portfolios must be carefully planned, and they suggest five steps for implementing them in the classroom:

1. Decide on the purpose for using portfolios for assessment (e.g., to encourage student self-assessment, to monitor the development of students' skills, to communicate learners' progress to family members).
2. Choose contents that match the purpose.
3. Include clear criteria for examining student work. If possible, involve students in identifying the criteria that will be used; at a minimum, make sure students understand the

criteria and what they mean in terms of the work they are expected to produce.

4. Set standards for performances. Samples of student work that meets these expectations are one way to help students "see" these targets.

5. Involve students. A major benefit of portfolios is the potential they carry for engaging students in the learning process and taking more responsibility for their learning. An important component of this involvement is students' self-reflections about the work they have chosen to include in a portfolio, including what they have learned and what they still need to improve.

By now it should be clear that many assessment tools that teachers use can also be used by students as long as students understand the criteria for their use and have opportunities to practice applying them. In fact, student participation in the assessment process can be considered a critical factor in supporting learning in the language classroom.

Teacher observations

An important assessment tool is observation. This activity takes place throughout the lesson as teachers watch their students engage in tasks, respond to teacher instructions, and interact with peers. Through these observations, teachers try to make sense of their students' moment-to-moment learning and the level of their engagement in instructional tasks. Because observation is ongoing, the challenge in using it for assessment purposes can be daunting.

Just as with other assessment tools, planning can help to systemize observations to make them more useful. Equally important is figuring out a way to record the observations. Following are suggestions for these two elements.

Planning. Since there are any number of things to be observed in the classroom, it is necessary to narrow the focus to make the task manageable.

- Decide on what aspect of teaching or learning is going to be observed. Will it be focused on students' use of a targeted language form? Amount of participation in a group task? Use of learned vocabulary? Will it provide information about whether students are ready to move on to the next unit or need more instruction?

- Choose whom to observe. Depending on the class size and the observation focus, observing all the students at one time is probably impossible. Some teachers select several students to observe at each class, eventually rotating through all the students, or monitor groups of students as they engage in a learning task.

- Decide on the timing for observations. Having a time line or schedule for the observations ensures that they do indeed take place and that all students are included in this assessment activity.

Recording. Tools for capturing observations include anecdotal notes, rating scales, and checklists. While it takes some thought to use these tools, they enable teachers to capture moments of classroom learning that can be reviewed and evaluated at a later date. Anecdotal notes are brief notes reporting on what has been observed. They can be recorded on pieces of paper, note cards, or even sticky notes that are then organized and stored for later reference. Since checklists and rating scales have already been described in the earlier section on assessing productive skills, only anecdotal notes are covered here. Anecdotal notes can focus on a specific aspect of instruction or be more open-ended so as to capture spontaneous moments that occur during class. They can be recorded during instruction as students engage in tasks and teachers are monitoring their work or at the end of a lesson while teachers reflect on the day's activities and interactions.

Whether anecdotal notes, rating scales, or checklists are used for observation, it is critical to include students' names and the observation date when recording information about the event. It is also helpful to reference the instructional activity being observed to make the connection between the observation and the instructional moment.

Student engagement in assessment

A basic tenet underlying current approaches to instruction and assessment is that each member of the classroom community contributes to transforming classrooms into rich learning environments. It is increasingly clear that students can and should take a more active role both in the learning process and in the assessment of that learning. When they participate in the assessment process, students can:

- develop a deeper understanding of what they are expected to learn and do with language

- look more closely at their own strengths and weaknesses as they progress in learning English
- gauge their current proficiency against targeted levels of language growth (in other words, compare where they are with where they want to be)

By gaining a clearer understanding of their own learning through assessment, students reap additional benefits such as developing a deeper sense of responsibility for learning and increasing their motivation to continue to learn. Just as important, students acquire skills that provide a basis for ongoing learning after leaving their instructional program. Self-assessment is particularly useful in documenting the development of receptive skills. Next I consider some tools that students can use to document and understand their language learning experiences.

Student journals or logs are kept by students as records of their learning experiences. In them, students can keep track of their language learning progress, the context for their use of language, and how successful (or not) they feel they have been. Figure 11 is an example of a student listening log.

Language use inventories or reports provide students with a way to keep track of how they use language in specific ways. Using a list of possible language performances, students can check what they can do and what they are still working on. Figure 12 is an example of a language use inventory focused on listening.

Self-assessment tools can also be used to document other kinds of learning in addition to specific language skills, for example, how students use strategies to extend their competence in communicating with others. Strategies, such as constructing hypotheses from cues, making inferences, and revising hypotheses, make up an important part of language instruction and do not lend themselves to more traditional assessment tools. Figure 13 is an example of a learning log that students can use to monitor their progress in using strategies.

		I can do this	I'm still working on this
Name:			
Date:			
1.	I understand what the teacher says in class.	_____	_____
2.	I understand what the students in my group are saying.	_____	_____
3.	I understand the main points of news stories I hear on TV.	_____	_____
4.	I understand the main points of news stories I hear on the radio.	_____	_____
5.	I understand the gist of conversations with others.	_____	_____
6.	I understand most of what people say to me on the telephone.	_____	_____

Figure 12. Sample listening inventory.[2]

Name: Date	What I read	Strategies I used
9/25	newspaper article	skimming for main ideas

Figure 13. Sample log of reading texts and reading strategies.

Grading

Up to now, I have concentrated on ways of measuring and understanding language performances during periods of instruction. Although each individual performance may be scored or graded, at some point in most educational contexts teachers draw on the accumulated information collected during a term of instruction to provide a summing up of their students' work in the guise of term grades. Yet this is not an easy process because a number of issues surround this essential teacher task (see Brown & Abeywickrama, 2010; O'Malley & Valdez Pierce, 1996, for extended discussions of grading and its issues).

To get a sense of some of these issues, let us consider the dilemma Ms. Aranda faced at the end

Name: Date	What I listened to	What I understood
10/12	A short video in class	The main points but not why people did what they did

Figure 11. Sample listening log.

of the teaching year, one common to many teachers of classes with students of varying proficiency and engagement levels. One of her students, Fuad, was an attentive student in class, participating in group work and engaging in class activities. He turned in all his homework assignments and most of his assignments met the criteria for success. He had difficulty, however, with the mid-term and final exams that were required by the department. Another of Ms. Aranda's students, Rosa, did well on the departmental exams but rarely completed homework assignments and was a reluctant participant in group work or class discussions. What grade provides a fair reflection of each student's achievement?

This is a tricky question, of course, since there are many factors that go into developing a grading policy. While some people believe that only achievement should be the basis for a grade, others feel that additional factors, such as effort or class behavior, should also be included in the calculation. Another consideration may be the departmental or school policy regarding how grades are to be calculated and distributed within a class. The disparity in calculating final grades becomes readily apparent when teachers talk about their individual grading policy or discuss student grades from previous classes.

Although it is not the intent of this chapter to endorse a particular approach to grading, Figure 14 lists some guidelines that can help teachers develop sound grading policies congruent with current instruction and assessment theories.

- Be aware of any institutional guidelines or requirements related to grading.
- Decide on the components of the final grade and the weighting of each component.
- Make sure that students know what "counts" in calculating their grades right from the beginning of class.
- Ensure that grades are based on solid evidence—that the assessments for each component are well designed and match their intended purpose.
- Use scoring guides, rubrics, or anecdotal notes to capture student performances on more qualitative components rather than relying on memory or gut feelings (e.g., a checklist for class participation).
- Consider ways of providing qualitative feedback about each component in addition to a letter or number grade.

Figure 14. Guidelines for developing a sound grading policy.

It is important to reiterate that clarity in communication about grades is paramount. Connecting with students, with other stakeholders, and with other teachers about a grading policy can help to ensure that the policy fulfills its intended aim of providing useful information about what students have accomplished during a grading period. Such communication is particularly important given that English learners may come from school systems with vastly different grading systems. These cultural expectations can impact how students interpret which aspects of their work or language performances will be "counted" among the many activities in a language classroom.

FUTURE TRENDS

Classroom assessment holds much promise for transforming language classrooms into more vital learning communities in several ways.

An increase in the use of assessment for formative purposes rather than summative ones can lead to classrooms that are focused on supporting student learning. When teachers and students work together to identify learning needs and learning targets and then to chart a path to those targets, assessment moves from documenting what students do not know to highlighting what they can do with instructional guidance from the teacher and peers.

The inclusion of performance assessments among the roster of assessment types further blurs the line between instruction and assessment. Rather than requiring teachers to take time out of the instructional day for a test, these kinds of classroom assessments can be integrated into the daily routine of classroom activities, thus enhancing learning opportunities while also providing feedback to teachers and learners.

In designing and using classroom assessment, teachers achieve more agency within the classroom, functioning as agents for change to promote learning. Students also become agents of their own learning, taking on a more active role in assessment as they identify criteria for achievement, provide feedback to others, and reflect on their own performances.

However, these promises are also accompanied by several questions that should be considered in implementing classroom assessment.

What is useful feedback and how do we know?

As the discussion in the section on Assessment and Learning suggests, providing feedback is an essential step if assessment is to be used to support learning. It is not always clear, though, what constitutes effective feedback. Broad guidelines may point teachers in useful directions, but teachers still need to take into account levels of student language proficiency as well as student learning needs when translating those guidelines into local practice.

Are teachers prepared to implement classroom assessment?

As noted throughout this chapter, teachers are critical to the success of translating new ideas about classroom assessment into effective practice, yet courses in assessment make up a relatively meager proportion of preservice teacher preparation programs. How well prepared are teachers with the knowledge and skills needed to implement these types of assessment practices and assume this new role? What attitudes do teachers hold about these practices and how comfortable are they conducting assessments? If teachers are to situate new ideas about assessment practice within local teaching contexts, they will need support via ongoing professional development that will help them reflect on their practice and nurture their emerging assessment skills. In-service support is needed to provide teachers with time for collaboration with peers and for using resources such as online networking spaces where they can share innovative assessment ideas.

How receptive are students to new forms of assessment?

New ideas about assessment envision an active role for students as they identify learning needs, engage in language performances, use criteria, provide feedback to others, and reflect on their own achievements. Such a role may not be congruent with students' previous schooling experiences or cultural expectations, and so teachers may face responses ranging from puzzlement to disgruntlement. Classrooms that nurture a supportive climate can help students in the transition to this new role.

How receptive are institutions to changes in assessment policies?

Just as students may be reluctant to embrace new forms of assessment, institutions responsible for education may also be slow to adopt changes in assessment policies and practices. Without the support of ministries or departments of education, it may be challenging for teachers to adopt new ideas about assessment, especially in the face of prescribed accountability measures such as school-leaving examinations.

CONCLUSION

Assessment has become an increasingly larger part of the daily practice of language classrooms. While much attention has been paid to the role of standardized tests in education, in particular for accountability uses, more recent interest has centered on how teachers can use classroom assessments to gather information about and support student learning. This chapter has articulated how these new approaches to language testing are congruent with current theories of teaching and learning that focus on learning processes as well as products, on making meaning within social contexts, and on students' active role in classroom learning. The assessment literature provides numerous examples of assessment tools that can be used to monitor and document students' use of language skills. Effective implementation of these tools, however, requires careful thought and planning to ensure that assessments align with instructional aims and pedagogical purposes. To this end, professional development that supports teachers in experimenting with and using new assessment ideas will play a critical role.

SUMMARY

➤ Well-planned classroom assessments that are aligned with instructional aims can provide teachers—and students—with information about learning taking place in the classroom.

- ➤ A myriad of assessment types provide teachers with a range of creative options for documenting student learning.
- ➤ Through formative-assessment processes, both teachers and students are active participants in the process of achieving learning targets.
- ➤ Communication between teachers and students about learning expectations and performance criteria is a cornerstone to effective assessment policies and practices.

DISCUSSION QUESTIONS

1. Recall your own experiences with assessment as a learner. Consider how you felt, what you think you learned from the assessment experience, and how others felt about the methods used. Now create two lists: one list describing methods with positive effects and the other describing methods with negative effects. Which practices do you feel helped you learn? Which ones were less helpful? Why?

2. This chapter has explored the use of assessment for formative purposes as well as for summative ones. Review the use of assessments in your setting. What purposes do they serve? How are learners involved in learning and assessment? What external factors (e.g., Ministry of Education guidelines or state-mandated assessments) impact your choices about assessment?

3. You are planning an intermediate writing class. What learning aims will you include in your objectives for the class? How will you assess them? How will students participate in your assessment plan? How will you use the information you and your students collect?

4. The discussion of grading suggests that several factors can influence how teachers decide on grades for their students. What criteria do you think should be included in a final grade? Are your beliefs congruent with those of your institution? With your colleagues? Do your students know these criteria?

SUGGESTED ACTIVITIES

1. Your students have read a text of about 125 words. The table below presents a plan for assessment to determine their understanding of the text. Would you use the assessments listed? Would you modify them, or use others? Use the last column of the table to record your ideas.

2. Choose a language test and comment on it. Use one from your own teaching setting or download one from the Internet. What skills are being assessed? What model of language and assessment do you think is being used to inform the test design? How effective are the items? What impact do you think this test will have on students? What information will you (and the students who take this test) gather from the test results?

3. Use the chart on p. 336 to analyze the current use of assessment in your classroom or a class you are familiar with. Begin by specifying your learning objective. Include both assessments that you have chosen or designed and those that are required by your institution or Ministry of Education. Do the assessments align with your learning aims? How are students engaged in the assessment process?

Learning Objective	Possible Assessments	Your Notes
To determine whether students understand the key points in the reading passage.	• A gap-filling exercise with key information deleted. Students fill in their answers and swap papers to check answers. • In pairs, students make up questions based on information from the text. Sitting with another pair of students, they take turns asking questions and checking answers. • Students write a brief summary of the text, highlighting key ideas.	

Learning Objective	Current Assessments	Role of Students	Pros and Cons of Current Assessments

FURTHER READING

Brown, H. D., & Abeywickrama, P. (2010). *Language assessment: Principles and classroom practices* (2nd ed.). White Plains, NY: Pearson.

This book provides a thorough discussion of assessment principles and how they can be applied when implementing assessments in language classrooms. In addition to many useful examples of language assessments at various proficiency levels in each skill area, it also offers a thoughtful analysis of factors impacting grading policies.

Coombe, C., Folse, K., & Hubley, N. (2007). *A practical guide to assessing English language learners.* Ann Arbor, MI: Michigan University Press.

The authors provide numerous examples of assessment types for each language skill along with useful tips for designing various types of tests.

Gottlieb, M. (2006). *Assessing English language learners.* Thousand Oaks, CA: Corwin Press.

For teachers working with English learners in U.S. K–12 schools, this book provides a blueprint for designing an assessment plan that focuses on academic achievement while remaining congruent with current theories of teaching and learning.

McKay, P. (2006). *Assessing young language learners.* Cambridge, UK: Cambridge University Press.

This volume addresses issues related to assessing a specific population of students—young learners—and provides useful suggestions for ensuring that the assessment practices used with that population are appropriate.

O'Malley, J. M., & Valdez Pierce, L. (1996). *Authentic assessment for English language learners.* Reading, MA: Addison-Wesley.

Also focused on U.S.-based K–12 classrooms, the authors provide a range of assessment models, including numerous examples of self-assessment tools.

APPENDIX: SAMPLE ANALYTIC WRITING TOOL

Assessment	Topic Sentence	Supporting Sentences	Concluding Sentence
4	Presents the main point clearly. Sentence is complete. There are no grammar or spelling errors.	There are three or more complete supporting sentences, with ideas that stick to the main idea presented in the topic sentence. There are no grammar or spelling errors.	There is a concluding sentence that reaffirms the main idea presented in the topic sentence and summarizes the ideas in the supporting sentences. There are no grammar or spelling errors.
3	Presents the main point clearly. Sentence is complete. There are a few grammar and/or spelling errors.	There are a couple of complete supporting sentences, with ideas that stick to the main idea presented in the topic sentence. There are a few grammar and/or spelling errors.	There is a concluding sentence that reaffirms the main idea presented in the topic sentence. There are a few grammar and/or spelling errors.
2	The main point is presented in an incomplete sentence. There are a few grammar and/or spelling errors.	There are a couple of supporting ideas presented. There are a few grammar and/or spelling errors.	The concluding sentence is presented in an incomplete sentence. There are a few grammar and/or spelling errors.
1	Grammar and spelling errors make it almost impossible to understand the main point.	Grammar and spelling errors make it almost impossible to identify supporting sentences.	Grammar and spelling errors make it almost impossible to identify the concluding sentence.
0	There is no topic sentence.	There are no supporting sentences.	There is no concluding sentence.

This rubric was developed by Adriana Scheidegger as part of the requirement for the Learner Assessment course at The New School. Used with permission.

ENDNOTES

[1] Ms. Aranda's alignment chart is based on one created by Jeff Puccini as part of the requirement for the Curriculum Development and Assessment course at SIT Graduate Institute.

[2] This listening inventory is based on one developed by Caroline Sayre as part of the requirement for the Learner Assessment course at The New School.

Skills for Teachers

22 | Tools and Techniques of Effective Second/Foreign Language Teaching

DONNA M. BRINTON

KEY QUESTIONS

➤ What are the basic tools and techniques of effective second/foreign language teaching?
➤ What evidence do we have that these techniques lead to more effective practice?
➤ What guidelines should teachers follow in implementing these techniques?

EXPERIENCE

Francina[1] is enrolled in a university Teaching English as a Second Language (TESL) practicum course that satisfies one of the requirements for a TESL Certificate. For the course requirements, she must complete 40 hours in an English as a second language (ESL) classroom (supervised by a mentor teacher) and attend weekly sessions at the university led by the practicum supervisor. During the term, the supervisor observes her three times. Following each observation, Francina and the supervisor fill out an observation/feedback form (see the Appendix) prior to their post-observation conference. During the conference, they debrief each other on the strengths of the lesson and discuss what Francina can focus on to improve her teaching. Figure 1 represents a part of the written feedback that Francina's supervisor has prepared in advance of the meeting.[2]

In the observation/feedback session, the practicum supervisor first asked Francina to give her overall impressions of the lesson and then to talk about her strengths. In response, Francina noted that she felt pleased with her use of an authentic text to contextualize her presentation of definite and indefinite articles and with the way in which her preparation of clip-art visuals motivated the students to complete the guided writing activity. However, she was concerned about the unhealthy group dynamics of the class and the tendency for students to form groups according to L1 and/or ethnicity. She also shared that the mentor teacher in the class tended to tolerate these dynamics and often seemed unaware of the negative impact they were having on student learning. In her lesson, Francina was aware that these dynamics played a similarly detrimental role. The supervisor, in turn, commended Francina for her pacing and timing of the lesson; for her creativity in using the crime scene context and the clip-art graphics to motivate students; and for her skillful use of elicitation, her well-honed classroom management skills, and her rapport with students. She then shared her questions about the lesson and elaborated on the written suggestions that she provided in the observation/feedback form.

As we will see in this chapter, many of the issues that the supervisor has noted in the observation/feedback form are factors that contribute to a successful second/foreign language lesson. They are also issues for which both novice and experienced teachers need continued guidance and feedback.

WHAT ARE THE TOOLS AND TECHNIQUES OF EFFECTIVE SECOND LANGUAGE TEACHING?

Richards and Rodgers (2001), in their seminal article on the nature of language teaching methods, delineate three main components of a method. (See also Celce-Murcia, this volume.)

OBSERVATION/FEEDBACK FORM

Teacher: *Francina Sena*   **Site**: *Santa Anita College*

Observer: *Donna Brinton*   **Class**: *ESL 1*

Teaching point(s): *definite & indefinite articles*   **Date**: *May 10*
(1st vs. 2nd mention)

LESSON QUALITY (achievement of objectives, organization, sequencing, pacing, use of audiovisual aids, technology, etc.)

The lesson achieved all its objectives and was both well organized and sequenced. As a context for teaching the first vs. second mention rule of article usage, Francina slightly adapted an authentic crime report from the local newspaper. This was very motivational for students and provided a natural context for presenting this aspect of English grammar. While delivering the lesson, Francina made good use of the projector and the whiteboard, as well as class handouts.

TEACHER PRESENTATION (clarity of presentation, knowledge of material, classroom management, speech clarity, etc.)

All aspects of the teacher's presentation were clear, and Francina showed thorough command of the material she was presenting. She is easily able to manage the class, although she needs to attend more to deliberately mixing students during group work (i.e., to break up unproductive group dynamics).

STUDENT PARTICIPATION (interest level, interaction with instructor, balance of student/teacher speech, opportunity to practice learning points, etc.)

Francina has excellent rapport with this group of students and is able to motivate them to participate in all aspects of the class. They particularly enjoyed the two activities that she designed (the crime scene report and a writing activity with clip-art picture prompts). There were multiple opportunities for students to practice the learning points, contribute to class, and work in their peer groups.

MAJOR STRENGTHS

1. *The use of the crime context and the authentic article from the local newspaper was a big plus in the lesson. Not only was this interesting to students, it also provided valuable cultural information such as what to look out for and where to call if they are witnesses to or victims of a robbery. Similarly, the writing activity using crime scene picture prompts seemed to perk students up and truly motivate them.*
2. *Francina is very poised and has good control of the class.*
3. *She was adept at explaining (and eliciting explanations of) unknown vocabulary in the reading passage and also answering extemporaneous student questions. I liked the fact that she took time to elaborate by giving examples (such as, when defining the word scar, telling students how she has a scar from falling on her chin when she was young).*
4. *She is also very adept at eliciting information from students during the grammar lesson. Students were eager to share the rules they had learned in the previous lesson, and Francina encouraged them to do so.*
5. *She made concerted efforts to equalize participation by calling on students who hadn't contributed (e.g., "Yoshiko, you want to do it?")*

QUESTIONS OR UNCERTAINTIES ABOUT THE LESSON

1. *When eliciting unknown vocabulary from the news article, some but not all words were written on the whiteboard. For example, the words 50s, kidnap, etc. were omitted. Was there a rationale behind the words that were put up on the board?*
2. *Do the students always cluster in ethnic groups during this class? Does the mentor teacher ever rearrange the groups to address this?*

SUGGESTIONS

1. *I thought Francina could have done a bit more warm-up prior to moving into having students read the news article.*
2. *I think the underlining activity could have been done in pairs. It would have helped to model this by going over the 1st paragraph together w/ students. [Francina ended up taking excess time to repeat the task directions to those students who hadn't understood what to do, as it was.]*
3. *In retrospect, I think the crime scene passage could have been shortened somewhat and some of the nontargeted article uses omitted (e.g., "with the word Salvador or El Salvador"). Student attention seemed to drop off a bit toward the end of the activity.*
4. *Don't forget the cardinal rules of group work: group students beforehand and give directions before handing out the task so as to keep student attention.*

(Continued)

Figure 1. Sample observation/feedback form.

5. *I thought a smoother transition to the writing activity was in order (e.g., explaining to students how this activity related to the activity that preceded it).*
6. *There is a definite uneven dynamic in this class. Several groups (in the back and the one side of class) do not participate actively and also appeared not to be fully on task during the group work or some other phases of the lesson. Don't be afraid to control these dynamics more actively (e.g., by moving students out of their ethnic groups, asking them not to use their first language [L1], etc.).*

CHRONOLOGICAL ACCOUNT OF LESSON[3]

2:30 *Pre-class: FS puts homework for Friday and Monday on whiteboard.*

2:35 *FS distributes handout: "Man attempts to kidnap local woman"*

Read this and see what it means. Take a couple of minutes and then we'll talk about it. [projects full text onto the screen]

2:40 *Checks to see if students are done: Okay, you're not done. . . . Read it? . . . Okay, everybody's read it, you're done?*

etc. . . .

POST-OBSERVATION COMMENTS

We discussed various aspects of the class, such as the low pass rate in ESL 1, which is causing some students to become demotivated. We also discussed the variation in student proficiency level and the challenges that this poses for the teacher. Finally, we discussed a few aspects that Francina should monitor in her own teaching, such as pacing and group management.

Figure 1. Sample observation/feedback form. *(Continued)*

1. *Approach:* the theories of language and language learning that guide the principles and practices of language teaching
2. *Design:* consideration of the objectives of a method; the selection and organization of language content (i.e., the course syllabus); the types of tasks and activities; and finally the role of the teacher, the learners, and the instructional materials
3. *Procedure:* the day-to-day classroom techniques and practices used in the teaching and learning of a language

In this chapter, I concentrate on the third of these components, the procedures used by classroom teachers on a daily basis. Included in this overview of the tools and techniques that contribute to effective second/foreign language teaching are the pairing and grouping of students, teacher classroom discourse, and the use of visuals and graphic organizers.[4]

CONCEPTUAL UNDERPINNINGS

Research into the ways in which classroom interaction patterns affect the teaching/learning process is referred to as *classroom research.* Such research is typically carried out in formal instructional settings and may be either quantitative (i.e., involving the collection and analysis of data) or qualitative (i.e., conducted largely through observation or introspection); it may also involve classroom discourse analysis or ethnography. Examples of typical research foci include teacher discourse patterns (e.g., question types or patterns of language used to provide feedback to students), peer-peer interaction patterns (e.g., in pair and group work), teacher and/or student use of the L1 versus the second language (L2) in the classroom, and the impact of wait time (i.e., the amount of time that is allowed to elapse after a question is asked) on student response rates. As Allwright (1983) noted:

> Classroom processes become the central focus. We want to understand why it is that things happen as they do in the classroom—how it is, for example, that some learners participate more and others less than planned by the teacher and how we might expect such factors to affect language learning itself. (pp. 191–192)

Beginning in the 1970s, applied linguists began researching L2 classrooms hoping to identify what constituted "good" teaching practice. This research was largely inconclusive due to the enormous complexity of classroom teaching and the resulting difficulty of reducing it to a few categories (Allwright, 1983; Tsui, 2001). As Allwright concluded: "It seemed that applications to teacher training were therefore premature, and that a major effort should first be put into trying to unravel the enormous complexities of classroom behavior" (p. 194). Subsequent classroom research, instead of focusing on the level of approach or design, began to focus on the level of procedure, or day-to-day classroom processes.

Over the decades, classroom researchers have continued their investigations of L2 classroom practice—especially in the areas of input (the language used by teachers), output (the language produced by learners), and classroom interaction. Although the brief summary of research findings provided next cannot begin to capture all the findings, we can see clearly emerging patterns in several key areas of L2 teaching practice.

Pairing and grouping of students

The rationale for pairing and grouping students in the language classroom is multifaceted. Some of the most compelling arguments are found in the literature on second language acquisition (SLA). (See also Ellis, this volume.)

- Coupled with the need in SLA for comprehensible input (i.e., access to the target language at a level that is both contextually rich and challenges learners but does not overwhelm or frustrate them; Krashen, 1981) is the need for ample opportunities for comprehensible output (i.e., meaningful opportunities to produce the target language).
- Controlled practice exercises (as typically found in L2 textbooks) do not provide the conditions for sustained or "pushed" output (i.e., output where the learner's linguistic repertoire is extended and stretched to communicate the message effectively), which is necessary for successful SLA (Swain, 1985).
- Pairing or grouping learners is the surest way to foster SLA in the classroom setting. This includes structuring tasks in such a way that learners are required to interact with their peers, negotiate for meaning, and formulate and share their opinions on topics.

Factoring into these arguments is the importance of the time dedicated to learner production. Often referred to as *time on task*, this can vary greatly, ranging from 30% in some classes to 90% in others, depending on the effectiveness of the teacher (Richards & Schmidt, 2010). Time on task

is significantly increased through the use of pair and group work.

Additional supporting evidence comes from research into the social aspects of the language classroom (McDonough & Shaw, 2003a; Senior, 1997, 2006). According to this research, experienced language teachers confirm the importance of developing and maintaining classes where students have bonded and there is a general climate of cohesiveness. Key to this process is what Senior (1997) terms "breaking down the barriers" (p. 6), creating an environment in which the whole class knows something about every class member. Also critical, according to Senior, is harnessing students' energy toward positive group-building and encouraging them to engage in new tasks harmoniously.

Finally, a compelling rationale for pairing and grouping students is found in the literature on Cooperative Learning, a learner-centered approach emphasizing the importance of student cooperation rather than competition. Proponents of Cooperative Learning (see Gillies, 2007; Kagan, 1994) emphasize that learning is dependent on socially structured exchanges and requires cooperative strategies. In the facilitative environment of the group, students are more apt to learn. Further, due to the accountability within the group, they are more apt to assume responsibility for their own learning.

Teacher classroom discourse

The term *teacher classroom discourse* encompasses different types of teacher talk, including prelesson chitchat, lesson warm-up, teacher questions, explanations and teacher-fronted instruction, modeling language use, error correction and feedback to students, and praise and acknowledgment of student contributions. Regardless of which of these discourse types we are considering, there is much in the literature on classroom research that can help to guide our practice. Next, we examine several areas that are especially significant for teachers to consider.

Lesson warm-up. Edelhoff (1981) identifies the information and motivation stage as the first of four stages of the lesson.[5] According to Edelhoff, in this warm-up stage the learners' background knowledge is tapped and their interest is aroused by being confronted with an experience that is novel and yet not totally unfamiliar. Crookes (2003) adds that the lesson warm-up is part of a larger framing of the lesson that includes its beginning and end, both of which assist in the learning process. (See also Purgason, this volume.)

The literature affirms the importance of the lesson warm-up in setting learner expectations and in creating a social event that motivates students and positively contributes to the learning process. Yet little empirical research on its effectiveness exists. As summarized by Lopes (as cited in Crookes, 2003), the following findings from questionnaires and interviews conducted with Brazilian English as a foreign language (EFL) learners indicate that learners recognize the value of the lesson warm-up:

- It sets a positive atmosphere via the teacher's affectionate greetings.
- The lesson review portion of the warm-up aids concentration.
- It establishes routines (such as the teacher asking what students have been doing and directing personal questions to individual students).
- It assists in getting attention, reducing anxiety, increasing motivation, and establishing the lesson theme.

To these, Crookes adds that lessons should be considered as speech events, embedded in the culture of pedagogy; as such, they require an opening and closing.

Error correction and feedback. Given the swings of the methodological pendulum, we are aware that the view of what constitutes an "error" and how the teacher should react to errors has varied widely from method to method. (See Celce-Murcia, this volume.) It is safe to say that today's communicative approaches are generally more tolerant of error than many previous methodologies (such as the audiolingual approach, with its behaviorist influences, resulting in a view of errors as negative habits that needed to be eradicated). Indicative of the more tolerant approach to errors today is the fact that the term *feedback* is preferred over the term *error correction*, with a further distinction made between explicit feedback (i.e., involving overt correction) and implicit feedback (i.e., involving a teacher recasting or rephrasing the learner's utterance).[6] Similarly, teachers now tend to interpret student errors much more

positively, for example, as an indication that the learner is formulating creative hypotheses about the L2 and is taking risks which will ultimately (with positive or negative feedback and the appropriate motivation on the part of the learner) lead to the acquisition and internalization of the linguistic item.

The research on error correction contributes to our understanding of how to frame feedback to learners. A few of the key research findings are worth highlighting.

Recasts. A recast is the reformulation of a learner's utterance, usually by the teacher, in an attempt to provide the correct target form. An example is the teacher recast "He is eighteen years old" in response to the learner utterance "He has eighteen years." Crookes and Chaudron (2001) note that, despite recasts being a highly prevalent form of teacher feedback, research shows them to be effective only 20–25% of the time. Often the learner interprets the teacher's recast as simply a confirmation of what he or she has said or as a clarification of meaning rather than as feedback on the form of the utterance.

Explicit correction. Conversely, Crookes and Chaudron (2001) report that research conducted in language immersion classrooms indicates that explicit correction leads to a considerably higher rate of learner uptake (immediate recognition and acceptance) of the corrected form. This finding, however, is contested by other researchers, who remain skeptical that negative feedback of this type really works (see Ortega, 2009).

Types of errors corrected. Teachers following a communicative approach are most likely to correct errors in content, followed by errors in vocabulary, and finally errors in grammar or pronunciation (Richards & Lockhart, 1994a).

Role of the instructional context. Overall, more explicit feedback is provided in contexts where the lesson focus is on language rather than in those where language is being acquired through content, as in the immersion classroom (Ortega, 2009).

Teacher-student interaction patterns. McDonough and Shaw (2003a) note that the typical teacher-fronted classroom follows a lockstep sequence of teacher stimulus, student response, and teacher evaluation. Add to this the fact that 70% of such classroom time consists of the teacher talking or asking questions (Richards & Lockhart, 1994), and we can see how important it is that teachers learn to make productive use of this time and avoid falling into the trap of lockstep sequences.

According to Lightbown and Spada (2006), the most common discourse sequence in the classroom is initiation-response-evaluation (IRE), a teacher-led discourse sequence (see Figure 2). This consists of a three-part exchange:

1. The teacher asks a student a display question (one to which there is one correct answer) to find out whether the student can respond.
2. A student responds (with correct or incorrect information).
3. The student answer is evaluated by the teacher, who makes a brief reply such as "Good," or "No, that's not right."

The interaction typically ends with Step 3 (Sinclair & Coulthard, 1975). According to Hall and Walsh (2002), in this pattern the teacher assumes the role of expert, eliciting information from students and evaluating their responses as either right or wrong. As the authors note, "It is the teacher who decides who will participate, when students can take a turn, how much they can contribute, and

Figure 3. The initiation-response-feedback (IRF) sequence.

whether their contributions are worthy or appropriate" (p. 188).

Closely related to IRE, but allowing for slightly more communicative classroom exchanges, is the initiation-response-feedback (IRF) sequence (Cullen, 2002; Hall & Walsh, 2002). This discourse sequence (see Figure 3) consists of this three-part exchange:

1. The teacher (or student) initiates the interaction by asking a referential question (one to which there are multiple possible answers) or introducing a topic.
2. A response is given.
3. The initiator uses the response to move the conversation forward.

The interaction can continue for multiple turns (i.e., with "chained" questions) and may include contributions from multiple class members.

The IRF sequence, though at first glance closely resembling the IRE sequence, represents an important reconceptualization of the teacher-student interaction pattern, allowing for more naturalistic

Figure 2. The initiation-response-evaluation (IRE) sequence.

interaction between teacher and student, a loosening of teacher control, and the chaining of student responses and contributions. As Hall and Walsh (2002) note, instead of closing down the interaction in the third move by providing an evaluation, the teacher's substitution of the feedback move invites students to expand on their response, justify or clarify their opinion, or share their personal experience.

Both IRE and IRF sequences are typical of teacher-student exchanges in the L2 classroom.[7] However, while the IRE sequence is an efficient way of conducting a lesson and provides a useful framework for controlled classroom practice and teacher feedback, it tends to restrict students from displaying their knowledge of the target language. For this reason, critics claim that it is typical of the transmission mode of learning in that it: (1) emphasizes the gatekeeper or controlling role of the teacher (Hall & Walsh, 2002); (2) prompts the learner to say what the teacher wants him or her to say; (3) is devoid of any real communicative intent; and (4) ultimately may reflect negatively on the teacher's ideology and notions of power (Richards & Farrell, 2011; Waring, 2009). It also deprives students of the opportunity to negotiate meaning, nominate topics, and ask questions that interest them (Cullen, 2002). In fact, as pointed out by Wong and Waring (2009), evaluative responses such as "very good" in IRE sequences can actually disrupt the communicative flow of classroom discourse because they close discussion or debate on a topic and prevent peers from contributing to the flow of discourse.

More recently proposed alternatives to the IRE and IRF sequences are the "instructional conversation" (Hall, 2001) and the "collaborative dialogue" (Richards & Farrell, 2011),[8] both of which entail scaffolded (or assisted) learning. In this process, the teacher or other more advanced peers provide supports, or scaffolds, to assist learners in acquiring and producing new aspects of the language, often modeling for them the desired outcome. The teacher also builds in opportunities for the learners to notice new language features and encourages them to practice using these features. As learners become more autonomous in their production of the targeted language, these scaffolds are gradually removed. As described by Richards and Farrell (2011):

> Learning is initially mediated and directed by the teacher or other more advanced learners and is gradually appropriated by the individual learner. Throughout, the teacher provides opportunities for noticing how language is used, experimenting with language use, practicing new modes of discourse, and restructuring existing language knowledge. (p. 136)

Inductive versus deductive presentation. One factor in making the most productive use of class time concerns whether to use a deductive or inductive approach when presenting new material (e.g., grammar or pronunciation rules). Deductive approaches (also known as rule-driven learning) involve the teacher first presenting the rules and then providing examples that illustrate the rule. Inductive approaches, on the other hand, involve the teacher first presenting examples and then guiding the students to arrive at the rule based on the examples presented. The inductive approach (also known as discovery learning) is favored in communicative language teaching due to the amount of interaction that it fosters, and it has been shown to be appropriate for the teaching of complex structures (Larsen-Freeman, 2009). However, DeKeyser (2009) cautions that there is little evidence in the psychological literature concerning its superiority.

Teacher questions. As noted before, in the realm of teacher questions an important distinction is made between display questions and referential questions. The former are questions that assume just one (or a small closed set of) possible answer(s) and are typically used to check student comprehension; the latter are questions that allow the learner to provide an authentic response or an original, creative answer. To understand the difference between these two types of questions, compare the classroom discourse sequences in Figure 4.

Traditional approaches such as grammar-translation and audiolingualism used display questions almost exclusively, while extreme versions of the communicative approach argued for the virtually exclusive use of referential questions in the classroom (e.g., Dobbs, 1995). More balanced analyses of pedagogical discourse (e.g., Celce-Murcia & Olshtain, 2000; Cullen, 1998; Koshik, 2010) have demonstrated that the question type should be matched to the pedagogical purpose; error correction, awareness raising, comprehension checks, and scaffolding require the strategic use of display

Display Questions	Referential Questions
T: Van. What's in the back of the van?	T: Da Sheng, have you been in an accident?
S: Milk, milk.	S: No.
T: Milk.	T: No? Good! Lucky.
Ss: Milk. Milk.	S: Lucky. [The other students laugh.]
T: A milk van.	T: Seng?
S: Milk van.	S: No.
T: What's this man? . . . Driver.	T: No? Little?
S: Driver	S: No.
T: The driver.	T: You must be a good driver. [There is more laughter from the students.]
S: The driver.	S: No good driver!
T: The milkman.	T: No? May Yu?

Figure 4. Display versus referential questions: T, teacher; S, student; Ss, students (adapted from Nunan & Lamb, 1996, pp. 90–91).

questions, while communicative practice and fluency training call for referential questions.

Crookes and Chaudron (2001) emphasize that if our goal is to produce communicative users of the L2, the language of the classroom should mirror that of real-life interactions outside the classroom. Yet, in the domain of teacher questions, research reveals that teachers' classroom questions deviate significantly from questions asked outside the classroom, with display questions vastly outnumbering referential questions. The implications of these research findings are clear: display questions not only deprive the learner of the opportunity to negotiate meaning but also place the focus squarely on form rather than on meaning. (See Ellis, this volume.) Note, however, that not all display questions serve the same function. McCormick and Donato (as cited in Lightbown & Spada, 2006) investigated the function of teachers' questions in an adult ESL class, discovering that some display questions served the purpose of scaffolding learning. This research suggests that display questions may serve more functions than previously thought and that their usefulness should be examined within the wider framework of social and pedagogical interaction in the classroom.

Wait time. Closely related to the issue of teacher questions is that of how much wait time teachers allow after posing a question. Given that L2 learners require significantly more processing time to formulate their responses, allowing adequate wait time is essential. Tsui (2001) reminds us that this is especially true in the teacher-fronted portion of the lesson (i.e., where shy or reticent students may feel that all eyes are on them and thus do not want to risk failure).

Nunan and Lamb (1996, citing research by Rowe, 1986) note that, on average, after posing a question teachers allow one second or less before calling on a student, and (assuming no answer on the part of the student) allow a further second to elapse before reformulating their question, calling on another student, or providing the answer themselves. Nunan and Lamb summarize the research findings as follows:

- Teachers become anxious when too much wait time elapses after their questions.
- One to two seconds of wait time is insufficient for L2 learners to process the question and formulate their response.
- When teachers are trained to increase their wait time, learners produce longer and more

complex utterances, though they have not been shown to master content better.

- When three to five seconds of wait time are allowed, learner failures to respond decrease, the length of learner responses increases, students participate more, and student-initiated questions and unsolicited responses increase.

Overall, researchers conclude that the effectiveness of questioning is at least partly dependent on the amount of wait time allowed (Richards & Schmidt, 2010).

Use of visuals

As a tool for language learning, visuals have probably always been present in the L2 classroom. Given the pervasiveness of media in the outside world today, students expect a visually rich learning environment. Visuals include, but are not limited to, photos or line drawings in the course textbook; stick figures, written text or other graphics on the black/whiteboard; student-generated posters; graphic organizers (such as a matrix or a Venn diagram); magazine pictures; digital photos; images or clip art downloaded from the Internet; slide shows (e.g., PowerPoint or Prezi); films; and, last but not least, streaming videos. Brinton (2001) notes that the use of visuals (along with other instructional media) not only lends authenticity to the language lesson but can also serve as an important contextualizing device; that is, a photo, a graphic organizer, or a video can serve as a springboard for the entire lesson. In addition, visuals provide a means of engaging students who are visual learners. (See Shin, this volume.)

According to S. Kang (2004, citing Avgerinou & Ericson, 1997) a very high proportion of sensory learning is visual. Thus, as educators, we cannot afford to ignore the educational significance of visual learning. As Kang noted:

> we are moving into an era in which visual literacy is as important as language/textual literacy. In this new reality, our ability to communicate ideas visually is as important as our ability to conceive them. As a result, EFL teachers should explore the potential of visuals, and exploit spatial instructional strategies to enhance learning and instruction. . . . (p. 58)

Much of the support for the use of visuals is found in the literature on learning style, especially Gardner's theory of multiple intelligences, which posits that individuals have eight types of intelligence, among them spatial intelligence, or the ability to use maps and other forms of visual/graphic information to access complex domains (H. Gardner, 2006). Yet another source of support is the literature on schema theory (McVee, Dunsmore, & Gavelek, 2005). According to this theory, learners' prior knowledge is stored in memory in the form of distinct categories (schemata) and the processing of new knowledge is enhanced by accessing or activating these schemata. Extrapolating from schema theory to the teaching of language, it is posited that visuals provide a powerful means of activating the learners' schemata, thus facilitating the presentation of new information.

One type of visual that has been well documented in the research literature is the graphic (or visual) organizer (see J. H. Clarke, 1991). Graphic organizers consist of diagrams or charts that help students to organize knowledge using structures such as grids or matrices, Venn diagrams, spider maps, time lines, causal chains, network trees, and storyboards.[9] Originating in the work of the cognitive scientist Ausubel (1967), graphic organizers were proposed as one form of advance organizer (i.e., an organizational framework presented in advance of a lesson to emphasize its central idea) that could improve students' levels of understanding and recall. According to S. Kang (2004), using graphic organizers in the ESL/EFL classroom can:

- allow users to develop a holistic understanding that words cannot convey
- provide users with tools to make thought and organization processes visible
- clarify complex concepts into a simple, meaningful, display
- assist users in processing and restructuring ideas and information
- promote recall and retention of learning through synthesis and analysis. (p. 60)

CLASSROOM APPLICATIONS

To examine the classroom applications of the techniques we have discussed so far, let us take another look at the various issues as they play out in the L2 classroom. In this section, we also return from time to time to Francina's lesson and her supervisor's assessment of the lesson.

Pairing and grouping of students

In Francina's lesson, we see that she is struggling with one of the most challenging aspects of classroom management—the pairing and grouping of students. Her supervising instructor comments on the uneven dynamic, noting that not all students are on task. To remedy this, she encourages Francina to be more assertive and move students out of their ethnic groupings. She also comments on Francina's decision to have students work independently to underline all articles and nouns in the newspaper article, suggesting that this activity might instead have been done in pairs.

As detailed in the Conceptual Underpinnings section, classroom-based research attests to the benefits of pairing and grouping students. Primary among these benefits is the fact that students have more opportunity to speak and interact, sharing their personal knowledge and experiences. Perhaps equally significant is the fact that pairing and grouping students creates a bonded class atmosphere. This recognizes that social cooperation and teamwork are valued attributes in the working world. The intentional pairing and grouping of students are aspects of classroom management that require careful forethought during the lesson-planning phase. (See Purgason, this volume.) Teachers need first to decide which portions of the lesson benefit from whole-class or individual work and which benefit from collaborative pair or group work. Having made this decision, they can determine whether to pair or group students and how to handle the dynamics involved.

According to K. Brown (1999), there is definite value in whole-class activities because these promote cohesion, especially in classes comprising learners from diverse cultural and/or L1 backgrounds. However, whole-class work needs to be carefully balanced with pair and group work, each of which offers unique opportunities (along with certain risks) for language learning (see Hayes, 1997; McDonough & Shaw, 2003a, for more details). Figure 5 summarizes the differences and similarities in the implementation of pair and group work.

Teachers can prevent potential misunderstandings by clearly delineating for students when they should work individually and when and how they should collaborate with peers. However, even with the best of planning, teachers need to monitor pair and group work closely, identifying issues that interfere such as excessive use of the L1 and noise levels that impede communication. The following are some issues to keep in mind for pairing and grouping students.

Pair Work	Group Work
Differences	
• Can be done in a short amount of time	• Typically requires more time, both for group setup and task execution
• Requires little pre-planning on the part of the teacher	• Requires careful pre-planning of the group configuration on the part of the teacher
• Requires minimal reorganization of the classroom because students can simply turn and talk to their neighbors	• Depending on the existing seating configurations, may require reorganization of the classroom
• Maximizes the chances that both members of the pair participate in the interaction	• Maximizes the chances that all members of the group participate; however, runs the risk that one or more group members will dominate the discussion

Similarities
- Reduces teacher dominance while enhancing student participation and time on task
- Allows for the simultaneous practice of both productive and receptive skills
- Allows for flexibility of pairings (e.g., homogeneous versus heterogeneous ability levels, L1s, cultural or ethnic backgrounds, etc.)
- Provides a natural opportunity for information exchange as a result of the student grouping
- Increases the likelihood of risk-taking due to fewer inhibitions on the part of the learner

Figure 5. Differences and similarities in the implementation of pair and group work.

Interpersonal dynamics. In the ESL/EFL classroom, linguistic and cultural issues often flare up. Teachers should diffuse these at the outset of the term by doing icebreaker activities where students learn each other's names, get to know more about their peers, and hopefully bond in the process. Also, seating and group configurations can be changed frequently (and in ESL settings, students can be mixed so there are different L1s in each group where possible). Ultimately, it is important to recognize that grouping students does not automatically lead to cooperation, and thus careful thought must be given to the dynamics involved.

Learner autonomy. Keeping in mind that one major goal of group work is to enable learners to work autonomously and to assume responsibility for their own learning, it is important to help them achieve this. Delegating authority to a group leader and assigning roles to others in the group (e.g., recorder, timekeeper, and language monitor) can assist in this process.

Use of the target language. Setting limits is essential, in this case, making clear to students that during pair and group work the goal is to maximize the use of the target language. As noted by Littlewood and Yu (2011), it is important to differentiate between L1 use that serves as a "crutch" and L1 use that scaffolds learning. However, despite the numerous facilitative effects that the L1 can play in the classroom, it remains the single biggest danger in the L2 classroom if it decreases the amount of input in the target language.

Role of the teacher. Once students are already working in pairs or groups, the teacher may assume multiple roles, depending on the needs of individual learners and or groups (Harmer, 2007b). Thus the teacher may feel that it is appropriate to sit down with a given group and assume the role of participant; alternatively, the teacher may serve as resource, moving from group to group to answer questions that arise.

Differences in proficiency level. In most classes, no matter how fine-tuned the placement procedure, teachers will notice differences in students' proficiency levels. The decision whether to group students of a similar proficiency level together or to mix proficiency levels is one that may depend on a variety of factors, such as the type of task, the personalities of the students involved, and the educational setting.

Attitudes toward pair and group work. Some students embrace pair or group work; others dislike it; and yet others view its implementation as the teacher abandoning his or her responsibility to teach. To some extent attitudes may be culturally conditioned; however, even within groups of students from the same cultural/linguistic background there are differences in attitude. For this reason, it is important for teachers to explain the rationale behind group work and define what they hope to achieve with it. It is also important for them to understand their learners' stances on pair and group work before aggressively implementing such groupings.[10]

Teacher classroom discourse

Warm-ups. One of the first things we note from Francina's supervisor's chronological account of activities in her lesson is that she launches immediately into the reading, making no attempt at introducing a warm-up activity or icebreaker. As previously outlined, the rationale for including a warm-up phase at the outset of the lesson (and a cool-down phase at its end, as well) is quite compelling. However, in teachers' defense, time is always the enemy; many teachers, pressed to address an often overwhelming number of curricular objectives, opt to forgo this stage of the lesson in favor of "getting down to business" and covering the material or objectives mandated in the curriculum.[11]

Chik (2003) notes that warm-ups are an essential part of the lesson for a variety of reasons:

- The boundary between the outside world and the world of the classroom is a sharply defined one, and students need time to transition from one to the other. The warm-up phase allows students the chance to relax and begin focusing on the time, place, and tasks at hand.
- Warm-ups help students bond as a social unit (Woodward, 2001). This is all the more important if the lesson contains pair or group work, which is the case with most lessons nowadays.
- Latecomers are a fact of classroom life. Starting the lesson with a warm-up helps ensure that they do not disturb the "serious" part of the lesson; it also ensures that they do

not miss out on the main focus of the lesson. Often, the teachers' natural inclination is to wait to begin class until there is a quorum. This tendency, however, reinforces that lateness is acceptable and expected. Starting class promptly with a warm-up helps reinforce the need for students to arrive on time.

■ Ideally, the warm-up phase should be connected to the main theme of the lesson. Chik (2003) suggests, for example, that if the lesson focus is on exchanging or returning items that have been purchased, the warm-up phase could involve asking students who went shopping over the weekend and what items they purchased.

To understand the possibilities that exist to tie the lesson warm-up to the theme of the lesson, let us assume a lesson in which the theme is "What is a friend?"[12] Figure 6 provides a range of possible warm-up activities for this lesson tied to the theme of friendship.

Error correction and feedback. Research on feedback shows that teachers respond to anywhere between 48 and 90% of the learner errors that occur (Ortega, 2009). Reading between the lines, we can assume there are widely different feedback practices and, no doubt, a need on the part of teachers for more guidance in how to provide effective feedback to students. Unfortunately, the problem of how, when, where, and why to provide feedback has no simple prescription. Much depends on the instructional approach and its view of error, the learners themselves, the teaching context, the curricular goals, the skills being addressed, the focus of the lesson (i.e., accuracy vs. fluency), the mode (oral or written), and a host of other factors, including even the teachers' own command of English and confidence level. (See Kamhi-Stein, this volume.)

Despite the lack of a definitive approach to teacher feedback, a few simple guidelines may help:

Usefulness of feedback. Overall, students appreciate feedback. Many, in fact, complain about not being corrected enough and remark that they often do not get constructive feedback outside the classroom since native speaker friends or colleagues may feel hesitant to point out mistakes.

Feedback options. There are multiple options for providing feedback, not all of which need to be provided in a formalized way (see Figure 3). Teachers should feel free to select those feedback

Type of Warm-Up	Procedures
Find someone who . . .	1. Give students a "find someone who" task sheet containing items such as find someone who (a) considers his or her pet to be a best friend, (b) thinks friends should have the same political beliefs, and (c) thinks true friendship never dies. 2. Ask students to stand up and mill around the room, asking and answering questions. 3. Explain that their goal is to "find someone who" fits the descriptors on the task sheet and get that person's signature. 4. The first person to collect a signature for all items on the task sheet "wins."
Interview	1. Explain to students that they will interview their classmates about an important question. Possible interview questions could include "Describe your best friend," "What quality in a friend is most important to you?" and "Can your parents be your friends?" 2. Ask students to first answer the question themselves. 3. Next, ask them to mill around the class interviewing two or three of their classmates to collect information and sharing their own answers to the interview questions. 4. Finally, have them share in whole-class format the most interesting answers they received.
Game	1. Explain the rules of the game Tic-Tac-Toe. 2. Pair students and provide each pair with a tic-tac-toe board on which incomplete idioms about friendship are written (e.g., "is a friend indeed" or "once a friend"). 3. Explain that to score, a student needs to provide the complete idiom (e.g., "A friend in need is a friend indeed"). 4. The student who completes the game squares in either a vertical, horizontal, or diagonal line wins.

(Continued)

Figure 6. Sample warm-up activities to introduce the lesson theme "What is a friend?"

Music	1. Select a song with the theme of friendship (e.g., Carole King's "You've Got a Friend").
	2. Locate a copy of the song, and provide copies of the lyrics to students.
	3. Play the song at the beginning of class and have students follow the lyrics as they listen.
	4. Ask students to share their impressions of the song.
Visualization	1. Ask students to close their eyes and visualize their best friend when they were growing up.
	2. Ask them to remember as many details about this friend as possible.
	3. After one minute, allow them to open their eyes again.
	4. Encourage students to share the details of what they experienced during the visualization activity with the whole class.
Ranking	1. Divide students into small groups.
	2. Provide each group with a list of 10 adjectives that characterize individuals (e.g., *honest, loyal, sincere, funny, creative*).
	3. Ask them to rank the adjectives from which characteristic they think is most important for friendship to which is least.
	4. Have student groups volunteer to share the results of their discussion with the whole class.
Brainstorming	1. Use the whiteboard or poster paper to draw a spider map.

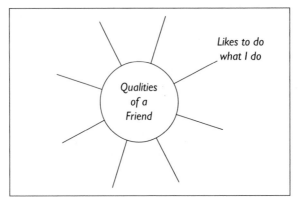

2. Elicit from students the qualities that make a good friend and add them to the spider map. As an alternative, use a T-graph to elicit the desirable versus undesirable qualities of a friend.

Desirable qualities	Undesirable qualities
remembers my birthday	_____
_____	_____
_____	_____
_____	_____
_____	

Magazine picture activity	1. Divide students into small groups.
	2. Provide each group with six or more magazine pictures of people who are roughly the same age (the age of the individuals depicted should match that of the students).
	3. Ask students to decide which of these people are close friends and why.
	4. In whole-class format, have students present their decisions and share their reasoning.

Figure 6. Sample warm-up activities to introduce the lesson theme "What is a friend?" *(Continued)*

options that they are most comfortable with (and that their learners respond to best).

Feedback focus. In general, when the focus of the lesson is on accuracy, feedback is called for; in contrast, when the focus is on fluency, it is best not to interrupt students but to allow a focus on meaning to prevail (though the teacher may keep notes on errors that occur during this fluency stage and address them at a later time).

Competence versus performance. A useful distinction to make is whether the error is one of competence (i.e., the student does not have command of the form) or one of performance (the student makes a mistake with the form because he or she is attending to other issues). In the former case, feedback is appropriate; in the latter, it is probably not.

Global versus local errors. Another useful distinction is that of global versus local error (Burt & Kiparsky, 1989). The former refers to a major error in sentence structure or lexical choice that makes an utterance difficult to understand (and thus warrants correction), whereas the latter refers to an error in one element of the sentence structure that does not cause problems in comprehension (and thus may not require correction). To illustrate the difference, Burt and Kiparsky cite the sentence "Since the harvest was good, was rain a lot last year" (p. 6). They note that *since* is attached to the wrong clause, thereby constituting a global error. However, the missing subject *it* in the second clause and the incorrect verb form *was rain* constitute local errors.

Slips, errors, and attempts. In addressing the type of feedback strategy to use, Edge (1989) distinguishes between the category of *slips* (mistakes that students can self-correct once the problem has been pointed out to them), *errors* (mistakes that students cannot correct themselves and that thus require explanation), and *attempts* (mistakes made when a student tries to explain something he or she does not know how to say). In the case of slips, the strategies of pinpointing, questioning, cueing, or using paralinguistics (see Figure 7) may be the most appropriate; on the other hand, in the case of errors, overt explanation maybe be called for followed by practice. And in the case of attempts, a simple recast by the teacher may serve the purpose best.

Type of Feedback	Teacher Behavior/Response
Overt correction	The teacher corrects the error.
Recast	The teacher repeats the word or phrase correctly.
Questioning	The teacher asks, e.g., "Is that correct?"
Denial	The teacher notes, e.g., "That's wrong."
Pinpointing	The teacher localizes the error using a pause and rising intonation to signal the need for an alternate form.
Oral cueing	The teacher provides various grammatical variations and allows student to select correct alternative.
Written cue	The teacher indicates the error by giving a written cue or by pointing to reminders placed around classroom (e.g., signs indicating frequent errors such as missing –s, –ing, and *be* copula).
Grammatical terms	The teacher notes the part of speech where the error occurred or otherwise gives a grammatical indication.
Paralinguistics	The teacher uses a facial expression, hand signal, or other gesture to signal the error.
Appeal to peers	The teacher appeals to other students to locate and repair error.

Figure 7. Types of teacher feedback.

Teacher-student interaction patterns. The importance that teacher-student interaction patterns play in the overall climate of the classroom is paramount. As seen in the discussion of IRE versus IRF sequences in the Conceptual Underpinnings section, the slight difference in these two teacher discourse patterns has been shown to make a significant difference in student participation, especially in the teacher's whole-group interactions with the class. In general, IRF sequences more closely mirror natural conversation and are therefore more authentic than the (often artificial) IRE sequences. Further, teacher responses that evaluate (as in the IRE) rather than encourage student responses (as in the IRF sequence) tend to suppress student contributions, while teacher responses that invite students or their peers to expand on the original contribution increase opportunities for further discussion, originality of language, and ultimately language learning. Teachers are therefore advised to monitor their use of these patterns. Whenever possible, they should use IRF sequences or collaborative dialogue in place of IRE sequences.[13]

Inductive versus deductive presentation. As noted previously, the inductive approach tends to be favored over the deductive approach in most current approaches to language teaching, despite the mixed research evidence supporting the inductive presentation of language. Nevertheless, there are definite advantages and disadvantages to both of these approaches, as summarized in Figure 8. Teachers are well advised to consider these advantages and disadvantages when deciding on how to present new material or review material that has been previously covered. Some lesson objectives lend themselves more to one pattern than the other, and varying the manner of presentation can also add interest to lessons. Above all, teachers should keep in mind that, while the inductive approach may be the currently favored one, there are legitimate reasons for deciding to use a deductive approach instead.

Teacher questions. One of the primary keys to an interactive classroom lies in the nature of questions that teachers ask and the sequencing of those questions within a given lesson. Questions serve a variety of roles, from classroom management (e.g., taking roll or controlling student behavior) to elicitation (a technique in which the teacher prompts students to provide examples or information) to the checking of comprehension.

As we have seen, display questions serve an important role in the controlled and guided practice stages of the lesson as well as in feedback and correction. However, if this pattern of question is used to the exclusion of referential questions in the communicative practice stage, learners are deprived of valuable opportunities to expand their linguistic repertoire and to receive teacher feedback on their creative use of language. One obstacle that many teachers face is that the questions in their textbooks tend to be overwhelmingly of the display variety. Consider, for example, the questions that

DEDUCTIVE (rule-driven learning)	INDUCTIVE (discovery learning)
Advantages	
1. Appeals to learners with a low tolerance for ambiguity	1. Requires more cognitive depth and may appeal to analytical learners
2. Gets straight to the point and may therefore be more time efficient	2. May make more of an impact on learners and thus information may be retained more easily
3. Acknowledges the role of cognitive processes in language learning	3. Actively engages learners and fosters learner autonomy
4. Fits with many students' classroom expectations	4. Involves problem-solving skills
Disadvantages	
1. May not catch students' attention	1. Focuses on working out the rules and may therefore lead learners to believe that rules are the sole objective of learning
2. Use of metalanguage (e.g., grammatical terminology) may be difficult for some	2. Time spent working out rules may be at the expense of time available for practice
3. Tends to be teacher-fronted	3. Students may work out the wrong rule or get frustrated
4. May not hold students' attention	4. Some aspects of language do not lend themselves easily to rule formulation
5. Reinforces the idea that language is rule driven rather than meaning driven	5. More difficult for teachers to manage

Figure 8. Advantages and disadvantages of deductive and inductive teacher presentations (adapted from Thornbury, 1999).

The **California Gold Rush** (1848–1855) began on January 24, 1848, when gold was discovered at Sutter's Mill in the foothills near Sacramento. News of the discovery soon spread, resulting in approximately 300,000 people coming to California in 1848 and 1849. These early gold-seekers, who were called "forty-niners," sailed around the tip of South America or crossed the U.S. continent in covered wagons through hostile Native American lands.

The effects of the Gold Rush were considerable. San Francisco grew from a tiny hamlet of tents to a boomtown, and roads, churches, schools, and other towns were built. A system of laws and a government were created, leading to the admission of California as a state in 1850. New methods of transportation developed as steamships navigated the Sacramento River and railroads were built. The business of agriculture, California's next major growth field, also began to prosper.

Task: Read the above passage. Then answer the questions below.

1. On what date did the California gold rush begin?
2. Where was gold first discovered?
3. How many people came to California?
4. What method of transportation did they use?
5. What were two effects of the Gold Rush?
6. When did California become a state?
7. What were two new methods of transportation that developed?
8. What business began to prosper in California after 1850?

Figure 9. Sample ESL/EFL reading passage with comprehension questions.

accompany the sample ESL/EFL reading passage in Figure 9. As can be seen, all the questions in Figure 9 require a specific answer, leaving little or no room for students to express personal opinions, share experiences, or exercise higher-level thinking skills. However, it is relatively simple for teachers to construct referential questions when they are missing from the textbook. For example, referential questions such as the following could also be asked for the "Gold Rush" passage:

1. Why do you think so many people caught "gold fever" and joined the gold rush?
2. Do you know of any similar situations in the history of your country where people left their homes to pursue opportunities in other regions?
3. Would you travel through hostile Native American territory to find gold? Why or why not?

Questions of this nature, when properly sequenced within the lesson (i.e., in the communicative practice phase, following more structured interactions of the IRE or IRF type), allow students to stretch their linguistic ability. They also lay the groundwork for the type of collaborative dialogue suggested by Richards and Farrell (2011).

In addition, as H. D. Brown (2007) suggests, teachers need to develop a wide repertoire of questioning strategies that foster classroom interaction, ideally augmenting display questions with referential questions wherever possible. These referential questions should span the range of higher-order thinking skills, including questions involving the application of knowledge and questions involving inference, analysis, synthesis, and evaluation.[14] A tip for teachers to keep in mind when doing this is to challenge students but not overwhelm them. To ensure variety in questions, teachers can consider taping a portion of their lesson and making a tally of the types of questions that they have asked (e.g., examining the ratio or pedagogical purpose of display vs. referential questions, or differentiating among simple comprehension checks, requests for clarification of meaning, requests for exemplification, and higher-order questions).[15]

Wait time.   Determining what constitutes adequate wait time is an aspect of classroom discourse that all teachers struggle with—no doubt because of the natural preference for a smooth flow of classroom discourse, without awkward pauses or interruptions. As we have seen in the Conceptual Underpinnings, allowing for more wait time is good practice and one that will be rewarded by students' being more forthcoming in their responses. The following are useful strategies for teachers:

- Count silently to three after asking a question before calling on a student or eliciting responses from the group as a whole.
- Decrease students' anxiety level by avoiding eye contact during the wait time. Try instead looking down (or elsewhere in the room) until you sense that the student is ready to answer; then make eye contact and wait for the student to volunteer the answer.
- Pose a question to the group as a whole, and announce that students have a minute to think about their responses before you call on them.

Use of visuals

In the case of Francina's lesson, we note that she has in fact planned visuals as part of her lesson, using downloadable clip-art images to motivate students and to prompt the guided writing activity. She also makes appropriate use of the whiteboard to list vocabulary elicited from students and to create a graphic organizer that reinforces and supports her lesson on article usage. However, as her supervisor notes, by not writing all the elicited vocabulary on the board, Francina may be missing an important opportunity to acknowledge her students' input.

Visuals remain one of the teacher's most precious and indispensable resources. In today's world of ready access to images (whether provided in the textbook, available as part of the text's ancillary materials, torn out of an old magazine, or downloaded from the Internet), there is really no excuse for students' being deprived of visual input or stimulation in class (Brinton, 2001). J. Crawford (2002, citing Hargreaves, 1994) notes that images are a pervasive feature of learners' lives. Often, however, the textbook, worksheets, and other ancillary materials lack images that conjure up the outside world

- Visuals provide a readily available, low-cost means of enhancing classroom instruction.
- They are an extremely flexible medium that can be used at virtually any stage of the lesson.
- They provide variety in the lesson and are motivational for students.
- They provide an easy means of addressing different learning styles and of individualizing instruction.
- They can help students process new information more readily and help to develop students' critical thinking skills.
- They can be used to teach all four skills as well as to introduce a new language focus (vocabulary, grammar, or pronunciation).
- They can provide a context for the lesson and enrich the learning situation.
- They add authenticity to the lesson by allowing the teacher to bring the outside world into the language classroom.
- They can help students call up background knowledge or existing schemata and thus maximize their prior knowledge in the language learning process.

Figure 10. Rationale for using visuals in the language classroom.

or that expose students to the authentic target culture. Figure 10 summarizes the rationale behind the use of visuals in the classroom.

One form of visual that is particularly suited to the ESL/EFL classroom is the graphic or visual organizer (Hill & Flynn, 2006). In terms of its application, the graphic organizer is not tied to any one segment of the lesson but, instead, can be used at any stage of the lesson and to teach any skill area. Thus graphic organizers are an extremely flexible, multipurpose tool for teachers and students alike. To cite just a few uses, they can be used to: (1) reveal text structure and highlight the rhetorical organization of a text; (2) "unpack" difficult ideas (e.g., cause-effect chains); (3) brainstorm ideas for a writing assignment; (4) present key content vocabulary at the outset of a lesson; (5) aid students in the recall of material previously learned; and (6) explore lexical fields. (See chapters by Grabe & Stoller and Zimmerman, this volume, for more examples of appropriate uses for graphic organizers.) Figure 11 presents a popular graphic organizer, the K-W-L chart (Ogle, 1986), that is often used in

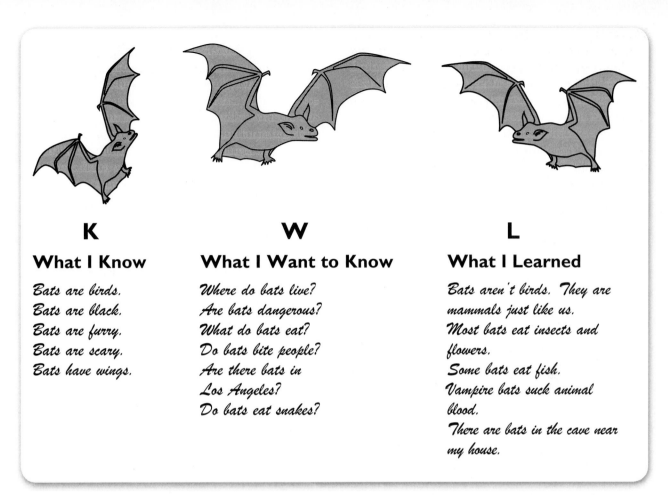

K

What I Know

Bats are birds.
Bats are black.
Bats are furry.
Bats are scary.
Bats have wings.

W

What I Want to Know

Where do bats live?
Are bats dangerous?
What do bats eat?
Do bats bite people?
Are there bats in
Los Angeles?
Do bats eat snakes?

L

What I Learned

Bats aren't birds. They are
mammals just like us.
Most bats eat insects and
flowers.
Some bats eat fish.
Vampire bats suck animal
blood.
There are bats in the cave near
my house.

Figure 11. Sample K-W-L chart for a theme-based unit on bats (adapted from Brinton, 2011b).

the sheltered content area classroom. (See Snow, this volume.) In the example depicted, students beginning a theme-based lesson on bats first fill in the left-hand column of the chart ("What I know") with facts they already know about bats. As the lesson proceeds, they reconvene to fill in the middle column ("What I want to know"). And finally, in the culminating stages of the lesson they fill in the right-hand column ("What I learned")—in some cases, correcting initial misconceptions (e.g., that bats are mammals rather than birds).

Ultimately, the availability of visuals along with the degree of teacher creativity and adaptability will determine the extent to which teachers select and use images in the language classroom. Above all, visuals should be used "to involve more students integrally in the learning process and to facilitate

language learning by making it a more authentic and meaningful process" (Brinton, 2001, p. 473).

FUTURE TRENDS

We can draw certain conclusions based on the research discussed in this chapter, such as the importance of pair and group work in creating a climate that fosters L2 development and the need for teachers to understand how various facets of teacher discourse impact learner responses. We also have fairly solid evidence of the importance of the students' rich, sustained exposure to the target language and the need for classroom activities involving the negotiation of meaning that "push" learners in generating output (Ortega, 2009).

Certainly, the prevailing paradigm at this time is communicative language teaching. (See Duff, this volume.) The popularity of many of the tools and techniques discussed in this chapter, while certainly attributable to the research evidence that supports them, can also be explained by their fit with the underlying approach and design of communicative language teaching.

In today's media-rich environment, the use of computer-mediated technology (including the widespread use of course management systems) has facilitated many aspects of classroom teaching practice. (See Sokolik, this volume.) Simple management tasks such as assigning homework and setting quiz dates can be facilitated through the use of the online course calendar, while instructor-to-student or student-to-student communication can be posted to the course forum so that all may read and benefit. Class quizzes can be administered through the management system's built-in quiz tool, while assignments can be checked for originality through built-in plagiarism software. Assignments can be easily tailored to appeal to a wider variety of student learning styles through the inclusion of podcasts, streaming video, and other links to outside sources. Finally, feedback to students can take a much more immediate form because many platforms today have online grading and feedback options.

As technology plays an ever-increasing role in and outside the language classroom and the brick-and-mortar classroom is either augmented through or replaced by online instruction, many new issues regarding effective L2 classroom practice are surfacing. How, for example, do we pair and group students effectively in an online platform? What is the optimal online wait time, and how do we account for the additional factor of the technological lag in response that may be caused by the platform itself? Are there differences in the types of teacher questions that elicit quality student responses when instruction is conducted online? And what about feedback? Given that online instruction provides a wider range of options via chat boxes, forum postings, course walls, and the like, how are teachers to frame their feedback and determine which feedback option to use? These, and other questions, will no doubt become hot topics of classroom research in the future.

The extent to which research will inform practice in the future is an open question. SLA researchers are careful to point out that the results of their studies do not necessarily translate directly to classroom teaching. Nonetheless, as has been shown in this chapter, a great many of the findings from this research *have* in fact found their way into the classroom and have positively informed L2 teaching practice. It is hoped that in the future, there will be greater convergence of research and practice, ideally with classroom practitioners joining ranks with their colleagues in academia to conduct applied research. (See Bailey, this volume.)

CONCLUSION

This chapter has examined L2 classroom practices with a rather narrow focus, looking at those classroom procedures that are generally agreed on as contributing significantly to the effectiveness of instruction. Though certainly not an exhaustive presentation, the practices discussed here include the pairing and grouping of students, teacher classroom discourse, and the use of visuals and graphic organizers. Other techniques certainly deserving of attention (but not included here due to space constraints) include input modification (the ways in which teachers alter their classroom language based on their perceptions of learners' proficiency level), dealing with learner diversity, coping with large classes, balancing teacher talk and student talk, encouraging the use of the L2, the individualization of learning tasks, and instructor modeling of the target language. These strategies, along with those discussed in this chapter, are crucial for novice teachers to master; they provide the cornerstones of effective teaching for novices and experienced teachers alike.

SUMMARY

➤ Over 40 years of classroom research carried out in formal instructional settings have provided insights into classroom interaction patterns that affect the teaching/learning process.

➤ This chapter concentrates on the procedures used by teachers on a daily basis in their classroom teaching with specific reference to the pairing and grouping of students, teacher classroom discourse, and the use of visuals.

➤ The use of pair and group work has numerous benefits, including increasing learners' time on task, providing ample time for students' communicative output and negotiation of meaning, increasing learner autonomy, and creating bonds among class members.

➤ Teacher classroom discourse encompasses a wide variety of issues, including pre-lesson chitchat, lesson warm-up, teacher-student interaction patterns, teacher questions, error correction and feedback, and wait time.

➤ The use of visuals and graphic organizers can significantly enhance classroom practice, lending context and authenticity to the lesson, addressing visually oriented students, helping learners to activate prior knowledge, and to recognize text structure.

➤ Online instruction provides a fascinating new context, both in terms of research into what constitutes effective second/foreign language teaching and in terms of applying new findings to our daily practice as teachers.

DISCUSSION QUESTIONS

1. Review the discussion of pair and group work. List the benefits cited. What additional advantages would you add from your own experiences as a language learner or teacher? Can you think of any disadvantages or challenges that you might face implementing pair or group work in a setting where you teach or have observed?

2. Look at the following two feedback sequences. In pairs or small groups, discuss how effective these sequences are. How might you deliver the feedback differently?

Feedback sequence 1

Student: I buyed it in New York.

Teacher: No, not buyed, bought.

Student: Yes.

Teacher: Okay, next question please. . . .

Feedback sequence 2

Teacher: Everybody repeat: "I bought it in New York on holiday."

Student 1: I buyed it New York yesterday.

Student 2: I bought it in New York holiday.

Student 3: I bought it in New York on holiday.

Student 4: I buyed it in New York on holiday.

Teacher: Good. . . .

3. Take another look at the feedback provided by Francina's supervisor. Are there aspects of effective teaching mentioned that are *not* included in this chapter? Explain.

4. How might you use the visual of the gold miner in Figure 9 as a pre-reading activity to help maximize learners' background? Can you think of other visuals or graphic organizers that might be used in class as well?

SUGGESTED ACTIVITIES

1. Visit an ESL resource site such as Dave's ESL Café[16] to locate possibilities for warm-up and icebreaker activities. If you are currently teaching or have access to ESL/EFL students, try out one or more of the icebreakers.

2. Select a unit from an ESL or EFL textbook. For each task, determine what type of classroom configuration (whole group, pair work, or group work) would be most appropriate. Be prepared to share the unit and your decision-making process with the class as a whole.

3. Arrange to observe an experienced ESL or EFL instructor. Using the observation/feedback form in the Appendix or another observation form of your choosing, focus your observation on the techniques that the teacher uses that you believe are most crucial to successful language teaching. After the observation, interview the instructor about his or her use of these techniques.

4. Select a text or a theme that you might use in the ESL/EFL classroom. (Alternatively, you may wish to use the Gold Rush reading passage in Figure 9.)

   a. Using the table on the next page as a model, write questions that conform to each question type.[17]

| Type of question | | | |
Form	Content	Purpose	Examples
1. Yes/no	Outside fact	Display	Are cats cheaper to own than dogs?
2. Wh–	Outside fact	Display	How much do dog owners spend on pet food each week?
3. Yes/no	Personal fact	Display	Do you have a dog at home?
4. Wh–	Personal fact	Display	Which of the pets mentioned in the text do you have?
5. Yes/no	Opinion	Display	Do you like dogs?
6. Wh–	Opinion	Display	Which kind of pet do you prefer?
7. Yes/no	Outside fact	Referential[18]	Do dogs usually live longer than cats?
8. Wh–	Outside fact	Referential	Why do dogs need insurance?
9. Yes/no	Personal fact	Referential	Do you have any pets at home?
10. Wh–	Personal fact	Referential	How much a year, roughly, do you spend on your pets?
11. Yes/no	Opinion	Referential	Do you find the information in the text surprising?
12. Wh–	Opinion	Referential	Why do you think people spend so much on their pets?

   b. Consider how you might sequence these questions in your lesson.

   c. Be prepared to discuss why an exercise of this type can help you improve your teaching.

5. Record a short (7- to 10-minute) teacher-led portion of an ESL or EFL lesson (either your own class or that of a teacher who has given you permission to record). Transcribe the teacher discourse and determine what type of interaction patterns (e.g., IRE, IRF, or collaborative dialogue) are used in the class. Be prepared to share your transcript with the class as a whole.

FURTHER READING

Harmer, J. (2007). *The practice of English language teaching* (4th ed.). Harlow, UK: Pearson Education.

This volume contains excellent coverage of managing the learning process, including providing feedback to learners, pairing and grouping students effectively, and promoting student autonomy; it is accompanied by a DVD of second language classroom vignettes suitable for discussion and self study.

Richards, J. C. (Ed.). (1998). *Teaching in action: Case studies from second language classrooms.* Alexandria, VA: Teachers of English to Speakers of Other Languages.

This edited volume consists of case studies of actual teaching contexts and the issues faced by teachers; each case study is accompanied by the teacher's proposed solution to the issue along with commentary by an expert suggesting alternate solutions.

Richards, J. C., & Farrell, T. S. C. (2011). *Practice teaching: A reflective approach.* Cambridge, UK: Cambridge University Press.

This volume focuses on novice teachers engaged in practice teaching; it has an excellent treatment of procedures that lead to effective teaching along with a thorough discussion teacher discourse and its effects on student learning.

APPENDIX: SAMPLE CLASSROOM OBSERVATION/FEEDBACK FORM

CLASSROOM OBSERVATION/FEEDBACK FORM

Date of observation:_____   Observation venue:_____   Class:_____

Teaching point(s):

Check one: ☐   Instructor_____
               ☐   Observer_____

LESSON QUALITY (achievement of objectives, organization, sequencing, pacing, use of AV aids, etc.)
Comment:

TEACHER PRESENTATION (clarity of presentation, knowledge of material, classroom management, speech clarity, etc.)
Comment:

STUDENT PARTICIPATION (interest level, interaction with instructor, balance of student/teacher speech, opportunity to practice learning points, etc.)
Comment:

MAJOR STRENGTHS
Comment:

QUESTIONS OR UNCERTAINTIES ABOUT THE LESSON
Comment:

SUGGESTIONS
Comment:

CHRONOLOGICAL DESCRIPTION OF CLASS ACTIVITIES

Time   Activity
         1.
         2.
         3.
         4. Etc.

ENDNOTES

1 Pseudonyms have been used for the practicum student and the observation site, and the observation date has been altered. However, the observation/feedback form is authentic and has been selected as representative of the type of feedback often given to novice teachers in a TESOL practicum course.

2 Many thanks to Kathi Bailey for inspiring this observation/feedback form, which has since undergone multiple revisions.

3 Given the length restrictions of the chapter, this portion of the feedback form does not appear in its entirety. Note that the chronological account is nonetheless an important part of the overall feedback provided by the supervising instructor because it sheds additional light on many of the pedagogical issues (e.g., time management and teacher feedback) that the instructor is dealing with.

4 In terms of its overall concept and content, this chapter owes much to the chapters by Brinton and by Crookes and Chaudron in the third (2001) edition of this book.

5 The other three stages, according to Edelhoff (1981), are input/control, focus/working, and transfer/application.

6 See, for example, VanPatten and Benati (2010).

7 In the literature on the topic, the IRE and IRF patterns are sometimes conflated and considered one and the same.

8 Collaborative dialogues are also sometimes referred to as *dialogic interaction*.

9 For examples, see http://www.enchantedlearning.com/graphicorganizers/

10 For a more thorough discussion of the dynamics of pair and group work, see McDonough and Shaw (2003a).

11 In Francina's case, since she is a guest in her mentor teacher's classroom, she may have been allocated a limited amount of time to teach her lesson. However, the lesson would undoubtedly have gone more smoothly and students would have been "hooked" into the lesson at the outset had she incorporated a warm-up phase.

12 See Brinton (2003) for a more thorough discussion of a content-based lesson using this theme.

13 Brinton (2011c) suggests that teachers monitor their classroom discourse patterns by periodically taping their lessons. After viewing the lesson and taking notes on general impressions of the lesson, they can identify a key issue (such as IRE vs. IRF sequences) and transcribe a short segment of the lesson to analyze and reflect on their practice.

14 A useful online reference is http://www.pgcps.pg.k12.md.us/~elc/isquestion2.html

15 The classic taxonomy of higher-order questions is that of Benjamin S. Bloom (1956); for a revision of Bloom's taxonomy see Anderson and Krathwohl (2001).

16 You can locate Dave's ESL Café at http://www.eslcafe.com/

17 For a more thorough discussion of this question typology, see Thompson (1997).

18 In Thompson's (1997) question typology, *referential* questions are referred to as *communicative*. We have opted here to use the more common term *referential* instead.

23 | Lesson Planning in Second/Foreign Language Teaching

KITTY B. PURGASON

KEY QUESTIONS

➤ What goes into lesson planning?
➤ Why should teachers plan lessons?
➤ How can planning in advance interact with on-the-spot classroom management and decision making?
➤ What are possible formats for lesson plans?

EXPERIENCE

Julie teaches a multiskills class in an intensive English program for international students in Los Angeles. In addition to teaching 15 hours a week, she is in a graduate program in Teaching English to Speakers of Other Languages and working part-time as a graphic designer to make ends meet. She has done some volunteer teaching in Guatemala and Thailand, but this is her first job as a teacher rather than as a conversation partner. Most of the time, her lesson planning consists of 30 minutes in a coffeeshop before class glancing over the in-house textbook she was given. She feels bad that she is not doing more, but she remembers what happened during her first term teaching here. She spent hours planning every lesson and searching the Internet for fun activities, yet her efforts did not seem to pay off. Half the time, something would go wrong, like the copier being broken or the students getting confused during a game. The students also complained that they were not using the book they had bought. And Julie knew she was spending way too much time on planning if she wanted to avoid burnout. This term's approach to lesson planning does not seem like a solution, however. She finds herself stumbling over things in the textbook she had not looked at carefully enough, and monotony seems to be settling in over the class. She is eager to find a balanced and effective approach to lesson planning.

WHAT IS LESSON PLANNING?

Lesson planning is the process of taking everything we know about teaching and learning, along with everything we know about the students in front of us, and putting it together to create a road map for what a class period will look like.[1] One reason why novice teachers often ask for help with lesson planning is because it involves all seven of the following interconnected elements.

1. *Second language acquisition theory.* A lesson informed by theories of scaffolding or teach-ability will sequence certain pieces in a certain order that are probably not the same as a lesson informed by behaviorism or a comprehension-based theory.[2]
2. *Methodology.* An oral skills lesson may consist of the three stages presentation, practice, and production. A task-based lesson may have completely different stages: pretask, task, report, and language analysis. (See Nunan, this volume.)
3. *Skill.* The stages of a lesson will vary depending on what skill is being taught. A reading lesson may consist of pre-reading, main idea, reading for details, and post-reading activities. A pronunciation lesson may include feature analysis, listening discrimination, controlled or guided practice, and communicative practice.
4. *Audience.* The number of objectives or activities in a lesson will be different in a lesson for

children than in one for adults or in a lesson for beginners than in one for advanced learners.

5. *Focus.* A different focus will result in a lesson with a different purpose. For example, a lesson in an intensive academic preparation program, a lesson in a vacation foreign language camp program, and a lesson in a test-preparation class may all have different purposes.

6. *Context.* Some programs allow for goals to emerge from a needs assessment or to be suggested by the learners themselves. In other contexts, the goals are specified by standards, external exams, or institutional rubrics.

7. *Philosophy of learning and teaching.* Should class be fun? Does a good teacher demand that students do lots of homework? Is the role of a teacher to allow students to control their own learning? Should the teacher do easy things first and build up to what is difficult or start out with the tough challenges while students are fresh? Lesson planning emerges from the teacher's view of what good teaching and learning consist of.

Knowing one's teaching context, students, and personal philosophy is a good foundation for lesson planning. However, teachers can also grow in their awareness of all these elements during the process of lesson planning.

Obviously this is a lot for teachers to consider the evening before they walk into class. This chapter assumes that either the teacher has thought about each of these elements and issues or the curriculum provided to the teacher accounts for them. The remaining question, and the focus of this chapter, is how to put the pieces together for a given day or week of classes.

CONCEPTUAL UNDERPINNINGS

Lessons have been described using many different metaphors. A lesson is like a film, with a plot, theme, rhythm, flow, and ending (Thornbury, 1999b). It is like jazz, with an initial chord sequence that players improvise on (Harmer, 2007b). It is like climbing a mountain, with hard work and a sense of satisfaction on reaching the goal (Ur, 2012). It is like a collection of playing cards that may be played one at a time, in suits, or other patterns (Woodward, 2001). It is like a road map or the signs on the highway that show us how to

get to where we are going (Spratt, Pulverness, & Williams, 2005).

A metaphor that I have found especially helpful is that of a meal. Teachers can satisfy their students with a pre-made meal heated up minutes before serving, can throw together something from random ingredients they happen to have in the kitchen, or can plan an elaborate multicourse meal. They may have to work with only a few items, or they may have access to markets full of a variety of foods. They can focus on nutrition, good taste, beautiful presentation, or a combination of these.

As Julie's experience reminds us, sometimes teachers plan a lesson while walking down the hall from the teachers' room to the classroom; at other times, they agonize for hours over what to do in class the next day. Other teachers do not plan at all, using the rationale that planning in advance is counterproductive given the unpredictability of classes. Harmer (2007b) calls this tension the "planning paradox" (p. 366). On the one hand, we need to think in advance about what we want to accomplish and how we will do it. On the one other hand, we want to be aware of the interaction among teachers, learners, and language and of what emerges minute by minute in our classes.

The way a cook plans a meal for a large group of people suggests a good way through this paradox. It is very sensible to prepare in advance a meal that will suit those coming to dinner, keeping in mind those who are vegetarian or eat *halal* (Muslim dietary restrictions) or cannot eat spicy food, and so on. However, there may be someone who forgot to tell the cook in advance that she is allergic to wheat or on a special diet. A good chef does not mind bringing out a fruit plate instead of the chocolate cake in such a situation.

Lesson plan as a term actually refers to three things. The first is what appears on paper, what I call the format for the plan (discussed later in the chapter). The second is a process occurring in the teacher's head (also discussed later). The third is a model of what is supposed to happen in a class. There are various models, from various experts, with various views of the learning/teaching process in general or of English language teaching in particular.

The *Hunter model* (Hunter 2004), sometimes known as five-step, seven-step, or nine-step model (depending on which of the steps are considered most deserving of emphasis), grew out of Madeline Hunter's work with American public school teachers. For advocates of this model, a good lesson starts with an anticipatory set, or hook, to attract students' attention. Next, the purpose of the lesson is stated. It is recommended that the instructional piece of the lesson include input, modeling, and checking for understanding. The next phase of the lesson is guided practice and monitoring. A closure statement reinforces the lesson before the final independent practice that helps students connect the lesson to the real world.

Aimed at language teaching in particular, rather than education in general, the *presentation-practice-production* (PPP) model contains three lesson stages (Harmer, 2001). The teacher presents a teaching point with new language to the students, the students practice the language teaching point (usually doing controlled activities), and finally the students produce the language on their own (doing communicative activities). This model is one that fits a beginning-level class of adults learning spoken English, for example.

In more recent editions of his methodology texts, Harmer (2007a, 2007b) suggests that the *engage-study-activate* (ESA) model is more versatile than PPP. During the engage phase, students' attention and interest are aroused. Next, during the study phase, students focus on language. Any number of different activities are appropriate here, from a teacher-centered explanation of grammar, to student discovery of lexical collocations while reading, to students' unconscious acquisition of intonation patterns through listening. Finally, students activate all their language knowledge and skill with communicative tasks during the activate phase. Although ESA reminds teachers of elements that need to be included in a lesson, the amount of time spent on each element and the sequence of elements can vary. A lesson for adults might consist of one ESA sequence during 50 minutes, while for children the 50-minute class could be made up of multiple ESA sequences, such as ESA-ESA-ESA. A lesson for beginners would probably be a straightforward ESA (similar to classic PPP). Other lessons, more task-based, might have the elements EASA. That is, after the engage phase, students plunge into a task using whatever language they have, and since the first activate phase has exposed gaps in what students are able to do in English, the teacher will be more focused and the students will

be more motivated to pay attention during the following study phase. Harmer (2007a, 2007b) calls this a "boomerang" lesson. Lessons, especially at the intermediate and advanced levels, can be patchworks, or combinations of various sequences, such as EAASASEA, reflecting the messy way that learning often occurs and providing variety in class.

The *Sheltered Immersion Observation Protocol* (SIOP) model was developed in classes in a U.S. kindergarten through 12th grade (K–12) context where children are learning language and content at the same time (Echevarria, Vogt, & Short, 2012). Although it started as a rubric for observing teachers (hence the name), it has evolved into a lesson-planning model. A good lesson in this model starts with motivation (building background for students through links to their experience, links to prior learning, and key vocabulary). The presentation would include language and content objectives, comprehensible input, strategies, interaction, and feedback. The lesson would then go on to practice and application. It would end with review and assessment, with an optional extension (contingency plan or homework assignment).

A model that was developed by teachers who wanted to focus more on the process of students' learning is *encounter, clarify, remember, internalize, and fluently use* (ECRIF) (Kurzweil & Scholl, 2007).[3] The encounter stage might include eliciting vocabulary from students, reading a text for the main idea, or having students in pairs talk about a topic. As students grasp the meaning and use of the new language during the clarify stage, the lesson could include finding out what students already know about a writing task, highlighting a grammatical feature, or explaining some vocabulary. Activities such as listen and repeat, drills, and quizzes are typical of those used during the remember phase as students move the new item from short-term to long-term memory. The purpose of the internalize phase is to enable students to personalize the new knowledge or skill. Finally, the fluently use phase is a time for communicative tasks in which students use language to spontaneously and automatically communicate their own ideas in different contexts.

These different models reflect different goals (language only, content only, or language plus content), different proficiencies (beginning versus intermediate or advanced), and different theories of teaching and learning (audiolingualism versus communicative approach). Teachers may be required by a supervisor or a school to use a particular model or be free to construct their lesson plans in any way they want. Regardless, it is hoped that this overview provides insight into which elements to include in a personal model of planning. To continue the cooking analogy, learning about these models is like learning about different chefs who espouse ideas such as "use local and seasonal ingredients" or "we love comfort food" or "whatever you have in your pantry."

CLASSROOM APPLICATIONS

What happens when teachers plan?

Lesson planning accomplishes several aims:

- Planning is a means of making decisions. As teachers anticipate their class, they think about content, materials, sequencing, and timing in light of who their students are and their objectives. Planning is actually a way that teachers develop expertise.
- The plan can act as a road map during the class itself. It enables teachers to confidently face the students, concentrating on their responses rather than mentally groping for what to do or say next. Students who sense that their teacher has planned the lesson also gain confidence.
- A plan can be part of a log of what has been covered and used in conjunction with a list of standards (statements of what students should know or be able to do, often provided by a school or educational body) or a needs assessment (a study of what students need to go from point A [where they are now] to point B [a particular goal]) to ensure that the necessary content has been included. It is also helpful for designing quizzes, tests, and exams.
- Finally, plans are useful when substitute teachers need to take over or when supervisors assess teachers or curriculum.

In the section that follows, lesson planning is viewed as a three-stage process: before, during, and after class.

Decision making before class

The first step in decision making involves looking at the curriculum and the materials and becoming familiar with them, especially with the objectives or student learning outcomes. What should students to be able to do at the end of the lesson? Why are we doing what we are doing in class? Objectives might include:

- Students will be able to greet others and introduce themselves.
- Students will be able to describe their weekend using the past tense.
- Students will be able to fill out an accident report form.
- Students will be able to write a topic sentence for a paragraph.

The second step involves answering this question: Can these objectives be accomplished with the materials provided? Teachers might need to bring in something else to supplement the materials (e.g., real objects, authentic print materials, pictures, or video clips). The materials might need to be adapted to make them more relevant and personal for their students (e.g., teachers can change the map of London to a map of Istanbul). There may be something that should be cut out because it does not match the objectives. There is often a need to add to the materials to give students more review, more practice, or more opportunities to communicate. This is where the teachers' knowledge of how students best learn will affect the plan. Richards and Bohlke (2011, pp. 42–43) have a useful section on adapting textbooks when planning. (See also Byrd & Schuemann, this volume.)

Third, it is good for teachers to look at more than the lesson in front of them. They should look back, considering how the lesson relates to previous work and how material can be reviewed and recycled. They should look ahead and see how related material might be coming up in the curriculum. They should also look outward to the lives of their students. How does this lesson relate to their concerns? How can it be connected to the real world so they are encouraged to use English outside class?

Those three steps will result in a variety of components, or dishes (to use the meal metaphor). The next stage involves matching these components to the class period. How much time should each component take? Is one of the activities a bonus if there is extra time, or is it something that can be cut or shortened if time is running short? Is it necessary to add an opener, or is one of the main activities suitable for starting the class? Which piece would make a good closing? How should the activities be sequenced for pedagogical effectiveness, variety, pacing, and management? What are the details for each activity? For example, should students listen to the dialogue with their books open or closed? Should they respond chorally or individually? Should they do a pair activity with someone sitting next to them or with teacher-assigned partners?[4] What will the teacher do, and what will the students do? This is a good time to think about how to give instructions so students will be clear on what they should be doing.

The final step in pre-class decision making involves appraisal, that is, looking over the plan one final time. Richards and Bohlke (2011, pp. 3–17) suggest that teachers evaluate their plans for the following: high professional standards, sound principles of language teaching, meaningful learning outcomes, opportunities for extended meaningful language practice and use, effective class management, a coherent sequence of activities, student motivation to learn given the opportunity to succeed, and the teacher's personal philosophy of teaching. Depending on the class, there may be other important questions, such as whether the plan incorporates the required standards.

There are several elements in a lesson that deserve a closer look. Starting the lesson well can be like serving a good appetizer in a meal. In a 45-minute lesson, the opener might take just 3 minutes, while in a 3-hour class, it could last 30 minutes. Specific ideas can be found in Figure 1.

Wrapping up the class well (not just with a rush to finish something or with an activity fizzling out) gives students a sense of accomplishment and teachers a sense of satisfaction. It might be like serving an elaborate cake or a simple after-dinner mint. See Figure 2 for ideas.

A good lesson planner is concerned with balance and variety the way is a cook is interested in serving a meal that is nutritious and has a nice blend of taste and texture. Variety helps keep the pace of the class lively. However, this does not mean selecting activities haphazardly just for variety's sake. Ways of varying activities and keeping

1. Establish the appropriate atmosphere for the day's class (e.g., "We're going to have fun today" or "It's time to work hard").
2. Warm students up so they are ready for class and focused on English (e.g., "Talk to your partner about three things you like and three things you don't like about cell phones").
3. Prepare students with ideas or vocabulary they will use in upcoming activities (e.g., "Check these five words in your dictionaries" or "What comes to mind when you hear after forgiveness?").
4. Review material from the previous lesson (e.g., "Yesterday we learned about the difference between excited and exciting. Amina, can you give an example with exciting?").
5. Reward early-arriving students with something useful and fun while you wait for others to trickle in (e.g., give students a chance to go over a composition with the teacher or play a game that reviews vocabulary).
6. Give students a preview of what the "meal" will consist of (e.g., by going over the list of the day's activities that has been written on the board). When we know how many courses we are going to eat and what type of food it is, we enjoy the meal more.

Figure 1. Ways to begin a lesson.

1. Give an assignment. (However, if the assignment will take a long time to explain and students are already thinking about catching the bus or eating lunch, it is better to give the instructions earlier in the class and just a reminder at the end of class.)
2. Make a positive comment about what has been learned to encourage the students (e.g., "You've learned the first step in writing a summary today" or "Your pronunciation of /ɪ/ has improved").
3. Preview the next class. Tell students what will happen in the next class can make them look forward to it.
4. Use a filler. It happens occasionally that you have come to a good stopping point—the goals have been met and the materials have been used—but there are still 5–10 minutes left in the class. Have a collection of five-minute activities (e.g., see Ur, 1992) ready that you can bring out so that the use of time is maximized by doing one or two.

Figure 2. Ways to end a lesson.

lessons from becoming monotomous are found in Figure 3. At the same time, too much variety might confuse beginning students, who are assisted by predictable routines. Finally, variety may also be implemented throughout the week, rather than in just one lesson.

1. Adjust the grouping of students (whole class, small groups, pairs, individual work) as appropriate for the given activity.
2. Integrate several skills, moving from one skill to another (speaking, listening, reading, and writing).
3. Mix up easy and challenging activities so all students can both experience success and feel that they are learning something new.
4. Appeal to different learning styles (auditory, visual, and kinesthetic/tactile).
5. Balance activities that are accuracy-oriented versus fluency-oriented, student-centered versus teacher-centered, serious versus light-hearted, low-tech versus high-tech, familiar versus new, and so on.

Figure 3. Ways of providing variety.

Good pacing is a challenge. It is important to go fast enough that activities do not drag and that students feel they have accomplished something by the end of the class. However, going too fast may mean that students feel they have been left behind, did not grasp the material, or did not accomplish the objectives. Pacing is not just about speed; variety also adds to pace. Ideal variety depends on the age of the students. Children may need to have a change in activity every few minutes, while adults may be able to focus longer on one activity.

It is helpful to make sure a clock is easily visible throughout the lesson. Teachers who have written in their plans estimated times (e.g., "When I start activity 3 it should be 10:30 a.m.") and glance at the clock frequently to know whether they are on track with their pacing, whether they need to pick things up a bit, whether they can relax the pace, or whether they are going to have to completely revise the timing of the lesson.

Classroom management through planning.   Issues such as students falling asleep in class or being disruptive are often thought of as management issues. However, to some extent, good planning can preemptively deal with some of them.

Activities can be thought of in terms of "stirring" and "settling."[5] A stirring activity gets students moving around, thinking hard, or talking a lot. A settling activity has students sitting quietly, listening, or writing. If students come to class all keyed up, starting with a settling activity can focus their minds on English. If students start to drag in the middle of an afternoon class, it is good to have a stirring activity at the halfway point. Teachers can build these into their plan as they get to know the personality and pace of the class.

Activities can also be thought of in terms of rewards and consequences. If students need the discipline of incentives and penalties, this could be accomplished by means of planning and sequencing activities, for example, "If you quietly finish your vocabulary notebooks, we'll have time for a game of Categories."

Objectives, standards, and outcomes.   Institutions often specify the objectives, aims, goals, or outcomes that they expect teachers to implement. Alternatively, teachers may be expected to develop their own course objectives or outcomes. Whether institution or teacher generated, these objectives or outcomes may entail levels from general to specific, or "terminal" (the ultimate aim) to "enabling" (steps that support the learner in getting to the final goal). When objectives are specific, they are easier to measure, and it is easier to determine whether students have achieved them. A simple way of thinking about objectives is to imagine what students will be able to do at the end of the class that they could not do when they walked in. Instead of "improve in reading," define a specific objective such as "students will defend their answers to comprehension questions by referring back to the text." Instead of "practice pronunciation," define a specific objective such as "students will use rising intonation for *would you like* questions in the context of offering hospitality to a guest." Another useful way to think about objectives and activities is with this framework: "If the students engage in X activity, then they will be able to do Y with the target language." (See Appendix A for more ideas on articulating objectives.)

Institutions may also have standards or learning outcomes specified for students at various levels, for example, seventh grade or pre-intermediate. Lesson plans help teachers tie class activities to these standards. Following are some examples from the China English as a Foreign Language project, adapted from China's Ministry of Education standards by an international team (Teachers of English to Speakers of Other Languages, 2007):

1.1—Learners will be motivated to learn, use, and enjoy English and have the courage to overcome challenges in learning.

2.2—Learners will convey information, attitudes, and ideas effectively, both in speech and in writing, in a variety of settings and for a variety of purposes.

3.1—Learners will show continually expanding knowledge, understanding, and appreciation of the cultural features and shared assumptions of both English-speaking and Chinese-speaking peoples.

The noncredit adult ESL program at Glendale Community College in California lists these among its student learning outcomes (Glendale Community College, 2011):

Level 1, 2.1—Using the Level 1 grammar structures, students will be able to write simple sentences about present and past situations and future plans.

Level 2, 2.4—Using the Level 2 grammar structures, students will be able to write guided paragraphs with simple and complex sentences about reasons and results.

ESL 080, 1—Students will demonstrate comprehension of conversations by responding appropriately to speakers' questions.

Some adult ESL programs in the United States use the standards developed by the Comprehensive Adult Student Assessment Systems (CASAS), a nonprofit organization that provides curricula and assessments.[6] Following are some example standards related to listening (Comprehensive Adult Student Assessment Systems, 2011):

L1.4—Distinguish basic stress and intonation patterns in English words and sentences (e.g., rising intonation for yes-no questions, emphasis)

L3.7—Recognize noun plurals

L4.1—Comprehend simple learned social exchanges

L5.1—Comprehend short emergency warnings and commands (e.g., *Stop! Wait!*)

Decision making during class

Given the dynamic nature of a group of students, plans can rarely be carried out in real life exactly as we had imagined them. Decision making and planning happen on the spot in class as well as at our desks in advance.[7] Three common reasons why we may abandon or adjust our plans include something has gone wrong and we need to recover, our timing is off and we need to recalibrate, or something has come up and we want to make the most of it.

There are lots of unanticipated problems that can disrupt lesson plans: Students did not do the homework that was foundational for the day's activities, the projector or the computer broke down, the material was too hard, the students told the teacher they just did something similar in another class, the discussion topic falls flat, and so on. Experienced teachers learn to anticipate such problems and, for example, always have a back-up activity that does not use technology. It is also helpful to have some generic back-up activities ready. If the back-up plan is "tried-and-true" and guaranteed to lead to a successful outcome and satisfied students, it can help teachers recover when something has gone wrong.

Because timing is so difficult to predict, it is likely that there will always be days when students understand quickly, finish a task soon, or run out of things to say—and there is extra time at the end. Thus, it is a good idea to have a supplement to the core activities or an additional activity on hand. It is also likely that things will go more slowly than anticipated. It is therefore advisable to make a notation on the lesson plan where activities might be shortened or which ones might be cut or postponed if time is running short.

The third reason to adjust the lesson plan is because of something special happening in the class. Teachers who are sensitive to students notice when a timely topic comes up and decide to let the class have a go at it or are willing to let students who seem especially engaged in an activity keep going. Harmer (2007b) calls these "magic moments" or "golden opportunities for real communication" (p. 366). Other situations—for example, when a student asks a question and the teacher decides the whole class can benefit from spending time on it, or the students seem confused and the teacher decides to insert an impromptu activity to help them find their way—require knowledge and experience, not just sensitivity to the moment.

Decision making after class

After the class, even though teachers have many urgent things to attend to, it is important to engage in one more bit of reflection. Going back over the lesson plan to assess what happened is a way to build up lesson-planning skills for the future. Typical questions that teachers might ask themselves include:

- How long did each activity take? What might have led to something going slower or faster than anticipated?
- How did the students respond? Were there any students who seemed left behind or left out?
- What did the students leave class with that they did not have before?

A starting point is Ur's (2012) checklist for evaluating lesson effectiveness. She recommends that teachers ask themselves whether learners are:

- actually learning the material well
- engaging with the target language
- attentive
- motivated and enjoying themselves
- active
- participating in real communication

However, since what is considered a "good" lesson will differ depending on the variables noted at the beginning of this chapter, teachers will have their own criteria for success for each class.

After several classes, say at the end of the week, it is good to reflect on the larger picture. What progress have students made? Are the lessons covering what is required? Are the lessons giving the students a sense of achievement and enjoyment?

Writing up a plan

Writing up a plan before the lesson is a way to discipline one's mind to think thoroughly about the class in advance. The template or format provided in Figure 4 is one option for writing up the plan. However, when teachers actually go into the class, they probably want to have a briefer version in hand, perhaps using sticky notes in the teacher's guide, 3 × 5 cards, or a single piece of paper. Something concise helps teachers remember the plan without tying them to a script that will prevent them from attending to the students. In addition, as teachers gain experience, they will probably be able to write less and rely on brief notes; novice teachers, however, benefit greatly from a formal detailed lesson plan.

Comments on the procedures section. Because procedures are the heart of the lesson plan, additional details are warranted (see Figure 4).

Activity/timing. In this column the name of the activity serves as a quick reminder of what is happening. An estimate of how long it will take is also valuable. This can be written in terms of the class hour (e.g., 3:15–3:30 p.m.) or in terms of minutes (e.g., 15 minutes). If particular stages of a lesson are important to name (e.g., introduction to new language, practice, communicative activities), they can be noted in this column too.

Objective(s). Objectives are the reason why each activity in the lesson needs to be clear. They may be related to the class itself (e.g., "help students relax" or "encourage students to do homework by checking it"). They may also be related to external standards (e.g., "meets Standard 3.7: Students will distinguish between fact and opinion"). As noted previously, most objectives should be framed in terms of what students will be able to do as a result of this activity (e.g., "Students will improve their ability to articulate /l/ and /r/ in the context of a fluency-focused activity"). This is also a good column in which to refer to specific language objectives (e.g., "simple present affirmative statements," "*can* to express ability," "collocations with *remember*," "listening to short conversations," "understanding warning labels found on common household items").

Materials/equipment. Writing down the exact materials and equipment will ensure that what is needed—from handouts to markers to puppets—has been gathered before going to class.

Step-by-step details. This will probably be the most detailed part of the lesson plan, unless the activity is a routine that is very familiar. It helps to imagine what will happen in class—what the teacher will do or say and what the students will do or say—and write it down in advance. Scripting something that may be tricky (e.g., instructions for a new activity, or an explanation of new language) will help prevent it from taking too much time or the language from being over the students' heads.

Interaction/seating. Are students interacting as a whole class with the teacher? Are students working on their own, in small groups, or in pairs? Putting

Context: *ESL or EFL setting*

Institution: *name of school, institute, or program*

Course/level: *e.g., Intermediate Reading, or Literacy & Citizenship, or ESL 2*

Students: *number of students (Ss), and relevant details such as male/female, first language, age, and education level*

Overall course goals: *e.g., prepare students for university level writing, or develop students' conversational fluency, or meet ____ standards*

Texts/materials: *details of textbooks, supplemental books, media, or websites used for this lesson*

Lesson aim(s): *e.g., students will learn ten housing-related words; students will be able to report a housing-related problem using the pattern, "The _stove_ is _broken_."*

Previous class work/what do Ss know that prepares them for the lesson: *e.g., Ss are familiar with vocabulary related to rooms and furniture*

Procedures

Activity/ timing	Objective(s)	Materials/ equipment	Step-by-step details	Interaction/ seating	Contingency plans/ other notes
Icebreaker 10 min	Ss will be able to . . . using x, y, z language	Handout I	T does: Ss do:	Ss in pairs, T + whole class, etc.	Be sure to. . . .
Etc.					

Follow-up, future ideas
What was not included in this lesson that will be covered soon?

Notes
What happened during the lesson? How long did things actually take? How did students respond? What could be improved next time? What worked well?

Figure 4. Lesson plan template or format.

this in a separate column allows teachers to prepare students to move around, check that the interactional pattern matches the activity (e.g., Do students need to be in pairs to fill out a worksheet?), and see at a glance whether there is variety.

Contingency plans/other notes. Teachers need to think in advance about potential problems that might arise (e.g., students are not interested in the discussion topic, students find the text too difficult or too easy, or Internet access is down) and plan for alternatives. This is a place to make notes about which activities can be skipped if time is short or note down a relevant extra contingency activity to add if there is extra time. It is also a good place to make any other notes that will help the class be run effectively and humanely (e.g., "Don't forget to collect the homework," or "Ask Tomiko about her father's health").

Sample lesson plan

Figure 5 presents a sample lesson plan for adult migrant students.

The planning process

Teachers initiate the planning process at different points. They may start with a page in the textbook, an activity that they like, some materials they think students will enjoy, a goal, or even a time frame they need to fill. Starting anywhere is fine. However, the end result must have strong connections between larger institutional standards or goals, overall course aims, lesson objectives, and class activities. If the activity does not have an objective or if the materials are not tied to the

Background:

Context: *Los Angeles area*

Institution: *MEND (a volunteer-based agency)*

Course/level: *ESL 2, 60-minute class MWF evenings (followed by computer class)*

Students: *8 to 15 adults, ages 19 to 59, Spanish-speaking*

Overall course goals: *prepare students for life and work in the U.S.*

Texts/materials: *teacher-created materials*

Lesson aim(s): *(1) Students will learn 10 housing-related words; (2) Students will be able to report a housing-related problem using the pattern, "The ___ stove ___ is ___ broken ___." The roof is leaking. The toilet is clogged. The carpet is dirty. The stove is broken. The faucet is dripping; (3) students will be able to talk about their personal housing-related issues. Ss are familiar with some vocabulary related to rooms and furniture.*

Previous class work/what do Ss know that prepares them for the lesson:

Procedures

Activity/ timing	Objective(s)	Materials/ equipment	Step-by-step details	Interaction /seating	Contingency plans/other notes
House vocab bingo 5–10 min	1. Review vocab from previous lessons 2. Allow late-comers to arrive Words: *living room, dining room table, chair, armchair, sofa,* etc.	Bingo cards	As students walk in, assign them to a group. Caller says vocab words. Other Ss put their markers on the words on their cards as they hear them. Ss take turns being the caller.	Ss in groups of 3 to 5	Place any new Ss in Tomas's group so he can orient them in Spanish.
Introduce new words 5 minutes	Ss learn new words *Roof, toilet, carpet, stove, faucet*	Picture cards, set 1	1a. Show pictures. Ss listen and repeat words. 1b. Write words next to pix. Ss listen and repeat. 2. Erase words and write numbers next to pix. T says word and Ss write number. T says number and Ss say word. 3. T says number and Ss say word. 4. Individual work on pronunciation as needed	T–Ss	Ss may already know these words; if so, go quickly.
Introduce grammar pattern 5 minutes	Ss learn the pattern *The ___ is ___.* Language: *The roof is leaking. The toilet is clogged. The carpet is dirty. The stove is broken. The faucet is dripping.*	Picture cards, set 2	As above, with listen and repeat, listen and choose, look and say.	T–Ss	Ss may wonder about *–ing* and *–ed.* Be ready to answer after class for those who are ready for grammatical details.
Choral drills 5–10 minutes	Ss practice the pattern *The ___ is ___*, developing accuracy and fluency.	Picture cards, set 3	1. Substitution. Key sentence on board: *The ___ is dirty.* T: cues with picture: *carpet* Ss: *The carpet is dirty.* T: *window* Ss: *The window is dirty* T: *stove* T: *floor* T: *fridge* Ditto with *The ___ is broken.*	T–Ss	

(continued)

Figure 5. Sample lesson plan for adult migrant education.

Activity / Time	Objectives	Materials	Procedure	Interaction	Notes
			2. Q&A Key dialogue on board: A: *What's wrong?* B: *The ___ is ___.* T cues with pictures. Ss are divided into two groups. Group A questions; Group B answers. Roles then reverse.		
Listen and draw 10 minutes	1. Ss get a rest from choral work. 2. Ss create materials for next activity. 3. Ss develop listening comprehension.	Blank 3×5 cards	T gives instructions for Ss to draw, e.g., "Take a card. Draw a house with a roof. Draw a hole in the roof. Take another card. Draw a window. Draw a crack in the window."	T-Ss	Ss will feel insecure about the drawing. Demonstrate on the board and tell them to draw quickly and simply.
Pair work 15 minutes	1. Ss practice the pattern *The ___ is ___,* developing accuracy and fluency. 2. T gives individual feedback.	Student-created cards. Colored candies.	Put model dialogues on board. Ask a pair of Ss to come up to the front to demo the dialogue. Put Ss in pairs. **1. What's the problem?** A: *What's the problem?* B [picks card and describes]: *The faucet is dripping.* Switch. **2. No, but . . .** A [picks card and asks]: *Is the roof leaking?* B [picks card and says]: *No, but the stove is broken.* Etc. **3. Guess** A [picks a card and doesn't show it to B] B: *Is the toilet clogged? Is the carpet dirty?* [until he guesses A's card] Switch.	S-S pairs	Tell Ss "Find the person with the same color candy as you" to mix up Ss in pairs. Walk among pairs to listen and give feedback. When most Ss have had a good round of #1, ring the bell and give instructions for #2, and so on for #3. Alternatively, if Ss are capable, put all three patterns on the board and let them move on when they're ready.
Discussion 5–15 minutes depending on available time	1. Ss talk about their own lives. 2. Ss ask about additional vocabulary of personal interest.	Spanish-English dictionary in case.	"Now let's talk about *your* house. Do you call the landlord when there's a problem? Do you repair your own house? What other problems with your house have you had? What's the best way to get repairs done?"	Ss	Ss are generally eager to talk, but if not, things to possibly bring up include: broken lock, AC, blinds, smoke alarm, insects, rats, mold. Be ready to explain without dominating the conversation; let Ss talk!

Follow-up, future ideas
Additional ways to request action, e.g., *We need a repairman right away.*

Notes
Things went pretty fast—we had almost 15 minutes for discussion at the end. The Ss ended up giving each other advice on how to get rid of ants.

Figure 5. Sample lesson plan for adult migrant education. (Continued)

overall course goals, then the lesson will most likely be less effective. In other words, "I will cover Chapter 3 in the textbook" or "we will play bingo" is not really good lesson planning.

Novice teachers are often advised to plan in great detail. As mentioned previously, scripting such things as the instructions used to introduce an information-gap activity to the students, how to transition from the warm-up to the main activity, how to group students for a given activity, or the details of a grammar explanation will ensure that things are clear and comprehensible. However, in the press of real-life teaching, it is rare to have time for such details in plans, and teachers should work at planning effectively but quickly.

One way to make planning more efficient is to think in terms of "chunks" (Woodward, 2001) or "game plans." An example is "dictation race." A novice teacher's plan might include:

> Post six texts up on the front board. Divide class into pairs [use matching color card method]. Identify writers and readers. Tell readers, "Come up to the board and read your text. Remember as much as you can. Go back to your partner. Tell your partner what to write." Tell writers, "Write what your partner tells you. You can ask questions about spelling and punctuation." Points will be given to teams who are fast and accurate. (p. 7)

Later, as this process becomes familiar, it is enough to just jot down "Dictation race with x, y, and z texts" in the plan. Smaller chunks combine to become larger units that teachers can carry out automatically. (However, too much reliance on chunks or routines makes teaching boring for experienced teachers or prevents them from doing new things that their students may benefit from.) To return to the cooking analogy: cooks often start by wanting a complete recipe with detailed instructions about how to perform a new technique such as braise or knead; later, their familiarity with cooking techniques means that a few brief notes about ingredients and processes will suffice.

FUTURE TRENDS

With publishers providing web-based supplements to textbooks, lesson planning for teachers using such materials may involve less imagining or searching and more choosing from the options provided by the publisher. Some schools use curricula that entail scripted lessons—if this is a future trend, lesson planning will entail familiarization with or even memorization of the scripts. As teachers develop specialties, for example, in content-based language teaching, business ESL, or online teaching, they will need to develop ways of integrating new content and technology into their lessons. Finally, with websites offering online lesson plans (see the online links), teachers need to hone their skills in adapting those ideas so that they work for their particular learners.

CONCLUSION

In the process of planning what to serve for lunch or dinner, we may stand at the freezer and decide which prepared meal to pull out and heat up, or we may make a trip to the farmer's market to see what is in season and start with fresh ingredients. We may go to the corner stand and pick up some ready-made kebabs or work all day preparing dozens of special dishes. In the same way, lesson planning can vary depending on the resources and time teachers have. However, just as a meal is converted from a raw ingredient to the energy a body needs, a lesson plan enables teachers to give students what they need to acquire the target language in an enjoyable and digestible way. It is also a tool that enables teachers to make decisions, solve instructional problems, deal with classroom management issues, record student progress, and be accountable.

Lesson planning can be facilitated with this series of questions asked before, during, and after the lesson planning process.

Before

1. What curriculum and materials do I have? What are the objectives?
2. Can the objectives be accomplished with what I have? What might I need to adapt, cut, or add?
3. How does this lesson relate to what students have already done in class, will do in the next lessons, or need to do outside class?

4. How can the various pieces of this lesson be put together in the time available?

   - Do I have good opener?
   - Do I have a good closing activity?
   - Is my lesson balanced?
   - Will my plan result in a well-paced class?
   - How can I use the plan to deal with classroom management issues?
   - Have I articulated objectives for each activity?

5. Does this lesson meet the criteria for quality?
6. Have I written down the plan in such a way that I can use it in class, in the future, and for any administrative requirements?

During

1. Have I formulated my plan to allow for flexibility once I am in class, anticipating problems, timing issues, or special teaching/learning opportunities?

After

1. Am I making notes on my lesson plans at the end of class to improve my teaching in the future?

SUMMARY

➤ Lesson planning is grounded in our overall understanding of language learning and teaching as well as the lesson context and the student population.

➤ Planning is a way to engage in advance decision making and develop teaching expertise. Plans give teachers the security to focus more intentionally on their students once they are in class. Plans also provide a mechanism for post-class assessment and reflection.

➤ Teachers can initiate the lesson-planning process at different starting points, write up their plans in different ways, or use different models of planning, as long as the end result is a coherent lesson with connections between objectives and activities, following good principles of teaching and learning.

➤ Teachers must also be mindful of objectives, standards, and learning outcomes to ensure that their lesson plans support overall curricular goals.

DISCUSSION QUESTIONS

1. Briefly describe a class you may have to plan in terms of several or all of the following: SLA theory, methodology, skill, audience, focus, context, standards/student learning outcomes, and teaching philosophy. Note whether these are given to you by the institution or are your personal choice. Compare notes with a classmate, and discuss how these will affect your lesson planning.

2. If you are a novice teacher, what is it about lesson planning that intimidates you the most? How do you plan to deal with these particular challenges?

3. What details do you find most important to include in your lesson plans? What are the pros and cons of writing out plans in detail?

4. Are you familiar with situations where teachers do not plan? The teachers may walk into class and just open the book to the next page, or they may just talk about whatever is on their mind. How do students react? What factors may underlie the lack of lesson planning, and what advice would you give such teachers about planning?

5. What effect does your plan have on what happens in your actual class? Give examples of inclass decision making that have resulted either from something you prepared in advance or that led to your changing your plan.

SUGGESTED ACTIVITIES

1. Examine the lesson plan in Appendix B.
   a. What model (or models) of lesson planning might underlie it? Is it a good match for the context and students?
   b. Critique the plan in light of the questions found in the Conclusion section of this chapter.

2. Using a textbook you teach from or are familiar with and a group of students you teach or have observed, write a lesson plan according to the template in this chapter.

3. Write a commentary on the decision making you engaged in while writing the plan (e.g.,

"The class is early in the morning and the students tend to arrive late, so I adjusted the opening activity in the book . . .").

4. Before observing an ESL/EFL class, ask the instructor for a copy of the day's plan and then sit in on the class. Compare the plan to the reality. What do you think led to any changes?

5. Interview some experienced teachers about how they plan their lessons, what they write down, and how long it takes. How do their strategies vary from class to class, and how have their strategies changed over the years?

6. Choose an aspect of lesson planning that you would like to improve, for example, preparing clear instructions for students or opening the class in a way that accomplishes both pedagogical and affective goals. Using the Further Reading resources, prepare a short paper or presentation.

FURTHER READING

Brown, H. D. (2007). *Teaching by principles* (3rd ed.). New York, NY: Pearson Longman.

Chapter 10, "Lesson Planning," is strong in the area of describing goals and objectives.

Harmer, J. (2007). *The practice of English language teaching* (4th ed.). Harlow, UK: Pearson Longman.

Chapter 21, "Planning Lessons," is very complete and has good examples of lesson plans.

Parrish, B. (2004). *Teaching adult ESL: A practical introduction.* New York, NY: McGraw-Hill.

Chapter 6, "Planning for Teaching and Learning," is excellent. Especially helpful are the anecdotes from actual adult ESL teachers and the lesson planning checklist.

Richards, J. C., & Bohlke, D. (2011). *Creating effective language lessons.* Cambridge, UK: Cambridge University Press. Available from http://www.cambridge.org/other_files/downloads/esl/fourcorners/Pedagogical_Books/Creating-Effective-Language-Lessons-Combined.pdf

This downloadable booklet is a thorough discussion of lesson planning, placed in the context of effective teaching, a positive learning environment, and learner-centered teaching.

Robertson, C., & Acklam, R. (2000). *Action plan for teachers: A guide to teaching English.* London, UK: BBC World Service. Available from http://www.teachingenglish.org.uk/transform/books/action-plan-teachers

This downloadable booklet contains a good chapter on lesson planning for novice teachers who use the engage-study-activate method.

Watkins, P. (2005). *Learning to teach English.* Surrey, UK: Delta Publishing.

Chapter 16, "Planning," has four samples that are especially helpful to novice teachers in short-course training programs.

Woodward, T. (2001). *Planning lessons and courses.* Cambridge, UK: Cambridge University Press.

This book contains a very complete coverage of planning lessons, written in an engaging style. The introduction and the final chapter on freedoms and constraints are especially helpful.

APPENDIX A: GUIDELINES FOR WRITING OBJECTIVES

Teachers are often urged to write objectives using verbs that match the levels in Bloom's taxonomy. The following websites are useful resources:

> http://www.celt.iastate.edu/teaching/RevisedBlooms1.html
> http://www.uwsp.edu/education/lwilson/curric/newtaxonomy.htm
> http://www.odu.edu/educ/roverbau/Bloom/blooms_taxonomy.htm

Helpful as these lists of verbs are, ESL teachers might need some verbs more applicable to English language teaching.

Useful action verbs for writing objectives related to ESL classes

1. related to the main skills: *read, write, speak, listen to, pronounce*
2. related to specific skills: *predict, scan, proofread, summarize, take notes, revise, participate in*
3. related to specific assignments or activities: *copy, complete, fill in, translate, correct, edit* (however, these tend to focus on things students do

in class rather than on things they need to do in the real world)

4. *produce* (sentences, paragraphs, essays, presentations)
5. *use* (words, patterns)
6. *identify* (ideas), *analyze* (texts), *interpret* (messages)
7. *comprehend* (texts), *recognize* (errors)
8. *organize, outline* (ideas, essays)
9. *apply* (rules, strategies)

Useful specifications

- texts at ___ level,
- TEXTS of _#_ words,
- ___ kinds of texts/tasks,
- topics related to ___, for ___ purposes, by means of ___
- with _% accuracy
- so that errors do not interfere with comprehension
- using the words ___, ___, and ___
- including _ and _ features

Typical weaknesses in writing objectives

- *Students will be able to comprehend short texts.* How do we know the students have comprehended? → *Students will comprehend short texts as demonstrated by means of multiple choice questions.*
- *Students will learn how to write an essay.* How do we know they know they have learned? → *Learn* is not a strong verb for objectives.
- *Students will write an essay.* What kind of essay? According to what standards? → *Students will write an essay following ___ format and including ___ thesis/supporting ideas and with fewer than __ errors per page.*
- *Student will practice the simple present tense.* Why? What will they be able to do with it after they practice? → *Practice* is not a strong verb for objectives.

APPENDIX B: SAMPLE LESSON PLAN (BUSINESS ESL)

This lesson is based on a public radio program, *On Being, with Krista Tippet*, American Public Media (http://being.publicradio.org/programs/godsofbusiness/index.shtml). The entire lesson can be found at TESOL Resources from Kitty (http://tesolresourcesfromkitty.pbworks.com).

Lesson plan for Business ESL

Background:

Context: *North Africa*

Institution: *Oasis (a private language institute)*

Course/level: *Business English (a ten-day elective). Class is 45 minutes long. Students (Ss) are supposed to be upper intermediate but there is a wide-range of abilities.*

Students: *15 adults; some Ss, some already in business. Most Ss enjoy speaking English and tend to be stronger in fluency than accuracy, but the lower-level Ss are weak in all skills.*

Overall course goals: *Develop accuracy and fluency in business-related English listening, reading, and speaking*

Texts/materials: *Teacher-created materials, based on a public radio show*

Lesson aim(s): *Ss will develop discussion and presentation oral skills; Ss will review vocabulary related to business ethics while reading and speaking*

Previous class work/what do Ss know that prepares them for the lesson: *Ss have spent three days on the listening portion of these materials, based on a recorded interview with a global business analyst and ethicist, Prabhu Guptara. The interview has talked about corruption, the effect of world religions and business practices, inequities fueled by the global economy, and possibilities for positive change. The vocabulary in the quotes for this lesson (e.g., "transcendent") is familiar.*

Procedures

Activity/ timing	Objective(s)	Materials/ equipment	Step-by-step details	Interaction /seating	Contingency plans/other notes
Opener/ review/ intro to the day's activity 5 min	1. Remind Ss of the topic; activate schema related to business ethics in a globalized world. 2. Get Ss ready for the discussion.	Recording of interview; listening worksheet from previous class, just in case.	T: "In our last class we heard the end of the interview. Guptara has four things on his agenda for better globalization. Who can remember them?" Ss: 1. "Create a culture where people are satisfied with enough." 2. "Restrain demands for higher wages and profits." 3. "Avoid economic expansion for its own sake." 4. "Encourage companies that take seriously concerns of the environment, labor, and civil society." T: "You've done a lot of listening and a little talking. Now it's time for more talking. Our activity today involves small-group discussions and presentations."	Whole class	If Ss don't remember anything, and are reluctant to talk, play the short segment of the interview in which Guptara's agenda is discussed.

(continued)

Lesson plan for Business ESL (*continued*)

Stage / Timing	Objectives	Materials	Procedure	Notes
Small group discussion of key quotes 15–20 minutes	1. Accurate reading: Ss will have a few sentences to examine carefully for detailed comprehension. 2. Speaking: Ss will articulate personal ideas related to business ethics. 3. Group work: Ss will get experience working in groups relevant to international business practice.	• Get-into-group cards • Quotation handouts for three groups [see below] • Board	T: "In small groups you'll be discussing a quotation related to global business ethics. Each group has a different quote, so after the discussion you'll be presenting your quote to the whole class." T hands out cards. T: "You will be in a group of five people who have the same color card as you. Each person has a different job in the group." [write on board]: • The leader gets the handout and reads the instructions and the quote. • The time-keeper makes sure the group is on track (about 3 minutes per question). • The English monitor makes sure everyone speaks English. • The secretary takes notes. • The presenter will organize the group to present ideas to the whole class. Try to let everyone participate. Groups will have about 15 minutes to look at the quote, discuss the four questions, and plan their presentation.	Three groups of five students each If students are absent and a group has only four people, combine leader and time-keeper roles. Higher proficiency Ss can explain the quote to the lower Ss, but T should be ready to help too if needed. Timing is tentative. Check groups after 10 minutes. If they seem ready to present, fine. If they need more time, tell the time-keeper. Encourage the presentation planners to include several people from the group, e.g., one person to read the quote, another to explain it, and another to expand on it.
Group presentation on quotes 5 min each = 15 min	1. Ss will gain confidence in speaking before a group. 2. Ss will consider the issues in all three quotations.	A projected version of each quote will be helpful.	T calls on each group to present. Encourage further class discussion on the quotes. T takes notes on Ss' English for future feedback.	Whole class Groups who are waiting to present will murmur among themselves instead of listening. Remind them that listening to colleagues is a good business practice. If the whole group is engaging in further discussion, consider extending this time.
Feedback/ Wrap-up 5 min	Ss will refine their pronunciation, vocabulary, or grammar	Board	T uses notes to give feedback that will be of benefit to the whole class, e.g., *make a difference, greed versus greedy.*	Whole class If there is no time for this, give individual Ss written feedback. (T should keep record of feedback.)

Follow-up, future ideas
The next (and last) lesson will involve jigsaw reading about what the following belief systems have to say about business ethics: Islam, Judaism, Christianity, Buddhism, Hinduism, Confucianism, and Atheism/Materialism.

Notes
It took at least five minutes to get the groups formed, organized, and oriented to their roles. Students were very eager to discuss but tended not to listen to each other well. A future lesson on turn-taking in discussions appropriate to an international business context would be helpful.

Handouts

Group 1

"The frightening thing about the Enron story is that it really wasn't about a few people doing the wrong thing; it was about almost no one associated with the company doing the right thing."

Bethany McLean, co-author *The Smartest Guys in the Room*

1. What does this quotation mean? Make sure everyone in your group understands it.
2. Can you think of other examples where a few people do the wrong thing and no one does the right thing, with the result being a disaster?
3. Who would you blame more, those who do the wrong thing or those who do not do the right thing?
4. Why is it hard to do the right thing?

Group 2

"There is no need to make an either/or choice between participating in the market economy and being a person of faith. Rather, the challenge is to live in the market but not be wholly possessed by the market."

Rebecca Blank, dean, Gerald Ford School of Public Policy

1. What does this quotation mean? Make sure everyone in your group understands it.
2. Do you agree that some people find it hard to be a sharp businessperson and a religious person at the same time?
3. Do you agree with Rebecca Blank that it is possible to do both at the same time?
4. What are some ways a person can "live in the market," that is, do business well, but not be "possessed by the market," that is, not be controlled by greed and profits?

Group 3

"The question I would leave us with . . . is where [and how] does my religious or transcendent orientation . . . relate to my individual ethics, to my group ethics in terms of the way my company operates, and then to global business ethics?"

Prabhu Guptara

1. What does this quotation mean? Make sure everyone in your group understands it.
2. How would you answer this question?
3. Can individuals make a difference?
4. How important are strong business ethics to the future of the world?

ENDNOTES

[1] This chapter draws on content from the lesson-planning chapters in the second edition (Purgason, 1991) and third edition (Jensen, 2001) of this book.

[2] For a concise treatment of second language acquisition theory, see Ellis (this volume).

[3] See also ECRIF: Seeing Learning, available at http://www.ecrif.com/planning-with-ecrif.html

[4] See Stevick (1986) for a discussion of the many choices teachers have.

[5] I first encountered these now widely used terms in Maclennan (1987).

[6] For more information on CASAS, visit https://www.casas.org/

[7] K. Bailey (1996) describes research into teachers' in-class decisions that depart from the lesson plans. For example: (1) a teacher spent extra time answering one student's question because she felt the whole class might benefit from the answer; (2) a teacher in an advanced speaking class, who began each lesson with a brief student-led discussion of current events, was prompted by student interest in one of those events to abandon her entire lesson plan; (3) a teacher who had originally planned to put students in groups to brainstorm ideas and take turns writing them on the board decided to let the most proficient student in one group take over for a less proficient student to "promote the substance and the progress of the lesson" (p. 29); and (4) seeing her writing students' difficulty with *in*, *on*, and *at*, a teacher took a detour from her original lesson on thesis statements to do a mini-lesson with a visual diagram explaining the prepositions.

[8] Some of this background information is usually included only when the lesson plan is an assignment for a class or is done for a supervisor or substitute teacher.

24 | English as a Second/Foreign Language Textbooks: How to Choose Them—How to Use Them

PAT BYRD AND CYNTHIA SCHUEMANN

KEY QUESTIONS

➤ What are useful ways to evaluate and select textbooks for particular classes?

➤ What is the role of textbooks in lesson planning and syllabus preparation?

➤ How can textbooks most appropriately be adapted or supplemented with additional materials?

EXPERIENCE

Mariah is in her second year as a full-time university English as a foreign language (EFL) instructor in Xi'an, China, in a U.S.-partnership dual-degree program. Her students will graduate with bachelor's degrees from two institutions, one Chinese and the other American. In China, she is responsible for teaching English to first- and second-year business and engineering students, who will then transfer to the U.S. university for their last two years. In this vignette, Mariah shares her textbook story to illustrate the real-life challenges of making selection decisions about materials and then implementing them.

> Here I find myself once again in the daunting shadow of a mountainous heap of English textbooks stacked before me. In my fourth semester, second year of teaching for this program, I have yet to find "the perfect textbook." Ironically, one of the textbooks before me is one that I had written myself, two years ago as a Peace Corps volunteer. But that was for a different group of Chinese students than the ones I am teaching now—at a different university, in a different province, and seemingly (in the age of ever-advancing technology) in a different era. It has some of what my students need, but by no means does it fit the bill. So now begins anew the painstaking process of evaluating, selecting, and adapting. Painstaking because my job

would be a lot easier, and I would have a lot more free time, if I could just select and follow a perfect-fit textbook. Well, you know what they say about things being too good to be true—they don't exist. So I begin to break away from the shadow by choosing from those books on my desk the ones which will be good enough. And, I then begin my work of adapting and supplementing so that my course will be unique, meaningful, useful, relevant, and hopefully even exciting for my students.

WHAT IS INVOLVED IN SELECTING AND USING TEXTBOOKS?

This chapter explores how teachers interact with English as a second language (ESL)/EFL textbooks that play an essential role in complementing instruction. Arguments have been presented both for and against using textbooks (Ur, 2012), but the reality of most ESL/EFL classroom settings provides clear evidence of a preference for teaching with textbooks. Because this is the case, it is important to learn about best practices for choosing and using textbooks. In this chapter, we consider six related topics: (1) textbook evaluation and selection; (2) textbook analysis for implementation; (3) textbook adaptation and supplementation; (4) the underpinnings of textbooks; (5) support for classroom applications, including textbook evaluation charts and checklists; and (6) some additional thoughts on textbooks and the future. We believe that reflecting on these critical areas of knowledge about textbooks in ESL/EFL classrooms can benefit language educators at all levels, as well as their students.

CONCEPTUAL UNDERPINNINGS

Any textbook is based on three kinds of theory (Byrd & Schuemann, 2013; McDonough & Shaw, 2003b; Mishan, 2004; J. C. Richards, 2001b, 2006b; Tomlinson, 1998, 2003). First, we have theories about the concept of textbook. In discussions about textbooks in general, focus is on the purposes and uses of published sets of materials. Second, any language teaching/learning textbook grows out of theories about the nature of language (Richards & Rodgers, 2001). Perhaps in our profession, we have more published theory in the third area, the relationship between textbooks and language teaching /language learning. Surely textbook writers might not be completely conscious of these traditions while preparing a textbook, but these conceptual underpinnings are deeply embedded in our approaches to the writing and use of published materials in textbook format.

What is a textbook? Teachers use many different kinds of materials in ESL/EFL classes, including handouts, various types of realia, and, in many contexts, computer and Internet resources of many kinds. While just about anything can be included under "language teaching materials," a textbook has a special status within that large category, not just in ESL/EFL but in most academic areas. There are many highly charged issues around these books, including fears that textbooks exploit students and that textbooks in many content areas include dumbed-down and/or biased content. Whatever the good or evil involved in the publication of textbooks, everyone seems to recognize what one is, although the actual books can be quite different in appearance from country to country. Generally, we expect a textbook to provide for a whole course information and learning activities that can be used to form and guide not just individual lessons but the entire length of time scheduled for a particular class.

What ideas about the nature of language or linguistics are directly or indirectly embodied in a textbook? Theories about language are always involved in language teaching textbooks (and materials). While the textbook writer can be fully conscious of trying to realize a particular set of beliefs about language in a set of materials, the focus of the writer can easily be on other aspects of language teaching with the ideas about language present but not fully articulated. In the United States, some language teachers view language based on their study of Chomskyan theoretical linguistics, with its focus on syntax and cognitive psychology (Chomsky, 1972). Other teachers have studied one of the many versions of sociolinguistics and see language as a social tool, and so they focus on how language is used in social groups (Hornberger & McKay, 2010). A third strand now found in ESL/EFL textbooks builds on corpus-analysis traditions that emphasize the interrelatedness of vocabulary and grammar and the specialized use of language in particular communicative settings (Biber, Johansson, Leech, Conrad, & Finegan, 1999; Moon, 2009; Sinclair, 2004). While theories about language can be very indirectly involved in a textbook, teachers need to watch carefully for those theories when they analyze textbooks during the selection process to be sure that there is a comfortable fit between their approaches to language and those embodied in the textbook selected for a particular course.

What ideas about language teaching/learning are reflected in the textbook? No single theory about language acquisition or language teaching dominates classroom practice. Thus, we can expect language teaching materials to involve a variety of ideas about effective practice, as can be seen in publications about the materials. As J. C. Richards (2006b) points out, while there is often a limited connection between published second language acquisition/teaching theory and published materials, all textbooks embody some core of ideas about what should happen in a language classroom, what the roles of the teacher should be, and what students need to be doing in a language class to achieve the language learning goals. These ideas are usually articulated for users of the textbook in the instructor's manual (as well as in any promotional materials provided by the publisher for potential adopters of the textbook).

CLASSROOM APPLICATIONS

Evaluating for selection

Evaluating and selecting textbooks for language instruction is a complex process carried out in different ways in different settings. Typically textbooks used in language classes strongly impact the teaching/learning experience on a daily basis; thus, in a practical sense, their selection is one of the most important decisions made. In some cases, especially in university settings, teachers make their own decisions about which books they want to use in their classes. For experienced teachers, this freedom might be preferred, while newer teachers are sometimes overwhelmed by the volume of choices available in today's textbook marketplace. In other cases, a committee of teachers contributes to a collaborative process of search, evaluation, and selection of books for piloting or use as primary texts. And a third scenario involves centralized decision making by a school district, administrative unit, or government seeking a unified system of language instruction. For example, in Egypt, the Ministry of Education created an English textbook series for use throughout the country rather than selecting one from a commercial publisher's collection. In the United States, national requirements do not exist, but at the state level, boards of education and school districts often develop lists of recommended books that meet state standards, and individual schools make selections within these established parameters. In Florida, for instance, there are statutes specifying the process in detail for primary and secondary school education. Textbook evaluation and selection committees are appointed and include teachers, laypeople, a district school board member, and teacher supervisors. Following bid submissions from publishers, the committee agrees on a list of a small number of textbook options for specific student levels or categories, and individual educators are required to teach using books on the list (Florida Department of Education, n.d.).

In actual practice, outside university settings, materials selection generally involves input from administrative authorities and others, and does not allow for an individual teacher to make personal decisions. This approach can be attributed to many factors, including the amount of time needed to learn a new language and the overlap of skills. English courses are not isolated. All programs seek to ensure some unity and coherence, and logical sequencing and recycling are important so that student learning will become more meaningful. Nonetheless, teachers can influence the decision-making process for textbooks, and they thus need to be aware of how instructional materials are selected in their own situations. That is, teachers not only have to be aware of their individual class realities but must also be knowledgeable about the larger system in which they work and about ways that the system allows for teacher participation in its administrative processes. Influencing the textbook-selection process in these situations is not just a matter of pedagogical knowledge but sometimes also of political considerations.

Systematic evaluation. Systems for evaluating textbooks and instructional materials generally include checklists built around specific aspects of teaching and student-teacher interactions (Ansari & Babaii, 2002; Byrd, 2001; Skierso, 1991; Ur, 2012). There are many published textbook-evaluation checklists, not only for ESL/EFL materials but for all discipline areas. While reviewing and updating our reference bank of textbook checklists, we recalled a case in which two colleagues sat down to make composition-revision checklists for their students. Their first list had over 100 items on it. Clearly, this was not going to be useful for most students. The pair quickly downsized the list to a more reasonable number of items that their students could handle. But they also realized that the checklist was useful only for a particular kind of writing; it worked reasonably well for personal essays being written for their own courses, but it would not have worked nearly so well if the students had been writing lab reports for science courses or literature reviews for history courses. Similarly, making a comprehensive yet reasonable checklist for evaluating language textbooks is an enormous challenge calling for flexible checklists useful in different types of courses and different settings. Like the previously suggested textbook-evaluation checklists, the models and templates proposed in this chapter need to be considered carefully and adapted to fit the particular situations in which they will be used. In the next section, we provide an overview and general rationale for three fundamental "fit" considerations when evaluating and selecting textbooks: fit with the curriculum, fit with the students, and fit with the teachers. A sample checklist structured around these three considerations follows.

Textbook fit 1: With the curriculum. Generally, the first area addressed in textbook evaluation and selection is an analysis of the fit between materials and curriculum. For large educational systems, publishing houses create materials based on published curriculum statements, and they provide tables or charts to show exactly how and where required standards or competencies are met in their textbooks. In U.S. states with large ESL populations such as California, New York, Texas, and Florida, publishers compete fiercely to provide materials that meet the stated curricular guidelines. For these educational systems with their considerable purchasing power and various methods of controlling content, the fit between textbooks and the curriculum is assumed to be a reasonable and achievable goal. In countries with centralized educational planning units, curricular fit is also more controlled. Such is the case in Egypt, for example, where the Ministry of Education arranges for publication of its own textbooks, and educators there can be sure that the materials are appropriate for the setting and that they carry out specified curricular goals. A third scenario of strong fit between curriculum and materials can be found in some private for-profit language programs such as Berlitz, which closely adhere to their own in-house instructional approaches.

For smaller programs and individual teachers, the fit between curriculum and textbooks can be harder to achieve for two reasons. First, all too many programs do not have clearly articulated curriculum statements; teachers have groups of students who want to learn English, but the program lacks general statements of purpose and methods (as Mariah encountered in China in our opening vignette). Second, when curriculum statements do exist in smaller ESL/EFL instructional settings, they may have features that are unique to a particular program, and publishers are not motivated to develop or sell limited-use textbooks because doing so would result in financial loss. In the first situation, the textbook must be selected based on features other than curriculum; therefore the textbook itself often *becomes* de facto the curriculum. In the second situation, textbooks that are completely congruent with the pedagogical goals of the program are unlikely to be found. The

purpose of the evaluation and selection process must be to find books that have as good a fit as possible with the expectation that the books will need to be adapted and supplemented with additional materials to support the curriculum.

Textbook fit 2: With the students. Textbooks are for students. An ESL/EFL textbook must have not just the English language or communication skill content demanded by the curriculum but also fit the needs of learners. Language textbooks are made up of three major elements: content (and explanations), examples, and exercises or tasks. In support of these three elements, textbooks also employ a variety of graphic features in their presentation and format, including print size and font style, color, white space, illustrations, and photo images. In the evaluation-for-selection process, the person or group making decisions needs to know enough about the student population to be able to answer the following questions:

Content/explanations. Is the content likely to be of interest or use to the students? Is there any chance that the content could be offensive or inappropriate for its intended audience? Do the explanations work for these learners—do they help the learners understand what they need to do to learn?

Examples. Are the examples appropriate to the lives and interests of students? Do the examples fit closely with the concepts they are supposed to be explaining? Are there enough examples included?

Exercises/tasks. Do the exercises or tasks provide enough variety to meet the needs of different kinds of learners in the class(es)? Will they be of interest to these students? Do they truly foster and support language learning? Are there worthwhile supplemental exercises for students provided by the publisher to reinforce learning? Does the book have complementary online resources for students who want to do additional work online?

Presentation/format. Does the book look right for the students? Visualize students walking down the hall with the textbook in their arms and then opening it at their desks. Are the design elements, including illustrations, appropriate for their age and instructional level? Is there an effective balance with the mix of print and white space and the use of color? Is readability enhanced? Does the book have appendices, an index, or other sections that are usable by students? Is the book well constructed—will it last through a term of hard use by students?

Textbook fit 3: With the teachers. Textbooks are also for teachers. As with students, teachers seek three things from textbooks: content/explanations, examples, and exercises or tasks. The evaluation-for-selection process needs to find out if the textbook can be used effectively by the teachers to whom it will be assigned. The basic questions will always be, can our teachers handle this material, and will our teachers find that the textbook meets their needs and preferences for teaching materials?

Questions such as the following should be included in the analysis of fit between a potential textbook and the teachers who will use it:

Content/explanations. In all settings, evaluators need to consider if the textbook provides content that teachers will find useful for carrying out the goals of the course and the program—is this a teacher-friendly book? In some settings, it is important to ask if teachers have adequate English to understand the content and to explain it to the students. A consideration of importance with content-based materials such as those used in advanced or English for specific purposes classes is to determine if there a reasonable fit between the content used and the knowledge base of the teacher. (See chapters by Snow and Johns & Price, this volume, for further discussion of this issue.) There are also other considerations: Is there an instructor's manual that helps the teacher better understand the content and ways of using the content with students? Does the textbook supply or require additional complementary materials (or ancillaries) such as audio or video components? Does it have a companion workbook? If these ancillaries exist, how accessible are they, and are they appropriate to and usable by teachers in the program?

Examples. Are the examples usable by the teacher—can they be expanded on or recast to be useful in lessons?

Exercises/tasks. Does the textbook provide enough activities for the teacher to satisfy students for the length of the course? Are the exercises and tasks doable in this setting? Do they provide for a variety of learning styles? Does an instructor's manual provide guidance on implementation or expansion of exercises and an answer key?

Presentation/format. Do the design and layout enhance teaching? Is there a close connection between the content and illustrations? Are there figures, tables, or charts that summarize the content effectively, and can they serve as introductory or review points for the lesson?

Analyzing textbooks to plan courses and lessons

While having rational and effective selection procedures is surely important for educational systems, programs, schools, teachers, and students, the selection process is one that is not open to all ESL/EFL teachers. Many teachers have no voice in textbook selection if they work in settings where textbooks are selected through an administrative process: at the ministerial or school board level, by the program director, by a committee of teachers that selects textbooks for the whole program, or even by the teacher who taught the course the previous semester but who is teaching something else this term. As a result, although information about evaluation for selection is important for teachers to understand, most teachers are mainly concerned with how to implement, adapt, and supplement materials in order to teach the most effective classes possible.

Although the evaluation-for-selection systems are created to make the selection process as rational as possible, encounters with textbooks in the selection process always involve a series of value judgments. Evaluation is about making judgment calls: yes or no, in or out, buy it or do not buy it, thumbs up or thumbs down. Because the types of analysis and decision making when using a textbook in the classroom are very different from those in the selection process, evaluating textbooks for classroom use involves different criteria. In the evaluation-for-selection process, the basic question is, does this book have the features that we want it to have so that we will adopt it? After adoption, the basic question changes to, how do teachers working with particular students in a particular class in a particular program make this book work to ensure effective and interesting lessons?

To avoid confusion over the type of evaluation required at this stage in the life of a textbook in a course or program, we now turn to a discussion of textbook analysis in the implementation process. The categories that a teacher can use here are the same as in the selection process—what is in the book and what is provided by the publisher to supplement the book. While the basic categories are the same, the purpose is much different and often much more urgent, since teachers can sometimes find themselves analyzing a textbook only hours before going into a class to teach a lesson that will be built around the materials in the textbook.

Getting an overview of the resources in the textbook to plan the course syllabus and individual lessons. Prior to using a textbook, a teacher needs to read the whole book from start to finish, including any appendices. In working with new teachers, we have found that one of their limitations in working with a textbook is that they do not see it as a whole and do not examine the textbook in detail before the first day of class. We have repeatedly had the experience of having a teacher tell us near the end of a term that he or she has just discovered some useful feature of the textbook, something that was in a later section of the book or in an appendix. A basic rule of textbook implementation thus is: Teachers can only make optimal use of materials if they know what features are at their disposal.

Teaching usually involves an overlapping cycle of presentation, practice, and evaluation. Presentation can involve the introduction of new materials or information or a reintroduction for a review session, and it can be direct or indirect. It is whatever the teacher does to get students started on a unit of study. Practice can be any type of activity, from a drill to writing an essay, from the least communicative form of repetition to an unscripted discussion; it is whatever the teacher sets up to help the students learn to do whatever it is they are studying in that unit. Evaluation is whatever the teacher does to find out what students have learned. This teaching cycle is bounded by the academic calendar of the school system in which the class is taught; a class is always limited in time to the number of hours a week it will be taught and to any additional time that might be added for homework, if homework is appropriate to the setting. This cycle provides a useful framework for the initial reading of a textbook and the making of plans for the use of that textbook. Those plans include both thinking about the overall pattern of the course that will result in a syllabus to guide the teacher and the students through the academic term and initial ideas about how individual lessons might be organized.

Initial reading of a textbook. Before undertaking a detailed analysis of the textbook to be used in a course, a teacher can benefit from conducting a general overview of the book. A reasonable series of questions that a teacher should ask during this initial reading should include the following.

Presentation/format. How many and what kinds of units does the book have? How many pages are there in each unit, and how can the number of pages be divided across the instructional time period while leaving sufficient class meeting time for review and testing too? How is each unit organized? What kinds of illustrations or other graphic elements are used? How many of these graphic elements are there? How are they connected to the rest of the materials in the unit? What additional features does the book have beyond the basic units—appendices? index? glossary? Are there any ancillary materials such as workbooks or audio/video supplements?

Content/information. What does each unit provide for presentation? What is each unit about? Ask these questions with regard to both topical content and language learning content. Are some units more relevant than others? Can some units be left out, or should only parts of some units be excluded? In general, it is better to underbook a syllabus because opportunities for supplementation and expansion readily present themselves. Overbooking a syllabus can result in stress when teachers feel as if they are falling behind or must catch up.

Practice. What type of practice does each unit provide for students? Where are the exercises or tasks placed, and how do they relate to the presentation of content? Are tasks and task items meaningfully sequenced? Do they follow a taxonomy of difficulty (e.g., from knowledge to evaluation) such as presented by Bloom (1956)?[1] Do task items reflect authentic use and contain episodically related elements rather than disconnected lists or sentences? Will the assignments demand a lot of time for correction? How much reinforcement and recycling do the assignments provide? What connections are made among activities provided in the various units?

Evaluation. What does each unit give the teacher to use for evaluation of student learning? When will assessment occur during the term? How long will each activity be? Are there supplemental testing materials provided by the publisher—test banks? unit-by-unit assessments? How much time is needed to spend on creating and correcting tests? If tests are provided, are there multiple forms? Are there interactive versions that are easy to modify and adapt?

Support. Is there an introduction printed in the textbook itself that has information on using the book? Is there an explicit scope and sequence? Is there an instructor's manual and answer key? If so, how does the teacher get copies? What online supplements and supports are provided by the publisher?

Analysis of the content of the textbook. Language textbooks differ considerably from those in other disciplinary areas. A biology textbook, for example, is dominated by the presentation of information about biology: theory, examples, recounting of famous experiments, and definitions of terminology. The purpose of the book is for students to learn a certain segment of the body of knowledge that makes up the disciplinary area of biology. Critiques of public school textbooks from other disciplines reveal two related problem areas: (1) inaccurate or incomplete content (e.g., see Suidan, Badenhoop, Glendening, & Weinhold, 1995); and (2) poor readability for the student audience because content experts do not necessarily understand how to present complex content for new, young learners (e.g., see Britton, Gulgoz, & Glynn, 1993). These problems should be of concern for ESL/EFL programs that use authentic materials as the basis for study, especially those that use content-area textbooks as resources for ESL/EFL materials. Analysis of authentic content selections should consider vocabulary load, expository style, and illustrations. Kearsey and Turner (1999) used genre analysis techniques to evaluate textbook materials written in Great Britain for secondary science courses; these techniques revealed that many texts had simple examples interspersed with hard nuggets of scientific writing to provide the content that was the real focus of the curriculum. Illustrations that may enhance the understanding of concepts for native speakers are not always accessible to newcomers to a society, especially if the examples include cultural or geographical references. When authentic materials are chosen, ESL/EFL instructors need to structure syllabi and plan lessons that foster language learning tied to disciplinary content. At the same time, they need to pay extra attention to potential barriers that the content and style may present for their students.

In contrast, traditional ESL/EFL textbooks tend to be made up of two strands of content: (1) the linguistic content (e.g., grammar, vocabulary, and skill areas); and (2) the thematic content ("school," "gender issues," "the environment," and other topic content used to present and practice the linguistic content). The teacher can expect the topics in content-based materials to be emphasized and clearly visible. In some materials, however, the teacher needs to look past the linguistic content to find out what themes have been included in the textbook. If, for example, the teacher notices in her or his initial analysis that a grammar textbook includes numerous examples and passages based on the biographies of famous people, then he or she can plan to supplement the text with other materials and activities (visits to local museums, readings about people famous in the cultures of the students, and so on). The analysis-for-implementation angle on content involves both the linguistic and the thematic content of the textbook. (See Figure 3 later in the chapter.)

Analysis of exercises/tasks in the textbook for implementation in classes. While planning the ways in which the textbook will be used for the whole academic term, a teacher needs to make concrete if tentative decisions about how different activities will be used, asking questions such as those in Figure 3. The primary issues considered in this figure include analyzing linguistic and thematic content; determining the purpose of activities for in-class instruction, homework, testing, or review; noting unit connections and review points; listing any special equipment needs; and prioritizing which sections to keep and which to skip. For example, with regard to analyzing linguistic content, the following questions are asked: "What language areas are being taught? In which chunks and what sequences? What adjustments must be made to fit the program's curriculum? Are there any adjustments that can be made in content and sequencing to provide a better fit with the course and the students?" Each section of the figure provides questions to guide reflection.

Seeking help in implementing a textbook. Teachers have both formal and informal sources of information and support as they analyze textbooks for implementation in particular classes. Formal sources include the instructor's manual as well as other written materials available in the school or program or online in websites provided by the publisher. In addition to suggestions for using individual activities in a textbook as part of lessons, textbook writers and publishers often provide sample course syllabi and scope and sequence charts that can be found in the instructor's manual (printed or online). These sample syllabi give teachers information about how the textbook author imagines the book will be used to structure a whole course. Another useful source of model course syllabi is samples of what other teachers in the program have done in the past or plan to do in the future. These materials can include a curriculum statement, course syllabi used in previous terms, pacing charts, and copies of handouts used by previous teachers. In addition, many schools provide teachers with formal help through structured interactions with senior teachers and supervisors.

Informal support is generally available if teachers seek it. When teaching a course for the first time or for the first time with a particular textbook, teachers can sometimes get help with implementation of materials in a course by talking with colleagues who are teaching the same course or who have taught it before. Another source of syllabus models can be found by simply doing an Internet search with the title of the book (enclosed in quotation marks) along with the word *syllabus*.

Adapting and supplementing

No published textbook will perfectly fit a particular teacher and a particular class of students in a particular setting. Teachers should expect to both adapt and supplement textbooks using principled approaches. Much of the published work on materials focuses on these actions of adapting and supplementing (e.g., Folse, 2006; N. Grant, 1987; McDonough & Shaw, 2003b; Mishan, 2004; J. C. Richards, 2001b, 2006; Savova, 2009; Tomlinson, 1998, 2003). Creating useful adaptations and supplements is a skill that depends both: (1) on planning ahead; and (2) on knowledge of options for making those changes. This skill is also one that develops over time. Teachers need to be patient; they will

become more skillful as they learn from their successes and failures in this important daily aspect of classroom teaching. One of the reasons that teachers generally like to use the same textbook over several years is that experience with the book means that they can build up collections of appropriate supplements and find ways to change what is in the book to fit their teaching styles as well as the learning styles of their students.

Basically, what teachers are trying to do when they adapt the textbook is what Madsen and Bowen (1978) call "achieving congruence" by adjusting the fit among a wide variety of factors: students, materials, methods, objectives/curriculum, target language, cultural context, teacher's personality, and teaching style. Savova (2009) includes useful discussions of adapting and supplementing textbooks in EFL settings. In general, adaptations may include:

- sequencing (doing the chapters in a different order or doing the subsets of materials in a chapter in a different order)
- being selective (using some chapters and activities and not others)
- changing the instructions (making them clearer or a better fit with the teacher's approach to the classroom or a better fit with the students' language skills or learning preferences)
- changing groupings (doing work individually, in pairs, or in small groups in ways not suggested in the original textbook instructions or the instructor's manual)

When supplementing a textbook, teachers bring in materials that are not provided by the textbook, including:

- different content (information required by the curriculum or needed by students that is not provided in the textbook)
- local examples (examples that better fit the lives of the students and the local setting)
- new activities that fit the content already found in the textbook or that support new content added to the textbook
- expansion exercises or tasks that fit students' needs and interests or that fit the teacher's philosophy of teaching and learning

To illustrate, if a grammar exercise asks students to change statements into *yes-no* questions, this could be expanded on with a game of Twenty

Questions where the students have to guess what object a teacher has secretly removed from a bag or box (a pencil, a pen, an eraser, a bookmark, etc.) by asking *yes-no* questions. Such supplements and adaptations enliven classes and make learning meaningful, fun, tactile, visual, and more long-lasting.

Effectively adapting and supplementing materials depends on prior planning. Making changes from the textbook on the fly can get teachers into trouble when they encounter difficulties with language, background knowledge, and cultural understanding that keep students from being able to do an activity successfully.

The rules of thumb for adapting and supplementing textbooks in Figure 1 grew out of discussions with experienced classroom teachers.

Checklist and guidelines for selecting and implementing ESL/EFL textbooks

Well before a teacher enters the classroom, decisions have to be made about what will happen when the teacher actually meets with the students. For many, a textbook-evaluation checklist can be a helpful tool in assessing the strengths and weaknesses of course texts and making textbook-adoption decisions. Once a text has been selected, a form that helps guide teachers in how to use the text can facilitate the effective use of the book.

The checklist for ESL/EFL textbook selection (Figure 2) and the guidelines for ESL/EFL textbook implementation (Figure 3) can be downloaded or printed without charge from Google Docs Template Gallery: Forms.[2] Working with electronic forms offers teachers the advantage of being able to compare responses from multiple reviewers of the same or different textbooks in a format that easily converts to a spreadsheet tally of the data. Having the findings managed this way also maintains a history. We hope these forms can be used both by individual teachers and by groups of teachers working together.

FUTURE TRENDS

What will a textbook be like in the future world of electronic books and online publications? The answer to this question is easier to imagine when the focus is on materials generally rather than

1. **Know yourself.** To use the activities in ways that fit your teaching style, you need to bring some of your preferences to a conscious level beyond "like" or "do not like" to "I believe in and am comfortable with XYZ."
2. **Know your students.** Analyze the students in your classes to understand how language skill, personality, and background knowledge influence the ways they learn in class.
3. **Know how the class fits into the larger curriculum.** No matter how clever an activity or how interesting and important some content, you should not use it unless you can clearly state how it fits the larger goals of the course and its place in the curriculum.
4. **Go slow.** Be careful about picking something that seems appealing but that has language that is too difficult or cultural knowledge that is not accessible to the students. Give yourself time to think through how the materials will fit with your students.
5. **Do not duplicate activities or content already in the textbook.** Be sure to know what is already in the textbook before you put the time and energy into creating materials.
6. **Be sure you can do a new activity yourself.** Try it out yourself before taking a new activity to class.
7. **Keep clear records.** Keep records about what worked and did not work in class and about your understanding of what changes might be needed in future classes.
8. **Find a like-minded colleague.** Share ideas and successes with colleagues; ask them to help analyze problems.
9. **Consider using additional or alternative media to complement a printed textbook.** For example, you might use music, film, computer software, Internet sites, field trips, or other nonprint materials that support learning of the linguistic or topic content of a textbook section.

Figure 1. Rules of thumb for adapting and supplementing a textbook for a particular class.

on the concept of a textbook as a unified whole that provides information for students and teachers along with activities to support and guide learning in classroom settings. Already we can see teachers reaching out to make use of diverse online resources.[3] Furthermore, many teachers are now enjoying the online "publication" of materials they have created for their own students and hope will be useful for others who find them on the Internet. Searches for almost any aspect of a language lesson can result in numerous hits, especially for topics on English.

Reviewer Name:

Course Name:

Text Name:

Author(s):

Publisher/Year of Publication:

Level and Skills Focus:

Note: For survey ranking of textbook fit, consider "0" poor fit/mismatch, "1" minimal fit, "2" average/potential fit, "3" good fit, and "4" superior fit.	0	1	2	3	4
Textbook Fitness Categories					
a) **CURRICULUM**: The textbook content is appropriate with respect to . . .					
1. overall program curriculum/goals	❑	❑	❑	❑	❑
2. language learning material for level/course	❑	❑	❑	❑	❑
3. thematic/topical content & course objectives	❑	❑	❑	❑	❑
4. pedagogical/SLA philosophy	❑	❑	❑	❑	❑
5. length & unit size versus program time frame	❑	❑	❑	❑	❑
CURRICULUM TOTAL _____ /5 items: _____					
b) **STUDENTS**: The textbook is appropriate and will foster student learning at this level with respect to . . .					
1. logically sequenced unit-by-unit presentation	❑	❑	❑	❑	❑
2. design & visual elements	❑	❑	❑	❑	❑
3. cultural & age-group sensitivities	❑	❑	❑	❑	❑
4. explanations & instructions	❑	❑	❑	❑	❑
5. activities/exercises/tasks for in-class and homework (varied and copious)	❑	❑	❑	❑	❑
6. examples in explanations & sample items in exercises	❑	❑	❑	❑	❑
7. periodic tests/learning checks	❑	❑	❑	❑	❑
8. multi-media support	❑	❑	❑	❑	❑
9. thematic/topical content & student interests	❑	❑	❑	❑	❑
10. cost	❑	❑	❑	❑	❑
STUDENTS TOTAL _____ /10 items: _____					
c) **TEACHERS**: The textbook is appropriate for the teachers of this program with respect to . . .					
1. teaching styles and preferences	❑	❑	❑	❑	❑
2. teaching experience levels	❑	❑	❑	❑	❑
3. level of English (for NNS teachers)	❑	❑	❑	❑	❑
4. designing a syllabus	❑	❑	❑	❑	❑
5. teaching from provided explanations	❑	❑	❑	❑	❑
6. ease of using & expanding examples & activities	❑	❑	❑	❑	❑
7. accessing & using ancillaries including guides with advice, tests, and answer keys, and/or multi-media supplements	❑	❑	❑	❑	❑
TEACHERS TOTAL _____ /7 items: _____					
TOTAL FOR ALL THREE CATEGORIES _____ /22 items: _____					
NOTES FOR FINAL SUMMARY/DECISION:					

Figure 2. Checklist for ESL/EFL textbook selection.

Reviewer Name:

Course Name:

Text Name:

Author(s):

Publisher/Year of Publication:

Level and Skills Focus:

1. **Analysis of Linguistic Content**	What language areas are being taught? In which chunks and what sequences? What adjustments must be made to fit the program's curriculum? Are there any adjustments that I would like to make in content and sequencing to better fit my course and my students?
	Comments:
2. **Analysis of Thematic Content**	What topics are used in each unit? What topics recur throughout the whole book? What connections can I make between these topics and the backgrounds/interests of my students? How can I enrich the use of these themes?
	Comments:
3. **Analysis of Activities for In-Class Use**	Which of the activities provided in the textbook will I do in class? I am looking for a variety of activities that can be used to meet the needs of different learners and to achieve the pedagogical goals of the course. Initial decisions can be made about using individual, pair, or small-group configurations for the activities. (Experienced teachers also look for change-of-pace activities—a high-energy task requiring a lot of moving around, balanced by something more contemplative.)
	Comments:
4. **Analysis of Activities for Homework**	Which of the activities provided in the textbook could be assigned as homework? This decision needs to be made on the basis of the purpose that homework has in this particular class. Generally, teachers use homework for follow-up practice and for activities that may have students engaging in "outside of class" use of English. Some teachers use homework to prepare students for new work, not just to review and practice things already presented.
	Comments:
5. **Analysis of Activities for Testing Purposes**	Which of the activities provided in the textbook could be held back to use for testing? If no tests are provided by the text or the publisher, some activities might be reserved to use for assessment.
	Comments:
6. **Analysis of Activities for Review Purposes**	Which of the activities provided in the textbook can be used for review later in the term? Some activities might be reserved for review, or a variation on an activity might be used for review later in the term.
	Comments:
7. **Analysis of Activities**	Which of the activities provided in the textbook require special equipment that has to be ordered ahead of time? In most settings specific equipment requires extra effort and planning time.
	Comments:

(continued)

Figure 3. Guidelines for ESL/EFL textbook implementation.

8. Analysis of Unit Connections & Review Points	Where are connections being made between various units of the book, connections that might require review? By reading the whole book prior to the beginning of the term, a teacher can become aware of topics and themes that recur in the book. Connections can be made that give more coherence and that deepen student knowledge of important topics
	Comments:
9. Analysis of What to Skip	Which activities in the textbook do I not want to use? Because the fit between any textbook and the curriculum of a program will seldom be perfect, some parts of the text might not be appropriate for a particular course. Additionally, some content and activities might not fit a particular group of students. Equally important, there are things that may not fit our personalities as teachers and that we may not be comfortable doing. (For example, some teachers make wonderful use of music and singing in their classes while others cannot sing well and would never try this in class.)
	Comments:
NOTES FOR FINAL SUMMARY/DECISION:	

Figure 3. Guidelines for ESL/EFL textbook implementation. *(Continued)*

In other academic areas, textbooks are being issued in electronic (ebook) formats by traditional publishers.[4] This trend will surely eventually influence the publication of classroom textbooks in ESL/EFL. Because of the worldwide nature of English teaching, there are reasonable concerns about access to such materials; these remain unresolved. In addition, textbook publishers do not yet seem to have settled on a uniform approach to ebook publication. Sometimes ESL/EFL textbooks have online or computer-based supplements that are open to the public, but more often access is under password control. The quality of these supplements varies, with some taking better advantage of the multimedia environment of the Internet than others. However, we have only to think back a few years to recognize that the concept of book is changing rapidly, and sooner rather than later these changes will influence the content as well as the purchasing of textbook materials.

CONCLUSION

In sum, the following fundamental questions should be asked by teachers as they choose and use textbooks: What can be done in class to achieve the goals of the program and of the students? What are the students going to do in class to achieve the goals of the program as well as their personal goals? What are students going to do for homework, and how does that connect to what they do in class?

In the evaluation-for-selection process, those with the responsibility for choosing textbooks need to consider not just the fit between the curriculum and the textbook but also the practical issues of usability by teachers and students. Once a textbook has been selected, teachers need to analyze the resources in the textbook to create a plan for daily lessons and for the whole course that will help them both adapt and supplement what is already in the textbook in the most efficient and effective way. (See Purgason, this volume, for a thorough treatment of lesson planning.)

On a final note, textbooks sometimes bring out two extremes of thought and emotion: (1) textbooks are always bad because they limit a teacher's creativity and freedom; versus (2) textbooks provide the school with a teacher-proof way to ensure that all students have exactly the same content and learning experiences. Of course, the reality for most teachers lies somewhere between these two extremes. Teachers are generally part of a larger system that does have legitimate concerns about students' receiving instruction that leads to a more or less uniform result. At the same time, each of us is different in our background knowledge and personalities, as are our students. Having a textbook with appropriate content and a variety of possible teaching activities can serve both needs, giving some uniformity to the information and activities in all classes while expecting that individual teachers will adapt, implement, and supplement the materials based on the needs of a particular class in a particular setting. When efforts are made to choose and use textbooks that truly form the right fit with a program's curricula, teachers, and groups of students, the best teaching and learning experiences result.

SUMMARY

➤ Textbooks should be selected through a process of systematic analysis.

➤ Textbook selection needs to focus on the essential features of a particular course. For instance, a composition book needs to have very different features from an oral communication textbook.

➤ Effective use of a textbook depends on a teacher's taking the time for a thoughtful analysis of the entire book as part of the planning process before a class begins.

➤ Adapting the materials in a textbook to fit a particular class of students (and a particular teacher) needs to be carried out in a principled way to ensure a good fit; the textbook needs to be adapted to the students, the teacher, and the curriculum.

➤ The choice of supplementary materials should be based on a thorough analysis of the materials already provided in a textbook. Supplements should cover missing content that is required by the course curriculum or should address the needs of a particular group of students.

DISCUSSION QUESTIONS

1. How are textbooks selected in the setting in which you teach or in the area where you live?

What involvement do classroom teachers have in that process?

2. If you are currently teaching an ESL/EFL class, explain how the textbook you are using was selected. If you are not sure, interview other teachers and the program administrator to find out about the process for textbook selection.

3. Compare the processes in Question 1 to those in Question 2. What features of the educational systems or programs lead to any similarities or differences between the processes?

4. This chapter presents differences between textbook selection and textbook use. What has your experience been with these two processes? How have they differed in your work with textbooks?

5. In the rules of thumb for adapting and supplementing a textbook (Figure 1), the first rule is "Know Yourself." Why do you think that is the first rule? Do you agree that it is the most important of the rules, or does another rule seem more important to you?

SUGGESTED ACTIVITIES

1. Work with a colleague or two to evaluate a textbook that is on the market for use in a specific potential class.
   a. Use the checklist provided in Figure 2. Compare and discuss your scores in each category.
   b. Evaluate the items on the checklist for ESL/EFL textbook selection (Figure 2). Which ones were most helpful in your decision-making process? If you were to evaluate another book at this time, how would you modify the checklist for your own purposes?

2. Create a checklist for an ESL/EFL textbook for a specific skill area such as reading, writing, oral communication, or grammar. What items on the checklist were added or revised depending on the focused skill? For example, for a reading textbook, it is especially important to add items that evaluate the vocabulary level and readability of passage selections.

3. Select a chapter or unit from a textbook, and analyze its features using Figure 3, guidelines for ESL/EFL textbook implementation. How can conducting a strategic reconnaissance of your textbook before you teach with it be

beneficial? What was the most surprising or important thing you learned from your textbook analysis?

4. Many teaching English to speakers of other languages (TESOL) and teaching English as a foreign language (TEFL) organizations publish newsletters that include book-review columns. Consider some examples from your region, and then contact the newsletter editor to offer your services as a book-review writer. You could ask the editor to provide either textbook suggestions or an examination copy for your review article, or you could submit a review of a recent textbook you are already familiar with.

FURTHER READING

Garinger, D. (2002). *Textbook selection for the ESL classroom.* Washington, DC: Center for Applied Linguistics.

Along with this useful discussion of textbook use and textbook selection, the Center for Applied Linguistics provides a selection of print publications and online downloadable teacher resources on a wide variety of issues of interest to classroom teachers. A digest of Garinger (2002) is available at http://www.cal.org/resources/digest/0210garinger.html

Harwood, N. (Ed.). (2010). *English language teaching materials: Theory and practice.* Cambridge, UK: Cambridge University Press.

The authors explore how today's materials do and do not apply theory to pedagogy, and they provide many sample illustrations of exercises, activities, and resources that can support teachers and textbook authors in developing effective materials.

Mishan, F., & Chambers, A. (Eds.). (2010). *Perspectives on language learning materials development: Intercultural studies and foreign language learning* (Vol. 1). Bern, Switzerland: Peter Lang.

This volume considers the use of real language and corpus-based materials with a focus on spoken rather than written applications. The book includes practical advice for teachers and materials writers, including guides and resources for creating and evaluating corpus-based lessons, and caveats for taking advantage of electronic media sources.

Richard-Amato, P. A. (2010). *Making it happen: From interactive to participatory language teaching—Evolving theory and practice* (4th ed.). White Plains, NY: Pearson Education.

This book includes a helpful chapter with selection guidelines for teachers who are evaluating materials, and it has an especially interesting consideration of nontext materials: computer programs, Internet sites, and videos/films.

ENDNOTES

[1] Bloom's (1956) work classifies educational objectives and activities into taxonomies associated with three domains: cognitive, affective, and psychomotor. With respect to language learning, the cognitive load difficulty should be paced in materials. Bloom's original taxonomy in the cognitive domain sequenced categories as knowledge, comprehension, application, analysis, synthesis, and evaluation.

[2] The following URLs lead to the forms in template format so that teachers can save the forms to use as they are or modify them to match their own purposes. Additional instructions are given with each form: checklist for ESL/EFL textbook selection (http://tinyurl.com/ESL-EFL-text-checklist); guidelines for ESL/EFL textbook implementation (http://tinyurl.com/ESL-EFL-text-use-guide).

[3] See, for example, Purdue University's Owl (http://owl.english.purdue.edu/), a well-known writing support site, or the University of North Carolina, Chapel Hill's website, (http://www.unc.edu/depts/wcweb/), a site with wonderfully organized sets of materials, including instructional videos.

[4] See, for example, the University of Michigan Press's list of ebooks at http://press.umich.edu/ebooks/

25 | Culture and Pragmatics in Language Teaching and Learning

ELI HINKEL

KEY QUESTIONS

➤ What is the role of culture in language teaching and learning?
➤ What is sociocultural competence?
➤ What are pragmatic norms of interaction?

EXPERIENCE

An international student who majors in engineering drops by the engineering department office and asks the secretary, "Can you tell me where the English department is?" The secretary smiles and responds, "I don't know, actually. It's probably somewhere in the Humanities Building. Do you have a campus map?" The student turns around and leaves. The secretary is taken aback and feels slightly uncomfortable. She wonders why the student left so abruptly.

WHAT IS CULTURE AND WHAT IS ITS ROLE IN LANGUAGE TEACHING AND LEARNING?

Two parallel types of research have been carried out to identify the role of culture in society and its influence on human behavior. The research on culture as it applies to social norms, beliefs, assumptions, and value systems that affect many (if not most) human activities is carried out in the domains of ethnography, anthropology, sociology, and intercultural communication. In these disciplines, culture is examined in terms that apply to most human societies and organizations, and research on culture seeks to determine the similarities and differences that exist in human constructions of reality. Applied linguistics (and specifically sociolinguistics and pragmatics) is concerned with the inextricable connection between

language and sociocultural norms and frameworks and also seeks to identify patterns that can lead to an understanding of how members of particular cultures use language to refer to, describe, or function within social organizations. For example, politeness is considered to be a universal feature of language use in social organizations, but its pragmatic, linguistic, social, intentional, and conceptual realizations vary substantially across different languages and cultures. Even speakers of the same language or speakers of different dialects may belong to different subcultures and thus have different concepts of what it means to be polite and how politeness should be realized in speech and behavior.

In addition, research in ethnography, anthropology, and applied linguistics also includes studies of specific cultures, such as American, Chinese, Japanese, and Mexican (e.g., Saville-Troike, 2003; Scollon & Scollon, 2001; Stewart & Bennett, 1991). These studies identify and describe ways of doing, speaking, and behaving in specific cultural communities without necessarily attempting to determine commonalities and differences among various cultures. Both research on culture in general and on specific cultures can be useful for teachers of second language (L2) students who wish to allow learners to become more aware of the connection between the culture of the community and the language of its speakers. In language teaching and research on language, the term *culture* includes many different definitions and considerations that deal with forms of speech acts, sociocultural behaviors, the rhetorical structure of text, and the ways in which knowledge is transmitted and obtained. Culture may find its manifestations in body language, gestures, concepts of time, hospitality customs, and even expressions of friendliness. While all these certainly reflect the cultural norms accepted in a particular society, the influence of culture on language use and on concepts of how language can be taught and learned is both broader and deeper. To a great extent, the culture into which an individual is socialized defines how that individual sees his or her place in society.

Although it is essential for learners to attain language proficiency to be linguistically competent, particularly in English as a second language (ESL) settings, language proficiency alone is not sufficient. On the whole, to become proficient and effective communicators, learners need to attain L2 sociocultural competence. Knowing how to say *thank you*, for example, does not automatically confer the knowledge of when to say *thank you*, how often to say *thank you*, and whether any additional action is called for. Quite reasonably, learners first tend to apply the standards that exist in the first or native language (L1) communities where they were socialized.

People who interact with ESL students have commented that some seem to express gratitude excessively for small considerations, even to the point of embarrassing the person they are speaking to. Others, like the student in the initial example, seem downright rude because they do not say *thank you* when they are expected to. If the receptionist in an office spends time and effort trying to help someone but fails to provide concrete help, it is not obvious to the student that a *thank you* is warranted. After all, she did not provide any real assistance, and it is her job to try to help. However, if no thanks is given, the receptionist may not be very likely to even attempt to help this student in the future. Not understanding the sociocultural expectations of the culture can negatively impact learners' ability to function in an L2 community.

In language teaching, focusing on the inextricable connections between a culture and its language uses should be a key characteristic of effective instruction in all language skills. At the present time, the ultimate goal of all cultural and cross-cultural education is to enable learners to become successful in an international community, in the global economy, and across national boundaries. Without instruction in and an understanding of L2 cultural and sociopragmatic norms, learners do not have and cannot make the essential choices needed to optimize their communicative competence.

CONCEPTUAL UNDERPINNINGS OF LANGUAGE LEARNING AND CULTURE LEARNING

Among many other researchers, Hymes (1996) emphasized that the learning of culture is an integral part of language learning and education because culture crucially influences the values of the community, everyday interaction, the norms of speaking and behaving, and the sociocultural expectations of an individual's roles. He further noted that those who do not follow the norms of appropriateness that are accepted in a community are often placed in a position that exacerbates social disparities and inequality.

Today, when the numbers of ESL and English as a foreign language (EFL) students have grown dramatically worldwide, it is becoming increasingly clear that the learning of a second culture does not take care of itself. Thus, L2 learners cannot always make the best of their educational, professional, and vocational opportunities unless they become familiar with fundamental L2 cultural concepts and constructs. Most important, an ability to recognize and employ culturally appropriate ways of communicating in speech or writing allows learners to make choices with regard to their linguistic, pragmatic, and other behaviors (Byram & Morgan, 1994; Hinkel, 1999).

Although traditionally courses and texts for language teachers have concentrated on teaching L2 language skills, it may be difficult to separate the teaching and learning of English from the culture of its speakers. For example, what represents polite ways of speaking and the appropriate ways of writing an essay depend on culturally dependent concepts that are closely bound up with the language skills needed to speak or write well in the L2.

The visible and the invisible culture

In L2 teaching, the term *culture* can and has been employed to refer to distinctly different domains of people's lives. It can be used to refer to the literature, the arts, the architecture, and the history of a particular people. When asked about their native culture, many L2 learners and ESL/EFL teachers alike describe the history or the geography of their country because these represent a popular understanding of the term *culture*. In addition, some definitions of *culture* can include the styles of dress, cuisine, customs, festivals, and other traditions. These aspects can be considered the *visible culture* in that they are readily apparent to anyone and can be discussed and explained relatively easily.

Yet another far more complex meaning of *culture* refers to sociocultural norms, worldviews, beliefs, assumptions, and value systems that find their way into practically all facets of language use, including the classroom. The term *invisible culture* applies to sociocultural beliefs and assumptions that most people are not even aware of and thus cannot examine intellectually. Scollon and Scollon (2001) state that the culturally determined concepts of what is acceptable, appropriate, and expected behavior are acquired in the process of socialization and, hence, become inseparable from an individual's identity. For example, in the classroom, the roles of the student and the teacher are defined by the sociocultural values of the larger community and the society. If students believe that the teacher is responsible for explaining the material and that speaking up in class is considered rude, presumptuous, and selfish, the teacher's simply instructing students to participate in discussions may do little to change learners' notions of what is appropriate and how they will be seen by others if they actually speak up in class. Most teachers, even those with minimal classroom experience or exposure, know how difficult it can be to convince some students to speak in front of their classmates, whereas other students may find it difficult to allow their classmates an opportunity to have their turn.

Why second culture learning is complex

The complexity of teaching culture lies in the fact that most people who engage in cross-cultural interactions are not aware of the indelible impact of the invisible culture—their own and that of other participants—on practically all social uses of language. In language learning, culture does not represent a separate domain of L2 skills, such as speaking or writing; instead, the learning of the L2 culture and its many manifestations in, for example, speech and writing makes learners better communicators. In language teaching and learning, crucial sociocultural principles determine the norms of appropriate language use and behavior within the frameworks of the society (Hall, 2012). These are likely to remain invisible unless they are taught and learned in conjunction with other language skills. As E. Stewart (1972) commented:

> [t]he typical person has a strong sense of what the world is really like, so that it is with surprise that he discovers that "reality" is built up out of certain assumptions commonly shared among members of the same culture. Cultural assumptions may be defined as abstract, organized, and general concepts which pervade a person's outlook and behavior. (p. 16)

To members of a particular community and culture, these assumptions appear to be self-evident and axiomatic. On the other hand, they are not always shared by members of other cultures whose values are similarly based on unquestioned and unquestionable fundamental assumptions and concepts. It is also important to note that ways of using language (e.g., speaking, listening, reading, and writing) and sociocultural frameworks in different communities may conflict to varying degrees (Hinkel, 1999).

Learners' awareness of sociocultural frameworks and the concepts they acquire as a part of their socialization into beliefs, assumptions, and behaviors remains predominantly first-culture-bound even for advanced and proficient L2 learners (Hinkel, 1999). Byram and Morgan (1994) pointed out that "[l]earners cannot simply shake off their own culture and step into another. . . . [T]heir culture is a part of themselves and created them as social beings . . ." (p. 43).

Identifying learners' needs and goals

There is little doubt that learners who live and/or study in English-speaking communities have a much greater need for developing their cultural competencies than those who study EFL as a part of their foreign language requirements. The learners' actual goals in attaining English proficiency may serve as guidelines for determining their needs in learning culture. In many settings, however, instruction highlighting the influence of culture on L2 use can be made effective and productive when working on particular L2 tasks or activities.

Learners who live, study, or work in English-speaking communities have a particularly acute need to be aware of how the use of English they are exposed to reflects the sociocultural norms of the L2 community. For these individuals, a lack of language skill that prevents them from speaking, listening, reading, and writing according to the norms accepted in the community can be particularly costly and even damaging in terms of lost opportunities for better grades, jobs, professional and economic advancement, or even social relationships. In general terms, the purpose of teaching culture together with other language skills is to increase learners' interactional as well as linguistic competence.

Teaching cross-cultural awareness in the language classroom

Because the culture of any community has many facets and manifestations, it would be practically impossible to deal with all of them in the classroom and prepare students for the many situations that they may encounter in the course of their functioning in ESL/EFL environments. However, many important aspects of teaching the second culture can be brought forth and addressed via classroom instruction, and some of these are exemplified next. The most important long-term benefits of culture teaching may be to provide learners with the awareness and the tools that will allow them to achieve their academic, professional, social, and personal goals and become successful in their daily functioning in L2 environments.

Recent studies, as well as the experiences of teachers, have shown that L2 students in colleges and universities in the United States, Canada, and other English-speaking countries do not always follow the norms of politeness and appropriateness commonly accepted in their L2 communities, despite having lived in their L2 environments for several years (Hinkel, 1996; Hymes, 1996).

Similarly, in their academic studies, L2 learners often experience difficulties because they do not always understand what is expected of them and do not have access to the necessary sociocultural concepts that are ubiquitously manifested in the academy (Schleppegrell, 2004). For example, when university students are assigned to read material at home, many professors expect that the students will actually "master" the content and come to class prepared to discuss and apply it. L2 students are often seen as coming to class unprepared because they may not always understand that achieving a relatively high degree of familiarity with the material is implicit when academic readings are assigned. To compound the problem, the learners may have difficulty understanding the text, or they may be unwilling to participate in class discussions. In any of these situations, the instructor (and even classmates) may form somewhat negative impressions of the non-native speakers' academic skills and preparation.

Causes and outcomes of sociocultural values

Because the sociocultural norms of politeness, appropriateness, and propriety are acquired during socialization, in their daily L2 interactions learners are exposed only to the outcomes of linguistic and other types of behaviors and not their causes. For example, when their classmates are reluctant to share lecture or textbook notes, many learners simply conclude that their classmates may not like them and are unwilling to help them. However, the reluctance to share notes may stem from several sociocultural constructs that are fundamental in many English-speaking communities: the value of intellectual property, self-reliance, and the right of an individual to refuse a request with which he or she is not comfortable. In addition, in many U.S. colleges and universities, students believe that they are expected to do their own work and are given credit based on their individual effort and achievement. However, in the situation where the learner wants to borrow class notes, neither the ESL learner nor the classmate who has the notes may even question the reasons why the request was made and refused. In general terms, the "behavioral prescriptions," a term coined by E. Stewart (1972), are assumed to be known to most (if not all) socially competent adults and, hence, are rarely overtly discussed; a need for such a discussion would imply a lack of basic and essential social competence.

The importance of noticing

In learning about the impact of sociocultural norms on language use, the first step is to understand that they exist in all languages, including learners' L1s. To become prepared for a practically infinite number of L2 interactions, learners need to become astute and consistent people watchers. Building on observations of their L1 sociocultural norms and behaviors, the next task in culture learning is to separate individual behaviors from those that are culturally determined. For example, repeated politeness routines, behaviors, and body language (e.g., eye contact) probably signal that these speech acts and behaviors are socioculturally acceptable (and/or expected) in a particular community. Once learners notice a particular routine or behavior on several occasions from several different individuals, they can be asked to investigate its sociocultural purposes and causes. An ability to identify the sociocultural purposes of L2 communicative behaviors in a community allows learners to identify cultural patterns in situations, to understand how they are realized in other situations, and to anticipate their manifestations in the future.

The fundamental factors to consider in all interactions include the genders of the speaker or the hearer, their respective ages, similarities or disparities in their social statuses (e.g., even if a professor wears blue jeans to class, it is not a good idea to pat him or her on the shoulder), the social distance between the speaker and the hearer (e.g., class friends, acquaintances, or strangers), the purposes of the speech events, the time available for the interaction, and its physical setting/location. In their investigations, learners should pay careful attention to politeness routines, expressions, and phrases that are employed by speakers or hearers and then should identify the reasons for the use of these language devices. For example, they could observe how a student asks the teacher to take a look at her paper (*Could you look at my paper and see if I am on the right track?*). Were the participants in the interaction of the same age, gender, and social status? What polite-ness expressions did the speaker use? How did the hearer respond? Why did the hearer give this particular response? What politeness devices were used in the response and why?

Practice, practice, practice

The tasks associated with training learners to be careful and sharp people watchers and observers of culturally appropriate and common interactional routines and expressions can serve as a basis for very productive and effective activities that are interesting and enjoyable for learners. For intermediate ESL learners, a teacher may choose to make a basic checklist of the linguistic and social features of speech events and interactions to encourage students to carry out their field research in cafeterias, restaurants, stores, and libraries. In EFL settings, a similar field study can take place in the students' L1 because the primary goal of this activity and of people watching is to make learners aware of the linguistic and social factors that play a crucial role in interactions in any language or culture. In teaching EFL, the next step is to compare the politeness and conversational routines in the learners' L1 to those found in English language materials (e.g., movie clips, recorded audio and video interviews, taped dialogues that accompany many student texts, or perhaps even materials for standardized test preparation).

When working with high-intermediate or advanced ESL learners, teachers can make similar checklists for expanded and more sophisticated linguistic, social, and behavioral features of interactions, such as the location where the interaction takes place (e.g., an office, a hallway, or a street), the availability of time (a scheduled appointment, a lunch hour, or a break between classes), and/or the complexity of the task entailed in the speech act. In addition, students can be assigned to investigate various types of speech acts, such as making appointments, seeking clarifications, or responding to requests, and even longer conversational exchanges, such as making small talk or negotiating the time and the place of meetings. High-intermediate and advanced EFL students can also participate in role plays, short skits, or mini-plays for which they write scripts centering on the linguistic features of particular speech acts or types of conversational exchanges in their L2.

In addition to learning to note the linguistic and situational variables in interactions, it is important that learners focus on the sociocultural features of speaking and behaving. In general, however, it would not be very comfortable or appropriate for the people interacting to become involved in discussing the reasons why a particular linguistic structure is used or a specific interactional behavior is displayed. To return to an earlier example, if the request to borrow someone's notes is refused, this may not be a good opportunity to ask why; however, it may be better, at a later time, to ask another individual, such as a different classmate, a roommate, or better yet, a teacher to explain the sociocultural causes for a particular behavior. Although many native speakers of English may not be aware of reasons for their own behaviors, they are usually aware of behavioral prescriptions in abstract terms. That is, most native speakers will be able to tell the difference between what is considered polite or even acceptable in a particular situation and, if asked, some may even be able say why some expression, phrase, or behavior will be perceived as more polite than another.

Teaching culture as pragmatics of interaction

According to Celce-Murcia and Olshtain (2000), "pragmatics deals very explicitly with the study of relationships holding between linguistic forms and the human beings who use these forms" (p. 19). The authors go on to say that "As such, pragmatics is concerned with people's intentions, assumptions, beliefs, goals, and the kind of actions they perform while using language. Pragmatics is also concerned with contexts, situations, and settings within which such language uses occur" (p. 19). In language learning and usage, pragmatic and cultural competence are closely related, and both require learners to "use language in socioculturally appropriate ways" (p. 20). One of the most challenging considerations in teaching L2 pragmatics is that socioculturally and contextually appropriate (or inappropriate) communication can take a number of forms; that is, there can be many pragmatically appropriate ways to ask for information or schedule an appointment.

In pragmatics, various sets of conventionalized, frequently repeated, and routinized expressions are called *speech acts*. These are typically classified by their pragmatic and communicative functions, such as requests, apologies, compliments, or complaints. Speech acts can be direct or indirect, and thus they vary in their degree of politeness or even comprehensibility. For example, on hearing, "Can you help me with this problem?" an interlocutor might respond, "I'm a little busy right now." This response is an indirect speech act, and it can mean, for example, that the speaker is in a hurry and does not have much time available. However, if the hearer does not fully grasp the pragmatic function of this speech act as a refusal, then the speaker's communicative goal may not be achieved. As Celce-Murcia and Olshtain (2000) noted the pragmatic context is crucial for the speaker's meaning to be understood.

Much research carried out in pragmatics and sociolinguistics over the past several decades has focused on the sociocultural norms of politeness and appropriateness in performing various types of speech acts. The linguistic and sociopragmatic forms of specific speech acts can be taught in the classroom, focusing on routine and conventionalized uses of language in context. The contextual factors that invariably affect speech act realization and interpretation include, as mentioned, the social status of the speaker and the hearer, social distance between them, their ages, their genders, and the situation where the interaction takes place (Celce-Murcia & Olshtain, 2000).

Most important, the key to productive teaching of culture and pragmatics is to provide learners with the tools that enable them to become aware of the sociolinguistic norms reflected in the ways of speaking in the target community. Thomas (1983) pointed out that violations of pragmatic and cultural norms of appropriateness in interactions often lead to sociopragmatic failure, uncomfortable breakdowns in communication, and the stereotyping of non-native speakers. She noted that, when many L2 learners display inappropriate language behaviors, they are often not even aware that they have done so. The teaching of interactional pragmatics in the L2 has to include developing learners' heightened awareness of the sociopragmatic features of interaction so as to provide them with appropriate choices.

Sociocultural variables in interaction

In the teaching of L2 speaking and pragmatics, two overarching goals lie at the core of instruction.

The *pragmatic function* (i.e., the sociocultural purpose/goal) of speech acts, such as requests, apologies, compliments, and complaints, can be found in practically every curriculum for teaching speaking skills. The linguistic form of speech acts and conversational routines is one of the most easily accessible and ubiquitous areas of teaching L2 speaking, for example, *Give me a penny* versus *Could you/would you give me a penny?* or *Do you have a penny?* The pragmatic function of these expressions is the same (i.e., request), but the speaker's choice of form may elicit different responses from the hearer. For example, to increase learners' linguistic repertoire, the majority of ESL/EFL textbooks for teaching speaking devote a great deal of attention to the forms of polite and casual expressions, idioms, short dialogues, and even their appropriate pronunciation and intonation because, for instance, the transfer of intonation from L1 to L2 can have very subtle negative consequences for interaction.

What makes a particular expression or speech act situationally appropriate is not so much the linguistic form or the range of the L2 speakers' linguistic repertoire but the sociocultural variables, which are rarely addressed in explicit instruction. Partly for this reason, it is not uncommon to hear learners say *How's it going, What's up,* or *Later* to peers, teachers and professors, and even principals and university deans. As Celce-Murcia and Olshtain (2000) pointed out, "pragmatics studies the context within which an interaction occurs as well as the intention of the language user. Who are the addressees, what is the relation between speakers/writers and hearers/readers, when and where does the speech even occur? . . ." (p. 20).

Socioculturally inappropriate greetings and conversational closures, as well as other speech acts mentioned in the earlier examples, are likely to raise an eyebrow or two, but as has been noted, their impropriety has little chance of being overtly discussed; thus, the learning value of the experience may be lost. The sociocultural variables and pragmatic forms that can make a perfectly acceptable expression unacceptable in different interactions or settings reflect the invisible aspects of L1 or L2 culture that do not easily lend themselves to textbook exercises or listings of expressions. Nonetheless, it is the sociocultural features, such as gender, age, and the social status of the

participants in the interaction, as well as the misuses of pragmatic functions and linguistic forms, that can lead to pragmatic failure (Thomas, 1983).

For example, a lesson on conversation openers is very common and can be found in many ESL/EFL textbooks. Usually, most lessons (or textbook chapters) start with a few models: *Good morning/afternoon. How are you (today/this evening)? How is it/everything going? What's up? How are you doing? How do you like this weather/Isn't this weather wonderful/terrible?* and *How do you like this city?* Few of these resources, however, distinguish between the pragmatic forms that are appropriate in peer-level interactions and those that should be used in conversational exchanges with hearers who have a different social status. Furthermore, in such examples, the contextual variables are rarely taken into account—while it is very appropriate to open a conversation with a brief mention of the weather with an acquaintance in the cafeteria, it may not be a good opener when asking a bank teller to cash a check or a bus driver for route details. Similarly, *What's up?* and *How's it going?* are used almost exclusively in short and casual encounters with friends, but they do not seem to be the best options when talking to a waiter, a store clerk, a receptionist in an office, or a doctor.

One activity for developing learners' awareness of the variability of politeness and appropriateness in interactions with different types of hearers and situations in which various conversational openers are used is to conduct field observations and experiments. In an experiment to determine the sociopragmatic and contextual appropriateness of a speech act, L2 learners can ask their native speaker friends or roommates to evaluate the degree of politeness entailed in each of the conversational openers and explain the factors that make one expression "softer" or more appropriate than another. For example, which expression seems more polite: *I want to make an appointment for 3 o'clock. I would like to make an appointment for 3 o'clock. May/Could I make an appointment for 3 o'clock?* or *Would it be okay for me to make an appointment for 3 o'clock?* What are the specific words and/or constructions that make one expression more polite than the other? Why is the question form used in two of these? Are there situations in which the least polite expression can be used? Who are the people (the speaker and the hearer) in these situations, and do they have equivalent social positions? The results of such experiments can be discussed in pairs or small groups so that, with the teacher's guidance, students learn to identify the linguistic, pragmatic, and situational features of language that come into play in conversational exchanges.

The pragmatic force and the linguistic form

Another important characteristic of real-life interactions is determining the *pragmatic force* (i.e., interactional/conversational purpose) of expressions used in daily interactions. For example, *How are you (today/this morning)?* and *How's it going?* are not intended to be real questions or conversation openers. Rather, their pragmatic force is to be a greeting to signal to hearers that they are recognized and acknowledged. As an outcome, these formulaic expressions do not require a response beyond the formulaic (*Fine, Great, Good, OK*). On the other hand, these expressions contrast with *How have you been?* or *How is everything/this term/your class going?* Because the linguistic form of formulaic expressions (e.g., *How are you?* vs. *How have you been [lately]?*) is similar, many learners interpret their pragmatic force to be equivalent as well. Setting up field research or experiments to be carried out by pairs or small groups of students to investigate the varying pragmatic force of such expressions can be very beneficial in making them aware of the divergences between the form and the conversational intent of pragmatic routines in English.

Other such investigations can include a great number of formulaic conversational expressions and exchanges in which the pragmatic force may be difficult for learners to determine and not always apparent from their linguistic form and content; examples are: *Call me some time* (no time specified) versus *Call me on Tuesday* (time specified); *Let's get together/have lunch sometime* (no time specified) versus *Let's get together/have lunch on Friday* (time specified); *Call me if you have any questions* (not mandatory to call; no time specified) versus *Call me any time; Do you have any questions?* (it is now time to ask questions, if you have them) versus *I'd be happy to answer your questions during office hours* (i.e., please do not ask me any questions now but come to my office at the designated time); *Your paper needs a little work* (this expression does not mean necessarily that the paper needs only a little bit of work to be improved) versus *Maybe you need to spend more time on your homework* (this does not mean that spending more time without greater effort will result in better grades).

Many conversational routines are closely tied to the pragmatic and sociocultural variables that affect the interactional effect of an expression or routine, and these can be taught to learners at practically all levels of proficiency, from beginning to highly advanced. For example, when and to whom to say *thank you* can be taught at the beginning level. In EFL settings, to raise learners' awareness of the important sociocultural dimensions of conversations, students can be asked to gather similar information in their native language. In pairs or small group discussions, learners can determine what characteristics of language (e.g., the pragmatic and linguistic form, stress, or tone) make one expression more polite than another. Then learners can be taught to identify parallel (but not necessarily similar) L2 features that can make a difference in the appropriateness of L2 conversational expressions and routines.

The sociocultural construction of writing and literacy

In English, what is appropriate and inappropriate in academic written discourse is highly conventionalized (Swales, 1990). In practically all ESL programs in colleges and universities in English-speaking countries, a great deal of attention, time, and resources are devoted to the teaching of academic writing. L2 writing instruction focuses on such fundamental features of written academic discourse as the organization (e.g., introduction, body, conclusion, and other discourse moves), the presence and the placement of the thesis statement, the structure of the paragraph (e.g., the topic sentence), the rhetorical support for the thesis included in every paragraph, and an avoidance of needless digressions, repetition, and redundancy, among many other factors. The reason that these features of academic writing need to be explicitly and persistently taught to ESL/EFL students is that they represent conventionalized (and prescribed) characteristics of the academic genre that are not necessarily found in written discourse in rhetorical traditions other than the Anglo-American one. For example, educated L2 learners who were socialized in other rhetorical traditions are rarely aware that a clear thesis statement should be placed close to the beginning of one's essay. Similarly, various sociocultural concepts and prescriptive behaviors play an important role in determining what can and cannot be included in academic discourse or even what can and cannot be discussed in an academic essay. For example, discussions of family disagreements, one's religious beliefs or political views, and ethnocentric attitudes are considered unacceptable in academic writing; on the other hand, descriptions of travels and vacations, celebrations of holidays and traditions, music, and literature are common and very appropriate in academic contexts.

In writing instruction, learners are typically presented with models and examples of paragraphs and essays to demonstrate the discourse paradigms commonly accepted in Anglo-American writing. However, as many teachers know from experience, learning to write in accordance with the rhetorical forms and norms expected in English academic discourse can be a difficult and tedious process. L1 socialization regarding written discourse paradigms usually has so much influence on learning to write in an L2 that often, even with explicit instruction, learners are not always able to recognize the rhetorical features of L2 discourse, much less produce them (Hinkel, 1994). In addition, as in most L2 interactions and communications, in the course of writing instruction, learners are faced with the outcomes and not the causes of the sociocultural norms and conventions prevalent in a second culture, which makes it harder for them to understand and apply what they are instructed to do. For example, students may wonder why the thesis statement should be placed at the beginning of an essay if they *know* that it should be in the conclusion or why the teacher says that this example is not clear when *to them* it is very clear. In many human societies, writing and literacy represent one of the most highly valued and prized domains of socialization and education. For this reason, many L2 learners may initially choose to adhere to the discourse frameworks they acquired in their L1 literacy socialization and the value associated with the appropriateness of writing in a particular way.

For example, in English, speakers are expected to present their points in a manner that is more direct than is common among speakers of many other languages (Scollon & Scollon, 2001). In particular, in many cultures, one is required to engage in social conversations to establish a relationship before making one's purpose known; the main point of the conversation comes closer to the end of discourse. Similarly, in some rhetorical traditions, the main point of the piece of writing usually does not come until the end because the writer needs to lead the reader gently to the conclusion, which is expected to be clear and obvious by the time it is stated at the end (or, sometimes, it is not even stated at all). If in speaking, vague and indirect hints are considered to be more socially acceptable, in writing, stating one's point directly and early may also be viewed as presumptuous and excessively forward. On the other hand, in the Anglo-American rhetorical tradition, it is important that the main idea or the purpose for writing is stated at the outset, and writers undertake to support their thesis with additional information, intended to validate their main points.

In the teaching of L2 writing, teachers may draw on many examples from speaking and establish parallels to help learners develop cultural awareness in language use. One of the typical problems in the teaching of writing in English is that learners often do not provide a sufficient amount of support and detail in their writing to make their points meaningful and convincing. In many cultures other than Anglo-American, the right to speak is considered to be the prerogative of those who have the authority to speak. Similarly, in writing, learners often believe that detailed support is excessive and unnecessary because readers are not really concerned with trivial descriptions. They may also think that they have little of value to say and that providing too much detail implies a lack of humility. To help learners take a different view of the necessary detailed support expected in L2 writing, teachers may need to provide explicit instruction about L2 reader expectations, the value of explicit explanations in the Anglo-American rhetorical tradition, and their uses in writing.

Cultural load in reading textbooks and authentic texts

In teaching reading, by and large, two main types of materials are employed: highly controlled and often simplified readings from textbooks, on the one hand, and authentic materials that vary in their level of difficulty, on the other. The materials from textbooks are most often used to develop learners' reading tactics and strategies and to improve their vocabulary base. In contrast, authentic texts can include a great variety of genres, such as introductory and advanced textbooks; scholarly articles; print media publications on hobbies, health, politics, and sports; how-to books; and literature for readers of all ages (see Celce-Murcia & Olshtain, 2005, for a thorough discussion). Because ESL/EFL textbooks present a limited and controlled range of ideas, vocabulary items, and culturally dependent concepts, they may not be the best means of explaining how the second culture affects language use. However, even within the limited thematic and lexical scope of textbook readings, learners may encounter comprehension difficulties that have to do with culture because cultural inferences often need to be made to understand text (and context).

Culture teaching in L2 reading goes far beyond instruction on vocabulary, idioms, and collocations, all of which are essential for understanding the meaning of the text. In addition, context- and culture-specific connotations and implications of word and phrase meanings also need to be addressed. More urgently, however, sociocultural meanings and values greatly affect the learners' ability to comprehend a text and the context in which it is employed. In the teaching of authentic texts, such as those excerpted from advanced print media (e.g., news magazines and literature), culture-specific references, allusions, metaphors, and symbolism play a prominent role. However, instructing learners to rely on their background knowledge and experience is not always productive or helpful.

In language teaching, it is relatively easy to obtain diverse reading materials and to gradually increase the degree of their cultural and linguistic complexity. Most important, however, the teaching of culture and its impact on text comprehension needs to be addressed at all levels of proficiency to build learners' awareness of cultural implications and references, without which few texts can be understood. For advanced learners, materials on popular hobbies, science, and even excerpts from introductory college textbooks can provide a relatively smooth transition to more complex readings such as authentic literature. For ESL/EFL purposes, literature should be chosen carefully to allow learners an opportunity to comprehend the text and enjoy it. However, the amount of work expended on pre-reading and preparing learners for reading literature must be sufficiently great for teachers to weigh its benefits relative to the cost (Birch, 2007). In EFL environments, in addition to textbooks, materials from many Internet sites, English-language newspapers, or free tourist and travel brochures can provide access to texts that contain fewer culture-bound and advanced metaphors and allusions because they are oriented to readers in various geographical locations and of varied language skills. Such materials allow the teacher to concentrate on culture-specific references and sociocultural values invariably present in most texts, but they may not become so numerous and complex that learners are unable to comprehend the reading material.

In general terms, readings selected for culture and L2 teaching combined can be effective in various ways and examined for discourse and text organization, cultural concepts, vocabulary, grammar, and the conventions of writing in English. The readings can be quite easily selected to be appropriate for various levels of reading proficiency and the range of attendant L2 skills. It is important, however, not to miss an opportunity to engage learners in a discussion of how culture impacts language use across skill levels.

CLASSROOM APPLICATIONS

Because manifestations of the influence of culture on language use are very common, activities and materials for teaching cultural concepts and implications are relatively easy to create. The following ideas for teaching L2 sociocultural and pragmatic concepts and their outcomes are just some suggestions. All these have been used for years with many different groups of learners in teaching ESL or EFL. Extensive culture-teaching projects and activities presented here may be adapted to a variety of contexts, and teachers can choose to use only portions of them.

ESL teaching

In teaching ESL, a highly effective activity that can be used for investigating L2 sociocultural norms and pragmatic linguistic forms is interviews of native speakers or experienced L2 users because they provide real-life testimonials and evidence that comes from real people (instead of teachers or textbooks). The greatest advantage in conducting interviews is that they allow learners to practice a variety of L2 skills in tandem; several productive assignments can be derived from them.

The first step is for learners to develop appropriate and focused questions. These can provide a fruitful avenue for working on various forms of polite speech acts, considerations of appropriateness (e.g., what represents personal information, what topics can be discussed, and how to approach them), as well as pragmatic forms of questions and requests. The questions should focus on the causal information that deals with L2 cultural concepts and sociocultural norms and behaviors that cannot be readily observed. Interviews allow learners access to the invisible aspects of L2 culture. Examples of questions can include:

- Why do people ask you *How are you?* and then not listen to the answer?
- Why do teachers say that students have to come on time if, when students come late, they know that the missed material is their own loss?
- Why do Americans smile so much?
- When and why is it okay to call teachers/professors by their first names?
- Why do strangers say *hello* to me on the street?
- Why is it necessary to explain everything in so much detail in writing, or if my essay explains everything (!), wouldn't readers think that I view them as a little slow?

It is strongly recommended that the instructor approve the questions before the actual interview.

In addition, learners can work at eliciting the polite and appropriate requests for appointments and meetings, "softening" devices (e.g., *maybe, possibly,* and *can/could*), appropriate telephone or email skills, negotiating the times and places for meeting, and seeking clarification. The interviews can be conducted in pairs, but it is preferable not to include more than two students on an interview team.

Following the interview, the information can be used for a presentation to other small groups of students or to an entire class. In a writing class, the outcomes can be turned into a short or long paper, depending on the learners' level of L2 proficiency. In any case, the presentations or written assignments should not turn into mere descriptions of the responses or behaviors but should set out

to determine their causes. When working on the presentation or writing assignments, the cultural conventions of L2 public speaking (e.g., eye contact, the organization of content, and demeanor) or L2 written discourse (e.g., the thesis statement, topic sentences, and their detailed support) can be addressed in conjunction with the work on the assignment content. In general, such a project can take approximately two or three weeks, depending on circumstances.

EFL teaching

In EFL settings, learners can work on short questionnaires that also have the goal of identifying the manifestations of culture in language use and heightening learners' awareness of politeness norms, sociocultural variables, pragmatic functions, and linguistic forms of speech acts (e.g., the types of "softening" devices and their variability) in their first language. The questionnaires can be administered in the learners' L1 to gather information that can be later used in L2 presentations or written assignments. The tasks can be simplified for intermediate-level learners or be made more complex for advanced L2 speakers.

ESL/EFL teaching

In ESL/EFL, home videos, movie clips, and videotaped excerpts from newscasts and TV programs (e.g., sitcoms, shows for younger learners, or interviews) can provide a practically inexhaustible resource for examining the influence of culture on language (e.g., routinized expressions, "softening" devices, questions, and requests), interactional practices, body language, turn-taking, and the length of pauses to signal the end of a turn. The information on sociocultural and politeness norms of the community obtained from such materials can be used in subsequent role plays, skits, or short plays that learners can script and present, as well as in formal presentations and writing assignments. In this case, written assignments can include the aspects of L2 speech acts and behaviors that learners found surprising, the descriptions of polite and routinized expressions that they noted, and culturally determined conventions displayed in the video excerpts. These projects can be worked on for one to two weeks, depending on the amount of material used in the videolesson.

Teacher, teach yourself

Because individuals are socialized into their first culture, they are usually unaware of the influence of culture on their language. To become effective, classroom teachers are often faced with the need to develop their professional knowledge of the fundamental sociocultural variables essential for L2 teaching. A great deal of literature has been published since the 1980s and 1990s on the impact of cultural awareness and knowledge on the overall language proficiency of learners. In addition, it has become apparent that cultural concepts affect how learners learn and teachers teach. Teaching adult learners to be or speak "like a native" (Saville-Troike, 2003, p. 31) is not likely to result in success because the sociocultural norms of language use are acquired during the socialization process. Thus, classroom teachers need to advance their own knowledge of how learners' first cultures work and how it impacts their ability to learn. For example, why is it that some students rarely speak in class, why do some learners memorize whole chapters instead of trying to "understand" the material, or why do some people never ask questions even if they need the teacher to provide more explanation?

Developing a sufficient knowledge base about learners' cultures does not mean that the teacher needs to become an expert ethnographer on the 15 different cultures represented in the classroom. For instance, the teacher does not necessarily need to be concerned with the roles and responsibilities of children and parents; religious rituals; or ways to celebrate holidays and life-cycle events, such as weddings and funerals. The ESL/EFL teacher is primarily concerned with cultural considerations that have a direct impact on his or her students' ability to learn and to do their best in a second language and in a second culture environment. If students from a particular culture (or several cultures) do not participate in a speaking activity, it would be interesting to find out why this is so. On the other hand, if the members of one culture seem to dominate most classroom interactions, it may be necessary to learn why they behave in this way, assuming that the teacher is seeking to make the classroom a productive learning place for all the students.

Thus, teachers' first priority is to identify their own needs in culture learning, in addition to those of their students. Another consideration is to investigate how teachers' own socioculturally determined beliefs, assumptions, and expectations affect their views on student learning and behaviors. For example, if a student does not want to speak up, the teacher may respectfully allow the student to maintain silence for the duration of the class or may take appropriate steps to make it more comfortable for all students to volunteer opinions in paired or small-group activities or other settings that are less threatening than speaking in front of the entire class. If, however, the student maintains polite silence and the teacher accommodates the student's choice of behaviors, the student is unlikely to improve his or her speaking proficiency and fluency.

Making choices

Teachers often need to develop their own approach to teaching L2 culture and pragmatics. One of the central objectives in developing effectiveness in sociopragmatic instruction is to address the causal knowledge about culture (Buttjes & Byram, 1991) and sociocultural reasoning that underlies practically all culturally determined ways of doing. Examining what causes members of a particular culture to do something in a particular way helps learners make choices in speaking, writing, and behaving. For example, in many English-speaking communities, students are expected to arrive to class on time or arrive at an appointment on time. In contrast, such an expectation may not be common in other cultures. The reason that students need to be punctual is that in English-speaking cultures the value placed on time is very high; it is considered to be a scarce and important commodity, similar to money. In fact, a number of sayings refer to time in ways similar to money (e.g., *spend time, waste time, to be short on time, time is money*). Therefore, when students arrive late, they disrupt the class, take other people's time, and display a certain amount of disrespect for the teacher and other students. Students make a choice whether to come on time or to take the liberty of coming late. To help learners make appropriate choices (or to make them aware that they are indeed making choices that have consequences), teachers need to develop their cultural knowledge and classroom effectiveness in dealing with culturally based problems.

FUTURE TRENDS

In the contemporary world, English predominates as a means of international communication. It is the language of technology, popular media and culture, business, and science. Intercultural interactions among speakers of many languages and members of many societies often take place in English. This does not necessarily imply, however, that learners and users of English as a medium of wider communication are obliged to follow Anglo-American sociocultural and pragmatic norms of interaction. For instance, in an L2 English communication between, for example, a speaker of a Central European language and a speaker of an Asian language, where both are non-native users of English, it does not seem reasonable to expect that they would attempt to follow Anglo-American sociocultural norms of politeness. However, learning about another culture and its social norms has already become more important in today's world, which keeps growing progressively smaller.

The dramatic advancement of technology, the rapid transmission of spoken and written language, and the expansion of English language teaching worldwide will continue to increase the ubiquity of cross-cultural interactions. In real-life interactions among speakers of various languages, including English, developing cross-cultural proficiency and familiarity with pragmatic norms of communication is likely to become a daily necessity on a par with other linguistic skills. As mentioned earlier, both linguistic and sociocultural proficiencies are essential for a successful communication to take place. In this light, teaching the language and the culture of speakers of the target language will probably become progressively more interdependent.

CONCLUSION

It is important for both teachers and learners to be aware of the manifestations and outcomes of L2 sociocultural values, concepts, and pragmatic norms on people's language usage. To this end, learners need to be taught to notice polite (and often routinized) expressions and behaviors common in the L2 community because, without becoming astute people watchers, learners will find it difficult, if not impossible, to become interactionally competent in the L2. Being aware of the sociocultural frameworks and the pragmatic features of language does not mean that learners have to become "nativelike." However, an awareness of the L2 sociocultural and pragmatic norms can allow learners to make their own informed choices of what to say and how to say it. The teacher's task is to provide learners with the tools that they need to recognize that they are indeed making choices.

Although ESL/EFL teachers devote a great deal of work, time, and attention to the teaching of L2 language skills, being linguistically competent is not enough for many learners to attain their educational, professional, and social goals. Because the way a language is used reflects the target language culture, the teaching of the L2 culture can be combined with the teaching of most L2 language skills. Teaching the L2 culture together with strategies for noticing while learners are speaking, listening, reading, and writing more adequately represents the connections between language and culture than teaching L2 language skills—or the culture—in isolation.

SUMMARY

➤ In L2 teaching and learning, the term *culture* can be used to refer to very different domains of human societies: (1) literature, the arts, architecture, festivals, and history; or (2) sociocultural norms, worldviews, beliefs, assumptions, and value systems that can be identified in practically all language use. Language teaching should focus on the latter.

➤ Teaching and learning a second culture do not represent a separate domain of L2 usage or instruction; instead, learning to follow L2 sociocultural norms makes learners better and more proficient communicators in a range of other skills, such as speaking, reading, or writing.

➤ L2 pragmatics deals with a crucial area in culture teaching and learning because it addresses intentions, assumptions, beliefs, goals, and actions that people perform by means of language in socioculturally appropriate ways.

- The most important long-term benefit of culture teaching is to provide learners with the awareness and tools that allow them an opportunity to achieve their academic, professional, social, and personal goals and to succeed in their daily L2 interactions.
- L2 teachers' primary focus is to work with the cultural aspects and pragmatic uses of language that have a direct impact on students' ability to learn and to do their best in L2 communications.
- A central objective of effective L2 sociopragmatic instruction is to address the causal knowledge about culture (why people do something in a particular way) and sociocultural reasoning that underlies practically all culturally determined ways of doing.

DISCUSSION QUESTIONS

1. The chapter mentions that culture teaching does not represent a separate domain of L2 teaching. If this is so, is it useful for teachers to develop lessons to deal with folk dances, festivals, facts, and foods when teaching culture?

2. The distinction between the visible and the invisible culture is described as one of the most important aspects of teaching the influence of culture on L2 use. What are the key features of the invisible culture, and what impact do they have on L2 learning and use?

3. Why does the teaching of L2 culture seem to be more directly relevant to ESL rather than to EFL learners? Why is contrasting culturally determined ways of speaking and writing useful for teaching second culture to EFL learners?

4. In many ways, cultural references are closely intertwined with reading, discourse, and text. What is the role of linguistic proficiency and cultural proficiency in ESL/EFL reading and/or writing? How important can L1 literacy be in learning to read and write in ESL/EFL?

5. Why is it that many teacher-training programs stay away from preparing teachers to work with the second culture? If you were in charge of an ESL/EFL program would you choose include the teaching of the culture as a component of teacher training? Why or why not?

SUGGESTED ACTIVITIES

1. Create lists of common linguistic expressions or behaviors, each associated with two or three types of speech acts (e.g., agreeing, disagreeing, inviting someone to do something or visit, or accepting or declining invitations) and arrange them from the least to the most polite expressions. What are the characteristics of the least or the most polite speech acts? What are the sociocultural variables that would make each of them acceptable or unacceptable in real-life interactions?

2. Different writing genres require the use of different conventions. Gather samples of different texts, for example, a personal letter, an email message, a blog posting, a popular magazine article, an excerpt from an introductory textbook, or a formal essay/academic paper. Identify the features of these texts that make them different in important ways. What are the culturally prescribed conventions common in personal, expressive, or formal academic writing? What do these genres share? What do the shared and different conventions say about the culture of the L2 community?

3. Observe a group of people who are engaged in a similar activity at the same time (e.g., standing in line, waiting for the teacher to arrive in class, or making small purchases in a drugstore). What do the verbal and nonverbal behaviors of these individuals have in common? How do they, for instance, maintain eye contact or use their hands? What do most of them say, and what do only some individuals say? How can culturally determined causes of ways of behaving and speaking in a community be identified and isolated from those that are based on individual choices?

4. To find out what represents a popular understanding of culture in the community, find five or six individuals who are about the same age and have similar social status and who are native speakers of the same language. Ask them to tell you about their culture. For example, ask several American or Japanese students to tell you about their culture. What do their responses include? How do these individuals identify the visible and the invisible aspects of their culture?

FURTHER READING

LoCastro, V. (2011). *Pragmatics for language educators: A sociolinguistic perspective*. New York, NY: Routledge.

This volume presents pragmatics as the study of language use in real-life social interaction and describes the effects of various language forms on communication. It concentrates on everyday conversation and the sociocultural variables that determine choices of language features made by participants in interactions.

Saville-Troike, M. (2003). *The ethnography of communication: An introduction* (3rd ed.). Malden, MA: Blackwell.

This volume describes how and why language is used in particular ways that differ in various cultures. It illustrates essential concepts in sociolinguistics and cites examples from many languages to outline frameworks of communication and cultural competence.

Scollon, R., & Scollon, S. W. (2001). *Intercultural communication* (2nd ed.). Oxford, UK: Blackwell.

This practical guide to the main concepts and problems of intercultural communication centers on principles of interactive sociolinguistics, the discourse of members of divergent cultures, pragmatics, and ethnography. It underscores the importance of language use in cross-cultural discourse and cultural norms of interaction.

Stewart, E., & Bennett, M. (1991). *American cultural patterns: A cross-cultural perspective* (Rev. ed.). Yarmouth, ME: Intercultural Press.

This book discusses fundamental concepts of American culture in terms of similar or different characteristics of other cultures. It also focuses on the impact of culture on communication and implications for cross-cultural interactions.

26 | Digital Technology in Language Teaching

MAGGIE SOKOLIK

KEY QUESTIONS

➤ What tools or techniques might be considered educational technology?
➤ How has educational technology changed over the past decades?
➤ Which computer applications are best suited for different learning skills and goals?

EXPERIENCE

In previous semesters, Professor Wong has asked her students not to use their cell phones or laptops during class because they created a distraction. This was a policy that worked well, and students had always cooperated. This semester, however, she finds that they increasingly have their laptops, tablet computers, and cell phones on their desks and use them frequently.

Further investigation reveals that her students are not texting their friends or checking their email. Several students have downloaded the course textbook onto their tablet computers, while others are consulting dictionaries and grammar references on their mobile phones. Professor Wong is now rethinking her policy against mobile technology in her classroom and is, instead, considering ways to make the best use of the tools students commonly carry in their backpacks or pockets.

WHAT IS DIGITAL TECHNOLOGY?

In the 2001 edition of this book, this chapter was titled "Computers in Language Teaching." The change in the title reflects a change in what we now understand as "computers." As stated in the *TESOL Technology Standards Framework* (Teachers of English to Speakers of Other Languages, 2009):

The term *technology* . . . refers to the use of systems that rely on computer chips, digital applications, and networks in all of their forms. These systems are not limited to the commonly recognized desktop and laptop computers: Almost all electronic devices these days include an embedded computer chip of some sort (DVD players, data projectors, interactive whiteboards, etc.). Mobile devices that employ a computer at their core (cell phones, personal digital assistants [PDAs], MP3 players, etc.) will undoubtedly occupy a more central role in language teaching and learning in the years to come. (p. 3)

For our purposes, we refer to this type of technology as *digital technology*—technology relying on computer chips—to distinguish it from more standard forms of educational technology, such as overhead projectors or even chalkboards. It is critical to recognize that, when we talk about classroom technology, we are no longer limited to thinking only about computers but an assortment of devices ranging from the smallest programmable smartpen[1] to the desktop tower computer.

In addition to the devices, digital technology also includes the software programs, databases, or webpages that users access. A tablet computer is not useful at all unless it has relevant applications (apps), such as word processing, dictionaries, and a web browser, available for use. In fact, in many ways, apps are more important than the devices in which they are housed. As we see in this chapter, it is not the technology alone that matters in the educational setting; it is how it is used.

CONCEPTUAL UNDERPINNINGS

Historical overview

Visionaries: The 1940s through 1980s. With the development of new technologies, there is an ongoing interest in applying these technologies to education and in making predictions about how they will affect the educational future of our classrooms and students. Although most people associate the birth of educational technology with the emergence of the personal computer in the 1970s and 1980s, the history of educational computing actually goes back to the 1940s. Writers such as Vannevar Bush (1945) foresaw a future in which communication and science would be enhanced with hyperlinked systems of information:

> Consider a future device for individual use, which is a sort of mechanized private file and library. It needs a name, and to coin one at random, "memex" will do. A memex is a device in which an individual stores all his books, records, and communications, and which is mechanized so that it may be consulted with exceeding speed and flexibility. It is an enlarged intimate supplement to his memory. (p. 106)

Of course, in the 1940s, the physical technology tied these ideas to microfilm, phonographic recordings, and punch card–style computing machines. In the 1950s and 1960s, the most powerful mainframe computers occupied entire rooms, not the corners of desktops or small briefcases. The development of the microchip and miniaturization of components enabled educational technology to move forward rapidly in the 1970s and 1980s.

By the 1980s, many of the technological restrictions of the 1940s had melted away, and financial barriers instead hampered (and continue to hamper) our visions of educational technology. And, by the late 1990s, the vision of the technological future described next was common (Young et al., 1997):

> What will happen is that in the university of the year 2000, students will be given a computer on their first day. Over the years that they spend at the university, a fixed cost will be assessed each term. This cost will pay for the computer, tuition, access to a myriad of database services, and online textbooks. (p. 259)

While the technology certainly exists to realize this vision today, the financial support and bureaucratic structures still do not. Some institutions have implemented programs such as these, but they remain rare.

The 1980s, however, did see the popularity and growth of email, which enhanced communication among connected instructors and students. Email enabled not only simple communication but expanded the boundaries of collaboration among researchers. It also enabled the easy distribution of manuscripts across distances and the growth of email discussion lists, sometimes called listservs after the LISTSERV software that enabled these discussions (L-Soft International, 1996). With tens of thousands of subscribers, the most popular email discussion list for English as a second language (ESL) and English as a foreign language (EFL) instructors was TESL-L, created in 1991 at Hunter College by Anthea Tillyer and other collaborators. On this list, and others like it, instructors were able to pose questions, share resources, and solve problems for each other. This list closed in April 2012, but other lists, such as those maintained by the interest sections of TESOL, continue to be avenues of communication for instructors. The closing of TESL-L, however, signaled ongoing changes in the way online communication takes place; it has increasingly moved to the web through blogs, specialized websites, or groups on Facebook, Yahoo!, or Google+ (among others).

Computer-assisted language learning and the web: The 1990s. In the 1990s, in addition to email communication, there was a growth of stand-alone programs that could be used in classrooms, in laboratories, or for individual learning. Examples of such programs included test-creation software, such as *TestMaster* (Wida Software, 1998); writing applications such as *HyperCard* (Apple Computer, 1989); video-based listening, such as *Real English Interactive* (Marzio, 1999); and game-like programs, such as *Oregon Trail* (Minnesota Educational Computing Consortium, 1974) and *Escape from Planet Arizona* (EF Education, 1995), which was one of the few simulation games intended for English learners. These programs (collectively called computer-assisted language learning [CALL]) represented a huge step forward in creativity and interactivity. However, due to the limitations of the technology at the time, in addition to network connections being slow and expensive, many of them focused on a limited band of skill development and relied on what the technology could do best at the time: fill-in-the-blank or multiple-choice type assessment items. As Buell (1994) noted:

> Tools, testers, tutors and toys: since the advent of CALL, these four categories have summed up the diversity of software available for language laboratory and individual use. The CD-ROM hasn't moved us beyond the four Ts, but it is bringing us bigger tools, testers, tutors and toys than ever before. (n.p.)

At the same time as the growth in stand-alone software, in 1990, a proposal for the World Wide Web was put forth by Sir Tim Berners-Lee and Robert Cailliau (Berners-Lee & Cailliau, 1990). By the end of 1994, the web was growing exponentially, with new websites being added daily. With this new technology came an enormous expansion of CALL; in fact, CALL began to take center stage in new pedagogical practices (Egbert & Hanson-Smith, 1999; Hanson-Smith, 2000).

One of the larger shifts in the use of technology came because of increasing user-friendliness of the technology. Until this point, most computer programs had to be written by professional programmers or by educators who learned to write programs on their own or through taking computer-programming courses. By comparison, webpages were easy to create. They required knowledge only of hypertext markup language (HTML), a rather unsophisticated word processing style code. Many educators and students found they could master HTML rather quickly with the help of a book or online tutorial.

As a result, CALL shifted from being teacher-centered (or, more accurately, program-centered), with stand-alone software delivering grammar drills or similar activities, to a more participatory medium. Teacher-created materials, now available on the web, became more popular, and even student-created projects, typically facilitated by teachers, popped up on sites around the globe (Isbell & Reinhardt, 2000). This change was generally seen as a positive one, but it created a

need for a new type of materials evaluation, one that took into account the new method of delivery and assessment of quality. With the nexus of control shifting away from traditional publishing, instructors and students grew wary of the quality of materials that were posted without having gone through traditional review processes (cf. Ciaffaroni, 2006; Sokolik, 2003). As Greene (2000) noted:

> There is an attraction in Japanese CALL instruction for software applications that demonstrate the power of computers to do graphic design rather than to learn English writing. This is evidence of the extent to which the "wow-factor" controls the Japanese post-secondary EFL agenda. (p. 241)

Although Greene was speaking specifically about Japanese students using writing software, most instructors experienced in using educational software would probably agree that this problem—attraction to graphically interesting programs over those that deliver sound educational experiences—continues to be an issue today.

Web 2.0, social media, and expanding mobility: The 2000s and now. What was not entirely foreseen in the 1990s was the emergence of Web 2.0, social networking, and social media along with their dramatic impact on educational practices and policies. Web 2.0 refers to a more interactive version of Internet capabilities. O'Reilly (2005) explains that it features "services, not software," functions "above the level of a single device," and harnesses "collective intelligence" (p. 5). Web 2.0 has meant that users are increasingly the creators of materials and that even the barrier of learning HTML has been eliminated.

Web 2.0 technologies have facilitated the growth of blogs, wikis (discussed later in this chapter), video sites like Vimeo and YouTube, social networking sites such as Facebook and LinkedIn, ebooks (both "print" and audio versions), and a host of other applications that have enabled direct communication between users, either *asynchronously* (at different times; e.g., email is asynchronous) through written comments or videos, or *synchronously* (at the same time; e.g., a telephone conversation is synchronous) via text, voice, and video chats. These tools have given students and instructors more control than ever over classroom materials and, as a result, have caused some turmoil in the print publishing world. The availability of a wide range of media, often freely available, has pushed traditional textbook publishers to change their own publishing practices and adapt to how students and teachers use materials.

As mentioned, Web 2.0 technologies are less and less platform-specific, meaning that they are available on laptops and mobile phones, as well as on an assortment of other connection tools such as tablet computers and ebook readers (e-readers). These tools make computing more ubiquitous and open up the possibilities of what can be used in the language classroom. No longer is the student or teacher tethered to a computer lab or even to a classroom computer.

Theoretical Basis for the Use of Digital Technology

The theoretical basis for the use of digital technology in the classroom comes from the various second language acquisition theories and classroom practices themselves, rather than any theory intrinsic to the technology. In other words, there are not any specific pedagogical theories suggested by the use of any medium or technology, whether it is a chalkboard, a pad of paper and pencil, a telephone, or a computer. Not surprisingly, studies done in the late 1990s and early 2000s (Pelgrum & Plomp, 2002; Wenglinski, 1998) showed that the mere presence of classroom computers, for example, did nothing to improve learning. Furthermore, according to the *TESOL Technology Standards Framework,* "At present, there is no clearly articulated theory specific to technology use in language teaching" (Teachers of English to Speakers of Other Languages, 2009, p. 13).

However, various studies (Grgurović & Chapelle, 2007; Warschauer, 1996) show that both student motivation and teacher instruction improve with the use of CALL in language learning. Similarly, "The use of technology in English language teaching and learning can also encourage the development of strategies necessary for modern survival: communication, collaboration, and information gathering and retrieval" (Teachers of English to Speakers of Other Languages, 2009, p. 15).

As Hanson-Smith (2003) noted, the development of methods and uses in CALL is a microcosm of the evolution of teaching practices in the field itself. When CALL features were limited by the technology, computer-based activities mimicked the audiolingual approach and grammar-based methods. As the technology developed, more opportunities for rich content and interaction developed as well. Web 2.0 applications, along with mobile telephones and computing, support the current focus on authentic materials and communicative learning tasks. The question arises, however: Did our methods evolve because the technology has developed to support them, or did the technology change, at least in part, to fulfill our demands for a more content-rich learning environment?

CLASSROOM APPLICATIONS

Reading and writing skills

Digital technology has traditionally had its strength in offering ways to mediate reading and writing. Vast amounts of authentic reading materials, not to mention English language teaching (ELT) materials, are available online. In addition, written exchanges between student and teacher have been made much simpler by email, instant messaging, and *course management systems* (CMSs), which offer an integrated set of tools to deliver course materials, send group emails, and track assignments and attendance, in addition to other functions (CMS technology is discussed in more detail later in the chapter). Given new platforms, such as ebook readers and mobile telephones, access to and opportunities for reading and writing have expanded even more dramatically.

Of course, along with these additional opportunities come complications; we might wonder which format is best for reading and writing, or whether any format is best. How do accessibility and usability figure into the use of different reading and writing platforms? How do we know which technologies our students can access? Can we predict which technologies are around the corner and plan accordingly? Teachers need to consider these questions as they learn about the details of various tools and techniques for digital reading and writing.

Online reading.   The type of reading we expect from students may not mesh well with what is generally known about online reading behavior.

According to Agger (2008, referencing various studies by J. Nielson):

■ Online readers tend to skip large blocks of text; shorter paragraphs and bulleted lists get more attention.

■ The reading pace for online reading is believed to be 25% slower than reading from paper.

If teachers assign reading that is to be read on a screen, these factors should be taken into consideration. For students who are interested in increasing their reading speed, several websites offer reading speed assessment online (cf. Minnesota Laboratory for Low-Vision Research, 1999).

On the other hand, the Internet has afforded instructors a nearly limitless supply of potential reading material.[2] Teachers can use search engines to locate topics of interest for students or assign students to research areas of interest. One way to do this is to provide a focus for Internet research and reading rather than having students simply look up material online. Consider the activity in Figure 1.

> You are teaching an intermediate reading course, and the theme for the week is "Choosing a Career." You go online and find three readings to assign to your students about three different careers: nursing, computer programming, and journalism. After having students read the articles you located, you ask them to participate in a discussion on a class discussion list, either by email or using other discussion platforms available to you. The question for discussion is: Which career seems most interesting?

Figure 1. Responding to assigned readings in an online discussion platform.

Writing: Email and chat. Much has been written about the use of email in the language classroom. Email has been used for communication between students, between students and teachers, and between students and others outside the classroom. Many instructors and researchers have designed email tasks to focus on language learning. International culture exchanges such as "key-pal"[3] programs help students to communicate authentically. However, email has in large part fallen out of favor as a method for communication between instructors and students in some circumstances. This is due to two main factors:

1. Many instructors feel they receive too much email and that student messages often become lost in the shuffle; email is a less efficient way of communicating when classroom matters affect more than an individual student. Messages can also be delayed, the answering time can be too long, or messages may end up in the spam folder.

2. Other platforms, such as social media (e.g., Facebook) or CMSs, have arisen to facilitate communication between teacher and student, or among students, more economically.

Chat, on the other hand, is real-time, or synchronous, communication. It has the informal feel of conversation, yet is mediated through writing. Chat has the added feature of immediate response rather than the time lag involved with email. Chat can be used to facilitate class discussions, for immediate feedback between students and teachers outside class time, or for communication between students outside class. Chat logs, or written records of a chat session, can be kept in most chat programs and used as data for future classroom work or research. At present, there is a host of programs that can facilitate synchronous chat sessions, many of them free applications available for computers, tablet computers, and mobile telephones.

But, just as email has fallen out of favor with many instructors, chat has become less popular with students, who prefer using their telephones for sending text messages. In fact, in many communities around the world, mobile telephones are more common than computers—thus, the applications and features of telephones are more popularly used. This fact need not be limiting—most smartphones have more computing capacity than the desktop computers of the early 1990s (using smartphones in the classroom is discussed later in the chapter).

Many instructors use chat to improve fluency in writing, but it can also be used to address issues in grammar and correctness. Consider the activity in Figure 2.

> You have an online chat to discuss a popular event in the media. You keep a chat log and have the file on your computer. You select some representative sentences, highlight the grammatical errors, print the file out or present it on a projector, and ask students to work in pairs to supply grammatically correct options.

Figure 2. Addressing accuracy in chat messages.

Blogs and wikis. *Blogs* (originally known as weblogs) have grown in popularity as a writing form. Blogs are usually kept by an individual writer who creates regular entries of ideas, descriptions of events, or other materials such as graphics or video. Blogs are typically built on Web 2.0 technology and, as such, are interactive, allowing visitors to leave comments. Blog assignments can be used for all levels of students; many different free software platforms are available for students to post their writing and other work.[4] Blogs can be public, that is, available to any reader on the Internet, or made more private, only for a specified, approved group of people. For educational purposes, there are probably good reasons for students' work to be kept private. Teachers who assign public blogs should be aware of the pitfalls—comments from strangers can range from encouraging to profane. On the other hand, many instructors believe that by making their work public, students will become more conscientious of the quality of their writing. As Mirtschin (2008) stated, "[Students are] no longer working for a teacher who checks and evaluates work but a potential global audience" (n.p.). In any event, if students' work is to be made public, their explicit permission should be sought in all cases.

A *wiki* is a website that allows the creation and editing of interlinked webpages via a browser using some type of built-in text editor. The most popular wiki is of course, Wikipedia (Wikipedia. org), a large cooperatively written and edited encyclopedia. Wikis are typically powered by wiki software and are useful in education because of their ability to facilitate collaboration. A wiki is usually a shared activity, allowing students to write information and other students to add to it or to amend it. Figure 3 is an example of wiki entries done by a group of advanced ESL students. This wiki was created to share cultural information about people, places, or things mentioned in the novel *Tales of the City*, by Armistead Maupin (2007).

Social networking. A social network is an online service or site that focuses on building and reflecting social relations among people, for example, those who share interests, backgrounds, and/or activities. Social networks usually have ways to share writing, photographs, personal information (e.g., birthdays and phone numbers), links to online resources, book reviews, political opinions, and just about anything else one can imagine. Although social networks have been typically used for noneducational purposes, instructors are increasingly using them to communicate with students, since students are usually familiar with them and how they work and often frequent these sites.

Two types of social networks are: (1) established networks such as Facebook; and (2) do-it-yourself networks, which provide the software so that users can build private networks. Instructors who use either type of network tend

---

Chapter 1. Taking the Plunge

- **The Buena Vista** - A reference to the Buena Vista Cafe, which claims to have invented Irish Coffee (coffee with whiskey and cream). More information about it is found at: http://thebuenavista.com
- **A Mood Ring** - A mood ring is a piece of jewelry which contains a thermochromic element, such as liquid crystal. The ring changes color in response to the body temperature of its wearer. The color is said, by some, to reflect the mood of the wearer. Mood rings were a fad in the 1970s. A picture is found at Wikipedia: http://en.wikipedia.org/wiki/File:Moodring1.jpg
- **McMillan & Wife** - McMillan & Wife was a popular 1970s television show. It revolved around a San Francisco police commissioner, Stewart McMillan (Rock Hudson) and his attractive, bright, and younger wife Sally (Susan Saint James). Often, the stories featured Mac and Sally attending fashionable parties and charity benefits before solving robberies and murders.
- **Patty Hearst** - Patricia Campbell Hearst (born February 20, 1954), now known as Patricia Campbell Hearst Shaw, is an American newspaper heiress, socialite, actress, kidnap victim, and convicted bank robber. She is the granddaughter of famous publisher William Randolph Hearst. She gained fame in 1974 when, following her kidnapping by the Symbionese Liberation Army (SLA), she joined her captors. She was apprehended after taking part in a bank robbery with other SLA members. She was imprisoned for almost two years before her sentence was commuted by President Jimmy Carter. She was later granted a presidential pardon by President Bill Clinton in his last official act before leaving office.

Figure 3. Excerpt from a student wiki.

to do so to share information with students and to facilitate communication among students.

In thinking about having students read and write online, consider the activity in Figure 4.

> You are teaching an intermediate writing course and decide to have students keep blogs about their English learning experience. You assign them to write 250 words minimum per week in a blog post. They must also respond in writing to at least three other classmates' blogs each week.

Figure 4. Online writing assignment.

Courseware or course management systems. CMSs are collections of online tools, usually presented in a password-protected area, where students can access course materials and assignments, and instructors can keep track of grades, post messages to the class, post assignments to the course calendar, and so on. There may also be integrated space for ebooks, student wikis, blogs, course glossaries, photo archives, and the like. Many schools host CMSs locally or subscribe to a CMS service. CMSs often have a more academic feel to them than do public social networking sites, and the added level of privacy usually makes them the medium of choice for institutions or individual instructors.

CMSs are used in two ways: as a supplement to a face-to-face course and as a platform on which a distance education course is built. Most CMSs (e.g., Moodle or Sakai) offer a variety of tools that can be implemented by the user, depending on the educational purpose each tool serves. In distance courses, typically more tools are used than in face-to-face courses. Consider the scenario in Figure 5.

> You are assigned to teach two courses—one meets regularly in a classroom, and one meets only online. Which of the following tools will you use for each?
> * announcements
> * calendar
> * assignments
> * online quizzes
> * anthology of course readings
> * discussion board
> * online chat area
> * photo database
> * gradebook
> * wiki

Figure 5. Deciding on possible CMS tools.

CMSs are convenient because they protect student privacy and gather tools in one location. However, a study by Papastergiou (2006) found that structuring online interactions using CMSs imposes a significant workload on faculty; furthermore, CMSs still fall short of providing collaborative knowledge-building environments and alternative forms of assessment.

Plagiarism. Writing in online environments has made it especially easy for students to plagiarize, either intentionally or unintentionally, through copying and pasting. Software such as turnitin.com, used by many institutions, requires students to submit their work to a database that checks it for originality. Even without access to this software, instructors can do online searches of suspected phrases or sentences in student writing. The outcomes of these searches, either through turnitin.com or a web search, can be used to teach about plagiarism and often provide good material for lessons on proper citation and quotation use.

Listening skills

Faster connection speeds have allowed for the greatly improved delivery of audio and video files over the Internet. Needless to say, this has increased listening opportunities for students as well. There are sites dedicated to teaching listening within an ELT context (e.g., esl-lab.com) and a variety of podcasts (lectures or talks produced for Apple's iPod but often accessible on other devices), lectures, talk radio broadcasts, interviews, audiobooks, and more. Students can listen to lectures about language learning, such as the podcasts developed by Grammar Girl (grammar.quickanddirtytips.com), or on any topic of interest. For instance, consider the classroom activity in Figure 6.

Pronunciation and speaking skills

Using digital technology for pronunciation and speaking instruction has been one of the last areas to develop fully. Partially, this has been because of the additional technology that was required with older computers, in particular the need for sound cards and external microphones. To make things more complicated, educational environments have not always been ideal for voice recording, which is usually a solitary activity done with one computer

In an advanced integrated skills course, you ask the students to read the poem "My Father on a Bicycle" by Patricia Clark (2003). You discover that there is a recording of the author reading the poem aloud,[5] and you play the recording of the poem to the students before they read it, asking them to note the author's pronunciation and emphasis, and to try to understand the poem before reading it.

Figure 6. Using a digital audio file to teach a poem.

You assign students to keep audio journals to focus on their pronunciation. Each week they record a short piece on a topic you assign. To respond to the journals, using Audacity (or similar audio editing software), you insert your spoken comments at relevant points, either to correct the pronunciation of key words or to comment on suprasegmental aspects such as stress or intonation.

Figure 7. Responding to student audio journals using audio software.

and one student. Schools and students often do not have this type of equipment; thus, instructors do not use this technology in class, since the solitary activity is not conducive to the group learning and interaction afforded by a classroom, nor do they assign it as homework unless they are certain that students have adequate access. Another reason it is not used may be the relative inattention given to pronunciation instruction (Derwing & Munro, 2005).

The changing technology, especially the popularity of mobile telephones, is altering the face of pronunciation and speaking instruction. With speakers and microphones integrated into the equipment, a telephone is an ideal instrument for these skills.

Voice over Internet protocol and audio-recording programs. Voice over Internet protocol (VoIP), also known as "Internet telephone," is an increasingly popular way to communicate for little or no cost. VoIP programs can be voice only or can integrate video. The uses of VoIP in language education have focused on individual tutoring—English instructors can offer one-to-one English instruction from any location; they need computers running a VoIP program and an Internet connection (Skype is the most popular VoIP at the time of writing).

Classroom instructors can also use such programs to offer additional help in aural/oral skills. For example, Audacity (http://audacity. sourceforge.net) offers a free program that allows instructors or students to record their voices, insert spoken comments, and edit the sound files. For example, take a look at the classroom application in Figure 7.

Voice recognition. *Voice recognition* is the capability of a computer or software program to accept and interpret spoken dictation or to understand and carry out voice commands. Voice recognition

is used to dictate text into the computer or to give commands to the computer (e.g., opening programs and menus, or saving files).

Bell Labs began a project for voice recognition in the 1960s, and voice recognition software has advanced greatly since that time. Modern programs can be trained to a high degree of accuracy, although most still find the process slow. Voice recognition software requires training—that is, the computer must "learn" the characteristics of the user's voice to interpret what is said and translate it into written English words. This task alone provides specific training in pronunciation and clarity. An additional voice recognition application is the recent introduction of applications that will recognize a spoken word and translate it into another language. Google Translate is one such application for the smartphone.

Presentation tools. Other digital tools that do not address speaking directly, but rather augment a presentation, have their history in *slideware*, originally software meant only to display slides at a presentation. The most common of these tools has been Microsoft PowerPoint, although other similar programs, as well as new approaches, have emerged recently, including slideware that has a nonlinear approach to organization, and easy-to-use animation programs that allow the user to create short videos with narration merely by typing in a written script or recording a narrative track.[6]

Grammar and vocabulary skills

Grammar checkers. Modern word processing software usually comes equipped with grammar-checking routines. Unfortunately, as most users will attest, this software generally falls short of the grammatical editing that is required for language instruction. The software is not sensitive to context or conventions of use, such as the difference between academic English written for the humanities and that written for the sciences. Consider the following sentence, written by a second language learner in an English writing class: "In *Typical American*, the Changs become Americanized in order to succeed." Since the current grammar-checking routines are sensitive to passive constructions, the word processing grammar program made the following suggestion: *Passive voice (consider revising)*. Unfortunately, two issues potentially confuse the language learner here. First, there has to be a full understanding of how to revise to eliminate passive voice. Unfortunately, the student must already understand English grammar to make full use of the suggestions offered by the grammar-checking software. But more troubling in this case is the fact that this sentence cannot be rewritten in the active voice given its syntactic constraints. Thus, the suggestion to revise may introduce additional difficulties for ESL/EFL students who may trust the software more than they trust their own judgments about English grammar. Sometimes the suggestions are not only misguided but also completely wrong. In fact, a good example of this happened in the writing of this chapter—my software suggested I change the phrase *more participatory* in an earlier section to *participatorier*, an incorrect comparative form.

Use of drills. Much of language learning is facilitated by repetition, whether it is the repetition of individual sounds, intonation patterns, conversational gambits, or other types of words and phrases. Computers are useful in delivering drills for practice, whether for grammar, vocabulary, pronunciation, or listening, because they are tireless in their delivery. Unlike human interlocutors, who may grow weary of repeating a word for a learner, a computer will repeat a word hundreds of times or as many as the user wishes. Digital technology in this regard has some specific advantages: organization of materials, including a large volume of material and random presentation; scoring and record-keeping; graphics and animation; student control of materials; audio-cueing; and recording and storage of student responses.

Furthermore, with increasing awareness of the value of collaborative learning and communicative competence, the state of current digital resources and applications is a vast improvement over the old-style CALL "drill and kill," moving beyond mere repetition to interaction with authentic texts and participants who are communicating in real environments for real purposes.

Corpora and concordances. Computers are expert at storing large amounts of information and categorizing or sorting it by user-determined categories. Concordance programs and linguistic corpora are types of tools and data that are increasingly being used in the language classroom. A *concordance* is a type of index that searches for occurrences of a word or combinations of words, parts of words, punctuation, affixes, phrases, or structures within a *corpus* (a large collection of text) and can show the immediate context of the search item.

The output from a concordance search can be used in the preparation of teaching materials, such as grammar and vocabulary activities. Teachers can gather examples of language usage for creating exercises. In an article about concordances, V. Stevens (1993) states that with concordance software and a corpus of natural English, language learners can short-cut the process of acquiring competence in the target language. This is because the computer is able to help students organize huge amounts of language data so that patterns are more easily discerned. (For more information on teaching with concordances and corpora, see McCarthy & O'Keeffe, this volume.)

Concordances can be used to look at the context in which a given word or phrase occurs in a database. The example in Figure 8 shows the use of the word *purpose* extracted from a corpus of the University Word List (Xue & Nation, 1984). These samples show the use of the phrase *purpose + of*, which students should notice is followed by a noun, frequently in the gerund form. In *Using Corpora in the Language Classroom*, Reppen (2010) states, "Corpus-informed teaching materials provide students with examples of real language use, helping learners to know how to use language that is appropriate in different contexts" (p. 20). In this way, corpora and concordance programs can complement the use of dictionaries and thesauruses.

her for a Town Meeting on Thursday, it will be for the sole PURPOSE OF deciding the fate of a 19th- century building, a

loss in alfalfa seed. The composition of the House for the PURPOSE OF exercising its judicial function is now

at this ship may be the 'Duncan' come to these seas for the PURPOSE OF taking you home again." "The 'Duncan!'" murmured

there was no port, vessels might have visited it for the PURPOSE OF renewing their store of water.

a really urgent work, since it was for the PURPOSE OF depositing, as soon as possible, at Tabor Island

of Medicine and principal investigator of the study. The PURPOSE OF this article is to discuss legal and ethical

is an hypothesis about a population parameter. The PURPOSE OF hypothesis testing is to test the viability of

her ambiguity. What needs more elucidation is the very PURPOSE OF her ambiguity, and I would like to propose

Figure 8. Concordance of the phrase *purpose of* from the University Word List.

Online and electronic dictionaries. Instead of picturing a dictionary as a print object to carry around, in an increasingly digital world, a dictionary is something found on one's phone, in a stand-alone unit, or built into an electronic text. This is especially the case with ebook readers; using an ebook text, a student needs only to click on a word to get its definition and often also a sound file with its pronunciation. Definitions pop up in context, allowing the student to see how the definition fits with the use of the word. Certain web browsers and word processing programs have similar functions.

Culture and cross-cultural awareness skills

As a skill area, cross-cultural awareness is sometimes ignored. Fortunately, digital environments give students access to online videos, blogs, and a host of cultural information that can assist in cross-cultural understanding. Brinton (2008) suggests using WebQuests, inquiry-based activities in which learners seek specific information from the Internet to locate cultural information. Some of the topics included by Brinton (2008) are:

1. US geography—Select a state and find its . . .
   - **a.** Nickname
   - **b.** Current population
2. US traditions
   - **a.** What is a rodeo? Name three typical events that take place at a rodeo.
   - **b.** What is a soap opera? Name two famous American soap operas. (n.p.)

For controversial issues in cultural understanding, WebQuests can be an excellent way to encourage students to discover both the facts and opinions about a topic and to report on their findings. As Brinton mentions, "This has obvious advantages over the more traditional U.S. culture lesson, where often stereotyped information about the U.S. is provided in the form of edited readings and follow-up discussion questions" (2008, n.p.).

Another approach is found in the activity in Figure 9.

Locate three or four blogs that deal with cultural issues, such as the growth of the organic farming movement or the impact of video games on adolescents. Ask students to read posts that interest them. Also find some video clips, such as news broadcasts, that demonstrate some of the cultural issues. As a follow-up, ask students what kinds of cultural questions they have or what problems they have had in understanding a behavior or habit. Have them conduct a WebQuest to find more information about the questions the class had and share the information with the class.

Figure 9. Incorporating an online WebQuest into class.

Creating and evaluating technology-based activities

Whether an instructor decides to create his or her own materials or to use materials found on the Internet or in commercially available software, it is important that several features be evaluated and addressed. First and foremost, however, an instructor needs to decide whether a particular digital technology is the answer to a particular classroom question. In this section,

I guide instructors through a series of questions they should ask themselves as they consider the classroom use of digital technology.

Do I need technology?

What activities in my classroom, or in the administration of my classroom, are more difficult to do without technology? For example, one instructor might find having an online gradebook system to be more convenient than adding up scores by hand, while another may like the flexibility of tracking scores in a paper gradebook given the necessity of sharing a computer with two other instructors.

What technologies are available for the level of students I teach? For the course material or skills? Can they be used with our school's capacity? Certain instructors may find that showing YouTube videos is a good way to demonstrate cultural concepts; another instructor's school may block YouTube from the institution's Internet servers.

Am I letting the technology drive the course, or is the course driving the technology? An article in *Education World* (Education World Tech Team, 2008) expressed this idea well:

> [I]n a classroom where technology is appropriately integrated, sometimes print will be the best format for a particular lesson; sometimes a video will be; sometimes a podcast. Instead of starting with a form of technology and making it fit what you do, successful educators first determine whether or not that technology is the best way to deliver the instruction. (n.p.)

How do I know if the technology is worthwhile?

What are the learning objectives for my course? What do we hope to achieve? How will this technology help bring those objectives about? This question is not intended to prevent instructors from using a form of technology that appeals to them. Consider an instructor who is teaching a low-level reading course and wants to introduce podcasts as a way of integrating listening into reading. How might she use podcasts to support reading? Connections between the course goals and technology need not be restricted to only the most *obvious*—frequently the less obvious ones are the most creative—but instructors must be able to articulate exactly how a particular technology will further course goals.

How do others feel about this technology? Instructors need to find out how a particular technology has been received. They can read reviews and comments by searching online. It can be helpful to look at educators' blogs or review sites for devices, media, and software. And, of course, talking to colleagues who may have experience with a similar student population is also important. One instructor's positive experience using Skype with students, for example, may not translate into another's success if the teaching conditions are completely different.

What if I want to create my own materials?

What if I do not have time to learn computer programming or even how to make webpages? Instructors should find out which tools have a manageable learning curve. Again, educator blogs and review sites can help in this respect. Another way to do this is to create an inventory of which tools and technology are *already* known to teachers. For example, what tools are on their mobile telephones? Do they use ebooks or podcasts? Instructors will find it easier to start by using the tools they know and then add new tools or applications.

FUTURE TRENDS

The great contradiction in the twenty-first century is that anyone writing for the print medium about digital technology fully realizes that the technology will be outmoded by the time that the book or article is published. Some of the sites listed in the companion website for this volume will probably disappear, some software programs mentioned will be outmoded, and companies will be bought and sold. What is new will become old.

Against this backdrop, it is clear that textbooks and classroom materials are also changing rapidly at this time. With numerous predictions about traditional textbooks disappearing and new models for electronic publishing and distribution of texts, it is likely we will continue to see changes in how students and instructors choose, buy, and use classroom materials. In addition, since e-readers and electronic texts allow a wider range of media to be embedded, textbooks are no longer just words and images on a page but can include interactivity through video and sound as well. Some experts predict that the print book will be "extinct" by 2025 (Biggs, 2011). A clear example of how this future is upon us is the fact that at a recent international TESOL conference, one major textbook publisher had *no* textbooks on display; instead, the publisher demonstrated its entire collection to potential customers using tablet computers.

However, the history of educational technology over the past 30-plus years has shown that the trend toward increasing control of materials by teachers and their students will continue, regardless of the changes in the technology. As students and teachers become both creators and consumers of the classroom experience, facilitated by a spectrum of digital tools, the future challenge will be in determining the successful integration of new technology into the curriculum.

CONCLUSION

The hope that computers would be a panacea for those trying to learn second languages has not been realized. However, it is clear that digital technology can provide instructors and students alike with a new battery of tools with which language can be learned effectively. The Internet has changed the way we look at CALL, now sometimes known as technology-assisted language learning (TELL). Computing devices, from laptops to mobile devices, are now used as tools for communication rather than simply as ways of delivering automated drills or exercises.

Reading on any topic and in many languages is available on the Internet, and the chance to participate in discussions with people from all walks of life is motivating for many learners. In addition, the speed and size of computers now allow large databases to be manipulated, offering insights into language that we did not have access to previously. Corpus linguistics and concordance programs can help provide the data and tools that students and instructors need to make sense out of the usage patterns of general English and to gain insight into the typical discourse patterns in specific settings such as academic lectures or in specific disciplines such as business.

Fortunately, the same principles that instructors and policymakers use to evaluate print materials can be brought to bear on technological materials as well. The advances in technology oblige us to ask and answer these questions: How can this tool be used to augment the language learning process? How can we fully implement and integrate it into the educational experience? In other words, technology should be the flour in the cake, not the icing on top of it.

SUMMARY

➤ Although the foundation for an interlinked online system had been envisioned since the 1940s, it was not been until the 1990s that we saw its implementation in a way that allowed for flexible educational uses.

➤ Mobile devices, such as smartphones and tablet computers, have allowed the integration of educational technology in diverse learning environments.

➤ The Internet offers vast opportunities for reading and writing in authentic environments, but it is not without problems. Online reading is for many a slower, less in-depth process than reading on paper, and online writing is susceptible to plagiarism through copy-and-paste techniques.

➤ Chat programs, email, and CMS programs are among the many ways that teachers can communicate with students and that students can communicate among themselves. These platforms can all be leveraged in an educational environment to achieve the goals of fluency in communication.

➤ Speaking tasks can be augmented with technology either directly, using voice recording or recognition tasks, or indirectly, through presentation applications.

➤ All educational technology use needs to be evaluated for its effective use; we should always tie instructional decisions about technology to the goals and objectives of the curriculum.

DISCUSSION QUESTIONS

1. Which of the technologies discussed in this chapter have you experienced in your own language learning? Why? Which would you want to use as a teacher? Which seem most useful? Are there any that seem impractical?

2. Return to the scenario presented on the first page of this chapter. What should Professor

Wong's new policy be about the use of smart-phones, laptops, and tablet computers in her class, given the new realities? Formulate a classroom policy that you believe would work.

3. Social media has created numerous new considerations for teaching with technology. Concerns about privacy accompany any consideration of social media use. How might you balance the concerns of privacy with the enthusiasm that students show for using social media? What restrictions might an instructor want to consider in an educational setting?

4. Given that mobile phones are globally the most ubiquitous technology, what uses not included in this chapter might they serve in an educational environment? Think of as many ways to incorporate smartphone technology as you can.

5. While many instructors applaud the use of turnitin.com or similar plagiarism checking software, others question its use, worrying that it sends a message of mistrust to students. What is your opinion of plagiarism checking software? Have you used it?

SUGGESTED ACTIVITIES

1. Search online for a blog intended for students learning English. Based on your understanding of good educational practices, list at least three positive features of the blog. List three things that you could do to improve the blog.

2. Create a syllabus for a beginning English grammar course for ESL/EFL learners in which you integrate at least three different types of technology use. Discuss how your use of technology will enhance the grammar learning experience.

3. Locate a website intended for ESL/EFL teachers. Provide a summary and review of what this site offers and how it is useful to ESL/EFL instructors.

4. Find an online resource that is a good source of authentic listening material for ELLs. How might you use the material in the context of an ESL or EFL course? What types of activities could you create to help students understand the material? What kinds of follow-up activities might be interesting and/or useful?

FURTHER READING

Cennamo, K., Ertmer, P., & Ross, J. (2009). *Technology integration for meaningful classroom use: A standards-based approach*. Belmont, CA: Wadsworth.

This text is organized around the International Society for Technology in Education standards, focusing on aspects of educational technology like computers as systems and technology integration as a systematic process; it addresses issues of integrating technology resources into teaching practices.

Egbert, J., & Hanson-Smith, E. (Eds.). (2007). *CALL environments* (2nd ed.). Alexandria, VA: Teachers of English to Speakers of Other Languages.

This book presents eight conditions for optimal computer-assissted learning environments and offers suggestions for projects and questions for reflection at the end of each chapter.

Teachers of English to Speakers of Other Languages. (2009). *TESOL technology standards framework*. Alexandria, VA: Author.

The TESOL Technology Standards Framework offers a focus on specific pedagogy for English language teaching. The standards are applicable to teachers and students at a range of English proficiency levels in a wide range of English language teaching and learning settings around the world.

ENDNOTES

[1] A smartpen is a pen with a digital recorder and microphone built into it. This enables students or others to record and take notes at the same time. Notes are taken on special paper that allows the user to play back segments of the audio file that are coordinated with the notes. It also has other functions, including a calculator, dictionaries, and other downloadable applications such as translation programs.

[2] But be aware that, if you want to copy online materials for students to read, you cannot assume they are free just because they are on the Internet. Copyright laws govern the educational use of materials written by others. You can learn more about this by reading about the TEACH (Technology, Education, and Copyright Harmonization) Act of 2002. A good source of information on this is found at http://fairuse.stanford.edu/primary_materials/legislation/teach.html

[3] *Keypal* is the modernization of *pen pal* now that users work on computer keyboards and send mail electronically.

[4] Currently, blogger.com, a Google company, and WordPress.com are two sites offering free space for keeping blogs.

[5] An audio recording of this poem can be found at http://www.theatlantic.com/past/docs/unbound/poetry/antholg/clark/bicycle.htm

[6] At the time of writing, Prezi is a cloud-based nonlinear presentation tool that is available (prezi.com) with a reduced educators' license fee. GoAnimate (goanimate.com) and Xtranormal (xtranormal.com) are tools for animated video creation; these two programs have a graduated pay plan and have discounts for educators.

UNIT IV

Integrated Approaches

27 | Teaching Language through Discourse

MARIANNE CELCE-MURCIA AND ELITE OLSHTAIN

KEY QUESTIONS

➤ What do language teachers and language learners need to know about discourse analysis?
➤ How can language teachers use a discourse perspective to organize and facilitate their students' language learning?

EXPERIENCE

Following up on a lecture describing the use of discourse in language teaching, an aspiring teacher asks her professor during his office hour to explain in more detail the concept of cohesion, which he had touched on briefly in the lecture. The professor shows his student the following excerpt from a brochure (Santa Monica Convention and Visitors Bureau, 1998): "Natural beauty plays a starring role in Santa Monica, and seaside is the perfect vantage from which to watch the performance. Early risers will notice that the show begins just after sunrise." The professor points out that this short text refers to the same event using three different noun phrases, all of which suggest a theatrical metaphor: *a starring role* (first mention, new information, thus the indefinite article is used); *the performance* (second mention and the use of the definite article points back to *starring role*); *the show* (third mention, also definite, and it points back to *performance* and *starring role*). While acknowledging that there are other types of cohesion, the professor comments that such networks of referential and lexical ties are very common in English writing. He tells his student that they will be focusing on cohesion in more detail in class and that they will also discuss ties of substitution, ellipsis, and conjunction, in addition to referential and lexical ties.

WHAT IS DISCOURSE? WHAT IS DISCOURSE ANALYSIS?

There have been various attempts to define *discourse*.[1] Formal definitions usually state that discourse is a unit of language consisting of more than one sentence; functionalists have defined discourse as a unit of language in use (Schiffrin, 1994). However, neither of these definitions is optimal since a piece of discourse, given the right context, can consist of just one or two words, for example, *Stop!* or *No Smoking*. A piece of discourse can also be a very long novel. However, generally a piece of discourse falls somewhere in between the very short and the very long. The phrase language in use is too general to be useful. A more satisfying definition of discourse combines both the formal and functional perspectives and gives some necessary attention to context (Celce-Murcia & Olshtain, 2000):

> A piece of discourse is an instance of spoken or written language with describable internal relationships of form and meaning (e.g., words, structures, cohesion) that relate coherently to an external communicative function or purpose and a given audience or interlocutor. (p. 4)

We should also keep in mind that the notion of sentence is not always relevant, especially if we are analyzing spontaneous spoken discourse, where the utterance (i.e., a word, phrase, or chunk that can serve as a turn in conversation) is a more suitable unit of analysis.

What then is *discourse analysis*? A variety of disciplines in the late 1960s and the 1970s developed two parallel disciplines: text linguistics, which focused on written texts from a variety of fields and genres, and discourse analysis, which entailed more cognitive and social perspectives on language use and communicative exchanges; the latter focused mainly on spoken rather than written discourse. Today discourse analysis is carried out in a number of disciplines and serves as an umbrella term for all issues that are dealt with in the study of text and discourse. Other terms that are sometimes used to refer to discourse analysis are *discourse linguistics*, *discourse studies*, and, simply, *discourse*.

There are many different types of discourse. Within spoken discourse, we have conversations, lectures, interviews, narratives, sermons, speeches, on-the-spot news reports, and so on. Within written discourse, we have journalism (news articles and editorials); academic writing (textbooks, research papers, and journal articles); literature (fiction, nonfiction, drama, and poetry); letters (personal, business, and professional); scripts for movies, television, and radio; and Internet writing (email, blogs, e-magazines, and entries on social networking sites such as Facebook, Twitter, etc.). The boundaries between speech and writing are not always clear-cut; some spoken discourse may be prepared in advance (written down to be read aloud), while spontaneous spoken discourse such as conversation can be recorded and transcribed to enable close analysis. Some written discourse is informal and spontaneous and thus somewhat speechlike (personal letters and much email), while other written discourse is carefully planned, formal in style, undergoing multiple revisions (e.g., doctoral dissertations and legal briefs). Some instances of oral discourse have a professional, vocational, or educational purpose and are sometimes recorded for subsequent analysis: doctor-patient interactions, waiter-customer interactions in restaurants, classroom discourse (lectures, teacher-student interactions, and student-student interactions), interviews, writing conferences, and so on.

Not surprisingly, there are also many different types of discourse analysis, including *genre analysis* (e.g., Hyland, 2002; Swales, 1990), *conversation analysis* (e.g., Schegloff, 2007; Wong & Waring, 2010), *rhetorical structure theory* (e.g., Mann & Thompson, 1988), *cohesion analysis* (e.g., Halliday & Hasan, 1976, 1989), and *critical discourse analysis* (e.g., Fairclough, 2010; van Leeuwen, 2010).

In language teaching contexts, we often examine oral interactions between native and non-native speakers of the target language (or between two or more non-native speakers) to see what problems or breakdowns occur in a given communicative situation. This is sometimes referred to as *pedagogical discourse analysis* since the purpose is to identify problems and develop activities to help learners overcome the communication problems thus identified. (See also McCarthy & O'Keeffe, this volume.)

An authentic example might be useful at this point. A guest from overseas in an American home is offered a cup of coffee:

Hostess: [holding a pot of coffee] Would you like a cup of coffee?
Guest: I don't care.

The guest's reply is puzzling to the hostess since it could mean "Don't mind if I do" or "Please don't bother on account of me; no thanks." Since the American hostess does not know if the guest's answer means "yes" or "no," she puts the coffee pot on the table without pouring coffee into the cups. Both the hostess and the guest seem uncomfortable until a third person joins the group and cheerfully says, "Oh, a pot of fresh coffee. I'd love some! Does anyone else want coffee?" at which point the foreign guest quickly reformulates his response, "Yes, I want coffee, please."

Sometimes communication breaks down because of errors in grammar, pronunciation, or lexical choice. In this example, however, all the language was formally accurate, yet the message was unclear since the guest's first response did not come close to any pragmatically appropriate way of accepting the offer of a cup of coffee in English. Pedagogical discourse analysis can pinpoint the cause of such communication breakdowns, allowing language teachers to incorporate an exchange like the example into their lessons.

They can then give an explanation of the problem followed by interactive practice regarding appropriate ways of accepting and declining offers.

CONCEPTUAL UNDERPINNINGS

Discourse-based approaches to language teaching have grown out of three prior strands of research: (1) linguistic theories that include the analysis of discourse as well as analysis of grammar, lexicon, and phonology; (2) work in communicative approaches to language teaching; and (3) theoretical models of communicative competence. We discuss each of these next.

For more than 40 years, discourse-inclusive models of language analysis have been developed partly as a reaction to the sentence-level paradigm, long dominant in Chomsky's context-free model of language, including the innate mechanisms for language acquisition that he posits (Chomsky, 1957, 1995). Both anthropological linguists such as Hymes (1967, 1972), who coined the term *communicative competence*, and socially oriented functional linguists such as Halliday (1973, 1978) challenged the narrowness of Chomsky's view of language as grammatical competence; they argue instead that language has social and cultural functions that include discourse and use, as well as grammar, lexicon, and phonology, as integral components.

What all discourse-inclusive approaches to language analysis have in common is that they seek to analyze entire coherent segments of authentic language, not simply decontextualized and artificially constructed sentences (as is the typical case in Chomskyan linguistics). This means that in addition to sentence-level grammar, vocabulary, and phonology (if data are oral), the analysis also covers features of language that manifest themselves over stretches of discourse, such as referential ties, discourse connectors, ellipsis, topic continuity, temporal frames or sequences of tense-aspect-modality forms, discourse connectives, ellipsis, and ordering of propositions.[2]

Proponents of communicative language teaching emerged in the mid- to late seventies, arguing that language should be taught as communication and for communication (e.g., Brumfit & Johnson, 1979; Widdowson, 1978). (See Duff, this volume.) They were reacting to

"building-block" approaches to language teaching such as audiolingualism, where sounds and letters are viewed as making up words and morphemes; these in turn are viewed as forming sentences, which learners can then try to use to communicate. With respect to achieving communicative competence, the past and current failures of the building-block approaches led some language methodologists to propose that it would be better to drop all teaching of grammar in favor of providing comprehensible input to learners (e.g., Krashen, 1981). Other methodologists proposed that, instead of being organized around points of grammar, language instruction should be organized around notions such as time, space, and quantity and around social functions such as requests, apologies, and complaints (e.g., van Ek, 1976; Wilkins, 1976).

Early communicative methodology as well as early immersion education (both of which focused on meaning largely to the exclusion of any focus on form) produced learners who often had good receptive skills but whose production, though fluent, was noticeably inaccurate (Harley & Swain, 1984; Larsen-Freeman & Long, 1991). In other words, language learners in such programs did not acquire the grammar of the target language to the same extent that children do when learning their first language (L1). Their acquisition of morphology, in particular, was markedly imperfect (Lightbown & Spada, 2006). Subsequent versions of communicative methodology have been finding ways to focus learners' attention on form and to integrate instruction dealing with specific errors of form and extensive meaning-based language use (Lyster & Mori, 2008; Swain & Lapkin, 2002).

This brings us back to Hymes's notion of communicative competence (Hymes, 1972). Language teachers need to understand the complex and integrated nature of this notion. Canale (1983), drawing on Hymes, described communicative competence in the second language (L2) context as having four major components: (1) *linguistic competence* (knowledge of morphology, syntax, phonology, and lexicon); (2) *sociolinguistic competence* (knowledge of social and cultural factors that influence or are expressed via linguistic choices); (3) *discourse competence* (knowledge of how to use linguistic resources and sociolinguistic competence to produce coherent discourse); and (4) *strategic competence* (knowledge of how to plan communication, compensate for linguistic deficits, elicit input, repair communication breakdowns, etc.).

These competencies are not independent and randomly ordered. The central competency, in our view, is discourse competence, with sociolinguistic competence providing the requisite top-down background knowledge. Top-down knowledge assists learners in getting the overall gist, important details, and social and cultural implications. At the same time, discourse competence interacts with linguistic competence, which provides the bottom-up resources such as key vocabulary, structural patterns, and prosodic or other important pronunciation or orthographic conventions. These competencies all interact in the production or interpretation of the discourse occurring during any given instance of communication. Strategic competence is an available set of cognitive and social strategies that allows language users to deploy the knowledge and resources at their disposal to plan, monitor, assess, and compensate—as needed—during any instance of communication (Canale & Swain, 1980; Celce-Murcia, Dörnyei, & Thurrell, 1995). Given this perspective, it is discourse (not grammar, vocabulary, speech acts, or strategies) that should function as the core organizer for language teaching and learning.

The other five chapters in this section of the book describe a variety of approaches to language teaching fully compatible with a discourse-based approach (content-based and immersion models, task-based and project-based language teaching, English for specific purposes, literature-based approaches, and bilingual education). In the remainder of this chapter, we propose that second and foreign language courses at all levels (even the most general) should be discourse-based, and we provide a description of how this can be accomplished along with teaching the bottom-up language resources (grammar, vocabulary, and pronunciation) and the four language skills (listening, reading, speaking, and writing).

Teaching the language resources

Within a discourse-based approach to language teaching, the bottom-up language areas are no longer taught as ends in themselves but as resources for creating and interpreting discourse.

Pronunciation. The teaching of pronunciation is highly relevant to the teaching of L2 oral dis-

course. Of particular importance are the prosodic or suprasegmental elements, which include the most common combinations of rhythm, stress, and intonation. (See Goodwin, this volume.) In English, the context determines appropriate prosody in any given utterance. The most frequent pragmatic strategy used by English speakers is: (1) to deemphasize given/known information by using lower pitch contours and weaker stress; and (2) to emphasize new or contrastive information by using higher pitch contours and stronger stress. Thus prosody plays a critical role in the management of information and interaction, which argues for highlighting the role of prosody in oral communication and teaching it as part of the productive and receptive oral skills. In fact, many applied linguists argue that prosodic features should have priority over the teaching of sounds (vowels and consonants) in discourse-based approaches (Gilbert, 2008; McNerney & Mendelsohn, 1992).

Grammar. A discourse-based approach to teaching L2 grammar gives importance to the written and spoken discourse segments within which grammatical points are presented or highlighted. It also helps to emphasize the role that grammar plays in "welding clauses, turns, and sentences into discourse" (McCarthy, 1991, p. 62). The vast majority of grammatical choices made in English are context-sensitive (e.g., using the definite versus indefinite article, using active versus passive voice, and choosing the appropriate tense-aspect-modality form). These choices are not sentence-level but discourse-level, context-determined choices. Of particular importance is *cohesion*, which can be usefully regarded as a major component of the grammar of discourse. Through the appropriate use of cohesive devices, textual cohesion facilitates discourse *coherence* (i.e., the manner in which individual sentences or utterances are connected to each other to form a meaningful whole) (Halliday & Hasan, 1976, 1989). It is thus important to give attention to cohesion as part of discourse-based grammar instruction. See Figure 1 for examples of cohesive devices (i.e., referential ties, substitute expressions, ellipsis, and logical connectors).

Vocabulary. Many language teachers and learners equate the learning of L2 vocabulary with memorizing lists of words along with one or two dictionary meanings and perhaps translating these words into the L1. This is a start. However,

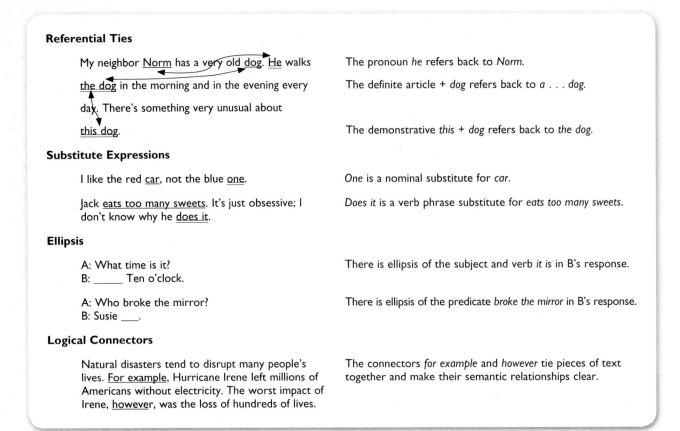

Referential Ties

My neighbor <u>Norm</u> has a very old <u>dog</u>. <u>He</u> walks <u>the dog</u> in the morning and in the evening every day. There's something very unusual about <u>this dog</u>.

The pronoun *he* refers back to *Norm*.

The definite article + *dog* refers back to *a . . . dog*.

The demonstrative *this* + *dog* refers back to *the dog*.

Substitute Expressions

I like the red <u>car</u>, not the blue <u>one</u>.

Jack <u>eats too many sweets</u>. It's just obsessive; I don't know why he <u>does it</u>.

One is a nominal substitute for *car*.

Does it is a verb phrase substitute for *eats too many sweets*.

Ellipsis

A: What time is it?
B: _____ Ten o'clock.

A: Who broke the mirror?
B: Susie ___.

There is ellipsis of the subject and verb *it is* in B's response.

There is ellipsis of the predicate *broke the mirror* in B's response.

Logical Connectors

Natural disasters tend to disrupt many people's lives. <u>For example</u>, Hurricane Irene left millions of Americans without electricity. The worst impact of Irene, <u>however</u>, was the loss of hundreds of lives.

The connectors *for example* and *however* tie pieces of text together and make their semantic relationships clear.

Figure 1. Grammatical cohesive devices.

L2 vocabulary must be experienced in context at the level of discourse for the meaning of any word or lexical phrase to become fully comprehensible to the learner. Etymologically related words in two different languages often function differently in terms of their collocations (the words they associate with), meanings, and discourse functions. For example, the English word *gift* and the German word *Gift* are both nouns that derive from the verbs that mean "give" in English and German. However, the English noun is a countable noun synonymous with "a present," while the German noun is a mass noun meaning "poison." These two words are a drastic case of false cognates (words that look the same and have the same etymology but different meanings). A less drastic example is English *library* and French *librarie*. In this case, the English word translates into French as *bibliotheque,* and the French word translates into English as *bookstore/bookshop*. While the meanings both involve books, they are clearly different.

Vocabulary can be used literally or figuratively, with figurative language including idiomatic and metaphorical uses (Lakoff & Johnson, 1980) that often do not readily translate. For example, *John kicked the bucket* can mean either: (1) "John moved/knocked over the bucket with his foot" or (2) "John died." The interpretation one arrives at depends on the context. However, a learner with no knowledge of the idiom will tend to go with the first meaning in all contexts. Teachers should thus give attention to familiarizing learners with the key L2 vocabulary items for comprehending reading texts or for carrying out assigned tasks and activities. Along with grammatical resources, the appropriate understanding and use of vocabulary items—including lexical phrases and collocations (Nattinger & De Carrico, 1992; Shin & Nation, 2008)—are important areas for the comprehension and production of L2 discourse.

Vocabulary is also a critical part of specialized subject matter where English is taught for specific academic or professional purposes. There can be three types of vocabulary to deal with in these contexts: (1) general academic/professional vocabulary; (2) more specific vocabulary for the general area (e.g., law or biology); and (3) a highly specialized vocabulary for the subfield (e.g., microbiology). Discourse analysis and concordance analysis (access to tokens of word forms used in context in an appropriate corpus[3]) can provide very useful information for teaching vocabulary to L2 learners who are studying a specific discipline. (See also Zimmerman, this volume.)

We should also mention lexical cohesion, which along with grammatical cohesion adds much to the coherence of any piece of discourse. The short example text at the beginning of this chapter illustrates lexical cohesion using synonyms. Lexical cohesion can also be signaled through the use of antonyms, exact or partial repetitions, words exhibiting part-to-whole relations, words that belong to the same semantic class, a class word and a member word, and so forth (Halliday & Hasan, 1976, 1989). See Figure 2 for examples of lexical cohesion.

It is thus worthwhile spending some time helping learners identify such lexical ties in well-selected pieces of discourse since different languages have different preferred conventions for signaling lexical ties, which form cohesive chains over a span of discourse.

Teaching language skills

Listening and reading. When using language for purposes of communication, we are either transmitting our ideas and intentions to an addressee or interpreting the text or message produced by an interlocutor. (Sometimes—as in a conversation—we do both in fairly rapid succession.) When producing discourse, we combine discourse knowledge with the use of strategies for speaking or writing and with audience-relevant contextual factors. When interpreting discourse, we combine discourse knowledge with the use of strategies for listening or reading and rely on our prior knowledge as well as our assessment of the context and topic at hand.

For receptive skills, prior and shared knowledge involve both schematic and contextual knowledge. *Schematic knowledge* consists of both *content schemata* (background information on the topic) and *formal schemata* (knowledge of how discourse

Use of Synonyms

Hurricane Irene was a major <u>calamity</u>. It created a pressing need in many eastern states for <u>disaster</u> relief.	*Calamity* and *disaster* are synonyms, both describing the effects of Irene and thus creating a lexical tie.

Use of Antonyms

Jack Spratt could eat no <u>fat</u>; his wife could eat no <u>lean</u>.	The antonyms *fat* and *lean* in this nursery rhyme create a lexical tie.

Use of Exact or Partial Lexical Repetitions

They asked me for the <u>length</u> and <u>width</u> of the painting, but I couldn't recall how <u>long</u> or <u>wide</u> it was.	Here the noun-adjective pairs *length/long* and *width/wide* help tie the discourse lexically.

Use of Part-Whole Relationships

That's a beautiful <u>house</u>. I especially like the French <u>windows</u>.	The fact that *windows* are a prototypical part of a *house* creates lexical cohesion.

Use of Words in the Same Semantic Class

Fred likes to travel by <u>plane</u>, but his wife is afraid to fly and will travel only by <u>car</u> or <u>train</u>.	Here *plane*, *car*, and *train* are all means of transportation, thus providing lexical cohesion.

Use of a Class/Genus Word and a Related Member/Species Word

Our neighbor died of acute <u>leukemia</u>. It's a very unforgiving <u>disease</u>.	The relationship between *leukemia* and *disease* helps make the text cohesive.

Figure 2. Examples of lexical cohesion.

is organized with respect to different genres, topics, or purposes) (Carrell & Eisterhold, 1983). *Contextual knowledge* is the listener's overall sense of the situation regarding the participants, the setting, the topic, and the purpose. In written discourse, Grabe (2009) reminds us, readers should learn to consider the title and subtitles of the text, the author's background, and the larger context in which the text appeared.

Teachers can provide learners with a variety of listening and reading activities that will engage them in interpreting language at the discourse level. Listeners need to combine aural recognition of words with the prosodic signals coming from stress, pauses, and intonation and then use lexicogrammatical signals such as discourse markers and word order to achieve an understanding of the spoken message. Listening materials should be varied and can include recorded lectures and speeches, recorded conversations, and radio/television broadcasts. Activities can include practice in getting the overall gist, noting details, doing a dictation of an excerpt, completing a cloze passage, and discussing what one has understood with classmates.

To process a written text rather than spoken discourse the reader needs to decode the written words to interpret the message by assigning meaning to strings of words and to figure out the author's purpose and intention. Effective readers know how to select and apply reading strategies skillfully, while poor readers often become confused or side-tracked. When the writer's intention and the reader's expectations match, a good interpretation of the text is more readily achievable.

A well-written text exhibits coherence and cohesion, both of which facilitate reader interpretation. Coherence is what organizes a text such that it conforms to a consistent worldview based on one's experience, culture, or knowledge of formal conventions regarding the order in which ideas and arguments are presented. Grammatical and lexical cohesion, which we have previously discussed, also provide links that help to shape words, phrases, and clauses into coherent discourse.

L2 reading teachers often start a reading unit by doing intensive in-class reading with their students, which involves going over a text in detail and helping students to interpret the meaning of words in context, having them use the dictionary sparingly but as needed, and having them summarize the gist of the text (segment by segment and then as a whole) as well as giving their personal responses to it. Such experiences, along with explicit focus on reading strategies, can encourage students to become independent readers, capable of doing extensive reading on their own. Learners need to engage with a variety of multipurpose reading materials so that they learn to develop effective reading strategies and to make wise strategic choices with respect to interpreting any given text.

Speaking and writing. Discourse-based approaches to L2 listening and reading provide a solid foundation for teaching L2 speaking and writing for communication. Speaking (unless planned in advance and written down to be read aloud) shares with live, unrecorded listening the fact that spoken language happens in the here and now and must be produced and processed in real time (Cook, 1989). Given time pressure, there are many possible causes of miscommunication: less than optimal L2 proficiency causes the speaker to produce inaccurate or inappropriate language; the speaker and hearer do not share the same culture, background information, and expectations; inappropriate or inaccurate transfer takes place from the speaker's (or listener's) L1; and so on. Following Grice (1975), we assume that in any oral interaction the speaker wants to communicate ideas, feelings, and attitudes to the hearer that are relevant to the situation at hand. If any of the aforementioned problems occur when speakers use their L2, the spoken discourse they produce can be misunderstood. Teachers need to provide L2 speakers with numerous and varied opportunities to communicate orally in their L2 by role-playing speech acts (e.g., requesting, complimenting, and complaining), by being polite or direct as needed, by making oral presentations, by interviewing or being interviewed, and by debating, among other activities. For classes teaching L2 speaking that focus primarily on conversational skills, Wong and Waring (2010) guide teachers in how to expose learners to authentic conversational openings, closings, topic shifts, repairs, and so on in English. By combining communication strategies with ever-improving linguistic and sociocultural knowledge, the L2 speaker's oral discourse will steadily improve.

When L2 writing is viewed as a skill needed for communication, it has much in common with discourse-based reading and speaking in the L2. It shares the features of written text with the reading process, and it shares with speaking the features of the production process. To facilitate communication, the writer is responsible for creating a text that is coherent and cohesive and for taking the reader's background knowledge and expectations into account. While much of spoken language is spontaneous and unplanned, much of written language is planned and less dependent on context. The teacher must get L2 writers to liberate themselves from dependence on context by continually reminding them to consider and accommodate to an absent reader/audience that does not share their immediate physical and temporal context (Flower, 1979; Ong, 1982).

The writing process has also usefully been viewed as socialized dialogic speech (e.g., a conversation) that becomes monologic speech as in an oral presentation (Vygotsky, 1962/1978) and that must then be adapted to conform to the conventions of the writing system (Myers, 1987). The two most universal written genres are narrative (event-telling) and exposition (informing, reporting, or persuading). Narrative is easier to start with. L2 writers can describe what they did last week or yesterday, keep diaries or journals, write accounts of field trips, and so on. These writings can be brief paragraphs or extended essays, depending on the writer's level of proficiency and literacy skills. Expository writing can begin by learners drawing on personal experience to write a review of a book they have read, a journalistic-style first-hand report of a sporting event, or a review of an artistic performance or exhibit they have attended. Eventually, as L2 writers gain advanced proficiency and need to use English for academic and professional purposes, this type of expository writing will involve the use of sources (employing appropriate citation conventions) to present information or argue for a position on a significant social or political issue.

L2 writing shares a great deal with L1 writing except that greater feedback and correction are typically needed in L2 writing in the areas of coherence and organization, cohesion, grammar, and lexical choice. When targeted preparatory work is done, some of the L2 problem areas can be minimized. This can be achieved by choosing carefully selected readings and related speaking activities, and by planning tasks prior to writing. Showing L2 learners how to compose, get feedback, rewrite, and edit is part of the recursive feedback and error-correction process that helps L2 learners improve their written discourse. (See also Weigle, this volume.)

Implementing discourse-based language programs

To implement a discourse-based approach to language teaching, we must first ensure that the course syllabus or program curriculum prioritizes the social context of learning and language use. A discourse-oriented curriculum gives special emphasis to three areas: (1) context; (2) text/discourse types; and (3) communicative goals. The specification of the goals, tasks, and procedures should always take the learning context into account. Expectations related to student achievement should carefully consider the learners' linguistic, educational, and cultural backgrounds. Texts, examples of authentic discourse, and other teaching materials should be selected or designed to be compatible with learners' needs and interests. The classroom activities developed around these materials should anticipate and simulate real-life communication needs outside the language classroom.

A discourse-oriented curriculum encompasses the dynamic relationships existing between discourse analysis, language resources, and language skills. It enables the teacher to operate like a well-equipped camera: He or she starts with a wide-angle lens, exposing learners to the larger context; then he or she zooms in on various details and features to enable the learners to analyze, practice, and acquire the linguistic and sociocultural knowledge inherent in the discourse, which in turn will help make them more competent users of the target language.[4]

This type of language curriculum requires discourse-based assessment tools. Thus, instead of assessing learners using discrete-point multiple-choice tests, teachers should use more holistic means of assessing mastery of learning goals. Essays and dictations can be used to evaluate content, grammar, lexical knowledge, spelling, and punctuation. Cloze (or gap) passages can be used to assess the learners' discourse-based ability to use articles, tenses, prepositions, and other grammatical forms correctly. Error detection and correction exercises can be presented as short coherent texts that contain the students' most frequent language errors, which they are asked to identify and correct (perhaps in pair or group work).

Achievement in oral skills should be assessed using face-to-face interviews, recorded small-group tasks, and short oral presentations made using only a minimal outline for cues. Often the best assessments consist of a set of integrated tasks, all of which have been previously practiced several times. For example, the students can listen to a lecture, take notes, summarize the lecture (to demonstrate comprehension), and then write a response to the lecture to express their opinion (whether or not they agree with the lecture's content and why).

Ideally, many discourse-based activities and tasks are done during the course of the school term, and the products of these activities should be kept in chronological order in each learner's individual portfolio to allow ongoing and course-final assessments of each learner's achievement as well as to permit feedback at regular intervals on individual strengths and weaknesses.

To remove what is perhaps the biggest obstacle to getting teachers to move beyond ad hoc communicative approaches, all language teachers and other related professionals (e.g., curriculum developers, textbook writers, and language testers) must receive a thorough grounding in the application of discourse analysis to language teaching. This, in turn, will assist them in arriving at a well-grounded discourse-based approach to L2 teaching. Although teachers in training often receive instruction in grammar and phonetics as well as training in teaching the language skills, few teacher education programs require a course in pedagogical discourse analysis. We see such a course as a much-needed addition to language-teacher preparation programs and encourage language educators to consider the following published resources for the development of an appropriate course: (1) for teachers in training with little or no background in discourse, we recommend Cook (1989) or Nunan (1993); (2) for those ready for more extensive and sophisticated grounding, we recommend McCarthy (1991), Celce-Murcia and Olshtain (2000), and Johnstone (2008).

As part of such a course, language teachers also need to learn how to impart awareness of relevant discourse features to their learners as both top-down and bottom-up processes (see Martinez, 2011, for suggestions). Both teachers and learners need to take responsibility for the collaborative teaching-learning process within the discourse community. Ideally, this process becomes established in the language classroom whenever a discourse-based approach is well implemented. Teachers, however, must be properly prepared so that they can enable such shared responsibility to take place.

CLASSROOM APPLICATIONS

When we translate the principles described here into classroom applications, we need to focus on two major elements: the relevant context and the relevant discourse features of the learning material (consisting of authentic spoken or written texts). In this section, we discuss three examples of discourse-based language lessons: (1) the teaching of the present perfect progressive in English, highlighting the teaching of grammar in a discourse-based approach; (2) the teaching of a written narrative text; and (3) the teaching of a written expository text. The objective of these teaching examples is to strengthen the connection between theory and practice while supplying some concrete instances of classroom teaching and learning.

Teaching the present perfect progressive within a discourse-based approach

The present perfect progressive (PPP) is a highly context-dependent form. After collecting 250 authentic discourse segments in which the PPP occurs, Celce-Murcia and Yoshida (2003) examined these spoken and written English tokens of PPP. Their analysis led to four important findings that describe the use of PPP:

1. The activity mentioned may have been completed just before, at, or after the moment of speech, depending on the context.
2. Temporal framing may occur overtly with the use of a time adverbial, or there may be an earlier sentence in the discourse indicating that the time frame is "recent."
3. The PPP is typically part of a three-move structure, with the first move providing background (in present or present perfect tense), the second and most crucial move highlighting an ongoing activity of concern (in PPP), and the third move giving some evaluation (in present tense).
4. The discourse context and the semantics of the entire verb phrase along with any accompanying temporal adverbs are all part of the meaning conveyed by the PPP.

Based on these features of the PPP, Celce-Murcia (2008) suggests teaching applications that are compatible with a discourse-based approach. The sequence of activities begins with learners' listening to an authentic segment from a radio talk show (the names of the participants have been changed):

Host: I'm Dr. Mary Smith and you're on talk radio. Hello?
Caller: Good afternoon, Dr. Smith. I'm Lucy and I'm 59. I'd just like to share a positive thing that I have found in the last year or so. I've been hiking and find that this is a wonderful way to keep your weight down and meet some people and just really feel good. (Celce-Murcia & Yoshida, 2003, p. 6)

The students may listen to the recording several times, retell the conversation in their own words and talk about the theme of weight loss or maintenance and fitness. Then the teacher shows them the transcript, pointing out that the caller's segment follows the typical pattern for use of PPP in having the three moves: (1) background in the present tense; (2) activity of the focus (hiking), the speaker's special concern, in PPP; and (3) evaluation in the present tense.

Staying within the theme of "physical activity for good health," the students now talk, in groups or individually, about their own activities, for example, *I've been jogging* or *I've been swimming every day*. This is a time when students can begin to attach an accurate meaning to the grammatical form and gain fluency in using this form. The discourse-level assignment that follows consists of students generating a segment like Lucy's, working with a partner who begins with the question: "What have you been doing lately to keep fit?" This activity should be generated and rehearsed orally and then written out as a dialogue with the question first and then the answer (as in the example discourse).

As an expansion of this use of the PPP, students can work with complaints, where this grammatical form is often used. When a request is made to address the source of a complaint, the justification for the request is often in PPP. For example, if the request that addresses the source of the complaint is *Don't get in line in front of me* or *Please turn down the volume on your radio*, the justification for the request could be something like *I've been waiting in line a long time* or *I've been trying to do my homework*, respectively. Instances of similar

situations involving complaints can be drawn from the students' real-life experiences and then role-played using sentences with the PPP.

These examples for teaching the use of the PPP in English have been embedded in a context and are drawn from naturalistic discourse. Such learning activities help students understand that grammar is a systematic resource for creating discourse. This is a direction that language teachers and material developers can take to improve grammar instruction within a discourse-based approach.

Reading narratives in the second or foreign language

The reading process involves at least three participants: the writer, the text, and the reader. The reader requires prior knowledge to activate schematic and contextual knowledge as well as linguistic and textual knowledge to process the text. The first and most important step that a novice reader has to make is to develop a drive for "making sense." In the interaction that takes place between reader and text, readers match new text-presented knowledge with their content schemata (or stored knowledge) and with their formal schemata (or knowledge regarding text structure, based on prior reading experience). Following a discourse-based approach, the students should receive ample exposure to a variety of text types. During the reading process, the teacher asks students to focus on elements of coherence and cohesion, on top-down strategies and on bottom-up features that they need to understand the text, and on the individual strategies that lead to making sense of a new text (Celce-Murcia & Olshtain, 2000).

The following short narrative (Heyer, 1996) serves as an example of how to teach L2 reading via a discourse-based approach.

John and Bobby

A long time ago, in a small house in Scotland, two friends lived together. Their names were John and Bobby. John and Bobby were not rich, but they were happy. They had a warm fire when it was cold outside. They had good food to eat when they were hungry. They were never lonely because they had each other.

John and Bobby liked to take long walks together. After their walk, John usually cooked dinner. John and Bobby ate dinner and then sat in front of the fire. They had a simple but good life.

Then, in the spring of 1858, John got sick and died. He was buried in a cemetery in Edinburgh, Scotland. After John was buried, Bobby stood at John's grave and cried. "Come on Bobby," friends said. "It's time to go home." Bobby went home, but later he returned to the cemetery. He sat down near John's grave. He stayed there all night. Bobby stayed at the cemetery for the next fourteen years. . . .

Finally, in 1872, Bobby died, too. Friends buried him in a little grave near John. (p. 31)

Prior to actually reading the text with the students, the teacher should develop an activity to build background knowledge on the topic of friendship and thus familiarize the learners with the vocabulary and grammar that are relevant to the text. It is important at this stage not to talk about dogs since this will be the special surprise in the passage. In fact, the teacher should talk about the title and ask students if they think that this is a passage about friends or perhaps brothers and what they might expect the text to be about.

During the first reading of the story, students can be asked some leading questions such as "What do John and Bobby do together?" and "How do they feel?" Then they can discuss at which point in the story they realized that Bobby was a dog and what made them think of this possibility. Since this is a typical narrative, students can be guided to look for the sequence of events and the appropriate time expressions and tenses that build the chronological sequence. They can also consider the main verbs, determining which are action verbs and which allow the reader to follow the plot.

At the stage of text evaluation, the students can discuss the language elements that help the writer keep the secret of Bobby's identity until the very end. They can also discuss language elements that engage the reader and make the story interesting.

At the end of the sequence of activities suggested here, the students will have become aware of the structure of narratives in English as well as of the way in which events within the story are presented with relevant time expressions. They will have paid attention to elements of cohesion such as word and name repetitions, the use of the definite article to indicate known information, and how the paragraphs were structured to make the story interesting. They will also have learned to evaluate the language used to add interest and feelings. This is very much in line with a discourse-based approach. Furthermore, the teacher can make good use of this reading passage to engage students in spoken interactions as well as in writing personal narratives on topics involving friendship or pets.

Reading expository texts

We read expository texts to gain new knowledge and information. Expository texts are typical of instructional settings at all levels, particularly in the academic world. Readers of expository texts acquire new information, interpret and analyze this information according to their needs, and use it in reasoning and action. Some expository texts might be ordered chronologically to present historical facts, personal accounts, or procedures for the reader to follow. More often, however, expository texts organize information in a logical manner, describing cause and effect; comparison and contrast; or processes, behaviors, or conditions.

Expository texts use language that suits a rather objective presentation of facts; therefore, passive verb forms are common in such texts. Vocabulary that is more academic in nature is used, and when the text represents a specific field of inquiry, some of the vocabulary may be specialized. All these facts tend to make the reading of expository texts more complicated than the reading of narratives.

When teaching expository texts according to a discourse-based approach, both careful preparation before reading and the activities that follow the reading are very important. The following example (Lahav, Barzel, & Shrire, 2003) illustrates some of these features:

A Coral Reef

Coral reefs are dynamic ecosystems, but they are also one of the most endangered living things on our planet. If the present rate of destruction continues, 70 percent of the world's coral reefs will be destroyed within our lifetime. Corals and coral reefs are very sensitive. Even the smallest change in the natural reef environment can have disastrous effects. (p. 34)

When students read such an expository passage (only a small section is given here for purposes of illustration), preparation before reading is important and will have two main objectives: (1) to allow students to encounter the key words of the passage and practice them; and (2) to build the background knowledge related to endangered species, in general, and coral reefs, in particular.

In the preparatory stage, the teacher discusses coral reefs to encourage students to use the knowledge they already have and perhaps motivate them to find out more about the topic. Thus leading questions such as "What do you know about coral reefs?" "Where do coral reefs exist?" and "Why are they considered endangered?" could lead to a discussion in class and/ or to individual searches for information. Words such as *endangered, dynamic, destruction, disastrous,* and *effect* should be discussed with respect to the environment in general; the word *ecosystem* can be viewed as a more specialized item. However, students need to understand all these words to get the message of the passage.

The second paragraph in the same passage presents a more specific description of processes related to coral reefs:

> Coral reefs have many important functions in the global ecosystem. First, the marine life removes and recycles carbon dioxide from the ocean. This process helps maintain the balance of gasses on our planet and reduces the threat of global warming. Second, the coral reefs slow down water before it reaches the shore. This helps protect coasts from strong currents and waves. Finally, many natural resources can be found in coral reefs. (p. 34)

Here students can be guided to pay attention to markers of sequence within the paragraph while also looking for connections with the previous paragraph. Features of both coherence and cohesion can be pointed out. The use of simple present tense is prominent here since we are talking about natural processes and phenomena. This can help students who are still uncertain about the distinction between simple and progressive aspect to grasp the use of the simple present to express timeless facts and states.

The reading of expository texts often leads to further investigation being carried out by the students themselves and to a variety of writing activities, all of which fit the discourse-based approach. In this case, students can seek out a short text about another endangered species to share with the class for reading and further discussion.

FUTURE TRENDS

Future research in discourse analysis will supply practitioners with improved knowledge about language use in authentic written and spoken texts. Such knowledge can serve as the basis for developing improved reading programs. It enables teachers to focus on discourse features that can facilitate reading in the learners' L1 as well as in their L2. Dewitz, Jones, and Leahy (2009) claim that, today, most reading programs are missing three crucial research-based features: (1) explicit teaching; (2) focus on critical skills related to relevant texts; and (3) a teaching process that gradually transfers the responsibility for reading comprehension from the teacher to the students. These three elements are fully compatible with a discourse-based approach, and it is hoped that they will become common practice in all reading programs.

Future classrooms will look different (many classrooms in the world already look different), with interactive white boards, computers, multimedia programs, and so on. The advantage of having a cutting-edge technological environment for a discourse-based approach to language teaching is first and foremost the possibility of creating a multifaceted learning context that exposes students to many authentic and dynamic texts simultaneously. The principles guiding the classroom applications discussed in this chapter will be the same, but the variation in activities and texts will be much greater. For instance, while teaching the PPP and using the theme of fitness, the teacher can bring to class a variety of interviews with people who can describe "how they have been keeping fit" from existing sites and available materials on the Internet.[5] Students will be able to look for their own materials, choose and select what is relevant, and then present the research to the whole class, all in a single classroom session.

When reading passages such as "John and Bobby," students can respond to ongoing questions as they read; they might also color-mark the story on their individual screens to highlight various discourse features and then project them on the interactive white board. Teachers will be able to show students pictures from Scotland and the actual graves of John and Bobby. They will be able to add other stories about dogs and friends and expand the classroom beyond its four walls. All this will require careful preparation and research on the part of teachers, and the students and teachers will have endless opportunities to share the responsibilities involved in the learning process. Some of these changes are already happening in English learning centers throughout the world, but there are still many classrooms where such positive change has not yet taken place.

CONCLUSION

This chapter argues that all contemporary instructional L2 programs should be communicatively oriented and discourse-based. This means that instruction begins with one or more carefully selected exemplars of spoken and/or written discourse that—in terms of topic and content—meet learners' needs and interests. The teacher first activates schemata and background knowledge and engages the students in top-down comprehension. There must also be attention to the relevant details of bottom-up language processing. There should be follow-up activities to practice any challenging language features that the learners are ready to tackle and more global communicative activities that allow for the consolidation of the language and content through skills-based activities for listening, reading, speaking, and writing.

SUMMARY

➤ The ability to comprehend and produce L2 discourse is a crucial part of communicative competence in an L2.

➤ Communicative approaches to language teaching should be discourse-centered and give attention to both top-down processing skills and bottom-up language resources.

➤ There are many different approaches to analyzing discourse as well as numerous types of

oral and written discourse. Teachers need to be eclectic and draw on the analytic approaches most useful for their learners while also exposing their learners to a variety of discourse types.

➤ Communicative language teaching allows for a variety of discourse-based approaches: content-based, immersion, literature-based, task-based, project-based, or a combination of these.

➤ Discourse-based approaches to L2 instruction require new and holistic forms of curriculum development and assessment.

➤ Language teachers must have basic competence in discourse analysis and explicit training in how to integrate discourse and pedagogy to promote L2 learning.

DISCUSSION QUESTIONS

1. What are the arguments the authors give in support of discourse-based L2 instruction? Are you convinced? Why or why not?

2. What are the differences between teaching L2 grammar, vocabulary, or pronunciation using a discourse-based approach and using more traditional approaches?

3. Have you ever experienced learning an L2 from a teacher who used (at least partially) a discourse-based approach? If so, describe the experience for your classmates.

4. As a prospective language teacher, what would you like to see included in a course to train L2 teachers in pedagogical discourse analysis?

SUGGESTED ACTIVITIES

1. Select an authentic paragraph-length text, and describe the discourse-based L2 teaching activities you could develop based on the text (consider grammar, vocabulary, and pronunciation and the four language skills).

2. Find a decontextualized drill in an L2 textbook, and discuss the ways in which the objective being drilled could be more effectively approached through discourse.

3. Choose a self-contained discourse segment from a subject-matter textbook. Design three different speaking activities using this discourse segment that involve learner input and pair or group work.

4. In a small group, brainstorm activities that could be used to help teachers in training to learn some aspect of pedagogical discourse analysis.

FURTHER READING

Celce-Murcia, M., & Olshtain, E. (2000). *Discourse and context in language teaching*. New York, NY: Cambridge University Press.

This source provides a more comprehensive account of many of the concepts and teaching suggestions made in this chapter.

Frodesen, J., & Holten, C. (Eds.). (2003). *The power of context in language teaching and learning*. Boston, MA: Thomson/Heinle.

This collection of 16 articles deals with discourse-based data analysis of grammar and lexicon and discourse-based pedagogy for language teaching.

McCarthy, M., Matthiessen, C., & Slade, D. (2010). Discourse analysis. In N. Schmitt (Ed.), *An introduction to applied linguistics* (2nd ed., pp. 53–68). London, UK: Hodder.

This is an article-length introduction to different types of discourse analysis for teachers.

McGroarty, M. (Ed.). (2002). Discourse and dialogue [Special issue]. *Annual Review of Applied Linguistics, 22*.

This volume of the *Annual Review of Applied Linguistics* is devoted to the role of discourse analysis in research and language teaching, with sections on approaches to discourse analysis, its applications in the classroom, and discourse-relevant assessment measures.

ENDNOTES

[1] This chapter draws on work we have done in Celce-Murcia and Olshtain (2000, 2005) and Olshtain and Celce-Murcia (2001).

[2] Referential ties, discourse connectors, and ellipsis are presented here in Figure 1. Topic continuity is an index of how long a given topic persists in a stretch of discourse. Temporal frames are established by the use of temporal adverbs (e.g., *yesterday, recently*) or verb forms (e.g., *be going to*, simple past tense). Tense-aspect-modality forms are often parts of a temporal frame. For example, a future scenario often begins with *be going to* and continues with *will/'ll: I'm going to Europe on vacation. I'll visit London, Paris, and Rome.* The ordering of propositions can be critical to interpretation. For example, compare *John came home when I turned off the computer* and *I turned off the computer when John came home.*

[3] A corpus is a searchable database, now generally online, of spoken and/or written texts, which can be used to research words and their collocations along with other discourse features.

[4] We are indebted to Howard Williams (person communication) for the camera analogy.

[5] There are, however, some places in the world where English teachers do not yet have access to advanced technology in their work environments. In such cases, teachers will need to use alternative strategies such as library research.

28 | Content-Based and Immersion Models of Second/Foreign Language Teaching

MARGUERITE ANN SNOW

KEY QUESTIONS

➤ How did content come to play such a prominent role in some forms of second and foreign language teaching?

➤ How do the various models of content-based language teaching differ from each other in terms of setting, student population, or goals?

➤ What strategies can teachers use to assist students to learn the second or foreign language and the targeted content?

EXPERIENCE

Kimiko Yamamoto was excited about studying English in a summer program in California. Upon her arrival, after studying English for four years in high school in Japan, she placed at the intermediate level. On the first day of the summer program, she met her teachers and fellow students, who, like her, came from different countries around the world. She was surprised to find out when she attended her first class—ESL 4—that she would be studying about earthquakes. She wondered what earthquakes had to do with improving her English. Her teacher went over the class syllabus for the first four weeks of the class, telling the students that they would learn a lot about the topic of earthquakes and a lot of language skills such as strategies for reading faster, listening for main ideas, expanding vocabulary, and practicing oral skills. Kimiko was curious about this new way of teaching and looked forward to the summer program. She hoped it would be more interesting than studying grammar, which she had done much of the time in her high school classes back home.

WHAT IS CONTENT-BASED LANGUAGE TEACHING?

To define *content-based language teaching* (CBLT), it is helpful to look back at the history of methods of second or foreign language (SFL) teaching. Historically, *content* has had many different interpretations. In methods such as grammar-translation, content was defined as the grammatical structures of the target language. In the audiolingual method, content consisted of grammatical structures, vocabulary, or sound patterns usually presented in dialogue form. More recently, communicative approaches have defined content as the communication purposes for which speakers use the SFL. Thus, in a class following a notional-functional syllabus, the content of a unit might be "celebrations" and a lesson might cover the notion of invitations, with students learning about typical question types, polite versus informal invitation forms, and ways to accept or decline invitations. Similarly, the content of a Natural Approach lesson might be a game in which students locate the person who matches a certain description by asking each other questions, thereby using language for problem solving. (See Celce-Murcia, this volume, for an overview of methods and approaches.)

By the 1980s, another definition of content emerged in an approach that is the focus of this chapter. Content, in this interpretation, is the use of subject matter for SFL teaching purposes (Brinton, Snow, & Wesche, 1989, 2003). Subject matter may consist of topics or themes based on student interest or need in an adult English as a second language (ESL) or English as a foreign language (EFL) setting, or it may be very specific, such as the subjects that students are currently studying in their elementary school class. This approach is in keeping with the English for specific purposes tradition, where the vocational or occupational needs of the learner are identified and used as the basis for curriculum and materials development. (See Johns & Price, this volume.) CBLT often has a strong English for academic purposes (EAP) orientation, in which the main instructional goal is to prepare second language (L2) students for the types of academic tasks they will encounter in school, college, or university.

More recently, Davison and Williams (2001) have defined *CBLT* as a "heuristic label for a diverse group of curriculum approaches which share a concern for facilitating language learning broadly defined, through varied but systematic linking of subject matter and language in the context of learning activities" (p. 57). The early work in CBLT originated in North America; more recently, CBLT has become popular in Europe under the label content and language integrated learning (CLIL), with the goal of assisting school children to become multilingual to facilitate the integration of the European Union (Coyle, Hood, & Marsh, 2010;

Dalton-Puffer, 2011). Thus, CBLT is an umbrella term for a multifaceted approach to SFL teaching that differs in terms of factors such as educational setting, program objectives, and target population but shares a common point of departure—the integration of language teaching aims with content instruction.

Models of CBLT

As CBLT has grown in popularity, a variety of models have emerged. In this section, I describe some of the key models in use in different settings and discuss characteristics that distinguish them from each other. One way to distinguish CBLT is the setting in which it is implemented, that is, in an L2 and or foreign language (FL) classroom. A second way to distinguish CBLT models is whether the approach serves *language majority* students or *language minority* students (Lightbown, 2014). Yet another way is by instructional level. There are many well-developed CBLT programs at the elementary school level; other models have typically been implemented successfully at the secondary or post-secondary levels with adolescents or adults (Brinton, Snow, & Wesche, 1989, 2003; M. A. Snow, 2013). Finally, another way to capture underlying differences in content-based models is to look at the degree of emphasis on language and content that underlies a particular course or program. As shown in Figure 1, Met (1999), places content-driven models at one end of a continuum and language-driven models at the other end. Five models of CBLT are described here to illustrate the continuum.

Immersion education. The *immersion model* of foreign language education is perhaps the prototypical content-based approach and is considered

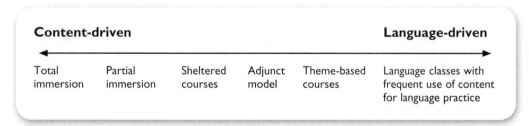

Figure 1. Content-based language teaching: A continuum of content and language integration.

content-driven according to Figure 1. The first immersion program was established in 1965, spearheaded by English-speaking parents in a suburb of Montreal, Canada, who wanted their children to acquire greater levels of proficiency in French than were typically achieved in traditional French classes. Immersion programs have since flourished in Canada. They are found in all Canadian provinces and offer a laboratory for the study of second language acquisition (SLA). The first immersion program in the United States, the Spanish immersion program in Culver City, California, started in 1972. In the United States, there has been a steady growth in immersion programs over the past 40 years. By the end of 2011, there were more than 440 immersion programs in 38 U.S. states, providing education in such foreign languages as Arabic, Chinese, French, German, Hawaiian, Japanese, and Mandarin, with Spanish being by far the most common (The Center for Applied Linguistics, 2011).

In the immersion model, English-speaking elementary school students receive the majority of their schooling through the medium of their FL. Immersion students in Culver City, for instance, learn to read, do mathematics problems, and conduct science experiments in Spanish; in fact, they go about the business of school like all other children—but in their FL. The immersion model is one of the most carefully researched language programs (Genesee 1987; Tedick, Christian, & Fortune, 2011). Immersion children consistently perform at or above grade level scholastically, they are on par with their monolingual peers in English language development, and by the end of elementary school, they are functional bilinguals.

The Culver City Spanish Immersion program is an example of *early total immersion* because the FL is used for most or all academic instruction beginning in kindergarten or grade 1. Other variations have developed over time; these programs differ with respect to the amount of time the FL is used for instruction and the grade in which the program begins. In *delayed immersion*, the onset of instruction in the FL begins in the middle elementary grades. *Late immersion* programs do not typically begin until the end of elementary school or the beginning of secondary school. *Partial immersion* typically involves devoting approximately 50% of instructional time to instruction taught in the L2. *Heritage language immersion* programs that promote Native American languages such as Ojibwe, Yup'ik, and Chinook can be found in the United States (Lenker & Rhodes, 2007); in Canada, there are also programs whose goal is restoring aboriginal languages such as Mohawk and Cayuga (Richards & Burnaby, 2008). *Double immersion* programs in which French and Hebrew serve as the FLs have been successful in Canada as well. The immersion model has also been implemented in international settings such as Hungary, Spain, and Finland (Johnson & Swain 1997) and, more recently, in Hong Kong (Hoare & Kong, 2008) and China (Hoare, 2010).

Theme-based model. On the other end of the continuum presented in Figure 1 are language classes with frequent use of content for language practice such as foreign language in the elementary school programs in the United States in which the FL is taught several times a week for short periods (e.g., 20 minutes) and the curriculum makes use of topics such as "holidays" and "culture" or draws on content from other school subjects such as science or geography (Curtain & Dahlberg, 2010).[1] Thematic curricula have been widely implemented in U.S. elementary schools serving native English-speaking (Walmsley, 1994) and L2 students (Gianelli, 1997). Such instruction is language-driven in that selected topics or themes provide the content from which teachers extract language learning activities. The theme-based model is also popular in language institutes at the post-secondary level, where classes are often composed of students of diverse language backgrounds or interests whose common goal is to attend college or university in an English-speaking country. The teacher's goal is to select topics suitable for a heterogeneous class of international students who need to improve their academic skills. A typical example is the theme-based course, *Animal Issues*, designed for students attending Kwansei Gakuin University, School of Policy Studies in Japan as a way to develop students' academic skills and language proficiency as well as increase their policy studies content knowledge (Evans, 2006). The semester-long course covered the subtopics of "endangered animals," "wildlife trafficking," "pets in society," "zoos," "whaling," and "animal research." Similarly, the ESL 4 class designed around the theme of "earthquakes" in which Kimiko (the student in the Experience section of this chapter), was enrolled covered subtopics such as "earthquake geology" and "earthquake preparedness."

Noting that many early theme-based courses lacked a principled basis for the selection of themes and activities, Stoller and Grabe (1997) offered the first systematic framework for theme-based instruction. Their Six T's Approach helps teachers organize content resources and select appropriate language learning activities:

1. *Themes* are the central ideas that organize major curricular units selected to meet student needs and interests, program resources, and teacher abilities and interests. "Insects" might constitute an elementary school theme, while "demography" might be chosen for a postsecondary ESL program.

2. *Topics* are the subunits of content that explore more specific aspects of the theme. A unit with the theme "Native Americans in the southwest" might include as topics the Navajo, the Hopi, and the Apache.

3. *Texts* could include readings from various genres, videos, audiotapes, maps, lectures, graphic representations, guest speakers, or field trips.

4. *Threads* are linkages across units that create greater curricular coherence. The thread responsibility, for example, might be used to link the units developed around the themes of "civil rights," "pollution," or "Native Americans."

5. *Tasks* are the day-to-day instructional activities. Tasks include debates and reading/writing activities across different rhetorical or academic genres (e.g., compare/contrast or classification).

6. *Transitions* are explicitly planned actions that provide coherence across the topics in a unit and across tasks within topics. An example of a transition in a unit on "demography" is shifting the emphasis from trends in global population to trends in developing countries to trends in developed countries and, finally, to trends in the students' home countries.

Sheltered model. Sheltered courses exist in a variety of secondary and post-secondary settings in both L2 and FL settings. The term *sheltered* derives from the model's deliberate separation of L2 students from native speakers of the target language for the purpose of content instruction. The original sheltered program was implemented at the University of Ottawa in 1982 as an alternative to the traditional university FL class (Edwards, Wesche, Krashen, & Clément, 1984). At the University of Ottawa, students could opt to take a content course, such as Introduction to Psychology, conducted in their L2 in lieu of taking a traditional language class. All instruction in the sheltered class was given in the L2 by content faculty. French sections were offered for native English-speaking students and English sections for native French-speaking students. At the beginning of each lecture, the language instructor held short sessions to go over key terms or provide students with useful expressions, such as polite ways to interrupt the professor to request clarification; however, there was no separate language class per se. Comparisons of the sheltered psychology students with students attending more traditional ESL and French as a second language classes found no significant differences in the gains of the two groups in L2 proficiency despite the fact that the sheltered students had not formally studied the L2. In addition to their gains in L2 proficiency, the sheltered students demonstrated content mastery at the same levels as the comparison students enrolled in native-speaker sections of the psychology course. Furthermore, the sheltered students reported greater self-confidence in their abilities to use their L2 as a result of participation in such a class.

The sheltered model has also been used extensively in middle and high school settings in the United States where ESL students are placed in classes such as *ESL Math* and *ESL Social Studies*. This model of CBLT is placed close to the content-driven end of the continuum because students are enrolled in an actual content class. These courses are frequently an alternative to courses taught in the students' native languages in settings where trained bilingual teachers are not available or where the student population is heterogeneous. Sheltered courses are an alternative to traditional ESL classes (which are often taught in isolation from the rest of the school curriculum) and give students access to school subjects from which they might otherwise be barred on the basis of their developing English proficiency. Sheltered classes follow the regular curriculum; however, instruction is geared to students' developing levels of L2 proficiency through the use of specific instructional strategies and materials such as visual aids, preteaching of vocabulary, and building students' background knowledge (Echevarria & Short, 2010; Rosen & Sasser, 1997). Sheltered courses can offer an effective approach to CBLT for ESL students whose language skills may not yet be developed enough for them to take regular content courses alongside native English speakers.

Adjunct model. The adjunct model is a content-based approach in which students are concurrently enrolled in a language class and a content course. This model is typically implemented in post-secondary settings where such linking or bridging between language and discipline departments is feasible. However, it has also been successfully implemented in paired biology/ESL and history/ESL classes in a California high school (Wegrzecka-Kowalewski, 1997) and, more recently, by secondary school teachers in Australia who met outside the classroom to discuss and plan their respective lessons (Arkoudis, 2006). In the Thai context, Hurst and Davison (2005) describe how secondary ESL and content teachers at the International School in Bangkok collaborated on the curriculum to meet the needs of students speaking English as a second or additional language.

A key feature of the adjunct model is the coordination of objectives and assignments by language and content instructors. The language class becomes content-based in the sense that the students' needs in the content class dictate the activities of the language class. An example of the adjunct model is Project LEAP: Learning English for Academic Purposes, a project at California State University, Los Angeles (M. A. Snow, 1997; Snow & Kamhi-Stein, 2002). In this model, language minority students were concurrently enrolled in two linked courses: an undergraduate course satisfying a general education requirement (e.g., *Introduction to Cultural Anthropology* or *Humans and their Biological Environment*) and a study group team taught by a peer study-group leader and a language specialist. Participating content faculty modified their syllabi and teaching methods to integrate language and content instruction with the aim of improving the academic literacy skills of the students enrolled in the adjunct courses. Evaluation of the project revealed that, overall, the performance of students in the adjunct courses approximated or exceeded that of the students who had not been enrolled in the courses in which content-based activities were introduced and practiced

(Kamhi-Stein; 1997; M. A. Snow, 1997).[2] Adjunct models of CBLT occupy the middle ground in the continuum in Figure 1 in that they are equally driven by language and content.

Expansion of content-based models

The content-based models described in the preceding section present well-documented prototypes of content-based instruction. Over time, the models have evolved into new formats, and different features have been borrowed, blurring many of the key distinctions. Brinton, Snow, and Wesche (1989) anticipated this trend: "The key point to be made is that depending on the setting, the configuration of the model may differ significantly, and the features of the three models [theme-based, sheltered, and adjunct] may tend to blend together" (p. 23). Numerous examples exist in the recent literature of the application of a model designed for one population to a different target population or of a program traditionally implemented at a particular educational level being used in another. One such example took place at the University of California, Los Angeles (UCLA) in the ESL service courses; the curriculum of the multiskill courses evolved from theme-based units used in the 1970s and 1980s to a "simulated" adjunct model (Brinton & Jensen, 2002). In this hybrid model, videotapes of actual lectures by UCLA content faculty along with their assigned course readings provided the content base for the ESL courses. More recently, Brinton (2007) has proposed language enhanced instruction (LEI), a variation of sheltered instruction offered in English for teachers in training. For example, at the Institute for English Teacher Education in Tashkent, Uzbekistan, the curriculum for students in the English teacher preparation program tended to emphasize language skills in the first two years and content knowledge in the third and fourth. LEI courses, therefore, were designed to integrate language and content in courses such as *American History* and *EFL Methods*, offering needed attention to the prospective English teachers' language development and more systematic feedback on language accuracy.

Another case is the theme-based model's growing popularity in the FL context. Owens (2002) describes the development of an EAP course at a Thai university that incorporated such topics as "the growth of advertising," "the movies," and "space exploration." Rosenkjar (2006) reports on the implementation of a theme-based course, *American English as Cultural Expression,* in a university EFL setting in Japan.

In the early 1990s, CBLT expanded to FL teaching at the post-secondary level in the United States (Krueger & Ryan, 1993). For example, at the University of Minnesota the CBLT program linked the major European languages with social science disciplines. Students enrolled in weekly seminars conducted in the FL and devoted to a comparison of news coverage in the American press and newspapers published in Spanish, French, or German. At the University of Pennsylvania, a content-based course, *Readings in Modern Chinese Literature,* seeks to instill a critical understanding of Chinese people, society, and culture along with facilitating the students' academic literacy skills (Dietrich, 2005). Interdisciplinary multilingual courses on a national security-related topic such as "nonproliferation" are offered at the Monterey Institute of International Studies in Chinese, Japanese, and Russian (Jourdenais & Springer, 2005).

One of the most dramatic examples of the changing configuration of CBLT models started in the United States in the mid-1980s when *two-way immersion* programs began to appear. Also called *dual language immersion,* these programs are a blending of immersion and developmental bilingual programs. For example, native Spanish-speaking students who are English learners and native English-speaking students are grouped in the same classroom with the goal of academic excellence and bilingual proficiency for both student groups (Lindholm-Leary, 2001; Lindholm-Leary & Genesee, 2010; Sohn & Merrill, 2008). By 2012, after approximately two decades of implementation, more than 240 two-way programs in 23 U.S. states have been established (The Center for Applied Linguistics, 2012).[3]

CONCEPTUAL UNDERPINNINGS

The theoretical foundations for CBLT can be drawn from a variety of sources, including SLA research and work in educational and cognitive psychology. Content-based instruction fulfills a number of conditions that have been posited as necessary for successful SLA. According to Krashen (1984), SLA occurs when the learner receives comprehensible input, not when the learner is memorizing vocabulary or completing grammar exercises. Therefore, methods that provide students with greater amounts of *comprehensible input,* according to Krashen, will be more successful. He argues that "comprehensible subject-matter teaching *is* language teaching" where the focus is on "*what* is being said rather than *how*" (p. 62).

Long's (1996) interaction model focuses on how input is made comprehensible. He argues that through interaction learners have the opportunity to use the L2 to negotiate meaning and benefit from the modified language of their interlocutors, who, in an effort to facilitate communication, often speak more slowly, repeat, or rephrase. Furthermore, through interaction L2 learners also learn to make clarification requests, confirmation checks, and comprehension checks as strategies for facilitating conversation and advancing their SLA.

Based on many large-scale studies of Canadian immersion programs, Swain (1993) advanced the position that to develop communicative competence learners must have extended opportunities to use the SFL productively. Thus, in addition to receiving comprehensible input, they must produce *comprehensible output;* in other words, explicit attention must be paid to the productive language skills of speaking and writing. Swain (1985) argues that, when L2 learners listen or read, they concentrate mainly on meaning, focusing on semantic processing of the message or text. When learners speak or write, they must undertake syntactic analysis; they must make grammatical and lexical choices and consider correctness. She maintains that learners need to be "pushed toward the delivery of a message that is . . . conveyed precisely, coherently, and appropriately" (p. 249). In Swain's 2005 update, she lists three functions of output: (1) noticing or triggering; (2) hypothesis testing; and (3) metalinguistic reflection.

Swain's work was a notable turning point in the way that CBLT theorists thought about the necessary conditions for SLA. It moved the field away from the long-standing belief that CBLT was simply a "two for one" approach, where through learning content students automatically learn language as an incidental by-product (Lightbown & Spada, 2006). It also explained why students in traditional immersion programs developed levels of receptive skills (e.g., listening and reading) equal to those of native speakers but exhibited speaking and writing skills that, even after hundreds of hours of instruction in the L2, contained persistent morphological and syntactic errors in areas such as person, tense, and gender, as well as errors in sociocultural forms (e.g., forms needed to address peers versus adults). Swain's position that "not all content teaching is necessarily good language teaching" (1988, p. 68) led to a rethinking of language learning as incidental in CBLT. Lyster and Ranta (1997) further note, "Subject-matter teaching does not on its own provide adequate language teaching: Language used to convey subject matter needs to be highlighted in ways that make certain features more salient to L2 learners" (p. 41).

Much of the current research in CBLT, therefore, examines ways to promote SLA. In a series of investigations with English-speaking students studying in French immersion classes in the upper elementary through secondary levels, Swain (2001) and Swain and Lapkin (1998) sought to test the output hypothesis and show how language instruction could be integrated into content instruction through systematic intervention. In these studies, collaborative tasks with the goal of linguistic accuracy were designed to assist students to extend their language output through speaking and writing activities. Collaborative tasks such as a dictogloss and jigsaw were used in the studies to help students focus on linguistic accuracy.[4] Results indicated that the collaborative tasks increased the amount of output, helped students focus attention on language as they formulated and tested hypotheses about their L2 and provided opportunities for students to engage in metatalk (use language to talk about their own language use).

Sociocultural approaches that draw theoretical support from the work of Vygotsky (1986) have been used to promote first language (L1) literacy development in multicultural elementary school settings and also offer promise for enhancing our understanding of SLA in the context of CBLT (Lantolf & Thorne, 2006). Vygotsky's notions of: (1) the zone of proximal development (in which learners are assisted by teachers or "more capable peers"); and (2) inner speech (internally directed speech as strategies for problem solving and rehearsing) can be effectively realized in content-based L2 settings where students have opportunities to negotiate not just language but also content in increasingly complex ways.

Language-focused instruction

More recently, Lyster (2007) has proposed *counterbalanced instruction*, where teachers assist students to vary their attentional focus between content learning, classroom discourse, and target language features. This approach includes pedagogical techniques that draw learner's attention to form-function relationships while also focusing on meaning-based tasks, differentiating it from traditional grammar lessons that tend to emphasize the memorization of forms out of context (Lyster, 2011). Form-focused options include: (1) enhanced input through noticing and awareness tasks; (2) practice activities for production; and (3) negotiation as feedback. Ranta and Lyster (2007) propose the awareness-practice-feedback sequence in which teachers make learners aware of what they need to learn or change, create practice opportunities, and provide feedback so that learners know whether their use of language forms and features has been successful or unsuccessful. It is also interesting to see the influence of DeKeyser's Skill-Acquisition theory (described in more detail by Ellis, this volume), which emphasizes the role of practice in the context of meaningful use of the language forms needed, for example, in a writing activity where students must express hypothetical ideas.

Academic language

Another major thrust of research in recent years is the focus on academic language in CBLT. Cummins (1980, 2000) made the well-known distinction between the type of language used in everyday conversation (basic interpersonal communication skills [BICS]) and that required in school (cognitive academic language proficiency [CALP]).[5] Chamot and O'Malley (1987), known for the cognitive academic language learning approach (CALLA), define *academic language* as "the language that is used by teachers and students for the purposes of acquiring new knowledge and skills . . . imparting new information, describing abstract ideas, and developing students' conceptual understanding" (p. 40).

More recently, there has been interest in further conceptualizing academic language. Anstrom et al. (2010) refer to academic English as a "variety of English, as a register, or as a style . . . typically used within specific sociocultural academic settings" (pp. iv–v). M. A. Snow (2005) emphasized the importance of language functions, distinguishing between social language functions (e.g., inviting or complimenting) and academic language functions where students have to use language for tasks such as defining, classifying, and sequencing. In addition, English learners must be exposed to the common discourse patterns in the content areas (Saunders & Goldberg, 2010). Carr, Sexton, and Lagunoff (2006), for instance, provided discourse functions of science such as formulating, hypothesizing, inferring, and predicting as well as common connectors in science used to show cause and effect like *because, since, consequently, as a result of,* and *so that.*

All conceptualizations suggest that it is necessary to broaden the discussion in CBLT to target the distinctive language patterns and discourse features in different content areas or disciplines. Schleppegrell (2004) noted that the academic language needed to read, write, and talk about science is different from the language required in mathematics. Bailey and Heritage (2008) break down academic language into "school navigational language" and "curriculum content language." For them, school navigational language is the language students use "to communicate with teachers and peers in the school setting in a very broad sense" and curriculum content language is "the language used in the process of teaching and learning content material" (p. 15).

Another perspective on academic language is Grabe and Stoller's (1997) claim that effective approaches to CBLT "combine coherent and interesting informational resources to create increasing, but manageable, task complexity" (p. 14). Stoller (2002) advocates adding "positive tension" to the CBLT classroom by selecting input with multiple perspectives and opposing viewpoints. She suggests that learners be exposed to "positive complexity," that is, tasks that require students to reinvest their language skills, cognitive skills, and content knowledge to negotiate tasks that become progressively more complex, thus requiring more sophisticated academic language and greater depth in processing the content material.[6]

Standards and accountability

A more recent development in CBLT is the standards and accountability movement. In the United States, national standards for the content areas have been developed for English, science, history, geography, civics and government, foreign languages, economics, and art (M. A. Snow, 2000). In 1997, the *ESL Standards for Pre-K–12 Students* was published by the professional association Teachers of English to Speakers of Other Languages (TESOL) (Teachers of English to Speakers of Other Languages, 1997), and a revised set, *Pre-K–12 English Language Proficiency Standards,* was released in 2006 (Teachers of English to Speakers of Other Languages, 2006). ESL standards for school-age learners have also been developed in Australia, Canada, and England (McKay, 2007) and in settings such as the Netherlands, where a national accreditation system for CLIL schools has established explicit quality parameters and teacher and school development measures (Dalton-Puffer, 2011). Content and language standards are meant to reflect what students should know and be able to do in the various subjects.

ESL standards make assumptions about requisite language skills that L2 learners must attain. TESOL's 1997 standards specify the language competencies needed by English language learners in elementary and secondary schools: "to become fully proficient in English, to have unrestricted access to grade-appropriate instruction in challenging academic subjects, and ultimately to lead rich and productive lives" (Teachers of English to Speakers of Other Languages, 1997, pp. 1–2). TESOL's 2006 *English Language Proficiency Standards* (Teachers of English to Speakers of Other Languages, 2006) reflect an increasingly explicit focus on the interface of language and content:

Standard 1: English language learners communicate for **social, intercultural**, and **instructional purposes within the school setting**.

Standard 2: English language learners communicate information, ideas, and concepts necessary for academic success in the area of **language arts**.

Standard 3: English language learners communicate information, ideas, and concepts necessary for academic success in the area of **mathematics**.

Standard 4: English language learners communicate information, ideas, and concepts necessary for academic success in the area of **science**.

: English language learners communicate information, ideas, and concepts necessary for academic success in the area of **social studies**. (p. 2)

These 2006 standards clearly reflect the integrated nature of school learning—namely that L2 students must develop language skills as they master subject matter—and illustrate this interface with a series of matrices addressing language development within each standard, at specific grade level spans, and for each of the four language skills at five levels of proficiency.

The forces that brought about the trend toward standards-based instruction also stress accountability. Gottlieb (2000) noted that, in the United States, "The success of the standards-based reform movement depends on the accurate and equitable measurement of students' achievement, which must be tied to challenging academic content" (p. 167). The issue is a complicated one for L2 learners, particularly because current language-assessment measures generally do not tap academic language. Stevens, Butler, and Castellon-Wellington (2000) found that, while the language proficiency and content tests used in their study overlapped in terms of high-frequency general vocabulary and grammatical structures, the vocabulary and sentence structures that appeared on the content tests were more complex, containing non-specialized academic words, specialized content words, and more embedded clauses.

Snow and Katz (2010) propose a process whereby teachers can situate instruction and assessment to plan for language and content instruction in a four-step framework:

1. Identify the learner's language proficiency level.
2. Select standards-based language objectives for English language development.
3. Design and enact activities.
4. Assess learning through standards-referenced assessments.

English language proficiency and content standards are used in this framework to ensure that grade-level content forms the basis for designing the targets for language learning. In the assessment step, teachers collect information that can help them determine whether students are meeting lesson objectives.

Preparing teachers to integrate language and content

Getting teachers to design lessons that truly integrate language and content in the manner proposed by current research has proven to be a difficult proposition. Fortune, Tedick, and Walker (2008), in their in-depth study of six Spanish immersion teachers, found that the "Vs" of language teaching (vocabulary and verbs) were the language components that the teachers typically targeted. Short (2002) conducted a study of four teachers who taught sheltered U.S. history in middle school. Two of the teachers were trained as ESL instructors, and two had social studies certification. The results of the study showed that all four teachers placed heavier emphasis on addressing content and tasks than on language. Even the trained ESL teachers devoted only one-fifth or less of their oral interactions to language, and when the teachers did address language issues, 95% of their comments related to vocabulary comprehension or pronunciation. While the teachers did develop activities for students to practice or apply their content knowledge, they rarely took language issues into consideration. At the university level, Pica (2002) investigated the ways that teachers modified classroom interaction around subject matter content in a literature class and a film class to assist the input, feedback, and production needs of L2 learners and to promote their attention to forms they had not yet fully acquired. She found numerous contexts in which the teachers could have drawn students' attention to developmentally difficult form-meaning relationships. There were, however, few instances where this actually occurred.

In a study with more positive results, Kong and Hoare (2011) investigated aspects of pedagogy in three middle schools in China that foster students' cognitive engagement with academic content that requires academic language use. They reported on results at one school where the course *Nature and Society* was taught only through English for two lessons each week. Focusing on the subtopics, "water and classification of living things," the researchers found that the teacher facilitated cognitive and academic language use through activities that required the students to process challenging content material deeply and to use the complex content-related academic language needed to explain, for instance, how a bat is classified as a mammal by referring to its defining features. The teacher also had clear content and language objectives.

One of the strongest research bases of CBLT is the Sheltered Instruction Observation Protocol (SIOP), a model of instruction for teaching subject matter content to students learning through a new language (Echevarria, Vogt, & Short, 2012). SIOP components include lesson preparation, building background, comprehensible input, strategies, interaction, practice and application, lesson delivery, and review and assessment. Numerous professional development programs in school districts across the United States serving large numbers of L2 students have adopted the SIOP model with positive results. Some SIOP studies have looked at implementation data to assess the teachers' skill level in sheltered instruction (Echevarria & Short, 2010); others have examined the achievement of students in classrooms with SIOP-trained teachers. For example, Short, Fidelman, and Louguit (2012) investigated the effects of SIOP instruction on the academic performance of middle and high school English learners. Results revealed that there were significant gains in the written and oral language of the English learners when their performance was compared to that of similar learners whose teachers had not received SIOP training.

CLASSROOM APPLICATIONS

CBLT provides a rich context for teaching all aspects of language: listening, speaking, reading, and writing, as well as grammar, vocabulary, pronunciation, and related discourse and pragmatic features. The types of instructional strategies, tasks, and activities presented in virtually every chapter of this volume can be adapted for use in content-based instruction.

Objectives, learning outcomes, and standards

In keeping with the conceptual underpinnings of CBLT, students need opportunities to gain input through listening and reading and to produce language through speaking and writing. They also need opportunities to interact in the L2 and negotiate meaning in the context of well-designed tasks (either for everyday life skills or academic use). In doing so, they can notice the particular grammatical and sociolinguistic conventions of the L2 and ultimately fine-tune their use of these features to better match the target language. As we have seen from the research cited, this does not take place incidentally. One way to help teachers in CBLT plan for effective integrated instruction is through the design of explicit language and content objectives. In addition, having teachers develop learning strategy objectives or study skill objectives assists students to become active learners—in other words, to "learn to learn," according to Kinsella (1997). Figure 2 provides examples of content, language, and strategy objectives designed by teachers who seek to maximize language and content mastery and to develop more strategic learners.

Another approach to making objectives explicit is to state learning outcomes so that

Example #1: These objectives are drawn from a thematic unit on earthquakes for intermediate level students (similar to the unit that Kimiko might have studied in the summer ESL program in California).[7]
<u>Content objectives:</u> By the end of the lesson, students will be able to:
 • distinguish between science and mythology.
<u>Language objective:</u> By the end of the lesson, students will be able to:
 • correctly form and answer *wh*-questions (*what, why, when, where, how*).
<u>Strategy objective:</u> By the end of the lesson, students will:
 • retell a myth about earthquakes from their country or another country in their own words.

Example #2: These objectives are drawn from an English-medium sheltered history course on the Lewis and Clark Expedition developed for use at the Uzbek State University of World Languages in Tashkent, Uzbekistan.[8]
<u>Content objective:</u> By the end of the lesson, students will:
 • learn details about key explorers in the Lewis and Clark Expedition.
<u>Language objective:</u> By the end of the lesson, students will improve their ability to:
 • comprehend a reading passage and summarize it.
<u>Strategy objective:</u> By the end of the lesson, students will:
 • employ a graphic organizer to chart the key dates and events of the expedition and make connections between the dates and events.

Figure 2. Examples of content, language, and strategy objectives.

Figure 3. Example of skills objectives and a learning outcome.

both the teacher and students can work toward a common goal. Figure 3 provides an example from a thematic unit called "What does it mean to be a global citizen?" in *Q: Skills for Success.*[9]

In addition to designing language, content, and strategy objectives and/or learning outcomes, teachers can build standards into their lesson plans to create explicit targets for language and content learning. Figure 4 illustrates how content-area and language standards are used in a thematic unit on ethnic conflict in society called "Me, My Neighbors, My World" designed for high school ESL students.[10] After students learn about genocide and ethnic cleansing in the unit, the culminating activity of the unit is for students to draw on the content they have learned and the language focus of persuasive writing to write letters to government leaders as a form of action against social injustice. The lesson incorporated California's *History–Social Science Content Standards* (California Department of Education, 2000) and *English Language Development Standards* (California Department of Education, 2002).

History Standard: (Historical Interpretation Standard #1)
• Students show the connections, causal and otherwise, between particular historical events and larger social, economic, and political trends and developments.

ELD Writing Standard for grades 9-12: Students
• recognize structured ideas and arguments and support with examples in persuasive writing
• edit writing for basic conventions (e.g., punctuation, capitalization, and spelling)

Figure 4. Example of history and English language development (ELD) standards in a thematic unit.

Instructional strategies

In all forms of CBLT, teachers must employ a variety of instructional strategies to integrate language and content instruction. To ensure that their language, content, and strategy objectives are carried out, teachers need to help student unpack difficult content in ways appropriate to the learner's developing language system. To do this, teachers must use a variety of techniques and strategies. These instructional techniques fall into five general categories.

Modifying input. Because L2 learners may have difficulty with the cognitively demanding language of content texts, it is critical that teachers adapt the delivery of instruction to their L2 learners' level of proficiency. The following techniques are useful ways to modify input:

- slower (yet natural) rate of speech
- clear enunciation
- controlled vocabulary with limited initial use of idioms
- clear explanation of tasks

Using contextual cues. Teachers must provide L2 learners with multiple cues to meaning so that they do not have to rely solely on the spoken or written word to understand difficult material. These contextual cues include:

- gestures
- dramatization of meaning through facial expressions, pantomime, or role play
- visuals, including pictures, posters, photographs, slides, maps, graphs, or diagrams
- realia (i.e., actual physical objects)
- bulletin boards, wall charts, or word banks (e.g., charts that associate math vocabulary with their corresponding symbols)
- building predictability into classroom procedures (e.g., having routines for opening and closing activities) so that students can figure out what to do from the context even if they do not completely understand the teacher's spoken instructions
- building redundancy into lessons through repetition, restatement, and exemplification

Checking for understanding. A variety of techniques can be used to ensure that students understand both the language used in instruction and the concepts being imparted:

- ask students to decide if information is true or false
- ask students to provide examples
- have students paraphrase important terms in their own words
- have students summarize key information
- ask students both factual questions (e.g., *Who?* and *What?*) and referential questions (*Why?* and *What would you do if . . . ?*)
- have students ask each other questions

Designing effective lessons. Gibbons (2009) suggests that teachers consider the following steps when developing a content-based unit: (1) decide on the "big questions" in the unit; (2) consider how the spoken language can be used to support both content and language learning; (3) identify what texts students will read; (4) identify the writing expectations; and (5) sequence activities broadly from speaking to writing.

In addition to these considerations, teachers should take extra measures in lesson planning in the following areas:

Vocabulary instruction. Vocabulary instruction must be systematic and give students multiple exposures. There are many aspects to word knowledge besides meaning or shades of meaning. These include knowing a word's derivations and word families, collocations, register, parts of speech, frequency, spelling, and pronunciation. Students must also be able to control the grammar (Scarcella, 2003). They must also learn the specialized vocabulary that characterizes academic texts such as the 570 word families found on *The Academic Word List* (Coxhead, 2006). (See also Zimmerman, this volume.)

Prioritizing objectives. In addition to teachers' writing course and lesson objectives, they must decide which key concepts should receive the most attention since covering all of the material may not always be possible.

Providing schema-building activities. Teachers should use techniques such as reviewing previously covered materials, relating ideas to the students' own experiences, and using brainstorming or clustering activities to help students develop a frame of reference for cognitively demanding content material. Graphic organizers such as outlines, charts, and study guides also help students see the inherent structure of content material.

Learner grouping strategies. A variety of grouping arrangements should be employed. Students can work in pairs, in small groups, and in Cooperative Learning groups where students are assigned specific roles (e.g., recorder, spokesperson, and praiser) to maximize different sources of input and output and to increase student interaction.

Designing language- and discourse-rich activities. Dutro and Moran (2003) advocate the "front loading" of language that students need to improve language and content understanding. Teachers first determine the language demands of the subject matter and then design activities that teach grammar, vocabulary, and language functions within the meaningful context of the content-based lesson. Gibbons (2006b) suggests that teachers create a language inventory, a list of the academic language features, for each unit of instruction. This language inventory can then be used to develop language objectives, to design learning activities that focus explicitly on the language connected to content tasks, and to guide the development of assessments to determine whether students are learning the L2 while developing content knowledge and skills. Additional strategies include:

- Identifying common discourse patterns highlighting the language associated with *inferring, hypothesizing, analyzing,* and so on
- Identifying common discourse patterns used, for example, to give a definition: *X means, X refers to,* and *X consists of*
- Designing form-focused activities to help students notice features of the L2, compare the L2 to their own language, and use metatalk to work toward more targetlike forms

Examples of content-based activities

In this section, I illustrate authentic activities used in different types of content-based classes.

The activity in Figure 5 comes from the theme-based *Animal Issues* course mentioned earlier, specifically from the "wildlife trafficking" unit (Evans, 2006). The goal of this unit is to have students rank and justify their opinions about wildlife traffickers, giving concrete reasons and reaching group consensus. Note that the teacher, Heidi Evans, has anticipated the kind of language students will need to state and justify their opinions by providing sentence starters.

Wildlife Trafficking Discussion Activity

Who Should Go to Jail?

The following people are involved in wildlife trafficking to some extent. Decide with your classmates who should go to jail and be prepared to support your opinion.

- ❑ I think _____ is the worst because _____.
- ❑ _____ is worse/better than _____ because _____.
- ❑ _____ should go to jail because _____.

1. Read each bio

Take turns reading aloud the short biographies of each person.

- **Marcio:** Marcio lives in Brazil and catches rare parrots. He sells them to zoos in Brazil and abroad, and he uses the money to take care of his family. He has seven children, and his oldest is pregnant.
- **Jan:** Jan hunts elephants in East Africa. His oldest son is attending medical school in America, and when he finishes, he will return to his village to replace the only doctor, who is retiring. Jan uses the money he gets from selling elephant tusks to pay for his son's education.
- **Yoko:** Yoko works twenty hours a week in her part-time job helping homeless people in Japan. She saves her small salary and spends it on collecting expensive name brand bags and shoes made of leather. She owns two fur coats and lots of jewelry made of animal shells and bones.
- **Lee:** Lee lives in China. He buys tiger bones and skins and uses them to make medicines that people in his village use for their health. Without his business, he cannot support his family. Recently, he used one of his medicines to cure his son who had malaria.
- **Atsushi:** Atsushi owns a shop that sells eyeglasses and jewelry in Japan. Many of his customers like eyeglass frames and accessories made of turtle shells and other animal products. Without these products, his business would collapse. Atsushi usually gets his products from black market smugglers.

2. Rank the people

Who should go to jail first? Second? Rank each person. (1 = mostly likely to go to jail, 5 = least likely to go to jail). If you don't think someone should go to jail, propose an alternative punishment.

WILDLIFE TRAFFICKING GROUP ASSESSMENT

Group Assessment #1 Who should go to jail?

Name: _____ #_____ Name: _____ #_____
Name: _____ #_____ Name: _____ #_____

Write your group answers and explain your reasons.

Name	Reason
1.	
2.	
3.	
4.	
5.	

Figure 5. Sample activity from "wildlife trafficking" unit.

The next activity (Figure 6) was devised by Professor Nadine Koch as part of the faculty development component in Project LEAP for use in her political science course, *Introduction to American Politics and Society*, at California State University, Los Angeles.[11] The aim was to assist her discipline-area colleagues to make the content of their courses more accessible to language-minority students.

Figure 7 is a sample planning document used by the content-area teacher and the FL teacher participating in team teaching in a primary-level CLIL project in Italy (Lopriore, 2009). It reflects a traditional lesson plan in many ways with objectives, use of the L2, classroom organization, and materials, but it also highlights the different functions and tasks performed by the two teachers.

FUTURE TRENDS IN CBLT

The selection, development, and adaptation of materials remain ongoing challenges in CBLT as teachers seek fresh and interesting topics around

Making Lectures Comprehensible

Objective: To make lectures more comprehensible by defining, simplifying, and recycling content-specific and noncontent vocabulary.

Rationale: Defining, embedding, and restating terminology helps students learn new content-specific terms (e.g., *communalist, democratic centralism*) and noncontent terms in new contexts (e.g., *the left, a watershed event*).

Procedures: It is very important to expose ESL students to sophisticated academic vocabulary during lectures.

1. Before the lecture, review lecture notes to anticipate difficult or unfamiliar content-specific and general academic vocabulary items.
2. During the lecture, monitor what you are saying to help yourself become aware of your use of difficult terminology. Use the strategies below to help students understand new terms and expand their academic vocabulary.
   - Define and explain new terms—whether or not they are content-specific.
   - Embed and restate new terms. For example: *the impetus for reform, that is, the driving force or stimulus for reform, was the Watergate scandal.*
   - Break down terms for the students so that they can understand the meanings.
     For example, *bicameral: bi*=two, *camera*=chamber.
   - Explain the meaning of colloquialisms or slang expressions. For example, take care to describe what a phrase like *to beat a dead horse* means and clarify its relevance to the conceptual point.

Figure 6. Tips for making content lectures accessible.

which to integrate language and content. And while interest in topics such as "Going Green: Merging Environmental Education and Language Instruction" (Hauschild, Poltavtchenko, & Stoller,

CLIL Collaboration Planning

Teachers:_____
Discipline/subjects: _____
Main topic:_____
Objectives: _____
Percentage of L1 and L2 use: _____
Activities:_____
Materials:_____
Classroom organisation:_____
Team-teaching model:_____
Content area teacher tasks: _____
Foreign language teacher tasks: _____
Assessment tools:_____

Figure 7. Sample planning document for CLIL teachers.

2012) still seems to be strong, teachers are also exploring other topics that resonate with students in the contemporary world. Grigoryan and King (2008), for example, have designed a course, *Critical Media Literacy*, in which students practice academic writing skills and learn how the media conceptualize race, class, and gender and promote social values through representations of beauty, prestige, family, love, success, sex, and freedom. In the past, instructors have usually developed their own curricula and materials for CBLT, a time-consuming process. The three sample exercises presented in this chapter reflect many hours of planning and preparation. In recent years, commercial publishers have developed theme-based series for use in both ESL and EFL settings, which has eased the burden somewhat on teachers, but the challenge of designing curricula and developing materials in CBLT will surely continue.[12]

A future trend in CBLT will undoubtedly be the expansion of standards and learning outcomes for all types of content-based programs. And while standards, benchmarks, and learning outcomes have already made a significant impact on content-based programs in SFL contexts, there is growing demand for evaluating and validating standards. P. McKay (2007) argues that English language proficiency standards lack an empirical foundation for describing classroom progress. Llosa (2011) notes that standards often separate language proficiency from content area knowledge, an ongoing dilemma in instruction and assessment. Bailey and Huang (2011) further question the relationship between English language proficiency standards and the construct of academic English, in particular how closely such standards represent the actual language demands found in classrooms across ages, grade levels, and content areas.

As CBLT expands to new settings around the world, the issue of teacher qualifications will gain further prominence. Language teachers are often called on to teach content areas in which they do not have sufficient expertise, and content teachers typically lack experience in addressing learners' language needs. Teacher-training programs need to assist teachers in mastering the skills needed to develop content objectives and language objectives that integrate the teaching of targeted concepts with the explicit teaching of the language skills and discourse patterns that support language development.

Further research is also needed to expand the work on academic language to a wider range of settings, age groups, and educational levels. Moreover, the findings of this research must be applied to the design of professional development programs for all teachers involved in the CBLT enterprise.

CONCLUSION

Content-based instruction differs from more traditional L2 language teaching methods in a number of ways. First, the roles of the language teacher and the content teacher are necessarily expanded. Since the content dictates the selection and sequence of teaching points, the language teacher must learn to exploit the content material for its language teaching potential. This means that the language teacher must select content material judiciously or, in the case where the materials are already selected (such as in adjunct classes or in courses using commercial theme-based texts), adapt materials to meet both student and programmatic needs. It also means that the language teacher must become familiar enough with the content material to put it to meaningful use. This is one of the most difficult, yet indispensable, requirements of CBLT. By the same token, the content teacher in CBLT needs to become sensitized to the language demands of the content and be familiar with effective pedagogy for maximizing content-based instruction. For the immersion teacher who wears two hats, both language and content considerations must stay at the forefront. No matter the model, content-based teaching entails systematic planning of integrated instruction using a rich repertoire of instructional strategies and techniques.[13]

Content-based instruction is a student-centered approach. The choice of content should revolve around considerations of students' current proficiency levels, academic or vocational objectives, interests, and needs. It may also be necessary to provide students with the rationale for CBLT. Students like Kimiko, who have initially learned English through more traditional approaches, may wonder, as she did, why she was studying earthquakes in an English class. Assessment also plays an important role on a number of levels. First, the needs of the learner must be determined. These may be very general, as in the case of students who are enrolled in college preparatory programs in intensive language institutes, or very specific, as in the case of ESL students in the public schools (who must be mainstreamed into regular content classes) or undergraduate or graduate students (who are pursuing degrees in their chosen field at English-medium universities). The needs of FL students must be considered as well, guided by the standards or learning outcomes developed for each particular teaching context. Second, the students' language proficiency levels must be carefully assessed in selecting the most appropriate type of content. Finally, once a content-based approach has been implemented, assessment must be carefully planned to take into consideration both language development and content mastery. With increasing accountability demands in CBLT, teachers will have to know how to design assessments that are reliable, valid, and fair. (See chapters by Kunnan & Grabowski and Katz, this volume.)

Just as we cannot expect students to learn the full range of language and discourse skills incidentally, we cannot expect teachers to be become effective teachers of CBLT without training. Thus, even after four-plus decades, we are still seeking to identify the requisite skills needed to be effective teachers of content-based instruction. Horn (2011) notes that there are four attributes that SFL teachers must possess to successfully implement content-based instruction: (1) language proficiency; (2) academic skills; (3) pedagogical knowledge and skills; and (4) an understanding of how different learners learn differently. While all SFL teachers need training in these four areas, a key area in CBLT is what he calls "content-language interface skills," which requires teachers to understand the links between emerging L2 proficiency and content learning. Models such as SIOP offer continued promise in assisting teachers to maximize the content-language interface.

The teaching of language through content is not so much a method as a reorientation to what is meant by *content* in language teaching. The literature offers strong theoretical support for content-based approaches and abundant examples of successful programs in SFL settings. As we have seen, content-based instruction crosses age groups and settings and is very much in keeping with the communicative approach to SFL teaching. As content-based instruction enters its fifth decade, we share Wesche's (2010) positive outlook that CBLT "is likely to continue to flourish, particularly in contexts where learners' main opportunity for developing advanced L2 proficiency is a school or post-secondary context and where they need to develop academic L2 ability" (p. 293).

SUMMARY

➤ CBLT is the integration of language and content teaching.

➤ There are many different models and configurations of CBLT, depending on the setting, age of the learners, and goals of the program.

➤ Some models of CBLT are more language-driven; others are more content-driven.

➤ CBLT is supported by the SLA literature, which demonstrates that CBLT offers students opportunities for plentiful input, output, and interaction.

➤ More recent research in CBLT focuses on the instructional conditions for creating learning opportunities that focus explicitly on language forms and discourse patterns.

➤ It is important in CBLT for teachers to develop language, content, and strategy objectives as part of systematic planning for instruction, taking into account learning outcomes and standards.

➤ A wide variety of instructional strategies for CBLT are available to the teacher to assist students with language development and content understanding.

➤ CBLT offers implications for assessment so that teachers can ensure that their students are learning the L2 as well as the targeted content.

➤ Preparing teachers for effective CBLT is an ongoing challenge for professional development.

DISCUSSION QUESTIONS

1. The chapter makes a number of points about ways in which CBLT differs from more traditional methods. Summarize the key points. Can you think of any other differences not discussed?

2. The author states that the immersion model might be considered the prototypical content-based program. Upon completion of elementary school, immersion students generally have native-like reading and listening skills, but they are typically not native-like in the productive skills of speaking and writing. How might these findings be explained in terms of the notions of comprehensible input, comprehensible output, and interaction?

3. If you were studying challenging content in your L2, which of the techniques and strategies listed in the chapter do you think would be particularly helpful in making the subject matter more comprehensible?

4. Consider Kinsella's (1997) notion of teaching students to be active learners through "learning to learn" strategies. What do you think she means by this? Give examples of these strategies from the chapter and from your own language teaching and learning experience.

SUGGESTED ACTIVITIES

1. The author describes several different models currently in use that integrate language and content instruction. Compare and contrast them in terms of:
   a. the degree to which they are language-driven or content-driven
   b. the degree of explicit language teaching
   c. the types of curricula and materials used
   d. the role of the language and/or content teacher
   e. the purpose of assessment

2. Imagine that you are a fourth-grade teacher and you have students who are English learners in your class. You are planning a unit on "Explorers of the New World." What steps might you take to conduct a language inventory as you plan the unit? Using the results from the inventory, design two language- or form-focused activities.

3. Gibbons (2009) states that in CBLT classrooms teachers must provide "high challenge" and "high support" for SFL learners. What do you think she means by this? Design a content-based lesson plan that illustrates these two features. Incorporate strategies described in the chapter and any others that you think might add challenge and support to the lesson.

4. Short (2002) observed, interviewed, and videotaped four middle school social studies teachers presenting sheltered lessons. She found that, out of 3,044 teacher utterances, 20% focused on language development, 35% revolved around content, and 44% addressed tasks. Discuss these findings in pairs or small groups. Based on the material presented in this chapter, speculate as to the reasons these results were obtained. What kind of teacher training might help these teachers to broaden their language focus?

FURTHER READING

California Department of Education. (2010). *Improving education for English learners: Research-based approaches.* Sacramento, CA: Author.

This volume presents a comprehensive, research-based review of the evidence available to inform instructional practices for K–12 English learners.

Nordmeyer, J., & Barduhn, S. (Eds.). (2010). *Integrating language and content.* Alexandria, VA: Teachers of English to Speakers of Other Languages.

This book presents interesting cases of how teachers around the world have designed and evaluated content-based courses.

Tedick, D. J., Christian, D., & Fortune, T. W. (Eds.). (2011). *Immersion education: Practices, policies, possibilities.* Clevedon, UK: Multilingual Matters.

This book is a collection of research studies on program design, implementation practices, and policies in one-way and two-way immersion programs and programs for indigenous languages.

ENDNOTES

1 The limited intensity of foreign language in the elementary school programs is often problematic for sustained language growth, but the programs do at least provide students with some exposure to the FL (Curtain & Dahlberg, 2010).

2 Cases of adjunct programs in both ESL and EFL contexts are described in detail in Crandall and Kaufman (2002) and Kaufman and Crandall (2005).

3 Another type of immersion program, structured immersion (also called English immersion), is a model implemented in some U.S. states to teach students with limited English proficiency. In this kind of program, students are typically immersed in English with no native language support and thus no goal of bilingual proficiency. According to Ovando and Collier (1998), structured immersion is a "misnamed program model that was promoted by English-only proponents with a political agenda in the 1980s" (p. 56). There are strong feelings in many quarters that structured immersion represents a misapplication of the original Canadian immersion model designed to teach French to English-speaking students.

4 *Dictogloss* (also called *dictocomp*) is an activity where the teacher reads aloud a text on a topic with which students have some familiarity. Students, working individually or in groups, reconstruct the text in their own words while retaining the overall gist. In a *jigsaw activity*, each student has a piece of text. Students are first grouped with other students who have the same piece of the text. They read and discuss the text, making sure that they fully comprehend it. Students are then regrouped such that each member of the new group has a different piece of the text, with all pieces present in each group. Students share their piece with their designated group members, working together to figure out the meaning of all parts of the text. This is often followed by a group task or assessment, such as a chart completion or quiz that requires all students in the group to work together toward successful completion.

5 In a more recent conceptualization, Schleppegrell (2004) argues that conversational language and academic language should not be viewed as a dichotomy since interactional spoken language can also be both complex and cognitively demanding. Further, A. L. Bailey (2007) argues that it is probably more accurate to speak of the difference between conversational and academic language as the relative frequency of complex grammatical structures, specialized vocabulary, and uncommon language functions, noting that formal oral language such as that used in lectures or debates can be highly academic.

6 See Grabe and Stoller (1997) for an early review of the contributions of research in educational and cognitive psychology.

7 This thematic unit was developed by Brian Bennitt, Misun Lee, Jackie Martinez, and Jose Rodriquez for TESL 564: Teaching English for Academic Purposes at California State University, Los Angeles.

8 The unit for Teaching American History: Language-Enhanced Content Instruction was designed by Donna Brinton and Barry Griner for use at the Institute for English Language Teacher Education at the University of World Languages in Tashkent, Uzbekistan.

9 This example comes from *Q: Skills for Success, Listening and Speaking: Book 5* (Unit 5, pp. 100–123) published by Oxford University Press (2011).

10 This thematic unit was developed by Inga Dabagian, Sheila Hudson, Yvette Romero, and Shelley Wood Goldstein for TESL 564: Teaching English for Academic Purposes at California State University, Los Angeles.

11 Other activities for teaching academic literacy in Project LEAP can be found in Brinton and Master (1997).

12 See Stoller (2008) for a more detailed discussion of ongoing challenges in CBLT in addition to developing materials, such as institutional resources, teacher and parent attitudes, teacher recruitment, and assessment.

13 There are many useful materials available to teachers that provide practical instructional strategies for CBLT. For useful sources, see Carrasquillo and Rodriguez (2002); Cloud, Genesee, and Hamayan (2009); Freeman and Freeman (2009); Gottlieb, Katz, and Ernst-Slavit (2009); Reiss (2005); Richard-Amato and Snow (2005). Also see Chapters 2–6 in *Improving Education for English Learners: Research-Based Approaches* (California Department of Education, 2010).

29 | Task-Based Teaching and Learning

DAVID NUNAN

> ## KEY QUESTIONS
>
> ➤ What is task-based language teaching?
> ➤ Where did task-based language teaching come from? That is, what are the conceptual and empirical wellsprings from which it evolved, and how does task relate to broader educational considerations?
> ➤ How is task-based language teaching realized in terms of materials development and classroom action?

EXPERIENCE

After graduating from Seoul National University, Sunyoung Kang worked in a local high school for five years before spending two years in Sydney, Australia, completing a master's degree in teaching English to speakers of other languages (TESOL), and teaching both Korean and English part-time. On returning to Seoul, she took a position as a teacher at a private language institute in Seoul. She has worked there for three years.

The class she is teaching consists of seven men and five women, all of whom are young professionals working in fields such as banking, travel, and technology. Although the class is oriented toward business, Sunyoung also likes to bring in aspects of social English. Because the students are all in full-time employment, the class takes place in the evening, and because her students are generally tired after a long day in the office, Sunyoung organizes lots of communicative group tasks that give the students opportunities to improve their spoken English through using it.

In the following Experience, the students are practicing the function of "making arrangements to meet." Sunyoung sets the scene by reminding the class of the objectives of the unit they have been working on. (The last class was based on several short conversations in which the people were making arrangements to meet.) She then divides the class into two. One group receives the Student

A Worksheet, while the other group receives the Student B Worksheet (see Figure 1).

Sunyoung: So, tonight we're going to do an information-gap task. You all know what an information-gap task is—we did one last week, remember? You're going to work in pairs, and you have the same task to do, but you have different . . . what? Different . . .?
Eunha: Informations.
Sunyoung: Right. Good, Eunha, different information. And you have to share your information. You have to share it. OK? So before we do that, I want you to look at your worksheet. I want to make sure you understand the words. Work together in your groups, and look at the activities on the worksheet. This is what people are doing on the weekend, on Friday, Saturday, and Sunday, OK? Now, which activities are related to work and which are not? Discuss among yourselves and decide. Some are work activities, and some are personal activities. If you don't know some words, you can ask me. I'll give you five minutes to make sure you know the words.

While the students are checking the words, she shuttles back and forth among the groups. When she is sure that the students understand the words, she claps her hands.

Sunyoung: OK, now, it's time to get into pairs. So I want one person from Group A

Student A Worksheet

	Friday evening	Saturday afternoon	Saturday evening	Sunday afternoon	Sunday evening
Bob	work late	_____	meet boss at airport	_____	prepare for a meeting
Karen	_____	free	_____	go shopping	_____
Philip	free	_____	free	_____	free
Joan	_____	take car to garage	_____	bake cookies	_____

Student B Worksheet

	Friday evening	Saturday afternoon	Saturday evening	Sunday afternoon	Sunday evening
Bob	_____	go to meeting	_____	free	_____
Karen	clean apartment	_____	visit aunt in hospital	_____	free
Philip	_____	play tennis	_____	study for exam	_____
Joan	free	_____	go to concert	_____	free

Figure 1. Sample task: Making arrangements to meet.

to pair up with one person from Group B. But don't show each other your worksheet—don't share your worksheets. This is an info-gap task. You have to share your information—not show it.

The students rearrange their chairs so that they are sitting in pairs.

Sunyoung: Right, so—ready? S. K., ready? Good. So this is what you have to do. Take a look at your worksheets. What are the names of your friends on the worksheets? Their names.
S.K.: Bob, Karen, Philip, and, er, Joan.
Sunyoung: Bob, Karen, Philip, and Joan. So, on the worksheets, you can see some of the things they have to do this weekend. Some of the things that they have to do are related to work, and some are not. You and your partner want to go to the movies some time over the weekend with your friends. Understand? Good—off you go.

As the students complete the task, the teacher circulates among the pairs and ensures that they are completing the task correctly. When all pairs have finished, she claps her hands together and points to one of the pairs.

Sunyoung: So, Eunha and Kelly. Did you manage to find a time slot when everyone is free?

Eunha: No, no slot, free slot.
Sunyoung: No free slot?
Eunha: No free slot.
Sunyoung: So what did you do? Decide not to go to the movies?
Kelly: We decide Sunday evening.
Sunyoung: Sunday evening. Why Sunday evening?
Kelly: Because only one person isn't free.
Sunyoung: Which one?
Kelly: Bob.
Eunha: Yes. Bob.
Sunyoung: So, poor Bob misses out! (laughs)
Eunha: Yes. Bob have to miss out.
Sunyoung: Do the rest of you agree?
Students: Yes, yes.
Sunyoung: OK. So, now I want you to change one thing about each person's schedule, just one thing, all right? Then I want you to change partners—find a new partner and do the task again.

WHAT IS TASK-BASED LANGUAGE TEACHING?

Task-based language teaching (TBLT) has its origin in a number of philosophical positions and empirical traditions in education, applied linguistics, and psychology. These include experiential learning and humanistic education, learner-centered instruction, and process-oriented and analytical approaches to syllabus design.

In this section, I build on the opening classroom Experience to describe and illustrate some key principles of TBLT, first showing how it fits into a larger historical curriculum framework and, second, offering a definition of the concept. I then look at its philosophical and empirical bases.

The Experience you just read is an extract from a lesson based on principles of TBLT. What do you notice about the extract? First, the learners are engaged in exchanging meanings, not memorizing and repeating utterances presented by the teacher or the textbook. In fact, the language they need to complete the task was practiced in a previous lesson. The learners exchange meanings based on the worksheet they have been given and do not simply repeat someone else's meaning. While the task is a pedagogical one (you would not see two people doing a task like this outside the classroom), there are clear connections between the in-class task and the real-world task of making plans and arrangements. Finally, the success of the task is assessed in terms of a communicative goal (negotiating and coming to an agreement about the best time to meet friends), not in terms of successfully manipulating linguistic forms. (For a discussion of these features, see Skehan, 1998.)

Any approach to pedagogy needs to take account of a number of broader curricular considerations before the actual process of designing courses and materials can begin. TBLT is no exception. Before turning directly to TBLT, I provide an overview of these curricular issues.

The term *curriculum* is a broad one, encompassing all the planned learning experiences provided by an institution or a course of study. The father of modern curriculum study is Ralph Tyler (1949), who presented his Rational Curriculum Model over 60 years ago. Since then, educators have staked out the curriculum terrain in different ways. Most, however, follow Tyler's argument that the curriculum needs to specify four essential elements: aim and objectives, content, learning experiences, and learning outcomes. Underlying Tyler's (1949) model were four key questions:

1. What educational purposes should the school seek to attain?

2. What educational experiences can be provided that are likely to attain these purposes?
3. How can these educational experiences be effectively organized?
4. How can we determine whether these purposes are being attained? (pp. 46–47)

These four questions equate to syllabus design, methodology, and assessment/evaluation, where: (1) syllabus design is concerned with specifying content and articulating this content in terms of goals and objectives; (2) methodology identifies, organizes, and sequences learning experiences; and (3) assessment and evaluation set out the means for determining whether the goals and objectives have actually been achieved (see Figure 2).

These three slices of the curriculum "pie" appear in some shape or form in most curricular proposals. However, they are sliced in different ways and have different degrees of prominence. In TBLT, for example, it is difficult to draw a strict separation between syllabus design and methodology, and the methodology slice is larger than in more traditional approaches, which give greater prominence to content.

Tyler's model, along with other similar models, represents a static product-oriented approach to curriculum design. At the end of the day, the designer has a set of products: lists of content, a set of goals and objectives, an inventory of task and activity types, assessment and evaluation instruments, and so on.

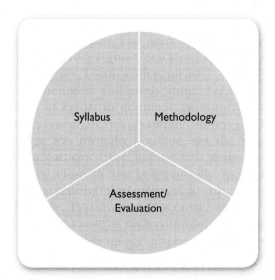

Figure 2. The three components of curriculum.

In the mid-1970s, an alternative, process approach to curriculum study was proposed by the British educator Lawrence Stenhouse (1975). Rather than emphasizing curriculum products, Stenhouse argued that the curriculum should articulate the processes and procedures for selecting content, learning experiences, and evaluation instruments. He argued that the curriculum should be formulated to make it accessible to critical scrutiny. Ideological positions should be made transparent. Teachers should have a greater say in curriculum design and development. The arguments for transparency and a greater say for teachers reflect Stenhouse's democratic, rather than elitist, approach to education. His approach takes a dynamic view of curriculum. The curriculum is a living entity that continues to change and evolve during the course of the instructional process, a notion that resonates strongly with my own views on curriculum.

To my mind, the development of content and objectives, learning experiences, and assessment and evaluation instruments is the beginning, not the end of the curriculum development process. This work, which is carried out before the instructional process begins, represents the planning phase of the curriculum and results in syllabuses, textbooks, tests, and so on. A second dimension, the curriculum in action, occurs as the curriculum is enacted in the moment-by-moment realities of the classroom. Finally, there is the curriculum as outcome, that is, what students actually learn as a result of instruction. We now know from classroom-based research and second language acquisition research that the relationships between planning, implementation, and outcomes are complex and asymmetrical. In other words, the traditional view that planning equals teaching and that teaching equals learning is simplistic and naïve.

Process-oriented views of curriculum resonated strongly with the emergence of communicative language teaching (CLT). Interestingly, this approach developed in applied linguistics at about the same time as Stenhouse's work was beginning to influence thinking and practice in general education. Language came to be seen not so much as a set of static products to be memorized but as a fluid set of procedures to enable human communication. It was out of these shifting perspectives on curriculum and communication that TBLT was born.

Before turning directly to TBLT, let us touch on the relationship between CLT and TBLT. (See Duff, this volume, for an expanded discussion.) CLT is a broad philosophical approach to language pedagogy. It draws on research in linguistics, anthropology, psychology, and sociology and rests on a view of language as a tool for communication rather than as a body of content to be mastered. TBLT is a realization of this philosophy at the levels of syllabus design and methodology. At the risk of oversimplifying a complex relationship, I would say that CLT addresses the question *why?* TBLT answers the question *how?*

Task defined

It is now time to look more directly at what we mean when we talk of tasks. TBLT belongs to a family of approaches to language pedagogy that are based on what is known as an analytical approach to language pedagogy (Wilkins, 1976). Here I describe this approach, contrasting it with the synthetic approach in the next section of this chapter. Before I look at the conceptual and empirical bases of TBLT, however, I need to clarify what I mean when I talk about tasks.

Tasks have been defined in various ways. As I mentioned when discussing the Experience that begins this chapter, I draw a basic distinction between pedagogical tasks, which are things that learners do in the classroom to acquire language, and real-world or target tasks, which are the uses to which individuals put language to do things in the world outside the classroom. In an early and rather programmatic definition, Long (1985) characterizes real-world tasks as "the hundred and one things people do in everyday life, at work, at play and in between" (p. 89). He provides a long list of these things, including domestic chores such as painting a fence, dressing a child, and writing a check and workplace tasks such as weighing a patient, typing a letter, and sorting correspondence.

Pedagogical tasks, on the other hand, are what learners do in the classroom to activate and develop their language skills. Creating an inventory of real-world tasks, that is, listing the actions that learners will actually or potentially need to perform outside the classroom, is a first step in the development of a TBLT curriculum. The next step is to turn these into pedagogical tasks. Such tasks involve learners in comprehending, manipulating, producing, or interacting in the target language to achieve a non-linguistic outcome. In Sunyoung's classroom the learners had to exchange and negotiate information to find the most suitable time to go to the movies with their friends. The learners, working in pairs, have access to related but different pieces of information. This is known as an information-gap task, a basic task type in TBLT. Other task types include problem solving, opinion exchange, and values clarification.[1] Notice that, although there is no explicit focus on pronunciation, grammar, or vocabulary, students need to mobilize their linguistic resources to achieve the goal of the task. Notice also that there is a concrete outcome that goes beyond the manipulation of linguistic forms. The task has a sense of completeness, and at the end of the task, learners are able to evaluate how well they have done.

In short, while pedagogical tasks should always have some kind of relationship to real-world tasks, the relationship may be somewhat tenuous. However tenuous the relationship might be, the link between the classroom and the world beyond the classroom should be clear to the learners.

Despite their diversity, most definitions of *task* in the literature have several characteristics in common. Skehan (1998) synthesizes the views of a number of writers and suggests that pedagogical tasks exhibit five key characteristics. If you refer back to the discussion of the Experience earlier in this chapter, you will find exemplification and elaboration of these features:[2]

- Meaning is primary.
- Learners are not given other people's meanings to simply repeat.
- There is some sort of relationship to comparable real-world activities.
- Task completion has some priority.
- The assessment of the task is in terms of outcome.

CONCEPTUAL UNDERPINNINGS

TBLT draws strength from the following six principles:

1. The point of departure for developing courses and materials is the development of an inventory of learner needs rather than an inventory of phonological, lexical, and grammatical items.

2. Learners develop the ability to communicate in a language through using the language rather than studying and memorizing bits of the linguistic system.

3. Learners' own personal experiences are central to the learning process.

4. There is a focus on learning processes and strategies as well as on language content.

5. Classroom language learning is systematically linked to learning outside the classroom (which I call task authenticity).

6. Learners are exposed to authentic listening and reading texts.

The point of departure for pedagogy

The traditional approach to pedagogy is rooted in the three language systems: the phonological, the lexical, and the grammatical. These systems are analyzed and broken down into their component parts, which are then taught separately, one at a time. The task for the language learner is subsequently to put these language bits back together to communicate. In other words, they have to synthesize the elements (Wilkins, 1976).

The alternative approach is to begin not with the language but with the learner. Under this approach, curriculum developers and materials designers begin with an inventory of the sorts of things that learners actually or potentially need to do with language. In the classroom, learners engage with authentic and/or naturalistic texts, and they are required to analyze the language into its component parts. Analytical approaches include TBLT, project-based language teaching, network-based, and content-based instruction (CBI) (Brinton, 2003). Project-based language teaching, network-based instruction, and CBI are discussed in the Classroom Applications section of this chapter. Wilkins (1976) provides the following articulation of analytical approaches:

> Prior analysis of the total language system into a set of discrete pieces of language that is a necessary precondition for the adoption of a synthetic approach is largely superfluous.... [Such approaches] are organized in terms of the purposes for which people are learning languages and the kinds of language that are necessary to meet these purposes. (p. 13)

Learning through doing

In TBLT, the learner acquires the language primarily through using the language in carefully structured situations. Proponents of a strong interpretation of TBLT argue that communicative engagement in tasks provides the necessary and sufficient condition for second language acquisition. In other words, there is no point in focusing on linguistic form because communicative engagement provides the necessary and sufficient condition for language acquisition (Krashen, 1981, 1982). Proponents of a weak interpretation (of which I am one) argue that a systematic focus on language systems is also healthy for language acquisition. Theoretical and empirical support for this position can be found in Doughty and Williams (1998a), an edited collection that presents original studies demonstrating the benefits of a focus on language form in CLT. Contributors to the collection argue that we need to move beyond the dichotomous notion that the only choice in second language teaching is either to adhere to a traditional grammar-only approach or to eschew the teaching of grammar altogether.

Learners' own experiences as a point of departure

The notion of learning through doing has its roots in experiential learning, which sees education as a process of building bridges between what learners already know and what they have to learn. Experiential learning has diverse origins, drawing on Dewey's (1938) progressive philosophy of education, Lewin's (1936) social psychology, and Piaget's (1972) developmental psychology. The work of Maslow (1970) and Rogers (1969) in humanistic psychology has also been influential.

The most articulate application of experiential learning to language teaching is provided by Kohonen (1992):

> Experiential learning theory provides the basic philosophical view of learning as part of personal growth. The goal is to enable the learner to become increasingly self-directed and responsible for his or her own learning. This process means a gradual shift of the initiative to the learner, encouraging him or her to bring in personal contributions and experiences. Instead of the teacher setting

the tasks and standards of acceptable performance, the learner is increasingly in charge of his or her own learning. (p. 37)

In many respects, his model can be seen as a theoretical blueprint for TBLT, as can be seen in the following principles for action, which are a synthesis of Kohonen's (1992) paper.:

- Encourage the transformation of knowledge within the learner rather than the transmission of knowledge from the teacher to the learner.
- Encourage learners to participate actively in small, collaborative groups.
- Embrace a holistic attitude toward subject matter rather than a static, atomistic, and hierarchical attitude.
- Emphasize process rather than product, learning how to learn, self-inquiry, and social and communication skills.
- Encourage self-directed rather than teacher-directed learning.
- Promote intrinsic rather than extrinsic motivation.

These principles see learning as a collaborative and transformative rather than a transmissive process, one in which the teacher creates an environment within which the learners take control of their own learning processes. Self-direction and learning how to learn are seen as central to the mastery of content.

Focus on learning strategies

While not a necessary component of TBLT, a focus on learning strategies and processes has emerged as an important concomitant of the approach.[3] Sensitizing learners to the processes underlying their learning is particularly important for learners who come to the TBLT classroom from a traditional classroom and who may not recognize or accept task-based language learning as legitimate. Learners' perceptions about what they should contribute to task completion, their views about the nature and demands of the task, and their perceptions of the situation in which the task takes place will all influence the task outcomes. We cannot know for certain how learners will actually go about completing a task, and it is certainly unwise to assume that the way we look at a task will be the way that learners look at it. There is evidence to suggest that, while we as teachers are focusing on one thing, learners may well be focusing on something else. For example, learners look for opportunities to practice grammar in tasks designed to focus them on exchanging meaning. Conversely, they may focus on meaning in activities designed to have them practice grammatical forms. Recent classroom research has also shown that learners consistently transform the nature, purpose, and outcomes of a task in the course of completing it (Chan, 2010).

One way to reconcile these mismatches between teachers' and learners' views is to add a focus on learning strategies and learning how to learn. (See also Purpura, this volume.) If learners develop a reflective attitude toward the intention of the task designer and toward their own preferences and attitudes about language learning, perceptual gaps may be reduced.

Task authenticity

As I indicated at the opening of this chapter, the point of departure for designing task-based curricula and materials is an inventory of the kinds of things that the learner actually or potentially needs to do in the world outside the classroom. There is thus an automatic link between the pedagogical world and the experiential world. There should be systematic links between the world of the classroom and the world beyond the classroom. The closer the link between the pedagogical and the experiential worlds, the greater the *task authenticity*.

Text authenticity

In addition to task authenticity, text authenticity is an important feature of TBLT. *Text authenticity* is the use of spoken and written material that has been produced for purposes of communication, not for purposes of language teaching. The issue here is not whether authentic materials should be used but which combination of authentic, simulated, and specially written materials will provide learners with optimal learning opportunities. Specially written texts display features of the phonological, lexical, and grammatical systems for learners. Input is simplified for beginning learners, and patterns are made explicit. While such texts are necessary,

they do not prepare learners for the challenge of coping with the language they will encounter in the real world outside the classroom. Scaffolded[4] in-class opportunities to process authentic aural and written texts are intended to assist learners to develop strategies for comprehending such texts in the world outside the classroom.

CLASSROOM APPLICATIONS

One issue that has surfaced many times since the development of CLT has been the place of grammar. At one extreme, as we have already seen, is the view that a focus on grammar is not necessary for successful SLA (Krashen, 1981, 1982). At the other extreme is the notion that grammar is central to the acquisition process (Doughty & Williams, 1998a). Somewhere in the middle is the notion that an incidental focus on form can be helpful (Long & Robinson, 1998).

R. Ellis (2008) draws a useful distinction between focused and unfocused tasks. *Unfocused tasks* are not designed with a particular grammatical form in mind, and learners are free to use whatever linguistic resources they have at their disposal to complete the task. Figure 3 illustrates a guided role play that exemplifies an unfocused task. Although some of the grammatical items that students taking part in the role play will need might be predictable, they are not required for the successful completion of the task. On the other hand, according to R. Ellis (2003), *focused tasks*:

> aim to induce learners to process, receptively or productively, some particular linguistic feature, for example, a grammatical structure. Of course, this processing must occur as a result of performing activities that satisfy the key criteria of a task, i.e. that language is used pragmatically to achieve some non-linguistic outcome. Therefore, the target form cannot be specified in the rubric of the task. Focused tasks, then, have two aims: one is to stimulate communicative language use (as with unfocused tasks), the other is to target the use of a particular predetermined target feature. (p. 16)

"Picture difference" tasks can be used to practice a wide variety of grammatical structures. In this task type, students work in pairs. Each student has a different version of a picture. (See also Bohlke,

Task: Work in pairs. One student looks at Card A. The other looks at Card B. Practice the conversation.	
Card A	**Card B**
You would like to arrange to go out with B this coming week. You call him/her up.	You receive a call from A who wants to make arrangements to do something during the coming week.
A Check if B has any free time during the coming week.	**A**
B	**B** Tell A you have some free time and ask what A has in mind.
A Tell B that you were thinking of Tuesday evening, which works well for you.	**A**
B	**B** Reply that Tuesday evening is not convenient. Give a reason.
A Try to persuade B to change his or her plans.	**A**
B	**B** Refuse. Suggest Wednesday or Thursday evening.
A Tell B that you can make Wednesday but not Thursday. Ask B if 7 pm works.	**A**
B	**B** Agree. Ask what A has in mind to do.
A Tell B there's a new Thai restaurant you've been wanting to try.	**A**
B	**B** Tell A that you love Thai food. Suggest meeting at the restaurant.
A Enthusiastically agree. Tell B that you will email him/her the address and directions to the restaurant.	**A**

Figure 3. Sample unfocused task.

this volume.) The differences may be subtle or not so subtle. Without looking at each other's picture, the students have to describe their picture to their partner and identify the differences. If you want your students to practice prepositions of place, the picture might show an untidy bedroom with certain items in different places. In Picture A, for example, there may be a backpack on the desk. In Picture B, the backpack is under the bed. This should lead to interactions such as the following:

A: Is there a backpack in your picture?
B: Yes, there is. It's under the bed.
A: Oh, in my picture, it's on the desk.

The task is a focused one because it cannot be completed successfully without the use of appropriate prepositions.

This type of task can readily be modified for learners at different proficiency levels or for mixed-ability classes simply by modifying the instructions. Weaker students can be instructed to find five differences and students with a slightly more advanced proficiency level to find nine differences. The better students might simply be told to "find as many differences as you can."

The examples of tasks provided so far have been relatively closed; that is, there is a single or limited number of correct answers. For students with beginning and lower levels of proficiency, it is best for tasks to be relatively closed because they provide a greater degree of security and the students are able to self-check whether they have the right answer. However, as students become more proficient, it is good to introduce more open-ended tasks where there is no one right answer. "Opinion exchange" tasks, such as the one illustrated in Figure 4, are typically open-ended.

Decision-making tasks can be more or less open-ended depending on the amount of information provided and the parameters within which the task must be completed. The decision-making task in the Experience at the beginning of this chapter is an example of a relatively closed task because there is really only one logical conclusion. The task in Figure 5, on the other hand, is much more open-ended. This task can encourage creativity, the use of personal experience, and occasionally considerable negotiation. I once observed a group completing a version of the task in which one student argued against the seemingly obvious choice of taking a cell phone.

She had been on a similar hike and had taken her cell phone, which proved to be useless because there was no service in the remote area where her group was hiking.

A. Work in groups of three to five. Brainstorm, and come up with a list of the five most helpful inventions and the five most annoying inventions.

Helpful inventions

Example: *Satellite navigation systems for cars*

1. _____
2. _____
3. _____
4. _____
5. _____

Annoying inventions

Example: *Downloadable cell phone ring tones*

1. _____
2. _____
3. _____
4. _____
5. _____

B. Share your lists with the class, and give reasons for your opinions.

Figure 4. Sample open-ended task.

A. You are going on a weekend hiking trip with your friends to a remote part of the countryside. The weather forecast is for hot sunny days and cold nights. Look at the following list of items and decide on 10 items to take.

flashlight	warm jacket
map of the area	energy bars
plastic rain coat	large plastic sheet
umbrella	spare pair of hiking
matches	shoes
cell phone	compass
first-aid kit	watch
1 bottle of water	pair of shorts
pair of sunglasses	flares
	hunting knife

B. Work with two other students. Share your lists and come up with a composite list of 10 items.

C. Now join with another group of students. Share your two composite lists and come up with a single composite list.

Figure 5. Sample open-ended decision-making task.

The decision-making task also exploits the principle of task repetition. The students get two opportunities to negotiate and come up with a single composite list. Although the actual substance of the discussion will vary from Phase B to Phase C, depending on the items chosen, the functional language will be similar (agreeing, disagreeing, raising objections, giving reasons, etc.). Plough and Gass (1993) have argued for task repetition, showing that the increased familiarity with the task can lead to greater fluency and more complex language, although if this is overdone it can also lead to boredom. Bygate (1996) has demonstrated that boredom can be avoided by making simple modifications, as in the exercise. Learners are, in effect, being given the opportunity to rehearse the task.

Relating TBLT to project-based, content-based, and network-based instruction

Project-based instruction. Projects are super-tasks that incorporate a number of self-contained but interrelated subsidiary tasks. In the real world, a project might be getting a job or renting an apartment. Subsidiary tasks in getting a job might include writing a resume, evaluating/rank-ordering the positions available in advertisements for their suitability (in terms of salary, location, and match to qualifications and experience), making an appointment, and taking part in an interview. Renting an apartment might involve deciding on a suitable suburb or neighborhood, identifying desirable facilities (proximity to public transportation, shops, or recreational facilities), rank-ordering the properties available to rent according to price or location, making an appointment to inspect an apartment, and so on.

In their book on project-based instruction, Ribe and Vidal (1993) argue that there have been three phases, or generations, in the evolution of TBLT. In the first generation, the focus was on developing communicative ability in a specific area of language through simulations and problem solving. The second generation included communicative development but extended it to cognitive development as well. Third-generation tasks involve language and cognitive development but go a step further, aiming at the development of the whole learner and using foreign language learning as a vehicle. Language learning thus transcends the utilitarian development of skills for communicating and becomes a truly educational endeavor.

Ribe and Vidal (1993) provide the following example of a third-generation task or project – to design an alternative world:

1. Students and teachers brainstorm aspects of their environment they like and those they would like to see improved. These may include changes to the geographical setting, nature, animal life, housing, society, family, leisure activities, politics, etc.
2. Students are put into groups according to common interests. The groups identify the language and information they need. The students carry out individual and group research on the selected topics. The students discuss aspects of this "alternative reality" and then report back. They decide on the different ways (stories, recordings, games, etc.) to link all the research and present their final projects.
3. Students present the topic and evaluate the activity. (Ribe & Vidal, 1993, p. 3)

Ribe and Vidal (1993, p. 4) then articulate the following characteristics of third-generation tasks.

- They are open and flexible, and it is the students who occupy center stage.
- They involve the teacher and students negotiating objectives, planning together, monitoring, and evaluating processes and results.
- They incorporate the students' previous knowledge and personal experiences.
- They appeal to the students' imagination, creativity, and affectivity.
- Their scope and length can be quite extensive.
- Their thematic content is related to the students' immediate environment and interests.
- They require the use of all the language skills and organizational strategies.
- They approach language globally, not sequentially, according to the needs created by the task.

In this list, you can see echoes of many of the principles already discussed. Language is seen as a dynamic, organic entity. An experiential approach is taken to learning, with learners' own experiences as the point of departure for learning. There is a strong focus on learning strategies. Finally, there is a linking of the classroom to the wider world beyond the classroom.

Content-Based Instruction. In CBI, all or part of the instructional content of a class is adapted from other subjects in the school curriculum, such as science, math, and social studies. (See Snow, this volume, for a detailed discussion of CBI and its origins in immersion education.) By integrating language and academic content, learners receive instruction that is both interesting and relevant; the subject content provides a rich context for the learning of language (Brinton, 2003).

Brinton (2003) and Snow (this volume) describe three different prototype models of CBI: theme-based language instruction, sheltered instruction, and adjunct instruction. These models vary according to the type of students and the setting in which they are learning, the lesson focus (whether the focus is on content, language, or both), the source of content, and the degree of coordination between the language and content teachers.

A *theme-based approach* is typically adopted in classes with students from diverse backgrounds. The themes therefore have to be broad enough to cater to this diversity as well as being age appropriate. For elementary or junior high school students, the theme might be "friendship" (from social science) or "endangered species" (from science). For older students preparing for college entry, themes might include "advertising" or "health." Courses following this model are very similar to TBLT courses for general purposes, where units of work are usually based on themes such as "entertainment," "transportation," and "neighborhoods."

The sample task in Figure 6 was designed for a group of older adolescents or young adults who are preparing for college entry. It is taken from a unit on "personal health."

Sheltered content courses exist at all educational sectors, although they are generally found in secondary and post–secondary school settings. The term *sheltered* refers to the second language learners' being separated from the native speakers of the language. Instruction is delivered by content teachers who have received special ESL training. The following scenario illustrates how, in a sheltered class, a task-based approach might be implemented. In a junior high school science class, ESL learners work in small groups. They have two sets of cards, one set showing pictures of insects, birds, and animals and the other with the names of the insects, birds, and animals. Step 1 of the task involves having the students match the

English for Architecture

How Healthy Are You?
1. Complete the following survey. Check the responses that are true for you, and then add up the numbers in the brackets.

Eats red meat
- ❑ every day [1]
- ❑ 3–5 times a week [2]
- ❑ once a week [3]
- ❑ once a month [4]
- ❑ 3–5 times a year [5]
- ❑ never [6]

Eats fruit and vegetables
- ❑ every day [6]
- ❑ 3–5 times a week [5]
- ❑ once a week [4]
- ❑ once a month [3]
- ❑ 3–5 times a year [2]
- ❑ never [1]

Eats dessert
- ❑ every day [1]
- ❑ 3–5 times a week [2]
- ❑ once a week [3]
- ❑ once a month [4]
- ❑ 3–5 times a year [5]
- ❑ never [6]

Walks
- ❑ every day [6]
- ❑ 3–5 times a week [5]
- ❑ once a week [4]
- ❑ once a month [3]
- ❑ 3–5 times a year [2]
- ❑ never [1]

Plays sports or exercises
- ❑ every day [6]
- ❑ 3–5 times a week [5]
- ❑ once a week [4]
- ❑ once a month [3]
- ❑ 3–5 times a year [2]
- ❑ never [1]

Smokes cigarettes
- ❑ every day [1]
- ❑ 3–5 times a week [2]
- ❑ once a week [3]
- ❑ once a month [4]
- ❑ 3–5 times a year [5]
- ❑ never [6]

2. Now compare your responses with three to four other students. Who is the healthiest person in the group? (The higher the score, the better!)

Figure 6. Sample task for a theme-based unit on "personal health."

English for Architecture

Assessment Task Guidelines

At the end of the course, you are required to give a 10-minute oral presentation based on your scale model. If you wish, you may accompany your talk with a slide presentation.

Your English instructor and the professor of Architectural Design will jointly assess you. Your presentation will be assessed in terms of the following:

- Language (grammar, vocabulary, fluency, and pronunciation)
- Content (mastery of architectural concepts and feasibility of the design)
- Organization (clear introduction and overview, body, and conclusion)
- Style (confidence and ability to maintain audience interest)

Detailed assessment criteria for each of these areas are attached.

Figure 7. Sample end-of-term task for an adjunct model class.

In the *adjunct model,* students are concurrently enrolled in both a language class and a content class. While the classes meet separately, the language and content instructors collaborate in planning their classes so that the instruction is coordinated. The task in Figure 7 is an end-of-semester assessment task for first-year architecture students at an English-medium university in Asia. All students are required to take a four-credit English for Architecture course. The major project in the course is to design and build a scale model of an architectural project. At the end of the course, the students are required to give a 10-minute oral presentation, for which they are assessed.

From these descriptions and examples, you can see that CBI and TBLT are closely related. I see CBI as a variant of TBLT. TBLT provides the pedagogical principles and methodology, while the academic subject areas provide the content (as opposed to types of TBLT courses described elsewhere in this chapter where, for example, content might be derived from a needs analysis of the everyday survival needs of immigrants).

Network-based language teaching and learning. Computer-assisted language learning (CALL), and particularly Internet-based instruction, have rapidly become an integral part of the design and delivery of education. This is particularly true of language

pictures with the vocabulary cards. Step 2 involves having them group or classify the pictures together according to the category to which they belong.

learning and teaching. Initial skepticism about the notion of learning language online has given way a broad acceptance that there are aspects of language learning and teaching that can be done online more effectively than in face-to-face instruction. Technology has four major roles to play in second language pedagogy (Nunan, 2011a):

1. as a carrier of content
2. as an instructional practice tool
3. as a learning management tool
4. as a communication device

As a carrier of content, technology gives learners access to authentic spoken and written data as well as information on the three linguistics systems (phonological, lexical, and grammatical). As an instructional practice tool, it provides opportunities for learners to practice the four skills (listening, speaking, reading, and writing) as well as to do a wide range of drills and exercises. As a learning management tool, it enables the teacher and learners to organize their learning in various ways, to monitor progress, and to keep records of achievement. Finally, as a communication device, it provides learners with opportunities for authentic spoken and written communication with other language users.

In this section, I focus on one form of CALL, *network-based language teaching* (NBLT). Warschauer and Kern (2000) define NBLT as follows:

> NBLT is language teaching that involves the use of computers connected to one another in either local or global networks. Whereas CALL has traditionally been associated with self-contained, programmed applications such as tutorials, drills, simulations, instructional games, tests, and so on, NBLT represents a new and different side of CALL, where human-to-human communication is the focus. Language learners with access to the Internet . . . can now potentially communicate with native speakers (or other language learners) all over the world twenty-four hours a day, seven days a week, from school, home, or work. (p. 1)

NBLT is pertinent to TBLT (as I have defined and discussed it in this chapter) for several reasons. First, it gives learner access to an enormous amount of authentic spoken and written data. Second, it enables learners to function autonomously and to develop their language skills through doing. And third, and probably most important, particularly for learners studying in foreign as opposed to second language contexts, it provides a means for authentic interaction. It thus fulfills three of the four roles for technology summarized here. It is as a communication device that NBLT becomes particularly potent, as Warschauer and Kern have made clear.

In a study of task-based language learning via audiovisual networks, Zahner, Fauverge, and Wong (2000) set out to evaluate the suitability of task-based language learning to networked environments. A group of university students in England who were studying French were teamed up with a group of French students in Paris who were studying English. They had to collaborate to complete two large-scale tasks, which were more like projects (one in English, the other in French). For example, one task (done in English) was to develop and present a marketing strategy for a French company trying to break into the British market. Student interactions were recorded and analyzed. The researchers concluded that networked environments were particularly suited to collaborative task-based learning.

FUTURE TRENDS

Crystal-ball gazing has always been an uncertain undertaking. In our increasingly uncertain era, it becomes even more problematic. However, here are my predictions of trends that are not specific to TBLT but that I believe will have an impact on TBLT.

Impact of English as a global language

The emergence of English as a global language has strengthened the rationale for a task-based approach to language pedagogy because it gives learners in English as a foreign language environments not only the opportunity but, indeed, the need to use the language for authentic communication. English becomes a tool for communication rather than an object of study. This trend is almost certain to increase. Millions of language learners around the world will have opportunities for the authentic use of language.

Greater focus on intercultural issues

Ownership of English can no longer be claimed by any one country or society. There are now more second language users than first language users. It is a truism that language and culture go hand in hand. The question, however, is *whose culture*? This question will come under increasing scrutiny in the years ahead and will have a significant impact on the nature of task-based language programs.

Increasingly important impact of technology

Technology has become an integral part of all aspects of life. In language education, it is also pervasive. In the past, it has given learners convenient access to authentic data. In the future, it will provide access to and opportunities for authentic interaction on a global scale. The Internet will provide opportunities for learners to engage in authentic communication with other users around the world.

CONCLUSION

In this chapter, I have provided an overview of TBLT. At the beginning of the chapter, I demonstrated TBLT in action using a classroom Experience and set out some general design considerations. The bulk of the chapter was then given over to defining *task* and summarizing the empirical and conceptual basis of TBLT while elaborating on a number of key principles. Although TBLT has been around since the 1980s, it is only in recent years that the concept has begun to gain traction at the level of classroom practice. This may seem surprising, but it should not be. The rule of thumb for any significant innovation to enter the bloodstream of an educational system is that it takes between 20 and 30 years.

SUMMARY

➤ TBLT is a methodological realization of communicative language teaching.
➤ The point of departure for TBLT is an inventory of the things that learners actually or

potentially need to be able to do in the target language rather than lists of phonological, lexical, and grammatical features of the language.
➤ TBLT belongs to a family of approaches to pedagogy that that are essentially process-rather than product-oriented. It is closely related to project-based learning and content-based instruction.

DISCUSSION QUESTIONS

1. How can you differentiate between pedagogical tasks and real-world tasks? Provide an example of each.
2. What do you see as the pros and cons of synthetic and analytical approaches to language teaching?
3. What is the relationship between TBLT and other related approaches, such as project-based, network-based, and content-based instruction? What do you see as the three most important principles connecting these different approaches?
4. What rationale is provided in the chapter for a focus on learning strategies?
5. What is meant by *text authenticity* and *task authenticity*?
6. What is your position on the place of form-focused instruction in TBLT?

SUGGESTED ACTIVITIES

1. Select three or four tasks that are familiar to you and evaluate them using the checklist in the Appendix. What strengths and weaknesses of the tasks emerged as a result of this exercise? What modifications would you make to the tasks in light of the evaluation?
2. Write a short narrative of your own language learning history. Analyze the narrative. Can you find evidence of some of the principles discussed in this chapter, such as a focus on learning strategies, activation through real-world language use, and exposure to authentic texts?
3. In small groups, brainstorm an idea for a student project (e.g., a trip to an unknown world, or an ideal weekend for a group of visitors in your town or city). Using the following template, sketch the idea for your project.

Idea for Student Project:	
Title of Project:	
Underlying Language Needs of Students:	• • • • • •
Themes and/or Subthemes:	• • • • • •
Potential Sources of Information:	• • • • • •
Materials Needed:	• • • • • •
Potential Obstacles to Implementing the Project:	• • • • • •

4. Design a unit of work based on the following model (adapted from Nunan, 2004, pp. 34–35).

Step 1. Scaffolding	**Example**
Create a number of schema-building tasks that introduce initial vocabulary, language, and context for the task.	Look at newspaper advertisements for rental accommodations. Identify key words (written as abbreviations), and match people with their accommodations.
Step 2. Controlled practice	**Example**
Give learners controlled practice in the target-language vocabulary, structures, and functions.	Listen to a model conversation between two people discussing accommodation options, and practice the conversation. Practice again using information from the advertisements in Step 1.

(continued)

Step 3. Authentic listening	Example
Give learners an authentic listening practice.	Listen to several native speakers inquiring about accommodations, and match the conversations with newspaper ads.
Step 4. Focus on linguistic elements	**Example**
Focus learners on an aspect of pronunciation, vocabulary, or grammar.	Listen again to conversations in Step 3, and note intonation contours. Use cue words to write complete questions and answers involving comparatives (*cheaper, closer, more spacious*, etc.).
Step 5. Free practice	**Example**
Provide free practice.	Pair-work information-gap role play. Student A: Play the part of a potential tenant. Make a note of your needs and then call a rental agent. Student B: Play the part of a rental agent. Use ads to gather information, and offer Student A suitable accommodations.
Step 6. Pedagogical task	**Example**
Have learners complete the target task.	Group-work discussion and decision-making task. Look at a set of advertisements, and decide on the most suitable place to rent.
Step 7. Learning strategies	**Example**
Focus learners on an aspect of the learning process.	Have students list 10 new words and 2 new grammar points. Have students review three learning goals and, on a 3-point scale, have them evaluate how well they performed these goals.

FURTHER READING

Ellis, R. (2003). *Task-based language learning and teaching.* Oxford, UK: Oxford University Press.

This volume provides a detailed examination of the research basis for task-based language learning and teaching, and it explores the relationship among research, teaching, and tasks.

Nunan, D. (2004). *Task-based language teaching.* Cambridge, UK: Cambridge University Press.

A comprehensive introduction to TBLT for practicing teachers and teachers in preparation, this book deals with the theory, research, and practice of TBLT.

APPENDIX: CHECKLIST FOR EVALUATING TASKS

The following checklist was designed to enable to comprehensive evaluation of pedagogical tasks (Nunan, 2004, pp. 174–175).

Goals and rationale

- To what extent is the goal or goals of the task obvious (a) to you (b) to your students?
- Is the task appropriate to the learners' proficiency level?
- To what extent does the task reflect a real-world or pedagogic rationale? Is this appropriate?
- Does the task encourage learners to apply classroom learning to the real world?
- What beliefs about the nature of language and learning are inherent in the task?
- Is the task likely to be interesting and motivating to the students?

Input

- What form does the input take?
- Is it authentic?
- If not, is it appropriate to the goal of the task?

Procedures

- Are the procedures appropriate to the communicative goals of the task?

- If not, can they be modified to make them more appropriate?
- Is the task designed to stimulate students to use bottom-up or top-town processing skills?
- Is there an information gap or problem that might prompt a negotiation of meaning?
- Are the procedures appropriate to the input data?
- Are the procedures designed in a way that will allow learners to communicate and cooperate in groups?
- Is there a learning strategies dimension, and is this made explicit to the learners?
- Is there a focus on form aspect, and if so, how is this realized?

Roles and settings

- What learner and teacher roles are inherent in the task?
- Are they appropriate?
- What levels of complexity are there in the classroom organization implicit in the task?
- Is the setting confined to the classroom?

Implementation

- Does the task actually engage the learners' interests?
- Do the procedures prompt genuine communicative interaction among students?
- To what extent are learners encouraged to negotiate meaning?
- Does anything unexpected occur as the task is being carried out?
- What type of language is actually stimulated by the tasks?
- Is this different from what might have been predicted?

Grading and integration

- Is the task at the appropriate level of difficulty for the students?
- If not, is there any way in which the task might be modified to make it either easier or more challenging?
- Is the task so structured that it can be undertaken at different levels of difficulty?

- What are the principles on which the tasks are sequenced?
- Do tasks exhibit the task continuity principle?
- Are a range of macro skills integrated into the sequence of tasks?
- If not, can you think of ways in which they might be integrated?
- At the level of the unit or lesson, are communicative tasks integrated with other activities and exercises designed to provide learners with mastery of the linguistic system?
- If not, are there ways in which such activities might be introduced?
- Do the tasks incorporate exercises in learning how to learn?
- If not, are there ways in which such exercises might be introduced?

Assessment and evaluation

- What means exist for the teacher to determine how successfully the learners have performed?
- Does the task have built into it some means whereby learners might judge how well they had performed?
- Is the task realistic in terms of the resources and teacher expertise it demands?

ENDNOTES

[1] *Values clarification* is a classroom activity in which students are asked to examine the values that they hold and to articulate why these values are important in their lives; often, the activity involves assigning a ranking (e.g., from 1 to 5) to a list of values.

[2] See also Bygate, Skehan, and Swain (2001); R. Ellis (2003); Willis and Willis (2001).

[3] Note, in the preceding section, the centrality of learning processes in Kohonen's scheme of things.

[4] A *scaffolded instructional sequence* is one in which the learning process is facilitated by supporting frameworks. (The term *scaffold* has been appropriated from the building industry and is used metaphorically.) In a reading lesson based on an authentic reading text, for example, the teacher might scaffold the learning by preteaching difficult vocabulary; he or she might also build up background knowledge of the topic by asking a series of leading questions and engaging students in a pre-reading discussion.

30 | English for Specific Purposes: International in Scope, Specific in Purpose

ANN M. JOHNS AND DONNA PRICE

KEY QUESTIONS

➤ How is English for specific purposes different from other approaches to second or foreign language teaching and curriculum design? What are its distinguishing characteristics?

➤ How has English for specific purposes evolved? What is its history?

➤ What happens in the English for specific purposes classroom?

EXPERIENCE

Antoine is from Haiti and has been living in the United States with his wife and children for nine months. He is getting financial assistance from the government, which will last for six more months. He began his program in the United States by studying in an intermediate English as a second language (ESL) class in a noncredit adult education program. However, he is worried that the topics and skills he is learning are too general, and he needs to get a job as soon as possible.

Antoine sits with a counselor, and they examine the class schedule together. The counselor presents one possibility—to enroll in a job skills class. However, for this path, Antoine needs to finish his intermediate ESL class and continue with two more semesters in advanced ESL. Then he can enroll in a career technical education (CTE) class, such as auto mechanics, welding, or nursing assistant. He looks at the counselor in desperation and says, "I don't have time to study for two more years before I get job training! My financial assistance will be cut in six months. What can I do?" The counselor suggests a second possibility—a vocational ESL (VESL) class, where students learn English for their career goals. In addition to the VESL class, he can enroll in a reading class that he can complete online in the computer lab. In the semester-long VESL class,

he will continue learning English, but it will be in the context of the career field he chooses, and this will prepare him for the CTE class, which will require 6–12 months. After completing the VESL class, Antoine will be more prepared to go into the CTE class of his choice. The VESL pathway reduces the amount of time for Antoine to meet his goal of obtaining job skills within one year; and in addition, with the language and vocabulary Antoine learns in this class, he can apply for a job and, if he's fortunate, be given on-the-job training.

WHAT IS ENGLISH FOR SPECIFIC PURPOSES?

English for specific purposes (ESP) is a pedagogical movement in applied linguistics devoted to creating research-based English language materials and instruction for (mostly adult) students with specific language learning goals directly related to their current or future academic, professional, or vocational lives and contexts. Before designing a course for a group of students—and while the course is being given—ESP practitioners conduct research into the students' language needs, their wants, and their academic and professional goals (needs assessment) as well as into the discourses and cultures where the students will be working or studying (target situation analysis). This intensive initial and reoccurring attention to a specific group of students' needs and language proficiencies and the contexts in which they will be using the language is "the cornerstone of ESP—and it leads to a very focused course" (Dudley-Evans & St John, 1998, p. 122). As a result of this focused research and the resulting focused curricula, ESP is often contrasted with teaching English for no apparent reason (TENAR) or general English instruction that is not based on a careful assessment of a particular group's specific language learning needs and target situation but instead is intended to cover the presumed fundamentals of the language.

ESP experts are in considerable agreement about its core characteristics. Strevens's (1988) list, later revised by Dudley-Evans and St John (1998), identifies the absolute and variable features of ESP curricula and teaching.

Absolute characteristics: ESP consists of English language teaching which is:

- Designed to meet the *specified* needs of the learner;
- Related in content (i.e., in its themes and topics) to particular disciplines, occupations and activities (and contexts);
- Centered on the language (and behaviors) appropriate to those activities in syntax, lexis, discourse, semantics (etc.) and analysis of this discourse;
- In contrast with General English.

Variable characteristics: ESP may be, but is not necessarily:

- Restricted as to the language skills to be learned (e.g., reading only);
- Not taught according to any *pre-ordained* methodology. (p. 2)

It can be seen, then, that ESP is a practitioners' movement based on the proposition that language teaching methodologies should be well researched and carefully focused—tailored to the specific learning and language use needs and goals of identified groups of students—and that curricula should be sensitive to the sociocultural and discourse contexts in which these students will use the language.

CONCEPTUAL UNDERPINNINGS

History of ESP

The creation of materials for and instruction in languages for specific purposes (LSP) have a long history, initiated in ancient times as people traveled and came into contact with speakers of other languages but had a limited amount of time to develop the competence needed to communicate, conduct their business, or study in their new contexts. In the twentieth century, as English became the predominant global language, the LSP for the world increasingly became ESP. According to Uber Grosse (1988), the modern ESP movement began in England in the 1920s and has continued apace, especially in the British colonies and, now, throughout the world.

John Swales, arguably the most prominent ESP scholar of the late twentieth century, has written a history of the modern movement, *Episodes in ESP* (1988). In this volume, he marks the beginning of the post–World War II, post-colonial ESP period with a research article by Barber (1962/1985) entitled "Some Measurable Characteristics of Modern Scientific Prose." He then proceeds to demonstrate, through other entries, the connections between the evolution of ESP research and pedagogical approaches. The close relationship among research into student needs and goals, their discourses of use, and the resulting pedagogy has continued throughout ESP's modern history. What has changed over the years is the diversity of approaches to research and pedagogies, paralleling similar developments in applied linguistics (Belcher, Johns, & Paltridge, 2011; Long, 2005).

The early years of ESP can be divided into at least five stages (Hutchinson & Waters, 1987):

1. *Register analysis.* In the 1960s and 1970s, the aim was to identify the grammatical and lexical features of the target discipline (e.g., electrical engineering) and then develop teaching materials around the linguistic features identified.
2. *Discourse analysis.* This stage moved beyond the sentence level as ESP practitioners used discourse analysis to examine the textual patterns in the targeted discipline. They were interested, for example, in how a biology text might be organized in terms of description, definition, classification, causality, and so on.

3. *Target situation analysis.* This stage was characterized by the use of target situation analysis and needs assessment to identify and elucidate learners' needs and wants. By the 1980s, the focus expanded to include not only the language that ESP learners needed for a particular target situation but also the thinking processes that underlie language use.

4. *Skills and strategies.* An emphasis on skills and strategies led to the development of materials that assisted learners to acquire strategic reading skills, such as guessing the meaning of unknown vocabulary from context and looking at how meaning is produced in spoken discourse.

5. *Learning-centered approach.* This stage moved beyond the different conceptualizations of language use in the earlier stages by offering a broader focus on understanding the processes of language learning.

As indicated in a study of the most prominent ESP publication, *English for Specific Purposes: An International Journal*, established in 1981, much of the published needs assessment and target situation research has dealt with the written discourse important to students' academic success, particularly in the sciences (Hewings, 2001). Since John Swales's ground-breaking work on written language, *Genre Analysis: English in Academic and Research Settings* (1990), ESP researchers have increasingly turned to the term *genre* for their discourse analyses to acknowledge that written and spoken discourses should be viewed as situated, purposeful, contextualized, communicative actions taken by a speaker or writer. Thus, for example, there are purposeful academic genres (e.g., research articles, proposals, abstracts, and lab reports), professional genres (e.g., legal briefs, business letters, and resumes), and vocational genres (e.g., application forms, accident reports, and work schedules), all of which can be researched to tease out their functions, discourse structures, grammar, vocabulary, and visual features as practitioners develop curricula and pedagogies for a particular group of students and a specified context (Paltridge, 2001).

The *English for Specific Purposes* journal continues to be the major research arm of the ESP movement; however, since ESP is an international initiative developed to meet the specific needs of students in local situations, research about ESP is also published in regional journals and publications throughout the world, and there are many unpublished studies and curricula as well (A. M. Johns, 2013).

Instructional settings

An increasing number of ESP practitioners live and work in English-speaking/medium countries, preparing curricula for VESL or English for occupational purposes (EOP) programs for new immigrant and refugee populations or in classrooms emphasizing English for academic purposes (EAP) or English for business purposes for students and professionals. However, ESP also continues to be common in English as a foreign language (EFL) contexts, where an increasing number of individuals are eager to learn business or academic English to pursue their careers or studies in English or in English-medium contexts. One remarkable example of the explosion of ESP programs in EFL contexts has taken place in China, but ESP continues to be strong in the Middle East and Latin America, as well.

ESP categories and instructional models

The main curricular areas of the ESP movement can be categorized in a number of ways (Dudley-Evans & St John 1998, p. 6). Figure 1 provides one possible classification.

It is important to note, however, that this figure is far from exhaustive, for there is a remarkable array of ESP courses offered throughout the world. In various cities in Italy, for example, there are project-oriented curricula for workers in the tourist industry (English for tourism). In Morocco, Hasan II University devotes its EAP courses to specific graduate majors, such as agronomy (e.g., advanced English for agronomy). There are also a considerable number of programs in various parts of Latin America (EAP, English for business, etc.). Even in French-medium universities, such as Antonine in Lebanon, the need for English in medicine, engineering, and business has become urgent, and focused materials have been developed by ESP experts to meet these needs (e.g., see Eid & Johns, 2011). In some countries, learning English to contribute to the development of a community or region is a central goal (Gueye, 1990). There are ESP courses in computer repair and other

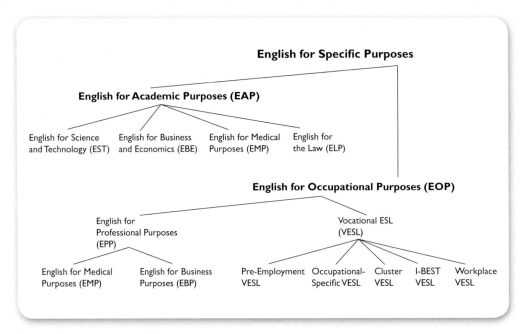

Figure 1. Classification of ESP categories.

areas of computer language and technology for the incarcerated in the United States. This extraordinary diversity of situations and curricula highlights the virtues and challenges of ESP. Programs are designed or adapted to the contexts and language learning needs of specific groups of students; therefore, each group may need a new or revised curriculum since each of these groups may be different in a variety of ways.

Despite this diversity, English for business and economics (EBE) and English for professional purposes (EPP) programs are the most popular ESP areas in the EFL world and in much of the ESL world, as well. Business professionals and students require instruction in negotiation, correspondence, proposal and report writing, uses of technology, and in supervising bilingual and ESL/EFL workers. Business students in academic programs need preparation to pass examinations, such as the Test of English as a Foreign Language (TOEFL), the Graduate Management Admissions Test (GMAT), or the International English Language Testing System (IELTS); and later, they may need support in their coursework or assistance in understanding the cultures of business English classrooms. Not surprisingly, EBE and EPP program design comes in many shapes and sizes, depending on the contexts and students served.[1]

With student and situational diversity and varied needs comes a variety of ESP instructional models. In this section, we describe models within two board categories, EAP and VESL.

EAP models. Among these models are:

Stand-alone EAP. This is the most common format. Stand-alone courses are reading and writing courses, most frequently taught at the undergraduate level, that enroll students from all academic disciplines. Typically, these courses are based on the research into common text types that cross disciplines (e.g., the summary and abstract) or on texts and writers in specified academic contexts (Wardle & Downs, 2011). Stand-alone courses are also offered at the graduate level. Many of the courses use a text like Swales and Feak (2012), written specifically for students in graduate stand-alone courses.

Adjunct EAP. A model that is closely related to a single-content course (e.g., biology or sociology) is the adjunct or linked model. In this model, the same group of students is enrolled in both an EAP literacy course and a content course. (See also Snow, this volume.) Instructors of the two linked courses often share objectives and topics for readings or collaborate on one or more of the assignments (A. M. Johns, 2001). For some EAP adjunct classes, students are encouraged to be researchers into the content course, viewing it as a microcosm for the study of college or university cultures and disciplines (A. M. Johns, 1997).

Team teaching. In this model, the content and language instructors team-teach a group of students, often within the same classroom. This is the ideal, though difficult to accomplish, because it enables the students, with the assistance of their EAP teacher, to reflect on their experiences with content, language, strategies, and assessments within the content classroom (T. Johns & Dudley-Evans, 1980).

VESL models. One of the best articulated and diverse sets of ESP models falls under the VESL rubric. This ESP area includes both *narrow-angled courses*, those focused on one type of job, and *wide-angled courses*, with a more general, comprehensive curriculum (Basturkmen, 2006). The most common VESL models are:

Pre-employment VESL. This is a modified version of a general English or wide-angled ESL model; the content is broadly defined and relates to a number of EOP areas. Instruction is devoted to job readiness and general "soft" job skills, as outlined in the SCANS Report (The Secretary's Commission on Achieving Necessary Skills, 1999). This report was written after a major data-gathering effort (that included analyzing information from employers, supervisors, and employees) to find a clear pattern of what it takes to be successful in the workplace. The commission concluded that a high-performance workplace demands workers who have a solid foundation in the traditional basic academic skills, in the thinking skills necessary to put knowledge to work, and in the personal characteristics that make a worker confident, trustworthy, and responsible. This list is called the "foundation" of workplace know-how. In addition, researchers found that high-performance workplaces also require the ability, or "competency," to manage resources, to work amicably and productively with others, to acquire and use information, to understand complex systems, and to work comfortably with a variety of technologies. In pre-employment VESL classes, students practice the language and pragmatics of general job functions such as responding to complaints, making requests, and answering the phone. They may also prepare

for job interviews and other skills for gaining employment. Technology integration is key to pre-employment VESL because the application process generally takes place online.

Occupation-specific VESL. This is a narrow-angled curriculum focusing on one particular job, such as nursing assistant or welder, and as such, it is closer to the ideal in ESP. The language, discourses, and pragmatics are often clearly and narrowly identified after the completion of a thorough needs assessment and target situation analysis. The course can be taught either as preparation for or concurrently with a vocational program. In most cases, there is frequent communication between the VESL and vocational instructors before the class is offered and while the students are enrolled.

Integrated basic education and skills training VESL. The integrated basic education and skills training (I-BEST) approach is an adjunct or sometimes a team-teaching model in which the ESL instructor is paired with the professional-technical instructor in the classroom to concurrently provide students with literacy education and workforce skills. An example of this model is a personal care assistant/caregiver class that is team-taught by an ESL instructor and a registered nurse. The ESL instructor teaches the language for personal care assistants/caregivers, and the registered nurse teaches the hands-on skills necessary for the job.

Cluster VESL. This popular model combines wide-angled and narrow-angled approaches. Initially, students from different vocations are in one classroom. They study all four skills (listening, speaking, reading, and writing), often in a theme-based program (e.g., *The World of Work*). In one class, for example, students read about how to meet people and make small talk in the workplace. Later, in a more narrow-angled approach, students work on individualized modules devoted to their chosen professions or vocations and are assessed on their progress in these specialized areas. This model is an example of the kind of class in which Antoine (from the Experience section at the beginning of this chapter) would enroll to expedite his entry into a career technical education class.

Workplace VESL. In this model, ESP classes are offered to employees at the job site. Often, the employer pays for some or all of the course, and employees are excused during their workday to attend. The goals of workplace instruction are often higher productivity on the job, improved safety, and increased use of English. Unfortunately, employers do not offer this training at worksites as much as in the past because of scheduling issues, cost, and a belief that teaching their employees English is not their responsibility (Burt, 2004).

Rationale and responsibilities of ESP practitioners

As has already been noted, the primary responsibilities of ESP practitioners are to develop, contextualize, evaluate, and/or revise ESL/EFL language curricula, classroom pedagogies, and assessments, making them appropriate for a *specific* group of students in a *specific* language learning environments by administering thorough and ongoing needs assessments and target situation analyses of the language, discourses, and contexts in which students will be using the language. This means that ideal ESP curricula are always in process as practitioner research continues and classroom pedagogies are made increasingly appropriate for a group of students with whom the instructor becomes more familiar. The specific tasks of ESP practitioners are discussed next.

Working closely with the those in the target situation. No matter what the students' goals may be, the ESP practitioner's close, continuous interaction with the experts and stakeholders in the target situation in which students will work or study is ideal for at least two reasons: students have more authentic practice, and they often are able to experience and reflect upon their immediate successes and roadblocks. Here are two examples:

Donna Price, in her VESL work with ESL for personal care assistants, team-teaches with a nurse in a classroom, using the I-BEST approach. Students are exposed to, and practice with, the texts, grammar, vocabulary, and communicative contexts of caregiving. As a result, students not only have immediate success in the jobs they plan to apply for but they also are prepared to move up to careers in the health field that go beyond the entry level, such as certified nursing

assistants, medical assistants, licensed vocational nurses, and registered nurses (Price, Carvajal, & McGee, 2010).

Ann M. Johns, whose focus is EAP, has been teaching and developing curricula for first-year university students at San Diego State University and at other universities for more than 35 years. She has been collaborating with instructors across disciplines who teach geography, history, biology, psychology, political science, business, and anthropology in an adjunct model approach. Her students are enrolled concurrently in her EAP class and a linked first-year class offered by a disciplinary instructor (A. M. Johns, 2001). In the EAP class, her students research the disciplinary class as an academic microcosm (A. M. Johns, 1997). In addition, they attempt to transfer their learning to other academic classes in which they are enrolled.

Conducting effective needs assessment and target situation research. First, and often, practitioners must determine as best they can the students' goals and their language and cultural needs as well as the nature of the language and genres of the context in which they will be using English. This careful pre- and ongoing research into students' needs, goals, and the discourses and contexts in which they will be using the language is what distinguishes ESP from other language teaching approaches. For this reason, the content (or topics) of a course is often not central to ESP instruction; instead, language and language learning strategies are the focus.

For some contexts and student populations, where the students are fairly homogeneous (e.g., all students are, or will be, lab technicians or electrical engineers) and narrow-angled courses can therefore be offered, this research may be fairly straightforward. It may involve interviews with the experts (instructors and managers), observation of classes or job shadowing in the workplace, collection of data and analysis of the language (vocabulary, grammar, and genres) and skills (reading, writing, listening, and speaking) that seem to predominate. For example, when teaching nursing assistants, EAP practitioners find it invaluable to shadow the students while they are doing their clinical training at a convalescent hospital to see what language skills they need. In addition, collecting charts and graphs that nursing assistants fill out on the job connects the classroom instruction to the workplace. Of course, the students must be directly involved as well, so part of the research may include a questionnaire distributed to the students so they can state their goals and assess their linguistic strengths and weaknesses.

On the other hand, ESP courses in many parts of the world must be wide-angled. These include English for (academic) business courses that enroll students in management, marketing, accounting, business ethics, or other fields. As in all needs assessments, those for wide-angled classes may produce some interesting results. For example, when planning an English for business professionals course in a Korean context, Huh (2006) found that there were tasks beyond the typical business correspondence (e.g., email) and genres (e.g., proposals, reports, and contracts) that should be included in a curriculum. Some of these involved understanding the language and culture of business meetings; the language of overseas travel, especially when visiting companies; attending to foreign guests; interpretation/translation; and gathering information on a foreign market. The results of Huh's needs assessment make clear how important *situating* an ESP course becomes.

Even broader are the EAP courses that abound, particularly in first-year programs in colleges and universities across the world. For these courses, practitioners need to concentrate on language that crosses disciplinary boundaries. Fortunately, corpus linguists have provided the EAP teacher with an academic word list (Coxhead, 2000),[2] and there is other research into the grammar and syntax that cross academic disciplines and registers (e.g., see Biber & Conrad, 1999; Conrad & Biber, 2004; Coxhead, 2000). (See also chapters by Snow and Zimmerman, this volume.) Interdisciplinary academic tasks have also been studied extensively. One of the most cited and respected of these studies was completed in 1986 by Horowitz. In his cross-disciplinary research, he found that the following tasks were common on his campus: summary/reaction to a reading, annotated bibliography, report on a participatory experience, making connections between theory and data, case study, synthesis of sources, and research project. The notion of research project has been further refined by M. Carter (2007), who found that research has four possible purposes, resulting in macro-genre responses within an academic context: to problem-solve (e.g., in business or social work), to report on empirical

inquiry (e.g., in the sciences), to investigate and discuss written or visual sources (e.g., in English or the humanities), and to review a performance (e.g., in the arts). Additional extensive research on EAP writing assignments has been completed by Melzer (2009) and research on reading by Grabe and Stoller (2011). After reviewing this research, those preparing an EAP curriculum can survey the courses on their own campus to situate the linguistic, discourse, and strategic features that cross disciplines in their specific context.

Adapting and developing methods and curricula. Experienced ESP teachers do not work solely with predetermined curricula or pedagogies. Instead, they assess their students, the context, and stakeholders to determine what is most appropriate. For example, when assisting teachers to develop EAP curricula for college students in China in the early 1980s, Johns studied not only the EAP demands on the students but the methods by which they had been taught English in the past. One method was intensive reading, a word-by-word approach to reading texts. As she and the teachers developed the materials, the approaches to intensive reading were incorporated—and then slowly revised within the curriculum—to ensure that students did not have to make too rapid a transition from the way they had been learning to newer, alternative approaches to teaching reading comprehension. (See chapters by Anderson, Ediger, and Grabe, & Stoller, this volume.)

More recently, Johns prepared a semester-long reading, writing, and critical thinking curriculum for students in a South African university. There, a drill-and-practice approach to writing had been in place since the early 1970s, and the students found this to be both easy and supportive of their high school literacy experiences. The university faculty, who were required to teach EAP but were much more interested in teaching literature, were also satisfied with the approach. Again, a consideration of the students' past experiences and faculty preferences was made to ensure a smooth transition to other types of instruction (Johns & Makalela, 2011).

It is not that ESP practitioners cannot introduce different classroom approaches; such changes must be made in a way, however, that considers the local contexts, the students' prior learning, and the stakeholders' interests and backgrounds.

Experienced ESP practitioners are not purists in terms of linguistic theories, research, curricula, or classroom pedagogy. They do not need to draw from one theory, one pedagogy, or one research tradition that happens to be in vogue. Instead, they are guided in their work by approaches that can assist them in determining their students' backgrounds, goals, and needs, and these findings determine the focus of the curriculum.

How do ESP practitioners proceed? What are the steps in ESP needs assessment and target situation research, curriculum design, and teaching? The topics presented by Swales in *Episodes in ESP* (1985) continue to be the principal focus of most ESP research—gaining a full understanding of the language features and discourses of a context and the roles that these will play in the lives of ESP students. In recent years, corpus linguistics has provided opportunities for researchers to study vast collections of authentic spoken and written discourse to use in curriculum design for a variety of ESP areas, and this has been a boon to ESP curriculum design (see Belcher, 2009b; Gavioli, 2005; Hyland, 2004a; Hyland & Tse, 2004; Paltridge, 2009). (See also McCarthy & O'Keeffe, this volume.)

As noted, ESP practitioners have adopted *genre* as a concept central to ESP research, conflating the context and language of a discourse community (Paltridge, 2001; Swales, 1990); like corpus linguistics, this concept and its implications should be integral to any ESP practitioner's repertoire. Once identified as text types by their structures and purposes, genres are now viewed as social actions realized in spoken or written discourses within occupational, academic, or social communities (Bawarshi, 2003; Bawarshi & Reiff, 2010; Belcher, 2006). What does this mean? The focus of genre is on the action that is being carried out within a context rather than, initially, on the features of the text itself. Devitt (2004) speaks of genre as "the nexus between individual actions and a socially defined context" (p. 163).

ESP practitioners conduct research into the contexts, functions ("moves"), and language of genres, noting what their findings imply about interactions between oral and written texts, communities, and writers (Hyland, 2000, 2005; Samraj, 2002; Swales, 1990). In this way, they can prepare students to not only employ appropriately the linguistic elements (e.g., vocabulary and grammar)

of their chosen occupation or academic field but to understand and exploit the genres that are valued in the context in this field as well.

Teaching skills and strategies for far transfer. A central goal for ESP programs should be to prepare students with skills and strategies that can be used in the future in different contexts (see Belcher, 2006; James, 2010). In the literature, this ability to adapt previously learned skills to new future tasks and contexts is called *far transfer*. Daniel Willingham (2009), a cognitive psychologist, notes that "when successful [far] transfer occurs, students can apply what they learn to different contexts, and recognize and extend that learning to a context which draws from prior experience but may appear to be completely new" (p. 212).

How can the skills for far transfer be enhanced in an ESP class? One way is to introduce students to learning with real-world situations and challenges, as practitioners do when they co-teach with experts. Ideally, students in these real-world situations can practice sorting out what they need to carry over and apply from the old learning to the new authentic situations and tasks (Svinicki, 2004). If working directly with experts is not possible, students in the ESP classroom can be presented with authentic materials and activities. Purcell-Gates, Degener, Jacobson, and Soler (2001) note that students who attend classes where real-world literacy activities and texts are used tend to increase their appropriate use of reading and writing skills outside the classroom. Based on their findings, these researchers recommend that VESL teachers include real-life activities and texts, such as job applications, work manuals, and newspapers in their instruction.

According to Willingham (2009), repeated practice of the types of strategies that transfer to a variety of situations is central to student success in the future. One EAP example of this approach is found in LeMaster's *Critical Reading* (2010), where students and teachers are first introduced to deep reading strategies (e.g., marking the text), and are then provided with opportunities to use the strategy repeatedly with different texts in several content areas (e.g., science, social science, and mathematics).[3] For students to recall the strategies they used, they are encouraged to reflect, assessing how they approached a task and how the strategy had to be adapted as new tasks arose (A. M. Johns, 1997).

Far transfer can also be enhanced through *problem-based learning* (PBL), an approach that assists students in solving the types of problems that they may have to face in their future careers (Barron, 2002; L. Flowerdew, 2005). One area where PBL has been particularly successful is nursing. Belcher (2009a) discusses how PBL is used in this field and advocates its adoption in other areas of ESP teaching. An example of PBL in a VESL personal care assistant class is the following hypothetical scenario:

> You have a client with dementia. She gives you $20 as a tip for helping her. You accept the money. When your client's daughter gets home, you show her the money that her mother had given you. Your client accuses you of stealing. What should you do?

Students work in groups to come up with options for resolving the problem. They practice problem solving, critical thinking, and negotiation skills at the same time that they are developing content knowledge.

CLASSROOM APPLICATIONS

What happens in the classroom after the needs assessment is completed and the curriculum is designed? Much depends on the results of the needs assessment and target situation analysis research, the students' backgrounds, the teaching context and teachers' abilities, and the administrative constraints and resources in which the teaching is taking place. The classroom-tested examples here are from EAP programs in different contexts and VESL/EOP programs. Other examples can be found in teacher guides (e.g., Dudley-Evans & St John, 1998).

EAP examples

Example 1. In 2007, the English Department at Limpopo University in northern South Africa was charged with creating a motivating first-year literacy course for students from all academic disciplines, that is, a wide-angled EAP program. One author of this chapter (Ann Johns) was invited to conduct a needs assessment on site and to develop a year-long curriculum. Johns and the English Department chair, Leketi Makalela, using ESP needs assessment and target situation analysis

---

Lesson 1: Proud to be South African

Reading: "Proud to be South African" from the *Mail & Guardian* online.

Objectives: Students will be able to

- Read and complete a short questionnaire relating to their experience as South Africans.
- Scan a text to answer comprehension questions.
- Identify, with a group, the methodology used and the results obtained in a paper discussing research.
- Accurately identify simple past, simple present, and present perfect tenses in a reading; and in a cloze passage, apply their knowledge by inserting the correct tense forms.
- With partners, identify the terms related to research in a short reading discussing a study.
- Given the introduction, methodology, results, and discussion (IMRD) model, convert the study discussed in a short reading into a research summary.
- Given questions about their learning, write at least four sentences about what they have learned during the lesson.

Lesson components:

- *Pre-reading*: Completing a short a questionnaire
- *Silent reading*: Scanning to answer questions
- *Group reading*: Identifying methodology and results
- *Grammar activities*: Using verbs in past and present tenses
- *Vocabulary activities*: Finding words for discussing research
- *Writing activity*: Writing a research summary
- *Reflecting upon learning*: Brainstorming goals achieved

Figure 2. EAP lesson organization.

approaches, developed a 15-lesson course that was then tested (and eventually revised) by instructors, based on the interests and current proficiency levels of the students. Figure 2 illustrates the lesson objectives and recurring lesson components, though the activities in each lesson varied.

An extensive guide for teachers and suggestions for organizing each activity accompanied the curriculum. One example of the activities comes from the Group Reading section in Lesson 1, based on three findings in the needs assessment: (1) that students enjoyed working in groups; (2) that the classes were large, and thus group activity was considered to be essential to student interaction and participation; and (3) that many of the students were majoring in the sciences, so methodology and results sections were central to their scientific papers. Figure 3 illustrates the group activity, followed by a related out-of-class writing activity and reflection questions.

Group reading: *Identifying methodology and results* (in-class, 20 minutes)

Task: In academic departments, experts conduct research. They pose a research question, which they study in depth. The method(s) used to conduct research is very important. In your groups, scan the reading for this information:
1) Who conducted this study?
2) How many people were surveyed?
3) What ethnic groups did the people belong to?
4) What were the most important results of the research?

As you answer these questions by working through the reading, ask one person to take notes. Each group will report answers to one of the questions.

Writing activity: *Writing a research summary* (out-of-class)

Task: Write up a summary of the research reported in this article. As a guide, below you are given the functions of each sentence in the summary and an example. Read the article and follow the directions:

Sentence 1: Tell what the study was about, the methods, and who conducted it.
> *Example:* In order to find out whether people like cheese and what kind, interviews were conducted at Woolworths by students from University of Limpopo.

Sentence 2: Tell who was involved in the research and what questions were asked.
> *Example:* The students asked 500 shoppers on a busy Saturday if they liked cheese and, if so, what type they were buying, who ate cheese in their families, and how much cheese they bought each week.

Sentence 3: Explain the results.
> *Example:* The researchers found that 100% of the shoppers questioned liked cheese. They prefer cheddar to the other kinds. The men in the family were the principal cheese eaters, and the average amount of cheese purchased each week was 2 kilos.

Sentence 4: Summarize what you, or the researchers, concluded from the study.
> *Example:* It can be concluded from this study of cheese preferences that South African shoppers are big cheese buyers and that men, rather than women, are the ones who eat most of the cheese.

Figure 3. Sample group reading and writing activity for an EAP lesson.

When the students completed these reading and the writing activities, they were asked to reflect on their learning with follow-up questions designed to promote transfer of learning (Figure 4).

Example 2. A second EAP example comes from a wide-angled, advanced course for international

Reflecting upon learning (in-class, 10 minutes)

Task: In your notebooks, reflect upon what you have learned in this lesson. Answer one or more of these questions:
1) What did you learn about South African people by reading this article? Were you surprised about what you learned?
2) What did you learn about research methods? How is a discussion of research organized in a summary?
3) What academic words that you learned have you seen elsewhere?
4) If you were going to conduct a survey of students on the Limpopo campus, what questions would you ask? Why?

Figure 4. Sample reflection activity from an EAP course.

graduate and undergraduate students offered by an intensive language institute in the United States. The needs assessment for this course was based on the types of tasks that the students were assigned in their university graduate classes, as determined by the syllabi for those classes and previous surveys of instructors across the disciplines. What the EAP instructor, Ann Johns, and her colleagues discovered was that in all the students' classes take-home, process-based papers were required; however, students had difficulty analyzing the prompts for these papers, that is, understanding what the required responses to the prompts were. Thus, throughout the class, students practiced prompt analysis. Figure 5 presents a sample activity.

VESL examples

Example 1: Contextualized instruction. One way to prepare adult learners for the workplace is by using contextualized instruction at all levels of adult education, including employment-related tasks as a large part of the context (Chisman, 2009). *Contextualized instruction* is defined as the development of skills, knowledge, and attitudes drawn from the context in which they will be used, based on real-life materials and situations from that context (National Institute for Literacy Workforce Education, 2005). In her VESL classes, Donna Price often asks her students to bring materials from their workplace that they have to read or write.

The following lesson is appropriate for beginning to intermediate adult education students in

Analyzing and Responding to a Take-Home Prompt

To the student: When you are given a writing prompt, you will need to carefully analyze the task at hand. What are you to do when writing? What is the important content? How should your writing be organized? Answer the questions below before beginning your reading or drafting your text.

Name _____ Date_____

Class _____ Period _____

Write the prompt from your class below: (a sample is provided here.)

You have recently read "Prison vs. education spending reveals California's priorities," and, as someone who has several incarcerated friends, you have become quite upset. Write a letter to the editor of the *San Francisco Chronicle* expressing your opinion of the priorities of the State of California. Follow the rules for a "letter to the editor" genre. Since you want this letter to be published, be sure that you understand the reading well—and that your writing is carefully edited.

With a partner, answer these questions about the above prompt (then individually, answer the same questions about the prompt from your own class).

1. What are you supposed to *do* as a writer when you are responding to this prompt? Are you asked to make an argument? To inform? To describe or list? If your "doing" word is vague, like *discuss* or *describe*, what do you think it means? If you don't know, how can you find out?
2. What content are you supposed to discuss in this prompt? Is the content related in some way?
3. Are you told anything about the language register or style you are to use? Can you guess?
4. Who are you supposed to *be* as a writer in this prompt? An ordinary student or someone else? (Some prompts tell writers to "speak" in the voice of an editorial writer, a leader, or. . . .)
5. Is your audience specified? If so, who is your audience? What will this mean in terms of the language you use or the content you include?
6. Are you told the genre of the text? Does this help you with how the text is supposed to be structured? For example, does the prompt indicate the order in which you are to discuss the content?
7. How are you to use sources, if at all? How many sources should you use? What kinds? Does the prompt specify whether the sources should be primary or secondary? What genres are appropriate? (Magazine or journal articles? Online sources? Textbooks? Newspapers? Full-length books?)
8. How long should your paper be? What other specifications are given? (The referencing style? The font size? The margin width?)
9. How will you be graded on this paper? What criteria will the instructor be using?
10. How will you organize your writing? On the back of this paper, write a draft plan for your response.

Figure 5. Sample activity for analyzing writing prompts in an EAP course.

pre-employment or cluster VESL classes, as well as general ESL classes. The objective of this lesson is for students to: (1) be able to read and interpret information from a chart in their textbook (the classroom inventory list in Figure 6); and (2) apply this skill to the authentic workplace task of reading a hotel worker's weekly maintenance schedule (Figure 7).

Figure 6 provides students with practice in interpreting information from a chart in their textbook. To connect school to work, an instructor first uses the chart to do chart reading and interpreting activities with the textbook material, asking, for example: "Where are the pens? What item is there only one of? What do they need to get more of?" The teacher actually teaches students how to read the chart by saying, "Put your finger on the eraser." Then the teacher asks, "How many erasers do we have?" The

teacher has students move their fingers across to the number of erasers. These kinds of questions and the accompanying scaffolding are important when dealing with students who have low literacy skills because they develop the students' skills in reading and interpreting information, which can then be transferred to the workplace.

The form from a local hotel (Figure 7) lists a hotel maintenance worker's daily job responsibilities. The worker is required to read and interpret the instructions and to perform certain specified tasks on a daily basis. To prepare students for this type of real-world task, the VESL teacher brings this type of form into the classroom and asks students, for example, "Which days does the worker have to clean the pool? Which days does he have to dust the cobwebs off the ceiling? What does he do on Mondays?" and so on. Skills that we teach in

Classroom Inventory List

Item		Number	Location
calculators		15	in the drawer
computers		1	on the desk
books		5	on the cabinet
erasers		20	in the box
pencils		20	on the table
pens		20	on the table
rulers		25	in the cabinet

Figure 6. Classroom inventory list (based on Bitterlin, Johnson, Price, Ramirez, & Savage, 2008a, p. 28.)

DUTIES	M	T	W	Th	F	Sa	S	Notes
Help housekeepers move carts up & down stairs	X	X	X	X	X	X	X	
Clean the entire pool area	X		X		X	X	X	
Clean the entire front lobby area & driveway	X	X	X	X	X	X	X	
Do a walk-thru of entire building and groups (am & pm)	X	X	X	X	X	X	X	
Clean all parking lots	X		X		X	X		
Clean entire lower level	X	X	X	X	X	X	X	
Clean entire upper level	X	X	X	X	X	X	X	
Clean laundry room	X		X		X			
All high dusting for cobwebs				X				
Put away linen delivery	X		X		X		X	
Clean BBQ grills	X		X		X	X	X	
Check & put away cots	X	X	X	X	X	X	X	
Clean all dirty stove pans and rims						X	X	

Figure 7. Hotel maintenance worker's weekly job inventory.

the classroom (e.g., such as reading the inventory chart) should transfer to the workplace (e.g., reading the hotel maintenance job chart).

Example 2: Problem-solving lesson—What should Yolanda do? Problem solving is a skill that is required in many jobs and is listed in workplace frameworks (Partnership for the 21st Century Skills, 2004; The Secretary's Commission on Achieving Necessary Skills, 1999). This lesson is appropriate for intermediate-advanced level adult education students (Bitterlin, Johnson, Price, Ramirez, & Savage, 2008b). It would be appropriate in a pre-employment VESL class or general ESL class.

The objectives of this lesson are for students to be able to:

- Identify solutions to and consequences of a workplace problem.
- Come to a consensus in their groups about the best solution.
- Use appropriate language for agreeing and disagreeing (i.e., *I agree; I don't agree; You're right; I think so, too*).

- Use appropriate language for giving suggestions (i.e., *She should; She ought to; I think it would be a good idea if she . . .*).

Teachers follow these procedures:

- Seat students in small groups of three to five students each.
- Ask students to number off within their groups.
- Designate Student 1 in each group as the group leader. This person will facilitate the group by asking group members' opinions.
- Designate Student 2 in each group as the reporter. This student will summarize the group's solution and the reasons why the group came to that decision to the whole class.
- Explain that all group members will write on the Problem-Solving Worksheet (Figure 8).
- Project the pictures (in Figure 9), and ask questions, for example:
  - How many pictures are there? (Answer: 3)
  - Where are they? (*Answer:* in a donut shop)
  - What is similar about all the pictures? (*Answer:* Yolanda is in all of them).

Problem-Solving Worksheet

Problem: David keeps leaving work early; Yolanda is tired of doing his share of the work.

Task:
a) What can Yolanda do?
b) What are the good and bad consequences of her actions?

1. Suggestion _____
   Good consequence _____
   Bad consequence _____

2. Suggestion _____
   Good consequence _____
   Bad consequence _____

3. Suggestion _____
   Good consequence _____
   Bad consequence _____

Solution: What will she do? Why?

1. Come to a consensus in your group.
2. Explain your decision to the class.

Yolanda will _____
because_____

Figure 8. Problem-solving worksheet.

Figure 9. Pictures to accompany the problem-solving lesson (based on Bitterlin, Johnson, Price, Ramirez, & Savage, 2008b, p. 96).

- (Pointing to picture 1) What is Yolanda doing here? (*Answer:* She's talking to David, who is leaving.)
- (Pointing to picture 2) What's Yolanda doing here? (*Answer:* She's leaving work after closing the shop.)

- (Pointing to picture 3) What is Yolanda doing here? (*Answer:* She's talking to her friends. She's upset.)

Students work in groups to discuss solutions and consequences to the problem. They then fill out the Problem-Solving Worksheet (Figure 8). The group must come to a consensus before reporting back. Table 1 presents some possible solutions and consequences that students might come up with and present to the class as a whole.

FUTURE TRENDS

ESP programs are developed because teachers, supervisors, government agencies, professionals, or students see a need for focused language courses in which certain skills, genres, motivations, processes, and/or values are identified and integrated into specialized, often short-term classes. As the world becomes more connected, this demand will undoubtedly grow; and as it does, practitioners need to be prepared. Concluding her 2006 survey article, Belcher notes that "ESP professionals should be able to face the prospect of reappraising the role of English language in a rapidly globalizing world with a ready array of professional resources" (p. 151).

Rethinking approaches to foundational ESP elements

The foundational elements of ESP—needs assessment, target situation analysis, pedagogical practices, reflection, and course and program

Table 1. Possible Solutions to the Problem-Solving Worksheet

Solutions	Good consequences	Bad consequences
1. She could quit.	She won't have to deal with David anymore.	She'll have to look for another job, which isn't easy. She might have the same problem in another job.
2. She should talk to her boss.	Her boss might help her solve the problem. He might talk to David in a nice way.	Her boss might tell her to solve this problem herself. He might tell David, and then David could make her life miserable at work.
3. She could talk to David.	He might listen to Yolanda and make some changes.	He might get mad at her and treat her badly at work.
4. She could make a checklist of duties. (This is a true story and this is actually what she did.)	A checklist of duties where each employee initials when the work is done would keep everyone accountable. There would be a record of who did what job.	The other employees might not take the checklist seriously. The boss might not enforce it.

assessment—will undoubtedly become increasingly complex and comprehensive in the future. In the case of needs assessments, for example, methodologies will be deeper and more triangulated[4] and critical (Jasso-Aguilar, 2005; Starfield, 2011); technology will be more thoroughly exploited; and spoken language will, in many cases, become more prominent in research in all ESP areas (Holmes, 2005; Long, 2005).

Incorporating digital literacies

Due to the rapid development and centrality of digital literacies, research and pedagogies will be increasingly devoted to this revolution in the ways that people communicate. The language and use of Internet sites, YouTube, blogs, and Twitter, or whatever succeeds these particular platforms and genres, will be an essential part of ESP research and ESP teaching for student success in a global context. One obvious area for research is in business English, for example, studying how social networking is exploited to brand a product (or person) or how advertising reaches certain target groups. Corpus linguistics, a well-established research methodology, will have an expanded use in ESP classrooms as the students themselves determine the predominant features of spoken or written text and how these features are employed in specific contexts.[5] As computers become the norm in ESP classrooms and labs, this trend will continue.

Re-orientating skill instruction

With the influence of the digital revolution on communication, we will need to reconsider the traditional skills of speaking, listening, reading, and writing for many ESP contexts. For instance, what does writing in the students' digital world require? What is involved in reading or writing a Twitter message, and who are the audiences? How do certain populations process a particular YouTube segment? What is encouraged in ESP literacies by the use of classroom management systems, such as Blackboard, WebCT, and PBWorks (Kolko, Regan, & Romano, 2001)?

Revising instructional models

Models for instruction may also require revision. One example, transition programs, comes from VESL. According to the National Center on Education and the Economy Workforce Development Strategies Group (2009), adult education should be redesigned to promote post-secondary and workplace readiness for all learners.

Thus, in today's educational and economic environment, program leaders need to prepare students to move quickly beyond intermediate ESL and into a higher level of ESL, ultimately transitioning into mainstream programs. For example, there is a trend in ESP to implement career pathways as systems of learning that move low-skilled adults rapidly through work-oriented adult education programs or into post-secondary programs. Some programs have described this effort as an educational transit system that must be collaboratively created by academic, administrative, and workforce education departments (National Institute for Literacy Workforce Education, 2005).

Expanding lingua franca studies

As additional native speakers of other languages use English as a lingua franca, or language of wider communication, more research and pedagogies will focus on those situations in which none of the participants in the ESP enterprise is a native speaker of English. This will provide opportunities to examine how ESP as a second (third, fourth) language is researched, produced, and taught by L2 speakers (Mauranen, 2011).

CONCLUSION

ESP requires of the practitioner an open mind; a willingness to conduct appropriate needs assessment and target situation research; knowledge of language and linguistics, corpus studies, and genres; and a broad understanding of curricular models and pedagogies, as well as new technologies. It requires that future researchers look beyond text products and consider more seriously learner processes, cognition, and target contexts and that they investigate the complexity and challenges that the online environment and other contexts present (Belcher, 2006). The future of ESP requires practitioners who will be true to the foundational principles but who will view their course design as ever more challenging as technologies, language use, and research practices become more complex.

SUMMARY

➤ ESP programs are designed for a specific group of ESL/EFL students, usually adults, who have limited time to develop the competence needed to work or study in identified contexts.

➤ ESP is distinguished not by a particular linguistic theory or teaching methodology but by its needs assessments and target situation analyses, which determine the focus of the curricula and pedagogy for a specific group of students in an identified context.

➤ Successful ESP teachers do not need to be content experts; however, they do need to have a solid linguistics background; to be skilled at various approaches to needs assessment and target situation analysis; to be adept at working with a variety of stakeholders in a variety of cultures; and to be open, observant, and flexible as their curriculum and instruction evolves.

DISCUSSION QUESTIONS

1. What questions do you have about ESP that have not been answered in this chapter? Where can you find the answers?
2. What do you feel is particularly appealing about ESP?
3. What are the challenges that an ESP practitioner faces as he or she designs and teaches courses?
4. What do you think the advantages and disadvantages are of teaching each are of the following classes: cluster VESL, I-BEST, and workplace VESL?

SUGGESTED ACTIVITIES

1. Observe an ESP class. What category (EAP, EBE, or VESL) does the class represent? What instructional model is in place? What ESP activities appear to be particularly useful for far transfer? Why?
2. Imagine that you are teaching a wide-angled EAP class for students who are also enrolled in college courses. Collect four or five syllabi from classes in different disciplines. Using the

descriptions of assignments, examinations, and readings in these, prepare at least five tasks (e.g., summarizing/abstracting) that will be appropriate for all the classes in the disciplines and thus for your wide-angled EAP class.

3. Consider the strategies for critical thinking that might be taught in secondary or post-secondary classes. Develop one or more activities that assist students to practice critical thinking skills. Or find activities in EAP textbooks that you believe will help students develop strategies for far transfer. Share them with the class.
4. You have been asked to teach a class for students who will be accountants and have recently completed their business degrees. What methods will you use to conduct a needs assessment and target situation analysis?
5. Imagine that you are teaching a pre-employment VESL class. You know from the SCANS Report and from what employers tell us that teamwork, sociability, and self-esteem are essential workplace skills. Develop several classroom activities that integrate these transferable skills.
6. In cluster VESL class, students have a variety of career goals. There are people who want to be auto techs, clerical workers, nurses, hotel managers, and so on. Make a list of transferable work skills that are necessary in all jobs (e.g., following directions). How would you integrate these skills into your teaching?

FURTHER READING

Basturkmen, H. (2006). *Ideas and options in English for specific purposes.* Mahwah, NJ: Lawrence Erlbaum Associates.

Taking a language acquisition approach, this author discusses how ESP relates to the conditions and processes of learning as well as teaching methods (e.g., input- and output-based strategies), and suggests a framework for curriculum analysis and development.

Bawarshi, A. S., & Reiff, M. J. (2010). *Genre: An introduction to history, theory, research, and pedagogy.* West Lafayette, IN: Parlor Press.

This volume presents a carefully explained and balanced overview of genre theories and their applications to pedagogical practices.

Belcher, D. (Ed.). (2009). *English for specific purposes in theory and practice.* Ann Arbor, MI: University of Michigan Press.

This is a useful introductory collection, with chapters relating to English for academic purposes (EAP), English for occupational purposes (EOP), and, a relatively new area, English for sociocultural purposes.

Belcher, D., Johns, A. M., & Paltridge, B. (Eds.). (2011). *New directions in ESP research.* Ann Arbor, MI: University of Michigan Press.

This volume includes chapters in which new approaches to needs assessment and target situation research are presented. New topics in research, such as critical ethnography, are also integral to this text.

Bitterlin, G., Johnson, D., Price, D., Ramirez, S., & Savage, K. L. (2010). *Ventures transitions.* New York, NY: Cambridge University Press.

This VESL textbook offers integrated-skills material to help prepare adult students for success at work or in academic settings.

English for Specific Purposes: An International Journal. Available from http://www.sciencedirect.com/

Founded in 1980, this Elsevier publication continues to lead the research field. Article topics include second language acquisition in specific contexts, needs assessment, curriculum development and evaluation, materials preparation, teaching and testing techniques, and the training and retraining of teachers for ESP.

Journal of English for Academic Purposes. Available from http://www.sciencedirect.com/

Also published by Elsevier, this journal was founded in 2001 to encourage continuing research and discussion among EAP practitioners. It encourages articles on a wide range of subjects, including classroom language, teaching methods, teacher education, language assessment, needs assessment, materials development and evaluation, and the sociopolitics of English uses and language planning.

Long, M. H. (Ed.). (2005). *Second language needs analysis.* Cambridge, UK: Cambridge University Press.

This book contains discussions of a variety of approaches to needs assessment research in the public, occupational, and academic sectors.

ENDNOTES

[1] For a more thorough treatment of this issue, see Nickerson and Planken (2009); Rogerson-Revell (2007).

[2] See the Academic Word List, http://www.uefap.com/vocab/select/awl.htm

[3] See the Literacy TA site, http://www.literacyta.com

[4] Triangulation refers to the use of at least three different types of data to support research findings (e.g., proficiency test scores, questionnaires, and classroom observations).

[5] See "Using Corpus Linguistics to Teach ESL," at http://www.catesol.org/Fagan.pdf

31 | Literature as Content for Language Teaching

SANDRA LEE MCKAY

KEY QUESTIONS

➤ Why use literature in English as a second or foreign language classes?
➤ What are key differences between literary and nonliterary texts?
➤ What are some ways to use literature in English as a second or foreign language classrooms?

EXPERIENCE

What they don't understand about birthdays and what they never tell you is that when you're eleven, you're also ten, and nine, and eight, and seven, and six, and five, and four, and three, and two, and one. And when you wake up on your eleventh birthday you expect to feel eleven, but you don't. You open your eyes and everything's just like yesterday, only it's today. And you don't feel eleven at all. You feel like you're still ten. And you are— underneath the year that makes you eleven. (Cisneros, 1996, p. 11)

So begins an excerpt from Sandra Cisneros's novel *Woman Hollering Creek*. A beginning teacher, working with middle school English as a second language (ESL) students, comes across the short excerpt and decides to use it in her ESL class. While excited about using it in class, she questions what she should do with it. The aim of this chapter is to help her answer this question.

There are those who maintain that, due to the special nature of literary texts, literature can contribute little to language learning (see McKay, 1982, for a summary of these arguments). However, in this chapter I argue that using literature as content in ESL and English as a foreign language (EFL) classes provides three major benefits. First, because literary texts depend on how the language is used to create a particular effect, literature demonstrates for learners the importance of form in achieving specific

communicative goals. Second, using literature as content in the second language (L2) classroom provides an ideal basis for integrating the four skills (Paran, 2006; Parkinson & Thomas, 2001). And finally, in an era when English is used in a great variety of cross-cultural encounters, literary texts are valuable in raising students' and teachers' cross-cultural awareness. (See Hinkel, this volume, on cross-cultural communication and pragmatics.) To demonstrate the benefits of using literature, I open this chapter with an examination of what is meant by *literary texts*. Then I examine in detail each of the advantages of using literature. Throughout the chapter, I provide examples of classroom activities to show how such activities can be designed.[1]

WHAT ARE LITERARY TEXTS?

The how of literary texts

Typically language is used to convey a message by relaying information. Whereas literary texts exemplify the features of normal communication, they generally lack this purpose. Rather, the aim of literary texts is to convey "an individual awareness of reality" (Widdowson 1975, p. 70). What makes literary texts unique is that in literature the *what* and *how* of the text are inseparable. As Widdowson (1975) puts it,

An understanding of what literature communicates necessarily involves an understanding of how it communicates: what and how are not distinct. It is for this reason that literary works cannot be satisfactorily paraphrased or explained by any single interpretation: to do so is to recast their essential ambiguity into the definite shape of conventional statement. The basic problem in the teaching of literature is to develop in the student an awareness of the what/how of literary communication and this can only be done by relating it to, without translating it into, normal uses of language. (p. 70)

The fact that in works of literature the "what and how are not distinct" makes them valuable for extending learners' awareness that how they say something is important in two ways. First, how something is said often contributes to speakers' achieving their purpose in communication; second, in deciding how something is said, speakers often communicate something about themselves—they establish a voice.

Kramsch (1993) offers a simple illustration of the importance of form in conveying information. She describes how, at a conference workshop she attended, the linguist A. L. Becker asked the participants to describe in one sentence what he was about to do. He then walked up the steps to the podium and laid a book on the desk. Following this, he asked a variety of participants to read their descriptions. After several participants had read their sentences, it was clear that, even in describing such a simple act, each text provided a unique perspective on what had been observed. Whereas some authors referred to Becker as "a linguist," others referred to him as "the man," "you," or "he." Whereas some stated that Becker "put" the book on the podium, others stated that he "slapped" or "placed" the book on the podium. Whereas some described the action in the simple past ("You stepped onto the stage."), others described it in the past continuous ("He was walking up the steps.") (p. 107).

For Kramsch, this exercise is significant in that it demonstrates that every writer has available a variety of choices for conveying a message. For example, the fact that the participants wrote rather than spoke affected the shape of their texts. The choice of grammatical form enabled the authors to relate the act to a particular time and place and to define what was new and what was old information. Perhaps most significantly, the participants had a choice of what to say and what not to say. For Kramsch, the particularity of literary texts rests on an author's use of six aspects of text development. Specifically, in creating literary texts, authors:

1. shape the medium of written texts
2. make grammatical and lexical choices that enable them to define spatial and temporal frames of references
3. negotiate interpersonal relationships with their readers
4. look through language to a believed world
5. evoke prior language
6. leave many things unsaid

These dimensions of literary texts contribute to the "what/how of literary communication," making it difficult to paraphrase literary texts.

R. Carter (1996) makes a case for extending the notion of literary texts to include such things as advertisements, newspaper headlines, jokes, and puns, in that they all provide examples of verbal play. As he points out, "the language used in such texts does not refer to activities, entities and events in the external world; it displays and creatively patterns its discourse in such a way as to invite readers to interpret how it represents that world" (pp. 7–8). As support, he provides several instances of the literary qualities present in everyday examples of language such as an advertisement from a British airline regarding its wider and more comfortable seating, stating, "Relief from aches on planes," or the advertisement for the Swiss chocolate bar, Toblerone, that reads "The one and Tobleronly." Such examples offer a convincing argument for introducing learners to the playfulness of literary language by drawing on selected instances of everyday language use.

CONCEPTUAL UNDERPINNINGS

Literary texts and the reader

Whereas Widdowson, Kramsch, and Carter define literary texts by their unique form, Rosenblatt (1978) defines literary texts primarily in terms of how readers interact with them. She maintains that the common way of distinguishing literary works of art from other types of texts has been to examine the text itself. For Rosenblatt, however, a text is merely an object of paper and ink until a reader interacts with the text. Hence, for Rosenblatt, the question of defining literary texts does not depend on examining how literary and nonliterary texts differ but, rather, on considering what a reader does in these different kinds of reading.

According to Rosenblatt, readers perform very different activities during aesthetic and nonaesthetic reading. To illustrate these differences, Rosenblatt relates the example of a mother whose child has just swallowed a poisonous liquid and is frantically reading the label to discover what course of action to follow. The mother's main concern is to get the essential information from the text. To describe the type of reading in which the main purpose of the reader is to decipher whatever message can be carried away from the text, Rosenblatt uses the term *efferent* from the Latin *efferre* ("to carry away"). In efferent reading, the author is focused on the message of the text. In contrast, in aesthetic reading, "the reader's primary concern is with what happens *during* the reading process" (p. 24).

For Rosenblatt the distinction between efferent and aesthetic reading rests on the stance a reader adopts in relation to a particular text. She maintains that the same text can be read either efferently or aesthetically. Hence, in reading a literary text, a reader can read it aesthetically so that "attention is centered directly on what he is living through during his relationship with that particular text" (p. 25) or he can read it efferently by gathering specific information. For Rosenblatt, too often literature classrooms focus on the latter type of reading, in that they analyze the form of the text and thus reduce learners' engagement with literature. Rosenblatt's concern with conscious attention to form in a literature class reflects an ongoing debate among teachers of literature.

There are many who argue that stylistics, or literary text analysis, can be of great value to language learners (e.g., Widdowson, 1975; R. Carter, 1996). Carter (1996), for example, summarizes the advantages of using stylistics in language classrooms:

(i) Stylistics provides students with a method of scrutinizing texts, a "way in" to a text, opening up starting points for fuller interpretation.

(ii) Basing interpretation on systematic verbal analysis reaffirms the centrality of language as the aesthetic medium of literature.

(iii) Non-native students possess the kind of conscious, systematic knowledge about the language which provides the best basis for stylistic analysis. In many respects, therefore, non-native students are often better at stylistic analysis than native speakers. (pp. 5–6)

Others, however, argue that a focus on stylistics undermines the reading of a literary text for enjoyment, for an aesthetic experience. Gower (1986), for example, poses the following question:

Can we, then in any sense, say that "stylistic analysis" helps the EFL student, when its declared aim is to illuminate the "mechanism" of a "text" under the microscope . . . ? This . . . is a very different thing from reading: the students operate on the "text" rather than let a poem or novel speak to them. (pp. 129–130)

Gower, like Rosenblatt, believes that literary texts should be read and enjoyed and that literary analysis by necessity will undermine this possibility.

The question of whether to use stylistics or language analysis in L2 classrooms depends on what is meant by *stylistics*. Clearly, if stylistics entails the mere analysis of literature to support one central meaning of a text (usually one arrived at by literary scholars), then there is little possibility that this will engage language learners or contribute to their enjoyment of reading a literary text. If, on the other hand, stylistics provides learners with the tools to justify their own opinions of a text, then the analysis of the text can be related to the student's own aesthetic reading of the text. Widdowson (1992) terms this approach one of *practical stylistics* in which the goal is "to stimulate an engagement with primary texts, to encourage individual interpretation while requiring that this should be referred back to features of the text" (p. xiv). R. Carter (1996) makes a distinction between what is traditionally thought of as stylistics and what he terms a language-based approach to literature. For Carter, a language-based approach is student-centered, activity-based, and process-oriented, in that classroom tasks help students support their interpretations of a text by engaging them in the process of meaning making.

How then can language analysis be productively used in L2 classrooms to enhance students' enjoyment in reading literature and develop their awareness of language?

CLASSROOM APPLICATIONS

To illustrate how literary texts might be approached in L2 classrooms, let us compare how two short stories might be used that recount the experience of young adolescents in their school environment: "Eleven" by Cisneros (an excerpt from a novel by Cisneros (1996) entitled *Woman Hollering Creek*) and "Out of Order" by William Saroyan (1984). "Eleven" tells the story of Rachel, a young girl on her 11th birthday. The story takes place at school where the teacher, Mrs. Price, asks who in the class owns a red sweater that has been "sitting in the coatroom for a month" (p. 13). No one in the class says it belongs to any of them until suddenly one student, Sylvia Saldivar, says, "I think it belongs to Rachel" (p. 13). Although Rachel states that it is not hers, the teacher answers, "Of course it's yours. . . . I remember you wearing it once" (p. 13). When Rachel shoves the sweater to the edge of her desk, Mrs. Price tells Rachel, "You put that sweater on right now and no more nonsense" (p. 13). The incident ends when, right before the bell rings for lunch, Phyllis Lopez, another student in the class, remembers that the sweater is hers, so Rachel takes it off and gives it to her.

"Out of Order" (Saroyan, 1984) tells the story of William Saroyan's his first day in seventh grade at Longfellow Junior High School. The story begins with the ancient history teacher, Miss Shenstone, telling the students to turn to page 192 in their books. William comments that "it would seem more in order to turn to page one for the first lesson" (p. 105). The teacher responds by telling William to be quiet and let her do the teaching. Then Miss Shenstone points to a photograph of Stonehenge on page 192 of the text—stones that she says are 20,000 years old. William then questions how she knows this. This leads Miss Shenstone to "fling" herself at William (p. 106), resulting in William leaving the room. He returns five minutes later when again Miss Shenstone "flings" herself at him (p. 106). This results in William going to see Mr. Monsoon, the principal of the school, to tell him why he left the class. Mr. Monsoon, meanwhile, wants to know William's name and who he is, specifically what nationality he is. When William tells him that he is Armenian, the principal replies, "Nobody but an Armenian would have asked a question like that" (p. 107). William's meeting with the principal ends with the principal telling him that he "must give him a thrashing" (p. 107). At this point, William leaves the school and goes home and tells his Uncle Alecksander what occurred at school. William then returns to the school accompanied by his uncle, who talks to the principal alone. After a short time, William is asked to come into the office to talk with the principal, Miss Shenstone, and his uncle, where he is told by his uncle that Miss Shenstone has agreed to look into the matter of how the age of the stones was determined. He is also told that it was with "admiration" (p. 108) that Mr. Monsoon commented that only an Armenian would ask a question like that. In the end, William has to spend the rest of the day away from school and then return to his classes as though "nothing had happened" (p. 108). The next day, William returns to school, apologizing to both the principal and Miss Shenstone. However, after four days, Miss Shenstone leaves the school. Meanwhile, Mr. Monsoon talks about manners at several student body meetings, but after a month he too leaves the school.

To promote aesthetic reading, it is important to begin by having students read and enjoy the stories. Obviously students will enjoy reading literature only if the text is accessible to them. Hence, it is important to select literary texts that have a theme that is engaging for the students and that are not too difficult for the students on either a linguistic or conceptual level. To encourage aesthetic reading, the initial discussion of the stories should focus on having students discuss what they enjoyed or did not enjoy about the story, what the story means to them, how it relates to their own personal experiences, and so on. However, it is this very kind of discussion that can lead to Widdowson's (1992) notion of practical stylistics, in which students are encouraged to express individual interpretations while being required to have their interpretations refer back to the text. To illustrate how this might occur in L2 classrooms, let us consider how students' individual interpretation of the characters in our two example stories can be the basis for a literary task.

Characterization

Readers assess each character in a story based on what the character says and does, what others in the story say about the character, and how the author describes the character. To encourage students' own response to the stories, a teacher might begin by having students describe both Rachel and William. This could involve having students list the adjectives they believe best describe each character, describe each in a short paragraph, gather pictures that depict their images of Rachel and William, or compare each character with someone they know.

The next part of the literary task should encourage students to return to the text to justify their own interpretation. One activity might be to have students complete a character web for each of the characters. In this activity (see Figure 1), students complete the following type of chart, citing specific details from the story. The list of what William says/thinks would include the passage from Saroyan's story in Figure 2. Similarly, the

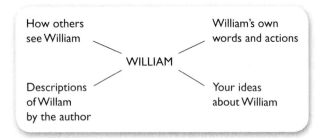

Figure 1. Character web for William (adapted from *Voices in Literature* by McCloskey & Stack, 1993, pp. 154–155).

> "How do you know?"
> "She said the rocks were twenty thousand years old. . . . All I said was, 'How do you know?' I didn't mean they *weren't* that old. I meant that maybe they were older, maybe thirty thousand years old. How old is the earth? Several million years old, isn't it? If the book can say the rocks are twenty thousand years old, somebody ought to be able to say how the book got that figure. This isn't Emerson School, it's Longfellow Junior High. I came here to learn. I don't expect to be punished because I want to learn."
> (p. 106)

Figure 2. William's response to the principal.

list of what Rachel says would include the phrases from Cisnero's story in which Rachel denies the sweater is hers (see Figure 3).

> "That's not, I don't, you're not. . . . Not mine."
> "But that's not." (p. 13).

Figure 3. Rachel's denial.

Once students complete their individual web, teachers can then encourage them to examine the language of the text. The mere contrast in the length of both characters' responses illustrates aspects of their personality. However, more subtle features, such as the false starts in Rachel's speech and the use of questions in William's speech, suggest differences in their character.

Because both stories are told from the first person point of view, students' interpretation of William and Rachel will undoubtedly be affected by what they learn about the characters from their thoughts. Hence, with these stories, the teacher may want to draw attention to the concept of first person point of view. In using literature in the classroom, exactly which tasks are developed should depend on the features of the text that are salient in the story and on the elements of the text that are relevant to students' interpretation of it. Let us consider how teachers might address the element of point of view in relation to these two stories.

Point of view

Fowler (1986) distinguishes three types of point of view: (1) spatiotemporal; (2) ideological; and (3) psychological. The *temporal* dimension refers to the sense of time that the author conveys by using such techniques as flashbacks or the interweaving of stories, whereas the *spatial* dimension refers to the manner in which the author depicts items such as objects, buildings, and landscapes in relation to one another. The *ideological point of view*, on the other hand, refers to the "set of values, or belief system, communicated by the language of the text" (p. 130).

The *psychological point of view* is the one most frequently referred to in literary analysis. According to Fowler (1986), this involves the question of "who is presented as the observer of the events of a narrative, whether the author or a participating character" (p. 134). Fowler delineates two types of psychological point of view: internal and external. In the internal *psychological point of view,* either the story is told from the first person point of view by a character who shares his or her feelings about the events and characters of the story or it is told by someone who is not a participating character but who has knowledge of the feelings of the characters—the so-called omniscient author. In the external point of view, the narrator describes the events and characters from a position outside the main characters with no access to the characters' feelings and opinions.

Psychological point of view. "Eleven" and "Out of Order" are both told from the first person point of view by Rachel and William, who share their feelings about the events. In both stories, the authors let the reader into the thoughts of the junior high student. The opening of each story illustrates this first person point of view.

"Eleven" (Cisneros, 1996) begins with the paragraph that opened the Experience section of this chapter. "Out of Order" (Saroyan, 1984), on the other hand, begins in the following way.

> Longfellow High was not strictly speaking a high school at all. It was the seventh and eighth grades of grammar school, and its full name was Longfellow Junior High School. The Longfellow in question was of course *the* Mr. Longfellow, or Henry Wadsworth, although nothing much was ever made of that.
>
> It was in ancient history class that I first astonished my class into an awareness that here was a truly original mind. It happened that this was the first class of the very first day. (p. 105)

To help students recognize how the difference in tone between the two openings is achieved, a teacher might pose a series of questions for students to consider such as those in Figure 4.

The aim of such questions is to help students recognize the way in which their assessment of the two characters has been influenced by how the author has used first person point of view to develop a childlike voice for Rachel and a self-confident and arrogant voice for William. In the case of "Out of Order," the relationship of the author

---

Questions about "Eleven"

1. Who does *they* refer to? Why do you think the author chose to use *they* rather than a specific reference? Who do you think *you* refers to? Why do you think the author chose to use *you*?
2. What effect does the author achieve by having Rachel list all the years of her life rather than just saying "when you're eleven, you're also all the other years of your life"? (p. 11)

Questions about "Out of Order"

1. William is in seventh grade yet points out the first and middle names of Longfellow. Why do you think William Saroyan (the adult author of the story) has William, the seventh grader, point this out?
2. What kinds of things "astonish" you? Why do you think Saroyan chose to describe himself as a seventh-grader using that word? Why do you think Saroyan described himself as a "truly original mind"? (p. 105)

Figure 4. Questions to promote students' understanding of point of view.

and narrator is even more complex since Saroyan, the author, is commenting on his own youth.

Another activity that could be used to highlight the manner in which the author depicts the characters is to have students list all the sentences in "Eleven" that sound childlike. This list might include sentences like those in Figure 5. Students might also make a list of any comments that William makes that demonstrate his outspoken self-confidence. This might include comments like those in Figure 6. The main point of such activities is to require students to return to the text to examine how the story is told and in what ways this has influenced their judgment of the characters.

1. "Like some days you might say something stupid, and that's the part of you that's still ten." (p. 11)
2. "Or maybe some days you might need to sit on your mama's lap because you're scared, and that's the part of you that's five." (p. 11)

Figure 5. Sample sentences for analysis of character depiction of Rachel.

Spatiotemporal point of view. Cisneros uses the present tense to recount the story, while Saroyan uses the past tense. To explore the difference that verb tense makes on telling a story, teachers might

1. "I remarked that it would seem more in order to turn to page one for the first lesson." (p. 105)
2. "I was asked my name, whereupon, I was only too glad to say honestly, 'William Saroyan.'" (p. 105)

Figure 6. Sample student list of comments demonstrating William's self-confidence.

refer to passages like the following and ask students which of the two accounts they felt they were actually witnessing.

From "Eleven":

> "Whose is this?" Mrs. Price says, and she holds the red sweater up in the air for all the class to see. "Whose? It's been sitting in the coatroom for a month?" (p. 11)

From "Out of Order":

> Miss Shenstone flung herself at me with such speed that I was scarcely able to get away. For half a moment she clung to my homeknit sweater, and damaged it before I got away. (p. 106)

Such comparisons help students recognize that the use of the present tense in story telling suggests the immediacy of events, inviting the reader to be a witness to these events.

The temporal point of view also involves the order in which the events of a story are told. In some instances the story time and real time are identical, whereas in others the author chooses to use flashbacks so that the story time and real time differ. One way of addressing the issue of the temporal point of view is to ask students to visualize key events in a story by completing a collage. Hence, in the case of "Out of Order" students could be asked to identify what they consider to be central events of the story, such as Miss Shenstone chasing William, the principal questioning William, and Uncle Alecksander coming to the principal's office. Then, individually or in small groups, students create a collage of these events using photographs, objects, line drawings, and texts.

As mentioned earlier, what Fowler (1986) calls the spatial point of view addresses how objects, buildings, and landscapes are described. For example, in "Eleven," the red sweater is introduced in the story when Mrs. Price "holds the sweater up in the air for all the class to see" (p. 13). Later she takes the "ugly sweater with red plastic buttons and a collar and sleeves all stretched out like you could use it for a jump rope" (p. 13) and puts it on Rachel's desk. This leads Rachel to "move the red sweater to the corner of my desk" (p. 13) until eventually she shoves "the red sweater to the tippy-tip corner" of her desk (p. 13) and "it's hanging all over the edge like a waterfall" (p. 14). To address this dimension of the story, teachers might begin by asking students why they think Rachel felt so humiliated by having the teacher insist that the sweater was hers. This undoubtedly will lead to a discussion of what the sweater was like. At this point, students might be asked to list all the descriptions of the sweater in the story. The goal of such an activity is to help students recognize that their opinion of the sweater has been influenced by how the author chose to describe the sweater.

Ideological point of view. Examining the ideological point of view of stories is closely related to what has been termed *critical literacy* or *critical reading*. Kress (1985) maintains that readers should approach all texts with three questions in mind: Why is the topic being written about, how is the topic being written about, and what other ways could the topic have been written about? In critical reading, readers are encouraged to examine the values and belief systems that underlie a text, or what Fowler (1986) refers to as the ideological point of view of a story. According to Fowler, in literary texts, the narrator or characters of a story frequently rely on certain grammatical structures to convey their beliefs and attitudes. These structures include such things as modal auxiliaries (e.g., *may, might,* and *should*); modal adverbs or sentence adverbs (e.g., *surely, perhaps,* and *It is certain that. . .*); evaluative adjectives and adverbs (e.g., *lucky, fortunate,* and *regrettably*); and verbs of knowledge, prediction, and evaluation (e.g., *seem, believe, foresee,* and *dislike*).

For example, teachers can encourage students to see the ideological point of view in "Out of Order" by asking why they think the story is entitled "Out of Order." As a follow-up to this question, teachers can have students underline all the references to the "old school" (i.e., where teachers ask the questions) and the "new school" (i.e., where students ask the questions) and use these references to determine whether they think the author is sympathetic to the old or the new school, citing sentences from the text to support their view. Such an approach might lead students to consider passages like the following, which occurs after William questions how Miss Shenstone knows the age of the stones at Stonehenge. William comments that "the truth of the matter is that neither Miss Shenstone . . . nor Mr. Monsoon himself, the principal, had anything like a satisfactory answer to any legitimate question of this sort, for they (and all the other teachers) had always accepted what they had found in the textbooks" (p. 106). The goal of this type of examination of a literary text is to help students see that authors often have a particular set of values that inform how they choose to tell a story.

It is important to emphasize several other points regarding the use of literary texts to develop students' language awareness. First, to promote students' enjoyment of reading literary texts, classroom activities should always begin with having students, individually or in small groups, share their personal reactions to a literary text. Second, as a way of developing students' awareness of how their interpretation of the text has been influenced by how the story is told, classroom tasks should encourage students to go back to the text for examples to support their interpretations of the text. Finally, the type of classroom tasks used should depend on which dimensions of the story are most salient (i.e., the spatiotemporal point of view, the ideological point of view, or the psychological point of view).

Using literary texts to integrate skills

Reading. Using literature as content provides an ideal way to integrate the development of the four skills. As the previous discussion makes clear, encouraging students to carefully examine a literary text to support their interpretations of the text promotes students' close reading of texts, a skill that will benefit their reading of other material. Literature, of course, is also ideal as content for extensive reading programs in L2 classrooms. Becoming engaged with a piece of literature will certainly increase students' interest in reading often and widely in English.[2]

Listening. When read aloud, literature also offers an excellent context for developing global listening skills. There are many books available in digital format that can be used as a basis for an extensive listening library. One clear advantage of encouraging students to listen to literature read by professionals is that such material exposes students to a variety of dialects and voice qualities.

Another type of listening task that can be used in L2 classrooms involves storytelling. Morgan and Rinvolucri (1983), in their book *Once upon a Time*, argue convincingly that the quality of listening that occurs when someone is telling a story

> is radically different from that during listening comprehension from a tape. The latter is always third-person listening, a kind of eavesdropping that is strangely uncompelling. To be told a story by a live storyteller, on the contrary, involves one in "I-thou" listening, where the listeners can directly influence the telling. (pp. 1–2)

Their book contains a variety of strategies for using storytelling to develop listening skills.

Speaking. Perhaps the greatest benefit of using literature in the language classroom lies in literature's potential for developing students' speaking skills, particularly their sociolinguistic and pragmatic competence. (See Hinkel, this volume.) Unlike dialogues written for traditional language learning texts, the dialogues included in stories typically offer a detailed account of the speakers' backgrounds and role relationships. Hence, such dialogues provide students with a basis for judging the appropriateness of language use. For example, in "Out of Order," William apologizes to the principal and his teacher, saying to Mr. Monsoon, "I've come to apologize. I don't want any special privileges" (p. 109), and to Miss Shenstone, "I'm sorry about the trouble I made. I won't do it again" (p. 109). Because the story itself has provided the background on why William is apologizing and who he is apologizing to, students have a context for evaluating the appropriateness of particular linguistic forms. Students also have a full context for determining when discourse is not appropriate as, for example, when Miss Shenstone tells William, "I might say, *Mister* William Saroyan, just shut up and let me do the teaching of the ancient history class" (p. 105).

Teachers can also use literary texts as a basis for having students write their own dialogues. For example, in "Out of Order," Saroyan leaves unsaid what William's uncle actually says to the principal regarding William's behavior and the principal's questioning of William's ethnic background. However, Saroyan does recount the agreement the uncle and principal reach at the conclusion of their meeting, providing learners with several clues as to what might have been said in their meeting. In addition, they have a sense of both the uncle's and Mr. Monsoon's personalities based on what has previously occurred. Hence, students have a great deal of relevant information to draw on to write a dialogue.

Plays provide another rich context for developing students' sociolinguistic and pragmatic awareness (see McKay, 2000). It is important, however, to recognize that plays differ in significant ways from natural conversation. As Simpson (1997) points out, drama and naturally occurring discourse are not identical types of communication:

> The most obvious difference between the two is that characters in plays are not real people in the way that interlocutors in conversation are. Another difference is that whereas naturally occurring conversation is straightforwardly "face to face," in drama dialogue the channel of communication is more complex. This is because there are two communicative layers at work in drama discourse. . . . On the one hand, there is interaction within a play: this is the character-to-character dialogue which is displayed on stage or in the text. On the other, there is communication between the dramatist and audience or reader. (p. 164)

Nevertheless, plays can be used to examine such things as the sequencing of conversation, stated and implied meanings, ellipsis, and so on.

Fish (1989) suggests a strategy for increasing students' awareness of the nature of conversation. He recommends giving students a list of the cast of characters in a play, which includes some background information on the characters (e.g., a journalist, a coach, an athlete, a sponsor). With this information and the title and setting of the play, students are asked to make hypotheses about the play in terms of the plot, theme, and so on. Then, Fish suggests giving students the lines from a short section of the play, with the characters' names deleted and the conversation out of order. Students first try to guess who is speaking based on the list of characters. Then, students are asked to sequence the lines from the play. In doing this, students can develop a sensitivity to the fact that, as Burton (1982) notes, "conversations are complicated, but orderly and rule-governed events" (p. 86).

Writing. Literature can be used to develop students' writing abilities by having students react to the literary texts they read via personal journals and formal essays. Using writing in this way offers two benefits. First, it provides students with a way to express their personal interpretation of a story, thus promoting the type of aesthetic response to reading literary texts referred to earlier. Second, to the extent that students are asked to refer to the text to justify their conclusions about the literary selection, students learn to support their opinions with relevant information, a skill that is important in various types of academic writing.

Using literary texts in writing classes is also valuable for helping students become aware of voice and point of view in written texts. For example, in "Out of Order" and "Eleven," one strategy for developing an awareness of point of view is to have students rewrite these stories from the point of view of the teacher in the stories. Another possibility is to have students rewrite "Eleven" as if told and experienced by William. In this case, students will need to consider how William, given what they know of him from the story, would react to being wrongly accused of owning an old red sweater and then assume the voice of William in recounting the story.

One excellent genre for developing fluency in writing, particularly for language learners with less proficiency, is poetry. Because poetry is less restricted by the grammatical and lexical constraints of other types of literary and written discourse, poems can provide learners with a medium for exploring and playing with language. Maley and Duff (1989) present a variety of strategies for encouraging students to create their own poems. For example, one strategy is to have students draw several familiar shapes, such as a ladder or staircase. Next students list words that they associate with this shape. Then they use some of these words to write a poem in the shape of the object itself. To increase students' awareness of the importance of word choice, Maley and Duff suggest giving students poems in which the descriptive words have been deleted and having students fill in the blanks. Students then compare their choices and discuss the differences in effect that arise from making specific word choices.

Widdowson (1992) makes a convincing argument for using poetry in the language classroom. He argues that, although the content of poems can often be reduced to ordinary observations (e.g., time passes; life is lonely), "the essentials of poetry lie in the way language is used to elaborate on such simple propositions so that they are reformulated in unfamiliar terms which somehow capture the underlying mystery of the commonplace" (p. 9). The simple themes of poetry and the unconventional method of expressing these themes thus provide an avenue for language learners to use the English they have to express sophisticated ideas, unrestricted by the typical constraints of conventional discourse.

Using literary texts to develop cultural awareness

A third important benefit of using literary texts in the language classroom rests in their potential for developing cross-cultural awareness. This is especially important in an era when learners communicate in English not only with native speakers of English but also with other non-native speakers around the globe. To discuss the benefits of using literary texts to develop cultural awareness, it is useful to distinguish various dimensions of culture. Adaskou, Britten, and Fahsi (1989) distinguish four dimensions of culture: (1) the aesthetic sense, in which a language is associated with the literature, film, and music of a particular country; (2) the sociological sense, in which language is linked to the customs and institutions of a country; (3) the semantic sense, in which a culture's conceptual system is embodied in the language; and (4) the pragmatic sense, in which cultural norms influence what language is appropriate for what context.

Frequently, a literary text exemplifies all four dimensions of culture. For example, if we consider "Out of Order" and "Eleven," the aesthetic sense of culture is evident in the mention of Henry Wadsworth Longfellow and Stonehenge. The sociological sense of culture is demonstrated in several ways: in the assumption in "Eleven" about the importance of clothes in American schools, in the accepted role of the teacher as someone who questions and commands students, and in the

ways birthdays are celebrated in the United States. The semantic sense of culture is clear in word choice when, for example, William reports that the teacher "flung herself" at him rather than saying she *chased* him or *ran after* him; it is also evident in the metaphorical use of language in "Eleven" when Rachel, for example, states "the way you grow old is kind of like an onion or like the rings inside a tree trunk or like my little wooden dolls that fit one inside the other, each year inside the next one" (p. 11). Finally, the pragmatic sense of culture is exemplified in the dialogue passages in "Out of Order" when, for example, the formal contractual sense of Uncle Alecksander's and Mr. Monsoon's agreement regarding William is sealed with the exchange in which Uncle Alecksander says, "I shall be interested in his progress," and Mr. Monsoon responds, "We all shall" (p. 108).

There are those who argue that a language cannot be taught without culture. Kramsch (1993), for example, maintains that if language "is seen as social practice, culture becomes the very core of language teaching. Cultural awareness must then be viewed both as enabling language proficiency and as being the outcome of reflection on language proficiency" (p. 8). She argues, however, that knowing about a culture (i.e., gaining cultural competence) does not mean that one has an obligation to behave in accordance with the conventions of that culture. Thus the goal of cultural learning is neither to convey information about a culture nor to promote the acquisition of culturally influenced ways of behaving; the goal is, rather, to help learners see their culture in relation to others to promote cross-cultural understanding.

If we accept this view of cultural learning, literary texts provide an ideal context for exploring cultural differences. However, approaching literature to develop cross-cultural understanding requires that teachers first carefully examine the cultural assumptions present in a particular literary work and then structure activities that help students gain an understanding of these assumptions. In the discussion of the literary text, teachers and students need to explore how their cultural assumptions differ both from each other and from those portrayed in the text. As a way of clarifying these aspects of using literary texts to develop cultural awareness, let us consider how a specific text might be approached in a L2 classroom to promote cross-cultural understanding.

In general, immigrant literature offers a rich context for exploring cultural differences since the stories frequently deal with individuals who have literally and figuratively crossed borders and, hence, experienced many cultural differences in their lives. A short story by Hisaye Yamamoto entitled "Seventeen Syllables" (Yamamoto, 1994) exemplifies this type of cultural border crossing. The story recounts the experience of a Japanese immigrant family working as tomato pickers in California. The Hayashi family is composed of Rosie, a young teenager, and her parents. Rosie is involved in many aspects of American culture and has acculturated to the extent of preferring to use English to Japanese. In the course of the story she falls in love with Jesus, another young immigrant worker, who is Hispanic. The story revolves around Rosie's mother, Tome, who assumes a pen name to write haiku poetry to submit to a contest being sponsored by *Mainichi Shimbu,* a newspaper. Mrs. Hayashi's talent for writing haiku results in her receiving an award from the editor of the newspaper, one of his favorite Hiroshiges[3] depicting four sampans on a pale blue sea. However, Rosie's father, upset by the disturbances that the haiku writing has caused the family, destroys the Hiroshige she receives. The story ends with Mrs. Hayashi admitting to her daughter that she came to the United States as part of an arranged marriage after having given birth to a stillborn son born out of wedlock. After this occurred, Mrs. Hayashi wrote to her favorite sister in America threatening to kill herself if her sister did not send for her. Her sister then arranged a marriage for her with a young man who had recently arrived from Japan. The story concludes when Rosie's mother kneels on the floor and takes Rosie by the wrists: "'Rosie,' she said urgently, 'Promise me you will never marry!'" (p. 38).

The story contains several cultural *schemata* (prior knowledge structures): the schema of the Japanese immigrant family in which various Japanese traditions like arranged marriages and particular gender roles are still upheld; the schema of U.S. popular culture, with references to movie stars like Shirley Temple and songs like "Red Sails in the Sunset"; and the schema of farmworkers with expectations about tomato picking and poor housing conditions. Which schemata are familiar to teachers and students depends on the cultural backgrounds of the teacher and learners. In using the story, however, the first step the teacher should take is to examine the cultural schemata portrayed in the story. This can be accomplished by simply clustering all the examples in the text that relate to a particular cultural schema.

Next, the teacher needs to design ways to make these differences accessible to students. One strategy for doing this is to merely present some of the assumed cultural information. Thus, in this case, the teacher might show pictures of U.S. farmworkers, read some examples of haiku poetry, or familiarize students with relevant aspects of U.S. popular culture. This level of cultural awareness is not difficult to exemplify. The significant cultural differences in the story, however, rest in such factors as the assumed gender roles of the Japanese father and mother, the acceptance of arranged marriages, and the entertaining of suicide in response to a significant loss of face. With these kinds of cultural assumptions, the goal should not be to evaluate these assumptions but, rather, to help students understand why the characters acted as they did. Ultimately, this should lead students to clarify their own understandings of such culturally bound phenomena as gender roles, loss of face, and marriage.

How these aspects of culture are approached in the classroom depends largely on the backgrounds of the teacher and students. If, for example, the story is taught in Japan with Japanese students and a Japanese teacher, the classroom participants already share many assumptions evident in the behavior of Mr. and Mrs. Hayashi. What might seem unusual to this class is that Rosie has not kept up her Japanese and is willing to meet secretly with Jesus. On the other hand, if the story is taught in the United States with an American teacher and some Japanese students, the teacher, while being familiar with many references to American culture and having an understanding of the farmworker community, may not understand the many references to Japanese culture or be willing to accept Mrs. Hayahsi's willingness at the end of the story to give up her writing of haiku. In short, to the extent that English classrooms represent individuals from diverse cultural backgrounds, the cultural information in particular literary texts may be known to and accepted by some of the classroom participants yet be unknown to others.

Ultimately, what the literary text provides is a medium for sharing and illuminating the cross-cultural differences exemplified in the text. The value of selecting texts that portray aspects of the culture of some of the classroom members is that those who come from this culture can explain many of the cultural elements that may not be understood by the members of other cultures. Ideally, the cultural discussion that occurs will illuminate why particular characters from a specific cultural background acted as they did. Such an approach, it is hoped, will avoid the cultural stereotyping that can occur in discussing cross-cultural differences, since these discussions will be grounded in specific behaviors portrayed in a particular literary context. This is one of the major benefits that literary texts can bring to cross-cultural L2 classrooms.

FUTURE TRENDS

As the popularity of English increases around the world and individuals from various cultures use English to communicate with one another, there is a need to develop among English users an awareness of the global diversity of cultures and beliefs, as well as a respect for and tolerance of cultural differences. Literature classrooms are a natural place for this to happen. What is presently needed are more materials and resources to help teachers do this. In addition, literature, because of the pleasure it can bring, is a productive way to encourage students to read extensively on their own. Indeed, the growing recognition of the importance of extensive reading suggests that teachers need to encourage more individual reading by language learners. What is needed are more materials and resources of literary texts, not just from the United Kingdom and the United States but also from around the world, to help language teachers do this.

CONCLUSION

Using literature as content in ESL/EFL classes, then, has a variety of benefits. While reading literature should be primarily an enjoyable aesthetic experience, using literature in L2 classrooms can also develop students' language awareness. Because literary texts are unique in their ability to illustrate that what is communicated cannot be separated from how it is communicated, they provide an ideal context for demonstrating the importance of form in language learning and language use. Exactly how they are used in a particular classroom depends on a great variety of factors. These include

students' language learning goals, proficiency level in English, and personal interests; they also include the teachers' knowledge of and interest in literature, teaching philosophy, and lesson objectives. Perhaps the greatest benefit of using literature as content in an era of increasing globalization is that literary texts provide an ideal context for examining cross-cultural differences and for exploring them in a manner that particularizes rather than stereotypes these differences.

SUMMARY

➤ In literary texts, what is conveyed is closely related to how a story is told.

➤ Because in literary texts form is essential to meaning, literary texts provide an excellent vehicle for developing students' language awareness.

➤ Literary texts can easily be used to develop all four language skills: reading, writing, listening, and speaking.

➤ Since literary texts typically contain various cultural schemata, they provide a context for developing cross-cultural awareness.

DISCUSSION QUESTIONS

1. Drawing on the ideas presented in this chapter, discuss what you believe are the essential differences between literary and nonliterary texts. Which of these types of texts do you read primarily and why?
2. Discuss what you believe are the major advantages and disadvantages of using literary texts with L2 students.
3. Do you think explicit attention should be given to examining the form of literary texts in L2 classrooms? What reasons do you have for your opinion? Do you believe this attention to form detracts from students' aesthetic experience with a text? Why or why not?
4. The author of this chapter has argued that, even though there are differences between dialogues in literary texts and natural conversation, such material is valuable in developing students' pragmatic competence? Do you agree? Why or why not?

5. Discuss ways in which you would find out about the cultural schemata in literary texts that you were not familiar with.

SUGGESTED ACTIVITIES

1. Select a short story that you believe will be engaging for a group of language learners you are familiar with. Then design one of the following activities:
    a. an activity that encourages students to draw on the text to support their opinion of a particular character in the story
    b. an activity that encourages students to explore how the text would be different if told from another point of view
    c. a series of activities that involves the development of all four skills: reading, writing, speaking, and listening
2. Select a piece of literature that exhibits several cultural schemata. Begin by analyzing the cultural schemata that exist in the text, listing specific details that contribute to each of the schemata. Then describe how you can make these schemata accessible to a particular group of language learners.
3. Select a second language textbook that uses literary texts as content. Then review the follow-up activities that are included in the text, and discuss whether you believe the activities contribute primarily to students' aesthetic reading of the text or to their efferent reading of the text.
4. Observe an ESL or EFL class that uses literary texts. Describe the activities in the class that contribute to students' awareness of the language in the text and activities that develop students' awareness of the cultural schemata in the text.

FURTHER READING

Carter, R., & McRae, J. (1996). *Language, literature and the learner*. London, UK: Addison Wesley Longman.

This collection of essays is derived from three international seminars on the teaching of literature in second and foreign language classrooms held at the University of Nottingham. The essays share a commitment to practical, classroom-based activities, particularly those that are language-based and student-centered.

Greenwood, C., & Walters, C. (2005). *Literature-based dialogue journals: Reading, writing, connecting, reflecting*. Norwood: MA: Christopher-Gordon.

This book connects journal writing with children's literature. Although it is intended for intermediate and advanced EFL learners in elementary and secondary school settings, the ideas could be adapted to other contexts as well. Student examples and self-assessment tools make this a very accessible resource.

Kay, J., & Gelshenen, R. (2004). *Adventures in literature: New pathways in reading*. Ann Arbor, MI: University of Michigan Press.

This is a thematically organized literature reader for beginning learners. The authors have adapted 15 stories by well-known authors into dialogue/script form to be used for role plays or reader's theater classroom activities. A major strength of the book is the strong focus on language-building exercises alongside the literature-related content.

Kramsch, C. (1993). *Context and culture in language teaching*. Oxford, UK: Oxford University Press.

This volume contains two excellent chapters that are particularly relevant to using literature as content. The first, "Stories and Discourse," elaborates on the dimensions of a text that contribute to its uniqueness. The second, "Teaching the Literary Text," describes various strategies for dealing with literary texts in the classroom.

Lazar, G. (1993). *Literature and language teaching*. Cambridge, UK: Cambridge University Press.

This book is addressed to language teachers who want to explore how they can use literature in their classroom. The book consists of a series of tasks and activities that teachers can do on their own or with other teachers to develop their skill in lesson planning using literary texts.

ENDNOTES

[1] Three excellent resources for using literature in the second language classroom are Collie and Slater (1988), Duff and Maley (2007), and Lazar (1993).
[2] For a good source of literature for language learners see Day and Bamford (1998), which includes 600 titles divided by levels of difficulty as well as by age group, genre, and region of the world.
[3] Hiroshige is one of the most famous Japanese woodblock print artists. He lived in the early 1800s. His woodblock prints such as the series "39 Views of Mt. Fuji" are known around the world.

32 Approaches to School-Based Bilingual Education

MARY MCGROARTY AND SHANNON FITZSIMMONS-DOOLAN

KEY QUESTIONS

➤ What does bilingual education mean?

➤ Is it possible to learn a second language well in school?

➤ Can bilingual language learning be combined with other school subjects such as math, history, science, and art?

➤ What determines the quality and effectiveness of bilingual instructional programs?

EXPERIENCE

It is the final period of the day in a middle school located in a small city on California's central coast. Señora Castillo presents the day's agenda to her eighth-grade math class: "Hoy vamos a resolver ecuaciones. Utilizaremos las propiedades de la igualdad al hacerlo." [*Today we are going to solve equations. To do this, we will use the properties of equality.*] Claire, Marisela, and the rest of their classmates take notes as Sra. Castillo provides some examples on the board. Claire is pleased. She had heard algebra would be difficult, but, although it is still early in the school year, she understands all the ideas her teacher has presented so far in this class. Sra. Castillo asks the students to get into groups of four. She passes out plastic bags filled with index cards. "Cada grupo tiene un rompecabeza en la bolsita. En la bolsa, hay un problema como los ejemplos que acabamos de discutir. Pero con ese problema, cada paso de la solución aparece en un papelito diferente. Trabajando con su grupo, tienen que ordenar todos los papelitos, línea por línea." [*Each group has a puzzle in the little plastic bag. In the bag, there is a problem like the examples that we have just finished discussing. But with this problem, each line of the solution is on a different strip of paper.*

Working with your group, you have to put the strips in order, line by line.] Marisela, Claire, Carlos, and Justin begin to work, speaking in low voices in Spanish with an occasional English term or question also heard. They want to put the pieces of the equation into the correct sequence faster than any other group in the class.

Marisela and Claire are best friends. They have attended school together since kindergarten but were not in the same class until third grade. Both girls are bilingual, although Marisela's family does not speak English and Claire's family does not speak Spanish. Both their families work in some aspect of agriculture, a dominant industry in this area. Now, in middle school, most of the girls' classes are together. In the morning, they take science, history, and language arts, all taught in English. Then, in fourth period, Marisela takes band and Claire takes P.E. After lunch, both girls take language arts, reading, and math, all delivered in Spanish. After seven years of consistent instruction following this model, the girls are testing above grade level in math and reading in both languages, a typical outcome for students who have spent all their elementary years in this school's Spanish-English two-way immersion bilingual education program.[1]

WHAT ARE BILINGUAL APPROACHES TO LANGUAGE LEARNING?

In many parts of the world, attainment of proficiency in two or more languages is viewed as a highly desirable goal. The development of bilingual skills sometimes takes place outside the bounds of formal education, propelled by factors in the sociocultural context or particular family environment. This chapter is not concerned with individuals who become bilingual outside the bounds of formal school instruction.[2] Readers interested in this and in the many ways people may become bilingual principally or entirely outside formal instruction should consult any of the several good discussions of bilingualism and language learning (e.g., Baker, 2011; Bhatia & Ritchie, 2004; Bialystok, 2004; Grosjean, 2010; Paradis, Genesee, & Crago, 2010). Rather, the emphasis here is on understanding how two (or more) languages can be used within an educational system to achieve the goal of proficiency in at least one, and often both, of the languages used for instruction.

Some definitions are in order because both the terms *bilingual* and *bilingual education* are used to refer to a great variety of phenomena (indeed, lack of uniformity regarding the term bilingual education is one of the many reasons it is difficult to compare data from programs that may be labeled "bilingual"; see García, 2009). In this chapter, bilingual, when used to refer to an individual, means a person with age-appropriate skills in two languages, although the nature and extent of skill in each language may vary according to multiple individual and situational influences. A person with bilingual oral skills may or may not be *biliterate*, that is, able to read and write two languages (Hornberger, 2003). A bilingual education approach is one in which two languages are used as media of classroom instruction for the same group of students so that students receive some of their instruction in one language and some in the other, with the proportion of each language varying according to program type, instructional goals, and various contextual influences. Bilingual programs may or may not have the goal of producing students with biliterate skills; this is one of the features on which they differ.

Before proceeding to describe bilingual approaches, a crucial clarification is in order: there is no necessary opposition between use of bilingual instruction and English as a second language (ESL) instruction. Indeed, in the United States and wherever the language of the dominant (wider or majority) society is English, it is generally expected that ESL will be a part of any bilingual program because a principal goal of any instructional program is the development of high-level academic language skills in the language(s) used to deliver instruction. Such development does not come about simply through exposure to a language; it requires instruction that is well-planned, engaging, and carefully sequenced. For this reason, it is important that any bilingual program include systematic attention to development of students' first language (L1) as well as second language (L2) skills; both necessitate sound, comprehensive curricula to support increasing proficiency in each language. Hence, English instruction should be a part of any bilingual program in an English-speaking context, although the timing, duration, nature, and amount of such teaching will vary by program model.

In bilingual programs at the school level, it is recommended that ESL as well as content instruction be presented through an approach known as sheltered instruction (Echevarria & Short, 2010; Howard, Sugarman, Christian, Lindholm-Leary, & Rodgers, 2007). (See also Snow, this volume.) Sheltered instruction approaches employ a variety of techniques to make any content, including the L2 but potentially including any other academic subject, comprehensible to learners. In this chapter, we summarize the research base for bilingual education, discussing, first, research findings on potential student participants in bilingual approaches, next the rationale for bilingual education programs as well as descriptive research on the most common bilingual program types, and then research findings related to the pedagogical features that help to determine the level of quality in bilingual instructional programs. Finally, we note some of the current educational concerns affecting the provision of bilingual education.

CONCEPTUAL UNDERPINNINGS: THE RESEARCH BASE FOR BILINGUAL EDUCATION

Who can benefit from bilingual instruction?

Research shows clearly that any student has the potential to benefit from bilingual education as long as the particular approach chosen suits the learner's linguistic profile and provides quality instruction. Bilingual education is not only for recent immigrants; there are also approaches aimed at monolingual students who speak only the majority language and wish to develop strong proficiency in another language (García, 2009; Howard et al., 2007). Therefore, it is potentially appropriate for *linguistic-majority students* (students whose native language is spoken in the larger national community, such as native speakers of English in the United States or in Anglophone Canada) (Genesee, 2004) and for *linguistic-minority students* (students whose native language is different from that used in the larger national community, such as native speakers of Spanish, Chinese, or Navajo in various parts of the United States) (J. Crawford, 2004; Lindholm-Leary & Genesee, 2010). There are also models of bilingual education that incorporate instruction for linguistic-majority and linguistic-minority speakers simultaneously (Howard et al., 2007). Furthermore, some bilingual approaches have also proven beneficial for *bidialectal students* (students who regularly use a dialect different from the mainstream standard, such as speakers of African American Vernacular English in U.S. schools) (Lightbown, 2007). The linguistic and sociocultural circumstances of bilingual and bidialectal students differ in many respects (Baugh, 2000; Ramírez, Wiley, de Klerk, Lee, & Wright, 2005), and it must be emphasized that bidialectal instruction may well be useful in its own right, particularly to support the initial literacy acquisition of dialect-using learners (Rickford & Rickford, 1995) and to expand the linguistic range of learners with a different home language. Hence, bilingual approaches are potentially useful for any student at any educational level. However, both the appropriateness and feasibility of bilingual approaches for particular instructional levels and settings vary, depending in part on school-related factors and in part on the larger social, economic, and political environment surrounding the school.

Why bilingual instruction?

Being bilingual can confer a host of benefits on an individual. Particularly for *balanced bilinguals* (individuals with relatively equal levels of proficiency in both languages), research seems to indicate positive correlations between bilinguality and divergent thinking, some metalinguistic skills, and communicative sensitivity (Baker, 2011). It is important to note, however, that several factors such as the relative language proficiencies and the characteristics of the languages being acquired affect comparisons between bilingual and monolingual individuals (Bialystok, 2004).

A major theoretical rationale underlying bilingual approaches to language learning is the concept of *positive transfer*—that the knowledge and specific linguistic skills developed in an individuals' L1 transfer to his or her developing L2 (Cummins, 2000; King & Benson, 2004). Although the findings of many studies have been consistent with theories of linguistic transfer, C. Snow (2008) notes that alternative explanations for second language development may also exist. That said, however, regardless of the theoretical mechanism, there is consistent evidence that L1 skills and knowledge have a strong relationship with L2 development and literacy attainment, evidence that supports bilingual approaches (Proctor, August, Carlo, & Barr, 2010; C. Snow, 2008). Another important practical rationale for bilingual approaches is their ability to keep students who are learning an L2 up to speed in the development of content-area knowledge (e.g., math) and graduation credits through instruction in the students' L1 (Hornberger, 2003; Lindholm-Leary & Genesee, 2010).

Types of bilingual programs

The following review of program types and related research provides some sense of the range of programs designated as bilingual. It is not exhaustive, and it is based on the program types most common in North America, drawing on descriptions in J. Crawford (2004) and Lindholm-Leary and Genesee (2010). We offer these descriptions with two caveats: (1) related terminology can differ from country to country and even from school district to school district (in Canada, from school board to school board), so it is essential to see how local participants define and implement all such programs; and (2) the degree to which an educational program in North America or elsewhere can accurately be called bilingual can be established definitively only by direct examination of the curriculum and firsthand observation of the materials and language-use patterns in the classrooms and schools so designated. Programs are labeled bilingual for a variety of reasons, only some of which have to do with the actual languages used for instruction, the criterion emphasized here. Each of the program models summarized in this section has different requirements for program length, curricular structure, materials needed, expected teacher qualifications, outcomes that can be justifiably anticipated, and nature of appropriate assessments. Most bilingual program types combine a consideration of the language(s) of instruction with the ages of the students enrolled. Thus it is common to see somewhat different types of bilingual programs at the elementary, secondary, and post-secondary levels. Program labels must always be interpreted in the local context in which they are used. Table 1 presents an overview of the models discussed.

Table 1. Bilingual Approaches

Program type	Educational level	Students served	Program goals
Early-exit (transitional)	Elementary	Language-minority	Proficiency in language of wider communication (L2)
Developmental (maintenance, late-exit)	Elementary	Language-minority	Literacy and academic language proficiency in language of wider communication (L2) and in home language (L1)
Immersion	Elementary Secondary Post-secondary	Language-majority	Literacy and academic language proficiency in L1 and L2
Two-way immersion	Elementary Secondary	Language-minority and language-majority	Literacy and academic language proficiency in language of wider communication and home language/foreign language
Early-exit (transitional); paired with ESL	Secondary	Language-minority	Proficiency in language of wider communication (L2)
Newcomer	Secondary	Language-minority	Proficiency in language of wider communication (L2) and content-area knowledge in home language
Vocational training	Post-secondary	Language-minority (often refugees)	Development of vocational knowledge in home language (L1) and/or language of wider communication (L2)
Content-based immersion	Post-secondary	Language-majority or language-minority	Literacy and academic language proficiency in language other than home language and access to content areas (e.g., psychology)
Heritage language	Post-secondary	Language-minority	Literacy and academic language proficiency in an L2/FL connected to the learner's family or community of origin
Language for specific purposes	Post-secondary	Language-majority	Literacy and academic language proficiency in language other than home language and content-area knowledge

Elementary-level program models. Bilingual programs found at the elementary school level are generally one of three types: (1) early-exit (or transitional) bilingual instruction; (2) developmental bilingual instruction (previously called maintenance or late-exit bilingual education (see Lindholm-Leary & Genesee, 2010); or (3) immersion/dual language/two-way immersion. Each of these is briefly explained next.

Early-exit, or transitional, bilingual education programs are usually developed to serve young students who are recent immigrants to a new country (and thus are likely to be language-minority students). These programs aim to use two languages for classroom instruction up until the point at which children have developed sufficient oral and literacy skills (i.e., reading and writing skills) to receive all classroom instruction in their second language. (Thus the label *transitional;* two languages, the children's native language and the dominant societal language, are used in classroom instruction only until the children can make the transition to receiving all instruction in the dominant language.) Early-exit programs always include the oral use of the children's native language in the classroom; they may or may not include the active teaching of literacy skills in the children's native language. To the degree that they do, they may aim to develop biliteracy, but only the degree of biliteracy needed to make a transition to literacy in the dominant language. Program length varies, usually from one to three years.

Most early-exit/transitional programs begin in kindergarten or first grade. The goals of transitional bilingual programs are to ensure the mastery of grade-appropriate academic content and facilitate the speedy acquisition of the dominant language so that children can move into mainstream classrooms within three years of program entry (Genesee, 1999). Transitional programs require: (1) a sufficient number of certified bilingual teachers able to teach at the corresponding grade level; (2) access to sufficient academic materials in the students' native language; (3) specialized instruction in the L2 (e.g., English, in most cases in the United States) so that students are prepared to move into classrooms using only that language, plus specialized linguistic support for students during and after the transition; (4) appropriate and regular assessment of student progress; and (5) support for and from students' family and community members.

Developmental (maintenance or late-exit) bilingual models also aim to serve young students who are either immigrants to a country or who are members of relatively large groups within a country that speak a native language different from the dominant one. Thus, such programs, too, have been established to serve language-minority students. The goals of such programs typically include the development of literacy skills in both the native language and the L2; the development of academic literacy skills in both languages theoretically continues for the duration of the program. Thus such programs explicitly aim to develop biliteracy. The designation *maintenance* refers to the program goal of maintaining the use of the children's native language all the way through the program. This goal does not in any way exclude the learning of academic literacy skills in the L2. On the contrary, maintenance bilingual programs are meant to develop age- and subject-matter-appropriate academic literacy skills in two languages. Because such programs aim to maintain and develop skills in two languages, there is no theoretical limit on the number of years they might extend. In practice, however, such programs are usually found at the elementary level and extend from kindergarten through sixth grade, depending somewhat on how the particular school system organizes the levels of instruction. In Texas, the Austin Independent School District began a program of rolling out Spanish-English dual language maintenance and two-way immersion programs (see discussion later in this chapter) districtwide in approximately 50 elementary schools in 2010–2011. The district, which serves 29% English language learners (ELL), is phasing in one instructional year (e.g., second grade) every academic year until 2015–2016, when all the programs will serve students pre-kindergarten through fifth grade.

Rachel Carson Elementary School in Chicago is an example of a Spanish-English instructional program in which the development of strong reading skills in both languages is a major goal across the entire pre-kindergarten to eighth-grade curriculum. Aspects of both a two-way immersion approach for preschoolers and a transitional approach for later grades, emphasizing creation of a language-rich environment in both languages and active incorporation of social and educational support for families, have been elaborated to better serve the student population, of which approximately two-thirds enter speaking little or no English. Additional attention has been given to the recruitment and ongoing training of teachers and administrators, nearly all of them also bilingual. The school has demonstrated consistent increases in reading comprehension and academic achievement that far exceed the results observed in other local schools with comparable populations (Hanson & Moore, 2003).

What kinds of resources are required to implement and sustain such programs? Like transitional bilingual programs, maintenance bilingual programs require: (1) a sufficient number of certified bilingual teachers to teach all the grade levels included in the program; (2) access to sufficient academic materials in the students' native language and in the second language (English, in the United States); (3) specialized second language instruction; (4) appropriate assessment; and (5) parental and community support. Because the programs extend longer in the students' educational experience than transitional programs, they require a greater number of certified bilingual teachers and academic materials in both languages that cover a wider range of grade levels. In maintenance bilingual education, teachers are encouraged to keep the languages separate, and the entire school staff and community are expected to create an atmosphere of equal status for both languages involved.

Maintenance bilingual programs depend to some degree on the interest of a particular language community in supporting the academic use of its language, along with the second language, and in insisting on high academic standards in both languages. This model can be extended and adapted to trilingual situations. One such example is found in a Lebanese school where a French-English bilingual curriculum is followed. For all students and most staff members, local colloquial Arabic is the native language, and the school also emphasizes the development of academic uses of standard Arabic as part of its instructional goals (Zakharia, 2010).

Immersion programs, pioneered in Canada to serve linguistic-majority students—in this case, native speakers of English desirous of developing high levels of skill in French (see also García, 2009; Genesee, 2004)—aim to immerse students in a language different from their native language. (See also Snow, this volume.) The ultimate goal is to build strong, age-appropriate oral skills and academic literacy skills in that language and to give students access to subject matter taught entirely through the L2. In the classic immersion model, students receive instruction completely or almost completely through the medium of the L2 for the first few years of their educational experience, with literacy instruction in their native language added once they have established a base of literacy in the L2. By the latter years of the program, they usually receive instruction in each language about half the time. This progression of time allocation is thus referred to as starting with 90/10 (most instruction initially takes place in the L2, with little or no use of the students' native language) and moving to 50/50. Immersion models may extend all the way through elementary and even secondary education. Immersion approaches have been implemented in various international contexts such as in Catalonia, Spain, and Japan (Baker, 2011); Taiwan and Argentina (García, 2009); and Hungary, Finland, and Singapore (Johnson & Swain, 1997).

In the United States, there is a great deal of interest in two-way immersion, a variant of the immersion model designed to serve both language-minority and language-majority children who wish to learn through the medium of two languages and develop literacy skills in both languages (see Christian, 1996; Howard et al., 2007; and the Experience that begins this chapter). Such programs typically begin in kindergarten or in first or second grade and extend all the way through elementary school. In the United States, immersion programs may also be realized within the structure of innovative educational programs such as *magnet schools*, schools that particularly emphasize curricular areas such as math and science or the performing arts (see Potowski, 2007, for discussion of a magnet Spanish immersion school in Chicago). Indigenous language groups, such as Navajo in the United States and groups elsewhere in the Americas, have shown tremendous interest in the immersion approach for both maintaining and revitalizing heritage languages as well as for improving overall educational success (Francis & Reyhner, 2002). An innovative elementary immersion program with Spanish-English and Navajo-English tracks is now operating in Flagstaff, Arizona. In immersion programs, the instructional allocation of languages follows one of several patterns. Allocation may be based on subject matter (i.e., math taught in one language, social studies in the other), on particular days of the week (e.g., two days per week are English days, three days are Spanish days, and then the allocation is reversed the following week), on parts of the day (e.g., mornings in Spanish and afternoons in English), or on weekly assignments (one week in Spanish and then one week in English).

Many, though not all, two-way immersion programs follow a 90/10 model for the first six years of elementary instruction. If the languages are Spanish and English, this means that, in kindergarten and first grade, 90% of the instruction occurs in Spanish and 10% in English; in second grade, 80% occurs in Spanish and 20% in English; in third grade, 70% occurs in Spanish and 30% in English; in fourth grade, 60% occurs in Spanish and 40% in English; and by fifth grade, each language is used 50% of the time (Lindholm-Leary & Block, 2010). Whatever pattern is chosen, the teaching staff and students know and follow it. Initially, children entering such programs are proficient in only one of the two languages, but, because some of the enrolled students are native speakers of each of the languages used, the children teach each other in addition to learning from the adult models around them. Because there are native speaker or highly proficient models of both languages among both teaching staff and student participants, the likelihood that students will in fact develop high levels of proficiency in both languages is increased.

Several studies document two-way immersion language programs. R. D. Freeman (1998) provides a comprehensive description of the history and function of a long-standing Spanish-English dual language program at Oyster School in Washington, D.C. Her account offers many insights into the confluence of parental and community interest, the presence of qualified and dedicated teachers and administrators, and other issues to be considered in implementing such programs. Lightbown (2007) describes a Spanish-English two-way immersion program in a northeastern city that supported the English language and math progress of all the enrolled students, many of whom came from disadvantaged families. The results for English and math achievement were comparable to those from English-only classrooms at the same school and, furthermore, showed that the students enrolled in the bilingual program had also acquired Spanish language literacy skills.

Secondary-level bilingual approaches. At the secondary level, issues of program model and choice of instructional language are affected by the departmentalized nature of instruction found in most secondary schools (Walqui, 2000). Moreover, the greater demands of secondary school instruction also create pressures for both students and teachers to cover more, and more challenging, content material in a limited period of time (Short & Fitzsimmons, 2007; Suárez-Orozco, Suárez-Orozco, & Todorova, 2008). Hence, bilingual programs found at the secondary level are usually some variant of early-exit or transitional bilingual programs, in which the students' native language is used just long enough to help them make a transition to the socially and politically dominant language, which they are then expected to use through the rest of secondary school. In addition, optimally, secondary students receive carefully targeted ESL instruction aimed at building the academic language skills and vocabulary needed in secondary-level subjects (Dutro & Kinsella, 2010; Saunders & Goldenberg, 2010). Because of the specialized nature of the instruction at the secondary school level, it is comparatively rare to find an entire program that is completely bilingual in a public school setting, although private schools offering instruction through bilingual approaches all the way through secondary education (often intended for the socially elite members of a society) are found the world over in such settings as Africa and Latin America (García, 2009).

Furthermore, some U.S. secondary schools serving students who come largely from a single-language background have been successful in establishing extended bilingual instruction that continues through high school (for an example of one such program in New York City serving Spanish speakers, most from the Dominican Republic, see García & Bartlett, 2007; for accounts of programs for Navajo students on the Navajo Nation in rural northeastern Arizona, see McCarty, 2002). These programs serve geographically concentrated student populations and depend on teaching-staff members who are predominantly bilingual and biliterate in both languages used in instruction, crucial factors that increase possibilities for high-quality bilingual instruction. While these conditions do not exist uniformly across the country, there is, nonetheless, growing interest in devising adaptations of the two-way immersion approach for secondary schools (Montone & Loeb, 2000).

Although the number of publicly funded two-way immersion programs in middle schools and secondary schools is still small, many districts around the United States, especially those in which elementary-level dual language immersion programs have become better established, are exploring the possibility of adapting this model to suit older students. Time and subject allocations vary considerably, according to the student population and teacher expertise. At Casey Middle School in Boulder, Colorado, the program-within-a-school model is followed; in this model, two-way immersion students are instructed together for two 1-hour blocks, one in science and social studies and the other in language arts. For all other classes, learners are mixed with other students (Montone & Loeb, 2000).

In addition, in some localities, notably in large cities where there are newcomer schools (or newcomer programs within schools) that serve large numbers of immigrant students from the same language background, bilingual content-area classes may be offered, depending on student numbers and the availability of qualified teachers (i.e, teachers certified in the appropriate subject areas who are also bilingual in the languages needed). For example, core secondary school classes such as social studies and science have been offered in Spanish and Chinese at Newcomers High School in Long Island City, New York (Center for Applied Linguistics, 2009). While particular classes may be offered predominantly in languages other than those used in the mainstream, there is still a program-wide emphasis on assisting students to develop the academic English language skills needed to make a rapid transition to English language instruction. Hence, while such programs are not called transitional bilingual programs, certain classes within them, along with the overall goal of transition to English for many academic subject areas, make them somewhat comparable to transitional programs. Nonetheless, regardless of program title, research clearly indicates that at the secondary level the development of strong English skills is paramount and a vital avenue for related progress.

A recent study of secondary school English learners in San Francisco, most from Asian language backgrounds, indicated that most of them saw the school environment as the one place where they had regular access to and support for English language development, while their out-of-school experiences were much more linguistically varied (Borrero & Yeh, 2010). The belief in the need to develop strong English skills and the essential role of school in that process was also articulated by both learners and teachers in the secondary bilingual program in New York studied by García and Bartlett (2007). While the separation of English language learners from large numbers of fluent English speakers in newcomer centers raises concerns among educators and members of the public, this approach has been used successfully in parts of California and in some other large U.S. cities with large numbers of secondary-level students from the same language groups. Therefore, it should figure among the options to be considered as teachers and administrators seek alternative paths toward academic success and high school completion for secondary-level students (Walqui, 2000).

Finally, immersion programs (e.g., French immersion) exist at the secondary level as well. As with other bilingual approaches at the secondary level, many of these immersion programs are "partial," with students being immersed in a minority language for only part of the day. For example, at Milton High School in Milton, Massachusetts, students who have completed grades 1–8 in French immersion classes may continue their French studies by taking literature and humanities classes with French as the medium of instruction.

Post-secondary-level bilingual approaches. Post-secondary institutions serve students beyond the age of compulsory attendance. In the United States, post-secondary students are an extremely diverse lot of traditional- and nontraditional-age students whose goals range from very specific occupational training to more general aims such as acquiring a liberal education to highly specialized preparation for further professional study. The role and extent of bilingual approaches observed for each such student group vary considerably. Because no national body or organization is charged with collecting related data, it is quite difficult to determine when and where bilingual approaches are used. Some bilingual programs for adults in the United States have been developed to provide short-term, highly focused vocational training for special populations, such as refugees who qualify for special government support. Where there are large numbers of English learners who share the same home language, native language instruction may be included as a part of relatively short (less than six months) programs aimed at helping participants find employment as soon as possible. Bilingual programs that include native language literacy instruction for adults tend to be found in the geographical areas with the largest proportional settlement of recent immigrants: New York, California, Texas, and Illinois (Gillespie, 1994). In addition, the U.S. Department of Labor certifies trainers for short-term (10- to 30-hour) construction-safety outreach classes to be delivered in Spanish.

Post-secondary students enrolled in degree programs may have access to academic instruction in a second language designed to accommodate various professional and personal goals. One such opportunity is the second language sections (for either Anglophone L2 French students or Francophone L2 English participants) of Canadian undergraduate university courses in areas such as psychology, sociology, political science, and Canadian history (described in Burger, Wesche, & Migneron, 1997). In these classes, the content is taught in the students' L2, and students may also have a separate support course (designed on the sheltered or adjunct model) in the L2 aimed at assisting them with the linguistic demands of the course. (See also Snow, this volume.) Some universities, notably in Canada, offer entire degree tracks in the two official languages, English and French.[3] It should be noted that at such universities individual students may complete a degree program using just one of the two official languages; however, the institutions are indeed bilingual in that full degree programs are offered using both English and French. Other universities, particularly in the United States, offer immersion programs that are best viewed as a variant of foreign language immersion programs.

There are many additional program variants that aim to help students achieve university-level language skills in two languages. In the United States, university foreign language immersion programs may combine intensive language instruction (instruction from four to six hours per day for a semester or summer term) with a period of residence in a country where the language is spoken (i.e., study abroad), with the goal of the students' rapidly building proficiency (Kinginger, 2008; Lafford & Collentine, 2006). (In such cases, the instruction is mainly in the L2, so these programs do not necessarily qualify as bilingual programs,

although their goal is to produce students who become bilingual to some degree as a result of participation.) In addition, many colleges and universities in the United States offer special language courses (in *heritage languages*) that may be taught either bilingually or entirely in Spanish for native speakers of Spanish, Chinese for those who speak some Chinese, and so on (see Brinton, Kagan, & Bauckus, 2008). In the case of Spanish speakers, the goal is often, though not always, the development of formal literacy skills and academic and professional vocabulary for the participants, who have received all or most of their formal education in U.S. schools and thus have not had the opportunity to build advanced literacy skills in Spanish (Valdés, Fishman, Chávez, & Pérez, 2006).

Finally, some post-secondary institutions in the United States offer language for specific purposes courses that combine language instruction with occupationally relevant material in courses designed for particular majors, such as education or business. Courses emphasizing Spanish for teachers or business people may or may not be taught bilingually, depending on the initial level of student proficiency, goals of the course, and the instructor's language capabilities. In Canada, some universities offer highly proficient students the option of taking content-area courses completely in the medium of their second language, either English or French; such courses, a kind of tertiary sheltered approach, offer the graduates of secondary-level immersion programs a way to maintain and develop their language proficiency while learning new subject matter (Brinton, Snow, & Wesche, 2003).

TEACHING IMPLICATIONS: FROM PROGRAM MODELS TO QUALITY INDICATORS

From the 1960s until about the mid-1990s, much of the discussion about bilingual education centered on possible program models, with most of the research literature emphasizing taxonomies, often elaborate, of various program types (e.g., Mackey, 1978). Increasingly, however, both researchers and practitioners have realized that, in the United States, for example, there are very few "pure" bilingual program models and that, in practice, most bilingual programs combine elements of different models found in the academic literature. Since the late 1990s, two other developments in U.S. education—an emphasis on accountability and the growing popularity of charter schools—have meant that any educational models, whether for bilingual instruction or any other possible goal, cannot be discussed without reference to the social, political, and economic contexts in which they are implemented (Brisk, Burgos, & Hamerla, 2004; García, 2009). All contemporary discussion of bilingual educational approaches (e.g., Genesee, 1999; Hakuta, 2011; Hornberger, 2003; Howard et al., 2007) emphasizes the match among the characteristics of an educational program; the sociocultural context of the students it serves; and the resources, tangible and intangible, available to support educational efforts. All these affect the choices of instructional approaches and outcomes to be expected in any educational program, bilingual or otherwise (Dolson & Burnham-Massey, 2011). We turn now to those quality indicators that bear most strongly on the quality of language and content teaching in bilingual approaches.

Qualified teachers and school staff

It is impossible to implement any sort of bilingual approach without qualified teachers who know the requisite languages well. For this reason, the availability of sufficient qualified staff members is the cornerstone of successful bilingual programs of all types (Cenoz & Genesee, 1998; García, 2009; García & Bartlett, 2007; Hakuta, 2011). Teachers must be both highly proficient in at least one of the instructional languages and appropriately certified to teach the grade level of the subject area for which they will be responsible. Program effectiveness is further enhanced if at least some teachers share the linguistic and cultural backgrounds of the students they teach (García & Bartlett, 2007; McCarty, 2002).

Although teachers are vital, they are not the only relevant personnel. The presence of school administrators who understand bilingual instruction, other bilingual instructional personnel such as classroom aides and librarians, and bilingual staff members in positions such as school secretary increase the likelihood of consistent and effective instruction. Furthermore, and more than in many conventional educational contexts, staff members in any variety of bilingual education must commit

themselves to practices that make ongoing professional learning and collaboration the norm (Freeman, Freeman, & Mercuri, 2005; Hanson & Moore, 2003). Engaged as they will be in innovative programs that demand high levels of linguistic expertise, subject-matter knowledge, pedagogical flexibility, and ability to deal with unexpected situations or other challenges, they will require related reserves of imagination and dedication (García, Skutnabb-Kangas, & Torres-Guzmán, 2006).

Sound curricula and instructional organization

The use of two languages is part of any bilingual program, but that is not enough by itself to create and sustain program quality (J. Crawford, 2004). Qualified staff members must implement high-quality, age-appropriate curricula. Too often, bilingual education programs have been viewed as remedial rather than enriching. Effective bilingual approaches exemplify the foundational characteristics of all effective instructional programs, including access to the core curriculum; careful articulation of subject instruction across grade levels; flexible student groupings; use of meaningful tasks and pedagogy that actively engages students in learning; teaching materials that are appropriate in quantity and quality for the subjects taught; team teaching, where appropriate; peer and cross-age tutoring; and collaborative staff planning (García, 2009; Hakuta, 2011; Hornberger, 2003). Such curricular matters demand careful planning and monitoring, and must be implemented sensibly and efficiently (Hanson & Moore, 2003), keeping in mind local conditions such as average class size, support for ongoing teacher training, and presence of other resources needed to maintain good bilingual instruction. To this must be added, specifically for bilingual approaches, the conscious selection and consistent implementation of a program- and schoolwide vision of the benefits of bilingualism along with a plan for language allocation throughout the school day and across the length of the school program (Baker, 2011). Appropriate decisions about language allocation depend greatly on the particular school, neighborhood, and community context (Dolson & Burnham-Massey, 2011; R. D. Freeman, 1998, 2004). If the two languages are to be developed appropriately, both must be unambiguously accorded the status of the medium of core academic instruction for a variety of curricular activities; depending on student age and program type, each language may also be a school subject in itself. (For further considerations related to sound pedagogical techniques for second language development and subject mastery in elementary and secondary classrooms, see Dutro & Kinsella, 2010; Snow & Katz, 2010.)

Appropriate regular assessment

Good bilingual programs demonstrate regular and systematic assessments of school subjects in the relevant languages. In ascertaining program quality, these two aspects of evaluation—subject-matter knowledge and types of language proficiency—are related but distinct. Each requires attention, although the nature and types of assessments used varies considerably according to local and national assessment traditions and practices. In the United States for the last several decades, public (and many private) schools have depended on large-scale, norm-referenced standardized tests given in English as high-stakes indicators of students' achievement, a trend that must be acknowledged (although it is subject to substantial and thoughtful critique; e.g., see Escamilla, 2006; Menken, 2008; Ravitch, 2010). In some U.S. states, standardized Spanish tests may also be used, particularly where elementary-level English-Spanish bilingual programs have existed for some time. Tests that rely on reading and writing typically have some role in most educational programs, particularly as learners move into the late elementary and the secondary levels and beyond; nonetheless, researchers caution that any test administered in a learner's L2 reflects, in some part, that learner's L2 proficiency as well as whatever other constructs or concepts are at issue (American Educational Research Association, 2000; Snow & Katz, 2013).

Considerable tension surrounds the use of such tests in all school programs in the test-driven environment of U.S. kindergarten to 12th-grade education at present, and bilingual programs are no exception. On the one hand, many politicians and state legislators are convinced that instituting large-scale testing programs (with tests administered mainly or only in English) will yield data that will lead to improvements in education. On the other hand, practicing educators, researchers,

and assessment professionals (e.g., Ravitch, 2010; Shepard, 2000a) express concerns about the inordinate importance accorded to standardized testing and the frequent exclusion of attention to other vital aspects of the educational experience. That exclusion applies to both academic subjects outside reading and math (e.g., where science has just begun to be tested and social studies/history has not yet been assessed) and, somewhat more controversially, to the myriad socially relevant areas of schooling such as attitudes toward peers different from oneself, ability to work with others, and willingness to engage proactively with civic and environmental responsibilities (Ladwig, 2010).

Experts concerned specifically with second language (Gottlieb, 2006; Snow & Katz, 2013) and bilingual assessment (Cummins, 2000; Durán, 2008; García & Baetens Beardsmore, 2009; Valdés & Figueroa, 1994) note the many gaps in the existing research related to the testing of bilinguals and call for a more diverse, curriculum-specific, and emergent philosophy of measurement of student progress. For example, although focused primarily on the problem of developing tests to identify language or learning disabilities in bilingual individuals, Langdon and Wiig (2009) note that problems in translation test development (e.g., developing a Spanish test from an existing English test) include: (1) word-for-word translation that alters constructs; (2) lack of accounting for dialectal variety in the L2; (3) introduction of cultural and linguistic bias via tasks and visuals; and (4) tasks that do not differentiate students in the L2 although they do so in the first language. Within the stream of informed L2 practice, then, there is growing consensus about the need for and value of alternative methods of student assessment, including portfolio systems, learning logs, and checklists of student learning. (See also chapters by Katz and Kunnan & Grabowski, this volume.) Schools need resources, time, and funding to collect and analyze available assessment data (Torres-Guzman, Abate, Brisk, & Minaya-Rowe, 2002).

Multiple channels of parent/ community input, outreach, and ongoing connections

In addition to having the strong and consistent leadership needed to recruit and retain qualified teaching staff and implement a sound curriculum, bilingual programs of all sorts must determine the most effective ways to establish and maintain links between school-level efforts and the daily activities and routines of students' families and communities (McGroarty, 1998, 2001). This is not merely the type of parent participation conventionally specified as important to the success of individual children but a serious ongoing program of reciprocal action and communication in which learners and families conduct research of all kinds in their own communities, forge new relationships and alliances while so doing, and find ways to report on their work both in and outside school classrooms. Moll (2010) describes three bilingual programs in different parts of the United States where educators, learners, families, and community members have developed innovative ways to engage in collaborative investigations that provide students with new skills, insights, and confidence; build trust between schools and community members; and generate invaluable current knowledge of local community conditions and priorities. Educators use this information to adapt curricula more effectively for their learners.

Optimally, all good educational programs do this; but the need for community linkages is particularly crucial when one of the instructional languages in a bilingual program represents a language that is customarily used by students' families but is not regarded as a prestige language by politically dominant groups. Individual teachers can take many steps within their own classrooms to draw on parents' interests in their children's education, but effective community connections also require schoolwide leadership and support. Explicit efforts to create such links are particularly crucial when most teachers do not share students' linguistic and cultural characteristics. The challenge is greater still when the students represent not one or even two distinct linguistic and cultural backgrounds but several different ones, as is often the case in large school districts. Very few teachers or other school personnel receive systematic training in community outreach, but community outreach shows up repeatedly as a characteristic of effective school programs for bilingual students and L2 learners (R. D. Freeman, 2004; Moll, 2010).

Political climate

One final contextual feature demands attention—explicit political and public support for or opposition to bilingual approaches to language learning and education. This is particularly true with respect to recent developments in the United States, where the implementation of bilingual programs, never without controversy, has grown more controversial since the late 1990s. Opposition to such programs, often spearheaded by individuals and organizations not involved professionally in education, frequently reflects a lack of awareness of the robust international research that documents the nature of bilingual development and its potential to enhance educational outcomes (Cummins, 2000, 2003; Ulloa & Crawford, 2007).

In 2002, the federal 1968 Bilingual Education Act (which provided some federal support for bilingual instruction) was repealed (Lo Bianco, 2004), and political measures to limit, often severely, support for elementary- and secondary-level bilingual instruction have, since then, been passed in a number of individual states, including California, Arizona, and Massachusetts. These policies may align with public sentiments expressing antipathy for immigrant groups and linguistic pluralism (Gándara et al., 2010). While such policies do not always entirely prohibit the implementation of bilingual approaches to language learning, they do greatly restrict the awareness, number, and influence of bilingual approaches. Studies of the effects of such restrictions suggest that these policies increase neither the rate of English acquisition (Mahoney, MacSwan, Haladyna, & García, 2010) nor levels of academic achievement for English learners. In California, furthermore, evidence has emerged that Hispanic students enrolled in well-established dual language programs, even those in highly segregated school districts, outperform peers enrolled in English-only classrooms at the same schools (Lindholm-Leary & Block, 2010). In states where restrictive language policies have been instituted, the disparities between fluent English speakers and those still acquiring English remained sizable, although there are indications that any form of special language assistance, whether bilingual or special ESL instruction, lessened them (Rumberger & Tran, 2010). Furthermore, such policies are reported to restrict the instructional practices (beyond the obvious choice to use a language other than English) available to teachers who have been systematically trained in bilingual educational approaches, which may be related to a reduced demand for bilingual teaching credentials in some U.S. states (Gándara & Orfield, 2010).

In international contexts, political and public support plays an important role in the success of bilingual education programs as well. King and Benson (2004) describe the climate for and issues concerning the implementation in Ecuador and Bolivia of bilingual education (providing instruction in one of various indigenous languages, such as Quichua and Spanish). They note that, though no fewer than a quarter of the citizens in each country are speakers of languages other than Spanish, it is only recently, following both internal and external political pressure, that bilingual programs were supported by formal policy. García (2009) describes how formal policy efforts in Wales in the latter half of the twentieth century promoted English-Welsh bilingual education efforts.

FUTURE TRENDS

It is one of the great ironies of the early twenty-first century that, even as the forces of globalization are everywhere recognized as powerful influences on individuals and society, bilingual approaches to education in the United States face such strong opposition, often based on ignorance and misunderstanding (J. Crawford, 2004; Gándara & Hopkins, 2010). Worldwide, it is clear that there is growing awareness of and interest in various forms of school-based bilingual education. Bilingual programs have been proposed and implemented for indigenous languages long neglected in the educational systems in their own countries (Hornberger & López, 1998; King & Benson, 2004; López, 2006). They have also been proposed for minority languages in Europe (Cenoz, 1998; Etxeberría-Sagastume, 2006) and the United States (J. Crawford, 2004) and for the children of the middle-class citizens and elites in many countries who are desirous of ensuring that their children become bilingual and biliterate. Yet neither bilingualism nor biliteracy represents a simple dichotomy (Cummins, 2003; Hornberger, 2003); both can be defined as continua. Their definitions and measurements are varied and, to some degree, contextually determined. In addition, research conducted with youth in varied sites of language contact around the world indicates that young people demonstrate a range of behaviors related to bilingual and multiple language use; many are eager to incorporate linguistic hybridity into their language repertoires, sometimes in ways that accord with conventional educational programs, sometimes in arenas beyond the purview of traditional school curricula (Cummins, 2006; Davis, 2009). Some communities are interested in the potential of bilingual approaches to strengthen indigenous language skills and revitalize knowledge of indigenous cultural practices (Francis & Reyhner, 2002; McCarty, Romero, & Zepeda, 2006). Social, political, and economic trends suggest that many educators, along with many parents, are eager to better equip the students they serve with strong abilities in multiple languages as an essential component of a high-quality education (Valdés, 2009). In addition, many stakeholders in the educational process hope to prepare young people for success in a globalized world where English undoubtedly has a place but a place that is, increasingly, co-equal with other local, national, and regional languages (Zakaria, 2011). Indeed, the Council of Europe (representing 48 nations) has, in recent decades, developed several policies supporting plurilingualism as a group right, an individual resource, and a mechanism for political cohesion and cross-cultural understanding. Among these policies is the Common European Framework, which is a tool for evaluating levels of proficiency in any given language (Baetens Beardsmore, 2009). Thus, as the present century unfolds, all whose lives are implicated in or touched by formal education urgently need the proactive planning, engaged and imaginative pedagogy, and ongoing research into school-based approaches to the attainment of bilingual skills described here.

CONCLUSION

Bilingual approaches to education all include instruction through two languages but have goals that vary from transition to the language of wider communication to biliteracy in each of the two languages of instruction. Bilingual approaches come in many models at each level of education (elementary through post-secondary), and both the choice of these models and the way in which they are actually manifested depend heavily on context-specific variables such as the language abilities of teachers, the native languages of students, and the language values of the wider polity. Like bilingualism itself, bilingual approaches to education are unusual in certain parts of the United States but are the dominant model of instruction for second language learners in others. Internationally, bilingual approaches to education have always been valued by the elite and are increasingly valued for all students.

SUMMARY

➤ School-based bilingual education can take many forms.

➤ Second language learning can be combined with other school subjects in different ways.

➤ The effectiveness of language learning in a bilingual program depends on the length and quality of the program as well as the perceived usefulness of the instructional languages outside the school context.

➤ Like other educational programs, bilingual approaches require skilled teachers; high-quality curricula; appropriate assessments; and continuing parental, public, and fiscal support.

DISCUSSION QUESTIONS

1. In your state, region, or country, what is meant by the term *bilingual*? Which languages does this term usually refer to, and which of these are found in the educational system? At what levels are they used/taught?

2. In your teaching context, why are teachers, students, and families interested in bilingual approaches to language learning? What kinds of goals do they hope to achieve?

3. In your locality, are there any other institutions, community groups, or broadcast media where the use of a language other than the dominant one is usual? Identify any settings where the use of another language is a regular occurrence; comment on whether and how the use of language in such a setting might promote an interest in bilingual instruction in that language.

4. In your view, is comprehensive academic literacy in two languages a reasonable goal for students enrolled in the bilingual programs you know about? Why or why not? What conditions are conducive to the development and maintenance of literacy in two languages?

5. U.S. instructors: Look at the content of propositions such as California's Proposition 227 (1998) or Arizona's Proposition 203 (2000). Then search for websites advocating English-only policies. Summarize the arguments presented. Based on the information provided in this chapter and your own experiences, how would you counter these arguments?

SUGGESTED ACTIVITIES

1. Call your local school district to find out whether they have any classrooms that follow a bilingual model. If they do, visit a class for an hour or two to observe some typical classroom activities and see how the teachers and students negotiate the use of two languages.

2. If there are any bilingual programs located at schools (public or private) near you, arrange to talk with one of the teachers in the program. Ask the teacher how the curricular design and materials are employed to develop proficiency in two languages. Examine the materials used for literacy instruction in each language to get some idea of the language models used to help students become biliterate.

3. Gather some information on student assessment from one or two schools or school districts with bilingual programs. What kinds of student assessments are regularly administered and in what language? If the district includes non-native speakers of English, are testing and assessment requirements modified or altered in any way to accommodate them? If so, how?

4. Ask staff members from schools serving different levels of students (elementary, middle school, or secondary) how they address issues of family contact and community outreach. Gather samples of any communications sent to students' homes. Find out which languages are used to communicate with families; also find out how often and why families are asked to come to the school. Do you think such modes of outreach are likely to engage students' families? Why or why not?

5. Contact the legislative analyst's office for your state or region to see whether any legislation affecting language use or study has been proposed within the last two years. Identify the

sponsors and the intent of this legislation. If it has passed, ask some bilingual and teachers of English language learners if it has affected their work in any way.

FURTHER READING

Baker, C. (2011). *Foundations of bilingual education and bilingualism* (5th ed.). Clevedon, UK: Multilingual Matters.

This book is the most recent edition of a comprehensive textbook offering a thorough discussion of many aspects of bilingualism, including individual, group, and national considerations. It also discusses multiple models of bilingual education suitable for various goals, including academic progress, language revitalization, literacy development in multiple languages, and potential to serve special populations.

Bhatia, T. K., & Ritchie, W. (Eds.). (2004). *The handbook of bilingualism*. Oxford, UK: Blackwell.

This handbook provides broad and timely coverage of the developmental, psycholinguistic, cognitive, and sociolinguistic aspects of bilingualism by international experts who discuss bilingual and multilingual contexts around the world.

California State Department of Education. (2010). *Improving education for English learners: Research-based approaches*. Sacramento, CA: Author.

This volume is particularly directed to educators working in North American educational settings where a variety of approaches to effective public education for English language learners is a high priority.

Crawford, J. (2004). *Educating English language learners: Language diversity in the classroom* (5th ed.). Los Angeles, CA: Bilingual Educational Services.

The most recent edition of a foundational teacher training textbook, this volume offers clear, concise accounts of some of the historical and contemporary bilingual education efforts in the United States. It includes information on more recent TWI bilingual models, along with considerations of the effects, intended and unintended, of educational reform efforts and the push for accountability through testing on various aspects of bilingual programs.

García, O. (with Baetens Beardsmore, H.). (2009). *Bilingual education in the 21st century: A global perspective*. Malden, MA: Wiley-Blackwell.

This comprehensive volume provides substantial information and a provocative reevaluation of existing research on bilingualism and bilingual education in the United States and around the world.

ENDNOTES

[1] This Experience is based on entries from the Center for Applied Linguistics *Directory of Two-Way Bilingual Immersion Programs in the United States*, which can be found online at http://www.cal.org/twi/directory/

[2] Also not discussed here are the possibilities for bilingualism: (1) when parents are native speakers of two different languages and want to raise their children bilingually despite lack of access to schooling in one or both languages; or (2) when parents are not themselves bilingual but want to give their children that asset. Some excellent and current handbooks with guidance for parents exist. See, for example, Baker (2007); King and Mackey (2007).

[3] See, for example, information about the University of Ottawa, http://www.uottawa.ca

Focus on the Learner

33 | Motivation in Second Language Learning

ZOLTÁN DÖRNYEI

> ## KEY QUESTIONS
>
> ➤ What does it mean when we say that a learner is motivated?
> ➤ What is the role of motivation in language learning, especially in classroom contexts?
> ➤ How can language teachers actively promote their students' motivation?

EXPERIENCE

When enthusiastic novice teacher Erin Gruwell started her teaching career in a high school in Long Beach, California, she soon realized that she had been assigned the lowest-performing students in the school, with all the students in her class labeled at-risk inner-city youths, also known as "unteachables." Cliques formed among the students according to their ethnic backgrounds, fights broke out, and the drop-out rate was high. Not only did school management not help in this situation of violence, racial tension, and underachievement, but the head of her department even refused to let her use actual books in class in case they got damaged or lost. To make a long story short, it is difficult to imagine a more desperate situation for a beginner teacher, yet Erin Gruwell not only survived the first year but became so successful that all 150 of her "unteachable" students graduated from high school and many went on to college. As a result, her inspirational story was turned into a Hollywood film in 2007, *Freedom Writers*, starring Oscar-winner Hilary Swank. After leaving her high school job, Erin Gruwell became a distinguished teacher in residence at California State University, Long Beach; published several teacher-training books based on her experience (e.g., Gruwell, 2007a, 2007b); and started the Freedom Writers Foundation, which aspires to spread the Freedom Writers method across the country.

How did Erin Gruwell achieve the almost unachievable? Of course, she had to have a natural gift for teaching with a uniquely compassionate and, at the same time, stubborn personality, but that would not have been enough to beat such impossible odds. As becomes clear from her writings and from the well-scripted film, with no available resources and support all she had at her disposal was a range of creative educational strategies to raise the students' motivation and promote group dynamics in her classes—and she used these to great effect. The ultimate lesson from Erin Gruwell's story is that motivational and group-building strategies can work even in such a tough environment, and therefore an understanding of the motivational dimension of classrooms can offer teachers very powerful tools to combat a range of possible problems, from student lethargy to an unproductive classroom climate.

WHAT IS MOTIVATION?

Motivation is a word that both teachers and learners use widely when they speak about language learning success or failure, and normally it is taken for granted that we understand what the term covers. This seemingly unambiguous understanding, however, contrasts starkly with the perception of motivation as a technical term in the psychological and applied linguistics literature. Although it is used frequently, the meaning of the concept can span such a wide spectrum that sometimes we wonder whether people are talking about the same thing at all. In fact, there have been serious doubts as to whether motivation is more than a rather obsolete umbrella term for a wide range of variables that have little to do with each other. Indeed, motivation has been considered as both affect (emotion) and cognition; it has been used as both a stable variable of individual difference (i.e., a trait) and a transient-state attribute; and it has even been characterized as a process that is in constant flux, going through ebbs and flows. Furthermore, motivation has been considered as both a factor internal to the learner (e.g., individual curiosity or interest) and a factor externally determined by the sociopolitical setup of the learner's environment (e.g., language attitudes influenced by the relationships within language communities).

Perhaps the only thing about motivation that most researchers would agree on is that it, by definition, concerns the fundamental question of why people behave as they do. Accordingly, motivation determines the direction and magnitude of human behavior or, in other words, the choice of a particular action, the persistence with it, and the effort expended on it. This seems to be fairly straightforward: Motivation is responsible for *why* people decide to do something, *how long* they are willing to sustain the activity, and *how hard* they are going to pursue it. So, what is the problem?

The complex relationship of motivation, cognition, and emotion

The basic problem with conceptualizing motivation as the foundation of human behavior lies with the fact that human behavior can be influenced and shaped in a wide variety of ways, ranging from external motives, such as rewards and incentives, to diverse types of pressure, threats, and punishments. From an internal point of view, there is also a broad spectrum of reasons for doing things: we can be motivated by the love of money or power, the love of people and the world around us, or the love of peace and freedom. Our principal motivation can also be centered around our faith, our family, our profession, or our car. To make things even more complex, several of these motives can affect us simultaneously, interacting with each other on a temporary or on a permanent basis.

There is, however, some good news amid all this perplexing complexity. In spite of what lies behind our motivation, the actual state of being motivated is clearly discernible from a phenomenological (i.e., experiential) perspective; we simply know and feel when we are motivated and when we are not, and we can even grade this distinct experience of wanting (e.g., "It wouldn't be bad" versus "I really-really-really want it!"). Further good news is that people typically have no problem distinguishing this motivational experience from emotional experiences such as feeling happy, sad, or angry, even though those experiences are also gradable (i.e., you can be a bit sad or really angry). Finally, both motivational and emotional states can be relatively easily separated from thoughts, which are not gradable in terms of their intensity either in a positive or negative direction and have therefore sometimes been referred to as the "cold intellect." Thus, it has long been established—ever since Plato, in fact—that phenomenologically we can separate three areas of mental functioning: cognition, motivation, and affect (or emotions). This warrants their use as primary organizing principles of learner characteristics.

So, we can safely conclude that motivation *does* exist but that, in accordance with the hardware of our human mind being a highly integrated neural network, motivation constantly interacts with cognitive and emotional issues and that complex motivation constructs usually include cognitive and affective components. For example, classic expectancy-value theories of motivation hold that individuals are motivated to do a task if they expect to do well on it and if they value the task outcome (Wigfield & Eccles, 2000). In this case, a key component is our appraisal of the task and its consequences, which is a primary cognitive function; for such reasons, most modern motivational theories have been largely cognitive in nature (for a review, see Dörnyei & Ushioda, 2011). In addition to the motivation-cognition link, motivation is closely related to affect; we do not need much justification to assert that emotions such as joy, happiness, fear, anger, and shame profoundly shape our behavior. And, of course, to close the circle, emotions also have a cognitive dimension, which can be clearly seen when we become angry, for example, after we have cognitively appraised a situation and come to the rational conclusion that some major injustice has been done. Indeed, R. Buck (2005) is clearly right when he concludes, "In their fully articulated forms, emotions imply cognitions imply motives imply emotions, and so on" (p. 198).

Motivational conglomerates

So, even if motivation is recognized as a valid category, it always manifests itself in a dynamic interplay with cognitive and emotional factors. I have suggested (Dörnyei, 2009b) that a particularly fruitful approach to conceptualizing motivation, rather than trying to identify individual motives in isolation (as has been the typical practice in motivation research in the past), is to focus on motivational conglomerates of motivational, cognitive, and emotional variables that form coherent patterns or amalgams that act as wholes. While this may sound very abstract, well-known concrete examples of conglomerates, such as interest, indicate that such patterns/amalgams do exist and have traditionally been seen as significant motivational factors. Interest, for example, is clearly a motivational concept and, accordingly, has been included as a key component in various mainstream theories (e.g., expectancy-value theories or self-determination theory), yet it also involves a salient cognitive aspect (curiosity about and the engagement with a specific domain) as well as a prominent affective dimension (the joy associated with this engagement). Therefore, when people say in everyday parlance that someone is "interested" in doing something, they actually are referring to this complex meaning using a single term as a shortcut because they intuitively know that the constituents of the concept hang together in a way that forms a whole. The validation of this assumption is that the interlocutors have no problem understanding what is meant. In the next section, I describe a new motivation theory for learning foreign or second languages that is based on a motivational conglomerate of this sort: the learners' visions of their future self-image.

CONCEPTUAL UNDERPINNINGS OF LANGUAGE LEARNING MOTIVATION

In a long-term learning process such as the mastery of a second language, the learner's ultimate success always depends on the level of motivation; therefore, the concept of second language (L2) learning motivation (L2 motivation) has been the target of intensive research in second language acquisition (SLA) for over five decades. During this period, several approaches have been pursued.

The first famous theory was R. C. Gardner's (1985) social psychological paradigm, in which attitudes toward the speakers of the target language community were seen to play a key role in determining the learner's *integrative motivation* (i.e., the desire to learn an L2 of a valued community to communicate with members of the community and sometimes even to become like them). In the subsequent cognitive period, the best-known theory was Noels's (2001) adaptation of self-determination theory to language learning contexts, highlighting two motivational dimensions: *intrinsic motivation*, performing a behavior for its own sake (e.g., to experience pleasure or to satisfy one's curiosity), and *extrinsic motivation*, pursuing something as a means to an end (e.g., to receive some extrinsic reward such as good grades or to avoid punishment). In the late 1990s, there was a growing interest in looking at motivation as a dynamic concept that is in constant change and displays ongoing ebbs and flows, the process-oriented approach (see Dörnyei, 2005); this has culminated in contemporary attempts to adopt a dynamic systems perspective in motivation research that integrates the various factors related to the learner, the learning task, and the learning environment into one complex system (for a review, see Dörnyei & Ushioda, 2011). Because motivation theories intend to answer the ultimate question of why people behave and think as they do, it is not at all surprising to find such a richness of approaches. In this chapter, however, I focus on one recent theory in particular, the *L2 motivational self system* (Dörnyei, 2005, 2009a). This is partly because this theory offers a comprehensive perspective that builds on several previous constructs and is compatible with the emphasis on motivational, cognitive, and emotional conglomerates discussed earlier and partly because the framework it provides is practical and lends itself to classroom application.

Possible selves and the L2 motivational self system

In 2005, I proposed a new approach to the understanding of L2 motivation (Dörnyei, 2005), conceived within an L2 motivational self system, which attempts to integrate a number of influential SLA theories with the findings of self research in psychology. The new initiative was rooted in the important psychological concept of possible selves (Markus & Nurius, 1986), which represents people's ideas of what they *might* become, what they *would like to* become, and what they *are afraid of* becoming. Thus, possible selves involve people's vision of their likely or hoped-for (or even dreaded) selves in future states, not unlike an athlete envisaging himself or herself stepping onto the Olympic podium one day in the future. In this sense, possible selves are more than mere long-term goals or future plans in that they involve tangible images and senses; if we have a well-developed possible future self, we can imagine this self within vivid and realistic future scenarios.

From the point of view of learning and teaching, one type of possible self, the *ideal self*, is of particularly relevance because it involves the characteristics that someone would ideally like to possess (i.e., it concerns hopes, aspirations, and wishes). If a person has a well-established and vivid ideal self—for example, a student envisions himself or herself as a successful business person—this self-image can act as a potent future self-guide with considerable motivational power. This is expressed in everyday speech when we talk about people following or living up to their dreams. A complementary self-guide that has educational relevance is the *ought-to self*, which involves the attributes that someone believes he or she ought to possess (i.e., it concerns personal or social duties, obligations, and responsibilities). This self-image is particularly salient in some Asian contexts where students are often motivated to perform well to fulfill some family obligation or to bring honor to the family's name (see Magid, 2012). These two self-guides form the basis of the proposed L2 motivational self system, but to make the theory comprehensive, a third dimension has been added, representing the motivational influence of the students' learning environment (i.e., the motivational impact of various facets of the classroom situation, such as the teacher, the curriculum, and the learner group). This is justified by the observation that for some language learners the motivation to learn a language does not come from internally or externally generated future self-images but from successful learning experiences—after all, nothing succeeds like success, as the saying goes.

Accordingly, the proposed L2 motivational self system consists of the following three main constituents (for a more detailed discussion, see Dörnyei, 2009a):

1. *Ideal L2 self*, which concerns the L2-specific facet of the learner's ideal self. If the person the learner would like to become speaks an L2 (e.g., the person is associated with traveling or doing business internationally), the ideal L2 self is a powerful motivator for the learner to succeed in learning the L2 because he or she would like to reduce the discrepancy between the actual and ideal selves.
2. *Ought-to L2 self*, which concerns the attributes that the learner believes he or she ought to possess to avoid possible negative outcomes and that, therefore, may bear little resemblance to his or her own desires or wishes.
3. *L2 learning experience*, which concerns the learner's situation-specific motives related to the immediate learning environment and experience (e.g., the positive impact of success or the enjoyable quality of a language course).

Theoretical and research support

Over the past five years, several studies have employed and tested the L2 motivational self system in a variety of learning environments (e.g., see the selection of papers in Dörnyei & Ushioda, 2009) and the emerging picture consistently supports the validity of the theoretical construct. In studies that specifically compared R. C. Gardner's traditional concept of integrativeness with the ideal L2 self, the latter was found to explain the criterion measures better (typically explaining more than 40% of the variance, which is an exceptionally high figure in motivation studies), and the construct seems to work equally well for different age groups, from secondary school pupils through university students to adult language learners. This is good news, but we need to ask a further theoretical question: Is the proposed system compatible with the dynamic and complex nature of motivation discussed earlier?

Although so far we have looked only at the motivational capacity of future self-guides and images, the possible selves present broad overarching constellations that blend together motivational, cognitive, and affective areas. Previously, the originator of the concept, Markus (2006), has pointed out that the possible self-structure could be seen as a "dynamic interpretive matrix for thought, feeling and action" (p. xi), and indeed, MacIntyre, MacKinnon, and Clément (2009) have underscored the emotional aspect of possible selves: "When emotion is a prominent feature of a possible self, including a strong sense of fear, hope, or even obligation, a clear path exists by which to influence motivation and action" (p. 47). Furthermore, as we see in the next section, the effective functioning of these self-guides is dependent on several cognitive components, most notably on the learners' appraisal of their own capabilities and their personal circumstances to anchor their vision in a sense of realistic expectations. Last but not least, learners also need a good repertoire of task-related strategies that can be activated by the ideal language self—after all, even Olympic athletes need coaches and training plans in addition to their vivid vision of achieving excellence. All this points to the conclusion that effective future self-guides come in a package with a vision component that activates appropriate emotions and a variety of task-specific cognitive plans, scripts, and self-regulatory strategies. As such, future vision can be seen as the ultimate motivational conglomerate.

Conditions for the motivational power of vision

It has been widely observed that, although visionary future self-guides have the capacity to motivate action, this does not always happen automatically but depends on a number of conditions. The following list contains some of the most important prerequisites; this list is highly relevant when we consider ways of generating an L2 vision in the learners because vision-enhancing strategies are geared at ensuring that these conditions are met.

- *The learner has a desired future self-image.* People differ in how easily they can generate a successful possible self, and therefore not everyone is expected to possess a developed ideal or ought-to self-guide.

- *The learner's future self is sufficiently different from the current self.* If there is no observable gap between current and future selves, no increased effort is felt to be necessary and no motivation emerges.

- *The learner's future self-image is elaborate and vivid.* People vary in the vividness of their mental imagery, and a possible self with insufficient specificity and detail may not evoke the necessary motivational response.

- *The learner's future self-image is perceived as plausible.* Possible selves are effective only to the extent that the individual does indeed perceive them as possible, that is, to be realistic within the person's individual circumstances. Thus, a sense of controllability (i.e., the belief that his or her action can make a difference) is an essential prerequisite.

- *The learner's future self-image is not perceived as being comfortably certain to be reached, that is, to be within his or her grasp.* The learner must believe that the possible self will not happen automatically, without a marked increase in expended effort.

- *The learner's future self-image is in harmony (or at least does not clash) with the expectations of his or her family, peers, and other elements of the social environment.* Perceived social expectations or group norms that are incongruent with the self-image (e.g., language learning is for girls) are obviously counterproductive, as are ideal and ought-to self-images that are in conflict with each other.

- *The learner's future self-image is regularly activated in his or her working self-concept.* Possible selves become relevant for behavior only when they are primed by frequent and varied reminders.

- *The learner's future self-image is accompanied by relevant and effective procedural strategies that act as a road map toward the goal.* Once the learner's vision generates energy, he or she needs productive tasks into which to channel this energy.

- *A learner's desired future self-image is offset by a counteracting feared possible self in the same domain.* Maximal motivational effectiveness is achieved if the learner also has a vivid image about the negative consequences of failing to achieve the desired end state.

CLASSROOM APPLICATIONS

Luckily, most teachers do not have to face teaching situations as adverse as Erin Gruwell did at the beginning of her career; nevertheless, research has shown that many teachers find that problems with motivating pupils are the second most serious source of difficulty (the first is maintaining classroom discipline), outranking other, obviously important issues such as the effective use of different teaching methods, a knowledge of the subject matter, and the competent use of textbooks and curriculum guides (Veenman, 1984). If you have ever tried to teach a language class with reluctant, lethargic, or uncooperative students, you know that the results of these surveys of the impediments to learning are quite accurate. This being the case, teacher skills in motivating learners need to be seen as central to teaching effectiveness. The key question is this: Can motivational skills be consciously developed, or is the motivational and inspirational capacity of a teacher solely the consequence of a natural talent that the person has been born with? My past research and experience suggests that, while having a natural flair always helps, there is no doubt that motivational skills can be developed in teachers as part of purposeful training. Furthermore, there is a growing body of research that shows that, once such skills are in place, they have a significant impact on student motivation (e.g., see Guilloteaux & Dörnyei, 2008; Papi & Abdollahzadeh, 2012). Let us start the exploration with several key motivational principles.

Three fundamental motivational principles

Principle 1: There is much more to motivational strategies than offering rewards and punishments. Although rewards and punishments are often seen as the only tools in the motivational arsenal of teachers, a closer look at the spectrum of other, potentially more effective motivational strategies reveals that we have an array of varied techniques at our disposal to increase our learners' enthusiasm for L2 learning. In fact, most educational psychologists would consider rewards and punishments too simplistic and rather undesirable tools. The "carrot and stick" approach may work in the short run, but rarely does it lead to real long-term commitment. For example, books have been written about the potential damage of grades, which are by far the most often used forms of rewards and punishments; getting rewards—and good grades in particular—can become more important than learning, and students can easily become grade-driven. Therefore, I encourage teachers to start experimenting with other motivational techniques, such as making the learning process more engaging or promoting the learners' language-related vision. The variety of ways by which human learning can be promoted is so rich that teachers should be able to find something that works in most learning situations.

Principle 2: Generating student motivation is not enough in itself—it also has to be maintained and protected. In everyday parlance, motivating someone equals generating the initial motivation in the person. In educational contexts, however, this is not the whole picture. Although generating motivation is a crucial aspect of any motivational teaching practice, unless motivation is actively maintained and protected during the lengthy process of L2 learning, the natural human tendency to lose sight of the goal, get tired or bored with an activity, and give way to attractive distractions will result in the initial motivation gradually petering out. Thus, motivation needs to be actively nurtured, which means that any motivational practice needs to be an ongoing activity.

Principle 3: It is the quality (not the quantity) of the motivational strategies that we use that counts. One of the challenges of looking at the richness of the motivational strategies in the literature is that we become aware of the great number of useful techniques available that we are not applying consistently in our own teaching practice. Is this a problem? Not necessarily. There is so much that requires our constant attention in the L2 classroom that we simply cannot afford to continuously strive to achieve super-motivator status; if we try to do so, we will end up being burned out. I have come to believe that what we need is quality rather than quantity. A few well-chosen strategies that suit both teachers and their learners may be sufficient to create a positive motivational climate in the classroom. Indeed, some of the most motivating teachers rely on only a handful of techniques.

The range of motivational strategies

As noted previously, there is a wealth of potential motivational techniques available to teachers for use in the language classroom; Figure 1 presents 20 motivational facets of motivational teaching

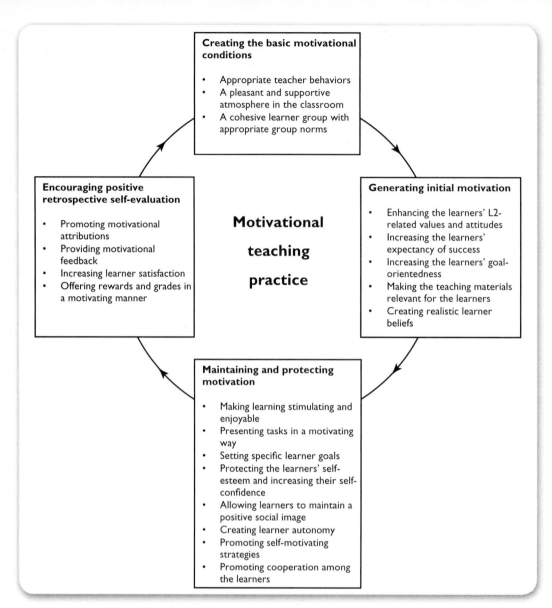

Figure 1. The main components of Dörnyei's (2001) framework of motivational teaching practice in the L2 classroom.

practice, grouped into four broad, successive stages (Dörnyei, 2001):

1. *Creating the basic motivational conditions.* Motivational strategies cannot be employed successfully in a motivational vacuum; certain preconditions must be in place before any further attempts to generate motivation can be effective.
2. *Generating initial motivation.* Unless we are singularly fortunate with the composition of our classes, student motivation will not be automatic for everybody, and we need to actively generate positive student attitudes toward L2 learning.

3. *Maintaining and protecting motivation.* We can initially whet the students' appetites with appropriate motivational techniques, but unless motivation is actively maintained and protected, it is likely to decrease in strength over time and can even disappear altogether (see Principle 2).
4. *Encouraging positive retrospective self-evaluation.* A large body of research has shown that the way learners feel about their past accomplishments significantly determines how they approach subsequent learning tasks. Strangely enough, the students' appraisal of their past

performance does not depend only on the absolute, objective level of the success they have achieved but also on how they subjectively interpret their achievement. Using appropriate strategies, teachers can help learners to evaluate their past performance in a more positive light, take more satisfaction in their successes and progress, and explain their past failures in a constructive way.

The introduction of the L2 motivational self system has further broadened the motivational repertoire at the disposal of language teachers because it highlights the significance of the learners' language learning vision. The possibility of harnessing the powerful motivational capacity of vision opens up a whole new avenue for promoting student motivation by means of increasing the elaborateness and vividness of self-relevant imagery in the students. The reality of such an approach has been evidenced in the field of sports psychology, where vision and imagery are generally seen as highly effective performance-enhancement techniques. Thus, language teachers interested in promoting their students' motivation can now choose from a variety of techniques based on their personal preferences as well as the needs and characteristics of their learners. The L2 motivational self system suggests that these motivational strategies can be divided into two main groups: (1) strategies focusing on the learners' vision of their ideal and the ought-to L2 selves; and (2) strategies that concern the improvement of the learning experience. Furthermore, it makes sense to subdivide Group 2 into two levels, the first associated with the individual learner and the second related to the learner group as a social unit. Let us take a closer look at these three clusters (vision, individual learner experience, and learner group experience).

Motivational strategies focusing on the learner's future vision. While virtually every successful athlete in the world applies some sort of imagery enhancement technique during training and competition, having the students in the area of language learning focus on vision is a relatively recent development. Dörnyei (2009b) has proposed a multicomponential framework to develop in the learners an attractive vision of their future language selves and thus to establish effective motivational self-guides for learning. This visionary program consists of six components. Moreover, Hadfield and Dörnyei (2013) have recently compiled a teachers' resource book that offers 100 practical classroom activities centered around the six stages.

Creating the vision. The first step in a motivational intervention that follows the self approach is to help learners to construct their ideal L2 self, that is, to create an L2-related vision. The verb *construct* here is, in fact, not entirely accurate because it is highly unlikely that any motivational intervention will lead students to generate an ideal self out of nothing. Realistically, the process is more likely to involve awareness raising about, and guided selection from, the multiple aspirations, dreams, and desires that the students have already entertained in the past while also presenting powerful role models to illustrate potential future selves.

Strengthening the vision. Even if a desired language self-image exists, it may not have a sufficient degree of elaborateness and vividness to act as an effective motivator. Methods of imagery enhancement have been explored in several areas of psychological, educational, and sports research, and the techniques of visualization and guided imagery can be used to promote the students' ideal L2 self-images.

Substantiating the vision. Effective visions share a mixture of imagination and reality; therefore, to go beyond mere fantasizing, learners need to anchor their future self-guides in a sense of realistic expectations. This substantiating process requires honest and down-to-earth reality checks as well as a consideration of any potential obstacles and difficulties that might stand in the way of learners' realizing the vision.

Operationalizing the vision. Future self-guides need to be part of a package consisting of an imagery component *and* a repertoire of appropriate plans, scripts, and specific learning strategies. This is clearly an area where L2 motivation research and language teaching methodology overlap.

Keeping the vision alive. Warm-up activities or ice-breakers and other classroom activities can all be turned into effective ways of reminding students of their vision and thus to keep the enthusiastic students going and the less-than-enthusiastic ones thinking.

Counterbalancing the vision. People do something both because they want to do it and because not doing it would lead to undesired results. Regular reminders of the limitations of not knowing foreign languages and highlighting the duties and obligations the learners have committed themselves to as part of their ought-to selves will help to counterbalance the vision with a feared self.

Motivational strategies focusing on the learning experience: Individual learner level. How can the L2 learning experience be made more attractive to individual learners? The following 10 strategies offer a representative selection of the techniques and approaches available to the teacher.

Whetting the students' appetite. The key in generating interest in learning is to whet the students' appetite, that is, to arouse the learners' curiosity and attention to create an attractive image for the L2 course. This is very much a "selling" task in which the teacher may point out challenging, exotic, or satisfying aspects of L2 learning; connect L2 learning with activities that students already find interesting or hold in esteem (e.g., computer-assisted learning); highlight the variety of activities that L2 learning may involve; and provide a demonstration of some particularly enjoyable tasks (e.g., games, simulations, or competitions).

Increasing the learners' expectancy of success. The notion of expectancy of success has been one of the most researched factors in motivational psychology for the past four decades. This is due to the undeniable fact that people do things best if they believe they can succeed in them. Whether a student expects success in a given task is a rather subjective matter; therefore an effective way of motivating learners is to put them in a more positive or optimistic mood. Of course, the best way of ensuring that students expect success is to make sure that they achieve it consistently; in addition, it also helps if the success criteria are clear, the students are provided with sufficient advance preparation, and they are aware that they can rely on ongoing assistance both from the teacher and their peers.

Making the teaching materials relevant to the learners. One of the most demotivating factors for learners is to have to learn something that has no apparent relevance to their lives. This experience is, unfortunately, more common than many of us would think. Accordingly, much of the motivational advice offered to teachers in the educational literature boils down to the following general principle: find out what students' goals are and what topics they want to learn about; then build these into the curriculum as much as possible.

Breaking the monotony of learning. Even in classes characterized by a mixture of interesting teaching approaches, there is a danger of settling into familiar routines, which then can easily turn into a monotonous daily grind. To prevent monotony, teachers need to vary as many aspects of the learning process as possible (e.g., the focus and nature of the tasks, the type of student involvement, the learning materials, and even the arrangement of the furniture). Of course, trying to continuously change all the aspects of teaching becomes the perfect recipe for teacher burn-out; rather, teachers should look at these factors as cooking ingredients and make sure that they do not serve exactly the same meal every day.

Making the learning tasks more interesting. Not even the richest variety of tasks will motivate students if their content is not attractive, that is, if the students find the activities boring. The literature contains an abundance of suggestions on how to make tasks interesting; for example, tasks that offer some challenge, contain interesting topics, or include novel, intriguing, exotic, humorous, or fantasy elements are always welcomed by learners.

Increasing the learners' self-confidence. Learning a new language is to a large extent a "confidence game." Confident learners can communicate using surprisingly limited L2 resources, whereas no amount of vocabulary and grammatical knowledge will help someone to speak if his or her confidence is lacking. Two key aspects of confidence building are providing regular encouragement and reducing language anxiety. Teachers should never forget that the language classroom is an inherently face-threatening environment where saying even a simple sentence carries the danger of making big mistakes. Helping learners to accept that mistakes are a natural part of the learning process is already half the battle.

Allowing learners to maintain a positive social image. For most schoolchildren, the main social arena in life is their school and their most important reference group is their peers. Adult learners can be similarly self-conscious. Therefore, it is unlikely that students will be keen to do a task that puts them in a situation where they are made to look small in front of their classmates. This might involve performances that require free, unscripted speech in front of the others; learners in some cultures might be particularly self-conscious about their accented pronunciation in such situations. On the other hand, if teachers provide an opportunity for everybody to play the protagonist's role in one way or another (e.g., by creating situations in which students can demonstrate their particular strengths), the "positive hero" image might work as a stimulant.

Creating learner autonomy. Students are more motivated to pursue tasks when they feel some sort of ownership. This can be achieved by teachers' allowing them to make real choices about as many aspects of the learning process as possible, handing over various leadership/teaching roles, and adopting the role of facilitator rather than drill sergeant. Autonomy and motivation go hand in hand.

Increasing learner satisfaction. I have noticed in myself, and also in many other teachers, a tendency to show far less emotion when something goes right than when it goes wrong. The problem with acknowledging accomplishments in such a cool manner, but making failures or difficulties tangible, is that teachers miss out on the celebratory part of learning and reduce the amount of satisfaction they may feel. Celebrations and satisfaction are crucial motivational building blocks because they validate past effort, affirm the entire learning process, and in general provide the bright spots along the road toward the ultimate goal. So teachers should take the time to celebrate any student victory.

Offering grades in a motivational manner. Although many teachers and researchers would love to get rid of assessment, realistically speaking, grades are likely to remain a fact of life for the foreseeable future. Therefore, an important task for teachers is to find ways of offering grades and rewards in a motivating manner. The following guidelines may take teachers some way toward this end: (1) make the assessment system completely transparent, with clear success criteria, and create opportunities for the students to also express their views; (2) make sure that grades reflect effort and improvement, and not just objective levels of achievement; (3) apply continuous assessment that does not rely solely on pencil-and-paper tests; and (4) encourage accurate student self-assessment by providing a variety of self-evaluation tools.

Motivational strategies focusing on the learning experience: Learner group level. When a teacher faces a motivationally challenging classroom situation (like Erin Gruwell did in Long Beach in the 1990s), it is usually evident that trying to cater to the individual learners' motivational needs is not enough because the learner group as a whole has such a powerful influence over the members that it can, and often does, override the individual students' personal preferences. Therefore, motivation also needs to be tackled at the group level. This is where lessons from group dynamics become invaluable (see Dörnyei & Murphey, 2003).

In the social sciences, group dynamics concerns the scientific analysis of the behavior of small groups and involves overlapping disciplines such as social, industrial, organizational, and clinical psychology; psychiatry; anthropology; sociology; and social work since all these fields involve groups as the focal points around which human relationships are organized. Because in instructional contexts most organized learning occurs in some kind of group (classes, seminars, workshops, discussion groups, etc.), group dynamics is highly relevant in education, including language education. An awareness of the principles of group dynamics can make classroom events less threatening to teachers and can help them develop more efficient methods of classroom management and thus consciously facilitate the development of creative, well-balanced, and cohesive groups. All this, of course, has a significant motivational impact.

Group dynamics

The two areas of group dynamics that most concern the motivational state of group members are group cohesiveness and group norms. Group cohesiveness is the strength of the relationships linking group members to one another and to the group itself; group norms are the implicit and explicit rules of conduct that regulate the life of the learner group and that make joint learning possible.

Group cohesiveness. The motivational significance of a cohesive classroom becomes obvious if we consider its opposite, a classroom with cliques and a lack of proper communication among students. So, how can we avoid such a situation and consciously promote a cohesive classroom climate? Here are some relevant points to consider.

Learning about each other. This is the most crucial and most general factor to foster inter-member relationships; it involves the students' sharing genuine personal information with each other. People do not accept others without knowing the other people well enough; images of others as enemies or a lack of tolerance very often stems from insufficient knowledge about the other people.

Proximity, contact, and interaction. Proximity is the physical distance between people, a contact is a situation where learners can meet and communicate spontaneously, and an interaction is a special contact situation in which the behavior of each person influences the behavior of others. These three factors are effective natural gelling agents that highlight the importance of classroom issues such as the seating plan, small-group work, and independent student projects.

Shared group history. The amount of time people have spent together and statements such as "Remember when we . . ." usually have a strong bonding effect.

The rewarding nature of group activities. Rewards may involve the joy of performing the activities, approval of the goals, success in achieving these goals, and personal benefits (such as grades or prizes).

Group legend. Successful groups often create a kind of group mythology that includes giving the group a name; inventing special group characteristics (e.g., a dress code) and group rituals; and creating group mottos, logos, and other symbols such as flags or coats of arms.

Public commitment to the group. Group agreements and contracts spelling out the common goals and rules of the group are types of such public commitment; wearing school colors or T-shirts is another way of achieving this.

Investing in the group. When members spend a considerable amount of time and effort contributing to the group goals, this increases their commitment toward these goals and, subsequently, to the group.

Extracurricular activities. These represent powerful experiences—indeed, even one successful outing may be sufficient to create the group,

partly because during outings students lower their "school filter" and relate to each other as civilians rather than students. A positive experience will prevail in students' memories, adding a fresh perception to their school relationships.

Cooperation toward common goals. Superordinate goals that require the cooperation of everybody to achieve them have been found to be an effective means of bringing together even openly hostile parties.

Intergroup competition. Games in which small groups compete with each other within a class can produce a powerful type of cooperation; people will unite in an effort to win. Teachers can group students together who would not normally make friends easily and mix up the subteams regularly.

Defining the group against another. Emphasizing the differences between "us" and "them" is a powerful but obviously dangerous aspect of group cohesiveness. While stirring up emotions against an out-group to strengthen in-group ties is definitely to be avoided, teachers might occasionally allow students to reflect on how special their class and the time spent together are compared to the experiences of other groups.

Joint hardship and common threat. Strangely enough, going through some difficulty or calamity together (e.g., carrying out some tough physical task together or being in a common predicament, such as having to take an exam) can have a beneficial group effect.

Teacher as role model. Friendly and supportive behavior by the teacher is infectious, and students are likely to follow suit.

Group norms. The best way to illustrate the motivational role of group norms is to consider a situation where things have gone wrong. In many contemporary classrooms, we come across the norm of mediocrity, that is, there is often peer pressure on fellow students not to excel academically; if they do excel, they will be made fun of and called names such as "nerd" or "brain." This is a clear-cut illustration of group norms directly affecting students' individual levels of motivation, sometimes in a dramatic way. So, how can we make sure that the norms in our classroom promote rather than hinder learning? The key is that real group norms are inherently social products; for a norm to be long-lasting and constructive, it needs to be explicitly discussed with and accepted by the students as right and proper. Therefore, it is beneficial for teachers to include an explicit norm-building procedure early in the group's life by:

- formulating potential norms
- justifying their purpose to enlist support for the norms
- having the norms discussed by the whole group
- eliciting further potential norms from the learners and subjecting these to discussion too
- explicitly addressing unproductive norms and changing them by consensus
- agreeing as a group on a mutually acceptable set of class rules that can be displayed on a wall chart

Norm-building efforts will really pay off for the teacher when someone breaks the norms, for example, by behaving inappropriately or not doing something expected. The more time a group spends setting, negotiating, and modeling the norms, the fewer people in the group will go astray; and when group members do break the norms, it is usually the group that brings them back in line. Having the group on the teacher's side when coping with deviations and maintaining discipline is a major help. Members can usually bring considerable group pressure to bear on errant members and enforce conformity with the group's norms. Teachers should never underestimate the potential power of the group.

FUTURE TRENDS

Contemporary research on L2 motivation is moving into a new phase characterized by a concern with the situated complexity of the L2 motivation process and its dynamic interaction with a multiplicity of internal, social, and contextual factors in our modern and increasingly globalized world. Indeed, over the past decades the world of the L2 learner has changed dramatically—it is now characterized by linguistic and sociocultural diversity and fluidity, where language use, ethnicity, and identity have become complex topical issues and the subjects of sociolinguistic and social psychological research. To address this changing global reality and, in particular, to account for the motivation to learn global English as a target language of people aspiring to acquire a global identity, L2 motivation is currently being radically reconceptualized in the context of contemporary notions of self and identity. The first part of this chapter provided a sense of the emerging new theoretical focus.

With regard to practical developments concerning the methods of increasing learner motivation, I believe that the concepts of vision and future self-guide will play a key role in the next decades. Techniques are currently being developed to use self-enhancing activities, visualization, and guided imagery in the language classroom (e.g., Arnold, Puchta, & Rinvolucri, 2007; Hadfield & Dörnyei, 2013; Magid & Chan, 2012), and the initial positive perception of the self-based approach by teachers in many settings suggests that this is a direction that may activate considerable creative energy at the classroom level. This will be very welcome because, as every reader of this chapter will probably agree, the way we currently approach classroom processes and events—and more generally, the psychological reality of the language classroom—has for some time been due for a major overhaul.

CONCLUSION

In an inherently social process such as language acquisition, the learner cannot be meaningfully separated from the social environment within which he or she operates, and therefore the challenge for future research on motivation is to adopt a dynamic perspective that allows us to consider simultaneously the ongoing multiple influences between environmental and learner factors in all their componential complexity. Erin Gruwell's response to the challenges she faced involved taking exactly such an integrated approach; she addressed motivational issues, at both the individual learner and group levels, that ranged from designing creative learning tasks and ensuring adequate resources to developing a classroom climate characterized by cohesiveness and a norm of tolerance. But she also knew that to turn around such hard-to-reach students (or "unteachables") she needed to impact the learners' whole identities by offering them a new, attractive vision. The Freedom Writers project showed that such goals are not merely idealistic fantasies but can actually work;

the L2 motivational self system described in this chapter offers a useful theoretical framework to pull together a wide range of issues concerning the internal desires of the learner, the social pressures exercised by significant or authoritative people in the learner's environment, and the learner's actual experience of being engaged in the learning process.

On a more practical level, my experience is that motivational issues still do not receive their due importance in language teacher education. One consequence of this is that teachers are expected to meet the challenging demands of managing complex classrooms without sufficient awareness and training to tackle the psychological level—this is a little bit like sending soldiers to war without enough ammunition. It is hoped that this situation will change, and this chapter has outlined a wealth of strategies and approaches that language teachers have at their disposal to motivate their learners. However, let me reiterate here that striving to achieve super-motivator status can easily lead a teacher to burnout; instead, it is sufficient for teachers to choose a few strategies that suit both them and their learners to create a positive motivational climate in the classroom. Some of the most motivating teachers rely on only a handful of techniques.

SUMMARY

➤ Motivation concerns the fundamental question of why people behave as they do, that is, the choice of a particular action, the persistence with it, and the effort expended on it.

➤ With a long-term learning process such as the mastery of a second language, learners' ultimate success will depend heavily on their level of motivation.

➤ Because motivation always manifests itself in a dynamic interplay with other personal and contextual factors, a particularly fruitful approach to conceptualizing motivation is by focusing on motivational conglomerates of various motivational, cognitive, and emotional variables that form coherent patterns and, as such, act as wholes.

➤ One motivational conglomerate that offers a particularly useful framework for language educators is the learners' future vision of themselves.

➤ Language-specific vision is operationalized within the broader construct of the L2 motivational self system, which highlights three primary sources of L2 motivation: the learners' vision of themselves as effective L2 speakers; the social pressure coming from the learner's environment; and the learners' positive learning experiences.

➤ Skills in motivating learners are central to effective teaching; relevant motivational strategies can be divided into three main clusters, focusing on: (1) the learner's future vision; (2) the individual's learning experience; and (3) the group's learning experience.

DISCUSSION QUESTIONS

1. Is it meaningful to use the term *motivation* to refer to such divergent purposes as learning an L2: (a) to be able to make more money and (b) to be able to read a sacred text in the original? Or (c) to get good grades and (d) to expand one's mental horizon?

2. What happens to a learner's overall motivation when the ideal language self and the ought-to language self come into conflict (e.g., the learner experiences conflict between personal and family plans, or faces negative peer pressure at school)? How can such a conflict be handled in a constructive way?

3. Why are most motivational strategies underutilized and most language teachers not overly concerned about motivating their students? What is your personal experience with this issue?

4. How universal are motivational strategies? Can some strategies be effective in one learning environment and counterproductive in another?

SUGGESTED ACTIVITIES

1. The following four strategies are part of the vision-building sequence described earlier in the chapter. Think of your past experiences as a language learner and/or teacher, and imagine how you might be able to apply some of these strategies:
   a. construction of the ideal L2 self: creating the vision
   b. imagery enhancement: strengthening the vision

c. developing an action plan: operationalizing the vision

d. activating the ideal L2 self: keeping the vision alive

2. You want to give your students controlled practice of a grammar point (e.g., *since/for* + present perfect tense). Think of ways to make the inherently boring drill task more interesting by exploiting the following elements:

a. some kind of a challenge

b. interesting content (i.e., related to the students' interest)

c. some novelty element

d. some exotic/fantasy element

e. some personal element (i.e., personalizing the content)

Factors promoting group cohesiveness	Current group	Past/future group
Learning about each other		
Proximity (physical distance)		
Social contact and interaction		
Cooperation		
The rewarding nature of group experience		
Joint hardship		
Intergroup competition		
The teacher's role in modeling		
Investing in the group		
Defining one's group compared to another group		

3. The chart on this page contains a list of factors that can positively contribute to group cohesiveness. Using a scale from 1 to 5 (where 1 = not relevant/applicable/practical and 5 = highly relevant/applicable/practical), mark how relevant/practical/applicable each factor is: (a) in the learner group you are currently a member of; and (b) in the context you have come from and/or where you are planning to teach in the future. Summarize the results together in class on the board and discuss them.

4. Watch the film *Freedom Writers* (2007, Paramount Pictures), and write down two examples of each of the following instructional strategies used by the teacher, Erin Gruwell:

a. group-building activities

b. vision-building activities and practices

c. creative learning techniques

FURTHER READING

Dörnyei, Z. (2009). The L2 motivational self system. In Z. Dörnyei & E. Ushioda (Eds.), *Motivation, language identity and the L2 self* (pp. 9–42). Bristol, UK: Multilingual Matters.

This is the most detailed description of the L2 motivational self system to date, discussing its genesis, theoretical validity, and main features.

Dörnyei, Z., & Ushioda, E. (2011). *Teaching and researching motivation* (2nd ed.). Harlow, UK: Longman.

This book offers an accessible overview of everything teachers want to know about motivation, from theory and research to applications and motivational strategies.

Markus, H., & Nurius, P. (1986). Possible selves. *American Psychologist, 41*, 954–969.

If you want to read one psychological work on possible selves and future self-guides, this is the one.

Ushioda, E. (2008). Motivation and good language learners. In C. Griffiths (Ed.), *Lessons from good language learners* (pp. 19–34). Cambridge, UK: Cambridge University Press.

This is a concise overview in a very useful volume.

34 | Language Learner Strategies and Styles

JAMES E. PURPURA

KEY QUESTIONS

➤ What strategies do language learners use when learning or using a second or foreign language?

➤ What are learner styles, and how do they relate to learner strategies?

➤ What has been learned from the research on learner strategies, and how can this information be used to inform language teaching and learning?

➤ How can teachers design tasks to promote strategic awareness and develop cognitive flexibility in their students?

EXPERIENCE

Imagine a teacher in an intermediate-level second or foreign language (SFL) class, in which students are having trouble with *break* expressions (e.g., *break in*).[1] She gives her students the task shown in Figure 1, asking them to infer the meaning(s) of the italicized words and phrases in the story from context and to choose the best paraphrase from the options given.

When they are finished, the students compare answers in groups, check the correct answers to verify their choices, and clarify any ongoing problems. Verifying and clarifying are strategies commonly used to understand new information. The students then discuss how they figured out the meanings from the context. They report using several strategies: deducing meanings from explicit explanations in the text; making associations and inferring meanings from context; and in the case of words they already knew, linking with prior word knowledge.

As the final step in the lesson, the teacher asks the students, in pairs, to write about a different break-in, after which they share stories. After both tasks, the students again list their strategies and report: remembering the original story, brainstorming ideas for a new story, examining the original story to plan the new one, generating a

Yesterday while Hal and Ann were at a restaurant, thieves (1) *broke down* the door of their house, went inside, (2) *broke into* their safe, and stole Ann's diamond ring. When they got home, the thieves were in the house. Hal grabbed one of them, but he hit Hal and (3) *broke* his nose. Ann almost (4) *had a nervous breakdown*. She took Hal to the hospital, but on the way the car (5) *broke down*, so they got a cab. When they got home, Ann calculated the cost of the (6) *break-in*. She felt like (7) *breaking out* in tears she was so upset. Hal said, "Gee! We've never spent so much money! We've (8) *broken all records*." Ann added, "We've spent all our money. We're totally (9) *broke!*" Hal replied, "Everything's either broken, broken down, or broken into, but we still love each other. We'll never (10) *break up.*"

__ a. become very upset	__ f. make into two or
__ b. pushed and destroyed	more pieces
__ c. got into something by	__ g. end a relationship
breaking	__ h. stopped working
__ d. entry for illegal	__ i. given a superlative
purposes	performance
__ e. have no money	__ j. start suddenly

Figure 1. Exercise for inferring the meanings of *break* expressions (adapted from Purpura & Pinkley, 1999, p. 82).

new story, evaluating and revising their story, using words and expressions with *break*, translating words, recalling the events in their story, sharing and helping each other, rehearsing the new story, and finding ways to reduce anxiety.

WHAT ARE LEARNER STRATEGIES AND LEARNER STYLES?

Language educators have long been intrigued by learners' inner mechanisms as they acquire and use a SFL to communicate. Alongside learners' knowledge of the language and of what they want to communicate, success in learning a SFL depends on students' ability to plan, ask questions, make associations, remember, prioritize, distinguish main ideas from details, monitor progress, reflect on successes, and flexibly shift their approaches to language learning or use. These thoughts and actions—*learner strategies*—are part of strategic competence and are critically important when learning and using a SFL.

Strategic competence is the information structures in working memory and long-term memory associated with the brain's information processing system; *strategies* are thoughts or behaviors used by learners to regulate SFL learning or use. *Metacognitive strategies* mentally regulate actions or behaviors (e.g., planning talk or monitoring SFL use).[2] *Cognitive strategies* are "doing" behaviors that learners invoke to understand, remember, retrieve, or use new information (e.g., clarifying, inferring meaning from context, categorizing words, correcting grammar). *Social strategies* are collaborative behaviors that promote positive interactions and relationships (e.g., helping and sharing). Finally, *affective strategies* are behaviors that allow learners to identify and adjust their feelings, beliefs, attitudes, and impulses while learning and using a SFL (e.g., coping with frustration).

Teachers need to know about strategic competence because it controls how learners notice and understand new SFL input (e.g., the *break* expressions), how they organize this new information mentally so it can be remembered, and then how they retrieve this information from memory to communicate. Strategic competence also helps learners understand and regulate the social, interactional, and emotional challenges of learning and communicating effectively in a SFL.

Many researchers believe that learners use strategies to regulate their thoughts, actions, interactions, and affect in a purely conscious, intentional, and goal-directed fashion, especially when confronted with SFL challenges. For example, before a SFL speaker volunteers to answer a question in class, she might consciously plan and rehearse her answer to the question. Such deliberate strategies are highly useful for learning and for the immediate attainment of goals.

Recent research, however, has shown that the regulation of strategy use may also occur without the learner's conscious knowledge or awareness of how he or she is learning a new language or using it to communicate. As Papies and Aarts (2011) state, "in most situations, such conscious control is neither necessarily present, nor indeed required to regulate one's behavior successfully in accordance with one's goals" (p. 126). This nonconscious use of strategies is called *automatic processing*.

Consider, for example, how an advanced SFL learner uses automatic processing to read an easy text. She automatically analyzes or parses words, structures, and parts of speech, associating these forms with their meanings; she also synthesizes the meanings within and across sentences, inferring any implied meanings to understand what is being communicated. Most learners move flexibly between conscious and automatic processing while performing tasks. In the Experience at the outset of this chapter, as students learn the different meanings of *break*, they first use the new words and expressions consciously; then, as the words and expressions are gradually acquired, they use them in nonconscious ways. Strategic competence thus refers to strategies that may be used either consciously and deliberately or unconsciously and automatically to further learners' processing while they are learning or performing SFL tasks (Purpura, 1999).

In fact, learners differ greatly in the strategic processes they invoke to learn or use a SFL. These differences appear across skill domains (e.g., reading), contexts (e.g., the classroom or the drugstore), topics and themes (e.g., "ecology" or "people watching"), and tasks (e.g., booking a flight). Strategic processes also vary across the stages of SFL processing (i.e., perceiving, understanding, remembering, or retrieving information) as learners progress from having no knowledge of a learning objective to the ability to use the new knowledge automatically.

In addition to strategy use, learners also vary in their "preferred and habitual modes of perceiving, remembering, organizing, processing, and representing information" (Dörnyei, 2005, p. 125). These somewhat fixed preferences involve a consistent clustering of strategies while learners complete learning tasks. These clustered strategies constitute a learner's cognitive style. For example, a learner who already knows some foreign languages (e.g., Spanish and Italian) might expedite her knowledge of the verb system of a third language (e.g., Catalan) by memorizing verb forms in a grammar book rather than going through the forms one by one in her lessons. This same learner might prefer the following cluster of strategies: noticing the new forms, comparing the forms across languages (e.g., transferring from the second to the third language), memorizing forms, and self-testing.

When strategic clusterings combine with a learner's affect (e.g., high versus low anxiety), motivation (e.g., high versus low willingness to devote time and effort), or personality characteristics (e.g., extroversion versus introversion) associated with specific instances of language learning or use, we refer to this as *learner style*, the natural, habitual, or acquired orientation toward learning or using a SFL in specific contexts. For example, a learner with an introverted style might develop listening skills by repeating an audio text alone over and over until the words are parsed and meanings discovered or decoded. In another context, the same learner might develop listening skills by assuming an extroverted learner style—for example, by interacting with others, asking for clarification of the speaker's meanings, or verifying what he or she had understood.

CONCEPTUAL UNDERPINNINGS

What is a "good" language learner?

While the inner mechanisms of learning have always been of concern to psychologists (see Piaget, 1954; Vygotsky, 1978), interest in SFL learner strategies began in the 1970s with research on the "good language learner" (e.g., Naiman, Fröhlich, Todesco, & Stern, 1978). The basic premise was that, if we could understand what "successful" learners do in contrast to "unsuccessful" learners, then we could better address the teaching and learning of a SFL. The focus of the early research was on identifying "good" language learning strategies so that links between strategy use and learning success could be established.

For example, Rubin (1975, as cited in Naiman et al., 1978) identifies the following seven characteristics of and strategies used by "good" language learners to achieve success:

(1) They are willing and accurate guessers.
(2) They have strong drives to communicate, or to learn from communication. They are willing to do many things to get their message across.
(3) They are not inhibited. They are willing to appear foolish if reasonable communication results. They are willing to make mistakes in order to learn or communicate. They can tolerate some vagueness.
(4) In addition to focusing on communication, they are prepared to attend to form and are constantly looking for patterns in the language.
(5) They practice.
(6) They monitor their own speech and that of others. That is, they are constantly attending to how well their speech is being received and whether their performance matches what they have learned.
(7) They attend to meaning. They know that in order to understand a message, it is not sufficient to pay attention to the grammar or to the surface form of incoming speech. (p. 228)

While many of Rubin's strategies have been empirically associated with proficient learners, the attribution of learning success to any one set of strategies for all learners is problematic. This is due to the large number of interacting variables involved in learning languages and the differences that individuals display in their learning patterns and preferences. What might be an effective complex of strategies for one learner could be ineffective for another. Similarly, what might work for a given learner in one situation might not work for him or her in another situation. The "good language learner" research, nonetheless, initiated a program of inquiry examining the relationships among strategy use, learning styles, and other factors contributing to successful SFL learning and use.

Learner styles: What kind of language learners are we?

Shortly after researchers began examining the strategies associated with "good" language learners, some researchers noticed the connection between learners' success and their general or preferred orientation toward learning—that is, their learning style. For example, Rubin (1975) noticed that SFL learners who were extroverted and unafraid to make mistakes also seemed to be good language learners, and Stern (1975) observed that differential success in learning a SFL might be influenced by the learner's ability to handle emotions. In fact, the notion that a learner's style might be a factor influencing success, or that a learner's style might help determine the strategies learners invoke in certain contexts, was intuitively appealing to teachers and researchers alike.

Consider the following scenario. A SFL teacher notices that his students need help writing a lab report, especially with: (1) the organization of the sentences; (2) the use of the passive and active voice; and (3) the use of logical connectors (e.g., *then, therefore*). He thus presents them with the following extract from a lab report.

> Small pieces of litmus paper were dipped into the solutions. The solutions marked 1 and 2 turned blue. These were, therefore, the two alkalis, sodium carbonate, and potassium hydroxide. Small pieces of blue litmus paper were then dipped into the remaining four solutions. The paper turned red in solutions 3 and 4. These were, therefore, the two acids. Hence, solutions 5 and 6 were the two chlorides.

The teacher first asks his students to read the text; underline sentences that convey actions, observed results, and inferences; and label each accordingly. He then asks them if they notice any patterns in the organization. After that, he asks them to circle the main verb phrases in each sentence, and indicate if they are in the active or passive voice by putting *A* or *P* above the verb phrase. He next asks them to make some generalizations about how the active and passive are used in writing lab reports. After that, he asks them to draw a box around the logical connectors, indicating if they refer to a subsequent action or conclusion. Finally, he asks them to analyze the example and summarize how to write a lab report.

Learners with an inductive learner style would probably benefit greatly from this lesson, since they prefer to examine samples of language to recognize patterns and draw generalizations from the patterns. However, learners with a deductive style might be confused or even overwhelmed because they prefer having the teacher give them the rules for organizing lab reports and using the appropriate grammar. This will allow them to then apply the rules in their own work.

Given the possibility that a learner's style might increase or decrease challenges to learning and impact success, several researchers (e.g., Ehrman & Leaver, 2003; Oxford, 1993; Reid, 1995) have investigated the nature and range of preferred and habitual styles that learners orient to while perceiving, remembering, organizing, processing, and representing information. In so doing, many researchers have proposed learner style taxonomies as a basis for designing questionnaires that help learners gain an awareness of their own learning styles. Drawing on the taxonomies proposed by Ehrman and Leaver (2003), Oxford (1993), and Reid (1995), we can outline three categories of learner styles thought to represent natural orientations of learners:

1. *Perceptual preferences.* This involves whether or when learners tend to learn by listening (auditory style), seeing (visual style), or doing things (kinesthetic style). For example, a learner with a visual style might prefer to learn vocabulary by reading new words rather than by hearing them.

2. *Personality preferences.* This involves learners' degree of openness to new experiences and their extroversion versus introversion. For example, learners might prefer to learn by looking outward in social contexts (extroverted style) or looking inward (introverted style). If asked to perform a role play in front of the class, learners with an introverted style might feel embarrassed, causing their performance to suffer.

3. *Processing preferences.* This concerns whether or when learners prefer to process information by seeing the big picture (global-oriented style) versus the specifics (detail-oriented style), by figuring out rules from examples (inductive style) versus learning the rules and applying them to examples (deductive style), or by bringing the parts together to determine the whole (synthetic style) versus disassembling the whole into parts (analytic style). For example, a learner with a global-oriented style might prefer to begin a new lesson by looking over the entire unit to get the big picture before attending to specifics.

Table 1. Common Learner Styles

Perceptual preferences		
Style	**Description**	**Example learner self-report**
Auditory	Prefers learning by hearing.	I learn better by hearing someone explain it.
Visual	Prefers learning by seeing.	I learn better by reading it.
Kinesethic	Prefers learning by doing.	I learn better when I experience doing it myself.
Personality preferences		
Style	**Description**	**Example learner self-report**
Extroverted	Prefers to learn by looking outward.	I learn better working with others.
Introverted	Prefers learning by looking inward.	I learn better by working alone.
Processing preferences		
Style	**Description**	**Example learner self-report**
Global-oriented	Prefers focusing on the big picture (top-down); gravitates first toward the main ideas, then the details.	I learn better by summarizing the information.
Detail-oriented	Prefers focusing on the specifics (bottom-up); gravitates first toward the details, then the main ideas.	I learn better by understanding the specifics.
Inductive	Prefers to start with examples so generalizations can be made from the patterns.	I learn better by figuring out the rules from examples in the language.
Deductive	Prefers to start with the rules or theories so they can be applied to examples.	I learn better when I have the language rules before applying them.
Synthetic	Prefers to bring the parts together to construct new ideas.	I learn better by summarizing what has been said.
Analytic	Prefers to break information down into components so the relationships can be identified and understood.	I learn better by looking at the parts so I can analyze and understand them.
Field-sensitive	Prefers to get information in context.	I learn better if I see new words, structures, or ideas in context.
Field-insensitive	Prefers to get information in the abstract rather than in concrete situations.	I learn better if new words, structures, or ideas are explained without reference to context.

These styles are summarized and exemplified in Table 1.

Research suggests that with information on learner styles, teachers might be better able to devise style-based teaching strategies to accommodate their students' learning styles (Dörnyei, 2005; Oxford, 1999). Alternatively, teachers can vary their teaching styles so that all learner styles will be accommodated at least some of the time. For example, teachers might vary the instructional input of the lesson so that one task requires students to listen, another requires them to read, and yet another requires them to work first independently and then in pairs. This research also suggests that teachers should become aware of their own learning style since they need to know: (1) that their learners may have another preferred style of learning; and (2) that, if mismatches occur, their students could experience learning difficulties.

An alternative approach to style mismatches, though, might be to view them as opportunities for learners to gain experience operating outside their preferred style. This is called *style stretching* (Ehrman, 1996), and it can be done by first providing learners with a learning-style questionnaire designed to raise their awareness of their preferred learning styles. Then, they could be given tasks explicitly designed to make them use a style they are not accustomed to. By developing the ability to respond flexibly in different situations, learners are more likely to achieve success.

How has strategic competence been conceptualized in SFL learning and use?

Since the early work on strategies, there has been considerable research on the nature of strategic competence itself and its relationship to learning outcomes. This is the focus of the current chapter; however, it should be noted that much work has also been done on strategies-based instruction, where strategies are taught either explicitly through direct instruction or implicitly through tasks designed to increase SFL proficiency, foster learner autonomy, or promote SFL processing.

Several researchers have proposed taxonomies of strategy use. In her early work, Oxford (1990) conceptualized strategy use in terms of direct and indirect strategies. The direct strategies (i.e., strategies assumed to have a direct impact on learning) include:

1. *Memory strategies* (e.g., *using memory aids* to learn Farsi, such as the "Rahat" sisters, Nora and Esther, to remember *Nourahat*, nervous, and *Esterrahat*, relax);
2. *Cognitive strategies* (e.g., *analyzing* the parts of a word, *un friend ly*);
3. *Compensation strategies* (e.g., *coining new words* such as **knowledgeful*).

Oxford's (1990) indirect strategies (i.e., strategies that indirectly support learning) are:

1. *Metacognitive strategies* (e.g., *evaluating* one's recent interaction, *planning* a conversation);
2. *Affective strategies* (e.g., *encouraging* oneself after a poor performance);
3. *Social strategies* (e.g., *cooperating* with classmates).

Oxford (1990) uses this conceptualization of strategic competence as a basis for her *Strategy Inventory for Language Learners* (SILL), which has been administered widely and adapted for use with different types of SFL learners to increase their awareness of strategy use.

Another popular conceptualization of strategy use, inspired by J. R. Anderson's (1995) serial processing model of cognition, was proposed by O'Malley and Chamot (1990). They define strategy use in terms of:

1. *Metacognitive strategies* (i.e., thinking actions designed to regulate learning and performances through planning, monitoring, evaluating, and organizing)
2. *Cognitive strategies* (i.e., doing actions designed to manipulate or transform materials or input through analysis, transformation, repetition, summarization, and imaging)
3. *Social/affective strategies* (i.e., interpersonal and feeling strategies designed to maintain productive interactions, or positive states of mind)

This taxonomy has also been widely used in research and practice, and it serves as the basis for strategy instruction in Chamot's (2009) cognitive academic language learning approach (CALLA), an approach designed to weave strategy instruction into content-based instruction.

These taxonomies are compared in Figure 2. While these taxonomies have increased learners' awareness of strategy use, some concerns have been expressed regarding their validity (Dörnyei, 2005). The most important concern is that the taxonomies claim to measure strategic competence; however, direct alignment with a model of information processing is not explicit (Purpura, 1999).

Oxford (2011) has recently proposed an updated model of strategic competence (see Figure 3). Inspired by several learning theories—especially sociocultural theory (Vygotsky, 1978)—this model focuses on how learners use strategies to regulate their language learning behaviors. It describes metastrategies that guide behavioral strategies, including: (1) *metacognitive strategies* (to guide the use of cognitive strategies such as analyzing the situation); (2) *meta-affective strategies* (to regulate strategies relating to emotion, attitude, motivation); and (3) *meta-sociocultural-interactive strategies* (to govern strategies related to how learners interact or communicate with each other, how they handle communicative deficiencies, or how they deal with sociocultural diversity).

Let us examine this process. Imagine a student is proofreading his essay and notices that a sentence is unclear. He decides to revise

Oxford (1990)

A. Direct

1. Memory strategies
   (e.g., creating mental images; grouping; applying images & sounds; semantic mapping; reviewing; employing action; using physical response)
2. Cognitive strategies
   (e.g., practicing; repeating; receiving & sending messages; getting the idea quickly; analyzing & reasoning; reasoning deductively; creating structure for input & output; highlighting)
3. Compensation strategies
   (e.g., guessing; overcoming limitations in production)

B. Indirect

1. Metacognitive strategies
   (e.g., centering learning; arranging & planning learning; evaluating learning)
2. Affective strategies
   (e.g., lowering anxiety; self-encouragement; taking one's emotional temperature)
3. Social strategies
   (e.g., questioning; cooperating; empathizing)

O'Malley and Chamot (1990)

A. Metacognitive strategies
   (e.g., attending selectively; planning; goal-setting; monitoring; evaluating)

B. Cognitive strategies
   (e.g., rehearsing; repeating; organizing; grouping/classifying; inferencing; summarizing; synthesizing; deducing; applying rules; using visual imagery; transferring from the first language; elaborating; linking ideas)

C. Social/affective strategies
   (e.g., cooperating; questioning for clarification; self-talk to reduce anxiety)

Figure 2. A comparison of Oxford's and O'Malley and Chamot's strategy taxonomies.

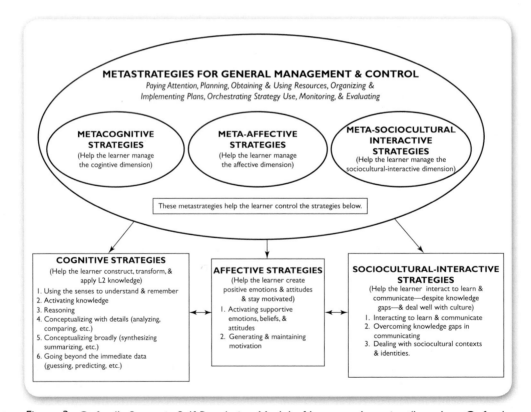

Figure 3. Oxford's Strategic Self-Regulation Model of Language Learning (based on Oxford, 2011, p. 24).

it. These regulatory actions (proofreading and deciding to revise) are metacognitive strategies. The student then changes the tense and corrects the word order. These implementation behaviors are cognitive strategies. Then, since he is writing the essay under time pressure, he notices that he is getting nervous, so he decides to calm himself down (regulation is a meta-affective strategy). He calms himself down by reminding himself that he knows the material and that he can finish on time (implementation with an affective strategy). A few days later, when the teacher returns the essay with feedback, he evaluates what he did well and where he needs to improve (regulation using metacognitive strategies). He decides to work with a partner (regulation using a meta-sociocultural-interactive strategy) to improve his essay. Finally, they work together collaboratively (implementation using sociocultural-interactive strategies) to revise some of their unclear sentences (implementation using cognitive strategies).

Oxford's (2011) model thus represents a significant reconceptualization of the regulatory function in SFL learning. Regulation is not just about cognitive strategies but also about affect and interaction in sociocultural contexts. An important question with respect to this model is how these strategies might operate at different stages of the learning process. In other words, how do they align with a processing model of second language acquisition (SLA)? After all, learners use different strategies when trying to understand new linguistic input than when trying to remember new input or use what they learned in communication. Furthermore, learners use different strategies at various stages of processing new learning objectives, which indicates that Oxford's (2011) model could benefit from a closer connection with a processing model for SLA.

How might strategic competence be conceptualized within a processing model of SFL learning and use?

The conceptualizations of strategic competence discussed so far treat strategies as behaviors that learners use to further their SFL learning. While this approach has provided many insights, strategy use is a function of both the language learning tasks we are asked to perform (Cohen & Macaro, 2007; Macaro, 2001) and the processing demands of these tasks.

To relate strategy use to SFL processing, Purpura (2004, 2012) proposes a conceptualization of strategic competence specifically designed to link strategies to different stages of information processing. Before describing this conceptualization, however, let us examine what information processing is in the context of learning a SFL and why it is important for teachers to understand how learners process such information.

What is information processing and how does it relate to SFL learning?

Information processing refers to the mental activities that humans engage in as they progress from developing a conceptual understanding of new information to being able to use this new information effortlessly and automatically in context. With regard to SLA, information processing relates to the developmental activities that learners engage in as they are exposed to new linguistic input and as they develop the competence to use new language features automatically in communication. This approach assumes that new linguistic input will be handled by the cognitive processing system of the brain, where memory plays a critical role in the developmental process (Baddeley, 1986; Gagné, Yekovich, & Yekovich, 1993; McLaughlin, 1987; Wenden, 1991). In this system, information processing involves several different types of memory: sensory memory, short-term memory, working memory, and long-term memory. (See Figure 4.)

In the first stage of processing, new linguistic input enters the sensory receptors (e.g., ears or eyes) and is stored momentarily in sensory memory (SM). The information is then attended to, perceived, and stored briefly in a learner's short-term memory (STM). In other words, when we hear a conversation or read a book, we perceive a lot of information, but we might actually attend to and notice a past tense form (e.g., *traveled*). As we focus on this input, we simultaneously ignore other input (e.g., background noise and distracting text). The noticed input is held only long enough (i.e., microseconds) for working memory (WM) to begin processing. Thus, learners need to pay attention and notice language if they wish to learn language.[3] Attending is an important strategy, to varying degrees, throughout the learning process.

It is in WM where the noticed information is held temporarily, so that the key processes of perceiving, understanding, remembering, and storing the new information in long-term memory (LTM) can occur. It is also in WM where information from LTM is retrieved and processed, so that responses can be prepared mentally before being generated through the effectors (i.e., voice or hands) in speaking or writing.

Let us illustrate this using the same past tense example (*traveled*). After seeing, attending to, and noticing the past tense morpheme (*–ed*) in a written dialogue, the second language (L2) learner holds this information temporarily in WM so that he can identify the form (i.e., an *–ed* added to the verb stem), relate the morpheme to past meaning, contrast the new input with previously stored information (e.g., present vs. past tense), and eventually remember and store the new information in LTM. In so doing, he is restructuring his knowledge of the English verb system to accommodate the new information in LTM. If he wishes to use the past tense later to perform a task, he retrieves this information from LTM to WM, where he plans a response using the new form-meaning information, and then generates the response.

Depending on what we are trying to learn, the processes in WM may include a host of identification strategies: (e.g., spotting similarities and differences, translating); association strategies (e.g., relating, categorizing); repetition or rehearsal strategies (e.g., saying words several times); summarization strategies (e.g., getting the gist); elaboration strategies (e.g., applying rules deductively or inductively); and retrieval strategies (e.g., inferencing, applying rules, synthesizing, transferring from a known language to another, paraphrasing). In sum, WM is where temporary maintenance and manipulation of information take place and where responses are prepared to perform language tasks.

Figure 4 also depicts how the regulatory processes control the stages of processing associated with memory. These metacognitive processes are often characterized in terms of goal-setting, planning, monitoring, and evaluating strategies, but as Oxford (2011) and others demonstrate, the metaprocesses control other aspects of language learning and use as well (e.g., affect and sociocultural interaction).

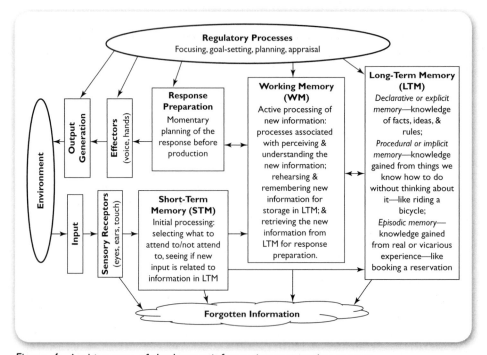

Figure 4. Architecture of the human information processing system.

Many researchers believe that WM provides only one storage resource and that this resource has limited capacity. In other words, our memory shortcomings can potentially interrupt what is processed, thereby impacting what is learned. An implication of this limitation for learners is that they cannot attend to too many things at once without experiencing cognitive overload. To avoid this, learners need to be exposed to new learning units gradually so that they have time to process the information without overly taxing their memory. Other researchers, especially those influenced by Baddeley's (2006) work, believe that WM contains multiple resource pools (e.g., memory for visual-spatial processing and for auditory processing). As a result, while learners might experience difficulty learning about the past tense through the auditory channel, they might be better at processing this information if it is also presented visually. Since this debate remains unresolved, teachers should consider presenting learners with new input in a variety of modes.

Whatever the process, the ultimate goal of language learning is to get new information into LTM, where it can be stored for long periods of time and where it is readily available for retrieval and use. Cognitive psychologists have identified several types of LTM. One type is referred to as declarative or explicit memory; this is where we store knowledge of facts, ideas, and rules. These items are usually represented in organized, hierarchical networks in which related items are stored together. They can also be stored in visual images or linear orderings (Dehn, 2006). For example, when thinking of crime investigation, a whole network of vocabulary comes to mind (e.g., *detective*, *investigate*, *butler*, *break-in*, *scream*). Grammatical structures (e.g., *could/might/ must have done it*) are also part of this network. Procedural or implicit memory is the knowledge of how to do things, such as ride a bike or have a routine conversation. With practice, performed procedures or skills become automated with fewer memory resources devoted to conscious processing. Finally, episodic memory is knowledge gained from lived or vicarious experience, that is, self-contained events in our lives like booking a plane reservation or ordering a meal at a restaurant.

Teachers need to be sensitive to the kinds of LTM they are asking learners to access when designing learning tasks. For example, if we expect students to use the past tense in narratives, we need to give them practice that will help them develop procedural knowledge. Similarly, if we want them to cite the rules for forming the past tense, then we should provide tasks that help them process and remember the rules as declarative knowledge. Finally, if we expect learners to perform role plays revolving around a job interview, which draws on episodic knowledge, then we need to ensure they have at least some notion of what is involved in applying for a job; otherwise, the task will be beyond their reach.

How does information processing relate to SFL learning?

To directly align strategic competence with how learners process information, Purpura (1999), drawing on Gagné, Yekovich, and Yekovich's (1993) model of information processing, proposes a taxonomy of strategy use specifically linked to the stages of information processing. Metacognitive strategy use includes strategies designed to assess the situation, monitor, evaluate, and self-test. Cognitive strategy use is involved in attending, comprehending, storing/memory, and retrieval/using (see Figure 5). This taxonomy was then used to produce Purpura's (1999) *Metacognitive and Cognitive Strategy Use Questionnaires.*

Research on these questionnaires and adaptations of them for special contexts (Phakiti, 2007; Purpura, 1999) show that specific clusters of strategies are associated with the different stages of information processing. In other words, the same strategy can be invoked in the comprehending stage of processing new language information (e.g., inferencing to understand), in the storing/memory stage (e.g., inferencing to remember), or in the retrieval stage (inferencing during retrieval/use). This research also shows that metacognitive strategies exert regulatory influence over the choice of cognitive strategies, which, in turn, impacts learning success. In sum, metacognitive strategy use is critical, and SFL learning success depends on the flexible use of both metacognitive and cognitive processes. Therefore, teachers need to provide opportunities for learners to become aware of their strategy use so that, with practice, they can flexibly and automatically invoke these strategies and use them for different processing goals.

Metacognitive Strategy Use

1. Metacognitive processes
   - Assessing the situation (e.g., goal-setting; planning)
   - Monitoring
   - Self-evaluating
   - Self-testing

Cognitive Strategy Use

1. Attending processes
   (e.g., focusing, paying attention)
2. Comprehending processes
   (e.g., clarifying, verifying)
3. Storing/memory processes
   (e.g., associating, repeating, rehearsing, summarizing, applying rules, transferring from the first language to the L2)
4. Retrieval/using processes
   (e.g., transferring from the first language to the L2, inferencing, linking with prior knowledge, practicing naturalistically)

Figure 5. Purpura's (1999) taxonomy of strategic competence.

While Purpura's early (1999) conceptualization of strategic competence related strategy use to information processing, it did not account for the regulatory processes associated with the (meta) affective strategies and (meta)sociocultural interactive strategies proposed by Oxford (2011). Given

the importance of these strategies in learning or using a SFL, Purpura (2012) has proposed an updated model of strategic competence that includes these meta(strategies) and describes the interface between strategy use and the processes underlying SFL learning and use (see Figure 6).

As seen in Figure 6, learning something new involves SFL processing supported by several strategies. Let us examine this model through an example. Imagine you want to introduce your lower-intermediate-level EFL class to modal auxiliaries. To contextualize the use of the auxiliaries, you have them read a one-page mystery story. One of your learners notices a new word, the modal auxiliary *might* (i.e., the new input) in the environment (i.e., the text). To decipher this word, input processing begins, thereby initiating several comprehending processes (Stage I). Seeing the new word activates the learner's first language and her prior SFL knowledge as she searches for clues to the meaning. It might also activate her prior knowledge of detective novels. In examining the input, she notices that *might* precedes main verbs. Given the context of the story, she infers that *might* means *possible*. When she understands the connection between the new form and its meaning, this is called intake, the result of the successful processing of input (VanPatten, 1996).

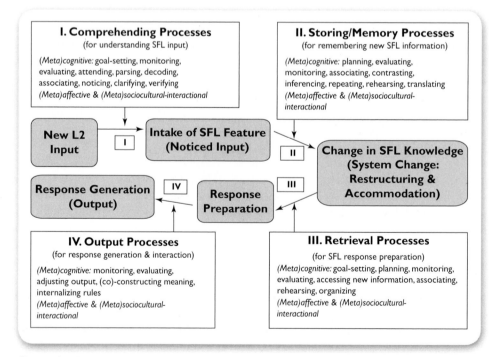

Figure 6. The interface between strategic competence and SFL processing.

In moving from "not understanding" to "understanding," however, the learner has to invoke strategic competence to understand the input; she therefore explicitly or implicitly invokes metacognitive strategies (e.g., evaluation strategies—I understand/or do not), together with several cognitive strategies to help her attend to the input and comprehend the meaning of the form (comprehending strategies—attending, comparing, associating, clarifying, inferencing, translating). If she has doubts about not understanding, she might also invoke (meta)affective strategies to calm herself down. Or she might use (meta)sociocultural-interactive strategies by asking a peer for assistance. To help learners check their understanding, the teacher can design tasks that require learners to infer the meaning of certain words or tasks that involve identifying synonymous sentences (e.g., *Possibly the butler is the murderer = the butler* [a. *might*/b. *must*] *be the murderer*).

Once intake has occurred, the learner's ability to use the modals is still likely to be developing. In other words, the learner needs to rethink what she knows, so that she can restructure what she already knows about modals and accommodate the new information into her SFL system. More specifically, she needs to remember that *might* means *possible* (in this case to speculate on who committed the crime), that *might* is followed by a base form of the verb, and that *might* does not take inflections. To help her remember, she may need to see the modal in several different contexts. Or she might need to compare modals in her SFL with those in her first language, distinguish between the meanings of different modals, or even use *might* to speculate about the story. As this new information is refined and stored in LTM, a change in the learner's SFL knowledge system occurs.

In progressing from intake to system change, however, the learner again invokes strategic competence by activating her storing and memory processes (Stage II) so that this information can be stored in LTM. When given tasks to restructure and accommodate this new information into LTM, she could again invoke the use of metacognitive strategies together with several cognitive strategies (e.g., associating, inferencing, linking with prior knowledge, translating). In addition, she could use (meta)affective strategies if she needs them, or (meta)sociocultural-interactive strategies if she decides to work with others.

Once the new information is to some extent stored in LTM, the learner might be asked to write a police report in which she has to speculate on who the murderer is. Or she might be asked to role play a meeting with other detectives in which they make similar speculations. Before producing a response, however, the learner has to prepare mentally—even if only for a split second. To do this, she needs to access LTM and retrieve information related to the detective story and to the modals. In other words, she needs to activate retrieval processes (Stage III) to prepare her response. This requires the use of retrieval strategies for response organization. The task might engage several metacognitive strategies (e.g., planning, organizing, evaluating) and cognitive strategies (linking with prior knowledge, imagining, associating, repeating, rehearsing, and translating). It could also engage (meta)affective strategies and, in the case of the role play, several (meta)sociocultural-interactive strategies. To promote response preparation, teachers might have learners mentally rehearse their response ("What might you say if you were the detective in this case?"). Such tasks help learners engage with context, retrieve information, and mentally organize responses. Response retrieval and organization occur, on some level, before learners can respond.

Finally, the learner needs to generate a response, hopefully using the newly learned modals. Generating a response activates output processing (Swain, 1995)—Stage IV. In other words, while the learner is constructing and conveying messages, she is managing how she is communicating and continuously adjusting the message. Along with the information about modals, she is also retrieving other information from LTM related to the context (i.e., the crime scene), the topic/theme (i.e., the murderer), and the task (i.e., speculating). To generate complex responses obviously requires the deployment of many strategies. In sum, output processes are also engaged in task performance— in complex tasks and even in simple multiple-choice or gap-fill tasks, where learners must generate responses.

While SFL processing is conceptualized in this discussion as independent stages, in reality these processes are closely intertwined, occurring at split-second speed. For pedagogical purposes, however, teachers should be familiar with these stages so that each process can be appropriately targeted in instruction and assessment. Also, while this discussion has mainly focused on processes related to individuals, SFL processing and strategic competence are commonly distributed across members of a class when the goal is to collectively understand new information, reason together, or solve problems. The role of the sociocultural context in processing a SFL is also a critical factor in SLA.

Practice serves to strengthen the efficiency and automaticity of response preparation and generation. However, learners also require feedback, not only on their performance but also on their process. Practice without timely feedback may result in learners' practicing and internalizing incorrect language. In other words, learners need to know what they are doing right and what they need to improve. They also need feedback on the strategies they are using. Feedback involves reflection and metacognitive strategy use. It may be self-generated, or it may come from others, for example, when a peer indicates the need for conversational repair (e.g., *I don't understand. Say that again, please*) or provides explicit corrective feedback (e.g., *broke* not *breaked*).

To promote the processing of feedback, teachers can design tasks that require learners to provide feedback, reflect on feedback given them, and figure out how feedback can serve as input for further processing. Learners should also reflect on the strategies they use when they apply the feedback they have received to their subsequent output.

CLASSROOM APPLICATIONS

After over 30 years of study, we can conclude that strategic competence plays an important role in SFL learning. In other words, learners' awareness of and ability to regulate their SFL learning and performance are likely to result in increased levels of achievement. While we still do not understand the exact mechanisms underlying these processes, we do know they are important. Teachers need to know how existing strategy research can be applied to language pedagogy by: (1) raising learners' awareness of strategy use; (2) promoting learners' strategy awareness through classroom activities; and (3) being aware of findings from strategy research.

Raising awareness of learner strategy use

An important first step in strategy instruction is to raise students' awareness of their strategy use. This assessment is done by means of questionnaires; interviews or written reports; observation by teachers while students are performing tasks; and students' verbal reports before, after, or while performing tasks.[4] A common form of strategy assessment involves questionnaires designed to elicit the learners' domain-specific or domain-general strategy use. *Domain-specific strategies* are those used when completing specific tasks. *Domain-general strategies* are used without reference to any specific task. When domain-specific strategies are ineffective for task completion, learners fall back on domain-general strategies. In reality, we continuously switch back and forth between domain-specific and -general strategies. For example, when reading an article about earthquakes, we invoke domain-specific strategies to understand (e.g., linking with prior knowledge about earthquakes, associating, and inferencing). If these strategies fail to help us understand, we revert to domain-general strategies such as translating, using a dictionary, or asking for help, which are nonspecific to the task.

Many questionnaires are available to teachers and learners to assess domain-general learning strategies. Of particular note, however, is Cohen, Oxford, and Chi's (2005) *Language Strategy Use Inventory* (LSUI).[5] This 90-item questionnaire, specifically designed for classroom use, asks learners to reflect on their strategy use and on the effectiveness of these strategies in achieving learning goals. It also aims to get learners to discover new learning strategies. In this questionnaire, learners report on the strategies used to learn vocabulary, translation skills, and the four language skills. Rather than asking learners to report on frequency or agreement (e.g., I use this strategy: always⟷never; strongly agree⟷strongly disagree), this survey elicits responses to four statements: (1) "I use this strategy and like it." (2) "I have tried this strategy and would try it again." (3) "I've never used this strategy, but am interested in it." and (4) "This strategy doesn't fit for me." Survey responses help make learners aware of their strategy use.

For example, imagine that a teacher wants to understand what domain-general strategies his students use to learn vocabulary, so he asks them to complete the vocabulary section of the LSUI. This section has students report on the strategies they use to learn and review new words, to recall and make use of vocabulary, and if relevant, to report on any other strategy they might use. When the teacher tallies the results, he realizes that 95% of the students said that they "used and liked" or "used and would try again" the strategies related to learning new words, recalling new vocabulary, and making use of new vocabulary. However, most students reported that they never used strategies for remembering new vocabulary (e.g., looking at meaningful parts of words, remembering words in situations, or visualizing spellings). Since such associations are likely to help students remember and store new vocabulary, the teacher now has justification for presenting students with tasks specifically designed to teach strategies for remembering new vocabulary.

Similarly, if the teacher wishes to understand his students' domain-specific strategy use, he can give students a short reading containing new vocabulary items. He then administers the same part of the LSUI, but, this time, he makes the statements specific to the assigned reading, such as: (1) "I used this strategy in this reading and liked it." and (2) "I tried this strategy while reading and would try it again." The teacher again has students report their responses to determine group patterns. He then compares the responses from the two surveys for a comprehensive assessment of strategy use.

Teachers wishing to understand the strategies that learners use to process new vocabulary input can adapt the LSUI. For example, they can ask students to report on the strategies they use while:[6]

- *Understanding new words* (i.e., comprehending processes): "I notice new words I don't know." or "I divide words into parts so I can understand them."
- *Remembering new words* (i.e., storing/memory processes): "I go over words often to help me remember them." or "I relate words to the situation in which I first saw them."
- *Retrieving new words* (i.e., retrieval processes): "I think of the words I will need to communicate." or "I try to predict what words I might hear before communicating."

- *Using new words* (i.e., output processes): "I try to use new words in a variety of contexts." or "I try to imagine how to use new words in different situations."

Promoting strategy awareness

Several researchers (e.g., Macaro, 2001) have provided guidelines on how to teach strategies explicitly. According to Dörnyei (2005), the general goal of strategy instruction is: (1) to increase the learners' awareness of and rationale for strategy use in SFL learning or use contexts; (2) to introduce learners to new strategies and model their use; (3) to give learners opportunities to use strategies; and (4) to allow learners to share reflections about strategy effectiveness.

The following synthesis of suggestions for explicit strategy instruction draws on guidelines from several researchers (e.g., Chamot, 2005; Macaro, 2001; Oxford, 2011):

- *Task completion.* The teacher asks students to complete a selected-response (e.g., multiple-choice), limited-production (e.g., gap-fill), or extended-production (e.g., problem-solving) task.
- *Awareness-raising.* Following task completion, learner(s) identify the strategies used to complete the task. They then share and compare.
- *Modeling.* The teacher (or a learner) demonstrates a strategy, names it, explains it, and comments on its value.
- *Practice.* Learners complete tasks to practice the strategy.
- *Evaluation.* Learners evaluate the use of the strategy in terms of goal achievement and degree of comfort.
- *Extension.* Learners complete a complex task requiring them to use a new strategy along with familiar ones.
- *Final evaluation.* Learners evaluate the effectiveness of the new strategy in terms of their learning or performance, and they share their experiences.

Findings from strategy research that teachers should know

Teachers need to remember the following key findings that can be extrapolated from the strategy research.

Finding 1: Strategy use correlates with learning success.

- All learners use strategies while learning or using a SFL. High- and low-ability learners use some strategies in the same way and other strategies in different ways. High-ability learners generally have greater meta-strategic awareness; therefore, teachers should consider ways to help students use metastrategies to regulate their SFL learning and use.

- Domain-specific and domain-general strategies provide a comprehensive picture of strategic competence. Therefore, teachers should consider strategy instruction that taps into both domains.

- Strategies are neither good nor bad. Rather, they are efficient or inefficient in achieving goals. Therefore, teachers should introduce learners to a wide range of strategies, so they can choose which ones work best for them.

- Strategies are engaged when learners are consciously aware of learning challenges, for example, when they are explicitly trying to decode texts. However, much of SFL learning and use happens in nonconscious ways. Therefore, teachers should bear in mind the kinds of strategies their tasks are likely to elicit.

- Strategies are not only used when learners have problems; they are also deployed in successful learning or performance. Therefore, teachers should systematically ask learners to report on and evaluate their strategy use.

- Learners often use short-lived transition strategies that become more enduring and automatic with repeated experience. Therefore, teachers should give students tasks that help them consolidate and automatize their strategy use.

- Good learners use strategies appropriate to the task at hand. These strategies often appear in clusters or sequences. Teachers should therefore ask learners to make explicit what these strategy clusters are and have them evaluate their use.

- Learners need to use strategies flexibly and efficiently to reflect the changing conditions of language learning and use. Therefore, teachers should provide learners with tasks that help them develop cognitive flexibility by varying domains, contexts, topic/themes, and tasks with respect to the same learning point.

Finding 2: Metacognition is important. The research clearly highlights the importance of metacognitive strategy use as a means of regulating SFL learning or use. Therefore, teachers should explicitly embed metacognitive strategy instruction into their lessons by telling learners. For example, teachers can state the following: "Before you respond, plan your response. After you finish, write down two things you think you did well. Compare your answers with those of your partner—then, resolve the differences or generate questions. What do you still find challenging, and what do you plan to do about it?"

The following are some ways in which (meta) cognitive strategy instruction can be embedded into SFL instruction. Ask learners to:

- set and/or prioritize goals
- plan their responses to tasks
- monitor their understanding in comprehension checks
- evaluate their own work and that of their peers
- identify what they know and do not know
- make a plan for addressing learning gaps
- predict other situations in which the learning point could be used
- list the strategies or strategy cluster used to complete tasks
- evaluate the effectiveness of strategy use
- share and compare strategy reflections with others

To sum up, teachers need to provide learners with opportunities to reflect on and report their strategy use in task completion.

Finding 3: Cognitive flexibility is critical. Learners need to develop a large repertoire of strategies for flexible deployment in meeting their SFL learning and use goals. Learning a SFL or being able to use it to understand or communicate effectively requires the ability to shift strategies on a moment-by-moment basis so that multiple sources of knowledge can be accessed, synthesized, and applied. *Cognitive flexibility* is the ability to adapt strategy use without rigidity to conform to unfamiliar or unexpected moments in SFL learning or use contexts, and it is critical for successful SFL learning or use (Meltzer & Sage Bagnato, 2010).

To help students develop cognitive flexibility, teachers need to design tasks that require learners to think flexibly. In other words, learners should be asked to make connections, consider alternative interpretations and positions, solve problems from different perspectives, and predict alternative outcomes. While doing this, they need to reflect on the strategy clusters they use to achieve task goals. To illustrate, imagine students have learned to use the past modals to speculate about the dinosaurs' demise (e.g., *they could/might/may/must have died from lack of food*). However, to promote the flexible use of these modals, the learners can be asked to speculate about other topics and contexts.

Consider the multistep task in Figure 7. As a concluding activity in this task, students are asked to evaluate their performance and report their strategy use. This complex task invokes several strategy clusters and encourages students to think flexibly.

1. Read the following situations. In which one(s) would you be likely to use *could/may/might/must have*. Write a sentence or two to support your decision.
   a. You and a friend are detectives at a crime scene. You are trying to piece together the crime and find the thief.
   b. You are applying for a job in a new wireless company.
   c. You're trying to figure out how humans survived during the last ice age.
   d. You are on a committee at work to propose new safety procedures in case of an emergency.
   e. You're reading a detective novel and wondering how it is going to end.
   f. An idea of your own (do an Internet search for "world mysteries")
2. Compare your answers with those of a partner. Then, select a situation, and write a dialogue, alone or with a partner, using *could have/may have/might have/must have*.
3. How satisfied are you with your dialogue? What is good about it? What needs work?
4. Think of the challenges you encountered in writing this dialogue. What strategies did you use to achieve your goal? How might you do this activity differently the next time?

Figure 7. Unsolved mysteries: Teaching for cognitive flexibility.

FUTURE TRENDS

First, Oxford's (2011) model of strategic self-regulation of language learning represents a significant reconceptualization of strategic competence. She clearly defines the components and states how they could be implemented. While this model has not yet been empirically tested, it is intuitively appealing and should be the focus of future research. From a pedagogical perspective, this model will help the field rethink strategy instruction and how it might be applied to classroom tasks.

Second, Purpura's (2012) sociocognitive model of SLA, also too new to have undergone empirical testing, takes Oxford's model one step closer to a model of human information processing by showing how the strategies might play out while learners are engaged in different stages of language processing. By looking at strategy use within different stages of the learning process, we may discover how strategies contribute to or inhibit learning. From a pedagogical perspective, teachers can apply this model and begin thinking about the stages of processing and the kinds of strategies that learners might use to achieve goals and overcome challenges.

Finally, both Oxford (2011) and Purpura (2012) acknowledge that much of learning is situated in a sociocultural context and is mediated through dialogic interactions among students and teachers. The nature of these interactions and the degree to which they further processing by encouraging strategy use are likely areas for future research and pedagogical application. Such research will involve discourse analysis of classroom interaction, including analysis of accompanying gestures and body language.

CONCLUSION

Strategy research is a vibrant area of applied linguistics. Many teachers are genuinely interested in applying this research so that learners can learn more language and learn it more quickly. It is now time to evaluate the curricula of language teacher-education programs with regard to whether they contain sufficient instruction in strategy research for prospective teachers to gain a solid understanding of what strategic competence is, how to assess it, and how to teach learners to use strategies effectively and flexibly.

SUMMARY

➤ Strategic competence can be defined in terms of (meta)cognitive, (meta)affective, and (meta)sociocultural-interactive strategies.

➤ The three dimensions of strategy use have a differential impact on how learners acquire and use SFLs as they process new input, store and remember new information, and retrieve information to respond and communicate.

➤ Learners differ widely in the strategies they use. In fact, strategy use is a function of what is being learned, under what conditions, and with what processing constraints.

➤ Metacognition is highly correlated with learning success.

➤ Learner styles, or a person's preferred or habitual ways of learning, can affect strategy use and learning outcomes. Therefore learners need to be aware of their styles so they can develop style-stretching skills for learning and using a SFL.

➤ Learners need to develop a repertoire of effective strategies that can be deployed flexibly in response to the changing conditions of learning and use.

➤ Teachers should structure tasks to advance SFL processing and to promote strategy awareness and implementation.

DISCUSSION QUESTIONS

1. Review the different learner styles presented in Table 1. Describe which learning styles generally apply to you as a SFL learner. Then, thinking about how you learned the new vocabulary in this article, describe which styles you preferred. Compare your preferred styles with those of a partner.

2. Review Oxford's (2011) model of strategic competence in Figure 3. How does this model compare with O'Malley and Chamot's (1990), Oxford's (1990), and Purpura's (1999) taxonomies?

3. How does Purpura's (2012) model of strategy competence and SFL processing in Figure 6 build on Oxford's (2011) model? How is it different?

4. Examine the lesson outline for teaching cognitive flexibility in Figure 7. How might you apply

or adapt this outline to teach a domain-specific and a domain-general strategy to a SFL learner?

SUGGESTED ACTIVITIES

1. Download Cohen, Oxford, and Chi's *Learning Style Inventory* in Cohen and Weaver's (2005) *Styles and Strategies-Based Instruction: A Teachers' Guide* (available at http://elechina.super-red.es/cohen-weaver.pdf). Take the survey on pp. 16–19. Do you think these styles accurately reflect your SFL preferences?

2. Download Cohen, Oxford, and Chi's *Language Strategy Use Inventory* in Cohen and Weaver's (2005) *Styles and Strategies-Based Instruction: A Teachers' Guide* (available at http://elechina.super-red.es/cohen-weaver.pdf). Take the survey on pp. 53–59. Do you feel these strategies accurately reflect your SFL strategy use? Why? Why not?

3. Look at Oxford's (2011) model of strategic competence in Figure 3. What kind of (meta)cognitive, (meta)affective, and (meta)sociocultural-interactive strategies did you use to read the current chapter? Make a list of strategies you used in each category. Then compare your list with a partner's. Discuss the similarities and differences.

4. Select a writing or speaking task in a SFL textbook. Using Oxford's model in Figure 3, think of some questions you can ask learners about their meta(strategies). Then ask one or more SFL learners to perform the task and respond to your questions. What did you and the learners find out about their metastrategic processes?

FURTHER READING

Cohen, A. D., & Macaro, E. (Eds.). (2007). *Language learner strategies.* Oxford, UK: Oxford University Press.

This book provides a useful review of strategy research and its applications.

Cohen, A. D., & Weaver, S. J. (2006). *Styles and strategies-based instruction: A teachers' guide.* Minneapolis, MN: Center for Advanced Research on Language Acquisition, University

of Minnesota. Retrieved from http://elechina.
super-red.es/cohen-weaver.pdf

This teacher's guide has style and strategy questionnaires as well as several excellent classroom activities
on learning styles and strategy instruction.

Hurd, S., & Lewis, T. (Eds.). (2008). *Language
learning strategies in independent settings.* Oxford,
UK: Oxford University Press.

This volume includes articles on strategy use in a
number of different contexts.

Macaro, E. (2006). Strategies for language learning and for language use: Revising the theoretical framework. *The Modern Language Journal,
90*(3), 320–337.

This article provides a useful review of the issues
and debates in strategies for language learning
and use.

Oxford, R. L. (2011). *Teaching and researching language learning strategies.* London, UK: Pearson.

This book thoroughly reviews strategy research
and proposes a new comprehensive model of self-
regulation.

ENDNOTES

[1] I thank Andrew Cohen, Steve Albanese, and Sian Morgan for their helpful feedback and comments on this chapter.

[2] The prefix *meta*– means "thinking about" rather than "doing." For example, evaluating an essay is a metacognitive strategy because learners think about the quality of the essay rather than doing something to improve the essay. Revising the essay is a cognitive strategy.

[3] This part of the process can obviously be problematic with children, who have a very short attention span, or with learners who have difficulties noticing the language input. In such cases, teachers may need to design tasks to help learners develop attending strat-egies or they may need to help them notice input by highlighting, underlying, or using some other noticing technique so that learn-ing is not compromised.

[4] For a comprehensive discussion of strategy assessment methods, see A. D. Cohen (2011) and Oxford (2011).

[5] To view the *Language Strategy Use Inventory*, visit http://elechina.super-red.es/cohen-weaver.pdf

[6] For more ideas on methods for assessing students' strategy use, see Cohen and Weaver (2006).

35 | Teaching Young Learners in English as a Second/Foreign Language Settings

JOAN KANG SHIN

KEY QUESTIONS

➤ Is starting earlier in a learner's life better when it comes to second or foreign language learning?

➤ How are the approaches to teaching children English as a second language and English as a foreign language the same? How are they different?

➤ How does the role of English as a global or international language affect the way we approach teaching English to young learners?

EXPERIENCE

Peanut, peanut butter . . . and jelly! Peanut, peanut butter . . . and jelly! Rosa, a young Peruvian English teacher, waves her hands in the air and shakes her hips to the rhythm of the song while her second-graders imitate her voice and body. Behind her on the wall are colorful pictures of peanuts, grapes, a piece of bread, and a sandwich. *First, you take the peanuts . . .* Rosa chants while pointing to the picture of peanuts. . . . *and you crunch 'em, you crunch 'em!* The students watch her pound her right fist into her open left palm and show the crunching motion to the beat of the chant. *First, you take the peanuts, and you crunch 'em, you crunch 'em!* Then they do it with her, pounding their right fist into their left palm on the beat while chanting about making peanut butter. *Peanut, peanut butter . . . and jelly! Peanut, peanut butter . . . and jelly! Then you take the grapes, and you squish 'em, you squish 'em!* The kids have the rhythm now, and they follow Rosa as she twists her right fist into her palm to show how to squish the imaginary grapes she is holding. What comes next? *Peanut, peanut butter . . . and jelly! Then you take the bread, and you spread it, you spread it!* All the students are brushing their left palm with the other hand because it is now a piece of bread. And finally? *Peanut, peanut butter . . . and jelly! Then you take the sandwich, and you eat it, you eat it!* As the children sing out loudly while waving their hands and shaking their hips *Peanut, peanut butter . . . and jelly!*

Rosa stops singing and looks at them confused and concerned as she chews on her imaginary peanut butter and jelly (PB&J) sandwich, pointing at her mouth. The kids stop to see what she is doing and laugh hysterically. Rosa sings the chorus with her mouth closed full of imaginary food waving her hands in the air and shaking her hips like before. *Mm mm, mm mm mm mm . . . mm mm mm!* She tells them, pointing at a picture of a sandwich on the wall, "You ate a PB&J sandwich!" Then she points to her mouth, "Your mouth is full! Let's do it again!" *Then you take the sandwich, and you eat it, you eat it! Mm mm, mm mm mm mm . . . mm mm mm!* The children imitate Rosa, and they end the song with rounds of laughter and lots of chatter. Rosa continues with the lesson. "OK, kids! Now let's make PB&J sandwiches!"[1]

WHAT IS INVOLVED IN TEACHING ENGLISH TO YOUNG LEARNERS?

What is the best way to teach young learners English as a second or foreign language? The example here shows a second-grade teacher who could be either an English as a second language (ESL) or an English as a foreign language (EFL) teacher. It is typical for both ESL and EFL young learner (YL) classrooms to use fun songs with humor, dancing, and movement for kinesthetic learning, and techniques to make input comprehensible like using gestures, pointing at visuals, explaining, demonstrating, and using realia, or real objects. An effective YL teacher, like Rosa, can combine many techniques into one activity, thus engaging children in the learning process. The better the YL teacher, the less the children realize that they are involved in a step-by-step English language lesson. In both ESL and EFL contexts, children learn through play. The challenge of teaching children an additional language or any other subject is that they often do not understand the importance of school and learning; therefore, teachers of young learners need to incorporate activities into the curriculum that are meaningful, engaging, and also fun. Of course teachers of young learners need guidance in accomplishing this. This chapter gives both ESL and EFL teachers the peanuts, grapes, and bread of teaching English with the instructions to make PB&J sandwiches to their own taste.

Defining the young learner

Before discussing teaching English to young learners (TEYL) further, it is necessary to define *young learner*. In EFL settings, TEYL has become its own field of study. However, not all professionals in the field define young learners the same way. Different experts (Cameron, 2001; Linse, 2005; Nunan, 2011b; Pinter, 2006) have defined them as ranging anywhere from 5 to 14 years old. A recent large-scale study on TEYL around the world by Garton, Copland, and Burns (2011) investigated global teaching practices for young learners ages 7–11. Others have defined *young learners* as 7–12 years old and have defined *very young learners* (VYLs) as under 7 years old (Shin, 2006; Slatterly & Willis, 2001). Based on educational practice, YLs can be defined as elementary school–age students ranging from 5 to 12 years old.

ESL in the United States is usually defined not by using the term *young learner* but, rather, by U.S. grade levels in elementary school. *Elementary ESL* therefore refers to kindergarten through grade 5 (K–5), or children 5–10 (or 11) years old. The U.S. education system also makes a distinction between elementary education and early childhood education. *Early childhood* is defined from birth to 8 years old. In education departments in U.S. universities and teacher preparation programs, there are courses and degrees specifically designed for early childhood education that focus on prekindergarten (preK) through grade 3.

The distinctions between YL and VYL and between elementary and early childhood have their roots in Piaget's (1963) four stages of cognitive development, which includes language learning capabilities:

1. *Sensorimotor stage* (0–2 years old). Knowledge or intelligence is based on physical interactions and experience with limited use of symbols, including language.
2. *Preoperational stage* (2–7 years old). Intelligence is increasingly demonstrated through the use of symbols and language development. This stage is marked with the development of memory and imagination. Children at this stage are very egocentric in the psychological sense and cannot see things from another's perspective. Their thinking is not logical, and they do not have the ability to reason.
3. *Concrete operations stage* (7–11 years old). Intelligence is increasingly demonstrated through logical and organized ways of relating to concrete objects. Children are able to use inductive reasoning and take a specific experience and apply it to a general principle. Children at this stage are less egocentric and can recognize another's perspective.
4. *Formal operations stage* (11 years old and older). Intelligence is demonstrated through the logical use of symbols related to abstract concepts. Adolescents are capable of hypothesizing and using both inductive and deductive reasoning.

There seems to be a distinction made in both EFL and ESL contexts between children younger than 7–8 years old (U.S. grades 2–3) and those who are at this age or older. In both EFL and ESL, the learners move toward the secondary level around 11–12 years old (grades 6–7). In this chapter, I therefore use YLs to refer to school-age children from 5 to 12 years old, that is, those in elementary school. To refer to only children under 7, I use VYLs.

Teaching YLs: ESL versus EFL

One of the main differences between teaching YLs in ESL as opposed to EFL settings is the role of English in that context. ESL contexts are found in places where English is the primary language of key institutions such as the government, schools, and the media, whereas EFL contexts are located in places where languages other than English are primarily spoken.

Teaching ESL to YLs.　ESL is actually a misnomer for many learners, who might be learning English as a third or fourth language or as a variation of their first language. ESL programs are embedded in a context where English is used on a regular basis. ESL students (typically referred to as an English learners [ELs] in the United States) may have plenty of chances to hear English being used for various purposes in school, at the store, in their neighborhood, or on television. More important, they may need this language to socialize and play games with their classmates and neighborhood children. The goal of most elementary ESL programs is to mainstream the student as quickly as possible into their grade-level class where they are no longer separated from their first-language (L1) peers.

Most elementary ESL programs in the United States use one of two program models. (See also McGroarty & Fitzsimmons-Doolan, this volume.)

ESL pull-out.　ESL pull-out is also known as English language development (National Clearinghouse for English Language Acquisition and Language Instruction Educational Programs, n.d.). Calderon, Slavin, and Sanchez (2011) describe this as a common practice for K–5 ESL in which ELs are pulled out of class for about 30 minutes but spend the rest of the day in their grade-level class. All instruction is in English and usually focuses on grammar, vocabulary, and communication skills rather than content (National Comprehensive Center for Teacher Quality, 2009). According to Quality Counts (as cited in Viadero, 2009), ESL pull-out is used in 42 of 50 states in the United States.

ESL push-in (or plug-in).　ESL push-in programs integrate ELs into the mainstream classroom and the ESL teacher comes to the class as well. The ESL teacher or instructional aide provides assistance through clarification, translation, or other ESL strategies (National Clearinghouse for English Language Acquisition and Language Instruction Educational Programs, n.d.). In some cases, the ESL teacher collaborates with the mainstream teacher. Using this model, the ESL and mainstream teacher may co-plan and co-teach lessons for all students together. Or the class could be divided into two groups, with one group taught by the mainstream teacher and the other taught by the ESL teacher; afterward, groups can be rotated so all students can benefit from language development instruction by the ESL teacher. This leveled teaching can provide an opportunity for students to have a focus on both content and language development.

Teaching EFL to YLs.　Teaching EFL differs from teaching ESL because EFL contexts typically lack an English-speaking environment outside the classroom and thus YLs may find little to hear and read in English in their immediate surroundings. With the spread of English as an international language, ministries of education in countries where English is not commonly spoken are consistently lowering the age of compulsory English education to the elementary grade levels—the majority now starting in grades 1–3. Extending the study of English to younger ages means that students around the world will study English for a longer period of time, thus increasing their facility in using English by the time they are adults and enter the workforce. This lowering of the age at which EFL instruction commences is a worldwide phenomenon, as noted by Enever, Moon, and Raman (2009): "The last three to four decades have seen a huge expansion in TEYL programmes across the world, mainly in response to the impact of rapid globalization" (p. 3).

Data collected in 2010–2011 about teaching EFL to YLs from teachers in 77 countries show that 82% of countries (63 of 77 countries) start English instruction in elementary school (see Figure 1). Approximately 66% begin English instruction for VYLs in grades preK–3 (51 of 77 countries) and 16% for YLs in grades 4–6 (12 of 77 countries). Students in these EFL programs average three contact hours per week, with a range of 30 minutes to 7.5 hours per week.[2] The majority of these countries offer English classes for two to four hours weekly in a program model similar to foreign language in the elementary school (FLES) programs in the United States. In these programs, foreign languages are studied as regular school subjects several times a week for 30 to 45 minutes a day. FLES programs in the United States have the goal of exposing children to a foreign language and building basic proficiency in all four language skills (Curtain & Dahlberg, 2010).

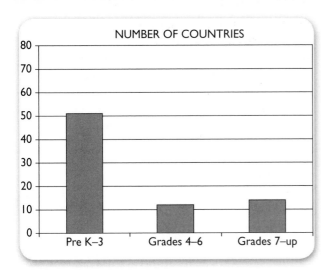

Figure 1. Starting grade levels for compulsory English education in 77 countries.

CONCEPTUAL UNDERPINNINGS

Is an earlier start better?

Whether the focus is on teaching ESL or EFL, many teachers, parents, and researchers are concerned with determining the optimal age for learning a second language (L2) or foreign language. Children seem to pick up languages quickly and effortlessly. However, does starting language learning earlier mean children will grow up speaking English as a second or foreign language better than those who start learning English as high school students or adults?

Early studies have argued that there is a critical period for language acquisition that lasts until puberty (Lenneberg, 1967; Penfield & Roberts, 1959), which typically occurs during the elementary school years. According to the *critical period hypothesis,* children's minds are still flexible and they can achieve nativelike proficiency in a foreign language. However, several more recent studies have shown that starting ESL at a younger age does not necessarily provide an advantage over a later start. For example, YLs are not considered the most efficient language learners. In terms of the rate of acquisition, with the length of exposure and instruction kept constant, adults and teenagers actually outperform YLs, with teenagers doing better than both children and adults, except in pronunciation (R. Ellis, 1985; Nunan, 1999, 2011b). In terms of pronunciation,

YLs are known to be good imitators and can achieve nativelike pronunciation; however, students who start English language instruction in high school can also attain nativelike proficiency (Singleton, 1995). Furthermore, a recent study conducted on the existence of a critical period concludes that "older learners have the potential to learn L2s to a very high level and that introducing foreign languages to very young learners cannot be justified on grounds of biological readiness to learn languages" (Marinova-Todd, Marshall, & Snow, 2000, p. 10). In fact, out of 35 studies in the past 30 years, only 14 show support for a critical period for L2 acquisition (Marinova-Todd et al., 2000). Thus, despite popular belief, it is not well documented by research that an early start to second or foreign language learning alone will result in higher levels of attainment.

Although an early start does not necessarily mean higher levels of L2 attainment and older learners may be just as successful in an effective language learning environment, there are some generally accepted advantages with an early start to ESL and EFL instruction. First, an earlier start means more time spent learning the language, an important factor in overall attainment. As Curtain and Dahlberg (2010) stated, "The amount of language to which the student has already been exposed is a critical element is his or her current and future levels of language acquisition. Time is a great ally in development of language proficiency" (p. 5). In addition, there are studies showing that YLs are more likely to attain nativelike pronunciation (Scovel, 1988), greater oral proficiency and confidence (Harley, 1986), and even higher attainment in pronunciation, morphology, and syntax (Harley & Wang, 1997). Although these studies do not discount the ability of older learners to achieve nativelike pronunciation or oral proficiency, YLs do show an advantage in these areas.

Naturally there is a difference in the expectation between an early start in ESL versus EFL situations. In ESL settings, "L1 minority children are expected to eventually become similar to native speakers of the majority L2, and with respect to conversational oral competence, they can become indistinguishable from monolinguals" (Genesee, Paradis, & Crago, 2011, p. 120). Although there is strong evidence that YLs of English in the

United States are likely to achieve nativelike pronunciation and oral proficiency, YLs in EFL settings are not surrounded by the use of English in their environment and may be in class only two to four hours weekly. Without broader exposure (i.e., resulting in large amounts of input and chances for interaction both in and outside class), it is not likely that these YLs can achieve high levels of proficiency in English. (See also Ellis, this volume.)

Can early dual language learning be detrimental to children?

Some people fear that YLs might experience detrimental effects from early L2 learning, such as psychological, social, linguistic, or cognitive issues. Genesee et al. (2011) dispute this, noting: "There is no significant theoretical reason to believe that learning, knowing, or using two languages should jeopardize children's development, yet this fear is harbored by some people" (p. 49). In fact, given the right environment and support for dual language learning, children can exhibit higher levels of cognitive ability. Cummins's (2000) research shows that "Cognitive advantages among bilingual children are usually associated with advanced levels of bilingual proficiency, whereas cognitive disadvantages (or relatively lower levels of cognitive ability relative to monolingual children) are often associated with low levels of bilingual proficiency" (as cited in Genesee et al., 2011, p. 52). Lower levels of cognitive ability are associated with the learning of one or both languages being cut off, which may be especially true in the case of children being educated in the L2 in ESL settings. Therefore, there is no cognitive disadvantage to dual language learning, especially if both languages are provided the support needed for development. The best-case scenario for English learners in all contexts is strong and continuous support for L1 language and culture.

What is the optimal environment for learning ESL or EFL?

Whether in an ESL or EFL setting, the optimum English language learning environment for YLs depends on their receiving *comprehensible input* (Krashen, 1981). According to Krashen, the language that students are exposed to should be just above their current level of understanding or, as Krashen terms it, "*i* + 1." As Curtain and Dahlberg (2010) stated, "An important part of a teacher's planning time for a classroom based on the principles of second-language acquisition will be devoted to strategies for making the target language comprehensible to the students" (p. 2). Teachers can use what is referred to as *child-directed speech* or *caregiver speech,* which is how a parent may talk to a child who is learning a language to aid in comprehension (Cattell, 2000, p. 104). Such speech, when used by a parent to a child or by a teacher to students, entails using clear pronunciation, a slower rate of speech, shorter and simpler utterances, rephrasing and repetition, meaning-focused error correction, and modeling when necessary (Collier, 2004). Ideally, the classroom environment should be rich in meaningful input in English that is comprehensible as well as interesting and relevant to the learner.

It is also important to provide plenty of opportunities for meaningful and *comprehensible output*—that is, to push students to produce comprehensible utterances in the L2 that allow learners to test their hypotheses about features of the target language (Swain, 2005). To encourage YLs to produce English, the teacher has to create a comfortable environment in which they will not feel inhibited to speak up. Children are spontaneous and uninhibited by nature, but they can also be easily embarrassed, and some can be shy about speaking up if the teacher has a habit of correcting every grammatical error. Instead of singling out individual learners to make grammatical corrections, teachers can instead focus corrections on meaning and also use choral repetition of certain forms, through songs, chants, or other appropriate activities for children, to practice the correct forms in meaningful ways.

What is the best approach for teaching English to YLs?

Early childhood programs support approaches for YLs that encourage developmentally appropriate teaching practices. As Nissani (1990) noted: "learning goes on developmentally as the child matures. Intellectual learning is fostered but not given priority over physical, social, and emotional learning. Self-discipline is encouraged as is self-esteem" (p. 4).

According to Nissani (1990), in this type of approach, children are encouraged to:

- become involved in purposeful and creative activities with other children;
- make major choices among hands-on learning activities;
- initiate and accomplish self-motivated tasks within a rich environment; and
- construct knowledge at their own individual pace by discovering and engaging in open-ended activities that reflect all areas of their development while dialoguing with supportive adults.(p. 4)

A developmentally appropriate approach puts the child at the forefront of the learning process and stresses the importance of nurturing YLs as they develop physically, cognitively, and personally. Teachers should explore the characteristics of children that affect the learning process. As most teachers will attest, YLs are talkative and spontaneous. They have lots of physical energy and are easily distracted. They need to have their interest, imagination, and curiosity sparked to keep their attention in the classroom. Teachers should harness these natural characteristics of YLs when planning their classes and use social, active, purposeful, creative, and hands-on activities that are interesting and relevant.

Developmentally appropriate approaches for TEYL have their roots in Piaget (1970), who emphasizes that children are active learners and thinkers who make sense of the world by interacting with their physical environment. YLs need a classroom environment that allows them to construct meaning and make discoveries on their own. In addition, these approaches emphasize that children learn through social interaction, in particular the interaction with a supportive adult (Vygotsky, 1962/1986). This interaction with an adult needs to support the learning process for the child to acquire new knowledge and skills within his or her *zone of proximal development* (ZPD), which is the difference between what a child can achieve alone and what he or she can achieve with the help of the adult (parent or teacher). As the adult in the classroom, the teacher must help YLs learn the new language and skills through a process of supporting or scaffolding. According to Bruner (1983), *scaffolding* is fine-tuned help to accomplish a particular task, which includes creating interest in the task, breaking it down into smaller steps, modeling it, showing alternate ways to accomplish it, and keeping the child on track by minimizing frustration and giving reminders of the purpose or goal.

In terms of language instruction, a developmentally appropriate approach should emphasize purposeful and meaningful activities rather than a focus on isolated grammatical structures. Teaching grammar explicitly should be limited in YL classes because young children are not easily able to attend to the underlying rules that govern language use. As Cameron (2003)pointed out, "children see the foreign language 'from the inside' and try to find meaning in how the language is used in action, in interaction, and with intention, rather than 'from the outside' as a system and form" (p. 107). It is important for teachers to help students "notice" the grammar by focusing on form holistically, without breaking the language into small parts for analysis; they also need to build grammatical accuracy through plenty of meaning-focused input and output (Cameron, 2001; Pinter, 2006). As Pinter (2006) stated, "Learning grammar is a messy process requiring the teacher to provide lots of meaningful practice, recycling, and guidance in attending to language form" (p. 85).

Coltrane (2003) emphasized that developmentally and linguistically appropriate learning for teaching ELs "should take into consideration the characteristics of young English language learners and their language development, the learning conditions that are most effective for these learners, and the kinds of instruction that best meet their needs" (p. 2).

One developmentally appropriate approach is the use of thematic units. Planning lessons around a theme is an effective approach for teaching YLs because it provides a meaningful context within which language can be used and practiced (Curtain & Dahlberg, 2010; Haas, 2000; Shin, 2006). Shin (2006) explained, "Thematic units, which are a series of lessons revolving around the same topic or subject, can create a broader context and allow students to focus more on content and communication than on language structure" (p. 4). When choosing an appropriate theme for YLs, it is important to consider what is relevant and interesting to them; it is also appropriate to consider developing units of instruction based on grade-level content from the students' other classes (Curtain & Dahlberg, 2010; Haas, 2000;

Shin, 2006, 2007). As Shin (2007) stated in reference to thematic-unit planning for the EFL context: "For school age students, it is highly recommended to make the learning process more holistic by connecting between the foreign language class and students' other classes since the most relevant topics for young learners revolve around their subject matter content" (p. 4). For ESL contexts, it is important to connect themes to subject-area content since the goal is to mainstream ELs and develop their English language proficiency so they can achieve in the content areas. In fact, "much of elementary school curriculum in all content areas is built around themes" (Curtain & Dahlberg, 2010, p. 150), so it is appropriate for ESL classes to be theme-based as well. In fact, if the push-in (or plug-in) model is being used, then the teacher will be developing instruction around the theme as planned in the grade-level curriculum.

What are some context-specific considerations for TEYL?

ESL-specific considerations for YLs. In an ESL context, YLs need English to communicate with their peers socially, understand the language found in their environment, and master grade-level content in their mainstream classes. ESL teachers need to ensure that both *basic interpersonal communication skills* (BICS) and *cognitive academic language proficiency* (CALP) are developed, which is the formal distinction between social and academic language first described by Cummins (1979). Genesee et al. (2011) describe a triple challenge that ELs in this setting have of "acquiring an L2 for academic purposes, integrating socially into a new community of peers, and acquiring new academic skills and knowledge" (p. 191). Beyond learning social and academic language, Genesee et al. emphasize the possible challenge to ELs of bridging the cultural and socioeconomic gap that might exist between their home and school, which can include academic skills and understanding the expectations of the school culture.

Even though YLs in the ESL classroom need to learn aspects of the target culture and school culture to be successful, Calderon et al. (2011) and Coltrane (2003) stress the importance of valuing and nurturing the home language and culture for learners' identity formation and success in school. Too often teachers view the ELs' native language use as a possible barrier to the learning of English. Believing that they are helping the child, they recommend that parents use English at home, thereby risking the loss of the child's heritage language. Coltrane (2003) emphasized that learning English is an "additive process" in which the native language and culture are an asset rather than a hindrance (p. 1). Calderon et al. (2011) went a step further by presenting support for using students' native language in class; they encourage students' cooperation with peers who speak the same language to help students build comprehension of a task and become more familiar with the school and classroom context.

Teachers, both ESL and mainstream, need to value, nurture, and use strategically students' native languages and cultures in the classroom. This can be a challenge because ELs can come from many different countries that are not familiar to teachers. Therefore, ESL teachers must develop intercultural sensitivity and deepen their understanding of cultural differences. In a diverse ESL classroom with ELs from many different linguistic and cultural backgrounds, this also means providing ELs the chance to explore their own cultures and encourage all students to learn about cultures around the world as represented by their classmates.

EFL-specific considerations for YLs. In the EFL context, YLs do not share the urgency of learning English to communicate with peers and succeed academically. The goal for early EFL programs as determined by ministries of education is typically to produce better speakers of English who can ultimately function in global markets and build their countries' economies. Parents often emphasize English in their children's education to increase their future socioeconomic prospects. While YLs themselves are not concerned with their future socioeconomic standing or their country's status in the global economy, motivation is a key factor. EFL teachers should take an approach that builds a positive attitude toward English in each student to create lifelong learners of English. Using fun, developmentally appropriate activities that are connected to the students' real lives will help students in EFL settings stay motivated and interested in learning English.

Because English is an international language and YLs will grow up using it to interact with people from all around the world, it is important to introduce diverse cultural materials into the EFL classroom. Curtain and Dalhberg (2010) stated that children under 10 are "at a maximum of openness to other cultures" (p. 7), so exposing students to other cultures at an early age is an ideal time to begin building their intercultural competence. EFL teachers can introduce students to three different types of cultural material: (1) the target culture (i.e., from English-speaking countries like the United States, the United Kingdom, and Australia); (2) the source culture (i.e., the students' home cultures); and (3) international target cultures (i.e., other non-English-speaking cultures) (S. L. McKay, 2002). In this fashion, students are exposed to other cultures around the world and learn how to express aspects of their own culture in English.

CLASSROOM APPLICATIONS

Whether teaching ESL or EFL, teachers need to make instruction developmentally appropriate by considering the characteristics of YLs and how children learn. Therefore, classroom instruction should be:

- enjoyable and interesting
- active and hands-on
- supported and scaffolded
- meaningful and purposeful
- culturally appropriate and relevant

Each of these aspects is explored using the PB&J song and the Food from around the World unit plan in the Appendix.[3] Additional practical ideas for teachers are also given. I highly recommend that teachers apply thematic unit planning in their classroom instruction. However, if teachers must follow a mandated curriculum that is not theme-based, the application of the recommended activities can be used to enhance instruction for YLs.

Enjoyable and interesting—capture their attention!

YLs get excited about learning when you present them with brightly colored visuals and fun activities. Choose topics and tasks that are engaging and relevant to young learners. Use stories, songs, chants, and other activities that will capture their

attention and make them want [...] YLs love to use their imagination. The[...] games and pretend. Activities that encoura[...] creativity and imagination can help engage th[...] in the learning process.

For example, in the PB&J lesson in the Experience section, the teacher used colorful pictures of peanuts, grapes, a piece of bread, and a sandwich to get the students' attention and increase their comprehension of vocabulary. In addition, the teacher used a song that students love singing to engage her YLs and get them to practice language without getting bored. In the "Food from around the World" unit plan in the Appendix, students make a mini-book called the Four-Step Book in class 2, which entails drawing colorful pictures of the ingredients, one for each step in the book: peanuts, grapes, bread, and sandwich. In class 3, students play a game of Charades to show their comprehension of newly learned actions for preparing food. Figure 2 summarizes these and other ideas for keeping YLs engaged.

Brightly colored visuals
- Photos
- Pictures
- Art work
- Cartoons
- Flash cards
- Posters
- Storybooks (picture books)
- Scrapbooks
- Coloring books
- Stickers

Engaging activities
- Singing
- Chanting
- Telling stories
- Role playing and acting
- Drawing, coloring, and painting
- Playing games, like Simon Says, I Spy, Hangman, and Charades (see www.eslkidstuff.com)
- Creating mini-books, like accordion books and four-step books (see www.makingbooks.com)

Figure 2. Ideas for capturing young learners' attention.

Active and hands-on—keep them moving!

YLs are kinesthetic learners and like to move their bodies. Sometimes they cannot sit still, so

...orate activities that get ...ound. Children learn by ...ed to have lots of hands- ...urage them to interact with ...ia. One method commonly ... that can keep even the liveliest ...Total Physical Response (TPR). ...nguage, particularly commands, to mo...sher, 1996). For instance, the teacher says, "St...up!" and stands up while uttering the words. Then the teacher says, "Sit down!" and then sits down. With the physical cues attached to the words, children can connect the language to the movement through repetition and demonstration and can follow the commands.

In the classroom Experience at the beginning of the chapter, the teacher used a song that incorporated TPR with movement and gestures. The teacher demonstrated how to *crunch*, *squish*, *spread*, and *eat* using actions. Not only is such movement engaging for students but the actions also illustrate the meaning of the verbs. In addition, the teacher in the Experience brought in peanut butter, jelly, and bread, so students could actually make PB&J sandwiches. Giving learners chances to interact with realia like food helps them build their understanding of language and makes for a tasty experience in the classroom. In the full unit plan in the Appendix, students play charades, an entertaining game that encourages students to get up and use their bodies to show the different actions for preparing food. Figure 3 summarizes kinesthetic activities that keep YLs moving and examples of realia that can be used for students to interact with.

Supportive and scaffolded—set them up for success!

It is important to support YLs by using a variety of techniques for making input comprehensible, such as visuals, realia, gestures, and caregiver speech. Teachers should also scaffold students' learning by breaking the activities into smaller steps that set up each student for success, offering praise and positive feedback every step of the way. Another aspect of being supportive is to cater to different learning styles, such as audio, visual, and kinesthetic. Some students learn well by just listening to the teacher and hearing the language input (auditory). Other students need more visual cues

Kinesthetic activities
- Songs with movement and dancing
- Body spelling (using the body to spell letters of the alphabet)
- Play sports (e.g., soccer or baseball)
- Games with movement (e.g., Charades, Simon Says)
- Hand-clapping songs (e.g., Pat-a-Cake, Say Say Oh Playmate)
- Arts and crafts (e.g., sock puppets, finger puppets, masks)
- Total physical response (TPR)

Possible realia to use
- Food
- Plates, cups, bowls
- Cans, bottles, boxes
- Kitchen utensils (e.g., spoons, chopsticks)
- Toys, puppets, and stuffed animals
- Clothes, hats, and accessories
- Purses, book bags, backpacks
- Paper, pens, and other school supplies
- Maps and globes
- Menus, food labels, and signs
- Clocks
- Telephones
- Flags
- Calendars
- Travel brochures and posters
- Newspapers and magazines
- Money

Figure 3. Ideas for keeping young learners active.

for comprehension or need to see language written out to understand it (visual). Still others need to move and touch objects to learn most effectively (kinesthetic). If teachers do not plan lessons that have a balance of these learning styles, this could cause stress for students or cause some students to perform better than others. Finally, instruction should support *multiple intelligences* as defined by H. Gardner (1983, 1999): spatial-visual or picture smart, bodily kinesthetic or body smart, musical or music smart, linguistic or word smart, logical-mathematical or number smart, interpersonal or people smart, intrapersonal or self smart, and naturalistic or nature smart. All students are individuals and may exhibit their own combination of the eight intelligences; therefore, teachers should try not to favor some kinds of intelligence over others.

In the Experience at the beginning of the chapter and in the full unit plan in the Appendix, the teacher chose to present language about food and prepare a dish using the PB&J song as input. The song is an example of comprehensible input that is just above the learners' level of English. The activities were prepared and sequenced to scaffold students' learning step by step. For example, Rosa introduced known words and then unknown words, she went from word level to sentence level through the song, and she showed the difference in spoken forms (e.g., *crunch 'em*) to written forms (e.g., *crunch them*). Every step of the lesson was scaffolded carefully to help YLs understand first and then produce successfully.

Rosa also used various activities and techniques to make input comprehensible and cater to different learning styles and intelligences. She started by teaching students key vocabulary using the pictures on the wall (spatial-visual and linguistic). Then she taught a song accompanied with gestures and dancing (bodily kinesthetic and musical). At the end of the lesson, Rosa had students make PB&J sandwiches together (bodily kinesthetic and interpersonal). Then students focused on writing the language by creating the four-step book (spatial-visual and linguistic). Next, students reviewed vocabulary for new food and actions through visuals, pictures, and gestures, including making their own flash cards to scaffold their use of language learning strategies and testing their understanding of the actions using the game charades (spatial-visual and bodily kinesthetic). To help facilitate students' comprehension of their classmates' song, students filled in a graphic organizer, which was a T-chart that listed the ingredients on one side and the actions on the other side (musical and spatial-visual).

Figure 4 presents additional techniques for making input comprehensible, a list of steps a

---

Techniques for making input comprehensible

- Use visual cues, like pictures and flash cards.
- Use gestures and body movement.
- Use realia.
- Use graphic organizers, such as T-charts, Venn diagrams, mind maps, and time lines.
- Translate difficult words (only when necessary).
- Give definitions, synonyms, and antonyms.
- Explain the word or expression.
- Demonstrate.
- Give an example.
- Use the item in a sentence.
- Pronounce words clearly.
- Speak more slowly (without distorting the natural flow).
- Repeat and rephrase.
- Use shorter and simpler sentences and phrases.
- Model expected utterances and responses.
- Connect to students' background knowledge.

Strategies for scaffolding the learning process

- Review known vocabulary.
- Preteach new vocabulary.
- Use a variety of techniques to make input comprehensible.
- Provide multiple opportunities during class to repeat and review.
- Teach how to make and use learning tools (e.g., mini-book or four-step book).
- Model expected outcomes and responses.
- Encourage student learning strategies (e.g., student-made flash cards).
- Use same language in different text types to reinforce new language (e.g., song and recipe).
- Recycle language within the same structure (e.g., different foods and actions using the same song format, like PB&J, sushi, and ceviche).
- Praise and encourage students throughout the process.

Activities that cater to both learning styles and intelligences

- Spatial-visual: brightly colored pictures, flash cards, photos, posters, maps, charts, and other graphic organizers (e.g., mind maps, T-charts, Venn diagrams)
- Audiovisual: storytelling, TV shows, movie clips, YouTube videos
- Auditory/musical: songs, chants, rhymes, tapping rhythms, listening activities
- Bodily kinesthetic/tactile activities: TPR, moving, dancing, gestures, miming, interacting with realia
- Logical-mathematical: mathematical and logical puzzles, keeping score in games, figuring out patterns in grammar, experiments, analysis
- Linguistic: noticing patterns in grammar, reading, writing, word and sentence analysis, word games (e.g., crossword puzzles, word searches, Scrabble)
- Interpersonal: cooperative activities, discussions, group work, teamwork, dialogues
- Intrapersonal: individual work like writing a poem or story, self-study, or reflection
- Naturalistic: field trips like the zoo, park, beach, or forest; topics related to plants, animals, and the environment

Figure 4. Ideas for supporting the learning process of YLs.

teacher can take to scaffold students' learning, and activities that combine learning styles and multiple intelligences.

Meaningful and purposeful—get them to communicate!

English grammar should be presented in context through meaning-focused input and output and not taught as isolated grammatical structures. Teachers can broaden the context by using thematic units that allow students to notice grammatical structures over several lessons and by encouraging the active use of these structures in the various modalities of listening, speaking, reading, and writing.

In the "Food from around the World" unit plan (see the Appendix), students used the same structure with different food and actions and also applied the same language to authentic text types such as recipes and demonstrating how to make food like on a television cooking show. In the lesson, the teacher focused on vocabulary, grammar, and pronunciation; however, students were encouraged to notice the grammar and different features of the language without their being taught explicitly, using grammatical terms. The grammatical structures *First you take the ___, and you ___ it* were repeated and recycled meaningfully using different kinds of food and actions. Students could notice and use the grammar through the four-step book activity and through the substitution of new foods and actions into the structure of the PB&J song. The focus throughout the unit was on teaching foods and actions through the context of songs and recipes. If it is possible to present language within a meaningful context, then YLs can see how language is used in real life. Figure 5 presents authentic text types appropriate for these learners.

Culturally appropriate and relevant—explore all cultures!

ESL and EFL instruction should build intercultural competence and provide opportunities for YLs to explore different cultures. There should be a multicultural approach that recognizes the students' home cultures and international cultures in addition to English-speaking cultures. It is important to teach YLs about cultures that are associated with the language being learned. With English becoming an

Authentic oral text types
- Songs
- Chants
- *Jazz Chants*®4
- Storytelling
- Plays
- TV shows
- Commercials
- News reports
- Weather reports
- Announcements
- Cartoons
- Movies
- Jokes and riddles
- Tongue twisters
- Dialogues (conversations)

Authentic written text types
- Stories
- Poems
- Letters
- Emails
- Text messages
- Shopping lists
- Schedules and calendars
- Menus
- Signs
- Flyers
- Labels
- Recipes
- Greeting cards
- Travel brochures and posters
- Comic strips
- Crossword puzzles, word jumbles, anagrams
- Newspapers articles
- Magazine articles
- Advertisements

Figure 5. Ideas for encouraging real-life communication.

international language, people in countries around the world are using English to communicate with each other. Therefore, teachers should develop a multicultural curriculum using target, source, and international target-culture materials (McKay, 2002).

In the introductory Experience and in the unit plan in the Appendix, the teacher introduced a popular food from U.S. culture, PB&J sandwiches. Then the teacher introduced other recipes such as sushi from Japan to expose children to cultures from around the world. Finally, students got a chance to create new English songs with recipes from their own

- **Food.** Have students pretend to be on a TV cooking show and teach, using imperatives, how to make simple dishes from various cultures.
- **Eating habits.** Have students compare and contrast table settings from different cultures by drawing posters of table tops with pictures of typical dishes, utensils (e.g., spoon, fork, chopsticks), and the placement of foods in individual versus shared plates for breakfast, lunch, dinner, or special occasions.
- **Dress.** Show clothes or pictures of clothes from different countries during a unit on clothing. Have students become familiar with the clothes of other countries and use the language to describe them.
- **Art.** Post prints of art from different countries around the room like an art exhibit. Have students learn about what country the artwork is from so they can appreciate the different ways to portray beauty. The artwork can be themed for a particular activity. For example, if all of the art work depicts animals, students can choose one to write a description using vocabulary relating to colors, shapes, and actions without using the names of animals. Have students read their descriptions out loud and have their classmates guess which piece of art is being described.
- **Holidays and celebrations.** Keep a calendar with world holidays in the classroom (see http://www.earthcalendar.net) and celebrate the holidays appropriately throughout the year. Use preparation for the different holidays as thematic units or classroom projects.
- **Folktales, fairy tales, and legends.** Create a thematic unit about "Cinderella Stories from around the World." Students can compare and contrast Cinderella stories from different countries/cultures (e.g., Russia, China, Egypt, Korea, Mexico, Cambodia, Caribbean, and Africa).
- **Music and dance.** Prepare videos of music and dance from English-speaking and international cultures. Have students put English lyrics to songs in other languages and have fun singing and dancing to new rhythms and melodies. Students can also put their own culture's rhythms to traditional English songs.
- **Wonders of the world.** Make a thematic unit about "Treasures of the World," which include the wonders of the world (e.g., the Egyptian pyramids, the Great Wall of China), and beautiful tourist attractions from different countries. The classroom can become a travel agency, and students can create posters and brochures for different countries.
- **Architecture, geography, animals.** Have students work in groups to create museum displays in the classroom for parents and other students to visit. Assign groups to research different countries or regions. Have students prepare maps and gather information about the country, such as the architecture, geography, native animals, and flags. They can include samples of the music, dress, food, and so on. This could be a large project that is the culmination of a thematic unit on countries.
- **Greeting customs.** Teach a dialogue about greeting friends and include demonstrations of different ways to greet people around the world.
- **Currency:** Have students role play traveling to another country, exchanging money, and going shopping.

Figure 6. Ideas for cultural activities for YLs.

culture. For example, in the Appendix students in Peru wrote a song about the most famous food from their country, ceviche. Food is one of many popular cross-cultural topics for YLs. Teachers should use mostly surface culture materials for children that are concrete, visible, and fun to learn about, such as food and eating habits, dress, art, holidays and celebrations, folktales, fairy tales and legends, music and dance, wonders of the world, architecture, geography and climate, animals, greeting customs, and currency. See Figure 6 for examples of different cultural activities based on these topics.

FUTURE TRENDS

The current trend of lowering the age for compulsory English education around the world has created a huge demand for trained teachers of YLs. The shortage of trained elementary school EFL teachers has prompted many countries to hire untrained native speaker teachers or elementary school teachers with qualifications in other subjects who have some English background (Garton et al. 2011; Nunan, 2003). In some cases, experienced English teachers at the secondary level have been recruited to teach at the elementary school level. These solutions frequently result in teachers who are not prepared to give developmentally appropriate instruction for YLs and/or who do not possess English proficiency or experience at levels needed to provide effective instruction using English. Therefore, ongoing in-service professional development programs are necessary for both language and pedagogical training.

In addition to providing training in linguistics and pedagogy for second/foreign language teaching, preservice English teacher education programs need to have a specific focus on methods for teaching children to prepare new teachers to apply developmentally appropriate approaches to the EFL classroom. Currently most TESOL teacher-preparation programs do not have extensive training specifically for teaching English at the elementary school level. However, the growth of TEYL as a field and the growing demand for trained teachers of YLs will necessitate both pre-service and in-service teacher-education programs tailored to this need.

Another future consideration for EFL contexts is reassessing how to teach English at the secondary level. If English language instruction starts at younger ages, then the curricula and teaching approaches at the secondary level will need to be revised. Students will enter secondary school with higher levels of English language proficiency and possibly better oral fluency and pronunciation in English than before. In addition, the approaches appropriate for elementary school students may create an expectation of more active and interactive approaches to teaching EFL. Additional training for secondary school English teachers may be necessary to implement changes in curricula and approaches and, possibly, to improve aspects of English language proficiency needed in the classroom to accommodate these changes.

Although I have focused in this chapter on approaches to teaching English to YLs that are developmentally appropriate, there is also the issue of cultural appropriateness that should be embedded in all the recommendations. Cultural appropriateness becomes an issue in ESL settings when an individual EL has difficulty adjusting to a particular U. S. cultural norm or a norm of another country where English is the dominant language; it may also figure into EFL contexts when the cultural norms shared by the teacher and students make a suggested activity either culturally inappropriate or not applicable. In fact, the ideas given in this chapter should be considered open for adaptation in local contexts. Variations based on class size or available resources need to be considered. More materials development and research related to TEYL should be shared and published by English-teaching professionals in local contexts that represent the perspectives of different countries, cultures, language groups, socioeconomic levels, and urban/rural contexts.

In ESL contexts, there is more awareness of and training on using the students' *funds of knowledge* in the classroom, that is, "the historically accumulated and culturally developed bodies of knowledge and skills essential for household or individual functioning and well-being" (Moll, Amanti, Neff, & Gonzalez, 2005, p. 73). To understand students' funds of knowledge, both ESL and mainstream teachers can conduct field visits to the ELs' neighborhoods and households and explore their culture and knowledge base. Teachers should do this for all their students but especially for their ELs whose diverse backgrounds are not familiar to them. With this approach, teachers can find ways to connect students' life experiences and home culture to the curriculum to increase the ELs' comprehension of concepts and to provide opportunities for them to make contributions that show the application of content through their funds of knowledge.

Finally, ESL teachers are increasingly becoming part of professional learning communities in their schools, meeting regularly with grade-level teachers, reading specialists and literacy coaches, and special education teachers to discuss ways of helping all students at that grade level meet the required standards and achieve learning outcomes. (See also Crandall & Finn-Miller, this volume.) The ESL teacher is no longer just someone to whom teachers send ELs for part of the day or someone who comes in and co-teaches certain lessons. He or she is increasingly becoming part of an instructional team focused on helping all children achieve and learn. This is a good model for all schools as it encourages a more holistic approach to educating YLs; and it provides critical opportunities for cross-disciplinary professional development, with all teachers learning from each other about both content and instructional strategies to try with all children.

CONCLUSION

It is important to remember that through the study of ESL and EFL, we are bringing up global citizens who learn English in addition to their own native language(s). Most important, elementary ESL and EFL teachers should remember that they are not just teaching English—they are teaching YLs! These learners are young citizens of our world. It is critical that teachers remember to:

- encourage and praise their YLs
- give all of them love and attention equally

- help them build good character and self-esteem
- nurture their home culture and language
- open their minds to other cultures

It is hoped that teachers will create lifelong learners of English who will be successful at using the world's dominant lingua franca in the future. Using the approaches described in this chapter, teachers will be able to create a classroom environment that will make YLs comfortable, confident, engaged, active, challenged, and, ultimately, successful in English. They will be able to create a learning environment that is as lively as the one created by Rosa in the introductory Experience and as pleasing to a YL's palate as a PB&J sandwich!

SUMMARY

➤ TEYL is a growing field of study in EFL contexts and focuses on learners from 5 to 12 years old, or elementary school-age children. YLs are usually defined as 7–12 years old, whereas VYLs are defined as under 7 years old.

➤ In ESL contexts, the study of YLs is often described in relation to elementary grades K–5. Some distinction is made for approaches based on the study of early childhood, which is birth to age 8.

➤ Older learners can achieve nativelike proficiency in English; however, YLs show advantages in oral fluency and pronunciation.

➤ An optimal environment for YLs of ESL or EFL should be developmentally appropriate and focus on meaning rather than grammatical forms; it should include plenty of comprehensible input and create a comfortable environment for interaction and production of comprehensible output.

➤ The ESL and EFL classroom for young learners should encourage real communication through enjoyable, interesting, active, hands-on, supportive, scaffolded, meaningful, purposeful, and culturally appropriate activities.

➤ Instruction in both ESL and EFL contexts should nurture the home language and culture and use a multicultural curriculum that includes both English-speaking cultures and other international cultures around the world.

DISCUSSION QUESTIONS

1. Do you think that starting to learn English as a second or foreign language earlier produces better speakers of English? Review the arguments presented in this chapter and be prepared to defend your position.

2. If English is studied as a foreign language at the elementary level only three or four hours per week, is it possible to produce better speakers of English rather than starting at the secondary level? Which approaches discussed in the chapter can help optimize the learning process in EFL contexts? Can you add any others from your experiences as a language learner or teacher?

3. The chapter emphasizes that children learn through play and interaction. In addition, it does not recommend teaching grammar explicitly. How can teachers ensure that YLs have fun and still learn language effectively at the same time? Look at the young learners unit in the Appendix, and give some specific examples of how language skills were taught.

4. Think about the differences between teaching ESL and EFL. What can an ESL teacher learn from an EFL teacher to improve his or her instruction? What can an EFL teacher learn from an ESL teacher to improve his or her instruction.

5. What are some consequences of using only target-language culture materials when teaching English to young learners? For example, what if an ESL class in the United States teaches YLs only about U.S. culture? Or what if an EFL class teaches YLs only about culture in the United States, the United Kingdom, Canada, Australia, and New Zealand?

SUGGESTED ACTIVITIES

1. Talk with a YL who is 5 years old. Ask him or her to show you what he or she likes to do. See what the YL likes to play, sing, read, write, and do on a day-to-day basis. Ask the child about his or her favorite school activities. Take notes, and decide what kinds of activities you can incorporate into an English lesson. Then do the same for YLs of different ages between 5 and 11 years old. Make a chart to show which activities are similar across the various ages and which activities are different.

2. Teachers of YLs can learn from each other about how to engage children in the learning process and manage them in the classroom. Observe an elementary school class that is not an English language class. What activities for teaching or classroom management does the teacher use? Are these activities developmentally appropriate for YLs? Are there useful activities or techniques that you can apply to your own ESL or EFL class (now or in the future)? Is there interesting and relevant content from the class you observed that you can use to teach English in your class? Are there developmentally appropriate activities that you can suggest to your colleagues?

3. Find a child to interact with. It could be your own child, a niece or nephew, or even a neighbor. Try to teach this child a list of new words through repetition and flash cards, and then teach him or her a new song or chant that includes the same number of new but different words. What were the child's reactions to the different activities? Did the child learn new words better through flash cards or the song/chant? What are the positive points and negative points for the two approaches?

4. Choose a popular song or story for YLs in English. Analyze the language structures, vocabulary, and expressions used in the song (or story). Then do the following:

   a. Describe how you would scaffold students' understanding of the song (or story).

   b. Develop a fun activity or game using the song (or story) that also encourages learners to notice the grammar without teaching it explicitly.

   c. Create an activity that encourages learners to use the language found in the song (or story) by applying that language to a real-life context.

   d. Describe some follow-up activities for the song (or story) that will introduce learners to an English-speaking culture, the students' native culture, and other international cultures.

   e. Design a lesson plan that incorporates the elements in Activity 4d. Designate the student population and the setting. Use a lesson plan format you are familiar with or one from the chapter on lesson planning. (See also Purgason, this volume.)

FURTHER READING

Curtain, H., & Dahlberg, C. A. (2010). *Languages and children—making the match: New languages for young learners* (4th ed.). Boston, MA: Pearson.

This textbook for teaching foreign languages to children K–8 focuses on foreign language instruction for the U.S. context, with references and examples in other languages, like Spanish and French. This book is well balanced between theory and practice and gives both teachers and administrators good information for program planning and classroom teaching.

Garton, S., Copland, F., & Burns, A. (2011). *Investigating global practices in teaching English to young learners.* Aston University, UK: British Council.

This is a report based on a project funded by the British Council and conducted through Aston University in Birmingham, United Kingdom, with the perspectives of teachers in over 142 countries. The study details findings related to teacher professional development and preparation, approaches used in the classroom, practices in planning lessons for YLs, use of course books, access to resources, and challenges in terms of class size, student motivation, and English language proficiency.

Li, G., & Edwards, P.A. (2010). *Best practices in ELL instruction.* New York, NY: Guilford.

This book provides a solid foundation in research on the instruction of ELLs in the United States as well as practical ideas for teachers at all levels working in different types of ELL programs in K–12 settings. Part II of the book, "Strategies for Teaching Young ELLs," includes chapters about teaching reading, teaching writing, and the main principles for teaching English to YLs.

Pinter, A. (2006). *Teaching young language learners.* Oxford, UK: Oxford University Press.

This book gives the basics for teaching English to YLs. It offers both theory and practices for TEYL and outlines the main principles for teaching all four language skills, teaching vocabulary and grammar, developing learning strategies, evaluating and developing materials, and assessing YLs.

APPENDIX: YOUNG LEARNER UNIT

The following unit, Food from Around the World, is designed for YLs who are 8–9 years old. The unit takes place over four lessons.

Class 1

1. Warm-up activity: Ask students what food they like. (Review food vocabulary learned in previous lesson.)
2. Introduce topic: Tell students that they will learn about your favorite food: PB&J sandwich.
3. Preteach new vocabulary: Teach students vocabulary in the context of a song using colorful photos (peanuts, grapes, peanut butter, jelly, sandwich).
4. Culture content: Tell students that PB&J sandwiches are popular in the United States and kids eat them every day.
5. Presentation of new language in context: Lead students in singing the PB&J Song with accompanying motions and gestures.
6. Reinforce new language: Have students make PB&J sandwiches together while explaining the ingredients and the process.
7. Practice: Have students sing the song again with accompanying motions and gestures.

PEANUT BUTTER AND JELLY SONG

Refrain:
Peanut, peanut butter ~ and jelly!
Peanut, peanut butter ~ and jelly!

First, you take the **peanuts,** and
you crunch 'em, you crunch 'em.
Refrain
Then you take the **grapes**, and
you squish 'em, you squish 'em.
Refrain
Then you take the **bread**, and
you spread it, you spread it.
Refrain
Then you take the **sandwich**,
and you eat it, you eat it.
Mm mm mm mm mm mm ~ mm mm mm!
Mm mm mm mm mm mm ~ mm mm mm!

Class 2

1. Review from previous class: Sing the PB&J Song.
2. Focus on vocabulary: Have students create a four-step book (see instructions). Ask them to write on each page only the key words and to draw a picture showing the meaning. (Key words: *peanuts/crunch; grapes/squish; bread/spread; sandwich/eat*)
3. Focus on structure: Model on each page how students should write each sentence using the key words. Example: "First, you take the peanuts and your crunch them." Ask, for example, "What is *them*?" and elicit *peanuts* while circling the pronoun *them* and drawing an arrow to the word *peanuts* in the sentence. Focus students on the pronoun without using the grammatical term *pronoun*.
4. Focus on pronunciation: Point out that in writing you use *them* and when singing you use *'em*.
5. Practice: Have students sing the song without looking at the words.

FOUR-STEP BOOK

1. Get two pieces of paper (8.5 × 11 or A4).
2. Put one piece of paper on top of the other.
3. Place the top piece of paper so it is lower by 1 inch.
4. Fold both pieces of paper until you have four layers.
5. Glue or staple the edge to make a book.

For instructions with pictures, see http://makingbooks.com/step.shtml

Class 3

1. Review from previous class: Have students sing the PB&J Song.
2. Review vocabulary: Review words for different food by showing students pictures (e.g., *rice*, *fish*, and *cucumber*).
3. Preteach new vocabulary: Teach new actions to prepare food using gestures (e.g., *crunch*, *squish*, *spread*, *cut*, *chop*, *slice*, *fry*, *roll*, and *pat*).
4. Check comprehension: Charades. Have one student pick an action word out of a bag and show it through gestures. Ask the class to guess which action it is.
5. Culture content: Tell students that they will learn recipes from different countries around the world.
6. Presentation of new language in context: Give each group of four students a new recipe from a different country, for example, sushi from Japan.
7. Reinforce language: In groups, have students create flash cards for the ingredients in their new recipe. Model how to make flash cards using peanuts, grapes, and bread.
8. Written practice: In groups, have students create a new song using the language in their recipes. Tell students that this new song will be based on the PB&J Song. Assign them to practice their song for homework, and tell them they should be prepared to sing their new song during the next class period.

Class 4

1. Oral practice: Have each group take a turn sharing their song. Instruct the other students that while they listen they should make two lists in a T-chart: (a) a list of ingredients and (b) a list of actions. After each group finishes singing its new song, have the students check their comprehension by providing the correct list of ingredients and corresponding actions. Write students' answers on the board.
2. Connection to home culture: Have students work in groups to make a new song and recipes from their own culture. (See The Ceviche Song created by students in Peru.)

RECIPE: MAKI SUSHI (JAPAN)

Ingredients:
Rice
Seaweed
Raw fish
Cucumber, avocado
Soy sauce

Directions:

Spread the rice on the seaweed.
Lay the fish (and vegetables) on the rice.
Roll the seaweed into maki.
Cut the maki into pieces.
Dip maki into soy sauce.

MAKI SUSHI SONG

Refrain: Maki, maki sushi ~ with soy sauce!

First you take the rice, and you spread it, you spread it.
Refrain.
Then you take the fish, and you lay it, you lay it.
Refrain.
Then you take the seaweed, and you roll it, you roll it.
Refrain.
Then you take the maki, and you cut it, you cut it.
Refrain.
Then you take the sushi, and you dip it in soy sauce.
Refrain.
Then you take the sushi, and you eat it, you eat it.
Mm mm mm mm mm mm ~ mm mm mm!
Mm mm mm mm mm mm ~ mm mm mm!

T-CHART EXAMPLE

Ingredients	Action
rice	*spread*
fish	*lay*
seaweed	*roll*
maki	*cut*
soy sauce	*dip*
sushi	*eat*

THE CEVICHE SONG

Refrain: Ceviche, ceviche ~ so yummy!

First you take the fish, and you cut it, you cut it.
Refrain.
Then you take the onion, and you slice it, you slice it.
Refrain.
Then you take the cilantro, and you chop it, you chop it.
Refrain.
Then you take the lemon, and you squeeze it, you squeeze it.
Refrain.
Then you take the ceviche, and you eat it, you eat it.

> *Mm mm mm mm mm mm ~ mm mm mm!*
> *Mm mm mm mm mm mm ~ mm mm mm!*

Follow-up project work

Have students work together to make a cookbook with recipes from their culture (and/or international cultures).

ENDNOTES

[1] Some children may be allergic to peanuts, so teachers should find out before conducting this activity.
[2] The data were collected in the U.S. Department of State's E-Teacher Scholarship Program through an online professional development course called Teaching English to Young Learners, which is offered by the University of Maryland, Baltimore County. The data came from the reports of teachers living in 77 countries in Africa, Asia, Central and South America, Europe, and the Middle East. Permissions to use the data were given by participants as regulated through the Institutional Review Board.
[3] More resources are available at https://sites.google.com/site/shinjin-shil/resources
[4] *Jazz Chants* are chants written by Carolyn Graham for teaching ESL/EFL. She wrote numerous books in the 1970s, 1980s, and 1990s that have been popular for teaching English to young learners. *Jazz Chants for Children* (1979), *Jazz Chant Fairy Tales* (1988), and *Mother Goose Jazz Chants* (1994) are a few of her popular books geared toward young learners.

36 | Adult Learners in English as a Second/Foreign Language Settings

JANET L. EYRING

KEY QUESTIONS

➤ What are unique characteristics of adult second language learners?

➤ What are major conceptual paradigms in adult literacy and second language learning?

➤ How do these paradigms affect instruction and classroom research?

EXPERIENCE

Picture a teacher at the end of a school term teaching a large multilevel, multiethnic adult English as a second language (ESL) class in a public school setting.[1] The teacher, who is enthusiastic, kind, and dedicated, works part-time and has no employment benefits. The class contains both beginning- and intermediate-level learners. After greeting the students and asking about their weekends, the teacher asks students to open their textbooks and review a short reading with accompanying photos about a woman taking a trip to a national park. She then gives a personal example about a trip she took to Yellowstone National Park in the U.S. state of Wyoming and describes what she saw there. She asks all the students to write down the names of local, state, or national parks they have visited. All students must list things they saw at one or more of the parks; the intermediate students must also write about their experience at one park, answering questions the teacher has written on the board about where they went, why they chose the place, and what they did there.

The teacher circulates throughout the room, complimenting and encouraging students as they write. After this, she pairs students from different language backgrounds but the same proficiency level to share their work. Then she asks one or two student volunteers to share their work orally with the whole class. At the end of the class, she summarizes what the class has done and bids the students good-bye, knowing that three or four of them will not be back the next class session because of family or work commitments. She also hands back to all students test-score reports for the competency exam they took the previous week (a program requirement). Two older intermediate students and one student with a reading disability will not be able to move to the advanced-level class because of insufficient progress in their current class.

WHO IS THE ADULT ESL/EFL LEARNER?

The class in the Experience is typical of many public or community-based classes for *adult learners* that are outside the normal credit or degree programs offered by colleges or universities. These students are ESL students in the United States, who live in an environment where English is widely spoken and who need English for daily living. But certain features are also characteristic of English as a foreign language (EFL) classrooms, where learners need to use English in the workplace or to prepare for further education.

To help us understand who these learners are and how they can be best served, in this chapter I explore in greater depth their backgrounds, motivations, and other unique features. I also identify three major conceptual paradigms of adult instruction that serve as a backdrop for distinguishing different types of ESL/EFL programs around the world. I then discuss program standards as well as other issues, such as teacher certification, staff development, and building learning communities. In the second part of the chapter, I focus on the more practical concerns related to classroom instruction and present several lesson plans based on different standards suitable for adult education classes. Finally, I discuss future trends in adult ESL/EFL.

Student backgrounds: ESL

Adult ESL students in the United States, English-speaking Canada, Australia, New Zealand, the United Kingdom, and other parts of the English-speaking world tend to be more varied than learners in EFL contexts. For teachers, this diversity provides an exciting and rich instructional context. Adult ESL learners may vary by age, ethnicity, educational background, literacy skills, occupation, and educational attainment. Their ages can span from 16 to 100. Students in ESL contexts can be from all parts of the world but often come from developing countries. They can be different races and religions and have very different educational backgrounds, from no formal education to advanced degrees. They usually juggle many responsibilities such as work and child care while they are going to school.

Adults in ESL classes can be subdivided into several categories. The first group consists of immigrants who have left their native countries because of various push-pull factors, which may include reuniting with family members, finding better employment, conducting business, or escaping natural disaster or discrimination. Many of these individuals are seeking economic opportunity, freedom, or human rights that they could not enjoy in their native countries.

Those who have left their native countries for low-skilled work, especially in agriculture, food services, or construction are called migrant workers. Some people in this group prepare for permanent residency once they have lived in a country for several years, depending on the laws of the land. Others, however, transmigrate back home or to

other countries during their adulthood in search of more work or better opportunities. Mexican laborers working on a seasonal basis in packing plants in Canada or Chinese fruit pickers working for fixed periods in Australia are examples.

Refugees are a special class of immigrants who have left their homes, often unwillingly, because of religious or ethnic persecution, political upheaval, or war. In addition to having to deal with a new language, refugees also deal with the psychological effects of their traumatic (often violent) departures from their countries. For example, the Hmong who fought with the U.S. military during the Vietnam War were assigned refugee status because they faced retaliation by the Vietnamese once U.S. troops left Southeast Asia. And an example of refugees facing religious persecution are Christians who were discriminated against in Malaysia and resettled in the United Kingdom.

Many immigrants go to English-speaking countries to search for opportunities they did not have in their native countries. Those mentioned previously have entered legally. However, there are large numbers in certain countries who enter the country illegally by walking or being transported in enclosed compartments in boats or trucks across the borders. In the United States, for example, there are an estimated 9.3 million undocumented workers, mostly from Latin American countries but also from Asia and other parts of the world (Passel, Capps, & Fix, 2004).

Immigrants are sometimes labeled by the length of time they have been in a country—from short term (several months) to long term (many years). The tendency for immigrants to settle in ethnic enclaves often reduces their contact with the mainstream English-speaking culture and causes other linguistic and cultural effects. Thus, the education of long-term immigrants has assumed more prominence in ESL settings, where not only linguistic but other sociocultural factors need to be considered. Some of these students may be continuing in adult ESL because they have dropped out of high school and did not graduate (Orfeld, 2004). Nearly half of the students in adult education are English language learners, some of whom also have learning disabilities (National Council of State Directors of Adult Education, 2009).[2]

On the other hand, some immigrants have been more successful in the academic system of their native countries. They may have had previous careers, possess academic literacy in their home language, and be learning English so that they can retrain in related professions in their new country. Others come on student or tourist visas to study English to matriculate into higher education (e.g., community colleges, universities, and private colleges) and then return home after their studies are completed. Adults who enroll in English language institutes or English immersion programs, such as a Spaniard learning English at a Berlitz school in Scotland, study English full-time to learn more about the target country's culture as well as improve their learning skills for academic purposes. Some students may also study English on temporary visitor visas; these study experiences are typically for very limited amounts of time, for example, a week-long cooking course in English for Japanese housewives or a two-week English Bible class for Korean ministers.

Student backgrounds: EFL

When English teachers teach adults in EFL contexts, it is important that they understand the sociopolitical context of the country in which they teach. B. B. Kachru (1989) characterizes the English teaching world using the metaphor of three concentric circles. The *inner-circle countries* are the countries where English is spoken as a native language, previously defined by their ESL contexts. *Outer-circle countries*, like India, Kenya, the Philippines, Singapore, Malaysia, and Zambia, where individuals may not be native speakers of a standard variety of English but speak an institutionalized second-language variety because of past colonial relationships with inner-circle countries. *Expanding-circle countries*, like China, Japan, Russia, Israel, Jordan, and Zimbabwe, are countries where English is considered a foreign language and is used in restricted domains. (See also the Celce-Murcia chapter on World Englishes, this volume.)

In this section, we focus on teaching adult EFL in the outer-circle and expanding-circle countries, and most particularly in noncredit adult public and private programs. EFL learners who pursue English language study are not always enamored with the language and culture. However, because English is often used in business, science, or politics, learners continue to study it because English language proficiency continues to be associated with greater knowledge, material gain, or higher social status in their communities.

For the most part, EFL learners take English to enhance their skills for work or future educational opportunities. In Thailand, for example, English is a required subject at vocational schools and a popular offering at many private institutions. Serbian workers living in Germany who want to communicate with international customers at hotels may take a course in hotel English. Business people from around the world who wish to improve their written communication skills with U.S. clients may take an English business correspondence class at their workplace. Also, students who want to study at a university in the United States, the United Kingdom, Australia, New Zealand, or Canada or at an English-medium university in such countries as Turkey or Qatar may take test preparation courses at an adult language center or private language school in their country to prepare for the Test of English as a Foreign Language (TOEFL) or the International English Language Testing System (IELTS). English proficiency is a prerequisite for admission to the University of the Philippines system, and in some countries, such as China and Japan, English is part of the national university entrance exam, so students may attend English cram schools to give themselves a better chance of being accepted.

EFL learners are quite similar to ESL learners in some respects, but they are very different in others. Like ESL learners, they vary by age, but they are more homogeneous in background. EFL learners, for the most part, are from the same native country and speak the same language as their classmates. Most are literate and have had some schooling. However, in some regions of the world, for example, in Europe and the Middle East, this has changed because war refugees or asylum seekers, with or without formal education, have brought more diversity to these settings. Unskilled laborers working in countries where English is the language of wider communication have also changed the balance.

Finally, with new opportunities to travel to English-speaking countries, many people are learning English for recreational and conversational purposes. Within the European Union, the new language passport encourages students to expand their knowledge of English and other languages based on the Common European Language Framework of Reference (CEFR) (2011). In countries like Cambodia, where English learning was restricted or illegal in the past, the study of English has even played a liberating function for some learners (Ellerington, 2000).

Motivation of adult learners

As suggested in the previous section, adults have various motivations for enrolling in ESL or EFL classes. Many students want to learn English to find jobs, keep jobs, or find better jobs, acknowledging that those proficient in English can earn higher wages than those who are not proficient. In the United States, for example, non-native English speaking male workers may expect to earn 14–28% more income if they develop English speaking fluency (Chiswick & Miller, 2002). In many EFL settings, someone who has better English skills is more likely to be retained or promoted if English is an important part of the daily operations of a company or organization.

Others have personal reasons for learning English, such as enjoyment, bettering themselves, or improving overall proficiency for communication. For example, in the United States, adult ESL learners may enroll with native speaker learners in adult basic education courses. In many cities, these classes run the gamut from professional continuing education courses like personal finance to leisure courses like flower arranging. In many EFL settings, English classes are geared to the special purposes of learners (e.g., basic teller transactions for bank employees) or general communication (e.g., intermediate multiskills instruction). Finland, for example, has a long established tradition (*kansanopisto*) of offering adult continuing education courses for lifelong learning, including language courses (Finnish National Board of Education, 2011).

Immigrants in ESL settings may also have a variety of other reasons for wanting to learn English. They may want to help their children with homework, make friends, or obtain medical information. Some may want to pass citizenship or naturalization exams or earn their high school diplomas. Some refugees who experienced psychological problems as a result of torture, trauma, or discrimination in their homelands may be looking for peace and acceptance in a new society.

Motivation has often been associated with persistence in adult programs. But lack of motivation is not the only reason for students' not attending classes or dropping out. Comings's (2007) study of 150 adults in ESL settings in the United States revealed three broad reasons for dropping out: life demands, relationships, and poor self-determination. Life demands include childcare needs, work demands, transportation difficulties, students' or family members' health issues, age, lack of time, fatigue, bad weather, rules set by welfare and other social programs, unfavorable conditions at home, moving, and lack of income. Problems associated with relationships include those with family members, friends, colleagues, and community or welfare workers who do not support persistence and fear of letting others down. Finally, poor self-determination issues such as thinking negative thoughts, apathy, and lack of confidence in their ability to succeed stop some students from continuing their adult education classes (Comings, 2007).

In addition, certain school factors in ESL settings may be to blame for students' losing the motivation to stay in class. Limited governmental funding may mean that fewer ESL classes are offered. Fewer classes may lead to overcrowding in the classes that remain. Also, as enrollment increases, classes become multilevel and students find them less relevant and lose motivation. As a result, they vote "with their feet." Once they stop coming to class, they may never return again.

Adult learners versus young learners

Compared to young learners, adult learners have several learning advantages and a few disadvantages. First, they are cognitively mature. This cognitive maturity based on life and school experiences helps them understand the contexts and rules of language learning better than young learners (Larsen-Freeman & Long, 1991). However, other research shows some disadvantages for adult learners in terms of acquiring the sound system of English and aural/oral skills (Harley & Wang, 1997; Singleton, 2001). Learners who immigrate after puberty or in their 20s may have more difficulty speaking without a foreign accent. Second, older learners may also face more illnesses associated with aging, like heart conditions, type 2 diabetes, hearing and eyesight problems, and arthritis. These can sometimes interrupt or interfere with their continuous attendance in a program and thus affect learning. Third, adult learners are self-directing. According to Comings and Cuban (2000, as cited in Burt, Peyton, & Adams, 2003), adult learners need to select their own literacy goals to maintain interest and motivation. Some of these goals may be instrumental (to fulfill a practical purpose) or integrative (to identify with the target group) or some combination of both (Peirce, 1995).

Fourth, adults have focused career paths. Knowles (1980) argues that adult learners learn best when they are learning something that has clear importance for them and their future goals. As previously mentioned, learners cease to attend class if they do not see the immediate relevance of the instruction. Fifth, adult learners are psychologically vulnerable. Many go to school even though they may feel embarrassed or self-conscious being in a language classroom at an older age. Sixth, as the chief supporters of their family, some adults are motivated to learn to obtain employment, pursue careers, and handle medical issues and financial transactions in their families. They also want to be more involved in the school lives of their children. Finally, Kegan (1994) identified something peculiar to adult learners—the hidden rules or changing developmental demands of modern culture that many adults struggle to deal with and the supports they need to accomplish their roles. Unlike children, they are obligated to keep up with new and sometimes unpredictable developments in their complex environments (e.g., at work, school, and home). In addition, they must access relationships or technical assistance to better meet their own daily needs and the needs of their families.

Literacy levels

Literacy instruction is often a key to academic success. As such, it is another consideration for learners in ESL situations and an increasing concern for learners in EFL situations. The teacher may have to deal with a wide range of literacy abilities within one class. Some learners may come from countries in which the oral language is not written. These learners are called preliterate learners. Hmong refugees from Laos or Bantu speakers from Somalia are examples of preliterate learners. They differ from learners who do not read or write a language for which there is a written system. Many Mexican immigrants to the United States are nonliterate or, if they can read Spanish or their indigenous native language, do so at only the elementary level and are semiliterate.

Further complications may relate to the type of alphabet that learners are familiar with in their home language. Birch (2007) distinguishes nonalphabet literates from non-Roman alphabet literates. For example, students who can read Chinese characters are nonalphabet literates, and students who can read the Cyrillic alphabet are non-Roman alphabet literates. Learning disabilities may affect the ability of some learners to learn to read. All these aspects of literacy exhibit themselves in many ESL classrooms and in some EFL classrooms.

ESL/EFL classroom settings

EFL programs generally fall into two main categories: general EFL (sometimes with a college-preparatory focus and other times with a travel or recreation focus) and workplace EFL (for vocational or paraprofessional purposes). On the other hand, ESL programs are more varied and fall into four broad categories: general ESL, family literacy, workplace programs, and civics education (Parrish, 2004; Spruck-Wrigley & Guth, 1992). These programs are offered in a wide range of settings, often with little or no articulation between segments. These settings include public kindergarten to 12th-grade (K–12) schools, adult schools, community colleges, continuing education programs, community-based organizations, correctional institutions, private colleges, public libraries, and departments of human services.

General ESL programs often follow a *competency-based syllabus* in which students learn functions and structures to accomplish practical daily tasks such as going to the bank, renting an apartment, or getting refills on prescriptions. Pre-employment instruction sometimes occurs in general ESL programs as well to teach some of the important "soft" skills (social, communication, and self-management behaviors) as well as "hard" skills (technical knowledge for a profession).

Family literacy (or intergenerational literacy) programs focus on strengthening the literacy skills of parents so that they can better assist with the education and development of their children while improving their own English proficiency. According to Quintero (2008), family literacy programs like Even Start in the United States include models with four main components: (1) intergenerational parent and child literacy activities directed at making literacy a meaningful part of parent-child relationships and communication; (2) adult education and adult literacy directed at assisting parents to obtain more information about becoming economically self-sufficient; (3) parenting education directed at helping parents support the educational growth of their children in the home and at school; and (4) age-appropriate education directed at preparing children for success in school and life.

Workplace programs are another important supplier of ESL instruction. According to Chisman (2009), these programs fall into four main categories: (1) training programs for particular occupations (e.g., cosmetology or car mechanics); (2) incumbent worker programs (e.g., programs offered to upgrade the basic and occupational skills of workers in response to problems the employer is having or because of new demands of the job); (3) post-secondary transition or "bridge" programs (e.g., preparatory courses for college, sometimes taken concurrently with classes at a college or university); and (4) career or academic preparation (e.g., occupational or academic preparation with an emphasis on workforce soft skills like workplace etiquette and problem solving or on academic skills like writing).

Finally, civics classes (sometimes called English literacy/civics) have three main goals: (1) to prepare students to take citizenship/naturalization exams; (2) to encourage new citizens to vote in a democratic election; and (3) to encourage students to participate as citizens to improve their communities (Weinstein, 2001). (See also Johns & Price, this volume.)

CONCEPTUAL UNDERPINNINGS OF ADULT LITERACY

Although many scholars may argue that there are innumerable ways to conceptualize adult literacy instruction, most fit into one of three camps. Taking the United States as an example, Demetrion (2005) points to three paradigms of literacy education: *functional literacy*, the *New Literacy Studies* (NLS), and *critical literacy*. He acknowledges that these paradigms sometimes overlap, but in this case, there is more overlap between functional literacy and NLS than between functional literacy and critical literacy. Functional literacy approaches are normally associated with preparing ESL learners with the knowledge and skills needed in the United States to obtain work in and assimilate into U.S. culture. Critical literacy, on the other hand, is associated with emancipatory goals in which reforms are sought by marginalized or oppressed groups to bring about change in society. According to Spring (2011), educational models are always political. The same is true in adult literacy programs. Functional literacy is often associated with a more capitalist orientation in that it helps learners obtain work so they can support themselves. In contrast, critical literacy is often associated with a more socialist orientation in that it helps learners solve social problems through government social programs. Educational ideologies vary based on whether the emphasis is on developing human capital to compete in the global marketplace or on educating individuals to bring about social justice (Spring, 2011).

The first paradigm, the functional literacy model, has been favored in the United States as a result of an influential report entitled *A Nation at Risk* (National Commission on Excellence in Education, 1983). This report argued that the U.S. educational system in the 1980s was failing and needed an overhaul to prepare for the global marketplace, with its shift from goods to services. Additional projects—Workforce 2000 and Jump Start—argued that the minority-based workforce was ill-equipped to meet the changing needs of the economy. This prompted the federal government to initiate the Secretary's Commission on Achieving Necessary Skills (SCANS) curriculum for the restructuring of K–12 public education (The Secretary's Commission on Achieving Necessary Skills, 1999). This framework of foundational skills and workplace competencies was borrowed and adapted for adult education. Advocates of this approach believe that contextualized instruction, which teaches basic skills applied to occupational tasks, produces the best results (Chisman, 2009). Similar initiatives have taken place in other ESL and EFL settings.

The second orientation, NLS, may represent a compromise between the functional and critical approaches to curriculum. Shirley Brice Heath's (1983) groundbreaking work, *Ways with Words*, used ethnographic methods to investigate the literacies used in three communities in the southern United States to accomplish real life goals. She shows that the impact of family structure and social goals expanded the notions of what literacy is. Now, literacy is considered a set of practices embedded within certain cultures and constructed relative to the needs and goals of the community. This is sometimes called a constructivist approach. Sociolinguistic and psycholinguistic factors heavily influence what kind of literacy is needed and how a learner can become a member of a particular field of knowledge (Ferris & Hedgcock, 2004). If the goal is to obtain a job, NLS suggests that a functional literacy curriculum might be appropriate since this curriculum focuses on the skills and competencies needed to succeed in the workplace. If the goal is to make changes in one's society, NLS offers a critical literacy curriculum to focus on the real needs of learners to change what is not right in their environments.

Critical literacy, the third paradigm, is based upon the philosophy of Paulo Freire, the Brazilian educator; this paradigm focuses on learner needs and on empowering learners to change systems that are not serving them. Freire's (1970) ideas have influenced professionals in the United States and in other parts of the world (Papen, 2005). According to Auerbach (1992a, 1992b), a proponent of critical literacy, the instructional process moves from the students to the curriculum rather than from the curriculum to the students. Needs assessment is ongoing. Students examine their own contexts through problem-posing (versus problem solving). According to Demetrion (2005), Auerbach's perspective shows: "It is not the individual that should change, but the social order that needs to become more responsive to the voices and concerns of those who suffer most from conditions perpetuated by the dominant power structure" (p. 9). This type of curriculum is very different from the means-end type we find in the functional approach with clear objectives and results.

According to Silver-Pacuilla (2007), "The New Literacy Studies model shares much with the Freirean model of literacy that embeds literacy learning and use in praxis of naming powers and working openly toward social justice" (p. 98). However, the NLS model also views "adult literacy as a complex form of personal assimilation within the mores and institutions of the prevailing

social order" (Demetrion, 2005, p. 241). The NLS perspective values the needs and goals of the learner in participatory literacy education, exemplified by the critical literacy, NLS, and the multiliteracies work of the New London Group.[3] However, those favoring participatory models have been pressured to conform to "standardized measures of accountability" with the "functional literacy" orientation of the United States since the late 1980s (Demetrion, 2005, p. ix). Both the critical literacy and the NLS orientations may be more attractive for long-term immigrant learners, especially those who did not do well under the more functional, competency-based K–12 model (Demetrion, 2005). However, federal laws and regulations often favor the more means-to-an-end and accountability orientation of the functional literacy paradigm, and consequently, this model is most prevalent.

According to Demetrion (2005, cited in Mertens, 1998), all three literacy orientations favor particular research methods based on their goals. Functional literacy corresponds to the positivist/post-positivist research tradition in which quantitative, experimental, and generalizable findings are preferred. Critical literacy is emancipatory and transformative and relies on qualitative description and case studies. The NLS model is interpretive/constructivist and uses anthropological ethnographic methods, preferring qualitative data and *thick description* (detailed and thorough description) (Geertz, 1973) to contextualize its findings. Table 1 shows some of the key features of each paradigm.

Standards for adult ESL/EFL students

D. Murray (2005) compares various expectations that Australia and other English-speaking countries such as Canada, Great Britain, New Zealand, and the United States have for non-native English-speaking immigrants. In all cases, individuals must demonstrate a familiarity or basic proficiency in English and knowledge of the culture to become citizens. This can mean anything from taking a course focusing on language and culture to demonstrating proficiency in an oral and/or written test.

Australia has been at the forefront of identifying goals for students to listen, speak, read, and write functional English through its three Certificates in Spoken and Written English (CSWE)

Table I. Three Paradigms of Adult ESL/EFL Literacy

	Paradigm Features		
	Functional Literacy	**New Literacy Studies**	**Critical Literacy**
Goal of research	Accept the existence of an objective reality, attempt to investigate reality through scientific experimental research	Identify and respect different discourses, attempt to describe social interaction within real human contexts	Identify discourses that are privileged or marginalized, and seek reform for oppressed social groups
Type of research	Positivist/post-positivist, neopositivism, behaviorist	Interpretive/constructivist, practitioner-based	Emancipatory, transformative
Methods	Quantitative, experimental, quasi-experimental, correlational, causal, comparative, generalizable	Qualitative, ethnographic, detailed description, naturalistic, phenomenological, hermeneutic, symbolic interaction	Qualitative and case studies
Political association	Capitalist, assimilationist	Liberal, humanist, acculturationist	Neo-Marxist, nonviolent revolution
Important works	*Reach Higher, America: Overcoming Crisis in the U.S. Workforce* (National Commission on Adult Literacy, 2008)	*Ways with Words: Language, Life, and Work in Communities and Classrooms* (Heath, 1983)	*Pedagogy of the Oppressed* (Freire, 1970)

(Adult Migrant English Program Research Centre, 2011). Since 1945, when large waves of immigrants began streaming into Australia, the country set up the Adult Migrant English Program (AMEP) to facilitate the settlement of people from many different countries (Allender, 1998). This program has provided social services as well as language training following the CSWE curriculum, which prepares students with beginning through intermediate proficiency to function in everyday life.

In Canada, the nationally funded program Language Instruction for Newcomers to Canada (LINC), which has been managed through Citizenship and Immigration Canada since 1994 (Citizenship and Immigration Canada, 2012), has provided instruction in English and French to help immigrants integrate into Canadian society. Canada has a national English for speakers of other languages (ESOL) curriculum and an assessment framework. Their benchmarks are descriptive scales of ESL proficiency and are used as a guide in syllabus design. The Canadian Benchmarks 2000 (Pawlikowski-Smith, 2000) are partially based on the Australian CSWE (Peirce & Stewart, 1997).

D. Murray (2005) noted that the United States and the United Kingdom historically have conflated adult ESL under the umbrella of adult education, with native English speakers not clearly distinguished from ESL speakers, thus leading to a diminished focus on the needs of non-native English-speaking learners. In the 1990s, the National Institute for Literacy (NIFL) in the United States initiated a standards project called Equipped for the Future (EFF). This project included a framework and performance assessment benchmarks by which adults could achieve national goals within a global economy. However, it was later abandoned in favor of collecting information through the National Reporting System of core outcome measures related to more basic educational gains, employment and attainments of secondary school diplomas or the equivalent, or placement in post-secondary training or education (Demetrion, 2005).

In 2001, the United Kingdom added the Adult ESOL Core Curriculum to the national standards for adult literacy (Excellence Gateway, 2012). Since 2004, the United Kingdom has had a systematic framework that defines the skills, knowledge, and understanding that non-native speakers will need to demonstrate to achieve national standards. An Adult ESOL Strategy has been developed for Scotland that includes information about teaching, learning, and assessment to prepare learners with the relevant skills to enter the workplace and participate more fully in Scottish society (The Scottish Government, 2007).

In 2003, New Zealand developed the Adult ESOL Strategy to provide increased opportunities for non-native English speakers to learn English and participate in New Zealand's cultural life. Increased national funding has improved the accessibility of a variety of programs, but there is still no national curriculum for adult ESOL (D. Murray, 2005).

For both ESL and EFL settings, the international association of Teachers of English to Speakers of Other Languages (TESOL) has published sets of standards that can be used around the world. The *Standards for Adult Education ESL Programs* (Teachers of English to Speakers of Other Languages, 2003) are best used in English-speaking settings and specify standards not only for learner achievement but also for other aspects of programs, including program structure, administration, and planning; curriculum and instructional materials; instruction; learner recruitment, intake, and orientation; learner retention and transition; assessment and learner gains; employment conditions and staffing; professional development and staff evaluation; and support services. The *Standards for ESL/EFL Teachers of Adults* (Teachers of English to Speakers of Other Languages, 2008) specify what teachers in English-speaking and non-English-speaking contexts should know about planning, instruction, assessment, identity and context, language proficiency, the learning process, content, and commitment and professionalism.

In Europe, the CEFR is a standard through which adolescents and adults (in adult schools or colleges) can move from one European country to another and establish a record of development through a language portfolio documenting proficiency in one or more languages (Council of Europe, 2012). This standard builds on previous work by the Council of Europe on the threshold level, the level at which learners could learn enough of a language to participate in everyday communication (van Ek, 1975). The CEFR expands this standard to span beginner through advanced proficiency levels of language competence, which are mutually recognized by all member nations of the Council of Europe.

In many other EFL settings, regardless of existing international standards or benchmarks, the ministry of education in any country may determine the level, type of English, and materials for English study for that country. For example, in Japan, reading, grammar, and translation are emphasized since this is the focus of the college entrance exam (S. L. McKay, 1992). In many countries, no oral exam is administered at all.

Teacher certification and staff development

ESL settings. The need for qualified adult ESL teachers is great, especially considering the cultural and logistical complexity of most adult ESL classrooms. However, countries, and even states and provinces within countries, differ in the kind of certification they require. This ranges from no requirement to a college degree. For many programs, staff development consists of voluntary attendance at workshops, conferences, or seminars rather than paid professional development; this is one of the reasons that teaching morale in many adult ESL settings can be quite low.

Various staff development models exist. Ziegler and Bingman (2007) found that in-service training that takes place with teachers in their own classrooms is most successful. Paid in-service training is even more motivating but not always feasible. In places where face-to-face staff development is not feasible, technical assistance networks often provide an alternative. Some countries operate literacy resource centers that provide training, information, and technical assistance to ESL teachers. In the United Kingdom, for example, the National Research and Development Centre for Adult Literacy and Numeracy focuses on promoting research and quality professional practice in national and international projects (Paton & Wilkins, 2009, for an example). The Centre provides consultancies, helpful publications, and practitioner resources.[4]

Listservs at schools or through local, regional, or national ESL or literacy organizations attune instructors to the latest developments in the field and provide them with opportunities to reflect and jointly solve important problems through the web. These types of supports are often appreciated by teachers who do not have sufficient training or time to do face-to-face training while at work. (See Crandall & Finn Miller, this volume, for more information on professional development.)

EFL settings. The same range of certification requirements, from limited to extensive, may apply in EFL settings. Individuals can apply for part-time and full-time jobs, but those with the appropriate certification and training will likely be hired for the best positions. Often native English speakers who have no formal training in TESOL are hired in EFL settings. However, these jobs may not be permanent or be at the most reputable schools. More demanding full-time jobs may require individuals to have a certificate or Master's degree in TESOL and apply for employment through a formal process.

Native English speakers without training may be fairly successful in tutoring students in small conversation groups but may be less successful in preparing college-bound students for the reading and writing demands of an academic environment. In these cases, native and near-native English-speaking individuals with formal pedagogical training are preferred.

CLASSROOM APPLICATIONS

How can the philosophical and research paradigms and standards discussed earlier be applied to the adult ESL classroom? Each paradigm (functional literacy, NLS, and critical literacy) suggests particular choices when planning ESL programs in terms of objectives, methods, techniques, materials, and assessments. There are also some commonalities in approaches. Needs assessment and tailoring instruction to learners' needs and interests are important to all three perspectives; however, these may be more prominent in the critical literacy orientation. Where proponents of a functional literacy approach may survey students on the first day of class about what they want to learn, proponents of a critical literacy model may require an ongoing student-negotiated syllabus throughout the school term. The communicative approach and using language for real purposes are characteristic of all three paradigms. Adult language pedagogy has moved past the drill and kill of the audiolingual method, although certain drilling techniques for learning vocabulary or memorizing important information at certain times might be acceptable in all three paradigms. (See Celce-Murcia on methods, this volume.)

Teachers working in all three paradigms may also address students' different learning styles. H. Gardner (1993) has identified multiple intelligences that different learners exhibit. (See also Shin, this volume.) They include verbal/linguis-tic, musical, logical/mathematical, spatial/visual, bodily/kinesthetic, intrapersonal, and natural/environmental intelligences. Students who learn best through pictures may have a spatial/visual preference. Students who learn best by demonstration and showing versus telling may have a bodily/kinesthetic preference. In addition to addressing learning styles, all three paradigms may also include a variety of assessments, including placement, diagnostic, and achievement measures.

The adult education ESL or EFL teacher (no matter the paradigm) also needs to have a good understanding of culture. Whether a bilingual Spanish-English speaker teaching English at a private ESL school in the United States or an English speaker teaching EFL at a language center in Thailand, the teacher must be familiar with the educational system and culture of the host country. Teachers should familiarize themselves with the customs and cultural values of the mainstream culture as well as the prominent subcultures in the areas where they teach. Doing this will prevent them from unknowingly making uninformed or unintentionally offensive comments when working with English materials in the classroom, such as making references to dating or drinking alcohol in Muslim areas of the EFL world or neglecting to teach international students what plagiarism is and its potential consequences in U.S. academic settings.

Each type of curriculum may lean toward certain instructional methods, materials, and tests more than the other. For example, the more culturally conservative, school-based programs may incorporate functionally and competency-based syllabi, skills-based activities, textbook materials, and commercial tests. In contrast, the more culturally liberal, community-based private programs may embrace task- or project-based syllabi, problem-posing materials, and portfolios.

Sample lessons for adult learners

To provide an understanding of the types of techniques and materials that may be appropriate for adult students in ESL/EFL settings in relation to the standards mentioned earlier, several sample 30–60 minute lessons are presented next for learners in beginning through advanced levels. The appropriate standard is mentioned as well as a

Table 2. Sample Activities for Adult ESL or EFL Classes

Level	Literacy paradigm	Setting	Type of class	Standard	Type of activity
Beginning	Functional literacy	ESL	Listening/speaking; survival	Canadian Benchmarks	Total Physical Response: the doctor's office
Low intermediate	New literacy studies	ESL	Multiskills; family literacy	TESOL Standards	Reading comprehension using multiple intelligences: school testing
Advanced	Critical literacy	EFL	Multiskills; general EFL	CEFR	Problem posing: housing issues

specific objective that describes the activity. Table 2 provides a summary of these activities.

Sample lesson 1: Applying the Canadian Benchmarks with a low-beginning-level class. The sample lesson "The Doctor's Office" (see Figure 1) uses a Canadian Benchmark standard for a beginning level class. The teacher uses the popular teaching method Total Physical Response (TPR), in which students are encouraged to listen to a series of commands and follow them (Larsen-Freeman & Anderson, 2011). They are not asked to say the commands at first but just to listen to the teacher's model. Because some students are not familiar with this nontraditional method, an introduction to the

---

ESL Lesson Plan Topic: The Doctor's Office (30 minutes)

Standard: Follow simple instructions and positive and negative commands and requests. (*Listening Canadian Benchmark 1:* Initial basic proficiency)

Objective: To demonstrate understanding of positive commands, the student will respond correctly to commands related to a visit to a doctor's office.

1. The teacher shows a picture of a patient checking in for an appointment at the doctor's office. (If all students speak one language, she briefly explains the picture in the students' native language. If the students speak multiple languages, she mimes what the situation is using the picture. In either case, she continues the rest of the lesson all in English.)
2. The teacher asks for four volunteers to sit beside her on four chairs at the front of the room. She tells the small group *not* to speak at this time but just to listen and watch what she does. She repeats the following commands several times while demonstrating them with gestures and exaggerated movements: *stand up, walk to a desk, sign your name, walk to a chair, sit down.* Students watch as the teacher performs the commands but they do not speak.
3. The teacher has the students in the small group listen and perform the commands, following her model three times without speaking. She asks them to use the accompanying gestures for each command (e.g., pretend they are holding a pencil when they sign their names). She asks the rest of the class to just watch and listen.
4. The teacher adds more commands and follows the same pattern as before but then mixes up the order. She again tells the students in the small group to perform the commands but not to speak. Commands: *stand up, walk to a desk, sign your name, walk to a chair, sit down, read a magazine* (new command), *listen for your name* (new command), *stand up, walk to a door* (new command), *say hello to the nurse* (new command).
5. The teacher reorders the commands in random sequences: *stand up, read a magazine, say hello to the nurse, sit down, stand up, walk to a desk, walk to a door, walk to a desk, read a magazine, sign your name, sit down,* and so on. Again, students perform the commands.
6. The teacher gives the commands again, but this time she remains seated. Students follow the commands, using the accompanying gestures.
7. The teacher asks for one volunteer in the small group to follow the same commands in random order. The teacher repeats the sequence three times.
8. The teacher turns to whole class and asks them to follow commands. She remains in her seat. She repeats random sequences several times.
9. The teacher demonstrates commands and asks all students to orally repeat the commands after her. She repeats the sequence several times until students are comfortable with the pronunciation of all the commands.
10. One volunteer student gives a random sequence of commands to the whole class, followed by paired students giving commands to each other. Those listening perform the commands with accompanying gestures to demonstrate comprehension.

Figure 1. Sample lesson plan: The doctor's office.

Lesson Plan Topic: School Testing (60 minutes)

Standard: Individual can read simple material on familiar subjects and comprehend with high accuracy simple and compound sentences in single or linked paragraphs containing familiar vocabulary. (*TESOL Standards for Low Intermediate ESL Literacy Level*)

Objective: To demonstrate reading comprehension of linked paragraphs, students will collaboratively read a short passage about learner performance on tests and then create lists, stories, skits, songs, or chants about promoting their children's academic success.

1. *Pre-reading.* The teacher shows students a sample achievement test and asks several questions, writing key words on the board or using pictures to clarify if necessary (spatial/visual strategy): "How well do you think English learners do on tests? How are test results reported? What does it mean to be reclassified? Who decides who should be reclassified?" Students indicate the names of tests, their characteristics, test results, and the reasons for the results, if they know.
2. The teacher continues to ask more questions: "Have your children taken achievement tests? What is contained in the test? What scores did your children get? Why did they get the scores they did? How do you feel about their performance? Do you think the scores fairly reflect what they can do? How will these scores affect their chances for college or advanced work opportunities?" (intrapersonal strategy). Students reflect on their children's performance on tests and how this may affect their future success; they share their ideas with a partner.
3. *During reading.* The teacher divides class into small groups and asks students to read a short passage about the performance of English language learners on the California English Language Development Test. They read it twice, first silently and then cooperatively in groups. They underline new words or mark concepts they do not understand. The teacher explains new words and concepts as needed. Each student in a group reads silently and then students take turns reading aloud and asking each other questions (interpersonal strategy). If they need help, they ask the teacher or consult a dictionary.
4. *Post-reading.* The teacher asks groups of students to demonstrate, in a method of their choice, what they have learned from the reading passage and how they might help their children succeed.
   - *Option 1.* Describe the steps you will follow to help your child succeed at school (logical/mathematical intelligence strategy).
   - *Option 2.* Write a story or skit about a student who was able to improve his or her test score with his or her parents' help (linguistic intelligence strategy).
   - *Option 3.* Write a song or rhythmic chant about what a student can do to go to college (musical intelligence strategy).
5. The teacher asks each student to stand up, stretch, and walk around before the group presentations. She also passes out candy to all students to energize them during their performances (bodily/kinesthetic strategy). Student groups present their lists, stories, skits, songs, or chants to the other groups in the class.

Figure 2. Sample lesson plan: School testing.

method in the students' native language (if it is a homogeneous group) sometimes precedes the instruction. The topic is a popular functional survival topic related to a doctor's office visit and works well with preliterate or semiliterate learners.

Sample lesson 2: Applying the TESOL standards with a low-intermediate-level class. The sample lesson "School Testing" (see Figure 2) is tailored for a low-intermediate class in an ESL family literacy setting. Parents, often mothers, take classes related to the education of their children. In this activity, students are reading a text taken from a local newspaper reporting on important test results that can affect the educational future of their children. Parents may be aware that their children are not performing well on tests, but they may not know how to help them. This lesson addresses a TESOL standard and uses multiple intelligences techniques to address the different learning styles and multiple literacies of the students.

Sample lesson 3: Applying the CEFR with an advanced-level class. The sample lesson "Complaining about Housing Issues" (see Figure 3) addresses an advanced-level objective of the CEFR. This lesson takes place in a location where there are many new immigrants and English is used as a lingua franca in an EFL setting. It is a critical literacy lesson because it relates to a housing problem that several students have reported. This lesson uses codes, dialogues, and action plans to help students resolve their problems in English.

Building learning communities

Based on the broad range of learner types and curricula in adult ESL/EFL programs discussed in this chapter, it is hard to generalize about what kind of classroom supports will work best for students. However, the large proportion of older students who have diverse cultural backgrounds, disabilities, and lack of school experience and success surely deserves attention. First and foremost, teachers should try to build a sense of community in their own classrooms. McKay and Tom (2001) suggest

EFL Lesson Plan Topic: Complaining about Housing Issues (45 minutes)

Standard: Can use language flexibly for social, academic, and professional purposes (*Common European Framework, Advanced Level, C1*)

Objective: To use language flexibly for social purposes, the students will develop an action plan to resolve a personal housing problem with their landlords.

1. *Presentation of code.* The teacher is aware that most students live in low-income apartment complexes that are managed by absentee landlords. English is the lingua franca between landlord and tenant. The teacher shows a photo (Figure 4) of a run-down apartment.
2. *Dialogue.* The teacher asks the students several questions to uncover their feelings about their housing situations: "What do you see in the photo? What seems to be the problem? Has anything similar happened to you? Why do you think this is a problem?" The teacher may ask additional questions (e.g., "What else is wrong? Does the electricity work? Are there leaky toilets or faucets? Is there an infestation of pests?"). If appropriate, the teacher may also add information about *slumlords* (landlords who often do not live on or near the property and do little maintenance because they are more interested in profit than the comfort of their tenants). Students talk about the problem of housing, small quarters, damaged property, leaky ceilings, and so on. If they have had similar problems, they may compare their apartments to the photo or talk about additional problems they have had.
3. *Action plan.* The teacher asks students what they would like to do about the problem. The teacher encourages students to share their stories and possible solutions. Students suggest complaining to the landlord and making specific requests. Other students state that this has not worked. Still others suggest filing a complaint with the city council or contacting a public attorney.
4. *Communication practice.* The teacher reminds students of the difference between short-term and long-term approaches to problems. The teacher creates a short dialogue on the blackboard that allows students to practice clearly stating their problem to their landlords to solve a short-term problem. She asks two students to read the dialogue.

   <u>On the Telephone</u>.

   Tenant: Hello, my name is Jan Wysocki, and I am calling to complain about lack of heat in my apartment.
   Landlord: I am sorry. That is not my responsibility.
   Tenant: Excuse me, but the legal code requires that owners are responsible for providing safe and habitable living conditions for their tenants. When will you be able to come out to check on this matter?
   Landlord: I will be in town at the end of the month.
   Tenant: I am sorry. That is too late. If you do not send someone to fix this in two days, I will be filing a complaint with the City Council.

5. Then the teacher asks students to write their own dialogues in pairs, inserting new information that suits their particular problems ("I am calling to complain about ___," e.g., *lack of water, a broken window, a broken lock*). Students perform their dialogues in front of the class, and the whole class discusses other, long-term solutions to their particular problems.

Figure 3. Sample lesson plan: Complaining about housing issues.

techniques like seating students in circles or semi-circles instead of rows to create a friendlier atmosphere. They also recommend using classroom furniture that moves easily to facilitate group work. If classrooms are too small, some student groups can move to the hallways so that they can hear each other and comfortably work together. Teachers can display photographs of students or activities on bulletin boards (or if the class is in borrowed space, they can display them on portable pieces of poster board).

Another idea is for teachers to use name tags to help students become better acquainted. Teachers can also establish regular routines to signal to students that class will begin or is coming

Figure 4. Photo of a run-down apartment.

to a close. Magy and Price (2011) suggest, at the beginning of class, designating students to perform the classroom jobs of trainer (greeter and mentor to new students), cell phone monitor, materials manager, and custodian to help prepare them for the soft skills of work. McKay and Tom (2001) suggest ways of closing the class, such as summarizing the day's lesson or previewing the next lesson.

Drago-Severson (2004a) and Weinstein (1999, 2004) recommend the use of student narratives and autobiographies to make it possible for learners to share their backgrounds and experiences and express their own voices with each other and their instructors. Peirce (1995) also believes that observations in diaries and journals can be useful to students to examine communicative interactions, breakdowns, surprising occurrences, and cross-cultural differences. In doing so, "learners may be able to critically engage their histories and their experiences from a position of strength rather than a position of weakness." She also suggests drama where students can learn to "claim the right to speak outside of the classroom" (pp. 27–28).

Blogs, social networks, email, texting, YouTube, and distribution lists make it possible for students to share their stories, photos, videos, and ideas and to give and solicit assistance with real-life needs. (See also Sokolik, this volume.) Adult schools can also arrange service-learning by matching college students with adult students in ESL classes, expanding communication networks and opportunities for friendship (Carr, Eyring, & Gallego, 2006). Some schools offer adult diplomas or sponsor adult graduation ceremonies to help learners celebrate their own and their classmates' accomplishments.

FUTURE TRENDS

Based on the large number of underserved adult learners, reduced funding in many areas, and the importance of educating all adults for the twenty-first century, growth in adult English programs should be a high priority. According to *Adult ESL Language and Literacy Instruction: A Vision and Action Agenda for the 21st Century* (Teachers of English to Speakers of Other Languages, 2000), adult ESL education "must take place within a system that is on a par with K-12 and higher education in terms of status, infrastructure, attention, and financial support" (p. 6). TESOL recommends five components that must work together toward a common goal:

1. *Program delivery.* Provide more classes for all types of adult ESL learners as well as greater facilitation of the noninstructional services whose absence hinders participation: child care, health care, transportation, social and legal counseling in human and civil rights, job counseling, placement and employment services, immigration service, and mental health counseling.
2. *Collaborations.* Interact with organizations and institutions outside the instructional programs, including community-based and volunteer organizations, labor unions, health-care organizations, businesses, public schools and community colleges, and immigrant advocacy organizations.
3. *Policies.* Be more active in making policies at national, state, and local levels responsive to the ever-changing population of adult ESL learners and in implementing them with all the stakeholders.
4. *Resources.* Generate funds for quality instruction and research.
5. *Research.* Establish research priorities related to adult ESL, and ensure that the results are clear, relevant, and accessible to practitioners.

Many of these goals are pertinent to adult EFL programs as well. More specifically, these might include new methods of program delivery (e.g., online and web-based instruction to reach larger numbers of students), greater articulation and collaboration between those offering instruction (e.g., to capitalize on limited target-language resources), new national language policies (e.g., college entrance exams with English components or higher standards for teachers), resources (e.g., expanded adult and vocational school funding for English), and targeted research (e.g., to identify effective instructional strategies and programs in EFL settings). Quigley (1993) emphasized the need to understand how learners themselves make sense of their experiences in adult programs to improve policy and practice. In both ESL and EFL settings, it will be important to include ways to collect data from learners themselves about these issues as we move to the future.

CONCLUSION

The need for quality adult ESL/EFL instruction around the world is great. Adults have many advantages over younger learners for successful language learning; however, motivational and practical factors sometimes hinder their progress. Different paradigms of instruction suggest different priorities for instruction in adult ESL/EFL programs, and variations in teacher certification and staff development sometimes affect the effective delivery of instruction. Whatever the approach, programs should support the development of learning communities sensitive to the time, real needs, and learning constraints of their participants.

SUMMARY

➤ Large numbers of adult ESL/EFL learners are enrolled in classes internationally.

➤ Many needs of diverse adult ESL/EFL learners are unmet due to insufficient opportunities for appropriate instruction as well as personal factors.

➤ Effective adult ESL/EFL programs provide opportunities for learner input in instruction.

➤ Common standards provide a way for teachers to deliver systematic and comprehensive English language instruction and assessment.

➤ Adult ESL learners and teachers work best in supportive learning communities.

➤ Future goals should include better program delivery, improved collaborations, appropriate policies, more resources, and better research.

DISCUSSION QUESTIONS

1. Dissect the Experience at the beginning of the chapter using the features of adult ESL classrooms discussed in this chapter. Would students be interested in the lesson? Which aspects of the lesson were done well? What could have been improved? How might the lesson have differed if it had been delivered to a group of EFL learners? Refer to sections in the chapter to explain your answers.

2. Discuss the three paradigms of adult literacy instruction. Which one seems most appropriate for an adult ESL/EFL class that you have observed or that you teach? In your response, cite information from this chapter to explain why.

3. What are the diverse types of backgrounds and concerns that adult learners bring to the classroom? How can the instructor help create a positive learning environment for all types of students? What methods and techniques work best in a complex learning environment of this type?

4. "Open-entry, open-exit" ESL programs have their advantages and disadvantages. On the one hand, they are responsive to students' family and work schedules and allow students to enter or exit at any time. However, they have also been criticized for their ineffectiveness in building student learning communities, which lead to increased student retention. Debate the pros and cons of open-enrollment versus managed-enrollment (i.e., programs with shorter terms of several weeks).

5. How can standards and staff development be used to improve instruction at a school with which you are familiar? Discuss specific recommendations you would make and explain the direct and indirect effects they could have on student learning.

SUGGESTED ACTIVITIES

1. Subscribe to a listserv or discussion list[5] which focuses on the issues of teaching English to adult learners. Participate in the discussion list over the course of a school term. Write a report summarizing some of the major concerns or interests of the participants.

2. Peruse the recordings of the Multimedia Adult English Learner Corpus from the ESOL Lab School at Portland State University.[6] Use these recordings to investigate classroom questions about adult ESL methodology and techniques, or compare ESL methodology and techniques to those used in EFL.

3. Write a research paper investigating adult ESL in one of the following English-dominant countries: the United States, Canada, Australia, New Zealand, England, Scotland, Ireland, or South Africa. Discuss the types of programs, learner characteristics, classroom settings, funding, standards, curriculum, and assessment that currently affect ESL instruction in the country you researched.

4. Divide the class into three groups and assign one literacy paradigm to each group: functional literacy, NLS, or critical literacy. Then, have each group research the paradigm it has been assigned and argue in favor of it. After the debate, each student should write a two-page essay arguing for the paradigm that is best for his or her particular ESL/EFL setting.

5. Select a set of standards approved or commonly used in your country. Then write a 50-minute lesson plan for a real or imaginary group addressing one objective. Include appropriate instructional sequences, materials, and assessments. Review the three sample lesson plans in this chapter for ideas.

FURTHER READING

Gunderson, L. (2009). *ESL (ELL) literacy instruction: A guidebook to theory and practice* (2nd ed.). New York, NY: Routledge.

This book provides an excellent discussion of current issues in ESL literacy instruction and proposes appropriate instructional approaches based on adult learners' proficiency levels and previous educational experiences.

Papen, U. (2005). *Adult literacy as social practice: More than skills.* London, UK: Routledge.

The author distinguishes different approaches to literacy in the United Kingdom and around the world and advocates a critical approach rather than a functional approach to teaching reading, writing, and numeracy to adults.

Parrish, B. (2004). *Teaching adult ESL.* Chicago, IL: McGraw Hill ELT.

This book provides an overview of programs, approaches, and techniques for teaching adult ESL learners. Information about standards, assessment, and materials are made accessible to individuals preparing to teach in school-based and community-based programs.

Teachers of English to Speakers of Other Languages. (2008). *Standards for ESL/EFL teachers of adults.* Alexandria, VA: Author.

This set of standards specifies what teachers of adult language learners around the world should know about planning, instructing, assessing, identity and context, language proficiency, learning, content, and commitment and professionalism.

ENDNOTES

[1] I am grateful for the time provided by a sabbatical at California State University, Fullerton, to conduct the research for this chapter. I also appreciate feedback on earlier drafts of this article from colleagues in the field: Doreen Doherty, Lori Howard, Robert Jenkins, Ronna Magy, and Donna Price.

[2] In the United States, 10–29.4% of high school dropouts have learning disabilities such as dyslexia, attention deficit disorder, and executive function disorder (Silver-Pacuilla, 2007). Of the overall population served in adult education, half of the adult students have learning disabilities.

[3] The New London Group is a group of 10 scholars who met in New London, New Hampshire, to discuss the emerging pedagogy that is accompanying the new literacies or multiliteracies engendered by globalization, technology, and social and cultural diversity (see The New London Group, 1996).

[4] The website for the National Research and Development Centre for Adult Literacy and Numeracy can be found at http://www.nrdc.org.uk/

[5] Good examples are the discussion lists at the Literacy Information and Communication System (LINCS) website, http://lincs.ed.gov/

[6] See the Multimedia Adult English Learner Corpus from the ESOL Lab School, Portland State University, available at http://www.labschool.pdx.edu

Focus on the Teacher

37 | Non-Native English-Speaking Teachers in the Profession

LÍA D. KAMHI-STEIN

KEY QUESTIONS

➤ How should the terms native speaker and non-native speaker be defined?

➤ How has the World Englishes movement contributed to the role and status of non-native English-speaking professionals?

➤ What are some strategies that non-native English teachers-in-preparation and their teacher educators may use to enhance the professional development of non-native English-speaking professionals?

EXPERIENCE

There was a sharp knock on the door of my university office. A graduate student whom I often see at departmental seminars and parties popped his head inside the door and said, "Do you know any native speakers [of English]?" He had a sheet of paper with approximately 20 sentences and phrases, and he wanted a native speaker to go over them. I offered to look at them. He reluctantly handed me the sheet, and I did not find it difficult to give him the "correct" answers. Indeed, the problems and questions were so simple that most teachers of English as a second language (ESL), particularly at the higher levels where there is emphasis on colloquialisms and where you are supposed to have a "feel" for the language, could easily have answered them. I pointed out a few phrases that I would not use and others that I considered to be acceptable. He thanked me and as he was leaving said, "Would a native speaker agree with you on these suggestions?" (Nuzhat Amin, 2004, a speaker of Pakistani English)

Once at a job interview for an English as a Foreign Language (EFL) teaching position in Seoul, Korea, an employer told me he did not know how to categorize me. "You sound like an American, yet you are a Korean. You don't sound like a Korean, but you can't be a Korean-American because you're not an American citizen. And to make matters worse, you don't hold a degree from an American university," he said. (Hee Jin Kim, in Kamhi-Stein, in press)

Are you a native speaker or a nonnative speaker of English? Well, my answer is neither one. How do I perceive myself? I perceive myself as a bilingual or a multicompetent speaker. I learned English and Tagalog at the same time, and I have been code-switching ever since I can remember. My fluency in these two languages has made me flexible, powerful, and skillful in responding to all of life's demands. (Veneza Angel Pablico, in Kamhi-Stein, in press)

The experiences of Nuzhat, Hee Jin, and Veneza Angel are not unique. Instead, they reflect those of many English language teachers working in a variety of settings. In this chapter, I discuss these teachers' experiences and identify factors that contribute to non-native English-speaking (NNES) teachers' success as language teachers.

WHAT IS A NON-NATIVE ENGLISH-SPEAKING PROFESSIONAL?

Traditionally, the term *native speaker* has been used to refer to "someone who learned a language in a natural setting from childhood as first or sole language" (Kachru & Nelson, 1996, p. 81). The validity of the *native speaker construct* (i.e., the notion that all native speakers share one and the same language and culture) has been challenged on the basis that it is an abstraction based on a person's linguistic and physical characteristics (Kramsch, 1998a). In fact, Amin (2004) argues that the construct of the native speaker "is not only about language competence but is deeply embedded in discourses of racism and colonialism" (p. 62). The term has also been challenged on the basis that it gives the impression—a false one indeed—that there is linguistic unity in the world (Kaplan, 1999) and that native speakers speak only a standard variety of their language (Kramsch, 1998a). The professional literature identifies three different positions on the native English speaker (NES)/NNES dichotomy, as represented in Figures 1, 2, and 3.

The first position, shown in Figure 1, is what J. Liu (1999) calls the "noninterface position" (p. 86). This position is best represented by the pioneering work of Medgyes (1994, 2001), who sees teachers as belonging in either the NES or NNES category. For the purposes of Medgyes's research these two groups are considered to be two completely different, and homogeneous, "species" (Medgyes, 2001, p. 434).

The second position, depicted in Figure 2, draws on the work of A. Davies (2003), who supports the idea that "the native speaker is a fine myth: we need it as a model, a goal, almost an inspiration" (p. 197). Davies (2003) further suggests that a second language (L2) learner "can become a native speaker of a target language" (p. 210), though with difficulty. However, Davies views the fundamental difference between NES and NNES as one of power; native speaker status is therefore an issue

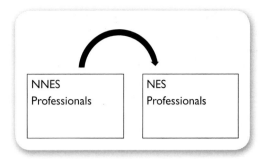

Figure 2. With difficulty, NNES professionals can become NES professionals.

of confidence and identity rather than an issue of which language the speaker learns as a first language (L1).

The final position, shown in Figure 3, draws on the ideas of researchers who argue that the labels native speaker and non-native speaker are in themselves problematic (e.g., Canagarajah, 1999; V. Cook, 1999; Jenkins, 2011, personal communication) since they emphasize the biological rather than the social factors affecting the L2 learning process. Researchers like Amin (2004) further argue that the native speaker construct—and by extension, the *native speaker fallacy* (i.e., the idea that the native speaker is the ideal language teacher)—should be eliminated because this construct "divides the profession according to a caste system" (p. 74). In this respect, researchers like Kramsch (1998b) and Velasco-Martin (2004) point out that the native and non-native speaker labels have no relevance in multilingual or multicultural settings such as the European Community, where teachers of English are perceived to be "intercultural speakers." V. Cook (1999) further proposes the use of the term "multicompetent language users" (p. 185) as a replacement for the terms native and non-native speaker since this term allows L2 users to be viewed in a positive light rather than as "failed native speakers" (p. 185).

| NNES professionals | ≠ | NES professionals |

Figure 1. NES professionals and NNES professionals are different.

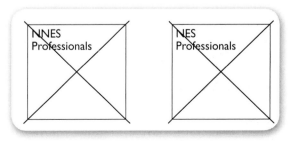

Figure 3. Labels are perceived as problematic.

The belief that native and non-native speakers are completely different (as represented in Figure 1) has been criticized in the field, most insightfully by Pasternak and Bailey (2004), who argue that being a native speaker of a language is not the same as being proficient in that language. They suggest that, rather than focusing on the native and non-native speaker constructs, the field of teaching English to speakers of other languages (TESOL) should place emphasis instead on issues of language proficiency and professionalism and that both constructs should be viewed on a continuum rather than as an either/or proposition. Figure 4 depicts Pasternak and Bailey's (2004) continua of language proficiency and professional preparation, with four possible combinations. As we see in the figure, teachers falling in Quadrant 1 are those who are proficient in the target language and are professionally prepared; conversely, teachers falling in Quadrant 4 are those who are neither proficient nor have professional preparation. Teachers falling in Quadrant 2 are professionally prepared and not proficient in the target language, and finally teachers falling in Quadrant 3 are proficient in the target language but not professionally prepared.

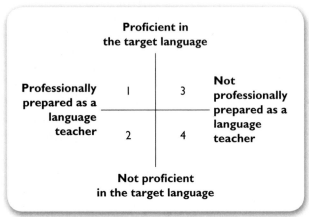

Figure 4. Continua of target-language proficiency and professional preparation.

Regarding the problematic nature of the terms, and more specifically, the term *NNES professional*, three additional points need to be made:

1. In spite of the fact that the terms native and non-native speaker have been challenged by researchers, as argued by Moussu and Llurda (2008), the same researchers still use the terms "in order to start constructing their supporting argumentation" (p. 318).

2. For years, the term *non-native English speaker* was used with negative connotations. In this view, being a non-native speaker is problematic because "it defines a group of people for what they are not" (Matsuda, 2003a, para. 2). Over the last few years, the term *non-native English-speaking professional* has begun to be reclaimed with a positive connotation—an idea that many support.[1] However, in no way does this mean that the term has become widely accepted by all NNES professionals. In fact, it is not uncommon to hear NNES professionals reject the term due to its negative historical connotations.

3. The label *non-native English-speaking teacher* is particularly problematic for novice ESL/EFL teachers who are visible minorities—those who do not resemble the stereotypical blond, blue-eyed American. In fact, it is not uncommon to find second-generation native speakers of English whose nativeness is challenged because they do not look like the idealized native speaker. Hee Jin Kim, whose scenario is presented at the beginning of this chapter, faced challenges to her native speaker status due to her appearance, in spite of the fact that she sounded like a NES. Like many other professionals, Hee Jin faced mistrust when she first started looking for teaching positions in and outside *inner-circle* countries (countries where English is the primary language) by administrators who require that applicants both *look* like native speakers and *be* native speakers of English[2] (Clark & Paran, 2007; Mahboob, Uhrig, Newman, & Hartford, 2004; Selvi, 2010). In this case, a change in how teachers present themselves, from non-native speaking professionals to multicompetent or bilingual professionals will allow them to see themselves in a positive light (Golombek & Jordan, 2005; Pavlenko, 2003).

While Pavlenko (2003) argues that the non-native speaker label is problematic, Medgyes (1994) argued that what is problematic is the "linguistic deficit" (p. 33) that NNES teachers suffer from. According to Medgyes, it is due to this deficit that non-native speakers have an "inferiority complex" (p. 40) and may implement instructional strategies that do not place them in a positive light vis-à-vis their NES counterparts[3] (see Medgyes,

2001, for a list of these strategies). Medgyes's (1983, 1994) view has been referred to as a "language as problem" perspective (Kamhi-Stein, 2005, p. 77).

Seidlhofer (1999) presents an alternative position, one that can be called a "language as resource" position (as cited in Kamhi-Stein, 2005, p. 77). Seidlhofer argues that NNES teachers should be viewed as "double agents" (p. 235) and that the dual role that NNES teachers play adds to their "value" (to use Seidlhofer's term). For Seidlhofer, these teachers perform their role as double agents by sharing their students' first language and culture and by helping to mediate between the two languages and cultures (a point also made by Velasco-Martin, 2004).

CONCEPTUAL UNDERPINNINGS

In this section I present an overview of selected research focusing on NNES professionals in relation to nativist and World Englishes perspectives; the intersection among race, language status, and hiring practices; the relationship among self-perceptions, language proficiency; instructional practices; and issues of teacher preparation. (See also the Celce-Murcia chapter on World Englishes, this volume.)

Nativist and World Englishes perspectives in the language classroom

When I started studying EFL in Argentina in 1965, my teachers, all NNES professionals, sought to provide me with native speaker models with the ultimate goal of having me sound like an idealized native speaker. Nowhere was this expectation more apparent than in the area of pronunciation. However, although my teachers had received professional preparation as EFL teachers and had taken several courses in English phonetics and phonology (with a strong emphasis on British Received Pronunciation), I sincerely doubt that they themselves truly had command of this variety of English.

The belief that a native speaker standard is the only acceptable standard is consistent with Quirk's (1990) "monocentric" view of the English language (as cited in Jenkins, 2006b, p. 171). This monocentric view, typical of nativist perspectives in place in the 1960s, applied to both users of *outer-circle* varieties (spoken in countries where English is widely used for educational, political, and business purposes) and to speakers of *expanding-circle*

varieties (spoken in countries where English is a foreign language, like Argentina). In the case of Amin, a speaker of an outer-circle variety of English (Pakistani English), the expectation that she sound like an idealized native speaker would not be relevant since outer-circle varieties have gone through a process of nativization in which these varieties have developed their own norms. In my own case, as a user of an expanding-circle variety of English, the expectation that my Argentinian teachers and I should sound like idealized native speakers was not realistic either. Expanding-circle users do not have their own norms but have instead traditionally relied on inner-circle norms (B. B. Kachru, 1985). In expanding-circle settings, factors like age, language aptitude, motivation, personality, affective variables, the learning setting, the amount of input received (as well as issues of identity) all contribute to the variety of English used and/or the level of proficiency attained.

Today, people who use English in the expanding and outer circles far outnumber those who use English as a native language in inner-circle settings (Kachru & Smith, 2008). English has become an "international commodity" (Burns, 2005, p. 2) and is no longer perceived as being the property of those in inner-circle settings (Widdowson, 1994). At the same time, the field of TESOL has experienced what B. B. Kachru (1992) calls a "paradigm shift" (p. 362), in that language teaching—at least in theory—no longer privileges the inner-circle varieties of English as the only acceptable standard. In contrast to a monocentric framework, in which only one standard is acceptable, what is appreciated from a World Englishes perspective is "the variation and cultural pluralism denoted by the term Englishes" (Kachru & Smith, 2008, p. 4).

In the language classroom, the most evident consequence of the paradigm shift is that, rather than having the emphasis of instruction placed on students acquiring a native-like pronunciation, emphasis is now placed on having them speak intelligibly. Intelligibility has been described by Smith (1992) as being one of three related components:

1. *Intelligibility*, involving the listener's ability to recognize words and utterances
2. *Comprehensibility*, involving the listener's ability to recognize the meaning of words or utterances
3. *Interpretability*, involving the listener's ability to understand the speaker's intentions

This shift in the goal of instruction from an idealized native speaker proficiency to intelligibility removes the burden from teachers and students of trying to sound like someone they are not; more important, it places emphasis on teaching students to communicate for real purposes rather than to imitate native speakers (Burns, 2005).

Research on intelligibility and comprehensibility supports two ideas. First, the more speakers (or students) listen to a particular variety of English, the more they become accustomed to that variety and the easier that variety becomes for them to understand.[4] In fact, a study by Moussu (2010) confirms that longer periods of exposure to NNES teachers positively affected ESL students' perceptions of their teachers' pronunciation (as well as their other skills). As Moussu (2010) notes, it could well be the case that students rate evidence of professionalism higher than issues of nativeness in English.

The second idea supported by the research is that teacher accentedness is independent of teacher intelligibility (Butler, 2007; Kim, 2008). In other words, language learners can in fact understand a teacher who is a non-native speaker. However, what a teacher's accent *has* been found to affect is students' perceptions of comprehensibility; that is, a teacher perceived to have a strong accent is also perceived to be difficult to understand (Kim, 2008). In turn, these perceptions lead students in EFL and ESL settings to have more positive attitudes toward teachers with a native speaker accent (Butler, 2007; Kim, 2008; Liang, 2002). However, it should be noted that, in spite of the EFL and ESL students' preference for NES teachers, ESL students have often been found to have difficulty differentiating between a NES and a NNES accent (Kelch & Santana-Williamson, 2002; Kim, 2008).

As previously suggested, the paradigm shift that changed the teaching goal from producing speakers with native-like accents to producing intelligible speakers has not been widely reflected in actual classrooms but has, instead, remained at the level of scholarship (a point that is discussed by Jenkins, 2006b). In fact, the notions that standard American and British English are the two prestigious varieties of English and that NES teachers are guardians of those varieties are still alive in many language classrooms around the world. In part, the mismatch between theory and practice can be attributed to the fact that the system in which teachers are educated plays an important role in shaping their self-perceptions and beliefs. More specifically, in expanding-circle settings, it is often the case that teacher preparation programs favor British and North American inner-circle language models along with inner-circle pedagogy (i.e., communicative language teaching). For these reasons, it is not unusual to find expanding-circle NNES teachers who measure their proficiency in relation to that of the idealized NES and who favor pedagogies that may not be the ones most appropriate to their setting or the ones most relevant to their students' needs and wants.

The intersection among race, language status, and hiring practices

Unfortunately, TESOL abounds with stories showing that the credibility of professionals who are visible minorities, regardless of whether they are native speakers of English, is challenged because they are perceived to be non-native speakers (Chacon, 2006; Govardhan, 2006; Nero, 2006). In fact, as noted by Nero (2006), the privilege of white teachers is "nowhere more evident than in hiring practices" (p. 29). This was the case for Hee Jin Kim (related in the Experience at the outset of this chapter), who sounded like a native speaker but did not look like one. As a result, a prospective employer chose not to hire her.

At this time, there is a small body of research focusing on the status of NNES teachers in relation to hiring practices in TESOL. Two such studies investigated hiring practices in: (1) U.S. intensive-English programs (Mahboob et al., 2004); and (2) a variety of institutions (private language schools, universities, and other educational institutions) in the United Kingdom (Clark & Paran, 2007). Taken together, both studies show that NES teachers far outnumbered NNES teachers in the programs investigated. In addition, both studies show that whenever great importance was accorded to native-speaker status by program administrators, there were fewer NES teachers on their staffs. Finally, both studies show that NES status was the most important hiring criterion and accounted for the high number of NES teachers in the programs (Clark & Paran, 2007; Mahboob et al., 2004).

In another study, Selvi (2010) analyzed the job advertisements on the TESOL association's Online Career Center[5] and on Dave's ESL Café,[6] a popular website that carries job advertisements from around the world. In his analysis, Selvi (2010) found that most of the advertisements called for "native or native-like/near-native proficiency" (p. 165). Moreover, in some instances, advertisements narrowed down the definition of *native speaker* to applicants with passports from countries such as Australia, Canada, Ireland, New Zealand, the United Kingdom, and the United States. In other instances, advertisers called for applications from American, Australian, South African, and Canadian teachers with European Union passports or from North Americans "whose first language is English (no heavy accents)" (Selvi, 2010, p. 170). The results of this study show that program administrators heavily favor NES over NNES teachers. Furthermore, the study shows that for these administrators, native-speaker status is equated to having been born in or having a passport from an English-dominant country.

Based on the results of these studies, it is clear that there is a need for NNES professionals to engage in advocacy activities to raise awareness about discriminatory hiring practices (Selvi, 2010). In other words, there is a need for advocacy designed to disabuse administrators of the notion that the native speaker is the ideal language teacher. In this respect, the TESOL association has produced two documents: *Statement on Nonnative Speakers of English and Hiring Practices* (1991)[7] and *Position Statement against Discrimination of Nonnative Speakers of English in the Field of TESOL* (2006).[8] The 1991 document stated that hiring decisions that are based solely on the native speaker criterion are discriminatory and are in "contradiction to sound linguistic research and pedagogical practice" (para. 3). The 2006 document also opposes discrimination against NNES teachers; it further argues that English language teachers should be proficient in English, regardless of status (native speaker or non-native speaker) and that hiring decisions should be made based on English language proficiency, teaching skills, teacher experience, and professional preparation. These statements have prompted discussion and raised awareness about discriminatory hiring practices. However, much still needs to be done to change hiring practices in the English language teaching profession.

While the findings discussed here may paint a somewhat grim picture, the reality is that NNES teachers do get hired. However, as explained by Amin (2004), teachers who are visible minorities (in the case of her research, female teachers) are often at a disadvantage in the hiring process because these teachers may lack confidence and thus not be able to present themselves as effective professionals. In turn, their negative self-perceptions may result in instructional practices that are not as strong as they could have been had the teachers been able to negotiate effective teacher identities. However, this is not to say that these visible minorities are not successful professionals in the field. In fact, the field also abounds with stories of visible minorities who have fought the challenges to their professional credibility and succeeded (Amin, 2004; Braine, 1999; Nero, 2006). Their successes can be attributed to several factors. First, they serve as inspirational role models for their students in that they reflect the local student population (Flynn & Gulikers, 2001). Second, they develop instructional materials that are anti-racist (Amin, 2004) and draw on their own status and experiences (de Oliveira, 2011). Third, they create classroom conditions that contribute to empowering their students (Kamhi-Stein, in press). Finally, with their presence in the classroom, they dispel the notion of the white native speaker as the ideal teacher (Amin, 2004).

The relationship among self-perceptions, language proficiency, and instructional practices

Why should we be concerned with teachers' self-perceptions? Self-perceptions are important because they affect how teachers position themselves in the classroom (Kamhi-Stein, in press), contribute (positively or negatively) to instructional practices, and ultimately affect students' motivation and learning (Butler, 2004). For example, Veneza Angel Pablico's quotation (in the Experience section) shows that she views her bilingualism as contributing to her flexibility, power, and skillfulness.

The relationship between self-perceptions and instructional practices is reflected in the experiences of two public school English teachers in South Korea, as reported by Kamhi-Stein and Mahboob (2005). The two subjects in their study used Korean and English in the classroom, but to different degrees and for different purposes. Specifically, Teacher A used Korean to translate terms that were not easy for the students to access and to joke with the students (as a means of creating a comfortable, relaxed atmosphere). Teacher B used Korean for most of the class time; in her case, classroom instruction was limited to having students listen and repeat sets of sentences in Korean and in English. Teacher B attributed her limited use of English in the classroom to her own lack of comfort in using the language.

The cases of these two teachers support research findings showing that NNES professionals in outer-circle settings such as Hong Kong or expanding-circle contexts (e.g., Japan, Korea, Taiwan, or Greece) may perceive their level of English language proficiency to be lower than that of NESs (Butler, 2004; Tang, 1997) and that, more important, some NNES professionals (in the case of the research reported here, teachers working in Japan, Korea, and Taiwan) may perceive their English language proficiency to be lower than it should be for them to provide effective instruction in English (Butler, 2004).

These findings may give the misleading impression that the relationship between language proficiency and language use in the classroom is a simple one. However, Kamhi-Stein and Mahboob (2005), in their investigation of Korean, Pakistani, and Argentine teachers (in which the two Korean teachers previously described participated) found that the use (or nonuse) of English in the classroom was affected by a complex interplay of factors. Specifically, the extent to which the teachers used their home language or English was affected by their perceived and actual proficiency in English (as measured by a battery of tests) *and* their beliefs about L2 teaching and learning. The researchers also found that the teachers' instructional practices reflected, to a large extent, the beliefs of the educational systems in which they had been brought up and were functioning. Based on this study, it appears inaccurate to say that language proficiency is the sole determining factor contributing to teachers' use of English in the language classroom.

While I have argued that self-perceptions affect how teachers position themselves in the classroom, self-perceptions cannot be considered to be fixed or stable. For example, in the case of NNES professionals, self-perceptions have been found to be negatively affected by changes in the setting in which teachers function, for example, from EFL to ESL (Kamhi-Stein, 1999; Samimy & Brutt-Griffler, 1999). Specifically, it is not uncommon to find that EFL professionals who travel to inner-circle countries to complete advanced degrees shift their self-perceptions, viewing themselves as accented minorities rather than as model professionals (Chacon, 2006). This shift in self-perception can have a debilitating effect on the NNES professionals if not properly addressed through the kinds of actions described in the Classroom Applications section.

Issues of language teacher preparation

Effective teachers have two types of knowledge: declarative and procedural (Pasternak & Bailey, 2004). *Declarative knowledge* consists of "knowledge about facts and things that we know" (O'Malley & Chamot, 1990, p. 229). In the case of an ESL/EFL teacher, this involves a teacher's ability to explain a grammatical rule, for example. *Procedural knowledge* consists of "knowledge of the things that we know how to do" (O'Malley & Chamot, 1990, p. 231). An example of procedural knowledge for the same teacher involves the teacher's ability to use the grammatical rule automatically in connected speech. TESOL teacher-preparation programs in EFL settings have shown great concern about NNES teachers' procedural knowledge as it relates to their ability to use the English language (e.g., Lavender, 2002). NNES teacher educators in inner-circle settings have the same concern about the language proficiency focus in TESOL teacher-preparation programs (J. Liu, 1999; Nemtchinova, Mahboob, Eslami, & Dogancay-Aktuna, 2010). More specifically, Nemtchinova et al. make the case for integrating a focus on teacher language proficiency across the curriculum of TESOL teacher-preparation courses. It could be argued that the rationale for this concern relies on the notion that "a teacher's confidence is most dependent on his or her own degree of language competence" (Murdoch, 1994, p. 258). Given this idea, a concern for English language proficiency is not surprising. Nevertheless, the idea that teacher educators are responsible for explicitly helping NNES professionals develop their language skills is often disregarded by teacher educators in inner-circle settings. In fact, a study by Frazier and Phillabaum (2011/2012) focusing on teacher educators in California showed that several of the participants argued that language training was not part of their job.

In inner-circle countries in North America, several studies have depicted a complex picture in relation to NNES teachers-in-preparation enrolled in teacher-preparation programs. Specifically, teacher-preparation programs in inner-circle settings have been found to place great cognitive and linguistic demands on the classroom participation of NNES students (especially in the areas of reading, writing, and oral classroom participation). These demands may lead to feelings of high anxiety (Lee & Lew, 2001; Morita, 2000). To deal with such feelings, NNES graduate students have been found to implement a variety of coping strategies, including turning to their NES peers for support; spending a lot of time writing, rewriting, and editing their papers (Lee & Lew, 2001); and extensively rehearsing and preparing for their oral presentations (Lee & Lew, 2001; Morita, 2000). NNES teachers-in-preparation have also reported going through a silent period (Kamhi-Stein, 1999; Thomas, 1999) and challenging themselves to participate in classroom discussions (J. Liu, 2004). While these strategies may give the impression that the burden of meeting the cognitive and linguistic expectations of language teacher-education programs lies solely with the NNES teachers-in-preparation, this is far from the truth. As shown by Morita (2004) in a study of female Japanese graduate students in a Canadian teacher preparation program, classroom participation (or nonparticipation) is co-constructed. This means that the teacher educators play a central role in creating conditions that allow teachers-in-preparation to see themselves as legitimate members of the classroom community—that is, as graduate students who have ideas to contribute and are worth being listened to by their NES peers. Conversely, teacher educators also play a role in creating negative conditions that place NNES teachers-in-preparation in the position of "the other," that is, students who are physically present in the classroom but, at the same time, marginalized in terms of participating in classroom discussions and activities.

The demands placed on NNES teachers-in-preparation are not minor. Their transition from the expanding-circle setting, where they are typically viewed as outstanding professionals, to graduate study in inner-circle settings, where (in the best-case scenario) they are often perceived as accented speakers (Samimy & Brutt-Griffler, 1999) or (in the worst) simply as language learners (G. Park, 2012), has an overall negative impact on their self-perception. Teacher preparation has been found to be instrumental in helping NNES professionals develop positive self-identities in teacher-preparation coursework, particularly through classroom assignments designed to help them demystify the notion of the native speaker. The work by Brutt-Griffler and Samimy (1999), Golombek and Jordan (2005), Pavlenko (2003), and Reis (2011) provides strong support for creating environments in which teachers-in-preparation engage in discussions about the native and non-native speaker constructs and issues of identity. As a result, NNES teachers-in-preparation who initially may not perceive themselves as legitimate owners of the English language come to recognize the native speaker fallacy and, as a consequence, are able to realign their self-perceptions. Through class discussions and classroom assignments, they can begin to view themselves as multicompetent language users and as members of multilingual communities rather than as disempowered non-native speakers of English.

To reach the goal of empowerment, Brutt-Griffler and Samimy (1999), for example, propose a seminar that focuses on issues related to NNES educators, with the objective of helping students understand the relationship between language and power and recognize the importance of creating a professional community. Another approach to empowerment is described by Kamhi-Stein (1999), who proposes a cross-curricular approach with a threefold purpose: (1) promoting reflection on issues related to NNES educators; (2) ensuring that discussions on issues related to NNES educators are not isolated to an individual course or to one group of teachers-in-preparation (in this case, the NNESs);

and (3) allowing NNES teachers-in-preparation to see themselves and the issues that concern them as an integral part of the teacher-preparation curriculum.

While clearly there are many positive practices in some inner-circle TESOL teacher-preparation programs, another issue is the practicum course, which has been an ongoing topic of concern for NNES teachers-in-preparation (Brinton, 2004; Llurda, 2005; Nemtchinova, 2005). Overall, work on the practicum course has shown that NNES teachers-in-preparation are often affected by concerns anchored in their status as non-native speakers and, at the same time, by concerns that are typical of all novice teachers. Drawing on these findings, Brinton (2004) argues that it is the responsibility of the teacher educator to create opportunities that are pedagogically meaningful and supportive for all teachers-in-preparation.

CLASSROOM APPLICATIONS

What does this discussion mean for NNES professionals? In this section, I describe a variety of strategies that can be implemented to enhance the English language skills, social-affective standing, and professional development/involvement of the NNES teachers-in-preparation. While reading this section, it is important to keep two points in mind. First, assuming that the strategies apply to *all* NNES teachers-in-preparation is problematic. Second, the strategies described in this section may and, in many cases, do apply to many NES teachers-in-preparation as well. In this section I discuss the strategies in terms of NNESs; however, readers should consider extending the ideas to their NES counterparts as well.

Strategies for English language development

The self-directed strategies discussed next are designed to help NNES teachers (both novice and experienced) enhance their English language skills. Central to the strategies is the idea that the teachers need to be motivated to implement them.

Work on sounding intelligible (if concerned about pronunciation). This involves NNES teachers being aware of the sounds or intonation patterns that may contribute to making their speech less intelligible and working to improve these speech features to enhance intelligibility. For example, in a conversation class, a student from Thailand said, "I will go to Las Vegas next mon. . . ." The teacher asked the student if he did not have a class the following Monday. The student replied: "no . . . no . . . next mon." At that point the teacher realized that the student wanted to say *month* and the problem was that he was not able to pronounce the *th* sound. Intelligibility can also be hindered by grammar and prosodic problems. If intelligibility is an issue, then it is important that the NNES teachers identify what is impeding their intelligibility and take steps to address the relevant issues. Some of these steps may involve the NNES teachers' engaging in a cyclical pattern of: (1) working on problematic sounds and intonation patterns in their speech by reading passages containing the features; (2) recording themselves reading the passages; and (3) then listening to their recordings and engaging in a process of self-correction.

Develop (or, as I prefer, enhance) conversational strategies. De Oliveira (2011) explains that NNES teachers may benefit from implementing questioning strategies designed to seek clarification, explanation, or examples. For example, rather than saying, "I don't understand" (i.e., a word or expression), she suggests using expressions like "I'm not sure I know what you mean. Would you mind clarifying that?" "I'm not sure what you're referring to. Would you mind giving me an example of that?" or "Would you mind explaining that again?" (de Oliveira, 2011, p. 233).

Another strategy that can be used to enhance NNES teachers' conversational skills involves learning about turn-taking (how a speaker takes and holds the floor in conversation). As explained by LoCastro (2012), speakers from different languages and cultures function under different assumptions about turn-taking; therefore, learning how and when to take and hold the floor may not be easy for NNESs. For this reason, LoCastro (2012) suggests a variety of cues to assist NNESs in recognizing that the speaker is getting ready to give up the floor. These cues include, but are not limited to, dropping one's pitch or loudness, slowing down the pace of one's speech, making unfilled pauses, inhaling audibly, making eye contact, nodding one's head, and changing one's body posture.[9] Therefore, it is important for NNES teachers to attend explicitly to how these cues are used in conversation to understand their interlocutors' intentions and expectations.

Prepare in advance to participate in classes and meetings. It is not uncommon to hear NNES teachers say that one of their fears is that their contributions (in a graduate class, in a meeting with an advisor, or as attendees at a professional meeting) may be overlooked. As explained by de Oliveira (2011), if NNES teachers want to be heard, they need to present themselves "in a professional manner" (p. 234). To help my NNES graduate students accomplish this in their graduate classes, I often counsel them to prepare what they are going to say and strategize how they are going to say it. Then, in managing group dynamics, I make eye contact with the students so that they can offer up their contribution. After students hear their voices a couple of times, they begin to see themselves as members of the classroom community and tend to increase their participation levels. Rehearsing what they are going to say and how they are going to say it contributes to decreasing the level of anxiety that some NNES graduate students or teachers may feel initially when they are expected to participate in class, meet with an advisor, or attend and make presentations at professional meetings.

Implement macro- and micro-text deconstruction strategies to understand how different text types are organized. *Macro-text deconstruction strategies* involve identifying the overall structure of a text (written or oral) as well the language features associated with that particular text. *Micro-text deconstruction strategies,* on the other hand, involve identifying vocabulary items, phrases, and clauses that authors use. Both strategies are helpful to NNESs as they seek to identify text structures, vocabulary, and phrases, and clauses that they can incorporate into their own written or spoken discourse. In my own case, I have found the use of these text deconstruction strategies particularly helpful both as a language user and a teacher. Specifically, as a graduate student, I used macro-text deconstruction strategies: (1) to understand how research articles in journals such as *TESOL Quarterly* were organized; and (2) to model my writing after more experienced authors. For example, as I read the introduction to a research study, I paid attention to how the section was organized (e.g., by understanding how the

authors established what the field had to say about their topic, how they gave a brief summary of prior research, how they showed gaps in the literature, and how they made a statement or asked questions designed to show how they intended to fill the gap). I also used micro-text deconstruction strategies, paying attention to the academic vocabulary that authors used (e.g., *analysis, benefit, conclude, data*) and interesting expressions the authors used to accomplish various discourse moves (e.g., *The results of prior research show that . . .* ; *X argues that . . .* ; *Central to this idea . . .* ; *However, X research suggests that . . .*). Then, in writing my own papers, I modeled my texts after the texts I had deconstructed—though I was, of course, careful not to plagiarize.

Use corpora to access authentic language usage. Corpora are large collections of authentic texts that are compiled and stored electronically and are processed by a search engine (D. Liu, 2010). Three examples of corpora are: (1) the Michigan Corpus of Academic Spoken English (MICASE),[10] a collection of data from a wide variety of speech events (e.g., lectures, classroom discussions, and lab sections) at the University of Michigan; (2) the Corpus of Contemporary American English (COCA),[11] which can be accessed through Brigham Young University and contains data for texts like fiction, popular magazines, newspapers, and academic texts; and (3) the Vienna-Oxford International Corpus of English (VOICE),[12] a corpus that contains naturally occurring data from non-native speakers communicating with other non-native speakers. By conducting searches in the various corpora and analyzing the results, teachers can become more aware of issues such as how English is used by non-native speakers interacting with other non-native speakers (in the case of VOICE), how American English is used in different genres (in the case of COCA), and how English is used in an academic settings (in the case of MICASE). (See also the McCarthy & O'Keeffe and Zimmerman chapters, this volume.)

Social-affective strategies

The strategies discussed next are designed to help NNES professionals enhance their self-perceptions (as and if needed). Employing these strategies will ultimately contribute to NNES teachers' positioning themselves as professionals.

Engage in a process of reimagining self-identity. For many professionals, calling themselves non-native English speakers is problematic since it relegates them to the position of "less competent" teacher (Pavlenko, 2003, p. 259). Reading the work of various authors (e.g., Braine, 2010; Pavlenko, 2003; Samimy & Brutt-Griffler, 1999) and reflecting on the native speaker fallacy will help NNES professionals understand how labels affect their self-perceptions. Using terms like *bilingual* or *multicompetent* to describe themselves may contribute to their view of self as being twice as competent. In practical terms, reimagining (using Pavlenko's 2003 term) themselves as bilingual professionals could, for example, result in job applications that highlight the professionals' *bilingual* skills (rather than *non-native* skills). This reimagination can also result in the identification of instructional practices that draw on the notion of bilingualism as a strength rather than NNES status as a weakness. One such instructional practice, in the case where the teacher knows the students' L1, is his or her ability to use the L1 to explain a term that students have difficulty understanding.

Buy into the notion that a teacher's accent does not necessarily imply a lack of intelligibility. Sometimes, NNES teachers' self-perceptions are negatively affected because they have a non-native accent. As noted throughout this chapter, self-perceptions affect how teachers present themselves in the classroom and vis-à-vis other professionals in the field. Therefore, developing an understanding of what the field has to say about accentedness and how accentedness differs from intelligibility can contribute to disabusing teachers of the notion that they need to sound like a native speaker to be accepted into the TESOL professional community.

Identify areas of professional strength. Rather than looking at what they are *not* (i.e., native speakers of English), it is important for NNES professionals to develop a strong understanding of the strengths they bring to the language classroom. I contend that teachers, regardless of their language status, can be effective professionals only if they have a sense of self-worth. To put it in simple terms, will students trust teachers who do not believe in themselves? The answer is *no*. One strategy that NNES teachers can use to develop awareness about their professional assets is to make a list of their professional strengths (as well as weaknesses) and to reflect on how these strengths contribute to their instructional practices. At the same time, teachers should consider developing a plan of action to work on their weaknesses.

Find NNES professionals who can serve as mentors. This is particularly important for NNES teachers working in inner-circle settings, where their professionalism can be challenged. While getting initiated into the profession in such settings is not easy for any teacher, it is usually more difficult for NNES professionals. For this reason, it is important for them to find mentors who can help them deconstruct the educational system of the inner circle. The model of mentoring I propose is one of "mentoring as transformational leadership" (Kamhi-Stein & de Oliveira, 2008, p. 40). In this model, mentoring involves: (1) engaging in a dyadic (two-way) relationship in which both mentor and mentee benefit from the relationship; (2) creating opportunities for professional and personal growth; and (3) engaging in a spiral process in which, as initial goals are met, new goals are established. Working with a mentor will help prepare NNES teachers to be successful professionals. In turn, based on the assumption that mentees may be newly graduated teachers, mentors will also benefit because they will be exposed to the latest developments in the field. How can NNES teachers find a mentor? Sometimes, NNES teachers (or NES professionals) are assigned to mentors through formal channels in professional associations such as TESOL. Other times, finding a mentor with whom a teacher would like to work requires initiative on the part of the potential mentee. However, in identifying a mentor, teachers should not attend solely to the professional qualifications of the potential mentor since, for the mentoring relationship to work, it is important that there be some level of personal comfort between the mentor and the mentee.

Develop strong support networks. Before the NNEST TESOL Interest Section (formerly a caucus) was founded, it was not uncommon for NNES professionals to feel marginalized and to be unable to find their experiences in TESOL reflected in those of NES teachers. At that time, finding support networks to exchange ideas and discuss issues related to their NNES status was difficult, if not impossible. Currently, access to professional groups like the TESOL association's NNEST Interest Section,[13] and interest sections that are part of TESOL's affiliates (e.g., the California affiliate [CATESOL][14] or the Washington area affiliate [WATESOL])[15] can help NNES professionals develop a sense of community and can provide contacts that they may not otherwise be able to make.

Professional-preparation programs in inner-circle settings

The strategies discussed next are classroom accommodation strategies that TESOL programs can implement to avoid the marginalization of NNES graduate students. The rationale for implementing these strategies is that (rather than lowering program standards) they will contribute to strengthening program quality by raising the visibility and contributions of the programs' NNES graduate students.

Provide an orientation for NNES graduate students from international backgrounds. International students who enroll in TESOL MA programs in inner-circle contexts may lack an understanding of how graduate classrooms function, what instructors' expectations are, and so on. In addition, as previously explained, the change in setting from EFL to ESL may affect the NNES professionals' self-perceptions. Therefore, it is important to provide NNES students with an orientation session so that their adjustment process is less traumatic. This orientation session can be followed up with individual meetings in which the NNES student and his or her advisor provide each other with an update on the former's process of adaptation. As a teacher educator, I hold individual meetings with all incoming students to learn about their professional goals and expectations. In addition, I meet with NNES students (as needed) to help them strategize their classroom participation.

Implement strategies designed to balance student participation in the classroom. One of the areas of greatest concern for NNES graduate students enrolled in teacher-preparation programs is oral classroom participation (Barratt, 2010; Kamhi-Stein, 1999). It is not uncommon to hear NNES

graduate students complain that class discussions move too fast and that they encounter difficulties entering conversations given their lack of familiarity with turn-taking conventions. Therefore, teacher educators need to implement balanced participation strategies (i.e., strategies that create an environment conducive to the participation of all students) as a solution, at least in part, to the problem described. Examples of balanced participation strategies include implementing a wait-time period so that all students have an opportunity to think about their answers before responding; inviting students to volunteer to respond, and calling on different volunteer students to hear different voices; making arrangements with individual students so that they conduct the warm-up/review at the beginning of class or the summary/closure activity at the end of class; and having students work in groups in which every person has to make a contribution. These strategies have two goals. First, they give all students an equal opportunity to be heard. Second, because they mirror strategies that are typically used in language classrooms, faculty can have students engage in reflection activities to create student awareness about classroom participation. In my own case, doing this usually contributes to my students' enhanced understanding of the important role that the teacher plays in creating classroom environments in which either all students feel accepted or some are put in the position of the "other."

Implement online asynchronous forum discussions. Forum discussions that exist as part of a course's website or course management system allow students to participate at their own pace. While these features may benefit all students, they have been found to be particularly helpful for NNES students since they promote active participation without putting students under pressure to perform. They allow students "to hear multiple voices and perspectives" (Kamhi-Stein, 2000, p. 448), voices that for linguistic, cultural, or personality reasons may not surface in face-to-face discussions.

Integrate discussions and activities designed to raise awareness about NNES teachers' issues across the curriculum of the TESOL program. Topics such as the native speaker fallacy, the relationship (or lack thereof) between accentedness and intelligibility, the reality of World Englishes, and the relevance of various teaching methodologies to different types of societies (e.g., Western, Asian, and African) are central to the preparation of English language teachers. An approach to instruction on NNES issues implemented across a variety of courses in TESOL programs will provide all future teachers, NES and NNES alike, with multiple opportunities to systematically examine these topics. In addition, implementing a cross-curricular approach to issues of interest to NNES professionals promotes meaningful dialogues between NESs and NNESs and prevents the latter from being marginalized. Some of the activities that raise awareness of NNES issues include writing linguistic autobiographies; researching hiring practices in various geographical areas, along with the beliefs supporting such practices; and analyzing exemplary practices implemented by NNES professionals.

Put NNESs in the position of consultants and experts. NNES graduate students bring to TESOL programs a wealth of knowledge and experience. Drawing on this knowledge and experience will benefit the graduate programs in which these students are enrolled. Therefore, it is important to view them as sources of knowledge rather than as individuals who bring deficiencies or gaps to the programs in which they are enrolled.

Work on issues of English language proficiency (both perceived and real). Sometimes, NNES teachers *believe* that their English language proficiency is not good enough to teach in an instructional setting. However, in many of these cases, the problem is one of self-perception. In this case, doing self-studies or getting hands-on experience teaching language learners will give teachers the security and confidence they need to succeed. On the other hand, in those cases where language proficiency really is a problem, it may be necessary to provide language support. The type of support provided will depend on the prospective teachers' needs. For example, such support could involve assigning conversation partners to those students who need to enhance their language fluency or integrating a language-development component into the classes that graduate students take (D. Liu, 1999). For example, in grammar or linguistics courses, students could work on their own use of structures, idioms, or word collocations;

in phonetics classes, they could investigate their articulations of speech sounds (D. Liu, 1999) or focus on their performance in planned and unplanned speech.

Professional development and/or involvement

The strategies discussed next are designed to raise the status of NNES professionals in the field while, at the same time, providing novice NNES teachers with models they can emulate. (See also Crandall & Finn-Miller, this volume.)

Serve as mentors for novice NNES teachers. Serving as mentors for new teachers is an important form of professional service. In addition, as I have already explained, the mentoring relationship brings benefits not only to the mentee but to the mentor too.

Participate in professional associations. Professional associations are always in need of new leaders. Given that NNES professionals have been language learners, they have an enhanced understanding of the language learning process as well as of the needs and wants of English language learners. Therefore, they can make excellent contributions to local, state, and international associations.

Monitor hiring practices, take action, and bring discriminatory practices to the attention of professional associations. This important advocacy activity has two goals: (1) to educate administrators about the myth that the native speaker is the ideal teacher; and (2) to work with professional associations to develop anti-discriminatory position statements and job-advertising practices.

FUTURE TRENDS

Just as language learners cannot be considered to be a monolithic group, neither can NNES professionals. Given the diversity among NNES professionals, there is a need to expand the research in four directions. First, it is important to continue presenting nuanced descriptions of NNES professionals. Such descriptions should not be limited to professionals in expanding-circle settings; instead, they should include professionals in inner-circle countries like the United States, where there are growing numbers of NNES language teachers who are long-term immigrants. Second, it is important to address the issue of hiring practices in inner- and expanding-circle countries related to NNES professionals. In this area, there is a need to identify hiring practices in various geographical areas and work within professional associations to develop advocacy action plans addressing discriminatory hiring practices. Third, in expanding-circle countries there is a need to look at teachers' and students' perceptions about the ownership of the English language as well the relationship between such perceptions and teachers' instructional practices. Finally, it is important to understand whether the English language is becoming nativized in specific expanding-circle settings and, where this is the case, to identify the features of these varieties of English (Seidlhofer, 2004).

CONCLUSION

In this chapter, I have argued that English is no longer perceived as the property of inner-circle speakers; however, the term non-native English-speaking teacher has continued to be used in TESOL. While some professionals argue for the need to find a new term, others have begun to reclaim the term. What is a fact in relation to the term non-native English-speaking teacher is that it continues to be problematic, particularly for novice teachers who find their credibility challenged because they may not sound or look like an idealized native English speaker. In this respect, there is an urgent need for advocacy activities designed to address discriminatory hiring practices and to educate administrators about the native speaker fallacy.

I have also argued that being a native speaker of English is different from being proficient in English. Teachers do not need to be native speakers of English to teach the language. Instead, what is needed is a high level of proficiency in English, although how high this level needs to be depends on a variety of factors, including but not limited to the setting in which the teachers function, the skill areas being taught, the purposes for which students are studying English, and the students' own level of proficiency in English.

SUMMARY

➤ Being a native speaker of English is not the same thing as being proficient in English.

➤ Issues of language proficiency and professional preparation need to be viewed as a continuum rather than as an either-or proposition.

➤ English is an international commodity and cannot be perceived as the property of inner-circle speakers. Language teaching can no longer privilege inner-circle varieties of English as the only acceptable standard.

➤ Often imbued with negative connotations in the past, the term non-native English speaker has begun to be reclaimed as having a positive connotation.

➤ Teachers who are members of visible minorities may find their professional credibility challenged simply because they do not look like an idealized native English speaker.

➤ There is a need for advocacy and action to educate administrators concerning the value that NNES professionals bring to the profession.

➤ The extent to which teachers use English in the classroom (when teachers and students share a L1) is affected by many factors, including teachers' actual and perceived proficiency in English, their beliefs about L2 teaching and learning, and the beliefs of the educational system in which they have been educated and function.

➤ Effective language teacher-preparation programs have been found to be instrumental in helping NNES teachers view themselves as multicompetent language users and as members of multilingual communities rather than as disempowered non-native speakers of English.

➤ Language teacher preparation programs in inner-circle settings need to more effectively integrate topics of relevance to NNES teachers into their courses.

DISCUSSION QUESTIONS

1. Are you convinced that the native speaker fallacy exists? If so, what are the arguments that have convinced you? Are there any additional arguments that should have been considered?

2. How do you perceive yourself (as a native speaker, a non-native speaker, a multilingual speaker, or some other category)? Does the label affect how you position yourself in the field of TESOL?

3. Have you ever experienced discriminatory hiring practices, or do you know someone who has? What were the circumstances? Do you agree with the idea that there have been some small, though positive, changes in hiring practices? What do you think needs to be done to change administrators' views about hiring highly qualified NNES teachers?

SUGGESTED ACTIVITIES

1. Identify the setting in which you teach (or are planning to teach). Then, make a list of the strengths you bring to the language classroom. In making the list, consider issues of teacher preparation, language proficiency, and socio-cultural knowledge. Then, identify the areas of concern to you; that is, make a list of your weaknesses. Finally, design an action plan. What strategies are you planning to implement to improve your skills?

2. Reflect on the strategies you have implemented to enhance your English or foreign language skills, social-affective standing in the field, and professional preparation. Are there other strategies you can add to the list? Share them with your colleagues or professional networks.

3. Find an exemplary teacher who has an accent that distinguishes him or her from the idealized native speaker. Interview the teacher, some of his or her students, and an administrator. What factors contribute to the teacher's success in the classroom from the points of view of the teacher, the students, and the administrator?

FURTHER READING

Braine, G. (2010). *Nonnative speaker English teachers: Research, pedagogy and professional growth.* New York, NY: Routledge.

This book, written by a founding member of TESOL's NNEST Caucus (now NNEST Interest Section), describes the roots of the NNES teachers' movement and provides a summary of the research focusing on NNES professionals.

Kubota, R., & Sun, Y. (Eds.) (2012). *Demystifying career paths after graduate school: A guide for second language professionals in higher education.* Charlotte, NC: Information Age Publishing.

This collection of articles provides a variety of practical suggestions on how to develop a successful academic career.

Morita, N. (2004). Negotiating participation and identity in second language academic communities. *TESOL Quarterly, 38*(4), 573–604.

This research study describes how six female graduate students from Japan negotiated their participation in the classes they took.

ENDNOTES

[1] See, for example, Matsuda's (2003a) article, in which he expresses his pride in being called a non-native speaker.

[2] I should note that oftentimes employers' idea of who is a native speaker is problematic since it is sometimes dependent on the applicant's last name, the country issuing the passport, or the applicant's place of birth (Selvi, 2010).

[3] One limitation of research on self-perceptions is that, as Medgyes (1994) explains, conclusions are made based on teachers' self-reported data. A review of the list of the perceived differences in teaching behavior between NES and NNES professionals suggests that the NNES professionals implement instructional practices that are not "valued" in the context of modern pedagogical practices. Therefore, a question that should be asked is: "What counts as good pedagogy *in specific sociocultural contexts?*" (Lin, Wang, Akamatsu, & Riazi, 2005, p. 210).

[4] See the summary of research findings in Pickering (2006).

[5] See http://careers.tesol.org/

[6] See http://www.eslcafe.com/

[7] See TESOL Matters, 2(4), 23.

[8] See http://www.tesol.org/s_tesol/bin.asp?CID=32&DID=5889&DOC=FILE.PDF

[9] These cues are not universal. For example, as explained by LoCastro (2012), in multicultural settings, misunderstandings may occur when participants in a conversation make eye contact to cue that they are ready to give up the floor, and because their interlocutors avoid making eye contact (due to cultural beliefs and practices), they may assume that their interlocutors are not ready to contribute to the conversation.

[10] Available at http://micase.elicorpora.info/

[11] Available at http://corpus.byu.edu/coca/

[12] Available at http://www.univie.ac.at/voice/

[13] Available at http://nnest.asu.edu/

[14] Available at http://nnlei.wordpress.com/

[15] Available at https://sites.google.com/site/watesolnnestcaucus/home

38 | Classroom Research, Teacher Research, and Action Research in Language Teaching

KATHLEEN M. BAILEY

KEY QUESTIONS

➤ What are classroom research, teacher research, and action research? How are they similar and how do they differ?

➤ Why should language teachers get involved in doing research in their classrooms?

EXPERIENCE

Imagine you are an English as a second language (ESL) teacher working with immigrant students in an English-speaking country.[1] Because there is a long waiting list for learners to get into the program, there is often a span of time between the intake assessment of the students' proficiency and the point at which they can actually enroll. When students finally do get into classes, their proficiency may not be accurately reflected in their somewhat-dated placement scores. As a result, you find the students in your classes typically have a wide range of English abilities.

How will the students' varied proficiency levels affect the classroom activities you plan? What grouping strategies should you use? What kind of investigation could you conduct to determine the usefulness of your choices? What does the literature have to say about teaching multilevel classes? These and other questions run through your mind as you walk to class at the beginning of the term, ready to meet your new students for the first time.

WHAT KINDS OF RESEARCH ARE CONDUCTED IN THE LANGUAGE CLASSROOM?

The purpose of this chapter is to introduce language teachers to research done in language classrooms. I consider some research findings as well as some research methods. I have structured the chapter around a series of questions, beginning with definitions of and a comparison of classroom research, teacher research, and action research. I include summaries of several studies directly related to the work of language teachers and end the chapter with some activities readers can do to enhance their understanding of the concepts presented. Although space constraints do not permit a comprehensive review of the available literature, I hope the studies cited here will encourage readers to learn more about these approaches to research and about their potential for having positive impact on teaching and learning.

In recent years there has been a marked increase in the frequency with which studies of classroom research, teacher research, and action research have been published in the field of language teaching. These research areas occur regularly in the program abstracts at language teachers' conferences too. But what do these three terms mean? They are sometimes used interchangeably, but are they in fact synonymous?

What is language classroom research?

Of these three concepts, the one with the longest tradition in language teaching is *classroom research* (or *classroom-centered research,* as it used to be called). As early as 1980, Long defined classroom research as "research on second language learning and teaching, *all or part of whose data are derived from the observation or measurement of the classroom performance of teachers and students*" (Long, 1980, p. 3). So, for example, a study about language learning for which students completed a questionnaire about their target language use outside of class, while interesting and potentially useful, would not fit Long's definition of *classroom research*. If, however, the researchers added an observation component to the study, visiting classrooms to document those same learners' in-class use of the target language, that would be classroom research, according to Long (1980).

Classroom research, however, is not just research where the data are collected within the confines of a physical classroom. As Allwright (1983) noted, classroom research is:

> research *centered* on the classroom, as distinct from, for example, research that concentrates on the *inputs to* the classroom (the syllabus, the teaching materials) or on the *outputs from* the classroom (learner achievement scores). It does not ignore in any way or try to devalue the importance of such inputs and outputs. It simply tries to investigate what happens inside the classroom when learners and teachers come together. At its most narrow, classroom-centered research is in fact research that treats the language classroom not just as the *setting for* investigation but, more importantly, as the *object of* investigation. Classroom processes become the central focus. (p. 191)

Classroom research, then, can be conducted by anyone as long as it fits Allwright's description. It is not the province of one school of thought, one group of researchers, or one methodological tradition (see also K. M. Bailey, 2005; Gieve & Miller, 2006).

What is teacher research?

Teacher research, in contrast, is research conducted by classroom teachers. The idea of teachers doing research has been gaining momentum in the past three decades, particularly in first language education. Teacher research is often connected with issues of teacher development and empowerment (Brindley, 1991), the idea being that, by investigating teaching and learning processes in our classrooms, we ourselves learn more about the craft and the science of teaching so that we may improve our work as teachers. For several examples, please see the series of edited volumes on language teacher research published by the Teachers of English to Speakers of Other Languages (TESOL) association. The series reports on studies conducted by teachers in Asia (Farrell, 2006), the Middle East (Coombe & Barlow, 2007), Australia and New Zealand (Burns & Burton, 2008), Europe (Borg, 2006a), the Americas (McGarrell, 2007), and Africa (Makelala, 2009).

Teacher research usually does take place in classrooms, and it typically focuses on some element(s) of classroom interaction, but it does not necessarily have to. For instance, Stewart and Lohon (2003) team-taught a course on cross-cultural communication in Japan. Their study focused on what the students learned from various tasks used during the lessons. They and their 38 students made diary entries eight times during the 16-week semester. This study is an example of teacher research because it was designed and carried out by teachers.

In teacher research, then, the agent conducting the research is the defining feature of the approach, regardless of the location involved or the research methods used. In our field, there are helpful discussions of teacher research written by D. Freeman (1998), K. E. Johnson (1999), and Richards and Farrell (2011), among others.

What is action research?

Finally, the term *action research* does indeed imply a particular methodological approach. The concept is sometimes confused with teacher research and classroom research because in our field action research is typically conducted by teachers in language classrooms and often focuses on particular features of classroom interaction. But action research is more than simply research conducted by teachers in classrooms.

Action research is an approach to collecting and interpreting data that involves a clear repeated cycle of procedures: planning, acting, observing, reflecting, and replanning. The researcher begins by planning an action to address a problem, issue, or question in his or her own context. This action (also called a "small-scale intervention") is then carried out. (This implementation is the source of the label action research.) The next step is the systematic observation of the outcomes of the action, which is done through a variety of data-collection procedures. These include audio- or video-recordings, test scores, teachers' diary entries, observers' notes, students' output (in speech or writing), and students' evaluations of lessons. Christison and Bassano (1995) provide examples of data-collection procedures that teachers can use in action research to gather information from students. After observing the apparent results of the action, the researcher reflects on the outcome and plans a subsequent action, after which the cycle begins again (Nunan & Bailey, 2009; van Lier, 1994). These steps are depicted in Figure 1, which also shows how the goals of action research may change as a study progresses.

The broad goals of action research are to seek local understanding and to bring about an improvement in the context under study. Kemmis and McTaggart (1989) describe action research as:

> a form of "self-reflective enquiry" undertaken by participants in social situations in order to improve the rationality and justice of their own social or educational practices, as well as their understanding of these practices and the situations in which these practices are carried out. (p. 2)

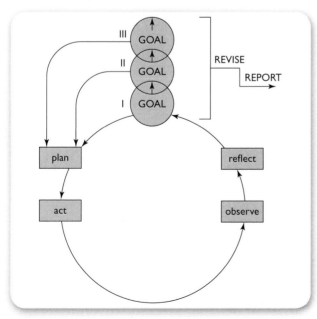

Figure 1. The cycles of action research (from van Lier, 1994, p. 34).

Thus, action research is particularly well suited as a research method that can be carried out in classrooms and can benefit teachers and learners.

Action research was begun in the United States by Lewin (1946) in the 1940s to address social problems. Although this approach was overshadowed in the United States for many years by psychometric research in the empirical tradition, it has been widely used for some time in the United Kingdom, Australia, and Hong Kong. A number of action research anthologies and a great deal of the methodological guidance have been published in general education, but in recent years, more and more books and articles have been published about action research in second or foreign language education contexts (see, for instance, Burns, 1998, 2004; Crookes, 2005; Mitchell, 2009). The TESOL association published a collection of action research studies conducted by language teachers (Edge, 2001). Calzoni (2002) investigated students' learning styles and homework using the action research approach. In Hong Kong, Mok (1997) used action research to study an English-enrichment program.

How do these three concepts fit together?

To summarize, then, the term *classroom research* refers to the location and the focus of the study. *Teacher research* refers to the agents who conduct the study. And *action research* denotes a particular research method, a codified but flexible set of reiterated procedures that participants use to conduct research in their own settings. Action research may or may not be conducted in classrooms, and it may or may not be done by teachers. Figure 2 depicts the possible overlapping relationship of classroom research, teacher research, and action research.

McPherson (1997) provides a good example of an action research project that she conducted as a language teacher investigating events in her own classroom. McPherson teaches adult ESL classes for recent immigrants to Australia. (In fact, it is her context that was introduced in the Experience section at the beginning of the chapter.) One year, her students had a very wide range of abilities, partly because many had had to wait a long time for a place in the course after the initial assessment of their English skills. McPherson and 25 other ESL

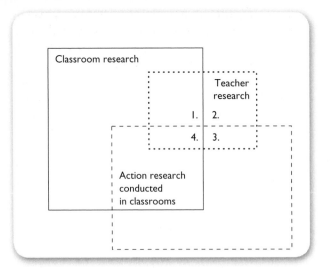

Figure 2. Classroom research, action research, and teacher research. I = classroom research conducted by teachers using approaches other than action research; 2 = research conducted by teachers outside classrooms using approaches other than action research; 3 = research conducted by teachers outside classrooms using the action research approach; 4 = classroom research conducted by teachers using the action research approach.

teachers in four states of Australia undertook related action research projects, all in their own contexts but each focusing on some aspect of teaching diverse learners. McPherson's article describes the three cycles of her own study, which is an example of teacher research. It uses the action research model and is situated within the wider approach of language classroom research.

In the first cycle, McPherson reviewed the literature on teaching mixed-ability classes, talked to other teachers, and tried various ways of grouping her students based on their proficiency levels. She discovered that the students appeared to have goals different from her own and sometimes resisted the group work and pair work she had organized.

In the second cycle, McPherson elicited the students' input about the activities. They were surprised that she saw mixed levels as a problem and said they were happy to work in mixed-ability groups. As a result of these discussions, McPherson gave the students more responsibility to select their own materials and activities. She then observed them making their own learning choices, which she carefully documented. She found that the students had reasons quite different

from her own for their choices. For instance, many students experienced intragroup tensions (e.g., in choosing partners for group work) related to their own ethnicity as well as to the political problems in their home countries. The students had developed strategies for maintaining civil relations in class, but the teacher's grouping efforts had inadvertently undermined that delicate balance. McPherson (1997) commented, "They had tried in subtle ways to make me aware of the sensitive and precarious nature of the classroom dynamics by declining to carry out the activities which they believed could upset the equilibrium" (p. 58). Allowing the students more choice was the teacher's first step toward resolving this issue.

The third cycle of McPherson's action research occurred near the end of the course. Although most of the learners had begun to work well together, there were still two students who were marginalized by the dominant ethnic group in the class. McPherson implemented a strategy of calling on these two students and validating their contributions to class discussions. As the term ended, even these two students had gotten more involved. Thus, McPherson's teacher research using the action research method in her classroom enabled her to teach better and, presumably, to create a better learning environment for the students.

CONCEPTUAL UNDERPINNINGS

Many topics have been studied in language classroom research. An extensive literature review by Chaudron (1988) identifies four main areas: (1) teacher talk in second language (L2) classrooms; (2) learner behavior in L2 classrooms; (3) teacher and student interactions; and (4) learning outcomes. These topics are still important areas of classroom research, but in some instances the focus of a topic has changed to keep up with developments in language teaching (Mitchell, 2009). For example, many early studies looked at patterns of student participation in teacher-fronted classes, but more recent investigations—influenced by communicative language teaching—have investigated small-group interaction (e.g., see Storch, 2002). In a further development, studies influenced by sociocultural theory and Swain's (1995) output hypothesis have examined small-group and dyadic interactions in the language classroom.

One of the basic precepts of sociocultural theory (Lantolf, 2000b) is that language mediates the interactions of human beings with their surroundings and with one another. As learning occurs, including language learning, scaffolding helps learners move to the next level of mastery. The term *scaffolding* is used here as a metaphor, based on the visual image of a building that is being painted or repaired. It refers to the idea that help may be needed initially by learners but is gradually removed as the learners take over more responsibility for accomplishing the task.

Swain (2000) discusses language learners scaffolding one another through collaborative dialogue, "in which speakers are engaged in problem solving and knowledge building" (p. 102). She gives an example of two French immersion students in Canada working on a task. Together, the students bolster each other's knowledge and complete the task successfully.

Two teachers of a course on English for medical congresses investigated the effects of repetition in a learning task called the "poster carousel." Lynch and Maclean (2000) describe this activity as a four-step process:

1. Pairs of participants are given one hour to make a poster about an article on medical research;
2. One partner (A) stands next to the poster and explains it to the "visitors," who must ask questions about the study it depicts. (The group of visitors is made up of the B partners from the other pairs.) The explanation takes about three minutes, and then a new group of visitors arrive and the process begins again;
3. Next the other partner (B) stands and explains the poster while the A partners circulate as visitors and ask questions about the posters;
4. After the second round, there is a whole-group discussion about the effectiveness of various posters. Meanwhile, the teachers take notes on the students' language, and that feedback is subsequently given to the students.

These teacher-researchers recorded the students' interactions using audio-recorders placed next to each poster and then transcribed the interactions. The students also completed a self-report questionnaire before they received the teachers' feedback. The questionnaire data indicated that half the students intentionally made changes as they explained and reexplained their posters. Many of these changes

had to do with vocabulary. Lynch and Maclean (2000) analyzed the transcripts in terms of the students' subject-verb structures, their lexical and grammatical accuracy, and their pronunciation, focusing on two participants with quite different proficiency levels. The two students "reacted to the communicative challenge in different ways," but "both showed evidence of making their English more native-like" during the activity (p. 241). The authors suggest that the changes in learner output are a result of "the poster carousel's configuration of input, interlocutors and repetition under time pressure" (p. 244).

The early topical focus on individual learner variables and language learners' behaviors has also broadened considerably. These topics have been studied through diary entries about the learners' experiences. Many early language learning diaries were kept by linguists who studied both a language and the processes of learning that language. This procedure has been criticized by Seliger (1983) because trained linguists do not represent the majority of language learners, so the learning processes they undergo may not be the same as those of the more typical language students. More recently, however, diaries have been kept by learners but analyzed by researchers. These studies include R. Ellis's (1989b) research on two adult learners of German and Hilleson's (1996) investigation of reticence and anxiety among secondary school students in Singapore. Curtis and Bailey (2009) review diary studies on both language teaching and learning.

Some classroom studies have used multiple data-collection procedures to investigate learner variables. For example, in Singapore, Allison (1998) analyzed questionnaires and journals kept by secondary school English learners. In Spain, Block (1996) compared students' tape-recorded journal entries with his own observations and the teacher's journal entries. Shaw (1996) used language learners' diary entries, his field notes, and interviews with teachers to investigate content-based language instruction at the graduate level in the United States. Katz (1996) used classroom observations, tape-recordings, and teacher interviews to document four different teaching styles used by four teachers working at the same level in the same program and using the same curriculum.

It is interesting to me, as a teacher-researcher and a reader of others' studies, to see how much development has occurred in language classroom research since the early 1980s. There have been new methodological developments, to be sure, but more impressive is the wide range of topics now being investigated. The traditional foci of classroom research are still studied, but other key topics have also appeared. Some of these issues, such as research on students' learning strategies (e.g., Chamot, 2005; Nunan, 1996b), have been influenced by second language acquisition research conducted outside classrooms. Some are related to sociolinguistic research on contextualized forms of competence, such as Rounds's (1987) investigation of the communication skills of non-native-speaking teaching assistants in U.S. universities. Other topics, such as those in the language awareness movement (e.g., van Lier, 1995), are closely related to developments in psycholinguistics. Three particularly interesting developments are: (1) investigations of teacher cognition; (2) the internationalization of language classroom research; and (3) empirical studies of washback. We next briefly examine these three areas, each of which is relevant to language teachers worldwide.

Classroom research on teacher cognition

Teacher cognition research investigates how teachers think about their work, what skilled decision making goes into effective teaching, and how novice teachers' thinking and teaching expertise develop over time (see Borg, 2006b; Woods, 1996). Teacher cognition is a vast and important topic, and we are just beginning to understand its richness and complexity.

Much of this research involves having teachers review data collected in their own classrooms by researchers. Then the teachers tell the researchers what they were thinking and what motivated their decision making at the time, using a procedure called *stimulated recall* (Gass & Mackey, 2000), in which a researcher uses some record of an event to prompt the recollections of that event by someone who participated in it. These data can include audio- or video-recordings of the class, observers' field notes, and transcripts of classroom interaction. The participants verbalize their recollections, and the researchers record those recollections as a new layer of data while the participants review and discuss the original data. For example, Nunan (1996a) and K. E. Johnson (1992) used stimulated recall to

prompt in-service and preservice teachers to explain the mental processes they used while teaching their lessons.

The topics of teacher cognition and development have been accessed in classroom research through the use of teachers' journals. Sometimes the journals have been analyzed by people other than the teachers themselves. For instance, Numrich (1996) analyzed the teaching journals kept by teachers-in-training who were enrolled in her practicum class. Pennington and Richards (1997) analyzed the teaching journals of five novice English as a foreign language (EFL) teachers in Hong Kong. In other instances, the journals have been analyzed by the teachers who kept them, thus providing us with examples of teacher research. These include Appel's (1995) book-length study based on a journal he kept for several years as he taught EFL in Germany. Brock, Yu, and Wong (1992) kept teaching journals of the university English classes they taught in Hong Kong, and they then met to read and discuss the journals. Their joint report documents both their journal findings and what they learned by sharing their journals.

The international scope of language classroom research

Language classroom research has been conducted in a wide variety of contexts in recent years. In the early 1980s, much of the published classroom research was done in Canada, Australia, the United Kingdom, and the United States. This is no longer the case. For instance, teachers' concerns about working with large classes have emerged as an important topic with serious practical consequences in many regions (H. Coleman, 2006): Nigeria (H. Coleman, 1989), Japan (LoCastro, 1989), Indonesia (Sabander, 1989), Pakistan (Shamim, 1996), and South Africa (Stein & Janks, 1996).

The language used by students and teachers during lessons, one of the early foci of language classroom research, has also been investigated internationally. These studies include research on students' English use in Sri Lankan classrooms (Canagarajah, 1993), the tasks performed in dual language programs in Hungary (Duff, 1995), and the use of language in Tunisian EFL classes using the communicative approach (Lili, 2007).

Washback studies in the language classroom

Research on washback also illustrates this international trend. *Washback,* broadly defined as the effects of testing on teaching and learning, has been studied in many countries. Much of this classroom research has been conducted by external observers rather than by teachers. For example, in Sri Lanka, Wall and Alderson (1993) collected baseline data at the beginning of a three-year observational study. *Baseline data* are "information that documents the normal state of affairs [and] provides the basis against which we make comparative claims about how different or unusual the phenomena we have seen may be" (Allwright & Bailey, 1991, p. 74). In the washback studies, baseline data are usually collected before the implementation of a new test so that the effects of adopting that test can be studied subsequently by collecting parallel data after the test has been used for some specific period of time.

Wall and Alderson's (1993) study involved classroom observers visiting English classes in five parts of Sri Lanka for six rounds of observations, before and after a new national English test was implemented. The new exam influenced the content of English lessons. For instance, many teachers used the textbook for the curriculum that the exam was meant to assess and added "questions and tasks of the sort that might appear on the exam" (p. 204). The exam also had some impact on how the teachers designed their own in-class exams. However, it had very little influence on how they taught or graded their students' performance on tests.

The effects of Japanese university entrance examinations were studied by Watanabe (1996), who found results similar to those of Wall and Alderson (1993). He observed two teachers, each of whom was teaching two test-preparation courses. Watanabe found that the grammar-translation questions on the university entrance exams did not influence the two teachers in the same way. Watanabe identified three factors that promoted or inhibited washback in these cases: (1) the teachers' educational background and/or experience; (2) the teachers' different beliefs about what constituted effective teaching; and (3) the timing of the researcher's observations relative to the date of the upcoming exam.

In Israel, Shohamy, Donitsa-Schmidt, and Ferman (1996) conducted classroom research on the washback created by introducing a new test of Arabic as a second language (ASL), as well as a new EFL test. When the new ASL test was implemented, the researchers observed that the teachers stopped covering new material and began to review intensively; worksheets based on the previous year's ASL test replaced the textbooks, class activities became test-like, and the atmosphere became tense. Once the test had been administered, these manifestations of washback stopped. In the case of the EFL test, which included an oral component, Shohamy et al. (1996) observed that the teachers increased the amount of class time spent on listening and speaking, using activities and tasks based on the EFL test. This study confirmed that, at the very least, washback influences what teachers emphasize in language classes.

Alderson and Hamp-Lyons (1996) observed two teachers as they both taught regular ESL classes and Test of English as a Foreign Language (TOEFL)–preparation classes in the United States. Their study found that the test-preparation classes included much more test taking, involved less time on pair work, entailed more teacher talk and less student talk, generated more metalanguage (talk about language), and elicited less laughter than did the non-TOEFL classes.

A parallel study comparing two International English Language Testing System (IELTS)–preparation classes at two different schools in New Zealand was conducted by Hayes and Read (2004). In School A, Teacher A had had 30 years of experience, including two years teaching the IELTS-preparation course. This person was also an official IELTS examiner. In School B, Teacher B had had seven years of experience, including three years teaching the IELTS-preparation course. This person was not an IELTS examiner. At School A, the course lasted four weeks, with a total of 22 hours of instruction. It emphasized the structure of the IELTS and test-taking strategies. At School B, the course also ran for four weeks, but it had a total of 28 hours of instruction. This course emphasized test familiarization and language development.

The students were all given a pre-test and a post-test using the IELTS. In School A, three of the nine students made no change, and the score of one student went down one-half band. Four students went up one-half band, and one went up a whole band, from 4 to 5 on the 9-point scale. In

School B, the score of one of the eight students went down one-half band, and the scores of three students stayed the same. The scores of two students went up one-half band, but the scores of two students went up a band and a half. Other findings were that, on average, the students in the IELTS preparation class at School A laughed once a day. In contrast, students in the IELTS preparation class at School B laughed eleven times per day. The data showed that students laughed most often in group or pair activities, which were more common at School B.

In Hong Kong, Cheng (2005) observed secondary school English teachers working with two groups of students preparing for their school-leaving examinations: One group of students was slated to take the old exam and the other group was slated to take the new exam. The old exam included the students' reading aloud, while the new test included role plays and group discussions instead. In the preparation classes for the new exam, Cheng found that the teachers did not have students practice reading aloud and that more time was spent on oral presentations and group discussions than had previously been the case. Like Wall and Alderson (1993), Cheng (2005) noted that the new exam changed the content of the courses but had a minimal impact on the teaching methods.

The existing classroom research studies on washback offer several insights and raise a number of interesting questions about how external tests influence teaching and learning. From what we have seen so far, tests seem to have considerable impact on *what* gets taught but less influence on *how* that content is taught. Future research in this area is needed, including more research by teachers and further investigations of students' opinions.

What topics have been investigated by teachers doing action research in language classrooms?

As previously noted, action research has seen a dramatic rise in popularity since 1980. The advent of action research as a legitimate approach to investigating phenomena in language classrooms has opened a wide range of new topics. It has also provided an accessible approach to doing research for the teachers who use this model.

In recent years, a number of action research studies have been published in which language teachers (sometimes working alone, sometimes collaborating with others) have used the action research approach to investigate issues in their own classrooms. For example, Tsui (1996) reports on a study in which several secondary school teachers in Hong Kong used action research to investigate their students' reticence to use oral English in their English classes. In the United Arab Emirates, Quirke (2001) used action research to elicit feedback systematically from his female university students about his teaching.

What is the teacher's role in language classroom research?

The teacher's role in classroom research has grown tremendously in the past three decades (Allwright, 1997). Experimental classroom investigations had been typically conducted by outside researchers to ensure objectivity in data collection and interpretation. Teachers were seen either as the subjects of a particular study or as the implementers of the treatment in the experiment. This situation is described by a teacher whose classroom was the site of just such an investigation (Schechter, 1997):

> That year, I had my first experience of sustained contact with university researchers in education, for they were in my classroom almost every day.... On the whole, I found them pleasant, even somewhat deferential, as they stood or sat, their bodies tightening at my approach so as not to impede my access to their subjects. I remember remarking to a friend that not one of the university people returned to tell me what they had found, as though I were not a critical consumer of these concepts. However, I didn't find it odd at the time that none of the visitors bothered to ask me what I thought. . . . In the environs in which I earned my livelihood, inside schools, I was an able teacher, not a person with ideas. It was only later that I would come to have a different perspective on these university researchers' lack of interest in my ideas, in my agency as a theory builder. (pp. 102–103)

In contrast, there is now a much more inclusive view of teachers as partners in the research enterprise, working in collaboration with researchers, such as in D. Freeman's (1992) study of a secondary school French class. It is also not uncommon these days for teachers in our field to be the producers as well as consumers of language classroom research (Crookes, 1998; D. Freeman, 1996). Pica (1997) has described the evolving relationship of language teaching and research as moving from coexistence to collaboration and complementarity (see also T. Stewart, 2006). The role of teachers in such research has been summed up nicely by S. L. McKay (2006):

> [T]hose involved in L2 teaching and learning . . . are in ideal positions to undertake classroom research. They are the ones who have a vested interest in better understanding L2 teaching and learning; they are aware of many of the classroom-based questions that need to be answered; and they have access to L2 classrooms. What they need is an understanding of the research process, as well as time and support to undertake research. (p. ix)

CLASSROOM APPLICATIONS

There are now many methodological resources available for conducting language classroom research in addition to the action research references already cited. For example, Allwright and Bailey (1991) discuss both the topics and the methods of classroom research for language teachers. Nunan and Bailey (2009) explain various data collection and analysis procedures used in language classroom research. Gass and Mackey (2000) provide step-by-step guidance and clear examples for researchers, including teacher researchers, who wish to use stimulated recall. Samway (1994) gives suggestions for teachers about recording data while they are teaching. D. Freeman (1998), K. E. Johnson (1999), and Tsui (1995) have all discussed ways to investigate language classroom interaction.

One sign of a field's professional maturity is its willingness to critique its own work. Recently many articles and books have been written that identify problematic issues. For example, each chapter of Nunan and Bailey (2009) discusses the pitfalls as well as the payoffs of particular approaches to classroom research. In addition,

Schachter and Gass (1996) have edited a collection of articles that candidly discuss the sorts of problems that arise in doing classroom research. Many of these resources will be helpful to language teachers who wish to get started on investigations in their own classrooms.

Should teachers make the effort to get involved in action research or in any form of classroom research, for that matter? Does it not take time to conduct such studies? Does research not require discipline and specialized training in research design to carry out? The answer to these questions is yes, certainly. In addition, in many situations, teachers are not given financial or strategic support, release time, or even recognition for conducting research. Allwright (1997) has addressed some of these concerns. Also, Allwright and Lenzuen (1997) have described an approach called exploratory practice, which is related to teacher research but allows both teachers and learners to explore and answer important questions about their practices in language classrooms (see also Allwright, 2005; Fanselow & Barnard, 2006).

There are many good reasons for teachers to conduct language classroom research, however. The processes involved in data collection and analysis can help them discover patterns (both positive and negative) in their interactions with students. They can discover interesting new puzzles and answers, both of which can energize their teaching. By reading or hearing accounts of other people's research, they can get new ideas for teaching and for their investigations, as well as becoming better connected with the profession at large. And by sharing the results of their own research (at conferences, in publications, in staff room lunch talks, etc.), they can get feedback from other teachers and learn from those colleagues' experiences.

Let me share an example based on a research project I did, primarily for my own professional development. During a sabbatical leave, I taught EFL at the Chinese University of Hong Kong for two semesters. While I was there, I kept a teaching journal. I wrote in it after every class, and sometimes after I'd been responding to students' dialogue journal entries. Originally I had planned to keep my teaching journal for the first three weeks of the first semester because I was anxious about how I would adjust to this new setting and I wanted to document my efforts to fit in as well as to resolve any difficulties that arose. But the diary writing took on a life of its own and would not let me stop. I continued keeping a journal for the entire academic year, a process that eventually resulted in 110 pages of single-spaced text (K. M. Bailey, 2001).

Why would a busy teacher voluntarily take on a data collection endeavor of this scope? What was it about the journal process that compelled me to write day after day?

First, my uncertainty about how my skills would work with these students was a matter of some concern. For many years, I had taught ESL to advanced graduate students and done language teacher training and administration, but it had been a long time since I had taught EFL to lower-intermediate learners, particularly to college freshmen. Also, the entire surrounding culture, the students' first language, the university bureaucracy, and the program's curriculum were all new to me. I was beset with doubts and questions, and writing in the teaching journal gave me a mechanism for dealing with those concerns.

Over the course of those two semesters, writing in my journal and rereading the entries, coupled with helpful support from my wonderful colleagues, led me to discover areas of my teaching that I could improve. For instance, for the first few weeks of the first term, my lessons felt sluggish. It was hard to get the students to talk. Rereading my journal entries showed me that I had been dominating the classroom interaction by overexplaining vocabulary items. When the journal revealed this pattern, I was able to take steps to cut back on the teacher talk and to develop techniques for getting the students to talk more. Over time, I documented what worked and what did not, and when the next semester began, the journal gave me a clear sense of direction about what I could do differently in teaching the course for the second time.

The process I engaged in that year was not a full-fledged action research project. I did not systematically go through the steps of planning, acting, observing, reflecting, and replanning. I did systematically collect data, which I later analyzed and interpreted, so this study is an example of teacher research in a language classroom. But, more important, as a teacher, I learned a great deal in the process (K. M. Bailey, 2001). Was keeping the journal time consuming and difficult? Well, yes, at first it took some discipline. Was the outcome worth the effort? Absolutely.

FUTURE TRENDS

What will the future hold for classroom research, particularly studies conducted by teachers, including those involving the action research approach? There are at least three predictable trends.

The first is that as videocameras become more accessible (i.e., cheaper and easier to use), teachers will use them more often to record data during language lessons. In the past, making a video-recording of classroom interaction often involved signing up in advance for the school's one videocamera and tripod. There might have even been a requirement that a trained audiovisual technician operate the camera. As a result, the hassle factor might have kept teachers from trying to videotape their lessons. And if teachers did go through these steps, the presence of the equipment and the stranger in the classroom could trigger the "observer's paradox" (Labov, 1972), the fact that, by openly observing human behavior, we may alter the very behavior we wish to observe. I expect that the threat of triggering the observer's paradox would be somewhat less severe if the teacher or one of the students were using a small hand-held videocamera to record the interaction rather than a stranger operating a large camera on a tripod.

The second likely trend is that online language lessons will be studied more frequently; there are two reasons for this. First, more language teaching will probably occur online as the number of technological options and tools increase. Second, some forms of technology provide automatic records of the online interaction, thus lessening the time and work involved in collecting and transcribing the data needed for studying lessons. For instance, Jepson (2005) investigated the differences between the typed chats and the voiced chats of English language learners participating in online chat rooms. He had to audio-record the interactions in the voiced chats and later transcribe them, but he was able to simply download the interactions in the typed chat sessions.

The third trend is related to the first two. The use of digital recording devices will make the analysis of classroom data easier. For example, after making a digital video-recording of students interacting in a lesson, teachers will be able to locate and isolate key episodes for transcription or other forms of analysis more easily than can be done with videotape. Synchronized multimedia integrated language resources can be used to connect video-recordings to particular lines of transcripts. Likewise, data from typed chats, such as those found in Moodle-based lessons,[2] can easily be searched with the electronic search function to locate key words, grammatical structures, and so on. Digital recording also permits the easier and more economical storage and retrieval of classroom data.

It is my hope that these developments, along with a growing recognition in the field that teachers have much to contribute, will lead to more teachers conducting research in their own classrooms. Such investigations can greatly increase our understanding of language learning and teaching in formal instructional settings.

CONCLUSION

In this chapter, I have discussed three related but separate constructs: classroom research, teacher research, and action research. To provide interested readers further avenues for exploration, I have cited several studies with different foci and/or research methods. Some studies have been described in greater detail to illustrate a particular approach to research. It is my hope that readers will find these ideas compelling, particularly the findings of teachers' classroom research.

In closing, I quote from McPherson's (1997) action research report, which was discussed earlier in this chapter:

> This action research project played a major role in helping *me* to understand the learning issues involved in *my class* and in developing systematic ways to investigate and address them. As a research method, action research was flexible enough to allow *me* to change the focus of *my* investigation from developing and trialing language learning materials and activities to addressing issues of difference and diversity. (p. 61; emphasis added)

I have added my own emphasis in these two sentences to stress the situated, localized nature of McPherson's research as well as what she personally gained from working on the project. Her positive attitude provides the impetus for all of us to think about conducting action research, teacher research, and classroom research in general. It is my belief that, for language teachers, conducting action research can "make our work more purposeful, interesting, and valuable, and as such it tends to have an energizing and revitalizing effect" (van Lier, 1994, p. 33).

SUMMARY

➤ Three approaches that are often confused are described: classroom research, teacher research, and action research.

➤ Classroom research is research conducted in language classrooms that focuses on the interaction in the lessons; it is defined by both the focus of the study and the setting in which the data are collected. Conducting classroom research can be beneficial for language teachers and for the profession in general.

➤ Teacher research is research conducted by the instructor; that is, it is defined by who conducts the study.

➤ Action research is a research method that consists of the iterative cyclic procedures of planning, acting, observing, reflecting, and replanning to solve problems and improve local practice.

DISCUSSION QUESTIONS

1. How do language classroom research, teacher research, and action research differ from one another? How do they differ from other forms of research with which you may be familiar (e.g., library research or quantitative or qualitative research methods)?

2. What are the advantages and disadvantages of language teachers conducting research in their own classrooms? What are the advantages and disadvantages of outsiders conducting research in language classrooms? Refer to examples from the chapter, and add your own.

3. What are two or three topics of interest to you as a teacher that have been investigated in language classroom research to date? Why are they of particular interest? What other topics do you think would be interesting or useful to investigate?

4. *Washback* has been defined as the effects of testing on language teaching and learning. Have you ever experienced washback, either as a teacher or as a language learner? If so, what were the circumstances? What was the test, and how did it influence your teaching or learning? If you had been able to do classroom research about the washback you experienced, what data would you have collected? What do you think the data would have shown you?

SUGGESTED ACTIVITIES

1. Record two or three consecutive lessons in the same language class. These tapes can provide baseline data. Listen to the recordings, and write down three to five questions that arise about the interaction in the class.
2. Think of some ways that you could go about answering your questions from Activity 1 by collecting additional data. How would your data collection procedures differ if you: (a) were teaching the class; or (b) were observing someone else teaching the class?
3. If you are currently teaching, identify an issue or problem that is puzzling to you. Then plan the initial steps of an action research project that you can conduct in your own class. Keep in mind that your goals may change as you work through the action research cycle of planning, acting, observing, reflecting, and replanning for the next iteration. Discuss your initial plans with a colleague or with a fellow student if you are in a teacher-training program.
4. Keep a diary of your own language teaching (or language learning) for a period of time, for instance, for two weeks. Try to write for at least 15 minutes each day. Write about both facts (what you and the students did) and your impressions (e.g., how you felt about the class). Do not reread your diary until the predetermined period is over. What patterns emerge in your diary entries? How can these issues be investigated further?

5. If you are currently teaching or doing your practice teaching, ask a trusted colleague or fellow student to observe you teaching a lesson and take notes on the interaction. What issues emerge from the observation that you were unaware of as the teacher? How could you and an observer investigate these issues further?

FURTHER READING

Burns, A. (1998). *Collaborative action research for English teachers.* Cambridge, UK: Cambridge University Press.
Wallace, M. J. (1998). *Action research for language teachers.* Cambridge, UK: Cambridge University Press.

These two books are comprehensive sources of information on action research.

Edge, J. (2001). *Action research.* Alexandria, VA: Teachers of English to Speakers of Other Languages.

This is a reader-friendly collection of action research reports.

Freeman, D. (1998). *Doing teacher research: From inquiry to understanding.* Boston, MA: Heinle & Heinle.
Johnson, K. E. (1999). *Understanding language teaching: Reasoning in action.* Boston, MA: Heinle & Heinle.

Freeman's (1998) and Johnson's (1999) books are ideal starting places for teachers who wish to do classroom research. They include examples of teacher research as well as teachers' comments on doing research.

ENDNOTES

[1] I am grateful to Mica Tucci, Courtney Pahl, Shani Abergel, Melanie Newman, and Ryan Damerow for their invaluable help and feedback during the preparation of this chapter.
[2] Moodle is a course management system. It is a free web application that educators can use to create effective online learning sites. It is available at https://moodle.org/.

39 | Reflective Teaching: Principles and Practices

JOHN M. MURPHY

> ## KEY QUESTIONS
>
> ➤ What does the idea of being a reflective language teacher bring to mind?
> ➤ How can language teachers continue to grow?
> ➤ What are some steps teachers can take to enhance awareness of their strengths and weaknesses?
> ➤ What are some strategies teachers could begin to develop now to avoid burnout in the future?

EXPERIENCE

Alice is in the third year of her teaching career. She serves as a full-time English as a second language (ESL) teacher at a U.S.-based intensive English program. Now in the 7th week of a 14-week semester, Alice is teaching a high-intermediate-level oral communication course. It is a course she has taught twice previously and one that Alice enjoys teaching. Listed in their order of representation, the 18 students in the course are from China, South Korea, two Middle Eastern countries, Vietnam, and two South American countries. The course features a wide range of communicative activity types that focus on developing students' speaking, listening, and pronunciation abilities. An overarching course goal is to develop learners' abilities in the kinds of academic speaking and listening tasks that will be expected of them once they become fully matriculated university undergraduates. To prepare for some of the challenges ESL learners encounter in academic settings, Alice uses assigned readings, brief instructor mini-lectures, and short video presentations to provide content for class discussions. Based on the content presented, she composes six to eight discussion prompts, which she arranges in a logical order and distributes as a class handout. In one recurring procedure, Alice then divides students into four small groups (of four to five students each) and instructs the students to have an interactive conversation supported by the discussion prompts.

Though this particular activity has worked well in the past and many of her current students responded enthusiastically during the initial weeks of the semester, recently Alice has noticed a marked decline in learner interest and participation. Lately, it seems that the same few students do most of the speaking in the groups, while the others do not seem to be contributing anything at all. Alice has tried her best to introduce topics that the learners have expressed interest in discussing, and she spends considerable time composing what she believes to be relevant and accessibly worded questions to prompt conversation. However, Alice recognizes that the classroom dynamic has degenerated to the point where less than a third of the class is contributing to the activity and even fewer seem to be benefiting from it. As well as feeling discouraged, Alice is at a loss as far as what else she might do to remedy this situation.

WHAT IS REFLECTIVE TEACHING?

As a language teacher, have you ever finished your teaching for the day only to find your mind racing with thoughts about lessons recently

613

completed? This is a recurring experience for me. My mind is filled with classroom images, including insights, memories of puzzling events, second guesses, resolutions, and plans for the future. I find myself responding with a full range of emotions that includes not only excitement, joy, and inspiration but also more troubling moments of boredom, annoyance, and even self-directed disappointments. There are occasions when something particularly intriguing might find its way into subsequent plans for teaching, but unless I take the step of writing my ideas down, such insights tend to dissipate into the evening.[1]

Richards and Lockhart (1994b) define *reflective teaching* as an approach to second language (L2) classroom instruction in which current and prospective teachers "collect data about teaching, examine their attitudes, beliefs, assumptions, and teaching practices, and use the information obtained as a basis for critical reflection" (p. 1). They posit five basic assumptions:

1. An informed teacher has an extensive knowledge base about teaching, particularly as connected with local contexts.
2. Much can be learned about teaching through self-inquiry.
3. Much of what happens in teaching is unknown to the teacher.
4. Teaching experience alone is insufficient as a basis for continuing development.
5. Critical reflection can trigger a deeper understanding of teaching.

Why should we spend the time and energy it takes to develop understandings through reflective teaching? We may find the answer by considering both our continuing needs as teachers and, even more important, the needs of the language learners we serve. What the five assumptions share is that reflective teachers (RTs) are capable of learning from, and further developing, their personal understandings and explanations of life within classrooms. A central reason for us to be interested in reflective teaching "is to gain awareness of our teaching beliefs and practices," to learn "to see teaching differently" (Gebhard & Oprandy, 1999, p. 4), and to develop and transform our professional practices. In addition to the reasons cited thus far, an integral dimension of reflective teaching is learning to take action, when possible, on whatever we might be

learning about ourselves as teachers and about students' responses with the goal of enhancing the quality of the language learning opportunities we are able to provide (Richards & Farrell, 2011). As language teachers, taking action might involve exploring instructional innovations, trying out alternatives, and modifying—or even breaking—teaching routines based on what we learn (Fanselow, 1988).

This chapter explores ways to help ensure that moments of self-reflection serve productive purposes. Gaining teaching experience, participating in teacher-development courses, thinking about and discussing published scholarship, attending conferences, consulting with colleagues, and getting to know students better are but some of the ways English language teachers grow as professionals (Richards & Farrell, 2005). This chapter adds to such resources by introducing ways for teachers to look inward, both within themselves and within the courses they offer, to access information and inspiration about their efforts in language classrooms. My purpose is to introduce reflective teaching since one of the more intriguing characteristics that distinguishes adults from children is the adult's increased capacities for self-reflective thought (Kohlberg, 1981). The challenge is to put such capacities to productive use.

Purposes of reflective teaching

The purposes of reflective teaching are: (1) to expand our understandings of the teaching-learning process; (2) to expand our repertoire of strategic options as language teachers; (3) to take ownership of our own theories of language teaching as informed by teaching practice; and (4) to enhance the quality of learning opportunities we are able to provide in language classrooms. To these ends, those of us interested in reflective teaching take steps to deepen our awareness of teaching and learning behaviors by working to improve our abilities to:

- gather and examine information on what is taking place within a language course
- identify anything puzzling about the teaching-learning process
- build awareness and deepen understanding of teaching-learning behaviors

- collaborate with others interested in processes of reflective teaching
- refine questions tied to teaching that are worth further exploration
- locate resources to help clarify questions being posed
- make informed changes in teaching-learning behaviors
- document changes and share emerging insights with others over time

CONCEPTUAL UNDERPINNINGS

The roots of reflective teaching extend at least as far back as John Dewey's contributions in the early twentieth century (J. Burton, 2009; Farrell, 2007; Zeichner & Liston, 1996). Dewey (1933) posits three essential characteristics of reflective teaching:

1. *Open-mindedness*—the ability to remain attentive and receptive to different points of view
2. *Responsibility*—staying aware and being responsive to the consequences of our actions
3. *Wholeheartedness*—doing our best to situate our engagements with open-mindedness and to accept responsibility as the core of our professional lives

Zeichner and Liston (1996) remind us that openmindedness, responsibility, and wholeheartedness are states of being to be aspired to, not qualities we ever fully possess. While being conscientious in working to embrace these characteristics is essential to our professional lives, we should also recognize that reflective practitioners, just like everyone else, are fallible. As teachers we will have many good days and growing numbers of rewarding classroom experiences, but we remain intimately acquainted with what it means to stumble, to fall, and at times to fail, as well. Our challenge is to learn as much as we can from all such experiences. What Dewey sets out as the landscape of reflective teaching features a horizon that we challenge ourselves to be attentively and wholeheartedly moving toward, though it remains a destination we may never reach. The rewards of reflective teaching can be discovered only through the process of continuing on our journey.

Not I, nor anyone else can travel that road for you.
You must travel it by yourself.
It is not far. It is within reach.
Perhaps you have been on it since you were born, and did not know.
Perhaps it is everywhere—on water and on land.

Walt Whitman, "Song of Myself"

Three cognitive dimensions commonly associated with reflective teaching are *reflection-in-action, reflection-on-action*, and *reflection-for-action* (Schön, 1983). The first is probably the most familiar to practicing teachers since reflecting-*in*-action involves the online, real-time decisions teachers are continually making while teaching. Teaching is, after all, a decision-making process (H. D. Brown, 2007; Richards & Lockhart, 1994b). When reflecting-*in*-action, teachers depend on previously assimilated forms of knowledge (e.g., knowledge schemata, maxims of teaching, and instructional routines) that they carry with them into the classroom. An example of reflection-*in*-action is the teacher's deciding what to do while an unplanned or unexpected event happens in the classroom (see Figure 1). Although experienced teachers may be better able to make efficient use of their repertoire of teaching routines when impromptu decisions are called for, "novice teachers may have [more of]

Soon after setting up a small-group activity in a class of adult ESL learners, you notice that someone left the classroom door partially open and the hallway has become noisy. Since you are assisting one of the groups while seated on the other side of the room, in a soft voice you call to Anna, a woman in her early 20s, who is seated closest to the door. Once you catch Anna's attention, you quietly mouth the words, "*Could you close the door?*" accompanied by a hand gesture mimicking the closing of a door. Rather than following through with what you thought was a politely worded request, you are surprised when she immediately begins to complain to the three students around her about being asked to do such a thing. Though her comments start off mildly, they soon escalate into an angry verbal scolding directed at you that everyone present hears. Her unexpected reaction seems way out of the proportion to what you thought was a normal request. Her animated scolding of you continues for well over three minutes. As the teacher you are stunned.

Figure 1. Reflection-*in*-action: An unexpected classroom event.

a problem reflecting-*in*-action because they have not built up such an advanced schema of teaching routine" (Farrell, 2007, p. 5).

In contrast, reflections-*on*-action are retrospective. These typically take place once a lesson is over and the teacher engages in thinking back on lesson events already completed when there is more time available to synthesize what happened during a lesson. When engaged with reflections-*on*-action, teachers can find it easier to activate a wider range of their experiences and knowledge about the teaching process since: (1) the pressure to perform in the classroom is suspended; and (2) more time is available to think (Bartels, 2009). Under these more relaxed, outside-the-classroom conditions, the teacher is better able to reconsider and build an awareness of the meaning, sources, and impacts of lesson events, including the actions and responses of everyone who was present in the room. Since different lengths of time available and degrees of need for immediate action are the factors distinguishing between them, reflection-*in*-action seems to be a more purely cognitive process, while reflection-*on*-action offers enhanced potential to draw from, and further develop, both cognitive and metacognitive reasoning processes (Borg, 2003).

The third reflection type, reflection-*for*-action, differs from the other two in that its purpose is more explicitly proactive and future-oriented. It is, in fact, the broader purpose and *raison d'être* of reflective teaching (Wilson, 2008). Through reflection-*for*-action, we recognize that our purpose goes beyond enhancing our awareness of past or present classroom events. Rather, we assimilate and move beyond these initial purposes and begin to develop action plans for what to do and for what to do differently in the future. Such are the practical implications of reflective teaching. While all of us want to increase our capacities for understanding and responding to live events in the classroom and for learning to make sense of past experiences, ultimately a more ambitious purpose envisions a future of what our classrooms, students' lives as learners, and our own lives as teachers have yet to become. In this sense, reflection-*for*-action represents a culminating dimension of reflective teaching as supported and informed by its other two dimensions (Conway, 2001). Figure 2 summarizes the three types of teacher reflection.

Alternative traditions of reflective teaching

In addition to the conceptual roots and tripartite dimensions of reflective teaching already discussed, there is another definitional matter that merits attention—specialists continue to debate the scope and

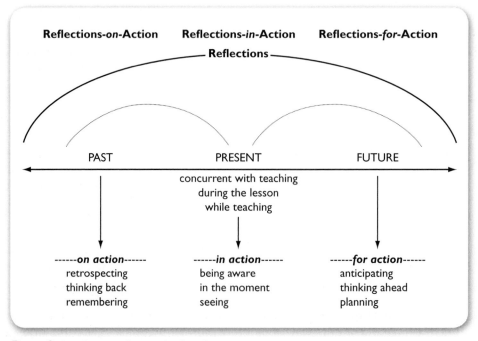

Figure 2. Landscape of a teacher's reflections.

parameters of reflective teaching. In one tradition, the focus is on the professional efforts of individual teachers working in particular settings. Illustrated in the work of many contemporary English language teachers, this first tradition involves the processes of self-observation, self-assessment, building awareness, and continuing professional development (Richards & Farrell, 2005). As individual teachers we take deliberate steps to examine and think about what we do in the classroom, why we do the things we do, what outside sources to consult, whether or not what we do benefits learners, and what plans to make for the future. Our reflective efforts often lead to modifications in our instructional routines combined with a recognized need for continuing exploration, refinement, further probing, and continuing change. An underlying premise is that sustained efforts of this kind eventually lead to improvements in the quality of our teaching. A point sometimes overlooked by those encountering discussions of reflective teaching for the first time is that its intended beneficiaries are the current and future language learners we meet since our aspiration is to provide learners with continually improving learning opportunities.

Although not the specific focus of this chapter, there is a second reflective teaching tradition that extends beyond the professional lives of individual teachers (Collin & Karsenti, 2011). This second tradition also features cycles of critical reflection, exploration, and change, but it differs in that it widens the focus of attention to include "broader historical, sociopolitical, and moral contexts of schooling" for the purpose of fostering change in these contexts (Farrell, 2007, p. 4). It is important to acknowledge this second tradition's potential to expand the scope of our attention to include the professional lives of larger teams of teacher-colleagues working in collaboration, including those working across whole programs, institutions, professional associations, national agencies, and beyond.[2]

CLASSROOM APPLICATIONS

Topics explored by reflective teachers

To examine some of the topics typically explored by RTs, we first need to acknowledge that every language course is unique. English language

teaching and learning are processes embedded in complex arrays of dynamic and socially interactive events. Early stages of reflective teaching begin with a teacher's desire to better understand the dynamics of a single language course as it is being experienced by a group of learners and their teacher (J. C. Richards, 1998). This is not to say that reflective teaching cannot extend beyond the scope of a single course; at later stages, it often does. But as a place to begin, most teachers find an individual course to be the most useful place to initiate what eventually becomes the systematic efforts of reflective teaching. Some general topic areas that RTs often explore are: (1) communication patterns in the classroom (e.g., turn-taking and the teacher's action zone); (2) teacher decision making; (3) ways in which learners apply knowledge; (4) the affective climate (i.e., the emotional comfort level of everyone in the classroom); (5) impacts of the classroom's physical environment; and (6) a teacher's self-assessment of growth and development as a professional (Richards & Farrell, 2011). In the next section, I focus on the first two of these six topic areas.

Reflection Break 1

In addition to these six general areas, what are some other areas you think RTs who work in English language teaching settings might profitably explore? Alternatively, what might be some specific examples of the six areas just listed?

Communication patterns in the classroom. Teachers interested in communication patterns might begin by exploring relatively broad topics such as: Who is doing what during lessons? Who are the sources of power and control? And do learners sometimes have an impact on what takes place? Later, more specific topics might be examined, such as teachers' ways of giving instructions, providing feedback, using language, encouraging language use beyond the classroom, working with reluctant learners, and responding to students' errors. With respect to students' behaviors, RTs might examine learners' ways of requesting clarifications, responding to feedback, interacting with their peers, responding to changes in teaching, using learning strategies, and so forth. A brief listing of additional classroom dimensions to explore include: the affective climate of the classroom; impacts of debilitative and facilitative anxiety; cultural considerations; the physical setup of the classroom; and the impact of textbooks, student-generated materials, and other instructional resources (including resources beyond the classroom).

Most of us are interested in better understanding of how communications among all participants in the classroom influence teaching and learning experiences (Allwright & Bailey, 1991). For example, a teacher might examine recurring instructional routines to better understand students' learning preferences. Or the teacher might analyze whether lessons usually begin and end in the same way or if there are recognizable patterns in how lessons are structured and organized. With video support, it is possible to divide a lesson into identifiable segments for analysis. Multiple viewings tend to reveal lesson openings, introductions to specific activities (e.g., setting things up, giving directions, and offering rationales), core lesson segments (e.g., guided practice activities and application tasks), transitions from one activity to another, sequencing of lesson segments (e.g., pre-, core-, and post-activity phases), students' responses to feedback, and the teacher's way of drawing a lesson to a close (e.g., calling for attention, assigning homework, or previewing upcoming events) (Richards & Farrell, 2011). Most language lessons feature identifiable segments of these kinds straddled by transitions from one segment to another. By generating and then examining a video-recording of one's own teaching multiple times, a teacher may gain a clearer understanding of how she or he structures, paces, and sequences recurring lesson segments (Bailey, Curtis, & Nunan, 2001b).

Close review of ways of teaching leads many teachers to consider ways of manipulating features embedded within lesson segments to increased effect. A particularly interesting dimension of classroom communication patterns is the nature of participant interactions. Who speaks to whom, how often, in what sequence, and for how long? How are speaking turns distributed? Is the teacher the only one who controls turn distribution? How are the topics and shifts in topic development introduced? What are some of the ways in which learners gain the floor as speakers in the midst of classroom communications? Are there learners who are relatively more or less participatory during particular lesson phases, and do patterns of classroom communication provide opportunities for learners to take initiative? Do male students speak more than female students?

Teacher decision making. This area for exploration includes a vast, and as yet poorly understood, dimension of language teaching. Acts of language teaching spring from sources within us that include our cognitive, behavioral, and emotional responses to external classroom events (Borg, 2003). Because all of us depend on knowledge, values, and beliefs about teaching and learning to function competently as teachers, our internal understandings and expectations contribute greatly to our teaching decisions and behaviors. Richards and Lockhart (1994) divide teacher decision making into pre-, during-, and post-lesson decisions. In the case of during-lesson decisions (i.e., reflection-*in*-action), teachers have very little time to follow through on what they decide to do since the process unfolds in collaboration with—and in front of—a group of learners. At such moments, a teacher's decisions may seem nearly instantaneous although they are informed by the teacher's background and previous experiences. Communication patterns in classrooms, lesson participant interactions, and teacher decision making are just a few of the topic areas often explored by RTs. They suggest the kinds of topics that most language teachers are interested in learning more about but that RTs take deliberate action to explore more closely.

Reflection Break 2

Generate a list of topics related to your own teaching that you think would be worth learning more about. See if you can come up with at least four examples not mentioned in the preceding section. Once your list is complete, compare it to that of one or more other language teacher(s). How might you set about increasing your understanding of at least some of the topics of interest to you?

Tools for reflective teaching: Gathering information

Just as there are many topics to be explored by RTs, there are also many different ways to gather such information. I refer to ways of gathering information included in this section as tools in a positive sense since these are the tools of the trade that growing numbers of RTs depend on to explore the teaching-learning process. Teachers use different tools to access different sorts of information. By combining two or more tools over the span of an entire course, a teacher gains access to alternative vantage points. While Figure 3 depicts a broader listing of some of the major tools RTs use, I now turn to five tools that should be useful to teachers interested in becoming more involved in the processes and procedures of reflective teaching.[3] These tools are five-minute papers, formative teacher assessment surveys, student focus groups, retrospective field notes, and formative feedback from peers.

Five-minute papers. The regular use of five-minute papers is a direct way of finding out how learners are perceiving and responding to our efforts as teachers. A few minutes before the end of the lesson, the teacher asks everyone to take out a sheet of paper and to write responses to just one or two open-ended prompts, such as (1) What is the one thing you are likely to remember from today's class? (2) What was the most confusing concept we covered? (3) Is there anything you would like to know more about? (4) Or is there anything you think we should be doing differently in class? Learner responses to such questions are especially useful if the teacher emphasizes that their function is to provide formative feedback on how the course is going. In many English language courses—especially in ESL settings—teachers can ask students to compose five-minute papers in English. With lower-level learners or in English as a foreign language settings, students might be given the option of writing five-minute papers in their first language. Though five-minute papers take brief periods of time away from the regular part of a lesson, using them at the end of class can better inform a teacher's post-lesson (i.e., reflection-*for*-action) decisions. When introducing these papers for the first time, I explain to students that:

- Their names should not appear on their papers (their writings will be kept in confidence).
- When reading the papers I will *not* be looking at things like grammar, spelling, or vocabulary choice but only for the ideas they convey.
- As their teacher, I will be reading to improve my teaching in the course and not to evaluate their progress.

Invariably, I find something of value in what students have to say. I occasionally ask a colleague to read the papers first and then discuss with me the gist of students' comments. Involving someone else is a small step toward gaining access to an outside perspective on my work. As well as providing an opportunity to talk about my teaching with another teacher, it helps to ensure that I will be more responsive to students' concerns. Experiences over the past few years have taught me that a teacher's sense of timing is essential since the use of five-minute papers can be overdone. If students are asked to compose them too often, they lose interest and may even become resentful. In courses that meet multiple times per week, I find that once every two or three weeks is enough. Using five-minute papers wisely can serve to remind students that their responses to the course are valued and given serious attention.

Formative feedback from learners
- Five-minute papers
- Teacher assessment surveys
- Questionnaires
- Dialogue journals
- Written assessments
- Student focus groups

Formative feedback from other teachers
- Peer collaborations (Richards & Farrell, 2005)
- Case interviews
- Field notes and classroom ethnographies
- Dialogue with a supervisor (Oprandy, 1999)
- Observation schedules
- Score charts
- Classroom observation

Self-generated sources of information
- Retrospective field notes
- Teaching journals and teaching logs
- Classroom diagrams and maps
- Lesson plans and lesson reporting
- Audio-recordings
- Video-recordings
- Transcript analysis
- Protocol analysis
- Stimulus recall

Course descriptions (Murphy & Byrd, 2001)

Summative feedback from learners at the end of the course

Action research (Burns, 2009)

Figure 3. Some tools of reflective teaching: Ways of gathering information.

Formative teacher assessment surveys. A complement to assigning five-minute papers is to implement several formative surveys of students' perceptions of how well the course is going. These might be scheduled in the syllabus on the first day of class so students know from the start that their impressions will be valued, when their opinions will be solicited, and what the survey will include. Some advantages of formative assessment surveys are that they can be designed in advance, it is easy to keep students' comments anonymous, a lot of information can be gathered at one time, and the procedure may be carried out at regular intervals. One option is to implement such surveys three times during a semester-length course. For example, in a 15-week course, the teacher can gather formative assessment information through student surveys after the 3rd, 8th, and 12th weeks of class. Giving a survey early on serves as a window into students' initial impressions. By the 8th week their impressions are even better informed. Although a student survey in the 12th week is useful, at this point the course is coming to a close and students' comments will have more of an impact on future course iterations. A practical strategy is to make the first survey sheet that students will be invited hand in the very last page of the course syllabus, to make the second survey the second-to-last page, and so on (see Appendices A and B for illustrations). For settings where student access to the requisite technology is available, an alternative to paper-based surveys is to use an online survey tool such as *SurveyMonkey,* which allows up to 10 survey questions for free.[4] When administering surveys either early or midway through the course, teachers can take time to discuss the survey findings with the class. This way, students are more likely to feel that their voices have been actually heard.

Reflection Break 3

Have you ever had an opportunity to receive learner feedback on your teaching? If so, what did you learn from the experience? If not, do you think such sources of information might be useful? Do you expect the quality of learner feedback to vary depending on the learners' cultural backgrounds? If so, what can you do to compensate for cultural differences?

Student focus groups. The use of student focus groups is a simple idea yet one that is underused in our field. The degree of requisite planning for focus groups is more involved than either five-minute papers or formative student surveys. With student focus groups, someone directly engages learners in a discussion of how well they feel a course is going. Although it is possible for the classroom teacher to serve as the focus group discussion leader, an even better procedure is to ask a colleague to perform this role. For example, teachers can make arrangements for a colleague they trust (and with whom they have a constructive working relationship) to serve as the focus group facilitator. In most settings, it is better to deliberately avoid working with a program administrator or supervisor for this since student focus groups are more useful when they are not used for formal evaluative purposes. I try to save my use of this procedure for a period in the course when things seem to be going relatively well (or at least normally).

Classroom teachers can arrange for their colleague to visit the class during a 30–45 minute time slot when they will not be present but for which students have been prepared in advance. As agreed on with the class, the colleague's role is to lead the whole class in a discussion of broad topics such as:

- What do students like about the course (or the teacher)?
- What are their least favorite things?
- Does the course textbook—or other instructional material—seem helpful?
- What are some characteristics of the teacher's instructional style that work well?
- Are there other teacher characteristics that students find to be less helpful?
- Do the assessment procedures seem fair?
- What are some of the ways in which the course might be improved?

The facilitator could distribute a list of such questions or use a modified version of the teacher assessment survey in Appendix B. Students can be invited to pick and choose their preferred topics for discussion. Prior to the agreed-on day and at the start of the actual focus group discussion, students should be assured that their comments will be kept in confidence. The facilitator's role is to listen carefully, keep the discussion on track, and take notes on what students have to say. When the class is finished, the facilitator composes a written report (*not* to be used for formal evaluation) that provides a synopsis of the students' comments that will be made available for the teacher to review. No student names should appear in the report, and it needs to be phrased to protect students' identities. Once the report has been completed, the visiting colleague gives the classroom teacher a copy and makes arrangements to discuss what took place in private.

An effective model for those interested in student focus groups is to build toward a reciprocal peer arrangement in which two teachers serve as the discussion facilitators for each other's classes. An alternative is to introduce the focus group process with the whole class but to ask for only a few students (e.g., 20–25% of the class) to volunteer to participate. Many language teachers find the kind of information that student focus groups reveal tremendously helpful for fine-tuning their planning decisions and increasing their awareness of their strengths and weaknesses as teachers. Focus groups can also be helpful when curriculum or textbook changes are being contemplated.

Retrospective field notes. An even less intrusive way to gather information on teaching is for teachers to document their understandings and explanations of what they are doing in the course through retrospective field notes. The word *retrospective* signals that such notes are not generated during lessons but only after a lesson has finished. Ideally a teacher's field notes should be generated within 30–60 minutes following the lesson. If too much time elapses, memories of classroom events fade quickly. The activity is similar to keeping a personal journal or diary, though field notes of this kind focus specifically on course-related events. To produce them, the teacher writes about whatever is fresh in her or his memory. General guidelines are to try to keep track of classroom issues that seem relevant to the lesson recently completed and to treat field notes as an ethnographer treats raw data. RTs using this procedure save their accumulated notes, review them on a regular basis, and examine their notes for recurring patterns. After a teacher has reworked her

or his notes by deleting or modifying anything that might be personally uncomfortable, a colleague might be invited to read them and discuss any relevant course concerns. Retrospective field notes are a valuable source of information about our understandings and can become a richly textured record of our explorations of teaching over time. Some general ways to frame field notes are to respond to questions about the teacher's role in the classroom, the teaching process, students in the class, the learning process, or anything tied to the dynamics of the lesson itself. A way to get started, and a useful task to return to whenever the RT has too little to write about, is to spend time generating a list of questions that might be useful as writing prompts for field notes in the future.

Reflection Break 4
Collaborate with someone else (a pre- or in-service teacher) to produce a list of five to eight questions you could use as prompts for composing retrospective field notes. Plan them so each writing prompt targets different dimensions of classroom teaching and learning.

Formative feedback from peers. There are many ways in which a teacher may collaborate with others to gain a deeper understanding and awareness of the teaching-learning process. I have mentioned earlier that colleagues may be consulted when examining materials such as five-minute papers, focus group discussions, retrospective field notes, and survey responses. A classic way of gaining access to formative feedback is for teachers to invite a peer—that is, another language teacher whose opinions they respect— to visit and observe one or more of their classes (Richards & Farrell, 2005). For reflective teaching, such visits should be planned to be different from the kinds of observations typically carried out by supervisors (see Murphy, 1992). For those interested in learning about more formal supervisory roles and practices, K. M. Bailey (2006) provides in-depth discussion of principles and practices of supervisory observation.

In setting up a peer's nonsupervisory visit to the classroom, it is important to discuss and clarify the visitor's purpose in advance (Cosh, 1999). Any potential visitor will have preconceptions, attitudes, and beliefs about what constitutes legitimate purposes for visiting another teacher's class. Some of these attitudes and beliefs may be compatible with the teacher's own, while others may not be. A primary purpose for observing another person teach is to gather descriptive information on what takes place during the lesson (Fanselow, 1988). Afterward, any information gathered may be examined, analyzed, discussed, or even ignored, but if some sort of record of what took place is never produced, meaningful discussions of the teaching are less likely to occur. A starting point to prepare for a peer's classroom visit is for both parties to be aware of the importance of staying attentive, interested in the lesson, open-minded, and nonjudgmental. Though some visitors may be able to gather useful information by merely observing what takes place, a visitor's recollections are more reliable and tend to be more helpful as starting points for later discussion if the visitor has taken notes. When clarifying the purpose for a peer visit, I emphasize my interest in engaging in discussions of teaching that are tied to descriptive information the visitor is able to gather during the lesson.

In a spirited yet thoughtful exchange, Master (1983, 1984) and Zuck (1984) debate the principles, purposes, and procedures of classroom observation that continue to be relevant today. In the language programs where I work, teachers have developed some useful procedures for observations that foster healthy professional relationships among those interested in collaborating as nonsupervisory visitors to each other's classes. Although the procedures are not intended as prescriptions for others to follow, they are offered here to illustrate the possibilities. I recommend they be viewed as prompts for discussing and clarifying what might be relevant procedures for either a "visiting" or a "visited" teacher in a given local instructional setting.

The "visited" teacher. Whenever a peer teacher (i.e., a nonsupervisor colleague) is coming to visit my class, we set time in advance to discuss the purpose for the classroom visit. A couple of classes prior to the visit, I explain to students that one of my colleagues will be coming to observe the class to assist me to become a more effective teacher. If the colleague comes to the class before I have had a chance to adequately prepare students, learners tend to get nervous and act differently, and the visitor misses what might have been a good opportunity to see a normal class. Prior to our pre-visit conversation, I make a list of anything I would like feedback on. These items become a focus of our pre-visit conversation. Together we rearrange the items in an agreed-on order of priority. Even at the early stage in the process, I find that the visitor's comments and questions can be helpful in clarifying some of my concerns about the course. During our pre-visit conversation, we also arrange a later time to meet after the class visit. I prefer to schedule this post-visit conversation for a couple of days following the observation since visitors tend to have more useful things to say if they have had a couple of days to reflect on what they witnessed. In anticipation of our post-visit discussion, I use the time between the lesson and our subsequent conversation to make notes about what I remember about the lesson. I also review the list of discussion topics we settled on and give careful consideration to what the lesson might have revealed. When we meet, I prefer my colleague's conversation opener to be something very general, intended to get me thinking and talking (e.g., "Well, what do you remember from the lesson?"; "What are some of the things you think went well?" . . . or not so well?). Although I try to be forthcoming when responding to my colleague's prompts, I am also interested in looking for opportunities to learn about the visitor's insights and perceptions. Once our scheduled discussion begins, I try to be patient and listen carefully whenever my collaborator has something to say.

The "visiting" teacher. Whenever I am asked to serve as a "visiting teacher," I try to figure out in anticipation of the class visit what my colleague would like me to look for. Otherwise, I might end up focusing on something of limited practical value. I ask my colleague things such as where in the room I should sit, whether or not he or she will be comfortable if I take notes, how long I should stay, and what I should do if small-group activities are used. Ideally, the teacher will have explained to the class ahead of time who I am and why I am visiting so that such explanations are unnecessary on the day of the actual visit. I am careful to arrive at least five minutes before the class begins. If possible, I find a seat near the back of the room, off to one side. I do not bring electronic devices or observation instruments unless my colleague has specifically asked me to use such supports. My usual procedure is to observe and listen carefully and to take brief written notes as unobtrusively as I can.

Since one of my purposes is to call as little attention to myself as possible, my preferred strategy is to have a book I really am interested in reading in front of me as students are entering the room. What students see if they glance in my direction is someone reading a book. Soon after the lesson begins, I quietly place the book aside and begin to watch, listen, and gather information discretely. When I write things down, I focus on nonjudgmental descriptions of classroom events. If I notice that I am writing down an opinion or suggestion, I place it between brackets as a reminder that such comments are different from my primary purpose. Eventually, my opinions and suggestions may end up being helpful as part of our follow-up discussion, but I keep these separate and clearly identified. If I notice that some students are paying an inordinate amount of attention to me, I suspend note-taking and simply watch and listen. If note-taking is impossible, immediately following the class I find a quiet place to write down my memories of the lesson as best I can. If I wait more than 30–60 minutes to do this, I find it increasingly difficult to access reliable memories.

Usually on the day following the lesson, I spend some time reviewing my notes, elaborating on what they include, and relating what seem to be important pieces of information to the themes the teacher and I agreed on as possible topics for discussion. For our post-visit conversation, I focus on what took place; what the teacher and students were doing; things I learned; and any personal beliefs about the teaching-learning process that I noticed being illustrated, extended, or challenged. I prioritize the items for discussion, and I look for opportunities to relate anything I have noticed to my own experiences in teaching. I often find myself saying things such as, "When you were doing X, Y, or Z as part of the lesson, it reminded me of things that I do, too" (see Fanselow, 1988). Comments that reveal connections to my own teaching are especially important since they help facilitate collaborative discussions relevant to our shared experiences and interests.

Reflection Break 5

Design a list of suggestions and guidelines you would like to follow when collaborating with another language teacher in ways similar to those discussed in this section. Include guidelines for both a "visited" and a "visiting" teacher. Are there any topics mentioned in this section that would not be of particular concern to you? Are there any topics left unmentioned that you would like to see given more attention?

Two underlying concerns

Now that we have examined some topics and tools, it is important to acknowledge two fundamental challenges facing those interested in the processes of reflective teaching. These challenges are the search for multiple perspectives and the question of learner involvement.

The search for multiple perspectives. To become more involved in processes of reflective teaching, an RT needs to ask, "How can I begin to see and examine my classroom efforts in ways similar to how others might be able to see and examine them?" Access to multiple perspectives makes it more likely that we will attain a deeper understanding of our work. The search for multiple perspectives relates to two essential stages of reflective teaching: gathering information (the data-collection stage) and making sense of the data (the interpretation stage).

As part of the first stage, RTs find ways of gathering information on teaching and learning that include outsider perspectives. Due to our immersion in the complex process of teaching, normally we are too close to the instructional process to form a realistic appraisal of our own strengths and weaknesses as teachers. By way of illustration, most of us are somewhat surprised the first time we view a video-recording of our teaching. Some common responses include "Oh, that's not what I sound like," "Is that what I really look like?" and "Oh, my directions really weren't very clear." A video-recording of teaching-in-action brings to the fore rather tangible evidence of how others probably view us. Such recordings surprise us because they serve as estrangement devices (i.e., any tool used to gain an outside perspective on what we do in the classroom). Anthropologists refer to such a vantage point as an *etic perspective* (an outsider's view). However, to complement the outsider perspectives, RTs are also interested in gathering information from course participants' perspectives. Anthropologists refer to the vantage point represented by course participants (e.g., learners) as an *emic perspective* (an insider's view). Some emic tools already discussed earlier include the use of five-minute papers, teacher assessment surveys, and student focus groups. As D. Freeman (1998) explains, etic perspectives provide us with information on "what outsiders see," while emic perspectives provide information on "what insiders know" (p. 70). Figure 4 summarizes etic versus emic distinctions that we can apply to either the collection or interpretation of classroom information. The effort to include multiple perspectives challenges RTs to find ways of gathering information on teaching-learning processes not only through their own perceptions and understandings but also through those of learners who are participating in the course and through those of their colleagues.

The question of learner involvement. In connection with emic perspectives, a second question for RTs to ask is, "Do I want to involve learners in my efforts as a reflective teacher, and if so, to what degree?" There are many ways to collect information about what goes on in language courses. A distinction we can make is between ways that are less intrusive and those that are relatively more intrusive with respect to their potential impacts on learners' normal classroom experiences. Less intrusive means of gathering information depend on little or no involvement from learners. Teachers interested in less intrusive means do their best to avoid direct impacts on inside-the-classroom events. For instance, a teacher might gather information about teaching on a near-daily basis but only after the completion of individual

lessons. To do this, some teachers keep private journals focused on their teaching, of which learners remain completely unaware (Gadsby & Cronin, 2012). Other nonintrusive options include writing retrospective field notes (discussed earlier) or other retrospective procedures such as writing a lesson report. Although similar in format to a lesson plan, a lesson report is generated soon after a lesson has been taught (see Appendix C for a lesson report template). Through adoption of such nonintrusive procedures, it is possible for teachers to gain considerable information about the teaching process without involving learners.

Even with less intrusive procedures, RTs will be able to incorporate multiple perspectives into their efforts by inviting colleagues whose opinions they respect to review and discuss whatever information the teachers gather from the classroom. Two or more teachers might collaborate to review a video- or audio-recording of teaching, transcripts of lesson segments, journal entries, lesson reports, samples of student work, or students' questionnaire survey responses. Some of these options do feature learner participation to some degree. A teacher might, for example, arrange for a lesson to be video-recorded for later review. It is worth mentioning that if a videocamera is in the room, the teacher has already taken a step in the direction of involving learners. However, a teacher can lessen the impact of such a recording device by taking steps ahead of time to familiarize students with whatever procedures are being followed (e.g., class discussion, seeking learners' permissions, and the early incorporation of a planned recording device as a normal part of classroom routines). In the case of videocameras, some suggestions are to work with as small a recorder as possible, position it out of students' direct lines of vision, and involve one or more members of the class in its operation. Through its early introduction and classroom use, learners may perceive the presence of recording equipment as a perfectly normal feature of what they have already come to anticipate from the course. The point is to be aware of the potential impacts of such devices and procedures and to make informed decisions on what all parties (i.e., the teacher, his or her colleagues, and the students) might consider to be (un)acceptable levels of learner involvement.

Although far from a comprehensive list of options and possibilities, Figure 5 provides a synopsis of several issues discussed in this section

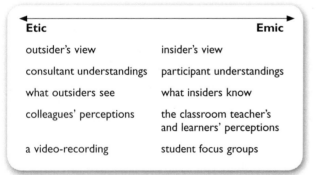

Figure 4. Continuum of vantage points for either the collection or interpretation of information on teaching-learning processes.

Etic

(A)

- A videorecording (video + audio) is made.
- A video- (or audio-) recording is made for the first time.
- A videocamera that is large and bulky is put at the front of the room.
- Learners participate in analyzing video-recordings during class time.
- A trained observer is inside the classroom.
- The in-class observer is someone unknown to learners.
- The in-class observer takes notes or completes an observation schedule live in the classroom.
- A supervisor gathers information on teaching for a formal assessment of teaching.

(B)

- An audio-recording only is made.
- A video- (or audio-) recording is made for the fifth time.
- A videocamera that is small is put out of sight of students.
- Learners participate in analyzing video-recordings of lessons only after a course has ended.
- A trained observer watches a video-recording of lesson.
- The in-class observer is someone learners know and are comfortable with.
- The in-class observer watches and listens, tries to blend into the background, and composes field notes only after the lesson has ended.
- A teacher gathers information on teaching through self-initiated collaborations with peers/colleagues.

Emic

(C)

- Students compose journals in which they discuss their experiences in the course and how they perceive the course.
- The teacher conducts student focus groups.
- Students are frequently interviewed.
- Whole-class, inside-the-classroom discussions about learners' perceptions and preferences are conducted while the course is in process.
- A student focus group, with the whole class participating, is held.
- The teacher serves as the focus group facilitator.
- Students complete several instructor assessment forms at different points during the course (formative).
- Five-minute papers are assigned frequently and on a regular basis.
- The teacher uses stimulated recall while the course is in process.
- The teacher and learners collaborate to gather information on the teaching-learning process.

(D)

- The teacher keeps a journal or engages in a regular practice of lesson reporting that focuses on course experiences and perceptions.
- A third party conducts student focus groups in which learners' comments are kept anonymous.
- Students are infrequently interviewed.
- Outside-of-class discussions with individual learners about their perceptions and preferences are conducted while the course is in process.
- A student focus group, with only some class members participating, is held.
- A teacher-colleague serves as the focus group facilitator.
- Students complete a single end-of-term instructor assessment form (summative).
- Transcripts are generated for discourse analysis of lesson events.
- The teacher uses stimulated recall only after the course is over.
- The teacher gathers information on teaching without learner participation (but may collaborate with colleagues).

Figure 5. Two-way matrix for gathering classroom information.

using a matrix of two intersecting continua for gathering information on teaching. As shown, the procedures in Quadrant A combine outsiders' perspectives with relatively more intrusive means for gathering information on teaching. Quadrant D is just the opposite; these procedures tap into insiders' perspectives through somewhat less intrusive means. Quadrant B is weighted toward outsider perspectives through less intrusive means. The procedures in Quadrant C involve the course participants sharing what they think about the course in ways that may impact students' learning experiences to varying degrees.

Teachers might set as a professional development goal to explore one or more of the options listed in each of the four quadrants over time. As we continue to learn more about these and other pathways to reflective teaching, as well as the particular topics we would like to explore within the language courses we teach, we will be reminded of the rewards of self-discovery, the importance of multiple perspectives, and the potentially facilitating impacts of learners' and colleagues' contributions to RTs' efforts.

FUTURE TRENDS

While resources to support reflective teaching abound, a disconcerting reality is that a majority of language teachers remain uninvolved (J. Burton, 2009). One impediment is that many teachers believe that the efforts of reflective teaching may drain valuable time and energy away from their primary professional roles as language teachers. While it is true that some procedures of reflective teaching may become time-consuming, several of the ones discussed in this chapter are not time-consuming at all (e.g., five-minute papers and periodic student surveys). In sum, a growing number of teachers affirm that self-initiated involvement with reflective teaching leads to processes of self-discovery that are well worth the effort.

Looking to the future, one need is to establish administrative structures within language programs that acknowledge and give professional credit for reflective teaching efforts. Teachers are more likely to become involved when they know they will be credited for the reflective teaching dimensions of their work. Such acknowledgment and credit can be accomplished through administrative support for in-house discussions, brown-bag presentations, and other local opportunities for RTs to share what they are exploring and learning about teaching. Minimally, such contributions should be acknowledged and credited as part of teachers' annual (or other professional) reviews. Likewise, RTs may pursue opportunities to disseminate some of their insights in professional forums beyond their academic homes (e.g., local, regional, and national conferences), which will also merit annual review credit. The annual TESOL conference, for example, features several less intimidating forums such as poster sessions and discussion groups that are natural places for those who are relatively new to sharing their work in conference presentations.

Also, reflective teaching will be very useful in more formal efforts, such as the supervision and mentoring of classroom teachers. Supervisors and mentors could be more closely involved as long as constructive working relationships have been established and clear distinctions are maintained between summative and formative support for teachers (Payant & Murphy, 2012). Increasingly in TESOL and applied linguistics, attention is being given to the processes and procedures of both individual and collaborative teacher development through exploratory practice, action research, teacher study groups, teacher support groups, and collaborative case analysis, in addition to the more conventional models of mentoring and supervision (Johnston, 2009). (See also Bailey, this volume.) Two future directions are: (1) to explore possibilities for incorporating elements of reflective teaching in teacher mentoring and supervision; and (2) to allow time for some of these other activities (e.g., action research, teacher study groups, etc.) to better inform the more individualized efforts of RTs.

CONCLUSION

As overworked as the phrases might sometimes seem, RTs' efforts are ultimately about self-empowerment, self-renewal, and continuing self-initiated professional development. A refrain often heard within the contemporary narrative of our field is that all instances of language teaching are necessarily localized in the contextual constraints and possibilities of particular settings (K. E. Johnson, 2009; Murphy & Byrd, 2001). It is the individual teacher who is better positioned than anyone else to fully understand and appreciate the conditions of her or his classroom as well as the needs and aspirations of the learners in it. Reflective teaching offers pathways for enhancing such local understandings. While broader discussions of teaching may also contribute to our expanding awareness of classroom possibilities, it is within local settings that more finely tuned applications are made and through which teachers develop more personalized context-sensitive insights.

SUMMARY

➤ Reflective teaching has a fascinating history worth learning more about. It traces back to educational reformers in the twentieth century, particularly to the work of John Dewey, David Schön, and others.

➤ Although collaborations with others are rewarding, valued, and to be encouraged, individual teachers are fully capable of initiating reflective teaching efforts on their own.

➤ Numerous tools and procedures are available to support reflective teachers' efforts.

➤ When teachers are conscientious in looking within their own classrooms for topics worth exploring, inevitably relevant topics arise.

- The future of reflective teaching lies in increasing teacher participation and in forging wider professional appreciation for its value.
- Some ways to gain much needed support from program administrators and colleagues are to model, discuss, and share the results of reflective teaching both in local settings and at professional venues.

DISCUSSION QUESTIONS

1. Imagine you have reached the midpoint of a course in which you have been conscientious in your teaching efforts. Nevertheless, you notice that many of the students seem uninterested in the course. How can you find out what some of the problems might be?

2. You are teaching an intermediate-level course that focuses on enhancing oral communication abilities in an English-dominant part of the world. The 18 students in the course are from a wide range of countries and ethnic backgrounds. You notice that a majority of the Asian students seem very reluctant to participate compared to other members of the class. What can you do to explore why this is so? How can you get them to become more involved?

3. You are teaching several sections of an entry-level ESL course for recent immigrants in a continuing education program in an English-dominant part of the world. You realize that students mainly use their first languages outside the classroom. A complication is that the city in which you live encompasses many ethnic neighborhoods, which provide easy access to community services and businesses in students' first languages. What can you do to encourage students to apply what they are learning to their life experiences beyond the classroom?

4. You have been hired by a large and well-organized program that places considerable emphasis on the role and importance of formal evaluations of teaching. All teachers in the program are observed three times per term by a trained supervisor. However, in addition to supervisory feedback, you are interested in learning more about your teaching through self-initiated means. Discuss with a partner some other things you might do to learn more about your teaching from both etic and emic perspectives.

5. You are teaching English as a foreign language in a secondary school setting in a non-English-dominant part of the world (or in some other setting). You are very excited about a series of innovative teaching procedures that you are trying out in the classroom. How can you document whether constructive changes are taking place? Who can you involve, and what specifically would you want them to do?

SUGGESTED ACTIVITIES

1. Make arrangements to consult two or more practicing language teachers. Ask if they have ever heard of the tradition of reflective (or exploratory) teaching. (Be aware that some teachers use different terms for similar concepts.) Find out if they have ever been involved in such efforts. If they have, gather as much information as you can about how their efforts have made a difference in their teaching. If they have not, explore what other things they might be doing to grow and develop as language teachers.

2. Make arrangements to meet with a classroom teacher soon after a lesson she or he has just taught (choose a time when the two of you can work uninterrupted for at least 30 minutes). At the meeting, interview the teacher on what the lesson was like. Begin by asking open-ended prompts (e.g., "What were you planning to teach?" "How did things turn out?" and "Was there anything unexpected that happened?") If the teacher you are interviewing consents, consider audio-recording the interaction for later review. Also, if you serve as a classroom teacher, follow similar procedures to collaborate with someone willing to interview you.

3. Imagine you are interested in producing a video-recording of someone else's class in a language program familiar to you. How would you secure the teacher's permission? How would you put the teacher at ease? What are likely to be some of the classroom teacher's and the learners' concerns? How do you suggest that learners be prepared? What are some of the steps you would follow while recording? What would you do with the recording once it was completed?

4. Place yourself in the position of a language learner. If you were studying with a teacher who was interested in reflective teaching, how would

you want the teacher to involve you in such efforts? Referring to Figure 5, make a list of the kinds of things you would (and would not) be willing to do. From a learner's perspective, what are some of the topics you think would be worthy ones for the teacher to explore? Arrange to meet with a language learner studying in a program with which you are familiar, and interview the student concerning these themes.

FURTHER READING

Farrell, T. S. C. (2004). *Reflective practice in action: 80 reflection breaks for busy teachers.* Thousand Oaks, CA: Corwin Press.

Addressed not only to language teachers, Farrell offers dozens of reflection topics and tasks intended as a basis for self-initiated professional development.

Farrell, T. S. C. (2007). *Reflective language teaching: From research to practice.* New York, NY: Continuum.

Farrell's book-length introduction and discussion of reflective teaching specifically targets a TESOL readership.

Reflective Practice: International and Multidisciplinary Perspectives. (2000). Available from http://www.tandf.co.uk/journals/RP

This is a must-read journal dedicated to explorations of reflection in practice that concerns personal knowledge and transformation, voice, values, negotiated meaning, identity, and community.

Schön, D. (1983). *The reflective practitioner: How professionals think in action.* London, UK: Temple Smith.

This highly influential book examines professional knowledge, professional contexts, reflection-in-action, and processes of professional reasoning.

The following journals have regular sections dedicated to teacher research:

- *Language Teacher Research.* Section titled: "Practitioner Research."
- *TESOL Journal.* Section titled: "Language Teacher Research."

APPENDIX A: FORMATIVE TEACHER ASSESSMENT SURVEY

This is an illustration for a high-intermediate-level ESL course.

Formative Feedback (1st of 3)
Please complete this survey and place it on the front desk at the end of our eighth day of class, [insert day of the week], [insert month]. (Alternatively, you are welcome to place it in my mailbox in the main office.)
Directions: Please do not sign your name. We are three weeks into the course. This is a time for some formative feedback from you as a course participant. You are welcome to use both sides of this page. Thanks.
1. What are some features of the course that you think are working out pretty well (features you would like to see continued for the remainder of the course)?
2. What are some possible changes you would like to see incorporated into the course from this point forward?

APPENDIX B: FORMATIVE TEACHER ASSESSMENT SURVEY

Please respond to the following items as follows by writing in a, b, or c:

a	b	c
Yes, I definitely agree.	I agree somewhat.	No, I do *not* agree.

In general, the textbooks, materials, and assignments in this course:
_____ are interesting and useful
_____ are at the right level
_____ help me to practice and improve my language skills
_____ require the right amount of homework

In general, the teacher of this course:
_____ presents well-organized lessons
_____ speaks in a way that is clear and easy to understand
_____ is knowledgeable about the subjects we cover
_____ answers my questions well
_____ grades assignments and tests fairly
_____ makes good use of class time
_____ returns work (that I hand in) on time
_____ gives me individual help when I need it (or when I ask for it)
_____ encourages me to do my best
_____ relates well to students
_____ provides appropriate opportunities for me to participate in class

[A final survey item might ask: If you were in a conversation with a friend, would you recommend taking a course from this teacher? Why or why not?]

APPENDIX C: FORMAT FOR A LESSON REPORT

The following is intended only as an illustration. Individual teachers will need to revise and modify it to better fit their personal teaching styles and preferences.

1. What did students do during today's lesson?
2. How did you open the lesson?
3. What materials were used? Were they effective? Next time, how might you modify the materials in any way?
4. What classroom configurations (e.g., student groupings) did you use? Were they effective? Next time, how might you modify them in any way?
5. Describe the first activity, the second activity, the third activity, etc.
6. Describe any transitions between activities.
7. Were you satisfied with the sequencing of activities?
8. Describe and discuss any new or different teaching strategy you used today.
9. Did any problems arise? If so, how did you address them?
10. Was the pacing of lesson events effective?
11. Describe and assess the affective climate in the classroom.
12. Did anything happen that surprised you?
13. What do you think students learned during the lesson? What did they take away?
14. What might have been some of their confusions? What did they ask you about?
15. How did you bring the lesson to a close?
16. Will you teach this lesson the same way the next time around? In not, what might you do differently?

ENDNOTES

[1] An inspiration for many of the principles and practices featured in this chapter has been John F. Fanselow's work on second language teacher development through self-awareness and reflection.

[2] For readers interested in reflective teaching's more expansive second tradition, Jay and Johnson (2002), Zeichner and Liston (1996), and contemporary literatures on critical pedagogy in English language teaching are useful starting points for learning more. Briefly, efforts in this second tradition involve similar processes of reflective teaching but operate on a larger scale.

[3] Unless otherwise indicated, resources for learning more about tools for reflective teaching are included in the Further Reading section.

[4] To access *SurveyMonkey* go to http://www.surveymonkey.com

40 | Effective Professional Development for Language Teachers

JOANN (JODI) CRANDALL AND SUSAN FINN MILLER

KEY QUESTIONS

➤ What are some characteristics of effective professional development for English as a second/foreign language teachers?

➤ What are some ways English teaching professionals can continue to learn both on their own and as part of a professional learning community?

➤ How has technology expanded professional learning opportunities?

That's the best part of teaching—the learning.

An experienced teacher serving as a Peace Corps volunteer in Kiribati

EXPERIENCE

During the summer break, Elena, who had been teaching adult English as a second language (ESL) for two years, attended a professional development seminar on learner-centered ESL practices. The seminar turned out to be a meaningful reminder of various practices that Elena had learned during her formal training. During the seminar, Elena valued the many opportunities she had to network and share ideas with colleagues, something she ordinarily had little chance to do. The seminar concluded with time set aside for participants to plan something they wanted to explore in their practice. Elena reflected on what she had learned and decided she wanted to find ways to incorporate learners' personal stories into her instruction. To follow up on the seminar, Elena was asked to post a message about her plans to an online discussion board for the teachers who participated in the seminar. Here's an excerpt of Elena's discussion board conversation with Maria, another participant.

Elena: I really liked the examples of students' stories shared during the seminar. Plus, there are so many ways to use the language in the stories to teach aspects of English. I'd love to get others' ideas for ways to get students to write their stories. I work with high beginners. Most of them can write a little, but some have limited literacy in their L1. How can I adapt this technique for these lower-level learners?

Maria: Elena, this is a great project. I've had students write stories, and it's worked well. I usually begin by writing my own story as a model. One time we wrote about a memory. My story was about my grandmother. I wrote about how she taught me all the words for flowers. Students followed my model and wrote about their own memories. For the lowest-level learners, you can help them to generate their stories orally first, and then you can write down the words for them. You know, using the Language Experience Approach. If they share the same home language, they can help each other understand. Let us know how it goes!

Elena: Thanks, Maria. Once I get the students who can write started on their stories, I can then work with the lower-level students in a small group. I plan to try this next week. I'll write back and let you know how it goes.

In addition to the online discussions, seminar participants were invited to be part of an online teacher inquiry group and to conduct a teacher research project. Elena decided to join the group to deepen her learning about ways to use student stories in her teaching. She especially valued the chance to share her discoveries along the way through the online learning community. She also planned to share the results of her inquiry project in a follow-up face-to-face session with her colleagues.

You may be about to complete or may have recently completed a program to prepare you as an ESL or English as a foreign language (EFL) teacher, and you have learned a lot about theories of teaching and learning, language acquisition and development, the structure of English, approaches and techniques for teaching and testing language proficiency, and cross-cultural communication. You probably also had the opportunity to read about, discuss, and research a number of specific topics related to second and foreign language teaching and learning. But this is only a beginning. If you have been able to teach during your program, you know how much more you learn when you can test out what you have been reading and thinking about. That testing and learning will now become a part of your daily routine. It was a wise person who said that teaching is lifelong learning.

It is that kind of learning ("the best part of teaching") that motivates many English language professionals to keep teaching when the benefits from other jobs would otherwise draw them away. Completing an academic program is really only the beginning of a lifelong quest to better understand our students, ourselves, our discipline, and the approaches and techniques we can use to help others to become competent users of English. If you are an experienced teacher, you may be feeling the need to find some new ways of connecting with professional colleagues and learning some fresh ideas for your teaching. This chapter is also addressed to you.

WHAT IS EFFECTIVE PROFESSIONAL DEVELOPMENT?

Over the past decades, our understanding of the best ways to help others and ourselves to continue to grow as professionals has changed substantially. In the past, the institutions where you worked often determined what you needed to learn and how you were going to learn that material. For instance, a mandatory in-service workshop might have been planned by administration with little input from teachers. While this practice is still common, you will now often have more input into your own professional development; in some cases, you will even be asked to develop a yearly plan for your professional learning. The most effective professional development begins with your concerns and your classroom. Just as effective language lessons address the needs of learners, professional development for language teachers should be relevant to your particular needs. All teachers have unique attributes and areas of need related to their teaching practice (e.g., Crandall, 1993; Crandall, Ingersoll, & Lopez, 2008; Richards & Farrell, 2005). If you are an experienced teacher, you probably have different needs and interests than someone just starting out in the profession. Moreover, studies of adult development (Kegan, 1994, as cited in Drago-Severson, 2004b) have shown that individual teachers tend to have different ways of knowing that influence the impact of professional development. Some adult learners are *instrumental knowers*, who are primarily interested in step-by-step procedures that are sure to succeed (Drago-Severson, 2004b, p. 25). *Socializing knowers* seek information and approval from experts and want to follow what has been shown to be best practice, while *self-authoring knowers* independently reflect on their practice and expect to take full responsibility for their instructional decisions (Drago-Severson, 2004b, pp. 25, 28). Regardless of which kind of knower you are, you may have a preference for professional development that involves engaging with other teachers or you may prefer independent professional learning. Not surprisingly, many teachers seek out a balance between the two types of professional development.

Looking to the research literature on the effectiveness of professional development can help you make decisions about what might best suit your particular needs and context. In one review of the research on professional development for kindergarten through 12th-grade (K–12) teachers, Darling-Hammond, Wei, Andree, Richardson, and Orphano (2009) define high-quality *professional development* as that which improves teachers' knowledge and instructional practices as well as accelerates students' learning. The studies that these researchers reviewed show that sustained, content-focused professional development was most effective when it actively involved teachers in concrete ways and concentrated on specific instructional practices rather than abstract discussions of teaching. In addition, professional development that focused on student learning (e.g., with groups of teachers analyzing student work samples together and seeking to understand how students process information) was shown to be effective. Other researchers (Desimone, 2009, 2011; Guskey & Yoon, 2009; Timperley, Wilson, Barrar, & Fung, 2007) have noted that the best professional development:

- involves learning opportunities over an extended period of time
- engages teachers in deepening and extending skills
- challenges teachers' assumptions about learning
- involves teachers in talking with one another
- has administrative support

The consensus is that the most effective professional learning is job-embedded, that is, immediately applicable to one's teaching practice (Croft, Coggshall, Dolan, & Powers, 2010; McCluskey, 2011/2012; Murphey et al., 2003; Takaki, 2005).

CONCEPTUAL UNDERPINNINGS

The research evidence (Ballantyne, Sanderman, & Levy, 2008; Darling-Hammond et al., 2009) suggests that educational institutions that align their performance goals to teachers' professional development through *professional learning communities* (i.e., groups of teachers who meet regularly to plan, problem solve, and learn together) achieve positive outcomes. Cochran-Smith and Lytle (1999; 2009) found that teachers working together in networks were better able to pose problems, identify discrepancies between theories and practices, and challenge common routine practices. Having the opportunity to reflect on your practice and question your assumptions (Farrell, 2007; Richards & Lockhart, 1994b; Schön, 1983), including those regarding traditional teaching methods (Stranahan, 2011/2012), may be particularly meaningful since, as Borg (2006b, 2011) has shown, our beliefs as teachers are not always aligned with our practice. Being trained to conduct research in a graduate program (Gonzalves, 2011/2012) and conducting research in your own classroom through inquiry-based approaches (Allwright & Hanks, 2009; Burns, 2011; D. Freeman, 1998; Johnson & Golombek,

2011a; Schaetzel, Peyton, & Burt, 2007) can also be important when seeking to more fully understand your teaching context.

Wallace (1991) has identified three major approaches to continued professional development of language teachers: (1) a craft or apprenticeship model, in which novice or less-experienced teachers learn from those with more experience; (2) an applied science or theory-to-practice model, in which teachers learn from research and explanations from experts and then apply what they have learned to their own contexts; and (3) a reflective approach, in which teachers critically analyze or research, reflect on, and adapt their own practice. As Wallace (1991) and others (e.g., D. Freeman, 1998; A. Murray, 2010) have indicated, however, critical reflection is an important component of any approach to professional learning. Reflective teachers routinely question their own beliefs about language teaching and are sensitive to the complex cultural contexts in which they practice (Burton, 2009; Zeichner & Liston, 1996, as cited in A. Murray, 2010). (See also Murphy, this volume.)

It is an exciting time to be an English language teaching (ELT) professional because not only have traditional opportunities for professional learning increased but the options have expanded exponentially with the Internet and the proliferation of Web 2.0 tools such as blogs, wikis, online courses, webinars, podcasts, study circles, book clubs, e-portfolios, and numerous other social networking tools (Chen, Chen, & Tsai, 2009; Davis, Kiely, & Askham, 2009; Flanigan, 2011; Huei-Tse, Kuo-En, & Yao-Ting, 2009; Jung Won & Brush, 2009; Meskill & Anthony, 2007; Meskill & Sadykova, 2011). In this chapter, you will learn about the many possibilities that should be both supported and appropriately challenged as a professional English teacher.

CLASSROOM APPLICATIONS: APPROACHES TO CONTINUED TEACHER LEARNING

A number of resources are available to stimulate new ideas and to help you reconsider old ideas or practices. Figure 1 displays some of the ways in which you can continue to grow as a teacher and become a better-informed ESL professional.

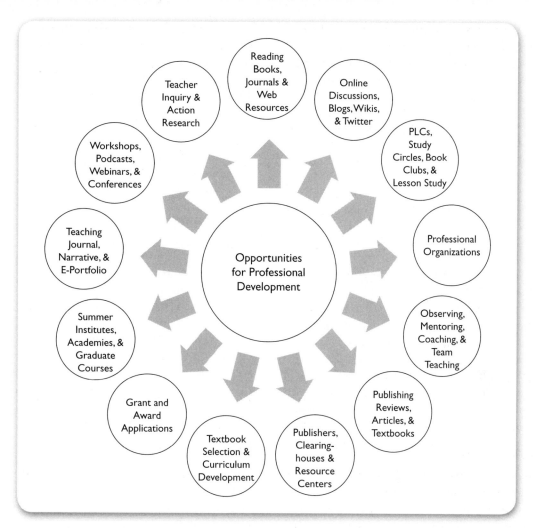

Figure 1. Professional development opportunities.

Professional associations and organizations

Professional associations and organizations offer an excellent means of keeping in touch with others in the field (see Appendix A for contact information). They provide a number of formal and informal channels (publications, conferences, podcasts, webinars, workshops, and classes) for teachers to learn what others in similar contexts or in different parts of the world are thinking and doing; they also offer the opportunity to share insights and ideas from your own experience. These associations publish a range of materials, including newsletters, journals, teacher reference books, and student texts or other materials, each of which provides a different way of keeping informed about new research, materials, or issues in the field. Most

associations also host conferences, both at the national and local level, that offer multiple avenues for professional growth. Plenary speakers often discuss emerging questions, presentations analyze research results, workshops introduce techniques or strategies, and book exhibits provide an opportunity to examine new student textbooks and teacher resource books. Professional conferences also offer opportunities for informal conversations with others who share similar interests or concerns, often leading to long-term professional correspondence and friendships.

There is perhaps no single experience with more potential for educating and refreshing a professional than an international ELT conference. But even at a smaller and more local, regional, or national level, these organizations (and their affiliates) are a great resource, sometimes providing information or assistance that is of more immediate use since professionals in the same geographical area are likely to share similar concerns. Through a professional association, you can also become more actively involved in improving the profession: in helping to set standards for instruction, in developing criteria for evaluating programs, or in recognizing exemplary research or practice. Most organizations also have a number of special interest groups (SIGs) that communicate regularly through publications, email, or conferences about specific aspects of the profession. For example, there are SIGs devoted to the use of technology and social media; the teaching of specific skill areas (e.g. pronunciation and oral communication); the teaching of specific educational levels (e.g., young learners and adult learners); teaching at specific educational levels (e.g., in the K–12 setting or in an intensive language institute); and finally the roles that ELT professionals can undertake (e.g,. as materials developers or program administrators). You may want to begin your involvement by volunteering with a local organization, serving on committees, working on publications, or getting involved with advocacy issues (Eisterhold, 2003; Lorimer & Schulte, 2011/2012). It is a good idea to become a member of a professional association during your teaching English to speakers of other languages (TESOL) program, but if this is not possible, then it should be one of the first things you do after you graduate.

But reading others' work, listening to what others are learning or doing, and taking courses is only a beginning. You also need to try out your ideas by presenting something you have learned through your experience, perhaps by giving a poster session, where you display the results of an action research project you have undertaken in your class; alternatively, you could participate in an informal "swap shop" or "what works" session or a mini-conference, where you join several colleagues in sharing teaching techniques that you have found particularly effective. Begin by presenting this at a local affiliate and then at a national or international conference. You may want to choose a co-presenter to help in developing and delivering the presentation. If you do not have access to a local, national, or international conference, consider starting a "grassroots professional development group" with your colleagues (Takaki, 2005). The more actively you participate, the more the professional association will offer you and the more you will learn (Murphey, 2000).

While there are many professional associations of interest to ELT professionals, the following are among the largest and most important.

Teachers of English to Speakers of Other Languages. Teachers of English to Speakers of Other Languages (TESOL) is an international professional association with several thousand individual members and more than 40,000 other professionals in 100 TESOL affiliate organizations around the world. The association publishes an online newsletter (*TESOL Connections*), an online practice-oriented journal (*TESOL Journal*), a research journal (*TESOL Quarterly*), some special-interest newsletters, and a range of teacher reference texts. It also maintains an extensive Online Resource Center at its website where members share instructional resources (e.g., lesson plans, activities, and quizzes) and professional development resources (e.g., articles or research briefs). In addition to an annual convention, which draws several thousand ELT professionals from around the world, TESOL also provides a range of face-to-face and online professional development opportunities, including yearly symposia on selected topics in several different countries, virtual seminars, online discussions, and a TESOL Leadership Development Certificate program where members learn about advocacy, strategic planning, and supervision. For prospective or current teachers or administrators with limited formal training in ELT, TESOL also offers a 130-hour online training program, the TESOL Core Certificate Program, providing a foundation in the theory and practice of ELT, with a focus on teaching adults in ESL or EFL contexts, or teaching young learners in EFL environments. TESOL also has 21 SIGs (e.g., Higher Education, Computer-Assisted Language Learning, and Teacher Education) with new ones forming as new interests emerge. Finally, it maintains a Directory of (Bachelor's, Master's, and Doctoral) Degree and Certificate Programs (both face-to-face and online) in TESOL and related fields on its website and articulates standards for ELT in diverse contexts. For example, TESOL has developed English language proficiency standards for pre-kindergarten through grade 12, standards for adult education, and technology standards (for teachers and learners).

The 100 TESOL affiliates around the world represent major metropolitan areas, states, provinces, regions, and countries, offering members an opportunity to link up with colleagues teaching in similar contexts. These more "local" language teaching associations (representing urban areas such as Washington, D.C.; states such as Michigan or California; and countries such as Australia, Korea, or Italy) are also important sources of professional development, sponsoring conferences, seminars, SIG meetings, career fairs, and publications (e.g., the *CATESOL [California TESOL] Journal* and Cam[bodia] TESOL's *Language Education in Asia*). A list of these affiliates and a worldwide calendar of events of interest to professionals are available on the TESOL website. Some support for attending the TESOL Convention is available through awards funded by organizations such as the Educational Testing Service TOEFL Grants and Awards or through sources such as U.S. embassies.

International Association of Teachers of English as a Foreign Language. International Association of Teachers of English as a Foreign Language (IATEFL) is a UK-based professional organization that hosts an annual conference of ELT professionals from around the world, often held in conjunction with one of the 100 national associated professional organizations. These associates and IATEFL's 14 SIGs also sponsor conferences (e.g., the Nepal ELT Conference), publish journals (e.g., IATEFL Poland's *Teaching English with Technology*), and provide professional development activities (e.g., Introduction to Qualitative Research or a Business English Summer Symposium), often in conjunction with the British Council or a TESOL affiliate. IATEFL members receive bimonthly issues of *IATEFL Voices* and an annual publication of conference selections. IATEFL also makes available at reduced rates teacher reference books and some professional journals, including the *ELT Journal, Modern English Teacher, Teacher Trainer, English Teaching Professional, World Englishes,* and *Annual Review of Applied Linguistics.* It also provides discounted access to the organization's website, which has one of the largest collections of activities, lesson plans, and other resources for ELT professionals working at any level.[1] The IATEFL website also provides an extensive ELT calendar of events, news of the association, and information on scholarships to attend its conference.

American Association for Applied Linguistics. The American Association for Applied Linguistics (AAAL) convenes an annual conference; publishes the online *AAALetter*, with notices about conferences, awards, and other association news; distributes the *Annual Review of Applied Linguistics* (the official journal of the organization, published by Cambridge University Press) and the *AILA Review* (published by the International Association for Applied Linguistics, of which AAAL is a member); and provides discounts on a number of journals and other publications in applied linguistics.

International Association of Applied Linguistics. The International Association of Applied Linguistics (AILA; also called the Association Internationale de Linguistique Appliquée) is a federation of national or regional associations of applied linguistics. Because it has no fixed secretariat, the easiest way to find out about AILA is through a national affiliate such as the AAAL or through the AILA website. AILA hosts a World Congress on Applied Linguistics in a different country every three years, providing an excellent opportunity for members to become acquainted with research and practice in more than 30 areas in applied linguistics. It also sponsors up to 15 research networks in areas of potential cross-disciplinary research. In addition, the association publishes the *AILA Review* (a thematic, guest-edited collections of papers) and the AILA Applied Linguistic Series of books.

National Association for Bilingual Education. Focusing on the education of language minority students in the United States, the National Association for Bilingual Education (NABE) offers a number of services of interest to ESL and EFL language professionals (teachers, administrators, policymakers, and researchers). It maintains an extensive website,[2] with back issues of the *Bilingual Research Journal,* featuring scholarly articles on bilingualism, bilingual education, and language policy, and *Language Learner* (formerly *NABE News*) with articles on legislative and policy issues. It hosts an annual convention that includes sessions by each of the organization's 20 SIGs, including a SIG for Parents.

NAFSA Association of International Educators. With a focus on international education and exchange, NAFSA (formerly the National Association for Foreign Student Advisers) includes among its members: the directors of international and study-abroad programs; international educational advisers and admissions officers; and English language teachers and program administrators working principally in higher education. The association hosts a national and several regional conferences; offers a series of online courses and webinars; and publishes *International Educator Magazine,* as well as a number of online publications, including *NAFSA News,* policy briefs, and (in cooperation with the Association for Studies in International Education) the *Journal of Studies in International Education.* It also provides an electronic news service to keep members current on legislation and policy.

Low Educated Second Language and Literacy Acquisition for Adults. Through annual symposia and online discussion groups, Low Educated Second Language and Literacy Acquisition (LESLLA) for Adults brings together linguists, psychologists, and educators interested in interdisciplinary, multicountry research on the language acquisition and literacy of adult immigrants. The website provides links to the proceedings of the annual symposia and related publications and research papers, websites, online databases and libraries, and other resources.

International Language Testing Association. The International Language Testing Association (ILTA) is an international group of language testing and assessment scholars and practitioners interested in providing leadership and disseminating information on language testing. The members meet annually at the Language Testing Research Colloquium. The association's website contains a number of links to publications, discussion groups (such as LTEST-L), conferences, and career opportunities.

Linguistic Society of America. An association comprised principally of theoretical and descriptive linguists, the Linguistic Society of America (LSA) publishes the journal *Language* and co-publishes a number of open-access online journals on its eLanguage website. It convenes an annual scholarly meeting, sponsors summer institutes for graduate students, and offers a number of journals at reduced rates to members. Its website provides a directory of programs and departments of linguistics.

Computer-Assisted Language Instruction Consortium. The Computer-Assisted Language Instruction Consortium (CALICO) is an association of linguists and educators interested in research on and development of technology in second language teaching. The organization hosts an annual conference, sponsors a number of SIGs, and publishes *CALICO Journal,* a book series, and software reviews.

Other benefits of joining professional organizations. While participation in language and linguistics professional associations might seem an obvious source of professional growth, what may be less obvious is the role that related professional organizations can play in helping to broaden and deepen your understanding of language teaching and learning. For example, attending a conference of reading or writing professionals or reading a journal concerned with cross-cultural communication or curriculum development can offer insights into ESL/EFL teaching. With expanding linguistic and cultural diversity in national populations and the increased study or use of English as an instructional medium for some portion of education in many countries of the world, links with still other professional associations will become increasingly important for ELT professionals. These organizations exist in many parts of the world.[3]

Professional journals

Another way to keep current is to read journals in the field (some of which are published by the professional associations just discussed) and submit comments, book reviews, and articles to them. Book reviews, especially, can be a good first publication (Kupetz, 2003). Because the number of journals relevant to the teaching and learning of language continues to grow, only the major representative ones are described here (see Appendix B for contact information). Many are now available online (some only in that format; others are available both in print and online).

Annual Review of Applied Linguistics. The *Annual Review of Applied Linguistics (ARAL)* offers a comprehensive, up-to-date review of research and practice in a different area of applied linguistics each year (e.g., language teaching, language testing, literacy, or language policy). Invited articles provide a critical summary, followed by an annotated bibliography of key references and a list of other references of interest.

Applied Language Learning. This journal, which can be downloaded from the website, focuses on the application of research from a number of fields to language teaching methods and techniques, curriculum and materials, and testing and evaluation.

Applied Linguistics. Published in cooperation with AAAL, and the British Association for Applied Linguistics (BAAL), and AILA, this journal includes theoretical and research articles and book reviews on topics such as first and second language acquisition, language teaching and testing, bilingualism and bilingual education, and discourse analysis.

ELT Journal. In addition to articles and reviews of publications relating theory to classroom practice in teaching ESL or EFL, *ELT Journal* also reviews a Key Concept in ELT in each issue, providing a synthesis and suggesting further readings. Recent key concepts have included the Common European Framework, learner autonomy, the non-native speaker-teacher, and corpus-aided language learning.

English for Specific Purposes. This journal is the major source of information about research, program design, curriculum, materials, assessment, teacher education, and other issues in the teaching of English for specific purposes around the world, including content-based language instruction and vocational ESL.

English Teaching Forum. While intended for teachers of English outside the United States, the *Forum* is also a major source of information on practical issues in language teaching and teacher education for U.S. ESL/EFL professionals, especially those interested in international perspectives on language teaching and learning. It is available via subscription or can be downloaded free of charge at the website.

English Teaching Professional. A practical magazine for ESL and EFL teachers, *English Teaching Professional* provides teaching tips, reviews of books and teaching materials, and articles on personal and professional development. Past issues are archived on the website.

Journal of Language, Identity and Education. A forum for international research, this journal focuses on educational, cultural, and literacy policies along with practices that address diversity and linguistic rights, promote educational equity, and discuss the consequences of education on identity and socialization.

Journal of Second Language Writing. This journal features theoretically grounded reports of research and discussion of issues central to second and foreign language writing and writing instruction, including characteristics and attitudes of second language writers and their texts, and readers' responses to and evaluation of their writing in a variety of contexts.

Language Learning. *Language Learning* includes research and theoretical articles on child, second, and foreign language acquisition and learning, language education, bilingualism, literacy, pragmatics, and culture, as well as book reviews, notes, and announcements.

Language Teaching. Published in association with the National Centre for Languages (CILT) and the British Council, *Language Teaching* offers research and survey articles by prominent researchers in ELT and includes surveys of doctoral dissertations, conference plenary addresses, and book reviews.

Language Testing. *Language Testing* is an international journal concerned with issues of testing and assessment of first, second, and foreign languages of interest to researchers and practitioners. Also included are reviews of book and tests.

Modern English Teacher. This magazine provides articles and reviews covering the latest ideas and trends in ELT. The focus is on practical ideas for teaching, with substantial attention to technology tools and professional development. Also included are a calendar of conferences and events, and reviews of materials, teacher reference books, and tests.

The Modern Language Journal. A publication of the National Federation of Modern Language Teachers Associations, *The Modern Language Journal* (*MLJ*) provides research and discussion about the teaching and learning of foreign and second languages. Research, reviews, and response articles; publication and media reviews; and articles from other journals of interest to *MLJ* readers are also included.

Reading in a Foreign Language. A free international online journal focusing on research and instructional issues in foreign language reading and literacy, *Reading in a Foreign Language* also includes discussions, conference reports, and reviews of teacher reference books and teaching materials.

Studies in Second Language Acquisition (SSLA). This journal publishes articles on theory and research in second and foreign language acquisition, some of which have pedagogical implications. Review articles, book reviews, and notices are also included.

TESL Canada Journal. A free online publication of the professional association, TESL Canada, this journal for teachers, teacher educators, and researchers focuses on the teaching and learning of official languages, second language teacher education, and minority language maintenance.

TESL-EJ. This free online journal, with feature articles and extensive reviews of classroom texts, media, and teacher education resources, is refereed by internationally recognized scholars.

TESOL Journal. An online practitioner-oriented publication with full access available only to TESOL members, *TESOL Journal* (*TJ*) publishes articles on theory and research in second and foreign language teaching. A sample free issue is available on the website.

TESOL Quarterly. Of interest to researchers, teacher educators, and teachers, *TESOL Quarterly* (*TQ*) publishes scholarly articles on ELT and standard English as a second dialect. Articles reflect a range of scholarly perspectives and focus on a number of issues in ELT.

World Englishes. *World Englishes* publishes theoretical and applied studies on language, literature, and ELT, focusing on the many varieties of English and their global, cultural, and sociolinguistic contexts.[4]

Publishers

To keep current on student textbooks, teacher reference materials, and technology tools, you will want to have your name and email or postal address added to the mailing lists of the major ESL/EFL and applied linguistics publishers so that you can receive regular announcements of new materials and professional development opportunities. You will also want to bookmark the websites of these publishers and consult them frequently for materials and other services they provide (e.g., newsletters, free materials, answers to questions, notices of upcoming or archived podcasts or online seminars, and even online courses).

The expanding role of English as an international or additional language has led to the development of an unprecedented quantity of ELT textbooks and reference materials, and their publishers, in turn, are providing an ever-increasing range of services. Since the publishing field is constantly changing, with mergers and acquisitions, we have not listed them in this section. A good way to get basic information about ELT and applied linguistics publishers and to browse some of their titles is to consult the Publishers section of Linguist List[5] or to visit the publishers' exhibits at conferences.

Clearinghouses and centers

A number of information clearinghouses and language research and service centers (see Appendix C for contact information) can provide timely answers to questions as well as opportunities for online or face-to-face learning through webinars/seminars, podcasts, summer institutes, and conferences. In ESL/EFL, some of these, such as the Center for Applied Linguistics or the SEAMEO Regional Language Centre, are long-standing; others develop as the need for them arises, only to dissolve when the issues are no longer as pressing or when funding is no longer available. If you find that such an organization is useful, you should ask to be placed on its regular or electronic mailing lists and consult the website for further information. Also be on the lookout for new clearinghouses or centers that may arise. Here are some of the most useful ones.

Center for Applied Linguistics. The Center for Applied Linguistics (CAL) seeks to improve communication through better understanding of language and culture by promoting and improving the teaching and learning of languages and by serving as a resource for information about language and culture. CAL carries out research, analysis, and the dissemination of information; designs and develops instructional materials; and provides technical assistance, teacher education, and policy analysis in a range of areas, including second, foreign, and heritage language education. It also operates a number of clearinghouses and provides a range of online resources, such as digests, frequently asked questions, and research reports (including documents developed by the ERIC Clearinghouse on Languages and Linguistics and the Center for Adult English Language Acquisition, both of which it formerly operated). Its website also provides searchable databases and directories and useful website links.

Centre for Educational Research on Languages and Literacies. The Centre for Educational Research on Languages and Literacies (CERLL; formerly the Modern Language Centre) offers courses, hosts seminars and colloquia, conducts research, and disseminates information on curriculum, instruction, and policies for second, foreign, minority and majority languages, with particular reference to English and French in Canada but also to other languages and settings.

CILT: The National Centre for Languages. CILT's objective is to provide leadership, quality, and excellence in the field of languages and intercultural skills. It partners with a number of organizations in collecting and disseminating information on all aspects of the teaching of modern languages, conducts research, and organizes courses and conferences. The website has an extensive set of helpful links.

National Clearinghouse for English Language Acquisition. The National Clearinghouse for English Language Acquisition (NCELA; formerly the National Clearinghouse for Bilingual Education) focuses on policy and practice in the education of language minority students in the United States. Its website provides access to timely information on legislative debates, policy, funding opportunities, and other information of interest to those teaching English language learners in the United States. NCELA also offers webinars, publishes an online quarterly review (*AccELLerate*), and answers questions through Ask NCELA.

SEAMEO Regional Language Centre. A regional educational project of the Southeast Asian Ministers of Education Organization (SEAMEO), the SEAMEO Regional Language Centre (RELC) is a center for research and information dissemination dedicated to language teacher education, with special attention to Southeast Asian contexts, and international cooperation among language professionals. RELC offers courses (on-site and distance), publications (including the *RELC Journal*), and an annual thematic conference on a state-of-the-art question in language teaching, the proceedings of which it publishes. It also maintains an excellent library and information center.

Other centers. The number of national and international centers focused on issues of language teaching and learning, policy, and research continues to grow, including a number within the European Union (e.g., the Mercator Research Centre on Multilingualism and Language Learning in the Netherlands).[6] A number of U.S. centers are partnerships, subject to funding constraints and thus may not continue functioning; however, even then, their publications are likely to still be available online. They include the Center for Advanced Research on Language Acquisition (CARLA), the Center for Research on Education, Diversity, and Excellence (CREDE), and the National Capital Language Resource Center (NCLRC).[7] As you read and visit websites, you will learn about still other clearinghouses and centers that can provide you with information and professional development opportunities.

Websites

The websites featured here are a representative sample of sites that provide a wide range of professional learning resources and opportunities for ESL and EFL teachers. These sites include articles and blogs, videos, podcasts, teaching and learning resources, and links to many other interesting and useful materials.

Linguist List. This extensive and easily navigated website[8] includes a conference calendar and calls for papers, an extensive list of linguistic associations with links, and a list of journals with descriptions. It also provides networking opportunities via information on subscribing to a number of electronic discussion groups.

The Education Alliance at Brown University. This website[9] includes a wide range of research articles, training materials and handbooks available for free download, including the following articles related to K–12 teaching: "Approaches to writing instruction for adolescent English language learners"; "Teachers' guide to diversity: Building a knowledge base"; and "Educating English language learners: Implementing instructional practices." The organization supports The Knowledge Loom website,[10] which focuses on critical thinking and equity in K–12 education.

New American Horizons. This site[11] currently features 10 teacher-training videos with footage from U.S. adult ESL classrooms with voice-over commentary and reflections from the teachers.

Topics covered in the videos include life skills, emergent readers, vocabulary, grammar, multi-level classes, listening skills, writing skills, reading skills, and assessment and critical thinking skills. More videos are always being added.

Larry Ferlazzo's Websites of the Day.   In addition to Larry Ferlazzo's interesting daily blogs and links to published articles on various topics related to ESL/EFL teaching, this site[12] includes an enormous assortment of links organized by topic and evaluated for their potential usefulness to language teachers. Of particular interest are the "Best of" series, which link to web resources for teachers and students, including the best websites for photos, for creating time lines, for Web 2.0 applications for students, and for online learning games.

Colorín Colorado!   This site[13] includes articles, research reports, webcasts, and podcasts, as well as guides and toolkits for teachers working with children or families. The site emphasizes the value of building on the first language and preserving heritage languages; it includes wonderful materials, including articles and tip sheets for parents available in both English and Spanish.

TTV by Russell Stannard.   Stannard's site[14] has won numerous awards for his teacher-training videos that focus on using technology to teach language. For example, the videos explain how to involve students in creating videos, blogs, wikis, or podcasts. Teachers can also learn to use a variety of online tools such as the Flickr photo website to create comic strips, SurveyMonkey to create online surveys, and an interactive website for using song lyrics[15] in creative ways.

Other websites.   The number of websites devoted to teaching language continues to expand daily. When you visit one site, you can easily find many more links to take you to additional high-quality resources. Visit the companion website for this volume at: www.NGL.Cengage.com/tesfl to find other recommended websites for K–12 teachers, for students and parents, for working with families, for teaching with technology, for free books online, and for web resources for learning English and other languages online.

Online discussion groups

The Internet has exploded with opportunities for teachers to engage in meaningful ways with colleagues and recognized experts from around the globe. A number of email lists and electronic discussion groups of interest to ESL/EFL professionals exist. They are excellent places to get quick responses to questions from colleagues with similar experiences. Some discussion lists regularly invite leaders in the field to facilitate discussions on specific topics (e.g., formative assessment, emergent readers, and multilevel classes). These facilitated discussions allow teachers to pose questions to experts and share ideas and resources with colleagues. (See Algren, 2003, for some guidelines on selecting and participating in email discussion lists.) What follows is information about a few of these lists.

- *LINCS LISTS.* A number of discussion lists that focus on adult education are described at this website,[16] along with subscription information. Of particular interest to adult ESL educators are the lists for Adult English Language Acquisition and Adult Literacy Professional Development. Although most subscribers are from the United States, practitioners from a number of other countries also participate in the discussions.
- *SLART-L.* This discussion list[17] on second language acquisition and teaching is of interest to researchers and teachers.

Blogs

Blogs have emerged as an important resource for teachers to find information, share it with others, and become members of virtual communities of practice with colleagues from around the world. Blogs include a range of useful resources, such as articles, videos, podcasts, lesson plans, handouts, game ideas, training resources, and approaches for using social media in teaching. Bloggers also welcome comments and suggestions from others, so a blog space allows you to participate in ongoing conversations, raise questions, and contribute ideas with others in an online community. Bloggers also list the blogs they follow on their websites, so you can easily locate other blogs of interest to check out. Two of the most useful language teaching blogs are OnlineDegrees.org[18] and bab.la.[19] You may also decide that creating a blog is something you'd like to try out.[20]

Twitter

Subscribing to Twitter[21] allows you to receive information from individuals who regularly share resources about ELT. You can select the individuals you want to follow based on your interests and the quality of the information being shared. Once you have identified one or two individuals you want to follow, you can expand the people you follow by checking out the list of language teachers your chosen individuals follow. For instance, if you teach high school students or ESP classes, you might want to follow Larry Ferlazzo since he routinely shares up-to-date resources about ways to effectively integrate content into language instruction. You can check out the list of language teachers that Larry Ferlazzo follows to determine if you want to add them to your own Twitter list.

Workshops, podcasts, seminars, webinars, institutes, academies, and graduate programs

One of the best ways of keeping up to date is to participate in local, state, national, or international workshops or seminars, some of which are provided online as podcasts or webinars. These continuing education programs may be sponsored by a professional association, a university-based teacher education program, a clearinghouse or center, a publisher, or a ministry of education. They may offer graduate credit or help lead to employment advancement. Of equal importance, they provide a forum for sharing problems and potential solutions, as well as ways of expanding one's teaching repertoire or identifying areas of potential classroom-based research. While you may begin participating as a learner, over time, you are likely to find yourself increasing your contributions to the discussion, participating as a member of a colloquium or panel, or leading one of the professional development programs yourself.

Deserving special mention are the summer professional development institutes for students and teachers that are hosted by a variety of professional associations and universities. It is also possible to enroll in intensive, short courses with ELT colleagues or in graduate classes (face-to-face and online) to learn from other teachers as well as from the instructor, in what is usually an informal, collaborative learning experience. The opportunity to participate in one of these intensive programs should not be missed; you are likely to emerge from the experience feeling renewed as a professional and reassured that you have chosen the right profession. You will also undoubtedly meet professional colleagues with whom you will correspond or collaborate for many years to come.

Materials review, textbook selection committees, and curriculum development teams

Publishers and journal editors are continually in need of professionals to review manuscripts, teacher reference books, or student texts and materials. If you wish to serve as a reviewer, contact the publishers, usually through their ESL/EFL editors, or contact book review editors of newsletters or journals to let them know of your interest. Indicate the skill, level, or focus that you are particularly interested in and your qualifications, and you may find yourself regularly keeping up to date by reading new books or manuscripts even before they are published. An additional benefit is that you will usually be able to keep the book for your own professional library. To get started, you may want to write reviews for a newsletter or a publication of a local affiliate of one of the professional associations discussed in this chapter.

Textbook and materials selection committees of your program or textbook-adoption committees for local, state, or regional educational agencies offer another source of professional growth. These committees usually request copies of new relevant publications from a number of publishers for the committee to review. By participating in these committees, you have an opportunity to keep current on the kinds of techniques and strategies that are included in the latest ESL/EFL materials and to enrich your own teaching, lesson planning, and materials writing projects. You are also likely to broaden your circle of ELT colleagues and to benefit from their unique educational backgrounds and experiences.

You may find, after reviewing manuscripts and books and serving on materials selection committees, that you want to edit a collection or create materials or books of your own or perhaps serve as a member of a curriculum writing team that is preparing new materials. In the process of researching, developing, and field-testing these materials, you will learn a great deal about current practice in ESL/EFL classrooms and will undoubtedly adapt some of your own teaching accordingly. You will also have the benefit of working with and learning from other professionals as you collaborate on the writing project. You may also want to enlist the aid of your learners in identifying themes or cultural issues to include in creating a learner-centered curriculum (Gordon, 2003).

Teacher observation, coaching, mentoring, and team-teaching

If this is your first teaching assignment, you may find it helpful to identify an experienced colleague who can provide you with guidance and advice, someone to act as a sounding board as you think through challenging situations or students. You may want to observe that teacher's classes or discuss homework or grading policies with him or her. As you become more experienced, you are likely to notice the challenges facing new colleagues and to remember how you felt early in your assignment or career. Offer to mentor beginning teachers or colleagues new to your institution. Meeting regularly with them, inviting them to observe your classes, co-teaching with them, or helping with paperwork, policies, or procedures may not only alleviate some of their burden but also illuminate some of your own growth as a professional, helping you to articulate more clearly your own teaching assumptions and practice (Bailey, Curtis, & Nunan, 2001; Malderez, 2009; Orland-Barak, 2001). Ongoing coaching and mentoring are also likely to help pinpoint areas of your own teaching that you may want to research (Deacon, 2003); in addition, it may lead you to search for instructional materials or reference works on topics that you may not have considered previously. You may also want to team-teach with another ELT colleague or even with colleagues in other disciplines who have English learners in their classes (Crandall, 1998; Dove & Honigsfeld, 2010). The latter is an excellent way for you to learn more about the actual language demands of another discipline and to help colleagues in that discipline adapt instruction to make it more accessible to English learners.

Teacher research, teaching journals, narrative inquiries, and e-portfolios

Teacher research can be highly formalized (as in quantitative and empirical research) or less formal and organic (as you might discover in action research and exploratory practice) (see Allwright, 2003; Bailey, Curtis, & Nunan, 2001a; Burns, 2009; Wallace, 1998).

In any case, the hallmark of teacher research is focusing on something you are curious about in your classroom. You can engage in an individual research project or collaborate with others on a question of interest or concern. For a discussion of an intercultural collaborative development project, see Field and Nagai (2003); for cross-disciplinary collaboration, see Crandall (1998). (See also Bailey, this volume.)

The more you teach, the more likely you will be asking questions about your own classroom, learners, or teaching practices. These questions can serve as the basis for a series of ongoing research projects of your own. Consider keeping a teaching journal or diary in which you record some of the episodes in your classes and some of your emerging insights about yourself, your teaching, or your students. That journal may highlight some areas for action research, beginning, perhaps, with studying the progress or problems of a few students in your classes. You might want to see how a change in your approach to teaching (e.g., substituting some extensive reading for the intensive reading in your syllabus, introducing electronic discussion in your writing class, or involving students in projects in your conversation class) affects your students' motivation or proficiency. You might want to share the results of your research in a blog, on a discussion list, in a conference presentation, or in an article in a teaching journal. You may also want to participate in an inquiry or reflection group where you can discuss your concerns with others, inviting their insights and suggestions, leading to your decision on a possible course of action. (See also Murphy, this volume.)

Teacher autobiographic *narrative inquiries*, crafted in the form of stories, have been recognized as a powerful means for reflection and "knowledge building" (Johnson & Golombek, 2011b, p. 486; Nelson, 2011). Oral and written narratives also enhance teacher confidence and self-efficacy. When you share your stories with colleagues through various means such as writing a blog, participating in a professional learning community, or even creating a digital story, you are able to give a voice to what you perceive, creating opportunities for introspection, explanation, and sense-making (Johnson & Golombek, 2011b, p. 491). The topic of a narrative may involve a classroom dilemma, such as why learners are reluctant to participate in whole-class discussions, or how students are using their first language to support their learning of English.

Similar to journaling, narratives may serve as a source for pursuing teacher research projects on a variety of topics; on the other hand, narratives can sometimes evolve into meaningful teacher research in and of itself (Barkhuizen, 2011) as well as becoming a means of involving learners in the engaging act of storytelling (Holmes & Marra, 2011). For example, the 2011/2012 issue of *CATESOL Journal* included a "theme section" on graduate student professional development in which authors use narrative as the principal approach (Lorimer, 2011/2012).

It is also possible to include your students as co-researchers in the issue you explore in your classroom, using an *exploratory research process* (Allwright & Hanks, 2009). Your research may take a surprising direction as learners are empowered to share their thoughts and ideas with you and with one another. You may also want to become part of a larger research group or project that is investigating questions of interest to you (Johnston, 2009). You can identify potential research collaborators or ongoing research projects through your participation in online discussion groups or SIGs, or in talking with colleagues in your workplace. You might be surprised to learn that some university researchers have difficulty identifying teachers with whom to collaborate or classrooms in which to work. They are likely to welcome your interest in some kind of joint project, one that will have as its objectives something that can be applied to your classroom or your particular teaching situation.

You might want to consider engaging with your colleagues in *lesson study*, which involves a group of teachers examining student data and together designing a lesson to improve student learning. One teacher teaches the lesson, while the others observe. The teachers meet again to reflect on the lesson and discuss their observations and then collaborate on revising the lesson and reteaching it (Fernandez, 2002). The lesson study process honors the knowledge and skills teachers bring related to their learners, teaching methodology and content and empowering teachers to address students' learning through effective collaboration.

Collaborations such as these are valuable at elementary, secondary, or tertiary level and across the curriculum, especially where English is used as an instructional medium. A brief exchange in the hall about a particular student or assignment can grow into ongoing collaborative research, curriculum development, or even team-teaching, all of which are likely to be professionally rewarding experiences.

Keeping an *e-portfolio* of your professional learning can be especially meaningful as you identify your needs and develop a plan, engage in professional learning, and reflect on the processes and outcomes for yourself and your learners (Tanner, 2003). Increasingly, teachers are taking advantage of online platforms to maintain an e-portfolio. You can capture and reflect on your learning through the inclusion of various multimedia artifacts (e.g., text, photos, audio-recordings, and videos). Ideally the e-portfolio tells the dynamic and evolving story of your professional learning through your own voice as a teacher. And while it may be one component of your evaluation, it can also serve as a means for you and fellow teachers to support and provide feedback to one another. Once you get started with your own e-portfolio, you may be eager to introduce this learning technique to your students.

Professional learning communities, study circles, book clubs, and wikis

There are a number of ways you can collaborate and learn from colleagues or other professionals, both face-to-face or in online communities. *Professional learning communities* (PLCs) are formal or informal gatherings of teachers who meet together over a period of time for any number of purposes (Calderon, 1999; Wenger, 1998). They might be called together by administrators or be created by teachers. As part of a learning community, you might focus on the goals of your institution, such as examining student learning gains and deciding on a course of action as a team, or you might focus on a particular area of interest or concern to you and the other members of the group (Murphey & Sato, 2005).

You and a group of colleagues may decide to form a *study circle* or a *professional book club*, either face-to-face or online, focusing on a topic of common interest. In a study circle, teachers typically read materials from the research literature and discuss the implications for their practice; as such, study circles can help to bridge the gap between research and practice. A professional book club involves teachers' choosing a book to read and discuss together. Your study circle or book club may choose an outside facilitator, or the group may decide on one member to serve as the facilitator or to rotate the facilitation duties among the group members.

Some teachers or groups set up wikis to create a collaborative online workspace. When you visit a wiki (or create your own), you can add, delete, or edit the site content without specialized knowledge or tools. A *wiki* is a dynamic space that is continually under revision, with the creative process shared among many individuals.[22] In addition, more and more professional learning communities or networks are springing up online through the many social networking tools now available, such as Ning, Wiggio, and Facebook. Teachers have started their own online networks to connect with colleagues across town, all over the nation, and throughout the world.

One example of an online network or PLC that includes both structured activities (i.e., book clubs and study circles) and unstructured activities (i.e., discussion boards and chat rooms) is the ELL-U ESL Professional Development Network,[23] designed to serve adult ESL teachers who work with immigrants and refugees in the United States. The network features free self-paced online courses, facilitated study circles, and clubs. Online courses are available on second language acquisition, teaching adult emergent readers, and formative assessment. The ELL-U study circles feature a variety of topics, including teaching vocabulary, developing listening and speaking skills, the role of the home language in learning English, learner-centered practices, teaching adult emergent readers, learner persistence in adult ESL, and assessing the reading skills of intermediate ESL readers. Through ELL-U's clubs, you can also participate in a book-study experience or virtual field trip, as well as complete a personal learning plan to deepen your understanding of a particular topic, such as teaching vocabulary or working with adult emergent readers.

FUTURE TRENDS

It is clear that in the future the use of innovative technologies will increase, and online professional development opportunities will grow. When teachers participate in new technologies as part of their own professional learning, they will become increasingly comfortable integrating these technologies into their own practice. (The authors' experiences in devel-

oping and delivering online courses or study circles is a case in point.) (See also Pawan & Jacobson, 2005.) Current research demonstrates that job-embedded professional learning that is sustained over time is most effective; this awareness and the trend toward teachers participating in communities of practice with colleagues locally or even throughout the world online is also likely to increase. These learning communities and other opportunities for teacher research and decision making are likely to continue the shift from administrator-designed to teacher-led professional development, with the goal of developing teacher leaders becoming more important. Furthermore, interest in teacher cognition and how teachers' beliefs influence practice is likely to grow (Borg, 2006b, 2011). And finally, a central focus on teacher reflection as the essence of teacher learning and change is likely to remain at the heart of future professional development for teachers, as is the use of teacher narratives as a way of structuring experience and reflection (Lorimer, 2011/2012). (See also Murphy, this volume.)

CONCLUSION

As A. Murray (2010) noted, "Effective professional development is self-empowerment" (p. 10), and when you are empowered as a teacher, this can lead to improvement in learners' attitudes and achievement. There are many ways in which being an ESL or EFL teacher is a growth experience. If you are just now completing a TESOL program, you will find that this is the beginning of a lifetime of professional learning. Experienced teachers know that teaching is, in itself, a continual growth experience since one really "learns" something only when asked to explain or teach it to others. Students are often our best teachers, and you will learn from new students each term. If you have the opportunity to teach different courses, grades, or levels or to add a new role or responsibility as a tester, program administrator, resource center coordinator, or mentor, you will find that your understanding of the field and of your own practice will be enhanced. The professional learning options offered here are only some of the many ways to keep up to date and to stay energized and empowered as a language teacher.

SUMMARY

As this chapter has shown, there are many exciting and meaningful ways to stay current with your field and continue learning as a professional ESL or EFL teacher. You might want to:

➤ join a professional organization and attend a conference, sign up for electronic discussion lists, or subscribe to periodicals of interest

➤ submit reviews of books or materials to journals

➤ become familiar with publishers, resource centers, and clearinghouses and what they have to offer

➤ participate in professional development workshops, seminars, webinars, summer institutes, or graduate courses, both face-to-face and online

➤ explore the vast number of ESL/EFL resources online, especially bloggers who generously share their materials and expertise

➤ volunteer to serve on textbook-selection committees or curriculum-development teams

➤ observe or collaborate with other teachers through mentoring, coaching, or team-teaching

➤ become part of a professional learning community through a teacher inquiry group, study circle, action research, or lesson study

➤ reflect on your teaching through writing a narrative inquiry, journaling, or creating an e-portfolio

DISCUSSION QUESTIONS

1. Take another look at the professional development wheel (Figure 1), which highlights the many ways an ESL/EFL professional can keep current in the field. From these various options for professional learning, what are you already doing? What other ideas do you think will be most helpful to you?

2. Why is it important to belong to a professional association in your field? What kinds of professional development opportunities do they offer? If you cannot belong to one of these associations, are there other ways in which you can benefit from their services?

3. How has the Internet increased your access to professional development? What resources have you accessed? How effective have they been?

4. Why do you think that it can be so difficult for teachers to keep current in their fields? What are some of the factors that might affect your ability to keep up to date?

5. What are some ways that you can collaborate with colleagues in your institution, in other institutions, or in other parts of the world or with your students?

SUGGESTED ACTIVITIES

1. Even if you are not a member, attend an international, national, or local (affiliate) convention or meeting of one of the ESL/EFL professional associations. Try to attend some plenary (large-group) sessions, some presentations and workshops, and the book exhibits. If there are poster sessions where colleagues informally share their teaching ideas or research, spend some time there, talking with the presenters and getting ideas for related posters that you might develop to share with colleagues back home. Allow yourself time to get to know some of your colleagues by attending social activities, engaging in informal discussion groups, or spending time at the poster sessions.

2. Visit a language teaching information center, either in person or online. Find out about the services they provide and the publications they offer. Have your name added to any mailing lists they maintain.

3. Choose recent issues of three of the journals listed in this chapter to examine more closely. What articles are included? What kinds of columns or information does the journal provide? Who is the intended audience? Do you think the journal will be useful to you? In what ways? Share your findings with a colleague.

4. Identify a relevant professional development network (a discussion group, study circle, blog, wiki, book club, etc.). Join and keep a journal of the insights you gain.

5. Make a list of individuals or groups with whom you might collaborate, and indicate some of the ways in which you might work together or share ideas about language teaching and learning.

FURTHER READING

Borg, S. (2006). *Teacher cognition and language education.* New York, NY: Continuum.

Borg reviews the research on teacher cognition (what teachers think, know, and believe) and examines the ways in which cognition influences teachers' practice.

Burns, A. (2011). *Doing action research in English language teaching: A guide for practitioners.* New York, NY: Routledge.

Both teachers and facilitators of action research will find this volume a useful guide to conducting action research. The book outlines each step in the action research process, from generating ideas for research questions to analyzing, reflecting on, and reporting findings.

Foord, D. (2009). *The developing teacher: Practical activities for professional development.* Surrey, UK: Delta ELT.

This book, designed for both novice and experienced teachers, is unique since its aim is not reading but doing. It is organized in concentric circles with an initial focus on oneself as a teacher; then on engagement with learners, colleagues, institution or school; and finally on the larger professional community of language teachers. Within each circle are reflective activities and practical suggestions for professional learning.

Richards, J. C., & Farrell, T. S. C. (2005). *Professional development for language teachers.* Cambridge, UK: Cambridge University Press.

This volume outlines various approaches to professional learning, including teaching journals and portfolios, peer observation, critical incident and case analysis, and peer coaching. Each chapter includes vignettes and practical examples from countries around the world.

APPENDIX A: PROFESSIONAL ASSOCIATIONS AND ORGANIZATIONS

Teachers of English to Speakers of Other Languages (TESOL)

1925 Ballenger Avenue, Suite 550
Alexandria, VA 22314-6820
Website: http://www.tesol.org
Phone: (703) 836-0774; or toll free in the United States at (888) 547-3369

Fax: 703 836-7864
E-mail: info@tesol.org

International Association of Teachers of English as a Foreign Language (IATEFL)

Darwin College
University of Kent
Canterbury, Kent, CT2 7NY UK
Website: http://www.iatefl.org
Phone: 0044 1227 824430
Fax: 0044 1227 824431
Email: generalenquiries@iatefl.org

American Association for Applied Linguistics (AAAL)

PMB 321
2900 Delk Road, Suite 700
Marietta, GA 30067-5350 USA
Website: http://www.aaal.org
Phone: (678) 229 2892
Toll free in the United States: (866) 821-7700
Fax: (678) 229-2777
E-mail: info@aaal.org

International Language Testing Association (ILTA)

3416 Primm Lane
Birmingham, AL 35216
Website: http://www.iltaonline.com
Phone: (205) 823-6106
E-mail: Info@iltaonline.com

International Association of Applied Linguistics (AILA)

Website: http://www.aila.info/

National Association for Bilingual Education (NABE)

8701 Georgia Avenue, Suite 611
Silver Spring, MD 20910
Website: http://www.nabe.org
Phone: (240) 450-3700
Fax: (240) 450-3799
Email: nabe@nabe.org

NAFSA: Association of International Educators

1307 New York Avenue, NW, 8th Floor
Washington, DC 20005-4701
Website: http://www.nafsa.org
Phone: (202) 737-3699
Fax: (202) 737-3657
E-mail: inbox@nafsa.org

Low Educated Second Language and Literacy Acquisition (LESLLA) for Adults

Website: http://www.leslla.org

International Language Testing Association (ILTA)

3416 Primm Lane
Birmingham, AL 35216
Website: http://www.iltaonline.com
Phone: (205) 823-6106

Linguistic Society of America (LSA)

1325 18th Street, NW, Suite 211
Washington, DC 20036-6501
Website: http://www.lsadc.org
Phone: (202) 835-1714
E-mail: lsa@lsadc.org

Computer-Assisted Language Instruction Consortium (CALICO)

Texas State University
214 Centennial Hall
San Marcos, TX 78666
Website: http://www.calico.org
Phone: (512) 245-1417
E-mail: info@calico.org

APPENDIX B: PROFESSIONAL JOURNALS

Annual Review of Applied Linguistics (ARAL)

Cambridge University Press
32 Avenue of the Americas
New York, NY 10013-2473
Website: http://journals.cambridge.org/action
/displayJournal?jid=APL

Applied Language Learning

Defense Language Institute
Foreign Language Center
Presidio of Monterey
Monterey, CA 93944-5006
Website: http://www.dliflc.edu/publications.aspx

Applied Linguistics

Oxford University Press
2001 Evans Road
Cary, NC 27513
Website: http://applij.oxfordjournals.org/

ELT Journal

Oxford University Press
2001 Evans Road
Cary, NC 27513
Website: http://eltj.oxfordjournals.org/

English for Specific Purposes

Elsevier Science
P.O. Box 945
New York, NY 10159-0945
Website: http://www.journals.elsevier.com
/english-for-specific-purposes/

English Teaching Forum

U.S. Department of State
301 4th Street, SW, Room 312
Washington, DC 20547
Website: http://exchanges.state.gov/englishteaching
/forum-journal.html

English Teaching Professional

Pavilion PO Box 100
Chichester PO18 8HD
UK
Website: http://www.etprofessional.com

Journal of Language, Identity and Education

Taylor & Francis, Inc.
325 Chestnut Street, Suite 800
Philadelphia, PA 19106

Website: http://www.tandf.co.uk/journals
/titles/15348458.asp

Journal of Second Language Writing

Elsevier Science
P.O. Box 945
New York, NY 10159-0945
Website: http://www.journals.elsevier.com
/journal-of-second-language-writing/

Language Learning

John Wiley & Sons, Inc.
432 Elizabeth Avenue
Somerset, NJ 08875
Website: http://www.blackwellpublishing.com/journal
.asp?ref=0023-8333

Language Teaching

Cambridge University Press
32 Avenue of the Americas
New York, NY 10013-2473
Website: http://journals.cambridge.org/jid_LTA

Language Testing

SAGE Publications
2455 Teller Road
Thousand Oaks, CA 91320
Website: http://ltj.sagepub.com/

Modern English Teacher

Pavilion PO Box 100
Chichester, West Sussex PO18 8HD
UK
Website: http://www.onlinemet.com/

The Modern Language Journal

John Wiley & Sons Inc.
350 Main Street
Malden, MA 02148
Website: http://mlj.miis.edu/

Reading in a Foreign Language

Website: http://nflrc.hawaii.edu/rfl/

Studies in Second Language Acquisition

Cambridge University Press
32 Avenue of the Americas
New York, NY 10013-2473
Website: http://www.esaim-cocv.org/action
/displayJournal?jid=SLA

TESL Canada Journal

104 - 8557 Government Street
Burnaby, British Columbia V3N 4S9
Canada
Website: http://www.teslcanadajournal.ca

TESL-EJ

Website: http://www.tesl-ej.org/wordpress/

TESOL Journal

TESOL
1925 Ballenger Avenue, Suite 550
Alexandria, VA 22314
Website: http://www.tesol.org/read-and-publish/journals
/tesol-journal

TESOL Quarterly

TESOL
1925 Ballenger Avenue, Suite 550
Alexandria, VA 22314
Website: http://www.tesol.org/read-and-publish/journals/tesol-quarterly

World Englishes

John Wiley & Sons, Inc.
432 Elizabeth Avenue
Somerset, NJ 08875

Website: http://www.blackwellpublishing.com/journal.asp?ref=0883-2919

APPENDIX C: CLEARINGHOUSES AND CENTERS

Center for Applied Linguistics (CAL)

4646 40th Street, NW
Washington, DC 20016
Website: http://www.cal.org

Centre for Educational Research on Languages and Literacies (CERLL)—formerly the Modern Language Centre

Ontario Institute for Studies in Education
University of Toronto
252 Bloor Street
West Toronto, Ontario M5S 1V6
Canada
Website: http://www.oise.utoronto.ca/cerll/

CILT: The National Centre for Languages

CfBT Education Trust
60 Queens Road
Reading RG1 4BS
UK
Website: http://www.cilt.org.uk

National Clearinghouse for English Language Acquisition (NCELA)

2011 Eye St. NW, Suite 300
Washington, DC 20006
Website: http://www.ncela.gwu.edu

SEAMEO Regional Language Centre (RELC)

30 Orange Grove Road
Singapore 258352
Republic of Singapore
Website: http://www.relc.org.sg

ENDNOTES

1 Visit http://www.onestopenglish.com
2 Visit http://www.nabe.org/
3 In the United States, the International Reading Association (www.reading.org), the National Council of Teachers of English (www.ncte.org), the American Council on the Teaching of Foreign Languages (www.actfl.org), the Society for Intercultural Education, Training, and Research (www.sietarusa.org), the Commission on Adult Basic Education (www.coabe.org), and the Association for Supervision and Curriculum Development (www.ascd.org) all provide publications, conferences, and professional development opportunities relevant to ESL and EFL professionals. Their websites, as well, are excellent sources of information about relevant topics. Most of these organizations also have regional, state, or local affiliates for professional relationships or collaborations closer to home.
4 Other periodicals that deserve mention include the *RELC Journal* (a publication of the SEAMEO [Southeast Asian Ministers of Education Organization] Regional Language Centre [RELC] in Singapore, which focuses on language teaching and learning in Southeast Asia), the *JALT Journal* and *The Language Teacher* (research and practice-oriented publications of the Japan Association of Language Teachers), the *Canadian Modern Language Review* (a journal with parallel articles in English and French concerned with language teaching and learning), and *Language Teaching Research* (which publishes both quantitative and qualitative research related to the teaching of second and foreign languages). In addition, professional associations in the fields of reading, writing, foreign languages, teacher education, and curriculum development publish journals and magazines of relevance to ELT. For example, the International Reading Association publishes *Reading Research Quarterly*, with theoretical articles and reviews of research of interest to reading researchers; the *Journal of Adolescent and Adult Literacy*, with theoretical and practical articles relevant to ESL/EFL literacy teachers; and *The Reading Teacher*, for elementary school teachers. The National Council of Teachers of English, which has an ESL Assembly at its annual conference, publishes journals on writing with discussion of second language issues, including *Research in the Teaching of English*, *Teaching English in the Two-Year College*, and *College Composition and Communication*. The Association for Supervision and Curriculum Development publishes *Educational Leadership*, an excellent magazine for keeping current on programmatic and political issues confronting public school education in the United States.
5 Visit http://linguistlist.org/pubs/publishers.cfm
6 Visit http://www.mercator-research.eu
7 Visit http://www.carla.umn.edu, http://crede.berkeley.edu, and http://www.nclrc.org, respectively.
8 Visit http://www.linguistlist.org
9 Visit http://www.lab.brown.edu/ae_ells.php
10 Visit http://knowledgeloom.org/index.jsp
11 Visit http://www.newamericanhorizons.com
12 Visit http://larryferlazzo.edublogs.org/
13 Visit http://www.colorincolorado.org/
14 Visit http://www.teachertrainingvideos.com/
15 Visit http://www.lyricstraining.com/
16 Visit http://lincs.ed.gov/lincs/discussions/list_events.html
17 Visit https://groups.google.com/forum/?fromgroups#!forum/bit.listserv.slart-l
18 Visit http://www.onlinedegrees.org/blog/
19 The English version of bab.la is available at http://en.bab.la/news/top-10-language-teaching-blogs-2010
20 Visiting several blogs can be a useful first step; the following link provides videos outlining the steps for creating your own blog and wiki as well as ways to expand your knowledge of other technology resources: http://www.freetech4teachers.com/2010/08/11-techy-things-for-teachers-to-try.html
21 To subscribe, visit http://twitter.com/
22 At http://wikisinefl.wikispaces.com/Wikis+in+EFL you can learn about using wikis in EFL. Another wiki designed for use by adult ESL teachers can be found at http://wiki.literacytent.org/index.php/English_for_Speakers_of_Other_Languages
23 Visit http://www.ell-u.org

References

Adamson, B. (2004). Fashions in language teaching methodology. In A. Davies & C. Elder (Eds.), *The handbook of applied linguistics* (pp. 604–622). Malden, MA: Blackwell.

Adaskou, K., Britten, D., & Fahsi, B. (1989). Cultural content in a secondary English course for Morocco. *ELT Journal, 44*(1), 3–10.

Adult Migrant English Program (AMEP) Research Centre. (2011). *Certificates in spoken and written English.* Sydney, Australia: Macquarie University. Retrieved from http://www.ameprc.mq.edu.au/resources/ cswe_2008

Afflerbach, P., Pearson, P., & Paris, S. (2008). Clarifying differences between reading skills and reading strategies. *The Reading Teacher, 61*(5), 364–373.

Agger, M. (2008). Lazy eye: How we read online. *Slate.* Retrieved from http://www.slate.com/id/2193552/

Agosti, C. I. (2006). Seizing the opportunity for change: The business preparation program, a new pathway to gain direct entry into Macquarie University. In M. A. Snow & L. Kamhi-Stein (Eds.), *Developing a new course for adult learners* (pp. 99–122). Alexandria, VA: Teachers of English to Speakers of Other Languages.

Akbari, R. (2008). Postmethod discourse and practice. *TESOL Quarterly, 42*(4), 641–652.

Alderson, C. (2000). *Assessing reading.* Cambridge, UK: Cambridge University Press.

Alderson, J. C., & Hamp-Lyons, L. (1996). TOEFL preparation courses: A study of washback. *Language Testing, 13*(3), 280–297.

Alexander, P. A. (2008). Why this and why now? Introduction to the special issue on metacognition, self-regulation, and self-regulated learning. *Educational Psychology Review, 20*(4), 369–372.

Algren, M. (2003). Developing through e-mail discussion groups. In J. Egbert (Ed.), *Becoming contributing professionals* (pp. 89–95). Alexandria, VA: Teachers of English to Speakers of Other Languages.

Aljaafreh, A., & Lantolf, J. (1994). Negative feedback as regulation and second language learning in the zone of proximal development. *The Modern Language Journal, 78*(4), 465–483.

Allen, J. (1999). *Words, words, words: Teaching vocabualry in grades 4–12.* York, ME: Stenhouse.

Allen, P., Swain, M., Harley, B., & Cummins, J. (1990). Aspects of classroom treatment: Toward a more comprehensive view of second language education. In B. Harley, P. Allen, J. Cummins, & M. Swain (Eds.), *The development of second language proficiency* (pp. 57–81). Cambridge, UK: Cambridge University Press.

Allender, S. (1998). *Adult ESL learners with special needs: Learning from the Australian perspective.* Washington, DC: Center for Adult English Language Acquisition. Retrieved from http://www.cal.org/caela/esl_resources/digests/AUSQA.html

Allison, D. (1998). Investigating learners' course diaries as explorations of language. *Language Teaching Research, 2*(1), 24–47.

Allwright, D. (1983). Classroom-centered research on language teaching and learning: A brief historical overview. *TESOL Quarterly, 17*(2), 191–204.

Allwright, D. (1997). Quality and sustainability in teacher-research. *TESOL Quarterly, 31*(2), 368–370.

Allwright, D. (2003). Exploratory practice: Rethinking practitioner research in language teaching. *Language Teaching Research, 7*(2), 113–141.

Allwright, D. (2005). Developing principles for practitioner research: The case of exploratory practice. *The Modern Language Journal, 89*(3), 353–363.

Allwright, D., & Bailey, K. M. (1991). *Focus on the language classroom: An introduction to classroom research for language teachers.* Cambridge, UK: Cambridge University Press.

Allwright, D., & Hanks, J. (2009). *The developing language learner: An introduction to exploratory practice.* New York, NY: Palgrave Macmillan.

Allwright, D., & Lenzuen, R. (1997). Exploring practice: Work at the Cultura Inglesa, Rio de Janeiro, Brazil. *Language Teaching Research, 1*(1), 71–79.

American Council for the Teaching of Foreign Languages (ACTFL). (n.d.a). *Standards for foreign language learning: Preparing for the 21st century.* Washington, DC: Author. Retrieved from http://www.actfl.org/files/public/StandardsforFLLexecsumm_rev.pdf

American Council on the Teaching of Foreign Languages (ACTFL). (n.d.b). *Testing for proficiency: The ACTFL oral proficiency interview.* Washington, DC: Author. Retrieved from http://www.actfl.org/professional-development/certified-proficiency-testing-program/testing-proficiency

American Council on the Teaching of Foreign Languages (ACTFL). (2012). *ACTFL proficiency guidelines.* Washington, DC: Author. Retrieved from http://actflproficiencyguidelines2012.org/

American Educational Research Association (AERA). (2000). Position statement of the American Educational Research Association concerning high-stakes testing in pre-K–12 education. *Educational Researcher, 29*(8), 24–25.

American Psychological Association, American Educational Research Association, National Council for Measurement in Education. (1999). *Standards for educational and psychological tests and testing.* Washington, DC: Author.

Amin, N. (2004). Nativism, the native speaker construct, and minority immigrant women teachers of English as a second language. In L. D. Kamhi-Stein (Ed.), *Learning and teaching from experience: Perspectives on nonnative English-speaking professionals* (pp. 61–80). Ann Arbor, MI: University of Michigan Press.

Anderson, A., & Lynch, T. (1988). *Listening.* Oxford, UK: Oxford University Press.

Anderson, J. R. (1990). *Cognitive psychology and its implications* (3rd ed.). New York, NY: W. H. Freeman.

Anderson, J. R. (1995). *Cognitive psychology and its implications* (4th ed.). New York, NY: Freeman.

Anderson, L. W., & Krathwohl, D. (Eds.). (2001). *A taxonomy for learning, teaching, and assessing: A revision of Bloom's taxonomy of educational objectives.* New York, NY: Longman.

Anderson, N. J. (1999). *Exploring second language reading: Issues and strategies.* Boston, MA: Heinle.

Anderson, N. J. (2005). L2 strategy research. In E. Hinkel (Ed.), *Handbook of research in second language teaching and learning* (pp. 757–772). Mahwah, NJ: Lawrence Erlbaum Associates.

Anderson, N. J. (2007). *ACTIVE skills for reading: Book 1* (2nd ed.). Boston, MA: Heinle.

Anderson, N. J. (2008). *Practical English language teaching: Reading.* New York, NY: McGraw-Hill.

Anderson, N. J. (2009). ACTIVE reading: The research base for a pedagogical approach in the reading classroom. In Z.-H. Han & N. J. Anderson (Eds.), *Second language reading research and instruction: Crossing the boundaries* (pp. 117–143). Ann Arbor, MI: University of Michigan Press.

Anderson, N. J. (2012). Metacognition: Awareness of language learning. In S. Mercer, S. Ryan, & M. Williams (Eds.), *Psychology for language learning: Insights from research, theory and pedagogy* (pp. 169–187). Basingstoke, UK: Palgrave.

Ansari, H., & Babaii, E. (2002). Universal characteristics of EFL/ESL textbooks: A step towards systematic textbook evaluation. *Internet TESL Journal, 8*(2). Retrieved from http://iteslj.org/Articles/Ansary-Textbooks/

Anstrom, K., DiCerbo, P., Butler, F., Katz, A., Miller, J., & Rivera, C. (2010). *A review of the literature on academic English: Implications for K–12 English language learners.* Arlington, VA: The George Washington University Center for Equity and Excellence in Education.

Anthony, E. M. (1963). Approach, method, and technique. *ELT Journal, 17*(2), 63–67.

Appel, J. (1995). *Diary of a language teacher.* Oxford, UK: Heinemann.

Apple Computer. (1989). *HyperCard* [computer software]. Cupertino, CA: Author.

Arkoudis, S. (2006). Negotiating the rough ground between ESL and mainstream teachers. *International Journal of Bilingual Education, 9,* 415–433.

Arkoudis, S., & O'Loughlin, K. (2004). Tensions between validity and outcomes: Teacher assessment of written work of recently arrived immigrant ESL students. *Language Testing, 21*(3), 284–304.

Arnold, J., Puchta, H., & Rinvolucri, M. (2007). *Imagine that! Mental imagery in the EFL classroom.* Cambridge, UK: Cambridge University Press.

Asher, J. (1996). *Learning another language through actions: The complete teacher's guidebook* (5th ed.). Los Gatos, CA: Sky Oak Productions.

Auerbach, E. (1992a). Literacy and ideology. *Annual Review of Applied Linguistics, 12,* 71–85.

Auerbach, E. (1992b). *Making meaning, making change: Participatory curriculum development for adult ESL literacy.* McHenry, IL: Center for Applied Linguistics/Delta Systems.

August, D., Carlo, M., Lively, T., McLaughlin, B., & Snow, C. (2006). Promoting the vocabulary growth of English learners. In T. Young & N. Hadaway (Eds.), *Supporting the literacy development of English learners* (pp. 96–112). Newark, DE: International Reading Association.

August, D., & Shanahan, T. (2006). *Developing literacy in second-language learners: Report of the National Literacy Panel on Language-Minority Children and Youth.* Mahwah, NJ: Lawrence Erlbaum Associates.

August, D., & Shanahan, T. (2010). Effective English literacy instruction for English learners. In California Department of Education, *Improving education for English learners: Research-based approaches* (pp. 209–250). Sacramento, CA: California Department of Education.

Ausubel, D. P. (1967). *Learning theory and classroom practice.* Ontario, Canada: Ontario Institute for Studies in Education.

Bachman, L. (1990). *Fundamental considerations in language testing.* Oxford, UK: Oxford University Press.

Bachman, L. F., & Palmer, A. S. (2010). *Language assessment in practice.* Oxford, UK: Oxford University Press.

Baddeley, A. (1986). *Working memory.* Oxford, UK: Oxford University Press.

Baddeley, A. D. (2000). The episodic buffer: A new component of working memory? *Trends in Cognitive Sciences, 4*(11), 417–423.

Baddeley, A. (2006). Working memory: An overview. In S. Pickering (Ed.), *Working memory and education* (pp. 3–26). Boston, MA: Academic Press.

Baetens Beardsmore, H. (2009). Language promotion by European supra-national institutions. In O. García (with H. Baetens Beardsmore), *Bilingual education in the 21st century: A global perspective* (pp. 197–217). Malden, MA: Wiley-Blackwell.

Bahrain Directorate of Curriculum. (2004). *Syllabus for basic education.* Bahrain: Author.

Bailey, A. L. (Ed.). (2007). *The language demands of school: Putting academic English to the test.* New Haven, CT: Yale University Press.

Bailey, A. L., & Heritage, H. M. (2008). *Formative assessment for literacy, grades K–6: Building reading and academic language skills across the curriculum.* Thousand Oaks, CA: Corwin Press.

Bailey, A. L., & Huang, B. H. (2011). Do current English language development/proficiency standards reflect the English needed for success in school? *Language Testing 28*(3), 343–365.

Bailey, K. (1996). The best-laid plans: Teachers' in-class decisions to depart from their lesson plans. In K. Bailey & D. Nunan (Eds.), *Voices from the language classroom* (pp. 15–40). New York, NY: Cambridge University Press.

Bailey, K. M. (2001). What my EFL students taught me. *The PAC Journal, 1*(1), 7–31.

Bailey, K. M. (2005). Looking back down the road: A recent history of language classroom research. *Review of Applied Linguistics in China, 1,* 6–47.

Bailey, K. M. (2006). *Language teacher supervision: A case-based approach.* Cambridge, UK: Cambridge University Press.

Bailey, K. M., Curtis, A., & Nunan, D. (2001a). *Pursuing professional development: The self as source.* Boston, MA: Heinle and Heinle.

Bailey, K. M., Curtis, A., & Nunan, D. (2001b). Video: Seeing ourselves as others see us. In *Pursuing professional development: The self as source* (pp. 117–132). Boston, MA: Heinle and Heinle.

Baker, C. (2007). *Parents' and teachers' guide to bilingualism* (3rd ed.). Clevedon, UK: Multilingual Matters.

Baker, C. (2011). *Foundations of bilingual education and bilingualism* (5th ed.). Clevedon, UK: Multilingual Matters.

Bakhtin, M. M. (1981). *The dialogic imagination: Four essays by M. M. Bakhtin* (M. Holquist, Ed.; C. Emerson & M. Holquist, Trans.). Austin, TX: University of Texas Press.

Ballantyne, K. G., Sanderman, A. R., & Levy, J. (2008). *Educating English language learners: Building teacher capacity.* Washington, DC: National Clearinghouse for English Language Acquisition.

Barber, C. L. (1985). Some measurable characteristics of modern scientific prose. In J. M. Swales (Ed.), *Episodes in ESP* (pp. 3–14). New York, NY: Prentice Hall. (Reprinted from *Contributions to English syntax and philology,* pp. 21–43, by C. L. Barber & F. Behre (Eds.), 1962, Göteborg, Sweden: Almqvist & Wiksell.)

Bargfrede, A. (1996). *Don't hang up yet! NNS negotiation of telephone closings.* (Unpublished master's thesis). Pennsylvania State University, State College, PA.

Barkhuizen, G. (2011). Narrative knowledging in TESOL. *TESOL Quarterly, 45*(3), 391–414.

Barratt, L. (2010). Strategies to prepare teachers equally for equity. In A. Mahboob (Ed.), *The NNEST lens: Non native English speakers in TESOL* (pp. 180–201). Newcastle, UK: Cambridge Scholars Publishing.

Barron, C. (2002). Problem-solving and EAP: Themes and issues in a collaborative teaching venture. *English for Specific Purposes Journal, 22*(3), 297–314.

Bartels, N. (2009). Knowledge about language. In A. Burns & J. C. Richards (Eds.), *The Cambridge guide to second language teacher education* (pp. 125–134). New York, NY: Cambridge University Press.

Bartholomae, D., & Petrosky, A. R. (1986). *Facts, artifacts and counterfacts: Theory and method for a reading and writing course.* Upper Montclair, NJ: Boynton/Cook.

Basturkmen, H. (2006). *Ideas and options in English for specific purposes.* Mahwah, NJ: Lawrence Erlbaum Associates.

Baugh, J. (2000). *Beyond Ebonics: Linguistic pride and racial prejudice.* New York, NY: Oxford University Press.

Bawarshi, A. (2003). *Genre and the invention of the writer: Reconsidering the place of invention in composition.* Logan, UT: Utah State University Press.

Bawarshi, A., & Reiff, M. J. (2010). *Genre: An introduction to history, theory, research, and pedagogy.* West Lafayette, IN: Parlor Press.

Bechtel, W., & Abrahamsen, A. (1991). *Connectionism and the mind: An introduction to parallel processing in networks.* Oxford, UK: Blackwell.

Beck, I., & McKeown, M. (2006). *Improving comprehension with Questioning the Author: A fresh and expanded view of a powerful approach.* New York, NY: Scholastic.

Beckett, G. H. (2006). Project-based second and foreign language education: Theory, research and practice. In G. H. Beckett & P. C. Miller (Eds.), *Project-based second and foreign language education* (pp. 3–16). Greenwich, CT: Information Age Publishing.

Beckett, G. H., & Miller, P. C. (Eds.). (2006). *Project-based second and foreign language education.* Greenwich, CT: Information Age Publishing.

Belcher, D. (2006). English for specific purposes: Teaching to the perceived needs and imagined futures in worlds of work, study, and everyday life. *TESOL Quarterly, 40*(1), 133–156.

Belcher, D. (Ed.). (2009a). *English for specific purposes: Theory and practice.* Ann Arbor, MI: University of Michigan Press.

Belcher, D. (2009b). Problem-solving for nursing purposes. In D. Belcher (Ed.), *English for specific purposes: Theory and practice* (pp. 229–242). Ann Arbor, MI: University of Michigan Press.

Belcher, D., & Hirvela, A. (2001). *Linking literacies: Perspectives on L2 reading-writing connections.* Ann Arbor, MI: University of Michigan Press.

Belcher, D., Johns, A. M., & Paltridge, B. (Eds.). (2011). *New directions in English for specific purposes research.* Ann Arbor, MI: University of Michigan Press.

Belluck, P. (2011, April 19). To tug hearts, music must tickle the neurons. Retrieved from http://www.nytimes.com/2011/04/19/science/19brain.html/

Benesch, S. (1993). Critical thinking: A learning process for democracy. *TESOL Quarterly, 27*(3), 545–548.

Benesch, S. (2001). *Critical English for academic purposes: Theory, politics and practice.* Mahwah, NJ: Lawrence Erlbaum Associates.

Bereiter, C., & Scardamalia, M. (1987). *The psychology of written composition*. Hillsdale, NJ: Lawrence Erlbaum Associates.

Berners-Lee, T., & Cailliau, R. (1990). *WorldWideWeb: Proposal for a HyperText project*. Retrieved from http://www.w3.org/Proposal.html

Berns, M. (2008). World Englishes, English as a lingua franca, and intelligibility. *World Englishes, 27*(34), 327–334.

Bhatia, T. K., & Ritchie, W. (Eds.). (2004). *The handbook of bilingualism*. Oxford, UK: Blackwell.

Bialystok, E. (2004). The impact of bilingualism on language and literacy development. In T. K. Bhatia & W. Ritchie (Eds.), *The handbook of bilingualism* (pp. 577–601). Oxford, UK: Blackwell.

Biber, D. (1988). *Variation across speech and writing*. Cambridge, UK: Cambridge University Press.

Biber, D., & Conrad, S. (1999). Lexical bundles in conversation and academic prose. In H. Hasselgard & S. Oksefjell (Eds.), *Out of corpora: Studies in honour of Stig Johansson* (pp. 181–190). Amsterdam, The Netherlands: Rodopi.

Biber, D., Conrad, S., & Reppen, R. (1998). *Corpus linguistics: Investigating language structure and use*. Cambridge, UK: Cambridge University Press.

Biber, D., Johannson, S., Leech, G., Conrad, S., & Finegan, E. (1999). *Longman grammar of spoken and written English*. Harlow, UK: Pearson Education.

Biggs, J. (2011, September 27). The future of books: A dystopian timeline. *TechCrunch*. Retrieved from: http://techcrunch.com/2011/09/27/the-future-of-books-a-dystopian-timeline/

Birch, B. M. (2007). *English L2 reading: Getting to the bottom* (2nd ed.). Mahwah, NJ: Lawrence Erlbaum Associates.

Bitterlin, G., Johnson, D., Price, D., Ramirez, S., & Savage, K. L. (2008a). *Ventures: Student book 1*. New York, NY: Cambridge University Press.

Bitterlin, G., Johnson, D., Price, D., Ramirez, S., & Savage, K. L. (2008b). *Ventures: Student book 4*. New York, NY: Cambridge University Press.

Blachowicz, C., & Ogle, D. (2008). *Reading comprehension: Strategies for independent learners* (2nd ed.). New York, NY: Guilford Press.

Black, P., & Wiliam, D. (1998). Assessment and classroom learning. *Assessment in Education, 5*(1), 7–68.

Black, P., & Wiliam, D. (2009). Developing the theory of formative assessment. *Educational Assessment, Evaluation and Accountability, 21*(5), 6–31.

Blanche-Benveniste, C. (1995). De la rareté de certains phénomènes syntaxiques en français parlé. *French Language Studies, 5*(1), 17–29.

Bloch, J. (2007). *Technologies in the second language composition classroom*. Ann Arbor, MI: University of Michigan Press.

Block, D. (1996). A window on the classroom: Classroom events viewed from different angles. In K. M. Bailey & D. Nunan (Eds.), *Voices from the language classroom* (pp. 168–194). Cambridge, UK: Cambridge University Press.

Block, D. (2003). *The social turn in second language acquisition*. Edinburgh, UK: Edinburgh University Press.

Bloom, B. S. (Ed.). (1956). *Taxonomy of educational objectives: The classification of educational goals: Handbook I. Cognitive domain*. New York, NY: Longman.

Bloomfield, L. (1933). *Language*. New York, NY: Holt, Rinehart, and Winston.

Blyth, M. C. (1996). Designing an EAP course for postgraduate students in Ecuador. In K. Graves (Ed.), *Teachers as course developers* (pp. 86–118). Cambridge, UK: Cambridge University Press.

Bollati, A. (2007). From back door to center stage: The evolution of an ESL program. In M. Carroll (Ed.), *Developing a new curriculum for adult learners* (pp. 13–32). Alexandria, VA: Teachers of English to Speakers of Other Languages.

Bonfanti, P., & Watkins, M. (2007). Revitalizing and strengthening an ESL program: Meeting the needs of students and the host institution. In A. Rice (Ed.), *Revitalizing an established program for adult learners* (pp. 35–56). Alexandria, VA: Teachers of English to Speakers of Other Languages.

Borg, S. (1999). The use of grammatical terminology in the second language classroom: A qualitative study of teachers' practices and cognitions. *Applied Linguistics, 20*(1), 95–124.

Borg, S. (2003). Teacher cognition in language teaching: A review of literature on what language teachers think, know, believe, and do. *Language Teaching, 36*, 81–109.

Borg, S. (Ed.). (2006a). *Language teacher research in Europe*. Alexandria, VA: Teachers of English to Speakers of Other Languages.

Borg, S. (2006b). *Teacher cognition and language education: Research and practice*. London, UK: Continuum.

Borg, S. (2011). The impact of in-service teacher education on language teachers' beliefs. *System, 39*(3), 370–380. doi:10.1016/j.system.2011.07.009

Borkowski, J. (1996). Metacognition: Theory or chapter heading? *Learning and Individual Differences, 8*(4), 391–402.

Borrero, N., & Yeh, C. (2010, November). Ecological English language learning among ethnic minority youth. *Educational Researcher, 39*(8), 571–581.

Braddock, R., Lloyd-Jones, R., & Schoer, L. (1963). *Research in written composition*. Urbana, IL: National Council of Teachers of English.

Bradley, J. (2009, March 30). Can Second Life help teach doctors to treat patients? *CNN Tech*. Retrieved from http://articles.cnn.com/2009-03-30/tech/doctors.second.life_1_second-life-medical-students-virtual-hospital?_s=PM:TECH

Bradlow, A. R., Pisoni, D. B., Akahane-Yamada, R., & Tokhura, Y. (1997). Training Japanese listeners to identify English /r/ and /l/. Some effects of perceptual learning on speech production. *Journal of the Acoustical Society of America, 101*(4), 2299–2310.

Braine, G. (Ed.). (1999). *Non-native educators in English language teaching*. Mahwah, NJ: Lawrence Erlbaum Associates.

Braine, G. (2010). *Nonnative speaker English teachers: Research, pedagogy and professional growth*. New York, NY: Routledge.

Brazil, D. (1995). *A grammar of speech*. Oxford, UK: Oxford University Press.

Breen, M. P. (1987a). Contemporary paradigms in syllabus design: Part 1. *Language Teaching, 20*(1), 81–92.

Breen, M. P. (1987b). Contemporary paradigms in syllabus design: Part 2. *Language Teaching, 20*(2), 157–174.

Breen, M. P., & Candlin, C. N. (1980). The essentials of a communicative curriculum in language teaching. *Applied Linguistics, 1*(2), 89–112. doi:10.1093/applin/I.2.89

Breen, M. P., & Littlejohn, A. (2000). *Classroom decision-making: Negotiation and process syllabuses in practice*. Cambridge, UK: Cambridge University Press.

Brindley, G. (1991). Becoming a researcher: Teacher-conducted research and professional growth. In E. Sadtono (Ed.), *Language acquisition and the second/foreign language classroom* (RELC Anthology Series 38, pp. 16–35). Singapore: SEAMEO Regional Language Centre.

Brinton, D. (2001). The use of media in language teaching. In M. Celce-Murcia (Ed.), *Teaching English as a second or foreign language* (3rd ed., pp. 459–476). Boston, MA: Heinle and Heinle.

Brinton, D. (2003). Content-based instruction. In D. Nunan (Ed.), *Practical English language teaching* (pp. 199–224). New York, NY: McGraw-Hill.

Brinton, D. M. (2004). Nonnative English-speaking student teachers: Insights from dialogue journals. In L. D. Kamhi-Stein (Ed.), *Learning and teaching from experience: Perspectives on nonnative English-speaking professionals* (pp. 190–205). Ann Arbor, MI: University of Michigan Press.

Brinton, D. M. (2007). Two for one? Language-enhanced content instruction in English for academic purposes. In *A symposium: Teaching English for specific purposes*. Alexandria, VA: Teachers of English to Speakers of Other Languages.

Brinton, D. (2008). Using WebQuests to foster cultural autonomy in international teachers. *TESOL Applied Linguistics Interest Section Newsletter, 28*(2).

Brinton, D. M. (2011a, October). *English language teaching methods: What's new under the sun?* Plenary address presented at the TESL Ontario Convention, Toronto, Canada.

Brinton, D. M. (2011b, May 27). *Into, through, and beyond* [webinar]. São Paulo, Brazil: Regional English Language Office, U.S. Embassy.

Brinton, D. M. (2011c, April–June). Promoting teacher reflection through critical incident analysis. *TESOL Greece Newsletter, 110*, 14–18.

Brinton, D. M., & Jensen, L. (2002). Appropriating the adjunct model: English for academic purposes at the university level. In J. Crandall & D. Kaufman (Eds.), *Content-based instruction in higher education settings* (pp. 125–137). Alexandria, VA: Teachers of English to Speakers of Other Languages.

Brinton, D. M., Kagan, O., & Bauckus, S. (Eds.). (2008). *Heritage language education: A new field emerging*. New York, NY: Routledge.

Brinton, D. M., & Master, P. (Eds.). (1997). *New ways in content-based instruction*. Alexandria, VA: Teachers of English to Speakers of Other Languages.

Brinton, D. M., Snow, M. A., & Wesche, M. (1989). *Content-based second language instruction*. New York: NY: Newbury House.

Brinton, D. M., Snow, M. A., & Wesche, M. (2003). *Content-based second language instruction* (Michigan Classics ed.). Ann Arbor, MI: University of Michigan Press.

Brisk, M. E., Burgos, A., & Hamerla, S. (2004). *Situational context of education: A window into the world of bilingual learners*. Mahwah, NJ: Lawrence Erlbaum Associates.

Britton, B. K., Gulgoz, S., & Glynn, S. (1993). Impact of good and poor writing on learners: Research and theory. In B. K. Britton, A. Woodward, & M. Binkley (Eds.), *Learning from textbooks: Theory and practice* (pp. 1–46). Hillsdale, NY: Lawrence Erlbaum Associates.

Brock, M. N., Yu, B., & Wong, M. (1992). "Journaling" together: Collaborative diary-keeping and teacher development. In J. Flowerdew, M. N. Brock, & S. Hsia (Eds.), *Perspectives on second language teacher development* (pp. 295–307). Hong Kong: City University of Hong Kong.

Broeder, P., & Martyniuk, W. (2008). Language education in Europe: The Common European Framework of Reference. In N. Van Deusen-Scholl & N. H. Hornberger (Eds.), *Encyclopedia of language and education: Second and foreign language education* (2nd ed., Vol. 4, pp. 209–226). New York, NY: Springer.

Brown, A. (1991a). Functional load and the teaching of pronunciation. In A. Brown (Ed.), *Teaching English pronunciation: A book of readings* (pp. 211–224). London, UK: Routledge.

Brown, A. (1991b). *Pronunciation models*. Singapore: Singapore University Press.

Brown, D. (2011). What aspects of vocabulary knowledge do textbooks give attention to? *Language Teaching Research, 15*(1), 83–97.

Brown, G. (1987). Twenty-five years of teaching listening comprehension. *English Teaching Forum, 25,* 11–15

Brown, G. (1990). *Listening to spoken English* (2nd ed.). London, UK: Longman.

Brown, H. D. (2002). English language teaching in the "post-method" era: Toward better diagnosis, treatment, and assessment. In J. C. Richards & W. A. Renandya (Eds.), *Methodology in language teaching* (pp. 9–18). New York, NY: Cambridge University Press.

Brown, H. D. (2007). *Teaching by principles: An interactive approach to language pedagogy* (3rd ed.). Englewood Cliffs, NJ: Prentice Hall Regents.

Brown, H. D., & Abeywickrama, P. (2010). *Language assessment: Principles and classroom practices* (2nd ed.). White Plains, NY: Pearson.

Brown, J. D. (1995). *The elements of language curriculum*. Boston, MA: Heinle and Heinle.

Brown, K. (1999). *Teaching disparate learner groups*. Sydney, Australia: Macquairie University, National Centre for English Language Teaching and Research.

Brown, P., & Levinson, S. (1987). *Politeness: Some universals in language usage*. Cambridge, UK: Cambridge University Press.

Brumfit, C. (1984). *Communicative methodology in language teaching: The roles of fluency and accuracy*. Cambridge, UK: Cambridge University Press.

Brumfit, C., & Johnson, K. (1979). *The communicative approach to language teaching*. Oxford, UK: Oxford University Press.

Bruner, J. (1983). *Child's talk: Learning to use language*. Oxford, UK: Oxford University Press.

Brutt-Griffler, J., & Samimy, K. K. (1999). Revisiting the colonial in the postcolonial: Critical praxis for nonnative English-speaking teachers in a TESOL program. *TESOL Quarterly, 33*(3), 413–432.

Bublitz, W. (1988). *Supportive fellow-speakers and cooperative conversations*. Amsterdam, The Netherlands: John Benjamins.

Buck, G. (1995). How to become a good listening teacher. In D. Mendelsohn & J. Rubin (Eds.), *A guide for the teaching of second language listening* (pp. 113–128). San Diego, CA: Dominie Press.

Buck, G. (2001). *Assessing listening*. Cambridge, UK: Cambridge University Press.

Buck, R. (2005). Adding ingredients to the self-organizing dynamic system stew: Motivation, communication, and higher-level emotions—and don't forget the genes! *Behavioral and Brain Science, 28*(2), 197–198.

Buell, J. (1994). Review of *Learn to speak English for the multimedia PC, Ver. 3.0. TESL-EJ, 1*(1). Retrieved from http://www.tesl-ej.org/wordpress/issues/volume1/ej01/ej01mr1/

Burger, S., Wesche, M., & Migneron, M. (1997). "Late, late immersion": Discipline-based second language teaching at the University of Ottawa. In K. Johnson & M. Swain (Eds.), *Immersion education: International perspectives* (pp. 65–84). Cambridge, UK: Cambridge University Press.

Burns, A. (1998). *Collaborative action research for English language teachers*. Cambridge, UK: Cambridge University Press.

Burns, A. (2004). Action research. In E. Hinkel (Ed.), *Handbook of research in second language teaching and learning* (pp. 241–256). Mahwah, NJ: Lawrence Erlbaum Associates.

Burns, A. (2005). Interrogating new worlds of English language teaching. In A. Burns (Ed.), *Teaching English from a global perspective* (pp. 1–15). Alexandria, VA: Teachers of English to Speakers of Other Languages.

Burns, A. (2009). Action research in second language teacher education. In A. Burns & J. C. Richards (Eds.), *The Cambridge guide to second language teacher education* (pp. 289–297). Cambridge, UK: Cambridge University Press.

Burns, A. (2011). *Doing action research in English language teaching: A guide for practitioners*. New York, NY: Routledge.

Burns, A., & Burton, J. (Eds.). (2008). *Language teacher research in Australia and New Zealand*. Alexandria, VA: Teachers of English to Speakers of Other Languages.

Burns, A., Joyce, H., & Gollin, S. (1996). *"I see what you mean." Using spoken discourse in the classroom: A handbook for teachers*. Sydney, Australia: National Centre for English Language Teaching and Research.

Burt, M. (2004). *Issues with outcomes in workplace ESL programs*. Washington, DC: National Center for ESL Literacy Education. Retrieved from http://www.workandeconomy.org/images/Issues_in_Improving_Immigrant_Workers_English_Language_Skills_-_Burt.pdf

Burt, M., & Kiparsky, C. (1989). *The gooficon: A repair manual for English*. Boston, MA: Heinle and Heinle.

Burt, M., Peyton, J., & Adams, R. (2003) *Reading and adult English language learners: A review of the research*. Washington, DC: Center for Applied Linguistics.

Burton, D. (1982). Conversation pieces. In R. Carter & D. Burton (Eds.), *Literary texts and language study* (pp. 86–111). London, UK: Edward Arnold.

Burton, J. (2009). Reflective practice. In A. Burns & J. C. Richards (Eds.), *The Cambridge guide to second language teacher education* (pp. 298–307). New York, NY: Cambridge University Press.

Bush, V. (1945, July). As we may think. *The Atlantic Magazine*. Retrieved from http://www.theatlantic.com/magazine/archive/1969/12/as-we-may-think/3881/

Butler, Y. G. (2004). What level of English proficiency do elementary school teachers need to attain to teach EFL? Case studies from Korea, Taiwan, and Japan. *TESOL Quarterly, 38*(2), 245–278.

Butler, Y. G. (2007). How are non-native English speaking teachers perceived by young learners? *TESOL Quarterly, 41*(4), 731–755.

Buttjes, D., & Byram, M. (1991). *Mediating languages and cultures*. Clevedon, UK: Multilingual Matters.

Bybee, J. (2006). From usage to grammar. *Language, 82,* 711–733.

Bygate, M. (1996). The effect of task repetition: Appraising the developing language of learners. In J. Willis & D. Willis (Eds.), *Challenge and change in language teaching* (pp. 136–146). London, UK: Heinemann.

Bygate, M. (2001). Speaking. In R. Carter & D. Nunan (Eds.), *The Cambridge guide to teaching English to speakers of other languages* (pp. 16–19). Cambridge, UK: Cambridge University Press.

Bygate, M., Skehan, P., & Swain, M. (2001). *Researching pedagogic tasks: Second language learning, teaching and testing*. London, UK: Longman.

Byram, M., & Morgan, C. (1994). *Teaching-and-learning language-and-culture*. Clevedon, UK: Multilingual Matters.

Byrd, P. (2001). Textbooks: Evaluation for selection and analysis for implementation. In M. Celce-Murcia (Ed.), *Teaching English as a second or foreign language* (3rd ed., pp. 415–427). Boston, MA: Heinle and Heinle.

Byrd, P., & Schuemann, C. (2013). Materials publication. In C. A. Chapelle (Ed.), *The encyclopedia of applied linguistics* (pp. 3604–3609). Malden, MA: Wiley-Blackwell.

Byrne, D. (1988). *Teaching writing skills*. London, UK: Longman.

Byrnes, H. (Ed.). (2006). *Advanced language learning: The contribution of Halliday and Vygotsky*. London, UK: Continuum.

Cahnmann, M. (1998). Over thirty years of language-in-education policy and planning: Potter Thomas Bilingual School in Philadelphia. *Bilingual Research Journal, 22*, 65–81.

Calderón, M. (1999). Teachers' learning communities for cooperation in diverse settings. *Theory into Practice, 38*(2), 94–99.

Calderón, M., Slavin, R., & Sanchez, M. (2011). Effective instruction for English learners. *The Future of Children, 21*(1), 103–127.

California Department of Education. (2000). *History-social science content standards for California public schools: Kindergarten through grade twelve*. Sacramento, CA: Author. Retrieved from http://www. cde .ca.gov/be/st/ss

California Department of Education. (2002). *English language development standards for California public schools: Kindergarten through grade twelve*. Sacramento, CA: Author. Retrieved from http://www.cde .ca.gov/be/st/ss

California Department of Education. (2010). *Improving education for English learners: Research-based approaches*. Sacramento, CA: Author.

California Department of Education. (2011). *California Department of Education: Overview of the California High School Exit Examination*. Sacramento, CA: Author. Retrieved from http://www.cde.ca.gov /ta/tg/hs/overview.asp

California State University, Stanislaus. (n.d.). *The writing process diagram*. Retrieved from http://www.csustan.edu/teachered/FacultyStaff /betts/Handouts/DOCs/Writing%20Process%20Diagram.doc

Calzoni, D. (2002). Action research & teacher development: How to make homework more motivating if we take care of the learners' different learning styles. *Perspectives: A Journal of TESOL-Italy, 29*, 99–108.

Cambridge Michigan Language Assessments. (2012). *MELAB: Michigan English Language Assessment Battery*. Ann Arbor, MI: Author. Retrieved from http://www.cambridgemichigan.org/melab.

Cameron, L. (2001). *Teaching languages to young learners*. Cambridge, UK: Cambridge University Press.

Cameron, L. (2003). Challenges for ELT from the expansion in teaching children. *ELT Journal, 57*(2), 105–112.

Canagarajah, A. S. (1993). Critical ethnography of a Sri Lankan classroom: Ambiguities in student opposition to reproduction through ESOL. *TESOL Quarterly, 27*(4), 601–625.

Canagarajah, A. S. (1999). Interrogating the "native speaker fallacy": Non-linguistic roots, non-pedagogical results. In G. Braine (Ed.), *Non-native educators in English language teaching* (pp. 77–92). Mahwah, NJ: Lawrence Erlbaum Associates.

Canagarajah, A. S. (2006). TESOL at 40: What are the issues? *TESOL Quarterly, 40*(1), 9–34.

Canale, M. (1983). From communicative competence to communicative language pedagogy. In J. Richards & R. Schmidt (Eds.), *Language and communication* (pp. 2–27). London, UK: Longman.

Canale, M., & Swain, M. (1980). Theoretical bases of communicative approaches to second language teaching and testing. *Applied Linguistics, 1*(1), 1–47.

Carr, J., Sexton, U., & Lagunoff, R. (2006). *Making science accessible to English learners: A guidebook for teachers*. San Francisco, CA: WestEd.

Carr, N., Eyring, J., & Gallego, J. (2006). What is the value of service-learning for ESL teacher preparation? *The CATESOL Journal, 18*(1), 66–80.

Carrasquillo, A. L., & Rodríguez, V. (2002). *Language minority students in the mainstream classroom* (2nd ed.). Clevedon, UK: Multilingual Matters.

Carrell, P. L., & Eisterhold, J. C. (1983). Schema theory and ESL reading pedagogy. *TESOL Quarterly, 17*(4), 553–574.

Carrier, K. (2003). Improving high school English language learners' second language listening through strategy instruction. *Bilingual Research Journal, 27*(3), 383–408.

Carroll, S., & Swain, M. (1993). Explicit and implicit negative feedback: An empirical study of the learning of linguistic generalizations. *Studies in Second Language Acquisition, 15*(3), 357–386.

Carson, J., & Leki, I. (1993). *Reading in the composition classroom: Second language perspectives*. Boston, MA: Heinle and Heinle.

Carter, M. (2007). Ways of knowing, doing, and writing in the disciplines. *College Composition and Communication, 58*, 385–418.

Carter, R. (1996). Look both ways before crossing: Developments in the language and literature classroom. In R. Carter & J. McRae (Eds.), *Language, literature and the learner* (pp. 1–16). London, UK: Addison-Wesley Longman.

Carter, R., & McCarthy, M. (1995). Grammar and the spoken language. *Applied Linguistics, 16*(2), 141–158.

Carter, R., & McCarthy, M. (1997). *Exploring spoken English*. Cambridge, UK: Cambridge University Press.

Carter, R., & McCarthy, M. (2006). *Cambridge grammar of English: A comprehensive guide: Spoken and written English grammar and usage*. Cambridge, UK: Cambridge University Press.

Carter, R., McCarthy, M., Mark, G., & O'Keeffe, A. (2011). *English grammar today*. Cambridge, UK: Cambridge University Press.

Carver, R. P. (1990). *Reading rate: A review of research and theory*. San Diego, CA: Academic Press.

Carver, R. P. (1992). Reading rate: Theory, research, and practical implications. *Journal of Reading, 32*, 84–95.

Carver, R. P. (2000). *The causes of high and low reading achievement*. Mahwah, NJ: Lawrence Erlbaum Associates.

Catford, J. C. (1987). Phonetics and the teaching of pronunciation. In J. Morley (Ed.), *Current perspectives on pronunciation: Practices anchored in theory* (pp. 87–100). Alexandria, VA: Teachers of English to Speakers of Other Languages.

Cattell, R. (2000). *Children's language: Consensus and controversy*. New York, NY: Cassell.

Celce-Murcia, M. (1991). Discourse analysis and grammar instruction. *Annual Review of Applied Linguistics, 11*, 135–151.

Celce-Murcia, M. (2001). Language teaching approaches: An overview. In M. Celce-Murcia (Ed.), *Teaching English as a second or foreign language* (3rd ed., pp. 3–11). Boston, MA: Heinle and Heinle.

Celce-Murcia, M. (2002). Why it makes sense to teach grammar in context and through discourse. In E. Hinkel & S. Fotos (Eds.), *New perspectives on grammar teaching in second language classrooms* (pp. 119–134). Mahwah, NJ: Lawrence Erlbaum Associates.

Celce-Murcia, M. (2008). The importance of context and discourse in teaching grammar: The case of the present perfect progressive in English. In A. Stavans & I. Kupferberg (Eds.), *Studies in language and language education: Essays in honor of Elite Olshtain* (pp. 231–242). Jerusalem, Israel: The Hebrew University Magness Press.

Celce-Murcia, M., Brinton, D., & Goodwin, J. (with Griner, B.). (2010). *Teaching pronunciation: A reference for teachers of English to speakers of other languages* (2nd ed.). New York, NY: Cambridge University Press.

Celce-Murcia, M., Dörnyei, Z., & Thurrell, S. (1995). Communicative competence: A pedagogically-motivated model with content specifications. *Issues in Applied Linguistics, 6*(2), 5–35.

Celce-Murcia, M., & Larsen-Freeman, D. (with Williams, H.). (1999). *The grammar book: An ESL/EFL teacher's course* (2nd ed.). Boston, MA: Heinle and Heinle.

Celce-Murcia, M., & Olshtain, E. (2000). *Discourse and context in language teaching: A guide for language teachers*. New York, NY: Cambridge University Press.

Celce-Murcia, M., & Olshtain, E. (2005). Discourse-based approaches: A new framework for second language teaching and learning. In E. Hinkel (Ed.), *Handbook of research in second language teaching and learning* (pp. 729–741). Mahwah, NJ: Lawrence Erlbaum Associates.

Celce-Murcia, M., & Yoshida, N. (2003). Alternatives to current pedagogy for teaching the present perfect progressive. *English Teaching Forum, 41*(1), 2–9, 21.

Cenoz, J. (1998). Multilingual education in the Basque Country. In J. Cenoz & F. Genesee (Eds.), *Beyond bilingualism: Multilingualism and multilingual education* (pp. 175–191). Clevedon, UK: Multilingual Matters.

Cenoz, J., & Genesee, F., (Eds.). (1998). *Beyond bilingualism: Multilingualism and multilingual education*. Clevedon, UK: Multilingual Matters.

The Center for Applied Linguistics. (2009). *Secondary newcomer programs in the U.S.* Retrieved from http://www.cal.org/CALWebDB /Newcomer/Default.aspx

The Center for Applied Linguistics. (2011). *Directory of foreign language immersion programs*. Retrieved from www.cal.org/resources/immersion

The Center for Applied Linguistics. (2012). *Directory of two-way bilingual immersion programs*. Retrieved from www.cal.org/twi/directory

Centre for Canadian Language Benchmarks. (2000). *Canadian language benchmarks 2000*. Ottawa, Canada: Author. Retrieved from http://www.language.ca/

Chacon, C. T. (2006). My journey into racial awareness. In A. Curtis & M. Romney (Eds.), *Color, race, and English language teaching:*

Shades of meaning (pp. 45–63). Mahwah, NJ: Lawrence Erlbaum Associates.

Chall, J. S. (1967). *Learning to read: The great debate.* New York, NY: McGraw-Hill.

Chambers, A. (2010). What is data-driven learning? In A. O'Keeffe & M. McCarthy (Eds.), *The Routledge handbook of corpus linguistics* (pp. 345–358). London, UK: Routledge.

Chamot, A. U. (1995). Learning strategies and listening comprehension. In D. Mendelsohn & J. Rubin (Eds.), *A guide for the teaching of second language listening* (pp. 13–30). San Diego, CA: Dominie Press.

Chamot, A. U. (2005). Language learning strategy instruction: Current issues and research. *Annual Review of Applied Linguistics, 25,* 112–130.

Chamot, A. U. (2009). *The CALLA handbook: Implementing the cognitive academic language learning approach* (2nd ed.). White Plains, NY: Pearson Education.

Chamot, A. U., & O'Malley, J. M. (1987). The cognitive academic language learning approach: A bridge to the mainstream. *TESOL Quarterly, 21*(2), 227–249.

Chamot, A. U., & O'Malley, J. M. (1994). *The CALLA handbook: Implementing the cognitive academic language learning approach.* Reading, MA: Addison-Wesley.

Chan, C. (2010). *A sociocultural study of second language tasks in business English contexts: An activity theory perspective on task processes and outcomes.* (Unpublished doctoral dissertation). University of Hong Kong.

Chang, A., & Read, J. (2006). The effects of listening support on the listening performance of EFL learners. *TESOL Quarterly, 40*(2), 113–127.

Charles, M. (2007). Reconciling top-down and bottom-up approaches to graduate writing: Using a corpus to teach rhetorical functions. *Journal of English for Academic Purposes, 6*(4), 289–302.

Chaudron, C. (1988). *Second language classrooms: Research on teaching and learning.* Cambridge, UK: Cambridge University Press.

Chaudron, C., & Richards, J. C. (1986). The effect of discourse markers on the comprehension of lectures. *Applied Linguistics, 7*(2), 113–127.

Chen, Y., Chen, N., & Tsai, C. (2009). The use of online synchronous discussion for web-based professional development for teachers. *Computers & Education, 53*(4), 1155–1166. doi:10.1016/j.compedu.2009.05.026

Cheng, L. (2005). *Changing language teaching through language testing: A washback study.* Cambridge, UK: Cambridge University Press.

Cheville, J. (2004). Automated scoring technologies and the rising influence of error. *English Journal, 93*(4), 47–52.

Chien, C. N., & Wei, L. (1998). The strategy use in listening comprehension for EFL learners in Taiwan. *RELC Journal, 29*(1), 66–91.

Chik, C. (2003). *Warm-ups.* Unpublished manuscript. Department of Applied Linguistics & TESL, University of California, Los Angeles, CA, United States.

Chisman, F. (2009). *Expanding horizons: Pacesetters in adult education for work.* New York, NY: Council for Advancement of Adult Literacy. Retrieved from http://www.caalusa.org/Expanding.pdf

Chiswick, B. R., & Miller, P. W. (2002). Immigrant earnings: Language skills, linguistic concentrations and the business cycle. *Journal of Popular Economics, 15*(1), 31–57.

Chomsky, N. (1957). *Syntactic structures.* The Hague, The Netherlands: Mouton.

Chomsky, N. (1959). [Review of the book *Verbal behavior* by B. F. Skinner]. *Language, 35,* 26–58.

Chomsky, N. (1965). *Aspects of the theory of syntax.* Cambridge, MA: MIT Press.

Chomsky, N. (1972). *Language and mind (*2nd ed.). San Diego, CA: Harcourt Brace.

Chomsky, N. (1995). *The minimalist program.* Cambridge, MA: MIT Press.

Chomsky, N., & Halle, M. (1968). *The sound patterns of English.* New York, NY: Harper and Row.

Christian, D. (1996). Two-way immersion education: Students learning through two languages. *The Modern Language Journal, 80*(1), 66–76.

Christian, D., Howard, K., & Loeb, M. (2000). Bilingualism for all: Two-way immersion education in the United States. *Theory into Practice, 39*(4), 258–266.

Christison, M. A., & Bassano, S. (1995). Action research: Techniques for collecting data through surveys and interviews. *The CATESOL Journal, 8*(1), 89–103.

Chun, D. M. (2002). *Discourse intonation in L2: From theory and research to practice.* Amsterdam, The Netherlands: John Benjamins.

Ciaffaroni, M. T. (2006). How good are ESL/EFL websites? *The Journal of Teaching English with Technology, 6*(4). Retrieved from http://www.tewtjournal.org/VOL%206/ISSUE%204/06_HOWGOODARE.pdf

Cisneros, S. (1996). Eleven. In M. L. McCloskey & L. Stack (Eds.), *Voices in literature gold—A standards-based program* (pp. 11–15). Boston, MA: Heinle and Heinle.

Citizenship and Immigration Canada (2012). *Welcome to Canada: What you should know.* Ottawa, Ontario: Author. Retrieved from http://www.cic.gc.ca/english/resources/publications/welcome/wel-03e.asp#more

Clark, E., & Paran, A. (2007) The employability of non-native-speaker teachers of EFL: A UK survey. *System, 35*(4), 407–430.

Clark, P. (2003, July/August). My father on a bicycle [poem]. *The Atlantic Monthly.* Retrieved from http://www.theatlantic.com/past/docs/unbound/poetry/antholog/clark/bicycle.htm

Clarke, J. H. (1991). Using visual organizers to focus on thinking. *Journal of Reading, 34*(7), 526–534.

Clarke, M. (1982). On bandwagons, tyranny, and common sense. *TESOL Quarterly, 16*(4), 437–448.

Cloud, N., Genesee, F., & Hamayan, E. (2009). *Literacy instruction for English language learners: A teacher's guide to research-based practices.* Portsmouth, NH: Heinemann.

Cochran-Smith, M., & Lytle, S. L. (1999). Relationships of knowledge and practice: Teacher learning in communities. *Review of Research in Education, 24,* 249–305.

Cochran-Smith, M., & Lytle, S. L. (2009). *Inquiry as stance: Practitioner research in the next generation.* New York, NY: Teachers College Press.

Cohen, A. D. (2011). *Strategies in learning and using a second language* (2nd ed.). New York, NY: Longman.

Cohen, A. D., & Macaro, E. (Eds.). (2007). *Language learner strategies.* Oxford, UK: Oxford University Press.

Cohen, A., Oxford, R. L., & Chi, J. C. (2005). *Language strategy use inventory.* Minneapolis: MN: University of Minnesota Center for Advanced Research on Language Acquisition. Retrieved from http://www.carla.umn.edu/maxsa/documents/langstratuse_inventory.pdf

Cohen, A. D., & Weaver, S. J. (2006). *Styles and strategies-based instruction: A teachers' guide.* Minneapolis, MN: Center for Advanced Research on Language Acquisition, University of Minnesota. Retrieved from http://elechina.super-red.es/cohen-weaver.pdf

Cohen, J. (2011). Building fluency through the repeated reading method. *English Teaching Forum, 49*(3), 20–27.

Coleman, A. (1929). *Teaching of modern foreign languages in the United States.* New York, NY: Macmillan.

Coleman, H. (1989). *Large classes in Nigeria: Lancaster-Leeds language learning in large classes research project* (Report No. 6). Leeds, UK: Lancaster-Leeds Language Learning.

Coleman, H. (2006). Darwin and the large class. In S. Gieve & I. K. Miller (Eds.), *Understanding the language classroom* (pp. 115–135). Basingstoke, UK: Palgrave Macmillan.

The College Board. (2012). *Scholastic Achievement Test (SAT).* New York, NY: Author. Retrieved from http://sat.collegeboard.org/home

Collie, J., & Slater, S. (1988). *Literature in the language classroom: A resource book of ideas and activities.* Cambridge, UK: Cambridge University Press.

Collier, V. (2004). Teaching multilingual children. In O. Santa Ana (Ed.), *The lives of multilingual children in public education* (pp. 222–235). Lanham, MD: Rowman & Littlefield.

Collin, S., & Karsenti, T. (2011). The collective dimension of reflective practice: The how and why. *Reflective Practice: International and Multidisciplinary Perspectives, 12,* 569–581.

Coltrane, B. (2003). *Working with young English language learners: Some considerations.* Washington, DC: Center for Applied Linguistics. (ERIC Document Reproduction Service No. EDO-FL-03-01.)

Comings, J. (2007) Persistence: Helping adult education students reach their goals. In J. Comings, B. Garner, & C. Smith (Eds.), *Review of adult learning and literacy: Connecting research, policy, and practice* (Vol. 7, pp. 23–46). Mahwah, NJ: Lawrence Erlbaum Associates.

Common European Framework of Reference. (2011). *Common European framework of reference for languages: Learning, teaching, assessment*. Cambridge, UK: Cambridge University Press. Retrieved from http://www.coe.int/t/dg4/linguistic/Source/Framework_EN.pdf

Comprehensive Adult Student Assessment Systems (CASAS). (2011). *CASAS basic skills content standards*. Retrieved from https://www.casas.org/product-overviews/curriculum-management-instruction/casas-basic-skills-content-standards

Condon, W. S. (1982). Cultural microrhythms. In M. Davis (Ed.), *Interaction rhythms: Periodicity in communicative behavior* (pp. 53–77). New York, NY: Human Sciences Press.

Conrad, S., & Biber, D. (2004). The frequency and use of lexical bundles in conversation and academic prose. In W. Teubert & M. Mahlberg (Eds., Thematic Section), The corpus approach to lexicography. *Lexicographica: International Annual for Lexicography, 20*, 56–71.

Conway, P. F. (2001). Anticipatory reflection while learning to teach: From a temporally truncated to a temporally distributed model of reflection in teacher education. *Teaching and Teacher Education, 17*, 89–106.

Cook, G. (1989). *Discourse*. Oxford, UK: Oxford University Press.

Cook, V. (1999). Going beyond the native speaker in language teaching. *TESOL Quarterly, 33*(2), 185–209.

Cook, V. (2008). *Second language learning and language teaching* (4th ed.). London, UK: Hodder.

Coombe, C., & Barlow, L. (Eds.). (2007). *Language teacher research in the Middle East*. Alexandria, VA: Teachers of English to Speakers of Other Languages.

Coombe, C., Folse, K., & Hubley, N. (2007). *A practical guide to assessing English language learners*. Ann Arbor, MI: Michigan University Press.

Corder, S. P. (1967). The significance of learners' errors. *International Review of Applied Linguistics, 5*, 161–170.

Cortes, V. (2007). Exploring genre and corpora in the English for academic writing class. *The ORTESOL Journal, 25*, 8–14.

Cosh, J. (1999). Peer observation: A reflective model. *ELT Journal, 53*(1), 22–27.

Council of Europe. (2001). *Common European Framework of reference for languages: Learning, teaching and assessment*. Cambridge, UK: Cambridge University Press.

Council of Europe. (2012). *European language portfolio*. Retrieved from http://www.coe.int/t/DG4/Portfolio/?L=E&M=/main_pages/introduction.html

Couper, G. (2003). The value of an explicit pronunciation syllabus in ESOL teaching. *Prospect, 18*(3), 53–70.

Couper, G. (2006). The short and long-term effects of pronunciation instruction. *Prospect, 21*(1), 46–66.

Coxhead, A. (2000). A new academic word list. *TESOL Quarterly, 34*(2), 213–238.

Coxhead, A. (2006). *Essentials of teaching academic vocabulary*. Boston, MA: Houghton Mifflin.

Coyle, D., Hood, P., & Marsh, D. (2010). *Content and language integrated learning*. Cambridge, UK: Cambridge University Press.

Crandall, J. A. (1993). Professionalism and professionalization of adult ESL literacy. *TESOL Quarterly, 27*(3), 497–515.

Crandall, J. A. (1998). Collaborate and cooperate: Teacher education for integrating language and content instruction. *English Teaching Forum, 36*(10), 2–9.

Crandall, J. A., Ingersoll, G., & Lopez, J. (2008). *Adult ESL teacher credentialing and certification*. Washington DC: Center for Adult English Language Acquisition.

Crandall, J., & Kaufman, D. (Eds.). (2002). *Content-based instruction in higher education settings*. Alexandria, VA: Teachers of English to Speakers of Other Languages.

Craven, M., & Sherman, K. D. (2011). *Q: Skills for success—listening and speaking: Book 3*. New York, NY: Oxford University Press.

Crawford, J. (2002). The role of materials in the language classroom: Finding the balance. In J. C. Richards & W. A. Renandya (Eds.), *Methodology in language teaching: An anthology of current practice* (pp. 80–91). New York, NY: Cambridge University Press.

Crawford, J. (2004). *Educating English language learners: Language diversity in the classroom* (5th ed.). Los Angeles, CA: Bilingual Educational Services.

Crawford, M. (2005). Adding variety to word recognition exercises. *English Teaching Forum, 43*(2), 36–41.

Crawford Camiciottoli, B. C. (2005). Adjusting a business lecture for an international audience: A case study. *English for Specific Purposes, 24*(2), 183–199.

Crawford Camiciottoli, B. C. (2007). *The language of business studies lectures: A corpus-assisted analysis*. Amsterdam, The Netherlands: John Benjamins.

Crawford Camiciottoli, B. C. (2010). A corpus-informed approach to teaching lecture comprehension skills in English for business studies. In M. C. Campoy-Cubillo, B. Bellés Fortuño, & L. Gea-Valor (Eds.), *Corpus-based approaches to ELT* (pp. 95–106). New York, NY: Continuum.

Croft, A., Coggshall, J. G., Dolan, M., & Powers, E. (with Killion, J.). (2010, April). *Job-embedded professional development: What it is, who's responsible, and how to get it done well* (Issue Brief). Washington, DC: National Comprehensive Center for Teacher Quality.

Crookes, G. (1998). On the relationship between second and foreign language teachers and research. *TESOL Journal, 7*(3), 6–11.

Crookes, G. (2003). *A practicum in TESOL: Professional development through teaching practice*. Cambridge, UK: Cambridge University Press.

Crookes, G. (2005). Resources for incorporating action research as critique into applied linguistics graduate education. *The Modern Language Journal, 89*(3), 467–475.

Crookes, G., & Chaudron, C. (2001). Guidelines for language classroom instruction. In M. Celce-Murcia (Ed.), *Teaching English as a second or foreign language* (3rd ed., pp. 29–42). Boston, MA: Heinle and Heinle.

Cross, J. (2010). Raising L2 listeners' metacognitive awareness: A sociocultural theory perspective. *Language Awareness, 19*, 281–297.

Crystal, D. (2003). *English as a global language* (2nd ed.). Cambridge, UK: Cambridge University Press.

Cullen, R. (1998). Teacher talk and the classroom context. *ELT Journal, 52*(3), 179–187.

Cullen, R. (2002). Supportive teacher talk: The importance of the F-move. *ELT Journal, 56*(2), 117–127.

Cullen, R., & Kuo, I.-C. (2007). Spoken grammar and ELT course materials: A missing link? *TESOL Quarterly, 41*(2), 361–386.

Cumming, A. (2009a). The contribution of studies of foreign language writing to research, theories, and policies. In R. Manchon, (Ed.), *Writing in foreign language contexts* (pp. 209–231). Tonawanda, NY: Multilingual Matters.

Cumming, A. (2009b). What needs to be developed to facilitate classroom-based assessment? *TESOL Quarterly, 43*(3), 515–519.

Cummins, J. (1979). Cognitive/academic language proficiency, linguistic interdependence, the optimum age question and some other matters. *Working Papers on Bilingualism, 19*, 121–129.

Cummins, J. (1980). Psychological assessment of immigrant children: Logic or intuition? *Journal of Multilingual and Multicultural Development, 1*, 97–111.

Cummins, J. (1981). The role of primary language development in promoting educational success for language minority students. In California State Department of Education, *Schooling and language minority students: A theoretical framework* (pp. 3–50). Los Angeles: California State University, Evaluation, Dissemination and Assessment Center.

Cummins, J. (1984). *Bilingualism and special education: Issues in assessment and pedagogy*. Clevedon, UK: Multilingual Matters.

Cummins, J. (2000). *Language, power, and pedagogy: Bilingual children in the crossfire*. Clevedon, UK: Multilingual Matters.

Cummins, J. (2003). Foreword. In N. Hornberger (Ed.), *Continua of biliteracy: An ecological framework for educational policy, research, and practice in multilingual settings* (pp. vii–xi). Clevedon, UK: Multilingual Matters.

Cummins, J. (2006). Identity texts: The imaginative construction of self through multiliteracies pedagogy. In O. García, T. Skutnabb-Kangas, & M. E. Torres-Guzmán (Eds.), *Imagining multilingual schools: Language in education and glocalization* (pp. 51–68). Clevedon, UK: Multilingual Matters.

Curran, C. A. (1976). *Counseling-learning in second-language learning*. East Dubuque, IL: Counseling Learning Publications.

Currie, P. (1998). Staying out of trouble: Apparent plagiarism and academic survival. *Journal of Second Language Writing, 7*(1), 1–18.

Curtain, H., & Dahlberg, C. A. (2010). *Languages and children—making the match: New languages for young learners, grades K–8* (4th ed.). Boston, MA: Pearson.

Curtis, A., & Bailey, K. M. (2009). Diary studies. *On CUE Journal, 3*(1), 67–85.

Cutting, J. (Ed.). (2007). *Vague language explored.* Basingstoke, UK: Palgrave.

Dalton, C., & Seidlhofer, B. (1994). *Pronunciation.* Oxford, UK: Oxford University Press.

Dalton-Puffer, C. (2011). Content-and-language integrated learning: From practice to principles? *Annual Review of Applied Linguistics, 31,* 182–204. doi:10.1017/S0267190511000092

Darley, J. M., & Latané, B. (1973). Bystander "apathy." In J. Helmer & N. A. Eddington (Eds.), *Urbanman: The psychology of urban survival* (pp. 62–91). New York, NY: The Free Press.

Darling-Hammond, L., Wei, R. C., Andree, A., Richardson, N., & Orphanos, S. (2009). *Professional learning in the learning profession: A status report on teacher development in the United States and abroad.* Dallas, TX: National Staff Development Council.

Dauer, R. (2005). The lingua franca core: A new model for pronunciation instruction? *TESOL Quarterly, 39*(3), 543–550.

Davies, A. (2003). *The native speaker: Myth and reality.* Clevedon, UK: Multilingual Matters.

Davies, D. (2005). *Varieties of modern English: An introduction.* Harlow, UK: Pearson Longman.

Davis, K. (2009). Agentive youth research: Towards individual, collective, and policy transformations. In T. Wiley, J. S. Lee, & R. Rumberger (Eds.), *The education of language minority immigrants in the United States* (pp. 202–239). Bristol, UK: Multilingual Matters.

Davis, M., Kiely, R., & Askham, J. (2009). InSITEs into practitioner research: Findings from a research-based ESOL teacher professional development programme. *Studies in the Education of Adults, 41*(2), 118–137.

Davison, C., & Leung, C. (2009). Current issues in English language teacher-based assessment. *TESOL Quarterly, 43*(3), 393–415.

Davison, C., & Williams, A. (2001). Integrating language and content: Unresolved issues. In B. Mohan, C. Leung, & C. Davison (Eds.), *English as second language in the mainstream: Teaching, learning and identity* (pp. 51–70). Harlow, UK: Longman.

Day, R., & Bamford, J. (1998). *Extensive reading in the second language.* New York, NY: Cambridge University Press.

Day, R., & Bamford, J. (2002). Top ten principles for teaching extensive reading. *Reading in a Foreign Language, 14,* 136–141.

Deacon, B. (2003). Priceless peer-mentor observation. In J. Egbert (Ed.), *Becoming contributing professionals* (pp. 81–88). Alexandria, VA: Teachers of English to Speakers of Other Languages.

DeCapua, A., Smathers, W., & Tang, F. (2009). *Meeting the needs of students with limited or interrupted schooling.* Ann Arbor, MI: University of Michigan Press.

Dehn, M. J. (2006). *Essentials of processing assessment.* Hoboken, NJ: John Wiley & Sons.

DeKeyser, R. (1998). Beyond focus on form: Cognitive perspectives on learning and practicing second language grammar. In C. Doughty & J. Williams (Eds.), *Focus on form in classroom second language acquisition* (pp. 42–63). New York, NY: Cambridge University Press.

DeKeyser, R. (Ed.). (2007). *Practice in a second language.* New York, NY: Cambridge University Press.

DeKeyser, R. M. (2009). Cognitive-psychological processes in second language learning. In M. H. Long & C. J. Doughty (Eds.), *The handbook of language teaching* (pp. 119–138). Malden, MA: Wiley-Blackwell.

Demetrion, G. (2005). *Conflicting paradigms in adult literacy education: In quest of a U.S. democratic politics of literacy.* Mahwah, NJ: Lawrence Erlbaum Associates.

de Oliveira, L. C. (2011). Strategies for nonnative-English-speaking teachers' continued development as professionals. *TESOL Journal, 2*(2), 229–238.

Derwing, T. M., & Munro, M. J. (2001). What speaking rates do nonnative listeners prefer? *Applied Linguistics, 22*(3), 324–337.

Derwing, T. M., & Munro, M. J. (2005). Second language accent and pronunciation teaching: A research-based approach. *TESOL Quarterly, 39*(3), 379–397.

Derwing, T. M., Munro, M. J., & Wiebe, G .E. (1998). Evidence in favor of a broad framework for pronunciation instruction. *Language Learning, 48*(3), 393–410.

Desimone, L. M. (2009). Improving impact studies of teachers' professional development: Toward better conceptualizations and measures. *Educational Researcher, 38*(3), 181–199.

Desimone, L. M. (2011). A primer on effective professional development. *Kappan Magazine, 92*(6), 68–71.

Devitt, A. (2004). *Writing genres.* New York, NY: Pearson Education.

Dewey, J. (1933). *How we think: A restatement of the relation of reflective thinking to the educative process.* Boston, MA: Heath.

Dewey, J. (1938). *Experience and education.* New York, NY: Collier Macmillan.

Dewitz, P., Jones, J., & Leahy, S. (2009). Comprehension strategy instruction in core reading programs. *Reading Research Quarterly, 44,* 102–126.

Dietrich, M. S. (2005). Integrating content into the language classroom. In R. M. Jourdenais & S. E. Springer (Eds.), *Content, tasks and projects in the language classroom: 2004 conference proceedings* (pp. 7–60). Monterey, CA: Monterey Institute of International Studies.

Dixon, C., & Nessel, D. (1983). *Language experience approach to reading and writing: Language experience reading for second language learners.* Hayward, CA: Alemany Press.

Dobbs, J. (1995). Assessing our own patterns of discourse. *TESOL Journal, 4*(3), 24–26.

Dolson, D., & Burnham-Massey, L. (2011). *Redesigning English-medium classrooms: Using research to enhance English learner achievement.* Covina, CA: California Association for Bilingual Education.

Donato, R. (1994). Collective scaffolding in second language learning. In J. Lantolf & G. Appel (Eds.), *Vygotskian approaches to second language research* (pp. 33–56). Norwood, NJ: Ablex.

Doolan, S., & Miller, R. (2012). Generation 1.5 written error patterns: A comparative study. *Journal of Second Language Writing, 21*(1), 1–22.

Dörnyei, Z. (2001). *Motivational strategies in the language classroom.* Cambridge, UK: Cambridge University Press.

Dörnyei, Z. (2005). *The psychology of the language learner: Individual differences in second language acquisition.* Mahwah, NJ: Lawrence Erlbaum Associates.

Dörnyei, Z. (2009a). The L2 motivational self system. In Z. Dörnyei & E. Ushioda (Eds.), *Motivation, language identity and the L2 self* (pp. 9–42). Bristol, UK: Multilingual Matters.

Dörnyei, Z. (2009b). *The psychology of second language acquisition.* Oxford, UK: Oxford University Press.

Dörnyei, Z., & Csizér, K. (1998). Ten commandments for motivating language learners: Results of an empirical study. *Language Teaching Research, 2*(3), 203–229.

Dörnyei, Z., & Murphey, T. (2003). *Group dynamics in the language classroom.* Cambridge, UK: Cambridge University Press.

Dörnyei, Z., & Ottó, I. (1998). Motivation in action: A process model of L2 motivation. *Working Papers in Applied Linguistics* (Thames Valley University, London), *4,* 43–69.

Dörnyei, Z., & Ushioda, E. (Eds.). (2009). *Motivation, language identity and the L2 self.* Bristol, UK: Multilingual Matters.

Dörnyei, Z., & Ushioda, E. (2011). *Teaching and researching motivation* (2nd ed.). Harlow, UK: Longman.

Doughty, C., & Williams, J. (Eds.). (1998a). *Focus on form in classroom second language acquisition.* Cambridge, UK: Cambridge University Press.

Doughty, C., & Williams, J. (1998b). Pedagogical choice in focus on form. In C. Doughty & J. Williams (Eds.), *Focus on form in classroom second language acquisition* (pp. 197–261). New York, NY: Cambridge University Press.

Dove, M., & Honigsfeld, A. (2010). ESL coteaching and collaboration: Opportunities to develop teacher leadership and enhance student learning. *TESOL Journal, 1*(1), 3–23.

Drago-Severson, E. (2004a). *Becoming adult learners: Principles and practices for effective development.* New York, NY: Teachers College Press.

Drago-Severson, E. (2004b). *Helping teachers learn: Principal leadership for adult growth and development.* Thousand Oaks, CA: Corwin Press.

Drew, P., & Heritage, J. (Eds.). (1992). *Talk at work: Interaction in institutional settings.* Cambridge, UK: Cambridge University Press.

Dubois, S., & Horvath, B. (2003). Verbal morphology in Cajun vernacular English. *Journal of English Linguistics, 31,* 34–59.

Dudeney, G. (2007). *The Internet and the language classroom: A practical guide for teachers* (2nd ed.). Cambridge, UK: Cambridge University Press.

Dudeney, G., & Hockly, N. (2007). *How to teach English with technology.* Harlow, UK: Pearson Education.

Dudley-Evans, T., & St John, M. J. (1998). *Developments in ESP: A multi-disciplinary approach.* Cambridge, UK: Cambridge University Press.

Duff, A., & Maley, A. (2007). *Literature* (2nd ed.). New York, NY: Oxford University Press.

Duff, P. A. (1995). An ethnography of communication in immersion classrooms in Hungary. *TESOL Quarterly, 29*(3), 505–537.

Duff, P. A. (2008). *APEC second/foreign language standards and their assessment: Trends, opportunities, and implications* (APEC #208-HR-01.1). Singapore: APEC EdNET Human Resources Development Working Group, APEC Secretariat. Retrieved from http://www.apecknowledgebank.org/file.aspx?id=1943

Duff, P. A. (2012). Identity, agency, and SLA. In A. Mackey & S. Gass (Eds.), *The Routledge handbook of second language acquisition* (pp. 410–426). London, UK: Routledge.

Duff, P., & Zappa-Hollman, S. (2013). Critical discourse analysis of popular culture. In C. Chapelle (Ed.), *The encyclopedia of applied linguistics* (pp. 1471–1475). Malden, MA: Wiley-Blackwell.

Dunkel, P. (1991). Listening in the native and second/foreign language: Toward an integration of research and practice. *TESOL Quarterly, 25*(3), 431–457.

Durán, R. P. (2008). Assessing English learners' achievement. *Review of Research in Education, 32,* 292–327.

Dutro, S., & Kinsella, K. (2010). English language development: Issues and implementation in grades six through twelve. In California Department of Education, *Improving education for English learners: Research-based approaches* (pp. 151–207). Sacramento, CA: California Department of Education.

Dutro, S., & Moran, C. (2003). Rethinking English language instruction: An architectural approach. In G. Garcia (Ed.), *English learners: Reaching the highest levels of English literacy* (pp. 227–258). Newark, DE: International Reading Association.

Echevarria, J., & Short, D. (2010). Programs and practices for effective sheltered content instruction. In California Department of Education, *Improving education for English learners: Research-based approaches* (pp. 251–321). Sacramento, CA: California Department of Education.

Echevarria, J., Vogt, M. E., & Short, D. (2012). *Making content comprehensible to English language learners: The SIOP model* (4th ed.). Boston, MA: Pearson.

Eckersley, C. E. (1955). *Essential English for foreign students* (Vols. 1–4). London, UK: Longman, Green.

Eckerth, J. (2008a). Investigating consciousness-raising tasks: Pedagogically targeted and non-targeted learning gains. *International Journal of Applied Linguistics, 18*(2), 119–145.

Eckerth, J. (2008b). Task-based language learning and teaching—Old wine in new bottles? In J. Eckerth & S. Siekmann (Eds.), *Task-based language learning and teaching: Theoretical, methodological, and pedagogical perspectives* (pp. 13–46). Frankfurt am Main, Germany: Peter Lang.

Edelhoff, C. (1981). Theme-oriented English teaching: Text-varieties, media skills and project work. In C. N. Candlin (Ed.), *The communicative teaching of English: Principles and an exercise typology* (pp. 49–62). Essex, UK: Longman.

Edge, J. (1989). *Mistakes and correction.* London, UK: Longman.

Edge, J. (Ed.). (2001). *Action research: Case studies in TESOL practice.* Alexandria, VA: Teachers of English to Speakers of Other Languages.

Edge, J., & Garton, S. (2009). *From experience to knowledge in ELT.* Oxford, UK: Oxford University Press.

Ediger, A. M. (2006). Developing strategic L2 readers . . . by reading for authentic purposes. In E. Uso-Juan & A. Martínez-Flor (Eds.), *Current trends in the development and teaching of the four language skills* (pp. 303–328). New York, NY: Mouton de Gruyter.

Education World Tech Team. (2008). Assessing classroom technology integration. *Education World.* Retrieved from http://www.educationworld.com/a_tech/tech/tech243.shtml

Educational Testing Service. (2011). *Standardized testing and reporting system: California Standards Tests (CSTs).* Princeton, NJ: Author. Retrieved from http://www.startest.org/cst.html

Educational Testing Service. (2012a). *About the e-rater® scoring engine.* Princeton, NJ: Author. Retrieved from http://www.ets.org/erater/about

Educational Testing Service. (2012b). *TOEFL.* Princeton, NJ: Author. Retrieved from http://www.ets.org/toefl/

Educational Testing Service. (2012c). *TOEFL: About the TOEFL iBT test.* Princeton, NJ: Author. Retrieved from http://www.ets.org/toefl/ibt/about

Educational Testing Service. (2012d). *TOEIC.* Princeton, NJ: Author. Retrieved from http://www.ets.org/toeic

Edwards, H. P., Wesche, M. B., Krashen, S., & Clément, R. (1984). Second language acquisition through subject matter learning: A study of sheltered psychology classes at the University of Ottawa. *Canadian Modern Language Review, 41*(2), 268–282.

EF Education. (1995). *Escape from planet Arizona: An EF multimedia language game* [Computer software]. Stockholm, Sweden: Author.

Egbert, J., & Hanson-Smith, E. (1999). *CALL environments: Research, practice, and critical issues.* Alexandria, VA: Teachers of English to Speakers of Other Languages.

Ehrman, M. (1996). *Understanding second language difficulties.* Thousand Oaks, CA: Sage.

Ehrman, M., & Leaver, B. (2003). Cognitive styles in the service of language learning. *System, 31,* 391–415.

Eid, C., & Johns, A. (2011). *Teachers' guide to English language courses (2010–2015).* Beirut, Lebanon: Antonine University Press.

Eilam, B., & Ben-Peretz, M. (2010). Revisiting curriculum inquiry: The role of visual representations. *Journal of Curriculum Studies, 42*(6), 751–774.

Eisner, E. (1985). *The educational imagination* (2nd ed.). New York, NY: Macmillan.

Eisterhold, J. (2003). Making new friends: Becoming involved in a TESOL organization. In J. Egbert (Ed.), *Becoming contributing professionals* (pp. 1–7). Alexandria, VA: Teachers of English to Speakers of Other Languages.

Ellerington, K. (2000). English language learning in Cambodia: The quest for an international language. *English Australia Journal, 18*(1), 79–86.

Elley, W. B. (1991). Acquiring literacy in a second language: The effect of book-based programs. *Language Learning, 41*(3), 375–411.

Ellis, G., & Sinclair, B. (1989). *Learning to learn English.* Cambridge, UK: Cambridge University Press.

Ellis, N. (1996). Sequencing in SLA: Phonological memory, chunking, and points of order. *Studies in Second Language Acquisition, 18*(1), 91–126.

Ellis, N. (1998). Emergentism, connectionism, and language learning. *Language Learning, 48*(4), 631–644.

Ellis, N., & Larsen-Freeman, D. (Eds.). (2009). *Language as a complex adaptive system.* Malden, MA: Wiley-Blackwell.

Ellis, R. (1984). *Classroom second language development.* Oxford, UK: Pergamon.

Ellis, R. (1985). *Understanding second language acquisition.* Oxford, UK: Oxford University Press.

Ellis, R. (1989a). Are classroom and naturalistic acquisition the same? A study of the classroom acquisition of German word order rules. *Studies in Second Language Acquisition, 11*(3), 305–328.

Ellis, R. (1989b). Classroom learning styles and their effect on second language acquisition: A study of two learners. *System, 17,* 249–262.

Ellis, R. (1991). *Second language acquisition and language pedagogy.* Clevedon, UK: Multilingual Matters.

Ellis, R. (1993). The structural syllabus and second language acquisition. *TESOL Quarterly, 27*(1), 91–113.

Ellis, R. (1994a). *The study of second language acquisition.* Oxford, UK: Oxford University Press.

Ellis, R. (1994b). A theory of instructed second language acquisition. In N. Ellis (Ed.), *Implicit and explicit learning of languages* (pp. 79–114). San Diego, CA: Academic Press.

Ellis, R. (1998). Teaching and research: Options in grammar teaching. *TESOL Quarterly, 32*(1), 39–60.

Ellis, R. (1999). Making the classroom acquisition-rich. In R. Ellis (Ed.), *Learning a second language through interaction* (pp. 211–229). Amsterdam, The Netherlands: John Benjamins.

Ellis, R. (2002). The place of grammar instruction in the second/foreign language curriculum. In E. Hinkel & S. Fotos (Eds.), *New perspectives on grammar teaching in second language classrooms* (pp. 17–34). Mahwah, NJ: Lawrence Erlbaum Associates.

Ellis, R. (2003). *Task-based language learning and teaching.* Oxford, UK: Oxford University Press.

Ellis, R. (2004). The definition and measurement of explicit knowledge. *Language Learning, 54*(2), 227–275.

Ellis, R. (2005). Measuring implicit and explicit knowledge of a second language: A psychometric study. *Studies in Second Language Acquisition, 27*(2), 141–172.

Ellis, R. (2006). Current issues in the teaching of grammar: An SLA perspective. *TESOL Quarterly, 40*(1), 83–107.

Ellis, R. (2008). *The study of second language acquisition* (2nd ed.). Oxford, UK: Oxford University Press.

Ellis, R. (2009a). Corrective feedback and teacher development. *L2 Journal, 1*(1), 3–18.

Ellis, R. (2009b). Task-based language teaching: Sorting out the misunderstandings. *International Journal of Applied Linguistics, 19*(3), 221–246.

Ellis, R. (2010). Second language acquisition and language-teaching materials. In N. Harwood & J. C. Richards (Eds.), *English language teaching materials: Theory and practice* (pp. 33–57). New York, NY: Cambridge University Press.

Ellis, R., Basturkmen, H., & Loewen, S. (2001). Learner uptake in communicative ESL lessons. *Language Learning, 51*(2), 281–318.

Ellis, R., & Wells, G. (1980). Enabling factors in adult-child discourse. *First Language, 1*, 46–82.

Enever, J., Moon, J., & Raman, U. (Eds.). (2009). *Young learner English language policy and implementation: International perspectives.* Reading, UK: Garnet Education.

Erteschik-Shir, N. (1979). Discourse constraints on dative movement. In T. Givón (Ed.), *Syntax and semantics: Volume 12. Discourse and syntax* (pp. 441–467). New York, NY: Academic Press.

Escamilla, K. (2006). Monolingual assessment and emerging bilinguals: A case study in the USA. In O. García, T. Skutnabb-Kangas, & M. E. Torres-Guzmán (Eds.), *Imagining multilingual schools* (pp. 184–199). Clevedon, UK: Multilingual Matters.

Etxeberría-Sagastume, F. (2006). Attitudes towards language learning in different linguistic models of the Basque Autonomous Community. In O. García, T. Skutnabb-Kangas, & M. E. Torres-Guzmán (Eds.), *Imagining multilingual schools* (pp. 111–133). Clevedon, UK: Multilingual Matters.

Evans, H. (2006). Animals in the language classroom? Teaching English and critical thinking in a social issues class. In M. A. Snow & L. D. Kamhi-Stein (Eds.), *Developing a new course for adult learners* (pp. 167–195). Alexandria, VA: Teachers of English to Speakers of Other Languages.

Evans, N. W., Hartshorn, K. J., & Anderson, N. J. (2010). A research based approach to materials development for reading. In N. Harwood (Ed.), *Materials in ELT: Theory and practice* (pp. 131–156). Cambridge, UK: Cambridge University Press.

Excellence Gateway (2012). Adult ESOL core curriculum. Coventry, UK: Learning and Skills Improvement Service. Retrieved from http://rwp.excellencegateway.org.uk/ESOL/Adult%20ESOL%20core%20curriculum/

Eyraud, K., Giles, G., Koenig, S., & Stoller, F. L. (2000). The word wall approach: Promoting L2 vocabulary learning. *English Teaching Forum, 38*(3), 2–11.

Fairclough, N. (1992). Discourse and text: Linguistic and intertextual analysis within discourse analysis. *Discourse and Society, 3*(2), 193–217.

Fairclough, N. (2010). *Critical discourse analysis: The critical study of language* (2nd ed.). New York, NY: Pearson.

Fanselow, J. F. (1988). "Let's see": Contrasting conversations about teaching. *TESOL Quarterly, 22*(1), 113–130.

Fanselow, J. F., & Barnard, R. (2006). Take 1, take 2, take 3: A suggested three stage approach to exploratory practice. In S. Gieve & I. K. Miller (Eds.), *Understanding the language classroom* (pp. 175–199). Basingstoke, UK: Palgrave Macmillan.

Farrell, T. S. C. (Ed.). (2006). *Language teacher research in Asia*. Alexandria, VA: Teachers of English to Speakers of Other Languages.

Farrell, T. S. C. (2007). *Reflective language teaching: From research to practice*. London, UK: Continuum Press.

Feez, S. (1998). *Text-based syllabus design*. Sydney, Australia: National Centre for English Language Teaching and Research.

Feez, S. (2001). Curriculum evolution in the Australian adult migrant English program. In D. Hall & A. Hewings (Eds.), *Innovation in English language teaching* (pp. 208–228). London, UK: Routledge.

Ferguson, C. A. (1971). *Language structure and language use: Essays by Charles A. Ferguson selected by A. S. Dil*. Palo Alto, CA: Stanford University Press.

Fernandez, C. (2002). Learning from Japanese approaches to professional development: The case of lesson study. *Journal of Teacher Education, 53*(5), 393–405.

Ferne, T., & Rupp, A. (2007). A synthesis of 15 years of research on DIF in language testing: Methodological advances, challenges, and recommendations. *Language Assessment Quarterly, 4*, 113–148.

Ferris, D. (1999). The case for grammar correction in L2 writing classes: A response to Truscott. *Journal of Second Language Writing, 8*, 1–11.

Ferris, D. R. (2003). *Response to student writing: Implications for second language students*. Mahwah, NJ: Lawrence Erlbaum Associates.

Ferris, D. R. (2011). *Treatment of error in second language student writing* (2nd ed.). Ann Arbor, MI: University of Michigan Press.

Ferris, D., & Hedgcock, J. (2004). *Teaching ESL composition: Purpose, process, and practice* (2nd ed.). Mahwah, NJ: Lawrence Erlbaum Associates.

Field, J. (1998). Skills and strategies: Towards a new methodology for listening. *ELT Journal, 52*(2), 110–118.

Field, J. (2004). An insight into listeners' problems: Too much bottom-up or too much top-down? *System, 32*(3), 363–377.

Field, J. (2005). Intelligibility and the listener: The role of lexical stress. *TESOL Quarterly, 39*(3), 399–423.

Field, J. (2008). *Listening in the language classroom*. Cambridge, UK: Cambridge University Press.

Field, M. L., & Nagai, N. (2003). The "dead hand" project: Intercultural collaboration and professional development. In T. Murphey (Ed.), *Extending professional development* (pp. 11–18). Alexandria, VA: Teachers of English to Speakers of Other Languages.

Fillmore, C. J. (1979). On fluency. In C. J. Fillmore, D. Kempler, & W. S. Y. Wang (Eds.), *Individual differences in language ability and language behavior* (pp. 85–101). New York, NY: Academic Press.

Finnish National Board of Education. (2011). *Adult education*. Helsinki, Finland. Retrieved from http://www.oph.fi/english/education/adult_education

Firth, J. R. (1957). *Papers in linguistics: 1934–1951*. Oxford, UK: Oxford University Press.

Fish, H. (1989). Playing with plays: Increasing student involvement with dramatic texts. In C. Carter, R. Walker, & C. Brumfit (Eds.), *Literature and the learner: Methodological approaches* (pp. 68-74). Hong Kong, China: Modern English Publications/British Council.

Flanigan, R. L. (2011). Networking professionals. *Education Week, 31*(9), s10-s12.

Flavell, J. H. (1979). Metacognition and cognitive monitoring: A new area of cognitive developmental inquiry. *American Psychologist, 34*(10), 906–911.

Florida Department of Education, Bureau of Curriculum and Instruction. (n.d.). Florida statutes: *K–20 education code—Excerpts pertaining to instructional materials*. State of Florida: Author. Retrieved from http://www.fldoe.org/bii/instruct_mat/pdf/statutes.pdf

Flower, L. S. (1979). Reader-based prose: A cognitive basis for problems in writing. *College English, 41*, 19–37.

Flowerdew, J. (1994). Research of relevance to second language lecture comprehension: An overview. In J. Flowerdew (Ed.), *Academic listening: Research perspectives* (pp. 55–74). Cambridge, UK: Cambridge University Press.

Flowerdew, J., & Miller, L. (1992). Student perceptions, problems and strategies in second language lecture comprehension. *RELC Journal, 23*(2), 60–80.

Flowerdew, J., & Miller, L. (1995). On the notion of culture in L2 lectures. *TESOL Quarterly, 29*(2), 345–373.

Flowerdew, J., & Miller, L. (1996a). Lecturer perceptions, problems and strategies in second language lectures. *RELC Journal, 27*(1), 23–46.

Flowerdew, J., & Miller, L. (1996b). Lectures in a second language: Notes towards a cultural grammar. *English for Specific Purposes, 15*(2), 121–140.

Flowerdew, J., & Miller, L. (1997). The teaching of academic listening comprehension and the question of authenticity. *English for Specific Purposes, 16*(1), 27–46.

Flowerdew, J., & Miller, L. (2005). *Second language listening: Theory and practice*. Cambridge, UK: Cambridge University Press.

Flowerdew, J., Miller, L., & Li, D. C. S. (2000). Chinese lecturers' perceptions, problems and strategies in lecturing in English to Chinese speaking students. *RELC Journal, 31*(1), 116–138.

Flowerdew, J., & Peacock, M. (2001). Issues in EAP: A preliminary perspective. In J. Flowerdew & M. Peacock (Eds.), *Research perspectives on English for academic purposes* (pp. 8–24). Cambridge, UK: Cambridge University Press.

Flowerdew, J., & Tauroza, S. (1995). The effect of discourse markers on second language lecture comprehension. *Studies in Second Language Acquisition, 17*(4), 435–458.

Flowerdew, L. (2005). Integrating traditional critical approaches to syllabus design: The "what," "how," and the "why"? *English for Academic Purposes, 4*, 135–147.

Flynn, K., & Gulikers, G. (2001). Issues in hiring nonnative English speaking professionals to teach English as a second language. *The CATESOL Journal, 13*(1), 151–160.

Folse, K. S. (2004). *Intermediate reading practices: Building reading and vocabulary skills* (3rd ed.). Ann Arbor, MI: University of Michigan Press.

Folse, K. S. (2006). The effect of type of written exercise on L2 vocabulary retention. *TESOL Quarterly, 40*(2), 273–293.

Folse, K. (2010). Is explicit vocabulary focus the reading teacher's job? *Reading in a Foreign Language, 22*, 139–160.

Fortanet, I. (2004). The use of "we" in university lectures: Reference and function. *English for Specific Purposes, 23*(1), 45–66.

Fortanet-Gomez, I. (2004). Verbal stance in spoken academic discourse. In G. Del Lungo Camiciotti & E. Tognini Bonelli (Eds.), *Academic discourse: New insights into evaluation* (pp. 99–119). Bern, Switzerland: Peter Lang.

Fortune, T. W., Tedick, D. J., & Walker, C. L. (2008). Integrated language and content teaching: Insights from the immersion classroom. In T. W. Fortune & D. J. Tedick (Eds.), *Pathways to multilingualism: Evolving perspectives on immersion education* (pp. 71–96). Clevedon, UK: Multilingual Matters.

Foster, P. (1998). A classroom perspective on the negotiation of meaning. *Applied Linguistics, 19*(1), 1–23.

Foster, P. (2001). Rules and routines: A consideration of their role in task-based language production of native and non-native speakers. In M. Bygate, P. Skehan, & M. Swain (Eds.), *Researching pedagogic tasks: Second language learning, teaching, and testing* (pp. 75–97). Harlow, UK: Pearson Education.

Foster, P., & Skehan, P. (1996). The influence of planning and task type on second language performance. *Studies in Second Language Acquisition, 18*(3), 299–323.

Fotos, S., & Ellis, R. (1991). Communicating about grammar: A task-based approach. *TESOL Quarterly, 25*(4), 605–628.

Foucault, M. (1980). *Power/knowledge: Selected interviews and other writing, 1927–1977*. New York: NY: Pantheon.

Fowler, R. (1986). *Linguistic criticism*. Oxford, UK: Oxford University Press.

Francis, N., & Reyhner, J. (2002). *Language and literacy teaching for indigenous education: A bilingual approach*. Clevedon, UK: Multilingual Matters.

Frazier, S., & Phillabaum, S. (2011/2012). How TESOL educators teach nonnative English-speaking teachers. *The CATESOL Journal, 23*(1), 155–181.

Freeman, A. (2000). *Selection of culturally relevant text*. Tucson, AZ: University of Arizona.

Freeman, D. (1992). Collaboration: Constructing shared understandings in a second language classroom. In D. Nunan (Ed.), *Collaborative language learning and teaching* (pp. 56–80). Cambridge, UK: Cambridge University Press.

Freeman, D. (1996). Redefining the relationship between research and what teachers know. In K. M. Bailey & D. Nunan (Eds.), *Voices from the language classroom* (pp. 88–115). Cambridge, UK: Cambridge University Press.

Freeman, D. (1998). *Doing teacher research: From inquiry to understanding*. Boston, MA: Heinle and Heinle.

Freeman, R. D. (1998). *Bilingual education and social change*. Clevedon, UK: Multilingual Matters.

Freeman, R. D. (2004). *Building on community bilingualism*. Philadelphia, PA: Caslon Publishing.

Freeman, Y. S., & Freeman, D. E. (2009). *Academic language for English language learners and struggling readers: How to help students succeed across content areas*. Portsmouth, NH: Heinemann.

Freeman, Y., Freeman, D., & Mercuri, S. (2005). *Dual language essentials for teachers and administrators*. Portsmouth, NH: Heinemann.

Freire, P. (1970). *Pedagogy of the oppressed*. New York, NY: Herder and Herder.

Fries, C. C. (1945). *Teaching and learning English as a foreign language*. Ann Arbor, MI: University of Michigan Press.

Frodesen, J., & Holten, C. (2003). Grammar in the ESL writing class. In B. Kroll (Ed.), *Exploring the dynamics of second language writing* (pp. 141–161). New York, NY: Cambridge University Press.

Fulcher, G., & Davidson, F. (2009). Test architecture, test retrofit. *Language Testing, 26*(1), 123–144.

Fung, L., & Carter, R. (2007). Discourse markers and spoken English: Native and learner use in pedagogic settings. *Applied Linguistics, 28*, 410–439.

Gadsby, H., & Cronin, S. (2012). To what extent can reflective journaling help beginning teachers develop masters level writing skills? *Reflective Practice: International and Multidisciplinary Perspectives, 13*, 1–12.

Gagné, E. D., Yekovich, C. W., & Yekovich, F. R. (1993). *The cognitive psychology of school learning*. New York, NY: HarperCollins.

Gagné, R., & Medsker, K. (1996). *The conditions of learning*. Fort Worth, TX: Harcourt Brace.

Gándara, P., & Hopkins, M. (Eds.). (2010). *Forbidden language: English learners and restrictive language policies*. New York, NY: Teachers College Press.

Gándara, P., Losen, D., August, D., Uriarte, M., Gómez, M., & Hopkins, M. (2010). Forbidden language: A brief history of U.S. language policy. In P. Gándara & M. Hopkins (Eds.), *Forbidden language: English learners and restrictive language policies* (pp. 20–33). New York, NY: Teachers College Press.

Gándara, P., & Orfield, G. (2010). Moving from failure to a new vision of language policy. In P. Gándara & M. Hopkins (Eds.), *Forbidden language: English learners and restrictive language policies* (pp. 216–226). New York, NY: Teachers College Press.

García, O. (with Baetens Beardsmore, H.). (2009). *Bilingual education in the 21st century: A global perspective*. Malden, MA: Wiley-Blackwell.

García, O., & Baetens Beardsmore, H. (2009). Assessment of bilinguals. In O. García, *Bilingual education in the 21st century: A global perspective* (pp. 366–379). Malden, MA: Wiley-Blackwell.

García, O., & Bartlett, L. (2007). A speech-community model of bilingual education: Educating Latino newcomers in the U.S.A. *The International Journal of Bilingual Education and Bilingualism, 10*, 1–25.

García, O., Skutnabb-Kangas, T., & Torres-Guzmán. M. (Eds.). (2006). *Imagining multilingual schools: Language in education and glocalization*. Clevedon, UK: Multilingual Matters.

Gardner, D. (2004). Vocabulary input through extensive reading: A comparison of words found in children's narrative and expository reading materials. *Applied Linguistics, 25*(1), 1–37.

Gardner, D., & Miller, L. (1999). *Establishing self-access: From theory to practice*. Cambridge, UK: Cambridge University Press.

Gardner, H. (1983). *Frames of mind: The theory of multiple intelligences*. New York, NY: Basic Books.

Gardner, H. (1993) *Multiple intelligences: The theory in practice*. New York, NY: Basic Books.

Gardner, H. (1999). Are there additional intelligences? The case for naturalist, spiritual, and existential intelligences. In J. Kane (Ed.), *Education, information and transformation* (pp. 111–131). Englewood Cliffs, NJ: Prentice Hall.

Gardner, H. (2006). *Multiple intelligences: New horizons*. New York, NY: Basic Books.

Gardner, R. C. (1985). *Social psychology and second language learning: The role of attitudes and motivation*. London, UK: Edward Arnold.

Garton, S., Copland, F., & Burns, A. (2011). *Investigating global practices in teaching English to young learners*. Birmingham, UK: British Council.

Gary, J., & Gary, N. (1981). Caution: Talking may be dangerous to your linguistic health: The case for a much greater emphasis on listening comprehension in FL instruction. *International Review of Applied Linguistics in Language Teaching, 19*(1), 1–14.

Gass, S. (1982). From theory to practice. In M. Hines & W. Rutherford (Eds.), *On TESOL '81,* (pp. 129–139). Washington, DC: Teachers of English to Speakers of Other Languages.

Gass, S. L., & Mackey, A. (2000). *Stimulated recall methodology in second language research.* Mahwah, NJ: Lawrence Erlbaum Associates.

Gass, S. L., & Madden, C. (1985). *Input in second language acquisition.* Rowley, MA: Newbury House.

Gatbonton, E., & Segalowitz, N. (1988). Creative automatization: Principles for promoting fluency within a communicative framework. *TESOL Quarterly, 22*(3), 473–492.

Gatbonton, E., Trofimovich, P., & Magid, M. (2005). Learners' ethnic group affiliation and pronunciation accuracy: A sociolinguistic investigation. *TESOL Quarterly, 39*(3), 489–511.

Gattegno, C. (1976). *The common sense of teaching foreign languages.* New York, NY: Educational Solutions.

Gavioli, L. (2005). *Exploring corpora for ESP learning.* Amsterdam, The Netherlands: John Benjamins.

Gebhard, J., & Oprandy, R. (1999). *Language teaching awareness: A guide to exploring beliefs and practices.* New York, NY: Cambridge University Press.

Geddes, M. (1981). Listening. In K. Johnson & K. Morrow (Eds.), *Communication in the classroom: Applications and methods for a communicative approach* (pp. 78–86). London, UK: Longman.

Gee, J. (1996). *Social linguistics and literacies: Ideology in discourses* (2nd ed.). London: Taylor & Francis.

Geertz, C. (1973). *The interpretation of cultures: Selected essays.* New York, NY: Basic Books.

Genesee, F. (1987). *Learning through two languages: Studies of immersion and bilingual education.* Rowley, MA: Newbury House.

Genesee, F. (Ed.). (1999). *Program alternatives for linguistically diverse students.* (Educational Practice Report No. 1). Washington, DC: Center for Research on Education, Diversity, and Excellence /Center for Applied Linguistics. Retrieved from http://www.cal .org/crede/pdfs/epr1.pdf

Genesee, F. (2004). What do we know about bilingual education for majority-language students? In T. K. Bhatia & W. Ritchie (Eds.), *The handbook of bilingualism* (pp. 547–576). Oxford, UK: Blackwell.

Genesee, F., Lindholm-Leary, K., Saunders, W., & Christian, D. (Eds.). (2006). *Educating English language learners.* New York, NY: Cambridge University Press.

Genesee, F., Paradis, J., & Crago, M. B. (2011). *Dual language development and disorders: A handbook on bilingualism and second language learning.* Baltimore MD: Brooks Publishing.

Genesee, F., & Upshur, J. A. (1996). *Classroom-based evaluation in second language education.* Cambridge, UK: Cambridge University Press.

Geranpayeh, A., & Kunnan, A. J. (2007). Differential item functioning in terms of age in the Certificate of Advanced English Examination. *Language Assessment Quarterly, 4*(2), 190–222.

Gershon, S. (2008). *Present yourself 2: Viewpoints.* New York, NY: Cambridge University Press.

Gersten, R., Baker, S., Shanahan, T., Linan-Thompson, S., Collins, P., & Scarcella, R. (2007). Effective literacy and English language instruction for English learners in the elementary grades. Washington, DC: National Center for Education Evaluation. Retrieved from: http://ies.ed.gov/ncee/wwc/pdf/practice-guides/20074011.pdf

Gianelli, M. C. (1997). Thematic units: Creating an environment for learning. In M. A. Snow & D. M. Brinton (Eds.), *The content-based classroom: Perspectives on integrating language and content* (pp. 142–148). New York, NY: Longman.

Gibbons, P. (1991). *Learning to learn in a second language.* Portsmouth, NH: Heinemann.

Gibbons, P. (2002). *Scaffolding language, scaffolding learning.* Portsmouth, NH: Heinemann.

Gibbons, P. (2006a). *Bridging discourses in the ESL classroom: Students, teachers and researchers.* London, UK: Continuum.

Gibbons, P. (2006b). Steps for planning an integrated program for ESL learners in mainstream classes. In P. McKay (Ed.), *Planning and teaching creatively within a required curriculum for school age learners* (pp. 215–233). Alexandria, VA: Teachers of English to Speakers of Other Languages.

Gibbons, P. (2009). *English learners, academic literacy, and thinking: Learning in the challenge zone.* Portsmouth, NH: Heinemann.

Gieve, S., & Miller, I. K. (Eds.). (2006). *Understanding the language classroom.* Basingstoke, UK: Palgrave Macmillan.

Gilbert, J. (1994). Intonation: A navigation guide for the listener. In J. Morley (Ed.), *Pronunciation pedagogy and theory* (pp. 36–48). Alexandria, VA: Teachers of English to Speakers of Other Languages.

Gilbert, J. (2008). *Teaching English using the prosody pyramid.* Cambridge, UK: Cambridge University Press. Retrieved from http://www.cambridge. org/other_files/downloads/esl/booklets/Gilbert-Teaching-Pronunciation.pdf

Gilbert, J. (2012). *Clear speech—pronunciation and listening comprehension in North American English: Student's book* (4th ed.). New York, NY: Cambridge University Press.

Gillespie, M. (1994). *Native language literacy for adults: Patterns, issues, and promises.* Washington, DC: National Clearinghouse for ESL Literacy Education/National Center for Adult Literacy.

Gillies, R. M. (2007). *Cooperative learning: Integrating theory and practice.* Thousand Oaks, CA: Sage.

Gilman, R. A., & Moody, L. M. (1984) What practitioners say about listening: Research implications for the classroom. *Foreign Language Annals, 17*(4), 331–333.

Gilmore, A. (2004). A comparison of textbook and authentic interactions. *ELT Journal, 58*(4), 363–374.

Gleick, J. (1987). *Chaos: Making a new science.* New York, NY: Penguin Books.

Glendale Community College (2011). *Student learning outcomes for non-credit ESL.* Retrieved from http://www.glendale.edu/index .aspx?page=4689

Godwin-Jones, R. (2009). Speech tools and technologies. *Language Learning & Technology, 13*(3), 4–11. Retrieved from http://llt.msu .edu/vol13num3/emerging.pdf

Goh, C. (1997). Metacognitive awareness and second language listeners. *ELT Journal, 51*(4), 361–369.

Goh, C. (2000). A cognitive perspective on language learners' listening comprehension problems. *System, 28*(1), 55–75.

Goh, C. C. M. (2007). Teaching speaking in the language classroom. In W. A. Renandya & J. C. Richards (Eds.), *RELC portfolio series* (pp. 1–48). Singapore: SEAMO Regional Language Centre.

Goh, C. (2010). Listening as process: Learning activities for self-appraisal and self-regulation. In N. Harwood (Ed.), *Materials in ELT: Theory and practice* (pp. 179–206). Cambridge, UK: Cambridge University Press.

Goh, C., & Taib, Y. (2006). Metacognitive instruction in listening for young learners. *ELT Journal, 60*(3), 222–232.

Goldenberg, C. (2008). Teaching English language learners: What the research does—and does not—say. *American Educator, 32*(2), 8–44.

Golombek, P., & Jordan, S. R. (2005). Becoming "black lambs" not "parrots": A poststructuralist orientation to intelligibility and identity. *TESOL Quarterly, 39*(3), 513–533.

Gomez, I. (2006). Interaction in academic spoken English: The use of "I" and "you" in the MICASE. *Educational Linguistics, 7,* 35–51.

Gonzalves, L. (2011/2012). Professional development through graduate study: Using graduate research to inform professional practices. *The CATESOL Journal, 23*(1), 92–98.

Goodwin, J. (2005). The power of context in teaching pronunciation. In J. Frodesen & C. Holten (Eds.), *The power of context in language teaching and learning* (pp. 225–236). Boston, MA: Heinle.

Gordon, T. (2003). Learning from our students: Using students to develop curricula. In J. Egbert (Ed.), *Becoming contributing professionals* (pp. 59–66). Alexandria, VA: Teachers of English to Speakers of Other Languages.

Gottlieb, M. (2000). Standards-based, large-scale assessment of ESOL students. In M. A. Snow (Ed.), *Implementing the ESL standards for pre-K–12 students through teacher education* (pp. 167–186). Alexandria, VA: Teachers of English to Speakers of Other Languages.

Gottlieb, M. (2006). *Assessing English language learners: Bridges from language proficiency to academic achievement.* Thousand Oaks, CA: Corwin Press.

Gottlieb, M., Katz, A., & Ernst-Slavit, G. (2009). *Paper to practice: Using the TESOL English language proficiency standards in PreK–12 classrooms*. Alexandria, VA: Teachers of English to Speakers of Other Languages.

Govardhan, A. K. (2006). English teaching and ethnic origin. In A. Curtis & M. Romney (Eds.), *Color, race, and English language teaching: Shades of meaning* (pp. 137–147). Mahwah, NJ: Lawrence Erlbaum Associates.

Gower, R. (1986). Can stylistic analysis help the EFL learner to read literature? *ELT Journal, 40*(2), 125–130.

Grabe, W. (2002). Narrative and expository macro-genres. In A. Johns (Ed.), *Genre in the classroom* (pp. 236–258). Mahwah, NJ: Lawrence Erlbaum Associates.

Grabe, W. (2009). *Reading in a second language: Moving from theory to practice*. New York, NY: Cambridge University Press.

Grabe, W., & Stoller, F. L. (1997). Content-based instruction: Research foundations. In M. A. Snow & D. M. Brinton (Eds.), *The content-based classroom: Perspectives on integrating language and content* (pp. 5–21). New York, NY: Longman.

Grabe, W., & Stoller, F. L. (2011). *Teaching and researching reading* (2nd ed.). New York, NY: Pearson Longman.

Graddol, D. (1997). *The future of English?* London, UK: British Council.

Graham, C. (1979). *Jazz chants for children: Rhythms of American English through chants, songs and poems*. New York, NY: Oxford University Press.

Graham, C. (1986). *Small talk*. New York, NY: Oxford University Press.

Graham, C. (1988). *Jazz chant fairy tales*. New York, NY: Oxford University Press.

Graham, C. (1994). *Mother Goose jazz chants*. New York, NY: Oxford University Press.

Graham, S. (2006). Listening comprehension: The learners' perspective. *System, 34*(2), 165–182.

Grant, L. (2009). *Well said: Pronunciation for clear communication* (3rd ed.). Boston, MA: Heinle.

Grant, N. (1987). *Making the most of your textbook*. London, UK: Longman.

Graves, K. (Ed.) (1996). *Teachers as course developers*. Cambridge, UK: Cambridge University Press.

Graves, K. (2000). *Designing language courses: A guide for teachers*. Boston, MA: Heinle and Heinle.

Graves, K. (2006). Preface to P. McKay (Ed.), *Planning and teaching creatively within a required curriculum for school-age learners* (pp. v–vii). Alexandria, VA: Teachers of English to Speakers of Other Languages.

Graves, K. (2008). The language curriculum: A social contextual perspective. *Language Teaching, 41*(2), 149–183.

Graves, M. F. (2006). *The vocabulary book*. New York, NY: Teachers College Press.

Greaves, C., & Warren, M. (2010). What can a corpus tell us about multi-word units? In A. O'Keeffe & M. McCarthy (Eds.), *The Routledge handbook of corpus linguistics* (pp. 212–226). London, UK: Routledge.

Green, J. (2003). *The word wall: Teaching vocabulary through immersion* (2nd ed.). Ontario, Canada: Pippin.

Greene, D. (2000). A design model for beginner-level computer-mediated EFL writing. *Computer Assisted Language Learning, 13*(3), 239–252.

Grgurović, M., & Chapelle, C. (2007). *Effectiveness of CALL: A meta-analysis and research synthesis*. Paper presented at CALICO 2007, San Marcos, TX.

Grice, P. H. (1975). Logic and conversation. In P. Cole & J. L. Morgan (Eds.), *Syntax and semantics: Speech acts* (Vol. 3, pp. 41–58). New York, NY: Academic Press.

Grigoryan, A., & King, J. M. (2008). Adbusting: Critical media literacy in a multi-skills academic writing lesson. *English Teaching Forum, 46*(4), 2–9.

Grosjean, F. (2010). *Bilingual: Life and reality*. Cambridge, MA: Harvard University Press.

Grundy, P. (2008). *Doing pragmatics* (3rd ed.). London, UK: Hodder Education.

Gruwell, E. (2007a). *The Freedom Writers diary: Teacher's guide*. New York, NY: Broadway Books.

Gruwell, E. (2007b). *Teach with your heart: Lessons I learned from the Freedom Writers*. New York, NY: Broadway Books.

Gueye, M. (1990). One step beyond ESP: English for development purposes (EDP). *English Teaching Forum, 28*, 31–34.

Guilloteaux, M. J., & Dörnyei, Z. (2008). Motivating language learners: A classroom-oriented investigation of the effects of motivational strategies on student motivation. *TESOL Quarterly, 42*(1), 55–77.

Guskey, T. R., & Yoon, K. S. (2009). What works in professional development? *Phi Delta Kappan, 90*(7), 495–500.

Guthrie, J., McRae, A., & Klauda, S. (2007). Contributions of concept-oriented reading instruction to knowledge about interventions for motivation in reading. *Educational Psychologist, 42*, 237–250.

Haas, M. (2000). Thematic, communicative language teaching in the K–8 classroom. *ERIC Digest*, EDO-FL-00-04. Retrieved from http://www.cal.org/resources/digest/0004thematic.html

Hadfield, J., & Dörnyei, Z. (2013). *Motivating learning*. Harlow, UK: Pearson.

Hafner, C., & Miller, L. (2011) Fostering learner autonomy in English for science: A collaborative digital video project in a technological learning environment. *Language Learning and Technology, 15*(3), 201–223.

Hahn, L. (2004). Primary stress and intelligibility: Research to motivate the teaching of suprasegmentals. *TESOL Quarterly, 38*(2), 201–223.

Hakuta, K. (2011). Educating language minority students and affirming their equal rights. *Educational Researcher, 4*(4), 163–174.

Hall, J. K. (2001). *Methods for teaching foreign languages: Creating a community of learners in the classroom*. Columbus, OH: Prentice-Hall.

Hall, J. K. (2012). *Teaching and researching language and culture* (2nd ed.). Harlow, UK: Pearson Education.

Hall, J. K., & Walsh, M. (2002). Teacher-student interaction and language learning. *Annual Review of Applied Linguistics, 22*, 186–203.

Halliday, M. A. K. (1973). *Explorations in the functions of language*. London, UK: Edward Arnold.

Halliday, M. A. K. (1978). *Language as a social semiotic: The social interpretation of language and meaning*. London, UK: Edward Arnold.

Halliday, M. A. K., & Hasan, R. (1976). *Cohesion in English*. London. UK: Longman.

Halliday, M. A. K., & Hasan, R. (1989). *Language, context, and text: Aspects of language in a socio-semiotic perspective*. New York, NY: Oxford University Press.

Halliday, M. A. K., & Matthiessen, C. (2004). *An introduction to functional grammar*. London, UK: Arnold.

Han, Z.-H. (2004). *Fossilization in adult second language acquisition*. Clevedon, UK: Multilingual Matters.

Han, Z.-H., & Anderson, N. (Eds.). (2009). *Second language reading: Research and instruction*. Ann Arbor, MI: University of Michigan Press.

Hancock, M. (1995). *Pronunciation games*. Cambridge, UK: Cambridge University Press.

Hanson, M., & Moore, D. (2003). *Study summary: Rachel Carson Elementary School: An exemplary urban school that teaches children to read*. Chicago, IL: Designs for Change. Retrieved from http://www.designsforchange.org/pdfs/Carsonsept03.pdf

Hanson-Smith, E. (Ed.). (2000). *Technology-enhanced learning environments*. Alexandria, VA: Teachers of English to Speakers of Other Languages.

Hanson-Smith, E. (2003). A brief history of CALL theory. *The CATESOL Journal, 15*(1), 21–30.

Harada, T. (1997/98). The mishearing of content words by ESL learners. *The CATESOL Journal, 10*, 51–70.

Hardison, D. (2004). Generalization of computer-assisted prosody training: Quantitative and qualitative findings. *Language Learning and Technology, 8*(1), 34–52. Retrieved from http://llt.msu.edu/vol8num1/hardison/default.html

Hardison, D., & Sonchaeng, C. (2005). Theatre voice training and technology in teaching oral skills: Integrating the components of a speech event. *System, 33*(4), 593–608.

Harklau, L., Losey, K. M., & Siegal, M. (Eds.). (1999). *Generation 1.5 meets college composition: Issues in the teaching of writing to U.S.-educated learners of ESL*. Mahwah, NJ: Lawrence Erlbaum Associates.

Harley, B. (1986). *Age in second language acquisition*. Clevedon, UK: Multilingual Matters.

Harley, B. (1989). Functional grammar in French immersion: A classroom experiment. *Applied Linguistics, 10*(3), 331–359.

Harley, B., & Swain, M. (1984). The interlanguage of immersion students and its implications for second language teaching. In A. Davies, C. Criper, & A. P. R. Howatt (Eds.), *Interlanguage* (pp. 291–311). Edinburgh, UK: Edinburgh University Press.

Harley, B., & Wang, W. (1997). The critical period hypothesis: Where are we now? In A. M. B. de Groot & J. F. Kroll (Eds.), *Tutorials in bilingualism: Psycholinguistic perspectives* (pp. 19–51). Mahwah, NJ: Lawrence Erlbaum Associates.

Harmer, J. (2001). *The practice of English language teaching* (3rd ed.). Harlow, UK: Pearson Longman.

Harmer, J. (2007a). *How to teach English* (2nd ed.). Harlow, UK: Pearson Longman.

Harmer, J. (2007b). *The practice of English language teaching* (4th ed.). Harlow, UK: Pearson Longman.

Hartmann, R. R., & Stork, F. C. (1976). *Dictionary of languages and linguistics.* New York, NY: Wiley.

Hasanova, D., & Shadieva, T. (2008). Implementing communicative language teaching in Uzbekistan. *TESOL Quarterly, 42*(1), 138–143.

Hatch, E. (1978). Discourse analysis and second language acquisition. In E. Hatch (Ed.), *Second language acquisition* (pp. 401–435). Rowley, MA: Newbury House.

Hatch, E. (1979). Apply with caution. *Studies in Second Language Acquisition, 2*(1), 123–143.

Hauschild, S., Poltavtchenko, E., & Stoller, F. L. (2012). Going green: Merging environmental education and language instruction. *English Teaching Forum, 50*(2), 2–7.

Hayes, B., & Read, J. (2004). IELTS test preparation in New Zealand: Preparing students for the IELTS academic module. In L. Cheng, Y. Watanabe, & A. Curtis (Eds.), *Washback in language testing: Research contexts and methods* (pp. 97–111). Mahwah, NJ: Lawrence Erlbaum Associates.

Hayes, D. (1997). Helping teachers to cope with large classes. *ELT Journal, 51*(2), 106–116.

Healy, M., & Onderdonk-Horan, K. (in press). Looking at language in hotel management education. In F. Farr & M. Moriarty (Eds.), *Language, learning and teaching: Irish research perspectives.* Berlin, Germany: Peter Lang. Retrieved from http://www.shannoncollege.com/wp-content/uploads/2009/12/THRIC-2010-Full-Paper-M.Healy-and-K.-Onderdonk-Horan-pdf.pdf

Heath, S. B. (1983). *Ways with words: Language, life, and work in communities and classrooms.* Cambridge, UK: Cambridge University Press.

Hedgcock, J. S., & Ferris, D. R. (2009) *Teaching readers of English: Students, texts, and contexts.* New York, NY: Routledge.

Hedge, T. (1993). Key concepts in ELT. *ELT Journal, 47*(3), 275–277.

Herrington, A., & Moran, C. (2001). What happens when machines read our students' writing? *College English, 63*(4), 480–499.

Hess, N. (2001). *Teaching large multilevel classes.* Cambridge, UK: Cambridge University Press.

Hewings, M. (2001). A history of ESP through *English for Specific Purposes. English for Specific Purposes World: A Web-Based Journal, 1*(3). Retrieved from http://www.esp-world.info/Articles_3/Hewings_paper.htm.

Heyer, S. (1996). *A beginning reader* (2nd ed.). White Plains, NY: Addison Wesley Longman.

Higgs, T., & Clifford, R. (1982). The push toward communication. In T. Higgs (Ed.), *ACTFL Foreign Language Education Series: Curriculum, competence, and the foreign language teacher* (Vol. 13, pp. 57–79). Lincolnwood, IL: National Textbook Company.

Hill, J., & Flynn, K. (2006). Cues, questions, and advance organizers. In *Classroom instruction that works with English language learners* (pp. 44–54). Alexandria, VA: Association for Supervision and Curriculum Development.

Hilleson, M. (1996). "I want to talk to them but I don't want them to hear": An introspective study of second language anxiety in an English-medium school. In K. M. Bailey & D. Nunan (Eds.), *Voices from the language classroom* (pp. 248–275). Cambridge, UK: Cambridge University Press.

Hinkel, E. (1994). Native and nonnative speakers' pragmatic interpretation of English text. *TESOL Quarterly, 28*(2), 353–376.

Hinkel, E. (1996). When in Rome: Evaluations of L2 pragmalinguistic behaviors. *Journal of Pragmatics, 26,* 51–70.

Hinkel, E. (1999). *Culture in second language teaching and learning.* Cambridge, UK: Cambridge University Press.

Hinkel, E. (2002). *Second language writers' texts: Linguistic and rhetorical features.* Mahwah, NJ: Lawrence Erlbaum Associates.

Hinkel, E. (2003). Simplicity without elegance: Features of sentences in L1 and L2 academic texts. *TESOL Quarterly, 37*(2), 275–301.

Hinkel, E. (2004). *Teaching academic ESL writing: Practical techniques in vocabulary and grammar.* Mahwah, NJ: Lawrence Erlbaum Associates.

Hinkel, E., & Fotos, S. (Eds.) (2002). *New perspectives on grammar teaching in second language classrooms.* Mahwah, NJ: Lawrence Erlbaum Associates.

Hirvela, A. (2004). *Connecting reading and writing in second language writing instruction.* Ann Arbor, MI: University of Michigan Press.

Hoare, P. (2010). Content-based language teaching in China: Contextual influences on implementation. *Journal of Multilingual and Multicultural Development, 31,* 69–86.

Hoare, P., & Kong, S. (2008). Late immersion in Hong Kong: Still stressed or making progress? In T. W. Fortune & D. J. Tedick (Eds.), *Pathways to multilingualism: Emerging perspectives on immersion education* (pp. 242–263). Clevedon, UK: Multilingual Matters.

Holmes, J. (2005). When small talk is a big deal: Sociolinguistic challenges in the workplace. In M. H. Long (Ed.), *Second language needs analysis* (pp. 344–372). Cambridge, UK: Cambridge University Press.

Holmes, J., & Marra, M. (2011). Harnessing storytelling as a sociopragmatic skill: Applying narrative research in workplace English courses. *TESOL Quarterly, 45*(3), 510–534.

Hopper, P. (1998). Emergent grammar. In M. Tomasello (Ed.), *The new psychology of language* (pp. 155–175). Mahwah, NJ: Lawrence Erlbaum Associates.

Horn, B. (2011). The future is now: Preparing a new generation of CBI teachers. *English Teaching Forum, 49*(3), 2–9.

Hornberger, N. (Ed.). (2003). *Continua of biliteracy: An ecological framework for educational policy, research, and practice in multilingual settings.* Clevedon, UK: Multilingual Matters.

Hornberger, N., & López, L. E. (1998). Policy, possibility, and paradox: Multilingualism and education in Peru and Bolivia. In J. Cenoz & F. Genesee (Eds.), *Beyond bilingualism: Multilingualism and multilingual education* (pp. 206–242). Clevedon, UK: Multilingual Matters.

Hornberger, N., & McKay, S. (Eds.). (2010). *Sociolinguistics and language education.* Bristol, UK: Multilingual Matters.

Horowitz, D. (1986). What professors actually require: Academic tasks for the classroom. *TESOL Quarterly, 30*(3), 445–462.

Howard, E. R., Sugarman, J., Christian, D., Lindholm-Leary, K., & Rodgers, D. (2007). *Guiding principles for dual language education* (2nd ed.). Washington, DC: Center for Applied Linguistics.

Howard, R. M. (2007). Understanding "internet plagiarism." *Computers and Composition, 24*(1), 3–15.

Howatt, A. P. R. with H. G. Widdowson (2004). *A history of English language teaching* (2nd ed.). Oxford, UK: Oxford University Press.

Hu, M., & Nation, I. S. P. (2000). Vocabulary density and reading comprehension. *Reading in a Foreign Language, 23*(1), 403–430.

Huang, J. (2004, June). Voices from Chinese students: Professors' use of English affects academic listening. *College Student Journal.* Retrieved from http://findarticles.com/p/articles/mi_m0FCR/?tag=content;col1

Hubbard, A. L., Wilson, S., Callan, D. E., & Dapretto, M. (2009). Giving speech a hand: Gesture modulates activity in auditory cortex during speech perception. *Journal of Human Brain Mapping, 30,* 1028–1037.

Hudson, T. (2007). *Teaching second language reading.* New York, NY: Oxford University Press.

Huei-Tse, H., Kuo-En, C., & Yao-Ting, S. (2009). Using blogs as a professional development tool for teachers: Analysis of interaction behavioral patterns. *Interactive Learning Environments, 17*(4), 325–340.

Hughes, A. (2003). *Testing for language teachers* (2nd ed.). Cambridge, UK: Cambridge University Press.

Hughes, R., & McCarthy, M. (1998). From sentence to discourse: Discourse grammar and English language teaching. *TESOL Quarterly, 32*(2), 263–287.

Huh, S. (2006). A task-based needs analysis for business English. *Second Language Studies, 24*(2), 1–64. Retrieved from http://www.hawaii.edu/sls/uhwpesl/24%282%29/Huh,Sorin.pdf

Hunter, R. (2004). *Madeline Hunter's mastery teaching.* Thousand Oaks, CA: Corwin Press.

Hurst, D., & Davison, C. (2005). Collaborating on the curriculum: Focus on secondary ESOL. In D. Kaufman & J. Crandall (Eds.), *Content-based instruction in primary and secondary school settings* (pp. 41–66). Alexandria, VA: Teachers of English to Speakers of Other Languages.

Hutchinson, T., & Waters, A. (1987). *English for specific purposes: A learning-centred approach.* Cambridge, UK: Cambridge University Press.

Hyland, K. (2000). *Disciplinary discourses: Social interactions in academic writing.* Harlow, UK: Longman.

Hyland, K. (2002). Genre: Language, context, and literacy. *Annual Review of Applied Linguistics, 22,* 113–135.

Hyland, K. (2004a). *Disciplinary discourses: Social interactions in academic writing.* Ann Arbor, MI: University of Michigan Press.

Hyland, K. (2004b). *Genre and second language writing.* Ann Arbor, MI: University of Michigan Press.

Hyland, K. (2004c). Patterns of engagement: Dialogic features and L2 undergraduate writing. In L. J. Ravelli & R. A. Ellis (Eds.), *Analysing academic writing: Contextualized frameworks* (pp. 5–23). New York, NY: Continuum.

Hyland, K. (2005). Stance and engagement: A model for interaction in academic discourse. *Discourse Studies, 7,* 173–192.

Hyland, K., & Tse, P. (2004). Metadiscourse in academic writing: A reappraisal. *Applied Linguistics, 25*(2), 156–177.

Hymes, D. (1967). Models of the interaction of language and social setting. *Journal of Social Issues, 23,* 8–38.

Hymes, D. (1971). *On communicative competence.* Philadelphia, PA: University of Pennsylvania Press.

Hymes, D. (1972). On communicative competence. In J. B. Pride & J. Holmes (Eds.), *Sociolinguistics: Selected readings* (pp. 269–293). Harmondsworth, UK: Penguin.

Hymes, D. (1996). *Ethnography, linguistics, narrative inequality.* Bristol, PA: Taylor and Francis.

Ingels, S. (2010). The effects of self-monitoring strategy use on the pronunciation of learners of English. In J. Levis & K. LeVelle (Eds.), *Proceedings of the 1st Pronunciation in Second Language Learning and Teaching Conference,* Iowa State University, Sept. 2009 (pp. 67–89). Ames, IA: Iowa State University.

Isbell, K., & Reinhardt, J. (2000). Web integration: A model for task-based learning. In E. Hanson-Smith (Ed.), *Technology enhanced learning environments* (pp. 45–56). Alexandria, VA: Teachers of English to Speakers of Other Languages.

Ishihara, N., & Cohen, A. D. (2010). *Teaching and learning pragmatics: Where language and culture meet.* Harlow, UK: Pearson Education.

James, M. A. (2010). Transfer climate and EAP education: Students' perceptions of challenges to learning transfer. *English for Specific Purposes, 29,* 133–147.

Jamieson, J., Eignor, D., Grabe, W., & Kunnan, A. J. (2008). The frameworks for the re-conceptualization of TOEFL. In C. Chapelle, J. Jamieson, & M. Enright (Eds.), *Building a validity argument for the new TOEFL* (pp. 55–95). Mahwah, NJ: Lawrence Erlbaum Associates.

Janzen, J. (1996). Teaching strategic reading. *TESOL Journal, 6*(1), 6–9.

Janzen, J. (2007). Preparing teachers of second language reading. *TESOL Quarterly, 41*(4), 707–729.

Jaschik, S. (2011). Can you trust automated grading? *Inside Higher Education.* Retrieved from http://m.insidehighered.com/news/2011/02/21/debate_over_reliability_of_automated_essay_grading

Jasso-Aguilar, R. (2005). Sources, methods and triangulation in needs analysis: A critical perspective in a case study of Waikiki hotel maids.

In M. H. Long (Ed.), *Second language needs analysis* (pp. 127–168). Cambridge, UK: Cambridge University Press.

Jay, J. K., & Johnson, K. L. (2002). Capturing complexity: A typology of reflective practice for teacher education. *Teaching and Teacher Education, 18*(1), 73–85.

Jeffries, L., & Mikulecky, B. S. (2009a). *Basic reading power 1: Extensive reading, vocabulary building, comprehension skills, thinking skills* (3rd ed.). New York, NY: Pearson Longman.

Jeffries, L., & Mikulecky, B. S. (2009b). *Basic reading power 2: Extensive reading, vocabulary building, comprehension skills reading faster* (4th ed.). New York, NY: Pearson Longman.

Jenkins, J. (2000). *The phonology of English as an international language.* Oxford, UK: Oxford University Press.

Jenkins, J. (2002). A sociolinguistically based, empirically researched syllabus for English as an international language. *Applied Linguistics, 23*(1), 83–103.

Jenkins, J. (2006a). Attitudes toward (proposed) changes in pronunciation standards. *Speak Out! 36,* 43–46.

Jenkins, J. (2006b). Current perspectives on teaching World Englishes and English as a lingua franca. *TESOL Quarterly, 40*(1), 157–181.

Jensen, L. (2001). Planning lessons. In M. Celce-Murcia (Ed.), *Teaching English as a second or foreign language* (3rd ed., pp. 403–413). Boston, MA: Heinle and Heinle.

Jepson, K. (2005). Conversations—and negotiated interaction—in text and voice chat rooms. *Language Learning and Technology, 9*(3), 79–98.

Jiang, X., & Grabe, W. (2007). Graphic organizers in reading instruction: Research findings and issues. *Reading in a Foreign Language, 19,* 34–55.

Jiang, X., & Grabe, W. (2009). Building reading abilities with graphic organizers. In R. Cohen (Ed.), *Explorations in second language reading* (pp. 25–42). Alexandria, VA: Teachers of English to Speakers of Other Languages.

Johns, A. M. (1997). *Text, role, and context: Developing academic literacies.* New York, NY: Cambridge University Press.

Johns, A. M. (2001). An interdisciplinary, interinstitutional learning communities program: Student involvement and student success. In I. Leki (Ed.), *Academic writing programs* (pp. 61–72). Alexandria, VA: Teachers of English to Speakers of Other Languages.

Johns, A. M. (2013). The history of English for specific purposes research. In B. Paltridge & S. Starfield (Eds.), *The handbook of English for specific purposes* (pp. 5–30). Malden, MA: Wiley-Blackwell.

Johns, A. M., & Makalela, L. (2011). Needs analysis, critical ethnography, and context: Perspectives from the client—and the consultant. In D. Belcher, A. M. Johns, & B. Paltridge (Eds.), *New directions in English for specific purposes research* (pp. 197–221). Ann Arbor, MI: University of Michigan Press.

Johns, T. (1994). From printout to handout: Grammar and vocabulary teaching in the context of data-driven learning. In T. Odlin (Ed.), *Perspectives on pedagogical grammar* (pp. 293–313). New York, NY: Cambridge University Press.

Johns, T. F., & Dudley-Evans, A. (1985). An experiment in team-teaching of overseas postgraduate students of transportation and plant biology. In J. Swales (Ed.), *Episodes in ESP* (pp. 137–155). Hempstead, UK: Prentice-Hall International. (Reprinted from *ELT Documents 106: Teaching in ESP,* pp. 6–23, 1980, London, UK: The British Council.)

Johnson, K. E. (1992). Learning to teach: Instructional actions and decisions of preservice ESL teachers. *TESOL Quarterly, 26*(3), 507–535.

Johnson, K. E. (1995). *Understanding communication in second language classrooms.* Cambridge, UK: Cambridge University Press.

Johnson, K. E. (1999). *Understanding language teaching: Reasoning in action.* Boston, MA: Heinle and Heinle.

Johnson, K. E. (2009). *Second language teacher education: A sociocultural perspective.* New York, NY: Routledge.

Johnson, K. E., & Golombek, P. (2011a). *Research on second language teacher education: A sociocultural perspective on professional development.* New York, NY: Routledge.

Johnson, K. E., & Golombek, P. (2011b). The transforming power of narrative in second language teacher education. *TESOL Quarterly, 45*(3), 486–508.

Johnson, M. (2004). *A philosophy of second language acquisition*. New Haven, CT: Yale University Press.

Johnson, R. K. (1989). A decision-making framework for the coherent language curriculum. In R. K. Johnson (Ed.), *The second language curriculum* (pp. 1–23). Cambridge, UK: Cambridge University Press.

Johnson, R. K., & Swain, M. (1997). *Immersion education: International perspectives*. Cambridge, UK: Cambridge University Press.

Johnston, B. (2009). Collaborative teacher development. In A. Burns & J. C. Richards (Eds.), *The Cambridge guide to second language teacher education* (pp. 241–249). New York, NY: Cambridge University Press.

Johnstone, B. (2008). *Discourse analysis*. Malden, MA: Blackwell.

Jones, L. (2007). *The student-centered classroom*. Cambridge, UK: Cambridge University Press.

Jourdenais, R. M., & Springer, S. E. (Eds.). (2005). *Content, tasks and projects in the language classroom: 2004 conference proceedings*. Monterey, CA: Monterey Institute of International Studies.

Jung Won, H., & Brush, T. A. (2009). Teacher participation in online communities: Why do teachers want to participate in self-generated online communities of K–12 teachers? *Journal of Research on Technology in Education, 41*(3), 279–303.

Kachru, B. B. (1985). Standards, codification, and sociolinguistic realism: The English language in the outer circle. In R. Quirk & H. G. Widdowson (Eds.), *English in the world: Teaching and learning the language and literatures* (pp. 11–30). Cambridge, UK: Cambridge University Press.

Kachru, B. (1989). Teaching World Englishes. *Indian Journal of Applied Linguistics, 15*(1), 85–95.

Kachru, B. B. (1992). Teaching World Englishes. In B. B. Kachru (Ed.), *The other tongue: English across cultures* (2nd ed., pp. 356–364). Chicago, IL: University of Illinois Press.

Kachru, B. B., & Nelson, C. L. (1996). World Englishes. In S. L. McKay & N. H. Hornberger (Eds.), *Sociolinguistics and language teaching* (pp. 71–102). Cambridge, UK: Cambridge University Press.

Kachru, Y. (2005). Teaching and learning World Englishes. In E. Hinkel (Ed.), *Handbook of research in second language teaching and learning* (pp. 155–173). Mahwah, NJ: Lawrence Erlbaum Associates.

Kachru, Y., & Smith, L. E. (2008), *Cultures, contexts, and World Englishes*. New York, NY: Routledge.

Kagan, S. (1994). *Kagan cooperative learning*. San Clemente, CA: Kagan Publishing.

Kamhi-Stein, L. D. (1997). Enhancing student performance through discipline-based summarization-strategy instruction. In M. A. Snow & D. M. Brinton (Eds.), *The content-based classroom: Perspectives on integrating language and content* (pp. 248–273). New York, NY: Longman.

Kamhi-Stein, L. D. (1999). Preparing non-native professionals in TESOL: Implications for teacher education programs. In G. Braine (Ed.), *Non-native educators in English language teaching* (pp. 145–158). Mahwah, NJ: Lawrence Erlbaum Associates.

Kamhi-Stein, L. D. (2000). Looking to the future of TESOL teacher education: Integrating web-based bulletin board discussions into the methods course. *TESOL Quarterly, 34*(3), 423–456.

Kamhi-Stein, L. D. (Ed.). (2004). *Learning and teaching from experience: Perspectives on nonnative English-speaking professionals*. Ann Arbor, MI: University of Michigan Press.

Kamhi-Stein, L. D. (2005). Research perspectives on non-native English-speaking educators. In P. Bruthiaux, D. Atkinson, W. G. Eggington, W. Grabe, & V. Ramanathan (Eds.), *Directions in applied linguistics: Essays in honor of Robert B. Kaplan* (pp. 72–83). Clevedon, UK: Multilingual Matters.

Kamhi-Stein, L. D. (in press). *English language teachers narrating their lives: From the construction of professional identities to the construction of the language classroom*. Ann Arbor, MI: University of Michigan Press.

Kamhi-Stein, L. D., & de Oliveira, L. C. (2008). Mentoring as a pathway to leadership: A focus on nonnative English-speaking professionals. In C. Coombe, M. L. McCloskey, N. Anderson, & L. Stephenson (Eds.), *Leadership skills for English language educators* (pp. 38–49). Ann Arbor, MI: The University of Michigan Press.

Kamhi-Stein, L. D., & Mahboob, A. (2005, March/April). *The relationship between teachers' English proficiency and instructional practices in EFL settings and settings where English is an institutionalized language.*

Paper presented at the annual convention of Teachers of English to Speakers of Other Languages, San Antonio, TX.

Kane, M. (1992). An argument-based approach to validation. *Psychological Bulletin, 112*(3), 527–535.

Kang, O. (2010). Relative salience of suprasegmental features on judgments of L2 comprehensibility and accentedness. *System, 38*(2), 301–315.

Kang, S. (2004). Using visual organizers to enhance EFL instruction. *ELT Journal, 58*(1), 58–67.

Kaplan, R. B. (1999, March). The ELT: Ho(NEST) or not Ho(NEST)? *NNEST Newsletter: The Newsletter of the Nonnative English Speakers in TESOL Caucus, 1*(1), 1, 5–6.

Kasper, G., & Rose, K. R. (2002). *Pragmatic development in a second language*. Oxford, UK: Blackwell.

Katz, A. (1996). Teaching style: A way to understand instruction in language classrooms. In K. M. Bailey & D. Nunan (Eds.), *Voices from the language classroom: Qualitative research on language education* (pp. 57–87). Cambridge, UK: Cambridge University Press.

Katz, A. (2012). Linking assessment with instructional aims and learning. In C. Coombe, P. Davidson, S. Stoynoff, & B. O'Sullivan. (Eds.), *The Cambridge guide to second language assessment* (pp. 66–73). New York, NY: Cambridge University Press.

Katz, A., & Snow, M. A. (2009). Standards and second language teacher education. In A. Burns & J. C. Richards (Eds.), *The Cambridge guide to second language teacher education* (pp. 66–77). Cambridge, UK: Cambridge University Press.

Kaufman, D., & Crandall, J. (Eds.). (2005). *Content-based instruction in primary and secondary school settings*. Alexandria, VA: Teachers of English to Speakers of Other Languages.

Ke, C. (1996). An empirical study on the relationship between Chinese recognition and production. *The Modern Language Journal, 80*(3), 340–349.

Kealey, J., & Inness, D. (1997). *Grammar-focused shenanigames*. Brattleboro, VT: Pro Lingua.

Kearsey, J., & Turner, S. (1999). Evaluating textbooks: The role of genre analysis. *Research in Science and Technological Education, 17*(1), 35–44.

Keck, C. (2006). The use of paraphrase in summary writing: A comparison of L1 and L2 writers. *Journal of Second Language Writing, 15*, 261–278.

Kegan, R. (1994). *In over our heads: The mental demands of modern life.* Cambridge, MA: Harvard University Press.

Kelch, K., & Santana-Williamson, E. (2002). ESL students' attitudes toward native- and nonnative speaking instructors' accents. *The CATESOL Journal, 14*, 57–72.

Kelley, M. J., & Clausen-Grace, N. (2007). *Comprehension shouldn't be silent: From strategy instruction to student independence*. Newark, DE: International Reading Association.

Kelly, L. G. (1969). *Twenty-five centuries of language teaching*. Rowley, MA: Newbury House.

Kemmis, S., & McTaggart, R. (1989). Action research. *IATEFL Newsletter, 102*, 2–3.

Kendeou, P., van den Broek, P., White, M. J., & Lynch, J. (2007). Comprehension in preschool and early elementary children: Skill development and strategy interventions. In D. McNamara (Ed.), *Reading comprehension strategies* (pp. 27–45). New York, NY: Lawrence Erlbaum Associates.

Kern, R. (2000). *Literacy and language teaching*. New York, NY: Oxford University Press.

Kim, S., & Elder, C. (2005). Language choices and pedagogic functions in the foreign language classroom: A cross-linguistic functional analysis of teacher talk. *Language Teaching Research, 9*(4), 355–380.

Kim, T. (2008). Accentedness, comprehensibility, intelligibility, and interpretability of NNESTs. *The CATESOL Journal, 20*(1), 7–26.

King, K., & Benson, C. (2004). Indigenous language education in Bolivia and Ecuador: Contexts, changes, and challenges. In J. W. Tollefson & A. B. M. Tsui (Eds.), *Medium of instruction policies: Which agenda? Whose agenda?* (pp. 241–261). Mahwah, NJ: Lawrence Erlbaum Associates.

King, K., & Mackey, A. (2007). *The bilingual edge: Why, when, and how to teach your child a second language*. New York, NY: Harper Collins.

Kinginger, C. (2008). Language learning in study abroad: Case studies of Americans in France [monograph]. *The Modern Language Journal, 92*, 1–131.

Kinsella, K. (1997). Moving from comprehensible input to "learning to learn" in content-based instruction. In M. A. Snow & D. M.

Brinton (Eds.), *The content-based classroom: Perspectives on integrating language and content* (pp. 46–68). New York, NY: Longman.

Kirkpatrick, A. (2007). *World Englishes: Implications for international communication and English language teaching*. Cambridge, UK: Cambridge University Press.

Klingner, J., & Vaughn, S. (2000). The helping behaviors of fifth graders while using collaborative strategic reading during ESL content classes. *TESOL Quarterly, 34*(1), 69–98.

Klingner, J., & Vaughn, S. (2004). Strategies for struggling second-language readers. In T. Jetton & J. Dole (Eds.), *Adolescent literacy research and practice* (pp. 183–209). New York, NY: Guildford Press.

Knowledge Technologies. (2011). *Versant*. New York, NY: Pearson Education. Retrieved from http://www.versanttest.com/

Knowles, M. S. (1980). *The modern practice of adult education: From pedagogy to andragogy*. New York, NY: Association Press.

Koda, K. (2005). *Insights into second language reading*. New York, NY: Cambridge University Press.

Kohlberg, L. (1981). *Essays on moral development*. San Francisco, CA: Harper and Row.

Kohonen, V. (1992). Experiential language learning: Second language learning as cooperative learner education. In D. Nunan (Ed.), *Collaborative language learning and teaching* (pp. 14–39). Cambridge, UK: Cambridge University Press.

Kolko, B. E., Regan, A. E., & Romano, S. (2001). *Writing in an electronic world: A rhetoric with readings*. New York, NY: Longman.

Komiyama, R. (2009). CAR: A means for motivating students to read. *English Teaching Forum, 47*(3), 32–37.

Kong, S., & Hoare, P. (2011). Cognitive content engagement in content-based language teaching. *Language Teaching Research, 15*(3), 307–324. doi:10.1177/1362168811401152

Koponen, M., & Riggenbach, H. (2000). Overview: Varying perspectives on fluency. In H. Riggenbach (Ed.), *Perspectives on fluency* (pp. 5–24). Ann Arbor, MI: University of Michigan Press.

Koshik, I. (2010). Questions that convey information in teacher-student conferences. In A. F. Freed & S. Ehrlich (Eds.), *"Why do you ask?": The function of questions in institutional discourse* (pp. 159–186). Oxford, UK: Oxford University Press.

Krahmer, E., & Swerts, M. (2007). The effects of visual beats on prosodic prominence: Acoustic analyses, auditory perception and visual perception. *Journal of Memory and Language, 57*(3), 396–414.

Kramsch, C. (1993). *Context and culture in language teaching*. Oxford, UK: Oxford University Press.

Kramsch, C. (1998a). *Language and culture*. Oxford, UK: Oxford University Press.

Kramsch, C. (1998b). The privilege of the intercultural speaker. In M. Byram & M. Fleming (Eds.), *Language learning in intercultural perspective: Approaches through drama and ethnography* (pp. 16–31). Cambridge, UK: Cambridge University Press.

Krashen, S. (1989). We acquire vocabulary and spelling by reading: Additional evidence for the input hypothesis. *The Modern Language Journal, 73*(4), 440–464.

Krashen, S. D. (1981). *Second language acquisition and second language learning*. Oxford, UK: Pergamon Press.

Krashen, S. D. (1982). *Principles and practice in second language acquisition*. Oxford, UK: Pergamon Press.

Krashen, S. D. (1984). Immersion: Why it works and what it has taught us. *Language and Society, 12*, 61–64.

Krashen, S. D., & Terrell, T. D .(1983). *The natural approach: Language acquisition in the classroom*. New York, NY: Pergamon Press.

Kress, G. (1985). *Linguistic processes in sociocultural practice*. Oxford, UK: Oxford University Press.

Kroll, B. (2001). Considerations for teaching an ESL/EFL writing course. In M. Celce-Murcia (Ed.), *Teaching English as a second or foreign language* (3rd ed., pp. 219–232). Boston, MA: Heinle and Heinle.

Krueger, M., & Ryan, F. (Eds.). (1993). *Language and content: Discipline- and content-based approaches to language study*. Lexington, MA: D.C. Heath.

Kuhn, T. S. (1970). *The structure of scientific revolutions*. Chicago, IL: University of Chicago Press.

Kumaravadivelu, B. (1994). The postmethod condition: (E)merging strategies for second/foreign language teaching. *TESOL Quarterly, 28*(1), 27–48.

Kumaravadivelu, B. (2001). Toward a postmethod pedagogy. *TESOL Quarterly, 35*(4), 537–560.

Kumaravadivelu, B. (2003). *Beyond methods: Macrostrategies for language teaching*. New Haven, CT: Yale University Press.

Kumaravadivelu, B. (2006). TESOL methods: Changing tracks, challenging trends. *TESOL Quarterly, 40*(1), 59–81.

Kunnan, A. J. (1999). Recent developments in language assessment. *Annual Review of Applied Linguistics, 19*, 235–253.

Kunnan, A. J. (2004). Test fairness. In M. Milanovic & C. Weir (Eds.), *European year of languages conference papers, Barcelona, Spain* (pp. 27–48). Cambridge, UK: Cambridge University Press.

Kunnan, A. J. (2008). Towards a model of test evaluation: Using the test fairness and wider context frameworks. In L. Taylor & C. Weir (Eds.), *Multilingualism and assessment: Achieving transparency, assuring quality, sustaining diversity. Papers from the ALTE Conference in Berlin, Germany* (pp. 229–251). Cambridge, UK: Cambridge University Press.

Kunnan, A. J. (2009a). Politics and legislation in citizenship testing in the U.S. *Annual Review of Applied Linguistics, 29*, 37–48.

Kunnan, A. J. (2009b). The U.S. Naturalization Test. *Language Assessment Quarterly, 6*, 89–97.

Kunnan, A. J., & Jang, E. (2009). Diagnostic feedback in language assessment. In M. H. Long & C. Doughty (Eds.), *The handbook of language teaching* (pp. 610–627). Malden, MA: Wiley-Blackwell.

Kupetz, M. (2003). Having dessert first: Writing book reviews. In J. Egbert (Ed.), *Becoming contributing professionals* (pp. 25–31). Alexandria, VA: Teachers of English to Speakers of Other Languages.

Kurzweil, J., & Scholl, M. (2007). *Understanding teaching through learning*. New York, NY: McGraw-Hill.

Labov, W. (1972). Some principles of linguistic methodology. *Language in Society, 1*(1), 97–120.

Ladwig, J. G. (2010). Beyond academic outcomes. *Review of Educational Research, 34*, 113–141.

Lafford, B., & Collentine, J. (2006). The effects of study abroad and classroom contexts on the acquisition of Spanish as a second language. In R. Salaberry & B. Lafford (Eds.), *The art of teaching Spanish*. Washington, DC: Georgetown University Press.

Lahav, D. (2005). Recycling an "old idea": Dialogue journals in the digital age. *ETAI Forum*. Retrieved from http://associates.iatefl.org/pages/materials/i4c1.pdf

Lahav, D., Barzel, S., & Shrire, S. (2003). *Earth matters: English outline series*. Tel Aviv, Israel: Center for Educational Technology.

Lakoff, G., & Johnson, M. (1980*). Metaphors we live by*. Chicago, IL: University of Chicago Press.

Lancaster University. (2006–2012). *Information about DIALANG*. Lancaster, UK: Author. Retrieved from http://www.lancs.ac.uk/researchenterprise/dialang/about.htm

Langdon, H. W., & Wiig, E. H. (2009). Multicultural issues in test interpretation. *Seminars in Speech and Language, 30*(4), 261–278.

Lankshear, C., & Knobel, M. (2006). *New literacies: Everyday practices & classroom learning* (2nd ed.). New York, NY: Open University Press.

Lantolf, J. (1996). SLA theory building: Letting all the flowers bloom! *Language Learning, 46*(4), 713–749.

Lantolf, J. (2000a). Second language learning as a mediated process. *Language Teaching, 33*, 79–96.

Lantolf, J. (Ed.). (2000b). *Sociocultural theory and second language learning*. Oxford, UK: Oxford University Press.

Lantolf, J. P., & Thorne, S. L. (2006). *Sociocultural theory and the genesis of second language development*. New York, NY: Oxford University Press.

Larsen-Freeman, D. (1991). Consensus and divergence on the content, role, and process of teaching grammar. In J. E. Alatis (Ed.), *Georgetown University roundtable on languages and linguistics 1991. Linguistics and language pedagogy: The state of the art* (pp. 260–272). Washington, DC: Georgetown University Press.

Larsen-Freeman, D. (1995). On the teaching and learning of grammar: Challenging the myths. In F. Eckman, D. Highland, P. Lee, J. Mileham, & R. Rutkowski Weber (Eds.), *Second language acquisition theory and pedagogy* (pp. 131–148). Mahwah, NJ: Lawrence Erlbaum Associates.

Larsen-Freeman, D. (1997). Chaos/complexity science and second language acquisition. *Applied Linguistics, 18*(2), 141–165.

Larsen-Freeman, D. (2000, January/February). Grammar: Reasons and rules working together. *ESL Magazine*, 10–12.

Larsen-Freeman, D. (2002). The grammar of choice. In E. Hinkel & S. Fotos (Eds.), *New perspectives on grammar teaching in second language classrooms* (pp. 105–118). Mahwah, NJ: Lawrence Erlbaum Associates.

Larsen-Freeman, D. (2003). *Teaching language: From grammar to grammaring*. Boston, MA: Heinle/Cengage.

Larsen-Freeman, D. (Ed.). (2007). *Grammar dimensions: Form, meaning, and use—Books 1–4* (4th ed.). Boston, MA: Thomson Heinle.

Larsen-Freeman, D. (2009). Teaching and testing grammar. In M. H. Long & C. J. Doughty (Eds.), *The handbook of language teaching* (pp. 518–542). Malden, MA: Wiley-Blackwell.

Larsen-Freeman, D. (in press). Complex systems and technemes. In J. Arnold & T. Murphey (Eds.), *Inside and between the people: Reflections on language learning and teaching*. Cambridge, UK: Cambridge University Press.

Larsen-Freeman, D., & Anderson, M. (2011). *Techniques and principles in language teaching* (3rd ed.). New York, NY: Oxford University Press.

Larsen-Freeman, D., & Cameron, L. (2008). *Complex systems and applied linguistics*. Oxford, UK: Oxford University Press.

Larsen-Freeman, D., & Long, M. (1991). *An introduction to second language acquisition research*. New York, NY: Longman.

Laufer, B. (1989). What percentage of text-lexis is essential for comprehension? In C. Lauren & M. Nordman (Eds.), *Special language: From humans to thinking machines* (pp. 316–323). Clevedon, UK: Multilingual Matters.

Laufer, B., & Ravenhorst-Kalovski, G. C. (2010). Lexical threshold revisited: Lexical text coverage, learners' vocabulary size and reading comprehension. *Reading in a Foreign Language, 22*(1), 15–30.

Lavender, S. (2002). Towards a framework for language improvement within short in-service teacher development programmes. In H. Trappes-Lomax & G. Ferguson (Eds.), *Language in language teacher education* (pp. 237–250). Amsterdam, The Netherlands: John Benjamins.

Lazaraton, A. (2002). *A qualitative approach to the validation of oral language tests*. Cambridge, UK: Cambridge University Press.

Leany, C. (2007). *Dictionary activities*. Cambridge, UK: Cambridge University Press.

Lebauer, R. S. (2010). *Learn to listen, listen to learn: Academic listening and notetaking—Books 1 & 2* (3rd ed.). White Plains, NY: Pearson.

Lee, D., & Swales, J. (2006). A corpus-based EAP course for NNS doctoral students: Moving from available specialized corpora to self-compiled corpora. *English for Specific Purposes, 25*, 56–75.

Lee, E., & Lew, L. (2001). Diary studies: The voices of nonnative English speakers in a master of arts program in teaching English to speakers of other languages. *The CATESOL Journal, 13*(1), 135–149.

Leech, G. (2000). Grammars of spoken English: New outcomes of corpus-oriented research. *Language Learning, 50*(4), 675–724.

Leki, I., Cumming, A., & Silva, T. (2008). *A synthesis of research on second language writing*. London, UK: Routledge.

LeMaster, J. (2010). *Critical reading*. San Diego, CA: AVID Center.

Lenker, A., & Rhodes, N. (2007, February). Foreign language immersion programs: Features and trends over 35 years. *CALdigest*, 1–4.

Lenneberg, E. H. (1967). *Biological foundations of language*. New York, NY: John Wiley.

Leu, D., Kinzer, C., Coiro, J., & Cammack, D. (2004). Toward a theory of new literacies emerging from the Internet and other information and communication technologies. In R. B. Ruddell & N. J. Unrau (Eds.), *Theoretical models and processes of reading* (5th ed., pp. 1570–1613). Newark, DE: International Reading Association.

Leu, D., Zawilinski, L., Castek, J., Banerjee, M., Housand, B., Liu, Y., & O'Neil, M. (2007). What is new about the new literacies of online reading comprehension? In *Secondary school literacy: What research reveals for classroom practice* (pp. 37–68). Retrieved from http://teachers.westport.k12.ct.us/ITL/wkspmaterials/NCTE%20chapter.pdf

Leung, C., & Mohan, B. (2004). Teacher formative assessment and talk in classroom contexts: Assessment as discourse and assessment of discourse. *Language Testing, 21*(3), 335–359.

Levelt, W. J. M. (1989). *Speaking: From intention to articulation*. Cambridge, MA: MIT Press.

Levinson, S. (1983). *Pragmatics*. Cambridge, UK: Cambridge University Press.

Levis, J. (1999). Intonation in theory and practice, revisited. *TESOL Quarterly, 33*(1), 37–63.

Levis, J. (2007). Computer technology in teaching and researching pronunciation. *Annual Review of Applied Linguistics, 27*, 184–202.

Levis, J., & Grant, L. (2003). Integrating pronunciation into ESL/EFL classrooms. *TESOL Journal, 12*(2), 13–19.

Levis, J., & Pickering, L. (2004). Teaching intonation in discourse using speech visualization technology. *System, 32*(4), 505–524.

Lewin, K. (1936). *Principles of topological psychology*. New York, NY: McGraw-Hill.

Lewin, K. (1946). Action research and minority problems. *Journal of Social Issues, 2*, 34–46.

Lewis, M. (1993). *The lexical approach*. Hove, UK: Language Teaching.

Lewis, M. (1997). *Implementing the lexical approach*. Hove, UK: Language Teaching.

Lewis, M. (2001). Lexis in the syllabus. In D. R. Hall & A. Hewings (Eds.), *Innovation in English language teaching: A reader* (pp. 46–54). London, UK: Routledge

Li, S. (2010). The effectiveness of corrective feedback in SLA: A meta-analysis. *Language Learning, 60*(2), 309–365.

Liang, K. Y. (2002). *English as a second language (ESL) students' attitudes towards non-native English-speaking teachers' accentedness*. (Unpublished master's thesis). California State University, Los Angeles.

Lightbown, P. (1985). Great expectations: Second-language acquisition research and classroom teaching. *Applied Linguistics, 6*(2), 173–189.

Lightbown, P. (1998). The importance of timing in focus on form. In C. Doughty & J. Williams (Eds.), *Focus on form in classroom second language acquisition* (pp. 177–196). New York, NY: Cambridge University Press.

Lightbown, P. (2000). Anniversary article: Classroom SLA research and second language teaching. *Applied Linguistics, 21*(4), 431–462.

Lightbown, P. (2007). Fair-trade: Two-way bilingual education. *Estudios de Lingüística Inglesa Aplicada, 7*, 9–34.

Lightbown, P. (2014). *Focus on content-based language teaching*. Oxford, UK: Oxford University Press.

Lightbown, P. M., & Spada, N. (2006). *How languages are learned* (3rd ed.). New York, NY: Oxford University Press.

Lili, M. (2007). The culture of learning and the relevance of CLT to the Tunisian context. In S. Midraj, A. Jendli, & A. Sellami (Eds.), *Research in ELT contexts* (pp. 132–157). Dubai, UAE: TESOL Arabia.

Lim, P., & Smalzer, W. (2005). *Noteworthy: Listening and notetaking skills* (3rd ed.). Boston, MA: Thompson Heinle.

Lin, A., Wang, W., Akamatsu, N., & Riazi, M. (2005). International TESOL professionals and teaching English for glocalized communication (TEGCOM). In A. S. Canagarajah (Ed.), *Reclaiming the local in language policy and practice* (pp. 197–225). Mahwah, NJ: Lawrence Erlbaum Associates.

Linderholm, T., & van den Broek, P. (2002). The effects of reading purpose and working memory capacity on the processing of expository text. *Journal of Educational Psychology, 94*, 778–784. doi: 10.1037/0022-0663.94.4.778

Lindholm-Leary, K. J. (2001). *Dual language education*. Avon, UK: Multilingual Matters.

Lindholm-Leary, K., & Block, N. (2010). Achievement in predominantly low SES/Hispanic dual language schools. *International Journal of Bilingual Education and Bilingualism, 13*(1), 43–60.

Lindholm-Leary, K. J., & Genesee, F. (2010). Alternative educational programs for English learners. In California Department of Education, *Improving education for English learners: Research-based approaches* (pp. 323–382). Sacramento, CA: California Department of Education.

Linse, C. (2005). *Practical English language teaching: Young learners*. New York, NY: McGraw-Hill International.

Lippi-Green, R. (1997). *English with an accent: Language, ideology, and discrimination in the United States*. New York, NY: Routledge.

Little, D. (1994). Words and their properties: Arguments for a lexical approach to pedagogical grammar. In T. Odlin (Ed.), *Perspectives on pedagogical grammar* (pp. 99–122). New York, NY: Cambridge University Press.

Little, D. (2007). The Common European Framework of Reference for Languages: Perspectives on the making of supranational language education policy. *The Modern Language Journal, 91*(4), 645–655.

Littlewood, W. (2011). Communicative language teaching: An expanding concept for a changing world. In E. Hinkel (Ed.), *Handbook of research in second language teaching and learning* (Vol. 2, pp. 541–557). New York, NY: Routledge.

Littlewood, W., & Yu, B. (2011). First language and target language in the foreign language classroom. *Language Teaching, 44*(1), 64–77.

Liu, D. (1999). Training non-native TESOL students: Challenges for TESOL teacher education. In G. Braine (Ed.), *Non-native educators in English language teaching* (pp. 159–176). Mahwah, NJ: Lawrence Erlbaum Associates.

Liu, D. (2010). Using corpora for language enhancement, teaching and research. In A. Mahboob (Ed.), *The NNEST lens: Non native English speakers in TESOL* (pp. 305–324). Newcastle, UK: Cambridge Scholars Publishing.

Liu, D., & Jiang, P. (2009). Using a corpus-based lexicogrammatical approach to grammar instruction in EFL and ESL contexts. *The Modern Language Journal, 93*, 61–78.

Liu, J. (1999). Nonnative-English-speaking-educators. *TESOL Quarterly, 33*(1), 85–102.

Liu, J. (2004). Confessions of a nonnative English-speaking professional. In L. D. Kamhi-Stein (Ed.), *Learning and teaching from experience: Perspectives on nonnative English-speaking professionals* (pp. 25–39). Ann Arbor, MI: University of Michigan Press.

Liu, J., & Hansen, J. G. (2002). *Peer response in second language writing classrooms.* Mahwah, NJ: Lawrence Erlbaum Associates.

Liu, X. L., & Goh, C. (2006). Improving second language listening: Awareness and involvement. In T. S. C. Farrell (Ed.), *Language teacher research in Asia* (pp. 91–106). Alexandria, VA: Teachers of English to Speakers of Other Languages.

Llosa, L. (2011). Standards-based classroom assessments of English proficiency: A review of issues, current developments, and future directions for research. *Language Testing, 28*(3), 367–382.

Llurda, E. (2005). Non-native TESOL students as seen by practicum supervisors. In E. Llurda (Ed.), *Non-native language teachers: Perceptions, challenges and contributions to the profession* (pp. 131–154). New York, NY: Springer.

Lo Bianco, J. (2004). Uncle Sam and Mr. Unz: Language needs, politics, and pressures in the United States. *English Today, 20*(3), 16–22.

LoCastro, V. (1989). *Large size classes: The situation in Japan: Lancaster-Leeds language learning in large classes research project* (Report No. 5). Leeds, UK: Lancaster-Leeds Language Learning.

LoCastro, V. (2012). *Pragmatics for language educators: A sociolinguistic perspective.* New York, NY: Routledge.

Loewen, S. (2005). Incidental focus on form and second language learning. *Studies in Second Language Acquisition, 27*(3), 361–386.

Long, M. H. (1980). Inside the "black box": Methodological issues in research on language teaching and learning. *Language Learning, 30*(1), 1–42.

Long, M. H. (1983). Does second language instruction make a difference? A review of the research. *TESOL Quarterly, 17*(3), 359–382.

Long, M. H. (1985). A role for instruction in second language acquisition. In K. Hyltenstam & M. Pienemann (Eds.), *Modelling and assessing second language acquisition* (pp. 77–99). Clevedon, UK: Multilingual Matters.

Long, M. H. (1990). Maturational constraints on language development. *Studies in Second Language Acquisition, 12*(3), 251–285.

Long, M. H. (1991). Focus on form: A design feature in language teaching methodology. In K. de Bot, R. Ginsberg, & C. Kramsch (Eds.), *Foreign language research in cross-cultural perspective* (pp. 39–52). Amsterdam, The Netherlands: John Benjamins.

Long, M. H. (1996). The role of the linguistic environment in second language acquisition. In W. Ritchie & T. Bhatia (Eds.), *Handbook of second language acquisition* (pp. 413–468). San Diego, CA: Academic Press.

Long, M. H. (2005). *Second language needs analysis.* Cambridge, UK: Cambridge University Press.

Long, M. H. (2007). *Problems in second language acquisition.* Mahwah, NJ: Lawrence Erlbaum Associates.

Long, M. H., & Porter, P. (1985). Group work, interlanguage talk, and second language acquisition. *TESOL Quarterly, 19*(2), 207–228.

Long, M. H., & Robinson, P. (1998). Focus on form: Theory, research and practice. In C. Doughty & J. Williams (Eds.), *Focus on form in classroom second language acquisition* (pp. 15–41). Cambridge, UK: Cambridge University Press.

López, L. E. (2006). Cultural diversity, multilingualism, and indigenous education in Latin America. In O. García, T. Skutnabb-Kangas, & M. E. Torres-Guzmán (Eds.), *Imagining multilingual schools: Language in education and glocalization* (pp. 238–261). Clevedon, UK: Multilingual Matters.

Lopriore, L. (2009). Content learning in English: Issues and perspectives. In K. Graves & L. Lopriore (Eds.), *Developing a new curriculum for school-age learners* (pp. 173–196). Alexandria, VA: Teachers of English to Speakers of Other Languages.

Lorimer, C. (2011/2012). Introduction to the theme section: Graduate student professional development. *The CATESOL Journal, 23*(1), 28–30.

Lorimer, C., & Schulte, J. (2011/2012). Reimagining TESOL professionalism: The graduate student perspective. *The CATESOL Journal, 23*(1), 31–44.

Loschky, L., & Bley-Vroman, R. (1993). Grammar and task-based methodology. In G. Crookes & S. Gass (Eds.), *Tasks and language learning: Integrating theory and practice* (pp. 123–167). Clevedon, UK: Multilingual Matters.

Low, G., Littlemore, J., & Koester, A. (2008). Metaphor use in three UK university lectures. *Applied Linguistics, 29*(3), 428–455.

Lozanov, G. (1978). *Suggestology and outlines of suggestopedy.* New York, NY: Gordon and Breach.

L-Soft International. (1996). Early history of LISTSERV®. Retrieved from http://www.lsoft.com/products/listserv-history.asp

Luoma, S. (2004). *Assessing speaking.* Cambridge, UK: Cambridge University Press.

Lynch, T. (1997). Nudge, nudge: Teacher interventions in task-based learner talk. *ELT Journal, 55*(2), 317–325.

Lynch, T. (2004). *Study listening: A course in listening to lectures and note taking.* Cambridge, UK: Cambridge University Press.

Lynch, T. (2009). *Teaching second language listening.* Oxford, UK: Oxford University Press.

Lynch, T., & Maclean, J. (2000). Exploring the benefits of task repetition and recycling for classroom language learning. *Language Teaching Research, 4*(3), 221–250.

Lyster, R. (2004). Differential effects of prompts and recasts in form-focused instruction. *Studies in Second Language Acquisition, 26*(3), 399–432.

Lyster, R. (2007). *Learning and teaching languages through content: A counterbalanced approach.* Amsterdam, The Netherlands: John Benjamins.

Lyster, R. (2011). Content-based second language teaching. In E. Hinkel (Ed.), *Handbook of research in second language teaching and learning* (Vol. 2, pp. 611–630). New York, NY: Routledge.

Lyster, R., & Mori, H. (2006). Interactional feedback and instructional counterbalance. *Studies in Second Language Acquisition, 28*(2), 269–300.

Lyster, R., & Mori, H. (2008). Instructional counterbalance in immersion pedagogy. In T. W. Fortune & D. J. Tedick (Eds.), *Pathways to multilingualism: Evolving perspectives on immersion education* (pp. 133–151). Clevedon, UK: Multilingual Matters.

Lyster, R., & Ranta, L. (1997). Corrective feedback and learner uptake: Negotiation of form in communicative classrooms. *Studies in Second Language Acquisition, 19*(1), 37–66.

Macaro, E. (2001). *Learning strategies in foreign and second language classroom.* London, UK; New York, NY: Continuum.

Macaro, E., Graham, S., & Vanderplank, R. (2007). A review of listening strategies: Focus on sources of knowledge and on success. In E. Macaro & A. Cohen (Eds.), *Language learner strategies: 30 years of research and practice* (pp. 165–185). Oxford, UK: Oxford University Press.

MacIntyre, P. D., MacKinnon, S. P., & Clément, R. (2009). The baby, the bathwater, and the future of language learning motivation research. In Z. Dörnyei & E. Ushioda (Eds.), *Motivation, language identity and the L2 self* (pp. 43–65). Bristol, UK: Multilingual Matters.

Mackey, A., & Gass, S. (2006). Introduction to special issue. *Studies in Second Language Acquisition, 28*(2), 169–178.

Mackey, W. (1978). Appendix F: A typology of bilingual education. In T. Andersson & M. Boyer (Eds.), *Bilingual schooling in the United States* (2nd ed., pp. 264–283). Austin, TX: National Educational Laboratory.

Maclennan, S. (1987). Integrating lesson planning and class management. *ELT Journal, 41*(3), 193–197.

Madsen, H. S. (1979). Innovative methodologies applicable to TESL. In M. Celce-Murcia & L. McIntosh (Eds.), *Teaching English as a second or foreign language* (pp. 26–37). Rowley, MA: Newbury House.

Madsen, H., & Bowen, J. D. (1978). *Adaptation in language teaching.* Rowley, MA: Newbury House.

Magid, M. (2012). The L2 motivational self system from a Chinese perspective: A mixed methods study. *Journal of Applied Linguistics, 6*(1), 69–90.

Magid, M., & Chan, L. H. (2012). Motivating English learners by helping them visualise their ideal L2 self: Lessons from two motivational programmes. *Innovation in Language Learning and Teaching, 6*(2), 113–125.

Magy, R., & Price, D. (2011, April). *Integrating workplace skills in ESL classes.* Paper presented at the 2011 CATESOL State Convention, Long Beach, CA.

Mahboob, A., Uhrig, K., Newman, K., & Hartford, B. (2004). Children of a lesser English: Status of nonnative English speakers as college-level ESL teachers in the United States. In L. D. Kamhi-Stein (Ed.), *Learning and teaching from experience: Perspectives on nonnative English-speaking professionals* (pp. 100–120). Ann Arbor, MI: University of Michigan Press.

Mahoney, K., MacSwan, J., Haladyna, T., & García, D. (2010). Castañeda's third prong: Evaluating the achievement of Arizona's English learners under restrictive language policy. In P. Gándara & M. Hopkins (Eds.), *Forbidden language: English learners and restrictive language policies* (pp. 50–64). New York, NY: Teachers College Press.

Major, R. (2008). Transfer in second language phonology: A review. In J. Edwards & M. Zampini (Eds.), *Phonology and second language acquisition* (pp. 63–94). Philadelphia, PA: John Benjamins.

Makelala, L. (Ed.) (2009). *Language teacher research in Africa.* Alexandria, VA: Teachers of English to Speakers of Other Languages.

Malderez, A. (2009). Mentoring. In A. Burns & J. C. Richards (Eds.), *The Cambridge guide to second language teacher education* (pp. 259–268). New York, NY: Cambridge University Press.

Maley, A., & Duff, A. (1989). *The inward ear: Poetry in the language classroom.* Cambridge, UK: Cambridge University Press.

Manchón, R. (Ed.). (2009). *Writing in foreign language contexts.* Tonawanda, NY: Multilingual Matters.

Mann, W., & Thompson, S. A. (1988). Rhetorical structure theory: A framework for the analysis of text. *Text, 8,* 243–281.

Mareschal, C. (2007). *Student perceptions of a self-regulatory approach to second language listening comprehension development.* (Unpublished doctoral dissertation). University of Ottawa, Ottawa, Canada.

Marinova-Todd, S. H., Marshall, D. B., & Snow, C. E. (2000). Three misconceptions about age and L2 learning. *TESOL Quarterly, 34*(1), 9–34.

Markee, N. (1997). *Managing curricular innovation.* Cambridge, UK: Cambridge University Press.

Markus, H. R. (2006). Foreword. In C. Dunkel & J. Kerpelman (Eds.), *Possible selves: Theory, research and applications* (pp. xi–xiv). New York, NY: Nova Science.

Markus, H., & Nurius, P. (1986). Possible selves. *American Psychologist, 41,* 954–969.

Martinez, D. F. (2011). *Introducing discourse analysis in class.* Newcastle upon Tyne, UK: Cambridge Scholars.

Marzano, R. J. (2006). *Classroom assessment and grading that work.* Alexandria, VA: Association for Supervision and Curriculum Development.

Marzio, M. (1999). *Real English interactive.* [CD ROM]. Istres, France: The Marzio School/Ipse Communication.

Maslow, A. (1970). *Toward a psychology of being* (2nd ed.). New York, NY: Van Nostrand.

Massachusetts Department of Education, Adult and Community Learning Services. (2005, December). *Massachusetts adult basic education curriculum framework for English for speakers of other languages.* Malden, MA: Author. Retrieved from www.doe.mass.edu/acls/frameworks/esol.doc

Master, P. (1983). The etiquette of observing. *TESOL Quarterly, 17*(3), 497–501.

Master, P. (1984). The dynamics of classroom observation: Sharing the power. *TESOL Quarterly, 18*(2), 342–344.

Matsuda, P. K. (2003a). Proud to be a nonnative English speaker. *TESOL Matters, 13*(4), 15.

Matsuda, P. K. (2003b). Second language writing in the twentieth century: A situated historical perspective. In B. Kroll (Ed.), *Exploring the dynamics of second language writing* (pp. 15–34). New York, NY: Cambridge University Press.

Maupin, A. (2007). *Tales of the city.* New York, NY: Harper Perennial. (Original work published in 1978).

Mauranen, A. (2011). English as a *lingua franca* of the academic world. In D. Belcher, A. M. Johns, & B. Paltridge (Eds.), *New directions in English for specific purposes research* (pp. 94–117). Ann Arbor, MI: University of Michigan Press.

Maurice, K. (1983). The fluency workshop. *TESOL Newsletter, 17*(4), 29.

McCardle, P., Chhabra, V., & Kapinus, B. (2008). Motivation and engagement. In P. McCardle, V. Chhabra, & B. Kapinus (Eds.), *Reading research in action: A teacher's guide to student success* (pp. 207–222). Baltimore, MD: Brookes Publishing.

McCarthy, M. (1991). *Discourse analysis for teachers.* Cambridge, UK: Cambridge University Press.

McCarthy, M. (1998). *Spoken language and applied linguistics.* Cambridge, UK: Cambridge University Press.

McCarthy, M. J. (2008). Accessing and interpreting corpus information in the teacher education context, *Language Teaching, 41*(4), 563–574.

McCarthy, M. J. (2010). Spoken fluency revisited, *English Profile Journal Inaugural issue.* Retrieved from http://journals.cambridge.org/action/displayJournal?jid=EPJ

McCarthy, M., & Carter, R. (1995). Spoken grammar and how we should teach it. *ELT Journal, 49*(3), 207–218.

McCarthy, M., & Carter, R. (2001). Ten criteria for a spoken grammar. In E. Hinkel & S. Fotos (Eds.), *New perspectives on grammar teaching in second language classrooms* (pp. 51–75). Mahwah, NJ: Lawrence Erlbaum Associates.

McCarthy, M., & Carter, R. (2006). Ten criteria for a spoken grammar. In M. McCarthy (Ed.), *Explorations in corpus linguistics* (pp. 27–52). New York, NY: Cambridge University Press.

McCarthy, M., & Handford, M. (2004). "Invisible to us": A preliminary corpus-based study of spoken business English. In U. Connor & T. A. Upton (Eds.), *Discourse in the professions* (pp. 167–201). Amsterdam, The Netherlands: John Benjamins.

McCarthy, M. J., McCarten, J., & Sandiford, H. (2005). *Touchstone* (Student books 1–2). Cambridge, UK: Cambridge University Press.

McCarthy, M., McCarten, J., & Sandiford, H. (2005/2006). *Touchstone* (Books 1–4). New York, NY: Cambridge University Press.

McCarthy, M. J. McCarten, J., & Sandiford, H. (2006). *Touchstone* (Student books 3–4). Cambridge, UK: Cambridge University Press.

McCarthy, M., & O'Keeffe, A. (2004). Research in the teaching of speaking. *Annual Review of Applied Linguistics, 24,* 26–43.

McCarty, T. (2002). *A place to be Navajo: Rough Rock and the struggle for self-determination in indigenous schooling.* Mahwah, NJ: Lawrence Erlbaum Associates.

McCarty, T., Romero, M. E., & Zepeda, O. (2006). Reimagining multilingual America: Lessons from Native American youth. In O. García, T. Skutnabb-Kangas, & M. E. Torres-Guzmán (Eds.), *Imagining multilingual schools: Language in education and glocalization* (pp. 91–110). Clevedon, UK: Multilingual Matters.

McCloskey, M. L., & Stack, L. (1993). *Voices in literature.* Boston, MA: Heinle and Heinle.

McCluskey, C. (2011/2012). Professional development to work with low-educated adults ESL learners: Searching beyond the program. *The CATESOL Journal, 23*(1), 56–64.

McDonough, J., & Shaw, C. (2003a). Group and pair work. In *Materials and methods in ELT: A teacher's guide* (2nd ed.). Oxford, UK: Blackwell.

McDonough, J., & Shaw, C. (2003b). *Materials and methods in ELT: A teacher's guide* (2nd ed.). Oxford, UK: Blackwell.

McGarrell, H. M. (Ed.). (2007). *Language teacher research in the Americas.* Alexandria, VA: Teachers of English to Speakers of Other Languages.

McGroarty, M. (1998). *Partnerships with linguistic minority communities.* (TESOL Professional Paper No. 4). Alexandria, VA: Teachers of English to Speakers of Other Languages.

McGroarty, M. (2001). Bilingual approaches to language learning. In M. Celce-Murcia (Ed.), *Teaching English as a second or foreign language* (3rd ed., pp. 345–356). Boston, MA: Heinle and Heinle.

McGroarty, M. (Ed.). (2006). Lingua franca languages [Special issue]. *Annual Review of Applied Linguistics, 26.*

McKay, H., & Tom, A. (2001). *Teaching adult second language learners.* New York, NY: Cambridge University Press.

McKay, P. (2007). The standards movement and ELT for school-aged learners: Cross-national perspectives. In J. Cummins & C. Davidson (Eds.), *International handbook of English language teaching* (pp. 439–456). New York, NY: Springer.

McKay, S. (1982). Literature in the ESL classroom. *TESOL Quarterly, 16*(4), 529–536.

McKay, S. L. (1992). *Teaching English overseas: An introduction.* Oxford, UK: Oxford University Press.

McKay, S. (1994). Developing ESL writing materials. *System, 22*(2), 195–203.

McKay, S. (2000). "It's certainly been nice to see you": Using plays to develop sociolinguistic competence. *Guidelines, 22*(2), 24–29.

McKay, S. L. (2002). *Teaching English as an international language: Rethinking goals and approaches.* Oxford, UK: Oxford University Press.

McKay, S. L. (2006). *Researching second language classrooms.* Mahwah, NJ: Lawrence Erlbaum Associates.

McKay, S. L. (2012). English as an international language. In A. Burns & J. C. Richards (Eds.), *The Cambridge guide to pedagogy and practice in second language teaching* (pp. 15–22). New York, NY: Cambridge University Press.

McLaughlin, B. (1987). *Theories of second language acquisition.* London, UK: Edward Arnold.

McNerney, M., & Mendelsohn, D. (1992). Suprasegmentals in the pronunciation class: Setting priorities. In P. Avery & S. Ehrlich (Eds.), *Teaching American English pronunciation* (pp. 185–196). Oxford, UK: Oxford University Press.

McPherson, P. (1997). Action research: Exploring learner diversity. *Prospect: An Australian Journal of Teaching/Teaching English to Speakers of Other Languages (TESOL), 12*(1), 50–62.

McTighe, J., & Ferrara, S. (1998). *Assessing learning in the classroom.* Washington, DC: National Education Association.

McVee, M. B., Dunsmore, K., & Gavelek, J. R. (2005). Schema theory revisited. *Review of Educational Research, 75*(4), 531–566.

Meara, P. (1980). Vocabulary acquisition: A neglected aspect of language learning. *Language Teaching and Linguistics: Abstracts, 13*(4), 221–246.

Medgyes, P. (1983). The schizophrenic teachers. *ELT Journal, 37*(1), 2–6.

Medgyes, P. (1994). *The non-native teacher.* London, UK: Macmillan.

Medgyes, P. (2001). When the teacher is a non-native speaker. In M. Celce-Murcia (Ed.), *Teaching English as a second or foreign language* (3rd ed., pp. 429–442). Boston, MA: Heinle and Heinle.

Meltzer, L., & Sage Bagnato, J. (2010). Shifting and flexible problem solving. In L. Meltzer (Ed.), *Promoting executive function in the classroom* (pp. 140–159). New York, NY: The Guilford Press.

Melzer, D. (2009). Assignments across the curriculum: A survey of college writing. *Language and Learning across the Disciplines, 6*(1), 86–110. Retrieved from http://wac.colostate.edu/llad/v6n1/melzer.pdf

Mendelsohn, D. (1995). Applying learning strategies in the second/foreign language listening comprehension lesson. In D. Mendelsohn & J. Rubin (Eds.), *A guide for the teaching of second language listening* (pp. 132–150). San Diego, CA: Dominie Press.

Menken, K. (2008). *English learners left behind: Standardized testing as language policy.* Clevedon, UK: Multilingual Matters.

Mertens, D. M. (1998). *Research methods in education and psychology: Integrating diversity with qualitative and quantitative approaches.* Thousand Oaks, CA: Sage.

Meskill, C., & Anthony, N. (2007). Learning to orchestrate online instructional conversations: A case of faculty development for foreign language educators. *Computer Assisted Language Learning, 20*(1), 5–19.

Meskill, C., & Sadykova, G. (2011). Introducing EFL faculty to online instructional conversations. *Recall, 23*(3), 200–217. doi:10.1017/S0958344011000140

Met, M. (1999, January). Content-based instruction: Defining terms, making decisions. *NFLC Reports.* Washington, DC: The National Foreign Language Center.

Miller, L. (2002). Towards a model for lectures in a second language. *Journal of English for Academic Purposes, 1*(2), 145–162.

Miller, S. (2006). *Targeting pronunciation: Communicating clearly in English* (2nd ed.). Boston, MA: Houghton Mifflin.

Minnesota Educational Computing Consortium. (1974). *Oregon Trail* [Computer software]. Brooklyn Center, MN: Author.

Minnesota Laboratory for Low-Vision Research. (1999). *How fast can you read?* Retrieved from http://gandalf.psych.umn.edu/groups/gellab/MNREAD/DEMO_RS/

Mirtschin, A. (2008, March 14). 20 reasons why students should blog [Web log comment]. Message posted to http://murcha.wordpress.com/2008/03/14/20-reasons-why-students-should-blog/

Mishan, F. (2004). *Designing authenticity into language learning materials.* Bristol, UK: Intellect.

Mitchell, R. (2009). Current trends in classroom research. In M. H. Long & C. J. Doughty (Eds.), *The handbook of language teaching* (pp. 675–705). Chichester, UK: Wiley Blackwell.

Mok, A. (1997). Student empowerment in an English language enrichment programme: An action research project in Hong Kong. *Educational Action Research, 5*(2), 305–320.

Moll, L. C. (2010). Mobilizing culture, language, and educational practices: Fulfilling the promises of *Mendez* and *Brown. Educational Researcher, 39*(6), 451–460.

Moll, L. C., Amanti, C., Neff, D., & Gonzalez, N. (2005). Funds of knowledge for teaching: Using a qualitative approach to connect homes and classrooms. In N. Gonzalez, L. C. Moll, & C. Amanti (Eds.), *Funds of knowledge: Theorizing practices in households, communities, and classrooms* (pp. 71–88). Mahwah, NJ: Lawrence Erlbaum Associates.

Montone, C., & Loeb, M. (2000). *Implementing two-way immersion programs in secondary schools* [Educational Practice Report No. 5]. Washington, DC: Center for Research on Education, Diversity, and Excellence/Center for Applied Linguistics.

Moon, R. (Ed.). (2009). *Words, grammar, text: Revisiting the work of John Sinclair.* Amsterdam, The Netherlands: John Benjamins.

Morgan, J., & Rinvolucri, M. (1983). *Once upon a time.* Cambridge, UK: Cambridge University Press.

Morita, N. (2000). Discourse socialization through oral classroom activities in a TESL graduate program. *TESOL Quarterly, 34*(2), 279–310.

Morita, N. (2004). Negotiating participation and identity in second language academic communities. *TESOL Quarterly, 38*(4), 573–604.

Morley, J. (1979). *Improving spoken English.* Ann Arbor, MI: University of Michigan Press.

Morley, J. (1999). New developments in speech/pronunciation instruction. *As We Speak . . . , 2*(1), 1–5.

Morley, J. (2001). Aural comprehension instruction: Principles and practices. In M. Celce-Murcia (Ed.), *Teaching English as a second or foreign language* (3rd ed., pp. 69–85). Boston, MA: Heinle and Heinle.

Morrow, K. (2004). *Insights from the Common European Framework.* Oxford, UK: Oxford University Press.

Moskowitz, G. (1978). *Caring and sharing in the foreign language class: A sourcebook on humanistic techniques.* Rowley, MA: Newbury House.

Moss, C. M., & Brookhart, S. M. (2009). *Advancing formative assessment in every classroom.* Alexandria, VA: Association for Supervision and Curriculum Development.

Moussu, L. (2010). Influence of teacher-contact time and other variables on ESL students' attitudes toward native- and nonnative-English-speaking teachers. *TESOL Quarterly, 44*(4), 746–768.

Moussu, L., & Llurda, E. (2008). Non-native English-speaking English language teachers: History and research. *Language Teaching, 41*(3), 315–348.

Moyer, A. (2004). *Age, accent and experience in second language acquisition: An integrated approach to critical period inquiry.* Clevedon, UK: Multilingual Matters.

Mumford, S. (2008). An analysis of spoken grammar: The case for production. *ELT Journal, 63*(2), 137–144.

Munro, M. (2003). A primer on accent discrimination in the Canadian context. *TESL Canada Journal, 20*(2), 38–51.

Munro, M., & Derwing, T. (1995). Foreign accent, comprehensibility, and intelligibility in the speech of second language learners. *Language Learning, 45*(1), 73–97.

Munro, M., & Derwing, T. (2001). Modeling perceptions of the accentedness and comprehensibility of L2 speech: The role of speaking rate. *Studies in Second Language Acquisition, 23*(4), 451–468.

Munro, M., & Derwing, T. (2006). The functional load principle in ESL pronunciation instruction: An exploratory study. *System, 34*(4), 520–531.

Munsch, R. (1980). *The paper bag princess*. Toronto, Canada: Annick Press.

Murdoch, G. (1994). Language development provision in teacher training curricula. *ELT Journal, 48*(3), 253–265.

Murphey, T. (2000). Becoming contributing professionals: Nonnative-English-speaking teachers in an EFL environment. In K. E. Johnson (Ed.), *Teacher education* (pp. 105–118). Alexandria, VA: Teachers of English to Speakers of Other Languages.

Murphey, T., Connolly, M., Churchill, E., McLaughlin, J., Schwartz, S. L., & Krajka, J. (2003). Creating publishing communities. In T. Murphey (Ed.), *Extending professional contributions* (pp. 105–118). Alexandria, VA: Teachers of English to Speakers of Other Languages.

Murphey, T., & Sato, K. (Eds.) (2005). *Communities of supportive professionals*. Alexandria, VA: Teachers of English to Speakers of Other Languages.

Murphy, J. M. (1992). An etiquette for the non-supervisory observation of L2 classrooms. *Foreign Language Annals, 25*, 215–225.

Murphy, J. M., & Byrd, H. P. (Eds.). (2001). *Understanding the courses we teach: Local perspectives on English language teaching*. Ann Arbor, MI: University of Michigan Press.

Murray, A. (2010). Empowering teachers through professional development. *English Teaching Forum, 1*(1), 2–11.

Murray, D. (2005). ESL in adult education. In E. Hinkel (Ed.), *Handbook of research in second language teaching and learning* (pp. 65–84). Mahwah, NJ: Lawrence Erlbaum Associates.

Myers, M. (1987). The shared structure of oral and written language and the implications of teaching writing, reading and literature. In J. R. Squire (Ed.), *The dynamics of language learning* (pp. 121–146). Urbana, IL: ERIC Clearinghouse on Reading and Communication Skills.

Myles, F. (2004). From data to theory: The over-representation of linguistic knowledge in SLA. *Transactions of the Philological Society, 102*, 139–168.

Myles, F., Hooper, J., & Mitchell, R. (1998). Rote or rule? Exploring the role of formulaic language in classroom foreign language learning. *Language Learning, 48*(3), 323–364.

Myles, F., Mitchell, R., & Hooper, J. (1999). Interrogative chunks in French L2: A basis for creative construction? *Studies in Second Language Acquisition, 21*(1), 49–80.

Nagy, W. E., & Anderson, R. C. (1984). The number of words in printed school English. *Reading Research Quarterly, 19*, 204–330.

Nagy, W. E., Herman, P. A., & Anderson, R. C. (1985). Learning words from context. *Reading Research Quarterly, 20*(2), 233–253.

Naiman, N., Fröhlich, M., Stern, H., & Todesco, A. (1996). *The good language learner: Modern languages in practice* (Vol. 4). Clevedon, UK: Multilingual Matters.

Nakada, T., Fujii, Y., & Kwee, I. (2001). Brain strategies for reading in the second language are determined by the first language. *Neuroscience Research, 40*, 351–358.

Nation, I. S. P. (1990). *Teaching and learning vocabulary*. Boston, MA: Heinle and Heinle.

Nation, I. S. P. (2001). *Learning vocabulary in another language*. New York, NY: Cambridge University Press.

Nation, I. S. P. (2006). How large a vocabulary is needed for reading and listening? *Canadian Modern Language Review, 63*, 59–82.

Nation, I. S. P. (2008). *Teaching vocabulary: Strategies and techniques*. Boston, MA: Heinle Cengage.

Nation, I. S. P. (2009) *Teaching ESL/EFL reading and writing*. New York, NY: Routledge.

Nation, I. S. P., & Macalister, J. (2010). *Language curriculum design*. London, UK: Routledge.

Nation, I. S. P., & Newton, J. (2009). Developing fluency. In I. S. P. Nation & J. Newton (Eds.), *Teaching ESL/EFL listening and speaking* (pp. 151–164). New York, NY: Routledge.

Nation, I. S. P., & Newton, J. (Eds.). (2009). *Teaching ESL/EFL listening and speaking*. New York, NY: Routledge.

Nation, P. (2002). Best practices in vocabulary teaching and learning. In J. C. Richards, & W. A. Renandya (Eds.), *Methodology in language teaching: An anthology of current practice* (pp. 267–272). Cambridge, UK: Cambridge University Press.

National Center on Education and the Economy, Workforce Development Strategies Group. (2009). *Background and supporting evidence for adult education for work*. Boston, MA: Jobs for the Future. Retrieved from http://www.jff.org/publications/workforce/background-and-supporting-evidence-adult/906

National Clearinghouse for English Language Acquisition and Language Instruction Educational Programs (NCELA). (n.d.). *Types of language instruction educational programs (LIEPs)*. Washington, DC: Author. Retrieved from http://www.ncela.gwu.edu/files/uploads/5/Language_Instruction_Educational_Programs.pdf

National Commission on Adult Literacy. (2008). *Reach higher, America: Overcoming crisis in the U.S. workforce*. New York, NY: Council for Advancement of Adult Literacy. Retrieved from http://www.nationalcommissiononadultliteracy.org/ReachHigherAmerica/ReachHigher.pdf

National Commission on Excellence in Education. (1983). *A nation at risk: The imperative for educational reform*. Washington, DC: Author. Retrieved from http://www.channelingreality.com/un/education/nationatrisk/NATION_AT_RISK_Background.pdf

National Comprehensive Center for Teacher Quality. (2009). *Teaching English language learners: A complex system*. Washington, DC: Author.

National Council of State Directors of Adult Education. (2009, June). *The blue book: Legislator's resource book: Adult education services—the success, the impact and the need*. Retrieved from http://www.ncsdae.org/Final%20Blue%20-%207-1-09.pdf

National Institute for Literacy Workforce Education. (2005). *Glossary of workforce education terms*. Knoxville, TN: Center for Literacy Studies. Retrieved from http://worklink.coe.utk.edu/glossaryb.htm#c

Nattinger, J., & DeCarrico, J. (1992). *Lexical phrases and language teaching*. Oxford, UK: Oxford University Press.

Neisser, U. (1967). *Cognitive psychology*. New York, NY: Appleton-Century-Crofts.

Nelson, C. (2011). Narratives of classroom life: Changing conceptions of knowledge. *TESOL Quarterly, 45*(3), 463–485.

Nelson, G., Winters, T., & Clark, R. (2004). *Do as I say: Operations, procedures and rituals for language acquisition* (3rd ed.). Brattleboro, VT: Pro Lingua Associates.

Nemtchinova, E. (2005). Host teachers' evaluations of nonnative-English-speaking teacher trainees: A perspective from the classroom. *TESOL Quarterly, 39*(2), 235–261.

Nemtchinova, E., Mahboob, A., Eslami, Z., & Dogancay-Aktuna, S. (2010). Training non-native English speaking TESOL professionals. In A. Mahboob (Ed.), *The NNEST lens: Non native English speakers in TESOL* (pp. 222–238). Newcastle, UK: Cambridge Scholars Publishing.

Nero, S. (2006). An exceptional voice: Working as a TESOL professional of color. In A. Curtis & M. Romney (Eds.), *Color, race, and English language teaching: Shades of meaning* (pp. 23–36). Mahwah, NJ: Lawrence Erlbaum Associates.

The New London Group. (1996). A pedagogy of multiliteracies: Designing social futures. *Harvard Educational Review, 66*(1), 60–93.

Newton, J. (1993). *Task based interaction among adult learners of English and its role in second language development*. (Unpublished doctoral dissertation). Victoria University of Wellington, New Zealand.

Newton, J. (1995). Task based interaction and incidental vocabulary learning: A case study. *Second Language Research, 11*(2), 159–177.

New York State Education Department. (2011). *Office of Assessment Policy, Development, and Administration: New York State English as a Second Language Achievement Test (NYSESLAT)*. Albany, NY: Author. Retrieved from http://www.p12.nysed.gov/apda/nyseslat/

Nicholson, T. (2000). The flashcard strikes back. In T. V. Rasinski, N. D. Padak, B. W. Church, G. Fawcett, & J. Hendershop (Eds.), *Teaching word recognition, spelling, and vocabulary: Strategies from the Reading Teacher* (pp. 37–44). Newark, DE: International Reading Association.

Nickerson, C., & Planken, B. (2009). English for specific purposes: Written business English and the increasing influence of multimodality. In D. Belcher (Ed.), *English for specific purposes: Research and practice* (pp. 127–42). Ann Arbor, MI: University of Michigan Press.

Nissani, H. (1990). Early childhood programs for language minority students. Washington, DC: National Clearinghouse for Bilingual Education. (ERIC Document Reproduction Service No. ED337033.)

Noels, K. A. (2001). New orientations in language learning motivation: Toward a contextual model of intrinsic, extrinsic, and integrative orientations and motivation. In Z. Dörnyei & R. Schmidt (Eds.), *Motivation and second language acquisition* (pp. 43–68). Honolulu, HI: University of Hawai'i Press.

Noji, F., Ford, S., & Silva, A. (2009). Purposeful reading. In R. Cohen (Ed.), *Explorations in second language reading* (pp. 7–24). Alexandria, VA: Teachers of English to Speakers of Other Languages.

Norris, J. M., & Ortega, L. (2000). Effectiveness of L2 instruction: A research synthesis and quantitative meta-analysis. *Language Learning, 50*(3), 417–528.

Norton, B., & Toohey, K. (Eds.). (2004). *Critical pedagogies and language learning*. New York, NY: Cambridge University Press.

Numrich, C. (1996). On becoming a language teacher: Insights from diary studies. *TESOL Quarterly, 30*(1), 131–151.

Nunan, D. (1988). *Syllabus design*. Oxford, UK: Oxford University Press.

Nunan, D. (1989a). *Designing tasks for the communicative classroom*. Cambridge, UK: Cambridge University Press.

Nunan, D. (1989b). *Understanding language classrooms: A guide for teacher-initiated action*. Englewood Cliffs, NJ: Prentice-Hall.

Nunan, D. (1993). *Introduction to discourse analysis*. Harmondsworth, UK: Penguin.

Nunan, D. (1996a). Hidden voices: Insiders' perspectives on classroom interaction. In K. M. Bailey & D. Nunan (Eds.), *Voices from the language classroom* (pp. 41–56). Cambridge, UK: Cambridge University Press.

Nunan, D. (1996b). Learner strategy training in the classroom: An action research study. *TESOL Journal, 6*(1), 35–41.

Nunan, D. (1999). *Second language teaching and learning*. Boston, MA: Heinle-Cengage Learning.

Nunan, D. (2003). The impact of English as a global language on educational policies and practices in the Asia-Pacific region. *TESOL Quarterly, 37*(4), 589–613.

Nunan, D. (2004). *Task-based language teaching*. Cambridge, UK: Cambridge University Press.

Nunan, D. (2011a, February). *Enhancing 21st century learning with Internet technology*. Workshop presented at the Amazing Minds Conference, Penang, Malaysia.

Nunan, D. (2011b). *Teaching English to young learners*. Anaheim, CA: Anaheim University Press.

Nunan, D., & Bailey, K. M. (2009). *Exploring second language classroom research: A comprehensive guide*. Boston, MA: Heinle Cengage.

Nunan, D., & Lamb, C. (1996). *The self-directed teacher: Managing the learning process*. Cambridge, UK: Cambridge University Press.

Ogle, D. M. (1986). K-W-L: A teaching model that develops active reading of expository text. *Reading Teacher, 39*, 564–570.

O'Keeffe, A., & Farr, F. (2003). Using language corpora in language teacher education: Pedagogic, linguistic and cultural insights. *TESOL Quarterly, 37*(3), 389–418.

O'Keeffe A., & McCarthy, M. (Eds.). (2010). *The Routledge handbook of corpus linguistics*. London, UK: Routledge.

O'Keeffe, A., McCarthy M., & Carter, R. (2007). *From corpus to classroom: Language use and language teaching*. Cambridge, UK: Cambridge University Press.

Olshtain, E., & Celce-Murcia, M. (2001). Discourse analysis and language teaching. In D. Schiffrin, D. Tannen, & H. E. Hamilton (Eds.), *The handbook of discourse analysis* (pp. 706–724). Oxford, UK: Blackwell.

Olshtain, E., Crumlish, C., Goell, L., & Kneller, H. (1970). *English for speakers of Hebrew. Pre-reader workbook*. Tel Aviv, Israel: University Publishing Projects.

Olshtain, E., Feuerstein, T., Schcolnik, M., & Zerach, B. (1998). *Beginner's file one: Book and workbook*. Tel Aviv, Israel: University Publishing Projects.

Omaggio Hadley, A. (2001). *Teaching language in context* (3rd ed.). Boston, MA: Heinle and Heinle.

O'Malley, J. M., & Chamot, A. U. (1990). *Learning strategies in second language acquisition*. New York, NY: Cambridge University Press.

O'Malley, J. M., & Valdez Pierce, L. (1996). *Authentic assessment for English language learners*. Reading, MA: Addison-Wesley.

Ong, W. (1982). *Orality and literacy*. London, UK: Methuen.

Oprandy, R. (1999). Exploring with a supervisor. In J. Gebhard & R. Oprandy (Eds.), *Language teacher awareness* (pp. 99–121). New York, NY: Cambridge University Press.

O'Reilly, T. (2005, September 30). What is Web 2.0? Designing patterns and business models for the next generation of software [Web log comment]. Message posted to http://oreilly.com/web2/archive/what-is-web-20.html

Orfeld, G. (Ed.). (2004). *Dropouts in America: Confronting the graduation rate crisis*. Cambridge, MA: Harvard Education Press.

Orland-Barak, L. (2001). Learning to mentor as learning a second language of teaching: Conditions for development. *Cambridge Journal of Teacher Education, 31*(1), 53–68.

Ortega, L. (2009). *Understanding second language acquisition*. London, UK: Hodder Education.

Ortega, L. (2012). Language acquisition research for language teaching: Choosing between application and relevance. In B. Hinger, D. Newby, & E. M. Unterrainer (Eds.), *Sprachen lernen: Kompetenzen entwickeln? Performanzen (über) prüfen.* (pp. 24-38). Vienna, Austria: Präsens Verlag.

Ovando, C. J., & Collier, V. P. (1998). *Bilingual and ESL classrooms: Teaching in multicultural contexts* (2nd ed.). Boston, MA: McGraw-Hill.

Owens, C. (2002). Content-based English for academic purposes in a Thai university. In J. Crandall & D. Kaufman (Eds.), *Content-based instruction in higher education settings* (pp. 45–62). Alexandria, VA: Teachers of English to Speakers of Other Languages.

Oxford, R. L. (1990). *Language learning strategies: What every teacher should know*. Boston, MA: Heinle & Heinle.

Oxford, R. L. (1993). *Style analysis survey (SAS)*. Unpublished manuscript. University of Alabama, Tuscaloosa.

Oxford, R. L. (1999). "Style wars": As a source of anxiety in language classrooms. In D. J. Young (Ed.), *Affect in foreign language and second language learning* (pp. 216–237). Boston, MA: McGraw Hill.

Oxford, R. L. (2011). *Teaching and researching language learning strategies*. London, UK: Pearson.

Oxford University Press. (2011). *Oxford online placement test*. Oxford, UK: Author. Retrieved from http://www.oxfordenglishtesting.com/

Ozgungor, S., & Guthrie, J. (2004). Interactions among elaborative interrogation, knowledge, and interest in the process of constructing knowledge from text. *Journal of Educational Psychology, 96*, 437–443.

Palincsar, A., & Brown, A. (1984). Reciprocal teaching of comprehension-fostering and comprehension-monitoring activities. *Cognition and Instruction, 1*, 117–175.

Palmer, H. E. (1921/1964). *The principles of language study*. London, UK: Harrap. [Republished by Oxford University Press, Oxford, UK (1964) and edited by R. Mackin].

Paltridge, B. (2001). *Genre and the language learning classroom*. Ann Arbor, MI: University of Michigan Press.

Paltridge, B. (2009). Afterword: Where have we come from and where are we now? In D. Belcher (Ed.), *English for specific purposes in theory and practice* (pp. 289–296). Ann Arbor, MI: University of Michigan Press.

Papastergiou, M. (2006). Course management systems as tools for the creation of online learning environments: Evaluation from a social constructivist perspective and implications for their design. *International Journal on E-Learning, 5*(4), 593–622.

Papen, U. (2005). *Adult literacy as social practice*. New York, NY: Routledge.

Papi, M., & Abdollahzadeh, E. (2012). Teacher motivational practice, student motivation, and possible L2 selves: An examination in the Iranian EFL context. *Language Learning, 62*(2), 571–594.

Papies, E. K., & Aarts, H. (2011). Nonconscious self-regulation, or the automatic pilot of human behavior. In K. D. Vohs & R. F. Baumeister (Eds.), *Handbook of self-regulation: Research, theory, and applications* (2nd ed., pp. 125–142). New York, NY: Guilford Press.

Paradis, J., Genesee, F., & Crago, M. B. (2010). *Dual language development and disorders: A handbook on bilingualism and second language learning*. Baltimore, MD: Brookes Publishing.

Paradis, M. (1994). Neurolinguistic aspects of implicit and explicit memory: Implications for bilingualism and SLA. In N. Ellis (Ed.), *Implicit and explicit learning of languages* (pp. 393–420). London, UK: Academic Press.

Paran, A. (2006). *Literature in language: Teaching and learning*. Alexandria, VA: Teachers of English to Speakers of Other Languages.

Park, G. (2012). "I am never afraid of being recognized as an NNES": One teacher's journey in claiming and embracing her nonnative-speaker identity. *TESOL Quarterly, 46*(1), 127–150.

Park, J. K. (2000). *The effect of forms and meaning-focused instruction on ESL learners' phonological acquisition*. (Unpublished doctoral dissertation). University of Pennsylvania, Philadelphia. Retrieved from http://repository.upenn.edu/dissertations/AAI9976464/

Parkinson, B., & Thomas, H. R. (2001). *Teaching literature in a second language*. Edinburgh, UK: Edinburgh University Press.

Parrish, B. (2004). *Teaching adult ESL: A practical introduction*. New York, NY: McGraw Hill.

Partnership for 21st Century Skills. (2004). *A framework for 21st century learning*. Washington, DC: Author. Retrieved from http://www.p21.org/

Passel, J., Capps, R., & Fix, M. (2004, January). *Undocumented immigrants: Facts and figures*. Washington, DC: Urban Institute Immigration Studies Program. Retrieved from http://www.urban.org/UploadedPDF/1000587_undoc_immigrants_facts.pdf

Pasternak, M., & Bailey, K. M. (2004). Preparing nonnative and native English-speaking teachers: Issues of professionalism and proficiency. In L. D. Kamhi-Stein (Ed.), *Learning and teaching from experience: Perspectives on nonnative English-speaking professionals* (pp. 155–175). Ann Arbor, MI: University of Michigan Press.

Paton, A., & Wilkins, M. (2009). *Teaching adult ESOL: Principles and practice*. Maiden Head, UK: McGraw Hill.

Paulesu, E., McCrory, E., Fazio, F., Menoncello, L., Brunswick, N., Cappa, S., Cotelli, M., Cossu, G., Corte, F., Lorusso, M., Pesenti, S., Gallagher, A., Perani, D., Price, C., Frith, C. D., & Frith, U. (2000). A cultural effect on brain function. *Nature Neuroscience, 3*(1), 91–96.

Pavlenko, A. (2003). "I never knew I was a bilingual": Reimagining teacher identities in TESOL. *Journal of Language, Identity, and Education, 2*(2), 251–268.

Pawan, F., & Jacobson, A. (2003). Growing with the flow: Sustaining professionalism through online instruction of language teachers. In T. Murphey (Ed.), *Extending professional development* (pp. 67–75). Alexandria, VA: Teachers of English to Speakers of Other Languages.

Pawley, A., & Syder, F. (1983). Two puzzles for linguistic theory: Nativelike selection and nativelike fluency. In J. Richards & R. Schmidt (Eds.), *Language and communication* (pp. 191–226). London, UK: Longman.

Pawlikowska-Smith, G. (2000). *Canadian language benchmarks: English as a second language—for adults*. Ottawa, Ontario: Centre for Canadian Language Benchmarks. Retrieved from http://www.language.ca/pdfs/clb_adults.pdf

Pawlikowska-Smith, G. (2002). *Canadian language benchmarks: Theoretical framework*. Ottawa, Canada: Centre for Canadian Language Benchmarks. Retrieved from http://www.language.ca/display_page.asp?page_id=257

Payant, C., & Murphy, J. M. (2012). Cooperating teachers' roles and responsibilities in an MATESOL practicum. *TESL Canada Journal, 29*(2), 1–23.

Pecorari, D. (2003). Good and original: Plagiarism and patchwriting in academic second language writing. *Journal of Second Language Writing, 12*, 317–345.

Peirce, B. (1995). Social identity, investment and language learning. *TESOL Quarterly, 29*(1), 9–31.

Peirce, B., & Stewart, G. (1997). The development of the Canadian Language Benchmarks assessment. *TESL Canada Journal, 14*(2), 17–31.

Pelgrum, W., & Plomp, T. (2002). Indicators of ICT in mathematics: Status and covariation with achievement measures. In A. E. Beaton & D. F. Robitaille (Eds.), *Secondary analysis of the TIMSS data* (pp. 317–330). Dordrecht, The Netherlands: Kluwer.

Penfield, W., & Roberts, L. (1959). *Speech and brain mechanisms*. Princeton, NJ: Princeton University Press.

Pennington, M. C., & Richards, J. C. (1997). Reorienting the teaching universe: The experience of five first-year English teachers in Hong Kong. *Language Teaching Research, 1*(2), 149–178.

Pennycook, A. (1989). The concept of method, interested knowledge, and the politics of English language teaching. *TESOL Quarterly, 23*(4), 589–618.

Pennycook, A. (1996). Borrowing others' words: Text, ownership, memory, and plagiarism. *TESOL Quarterly, 30*(2), 201–230.

Pennycook, A. (Ed.). (1999). Critical approaches to TESOL [Special issue]. *TESOL Quarterly, 33*(3).

Peñuelas, A. (2008). A comparison of an effective and an ineffective writer's mental representations of their audience, rhetorical purpose and composing strategies. *Rael: Revista Electronica De Linguistica Aplicada, 7*, 90–104. Retrieved from http://dialnet.unirioja.es/servlet/articulo?codigo=2900631

PEP Curriculum Team. (2002). *PEP primary English: Student's book year 4*. Beijing, China: Lingo Media and People's Education Press.

PEP Curriculum Team. (2003a). *PEP primary English: Student's book year 5*. Beijing, China: Lingo Media and People's Education Press.

PEP Curriculum Team. (2003b). *Senior English for China: Student's book 2A*. Beijing, China: People's Education Press.

Petro, A. N. (2007). Finding the institutional logic for change. In A. Rice (Ed.), *Revitalizing an established program for adult learners* (pp. 119–134). Alexandria, VA: Teachers of English to Speakers of Other Languages.

Peyton, J. K., & Reed, L. (1990). *Dialogue journal writing with nonnative English speakers: A handbook for teachers*. Alexandria, VA: Teachers of English to Speakers of Other Languages.

Phakiti, A. (2007). *Strategic competence and EFL reading test performance*. New York, NY: Peter Lang.

Piaget, J. (1954). *The construction of reality in the child*. New York, NY: Basic Books.

Piaget, J. (1963). *The language and thought of the child*. New York, NY: W. W. Norton.

Piaget, J. (1970). *The science of education and the psychology of the child*. New York, NY: Oxford University Press.

Piaget, J. (1972). *The principles of genetic epistemology*. New York, NY: Basic Books.

Pica, T. (1983). Adult acquisition of English as a second language under different conditions of exposure. *Language Learning, 33*(4), 465–497.

Pica, T. (1997). Second language teaching and research relationships: A North American view. *Language Teaching Research, 1*(1), 48–72.

Pica, T. (2002). Subject-matter content: How does it assist the interactional and linguistic needs of classroom language learners? *The Modern Language Journal, 86*(1), 1–19.

Pickering, L. (2006). Current research on intelligibility in English as a lingua franca. *Annual Review of Applied Linguistics, 26*, 219–233.

Pienemann, M. (1989). Is language teachable? Psycholinguistic experiments and hypotheses. *Applied Linguistics, 10*(1), 52–79.

Pienemann, M., & Johnston, M. (1987). Factors influencing the development of language proficiency. In D. Nunan (Ed.), *Applying second language acquisition research* (pp. 45–141). Adelaide, Australia: National Curriculum Research Centre.

Piller, I. (2002). Passing for a native speaker: Identity and success in second language learning. *Journal of Sociolinguistics, 6*, 179–208.

Pinter, A. (2006). *Teaching young language learners*. Oxford, UK: Oxford University Press.

Plough, I., & Gass, S. (1993). Interlocutor and task familiarity: Effect on interactional structure. In G. Crookes & S. Gass (Eds.), *Tasks and language learning: Integrating theory and practice* (pp. 95–122). Clevedon, UK: Multilingual Matters.

Polio, C., & Duff, P. (1994). Teachers' language use in university foreign language classrooms: A qualitative analysis of English and target language alternation. *The Modern Language Journal, 78*(3), 313–326.

Postovsky, V. A. (1974). Effects of delay in oral practice at the beginning of second language learning. *The Modern Language Journal, 58*(5/6), 229–239.

Potowski, K. (2007). *Language and identity in a dual immersion school*. Clevedon, UK: Multilingual Matters.

Potts, D., & Park, P. (2007). Partnering with students in curriculum change: Students researching students' needs. In A. Rice (Ed.), *Revitalizing an established program for adult learners* (pp. 181–202). Alexandria, VA: Teachers of English to Speakers of Other Languages.

Powers, D., & Farnum, M. (1997). *Effects of mode of presentation on essay scores* (ETS-RM-97-08). Princeton, NJ: Educational Testing Service.

Prabhu, N. S. (1987). *Second language pedagogy.* Oxford, UK: Oxford University Press.

Prabhu, N. S. (1990). There is no best method—why? *TESOL Quarterly, 24*(2), 161–176.

Prater, K. (2009). Reading comprehension and English language learners. In S. E. Israel & G. G. Duffy (Eds.), *Handbook of research on reading comprehension* (pp. 607–621). New York, NY: Routledge.

Prator, C. H. (1974). Invited lecture on the history of language teaching, delivered in English 370K, University of California, Los Angeles.

Prator, C. H. (with Celce-Murcia, M.). (1979). An outline of language-teaching approaches. In M. Celce-Murcia & L. McIntosh (Eds.), *Teaching English as a second or foreign language* (pp. 3–5). Rowley, MA: Newbury House.

Pressley, M. (2002). Metacognition and self-regulated comprehension. In A. Farstrup & S. Samuels (Eds.), *What research has to say about reading instruction* (pp. 291–309). Newark, NJ: International Reading Association.

Pressley, M. (2006). *Reading instruction that works* (3rd ed.). New York, NY: Guilford Press.

Price, D., Carvajal, R., & McGee, A. (2010, Fall). ESL instructor and nurse team teach I-BEST class. *CALProgress Newsletter, 9,* 6–7. Retrieved from http://www.calpro-online.org/documents/CALPROgressFall2010.pdf

Proctor, C. P., August, D., Carlo, M., & Barr, C. (2010). Language maintenance versus language of instruction: Spanish reading development among Latino and Latina bilingual learners. *Journal of Social Issues, 66*(1), 79–94.

Pulido, D., & Hambrick, D. Z. (2008). The virtuous circle: Modeling individual differences in L2 reading and vocabulary development. *Reading in a Foreign Language, 20,* 164–190.

Purcell-Gates, V., Degener, S., Jacobson, E., & Soler, M. (2001, April). Taking literacy skills home. *Focus on Basics, 4*(D), 19–22. Retrieved from http://www.ncsall.net/?id=286

Purgason., K. (1991). Planning lessons and units. In M. Celce-Murcia (Ed.), *Teaching English as a second or foreign language* (2nd ed., pp. 419–431). New York, NY: Newbury House.

Purpura, J. E. (1999). *Learner strategy use and performance on language tests: A structural equation modeling approach.* Cambridge, UK: Cambridge University Press.

Purpura, J. E. (2004). *Assessing grammar.* Cambridge, UK: Cambridge University Press.

Purpura, J. E. (2012, March). *What is the role of strategic competence in a processing account of L2 learning or use?* Paper presented at the American Association for Applied Linguistics Conference, Boston, MA.

Purpura, J. E., & Pinkley, D. (1999). *On Target I.* White Plains, NY: Pearson Education.

Quigley, B. (1993). To shape the future: Towards a framework for adult education, social policy research and action. *International Journal of Lifelong Education, 12*(2), 117–127.

Quintero, E. A. (2008). A crossroads: Family education programs. In K. M. Rivera & A. Huerta-Macias (Eds.), *Adult biliteracy: Sociocultural and programmatic responses* (pp. 115–130). New York, NY: Lawrence Erlbaum Associates.

Quirk, R. (1990). Language varieties and standard language. *English Today, 21,* 3–10.

Quirke, P. (2001). Hearing voices: A robust and flexible framework for gathering and using student feedback. In S. Midraj, A. Jendli, & A. Sellami (Eds.), *Research in ELT contexts* (pp. 81–91). Dubai, UAE: TESOL Arabia.

Raimes, A. (1985). What unskilled ESL students do as they write: A classroom study of composing. *TESOL Quarterly, 19*(2), 229–258.

Raimes, A. (1991). Out of the woods: Emerging traditions in the teaching of writing. *TESOL Quarterly, 25*(3), 407–430.

Rajagopalan, K. (2007). From madness in method to method in madness. *ELT Journal, 62*(1), 84–85.

Ramírez, J. D., Wiley, T., de Klerk, G., Lee, E., & Wright, W. (2005). *Ebonics: The urban education debate* (2nd ed.). Clevedon, UK: Multilingual Matters.

Ranta, L., & Lyster, R. (2007). A cognitive approach to improving immersion students' oral language abilities: The awareness-practice-feedback sequence. In R. DeKeyser (Ed.), *Practicing for second language use: Perspectives from applied linguistics and cognitive psychology* (pp. 141–160). Cambridge, UK: Cambridge University Press.

Raphael, T. E., George, M., Weber, C. M., & Nies, A. (2009). Approach to teaching reading comprehension. In S. E. Israel & G. G. Duffy (Eds.), *Handbook of research on reading comprehension* (pp. 449–469). New York, NY: Routledge.

Rasinski, T. V. (2010). *The fluent reader: Oral & silent reading strategies for building fluency, word recognition and comprehension.* New York, NY: Scholastic Books.

Rasinski, T., Blachowicz, C., & Lems, K. (Eds.). (2006). *Fluency instruction: Research-based best practices.* New York, NY: Guilford Press.

Ravitch, D. (2010). *The death and life of the great American school system: How testing and choice are undermining education.* New York, NY: Basic Books.

Rea-Dickens, P. (2001). Mirror, mirror on the wall: Identifying processes of classroom assessment. *Language Testing, 18*(4), 429–462.

Reese, L., Garnier, H., Gallimore, R., & Goldenberg, C. (2000). Longitudinal analysis of the antecedents of emergent Spanish literacy and middle-school English reading achievement of Spanish-speaking students. *American Educational Research Journal, 37,* 633–662.

Reid, J. (1995). (Ed.), *Learning styles in the ESL/EFL classroom.* Boston, MA: Heinle and Heinle.

Reid, J. M. (1998a). "Eye" learners and "ear" learners: Identifying the language needs of international and U.S. resident writers. In P. Byrd & J. M. Reid (Eds.), *Grammar in the composition classroom: Essays on teaching ESL for college-bound students* (pp. 118–137). New York, NY: Heinle and Heinle.

Reid, J. M. (1998b). Learning styles and grammar teaching in the composition classroom. In P. Byrd & J. M. Reid (Eds.), *Grammar in the composition classroom: Essays on teaching ESL for college-bound students* (pp. 18–30). New York, NY: Heinle and Heinle.

Reid, J. (2001). Writing. In R. Carter & D. Nunan (Eds.), *The Cambridge guide to teaching English to speakers of other languages* (pp. 28–33). Cambridge, UK: Cambridge University Press.

Reid, J., & Kroll, B. (1995). Designing and assessing effective classroom writing assignments for NES and ESL students. *Journal of Second Language Writing, 4*(1), 17–41.

Reis, D. S. (2011). "I'm not alone": Empowering non-native English-speaking teachers to challenge the native speaker myth. In K. E. Johnson & P. R. Golombek (Eds.), *Research on second language teacher education: A sociocultural perspective on professional development* (pp. 31–49). New York, NY: Routledge.

Reiss, J. (2005). *Teaching content to English language learners: Strategies for secondary school success.* New York, NY: Pearson.

Renandya, W. A., & Jacobs, G. M. (2002). Extensive reading: Why aren't we all doing it? In J. C. Richards & W. A. Renandya (Eds.), *Methodology in language teaching: An anthology of current practice* (pp. 295–302). New York, NY: Cambridge University Press.

Reppen, R. (2010). *Using corpora in the language classroom.* Cambridge, UK: Cambridge University Press.

Reutzel, D. R., Fawson, P. C., & Smith, J. A. (2008). Reconsidering silent sustained reading: An exploratory study of scaffolded silent reading. *The Journal of Educational Research, 102*(1), 37–50.

Reutzel, D. R., Jones, C. D., & Newman, T. H. (2010). Scaffolded silent reading: Improving the conditions of silent reading practice in classrooms. In E. H. Hiebert & D. R. Reutzel (Eds.), *Revisiting silent reading: New directions for teachers and researchers* (pp. 129–150). Newark, DE: International Reading Association.

Reynolds, D. (2005). Linguistic correlates of second language literacy development: Evidence from middle-grade learner essays. *Journal of Second Language Writing, 14,* 19–45.

Ribe, R., & Vidal, N. (1993). *Project work step by step.* Oxford, UK: Heinemann.

Ricento, T. (1987). Clausal ellipsis in multi-party conversation in English. *Journal of Pragmatics, 11*(6), 751–775.

Richard-Amato, P. A., & Snow, M. A. (Eds.). (2005). *Academic success for English language learners: Strategies for K–12 mainstream teachers.* White Plains, NY: Longman.

Richards, I. A. (1942). *How to read a page: A course in efficient reading with an introduction to a hundred great words.* New York, NY: W. W. Norton & Company.

Richards, J. C. (1983). Listening comprehension: Approach, design, procedure. *TESOL Quarterly, 17*(2), 219–240.

Richards, J. C. (1984). The secret life of methods. *TESOL Quarterly, 18*(1), 7–23.

Richards, J. C. (1998). *Teaching in action: Case studies from second language classrooms.* Alexandria, VA: Teachers of English to Speakers of Other Languages.

Richards, J. C. (2001a). *Curriculum development in language teaching.* New York, NY: Cambridge University Press.

Richards, J. C. (2001b). *The role of textbooks in a language program.* Retrieved from http://professorjackrichards.com /work.htm

Richards, J. C. (2006a). *Communicative language teaching today.* Cambridge: Cambridge University Press. Retrieved from http:// www.cambridge.org/other_files/downloads/esl/booklets /Richards-Communicative-Language.pdf

Richards, J. C. (2006b). Materials development and research— Making the connection. *RELC Journal, 37*(1), 5–26. Retrieved from http://professorjackrichards.com /work.htm

Richards, J. C. (2008). *Teaching listening and speaking: From theory to practice.* Cambridge, UK: Cambridge University Press.

Richards, J. C., & Bohlke, D. (2011). *Creating effective language lessons.* Cambridge University Press. Retrieved from http://www .cambridge.org/other_files/downloads/esl/fourcorners /Pedagogical_Books/Creating-Effective-Language-Lessons-Combined.pdf

Richards, J. C., & Bohlke, D. (2012). *Four corners level 2: Student's book with self-study CD-ROM.* New York, NY: Cambridge University Press.

Richards, J. C., & Farrell, T. S. C. (2005). *Professional development of language teachers: Strategies for teacher learning.* Cambridge, UK: Cambridge University Press.

Richards, J. C., & Farrell, T. S. C. (2011). *Practice teaching: A reflective approach.* New York, NY: Cambridge University Press.

Richards, J. C. (with Hull, J., & Proctor, S.). (2012). *New interchange* (4th ed.). Cambridge, UK: Cambridge University Press.

Richards, J. C., & Lockhart, C. (1994a). Interaction in the second language classroom. In J. C. Richards (Ed.), *Reflective teaching in second language classrooms* (pp. 138–158). Cambridge, UK: Cambridge University Press.

Richards, J. C., & Lockhart, C. (1994b). *Reflective teaching in second language classrooms.* Cambridge, UK: Cambridge University Press.

Richards, J. C., & Rodgers, T. S. (2001). *Approaches and methods in language teaching: A description and analysis* (2nd ed.). New York, NY: Cambridge University Press.

Richards, J. C., & Sandy, C. (2008). *Passages* (2nd ed.). Cambridge, UK: Cambridge University Press.

Richards, J. C., & Schmidt, R. (2010). *Longman dictionary of language teaching and applied linguistics* (4th ed.). New York, NY: Pearson Education.

Richards, M., & Burnaby, B. (2008). Restoring aboriginal languages: Immersion and intensive language program models in Canada. In T. W. Fortune & D. J. Tedick (Eds.), *Pathways to multilingualism: Evolving perspectives on immersion education* (pp. 221–241). Clevedon, UK: Multilingual Matters.

Riches, C., & Genesee, F. (2006). Crosslinguistic and crossmodal issues. In F. Genesee, K. Lindholm-Leary, W. Saunders, & D. Christian (Eds.), *Educating English language learners* (pp. 64–108). New York, NY: Cambridge University Press.

Rickford, J., & Rickford, A. (1995). Dialect readers revisited. *Linguistics and Education, 7,* 107–128.

Rifkin, B. (2006). A ceiling effect for communicative language teaching? *The Modern Language Journal, 90*(2), 262–264.

Riggenbach, H. (1999). *Discourse analysis in the language classroom: The spoken language* (Vol. 1). Ann Arbor, MI: University of Michigan Press.

Rixon, S. (1981). *The design of materials to foster particular listening strategies.* London, UK: British Council.

Roberts, C., & Cooke, M. (2009). Authenticity in the adult ESOL classroom and beyond. *TESOL Quarterly, 43*(4), 620–642.

Robinson, P. (1996). Learning simple and complex second language rules under implicit, incidental, rule-search, and instructed conditions. *Studies in Second Language Acquisition, 18*(1), 27–67.

Roca de Larios, J., Murphy, L., & Marin, J. (2002). A critical examination of L2 writing process research. In S. Ransdell & M. Barbier (Eds.), *New directions in research on L2 writing* (Vol. 11, pp. 11–47). Dordrecht, The Netherlands: Kluwer.

Roediger, I., & Guynn, M. (1996). Retrieval processes. In E. Bork & R. Bork (Eds.), *Memory* (pp. 197–236). New York, NY: Academic Press.

Rogers, C. (1969). *Freedom to learn.* Columbus, OH: Charles Merrill.

Rogerson-Revell, P. (2007). Using English for international business: A European case study. *English for Specific Purposes, 26,* 103–120.

Roit, M. (2006). Essential comprehension strategies for English learners. In T. Young & N. Hadaway (Eds.), *Supporting the literacy development of English learners* (pp. 80–95). Newark, DE: International Reading Association.

Rolstad, K. (2005). Rethinking academic language in second language instruction. In J. Cohen, K. McAlister, K. Rolstad, & J. MacSwan (Eds.), *Proceedings of the 4th International Symposium on Bilingualism* (pp. 1993–1999). Somerville, MA: Cascadilla Press.

Römer, U. (2004). Comparing real and ideal language learner input: The use of an EFL textbook corpus in corpus linguistics and language teaching. In G. Aston, G. Bernardini, & D. Stewart (Eds.), *Corpora and language learners* (pp. 151–168). Amsterdam, The Netherlands: John Benjamins.

Römer, U. (2011). Corpus research applications in second language teaching. *Annual Review of Applied Linguistics, 31,* 205–225.

Rosen, N. G., & Sasser, L. (1997). Sheltered English: Modifying content delivery for second language learners. In M. A. Snow & D. M. Brinton (Eds.), *The content-based classroom: Perspectives on integrating language and content* (pp. 35–45). New York, NY: Longman.

Rosenblatt, L. (1978). *The reader, the text, the poem.* Carbondale, IL: Southern Illinois University Press.

Rosenkjar, P. (2006). American English as cultural expression: Designing a new course in linguistic analysis of culture for EFL undergraduates in Japan. In M. A. Snow & L. D. Kamhi-Stein (Eds.), *Developing a new course for adult learners* (pp. 123–142). Alexandria, VA: Teachers of English to Speakers of Other Languages.

Rost, M. (1990). *Listening in language learning.* London, UK: Longman.

Rost, M. (1994). *Introducing listening.* London, UK: Penguin English Applied Linguistics.

Rost, M. (2011). *Teaching and researching listening* (2nd ed.). London, UK: Longman.

Rounds, P. L. (1987). Characterizing successful classroom discourse for NNS teaching assistant training. *TESOL Quarterly, 21*(4), 643–671.

Royal, W. (2010). *The philosopher's teahouse: Implementing critical pedagogy in multicultural ESL academic preparation classes.* (Unpublished doctoral dissertation). University of British Columbia, Vancouver, Canada.

Royal, W., White, J., & McIntosh, H. (2007). Revitalizing a curriculum: The long and winding road. In A. Rice (Ed.), *Revitalizing an established program for adult learners* (pp. 57–78). Alexandria, VA: Teachers of English to Speakers of Other Languages.

Rubin, D. (1992). Nonlanguage factors affecting undergraduates' judgments of nonnative English-speaking teaching assistants. *Research in Higher Education, 33,* 511–531.

Rubin, J. (1975). What the "good language learner" can teach us. *TESOL Quarterly, 9*(1), 41–51.

Rumberger, R., & Tran, L. (2010). State language policies, school language practices, and the English learner achievement gap. In P. Gándara & M. Hopkins (Eds.), *Forbidden language: English learners and restrictive language policies* (pp. 86–101). New York, NY: Teachers College Press.

Russell, M., & Tao, W. (2004). Effects of handwriting and computer-print on composition scores: A follow up to Powers et al. *Practical Assessment, Research and Evaluation, 9.* Retrieved from http:// pareonline.net/getvn.asp?v=9&n=1

Rutherford, W. E. (1987). *Second language grammar: Learning and teaching.* London, UK: Longman.

Rutherford, W. E., & Sharwood Smith, M. (Eds.). (1988). *Grammar and second language teaching: A book of readings.* New York, NY: Newbury House.

Sabander, J. (1989). *Language learning in large classes in Indonesia: Lancaster-Leeds language learning in large classes research project* (Report No. 9). Leeds, UK: Lancaster-Leeds Language Learning.

Saito, K., & Lyster, R. (2011). Effects of form-focused instruction and corrective feedback on L2 pronunciation development of /ɹ/ by Japanese learners of English. *Language Learning.* doi:10.1111 /j.1467-9922.2011.00639.x.

Salehzadeh, J. (2009). *Academic listening strategies.* Ann Arbor, MI: University of Michigan Press.

Samimy, K. K., & Brutt-Griffler, J. (1999). To be a native or a non-native speaker: Perceptions of "non-native" students in a graduate TESOL program. In G. Braine (Ed.), *Non-native educators in English language teaching* (pp. 127–144). Mahwah, NJ: Lawrence Erlbaum Associates.

Samraj, B. (2002). Introductions in research articles: Variations across disciplines. *English for Specific Purposes, 21*, 1–17.

Samuda, V. (2001). Guiding relationships between form and meaning in task performance: The role of the teacher. In M. Bygate, P. Skehan, & M. Swain (Eds.), *Task-based learning: Language teaching, learning and assessment* (pp. 119–134). Harlow, UK: Pearson.

Samuels, S. J. (2006). Reading fluency: Its past, present, and future. In T. Rasinski, C. Blachowicz, & K. Lems (Eds.), *Fluency instruction: Research-based best practices* (pp. 7–20). New York, NY: The Guilford Press.

Samway, K. D. (1994). But it's hard to keep fieldnotes while also teaching. *TESOL Journal, 4*(1), 47–48.

Samway, K. D. (2006). *When English language learners write: Connecting research to practice, K–8.* Portsmouth, NH: Heinemann.

Santa Monica Convention and Visitors Bureau. (1998). *Santa Monica official visitors guide.* Santa Monica, CA: Author.

Saroyan, W. (1984). Out of order. In S. McKay & D. Pettit (Eds.), *At the door: Selected literature for ESL students* (pp. 104–109). Englewood Cliffs, NJ: Prentice-Hall.

Sasaki, M. (2000). Toward an empirical model of EFL writing processes: An exploratory study. *Journal of Second Language Writing, 9*, 259–291.

Sato, K., & Takahashi, K. (2008). Curriculum revitalization in a Japanese high school: Teacher-teacher and teacher-university collaboration. In D. Hayes & J. Sharkey (Eds.), *Revitalizing a curriculum for school-age learners* (pp. 205–238). Alexandria, VA: Teachers of English to Speakers of Other Languages.

Saunders, W., & Goldenberg, C. (2010). Research to guide English language development instruction. In California Department of Education, *Improving education for English learners: Research-based approaches* (pp. 21–82). Sacramento, CA: California Department of Education.

Savignon, S. (1983). *Communicative competence: Theory and classroom practice.* Reading, MA: Addison-Wesley.

Savignon, S. (2001). Communicative language teaching for the twenty-first century. In M. Celce-Murcia (Ed.), *Teaching English as a second or foreign language* (3rd ed., pp. 13–28). Boston, MA: Heinle and Heinle.

Savignon, S. (2005). Communicative language teaching: Strategies and goals. In E. Hinkel (Ed.), *Handbook of research in second language teaching and learning* (pp. 635–651). Mahwah, NJ: Lawrence Erlbaum Associates.

Savignon, S. (2007). Beyond communicative language teaching: What's ahead? *Journal of Pragmatics, 39*, 207–220.

Saville-Troike, M. (2003). *The ethnography of communication: An introduction* (3rd ed.). Malden, MA: Blackwell.

Savova, L. (Ed.). (2009). *Using textbooks effectively.* Alexandria, VA: Teachers of English to Speakers of Other Languages.

Scales, J., Wennerstrom, A., Richard, D., & Wu, S. H. (2006). Language learners' perceptions of accent. *TESOL Quarterly, 40*(4), 715–738.

Scarcella, R. (2003). *Accelerating academic English: A focus on the English learner.* Oakland, CA: Regents of the University of California. Retrieved from http://exstream.ucsd.edu/UCPDI/webtool/html/publications/ell_book_all.pdf

Scarcella, R., Andersen, E., & Krashen, S. (Eds.). (1990). *Developing communicative competence in a second language.* Boston, MA: Heinle and Heinle.

Schachter, J. (1986). Three approaches to the study of input. *Language Learning, 36*(2), 211–225.

Schachter, J., & Celce-Murcia, M. (1977). Some reservations concerning error analysis. *TESOL Quarterly, 11*(4), 441–449.

Schachter, J., & Gass, S. L. (Eds.). (1996). *Second language classroom research: Issues and opportunities.* Mahwah, NJ: Lawrence Erlbaum Associates.

Schaetzel, K., Peyton, J. K., & Burt, M. (2007). *Professional development for adult ESL practitioners: Building capacity.* Washington, DC: Center for Applied Linguistics.

Schane, S. (1970). Linguistics, spelling, and pronunciation. *TESOL Quarterly, 4*(2), 137–141.

Schecter, S. R. (1997). My professional transformation. In C. P. Casanave & S. R. Schecter (Eds.), *On becoming a language educator: Personal essays on professional development* (pp. 101–108). Mahwah, NJ: Lawrence Erlbaum Associates.

Schecter, S. R., & Bayley, R. J. (2002). *Language as cultural practice: Mexicanos en el Norte.* Mahwah, NJ: Lawrence Erlbaum Associates.

Schegloff, E. A. (2007). *Sequence organization in interaction: A primer in conversation analysis* (Vol. 1). Cambridge, UK: Cambridge University Press.

Schiffrin, D. (1994). *Approaches to discourse.* Oxford. UK: Blackwell.

Schleppegrell, M. J. (1992). Subordination and linguistic complexity. *Discourse Processes, 15*, 117–131.

Schleppegrell, M. J. (1998). Grammar as resource: Writing a description. *Research in the Teaching of English, 32*, 182–211.

Schleppegrell, M. J. (2004). *The language of schooling: A functional linguistics perspective.* Mahwah, NJ: Lawrence Erlbaum Associates.

Schleppegrell, M. J. (2009, October). *Language in academic subject areas and classroom instruction: What is academic language and how can we teach it?* Paper presented at the Workshop on the Role of Language in School Learning: Implications for Closing the Achievement Gap, Menlo Park, CA.

Schmidt, R. (1990). The role of consciousness in second language learning. *Applied Linguistics, 11*(2), 129–158.

Schmidt, R. (1994a). Deconstructing consciousness: In search of useful definitions for applied linguistics. *AILA Review, 11*, 11–26.

Schmidt, R. (1994b). Implicit learning and the cognitive unconscious: Of artificial grammars and SLA. In N. Ellis (Ed.), *Implicit and explicit learning of languages* (pp. 165–209). London, UK: Academic Press.

Schmidt, R. (2001). Attention. In P. Robinson (Ed.), *Cognition and second language instruction* (pp. 3–32). Cambridge, UK: Cambridge University Press.

Schmidt, R., & Frota, S. (1986). Developing basic conversational ability in a second language: A case study of an adult learner of Portuguese. In R. Day (Ed.), *Talking to learn: Conversation in second language acquisition* (pp. 237–326). Rowley, MA: Newbury House.

Schmitt, N. (1997). Vocabulary learning strategies. In N. Schmitt & M. McCarthy (Eds.), *Vocabulary: Description, acquisition and pedagogy* (pp. 199–227). Cambridge, UK: Cambridge University Press.

Schmitt, N. (2000). *Vocabulary in language teaching.* Cambridge, UK: Cambridge University Press.

Schmitt, N. (Ed.). (2004). *Formulaic sequences.* Amsterdam, The Netherlands: John Benjamins.

Schmitt, N. (2008). Instructed second language vocabulary learning. *Language Teaching Research, 12*(3), 329–363.

Schmitt, N., Jiang, X., & Grabe, W. (2011). The percentage of words known in a text and reading comprehension. *The Modern Language Journal, 95*(1), 26–43. doi:10.1111/j.1540-4781.2011.01146.x

Schön, D. (1983). *The reflective practitioner: How professionals think in action.* New York, NY: Basic Books.

Schramm, W. (1956). Why adults read. In N. B. Henry (Ed.), *Adult reading, Fifty-fifth yearbook of the National Society for the Study of Education* (Part II, pp. 55–88). Chicago, IL: University of Chicago Press.

Schwanenflugel, P., & Ruston, H. (2008). Becoming a fluent reader: From theory to practice. In M. Kuhn & P. Schwanenflugel (Eds.), *Fluency in the classroom* (pp. 1–16). New York, NY: Guilford Press.

Schwartz, M. (2006). For whom do we write the curriculum? *Journal of Curriculum Studies, 38*(4), 449–457.

Scollon, R., & Scollon, S. (2001). *Intercultural communication* (2nd ed.). Oxford, UK: Blackwell.

The Scottish Government. (2007). *The adult ESOL strategy for Scotland.* Retrieved from http://www.scotland.gov.uk/Publications/2007/05/09155324/0

Scovel, T. (1988). *A time to speak: A psycholinguistic inquiry into the critical period for human speech.* Rowley, MA: Newbury House.

Scovel, T. (2000). A critical review of the critical period research. *Annual Review of Applied Linguistics, 20*, 213–223.

The Secretary's Commission on Achieving Necessary Skill (SCANS). (1999). *Skills and tasks for jobs: A SCANS report for America 2000.* Washington, DC: U.S. Department of Labor. Retrieved from http://wdr.doleta.gov/opr/FULLTEXT/1999_35.pdf

Segalowitz, N. (2003). Automaticity and second languages. In C. J. Doughty & M. H. Long (Eds.), *The handbook of second language acquisition* (pp. 382–408). Malden, MA: Blackwell.

Seidlhofer, B. (1999). Double standards: Teacher education in the expanding circle. *World Englishes, 18*(2), 233–245.

Seidlhofer, B. (2001). Closing a conceptual gap: The case for a description of English as a lingua franca. *International Journal of Applied Linguistics, 11*(2), 133–158.

Seidlhofer, B. (2004). Research perspectives on teaching English as a lingua franca. *Annual Review of Applied Linguistics, 24,* 209–239.

Seidlhofer, B., Breiteneder, A., & Pitzl, M. L. (2006). English as a lingua franca in Europe: Challenges for applied linguistics. *Annual Review of Applied Linguistics, 26,* 3–34.

Seliger, H. W. (1983). The language learner as linguist: Of metaphors and realities. *Applied Linguistics, 4*(3), 179–191.

Selvi, A. F. (2010). All teachers are equal, but some teachers are more equal than others: Trend analysis of job advertisements in English language teaching. *WATESOLNNEST Caucus Annual Review, 1,* 156–181.

Senior, R. (1997). Transforming language classes into bonded groups. *ELT Journal, 51*(1), 3–11.

Senior, R. (2006). *The experience of language teaching.* Cambridge, UK: Cambridge University Press.

Setter, J. (2006). Speech rhythm in World Englishes: The case of Hong Kong. *TESOL Quarterly, 40*(4), 763–782.

Shamim, F. (1996). In or out of the action zone: Location as a feature of interaction in large ESL classes in Pakistan. In K. M. Bailey & D. Nunan (Eds.), *Voices from the language classroom* (pp. 123–144). Cambridge, UK: Cambridge University Press.

Sharkey, J., & Cade, L. (2008). Living things are interdependent: An ecological perspective on curriculum revitalization. In D. Hayes & J. Sharkey (Eds.), *Revitalizing a curriculum for school-age learners* (pp. 179–204). Alexandria, VA: Teachers of English to Speakers of Other Languages.

Sharwood Smith, M. (1993). Input enhancement in instructed SLA: Theoretical bases. *Studies in Second Language Acquisition, 15*(2), 165–179.

Shaw, P. A. (1996). Voices for improved learning: The ethnographer as co-agent of pedagogic change. In K. M. Bailey & D. Nunan (Eds.), *Voices from the language classroom* (pp. 318–337). Cambridge, UK: Cambridge University Press.

Sheen, R. (2003). Focus on form: A myth in the making? *ELT Journal, 57*(3), 225–233.

Sheen, Y. (2010). The role of corrective feedback in second language acquisition: An introduction to the special issue. *Studies in Second Language Acquisition, 32*(2), 169–179.

Sheerin, S. (1987). Listening comprehension: Teaching or testing? *ELT Journal, 41*(2), 126–131.

Shehadeh, A. (2003). Learner output, hypothesis testing, and internalizing linguistic knowledge. *System, 32,* 155–171.

Shepard, L. (2000). The role of assessment in a learning culture. *Educational Researcher, 29*(7), 4–14.

Shepard, L. (2000). *The role of classroom assessment in teaching and learning.* Washington, DC: Center for Research on Education, Diversity and Excellence/Center for Applied Linguistics.

Shermis, M. D., Burstein, J., Higgins, D., & Zechner, K. (2010). Automated essay scoring: Writing assessment and instruction. In P. Peterson, E. Baker, & B. McGraw (Eds.), *International encyclopedia of education* (3rd ed.). New York, NY: Elsevier.

Shi, L. (2004). Textual borrowing in second-language writing. *Written Communication, 21*(2), 171–200.

Shin, D., & Nation, I. S. P. (2008). Beyond single words: The most frequent collocations in spoken English. *ELT Journal, 62*(4), 339–348.

Shin, J. K. (2006). Ten helpful ideas for teaching English to young learners. *English Teaching Forum, 44*(2), 2–7, 13.

Shin, J. K. (2007). Developing dynamic units for EFL. *English Teaching Forum, 45*(2), 2–8.

Shiotsu, T. (2010). *Components of L2 reading: Linguistic and processing factors in reading test performances by Japanese EFL learners.* Cambridge, UK: Cambridge University Press.

Shohamy, E., Donitsa-Schmidt, S., & Ferman, I. (1996). Test impact revisited: Washback effect over time. *Language Testing, 13*(3), 298–317.

Short, D. J. (2002). Language learning in sheltered social studies classes. *TESOL Journal, 11*(1), 18–24.

Short, D. J., Fidelman, C. G., & Louguit, M. (2012). Developing academic language in English language learners through sheltered instruction. *TESOL Quarterly, 46*(2), 334–361.

Short, D. J., & Fitzsimmons, S. (2007). *Double the work: Challenges and solutions to acquiring language and academic literacy for adolescent English language learners* (Report to the Carnegie Corporation of New York). Washington, DC: Alliance for Excellent Education.

Shrum, J. L., & Glisan, E. W. (2010). *Teacher's handbook—Contextualized language instruction* (4th ed.). Boston, MA: Heinle Cengage.

Silva, T. (1993). Toward an understanding of the distinct nature of L2 writing: The ESL research and its implications. *TESOL Quarterly, 27*(4), 657–677.

Silver-Pacuilla, H. (2007) Assistive technology and adult literacy: Access and benefits. In J. Comings, B. Garner, & C. Smith (Eds.), *Review of adult learning and literacy: Connecting research, policy, and practice* (Vol. 7). Mahwah, NJ: Lawrence Erlbaum Associates.

Simpson, P. (1997). *Language through literature.* London, UK: Routledge.

Simpson-Vlach, R., & Ellis, N. (2010). An academic formulas list: New methods in phraseology research. *Applied Linguistics, 31*(4), 487–512.

Sinclair, J. (2004). *How to use corpora in language teaching.* Amsterdam, The Netherlands: John Benjamins.

Sinclair, J. M., & Coulthard, M. (1975). *Towards an analysis of discourse: The English used by teachers and pupils.* London, UK: Oxford University Press.

Sinclair, J., & Fox, G. (1990). *Collins COBUILD English grammar.* London, UK: Collins.

Singleton, D. (1995). Introduction: A critical look at the critical period hypothesis in second language acquisition research. In D. Singleton & Z. Lengyel (Eds.), *The age factor in second language acquisition* (pp. 1–29). Clevedon, UK: Multilingual Matters.

Singleton, D. (1999). *Exploring the second language mental lexicon.* Cambridge, UK: Cambridge University Press.

Singleton, D. (2001). Age and second language acquisition. *Annual Review of Applied Linguistics, 21,* 77–89. doi:10.1017/S0267190501000058

Siok, T., Zhen, J., Fletcher, P., & Tan, L. (2003). Distinct brain regions associated with syllable and phoneme. *Human Brain Mapping, 18,* 201–207.

Skehan, P. (1998). *A cognitive approach to language learning.* Oxford, UK: Oxford University Press.

Skierso, A. (1991). Textbook selection and evaluation. In M. Celce-Murcia (Ed.), *Teaching English as a second or foreign language* (2nd ed., pp. 432–453). New York, NY: Newbury House.

Skinner, B. F. (1957). *Verbal behavior.* New York, NY: Appleton-Century-Crofts.

Slatterly, M., & Willis, J. (2001). *English for primary teachers.* Oxford, UK: Oxford University Press.

Smith, L. E. (1992). Spread of English and issues of intelligibility. In B. B. Kachru (Ed.), *The other tongue: English across cultures* (2nd ed., pp. 75–90). Chicago, IL: University of Illinois Press.

Smith, L. E., & Nelson, C. L. (1985). International intelligibility of English: Directions and resources. *World Englishes, 4*(3), 333–342.

Snow, C. (2008). Cross-cutting themes and future research directions. In D. August & T. Shanahan (Eds.), *Developing reading and writing in second-language learners* (pp. 275–300). Washington, DC: Center for Applied Linguistics and International Reading Association.

Snow, M. A. (1997). Teaching academic literacy: Discipline faculty take responsibility. In M. A. Snow & D. M. Brinton (Eds.), *The content-based classroom: Perspectives on integrating language and content* (pp. 290–310). New York, NY: Longman.

Snow, M. A. (Ed.). (2000). *Implementing the ESL standards for pre-K–12 students through teacher education.* Alexandria, VA: Teachers of English to Speakers of Other Languages.

Snow, M. A. (2005). A model of academic literacy for integrated language and content instruction. In E. Hinkel (Ed.), *Handbook of research in second language teaching and learning* (pp. 693–712). Mahwah, NJ: Lawrence Erlbaum Associates.

Snow, M. A. (2013). Content-based language instruction. In C. A. Chapelle (Ed.), *The encyclopedia of applied linguistics* (pp. 906–911). Malden, MA: Wiley-Blackwell.

Snow, M. A., & Brinton, D. M. (Eds.). (1997). *The content-based classroom: Perspectives on integrating language and content*. White Plains, NY: Longman.

Snow, M. A., & Kamhi-Stein, L. D. (2002). Teaching and learning academic literacy through Project LEAP. In J. Crandall & D. Kaufman (Eds.), *Content-based instruction in higher education settings* (pp. 169–181). Alexandria, VA: Teachers of English to Speakers of Other Languages.

Snow, M. A., Kamhi-Stein, L. D., & Brinton, D. M. (2006). Teacher training for English as a lingua franca. *Annual Review of Applied Linguistics, 26*, 261–281.

Snow, M. A., & Katz, A. (2010). English language development: Foundations and implementation in kindergarten through grade five. In California Department of Education, *Improving education for English learners: Research-based approaches* (pp. 83–148). Sacramento, CA: California Department of Education.

Snyder, J., Bolin, F., & Zumwalt, K. (1992). Curriculum implementation. In P. W. Jackson (Ed.), *Handbook of research on curriculum* (pp. 402–435). New York, NY: Macmillan.

Sohn, S-O. S., & Merrill, C. C. (2008). The Korean/English dual language program in the Los Angeles Unified School District. In D. M. Brinton, O. Kagan, & S. Bauckus (Eds.), *Heritage language education: A new field emerging* (pp. 269–287). New York, NY: Routledge.

Sokolik, M. E. (2003). Student perceptions of classroom technology. *The CATESOL Journal, 15*(1), 43–50.

Spada, N. (1987). Relationships between instructional differences and learning outcomes: A process-product study of communicative language teaching. *Applied Linguistics, 8*(2), 137–161.

Spada, N. (1997). State of the art: A review of classroom and laboratory research. *Language Teaching, 30*, 73–87.

Spada, N. (2007). Communicative language teaching: Current status and future prospects. In J. Cummins & C. Davis (Eds.), *International handbook of English language teaching* (pp. 271–288). New York, NY: Springer.

Spada, N., & Lightbown, P. (1993). Instruction and the development of questions in L2 classrooms. *Studies in Second Language Acquisition, 15*(2), 205–224.

Spivey, M. (2007). *The continuity of mind*. Oxford, UK: Oxford University Press.

Spratt, M., Pulverness, A., & Williams, M. (2005). *The TKT (teaching knowledge test) course*. Cambridge, UK: Cambridge University Press.

Spring, J. (2011). *The politics of American education*. New York, NY: Routledge.

Spruck-Wrigley, H., & Guth, G. (1992) *Bringing literacy to life: Issues and options in adult ESL literacy*. San Mateo, CA: Aguirre International.

Starfield, S. (2007). New directions in student academic writing. In J. Cummins & C. Davison (Eds.), *The international handbook of English language teaching* (Vol. 2, pp. 875–890). Norwell, MA: Springer.

Starfield, S. (2011). Doing critical ethnographic research into academic writing: The theory of the methodology. In D. Belcher, A. M. Johns, & B. Paltridge (Eds.), *New directions in English for specific purposes research* (pp. 174–96). Ann Arbor, MI: University of Michigan Press.

Stein, P., & Janks, H. (1996). Collaborative teaching and learning with large classes: A case study from the University of Witwatersrand. *Perspectives in Education, 17*(1), 99–116.

Stenhouse, L. (1975). *An introduction to curriculum research and development*. London, UK: Heinemann.

Stern, H. H. (1975). What can we learn from the good language learner? *The Canadian Modern Language Review, 31*, 304–318.

Sternberg, R. (2002). The theory of successful intelligence and its implications for language aptitude testing. In P. Robinson (Ed.), *Individual differences and instructed language learning* (pp. 13–43). Amsterdam, The Netherlands: John Benjamins.

Stevens, R. A., Butler, F. A., & Castellon-Wellington, M. (2000). *Academic language and content assessment: Measuring the progress of ELLs*. University of California, Los Angeles: National Center for Research on Evaluation, Standards, and Student Testing (CRESST).

Stevens, V. (1993). Concordances as enhancements to language competence. *TESOL Matters, 2*(6), 11.

Stevick, E. (1986). *Images and options in the language classroom*. New York, NY: Cambridge University Press.

Stevick, E. W. (1990). *Humanism in language teaching: A critical perspective*. Oxford, UK: Oxford University Press.

Stewart, E. (1972). *American cultural patterns: A cross-cultural perspective*. Yarmouth, ME: Intercultural Press.

Stewart, E., & Bennett, M. (1991). *American cultural patterns: A cross-cultural perspective*. Yarmouth, ME: Intercultural Press.

Stewart, T. (2006). Teacher-researcher collaboration or teachers' research? *TESOL Quarterly, 40*(2), 421–430.

Stewart, T., & Lohon, E. (2003). Professional development through student and teacher reflection journals. In T. Murphey (Ed.), *Extending professional contributions* (pp. 19–27). Alexandria, VA: Teachers of English to Speakers of Other Languages.

Stillwell, C., Curabba, B., Alexander, K., Kidd, A., Kim, E., Stone, P., & Wyle, C. (2011). Students transcribing tasks: Noticing fluency, accuracy, and complexity. *ELT Journal, 64*(4), 445–455.

Stoller, F. L. (1993). Developing word and phrase recognition exercises. In R. Day (Ed.), *New ways in teaching reading* (pp. 230–233). Alexandria, VA: Teachers of English to Speakers of Other Languages.

Stoller, F. L. (2002a, March). *Content-based instruction: A shell for language teaching or a framework for strategic language and content learning?* Paper presented at the annual meeting of Teachers of English to Speakers of Other Languages (TESOL), Salt Lake City, UT.

Stoller, F. L. (2002b). Content-based instruction: Perspectives on curriculum planning. *Annual Review of Applied Linguistics, 24*, 261–283.

Stoller, F. L. (2006). Establishing a theoretical foundation for project-based learning in second and foreign language contexts. In G. H. Beckett & P. C. Miller (Eds.), *Project-based second and foreign language education* (pp. 19–40). Greenwich, CT: Information Age Publishing.

Stoller, F. L. (2008). Content-based instruction. In N. Van Deusen-Scholl & N. H. Hornberger (Eds.), *Encyclopedia of language and education* (2nd ed., Vol. 4, pp. 59–70). New York, NY: Springer.

Stoller, F. L., & Grabe, W. (1997). A six-T's approach to content-based instruction. In M. A. Snow & D. M. Brinton (Eds.), *The content-based classroom: Perspectives on integrating language and content* (pp. 78–94). New York, NY: Longman.

Storch, N. (2002). Patterns of interaction in ESL pair work. *Language Learning, 52*(1), 119–158.

Stranahan, S. (2011/2012). Professional development as a novice tutor: Navigating the process approach. *The CATESOL Journal, 23*(1), 45–50.

Strevens, P. (1977). *New orientations in the teaching of English*. Oxford, UK: Oxford University Press.

Strevens, P. (1988). ESP after twenty years: A re-appraisal. In M. Tickoo (Ed.), *ESP: State of the art* (pp. 1–13). Singapore: SEAMEO Regional Language Centre.

Strodt-Lopez, B. (1991). Tying it all in: Asides in university lectures. *Applied Linguistics, 12*(2), 117–140.

Suárez-Orozco, C., Suárez-Orozco, M., & Todorova, I. (2008). *Learning a new land: Immigrant students in American society*. Cambridge, MA: Harvard University Press.

Suidan, L., Badenhoop, J. K., Glendening E. D., & Weinhold, F. (1995). Common textbook and teaching misrepresentations of Lewis structures. *Journal of Chemical Education, 72*(7), 583–593.

Svinicki, M. D. (2004). *Learning and motivation in the postsecondary classroom*. San Francisco, CA: Anker/John Wiley and Sons.

Swain, M. (1985). Communicative competence: Some roles of comprehensible input and comprehensible output in its development. In S. M. Gass & C. Madden (Eds.), *Input and second language acquisition* (pp. 235–256). Rowley, MA: Newbury House.

Swain, M. (1988). Manipulating and complementing content teaching to maximize second language learning. *TESL Canada Journal, 6*(1), 68–83.

Swain, M. (1993). The output hypothesis: Just speaking and writing aren't enough. *Canadian Modern Language Review, 50*(1), 158–164.

Swain, M. (1995). Three functions of output in second language learning. In G. Cook & B. Seidlhofer (Eds.), *Principle and practice in applied linguistics: Studies in honor of H. G. Widdowson* (pp. 125–144). Oxford, UK: Oxford University Press.

Swain, M. (2000). The output hypothesis and beyond: Mediating acquisition through collaborative dialogue. In J. Lantolf (Ed.), *Sociocultural theory in second language learning* (pp. 97–114). Oxford, UK: Oxford University Press.

Swain, M. (2001). Integrating language and content teaching through collaborative tasks. *Canadian Modern Language Review, 58*(1), 44–63.

Swain, M. (2005). The output hypothesis: Theory and research. In E. Hinkel (Ed.), *The handbook of research in second language teaching and learning* (pp. 471–483). Mahwah, NJ: Lawrence Erlbaum Associates.

Swain, M., & Lapkin, S. (1998). Interaction and second language learning: Two adolescent French immersion students working together. *The Modern Language Journal, 82*(3), 320–337.

Swain, M., & Lapkin, S. (2002). Talking it through: Two French immersion learners' response to reformulation. *International Journal of Education Research, 37*, 285–304.

Swales, J. M. (1985). *Episodes in ESP*. New York, NY: Prentice Hall.

Swales, J. M. (1990). *Genre analysis: English in academic and research settings*. Cambridge, UK: Cambridge University Press.

Swales, J. M., & Feak, C. B. (2012). *Academic writing for graduate students: Essential tasks and skills* (3rd ed.). Ann Arbor, MI: University of Michigan Press.

Swan, E. A. (2003). *Concept-oriented reading instruction: Engaging classrooms, lifelong learners*. New York, NY: Guilford Press.

Swan, M. (2005). Legislation by hypothesis: The case of task-based instruction. *Applied Linguistics, 26*(3), 376–401.

Swan, M., & Smith, B. (Eds.). (2001). *Learner English: A teacher's guide to interference and other problems* (2nd ed.). Cambridge, UK: Cambridge University Press.

Takaki, N. (2005). Keeping a grassroots teacher development group growing. In T. Murphey & K. Sato (Eds.) *Communities of supportive professionals* (pp. 47–56). Alexandria, VA: Teachers of English to Speakers of Other Languages.

Tan, L., Liu, H., Perfetti, C., Spinks, J., Fox, P., & Gao, J. (2001). The neural system underlying Chinese logograph reading. *NeuroImage, 13*, 836–846.

Tanaka, K. (2004). *Language learning beliefs and language proficiency of Japanese learners of English in New Zealand*. (Unpublished doctoral dissertation). University of Auckland, New Zealand.

Tang, C. (1997). The identity of the nonnative ESL teacher: On the power and status of nonnative ESL teachers. *TESOL Quarterly, 31*(3), 577–580.

Tanner, M. W., & Landon, M. M. (2009). The effects of computer-assisted pronunciation readings on ESL learners' use of pausing, stress, intonation, and overall comprehensibility. *Language Learning and Technology, 13*(3), 51–65.

Tanner, R. (2003). Outside in, inside out: Creating a teaching portfolio. In P. Byrd & G. Nelson (Eds.), *Sustaining professionalism* (pp. 19–25). Alexandria, VA: Teachers of English to Speakers of Other Languages.

Tao, H., & McCarthy, M. J. (2001). Understanding non-restrictive *which*-clauses in spoken English, which is not an easy thing. *Language Sciences, 23*, 651–677.

Tarone, E., & Swierzbin, B. (2009). *Exploring learner language*. Oxford, UK: Oxford University Press.

Teachers of English to Speakers of Other Languages. (1997). *ESL standards for pre-K–12 students*. Alexandria, VA: Author.

Teachers of English to Speakers of Other Languages. (2000, October). *Adult ESL language and literacy instruction: A vision and action agenda for the 21st century*. Alexandria, VA: Author.

Teachers of English to Speakers of Other Languages. (2001). *Scenarios for ESL standards-based assessment*. Alexandria, VA: Author.

Teachers of English to Speakers of Other Languages. (2003). *Standards for adult ESL programs*. Alexandria, VA: Author.

Teachers of English to Speakers of Other Languages. (2006). *PreK–12 English language proficiency standards*. Alexandria, VA: Author.

Teachers of English to Speakers of Other Languages. (2007). *Integrating standards into Chinese classroom settings*. Retrieved from http://www.tesol.org/docs/pdf/5411.PDF

Teachers of English to Speakers of Other Languages. (2008). *Standards for ESL/EFL teachers of adults*. Alexandria, VA: Author.

Teachers of English to Speakers of Other Languages. (2009). *TESOL technology standards framework*. Alexandria, VA: Author.

Tedick, D. J., Christian, D., & Fortune, T. W. (Eds.). (2011). *Immersion education: Practices, policies, possibilities*. Clevedon, UK: Multilingual Matters.

Teschner, R. V., & Whitley, M. S. (2004). *Pronouncing English: A stress-based approach*. Washington, DC: Georgetown University Press.

Thomas, J. (1983). Cross-cultural pragmatic failure. *Applied Linguistics, 4*(2), 91–112.

Thomas, J. (1999). Voices from the periphery: Non-native teachers and issues of credibility. In G. Braine (Ed.), *Non-native educators in English language teaching* (pp. 5–14). Mahwah, NJ: Lawrence Erlbaum Associates.

Thompson, G. (1997). Training teachers to ask questions. *ELT Journal, 51*(2), 99–105.

Thornbury, S. (1999a). *How to teach grammar*. Harlow, UK: Pearson Longman.

Thornbury, S. (1999b). Lesson art and design. *ELT Journal, 53*(1), 4–11.

Thornbury, S. (2005). *How to teach speaking*. Harlow, UK: Pearson Longman.

Thornton, B., Touba, N. A., Bakr, S. M., & Ianuzzi, S. (2009). A new way for a new age: Developing a standards-based curriculum for young learners in Egypt. In K. Graves & L. Lopriore (Eds.), *Developing a new curriculum for school-age learners* (pp. 15–36). Alexandria, VA: Teachers of English to Speakers of Other Languages.

Tillitt, B., & Bruder, M. N. (1985). *Speaking naturally: Communication skills in American English*. New York, NY: Cambridge University Press.

Timperley, H. S., Parr, J. M., & Bertanees, C. (2009). Promoting professional inquiry for improved outcomes for students in New Zealand. *Professional Development in Education, 35*(2), 227–245. doi:10.1080/13674580802550094

Timperley, H., Wilson, A., Barrar, H., & Fung, I. (2007). *Teacher professional learning and development: Best evidence synthesis iteration*. Wellington, New Zealand: Ministry of Education.

Tomasello, M. (2003). *Constructing a language*. Cambridge, MA: Harvard University Press.

Tomasello, M., & Herron, C. (1988). Down the garden path: Inducing and correcting overgeneralization errors in the foreign language classroom. *Applied Psycholinguistics, 9*, 237–246.

Tomasello, M., & Herron, C. (1989). Feedback for language transfer errors: The garden path technique. *Studies in Second Language Acquisition, 11*(4), 385–395.

Tomlinson, B. (Ed.). (1998). *Materials development in language teaching*. Cambridge, UK: Cambridge University Press.

Tomlinson, B. (Ed.). (2003). *Developing materials for language teaching*. London, UK: Continuum.

Torres-Guzman, M., Abbate, J., Brisk, M. E., & Minaya-Rowe, L. (2002). Defining and documenting success for bilingual learners. *Bilingual Research Journal, 26*, 23–44.

Toth, P. (2006). Processing instruction and a role for output in second language acquisition. *Language Learning, 56*(2), 319–385.

Trabasso, T., & Bouchard, E. (2002). Teaching readers how to comprehend texts strategically. In C. Block & M. Pressley (Eds.), *Comprehension instruction: Research-based best practices* (pp. 176–200). New York, NY: Guilford Press.

Trofimovich, P., Lightbown, P. M., Halter, R. H., & Song, H. (2009). Comprehension-based practice: The development of L2 pronunciation in a listening and reading program. *Studies in Second Language Acquisition, 31*(4), 609–639.

Trudgill, P., & Hannah, J. (2008). *International English: A guide to the varieties of standard Englishes* (5th ed.). London, UK: Hodder.

Truscott, J. (1996). The case against grammar correction in L2 writing classes. *Language Learning, 46*(2), 327–369.

Truscott, J. (1999). "The case for grammar correction in L2 writing classes": A response to Ferris. *Journal of Second Language Writing, 8*, 111–122.

Truscott, J. (2007). The effect of error correction on learners' ability to write accurately. *Journal of Second Language Writing, 16*(4), 255–272.

Tsui, A. B. M. (1995). *An introduction to classroom interaction*. London, UK: Penguin.

Tsui, A. B. M. (1996). Reticence and anxiety in second language learning. In K. M. Bailey & D. Nunan (Eds.), *Voices from the language classroom* (pp. 145–167). Cambridge, UK: Cambridge University Press.

Tsui, A. B. M. (2001). Classroom interaction. In R. Carter & D. Nunan (Eds.), *The Cambridge guide to teaching English to speakers of other languages* (pp. 120–125). New York, NY: Cambridge University Press.

Tsui, A., & Fullilove, J. (1998). Bottom-up or top-down processing as a discriminator of L2 listening performance. *Applied Linguistics, 19*(4), 432–451.

Turnitin. (2010). Turnitin quick facts. Retrieved from http://turnitin.com/static/resources/documentation/turnitin/sales/Turnitin_Quick_Facts.pdf

Tyler, R. (1949). *Basic principles of curriculum and instruction.* New York, NY: Harcourt Brace.

Uber Grosse, C. (1988). The case study approach to teaching business English. *English for Specific Purposes Journal, 7*(2), 131–136.

Ullman, M. (2001). The declarative/procedural model of lexicon and grammar. *Journal of Psycholinguistic Research, 30*, 37–69.

Ulloa, T., & Crawford, J. (2007). Lost in translation: Bilingual education in the United States of America. *Revista de Lingüística Teórica y Aplicada, 45*, 87–99.

Underhill, N. (1987). *Testing spoken language: A handbook of oral testing techniques.* Cambridge, UK: Cambridge University Press.

Underwood, M. (1989). *Teaching listening.* London, UK: Longman.

University of Cambridge ESOL Examinations. (2009–2011). *IELTS.* Cambridge, UK: Author. Retrieved from http://www.ielts.org/

Ur, P. (1984). *Teaching listening comprehension.* Cambridge, UK: Cambridge University Press.

Ur, P. (1992). *Five-minute activities.* Cambridge, UK: Cambridge University Press.

Ur, P. (2009). *Grammar practice activities: A practical guide for teachers* (2nd ed.). Cambridge, UK: Cambridge University Press.

Ur, P. (2012). *A course in language teaching: Practice and theory* (2nd ed.). Cambridge, UK: Cambridge University Press.

Valdés, G. (2009). Commentary: Language, immigration, and the quality of education: Moving towards a broader conversation. In T. Wiley, J. S. Lee, & R. Rumberger (Eds.), *The education of language minority immigrants in the United States* (pp. 295–301). Bristol, UK: Multilingual Matters.

Valdés, G., & Figueroa, R. (1994). *Bilingualism and testing: A special case of bias.* Norwood, NJ: Ablex.

Valdés, G., Fishman, J., Chávez, R., & Pérez, W. (2006). *Developing minority language resources: The case of Spanish in California.* Clevedon, UK: Multilingual Matters.

van Ek, J. A. (1975). *The threshold level in a European unit/credit system for modern language learning by adults.* Strasbourg, France: Council for Cultural Co-operation of the Council of Europe.

van Ek, J. A. (1976). *The threshold level for modern language learning in schools.* London, UK: Longman.

Van Leeuwen, T. (2010). *Discourse and practice: New tools for critical discourse analysis.* Oxford, UK: Oxford University Press.

van Lier, L. (1994). Action research. *Sintagma, 6*, 31–37.

van Lier, L. (1995). *Introducing language awareness.* London, UK: Penguin.

van Lier, L. (1996). *Interaction in the language curriculum: Awareness, autonomy, and authenticity.* London, UK: Longman.

Vandergrift, L. (1997). The comprehension strategies of second language (French) listeners: A descriptive study. *Foreign Language Annals, 30*(3), 387–409.

Vandergrift, L. (2003). Orchestrating strategy use: Toward a model of the skilled second language listener. *Language Learning, 53*(3), 463–496.

Vandergrift, L. (2004). Learning to listen or listening to learn. *Annual Review of Applied Linguistics, 24*, 3–25.

Vandergrift, L., & Goh, C. (2009). Teaching and testing listening comprehension. In M. H. Long & C. J. Doughty (Eds.), *The handbook of language teaching* (pp. 395–411). Malden, MA: Blackwell.

Vandergrift, L., & Goh, C. (2012). *Teaching and learning second language listening: Metacognition in action.* New York, NY: Routledge.

Vandergrift, L., & Tafaghodtari, M. H. (2010). Teaching learners how to listen does make a difference: An empirical study. *Language Learning, 60*(2), 470–497.

VanPatten, B. (1996). *Input processing and grammar instruction in second language acquisition.* Norwood, NJ: Ablex.

VanPatten, B. (2002). Processing instruction: An update. *Language Learning, 52*(4), 755–803.

VanPatten, B., & Benati, A. G. (2010). *Key terms in second language acquisition.* New York, NY: Continuum.

Veenman, S. (1984). Perceived problems of beginning teachers. *Review of Educational Research, 54*, 143–178.

Velasco-Martin, C. (2004). The nonnative English-speaking teacher as an intercultural speaker. In L. D. Kamhi-Stein (Ed.), *Learning and teaching from experience: Perspectives on nonnative English-speaking professionals* (pp. 277–293). Ann Arbor, MI: University of Michigan Press.

Venezky, R. L. (1970). *The structure of English orthography.* The Hague, The Netherlands: Mouton.

Viadero, D. (2009). Research hones focus on ELLs. *Education Week, 28*(17), 3–5.

Virtual Language Centre. (n.d). Virtual Language Centre, Hong Kong. Retrieved from http://vlc.polyu.edu.hk/

Vygotsky, L. S. (1978). *Mind in society: Development of higher psychological processes.* Cambridge, MA: Harvard University Press.

Vygotsky, L. S. (1986). *Thought and language* (A. Kozulin, Trans.). Cambridge, MA: The MIT Press. (Original work published 1962.)

Walker, R. (2010). *Teaching the pronunciation of English as a lingua franca.* New York, NY: Oxford University Press.

Wall, D., & Alderson, J. C. (1993). Examining washback: The Sri Lankan impact study. *Language Testing, 10*(1), 41–69.

Wallace, M. (1991). *Training foreign language teachers: A reflective approach.* Cambridge, UK: Cambridge University Press.

Wallace, M. (1998). *Action research for language teachers.* Cambridge, UK: Cambridge University Press.

Walmsley, S. A. (1994). *Children exploring their world: Theme teaching in elementary school.* Portsmouth, NH: Heinemann.

Walqui, A. (2000). *Access and engagement: Program design and instructional approaches for immigrant students in secondary school.* McHenry, IL: Center for Applied Linguistics/Delta Systems.

Wardle, E., & Downs, D. (2011). *Writing about writing.* Boston, MA: Bedford/St. Martin's.

Waring, H. Z. (2009). Moving out of IRF (initiation-response-feedback): A single case study. *Language Learning, 59*(4), 796–824.

Warschauer, M. (1996). Motivational aspects of using computers for writing and communication. In M. Warschauer (Ed.), *Telecommunication in foreign language learning: Proceedings of the Hawaii symposium* (pp. 29–46). Honolulu, HI: University of Hawai'i, Second Language Teaching & Curriculum Center.

Warschauer, M. (2007). Technology and writing. In J. Cummins & C. Davison (Eds.), *The international handbook of English language teaching* (Vol. 2, pp. 907–917). Norwell, MA: Springer.

Warschauer, M., & Kern, R. (Eds.). (2000). *Network-based language teaching: Concepts and practice.* New York, NY: Cambridge University Press.

Watanabe, Y. (1996). Does grammar translation come from the entrance examination? Preliminary findings from classroom-based research. *Language Testing, 13*(3), 318–333.

Waters, J. (2006). Local adaptations to meet national requirements: Using role-play and text-modeling strategies to enable young English learners to access the national curriculum. In P. McKay (Ed.), *Planning and teaching creatively within a required curriculum for school-age learners* (pp. 101–124). Alexandria, VA: Teachers of English to Speakers of Other Languages.

Watts, J. (2009). Task evaluation. (Unpublished MA paper). University of Auckland, Auckland, New Zealand.

Webb, S. (2007). The effects of repetition on vocabulary knowledge. *Applied Linguistics, 28*(1), 46–65.

Wegrzecka-Kowalewski, E. (1997). Content-based instruction: Is it possible in high school? In M. A. Snow & D. M. Brinton (Eds.), *The content-based classroom: Perspectives on integrating language and content* (pp. 319–323). New York, NY: Longman.

Weigle, S. C. (2005). Second language writing expertise. In K. Johnson (Ed.), *Expertise in language learning and teaching* (pp. 128–149). Hampshire, UK: Palgrave Macmillan.

Weigle, S. C. (2007). Teaching writing teachers about assessment. *Journal of Second Language Writing, 16*(3), 194–209.

Weigle, S. C. (2010). Validation of automated scores of TOEFL iBT tasks against non-test indicators of writing ability. *Language Testing, 27*(3), 335–353.

Weinstein, G. (1999). *Learners' lives as curriculum: Six journeys to immigrant literacy.* McHenry, IL: Delta Publishing.

Weinstein, G. (2001). Developing adult literacies. In M. Celce-Murcia (Ed.), *Teaching English as a second or foreign language* (3rd ed., pp. 171–186). Boston: Heinle and Heinle.

Weinstein, G. (2004). Immigrant adults and their teachers: Community and professional development through family literacy. *The CATESOL Journal, 16*(1), 1–13.

Wenden, A. (1991). *Learner strategies for learner autonomy.* New York, NY: Prentice Hall.

Wenger, E. (1998). *Communities of practice: Learning, meaning and identity.* Cambridge, UK: Cambridge University Press.

Wenglinski, H. (1998). *Does it compute? The relationship between educational technology and student achievement in mathematics.* Princeton, NJ: Educational Testing Service.

Wennerstrom, A. (1994). Intonational meaning in English discourse: A study of nonnative speakers. *Applied Linguistics, 15*(4), 399–420.

Wesche, M. (1981). Language aptitude measures in streaming, matching students with methods, and diagnosis of learning problems. In K. Diller (Ed.), *Individual differences and universals in language learning aptitude* (pp. 235–252). Rowley, MA: Newbury House.

Wesche, M. B. (2010). Content-based second language instruction. In R. B. Kaplan (Ed.), *Oxford handbook of applied linguistics* (2nd ed., pp. 275–293). Oxford, UK: Oxford University Press.

West, M. (1941). *Learning to read a foreign language.* London, UK: Longman.

West, M. (1953). *A general service list of English words.* London, UK: Longman, Green & Co.

White, L. (1987). Against comprehensible input: The input hypothesis and the development of second-language competence. *Applied Linguistics, 8*(2), 95–110.

White, L., Spada, N., Lightbown, P., & Ranta, L. (1991). Input enhancement and L2 question formation. *Applied Linguistics, 12*(4), 416–432.

Wida Software. (1998). *TestMaster* [Computer software]. London, UK: Author.

Widdowson, H. G. (1975). *Stylistics and the teaching of literature.* London, UK: Longman.

Widdowson, H. G. (1978). *Teaching language as communication.* Oxford, UK: Oxford University Press.

Widdowson, H. G. (1992). *Practical stylistics: An approach to poetry.* Oxford, UK: Oxford University Press.

Widdowson, H. G. (1994). The ownership of English. *TESOL Quarterly, 28*(2), 377–389.

Wigfield, A., & Eccles, J. S. (2000). Expectancy value theory of achievement motivation. *Contemporary Educational Psychology, 25*, 68–81.

Wiggins, G., & McTighe, J. (2005). *Understanding by design* (2nd ed.) Upper Saddle River, NJ: Prentice Hall.

Wilkins, D. A. (1976). *Notional syllabuses.* Oxford, UK: Oxford University Press.

Williams, J. [Jessica]. (2005). *Teaching writing in second and foreign language classrooms.* Boston, MA: McGraw Hill.

Williams, J. N. [John]. (2005). Learning without awareness. *Studies in Second Language Acquisition, 27*(2), 269–304.

Willingham, D. T. (2009). *Why don't students like school? A cognitive scientist answers questions about how the mind works and what it means for the classroom.* San Francisco, CA: Jossey-Bass.

Willis, D. (1990). *The lexical syllabus.* London, UK: Collins

Willis, D. (2003). *Rules, patterns and words.* Cambridge, UK: Cambridge University Press.

Willis, D., & Willis, J. (2001). Task-based language learning. In R. Carter & D. Nunan (Eds.), *The Cambridge guide to teaching English to speakers of other languages* (pp. 173–179). Cambridge, UK: Cambridge University Press.

Willis, J. R. (1996). *A framework for task-based learning.* Harlow, UK: Longman.

Willis, J. R. (2004). Perspectives on task-based instruction: Understanding our practices, acknowledging different practitioners. In B. L. Leaver & J. R. Willis (Eds.), *Task-based instruction in foreign language education* (pp. 3–46). Washington, DC: Georgetown University Press.

Wilson, J. P. (2008). Reflecting-on-the-future: A chronological consideration of reflective practice. *Reflective Practice: International and Multidisciplinary Perspectives, 9*, 177–184.

Winitz, H. (1981). *The comprehension approach to foreign language instruction.* Rowley, MA: Newbury House.

Wong, J., & Waring, H. Z. (2009). "Very good" as a teacher response. *ELT Journal, 63*(3), 195–203.

Wong, J., & Waring, H. Z. (2010). *Conversation analysis and second language pedagogy: A guide for ESL/EFL teachers.* New York, NY: Routledge.

Woods, D. (1996). *Teaching cognition in language teaching: Beliefs, decision-making and classroom practice.* Cambridge, UK: Cambridge University Press.

Woodward, T. (2001). *Planning lessons and courses.* Cambridge, UK: Cambridge University Press.

Wurr, A., & Hellebrandt, J. (Eds.). (2007). *Learning the language of global citizenship: Service-learning in applied linguistics.* San Francisco, CA: Jossey Bass.

Xue, G., & Nation, I. S. P. (1984). A university word list. *Language Learning and Communication, 3*(2), 215–229.

Yamamoto, H. (1994). Seventeen syllables. In K. K. Cheng (Ed.), *Seventeen syllables* (pp. 21–40). New Brunswick, NJ: Rutgers University Press.

Yim, K. Y-K. (2011). Second language students' discourse socialization in academic online communities. *Canadian Modern Language Review, 61*, 1–27.

Young, L., Thearling, K., Skiena, S., Robison, A., Omohundro, S., Mel, B., & Wolfram, S. (1997). Academic computing in the year 2000. In G. Hawisher & C. Selfe (Eds.), *Literacy, technology, and society: Confronting the issues* (pp. 248–261). Upper Saddle River, NJ: Prentice-Hall.

Yuan, F., & Ellis, R. (2003). The effects of pre-task and on-line planning on fluency, complexity and accuracy in L2 monologic oral production. *Applied Linguistics, 24*(1), 1–27.

Zahner, C., Fauverge, A., & Wong, J. (2000). Task-based language learning via audiovisual networks. In M. Warschauer & R. Kern (Eds.), *Network-based language teaching: Concepts and practice* (pp. 186–203). Cambridge, UK: Cambridge University Press.

Zakaria, F. (2011). *The post-American world: Release 2.0.* New York, NY: W. W. Norton.

Zakharia, Z. (2010). (Re)Constructing language policy in a Shi'i school in Lebanon. In K. Menken, & O. García (Eds.), *Negotiating language policies in schools* (pp. 162–181). New York, NY: Routledge.

Zechmeister, E. (1995). Growth of a functionally important lexicon. *Journal of Reading Behavior, 27*(2), 201–212.

Zeichner, K. M., & Liston, D. P. (1996). *Reflective teaching: An introduction.* Mahwah, NJ: Lawrence Erlbaum Associates.

Zhang, R. (2008). Learning English in China for today: Revitalizing a curriculum through task-based learning. In D. Hayes & J. Sharkey (Eds.), *Revitalizing a curriculum for school-age learners* (pp. 291–306). Alexandria, VA: Teachers of English to Speakers of Other Languages.

Zhang, X., & Head, K. (2009). Dealing with learner reticence in the speaking class. *ELT Journal, 64*(1), 1–9.

Ziegler, M., & Bingman, M. (2007) Achieving adult education program quality: A review of systematic approaches to program development. In J. Comings, B. Garner, & C. Smith (Eds.), *Review of adult learning and literacy: Connecting research, policy, and practice* (Vol. 7, pp. 47–91). Mahwah, NJ: Lawrence Erlbaum Associates.

Zielinski, B. (2006). The intelligibility cocktail: An interaction between speaker and listener ingredients. *Prospect, 21*(1), 22–45.

Zielinski, B. (2008). The listener: No longer the silent partner in reduced intelligibility. *System, 36*(1), 69–84.

Zimmerman, C. B. (1997a). Do reading and interactive vocabulary instruction make a difference? An empirical study. *TESOL Quarterly, 31*(1), 121–140.

Zimmerman, C. B. (1997b). Historical trends in second language vocabulary instruction. In J. Coady & T. Huckin (Eds.), *Second language vocabulary acquisition* (pp. 5–19). Cambridge, UK: Cambridge University Press.

Zimmerman, C. B. (2009). *Word knowledge: A vocabulary teacher's handbook.* New York, NY: Oxford University Press.

Zuck, J. G. (1984). Comments on Peter Master's "The etiquette of observing." A reader reacts. *TESOL Quarterly, 18*(2), 337–341.

Index

A small *n* following a page reference indicates the appearance of an entry in an endnote.

Clearinghouse, 638–639
    National Clearinghouse for English
        Language Acquisition, 639, 648
    SEAMEO Regional Language Centre,
        639, 648
Clément, R., 441, 522
Clifford, R., 12, 21
Closure (writing lessons), 230
Cloud, N., 160, 164, 169, 454n13
Cloze passages, 431
Clusters, 275
Cluster VESL, 475
Coaching, 642
Cochran-Smith, M., 632
Code-switching, 66
Coggshall, J. G., 632
Cognition, 12
    classroom research, 606
    relationship between emotion/
        motivation, 519
Cognitive academic language learning
        approach (CALLA), 444, 537
Cognitive academic language proficiency
        (CALP), 444, 556
Cognitive approach, 7, 9
Cognitive complexity, 45n4
Cognitive flexibility, 546–547
Cognitive perspectives, 224
Cognitive psychology, 7
Cognitive strategies, 240, 532, 537
Cohen, A. D., 107, 109, 120, 544, 548,
        549n1, 549n4, 549n5
Cohen, J., 205
Cohen, R., 186
Coherence, 427
    text, 242
Cohesion, 185, 242, 427
    analysis, 425
    creating, 248
    lexical, 429
Cohesive devices, 246
Cohesive learner groups, 527–529
Coiro, J., 155
Coleman, A., 6, 290
Coleman, H., 606
Coleman Report, 6
Collaboration, 124, 581
    artifacts, 276
    dialogues, 266
Collaborative strategic reading (CSR),
        203
Collecting data about learning, 324
Collocations, J., 509
Collications, 289
Collie, J., 500n1
Collier, V. P., 454n3, 554
Collin, S., 617
Collins, P., 158, 159, 160
Colorín Colorado!, 640
Coltrane, B., 555, 556
Comenius, Johann (Jan) Amos, 4
Comic strips, 147
Comings, J., 571, 572
Comity, 66, 67
Comments, 233
    procedures, 369

Committees, 641
Common European Framework of Reference
        for Languages (CEFR), 21–22, 50, 118,
        171, 317, 513, 571
Communicability, 145
Communication
    patterns in classrooms, 617–618
    with young learners (YLs), 560
Communication difficulties, 115
Communicative approach, 8–9. See also
        Communicative language teaching (CLT)
Communicative competence, 18
Communicative language teaching (CLT),
        15–16, 290, 458
    in the 21st century, 26–27
    classroom management and social organi-
        zation, 26
    concepts of, 18–20
    contexts for, 15, 16
    English as a lingua franca and, 26, 66–67
    in English for academic purposes, 24–25
    information and communication technolo-
        gies and, 27–28
    language education reforms in, 26
    theory vs. practice, 25
    young learners and, 23–24
Communicative practice, 146
Communities
    building learning, 579–581
    discourse, 223, 228
Compensation strategies, 537
Competency-based syllabus, 572
Competence
    strategic, 532
    versus performance, 353
Competition, intergroup, 528
Components of mechanics of writing, 209
Composition, 90
Comprehensibility, 589
Comprehensible input, 38, 443, 554
Comprehensible output, 443, 554
Comprehension-based approach, 8, 9
Comprehension monitoring, 84, 85, 196
Comprehension Shouldn't Be Silent (Kelley &
        Clausen-Grace), 183
Comprehension skills practice, 195–196
Comprehensive Adult Student Assessment
        Systems (CASAS), 368
Computational model, 42
Computer-adaptive testing (CAT), 316
Computer-assisted instruction, 144, 410
Computer-Assisted Language Instruction
        Consortium (CALICO), 636, 647
Computer-assisted language learning
        (CALL), 411, 412
Computer technology, effect on language
        assessment, 308, 316–317
Concept-of-definition maps, 194, 195n8,
        195n9
Concept-oriented reading instruction
        (CORI), 203
Concepts
    grammar, 240–244
    mechanics of writing, 210–213
    of time, 395, 398
Conceptualization in speech processing, 122

Concordances, 417
Concrete operations stage, 551
Conditions for power of vision, 522
Condon, W. S., 143
Conferences, individual writing, 233
Confirmation checks, 31, 32
Conjunctions, subordinate clauses, 274
Connected speech, 139, 152n1
Conrad, S., 243, 257, 281, 381, 477
Consciousness-raising, 265–266
Consequences of language assessment, 310, 314
Consistency of language assessment, 311
Consonants, 139–141
    English, 211–212
Constrained constructed response, 41
Constructed-response formats, 323
Constructions, learning techniques, 261
Construct-related evidence, 313
Contact, 528
Content, 452
    compacting clearly, 217
    descriptions, 217
    of language assessment, 315
    literature as, 488–500
    salience in course, 293–294
    of spoken language, 278–279
    textbook selection, 383, 384, 385
    unpacking meaning in, 246
Content and language integrated learning
        (CLIL) syllabus, 51, 439
Content-based instruction (CBI), 51, 155,
        203, 459. See also Language integrated
        learning environments
    syllabus, 51
Content-based language teaching (CBLT),
        22–23, 438–454
    classroom applications, 447–450
    concepts, 443–447
    definition of, 438–439
    examples of, 449–450
    expansion of, 442–443
    experience, 438
    future trends, 450–452
    instructional strategies, 448–449
    models, 439–442
Content-related evidence, 312
Content schemata, 429, 433
Context
    cues, 224
    English as a foreign language (EFL), 225
    face-to-face, 274, 280
    grammar, 241–244
    lesson planning, 362–363
    pragmatics, 258, 399
Context analysis, 49, 54, 56
Contextual cues, using, 448
Contextual dimension, 101
Contextualization, 79
Contextualized instruction, 144, 480
Contextualized listening, 94
Contextual knowledge, 429
Contingency plans, lesson planning, 370
Contrastive analysis, 142
Controlled practice, 145, 146
Conversational strategies, 594–595
Conversation analysis (CA), 110